D0928156

A Guide to the Study
of
MEDIEVAL HISTORY

EDITORS

Editorial Committee

Gray C. Boyce
A. C. Krey
F. P. Magoun, Jr.
W. A. Morris
P. B. Schaeffer
J. S. P. Tatlock

Dana C. Munro, Chairman

Contributing Editors

R. H. Bainton
C. S. Baldwin
Jean Birdsall
D. K. Bjork
Charles Bruneau
F. S. Cawley
S. H. Cross
E. T. DeWald
John Dickinson
J. D. M. Ford
H. Hermannsson
J. C. Hildt
A. C. Howland
Einar Joranson
R. J. Kerner
M. L. W. Laistner
George LaPiana
Louise R. Loomis
D. B. Macdonald
Kenneth McKenzie
R. P. McKeon
E. H. McNeal
R. B. Merriman
C. R. Morey
L. H. Motry
E. W. Nelson
R. A. Newhall
M. B. Ogle
E. K. Rand
W. M. Randall
I. W. Raymond
F. N. Robinson
W. W. Rockwell
R. J. Sontag
S. T. Starck
E. L. Stevenson
W. O. Strunk
A. H. Sweet
C. H. Taylor
J. W. Thompson
Lynn Thorndike
T. C. Van Cleve
A. A. Vasiliev
W. W. Westergaard

J. R. Williams

A Guide to the Study of MEDIEVAL HISTORY

BY

LOUIS JOHN PAETOW

Late Professor of Medieval History in the University of California

REVISED EDITION

Prepared under the auspices of

The Mediaeval Academy of America

KRAUS REPRINT CO.
Millwood, New York
1973

ALBRIGHT COLLEGE LIBRARY

COPYRIGHT, 1917,
BY
L. J. PAETOW

COPYRIGHT, 1931,
BY
F. S. CROFTS & CO., INC.

COPYRIGHT, 1959
BY
APPLETON-CENTURY-CROFTS, INC.

Paetow, Louis John, 1880-1928.
A guide to the study of medieval history.

"Prepared under the auspices of the Medieval Academy of America."

Reprint of the ed. published by Appleton-Century-Crofts, New York.

1. Middle Ages—Bibliography. 2. Middle Ages—History—Outlines, syllabi, etc. I. Medieval Academy of America. II. Title.
Z6203.P19 1973 016.9401 73-9705
ISBN 0-527-69100-3

Reprinted with the permission of
Appleton-Century-Crofts, Inc.

KRAUS REPRINT CO.
A U.S. Division of Kraus-Thomson Organization Limited

Printed in Germany

940.1
P126gK

146490

PREFACE TO FIRST EDITION

Ever since the fall of 1914 the stream of historical writing on the middle ages has become thinner and thinner, so that today it is comparatively easy to keep abreast with the literature on the subject due to the phenomenal decrease of new contributions by European scholars. This sudden lull, preceded by a period of almost feverish activity in book-making, is a peculiarly propitious time for the making of inventories of the wealth of historical literature which has been produced in the century since the close of the Napoleonic wars. Such a task for medieval history is attempted in this *Guide*.

The book has grown out of mimeographed syllabi prepared for two courses offered in the University of California, a general course in medieval history designed especially for juniors, and an advanced course in medieval culture for seniors and graduate students. These two syllabi have furnished the bases for parts II and III of this *Guide*. Part I, containing the most important general books useful in a study of medieval history, has been added in order to make the manual as complete and comprehensive as is possible within its limits. These general books are referred to constantly in parts II and III by cross references to the black-faced numbers by which they are designated. The table of contents furnishes an analysis of the general books in part I.

Part II is divided into thirty-five sections and part III into twenty-eight sections. The titles and Roman numbers of these sections are indicated by means of analytical page headings. A section comprises a well-defined subject which represents approximately one week's work in the courses mentioned above. Each section is divided into three parts: A, Outline; B, Special Recommendations for Reading; and C, Bibliography. "A," the Outline, aims to present the subject matter of the section in an orderly fashion, including the principal names and dates which readers will encounter in the books which are listed, and thus dispenses with the need of a text book. Under "B," Special Recommendations for Reading, are indicated such books and articles as are likely to appeal to undergraduates in college who have only a limited amount of time to give to the subject. The references are made as specific as possible and are graded and classified to suit various library conditions, individual tastes, and special requirements. Care has been taken to indicate, wherever possible, the original sources which are easily accessible and translated into English. "C," the Bibliography, presents a classified list of the most important special books and articles which will guide students in making reports and in preparing papers, but which is particularly designed for mature readers and for investigators who desire a survey of the most important literature in the fields in which

16.00

they are interested. Ordinarily the literature on a given subject is thus divided under "B," Special Recommendations for Reading, and "C," Bibliography, and should be sought for under both headings. At the end of each section are listed the special bibliographies which must be consulted by those who wish to pursue the subject to its ultimate limits.

While the mimeographed syllabi mentioned above were designed for only certain grades of college students, this printed *Guide* has been modified and augmented so as to appeal to all classes of students and readers who have advanced beyond the textbook stage and who have access to good libraries. It is hoped that teachers will find it useful and that librarians will give it a place among their books of reference. The task of selection, which is always difficult, has been rendered peculiarly delicate by the plan to make the book appeal to so wide a circle of readers. The present resources and the future needs of the University of California Library have been made the basis of selection. In this *Guide* there are listed all books, valuable for a study of medieval history, which now are in this library, and in addition, all others on this subject, which, in the opinion of the author, should be acquired by the library in the near future. It is hoped that this basis of selection will be considered as practical and as representative as any which might have been adopted to suit conditions in America.

The difficulty of choosing from the mass of literature in the various modern European languages has been met by selecting all the best material in English, French, and German, and by making a more limited selection from books in Italian and Spanish. Except in rare instances, all the other modern European languages have been neglected.

English history is not treated fully because in America the subject is usually taught in separate courses and because we have such admirable bibliographical guidance for the medieval period in the second edition of C. Gross, *The sources and literature of English history*.

In a book of this kind there is not much space for commentary and criticism of individual works. Confronted by the great difficulty of evaluating such a huge amount of literature, one is sorely tempted to give way to fear and to modesty by grouping books alphabetically in long unclassified lists. But this way out of the difficulty has been avoided because the average reader dislikes to choose altogether for himself, or at least he is curious to know another's choice before he makes his own. Critical notes have been inserted here and there, but the main task of criticism is revealed in the selection itself and in the order in which the books and articles are listed. Throughout the work classification has been made as minute as possible and with rare exceptions, as in the case of text books on pages 66–68, under each heading the books which are considered the most important are listed first. On the whole, books written in English are probably judged a little more leniently than those in foreign languages, because in all doubtful cases the English books were given the benefit of the doubt. The occasional advantage of the alphabetical arrangement of books is not entirely lost by this system of grouping because it is in large measure supplied by the index.

The index contains in one alphabet authors, editors, translators of medieval books, titles of large collections, and subjects on which there is special literature. All articles and papers, as well as books, are included. The black-faced figures refer to numbers in part I; the light-faced figures to pages in parts II and III. Reference is made to the place where the title of a work is given in full. If the reader wants complete information concerning the title of a work which he finds mentioned in abbreviated form he should turn to the index which indicates the place where he will find the desired details. Librarians will find that the information given about books is sufficient to locate them readily in the trade catalogues.

Again and again the author has been tempted to submit the manuscript to his friends who are specialists in this field of history, knowing full well how much the book would be benefited by their criticism; but sore experience in bibliographical work has convinced him that it would not be fair to impose even portions of this task upon his friends. Thus he decided to be content with whatever others had prepared for him in the form of printed books and syllabi and to do alone as much as his time, strength, patience, and the facilities at his command permitted. Perhaps this will induce those whom he spared and others to be all the more willing to point out mistakes and omissions and to offer suggestions for improvement.

L. J. PAETOW.

Berkeley, California,
October 17, 1917.

PREFACE TO REVISED EDITION

Scholars and students of medieval history and culture have long felt the need for a new edition of Professor Paetow's *Guide to the study of medieval history*. Issued in a limited edition in 1917, copies soon became scarce and have long since disappeared from trade lists of available books. At the time of his death in December 1928, Professor Paetow was at work formulating plans to meet this demand and to bring the volume abreast of current scholarship. His friends and colleagues were not surprised to learn that one who possessed such a rare combination of scholarly insight and methodical craftsmanship had left materials which might be used to save, in part at least, what promised to be another of his generous offerings to those whom he delighted to serve.

Through the kindness of Mrs. Paetow the Mediaeval Academy of America was authorized to direct the task of preparing the work for publication. In May 1929, the Academy appointed a committee to supervise this undertaking. It was immediately evident that the co-operation of many scholars would be required. Although a preliminary survey was attempted during the summer, it was not until the fall of 1929 that the arrangement of Professor Paetow's materials was begun. As the titles for each section were gathered they were criticized by scholars who are authorities in the various fields. The editors cannot praise too highly the services rendered by those who aided in this way and gave so willingly of their intimate knowledge, their time and energy, that the volume might be of greater service to others.

In preparing the new edition of the *Guide* an endeavor has been made to include the titles of all important contributions which appeared between the years 1917 and 1928 inclusive. In certain cases it was considered advisable to add titles which have appeared since 1928, although no systematic survey of the literature published since that date has been made. The arrangement of materials is usually the same as in the first edition. In a few instances the scope of the outline or section has been augmented. This is true especially of outline XXIV of part III which, as originally compiled, was devoted solely to medieval French language and literature. To supplement this and to satisfy a real need additional material has been inserted to cover other vernacular languages and literatures. In part I, chapter III, § 9 has been added for the study of place-names. It is hoped that this will be a useful supplement.

A list of contributors is given elsewhere. Others have given valuable assistance. Those to whom we are especially grateful are: Mr. M. O. Young and Miss Cecile Barsky of the Princeton University Library who have been of constant service; Mr. John Marshall, Secretary of the Mediaeval Academy, who has assisted in many ways; Mr. F. S. Crofts, the publisher, who has contributed so generously to this volume; and most of all, Mrs. M. S. Tignor, our secretary, whose conscientious care has prevented many a mistake. She has also prepared the index.

DANA C. MUNRO,
GRAY C. BOYCE.

Princeton University.

CONTENTS

Part I

GENERAL BOOKS

Chapter I

BIBLIOGRAPHICAL WORKS

Chapter II

BOOKS OF REFERENCE

CHAPTER III

SOME AUXILIARIES TO THE STUDY OF MEDIEVAL HISTORY

Chapter IV

GENERAL MODERN HISTORICAL WORKS

CHAPTER V

LARGE COLLECTIONS OF ORIGINAL SOURCES

Part II

GENERAL HISTORY OF THE MIDDLE AGES

Period I. 500–1100

Period II. 1100–1500

Part III

MEDIEVAL CULTURE

Period I. 500–1100

PAGE

Period II. 1100–1300

ABBREVIATIONS

Abh.m.n.G.	*Abhandlungen zur mittelalterlichen und neueren Geschichte.*
A.F.H	*Archivum franciscanum historicum.*
A.H.A	*American historical association.*
A.H.R.	*American historical review.*
B.E.C	*Bibliothèque de l'Ecole des chartes.*
B.Z	*Byzantinische Zeitschrift.*
C.M.H	*Cambridge medieval history.*
Diss.	Dissertation.
E.H.R.	*English historical review.*
Ency. Brit.	*Encyclopaedia Britannica.*
F.D.G	*Forschungen zur deutschen Geschichte.*
Heidelberg. Abh.	*Heidelberger Abhandlungen.*
H.V.J.S.	*Historische Vierteljahrschrift.*
H.Z.	*Historische Zeitschrift.*
M.A	*Le moyen âge.*
M.G.H.	*Monumenta Germaniae historica.*
M.I.O.G	*Mittheilungen des Instituts für oesterreichische Geschichtsforschung.*
Migne, *P.L*	*Patrologia latina.*
N.A.	*Neues Archiv der Gesellschaft für ältere deutsche Geschichtskunde.*
P.M.L.A	*Publications of the Modern language association.*
Prog	Programm.
Q.E.	*Quellen und Erörterungen zur bayerischen und deutschen Geschichte.*
R.D.M	*Revue des deux mondes.*
R.H.	*Revue historique.*
R.H.S.	*Royal historical society.*
R.Q.H.	*Revue des questions historiques.*
R.S.H.	*Revue de synthèse historique.*
S.B	*Sitzungsberichte* of the Berlin, Heidelberg, Munich, and Vienna Academies. Unless otherwise stated the philosophisch-historische Klasse is understood.
S.P.C.K. Helps.	Society for the promotion of Christian knowledge: Helps.
S.P.C.K. Texts.	Society for the promotion of Christian knowledge: Texts.

PART I

GENERAL BOOKS

CHAPTER I

BIBLIOGRAPHICAL WORKS

§ 1. Bibliographies of Bibliographies

1. STEIN, H. Manuel de bibliographie générale. Paris, 1898. (Manuels de bibliographie historique, II.)

Historical bibliographies are treated in ch. XIII, 401–66, but many other sections are of interest to the historian. Contains criticisms of some books. Much more useful than PETZHOLDT, but does not supersede it altogether.

1a. VAN HOESEN, H. B., with the collaboration of F. K. WALTER. Bibliography: practical, enumerative, historical. New York, 1928.

"The authors have made excellent general statements, illustrated by specific examples, and then have made running comment on leading bibliographies." Ch. IV is devoted to *Historical and social sciences.*

1b. COURTNEY, W. P. A register of national bibliography, with a selection of the chief bibliographical books and articles printed in other countries. 3 vols. London, 1905–12.

Vol. III is a supplement. The work is a dictionary index of bibliographies.

1c. SCHNEIDER, G. Handbuch der Bibliographie. Leipzig, 1923.

2. PETZHOLDT, J. Bibliotheca bibliographica: kritisches Verzeichniss der das Gesammtgebiet der Bibliographie betreffenden Literatur des In- und Auslandes. Leipzig, 1866.

Pages 771–875 deal with history and cartography.

2a. VALLÉE, L. Bibliographie des bibliographies. 2 vols. Paris, 1883–87.

Vol. II is a supplement.

§ 2. General Bibliographies; Catalogues of Large Libraries and Archives

3. British Museum. Catalogue of printed books in the library of the British Museum. London, 1881–1900. Supplement, 1900–05.

An alphabetical list according to authors, but also contains subject entries, some of which were sold as separates, e.g., "Dante." Since 1880 there has been published a *Catalogue of new books* which brings the printed catalogue up to date. G. K. FORTESCUE, *Subject-index of the modern works added to the library of the British Museum in the years 1881–1900*, 3 vols., London, 1902–03; works added in 1901–05, 1 vol., 1906; works added in 1906–10, 1 vol., 1911; works added in 1911–15, compiled by R. H. STREATFIELD and W. A. MARSDEN, London, 1918; works added in 1916–20, compiled by L. TAYLOR and others, London, 1922; and *idem* 1921–25, London, 1927. The following aids are valuable: *List of books forming the reference library in the reading room of the British Museum*, 4th edition, 2 vols., London, 1910; and G. W. PORTER, *List of bibliographical works in the reading room of the British Museum*, 2nd edition, revised by G. K. FORTESCUE, London, 1889. For guides to manuscript material in England consult GROSS, no. **36** below. See also H. C. SHELLEY, *The British Museum: its history and treasures*, Boston, 1911; and R. A. PEDDIE, *The British Museum reading room: a handbook for students*, London, 1912. Other useful volumes are GERTRUDE B. RAWLINGS, *The British Museum Library*, London, 1916; C. JOHNSON, *The Public Record Office*, London, 1919. (S.P.C.K. Helps, no. 4); H. JENKINSON, *Manual of archive administration*, Oxford, 1922; H. HALL, *Repertory of British archives*, London, 1920; G. F. BARWICK, *The reading room of the British Museum*, London, 1929; R. A. RYE, *Students' guide to the libraries of London*, 3rd edition, London, 1927; L. NEWCOMBE, *The university and college libraries of Great Britain and Ireland, a guide to the material available for the research student*, London, 1927.

4. Bibliothèque Nationale. Catalogue général des livres imprimés de la Bibliothèque Nationale. Paris, 1897ff. Vol. XC, to Le Basque, appeared in 1927.

This is an author catalogue; there are no subject entries. Three series are contemplated, of which this is the first: 1. Authors (including anonymous works whose authors are known); 2. Anonymous works; 3. Publications of a special nature. This catalogue is being supplemented by a *Bulletin mensuel des publications étrangères*, 1874ff.; and a *Bulletin mensuel des récentes publications françaises*, 1882ff. For other French libraries consult the *Catalogue général des bibliothèques publiques de France*, Paris, 1893–1924, which includes the departments of France and the libraries of Paris except the Bibliothèque Nationale.

See also the *Catalogue alphabétique des livres imprimés mis à la disposition des lecteurs dans la salle de travail* [of the Bibliothèque Nationale], *suivi de la liste des catalogues usuels du département des manuscrits*, Paris, 1895. This list [pp. 21–49 of the work just cited] is the most complete list of catalogues of manuscript material kept in libraries, such as the *Catalogue général des manuscrits des bibliothèques publiques de France*, Paris, 1885ff. Far more than a mere bibliography is the very extensive *Notices et extraits des manuscrits de la Bibliothèque Nationale et autres bibliothèques*, Paris, 1787ff., no. **885** below. The same is true of B. HAURÉAU, *Notices et extraits de quelques manuscrits latins de la Bibliothèque Nationale*, 6 vols., Paris, 1890–93.

For archive material see the exhaustive guide of C. V. LANGLOIS, *Etat des inventaires des Archives nationales au 1er janvier 1914*, Paris, 1914, 80 pp. A collection, by no means complete, of inventories of archives (French and foreign) is now on the shelves of the reading-room of the Archives Nationales in Paris, but no list of it has been printed yet. G. BOURGIN, "Les Archives nationales depuis la guerre" in *Revue des bibliothèques*, 36e année (1926), 381–400. See also nos. **20** and **25** below.

A. FRANKLIN, *Guide des savants, des littérateurs, et des artistes dans les bibliothèques de Paris*, Paris, 1908, is a valuable handbook for students of history. P. BOYER, etc. *La vie universitaire à Paris*, Paris, 1918.

4a. Catalogue général des manuscrits des bibliothèques publiques des départements. 7 vols. Paris, 1849–55.

4b. Catalogue des cartulaires des archives départementales. Paris, 1847.

5. MAZZATINTI, G. Inventari dei manoscritti delle biblioteche d'Italia. 37 vols. Forli, etc., 1891–1927.

See also MAZZATINTI, *Gli archivi della storia d'Italia*, Florence, 1897ff., and no. **41**. For the Vatican the best guide for American historians is still C. H. HASKINS, "The Vatican archives," in *A.H.R.*, II (1896), 40–58; see also G. BROM, *Guide aux archives du Vatican*, 2nd edition, Rome, 1911; C. R. FISH, *Guide to the materials for American history in Roman and other Italian archives*, Washington, D. C., 1911; E. BEGNI, *The Vatican: its history, its treasures*, New York, 1914.

6. GRAESEL, A. Handbuch der Bibliothekslehre. 2nd edition. Leipzig, 1902.

This standard handbook contains excellent bibliographies and a wealth of miscellaneous information of importance to all frequenters of libraries and archives. A. GRAESEL, *Führer für Bibliotheksbenutzer*, Leipzig, 1905; 2nd edition, 1913, is a primer for beginners. There is a short chapter (xv), "Library history and resources" in VAN HOESEN, no. **1a** above.

The article on "Libraries" in the *Ency. Brit.* is a valuable guide (with good bibliographies) for all the large libraries of the world; to be supplemented by *Minerva: Jahrbuch der gelehrten Welt*, no. **83**.

The most comprehensive periodical in this field is the *Centralblatt für Bibliothekswesen*, Leipzig, 1884ff., which no historian can afford to overlook. See also *Bibliothèques, livres et libraires: conférences faites à l'Ecole des Hautes Etudes Sociales sous le patronage de l'Association des Bibliothécaires français*, Paris, 1912ff.

For the literature on archives and libraries in Germany, see DAHLMANN-WAITZ, no. **28**, pp. 27–33.

7. SONNENSCHEIN, W. S. The best books. London, 1891. 3rd edition in four parts (entirely rewritten). London and New York, 1910–26.

7a. Standard books: an annotated and classified guide to all the best books in all departments of literature. 4 vols. London, 1919.

§ 3. Bibliographies of Periodical Literature

8. POOLE'S index to periodical literature, 1802–1906. Boston, 1882–1908.

9. Reader's guide to periodical literature. Minneapolis, 1905ff.

Covers material 1900ff.

9a. International index to periodicals, devoted chiefly to the humanities and science. New York, 1919ff.

From 1902–19 this appeared as *Reader's guide to periodical literature: supplement.*

9b. The art index. New York, 1930ff.

10. Bibliographie der deutschen Zeitschriftenliteratur. Leipzig, 1896ff. (Internationale Bibliographie der Zeitschriftenliteratur, Abteilung A.)

11. Bibliographie der fremdsprachigen Zeitschriftenliteratur. Gautzsch, near Leipzig, 1911ff. (*Ibid.*, Abteilung B.)

In some measure this continues the *Rêpertoire bibliographique des principales revues françaises*, 1897–99. 3 vols., Paris, 1898–1900.

11a. Union list of serials in the libraries of the United States and Canada. New York, 1927. Supplement, April, 1930ff.

§ 4. General Historical Bibliographies

12. LANGLOIS, C. V. Manuel de bibliographie historique. 2 vols., in one. Paris, 1901–04.

Part I, Instruments bibliographiques; part II, Histoire et organisation des études historiques. A work of fundamental value to every advanced student of history.

The "Enquêtes pour l'orientation des recherches dans la bibliographie historique des différents pays" which appear in the various issues of the *Bulletin of the International Committee of Historical Sciences* are very useful.

13. International yearbook of historical bibliography. (Annuaire international de bibliographie historique.)

The first issue of this bibliography was announced to appear in 1930. It is recognized as the successor to **13a**. The first issue will deal with works of 1926 and proposes to cover only general works or works that have to do with international relations of one sort or another.

13a. Jahresberichte der Geschichtswissenschaft. Berlin, 1880ff. 36 vols. in 1916.

Annual surveys of historical literature covering the years 1878–1913. The plan of this comprehensive work is explained by J. JASTROW, *Handbuch zu Literaturberichten*, no. **147**.

14. HERRE, P. Quellenkunde zur Weltgeschichte. Leipzig, 1910.

Includes both sources and modern works. C. K. ADAMS, *A manual of historical literature*, New York, 1882, 3rd edition, 1888. This volume will be superseded by *A guide to historical literature*, edited by W. H. ALLISON, S.B. FAY, A. H. SHEARER, and H. R. SHIPMAN, New York, to appear in 1931. C. M. ANDREWS, J. M. GAMBRILL, and LIDA L. TALL, *A bibliography of history for schools and libraries*, New York, 1910, reprinted with slight alterations, 1911, is a very handy little volume especially useful to teachers in high schools.

14a. COULTER, EDITH M. Guide to historical bibliographies, a critical and systematic bibliography for advanced students. Berkeley, 1927.

See VAN HOESEN, no. **1a.**

15. A union-list of collections on European history in American libraries [by the Committee on Bibliography of the A.H.A.]. Proof edition with locations, March, 1912. Copies added 1912–14. Princeton University library, 1915; also an index by A. H. SHEARER.

This list, although incomplete and imperfect, is of value to American scholars because it indicates in what American libraries the large sets of historical material for European history can be found.

15a. Gesamtkatalog der Wiegendrucke. Leipzig, 1925ff.

"The most comprehensive record of incunabula yet made, based on information collected during more than twenty years' work by the Kommission."

§ 5. General Bibliographies of the Middle Ages

16. CHEVALIER, U. Répertoire des sources historiques du moyen âge: bio-bibliographie. 2 vols. Paris, 1877–86. Supplément, 1888. 2nd edition, 1905–07.

17. CHEVALIER, U. Répertoire des sources historiques du moyen âge: topo-bibliographie. 2 vols. Paris, 1894–1903.

These two works cover the period from the beginning of the Christian era to 1500 A.D. They are invaluable guides for the literature on persons, places, and things in the middle ages, but are difficult to use because no attempt has been made to weed out worthless material. Good and bad, old and new, accounts are jumbled together in long alphabetical lists.

17a. LEES, BEATRICE A. Bibliography of mediaeval history, 400 to 1500 A.D. London, 1917. (Leaflets of the Historical Association, no. 40.)

18. POTTHAST, A. Bibliotheca historica medii aevi: Wegweiser durch die Geschichtswerke des europäischen Mittelalters bis 1500. Berlin, 1862. Supplement, 1868. 2nd edition, enlarged and improved, 2 vols., Berlin, 1896.

A stupendous undertaking devoted to the classification of the primary sources of medieval history. No modern works are mentioned except those which explain the sources. Only printed annals, chronicles, etc., written between 375 and 1500. Printed archive material is rigorously excluded.

Part I contains accurate titles and brief descriptions of all important printed collections of sources; part II is an alphabetical list of medieval authors and their works, with lists of the manuscripts, editions, translations and commentaries on each work. For criticisms of the second edition see the review by A. VIDIER, in *M.A.*, IX (1896), 73–83.

No. **949** plans to include *English translations of medieval sources* by JUDITH BERNSTEIN. [In preparation.] This bibliography will contain a list of medieval writings on literature, philosophy, theology, and science, as well as purely historical sources, produced between the years 300 and 1500, which have been translated into English. It will also include an analysis of **971** and **981.**

19. BRESSLAU, H. " Quellen und Hilfsmittel zur Geschichte der romanischen Völker im Mittelalter." In no. **305,** II, part IV (1896), 431–515.

20. OESTERLEY, H. Wegweiser durch die Literatur der Urkundensammlungen. 2 vols. Berlin, 1885–86.

The period covered is 500–1500 A.D. Naturally the work is best for Germany.

20a. THOMPSON, J. W. Reference studies in medieval history. Revised and enlarged edition. 3 vols. Chicago, 1923–24.

§ 6. Bibliographies of Various Countries

(*a*) FRANCE

21. MOLINIER, A. Les sources de l'histoire de France. Vols. I–VI on middle ages. Paris, 1901–06. (Manuels de bibliographie historique, III.)

This is now the standard bibliography of the history of France, devoted primarily to the original sources, but also including modern works which throw light on the sources and their authors. Vol. VI is the index for the middle ages. The first portion of vol. V contains an introduction to the work. See also H. BRESSLAU, no. **19.**

22. MONOD, G. Bibliographie de l'histoire de France: catalogue méthodique et chronologique des sources et des ouvrages relatifs à l'histoire de France depuis les origines jusqu'en 1789. Paris, 1888.

Until the appearance of no. **21,** this was the chief guide for the study of the history of France. Even now it still maintains a proper place beside MOLINIER because MONOD pays particular attention to modern works. For good recent bibliographical notes see no. **508.**

22a. Répertoire bibliographique de l'histoire de France. Edited by P. CARON and H. STEIN. Paris, 1923–27. Vol. I, 1920–21; vol. II, 1922–23.

A current bibliography of the history of France. Materials for all periods are included and biennial issues are planned.

23. FRANKLIN, A. Les sources de l'histoire de France: notices bibliographiques et analytiques des inventaires et des recueils de documents relatifs à l'histoire de France. Paris, 1877.

24. STEIN, H. Bibliographie générale des cartulaires français ou relatifs à l'histoire de France. Paris, 1907.

25. LANGLOIS, C. V., and STEIN, H. Les archives de l'histoire de France. 3 parts. Paris, 1891–93.

Supplemented by L. MIROT, "Les inventaires d'archives," *Congrès bibliographique internationale, compte rendu*, II. Paris, 1900, pp. 186–210; and the *Rapport au ministre sur l'administration des archives nationales, départementales*, etc., Paris, 1902. See also *Annuaire des bibliothèques et des archives*, Paris, 1886ff., and H. WAQUET, *Les sources de l'histoire religieuse de la France dans les archives départementales, communales, hospitalières et privées*, Paris, 1925.

26. LASTEYRIE, R. DE, A. VIDIER, and others. Bibliographie générale des travaux historiques et archéologiques publiés par les sociétés savantes de la France. Paris, 1888–1918.

26a. Bibliographie annuelle des travaux historiques et archéologiques publiés par les sociétés savantes de la France. Paris, 1906ff.

This supplements **26** for the literature published after 1900.

27. LELONG, J. Bibliothèque historique de la France, contenant le catalogue des ouvrages, imprimés et manuscrits, qui traitent de l'histoire de ce royaume ou qui y ont rapport. New edition, by FEVRET DE FONTETTE. 5 vols. Paris, 1768–78.

Still important for older books. Contents analyzed in A. FRANKLIN, no. **23**, 1–9.

27a. [HASKELL, D. C.] New York City Public Library. Provençal literature and language including the local history of southern France; a list of references in the New York Public Library. New York, 1925.

(*b*) GERMANY AND AUSTRIA

28. DAHLMANN-WAITZ. Quellenkunde der deutschen Geschichte. 8th edition by P. HERRE and many others. Leipzig, 1912. 1st edition by F. C. DAHLMANN, in 1830.

The most perfect of all bibliographies of national history. It covers both the medieval and the modern history of Germany and includes original sources and modern works. The comparative value of books is indicated to some extent by differences of type. It has a model index.

A survey of historical work in Germany during the period of the Great War is in K. L. HAMPE, *Mittelalterliche Geschichte*, Gotha, 1922. (Vol. VII of HÖNN, *Wissenschaftliche Forschungsberichte*.)

29. WATTENBACH, W. Deutschlands Geschichtsquellen im Mittelalter bis zur Mitte des dreizehnten Jahrhunderts. Berlin, 1858. 6th edition, 2 vols. Berlin, 1893–94. Vol. I in 7th edition by E. DÜMMLER. Stuttgart and Berlin, 1904.

30. LORENZ, O. Deutschlands Geschichtsquellen im Mittelalter seit der Mitte des dreizehnten Jahrhunderts. Berlin, 1870. 3rd edition, 2 vols., 1886–87.

These two model works of WATTENBACH and LORENZ supplement each other. They are not mere bibliographies of the original sources but are rather histories of medieval history writings which concern Germany. WATTENBACH is the best introduction to the *Monumenta Germaniae historica*, no. **978**.

31. VILDHAUT, H. Handbuch der Quellenkunde zur deutschen Geschichte. 2 vols. Arnsberg, 1898–1900. 2nd, revised edition. Werl, 1906, 1909.

Popularizes and supplements WATTENBACH and LORENZ, nos. **29** and **30**, and takes cognizance of the literature which appeared since the second edition of POTTHAST, no. **18**.

32. LOEWE, V. Bücherkunde der deutschen Geschichte: kritischer Wegweiser durch die neuere deutsche historische Literatur. Berlin, 1903. 4th edition. Altenburg, 1913.

The first edition, *Kritischer Wegweiser durch die neuere deutsche historische Literatur*, Berlin, 1900, appeared under the pseudonym "F. FÖRSTER."

32a. Jahresberichte für deutsche Geschichte. Edited by A. BRACKMANN and F. HARTUNG with the collaboration of V. LOEWE. Leipzig, 1927ff. Vol. I, 1925 (1927); vol. II, 1926 (1928); vol. III, 1927 (1929).

Note also *Jahresberichte der deutschen Geschichte*, edited by V. LOEWE and M. STIMMING, Breslau, 1920–25 (which **32a** supersedes) which covers materials published 1918–23.

33. JANSEN, M., and SCHMITZ-KALLENBERG, L. Historiographie und Quellen der deutschen Geschichte bis 1500. 2nd edition. Leipzig, 1914. (No. **331**, I:7.)

A book for students. Similar to VILDHAUT, no. **31**, but on a much smaller scale.

34. JACOB, K. Quellenkunde der deutschen Geschichte im Mittelalter [to 1400]. Leipzig, 1905. Vol. I, 3rd, revised and enlarged edition, Berlin and Leipzig, 1922, vol. II (1024–1250), 1926. (Sammlung Göschen, 279–80.)

Practically a short epitome of DAHLMANN-WAITZ, no. **28**, for schools.

35. CHARMATZ, R. Wegweiser durch die Literatur der österreichischen Geschichte. Stuttgart, 1913.

(*c*) ENGLAND AND IRELAND

36. GROSS, C. The sources and literature of English history from the earliest times to about 1485. New York and London, 1900. 2nd edition, revised and enlarged, 1915.

36a. HARDY, T. D. Descriptive catalogue of materials relating to the history of Great Britain and Ireland [to 1327]. Rolls Series. 3 vols. in 4 parts. London, 1862–71.

Convenient select bibliographies can be found in *History*, no. **185**.

36b. Kenney, J. F. The sources for the early history of Ireland: an introduction and guide. I. Ecclesiastical. New York, 1929.

A superior and indispensable aid for medievalists in many fields. Its broad scope and comprehensive character will invite scholars to await with keen anticipation the appearance of a complementary volume to cover "the Irish secular sources and such foreign records as do not relate chiefly to ecclesiastical affairs."

(*d*) Italy

37. Cipolla, C. Pubblicazioni sulla storia medioevale italiana. Venice, 1914.

37a. Pastorella, E. Indici per nome d'autore e per materie delle pubblicazioni sulla storia medioevale italiana (1899–1910) raccolte e recensite da Carlo Cipolla. Venice, 1916.

37b. Egidi, P. La storia medioevale. Rome, 1922.

Lists of works published from 1861–1921 covering the period from the middle of the 5th to the end of the 15th century.

38. Calvi, E. Biblioteca de bibliografia storica italiana. Rome, 1903. Supplement, 1907.

39. Lozzi, C. Biblioteca istorica della antica e nuova Italia, saggio di bibliografia analitico, comparato e critico. 2 vols. Imola, 1886.

40. Capasso, B. Le fonti della storia delle provincie napolitane dal 568 al 1500. Re-edited by E. O. Mastrjani. Naples, 1902.

41. Quellen und Forschungen aus italienischen Archiven und Bibliotheken. Issued by Preussisches historisches Institut in Rome. Rome, 1898ff.

Contains a yearly survey of new books on Italian history. See also H. Bresslau, no. **19.**

(*e*) Spain

42. Altamira, R. Historia de España, no. **628,** vol. IV (1914), 587–672.

This is a short bibliographical guide to the literature on Spanish history. See also Bresslau, no. **19,** pp. 450, 503–11. R. Altamira, *La enseñanza de la historia*, 2nd edition, Madrid, 1895, contains bibliographical matter of importance. For a description of the rich manuscript collections of Spain consult R. Beer, "Handschriftenschätze Spaniens," in *S.B.* Vienna Acad., 1891, 124ff. M. Menéndez y Pelayo was assigned the task of writing a bibliography of the history of Spain for the *Historia general de España*, no. **622,** but the book has not appeared.

See the important bibliographical notes, especially I, 42–50 in R. B. Merriman, *The rise of the Spanish empire in the old world and in the new*, no. **628a.**

42a. Ballester y Castell, R. Bibliografía de la historia de España; catálogo metódico y cronológico de las fuentes y obras principales relativas á la historia de España desde los orígenes hasta nuestros días. Gerona, 1921.

R. Konetzke, "Spanischer Literaturbericht," in *H.Z.*, CXXXVI (1927), 155–67, tells about the activities of the Centro de Estudios Históricos, Madrid, which has begun a Monumenta for Spain. It is to consist of four parts, Chronicles, Literary sources, Laws, Liturgical texts, and is devoted to the Latin texts of the middle ages. Two volumes in the first series appeared in 1918 and 1921.

This centro is also very active in editing and translating into Spanish the Mohammedan texts of medieval Spain. On page 158 Konetzke lists some of the recent work in this field.

42b. Sánchez, A. B. Fuentes de la historia española. Madrid, 1919.

42c. Foulché-Delbosc, R. Manuel de l'hispanisant. 2 vols. New York, 1920–26.

(*f*) Switzerland

43. Barth, H. Bibliographie der schweizer Geschichte enthaltend die selbständig erschienenen Druckwerke zur Geschichte der Schweiz. Vols. I–III, Basel, 1914–15. (Quellen zur schweizer Geschichte. Neue Folge, IV Abtlg., Handbücher.)

44. Burckhardt, F. Bibliographie der schweizer Geschichte. Jahrgang, 1913. Bern, 1915. (Beilage zu Bd. 12, N. F. des Anzeigers für schweizer Geschichte.)

(*g*) Belgium and Netherlands

45. Pirenne, H. Bibliographie de l'histoire de Belgique: catalogue méthodique et chronologique des sources et des ouvrages principaux relatifs à l'histoire de tous les Pays-Bas jusqu'en 1598 et à l'histoire de Belgique jusqu'en 1830. Ghent, 1893. 2nd edition, Brussels, 1902.

A third edition is being prepared.

Note H. Laurent, "Bulletin de bibliographie critique: le travail d'histoire du moyen âge en Belgique pendant la décade 1915–1925" in *M.A.*, 37ᵉ année (2ᵉ série, Vol. XXVII), 1926, and supplement for the period 1925–28, *ibid.* (XXX), 1929.

(*h*) Russia

46. Bestuschew, K. Quellen und Literatur zur russischen Geschichte von den ältesten Zeiten bis 1825. Translated into German by T. Schiemann. Mitau, 1876.

See Rambaud, no. **682**.

46a. Kerner, R. J. Slavic Europe; a selected bibliography in the western European languages, comprising history, languages, and literatures. Cambridge, 1918.

(*i*) BYZANTINE EMPIRE

46b. VASILIEV, A. A. History of the Byzantine Empire. 2 vols. Madison, 1928–30.

Chapter I. "A brief outline of works on Byzantine history," and the bibliographies at the end of each chapter are excellent guides.

(*j*) POLAND AND BOHEMIA

47. FINKEL, L. Bibliografia histori polskiej. 3 vols., in 7 parts. Crakow, 1891–1906. Supplement, 1914ff.

For Bohemia, see C. ZIBRT. *Bibliografie ceské historie*, 4 vols., Prague, 1900ff.

(*k*) SCANDINAVIA

48. SETTERWALL, N. K. Svensk historisk bibliografi, 1875–1900. Stockholm, 1907.

Supplemented by a yearly survey in a Supplement to the *Historisk Tidskrift*.

48a. AURIVILLIUS, P. F. Catalogus librorum impressorum bibliotheca regalis academiae upsaliensis. 2 vols. Uppsala, 1814.

48b. Bibliotheca danica. Edited by CHR. V. BRUNN. 4 vols. Copenhagen, 1877–1902.

A systematic account of the Danish literature from 1482 to 1830.

48c. Catalogus codicum latinorum medii aevi bibliothecae regiae hafniensis. Edited by ELLEN JÖRGENSEN. Copenhagen, 1926.

48d. ERICHSEN, B., and KRARUP, A. Dansk historisk bibliografi. 3 vols. Copenhagen, 1918–27. Well indexed.

48e. KLEMMING, G. E. Sveriges bibliografi, 1481–1892. 4 vols. Uppsala, 1889–92.

48f. NIELSEN, L. Dansk bibliografi, 1482–1550. Copenhagen, 1919.

48g. RUDBECK, G. Skrifter till Sveriges historia tryckta fôre år 1600. Uppsala, 1919. With index.

48h. WARMHOLTZ, C. G. Bibliotheca historica sueo-gothica, 15 vols. Stockholm, Uppsala, 1782–1817. Index volume by A. ANDERSON. Uppsala, Leipzig, 1889.

§ 7. Bibliographies of Various Subjects

(*a*) CHURCH

49. BRATKE, E. Wegweiser zur Quellen- und Literaturkunde der Kirchengeschichte: eine Anleitung zur planmässigen Auffindung der literarischen und monumentalen Quellen der Kirchengeschichte und ihrer Bearbeitungen. Gotha, 1890.

See the unfavorable review of it by C. MIRBT in *H.Z.*, LXV (1890), 117–20.

50. SMEDT, C. DE. Introductio generalis ad historiam ecclesiasticam critice tractandam. Ghent, 1876.

Still a serviceable elementary bibliography of ecclesiastical history. Beginners will find much additional material in the bibliographies in FLICK, no. **428.** See also J. F. HURST, *Literature of theology: a classified bibliography of theology and general religious literature*, New York, 1896.

51. HURTER, H. Nomenclator litterarius theologiae catholicae, theologos exhibens aetate, natione, disciplinis distinctos. 4 vols. 3rd edition. Innsbruck, 1903–10. 4th edition by F. PANGERL, Vienna, 1926ff.

Does for theological literature of the middle ages what POTTHAST, no. **18,** has done for chronicles and historical texts.

52. HÜBLER, B. Kirchenrechtsquellen. 4th edition. Berlin, 1902.

52a. CHIMINELLI, P. Bibliografia della storia della riforma religiosa in Italia. Rome, 1924.

Capitolo I. I precursori della riforma e l'inquisizione primitiva.

J. BURROW, librarian of the Day Missions Library of Yale University, is preparing a critical bibliography of the bibliographies of the Christian religion. He has collected 2500 titles. The critical work is complete only for the bibliographies of missions.

53. Bibliotheca hagiographica latina antiquae et mediae aetatis. 3 vols. Brussels, 1898–1911.

Supplements and completes the section "Vita" in POTTHAST, no. **18.** The best bibliography of hagiographical literature. See *Acta Sanctorum*, no. **963.**

54. Theologischer Jahresbericht. Freiburg, 1881–1913.

55. Archiv für Religionswissenchaft. Freiburg, 1898ff.

Publishes an annual Religionsgeschichtliche Bibliographie, 1917ff.

(*b*) PHILOSOPHY

56. Philosophisches Jahrbuch. Issued by the Görres-Gesellschaft. Fulda, 1888ff.

56a. BALDWIN, J. M. Dictionary of philosophy. Vol. III. Bibliography of philosophy. New York, 1905.

57. Die Philosophie der Gegenwart: eine internationale Jahresübersicht. Edited by A. RUGE. Heidelberg, 1910ff.

(*c*) Education

58. Historisch-pädagogischer Literaturbericht.

The *Bericht* for 1911 appeared as the 4th Beiheft of the *Zeitschrift für Geschichte der Erziehung und des Unterrichts*, Berlin, 1913.
See also *Pädagogischer Jahresbericht*, Leipzig, 1846ff.

59. Cubberley, E. P. Syllabus of lectures on the history of education, with selected bibliographies. New York, 1902.

Contains extensive bibliographies. Other similar syllabi are: P. Monroe, *Syllabus of a course of study on the history and principles of education*, New York, 1911; and W. J. Taylor, *A syllabus of the history of education*, Boston 1909.

(*d*) Law and Politics

60. Mühlbrecht, O. Wegweiser durch die neuere Literatur der Rechts- und Staatswissenschaften. 2nd edition. Berlin, 1893. Supplement, 1901.

See also *Uebersicht der gesammten staats- und rechtwissenschaftlichen Literatur*, edited by O. and H. Mühlbrecht, Berlin, 1869ff.

(*e*) War

61. Pohler, J. Bibliotheca historico-militaris: systematischer Übersicht der Erscheinungen aller Sprachen auf dem Gebiete der Geschichte der Kriege und Kriegswissenschaft seit Erfindung der Buchdruckerkunst bis 1880. 4 vols. Cassel, 1899.

(*f*) Jews

62. List of works in the New York Public Library relating to the history and condition of the Jews in various countries. New York Public Library, Bulletin XVII (1913).

(*g*) Geography

62a. Wright, J. K. Aids to geographical research: bibliographies and periodicals. New York, 1923.

CHAPTER II

BOOKS OF REFERENCE

§ 1. Miscellaneous Books of Reference

(a) Guide to Reference Books

63. Mudge, I. G. Guide to reference books. Chicago, 1929.

63a. Minto, J. Reference books: a classified and annotated guide to the principal works of reference. London, 1929.

(b) Historical Method

64. Bernheim, E. Lehrbuch der historischen Methode. 5th and 6th edition. Leipzig, 1908.

65. Langlois, C. V., and C. Seignobos. Introduction aux études historiques. Paris, 1899. 4th edition, Paris, 1909. Translated by G. G. Berry, Introduction to the study of history. London, 1898. Reprinted in a cheaper edition. London, 1912.

66. Wolf, G. Einführung in das Studium der neueren Geschichte. Berlin, 1910.

Contains much which interests the student of medieval history.

66a. Bauer, W. Einführung in das Studium der Geschichte. Tübingen, 1921.

67. Vincent, J. H. Historical research. New York, 1911.

Designed to be an introduction for beginners in historical research work in American universities. See also the article "History" by C. H. Haskins and H. E. Bourne in the *Cyclopedia of education*.

67a. Fling, F. M. The writing of history: an introduction to historical method. New Haven, 1920.

67b. Johnson, A. The historian and historical evidence. New York, 1926.

67c. Scott, E. History and historical problems. Oxford, 1925.

Advanced students of history will profit from a knowledge of the material presented in A. Morize, *Problems and methods of literary history, with special reference to modern French literature; a guide for graduate students*, Boston, 1922.

67d. Tardif, A. Notions élémentaires de critique historique. Paris, 1883.

67e. JOHNSON, C. The mechanical processes of the historian. London, 1922. (S.P.C.K. Helps, no. 50.)

67f. CRUMP, C. G. The logic of history. London, 1919. (*Ibid.*, no. 6.)

67g. CROCE, B. The theory and practice of history. New York, 1921.

67h. CRUMP, C. G. History and historical research. London, 1928.

67i. JUSSERAND, J. J., ABBOTT, W. C., COLBY, C. W., and BASSETT, J. S. The writing of history. New York, 1926.

67j. SHOTWELL, J. T. An introduction to the history of history. New York, 1921.

67k. BLACK, J. B. The art of history; a study of four great historians of the eighteenth century. London, 1926. (Voltaire, Hume, Robertson, Gibbon.)

67l. Histoire et historiens depuis cinquante ans; méthodes, organisation et résultats du travail historique de 1876 à 1926. 2 vols. Paris, 1927.

(*c*) CHRONOLOGICAL AND TABULAR AIDS

See no. **416.**

68. PLOETZ, C. Epitome of ancient, mediaeval and modern history. Translated from the German, and enlarged by W. H. TILLINGHAST. Revised under editorship of H. E. BARNES et al. 2nd edition. Boston, 1925.

69. HEILPRIN, L. The historical reference book: comprising a chronological table of universal history; a chronological dictionary of universal history; a biographical dictionary with geographical notes, for the use of students, teachers, and readers. 6th edition. New York, 1902.

70. HAYDN'S Dictionary of dates and universal information relating to all ages and nations. 25th edition. London, 1910.

See also E. F. SMITH, *A dictionary of dates*, London and New York, 1911 (Everyman's library).

71. LITTLE, C. E. Cyclopedia of classified dates. New York, 1900.

72. PUTNAM, G. P. Handbook of universal history: a series of chronological tables presenting in parallel columns a record of the more noteworthy events in the history of the world from the earliest times down to the present day. New York, 1928.

73. MORISON, M. Time-table of modern history, A.D. 400–1870. New York, 1901. 2nd edition. 1908.

74. NICHOL, J. Tables of European history, literature, science, and art, from A.D. 200 to 1909; and of American history, literature, and art. 5th edition. New York, 1909.

75. HASSALL, A. A handbook of European history, 476–1920, chronologically arranged. London, 1920.

76. The new Larned history for ready reference, reading, and research. The work of J. N. LARNED. Completely revised, enlarged and brought up to date under the supervision of the publishers, by D. E. SMITH, C. SEYMOUR, A. H. SHEARER, and D. C. KNOWLTON. 12 vols. Springfield, 1922–24.

(*d*) GUIDES TO HISTORICAL FICTION

77. BAKER, E. A. A guide to historical fiction. New edition, entirely rewritten and greatly simplified, with an index of 170 pages. London, 1914.

Note also HANNAH LOGASA, *Historical fiction suitable for junior and senior high schools*. Philadelphia, 1927. [Publications of the National Council for the Social Studies, No. 1] and, especially, C. H. FIRTH, "Historical novels," *Historical Association Leaflets*, no. 51, March, 1922.

78. NIELD, J. A guide to the best historical novels and tales. London, 1902. Latest edition, 1929.

79. BUCKLEY, J. A., and WILLIAMS, W. T. A guide to British historical fiction. London, 1912.

(*e*) WORDS AND EXPRESSIONS FAMOUS IN HISTORY

80. BÜCHMANN, G. Geflügelte Worte. 24th edition. Berlin, 1910.

81. HERTSLET, W. L. Der Treppenwitz der Weltgeschichte: geschichtliche Irrtümer, Entstellungen und Erfindungen. 8th edition. Berlin, 1912.

82. FOURNIER, E. L'esprit dans l'histoire: recherches et curiosités sur les mots historiques. Paris, 1857.

(*f*) GUIDES TO THE LEARNED WORLD

83. Minerva: Jahrbuch der gelehrten Welt. Strasburg, 1890ff.

Minerva-Zeitschrift, Berlin, 1924ff.

84. Minerva: Handbuch der gelehrten Welt. Vol. I. Die Universitäten und Hochschulen, etc.: ihre Geschichte und Organisation. Strasburg, 1911. Continued on an enlarged scale by *Minerva-Handbücher*. Berlin, 1927ff.

85. Index generalis: annuaire général des universités. Paris, 1919ff.

85a. Progress of medieval studies in the United States of America. J. F. WILLARD, editor. Boulder, Colo., 1923ff.

An annual bulletin which is of great service to all medievalists anxious to keep abreast of various undertakings in progress. Contains useful lists of medievalists in the United States, of their writings, and of doctoral dissertations in preparation.

(*g*) DICTIONARY OF NAMES

86. The century cyclopedia of names: a pronouncing and etymological dictionary of names in geography, biography, mythology, history, ethnology, art, archaeology, fiction, etc. Edited by B. E. SMITH. Revised and enlarged edition. New York, 1911.

(*h*) BOOK REVIEWS AND DIGESTS

87. Bibliographie der deutschen Rezensionen, mit Einschluss von Referaten und Selbstanzeigen. Supplement zur Bibliographie der deutschen Zeitschriftenliteratur. Leipzig, 1900ff. (Internationale Bibliographie der Zeitschriftenliteratur, Abteilung C.)

Two thousand to three thousand periodicals are scoured. Since 1912 the title is *Bibliographie der Rezensionen*, and each volume is published in two parts: 1, German periodicals; 2, periodicals in other languages.

88. Book review digest. White Plains, 1905ff. Vol. I is entitled, Cumulative book review digest.

Covers about fifty leading English and American periodicals. Gives extracts from reviews. The sign + indicates favorable comment; —, unfavorable comment.

88a. Social science abstracts. Menasha, Wisc., 1929ff.

§ 2. Biographical Dictionaries

89. Dictionary of national biography. Edited by L. STEPHEN and S. LEE. 63 vols. and 3 supplementary vols. London, 1885–1901. 2nd edition, 22 vols., 1908–09. 2nd Supplement, 1912; 3rd Supplement, 1912–21, 1927.

A model work of its kind. Confined to English biography, but that includes many men who made a reputation upon the continent in the middle ages, e.g., Roger Bacon. It contains signed articles with good bibliographies.

89a. Dictionary of American biography. Edited by A. JOHNSON. New York, 1928ff.

90. Allgemeine deutsche Biographie. 55 vols. Leipzig, 1875–1910. Vols. XLVII–LV are supplements.

Described by R. v. LILIENCRON, in *Götting. Gelehrten Anzeigen* (1898), 160, 655ff.

90a. Deutsches biographisches Jahrbuch. Stuttgart, 1925ff.

91. Biographisches Lexikon des Kaiserthums Österreich. Edited by C. v. WURZBACH. 60 vols. Vienna, 1856–91.

92. Biographie nationale, publiée par l'académie royale de Belgique. Brussels, 1866ff.

92a. Dictionnaire historique et biographique de la Suisse. Neuchâtel, 1921ff.

93. Biographie universelle. Edited by a society of literary men. 52 vols. with supplements. Paris, 1811–62. New edition, 45 vols. Paris, 1854–65.

Until **93a** is completed, this general biography must serve in the place of a national biography for France. See also the French encyclopedias, nos. **98–99**, for names.

93a. Dictionnaire de biographie française. Edited by J. BALTEAU, A. RASTOUL, and M. PRÉVOST. Paris, 1929ff.

The first fascicule appeared in May, 1929.

93b. Biografiskt Lexikon över namnkunniga svenska män. 10 vols. Uppsala, 1844ff. Örebro, 1861ff. Parts 5–8 revised by K. F. WERNER, Stockholm, 1875–76. New edition of parts 7–10. Edited by E. TEGNÉR. Stockholm, 1875–92.

93c. Dansk Biografisk Lexikon. Ed. by C. F. BRICKA. Copenhagen, 1888–1904.

93d. GEETE, R. Fornsvensk Bibliografi. Förteckning över Sveriges medeltida bokskatt på modersmålet. Stockholm, 1903, pp. 433. Supplement volume. Stockholm, 1919.

94. SMITH, W., and WACE, H. Dictionary of Christian biography, literature, sects, and doctrines. 4 vols. London and Boston, 1877–87.

Extends to the time of Charlemagne. A revised, but abridged, edition of the above is H. WACE and W. C. PIERCY, *A dictionary of Christian biography and literature to the end of the sixth century* A.D., London and Boston, 1911. This new edition does not supersede the old, which must still be consulted for the more extended articles and for all material falling in the seventh and eighth centuries.

95. Who's who: an annual biographical dictionary. London, 1848ff.

Students of medieval history have occasion to consult this and similar manuals when they desire information about living authors of books on the middle ages. For America, see *Who's who in America: a biographical dictionary of notable living men and women of the United States*, Chicago, 1899ff. For France, *Qui êtes-vous? Annuaire des contemporains*, Paris, 1908ff. For Germany, *Wer ist's?*, Leipzig, 1904ff.; *Deutsche Literaturkalender*, edited by J. KÜRSCHNER, Leipzig, 1878ff.; and *Biographisches Jahrbuch und deutscher Nekrolog*, edited by A. BETTELHEIM, Berlin, 1898ff. *Vem är det*, Stockholm, 1912ff. *Kraks blaa bog*, Copenhagen, 1928. *Catholic who's who and year book*, London, 1908ff. A. KEITNER (ed.), *Menschen und Menschenwerke: Men of today and their work: Hommes et oeuvres du temps présent.* Vol. I, Vienna, 1924. For further means of finding modern authors see *Centralblatt für Bibliothekswesen*, XII (1896), 115ff.

§ 3. Encyclopaedias

(*a*) GENERAL ENCYCLOPAEDIAS

96. Encyclopaedia Britannica: a new survey of universal knowledge. 14th edition, 24 vols. London and New York, 1929.

Vol. 24 consists of a very important index. Most of the articles are signed and some contain good bibliographies.

97. New international encyclopaedia. 2nd edition. 24 vols. New York, 1914–16. Supplements, 2 vols., 1925; 2 vols., 1930.

New international year book, New York, 1917 to date.

97a. The Encyclopedia Americana. 30 vols. New York, 1918–20.

American annual, New York, 1923ff.

98. La grande encyclopédie: inventaire raisonné des sciences, des lettres et des arts, par une société de savants et de gens de lettres. 31 vols. Paris, 1885–1903.

A very serviceable work of reference for students of history. It was not a mere publisher's venture, but was the work of a learned society headed by the famous chemist BERTHELOT. Subject entries are more numerous than in *Ency. Brit.* Many articles are signed. Its biographical articles are especially good and supplement no. **93.**

99. LAROUSSE grand dictionnaire universel du XIXe siècle. 17 vols. Paris, 1866–90. Smaller, not an abridged, edition by C. AUGÉ, Nouveau Larousse illustré, 7 vols. Paris, 1898–1904. Supplement, 1907.

A dictionary and an encyclopaedia combined. The very unique and compact *Petit Larousse illustré*, Paris, 1906, has been simmered down until it is little more than an ordinary dictionary.

99a. LAROUSSE du XXe siècle en six volumes. Paris, 1928ff. Vol. I has appeared.

100. Allgemeine Encyklopädie der Wissenschaften und Künste. Founded by J. S. ERSCH and J. G. GRUBER. 170 vols. Berlin, 1818–90.

Still incomplete. The most voluminous undertaking of its kind, addressed exclusively to the world of scholars.

101. BROCKHAUS Konversations-Lexikon: allgemeine deutsche Realencyklopädie. 14th edition. 16 vols. Leipzig, 1892–95. Vol. 17 is a supplement, 1897. 15th edition in progress, 1928ff.

Brockhaus kleines Konversations-Lexikon, 4 vols., Leipzig, 1921–23.

102. MEYERS Konversations-Lexikon: ein Nachschlagewerk des allgemeinen Wissens. 24 vols. 6th edition, revised and enlarged. Leipzig, 1902–13. 7th edition. 12 vols. Leipzig, 1924–30.

These two German works are similar in character and of about equal value to students of history. Perhaps MEYERS is slightly more serviceable on account of its excellent bibliographies and fine maps. Articles are not signed.

102a. Nordisk Familjebok, Konversationslexikon och Realencyklopedi. 38 vols. including supplement. Stockholm, 1904–26.

102b. Salmonsen Konversations leksikon. Second edition. 25 vols. Copenhagen, 1915–28.

103. Enciclopedia universal ilustrada Europeo-Americana. 67 vols. in 69. Barcelona, 1905ff.

103a. Lexicon Vallardi: Enciclopedia universale illustrate. Grande dizionario geografico, storico, artistico, letterario, politico, militare, tecnico, commérciali, industriale, agronomico, ecc. 10 vols. Milan [1887–98].

103b. Enciclopedia italiana di scienze, lettere ed arti, pubblicata sotto l'alto patronato di S. M. il Re d'Italia. Instituto Giovanni Treccani [Milan] 1929ff.

(*b*) History of the Church and Religion

104. Catholic encyclopedia: an international work of reference on the constitution, doctrine, discipline, and history of the Catholic Church. 15 vols. and an index. New York, 1908–14. Supplement, 1922.

Designed to serve as a general encyclopaedia with special emphasis on the part played by Catholics in the advancement of learning. Thus everything even remotely connected with the church is included. Scholars from all parts of the world have contributed. Articles are signed. It is handsomely illustrated. There are some excellent bibliographies appended to articles (e.g., Roger Bacon).

105. Encyclopaedia of religion and ethics. Edited by J. Hastings and others. 12 vols. and an index, 1927. Edinburgh and New York, 1908–27.

105a. A dictionary of religion and ethics. Edited by S. Mathews and G. B. Smith, New York, 1921.

106. The new Schaff-Herzog encyclopedia of religious knowledge. Based on the third edition of the Realencyklopädie founded by J. J. Herzog and edited by A. Hauck. Edited by S. M. Jackson and others. 12 vols. New York and London, 1908–12.

See no. **112.**

107. Encyclopédie des sciences religieuses.

Composed of the following separate works: 1. *Dictionnaire d'archéologie chrétienne*, no. **111**; 2. *Dictionnaire d'histoire et de géographie ecclésiastique*, by Baudrillart, no. **110**; 3. *Dictionnaire de théologie catholique* by Vacant and Mangenot, no. **109**; 4. *Dictionnaire de la bible*, by F. Vigouroux; 5 vols. Paris, 1907–12, and 5. *Dictionnaire du droit canonique*. When completed, this will be the largest work of reference on religion in any language. It incorporates the highest achievements of Roman Catholic scholarship in France.

108. Smith, W., and Cheetham, S. Dictionary of Christian antiquities. 2 vols. London, 1876–80.

Covers the period to the time of Charlemagne. Now being superseded by *Dictionnaire d'archéologie chrétienne*, no. **111.** See also J. S. Bumpus, *Dictionary of ecclesiastical terms*, Philadelphia, 1910.

Vírendra Vandyopádhyáya (Biren Bonerjea). *A dictionary of superstitions and mythology*, London, 1927.

109. Dictionnaire de théologie catholique, contenant l'exposé des doctrines de la théologie catholique, leurs preuves et leur histoire. Edited by A. VACANT and E. MANGENOT. Paris, 1909ff.

A very ambitious undertaking on a vast scale, distinctly Roman Catholic in tone. Good bibliographies, with special emphasis on the sources. Unfortunately the type is excessively small. Articles are signed.

110. Dictionnaire d'histoire et de géographie ecclésiastique. Edited by A. BAUDRILLART and others. Paris, 1912ff.

111. Dictionnaire d'archéologie chrétienne et de liturgie. Edited by F. CABROL and H. LECLERCQ. Paris, 1907ff.

112. Realencyklopädie für protestantische Theologie und Kirche, begründet von J. J. HERZOG. 3rd edition, edited by A. HAUCK. 24 vols. Leipzig, 1896–1913.

As its name implies, it is decidedly Protestant in tone. The articles dealing with history are particularly good. See no. **106.**

113. Kirchenlexikon oder Encyklopädie der katholischen Theologie. Edited by H. J. WETZER and B. WELTE. 12 vols. Freiburg-i-B, 1847–60. 2nd edition by J. HERGENRÖTHER and F. KAULEN, 13 vols., Freiburg, 1882–1903. French translation, with modifications by J. GOSCHLER, 26 vols., 1869.

Distinctly Roman Catholic in tone. A well-balanced work.

114. MORONI, G. Dizionario di erudizione storico-ecclesiastica da S. Pietro ai nostri giorni. 103 vols. Venice, 1840–61. Six index vols., 1878–79.

(*c*) POLITICAL ECONOMY

115. Palgrave's dictionary of political economy. Edited by H. HIGGS. 3 vols. London, 1925.

115a. Encyclopaedia of the social sciences. Edited by E. R. A. SELIGMAN and A. JOHNSON. New York, 1930ff.

116. Handwörterbuch der Staatswissenschaften. Edited by J. CONRAD and others. 4th edition. 8 vols. in 9. 1923–29.

See also *Wörterbuch der Volkswirtschaft*, edited by L. ELSTER, 2 vols., Jena, 1898; 3rd edition, 1911.

(*d*) EDUCATION

117. A cyclopedia of education. Edited by P. MONROE. 4 vols. New York, 1911–13.

117a. An encyclopaedia and dictionary of education. 4 vols. London, 1921–22. Edited by F. WATSON.

ALBRIGHT COLLEGE LIBRARY 146490

118. SCHMID, K. A. Enzyklopädie des gesammten Erziehungs- und Unterrichtswesens. 2nd edition by W. SCHRADER. 10 vols. Gotha and Leipzig, 1876–87.

See also *Enzyklopädisches Handbuch der Pädagogik*, edited by W. REIN. 2nd edition, 9 vols., Langensalza, 1902–09.

(*e*) JEWS

119. Jewish encyclopaedia: a descriptive record of the history, religion, literature, and customs of the Jewish people. 12 vols. New York, 1901–06.

(*f*) ISLAM

120. The encyclopaedia of Islam. Edited by M. T. HOUTSMA and others. London, 1913ff.

See also T. P. HUGHES, *A dictionary of Islam*, London, 1885; 2nd edition, 1896.

§ 4. Atlases and Other Geographical Aids

(*a*) GENERAL HISTORICAL ATLASES

121. SHEPHERD, W. R. Historical atlas. New York, Henry Holt, 1911. Seventh edition, revised and enlarged, 1929.

The best general atlas for the use of students in schools and undergraduates in college. R. MUIR, *Hammond's new historical atlas for students*, 2nd edition, New York, 1915, and E. W. DOW, *Atlas of European history*, New York, 1907, are fair substitutes. A very cheap *Atlas of historical geography: Europe*, New York, 1910, is published in the *Everyman's library series*. (See also the volumes on Asia and Africa.) The appearance of these recent atlases in English, with good indexes, makes it unnecessary for American students to refer to such popular German atlases as F. W. PUTZGER, *Historischer Schulatlas*, American edition, 1903; 35th edition, 1911; *Meyers historischer Handatlas*, Leipzig, 1911 (which, however, has a unique map for the Normans in Europe); and J. PERTHES, *Geschichts-Atlas*, Gotha, 1898; 2nd edition, 1904. S. R. GARDINER, *A school atlas of English history*, London, 1902. Putnam's historical atlas, London and New York, 1911. Sixth edition, revised and greatly enlarged, 1927, by R. MUIR, G. PHILIP, and R. M. McELROY.

Attention is called to the "Enquête sur les atlas historiques en préparation et sur la documentation cartographique" in *Bulletin of the international committee of historical sciences*, I, Pt. IV. No. 4, March, 1928, 497–523.

122. POOLE, R. L. Historical atlas of modern Europe from the decline of the Roman empire. Oxford, 1902.

123. DROYSEN, G. Allgemeiner historischer Handatlas. Leipzig, 1886.

124. SCHRADER, F. Atlas de géographie historique. Paris, 1896. New edition, Paris, 1907.

125. SPRUNER, K. VON, and MENKE, T. Handatlas für die Geschichte des Mittelalters und der neueren Zeit. 3rd edition, Gotha, 1880.

126. VIDAL DE LA BLACHE, P. Atlas générale: histoire et géographie. Paris, 1897. New edition, Paris, 1913.

(*b*) ATLASES FOR CHURCH HISTORY

127. HEUSSI, K., and MULERT, H. Atlas zur Kirchengeschichte. Tübingen, 1905.

128. MCCLURE, E. Historical church atlas. London, 1897.

(*c*) ATLASES FOR THE HISTORY OF MEDIEVAL FRANCE AND BELGIUM

129. LONGNON, A. Atlas historique de la France. Plates I–XV [to 1380 A.D.]. Paris, 1885–89.

The work was left incomplete. A valuable descriptive text is published under a separate cover.

129a. ESSEN, L. VAN DER, I. MAURY and F. L. GANSHOF, Atlas de géographie historique de la Belgique. Brussels and Paris, 1919ff.

(*d*) DICTIONARIES OF GEOGRAPHICAL NAMES

See the important section devoted to place-names, ch. III, § 9.

130. GRAESSE, J. G. T. Orbis latinus: oder Verzeichniss der lateinischen Benennungen der bekanntesten Städte . . . Meere, Seen, etc., in allen Teilen der Erde nebst einem deutschlateinischen Register. Dresden, 1861. New, revised, edition, 1909.

131. Dictionnaire de géographie ancienne et moderne à l'usage du libraire et de l'amateur de livres. Par un bibliophile [P. DESCHAMPS]. Paris, 1870.

For Gaul, up to the tenth century, there are excellent tables of Latin geographical names with their modern French equivalents in A. LONGNON, *Atlas historique de la France, Texte explicatif*, no. **129**.

132. EGLI, J. Nomina geographica: Sprach- und Sacherklärung von 42,000 geographischen Namen aller Erdräume. Leipzig, 1872. 2nd edition. Leipzig, 1893.

133. EGLI, J. Geschichte der geographischen Namenkunde. Leipzig, 1886.

134. OESTERLEY, H. Historisch-geographisches Wörterbuch des deutschen Mittelalters. 2 vols. Gotha, 1883.

135. BISCHOFF, H. T., and MÖLLER, J. H. Vergleichendes Wörterbuch der alten, mittleren, und neuen Geographie. Gotha, 1892.

136. GRÖHLER, H. Ueber Ursprung und Bedeutung der französischen Ortsnamen. Part I: Ligurische, iberische, phönizische, griechische, gallische, lateinische Namen. Heidelberg, 1913.

136a. Quicherat, J. De la formation française des anciens noms de lieu: traité pratique suivi de remarques sur les noms de lieu fournis par divers documents. Paris, 1867.

137. Chevin, l'abbé. Dictionnaire latin-français des noms propres de lieux ayant une certaine notoriété, principalement au point de vue ecclésiastique et monastique. Paris [1897].

138. Dictionnaire topographique de la France. Vols. I–XXVII. Paris, 1896–1912.

138a. Seyn, E. de. Dictionnaire historique et géographique des communes belges. 2 vols. Brussels, 1924–26.

(*e*) Historical Geographies

139. Freeman, E. A. The historical geography of Europe. 2 vols. London, 1881. 3rd edition, by J. B. Bury. London, 1903.

To be used in connection with his *Atlas of the historical geography of Europe*, 3rd edition, London, 1903.

E. W. Dann, *Historical geography on a regional basis: Europe*, London, 1908; K. Johnston, *A sketch of historical geography*, London, 1909; J. M. Thompson, *An historical geography of Europe (800–1789)*, Oxford, 1929, and J. K. Wright, *The geographical basis of European history*, New York, 1928. See also no. **110.**

140. Himly, A. Histoire de la formation territoriale des états de l'Europe centrale. 2 vols. Paris, 1876. 2nd edition, 1894.

141. Kretschmer, K. Historische Geographie von Mitteleuropa. Munich and Berlin, 1904. (Part IV of no. **330.**)

142. Kötzschke, R. Quellen und Grundbegriffe der historischen Geographie Deutschlands und seiner Nachbarländer. Leipzig and Berlin, 1906. In no. **331,** I, part II, 397–449.

A good short account of ground covered in Kretschmer, no. **141.**

143. Götz, W. Historische Geographie. Leipzig, 1904. (In *Die Erdkunde*, XIX.)

144. Hofmann, A. v. Das Land Italien und seine Geschichte: eine historisch-topographische Darstellung. Stuttgart, 1922.

145. Knüll, B. Historische Geographie Deutschlands im Mittelalter. Breslau, 1903.

146. Vidal de la Blache, P. Tableau de la géographie de la France. Vol. I. part I, of Histoire de France, no. **508.** Paris, 1908. New edition, illustrated, 1908.

§ 5 Historical Periodicals

147. Jastrow, J. Handbuch zu Literaturberichten. Berlin, 1891.

See pp. 177ff. for a list of periodicals pertaining to history. See also no. **13.** Stein, no. **1,** gives a list of historical societies and periodicals, pp. 697–708.

147a. Bulletin of the international committee of historical sciences. Paris, 1926ff.

(*a*) General Historical Periodicals

148. American historical review. New York, 1895ff. Index, vols. I–X, 1905; vols. XI–XX, 1915; vols. XXI–XXX, 1925.

149. English historical review. London, 1886ff. Index for vols. I–XX, 1906; vols. XXI–XXX, 1916.

149a. Bulletin of the institute of historical research. London, 1923ff.

149b. Bulletin of the John Rylands library. Manchester, 1903ff.

149c. Scottish historical review. Glasgow, 1903–28. No longer published.

149d. Economic history review. London, 1927ff.

149e. Journal of economic and business history. Cambridge, 1929ff.

149f. Catholic historical review. Washington, 1915ff.

150. Historische Zeitschrift. Munich, 1859ff. Index, vols. I–LVI, 1888; LVII–XCVI, 1906; XCVII–CXXX, 1924.

151. Historische Vierteljahrschrift. Freiburg, 1898ff.

A continuation of the *Deutsche Zeitschrift für Geschichtswissenschaft*, 1889–98. This continued the older and valuable "Bibliotheca historica" under the title "Bibliographie zur deutschen Geschichte," which is now continued in the *Hist. Vierteljahrschrift.* The *H.Z.* supplements the list in the *Hist. Vierteljahrschrift* mainly because it takes cognizance of a good deal of periodical literature, and because it reviews many books sent to it directly from different countries.

152. Historisches Jahrbuch. Munich, 1880ff.

Organ of the Roman Catholic Görresgesellschaft. It contains excellent reviews, and pays particular attention to eastern Europe. Index, vols. I–XXXIV, 1914.

153. Mitteilungen aus der historischen Literatur. Herausgegeben von der historischen Gesellschaft zu Berlin, 1873ff. Index, vols. I–XX (in XX); XXI–XXX (in XXX); XXXI–XL (in XL).

154. Historisches Literaturblatt: kritisch-bibliographisches Organ für Geschichte und ihre Hilfswissenschaften. 1898ff.

154a. Deutsche Vierteljahrschrift für Literaturwissenschaft und Geistesgeschichte. Halle, 1923ff.

155. Korrespondenzblatt des Gesamtvereins der deutschen Geschichts- und Altertumsvereine. Berlin, 1853ff.

156. Revue historique. Paris, 1876ff. Index vols. I–XIV, 1881; XV–XXIX, 1887; XXX–XLIV, 1891; XLV–LIX, 1896; LX–LXXIV, 1901; LXXV–LXXXIX, 1906; XC–CV, 1911; CVI–CXXXVI, 1922; CXXXVII–CLI, 1926 (1928).

Current issues frequently contain bibliographical essays of importance. See also the *Revue des études historiques*, publiée par la Société des études historiques, Paris, 1834ff; this title was adopted in 1899; it had varied considerably between 1834 and 1899.

157. Revue des questions historiques. Paris, 1866ff. Index for vols. I–XX, 1887; XXI–XL, 1889; XLI–LX, 1897; LXI–LXXX, 1906.

Pays exceptional attention to historical literature on Scandinavia and Russia.

158. Revue de synthèse historique. Paris, 1900ff. Index for the vols. covering the years 1900–1910, Paris, 1912.

158a. Revue belge de philologie et d'histoire. Brussels, 1922ff.

159. Revue critique d'histoire et de littérature. Paris, 1866ff. Index for the vols. covering the years 1866–90 in 1894.

Established "to enforce respect for method, to execute justice upon bad books, to check misdirected and superfluous work."

160. Archivio storico italiano. Florence, 1842ff. 5 series.

A vast collection of sources, essays, reviews, with special reference to Italian history. Indexes, first series, 1857; new series and third series, 1855–1872, 1874; fourth series, 1891; fifth series, 1900.

A list of 88 periodicals useful for workers in the field of Italian history is in *Bulletin of the international committee of historical sciences*, vol. I, part II, June, 1927, 238–46.

161. Rivista storica italiana. Turin, 1884ff. Index 1884–1901. 2 vols., 1904.

A *Nuova rivista storica*, edited by A. ANZILOTTI and others, was begun in Milan, January, 1917.

162. Bullettino dell' Istituto storico italiano. Rome, 1886ff.

163. Revista de archivos, bibliotecas y museos. Madrid, 1871–78; 1881–82; 3rd series, 1897ff. Index by R. GÓMEZ VILLAFRANCA. 1911.

Much broader in scope than its title would indicate. Covers all phases of Spanish history and the auxiliary studies, and contains the best current bibliographies of historical work in Spain.

163a. Revue hispanique. Paris, 1894ff.

(*b*) PERIODICALS DEVOTED ESPECIALLY TO MEDIEVAL HISTORY

164. Bibliothèque de l'Ecole des Chartes: revue d'érudition consacrée spécialement à l'étude du moyen âge. Paris, 1839ff. Indexes, 1839–49, Paris, 1849; 1870–79, Paris, 1888; 1880–89 [n. d.]; 1890–99 [n. d.]; 1900–09, Paris, 1911.

The contents of the first thirty-six volumes are analyzed in A. FRANKLIN, *Les sources de l'histoire de France*, no. **23**, 399–429. In the bibliographies, which are very full, special attention is given to palaeography and diplomatics. See *Livret de l'Ecole des Chartes*, 1901–13: *supplément au Livret publié en* 1902, Paris, 1913. See also M. PROU, "Nos grandes écoles: l'Ecole des Chartes" in *Revue des deux mondes*, XXXVII (1927), 372–96.

164a. Speculum: a journal of mediaeval studies. Cambridge, Mass., 1926ff.

164b. Aarböger for Nordisk Oldkyndighed og Historie. Published by Det Konglige Nordiske Oldskrift-Selskab. Copenhagen, 1866ff.

164c. Fornvännen. Published by K. Vitterhetshistorie och Antikvitets Akademien. Stockholm, 1906ff. A continuation of Svenska Fornminnesföreningens Tidskrift. Stockholm, 1871-1905.

164d. Historisk Tidsskrift. Published by the Danish Historical Society. Edited by E. MOLBECH, N. L. WESTERGAARD, E. HOLM, C. F. BRICKA, J. A. FRIDERICIA, and ELLEN JÖRGENSEN. 9 Raekke with 6 vols. in each Raekke. Copenhagen, 1840ff.

164e. Historisk Tidsskrift. Published by the Norwegian Historical Society. Christiania, 1870ff.

Contains an annual bibliography of Norwegian history.

164f. Historisk Tidskrift. Published by the Swedish Historical Society. Edited by E. HILDEBRAND, T. HÖJER, and S. TUNBERG. 49 vols. Stockholm, 1881ff.

165. Le moyen âge: revue d'histoire et de philologie. Paris, 1888ff.

Vol. VIII has bound with it: A. VIDIER, "Répertoire méthodique du moyen âge français . . . année 1895." The *Répertoire* for 1894 forms a regular part of this volume.

166. Mitteilungen des österreichischen Instituts für Geschichtsforschung. Innsbruck, etc., 1880ff.

Appeared formerly as Mitteilungen des Instituts für österreichische Geschichtsforschung.

Especially devoted to the middle ages and to the auxiliary sciences.

167. Neues Archiv der Gesellschaft für ältere deutsche Geschichtskunde. Hannover, 1876ff. A continuation of Archiv der Gesellschaft, etc., 12 vols., Hannover, 1824-74.

Reports on progress of work in connection with the *Monumenta Germaniae historica*, no. **978**.

168. Archivio Muratoriano. Città di Castello, 1904ff.

Supplements no. **988.**

(*c*) History of Culture and Literature

169. Archiv für Kulturgeschichte. Edited by G. Steinhausen. Berlin, 1902ff.

Follows the *Zeitschrift für Kulturgeschichte*, 1894–1901. For other predecessors, see Dahlmann-Waitz, no. **28,** no. 1693.

169a. Isis: international review devoted to the history of science and civilization. Brussels, 1913ff.

169b. Modern Language Association of America. Publications. (*P.M. L.A.*) 1884ff.

This periodical, in addition to frequent studies in the medieval field, has an "Annual American bibliography." The bibliography for 1928 appeared in the issue for March, 1929.

170. Archiv für Literatur- und Kirchengeschichte des Mittelalters. Edited by H. Denifle and F. Ehrle. Vols. I–VII. Berlin, 1885–1900.

171. Revue de l'histoire littéraire de la France. Paris, 1894ff.

A periodical which reports on work done in connection with no. **803.**

172. Bulletin critique de littérature, d'histoire et de philologie. 1880ff.

173. Studi medievali. Edited by F. Novati and R. Renier, Turin, 1904ff.

Was suspended during war. A new series began in 1928, edited by V. Crescini, etc.

173a. Nuovi studi medievali. Bologna, 1923ff.

Dedicated primarily to medieval Latin language and literature.

(*d*) Byzantine Empire and Near East

174. Byzantinische Zeitschrift. Founded by K. Krumbacher. Leipzig, 1892ff. Index of vols. I–XII, 1909.

Publication was suspended 1914–Aug. 1919, 1920–24. Issues now appear at regular intervals.

174a. Byzantion: revue internationale des études byzantines. Paris, 1924ff.

174b. Byzantinisch-neugriechische Jahrbücher: internationales wissenschaftliches Organ. Berlin, 1920ff.

175. Vizantijskij vremennik [Byzantine annals]. Published by the Russian Academy of Sciences. 1894–1923 (with interruption during the later years of publication).

Continued by *Vizantijskoe obozrienie* [*Byzantine review*], 1915ff. Contains articles, reviews, and texts. The new review publishes articles in Russian, French, English, Latin, and Greek, but not in German.

See A. A. Vasiliev, *Byzantine empire*, I, 51–54 for an excellent description of periodical literature available for Byzantine studies.

175a. Zeitschrift für osteuropäische Geschichte. Berlin, 1911ff.

175b. Slavonic review: a survey of Slavonic peoples, their history, economics, philology and literature. London, 1922ff.

Note also *Le monde slave*, Paris, 1917ff. and *Revue des études slaves*, Paris, 1921ff.

(*e*) Church History

176. Zeitschrift für Kirchengeschichte. Edited by T. Brieger and B. Bess. Gotha, 1877ff. See vols. XXVI–XXX (1905–09) for a bibliography of church history.

176a. Archief voor kerkelijke geschiedenis, inzonderheid van Nederland. 20 vols. Leyden, 1829–49. Vols. 12–20 also as N. S. Vols. 1–9 with added title page: Nederlandsch archief voor kerkelijke geschiedenis. Continued as Nieuw archief voor kerkelijke geschiedenis.

177. Analecta Bollandiana. Edited by C. de Smedt, etc. Paris, etc., 1882ff.

Reports on progress of work in connection with the *Acta sanctorum*, no. **963**.

178. Revue d'histoire ecclésiastique. Edited by A. Cauchie. Louvain, 1900ff. Bibliography, beginning with vol. V (1904). Index to vols. I–XXII, Louvain, 1928.

178a. Recherches de théologie ancienne et médiévale. Louvain, 1929ff.

178b. Oriens christianus. Vols. 1–8. Rome, 1901–11. New series, 1911ff.

179. Römische Quartalschrift für christliche Altertumskunde und für Kulturgeschichte. Rome, 1887ff.

180. Revue de l'histoire des religions. Paris, 1880ff.

180a. Archivum franciscanum historicum. Quaracchi, 1908ff.

180b. Revue d'histoire franciscaine. Paris, 1924ff.

180c. Revue d'histoire de l'église de France. Paris, 1910ff.

180d. Ricerche religiose. Rome, 1925.

(*f*) History of Philosophy

181. Archiv für Geschichte der Philosophie. Edited by L. Stein. Berlin, 1888ff.

As an appendix; *Jahresbericht über sämmtliche Erscheinungen auf dem Gebiete der Geschichte der Philosophie.*

181a. Revue d'histoire de la philosophie. Paris, 1927ff.

(*g*) History of Education

182. Mitteilungen der Gesellschaft für deutsche Erziehungs- und Schulgeschichte. Founded by K. Kehrbach. Berlin, 1891ff. Continued as Zeitschrift für Geschichte der Erziehung und des Unterrichts. Berlin, 1911ff. Includes Beihefte, which contain Historisch-pädagogische Literaturberichte in nos. **15, 17, 19, 21.** Berlin, 1906ff.

(*h*) History of Law

183. Zeitschrift der Savigny-Stiftung für Rechtsgeschichte. 3 parts: Germanic, canon, and Romanic Law. Weimar, 1880ff.

From 1861–80 it was published under the title: *Zeitschrift für Rechtsgeschichte.*

(*i*) Periodicals for Teachers of History

184. Historical outlook. Philadelphia, 1918ff.

From 1909–18 this journal appeared as *History teachers' magazine.*

185. History. London, 1912–16.

Since April, 1916, the organ of the Historical association [England]. A new series began with this number under the title *The quarterly journal of the Historical association*, new series, no. 1, April, 1916. The new journal is devoted chiefly to the teaching of history, and is edited by Miss E. Jefferies Davis.

186. Vergangenheit und Gegenwart: Zeitschrift für den Geschichtsunterricht und staatsbürgerliche Erziehung in allen Schulgattungen. Edited by F. Friedrich and P. Rühlmann. Leipzig, 1911ff.

§ 6. Pictorial Works

See also nos. **318, 775.**

187. Parmentier, A. Album historique. Publié sous la direction de M. Ernest Lavisse. 4 vols. Paris, 1897–1907. Edition de luxe, vols. I–III, 1901–02. Vol. I: Le moyen âge (du IVe au XIIIe siècle), 2nd edition, 1900. Vol. II: La fin du moyen âge (XIVe et XVe siècles), 1897.

188. Lacroix, P., and Séré, F. Le moyen-âge et la renaissance: histoire et description des moeurs et usages, du commerce et de l'industrie, des sciences, des arts et des littératures en Europe. 5 vols. Paris, 1847–52. Several later editions. Translated into English in 4 vols.: Manners, customs, and dress during the middle ages, and during the renaissance period, London, 1874; Science and literature in the middle ages and at the period of the renaissance, London, 1878; Military and religious life in the middle ages and at the period of the renaissance, London [1874]; Arts in the middle ages, and at the period of the renaissance, London, 1870.

189. KLEINPAUL, R. Das Mittelalter: Bilder aus dem Leben und Treiben aller Stände in Europa. 2 vols. Leipzig [1895].

190. ESSENWEIN, A. Kulturhistorischer Bilderatlas. Vol. II. Mittelalter. Leipzig, 1883.

191. RACINET, A. Le costume historique. 6 vols. Paris, 1876–88. 500 plates.

Vols. III and IV on the middle ages. The Brooklyn Public Library published a reading and reference list on costume, 1909.

192. LACROIX, P. Costumes historiques de la France d'après les monuments les plus authentiques . . . Avec un texte descriptif. 10 vols. Paris [1852].

193. PLANCHÉ, J. R. A cyclopaedia of costume, including a general history of costumes. [A.D. 1–1760.] 2 vols. London, 1876–79. Many illustrations.

194. HEFNER-ALTENECK, J. H. DE. Costumes du moyen-âge chrétien. 3 vols. Frankfort, 1840–54. 420 plates.

Now see also vol. III of C. ENLART, *Manuel d'archéologie française*, no. **299**.

195. Zur Geschichte der Costüme. Munich, 1874. New edition 1895. Colorierte Ausgabe. Munich, 1913.

196. ROSENBERG, A. Geschichte des Kostüms. Vol. I, Berlin, 1910.

197. DEMAY, G. Le costume au moyen-âge d'après les sceaux. Paris, 1880.

198. CLINCH, G. English costume from prehistoric times to the end of the eighteenth century. Chicago, 1910.

198a. PLANCHÉ, J. R. History of British costume from the earliest period to the close of the eighteenth century. 4th edition. London, 1913.

199. QUICHERAT, J. Histoire du costume en France. Paris, 1877.

200. BRETT, E. J. A pictorial and descriptive record of the origin and development of arms and armour. London, 1894. 133 good plates.

201. Longman's historical illustrations: England in the middle ages. 1910.

202. BELLOC, H. The book of the Bayeux tapestry, presenting the complete work in a series of colour facsimiles. London, 1914.

The Bayeux tapestry is also produced in color in vol. VI, 1819–23, of *Vetusta monumenta,* Society of Antiquaries of London, 7 vols., London, 1747–1906, which is interesting for many other fine illustrations. Another reproduction of the tapestry is in F. R. FOWKE, *The Bayeux tapestry,* London, 1898. See GROSS, no. **36,** no. 2139.

203. DIEDERICHS, E. Deutsches Leben der Vergangenheit in Bildern. 2 vols. Jena, 1908. Vol. I, 15th and 16th centuries.

203a. Monographien zur deutschen Kulturgeschichte herausgegeben von G. STEINHAUSEN. 12 vols. Leipzig, 1903.

204. DAERING, O. Deutschlands mittelalterliche Kunstdenkmäler als Geschichtsquelle. Leipzig, 1911.

205. LINDEN, H. VAN DER, and OBREEN, H. Album historique de la Belgique. Brussels, 1912.

206. HERRAD VON LANDSBERG (Abbess of Hohenburg, died 1195). Hortus deliciarum; publié aux frais de la Société pour la conservation des monuments historiques d'Alsace. Strasburg, 1901.

For other literature on this interesting book see DAHLMANN-WAITZ, *Quellenkunde,* no. 5723.

207. LABARTE, J. Histoire des arts industriels au moyen âge. 4 vols. Paris, 1864–66. 2nd edition, 3 vols., 1872–75. Many illustrations.

His *Handbook of the arts of the middle ages,* 1855, is a translation of a smaller work.

§ 7. Guides to Learned Societies

See also no. **83.**

208. Carnegie Institution of Washington. Handbook of learned societies and institutions: American. Washington, 1908.

A similar handbook for the rest of the world is in preparation. The material which is accumulating for it may be consulted at the Library of Congress in Washington, D. C. See "List of European historical societies," in *Annual Report, A.H.A.,* 1914, vol. I, 301–10. STEIN, no. **1**, pp. 642–49, gives a list of academies and miscellaneous learned societies and their publications.

208a. OGG, F. A. Research in the humanistic and social sciences, report of a survey conducted for the American Council of Learned Societies. New York, 1928.

209. Year-book of the scientific and learned societies of Great Britain and Ireland. London, 1884ff. 45th annual issue, 1929.

210. DELAUNAY, H. Les sociétés savantes de France. Paris, 1902.

See also no. **26.**

211. MÜLLER, J. Die wissenschaftlichen Vereine und Gesellschaften Deutschlands im neunzehnten Jahrhundert: Bibliographie ihrer Veröffentlichungen seit ihrer Begründung bis auf die Gegenwart. Berlin, 1883–87.

CHAPTER III

SOME AUXILIARIES TO THE STUDY OF MEDIEVAL HISTORY

§ 1. Latin Palaeography

(*a*) Handbooks

212. Thompson, E. M. An introduction to Greek and Latin palaeography. Oxford, 1912. 250 plates. The author regards it as an enlarged edition of his Handbook of Greek and Latin palaeography, London, 1893; 3rd edition, 1906.

In its enlarged form, the book is the best handbook in any language. See the bibliography at the end. Note also the excellent *Catalogue of works dealing with the study of western palaeography in the libraries of the University of London at its central buildings and at University College and King's College*, compiled by J. Wilks and A. D. Lacey, London, 1921. There is now a periodical *Palaeographia latina* edited by W. M. Lindsay, London, 1922ff.

The best book for the history of writing in the middle ages, apart from the form, is W. Wattenbach, *Das Schriftwesen im Mittelalter*, Leipzig, 1871; 3rd edition, 1896 (see outline XXVI in part III below). Wattenbach also has an *Einleitung zur lateinischen Palaeographie*, Leipzig, 1869; 4th edition, 1886.

Beginners will be interested in H. W. Johnston, *Latin manuscripts: an elementary introduction to the use of critical editions for high school and college classes*, Chicago, 1897; and E. E. Thoyts, *How to decipher and study old documents: being a guide to the reading of ancient manuscripts*, London, 1893; 3rd edition, revised, 1909. Now see also J. E. Sandys, *A companion to Latin studies*, Cambridge, 1910, 765–805; 2nd edition, 1913.

212a. Bauckner, A., and Hösl, I. Schrift und Urkunde im Geschichtsunterricht. Munich and Berlin, 1914.

212b. Clark, A. C. The descent of manuscripts. Oxford, 1918.

212c. Sinks, P. W. The reign of the manuscript. Boston, 1917.

212d. Mason, W. A. A history of the art of writing. New York, 1920.

A popular introduction to the study of palaeography. Cf. Van Hoesen, no. **1a,** ch. xii.

212e. Schramm, A. Schreib- und Buchwesen einst und jetz. Leipzig, 1922.

213. Paoli, C. Programma scolastico di paleografia latina e di diplomatica. 3 parts, Florence, 1883–98. 3rd edition of part 1, 1901. Translated by K. Lohmeyer, Grundriss der lateinischen Paläographie und der Urkundenlehre. Innsbruck, 1885ff. 3 parts. 3rd edition of part I, 1902.

213a. Schiaparelli, L. La scrittura latina nell' età romana. Como, 1921. (Auxilia ad res italicas medii aevi exquirendas in usum scholarum instructa et collecta. I.)

214. Prou, M. Manuel de paléographie latine et française suivi d'un dictionnaire des abréviations; avec 23 fac-similes. Paris, 1890. 3rd edition with an album of 24 plates. Paris, 1910. 4th edition revised, with A. de Bouärd. Paris, 1924.

See the bibliography on pp. 289–302.

215. Reusens, E. H. J. Eléments de paléographie. Louvain, 1891. Enlarged edition, Louvain, 1899.

See bibliography, pp. 468–79.

216. Steffens, F. Lateinische Paläographie: 100 Tafeln mit einer systematischen Darstellung der lateinischen Schrift. Fribourg, 1903. Supplement, 1906. 2nd edition, 125 plates, Trèves, 1907–09. French edition, by R. Coulon, Paléographie latine. Trèves, 1910. 125 plates.

See also his *Proben aus Handschriften lateinischer Schriftsteller zur ersten Einführung*, Trèves, 1907.

216a. Mentz, A. Geschichte der griechisch-römischen Schrift bis zur Erfindung des Buchdrucks mit beweglichen Lettern: ein Versuch. Leipzig, 1920.

217. Bretholtz, B. "Lateinische Palaeographie." In no. **331**, vol. I. Leipzig, 1906, pp. 21–30. 2nd edition, 1912. 3rd edition, 1926.

218. Traube, L. Zur Paläographie und Handschriftenkunde. Munich, 1909. In vol. II of his Vorlesungen und Abhandlungen (posthumous edition by F. Boll).

219. Hall, F. W. A companion to classical texts. Oxford, 1913.

See especially chapter ix, "The nomenclature of Greek and Latin mss. with the names of former possessors."

220. Loew, E. A. The Beneventan script: a history of the south Italian minuscule. Oxford, 1914.

220a. Clark, C. U. Collectanea Hispanica. Paris, 1920. (Transactions of the Connecticut Academy of Arts and Sciences. Vol. XXIV.)

Devoted to a study of the Visigothic hand.

220b. Rand, E. K. A survey of the manuscripts of Tours. 2 vols. Cambridge, 1929. (Studies in the Script of Tours, I.)

Vol. I, text; vol. II, plates.

220c. García Villada, Z. Paleografía española precedida de una introducción sobre la paleografía latina. 2 vols. Madrid, 1923.

220d. Muñoz y Rivero, D. J. Manuel de paleografía diplomática española de los siglos XII al XVII. Second revised edition. Madrid, 1917.

220e. Crons, E., and Kirchner, J. Die gothischen Schriftarten. Leipzig, 1928.

221. Chassant, A. Paléographie des chartes et des manuscrits du XIe au XVIIe siècle. 8th edition, Paris, 1885.

222. Wailly, N. de. Eléments de paléographie. 2 vols. Paris, 1838.

223. Marucchi, O. Epigrafia cristiana. Milan, 1910. Translated by A. Willis, Christian epigraphy. Cambridge, 1912.

223a. Sandys, J. E. Latin epigraphy. Cambridge, 1919. 2nd edition, 1927, revised by S. G. Campbell.

Note the "List of abbreviations," Appendix VI, 290–311.

(*b*) Abbreviations

See also nos. **214, 215, 223a, 244, 245.**

224. Cappelli, A. Dizionario di abbreviature latine ed italiene. Milan, 1899. German edition with additions, Lexicon abbreviaturarum: Wörterbuch lateinischer und italienischer Abkürzungen. Leipzig, 1901. 2nd edition, revised, 1912. A new printing, 1928.

E. K. Rand, "A nest of ancient notae," Speculum, II (1927), 160–76.

224a. Lindsay, W. M. Notae latinae: an account of abbreviations in Latin mss. of the early minuscule period (c. 700–850). Cambridge, 1915.

Very important.

224b. Schiaparelli, L. Avviamento allo studio delle abbreviature latine nel medioevo. Florence, 1926.

An important contribution.

225. Chassant, A. Dictionnaire des abréviations latines et françaises du moyen âge. Paris, 1846. 5th edition, 1884.

225a. Traube, L. Nomina sacra: Versuch einer Geschichte der christlichen Kürzung. In Quellen und Untersuchungen zur lateinischen Philologie des Mittelalters. II (1907).

Fundamental for history of abbreviations.

226. Chatelain, E. Introduction à la lecture des notes tironiennes. Paris, 1900.

227. Perugi, G. L. Le note tironiane. Rome, 1911.

228. Guenin, L. P., and E. Histoire de la sténographie dans l'antiquité et au moyen âge: les notes tironiennes. Paris, 1907.

229. ZIMMERMANN, A. Geschichte der Stenographie in kurzen Zügen vom klassischen Altertum bis zur Gegenwart. Vienna, 1912.

229a. Archiv für Stenographie. 63 vols. Berlin, 1862–1914.

(*c*) FACSIMILES

See also nos. **212** to **223a.**

230. The Palaeographical Society. Facsimiles of manuscripts and inscriptions. Edited by E. A. BOND, E. M. THOMPSON, G. F. WARNER, and W. WRIGHT. Series I–II; 465 facsimiles with descriptive text, transliteration, tables of contents, etc., and indices. London, 1873–1901. New Paleographical Society. Facsimiles of ancient manuscripts. Parts I–X. London, 1903–12. 250 plates. 2nd series, 1913ff.

231. Recueil de fac-similes à l'usage de l'Ecole des Chartes. 4 parts. 100 plates. Paris, 1880–87.

See also the *Album paléographique*, edited by L. DELISLE, for the *Société de l'Ecole des Chartes*. 50 plates. Paris, 1887.

In 1911 there was formed in Paris a society for the photographic reproduction of the most important medieval manuscripts, especially illuminated ones.

232. CHROUST, A. Monumenta palaeographica: Denkmäler der Schreibkunst des Mittelalters. 3 series. Munich, 1899ff.

233. Archivo paleografico italiano, edited by E. MONACI. Rome, 1882ff.

234. WILLIAMS, H. S. Manuscripts, inscriptions, and muniments, oriental, classical, mediaeval and modern, described, classified and arranged, comprehending the history of the art of writing. 200 facsimiles. 4 vols. London [about 1901].

235. SILVESTRE, J. B. Paléographie universelle, collection de fac-similes d'écriture de tous les peuples. 4 vols. Paris, 1839–41. Translated by F. MADDEN, Universal palaeography. 2 vols. London, 1850.

236. GALABERT, F. Album de paléographie et de diplomatique: facsimiles phototypiques de documents relatifs à l'histoire du Midi de la France, et en particulier de la ville de Toulouse. Paris, 1912ff.

237. ARNDT, W. Schrifttafeln zur Erlernung der lateinischen Paläographie. Berlin, 1897ff. 4th edition of parts I and II, Berlin, 1904–06. Part III, Berlin, 1903. 2nd edition, unchanged, 1908.

237a. KAALUND, K. Palaeografisk Atlas. Vol. I. Dansk Afdeling. Vols. II and III. Old-Norsk-Islandsk Afdeling. 3 vols. Copenhagen, 1903–07.

237b. DEGERING, H. Die Schrift: Atlas der Schriftformen des Abendlandes vom Altertum bis zum Ausgang des 18. Jahrhunderts. Berlin, 1929.

A convenient volume of facsimiles. Beautifully printed.

§ 2. Diplomatics and Sphragistics

238. MABILLON, J. De re diplomatica libri VI. Paris, 1681; supplement, 1704. 2nd edition, 1709. 3rd edition, 2 vols., Naples, 1789.

This book, together with TOUSTAIN and TASSIN, *Nouveau traitê de diplomatique*, 1750–65, laid the bases of this discipline. See also R. ROSENMUND, *Die Fortschritte der Diplomatik seit Mabillon, vornehmlich in Deutschland-Oesterreich*, Munich and Leipzig, 1897.

239. GIRY, A. Manuel de diplomatique. Paris, 1894; new printing, 1925.

For a very recent brief sketch see R. THOMMEN, L. SCHMITZ-KALLENBERG, and H. STEINACKER, *Urkundenlehre*, 2nd edition, Leipzig and Berlin, 1913 (in *Grundriss*, no. **331,** I, parts 2 and 2*a*). For information on weights and measures consult P. BURGUBURU, "Essai d'une bibliographie métrologique universelle," *Le bibliographe moderne*, XXIII (1926–27), 27–58; 105–69; XXIV (1928–29), 49–84 (to be concluded) and also *Select tracts and table books relatirg to English weights and measures* (1100–1742) edited by H. HALL and F. J. NICHOLAS, London, 1929 (Camden Miscellany, XV).

240. BRESSLAU, H. Handbuch der Urkundenlehre für Deutschland und Italien. Vol. I, Leipzig, 1889. 2nd edition, vol. I, 1912, vol. II, part I, 1915.

The second edition of vol. I covers only nine of the nineteen chapters of the first edition. Now see also the important book by R. L. POOLE, *Lectures on the history of the papal chancery down to the time of Innocent III*, Cambridge, 1915, and his *Chronicles and annals: a brief outline of their origin and growth*, Oxford, 1926, and "Seals and documents" in *Proceedings of the British Academy*, IX (1919–20), 319–39.

240a. PEITZ, W. M. Das Register Gregors I: Beiträge zur Kenntnis des päpstlichen Kanzlei- und Registerwesens bis auf Gregor VII. Freiburg, 1918.

241. LEIST, F. Urkundenlehre: Katechismus der Diplomatik, Paläographie, Chronologie, und Sphragistik. Leipzig, 1882. 2nd edition, 1893.

241a. BAUCKNER, A. Einführung in das mittelalterliche Schrifttum. Munich, 1923.

242. JOHNSON, C., and JENKINSON, H. English court hand, A.D. 1066–1500, illustrated chiefly from the public records. Oxford, 1915. One vol. together with an atlas of 44 plates.

See also H. JENKINSON, *Palaeography and the practical study of court hands*, Cambridge, 1915.

243. HALL, H. Studies in English official historical documents. Cambridge, 1908.

Supplemented by his *Formula book of English historical documents*, parts I–II, Cambridge, 1908–09. See also C. JOHNSON, *The care of documents*, London, 1919.

244. MARTIN, C. T. The record interpreter: a collection of abbreviations, Latin words, and names used in English historical manuscripts and records. London, 1892. 2nd edition, 1910.

245. WALTER, J. L. Lexicon diplomaticum: abbreviationes vocum in diplomatibus exponens. 3 parts. Göttingen, 1745–47. Another edition, Ulm, 1756.

Still the most complete list of abbreviations in official documents of the middle ages.

246. ROMAN, J. Manuel de sigillographie. Paris, 1913.

246a. NICODÈME, MARIETTE. "Bibliographie générale de la sigillographie." *Le bibliographe moderne*, XXII (1924–25), 130–61, 203–21 (to be concluded).

246b. COULON, A. Le service sigillographique et les collections d'empreintes de sceaux des Archives nationales; notice suivie d'un catalogue du musée sigillographique. Paris, 1916.

247. ILGEN, T. Sphragistik. 2nd edition, 1912. (In Grundriss, no. **331,** I, part 4, pp. 1–58.)

Has a very full bibliography.

248. Archiv für Urkundenforschung in zwanglosen Heften herausgegeben von K. BRANDI, H. BRESSLAU, and M. TANGL. Leipzig, 1907ff.

249. Kaiserurkunden in Abbildungen. Edited by H. v. SYBEL and T. v. SICKEL. Berlin, 1880–91.

249a. Facsimiles of royal and other charters in the British Museum. Edited by G. F. WARNER and H. J. ELLIS. Vol. I. Oxford, 1903.

§ 3. Chronology

250. GROTEFEND, H. Zeitrechnung des deutschen Mittelalters und der Neuzeit. 2 vols. Hanover, 1891–98.

250a. POOLE, R. L. Medieval reckonings of time. London, 1918. (S.P.C.K. Helps, no. 3.)

250b. POOLE, R. L. The beginning of the year in the middle ages. Oxford, 1921.

250c. HART, R. J. Chronos, a handbook of comparative chronology. London, 1921.

250d. CAVAIGNAC, E. Chronologie. Paris, 1925.

251. GROTEFEND, H. Taschenbuch der Zeitrechnung des deutschen Mittelalters und der Neuzeit. Hanover and Leipzig, 1898. 3rd edition, 1910.

This is a condensation of the previous work. A still briefer account, but the most recent of all, is the following:

252. GROTEFEND, H. Abriss der Chronologie des deutschen Mittelalters und der Neuzeit. 2nd edition. Leipzig, 1912. (In no. **331**, vol. I, part 3.)

253. IDELER, L. Handbuch der mathematischen und technischen Chronologie. Berlin, 1825–26. 2 vols. 2nd edition. Breslau, 1883.

254. RÜHL, F. Chronologie des Mittelalters und der Neuzeit. Berlin, 1897.

A very convenient general account. The same is true of GIRY, *Manuel de diplomatique*, no. **239**. See also B. M. LERSCH, *Einleitung in die Chronologie*, 2 parts, 2nd edition, Freiburg, 1899.

255. L'art de vérifier les dates. 2nd part. Depuis la naissance de Jésus-Christ [to 1770?]. Paris, 1750. 3rd edition, 3 vols., 1783–87. 4th edition by SAINT-ALLAIS, 18 vols., 1818–19.

256. MAS-LATRIE, L. DE. Trésor de chronologie, d'histoire et de géographie pour l'étude et l'emploi des documents du moyen âge. Paris, 1889.

257. GINZEL, F. K. Handbuch der mathematischen und technischen Chronologie. 3 vols. Leipzig, 1906–14.

257a. GINZEL, F. K. Beiträge zur Kenntniss der historischen Sonnenfinsternisse und zur Frage ihrer Verwendbarkeit. (Abh. Berlin Acad. Physik-math. Kl. no. 4, 1918.)

258. KELLNER, K. A. H. Heortologie: oder die geschichtliche Entwicklung des Kirchenjahres und der Heiligenfeste von den ältesten Zeiten bis zur Gegenwart. Freiburg, 1901. 2nd edition, 1906. Translated from the 2nd German edition, Heortology: a history of the Christian festivals from their origin to the present day. London, 1908.

259. HAMPSON, R. T. Medii aevi kalendarium: or dates, charters, and customs of the middle ages. 2 vols. London, 1841.

260. SCHMID, J. Die Osterfestberechnung in der abendländischen Kirche bis zum Ende des VIII. Jahrhunderts. Freiburg, 1907.

261. SCHRAM, R. Kalendariographische und chronologische Tafeln. Leipzig, 1908.

262. CAPPELLI, A. Cronologia e calendario perpetuo: tavole cronografiche e quadri sinottici per verificare le date storiche dal principio dell' era cristiana ai giorni nostri. Milan, 1906.

263. BOND, J. J. Handybook of rules and tables for verifying dates with the Christian era: giving an account of the chief eras and systems used by various nations, etc. London, 1866. 4th edition, London, 1889.

Especially valuable for English history.

264. WISLICENUS, W. F. Astronomische Chronologie: ein Hilfsbuch für Historiker, Archäologen, etc. Leipzig, 1895.

265. WISLICENUS, W. F. Der Kalender. Leipzig, 1905.

266. Brinckmeier, E. Praktisches Handbuch der historischen Chronologie aller Zeiten und Völker, besonders des Mittelalters. 2nd edition. Berlin, 1882.

267. Bilfinger, G. Die mittelalterlichen Horen und die modernen Stunden: ein Beitrag zur Kulturgeschichte. Stuttgart, 1892.

§ 4. Genealogy

268. Lorenz, O. Lehrbuch der gesamten wissenschaftlichen Genealogie. Berlin, 1898.

269. Lorenz, O. Genealogisches Handbuch der europäischen Staatengeschichte. 3rd edition. Stuttgart, 1907.

270. Stockvis, A. M. H. J. Manuel d'histoire de généalogie et de chronologie de tous les états du globe. 3 vols. Leyden, 1888–91.

271. Forst-Battaglia, O. Genealogie. Leipzig and Berlin, 1913. In no. **331,** I, part 4*a*.

See also his *Genealogische Tabellen zur Geschichte des Mittelalters und der Neuzeit: Abteilung Mittelalter*, erste Lieferung, Vienna, 1914.

272. Heydenreich, E. Handbuch der praktischen Genealogie. 2nd edition. 2 vols. Leipzig, 1913.

273. Devrient, E. Genealogisches Handbuch der europäischen Staatengeschichte. 3rd edition. Stuttgart, 1908.

274 Hübner, J. Genealogische Tabellen. 5 vols., with appendix, Leipzig, 1725–33. 2nd edition with continuation, 1737–66. Supplements, 6 numbers, Copenhagen, 1822–24.

275. Grote, H. Stammtafeln. Leipzig, 1877.

276. George, H. B. Genealogical tables illustrative of modern history. 5th edition, revised, Oxford, 1916.

277. Almanach de Gotha: annuaire généalogique, diplomatique et statistique. Gotha, 1763ff.

Since 1871 published in both French and German.

277a. Almanach de Bruxelles: pour prendre la place de l'Almanach de Gotha qui est allemand. Paris, 1918.

278. Allström, C. M. Dictionary of royal lineage of Europe, etc. 2 vols. Chicago, 1902–04.

279. Rye, W. Records and record searching: a guide to the genealogist and topographer. London, 1888. 2nd edition, 1897.

280. Marshall, G. W. The genealogist's guide. London, 1879. 4th edition, Guildford, 1903.

281. HOFMEISTER, A. "Genealogie und Familienforschung als Hilfswissenschaft der Geschichte." In *H.V.J.S.* XV (1912), 457–92.

282. WOODS, F. A. Mental and moral heredity in royalty: a statistical study in history and psychology. With 104 portraits. New York, 1906.

283. BRACHET, A. Pathologie mentale des rois de France: Louis XI et ses ascendants; une vie humaine étudiée à travers six siècles d'hérédité (852–1483). Paris, 1903.

283a. LITTA, P. Famiglie celebri italiane. 16 vols. Milan, 1819–99.

§ 5. Heraldry

284. BOUTELL, C. A manual of heraldry. London, 1863. 3rd edition, Heraldry, historical and popular. London, 1864. Abridged under the title, English heraldry. London, 1867; 10th edition, with 464 illustrations, by A. C. FOX-DAVIES, 1908; 11th edition, revised as Handbook of English heraldry, 1913.

See also W. A. SHAW, *The knights of England*, 2 vols., London, 1906.

285. FOX-DAVIES, A. C. A complete guide to heraldry. London, 1909.

See also his *The art of heraldry: an encyclopaedia of armory*, London, 1904.

286. WOODWARD, J., and BURNETT, G. A treatise on heraldry, British and foreign. 2 vols. Edinburgh, 1892. New edition, 1896.

287. GRITZNER, M. Handbuch der heraldischen Terminologie in zwölf Zungen. Nuremberg, 1890.

See his *Heraldik*, 2nd edition, Leipzig and Berlin, 1912, in no. **331,** I, part 4, pp. 59–97.

288. SEYLER, G. A. Geschichte der Heraldik. Nuremberg, 1890.

289. GOURDON DE GENOUILLAC, H. L'art héraldique. Paris, 1889.

290. SACKEN, E. Katechismus der Heraldik. 6th edition, 1899.

291. [HOZIER, L. P. D']. Armorial général de la France. 12 vols. Paris, 1865ff.

291a. HILDEBRAND, H. Heraldiska studier. 2 vols. Stockholm, 1883, 1887. Volume I. Det Svenska Riksvapnet, Stockholm, 1883. Volume II. Landskapens vapen, Stockholm, 1887.

291b. JÖRGENSEN, A. D. Det Gamle Danske Kongevaaben. Historiske Avhndlinger, I. 1898, 52–79.

291c. PETERSEN, H. Danske gejstlige Sigiller fra middelalderen. Edited by Th. Bergh. Copenhagen, 1886.

291d. STORCK, H. Dansk Vaabenbog. Copenhagen, [1906–] 1910.

291e. WRANGEL, F. U. En vapenbok från medeltiden, in Sv. Autografsällskapets Tidskrift, 1893, vol. II, pp. 121–28 (with facs.).

§ 6. Numismatics

292. ENGEL, A., and SERRURE, R. Traité de numismatique de moyen âge. 3 vols. Paris, 1891–95.

Contains comprehensive bibliographies. Note also "List of works in the New York Public Library relating to numismatics" in *Bulletin of the New York Public Library*, XVII (1913), 981–1049; XVIII (1914), 59–86, 149–75, 404–28.

293. LUSCHIN VON EBENGREUTH, A. Allgemeine Münzkunde und Geldgeschichte des Mittelalters und der neueren Zeit. Munich, 1904. In no. **330.** 2nd edition, 1926.

See also elementary books on the subject: H. HALKE, *Einleitung in das Studium der Numismatik*, 3rd edition, Berlin, 1908; H. DANNENBERG, *Grundzüge der Münzkunde*, 1891; 2nd edition, 1899, and G. F. HILL, *Coins and medals*, London, 1920.

294. BLANCHET, J. A., and DIEUDONNÉ, A. Manuel de numismatique française. Vol. I, Paris, 1912. Vol. II, 1916.

294a. Corpus nummorum italicorum: primo tentativo di un catalogo generale delle moneta medioevali e moderne coniate in Italia o da Italiani in altri paesi. Rome, 1910ff.

295. FRIEDENSBURG, F. Deutsche Münzgeschichte. 2nd edition. Leipzig and Berlin, 1912. In no. **331,** I, part 4, pp. 98–132.

296. FRIEDENSBURG, F. Die Münze in der Kulturgeschichte. Berlin, 1909.

297. POOLE, S. L. Coins and medals: their place in history and art. London, 1885. 3rd edition, 1894.

298. KEARY, C. F. Coinages of western Europe, Honorius to Charles the Great. London, 1879. 3rd edition, 1894.

298a. HILDEBRAND, H. De öster- och västerlänska mynten i Sveriges jord. Stockholm, 1897.

298b. HILDEBRAND, H. Sveriges mynt under medeltiden. Stockholm, 1887.

§ 7. Archaeology

See also no. **754.**

299. ENLART, C. Manuel d'archéologie française depuis les temps mérovingiens jusqu'à la renaissance. Vols. I–III. Paris, 1902–16. 2nd edition. Vol. I, parts 1–2, 1919–23.

See also J. A. BRUTAILS, *Précis d'archéologie du moyen âge*, Paris, 1908.

300. GAY, V. Glossaire archéologique du moyen âge et de la renaissance. 2 vols. Paris, 1887–1928.

301. LECLERCQ, H. Manuel d'archéologie chrétienne depuis les origines jusqu'au VIII siècle. 2 vols. Paris, 1907.

301a. SCAGLIA, P. S. Manuel d'archéologie chrétienne. Turin, 1916.

302. KAUFMANN, K. Handbuch der christlichen Archäologie. Paderborn, 1905. 2nd edition, enlarged, 1913.

§ 8. Philology

303. BÖCKH, A. Enzyklopädie und Methodologie der philologischen Wissenschaften. Leipzig, 1886.

This handbook does for philology what BERNHEIM, no. **64**, does for history.

304. KÖRTING, G. Enzyklopädie und Methodologie der romanischen Philologie. Heilbronn, 1884–88.

His *Enzyklopädie und Methodologie der französischen Philologie*, Leipzig, 1894; and *Handbuch der romanischen Philologie*, Heilbronn, 1896, are little more than extracts from the above.

305. Grundriss der romanischen Philologie. Edited by G. GRÖBER. 2 vols. Strasburg, 1888–1902. Vol. I, 2nd edition, 1904–06; vol. II, 1914.

Supplemented by *Kritischer Jahresbericht über die Fortschritte der romanischen Philologie*, Munich and Leipzig, 1892ff.; as well as by the *Répertoire des travaux historiques contenant l'analyse des nouvelles publications faites sur l'histoire des monuments et de la langue de France*, Paris, 1882ff.

For further details on the French language and literature in the twelfth and thirteenth centuries, see outline XXIV in part III.

306. MORF, H. Die romanischen Literaturen, and W. MEYER-LÜBKE, Die romanischen Sprachen. Berlin and Leipzig, 1909.

Part of vol. I of no. **729.**

307. Grundriss der germanischen Philologie. Edited by H. PAUL. 2 vols. in 3. Strasburg, 1891–93. 2nd edition, 3 vols. in 4, 1900–09; 3rd edition, many vols., 1911ff.

Supplemented by the *Jahresbericht über die Erscheinungen auf dem Gebiete der germanischen Philologie*, Berlin, 1800ff.

308. The Oxford English dictionary: a new English dictionary on historical principles, founded mainly on the materials collected by the Philological society. Edited by J. A. H. MURRAY. Oxford, 1888–1928.

309. Thesaurus linguae latinae editus auctoritate et concilio academiarum quinque Germanicarum: Berolinensis, Gottingensis, Lipsiensis, Monacensis, Vindobonensis. Leipzig, 1900ff.

Extends to the end of the sixth century. For DU CANGE and medieval Latin language and literature in general, see outline XXIII in part III and *Bulletin Du Cange: archivum latinitatis medii aevi.* (ALMA), Paris, 1924ff.

310. Münchener Archiv für Philologie des Mittelalters und der Renaissance. Munich, 1913ff.

311. Archiv für slavische Philologie. Berlin, 1876ff.

312. Die osteuropäischen Literaturen und die slawischen Sprachen. Berlin and Leipzig, 1908.

Part of no. **729.**

§ 9 Place-Names

(*a*) British

Bibliography. The nearest approach to a bibliography of this subject is in the scattered lists appearing in A. G. Kennedy, *A bibliography of writings on the English language from the beginning of printing to the end of 1922*, Cambridge and New Haven, 1927; see in this Index, p. 515 under "Place-Names." This may be consulted for early publications, for various detailed studies of single names, and above all for reviews of many books cited below. For current work see the *Annual bibliography of English language and literature*, 1920ff., under "Name Study," the *Zeitschrift für Ortsnamenforschung*, 1925ff. (abbreviated below *ZONF*), *Namn och Bygd*, 1913ff. (abbreviated below *NoB*), and *Studia neophilologica*, Uppsala, 1928ff. *passim.*

ENGLAND

English Place-Name Study. H. Alexander, "The new advance in place-study," *Queen's quarterly*, XXXIII (1925), 194–201. E. Björkman, "Engelska Ortsnamn och deras Betydelse som historiska Minnesmärken," *Nordisk Tidskrift för Vetenskap, Konst och Industri*, 1911, 553–70. O. G. S. Crawford, *The Andover district*, Oxford, 1922. E. Ekwall, "Die Ortsnamenforschung ein Hilfsmittel für das Studium der englischen Sprachgeschichte," *German Roman. Monatschrift*, V (1913), 592–608; "Über Ortsnamenforschung," Allgemein. Deutsch. Neuphilologen-Verband, *Bericht über die Verhandlungen d. 19. Tagung*, Berlin, 1925, 97ff., revised as "Englische Ortsnamenforschung," in *Anglica; Untersuchungen z. englischen Philol., Alois Brandl . . . überreicht*, I (1925), 19–40. A. Mawer, "English place-name study: its present condition and future possibilities," *Proceedings British Acad.*, X (1921–23), 31–44; *Place-names and history*, Liverpool, 1922; *Place-names: an essay in co-operative study*, Liverpool, 1922. M. J. C. Meiklejohn, *The place names of the English people at home and overseas*, London, 1929. W. J. Sedgfield, "Methods of place-name study," in A. Mawer and F. M. Stenton, editors, *Introduction to the survey of English place-names* (English Place-Name Soc.), Cambridge, 1923, Pt. i, pp. 1–4. I. Taylor, revised by A. S. Palmer, *Words and places*, London, 1909. E. Weekly, "English place-names," *Edinburgh rev.*, CCXLII (1925), 83–93. R. E. Zachrisson, "Five years of English place-name study (1922–27): a critical study," *Englische Studien*, LXII (1927–28), 64–105.

Place-Names (General). H. BRADLEY, "English place-names," *Essays and studies by members of the English Ass'n*, I (1910), 7–41, and reprinted (with other place-name articles) in *The collected papers of Henry Bradley*, Oxford, 1928, 80–109. O. G. S. CRAWFORD, "Place-names," *Archaeolog. journ.*, N. S., XXVIII (1921), 31–46. E. EKWALL, *English river-names*, Oxford, 1928; "Förklaring av några engelska Ortnamn," *Studier tillägnade Esaias Tegnér*, Lund, 1918, 435–443. T. B. F. EMINSON, "Some deceptive place-names in England and Normandy," *Antiquary*, LI (1915), 100–05, 173–78. O. GEVENICH, *Die englische Palatisierung von k>č im Lichte der englischen Ortsnamen* (MORSBACH's Studien z. engl. Philol., vol. LVII, Halle, 1918). H. JELLINGHAUS, "Englische und niederdeutsche Ortsnamen," *Anglia*, XX (1897–98), 257–334. J. B. JOHNSTON, *The place-names of England and Wales*, London, 1915. R. KLEINPAUL, *Die Ortsnamen im Deutschen: Ihre Entwicklung und ihre Herkunft* (Sammlung Göschen, No. 573); 2nd edition, Berlin, 1919. A. MAWER, "Some types of English place-names," *Discovery*, IV (1923), 94–97, 168; "English place-names and their pronunciation," *Discovery*, V (1924), 284–85; "Place-names," *Ency. Brit.*, fourteenth edition. E. MCCLURE, *British place-names in their historical setting*, London, 1910. A. F. C. RITTER, *Die Verteilung der ch- und k-Formen in Mittelenglischen*, Marburg, 1904 (Diss.). O. RITTER, *Vermischte Beiträge z. englischen Sprachgeschichte; Etymologie, Ortsnamenkunde, Lautlehre*, Halle, 1922, 68ff. R. E. ZACHRISSON, "Six groups of English river-names," *ZONF*, II (1927), 134–47; "Some English place-name etymologies," *Studier i modern Språkvetenskap*, IX (1924), 113–146; "Romans, Kelts, and Saxons in Ancient Britain," Uppsala, Kungl. Humanistika Vetenskapssamfundet, *Skrifter*, vol. XXIV (1927), no. 12.

Elements. H. ALEXANDER, "The genitive suffix in the first element of English place-names," *Modern lang. rev.*, VII (1912), 64–73. A. ANSCOMBE, "*Bug* in place-names," *Notes and queries*, Ser. 12, VII (1920), 77. H. ASKEW, "*Dragon* in place-names: Drakehord, Drakestone, Drakelow," *Notes and queries*, CL (1926), 124. W. ST. C. BADDELEY, "*Dragon* in place-names," *Notes and queries*, CXLIX (1925), 420–21. E. EKWALL, "Ae. *botl, bold, boðl* in englischen Ortsnamen," *Beiblatt z. Anglia*, XXVIII (1917), 82–91. G. T. FLOM, "Place-name tests of racial mixture in Northern England," *Modern lang. notes*, XXXIX (1924), 203–12. A. MAWER, "Animal and personal names in Old-English place-names," *Modern lang. rev.*, XIV (1919), 233–44; *The chief elements used in English place-names* (English Place-Name Soc., vol. I, Pt. ii), Cambridge, 1924; "Some unconsidered elements in Old-English place-names," *Essays and studies by members of the English Ass'n*, IV (1913), 55–71; "*Hamble-humble* in English place-names," *NoB*, IX (1921), 36–38; "English *head* 'source,'" *NoB*, XV (1927), 88–90. F. M. STENTON, "Personal names in place-names," in A. MAWER and F. M. STENTON, editors, *Introduction*, I, i, 165–89. H. R. WATKINS, "*Blag, blache, blach,* and *blake* in Place-Names," *Journ. Torquay Natural Hist. Soc.*, III (1922), 84–112. R. E. ZACHRISSON, "English place-names and river-names containing the primitive Germanic roots *vis, vask*," *Uppsala Universitets*

Årsskrift, 1926, vol. I, 67 pp.; "The French definite article in English place-names," *Anglia*, XXXIV (1911), 308–53; "Topographical names containing primitive Germanic *geb-*," *NoB*, XIV (1926), 51–64.

Suffixes. H. ALEXANDER, "The particle *-ing* in English place-names," *Essays and studies by members of the English Ass'n*, II (1911), 158–82. A. ANSCOMBE, "Sussex place-names in Domesday Book which end in *-intun*," *Sussex archaeolog. collections*, LIX (1918), 76–83; "Place-names in Domesday Book which end in *-intun*," London *Times*, *Liter. Suppl.*, 1921, p. 484. J. BIELEFELD, *Untersuchungen z. zweiten Teil d. englischen Ortsnamen*, Münster, 1926 (Diss.). H. CORNELIUS, "Englische Ortsnamen in *-wick*, *-wich*," MORSBACH'S *Studien z. englischen Philol.*, L (1913), 353–416. E. EKWALL, "English place-names in *-ing*," Lund, Kungl. Humanistika Vetenskapssamfundet, *Skrifter*, vol. VI (1923), xix, 190 pp. S. KARLSTRÖM, *Old-English compound place-names in -ing*, Uppsala, 1927 (Diss.). G. LANGENFELDT, *Toponymics, or derivations from local names in English*, Uppsala, 1920 (Diss.). P. H. REANEY, "Essex place-names in *-ing*," *Modern lang. rev.*, XIX (1924), 466–69. O. SCHRAM, "Place-Names in *-sett* in the East of England," *ZONF*, III (1928), 200–11. B. WALKER, "Interchange and substitution of second elements in place-names," *Englische Studien*, LI (1917–18), 25–36. G. H. WHEELER, "The method of formation of Old English place-names in *-hǽme*, *-sǽtan*, *-túningas*," *Modern lang. rev.*, XI (1916), 218, 219. R. E. ZACHRISSON, "English place-names in *-ing* of Scandinavian origin," *Uppsala Universitets Årsskrift*, 1924, vol. II (Språkvetenskapliga Sällskapet, pp. 107–30).

Old-English (Pre-Conquest). A. ANSCOMBE, see under Suffixes. A. BRANDL, "Zur Geographie d. altengl. Dialekte," *Abh. Preuss. Acad.*, no. 4, 1915. G. BINZ, "Zeugnisse z. german. Sage in England," PAUL and BRAUNE'S *Beiträge*, XX (1895), 141–223. W. DE G. BIRCH, "An unpublished MS. list of some early territorial names in England," *Journ. Brit. Archaeolog. Ass'n*, XL (1884), 28–46. H. BRADLEY, "Some Old English place-names," *Academy*, XLV (1894), 457, 458; "Some place-names in SWEET'S *Anglo-Saxon reader*," HERRIG'S *Archiv*, CXXXI (1913), 427, 428. J. B. DAVIDSON, "On some Anglo-Saxon charters at Exeter," *Journ. Brit. Archaeolog. Ass'n*, XXXIX (1883), 259–303. E. EKWALL, "Notes on the inflection of Old-English place-names," *NoB*, XVI (1928), 59–77. A. GOODALL, "The tribal Hidage," *ZONF*, I (1926), 161–76. G. B. GRUNDY, "On the meaning of certain terms in the Anglo-Saxon charters," *Essays and studies by members of the English Ass'n*, VIII (1922), 37–69; "The evidence of Saxon land charters on the ancient road system of Britain," *Archaeolog. journ.*, N. S., XXIV (1917), 79–105. See also *idem* under Berks., Hants., and Wilts. F. HAVERFIELD, "English topographical notes," *E.H.R.*, X (1895), 710–12. S. KARLSTRÖM, see under Suffixes above. A. MAWER, "Some place-name identifications in the Anglo-Saxon Chronicles," *Anglica; Untersuchungen z. englischen Philol., Alois Brandl . . . überreicht* (Berlin, 1925), 1, 41–54. See *idem* under Elements above. K. MALONE, "A note on *Brunanburh*," *Modern lang. notes*, XLII (1927), 238, 239. F. MEZGER, *Angelsächsische Völker- und Länderna-*

men, Berlin, 1921 (Diss.). H. MIDDENDORFF, *Altenglisches Flurnamenbuch*, Halle, 1902. TH. MILLER, *Place-names in the English Bede* (Quellen und Forschungen zur Sprach- und Culturgeschichte, vol. LXXVIII). F. C. MOORMAN, "English place-names and Teutonic sagas," *Essays and studies by members of the English Ass'n*, V (1914), 75–103. O. RITTER, "Beiträge zur altenglischen Wort- und Namenkunde," *Englische Studien*, LXII (1927–28), 106–12. J. SEPHTON, see Lancs. below. M. STOLZE, *Zur Lautlehre d. altengl. Ortsnamen im Domesday Book*, Berlin, 1902 (Diss.). C. W. VON SYDOW, "Grendel i anglosaxiska Ortnamn," *Nordiska Ortnamn: Hyllningsskrift tillägnad Adolf Noreen*, Uppsala, 1914, 160–64. W. H. STEVENSON, *Asser's Life of King Alfred*, Oxford, 1904, notes, pp. 147ff. *passim*. C. S. TAYLOR, see under Gloucestershire below. E. A. PHILIPPSON, *Germanisches Heidentum bei den Angelsachsen* (Kölner anglistische Arbeiten, vol. IV), Leipzig, 1930.

Foreign Influences. Celtic. O. G. S. CRAWFORD, "Celtic place-names in England," *Archaeolog. Journ.*, N. S., XXVII (1920), 137–47. E. EKWALL, "The Celtic element" in A. MAWER and F. M. STENTON, editors, *Introduction*, I, i, 15–35; "An Old English sound-change and some English forest-names," *Beiblatt z. Anglia*, XXXVI (1925), 146–51; "Scandinavians and Celts in the North-West of England," *Lunds Universitets Årsskrift*, N.F., afd. 1, vol. XIV, no. 27, 1918. M. FÖRSTER, *Keltisches Wortgut im Englischen*, Halle, 1921. Cf. *idem*, "Proben eines englischen Eigennamen-Wtb.," *German.-Roman. Monatschrift*, XI (1923), 86–110. A. H. SMITH, see under Yorks. below.

French. R. E. ZACHRISSON, "A contribution to the study of Anglo-Norman influence on English place-names," *Lunds Universitets Årsskrift*, N.F., afd. 1, vol. IV, 1908, no. 3, 171 pp.; "The French definite article in English place-names," *Anglia*, XXXIV (1911), 308–53; "French *le* for English *the*," HERRIG'S *Archiv*, CXXXV (1916), 69–79; "The French element" in A. MAWER and F. M. STENTON, *Introduction*, I, i, 93–114; "Some English place-names in a French garb," *Mélanges de philologie offerts à M. Johan Vising*, Göteborg-Paris, 1925, 179–201; "Two instances of French influence on English place-names," *Studier i modern Språkvetenskap*, V (1914), 1–23.

For French place-names see pp. 53–55 below.

Frisian. J. M. LYONS, "Frisian place-names in England," *Publ. Modern Language Association*, XXXIII (1918), 644–55.

For Frisian place-names see p. 58 below.

Latin. R. E. ZACHRISSON, "Some instances of Latin influence on English place nomenclature," *Lunds Universitets Årsskrift*, N. F., afd. 1, vol. VII, 1910, no. 2, 35 pp.

Scandinavian. E. BJÖRKMAN, *Nordische Personennamen in England in alt-und frühmittelenglischer Zeit* (MORSBACH'S *Studien z. englisch. Philolog.*, Bd. XXXVIII, Halle, 1910); "Nordische Wörter in englisch. Ortsnamen,"

Herrig's *Archiv*, CXXV (1910), 400, 401. E. Ekwall, "Något om nordiska Ortnamn i England," *Sydsvenska Ortnamnssällskapets Årsskrift*, <II> (1926), 1–13; "Några nordiska Ortnamn i England," *NoB*, VIII (1920), 85–96; "Nord. á 'å' i engelska namn," *NoB*, XIV (1926), 145–61; "Scandinavians and Celts in the North-West of England," *Lunds Universitets Årsskrift*, N.F. avd. 1, vol. XIV, 1918, no. 27; "The Scandinavian element," in A. Mawer and F. M. Stenton, *Introduction*, I, i, 55–92; "The Scandinavian suffixed article in English place-names," *NoB*, V (1917), 104, 105; "Trenne Nordiska ord i engelska Ortnamn," *Nordiska Ortnamn, cit. supra*, 151–54. G. T. Flom, "Place-name tests of racial mixture in Northern England," *Modern lang. notes*, XXXIX (1924), 203–12. A. Goodall, see Yorks. below. F. W. Hardman, see Kent below. J. Köpke, *Altnordische Personennamen bei den Angelsachsen*, Berlin, 1909 (Diss.). H. Lindkvist, *Middle-English place-names of Scandinavian origin*, part I, Uppsala, 1912 (Diss.), also in *Uppsala Universitets Årsskrift*, 1911, vol. I, lxiii + 227 pp. W. H. Stevenson, see London below. A. Wall, "A contribution towards the study of the Scandinavian element in the English dialects," *Anglia*, XX (1897–98), 45–135. R. E. Zachrisson, see under Suffixes above. W. Rye, see Norfolk, below.

For Scandinavian place-names see pp. 59–60 below.

English Counties. Bedfordshire. G. H. Fowler, "Some Saxon charters," *Bedfordshire Histor. Record Soc. Publ.*, V, i (1919), 39–57. W. W. Skeat, "The place-names of Bedfordshire," *Cambridge Antiq. Soc.*, Octavo Ser. No. 42 (1906). A. Mawer and F. M. Stenton, *The place-names of Bedfordshire and Huntingdonshire* (Engl. Place-Name Soc., vol. III), Cambridge, 1926. **Berkshire.** W. W. Skeat, *The place-names of Berkshire*, Oxford, 1911. F. M. Stenton, *Place-names of Berkshire*, Reading, 1911. G. B. Grundy, "Berkshire charters," *Berks., Bucks., and Oxon. Archaeolog. Journ.*, XXVII (1922–23), 137–71, 193–247; XXVIII (1924); 64–80; XXIX (1925), 87–128, 196–220; XXX (1926), 48–63, 102–20; XXXI (1927), 31–62, 111–45; XXXII (1928), 16–30. See also Grundy under Wilts. below. **Bucks.** A. Mawer and F. M. Stenton, *The place-names of Buckinghamshire* (Engl. Place-Name Soc., vol. II), Cambridge, 1925. C. F. J. Bourke, "Notes on place-name endings in Buckinghamshire," *Architect. and Archaeolog. Soc. of Bucks., Records of Bucks.*, VIII (1903), 327–41. See also Grundy under Berks. **Cambridgeshire.** W. W. Skeat, "The place-names of Cambridgeshire," *Cambridge Antiquar. Soc.*, Octavo Publ. no. 36 (1901). W. H. Evans and A. L. Williams, "Cambridgeshire place-names: Steeple Morden and Guilden Morden," *Notes and queries*, Ser. 13, I (1923), 32. C. Schererz, "Studien zu den Ortsnamen von Cambridgeshire," *ZONF*, III (1928), 13–26, 176–99. **Cheshire,** E. Ekwall, "Etymological notes," *Englische Studien*, LXIV (1929), 219–26. **Cornwall.** T. F. G. Dexter, *Cornish names*, London, 1926. M. Förster, "Die alten Namen von Kap Land's End," *NoB*, XII (1924), 41–49. **Cumberland.** W. J. Sedgfield, *Place-names of Cumberland and Westmoreland*, Manchester, 1915; also issued as vol. XIV of Cumberland and Westmoreland Antiquar. and Archaeolog.

Soc., Extra Ser. W. G. COLLINGWOOD, "Mountain-names [in Cumberland and Westmoreland]," *Cumberland and Westmoreland Antiquar. and Archaeolog. Soc., Transactions*, New Ser., XVIII (1918), 93–104. **Derbyshire.** B. WALKER, "Place-names of Derbyshire," *Journ. Derbyshire Archaeolog. and Natural Hist. Soc.*, XXXVI (1914), 123–284; XXXVII (1915), 97–244. **Devonshire.** B. BLOMÉ, *The place-names of North Devonshire*, Uppsala, 1929 (Diss.). **Durham.** C. E. JACKSON, *The place-names of Durham*, London, 1916. A. MAWER, "Notes on some place-names of Northumberland and County Durham," *Archaeologia Aeliana*, Ser. 3, XVI (1919), 89–102; *The place-names of Northumberland and Durham*, Cambridge, 1920. **Essex.** B. A. MACKENZIE, "Unfractured forms in thirteenth-century Essex place-names," *Rev. English Studies*, III (1927), 453–55. P. H. REANEY, "Essex place-names," *English*, III (1921), 508, 509, 524–26; "Essex place-names in -ing," *Modern lang. rev.*, XIX (1924), 466–69. **Gloucestershire.** W. ST. C. BADDELEY, *Place-names of Gloucestershire: a handbook*, Gloucester, 1913. C. S. TAYLOR, "Cotswold in Saxon times," *Bristol and Gloucestershire Archaeolog. Soc., Transactions*, XX (1895–97), 267–306. **Hampshire.** G. B. GRUNDY, "The Saxon land charters of Hampshire with notes on place and field names," *Archaeolog. Journ.*, New Ser., XXVIII (1921), 53–173; XXXI (1924), 31–126; XXXIII (1926), 91–253; "On place-names in general, and the Hampshire place-names in particular," *Hants Field Club and Archaeolog. Soc., Papers and Proceedings*, IX (1922), 221–61. See also GRUNDY under Wilts. below. **Herefordshire.** W. ST. C. BADDELEY, "Place-names of Herefordshire," *Bristol and Gloucestershire Archaeolog. Soc., Trans.*, XXXIX (1913), 87–200. A. T. BANNISTER, *The place-names of Herefordshire; their origin and development*, Cambridge (priv. printed), 1916. **Hertfordshire.** W. W. SKEAT, *The place-names of Hertfordshire*, East Herts Archaeolog. Soc., Hertford, 1904. **Huntingdonshire.** W. W. SKEAT, "The place-names of Huntingdonshire," *Cambridge Antiquar. Soc., Proceedings and Transactions*, X (1898–1903), 317–60. See also Bedfordshire above. **Kent.** J. W. HORSLEY, *Place-names in Kent*, Maidstone, 1921. F. W. HARDMAN, *The Danes in Kent: a survey of Kentish place-names of Scandinavian origin* (a lecture delivered at Walmer, 7 Feb., 1927, and privately printed). **Lancashire.** H. C. WYLD and T. O. HIRST, *The place names of Lancashire: their origin and history*, London, 1911. J. SEPHTON, "Notes on the South Lancashire place-names in Domesday Book," *Otia Merseiana*, IV (1904), 65–74. O. RITTER, "Über einige Ortsnamen aus Lancashire," *Englische Studien*, LIV (1920), 187–93. E. EKWALL, *The place-names of Lancashire*, Manchester, 1922. W. F. IRVINE, "Place-names in the Hundred of Wirral," *Historic Soc. of Lancs. and Cheshire, Trans.*, New Ser., VII–VIII (1891–92), 279–304. H. HARRISON, *The place-names of the Liverpool District; or, the history and meaning of the local and river-names of South-West Lancashire and of Wirral*, London, 1898; *Lancashire place-names*, London, 1911. **Lincolnshire.** C. W. FOSTER and T. LONGLEY (with Introduction by F. M. STENTON), *The Lincolnshire Domesday and Lindsey Survey* (Lincs. Record Soc., Publ. no. 19, 1924). **London** and **Middlesex.** J. E. B. GOVER,

The place-names of Middlesex (including those parts of the County of London formerly contained within the boundaries of the Old County), London, 1922. L. ZETTERSTEN, *City street-names. The origin and history of the names of streets, lanes, alleys, and courts of the City of London*, 3d edition, London, 1926. See also HOPWOOD under Surrey below. W. H. STEVENSON, "Danish place-names around London," *Academy*, XXXIII (1888), 189, 190. **Norfolk.** W. RYE, *Scandinavian names in Norfolk* (RYE'S Norfolk Hand-Lists, no. 1), Norwich, 1916; *A list of Norfolk place-names*, Norwich, 1922; *Some historical essays chiefly relating to Norfolk*, Norwich, 1927. **Northumberland,** see Durham above. **Nottinghamshire.** H. MUTSCHMANN, *The place-names of Nottinghamshire: their origin and development*, Cambridge, 1913. **Oxfordshire.** H. ALEXANDER, *The place-names of Oxfordshire: their origin and development*, Oxford, 1912. **Shropshire.** E. W. BOWCOCK, *Shropshire place-names*, Shrewsbury, 1923. **Somersetshire.** J. S. HILL, *The place-names of Somerset*, Bristol, 1914. G. B. GRUNDY, "The Saxon charters of Somerset," *Somersetshire archaeological and natural history society, Proceedings*, LXXIV (1928), 33ff. **Staffordshire.** W. H. DUIGNAN, *Notes on Staffordshire place names*, London, 1902. O. RITTER, under Place-Names (General) above, pp. 69–84. **Suffolk.** W. W. SKEAT, "The place-names of Suffolk," *Cambridge Antiquar. Soc.*, Octavo Publ. no. 46 (1913). O. RITTER, under Place-Names (General) above, pp. 84–94. **Surrey.** G. S. DAVIES, *Surrey local names; a paper read before the Charterhouse science and art society*, Godalming: R. B. STEDMAN, 1881. D. HOPWOOD, *The place-names of the County of Surrey including London in Surrey* (Annals of the Univ. of Stellenbosch, So. Africa, vol. IV, sec. B, no. 2, October, 1926). **Sussex.** R. G. ROBERTS, *The place-names of Sussex*, Cambridge, 1914. A. MAWER, F. M. STENTON, J. E. B. GOVER, *The place-names of Sussex*, pt. I (English Place-Name Society, vol. VI), Cambridge, 1929. A. ANSCOMBE, "Sussex place-names in Domesday Book which end in *-intun*," *Sussex Archaeolog. Collections*, LIX (1918), 76–83. O. RITTER, under Place-Names (General) above, 94–113. **Warwickshire.** W. H. DUIGNAN, *Warwickshire place-names*, Oxford, 1912. O. RITTER, under Place-Names (General) above, 114–30. **Westmoreland** see Cumberland above. **Wiltshire.** E. EKBLOM, *The place-names of Wiltshire: their origin and history*, Uppsala, 1917 (Diss.). G. B. GRUNDY, "The ancient highways and tracks of Wiltshire, Berkshire, and Hampshire, and the Saxon battlefields of Wiltshire," *Archaeolog. Journ.*, New Ser., XXV (1918), 69–194; "Saxon land charters of Wiltshire," *ibid.*, XXVI (1919), 143–301; XXVII (1920), 8–126. **Worcestershire.** W. H. DUIGNAN, *Worcestershire place-names*, London, 1905. A. MAWER and F. M. STENTON (with F. T. S. HOUGHTON), *The place-names of Worcestershire* (Engl. Place-Name Soc., vol. IV), Cambridge, 1927. O. RITTER, under Place-Names (General) above, 130–36. **Yorkshire.** J. H. TURNER, *Yorkshire place-names, or toponomy as recorded in the Yorkshire Domesday Book, 1086*, Bingley, n.d. F. W. MOORMAN, *The place-names of the West Riding of Yorkshire* (Thoresby Soc. Publ., vol. XVIII), Leeds, 1911. A. GOODALL, *Place-names of South-West Yorkshire, that is, of so much of the West Riding as lies South of the Aire from Keighley onwards*, revised edition,

Cambridge, 1914; "The Scandinavian suffixed article in Yorkshire place-names," *NoB*, V (1917), 102, 103. A. MAWER, "Yorkshire history in the light of its place-names," *Yorks. Philosophical Soc., Annual Report and Proceedings*, 1923. E. V. GORDON and A. H. SMITH, "The river names of Yorkshire," *Yorks. Dialect Soc., Transactions*, Pt. xxvi, vol. IV (1925), 5–30. A. H. SMITH, *The place-names of the North Riding of Yorkshire* (Engl. Place-Name Soc., vol. V), Cambridge, 1928; "Some aspects of Irish influence on Yorkshire," *Revue celtique*, XLIV (1927), 34–58; "The place-names of North Yorkshire," *Yorks. Dialect Soc., Transactions*, Pt. xxvii, vol. IV (1926), 7–19. H. LINDKVIST, "A study on early mediaeval York," *Anglia*, LX (1926), 345–94. South-West Yorkshire, see O. RITTER, under Place-Names (General) above, 136–47.

IRELAND

In general consult Kennedy, *op. cit.*, 343, 344, under Bibliography. The most comprehensive work on Irish place-names is P. W. JOYCE, *The origin and history of Irish names of places*, 3 vols., London, 1910–13. For current items see the periodicals cited under Celtic Literatures.

SCOTLAND

In general consult KENNEDY, *op. cit.*, 345–47, under Bibliography above. Add A. R. FORBES, *Place-names of Skye and adjacent islands*, Paisley, 1923. J. IRVING, *Place-names of Dumbartonshire*, Dumbarton, 1928. J. MEIKLE, *Places and place-names round Alyth*, Paisley, 1925. E. BEVERIDGE, *The 'Abers' and 'Invers' of Scotland*, Edinburgh, 1923. W. J. WATSON, *The history of the Celtic place-names of Scotland*, Edinburgh and London, 1926. See also 'Western Isles,' p. 60 below.

WALES

See KENNEDY, *op. cit.*, 348, under Bibliography above.

ISLE OF MAN

J. J. KNEEN, *The place names of the Isle of Man*, Pts. i–vi, The Manx Soc., Douglas, 1925–29.

FRANCIS P. MAGOUN, JR.

(*b*) FRENCH

(Including *la Belgique wallonne* and *la Suisse romande*)

Bibliography. A recent bibliography will be found in A. DAUZAT, *Les noms de lieux, etc.*, Paris, 1926, reviewed by M. NIEDERMANN in *Zeitschrift für Ortsnamenforschung* (*ZONF*), III (1927), 212–18, especially page 218. Beginning in 1925 the *ZONF* (under the direction of J. SCHNETZ, Munich and Berlin, Oldenburg) gives a classified bibliography of current works on toponomy.

Special bibliographies. Burgundy. A. DAUZAT, "Bibliographie toponymique de la Bourgogne," *ZONF*, V (1929), 245–51. **Lorraine.** Works on toponomy concerning Lorraine are noted and criticized in *Bibliographie lorraine des annales de l'Est*, publiée par la Faculté des lettres de l'Université de Nancy. **Alsace.** Similar works concerning Alsace are in *Bibliographie alsacienne*, publiée par la Faculté des lettres de l'Université de Strasbourg. **Champagne.** See " Les parlers anciens et modernes de la Champagne," by C. BRUNEAU, *Revue de linguistique romane*, V (1929). **Belgium.** *Bulletin de la commission de toponymie et dialectologie*, I (1927), Liége. **Switzerland.** *Glossaire des patois de la Suisse romande* by LOUIS GAUCHAT and JULES JEANJAQUET, Vol. II, *Noms de lieux et de personnes*, Neufchâtel, 1920.

General works. A list of names of inhabited places for the modern period is found in *Dictionnaire de l'administration des postes, télégraphes et téléphones* (use the most recent edition). For earlier periods, *Les dictionnaires topographiques*, publiés dans la Collection des documents historiques. This collection is still incomplete; dictionaries are lacking for several departments, but for those already published refer to one of the recent volumes in the series. For France as a whole the essential work is A. LONGNON; *Les noms de lieux de la France, leur origine, leur signification, leurs transformations*, publié par P. Marichal et L. Mirot, Paris, 1920–29 (Résumé des conférences de toponomastique générale faites à l'Ecole pratique des hautes études). See also H. GRÖHLER, *Über Ursprung und Bedeutung der französischen Ortsnamen.* I. *Ligurische, iberische, phönizische, griechische, gallische, lateinische Namen.* Heidelberg, 1913ff. Collection de manuels publiés sous la direction de M. Meyer-Lübke; see a review by P. SKOK, *Zeitschrift für romanische Philologie*, XXXIX, 111–21 (vol. II has never appeared). L. BERTHOUD and L. MATRUCHOT, "Etude historique et étymologique des noms de lieux habités du département de la Côte d'or," Semur (Extract from *Mémoires de la société des sciences historiques et naturelles de Semur*, 1901, 1902, 1905, 1915). A. DAUZAT, *Les noms de lieux*, Paris; popular work. A. VINCENT, *Les noms de lieux de la Belgique*, Brussels, 1927. G. KURTH, *La frontière linguistique en Belgique et dans le nord de la France*, 2 vols., Brussels, 1895–96. C. G. ROLAND, *Toponymie namuroise*, Namur, 1899 (*Annales de la Société archéologique de Namur*, XXIII). For Belgian Luxembourg see a series of articles by L. ROGER in *Annales de l'Institut archéologique du Luxembourg*, Arlon, XLV, 1910ff. For Switzerland note *Le glossaire des patois de la Suisse romande*, in course of publication.

Special Works. Celtic period. P. AEBISCHER, "Survivance du culte des eaux en pays fribourgeois," *Schweizerisches Archiv für Volkskunde*, XXVII (1926), 27–41. P. MARCHOT, "Note sur un suffixe gaulois -inos, -a, -on, de noms de lieu," *Zeitschrift für französische Sprache und Literatur*, XLVII (1924), 455–61. F. LOT, "Nouveaux exemples d'Igoranda," *Romania*, XLV, 492–96. P. MARCHOT, "Le gaulois archaïque apia," *Zeitschrift für romanische Philologie*, XLIV (1924), 206–15. J. VANNÉRUS, "Les 'chaumont' germaniques: notes de toponymie," *Revue belge de philologie et d'histoire*, I, 283–292. U. HUBSCHMEID, "Drei Ortsnamen gallischen Ursprungs: Ogo, Château d'Oex, Uechtland," *Zeitschrift für deutsche Mundarten*, XIX (1924), *Festschrift Bachmann*. **Gallo-Roman period.** P. SKOK, *Die mit den*

Suffixen -acum, -anum, -ascum und -uscum gebildeten südfranzösischen Ortsnamen, Halle, 1906. (Beiheft 2 zur *Zeitschrift für romanische Philologie.*) W. KASPERS, *Etymologische Untersuchungen über die mit -acum, -anum, -ascum und -uscum gebildeten nordfranzösischen Ortsnamen*, Halle, 1918; "Lateinische Personennamen aus französischen Ortsnamen erschlossen," *Wörter und Sachen*, IX (1926), 89–105. A. DAUZAT, "Notes de toponymie gallo-romaine," *ZONF*, IV (1928), 257–69. C. BRUNEAU, "Solimariaca, Solicia, Soulosse," *Mélanges offerts à M. Antoine Thomas*, Paris, 1927. **Place-names of Germanic origin.** P. MARCHOT, "Le germanique *awia* 'eau courante,' ou 'prairie avec eau courante' en français," *Archivum romanicum*, VIII (1924), 305ff. E. MURET, "Le suffixe germanique -ing dans les noms de lieu de la Suisse française et des autres pays de langue romane," *Mélanges de Saussure*, Paris, 1908, 269–308; "Les noms de lieux germaniques en -ens ou -ans, -enges ou -anges dans les pays de domination burgonde," *Revue de linguistique romane*, IV (1928), 209–21. **Roman period.** A. VINCENT, "Les diminutifs de noms propres de cours d'eau, particulièrement dans le domaine français," *Revue belge de philologie et d'histoire*, IV (1925), 35–76. H. ANDRESEN, "Villeneuve und Neuville," *Zeitschrift für romanische Philologie*, XXXVII (1913), 355–57. C. BRUNEAU, "Quelques noms de cantons de la forêt de Haye: les Rapailles de Maron; le plateau des Rays; au Haouï (étude de toponymie)" (Extract from *Bulletin de la société d'archéologie lorraine*, 1929). **Regional studies.** A. VINCENT, "L'Escaut, étude toponymique," Brussels, 1922 (Extract from *Revue de l'Université de Bruxelles*, 1922). E. MURET, "De quelques noms de lieu particulièrement fréquents dans la Suisse romande et en Savoie," *Romania*, XXXVII (1908), 1–46, 378–420, 540–69. M. NIEDERMANN, "Note de toponymie française," *Mélanges linguistiques offerts à M. J. Vendryes*, Paris, 1925, 301–07. P. SKOK, "Ortsetymologische Miszellen," *Zeitschrift für romanische Philologie*, XXXIX (1919), 608–17 (devoted primarily to the South of France). F. LANGENBECK, Beiträge zur elsässischen Siedlungsgeschichte und Ortsnamenkunde. I. Die elsässischen -ingen, -ach, und -heim Siedlungen, *Elsässisch-Lothringisches Jahrbuch*, VI (1927), 76–115. **Linguistic studies with special significance for toponomy.** E. HOCHULI, *Einige Bezeichnungen für den Begriff "Strasse," "Weg," "Kreuzweg" im Romanischen*, Zurich, 1926 (Diss.). P. SCHEUERMEIER, *Einige Bezeichnungen für den Begriff "Höhle" in den romanischen Alpendialekten* (*Balma, Spelunca, Crypta, Tana, Cubulum*). *Ein wortgeschichtlicher Beitrag zum Studium der alpiner Geländeausdrücke*, Heidelberg, 1920 (*Beiheft 69 zur Zeitschrift für romanische Philologie*). W. KAUFMANN, *Die galloromanischen Bezeichnungen für den Begriff "Wald,"* Zurich, 1913 (Diss.).

CHARLES BRUNEAU.

(*c*) HIGH AND LOW GERMAN

Bibliography. Current bibliographies may be found in *Zeitschrift für Ortsnamenforschung*, 1925ff. and *Volkskundliche Bibliographie*, 1917ff. Partial and special bibliographies are numerous. Some are cited below under the appropriate geographical heading. The most comprehensive is that edited by H. BESCHORNER, *Handbuch der deutschen Flurnamenliteratur bis Ende 1926*, Frankfurt a.M., 1928. Nearly every work has a bibliography of from one to ten pages.

General. *Zeitschrift für Ortsnamenforschung*, supra. *Zeitschrift für deutsche Mundarten*, 1906ff. as continuation of *Zeitschrift für hochdeutsche Mundarten*, vols. I–VI, Heidelberg, 1900–05. Many special articles and bibliographies may be found in the various folklore periodicals cited in the *Volkskundliche Bibliographie*. E. FÖRSTEMANN, *Die deutschen Ortsnamen*, Nordhausen, 1863. *Ortskunde und Ortsnamenforschung im Dienste der Sprachwissenschaft und Geschichte*, Halle, 1895. F. PFAFF, *Deutsche Ortsnamen*, Berlin, 1896. E. SCHROEDER, "Über Ortsnamenforschung," *Zeitschrift des Harzvereins*, XLI (1908), 76–92. O. WEISE, "Die deutsche Ortsnamenforschung im letzten Jahrzehnt," *Germanisch-Romanische Monatsschrift*, II (1910), 433ff. E. FÖRSTEMANN, *Altdeutsches Namenbuch*, 3d edition by H. JELLINGHAUS, Bd. II (2 Parts), *Ortsnamen*, Bonn, 1913–16. J. FELDMANN, *Ortsnamen: Ihre Entstehung und Bedeutung*, Halle, 1925. J. MEIER, *Deutsche Volkskunde*, 125–68 and 321ff., Berlin and Leipzig, 1926. K. BOHNENBERGER, "Zu den Ortsnamen," *Germanica. Festschrift für E. Sievers*, 129–202, Leipzig, 1925. R. KLEINPAUL, *Länder-und Völkernamen* (Sammlung Göschen, No. 478), 3d ed., Berlin, 1922. R. KLEINPAUL, *Die Ortsnamen im Deutschen*, (Sammlung Göschen 573), 2d ed., Berlin, 1919.

Prussia. G. GERULLIS, *Die altpreussischen Ortsnamen*, Berlin, 1922. H. PATZIG, *Alte Ortsnamen im Westen Gross-Berlins*, Berlin, 1926. A. BUTTMANN, *Die deutschen Ortsnamen mit besonderer Berücksichtigung der ursprünglich wendischen in der Mittelmark und Niederlausitz*, Berlin, 1856. G. WEISKER, *Slavische Sprachreste, insbesondere Ortsnamen, aus dem Havellande und den angrenzenden Gebieten, I u. II Teil*, Rathenow, 1890–96. F. CURSCHMANN, *Die deutschen Ortsnamen im nordostdeutschen Kolonialgebiet*, Stuttgart, 1910. J. RINK, *Die Orts- und Flurnamen der Koschneiderei* (*Quellen und Darstellungen zur Geschichte Westpreussens*, hrsg. v. Westpreussischen Geschichtsverein, 12), Danzig, 1926. *Schlesische Bibliographie*, hrsg. von der Historischen Kommission für Schlesien, Bd. III. *Bibliographie der schlesischen Volkskunde*, 289–342, "Die Namengebung," Breslau, 1929. P. DOHM, *Holsteinische Ortsnamen*, Kiel, 1908 (Diss.). J. SÖRENSEN, *Südschleswigsche Ortsnamen* (*Schriften zur schleswigschen Geschichte*, no. 4), Flensburg, 1923. J. SCHMIDT-PETERSEN, *Die Orts- und Flurnamen Nordfrieslands. Text und Atlas*, Husum, 1925; *Die Orts- und Flurnamen der Insel Föhr*, Husum, n.d.; *Die Orts- und Flurnamen der Insel Amrum*, Husum, n.d. L. BÜCKMANN, "Orts- und Flurnamen des Regierungsbezirks Lüneburg," *Lüneburger Heimatbuch*, hrsg. von O. und TH. BENECKE, 2 Aufl., II, 93–167, Bremen, 1926. H. JELLINGHAUS, *Die westfälischen Ortsnamen*, 3 Ausg., Osnabrück, 1923. Müller, *Die Ortsnamen im Regierungsbezirk Trier*, in *Jahresbericht der Gesellschaft für nützliche Forschungen zu Trier*, I, 1900 to 1905, and II, 1909. H. MARJAN, *Keltische Ortsnamen in der Rheinprovinz*, I–IV, Aachen, 1880–84. F. CRAMER, *Rheinische Ortsnamen aus vorrömischer* *und römischer Zeit*, Düsseldorf, 1901. W. KASPERS, *Die Acum-Ortsnamen des Rheinlandes*, Halle, 1921. W. STURMFELS, *Die Ortsnamen Hessens*, Leipzig, 1910. E. ZIEHEN, *Ortsnamen in und um Frankfurt*, Frankfurt a.M., 1926. A. WREDE, *Eifeler Volkskunde*, 2nd edition, p. 24ff. and notes, Bonn, 1924. J. GOTZEN, *Die Ortsnamen des Kreises Geilenkirchen*, Geilenkirchen, 1926.

Thuringia. H. HEINE, "Über thüringisch-sächsische Ortsnamen," *Pädagogisches Magazin*, no. 274, Langensalza, 1906. P. CASSEL, *Ueber thüringische Ortsnamen*, Erfurt, 1856; *Thüringische Ortsnamen*, Erfurt, 1858.

Mecklenburg. D. RAHN, *Die Orts- und Flurnamen des Staat- und Landkreises Greifswald*, Greifswald, 1923. (Bibliography.)

Saxony. P. KNAUTH, *Ortsnamenkunde des östlichen Erzgebirges*, Freiberg (Saxony), 1927.

Lübeck. W. OHNESORGE, *Deutung des Namens Lübeck*, Lübeck, 1910. (Pp. 8ff. *Bibliographie über die Forschungen zur slawischen Ortsnamenkunde.* Arranged geographically.)

Hamburg. L. BÜCKMANN, "Orts- und Flurnamen des Kreises Harburg," *Zwischen Elbe, Seere und Este*, hrsg. von H. LAVE und H. MEYER, I (1925), 298–318.

Bavaria. M. R. BUCK, *Oberdeutsches Flurnamenbuch*, Stuttgart, 1880. T. ZINK, *Pfälzische Flurnamen*, Kaiserslautern, 1923. (Bibliography.) E. EBERL, *Die bayerischen Ortsnamen als Grundlage der Siedlungsgeschichte*, I. und II. Teil, Munich, 1925–26. R. VOLLMANN, *Flurnamensammlung*, 4te verbesserte und vermehrte Auflage, Munich, 1926. (Pp. 65–70, Bibliography.) C. BECK, *Die Ortsnamen des Aischtales und der Nachbarländer*, Neustadt a.d. Aisch, 1926. (Bibliography.) J. MIEDEL, "Bayerische Ortsnamenforschung," 1910–20, *Bayerische Hefte für Volkskunde*, 1920, pp. 2 ff. G. BUCHNER, *Die Ortsnamenkundliche Literatur von Südbayern.* Prog., Munich, Piloty & Soehle, 1920. G. BUCHNER, "Schriftenverzeichnis zur Ortsnamenkundlichen Literatur Bayerns" (continued from *Bayerische Hefte für Volkskunde*, vols. IX and X), *Bayerischer Heimatschutz* (*Zeitschrift des bayerischen Vereins für Heimatschutz*), XXII (1926), 122–24; XXIII (1927), 203–07; XXIV (1928), 112–13.

Baden. O. HELIIG, *Die Ortsnamen des Grossherzogtums Baden*, Karlsruhe, n.d. (Bibliography.) A. GOTZE, *Die alten Namen der Gemarkung Waldshut*, Freiburg i.B., 1923 (pp. 5–7, Bibliography).

Wurttemberg. J. MIEDEL, *Oberschwäbische Orts- und Flurnamen*, Memmingen, 1906. W. KEINATH, *Württembergisches Flurnamenbüchlein*, Tübingen, 1926. K. BOHNENBERGER, *Die Ortsnamen Württembergs*, Tübingen, 1926.

OTHER COUNTRIES

Switzerland. W. GÖTZINGER, *Die romanischen Ortsnamen des Kantons St. Gallen*, St. Gall, 1891. H. BÄCHTOLD, *Die Flurnamen der schaffhauserischen Enklave Stein am Rhein*, Frauenfeld, 1916. (Bibliography, pp. 34–35.) M. KOCH, *Die Flurnamen der Gemarkung Thayngen im Kanton Schaffhausen*,

Bern, 1926. (Bibliography, pp. 7–14.) A. KÜBLER, *Die romanischen und deutschen Örtlichkeitsnamen des Kantons Graubünden*, Heidelberg, 1926.

Austria. C. v. ETTMAYER, "Geographica raetica. Versuch einer kritischen Ortsnamensystematik," *G.R.M.* II (1910), 299ff., 357ff. J. STUR, *Die slawischen Sprachelemente in den Ortsnamen der deutsch-österreichischen Alpenländer zwischen Donau und Drau, S.B., Vienna Acad.*, 1914. C. SCHNELLER, *Beiträge zur Ortsnamenkunde Tirols*, Innsbruck, 1893. K. SCHIFFMANN, *Das Land ob der Enns*, Munich and Berlin. (Bibliography.) G. PROSCH, *Die Hof- und Flurnamen in Lüsen*, Innsbruck, 1924. C. BATTIST, "Die Erforschung der Ortsnamen in Oberetsch während der Jahre 1914–1924," *ZONF*, I (1925), 140–55; 223–31. E. SCHWARZ, *Die Ortsnamen des östlichen Oberösterreich*, Reichenberg i.B., 1926. G. BUCHNER, *Bibliographie zur Ortsnamenkunde der Ostalpenländer*, Munich, 1927. E. SCHWARZ, "Die oberösterreichische Ortsnamenforschung," *ZONF*, III (1927), 53–61. W. VAN LINXTHOUDT, "Die niederösterreichische Ortsnamenforschung," *ZONF*, III (1927), 123–37; IV (1928), 193.

Czechoslovakia. E. SCHWARZ, *Flurnamenforschung in den Sudetenländern. Mitteilungen des Vereins für Geschichte der Deutschen in Böhmen*, 64 (1926), 93–110; 133–47; "Die Ortsnamenforschung in den Sudetenländern," *ZONF*, IV (1928), 64–77.

Hungary. V. LUG, *Deutsche Ortsnamen in Ungarn*, Reichenberg i.B., 1917.

Rumania. O. LIEBHART, *Die Ortsnamen des Seklergebietes in Siebenbürgen*, Leipzig, 1927. (Bibliography, pp. 86–89.) S. ORPEANU, *Beiträge zur Toponomie des Seklerlandes*, Klausenburg, 1926. I. IORDAN, "Bezeichnungen für 'Rodeland' in der rumänischen Toponomastik," *ZONF*, IV (1928), 48–60 (brief bibliography, p. 51f.), 171–83.

Holland and Belgium. W. NIJHOFF, *Bibliographie van Noord-Nederlandsche plaatsbeschrijvingen tot op het einde der XVIIIe eeuw*, Amsterdam, 1894. JOURDAIN and VAN STALLE, *Dictionnaire encyclopédique de géographie historique du royaume de Belgique*, 2 vols., Brussels, 1896. J. WINKLER, *Friesche Naamlijst*, Leeuwarden, 1898. K. DEFLOU, *Woordenboek der Toponymie van westlijk Vlaanderen*, Ie en IIe deel, Ghent, 1914–21. *Nomina geographica Neerlandica*, onder redactie van I. DORNSEIFFEN, J. H. GALLÉE et al. I–VI, Leyden, 1885–1928. J. MANSION, *Oud-gentsche Naamkunde*, The Hague, 1924. M. SCHÖNFELD, "Overzicht van het Onderzoek der Plaatsnamen in de Nederlanden, voornamelik in de laatste tien Jaren," *Nomina geographica Neerlandica*, VI, 9–21; "Die Ortsnamenforschung in den Niederlanden hauptsächlich während des letzten Jahrzehnts," *ZONF*, II (1927), 168–78. H. J. VAN DE WIJER, "Bibliographie van de Vlaamsche Plaatsnaamkunde," *Nomina geographica Flandrica*, I, Brussels, 1928. J. MANSION, "De huidige stand van het toponymisch onderzoek vooral in Belgie," *Leuvensche Bijdragen*, XIV (1922), 1–18. H. J. VAN DE WIJER, "Ons Toponymisch Onderzoek," *Leuvensche Bijdragen*, XVIII, 1 (1926), Bijblad, pp. 1–15; XX (1928), 48–59. A. VINCENT, *Les noms de lieux de la Belgique*, Brussels, 1927. Vlaamsche Toponymische Vereeniging te Leuven, *Mededeelingen*,

1925ff. contains an annual bibliography. *Bulletin de la commission de (Handelingen van de Commissie voor) toponymie et dialectologie*, 1927ff.

Luxemburg. J. Vannérus, "Notes d'histoire et de toponymie luxembourgeoises" *Ons Hemecht*, XXXI (1925), 18–44, 148–59. J. Vannérus, "A propos de noms de lieux luxembourgeoises en *-ing* ou en *-ingen*," *Bulletin de la Commission de Toponymie et Dialectologie*, II (1928), 225–63.

Latvia. E. Blesse, "Die Ortsnamenforschung in Lettland," *ZONF*, II (1927), 159–68.

Taylor Starck.

(*d*) Scandinavian

General. M. Kristensen, "Nordisk Stednavnegranskning," *Danske Studier* (1905), 177–93. H. Falk, "Die skandinavischen Ortsnamen und ihre Erforschung," *German.-Roman. Monatsschrift*, II (1910), 374–82. G. T. Flom, "The study of place-names with special reference to Norway," *Journ. English and Germanic Philol.*, XXIII (1924), 199–216. Current bibliographies may be found in *Namn och Bygd*, 1913–20; *Volkskundliche Bibliographie*, 1919ff. (for 1917ff.); *Zs. für Ortsnamenforschung*, 1925ff.; *Arkiv för nordisk Filologi*, 1883ff.; *Acta philologica Scandinavica*, 1926ff. See also O. Lundberg, *Nordisk Ortnamnlitteratur i bibliografisk Förteckning, År 1912*, Uppsala, 1917.

Denmark. *Danmarks Stednavne*, 1922ff. (official publication). Articles in *Danske Studier*, 1904ff.

Norway. *Norske Gaardnavne*, vols. I–XVII, Supplement, 1898–1924 (official publication). G. Indrebö, "Die Ortsnamenforschung in Norwegen," *Zs. für Ortsnamenforschung*, IV (1929), 273–82. Articles in *Maal og Minne*, 1909ff. M. Olsen, *Farms and fanes of ancient Norway: the place-names of a country discussed in their bearings on social and religious history*, Oslo and Cambridge, Mass., 1928.

Sweden. *Sverges Ortnamn*, 1906ff. (official publication). *Skrifter utg. av Institutet för Ortnams- och Dialektforskning vid Göteborgs Högskola*, Göteborg, 1918ff. *Sydsvenska Ortnamnsällskapets Årskrift*, 1925ff. Many articles and monographs in *Svenska Landsmålen*, 1879ff., *Namn och Bygd*, and in the publications of local antiquarian societies.

Finland. T. E. Karsten, *Svensk Bygd i Österbotten:* I, *Naturnamn;* II, *Kulturnamn* (Skrifter utg. av svenska Litteratursällskapet i Finland, vols. CLV, CLXXI), Helsingfors, 1921–23; G. Hausen, *Nylands Ortnamn* (*ibid.*, vols. CLII, CLX, CLXXVII), Helsingfors, 1920–24; *Ålands Ortnamn* (*ibid.*, vol. CXCIV), Helsingfors, 1927.

Iceland. K. Kaalund, *Bidrag til en historisk-topografisk Beskrivelse af Island*, Copenhagen, 1877–82. F. Jónsson, "Bæjanöfn á Íslandi," *Safn til Sögu Islands ok islenzkra Bókmenta*, IV (1911), 412–584; *Kort Oversikt over islandske Gaardnavne* (= Oversikt over det kgl. Danske Vidensk. Selskabs Forhandlinger, 1911, No. 4); "Islandske Elvenavne," *Namn och Bygd*, II (1913), 18–28.

Western Isles and Normandy. J. JAKOBSEN, *The dialect and place-names of Shetland*, Lerwick, 1897; "Shetlandsøernes Stednavne," *Aarbøger for nordisk Oldkyndighed og Historie* (1901), pp. 55–258; "Strejflys over færøske Stednavne," *Nordisk Tidsskrift for Filologi*, 3rd Ser., XVII (1908–09), 64–85; "Om Orknøernes Historie og Sprog," *Danske Studier* (1919), pp. 143–52; "Stednavne og Personnavne i Normandiet med særligt Hensyn til den nordiske Bosættelse," *Danske Studier* (1911), pp. 59–84. A. W. BRØGGER, *Ancient emigrants: a history of the Norse settlements of Scotland*, Oxford, 1929, pp. 68–93.

GREAT BRITAIN. See 'Scandinavian,' pp. 49–50 above.

F. S. CAWLEY.

(*e*) SLAVIC

General. W. OHNESORGE, *Deutung des Namens Lübeck*, esp. pp. 8–14: "Bibliographie über die Forschungen zur slavischen Ortsnamenkunde" (for all basic works prior to 1910). M. VASMER, "Die slavische Ortsnamenforschung in Deutschland," *Zeitschrift für slav. Philol.*, VI (1929), 173. F. MIKLOSICH, *Die Bildung der slavischen Personen- und Ortsnamen*, Heidelberg, 1927. N. P. BARSOV, *Očerki russkoi istoričeskoi Geografii*, Warsaw, 1885.

Recent special articles and monographs. S. KOZIEROWSKI, *Badania Nazw Topograficzñych Dzisiejszej Archidyecezyi Gnieźnieńskiej*, Posen, 1914; *Badania Nazw Topograficznych Dzisiejszej Archidyecezyi Poznańskiej*, Posen, 1916; *Badania Nazw Topograficznych na Obsarze Dawnej Zachodniej i Środkowej Wielkopolski*, 2 vols., Posen, 1921–22; "Pierwotne Osiedlenie Ziemi Gnieźnieńskiej w Swietle Nazw Geograficznych," *Slavia Occidentalis*, III–IV (1923–24), 1–129; *Badania Nazw Topograficznych na Obsarze Dawnej Wschodniej Wielkopolski*, Posen, 1926; *Pierwotne Osiedlenie Dorzecza Warty od koła do Ujścia*, Posen, 1926. S. PIRCHEGGER, *Die slavischen Ortsnamen im Mürzgebiet*, Leipzig, 1927. L. PINTAR, "Zur slavischen Ortsnamenkunde," *Archiv slav. Philol.*, XXXV (1914), 610. M. VASMER, "Zur slavischen Ortsnamenforschung," *ibid.*, XXXVIII (1924), 82; "Nochmals der russische Name von Narva," *ibid.*, XXXVIII (1924), 282. J. SCHNETZ, "Die *-ika* Flussnamen Oesterreichs," *ibid.*, XXXIX (1925), 153. E. EKBLOM, "Die Waräger im Weichselgebiet," *ibid.*, XXXIX (1925), 185. F. LIEWEHR, "Ein Bitrag zu česchischen Namenkunde," *ibid.*, XLI (1927), 156. W. TASZYCKI, "O Pochodzenie Nazwy Miejscowej *Bratislava*," *Slavia*, V (1926), 136. P. SKOK, "Dunaj et Dunav," *ibid.*, VII (1929), 721. J. MELIĆ, "Die Namen von Pressburg," *Zeitschrift für slav. Philol.*, I (1924), 79. R. HOLTZMANN, "Die älteste Namensform für *Pressburg*," *ibid.*, I (1924), 372. J. MELIĆ, "Ueber den serbischen und kroatischen Namen *Fruška Gora*," *ibid.*, II (1925), 35. A. SOBOLEVSKI, "Zur russischen Ortsnamenforschung," *ibid.*, II (1925), 51. H. WITTE, "Die Quellen zur slavischen Ortsnamenforschung in Mecklenburg," *ibid.*, II (1925), 521. M. VASMER, "Neuere Beiträge zur slavischen Ortsnamenforschung," *ibid.*, II (1925), 524; "Zu den slavischen Ortsnamen in Griechenland," *ibid.*, III (1926), 385.

R. KÖTZSCHKE, "Die Quellen zur slavischen Namenforschung in Thüringen und dem Freistaat Sachsen," *ibid.*, III (1926), 438. G. ILJINSKI, "Nochmals der Name von Moskau," *ibid.*, IV (1927), 104. R. HOLTZMANN, "Die Quellen zur slavischen Namenforschung in der Provinz Sachsen und dem Freistaat Anhalt," *ibid.*, IV (1927), 435. A. BRÜCKNER, "Zur slavischen und slavodeutschen Ortsnamenforschung," *Zs. f. Ortsnamenforschung*, II (1926), 67. S. MLADENOV, "Die Ortsnamenforschung bei den Bulgaren 1914–1925," *ibid.*, III (1927), 138. T. TOMICKI, *Słowiańskie Rzeki w Europie*, Crakow, 1925.

S. H. CROSS.

(*f*) SPANISH AND PORTUGUESE

The study of Spanish and Portuguese place-names has not been taken up in a systematic way. No comprehensive collections or special analyses exist. A full bibliography can easily be prepared with the help of the works listed chronologically below. Current bibliographies may be found in the *Bulleti de dialectología catalana*, Barcelona, 1913ff. and especially in the *Revista de filología española*, Madrid, 1914ff. J. DE JAURGAIN, "Toponimie basque," *Revista internacional de estudios bascos*, VIII, Paris, 1914. A. GOMES PEREIRA, *Toponimia dos concelhos de terra de Bouro, Povoa de Varzim e Villa do Conde*, Espozenda, 1914. J. MIRET Y SANS, "Los noms personals y geografìcho de la encontrada de Terrasa en los segles Xe y XIe," *Boletín de la real academia de buenas letras*, XIV, 385–407, 485–509, Barcelona, 1914. J. DA SILVERIA, "Toponímia portuguesa," *Revista lusitana*, XVII, 114–34, Lisbon, 1914. J. ALTADILL, "Nombres geográficos," *Boletín de la Comisión provincial de monumentos de Navarra*, VII, 101–7, Pamplona, 1916. A. MARTÎNEZ PAJARES, *Estudio sobre apellidos y nombres de lugar hispanomarroquês*, 1918. E. ASSMANN, "Altspanische Ortsnamen als Zeugen babylonischer Kolonisation," *Spanien*, III, 92–6, Hamburg, 1921. M. DE MONTOLIU, "Els noms de rius i els noms fluvials en la toponímia catalana," *Bulleti de dialectología catalana*, X, 1–33, Barcelona, 1922. A. M. ALCOVER, "Els noms de lloch," *Bolleti del diccionari de la llengua catalana*, XIV, 16–65, Palma de Mallorca, 1925. J. DA SILVEIRA, "Toponímia portuguesa," *Revista lusitana*, XXIV, 189–226, Lisbon, 1921–2. D. LOPES, "Toponímia árabe de Portugal," *Revista lusitana*, XXIV, 257–73, Lisbon, 1921–2. A. DE ALBUQUERQUE, "O nome de Portugal," *Nação portuguesa*, II, 241–9, Lisbon, 1927.

TAYLOR STARCK.

CHAPTER IV

GENERAL MODERN HISTORICAL WORKS

§ 1. Universal Histories

313. Allgemeine Geschichte in Einzeldarstellungen. Edited by W. ONCKEN. 45 vols. Berlin, 1879–93.

Commonly known as the "ONCKEN" series.

Part II, *History of the middle ages*, 10 works are noted in appropriate places.

313a. Histoire générale. Edited by G. GLOTZ, Paris, [in progress. Fasc. I of Sect. II: Western Roman Empire from 395 to 888, appeared in 1928].

314. History of all nations. 24 vols. Philadelphia, 1902–05.

Vols. VI–VII by J. v. PFLUGK-HARTTUNG; and vols. VIII–X, by H. PRUTZ, are on the middle ages.

315. Weltgeschichte. Edited by H. F. HELMOLT. 9 vols. Leipzig and Vienna, 1899–1907. 2nd, revised, edition by A. TILLE, 10 vols., 1913ff. Translated into English, The history of the world. 8 vols. New York, 1902–07.

A co-operative work arranged anthropologically and ethnologically, not chronologically. Based on the ideas of F. RATZEL. It is rather confusing. The portions on the middle ages are not so good as other parts of the work.

316. RANKE, L. v. Weltgeschichte. 9 vols. 5th edition, Leipzig, 1896–98. Popular edition, without notes, 4 vols. Leipzig, 1895.

Extends to the end of the 15th century.

317. WEBER, G. Allgemeine Weltgeschichte. 15 vols. and 4 index vols. 2nd edition, Leipzig, 1882–89. 3rd edition, 16 vols., Leipzig, 1922.

318. Weltgeschichte: die Entwickelung der Menschheit in Staat und Gesellschaft, in Kultur- und Geistesleben. 6 vols. Berlin, 1907–10. Edited by J v. PFLUGK-HARTTUNG. Vol. II, Geschichte des Mittelalters. Berlin, 1909.

Beautifully illustrated. See facsimiles of bulls and charters, with translations.

319. L'évolution de l'humanité. Edited by H. BERR. Paris, 1915ff.

319a. The history of civilization. New York, 1924ff.

This American series contains, in translation, many of the volumes which are published in **319**.

319b. Peuples et civilisations, histoire générale. Edited by L. HALPHEN and P. SAGNAC, Paris, 1926ff.

320. Bibliothek der Geschichtswissenschaft. Edited by E. BRANDENBURG. Leipzig, 1908ff.

The various volumes pertaining to the middle ages in this set and in nos. **321–27** will be mentioned in appropriate places.

321. Story of the nations series. New York, G. P. Putnam's Sons.

322. The making of the nations series. London, Adam and Charles Black.

323. The great peoples series. New York, Appleton.

324. Heroes of the nations series. New York, G. P. Putnam's Sons.

325. The world's epoch makers. Edited by O. SMEATON. New York, Charles Scribner's Sons.

326. Monographien zur Weltgeschichte. Edited by E. HEYCK and others. Bielefeld, 1897ff. Illustrated.

327. Weltgeschichte in Karakterbildern. Edited by F. KAMPERS and others. Part II on the middle ages. Illustrated.

§ 2. Medieval and Modern History

328. Histoire générale du IVe siècle à nos jours. Edited by E. LAVISSE and A. RAMBAUD. 12 vols. Paris, 1893–1901. New edition with revised bibliographies. Paris, 1927.

Vols. I–III cover the period 395–1492 A.D. A co-operative work of fundamental importance. About a dozen scholars have contributed to each volume.

E. LAVISSE, *Vue générale de l'histoire politique de l'Europe*, 2nd edition, Paris, 1890; translated by C. GROSS, *General view of the political history of Europe*, New York, 1897, is a remarkably lucid and stimulating summary of a couple of hundred pages.

329. Periods of European history. 8 vols. London and New York, Macmillan.

C. W. C. OMAN, *The dark ages, 476–918*, 1893; 2nd edition, 1894. T. F. TOUT, *The empire and papacy, 918–1273*, 1898. R. LODGE, *The close of the middle ages, 1273–1494*, 1901.

330. Handbuch der mittelalterlichen und neueren Geschichte. Edited by G. v. BELOW and F. MEINEKE. Munich and Berlin, 1903ff.

An undertaking like the *Handbuch der klassischen Altertumswissenschaft*, edited by I. MÜLLER, but broader in scope. The volumes are appearing irregularly. In a measure this publication is supplemented by the *Grundriss* edited by MEISTER, no. **331,** and by the *Bibliothek der Geschichtswissenschaft*, no. **320.**

331. Grundriss der Geschichtswissenschaft: zur Einführung in das Studium der deutschen Geschichte des Mittelalters und der Neuzeit. Edited by A. MEISTER. Leipzig and Berlin, 1906ff.

Not confined to German history. Special attention is given to sciences auxiliary to history. The various numbers which have appeared will be mentioned in their appropriate places.

332. Allgemeine Staatengeschichte. Hamburg, 1829ff. Gotha, 1855ff. Founded by A. H. L. HEEREN and F. A. UKERT and was continued by W. v. GIESEBRECHT and K. LAMPRECHT. Part I. Geschichte der europäischen Staaten.

Started by the same impulses which created the *Monumenta Germaniae historica*, no. **978.** WOLF, no. **66,** pp. 459–62, gives a good description of it and mentions some of the more useful works included. A complete list of the volumes is given by LOEWE, *Bücherkunde*, no. **32,** Anhang.

333. LINDNER, T. Weltgeschichte seit der Völkerwanderung. 7 vols., Stuttgart and Berlin, 1901–10.

334. KLOPP, O. Politische Geschichte Europas seit der Völkerwanderung. 2 vols. Mainz, 1912.

335. Epochs of modern history. Longmans.

R. W. CHURCH. *The beginnings of the middle ages*, 1885; A. H. JOHNSON, *The Normans in Europe*, 1877; G. W. COX, *The Crusades*, 1875.

336. FORREST, J. The development of western civilization. Chicago, 1907.

337. DEWE, J. A. Mediaeval and modern history: its formative causes and broad movements. London, 1907.

338. HILL, D. J. A history of diplomacy in the international development of Europe. 2 vols. London, 1905.

339. WOOLEY, R. M. Coronation rites. Cambridge, 1915. (Cambridge handbooks of liturgical study.)

§ 3. Medieval History

(*a*) STANDARD GENERAL SURVEYS

340. The Cambridge medieval history. Planned by J. B. BURY. London and New York, 1911ff. Vol. VI appeared in 1929.

Vol. I, *The renaissance*, of the *Cambridge modern history*, 12 vols., London, 1902ff., is important for the history of the fifteenth century and some chapters reach back even farther.

341. GIBBON, E. [1737–94]. The history of the decline and fall of the Roman empire. Edited with introduction, notes, appendices and index by J. B. BURY. 7 vols. London, 1896–1900.

The first edition appeared 1776–81. It covers the period from the 2nd century A.D. to the late 15th century. The scope of the work is so broad that it practically is a general history of the middle ages. BURY's edition was reprinted in 12 vols. by Fred de Fau and Company of New York in 1906, in *The works of Edward Gibbon*, vols. I–XII. This reprint is in large clear type on good white paper which adds much to the enjoyment of reading GIBBON. A very cheap new edition in six volumes, is now in *Everyman's library*, no. **944.** It is edited by A. SMEATON, who has utilized the notes of GUIZOT, MILMAN, WENDT, SMITH, and BURY, besides adding some of his own. The notes of GIBBON are given in full.

342. ASSMANN, W. Geschichte des Mittelalters. Parts I and II [to 1273] in 2nd edition by E. MEYER. Brunswick, 1875–79. Part III [Germany from 1273 to 1517] in 3rd edition by A. v. R. FISCHER, B. SCHEPPING and L. VIERECK. Brunswick, 1902–06.

343. PRUTZ, H. Staatengeschichte des Abendlandes im Mittelalter von Karl dem Grossen bis auf Maximilian. 2 vols. Berlin, 1885–87.

Part of no. **313.**

344. PRUTZ, H. and PFLUGK-HARTTUNG, J. v. Geschichte des Mittelalters. Berlin, 1889.

344a. KOEPPEN, A. L. The world in the middle ages: an historical geography, etc. New York, 1854.

(*b*) LARGE SECTIONS OF THE MIDDLE AGES

345. HODGKIN, T. Italy and her invaders. 8 vols. in 9. Oxford, 1880–99. 2nd thoroughly revised edition of vols. I and II, Oxford, 1892; 2nd slightly revised edition of vols. III and IV, Oxford, 1896; 2nd slightly revised edition by R. H. HODGKIN of vols. V and VI, Oxford, 1916.

In spite of its restricted title, this work is practically a general history of Europe from the 4th to the 9th century.

345a. LOT, F. La fin du monde antique et le début du moyen âge. Paris, 1927.

345b. CARTELLIERI, A. Weltgeschichte als Machtgeschichte, 382–911. Munich, 1927.

346. LOSERTH, J. Geschichte des späteren Mittelalters von 1197 bis 1492. Munich, 1903.

Part of no. **332.** It contains excellent bibliographies.

347. ABBOT, W. C. The expansion of Europe: a history of the foundations of the modern world. 2 vols. New York, 1918.

First four chapters deal with the middle ages, 1200–1500.

(*c*) IMPRESSIONISTIC SURVEYS OF THE MIDDLE AGES

348. HALLAM, H. View of the state of Europe during the middle ages. 2 vols. London, 1818. 11th edition, 3 vols., 1855. Often reprinted.

349. Souttar, R. A short history of mediaeval peoples: from the dawn of the Christian era to the fall of Constantinople. New York, 1907.

350. Del Mar, A. The middle ages revisited or the Roman government and religion and their relation to Britain. New York, 1900.

Contains a curious bibliography.

351. Sheppard, J. G. The fall of Rome and the rise of new nationalities. London, 1861.

A series of lectures.

352. Seignobos, C. Le moyen âge. Paris, 1911.

353. Brown, W. E. The achievement of the middle ages. London, 1928.

354. Osborn, E. B. The middle ages. New York, 1928.

355. Huizinga, J. The waning of the middle ages, a study of the forms of life, thought and art in France and the Netherlands in the XIVth and XVth centuries. London, 1924.

(*d*) Selections from Modern Historians

356. Langlois, C. V. Lectures historiques: histoire du moyen âge (395–1270). Paris, 1901. 5th edition, 1912.

Short selections from French historians, together with good bibliographies.

357. Mariéjol, J. H. Lectures historiques: histoire du moyen âge et des temps modernes, Paris, 1891.

358. Munro, D. C., and Sellery, G. C. Medieval civilization. New York, 1904. Enlarged edition, 1907.

A collection of comparatively short selections, most of them translated and adapted from standard French and German works.

(*e*) The Mediterranean

359. Manfroni, C. Il dominio del Mediterraneo durante il medio evo. Rome, 1900. (Reprint from Rivista marittima, 1900.)

360. Herre, P. Der Kampf um die Herrschaft im Mittelmeer. Leipzig, 1909. (Wissenschaft und Bildung, 46.)

361. Philippson, A. Das Mittelmeergebiet, seine geographische und kulturelle Eigenart. Leipzig, 1907.

§ 4. Text Books of Medieval History in English

362. Adams, G. B. Civilization during the middle ages. New York, 1896. New, revised, edition, 1914.

363. Beazley, C. R. A notebook of medieval history A.D. 323–A.D. 1453. Oxford, 1917.

364. Bémont, C., and Monod, G. Histoire de l'Europe et en particulier de France de 395 à 1270. Paris, 1891. Translated by Mary Sloan and G. B. Adams, Medieval Europe, 395–1270. New York, 1902.

365. Duruy, V. Histoire du moyen âge. Paris, 1861. Translated and abridged from the 12th edition by E. H. and M. D. Whitney, with notes and revisions by G. B. Adams, The history of the middle ages. New York, 1891.

366. Emerton, E. Introduction to the middle ages (375–814). Boston, 1888.

367. Emerton, E. Mediaeval Europe (814–1300). Boston, 1894.

368. Emerton, E. Beginnings of modern Europe (1250–1450). Boston, 1917.

369. Mowat, R. B. Later middle ages, 1254–1494. Oxford, 1917.

370. Hulme, E. M. The middle ages. New York, 1929.

371. Previté-Orton, C. W. Outlines of medieval history. Cambridge, 1916.

372. Munro, D. C., and Sontag, R. J. The middle ages: 395–1500. New York, 1928.

The first edition (by Munro alone) appeared in 1921 and covered the period 395–1270.

373. Robinson, J. H. Medieval and modern times: an introduction to the history of western civilization from the dissolution of the Roman empire to the present time. Boston, new and revised edition, 1926.

374. Seignobos, C. History of mediaeval and modern civilization. New York, 1907.

375. Sellery, G. C., and Krey, A. C. Medieval foundations of western civilization. New York, 1929.

376. Thatcher, O. J., and McNeal, E. H. Europe in the middle age. New York, 1920.

377. Thorndike, L. A history of medieval Europe. New York, 1917. Revised edition, 1928.

§ 5. "Source Books": Short Selections from the Sources

These books are included here rather than under Sources, nos. **949–1013**, because they are so closely associated with text books in the schools.

378. Ayer, J. C. Source book of church history for the first six centuries. New York, Scribner's Sons, 1913.

A similar source book which covers about the same ground but prints documents in the original Greek and Latin is the *Enchiridion fontium historiae ecclesiasticae antiquae*, edited by C. Kirch, Freiburg, 1910.

379. KIDD, B. J. Documents illustrative of the history of the church. 2 vols., New York, 1920–23.

Vol. I, to A.D. 313; vol. II, 313–461.

380. COULTON, G. G. A mediaeval garner. London, 1910.

A new edition of this work has appeared as *Life in the middle ages*, 4 vols. Cambridge, 1928–30. I. Religion, folklore, superstition. II. Chronicles, science and art. III. Men and manners. IV. Monks, friars, and nuns.

381. COULTON, G. G. Social life in Britain from the conquest to the reformation. Cambridge, 1918.

382. DUNCALF, F., and KREY, A. C. Parallel source problems in mediaeval history. New York, 1912.

383. FLING, F. M. European history studies: civilization during the middle ages. Selections made by G. JONES. Ten numbers. Chicago, 1900.

The Teutonic barbarians; Monasticism; Extracts from the Koran; Chivalry and the mode of warfare, etc.

384. HENDERSON, E. F. Select historical documents of the middle ages. London and New York, 1892.

385. MATHEWS, S. Select mediaeval documents and other material, illustrating the history of church and empire, 754–1254. Boston and Chicago, 1892. 2nd edition, 1900.

The documents are printed in the original Latin.

386. OGG, F. A. A source book of mediaeval history. New York, 1908.

387. REICH, E. Select documents illustrating mediaeval and modern history. London, 1905.

Documents are in Latin.

388. ROBINSON, J. H. Readings in European history. 2 vols. Boston, 1906. Abridged in one vol., 1906.

Contains good critical bibliographies at the end of chapters. Vol. I covers the middle ages.

389. THATCHER, O. J., and MCNEAL, E. H. A source book of mediaeval history. New York, 1905.

390. Texts for students. General editors: CAROLINE A. J. SKEEL, H. J. WHITE, J. P. WHITNEY. S.P.C.K. London, 1918ff.

391. Translations and reprints from original sources in European history. Department of history, University of Pennsylvania. Philadelphia, 1894–99.

The following numbers pertain to medieval history: vol. I, nos. 2 and 4; vol. II, nos. 3, 4, and 7; vol. III, nos. 2, 3, 4, 5; vol. IV, nos. 2, 3, 4; vol. VI, nos. 3, 4, 5.

392. WEBSTER, H. Historical selections. Boston, 1929.

§ 6. Histories of the Church

(a) General Histories of the Church

(1) *History of Religions*

393. Reinach, S. Orpheus: histoire générale des religions. 3rd edition, Paris, 1909. Translated by Florence Simmonds, Orpheus: a general history of religions. New York, 1909. New edition, New York, 1930.

Since no attempt is made in this *Guide* to list books on the history of religions, this popular little manual, with its bibliographical notes at the end of chapters, will serve as an introduction to those who wish to go deeper into the subject.

394. Moore, G. F. History of religions. 2 vols. New York, 1919–27.

(2) *Voluminous Standard Accounts*

395. Fleury, C. Histoire ecclésiastique. Last edition, 20 vols. Paris, 1836–37.

This is one of the great church histories and is still important.

395a. Moeller, W. Lehrbuch der Kirchengeschichte. 3 vols. Freiburg, 1889–94. 2nd edition, in 4 vols., 1893–1902. Vol. III in 3rd edition, 1907. Translated by A. Rutherford and J. H. Freese, History of the Christian church. 3 vols. London and New York, 1893–1902.

Vol. II on the middle ages.

396. Schaff, P. History of the Christian church. New edition in 7 vols. New York, 1882–1910.

Vol. V, which is by D. S. Schaff, his son, extends to 1517.

397. Hergenröther, J. von. Handbuch der allgemeinen Kirchengeschichte. 3 vols. 5th edition, by J. P. Kirsch. Freiburg, 1911ff. (Theologische Bibliothek).

There is a French translation by Belet.

398. Mourret, F. Histoire générale de l'église. 9 vols. Paris, 1909–20.

398a. Mourret, F., and Carreyre, J. Précis d'histoire de l'église. 3 vols. Paris, 1924.

399. Neander, J. A. W. Allgemeine Geschichte der christlichen Religion und Kirche [to 1430], 6 vols. Hamburg, 1826–52. Translated by J. Torrey, General history of the Christian religion and church. 9 vols. London, 1847–55.

400. Gieseler, J. C. L. Lehrbuch der Kirchengeschichte. 3 vols. Bonn, 1824ff. 6 vols. in 5, 1828–57. Translated by S. Davidson, A text book of church history. 5 vols. Edinburgh, 1854; American edition, New York, 1876–80.

401. ALZOG, J. Universalgeschichte der Kirche. Mainz, 1841. 10th edition, by F. X. KRAUS, 1882. Translated from the 9th German edition by F. J. PABISCH and T. S. BYRNE, Manual of universal church history. 4 vols. Dublin, 1889–1902.

402. SHELDON, H. C. History of the Christian church. 5 vols. New York, 1894.

403. BAUR, F. C. Geschichte der christlichen Kirche. 5 vols. 3rd edition of vol. I; 2nd edition of vols. II, III, IV. Tübingen, 1863–77.

404. MÖHLER, J. A. Kirchengeschichte, edited by P. B. GAMS. 3 vols. Regensburg, 1867–70.

(3) *Shorter Accounts and Text Books*

405. FISHER, G. P. History of the Christian church. New York, 1888.

A guide to the study of the Christian religion, edited by G. B. SMITH, Chicago [1916]. W. HOBHOUSE, *The church and the world in idea and in history*, London, 1910; 2nd edition, revised, 1911. A. BAUDRILLART, *L'église catholique, la renaissance, le protestantisme*, Paris, 1904, translated by Mrs. P. GIBBS, *The Catholic church, the renaissance and protestantism*, London, 1908, a series of lectures. A. MATER, *L'église catholique: sa constitution, son administration*, Paris, 1906, is historical in treatment.

405a. WALKER, W. A history of the Christian church. New York, 1918.

406. MÜLLER, K. Kirchengeschichte. 2 vols. [to 1555]. Tübingen, 1892–1902. In Grundriss der theologischen Wissenschaften, 4, 2.

See the author's short sketch entitled, "Christentum und Kirche Westeuropas im Mittelalter," in *Kultur der Gegenwart*, no. **729**, part I, IV, 2nd edition, Berlin and Leipzig, 1909.

407. KURTZ, J. H. Lehrbuch der Kirchengeschichte. Mitau, 1894. 14th edition, by N. BONWETSCH and T. TSCHACKERT. 2 vols. Leipzig, 1906. Translated from the 9th German edition by J. MACPHERSON, Church history. 3 vols. London, 1888–93.

408. KNÖPFLER, A. Lehrbuch der Kirchengeschichte auf Grund der akademischen Vorlesungen von K. J. v. HEFELE. 5th edition, Freiburg, 1910.

409. FUNK, F. X. Lehrbuch der Kirchengeschichte. 5th edition. Paderborn, 1907.

410. KRAUS, F. X. Lehrbuch der Kirchengeschichte. 6th edition. Trier, 1909.

411. SCHUBERT, H. v. Grundzüge der Kirchengeschichte. 4th edition. Tübingen, 1909.

412. SOHM, R. Grundriss der Kirchengeschichte. Leipzig, 1887. 16th edition, 1909. Translated by MAY SINCLAIR, from the 8th German edition, Outlines of church history. London, 1901.

413. LOOFS, F. Grundlinien der Kirchengeschichte. Halle, 1901. 2nd edition, 1909.

414. HEUSSI, K. Kompendium der Kirchengeschichte. Tübingen, 1909. 6th edition, 1928.

See also his *Abriss der Kirchengeschichte*, 3rd edition, Tübingen, 1925. (Hilfsbuch für den evangelischen Religionsunterricht an höheren Lehranstalten, Teil 2.)

415. HURST, J. F. A history of the Christian church. 2 vols. New York, 1897–1900 (Library of biblical and theological literature, vols. VII and VIII).

416. WEINGARTEN, H. Zeittafeln und Ueberblicke zur Kirchengeschichte. 6th edition, by C. F. ARNOLD. Leipzig, 1905.

417. Unsere religiösen Erzieher: eine Geschichte des Christentums in Lebensbildern. Edited by B. BESS. 2 vols. Leipzig, 1908.

(4) *Miscellaneous*

418. Epochs of church history. Edited by M. CREIGHTON. London, Longmans, Green and Co.

A. PLUMMER, *The church of the early fathers;* A. CARR, *The church and the Roman empire;* H. M. GWATKIN, *The Arian controversy;* H. F. TOZER, *The church and the eastern empire;* W. R. STEPHENS, *Hildebrand and his times;* U. BALZANI, *The popes and the Hohenstaufens.*

419. RENAN, E. Etudes d'histoire religieuse. 7th edition. Paris, 1864. Nouvelles études d'histoire religieuse. Paris, 1884.

419a. BARTLET, J. V., and CARLYLE, A. J. Christianity in history: a study of religious development. London, 1917.

420. VACANDARD, E. Etudes de critique et d'histoire religieuse. 3 vols. Paris, 1909–12. Vol. I, 4th edition, vol. II, 2nd edition, 1909–10; vol. III, 2nd edition, 1912.

421. Kirchengeschichtliche Festgabe ANTON DE WAAL zum goldenen Priester-Jubiläum (11 October, 1912) dargebracht. Edited by F. X. SEPPELT. Freiburg, 1913. (In Römische Quartalschrift, Supplementheft XX.)

Analyzed in *R.H.*, CXXII (1916), 322.

(*b*) THE ECCLESIASTICAL HIERARCHY

422. EUBEL, C. Hierarchia catholica medii aevi. 3 vols. Münster, 1898–1910. Vol. I, 2nd edition, Münster, 1913.

Extends from 1198 to 1600 A.D.

423. GAMS, P. B. Series episcoporum ecclesiae catholicae. Ratisbon, 1873. Supplement, 1886.

(*c*) THE LATIN CHURCH IN THE MIDDLE AGES

(1) *Extensive Standard Accounts*

424. MILMAN, H. H. History of Latin Christianity. 6 vols. London, 1854–55. Latest edition, 9 vols., London, 1883.

Extends to the middle of the fifteenth century. See also J. C. ROBERTSON, *History of the Christian church to the reformation*, 6th edition, 8 vols., London, 1874–75.

425. BARONIUS, C. (died 1607). Annales ecclesiastici a Christo nato ad annum 1198. 12 vols. Rome, 1588–93. Edited by J. D. MANSI. 35 vols. Lucca, 1738–59. Apparatus, 1 vol., 1740. Index, 4 vols., 1757–59. New edition, with all continuations, 37 vols. Bar-le-Duc and Paris, 1864–83. This edition was to comprise about 50 vols., but was not completed.

Fragmentary translations of this work have been made into French, Italian, German, Polish, and Arabic. BARONIUS printed many extensive selections from the sources.

426. DUFOURCQ, A. L'avenir du christianisme. 8 vols. Paris, 1908ff.

427. LANGEN, J. Geschichte der römischen Kirche. 4 vols. (to Innocent III). Bonn, 1881–93.

427a. SCHUBERT, H. v. Geschichte der christlichen Kirche im Frühmittelalter. Tübingen, 1921.

(2) *Text Books*

428. FLICK, A. C. The rise of the mediaeval church. New York, 1909.

428a. JACKSON, F. J. An introduction to the history of Christianity, A.D. 590–1314. New York, 1921.

429. FICKER, G., and HERMELINK, H. Handbuch der Kirchengeschichte für Studierende: das Mittelalter. Tübingen, 1912. 2nd edition, 1929.

430. SELL, K. Christentum und Weltgeschichte bis zur Reformation. Leipzig, 1910 (Aus Natur und Geisteswelt, 297).

431. LAGARDE, A. The Latin church in the middle ages. Translated by A. ALEXANDER. New York, 1915 (International Theological Library).

432. HARDWICK, C. A history of the Christian church: middle age. 4th edition, revised, and edited by W. STUBBS. London, 1874.

433. GUIGNEBERT, C. Christianity, past and present. New York, 1927.

Devoted primarily to origins and middle ages.

(3) *Miscellaneous*

434. LEA, H. C. A history of auricular confession and indulgences in the Latin church. 3 vols. Philadelphia, 1896.

434a. PAULUS, N. Geschichte des Ablasses im Mittelalter. 3 vols. Paderborn, 1923.

435. LEA, H. C. An historical sketch of sacerdotal celibacy in the Christian church. 2 vols. Philadelphia, 1867. 3rd edition, 2 vols., London, 1907.

436. LEA, H. C. Studies in church history: the rise of the temporal power; benefit of clergy; excommunication; the early church and slavery, etc. Philadelphia, 1883.

437. MORIN, G. Etudes, textes, découvertes: contributions à l'histoire des douze premiers siècles. Vol. I. Paris, 1913.

438. TRENCH, R. C. Lectures on medieval church history. New York, 1878.

(*d*) THE MEDIEVAL PAPACY

439. MANN, H. K. The lives of the popes in the early middle ages. 15 vols. in 16. London, 1906–29.

Through the pontificate of Gregory X. For the history of the papacy in the later middle ages, see CREIGHTON, PASTOR, etc., under outline XXIX of part II below.

440. GREGOROVIUS, F. Geschichte der Stadt Rom im Mittelalter. 8 vols. Stuttgart, 1859–72. 5th edition, Stuttgart, 1903ff. Translated from 4th German edition by ANNIE HAMILTON, History of the city of Rome in the middle ages. 8 vols. in 13. London, 1894–1902.

441. GRISAR, H. Geschichte Roms und der Päpste im Mittelalter. Freiburg, 1898ff. Translated by L. CAPPADELTA, History of Rome and the popes in the middle ages. 3 vols. St. Louis, 1911–13.

442. REUMONT, A. v. Geschichte der Stadt Rom. 3 vols. Berlin, 1867–70.

Chiefly on the middle ages.

443. GREENWOOD, T. Cathedra Petri: a political history of the great Latin patriarchate. 14 books in 6 vols. London, 1856–72.

Extends to the reformation.

444. BARRY, W. The papal monarchy from St. Gregory the Great to Boniface VIII (590–1303). London, 1902 (Story of nations).

445. DÖLLINGER, J. J. I. v. Die Papstfabeln des Mittelalters. Munich, 1863. 2nd edition by J. FRIEDRICH. Stuttgart, 1890. Translated by H. B. SMITH, Fables respecting the popes in the middle ages. New York, 1872.

446. Döllinger, J. J. I. v. [Pseudonym, Janus]. Der Papst und das Konzil. Leipzig, 1869. 2nd edition, by J. Friedrich, under the title, Das Papsttum, Munich, 1892. Translated into English, The pope and the council. Boston, 1870.

See J. Hergenröther, *Anti-Janus*, Freiburg, 1870. Although these books reflect the ecclesiastical politics in Germany of the time when they were written, they are full of interest to the student of medieval history.

447. Norden, W. Das Papsttum und Byzanz: die Trennung der beiden Mächte und das Problem ihrer Wiedervereinigung bis 1453. Berlin, 1903.

448. Seppelt, F. X. Das Papsttum und Byzanz. Breslau, 1904 (Kirchengeschichtliche Abhandlungen, ed. by M. Sdralek, 2).

449. McKilliam, A. E. A chronicle of the popes from St. Peter to Pius X. London, 1912.

See also the old but detailed Artaud de Montor, *Histoire des souverains pontifes romains*, 8 vols., Paris, 1847 and R. L. Poole, "The names and numbers of medieval popes," *E.H.R.*, XXXII (1917), 465–78.

450. McCabe, J. Crises in the history of the papacy. New York, 1916.

451. Rocquain, F. La papauté au moyen âge: Nicolas I., Grégoire VII., Innocent III., Boniface VIII. Paris, 1881.

452. Krüger, G. Das Papsttum: seine Idee und ihre Träger. Tübingen, 1907. Translated by F. M. S. Batchelor and C. A. Miles, The papacy: the idea and its exponents. New York, 1909.

453. Wurm, H. Die Papstwahl: ihre Geschichte und Gebräuche. Cologne, 1902.

See also L. Lector, *Le conclave: origines, histoire, organisation, législation ancienne et moderne*, Paris, 1902.

454. Beet, W. E. The medieval papacy, and other essays. London, 1914.

454a. Gregorovius, F. Die Grabdenkmäler der Päpste. 3rd edition. 3 vols. Leipzig, 1911.

(*e*) Church and State in the Middle Ages

See also nos. **499–504, 670, 725.**

455. Eichmann, E. Kirche und Staat. Vols. I–II [750–1350 A.D.]. Paderborn, 1912–14, is part I of no. **955.**

456. Scaduto, L. Stato e chiesa negli scritti politici dalla fine della lotta per le investiture sino alle morte di Ludovico il Bavaro (1122–1347). Florence, 1882.

456a. Solmi, A. Stato e chiesa secondo gli scritti politici da Carlomagno fino al Concordato di Worms. Modena, 1901.

456b. PIRANO, S. Stato e chiesa, 888–1015. Turin, 1908.

457. NIEHUES, B. Geschichte des Verhältnisses zwischen Kaiserthum und Papstthum im Mittelalter. 2 vols. 2nd edition, Münster, 1877–87.

To the time of Otto the Great.

458. FRIEDBERG, E. Die mittelalterlichen Lehren über das Verhältniss von Staat und Kirche. Part I. Leipzig, 1874.

See also his *Die Grenzen zwischen Staat und Kirche*, Tübingen, 1872.

459. GREENWOOD, ALICE D. The empire and the papacy in the middle ages. 3rd edition, London, 1901.

It practically is a short general history of the middle ages.

(*f*) THE CHURCH IN FRANCE IN THE MIDDLE AGES

460. Gallia Christiana in provincias ecclesiasticas distributa. Begun by the Benedictines of St. Maur and continued by the Académie des inscriptions et belles-lettres. 16 vols. Paris, 1715–65. Gallia Christiana novissima. 1899ff.

Contents analyzed by A. FRANKLIN, no. **23,** 465–85. See also P. DESLANDRES, *Histoire de l'église catholique en France*, Paris, 1913; and H. FISQUET, *La France pontificale*, 2 vols., Paris [1864–66].

460a. DUCHESNE, L. Fastes épiscopaux de l'ancienne Gaule. 3 vols. Paris, 1894–1915.

For the history of bishops it replaces *Gallia Christiana* to the end of the 9th century.

(*g*) THE CHURCH IN GERMANY IN THE MIDDLE AGES

461. HAUCK, A. Kirchengeschichte Deutschlands. 5 vols. in 6. Leipzig, 1887–1920. Vols. I–IV in 3rd and 4th edition.

See also A. NAEGLE, *Kirchengeschichte Böhmens: quellenmässig und kritisch dargestellt*, vol. I (on the introduction of Christianity), Vienna, 1915; and W. MOLL, *Kerkgeschiedenis van Nederland voor de hervorming*, 2 vols., Arnheim and Utrecht, 1869, index 1871; German edition by P. ZUPPKE, *Die vorreformatorische Kirchengeschichte der Niederlande*, 2 vols., Leipzig, 1895.

462. HINSCHIUS, P. Das Kirchenrecht der Katholiken und Protestanten in Deutschland. Part I. Das katholische Kirchenrecht. 6 vols. in 7. Berlin, 1869–97.

Incomplete. Although a book on church law, this vast work is placed here because it is a mine of trustworthy details on all phases of the church.

463. WERMINGHOFF, A. Geschichte der Kirchenverfassung Deutschlands im Mittelalter. Vol. I. Leipzig, 1905.

Verfassungsgeschichte der deutschen Kirche im Mittelalter, Leipzig, 1907, in no. **331,** vol. II, 6, is essentially an abridgment of the above.

(*h*) THE CHURCH IN ITALY IN THE MIDDLE AGES

464. SAVIO, F. (S. J.). Gli antichi vescovi d'Italia dalle origini al 1300 descritti per regioni, il Piemonte. Turin, 1898. La Lombardia, parte I, Milano. Florence, 1913.

The beginning of a very important Italia sacra, which will supersede F. UGHELLI, *Italia sacra*, 9 vols., Rome, 1644–62; 2nd edition, 10 vols., Venice, 1717–22.

465. DRESDNER, A. Kultur- und Sittengeschichte der italienischen Geistlichkeit. Breslau, 1890.

466. CAPPELLETTI. Le chiese d'Italia dalla loro origine sino ai nostri giorni. 21 vols. Venice, 1844–70.

(*i*) THE CHURCH IN SPAIN IN THE MIDDLE AGES

467. España sagrada. Edited by H. FLOREZ et al. 51 vols. Madrid, 1747–1879. See no. **997b.**

Contains many original sources. Index of the first 49 vols. in vol. XXII of *Colección de documentos inéditos para la historia de España*, no. **997.** See also V. DE LA FUENTE, *Historia ecclesiastica de España*, 2nd edition, 6 vols., Madrid, 1873–75. P. KEHR, Papsturkunden in Spanien: Vorarbeiten zur *Hispania pontificia*, I. Katalonien, Berlin, 1926 (Abh. Göttingen Acad. XVIII, 2).

468. GAMS, P. B. Die Kirchengeschichte von Spanien. 3 vols. in 5. Regensburg, 1862–79. See no. **627a.**

(*j*) HISTORY OF CHURCH COUNCILS

469. HEFELE, C. J. v. Conciliengeschichte. 7 vols. Freiburg, 1855–74; 2nd edition, 6 vols., 1873–90. Continued by J. A. C. HERGENRÖTHER, vols. VIII–IX, 1887–90. Translated by W. R. CLARK, History of the Christian councils, vols. I–V [to 787], Edinburgh, 1871–96. Translated and augmented by H. LECLERQ, Histoire des conciles. 8 vols. Paris, 1907–21.

470. LANDON, E. H. A manual of councils of the holy catholic church. 1845. New and revised edition by his son, P. LANDON. 2 vols. Edinburgh, 1893.

Arranged in dictionary form, thus constituting a handy work of reference.

471. DESLANDRES, P. Les grands conciles de Latran. Paris, 1913. (Questions historiques, science et religion.)

E. CECCHUCHI, *Histoire des conciles oecuméniques*, Lyons, 1901.

(*k*) History of Dogma

472. Harnack, A. Lehrbuch der Dogmengeschichte. 3 vols. Freiburg, 1886ff. 4th edition, revised, in 3 vols. Tübingen, 1909–10. Translated from the 3rd edition, by N. Buchanan, History of dogma, 7 vols., London, 1897–99.

See also his *Dogmengeschichte*, 4th edition, Tübingen, 1905.

472a. Thomasius, D. Die christliche Dogmengeschichte. 2 vols. Erlangen, 1886–87.

473. Tixeront, J. Histoire des dogmes. 3 vols. 2nd to 4th editions. Paris, 1906–12. Translated by H. L. B., History of dogmas. St Louis, 1910ff.

Extends to 800 A.D.

474. Fisher, G. P. History of Christian doctrine. New York, 1896 (The international theological library, IV).

A history of dogmas as well as of doctrine. See also K. R. Hagenbach, *A history of Christian doctrines* [English translation], Edinburgh, 1883–85.

475. Loofs, F. Leitfaden zum Studium der Dogmengeschichte. Halle, 1889. 4th edition, 1906.

476. Seeberg, R. Lehrbuch der Dogmengeschichte. 2 vols. 2nd edition. Leipzig, 1908–10. Translated into English by C. E. Hay. 2 vols., Philadelphia [c. 1905].

See also his *Grundriss der Dogmengeschichte*, 3rd edition, Leipzig, 1910.

477. Bonwetsch, G. N. Grundriss der Dogmengeschichte. Munich, 1908.

478. Bach, J. Die Dogmengeschichte des Mittelalters vom christologischen Standpunkt. 2 vols. Vienna, 1873–75.

(*l*) Monasticism

479. Montalembert, Comte de [C. F. R. de Tryon]. Histoire des moines d'occident depuis S. Benoît jusqu'à S. Bernard. 7 vols. Paris, 1860–77. Authorized translation, The monks of the west, 7 vols., Edinburgh, 1861–79; another edition, with introduction by F. A. Gasquet, 6 vols., London, 1896.

480. Helyot, P. Histoire des ordres monastiques, religieux et militaires, et de congrégations séculaires. 8 vols., Paris, 1711–21.

481. Workman, H. B. The evolution of the monastic ideal: from the earliest times down to the coming of the friars. London, 1913.

481a. Hannah, I. C. Christian monasticism. New York, 1925.

482. Eckenstein, Lina. Women under monasticism: chapters on saint-lore and convent life between A.D. 500 and A.D. 1500. Cambridge, 1896.

See also ETHEL R. WHEELER, *Women of the cell and cloister*, London [1913]; and AGNES B. C. DUNBAR, *A dictionary of saintly women*, 2 vols., London, 1904–05.

483. HEIMBUCHER, M. Die Orden und Kongregationen der katholischen Kirche. 2 vols. Paderborn, 1896–97. 2nd edition, 3 vols., 1907–08.

484. ZÖCKLER, O. Askese und Mönchthum. 2 vols. 2nd edition. Frankfurt, 1897.

These two books contain excellent bibliographies.

484a. SCHJELDERUP, K. V. Die Askese. Berlin, 1928.

485. MORIN, G. L'idéal monastique et la vie chrétienne des premiers jours. 2nd edition, revised. Paris, 1914.

485a. BUONAIUTI, E. Le origini dell' ascetismo cristiano. Pinerolo, 1928.

486. WOODHOUSE, F. C. Monasticism, ancient and modern. London [1896].

487. JAMESON, ANNA. Legends of the monastic orders. Corrected and revised edition. Boston [1884].

(*m*) COLLECTIONS OF CHURCH HISTORY

488. Freiburger historische Studien. Edited by A. BÜCHI et al. Fribourg (Switzerland), 1905ff.

489. Forschungen zur christlichen Literatur- und Dogmengeschichte. Edited by A. EHRHARD and J. P. KIRSCH. Paderborn, 1900ff.

490. Kirchengeschichtliche Abhandlungen. Edited by SDRALEK. Breslau, 1902ff.

491. Kirchenrechtliche Abhandlungen. Edited by U. STUTZ. Stuttgart, 1902ff.

492. Kirchengeschichtliche Studien. Edited by A. KNÖPFLER et al. 6 vols. Münster, 1891ff.

493. Papers of the American society of church history. 1st series edited by S. M. JACKSON, 1888–97. 2nd series. Edited by W. W. ROCKWELL. New York, 1908ff.

494. Studien und Mitteilungen aus dem kirchenhistorischen Seminar der theologischen Fakultät zu Wien. Vienna, 1908ff.

495. Studien zur Geschichte der Theologie und der Kirche. Edited by N. BONWETSCH and R. SEEBERG. Leipzig, 1897ff. Neue Studien, etc. Same editors. Berlin, 1907ff.

496. Veröffentlichungen aus dem kirchenhistorischen Seminar zu München. Edited by A. KNÖPFLER. Munich, 1899ff.

497. Funk, F. X. v. Kirchengeschichtliche Abhandlungen und Untersuchungen. Vols. I–III. Paderborn, 1897–1907.

498. Harnack, A. Reden und Aufätze. 2 vols. Giessen, 1904. 2nd edition, 1906.

§ 7. The Medieval Empire in the West

See also no. **538**; and the general books on Germany and Italy, nos. **560–621.**

499. Bryce, J. The holy Roman empire. Oxford, 1864. A new edition, enlarged and revised, London and New York, 1904.

This is the best book on the subject in any language. See E. A. Freeman's enthusiastic review of the 1st edition, with some references to the 3rd edition, 1871, in his *Historical essays*, first series, London, 1871, pp. 126–60. For Gibbon, *Decline and fall*, see no. **341.**

500. Fisher, H. The medieval empire. 2 vols. London, 1898.

From Otto I to the end of the Hohenstaufen. This is not a systematic narrative of events, but rather a series of essays, mostly constitutional.

501. Giesebrecht, W. v. Geschichte der deutschen Kaiserzeit. 5 vols. Brunswick and Leipzig, 1855–88. Vols I–III, 5th edition, Leipzig, 1881–90; vol. IV, 2nd edition, Brunswick, 1877; vol. VI, edited and continued by B. v. Simson, Leipzig, 1895.

502. Zeumer, K. Heiliges römisches Reich deutscher Nation: eine Studie über den Reichstitel. Weimar, 1910 (Quellen und Studien, by K. Zeumer, IV, 2).

503. Ficker, J. Das deutsche Kaiserreich in seinen universalen und nationalen Beziehungen. Innsbruck, 1861. 2nd edition unaltered, 1862.

504. Birot, J. Le saint empire du couronnement de Charlemagne au sacre de Napoléon. Paris, 1903.

505. Stengel, E. E. Den Kaiser macht das Heer: Studien zur Geschichte eines politischen Gedankens. Weimar, 1910.

506. Hahn, L. Das Kaisertum. Leipzig, 1913 (Das Erbe der Alten, vol. VI).

See ch. VIII, "Die Erben der römischen Kaiser."

507. Guglia, E. Die Geburts-, Sterbe- und Grabstätten der römisch-deutschen Kaiser und Könige. Vienna, 1914.

See also M. Kemmerich, "Die Porträts deutscher Kaiser und Könige bis auf Rudolf von Habsburg," *N.A.* XXXIII (1907), 461–513.

§ 8. France

(a) General Histories of France

(1) *Monumental Works*

508. Histoire de France depuis les origines jusqu'à la révolution. Edited by E. Lavisse. 9 vols. in 18. Paris, 1900–11.

This monumental co-operative work is now the standard history of France and has in large measure superseded the following older histories of France, nos. **509–13.** Good bibliographies are scattered in footnotes. This same edition appears also under the title *Histoire de France illustrée depuis les origines jusqu'à la révolution.*

A very handy condensed history of France for the general reader is being published under the title *Histoire de France racontée à tous,* edited by F. Funck-Brentano. As they appear, these volumes are translated into English.

508a. Hanotaux, G. Histoire de la nation française. 15 vols. Paris, 1920–29.

509. Sismondi, J. C. L. S. de. Histoire des Français depuis l'origine jusqu'en 1789. 31 vols. Paris, 1821–44.

510. Martin, H. Histoire de France depuis les temps les plus reculés jusqu'en 1789. 19 vols. Paris, 1838–54. 4th edition in 17 vols., 1855–65. Popular, illustrated, edition, 7 vols., 1867–85.

511. Dareste, M. C. Histoire de France depuis les origines jusqu'à nos jours. 3rd edition. 9 vols. Paris, 1884–85.

512. Michelet, J. Histoire de France depuis les origines jusqu'en 1789. 17 vols. Paris, 1833–67. New edition, 19 vols., 1879. Abridged translations by G. H. Smith, History of France, 2 vols., New York, 1845–47.

513. Lavallée, T. Histoire des Français depuis les temps des Gaulois jusqu'en 1873. 7 vols. Paris, 1864–73.

513a. Jullian, C. Histoire de la Gaule. 8 vols. Paris, 1908–26.

(2) *Shorter Accounts*

514. Kitchin, G. W. A history of France (to 1793). 3 vols. Oxford, 1873–77. Vol. I, 4th edition, revised, 1899.

Vol. I extends to 1453.

514a. Hudson, W. H. France: the nation and its development from earliest times to the establishment of the third republic. New York, 1917.

515. Macdonald, J. R. M. A history of France. 3 vols. New York, 1915.

516. Crowe, E. E. The history of France (to 1815). 3 vols. London, 1830. Enlarged edition. 5 vols. 1858–68.

517. Guizot, F. P. G. A popular history of France from the earliest times. Translated by R. Black. 6 vols. Boston [187–?].

(3) *Brief histories*

518. Adams, G. B. The growth of the French nation. New York, 1896.

519. Belloc, H. A history of the French people. Vol. 1. London, 1913.

519a. Duclaux, Mary, and Robinson, A. Mary F. A short history of France. London and New York, 1918.

520. Van Dyke, P. The story of France from Julius Caesar to Napoleon and the republic. New York, 1928.

521. Headlam, C. France. London, 1913 (The making of the nations).

522. Duruy, V. Histoire de France. New edition, 2 vols., Paris, 1884. Translated and abridged from the 17th French edition by Mrs. N. Carey; with an introduction by J. F. Jameson, A history of France. New York, 1889. Translated by L. C. Jane and Lucy Menzies. A short history of France. 2 vols. London and New York, 1917.

523. Cavaignac, E. Esquisse d'une histoire de France. Paris, 1910.

524. Jervis, W. H. The student's France: a history of France from the earliest times to the establishment of the second empire in 1852. New York [no date, ca. 1862].

(*b*) General Histories of Medieval France

525. Masson, G. The story of mediaeval France: from Hugh Capet to the beginning of the 18th century. New York, 1888 (Story of nations).

526. Guérard, A. L. French civilization from its origins to the close of the middle ages. Boston and New York, 1921.

526a. Evans, Joan. Life in mediaeval France. London, 1925.

(*c*) French Institutions

See also no. **584.**

527. Declareuil, J. Histoire générale du droit français des origines à 1789. Paris, 1925.

528. Glasson, E. Histoire du droit et des institutions de la France. 8 vols. Paris, 1887–1903.

Extends to the end of the middle ages.

529. Viollet, P. Droit public: histoire des institutions politiques et administratives de la France. 3 vols. Paris, 1890–1903.

Extends to the end of the middle ages. See also his *Histoire du droit civil français*, 3rd edition, Paris, 1905.

530. Luchaire, A. Manuel des institutions françaises, période de Capétiens directs. Paris, 1892.

531. Brissaud, J. Manuel d'histoire du droit français. Issued in 5 parts. Paris, 1898–1904. Translated in part by J. W. Garner, History of French public law. Boston, 1915.

Sums up the researches of Viollet, Flach, Luchaire, Esmein, Fustel de Coulanges, and others.

532. Esmein, A. Cours élémentaire d'histoire du droit français. Paris, 1892. 8th edition, 1907.

533. Holtzmann, R. Französische Verfassungsgeschichte von der Mitte des neunten Jahrhunderts bis zur Revolution. Munich and Berlin, 1910.

Part of no. **330.**

534. Cam, Helen M. Local government in France and England. London, 1912.

535. Funck-Brentano, F. L'ancienne France: le roi. 3rd edition. Paris, 1913.

See also H. Schreuer, *Die rechtlichen Grundlagen der französischen Königskrönung*, Weimar, 1911.

536. Mayer-Homberg, E. Die fränkischen Volksrechte im Mittelalter: eine rechtgeschichtliche Untersuchung. Vol. I, Die fränkischen Volksrechte und das Reichsrecht. Weimar, 1912.

(*d*) Foreign Relations of France

537. Corbin, P. Histoire de la politique extérieure de la France. Vol. I. Les origines et la période anglaise (jusqu'en 1483). Paris, 1912.

537a. Madelin, L. L'expansion française: de la Syrie au Rhin. Paris, 1918.

A series of popular lectures.

538. Leroux, A. Les conflits entre la France et l'empire pendant le moyen âge. Paris, 1902.

Contains a very important bibliography. See also, H. Otto, "Das Streben der Könige von Frankreich nach der römischen Kaiserkrone," in Kgl. Gymnasium zu Hadamar, *Bericht über das Schuljahr 1898–99, Beigabe.*

539. Langlois, C. V. "The comparative history of England and France in the middle ages." *E.H.R.*, V (1890), 259–63.

(*e*) Great Regions of France

540. Devic, C., and Vaissette, J. Histoire générale de Languedoc par deux religieux Bénédictins de la Congrégation de S. Maur. 5 vols. Paris, 1730–45. New edition in 16 vols. Toulouse, 1872–1905.

541. Moyne de la Borderie, A. le. Histoire de Bretagne [to 1715]. Vols. I–V. Paris, 1896–1913.

542. Febvre, L. Histoire de Franche-Comté. Paris, 1912 (Vieilles provinces de France).

542a. Poupardin, R. Le royaume de Bourgogne (888–1038), étude sur les origines du royaume d'Arles. Paris, 1907.

542b. Poupardin, R. Le royaume de Provence sous les Carolingiens (855–933?). Paris, 1901.

542c. Fournier, P. E. L. Le royaume d'Arles et de Vienne (1138–1378). Paris, 1891.

(*f*) Miscellaneous

543. Langlois, C. V. The historic rôle of France among the nations. An address delivered at the University of Chicago. Chicago, 1905.

543a. Tilley, A. A. Medieval France: a companion to French studies. Cambridge, 1922.

544. Stephen, Sir J. Lectures on the history of France. 2 vols. London, 1851.

545. Collection des meilleurs dissertations, etc., relatifs à l'histoire de France: composée en grande partie de pièces rares, etc. Edited by C. Leber. 20 vols. Paris, 1838.

For an analysis of its contents, see Franklin, no. **23,** 343ff.

546. La Roncière, C. Histoire de la marine française. 5 vols. Paris, 1889–1920.

547. Chevalier, E. Histoire de la marine française depuis les débuts de la monarchie jusqu'au traité de paix de 1763. Paris, 1902.

547a. Tramond, J. Manuel d'histoire maritime de la France. Paris, 1916.

Has but two introductory chapters on the middle ages, which, however, are accurate.

548. Molinier, A. Les obituaires françaises au moyen âge. Paris, 1890.

§ 9. Belgium and the Netherlands

549. Pirenne, H. Histoire de Belgique. 7 vols. Brussels, 1900ff. Vols. I–III [to 1567], 2nd edition, 1901–12. 3rd edition of vol. I, 1909.

550. Pirenne, H. Les anciennes démocraties des Pays-Bas. Paris, 1910. Translated by J. V. Saunders, Belgian democracy: its early history. London and New York, 1915. (In Publications of the University of Manchester, Historical series, XXVII.)

A very convenient manual for those who cannot master Pirenne's larger works.

551. LINDEN, H. VAN DER. Manuel d'histoire de Belgique. With a preface by H. PIRENNE. 2 vols. Brussels, 1910.

551a. LINDEN, H. VAN DER. Vue générale de l'histoire de Belgique. Paris, 1918.

551b. CAMMAERTS, E. A history of Belgium. 1921.

551c. KALKEN, F. VAN. Histoire de Belgique. Brussels, 1920.

552. VANDERKINDERE, L. La formation territoriale des principautés belges au moyen âge. 2 vols. 1st and 2nd editions. Brussels, 1902.

553. MILLARD, E. Les Belges et leurs générations historiques. Brussels, 1902.

554. BOULGER, D. C. The history of Belgium. 2 vols. London, 1902–09.

See also his *Belgium*, Detroit, 1913.

554a. HORNE, C. F., and KELLER, A. R. History of the Belgian people. 3 vols. New York, 1917.

555. ESSEN, L. VAN DER. A short history of Belgium. Chicago [1916].

556. ENSOR, R. C. K. Belgium. New York, 1915. (In Home university library, 95.)

557. BLOK, P. J. Geschiedenis van het Nederlandsche Volk. 8 vols. Groningen, 1892–1908. Translated by O. A. BIERSTADT and RUTH PUTNAM, History of the people of the Netherlands. 5 vols. New York, 1898–1912. Vol. I, to the beginning of the fifteenth century. Vols. I–IV (to 1648) translated into German by A. G. HOUTROUW, Gotha, 1901–09, part of no. **332.**

558. ROGERS, J. E. T. Holland. New York, 1900 (Story of nations).

559. WENZELBURGER, K. T. Geschichte der Niederlande. 2 vols. [to 1648]. Gotha, 1878–86.

Part of no. **332.**

§ 10. Germany

(*a*) GENERAL HISTORIES OF GERMANY

(1) *Monumental Works*

See also nos. **499–507.**

560. Bibliothek deutscher Geschichte. Edited by H. v. ZWIEDENECK-SUDENHORST. Stuttgart, 1876ff.

A general work something like the *Histoire de France*, no. **508,** but published in separate volumes which will be mentioned in their proper places. A list of them is given by LOEWE, *Bücherkunde*, no. **32,** Anhang.

561. LAMPRECHT, K. Deutsche Geschichte. 12 vols. in 16 parts. Berlin, 1891–1909. Partly in 2nd to 4th editions, 3 supplements, 1902–04.

For literature on this and other works of LAMPRECHT, see no. **28,** DAHLMANN-WAITZ, no. 1451.

561a. HOFMANN, A. Politische Geschichte der Deutschen. 4 vols. Stuttgart, 1921–25.

(2) *Shorter Accounts and Text Books*

562. Handbuch der deutschen Geschichte. Edited by B. GEBHARDT. 2 vols. Stuttgart, 1891. 6th edition by A. MEISTER. 3 vols., 1922–23.

This co-operative history is the best short general one on Germany.

563. HENDERSON, E. F. A short history of Germany. 2 vols. in 1. New York, 1902. New edition in 2 vols., 1916.

564. HOLLAND, A. W. Germany. London, 1914 (part of no. **322**).

565. LEWIS, C. T. A history of Germany from the earliest times. Founded on D. MÜLLER, History of the German people. New York, 1886.

566. HEYCK, E. Deutsche Geschichte: Volk, Staat, Kultur- und Geistesleben. 3 vols. Bielefeld, 1905–06.

567. JÄGER, O. Deutsche Geschichte. 2 vols. Munich, 1909.

568. KÄMMEL, O. Deutsche Geschichte. 2 vols. 2nd edition. Dresden, 1905. 3rd edition, Leipzig, 1910.

See also his *Der Werdegang des deutschen Volkes,* 2 vols., 3rd edition, Leipzig, 1911–12.

569. SCHÄFER, D. v. Deutsche Geschichte. 2 vols. Jena, 1910. 9th edition, 1922.

(*b*) GERMANY IN THE MIDDLE AGES

570. Jahrbücher der deutschen Geschichte [to 1250]. Under the auspices of the Munich Academy. Berlin and Leipzig, 1862ff.

571. RICHTER, G., and KOHL, H. Annalen der deutschen Geschichte im Mittelalter von der Gründung des fränkischen Reichs bis zum Untergang der Hohenstaufen. Mit fortlaufenden Quellenauszügen und Literaturangaben [to 1137]. 4 vols. Halle, 1873–98.

572. ZELLER, J. Histoire d'Allemagne. 7 vols. [to Luther]. Paris, 1872–92. Vol. III, L'empire germanique et l'église au moyen âge, in 2nd edition, 1884.

573. NITZSCH, K. W. Geschichte des deutschen Volkes bis zum Augsburger Religionsfrieden. Nach dessen hinterlassenen Papieren und Vorlesungen. 3 vols. Leipzig, 1883–85. 2nd edition by G. MATTHÄI, Leipzig, 1892.

574. GERDES, H. Geschichte des deutschen Volkes und seiner Kultur im Mittelalter. 3 vols. [to 1250]. Leipzig, 1891–1908.

575. HENDERSON, E. F. A history of Germany in the middle ages. London, 1894.

575a. THOMPSON, J. W. Feudal Germany. Chicago, 1928.

576. STUBBS, W. Germany in the early middle ages (476–1250). London and New York, 1908.

577. STUBBS, W. Germany in the later middle ages (1200–1500). Edited by A. HASSALL. London and New York, 1908.

(*c*) GERMAN INSTITUTIONS

578. WAITZ, G. Deutsche Verfassungsgeschichte. 8 vols. [to the 12th century]. Kiel and Berlin, 1844–78. 6 vols., 2nd and 3rd editions, Berlin, 1880–96.

W. ALTMANN and E. BERNHEIM, *Ausgewählte Urkunden zur . . . Verfassungsgeschichte Deutschlands im Mittelalter*, 4th edition, Berlin, 1909, serves the same purpose for German as W. STUBBS, *Select charters*, does for English constitutional history. See also W. STUBBS, *Constitutional history of England*, in no. **36**, GROSS, no. 643.

578a. KEUTGEN, F. Der deutsche Staat des Mittelalters. Jena, 1918.

579. BRUNNER, H. Deutsche Rechtsgeschichte. 2 vols. Leipzig, 1887–92. Vol. I, 2nd edition, 1906; vol. II, 2nd edition, by C. SCHWERIN. Munich and Leipzig, 1928.

A very good text is his *Grundzüge der deutschen Rechtsgeschichte*, Leipzig, 1901; 4th edition, 1910. See also his *Forschungen zur Geschichte des deutschen und französischen Rechtes*, Stuttgart, 1894.

580. GIERKE, O. Das deutsche Genossenschaftsrecht. 4 vols. Berlin, 1868–1914.

Part of vol. III translated by F. W. MAITLAND, *Political theories in the middle ages*. London, 1900.

581. BELOW, G. v. Der deutsche Staat des Mittelalters: ein Grundriss der deutschen Verfassungsgeschichte. Leipzig, 1914.

See also A. HEUSLER, *Deutsche Verfassungsgeschichte*, Leipzig, 1905.

582. MEISTER, A. Deutsche Verfassungsgeschichte, von den Anfängen bis ins 15 Jahrhundert. Leipzig, 1907.

Part of no. **331**.

583. SCHRÖDER, R. Lehrbuch der deutschen Rechtsgeschichte. 6th edition. Berlin and Leipzig, 1922.

584. MAYER, E. Mittelalterliche Verfassungsgeschichte: deutsche und französische Verfassungsgeschichte vom 9 bis zum 14 Jahrhundert. 2 vols. Leipzig, 1899.

585. DUNGERN, O. D. War Deutschland ein Wahlreich? Leipzig, 1913.

586. PFLEIDERER, O. Das deutsche Nationalbewusstsein in Vergangenheit und Gegenwart. Berlin, 1896.

587. HOOPS, J. Reallexicon der germanischen Altertumskunde. 4 vols. Strasburg, 1911–19.

(*d*) AUSTRIA

588. KRONES, F. v. Handbuch der Geschichte Oesterreichs von der ältesten bis zur neuesten Zeit. 6 vols. Berlin, 1879–81.

See also his *Grundriss der österreichischen Geschichte*, Vienna, 1882; and *Österreichische Geschichte*, 2 vols., Leipzig, 1899–1900 (*Sammlung Göschen*); and A. DUDAN, *La monarchia degli Absburgo, 800–1915*, 2 vols., Rome, 1915.

589. HUBER, A. Geschichte Oesterreichs. Vols. I–V [to 1648]. Gotha, 1885–95.

Part of no. **332.**

590. LEGER, L. Histoire de l'Autriche-Hongrie depuis ses origines jusqu'à l'année 1894. 5th edition. Paris, 1907. Translated by B. HILL, History of Austro-Hungary. London, 1889. Also translated by W. E. LINGELBACH in no. **314.**

591. KRALIK, R. Österreichische Geschichte. Vienna, 1914.

592. MAYER, F. M. Geschichte Österreichs mit besonderer Rücksicht auf das Kulturleben. 2 vols. 3rd edition. Vienna and Leipzig, 1909–10.

593. HUBER, A. Österreichische Reichsgeschichte. Leipzig, 1895. 2nd edition by A. DOPSCH, 1901.

594. LUSCHIN VON EBENGREUTH, A. Österreichische Reichsgeschichte. 2 vols. Bamberg, 1895–96.

See also his *Grundriss der österreichischen Reichsgeschichte*, Bamberg, 1899.

(*e*) PRUSSIA

595. RANKE, L. v. Zwölf Bücher preussischer Geschichte. 5 vols. in 3. Leipzig, 1874. 2nd edition, Leipzig, 1878–79. (Vols. XXV–XXIX of his complete works.)

596. PRUTZ, H. Preussische Geschichte. 4 vols. Stuttgart, 1899–1902.

H. TUTTLE, *History of Prussia*, 4 vols., Boston, 1884–96 (vol. I, A.D. 1134–1740, in second edition), touches but slightly on the middle ages.

(*f*) ALSACE-LORRAINE

597. DERICHSWEILER, H. Geschichte Lothringens: der tausendjährige Kampf um die Westmark. 2 vols. Wiesbaden, 1901.

Condensed in his *Geschichte Lothringens,* Leipzig, 1905 (*Sammlung Göschen*).

597a. BATIFFOL, L. Les anciennes républiques alsaciennes. Paris, 1918.

598. PUTNAM, RUTH. Alsace and Lorraine from Caesar to Kaiser. New York, 1915.

§ 11. Italy

(*a*) GENERAL HISTORIES OF ITALY

(1) *Political History*

Many of the general works on Germany just listed above must be consulted for the history of Italy in the time when German emperors were constantly crossing the Alps.

599. Storia politica d'Italia scritta da una società di professori. Edited by P. VILLARI. Milan, 1897ff.

Note—A distinction should be made between the *Storico politica d'Italia scritta da una società d'amici,* 1875ff. and its successor . . . *scritta da una società di professori,* 1897ff.

600. CANTU, C. Storia degli Italiani. 6 vols. Turin, 1854. 4th edition, 1892. Translated into French by A. LACOMBE under the supervision of the author and from the 2nd edition, Histoire des Italiens. 12 vols. Paris, 1859–62.

601. CAPPELLETTI, L. Storia d'Italia (476–1900). Genoa, 1902. 2nd edition of vol. I (476–1559). Milan, 1917.

See also E. BESTA, *La Sardegna medioevale,* 2 vols., Palermo, 1908–09 (to 1324 A.D.).

601a. MANNO, G. Storia di Sardegna. 3rd edition. 2 vols. Milan, 1835.

601b. SOLMI, A. Studi storici sulle istituzioni della Sardegna nel medio evo. Cagliari, 1917.

602. SEDGWICK, H. D. A short history of Italy (476–1900). Boston, 1905.

602a. JAMISON, EVELYN M., ADY, C. M., VERNON, K. D., and TERRY, C. S. Italy, mediaeval and modern: a history. Oxford, 1917.

Lays chief stress on modern Italy since 1789.

602b. TREVELYAN, J. P. (MRS. GEORGE M.). A short history of the Italian people: from the barbarian invasions to the attainment of unity. New York, 1920. 2nd edition, 1926.

603. Belviglieri, C. Tavole sincrone e genealogiche di storia italiana dal 306 al 1870. Florence, 1885.

604. Fedele, P. "La coscienza della nazionalità in Italia nel medio evo." Nuova Antologia (1915).

(2) *Constitutional History*

605. Pertile, A. Storia del diritto italiano. 6 vols. and index. Padua, 1873–87. 2nd edition by P. del Giudice, Turin, 1891–1903.

606. Besta, E. Storia del diritto italiano. Pisa, vol. II, 1914.

Vol. II relates to the Lombard period.

607. Ficker, J. Forschungen zur Reichs- und Rechtsgeschichte Italiens. 4 vols. Innsbruck, 1868–74.

See also Waitz, no. **578.**

608. Mayer, E. Italienische Verfassungsgeschichte von der Gothenzeit zur Zunftherrschaft. 2 vols. Leipzig, 1909.

609. Schupfer, F. Manuale di storia del diritto italiano. 4th edition. Città di Castello, 1908.

(3) *Maritime History*

610. Manfroni, C. Storia della marina italiana dalle invasioni barbariche al trattato di Ninfeo (1261). Leghorn, 1899. Continued by his Storia della marina italiana (1261–1453). 2 vols. Leghorn, 1902.

(*b*) Medieval History of Italy

(1) *Monumental Works*

See also no. **345.**

611. Hartmann, L. M. Geschichte Italiens im Mittelalter. 4 vols. Leipzig, 1897–1915. Vol. I. Das italienische Königreich. 2nd revised edition. Gotha, 1923.

Now the most reliable and scholarly work on medieval Italy. Part of no. **332.**

612. Muratori, L. A. Annali d'Italia. 12 vols. Rome, 1744–49. Often reprinted. Translated into German by Bandis. 9 vols. Leipzig, 1745–50.

From the beginning of the Christian era to 1749. See C. Troya, *Studi intorno agli "Annali d'Italia" del Muratori*, 2 vols., Naples, 1877.

613. Sismondi, J. C. L. S. de. Histoire des républiques italiennes du moyen âge. 16 vols. Paris, 1809–18. 5th edition, 8 vols. Brussels, 1838–39. Translated, condensed, and revised by W. Boulting, History of the Italian republics in the middle ages. London [ca. 1905].

This is practically a general history of medieval Italy. In large measure it supersedes Muratori, no. **612.**

614. TROYA, C. Storia d'Italia del medio evo. 17 vols. Naples, 1839–59.

Extends from the fall of the Roman empire in the west to the end of the Lombard kingdom. The author had planned to carry it to 1321. It is still of importance and is not entirely superseded by HODGKIN, *Italy and her invaders*, no. **345**, and perhaps not wholly even by HARTMANN, no. **611.**

(2) *Shorter Works and Text Books*

615. VILLARI, P. Le invasioni barbariche in Italia. Milan, 1901. Translated by LINDA VILLARI, The barbarian invasions of Italy. 2 vols. London, 1902.

616. VILLARI, P. L'Italia da Carlo Magno alla morte di Arrigo VII. Milan, 1910. Translated by his daughter, Mrs. C. HULTON, Mediaeval Italy from Charlemagne to Henry VII. London, 1910.

These two works form the best general history of medieval Italy available in English.

617. COTTERILL, H. B. Mediaeval Italy during a thousand years (305–1313). London, 1915 (Great nations series).

617a. COTTERILL, H. B. Italy from Dante to Tasso. London, 1919 (Great nations series).

618. BROWNING, O. Guelfs and Ghibellines: a short history of mediaeval Italy from 1250–1409. London, 1893. The age of the condottieri: a short history of mediaeval Italy from 1409–1530. London, 1895.

619. GABOTTO, F. Storia dell' Italia occidentale nel medio evo, 395–1313. Vols. I and II [to 568 A.D.], 1912.

620. LANZANI, F. I comuni, da Carlomagno al Henrico VII. Milan, 1880.

Part of no. **599.**

621. KLEIN, V. Italiens historie i middelalderen med saerlight blik paa kulturudviklingen. Copenhagen, 1907.

§ 12. Spain and Portugal

(*a*) GENERAL HISTORY OF SPAIN

(1) *Monumental Works*

622. Historia general de España. By members of the Real Academia de la Historia. 18 vols. Madrid, 1890–98.

623. LAFUENTE, M. Historia general de España. 30 vols. Madrid, 1850–67. 2nd edition continued by J. VALERA. 24 vols. Barcelona, 1888-90.

624. Ballesteros y Beretta, A. Historia de España y su influencia en la historia universal. 5 vols. Barcelona, 1918–29.

This work, which supersedes all the older ones on the same subject, goes down, so far, to the year 1808. There are full references at the end of every chapter; also indices, tables of contents, and illustrations.

625. Mariana, J. de. Historia general de España. Toledo, 1601; Madrid, 1623. New editions, 8 vols., Madrid, 1819; 10 vols., Barcelona, 1839.

The original work was published in Latin, *Historiae de rebus Hispaniae libri XX*, Toledo, 1592, with ten additional books in 1616, and was translated into Spanish by the author himself. English translation, abridged, by J. Stevens, London, 1699.

626. Lembke, F. W. Geschichte von Spanien. Vol. I, Hamburg, 1834; vols. II and III by H. Schäfer, Hamburg, 1844, and Gotha, 1861; vols. IV–VII (to 1516), by F. W. Schirrmacher, Gotha, 1881–1902. Vol. VIII (end of reign of Charles V) by K. Häbler.

Part of no. **332.** Rather antiquated.

627. Zurita, J. Anales de la corona de Aragón. Second edition, Saragossa, 1610. 6 vols.

The last two volumes of this edition have the subsidiary title of *Historia del rey Hernando el Católico.*

This work, written in the middle of the sixteenth century, is largely based on the sources, and marks a great advance over any work previously produced in Aragon. It is still a standard authority, which becomes increasingly valuable as it approaches the period in which the author lived.

627a. Gams, P. B. Die Kirchengeschichte von Spanien. 3 vols. in 5. Ratisbon, 1862–79.

Unsatisfactory in many respects, but still the standard ecclesiastical history of Spain.

(2) *Shorter Works and Text Books*

628. Altamira, R. Historia de España y de la civilización española. 4 vols. Barcelona, 1900–11. 3rd edition, 1913–14.

Note also C. E. Chapman, *A history of Spain founded on the Historia de España y de la civilización española of Rafael Altamira*, New York, 1918.

628a. Merriman, R. B. The rise of the Spanish Empire in the old world and in the new. 3 vols. New York, 1918–25.

The first of these three volumes covers medieval Spain; the second the period of the Catholic Kings; the third that of the Emperor Charles V.

629. Burke, U. R. A history of Spain from the earliest time to the death of Ferdinand the Catholic. 2 vols. London, 1895. 2nd edition, with additional notes, and an introduction by M. A. S. Hume. 2 vols. London, 1900.

629a. HANNAY, D. Spain. London and New York, 1917 (The nations' stories).

630. DIERCKS, G. Geschichte Spaniens von den frühesten Zeiten bis auf die Gegenwart. 2 vols. Berlin, 1895–96.

See also his *Spanische Geschichte*, Leipzig, 1905 (*Sammlung Göschen*, 266).

631. HUME, M. A. S. The Spanish people, their origin, growth and influence. London, 1901. (The great peoples series.)

See the Bibliography.

632. PERKINS, CLARA C. Builders of Spain. New York, 1909.

(3) *Constitutional History of Spain*

633. COLMEIRO, M. De la constitución y del gobierno de los reinos de León y Castilla. 2 vols. Madrid, 1855. 2nd edition, 1873–75.

See also his *Derecho administrativo español*, 3 vols., 4th edition, Madrid, 1876–80; J. M. ANTEQUERA, *Historia de la legislación española*, Madrid, 1849, 4th edition, 1895; F. MARTINEZ MARINA, *Ensayo histórico-crítico sobre la antiqua legislación . . . de León y Castilla*, Madrid, 1808, 2 vols., 1834; and A. MARICHALAR and C. MANRIQUE, *Historia de la legislación y recitaciones del derecho civil de España*, 9 vols., Madrid, 1861–76.

633a. CASTILLO DE BOBADILLA, J. Politica para corregidores y señores de vassallos. 2 vols. Madrid, 1597; Medina del Campo, 1608; Barcelona, 1616; Antwerp, 1750; Madrid, 1759; *id.* 1775.

A mine of information by a most learned lawyer on the whole question of local administration in Spain.

633b. HINOJOSA, E. DE. Historia general del derecho español. Madrid, 1887; and Estudios sobre la historia de derecho español. Madrid, 1903.

634. DANVILA Y COLLADO, M. El poder civil en España. 6 vols. Madrid, 1885–87.

The introduction to vol. I is a long and important survey of the middle ages.

634a. PIDAL, J. P., MARQUIS DA. Lecciones sobre la historia del gobierno y legislación de España. Madrid, 1880.

634b. ALTAMIRA Y CREVEA, R. Cuestiones de historia de derecho y de legislación comparada. Madrid, 1914.

635. CARDENAS, F. DE. Ensayo sobre la historia de la propriedad territorial en España. 2 vols. Madrid, 1873–75.

635a. COSTA, J. Derecho consuetudinario y economia popular de España. 2 vols. Barcelona, 1902.

635b. COLMEIRO, M. Historia de la economia politica en España. 2 vols. Madrid, 1863.

(*b*) PORTUGAL

636. HERCULANO, A. Historia de Portugal desde ó començo da monarchia até ó fin do reinado de Alfonso III. 4 vols. Lisbon, 1846–53. 4th edition, 1868ff.

See also the more popular book by J. P. OLIVEIRA MARTINS, *Historia de Portugal*, 2 vols., 6th edition, Lisbon, 1901.

637. RIBEIRO, J. P. Dissertações chronologicas e criticas sobre a historia e iurisprudencia ecclesiastica e civil de Portugal. 5 vols. in 7. Lisbon, 1810–36.

638. STEPHENS, H. M. Portugal. London, 1891 (Story of nations).

638a. YOUNG, G. Portugal old and young: an historical study. Oxford, 1917.

639. SCHÄFER, H. Geschichte von Portugal. 5 vols. Hamburg and Gotha, 1836–54.

Part of no. **332.**

640. MACMURDO, E. The history of Portugal from the commencement of the monarchy to the reign of D. João V. 3 vols. London, 1888–89. First volume is a bad translation of Herculano.

641. GAMA BARROS, H. DA. Historia da administração publica em Portugal nos seculos 12 a 15. 2 vols. Lisbon, 1885–97.

642. MICHEL, F. Les Portugais en France et les Français en Portugal. Paris, 1882.

§ 13. The Byzantine Empire

(*a*) GENERAL ACCOUNTS

See also no. **418** [TOZER].

643. VASILIEV, A. A. History of the Byzantine empire. 2 vols. Madison, 1928–30.

643a. BURY, J. B. A history of the later Roman empire 395–800 A.D. 2 vols. New York, 1889.

643b. BURY, J. B. History of the later Roman empire from the death of Theodosius I. to the death of Justinian. 2 vols. London, 1923.

N. H. BAYNES, *A bibliography of the work of J. B. Bury*, Cambridge, 1929.

644. BURY, J. B. A history of the eastern Roman empire from the fall of Irene to the accession of Basil I (A.D. 802–867). London and New York, 1912.

These works form the standard history of the period which they cover.

645. FINLAY, G. "History of the Byzantine empire, from DCCXVI to MLVII." New York, 1906 (Everyman's library).

This is a reprint of vol. II of his *History of Greece*, no. **656.**

646. OMAN, C. Story of the Byzantine empire. New York, 1892 (Story of nations).

647. FOORD, E. A. The Byzantine empire: the rearguard of European civilization. London, 1911.

Very inadequate.

648. BUSSELL, F. W. The Roman empire: essays on the constitutional history, 81–1081 A.D. 2 vols. London, 1910.

Very disappointing.

649. GELZER, H. Byzantinische Kulturgeschichte. Tübingen, 1909.

See also his *Ausgewählte kleine Schrifter*, Leipzig, 1907; and "Abriss der byzantinischen Kaisergeschichte," Appendix to no. **800.**

650. HESSELING, D. C. Byzantium: Studien over onze Beschaving na de Stichting van Konstantinopel. Haarlem, 1902. French translation, Essai sur la civilization byzantine, with a preface by G. SCHLUMBERGER. Paris, 1907.

651. GRENIER, P. L'empire byzantin, son évolution sociale et politique. 2 vols. Paris, 1904.

652. HERTZBERG, G. F. Geschichte der Byzantiner und des osmanischen Reiches bis gegen Ende des sechszehnten Jahrhunderts. Berlin, 1883.

Part of no. **313.**

653. ROTH, K. Geschichte des byzantinischen Reiches. Leipzig, 1904 (Sammlung Göschen).

654. KRAUSE, J. H. Die Byzantiner des Mittelalters in ihrem Staats-, Hof- und Privatleben, insbesondere vom Ende des 10ten bis gegen Ende des 14ten Jahrhunderts nach den byzantinischen Quellen. Halle, 1869.

655. LE BEAU, C. Histoire du Bas-Empire. 28 vols. Paris, 1757–1817, New edition by ST. MARTIN. 21 vols. Paris, 1824–36.

(*b*) GREECE IN THE MIDDLE AGES

656. FINLAY, G. History of Greece from its conquest by the Romans to the present time. Edited by H. F. TOZER. 7 vols. Oxford, 1877.

657. MILLER, W. The Latins in the Levant, a history of Frankish Greece (1204–1566). London, 1908.

658. HERTZBERG, G. F. Geschichte Griechenlands seit dem Absterben des antiken Lebens bis zur Gegenwart. 4 vols. Gotha, 1876–79.

Part of no. **332.**

659. Hopf, K. Geschichte Griechenlands vom Beginn des Mittelalters bis auf unsere Zeit (395–1821). 2 vols. Leipzig, 1867–68.

Vols. 85–86 in no. **100.** See also D. Bikélas, *La Grèce byzantine et moderne*, Paris, 1893.

660. Gregorovius, F. Geschichte der Stadt Athen im Mittelalter. 2 vols. 3rd edition, Stuttgart, 1889.

(*c*) Constantinople

661. Hutton, W. H. Constantinople: the story of the old capital of the empire. London, 1900. 3rd edition, 1907 (Mediaeval towns series).

See also J. Ebersolt, *Le grand palais de Constantinople et le livre des cérémonies*, Paris, 1910; and J. B. Bury, "The great palace," *B.Z.*, XX (1911).

661a. Ebersolt, J. Constantinople byzantine et les voyageurs du Levant. Paris, 1919.

662. Grosvenor, E. A. Constantinople. 2 vols. Boston, 1895.

663. Van Milligen, A. Byzantine Constantinople: the walls of the city and adjoining historical sites. London, 1899.

See also A. D. Mordtmann, *Esquisse topographique de Constantinople*, Lille, 1892; and W. J. Broadribb and W. Besant, *Constantinople: a sketch of its history from its foundation to its conquest by the Turks in 1453*, London, 1879.

664. Baker, B. G. The walls of Constantinople. London, 1910.

665. Dwight, H. G. Constantinople old and new. Illustrated. New York, 1915.

666. Clement, Clara E. Constantinople: the city of the Sultans. Boston, 1895.

667. Barth, H. Constantinople. Paris, 1906 (Les villes d'art célèbres).

668. Gurlitt, C. Konstantinopel. Berlin [1908] (Die Kultur).

669. Schultze, V. Konstantinopel. Berlin, 1913.

See also E. Oberhummer, *Constantinopolis: Abriss der Topographie und Geschichte*, Stuttgart, 1899.

(*d*) Miscellaneous

670. Sesan, V. Kirche und Staat im römisch-byzantinischen Reiche seit Konstantin dem Grossen bis zum Falle Konstantinopels. Czernowitz, 1911.

This volume extends to 380 A.D.

671. Cobham, C. D. Patriarchs of Constantinople. Cambridge, 1911.

672. ZACHARIAE VON LINGENTHAL, K. E. Geschichte des griechisch-römischen Rechts. 3rd edition, Berlin, 1892.

673. DIEHL, C. Figures byzantines. 2 vols. Vol. I in 4th edition; vol. II in 3rd edition. Paris, 1909. Translated by H. BELL as Byzantine portraits, New York, 1927.

674. DIEHL, C. Etudes byzantines. Paris, 1905.

674a. DIEHL, C. Dans l'orient byzantin. Paris, 1917. (Collections d'études d'histoire et d'archéologie.)

Assembles articles first published in *Revue de Paris* and *Journal des savants.*

675. KRUMBACHER, K. Populäre Aufsätze. Leipzig, 1909.

676. RAMBAUD, A. Etudes sur l'histoire byzantine. Paris, 1912.

677. GFRÖRER, A. F. Byzantinische Geschichten. 3 vols. Graz, 1872–77.

678. MCCABE, J. The empresses of Constantinople. London, 1913.

679. DIETERICH, K. Byzantinische Charakterköpfe. Leipzig, 1909 (Aus Natur und Geisteswelt, 244).

§ 14. Eastern Europe

(*a*) GENERAL ACCOUNTS

680. MARQUART, I. Osteuropäische und ostasiatische Streifzüge: ethnologische und historisch-topographische Studien zur Geschichte des 9. und 10. Jahrhunderts (ca. 840–940). Leipzig, 1903.

See also A. WIRTH, *Geschichte Asiens und Osteuropas*, vol. I, *Von den Anfängen bis 1790*, Halle, 1904.

680a. NIEDERLE, L. Manuel de l'antiquité slave. 2 vols. Paris, 1923–26.

(*b*) RUSSIA

681. KLUCHEVSKY, V. O. A history of Russia. Translated from the Russian by C. J. HOGARTH. 4 vols. London and New York, 1911–26.

A very poor translation of the best book we have on the history of Russia. M. BARING, *The Russian people*, London, 1911, is based largely on Kluchevsky's lectures, which form the basis of his book. Another reflection of Kluchevsky is the first volume of J. MAVOR, *An economic history of Russia*, 2 vols., London and New York, 1914.

681a. BEAZLEY, C. R., FORBES, N. and BIRKETT, G. A. Russia from the Varangians to the Bolsheviks. Oxford, 1918.

681b. PARES, B. A history of Russia. New York, 1928.

682. RAMBAUD, A. Histoire de la Russie depuis les origines jusqu'à nos jours. 6th edition, revised by E. HAUMANT. Paris, 1914. Translated by LEONORA B. LANG, A popular history of Russia, in 3 vols., Boston, 1882. New edition, 1886.

The best general history of medieval and modern Russia by a western scholar. See pp. 933–53 in the latest French edition for an extensive bibliography. See also F. P. GIORDANI, *Storia della Russia secondo gli studi più recenti*, 2 vols., Milan, 1916.

683. MORFILL, W. R. Russia. London, 1890 (Story of nations).

683a. FLOWE, SONIA E. A thousand years of Russian history. Philadelphia, 1916.

684. BRÜCKNER, A. Geschichte Russlands, bis zum Ende des 18 Jahrhunderts. 2 vols. Gotha, 1896–1913.

Part of no. **332.**

685. SCHIEMANN, T. Russland, Polen und Livland bis ins 17 Jahrhundert. 2 vols. Berlin, 1886–87.

Part of no. **313.**

686. PANTENIUS, T. H. Geschichte Russlands von der Entstehung des russischen Reichs bis zur Gegenwart. Leipzig, 1908.

687. BESTUSCHEW, K. Geschichte Russlands. A German translation from the Russian by T. SCHIEMANN. Mitau, 1874.

687a. GRUSHEVSKI (HRUSCHEWSKYJ), M. Geschichte der Ukraine. Translated from the Russian. Vol. I (9th–17th century). Lemberg, 1916. The Russian book was published in 1911. Translators made changes in earlier chapters in the interest of German propaganda. (See F. GOLDER in *A.H.R.*, XXIV (1919), 666–67.)

688. LEROY-BEAULIEU, A. L'empire des tsars et les Russes. Paris, 1881–82. Translated from the 3rd French edition by Z. A. RAGOZIN, The empire of the tsars and the Russians. 3 vols. New York, 1894–1902.

This book on modern Russia constantly reaches back to the middle ages to find explanations for present conditions.

689. REEB, W. Russische Geschichte. Leipzig, 1903 (Sammlung Göschen).

690. PIERLING, P. La Russie et le Saint-Siège. 4 vols. Paris, 1896–1907. Vol. I in 2nd edition, 1906.

(*c*) FINLAND AND THE BALTIC PROVINCES: LIVONIA, ESTHONIA, AND COURLAND

See also no. **717.**

691. SERAPHIM, E. Geschichte Liv-, Esth- und Kurlands von der "Aufsegelung" des Landes bis zur Einverleibung in das russische Reich. 2 vols. 2nd edition. Reval, 1897–1903.

See also his *Geschichte von Livland*, vol. I, Gotha, 1905, part of no. **332**; his *Baltische Geschichte im Grundriss*, Reval, 1908; and L. ARBUSOW, *Grundriss der Geschichte von Liv-, Esth- und Kurland*, 3rd edition, Riga, 1908. For Livonia see also no. **685.**

692. SCHYBERGSON, M. G. Finlands historia. 2 vols. Helsingfors, 1887–89. German edition by F. ARNHEIM. Gotha, 1896.

Part of no. **332.**

(*d*) POLAND

See also no. **685.**

693. ORVIS, JULIA S. A brief history of Poland. New York, 1916.

693a. LEWINSKI-CORWIN, E. H. The political history of Poland. New York, 1917.

694. MORFILL, W. R. Poland. London, 1893 (Story of nations).

S. A. DUNHAM, *The history of Poland*, London, 1834. L. LEPSZY, *Cracow, the royal city of ancient Poland: its history and antiquities*, translated by R. DYBOLSKI, London, 1912.

694a. SLOCOMBE, G. E. Poland. New York, 1916 (Nations' histories).

695. PHILLIPS, W. A. Poland. Home university library, 1915.

696. ROEPELL, R. Geschichte Polens. Vol. I. Continued by J. CARO, vols. II–V (to 1506). Hamburg and Gotha, 1840–86.

Part of no. **332.**

697. CARO, J. Geschichte Polens. Gotha, 1863.

698. BRANDENBURGER, C. Polnische Geschichte. Leipzig, 1907 (Sammlung Göschen).

(*e*) BOHEMIA AND MORAVIA

699. MAURICE, C. E. The story of Bohemia from the earliest times to the fall of national independence in 1620. New York, 1896 (Story of nations).

700. BRETHOLZ, B. Geschichte Böhmens und Mährens bis zum Aussterben der Premysliden (1306). Munich and Leipzig, 1912.

The old standard work on Bohemia was F. PALACKY, *Geschichte von Böhmen*, vols. I–V [to 1526], Prague, 1836–67, vols. I–III in 3rd, but unchanged edition, 1864–96. See also A. ZYCHA, *Ueber den Ursprung der Städte in Böhmen und die Städtepolitik der Premysliden*, Prague, 1914.

701. BACHMAN, A. Geschichte Böhmens. Vols. I and II. Gotha, 1899–1905.

Part of no. **332.** Vol. I extends to 1400 A.D.

702. LÜTZOW, F. H. H. v. Bohemia, an historical sketch. London [1909] (Everyman's library). First published in 1896.

See also his *Lectures on the historians of Bohemia*, London, 1905, and *The story of Prague*, London, 1907.

703. MONROE, W. S. Bohemia and the Čechs: the history, people, institutions, and the geography of the kingdom, together with accounts of Moravia and Silesia. Boston, 1910.

(*f*) HUNGARY

704. VÁMBÉRY, A. The story of Hungary. New York and London, 1886 (Story of nations).

705. SAYOUS, E. Histoire générale des Hongrois. 2 vols. Paris, 1876.

(*g*) BALKAN STATES

(1) *General*

706. MILLER, W. The Balkans: Roumania, Bulgaria, Servia, Montenegro. New York, 1896 (Story of nations).

N. FORBES, A. J. TOYNBEE, D. MITRANY, and D. G. HOGARTH, *The Balkans: a history of Bulgaria, Serbia, Greece, Rumania, Turkey*, Oxford, 1915. W. HOWARD-FLANDERS, *Balkania: a short history of the Balkan states*, London, 1909. L. LEGER, *Serbes, Croates et Bulgares*, Paris, 1913.

706a. SCHEVILL, F. The history of the Balkan peninsula from the earliest times to the present day. New York [c. 1922].

707. JIREČEK, K. J. Die Romanen in den Städten Dalmatiens während des Mittelalters. 3 vols. Vienna, 1901, 1903, 1905 (Denkschriften of the Vienna academy).

707a. ŠIŠIĆ, F. v. Geschichte der Kroaten. Vol. I (to 1102). Agram, 1917.

(2) *Rumania*

708. JORGA, N. Geschichte des rumänischen Volkes. Vols. I–III (to 1640). Gotha, 1905–10.

Part of no. **332**.

708a. JORGA, N. Histoire des Roumains de Transylvanie et de Hongrie. 2 vols. Bucharest, 1915–16.

709. XÉNOPOL, A. D. Histoire des Roumains. 2 vols. Paris, 1896.

Vol. I, 513–1633 A.D. See also his *Les Roumains: histoire, état matériel et intellectuel*, Paris, 1909.

(3) *Bulgaria*

710. SONGEON, R. P. G. Histoire de la Bulgarie depuis les origines jusqu'à nos jours (485–1913). Paris, 1913.

711. SAMUELSON, J. Bulgaria past and present: historical, political and descriptive. London, 1888.

712. BOUSQUET, G. Histoire du peuple bulgare depuis les origines jusqu'à nos jours. Paris, 1909.

713. JIREČEK, K. J. Geschichte der Bulgaren. Prague, 1876.

(4) *Serbia and Bosnia*

714. JIREČEK, K. J. Geschichte der Serben. 2 vols. Gotha, 1911–18.

See the review of this book by W. MILLER, "The mediaeval Serbian empire," *Quarterly review*, CCXXVI (1916), 488–507.

714a. TEMPERLEY, H. W. V. History of Serbia. London, 1917.

715. KANITZ, F. Das Königreich Serbien und das Serbenvolk von der Römerzeit bis zur Gegenwart. Vol. I. Leipzig, 1904.

716. THALLÓCZY, L. Studien zur Geschichte Bosniens und Serbiens im Mittelalter. Translated by F. ECKHART. Munich, 1914.

V. KLAIC, *Geschichte Bosniens*, Leipzig, 1885. S. NOVAKOVIC, "Les problèmes serbes," in *Archiv für slavische Philologie*, XXXIII–XXXIV (1912).

§ 15. Scandinavian Countries

(*a*) GENERAL

717. STEFANSSON, J. Denmark and Sweden with Iceland and Finland. New York, 1916 (Story of nations).

E. C. OTTÉ, *Scandinavian history*, London, 1874.

718. MAURER, K. v. Vorlesungen über altnordische Rechtsgeschichte. Vols. I–IV. Leipzig, 1906–09.

A posthumous work.

(*b*) DENMARK

719. Det Danske Folks Historie. Edited by A. FRIIS, A. LINVALD, M. MACKEBRANG. 8 vols. Copenhagen, 1927–30.

Vol. I. Det Danske Folk i Oldtiden. Vol. II. Det Danske Folk i den ældre Middelalder. Vol. III. Det Danske Folk i den yngre Middelalder.

720. Danmarks Riges Historie. By J. STEENSTRUP and others. Vols. I–VI. Copenhagen, 1896–1907.

721. ALLEN, C. F. Histoire de Danemark depuis les temps les plus reculés jusqu'à nos jours. French translation, by E. BEAUVOIS, from the 7th Danish edition. 2 vols., Copenhagen, 1878.

The French translation adds important bibliographies.

722. DAHLMANN, F. S. Geschichte von Dänemark. Vols. I–III. Vols. IV–V (to 1648) by D. SCHÄFER. Hamburg and Gotha, 1840–1902.

Part of no. **332**.

(c) NORWAY

723. Norges Historie, Fremstillet for det Norske Folk. A co-operative work by A. BUGGE, E. HERTZBERG, O. A. JOHNSEN, Y. NIELSEN, J. E. SARS, A. TARANGER, et al. 6 vols. published in 13 separate parts. Christiania, 1909–17.

723a. GJERSET, K. History of the Norwegian people from the earliest times to the present day. 2 vols. New York, 1915.

724. BOYESEN, H. H. The story of Norway. London, 1886 (Story of nations).

725. WILLSON, T. B. History of the church and state in Norway from the tenth to the sixteenth century. Westminster, 1903.

(d) SWEDEN

726. GEIJER, E. G. Geschichte Schwedens. Vols. I–III. Vols. IV–VI by F. F. CARLSON. Vol. VII (to 1772) by L. STAVENOW. Hamburg and Gotha, 1832–1908.

Part of no. **332**.

727. MONTELIUS, O. Sveriges Historia från äldsta Tid till vara Dagar. 6 vols. Stockholm, 1877–81.

727a. Sveriges Historia till våra Dagar. Edited by E. HILDEBRAND and L. STAVENOW, 14 vols. Stockholm, 1920ff.

Vol. I, Forntiden, by O. MONTELIUS; vol. II, Den äldre medeltiden, by S. TUNBERG; vol. III, Den senare medeltiden (not yet published).

727b. HILDEBRAND, H. Sveriges medeltid Kulturhistorisk Skildring. Vols. I–III. Stockholm, 1879–1903.

(e) ICELAND

728. HERRMANN, P. Island in Vergangenheit und Gegenwart: Reiseerinnerungen. 3 vols. Leipzig, 1907–10.

Vol. I, ch. III, "Geschichte Islands." See references to other works cited in the footnotes and especially J. BRYCE, "Primitive Iceland," I, 236–300, of *Studies in history and jurisprudence*, 2 vols., Oxford, 1901.

728a. KÅLUND, P. E. Kristian, Bidrag till en historisk-topografisk Beskrivelse of Island, 2 vols. Vol. II in two parts, a very complete index. Copenhagen, 1877.

728b. GJERSET, K. History of Iceland. New York, 1924.

728c. MAURER, K. Island von seiner ersten Entdeckung bis zum Untergang des Freistaats. Munich, 1874.

§ 16. History of Culture and Civilization

(a) General Histories of Civilization

See also nos. **187–207.**

729. Die Kultur der Gegenwart: ihre Entwickelung und ihre Ziele. Edited by P. Hinneberg. Berlin and Leipzig, 1905ff.

Most of the separate works in parts I and II have some bearing upon the middle ages. The most important of them will be mentioned in appropriate places.

730. Kulturgeschichtliche Bibliothek. Edited by F. Foy. 3 sections. Heidelberg, 1911ff.

731. Quellen und Forschungen zur Sprach- und Culturgeschichte der germanischen Völker. Edited originally by B. Ten Brink and W. Scherer. Strasburg, 1874ff.

732. Breysig, K. Kulturgeschichte der Neuzeit. Vols. I and II. Berlin, 1900–01.

Vol. II, part 2, is on the middle ages.

733. Hellwald, F. v. Kulturgeschichte in ihrer natürlichen Entwicklung bis zur Gegenwart. Augsburg, 1874. 4th edition, revised and enlarged by eighteen German scholars. 4 vols. Leipzig, 1896–98.

Vol. III is on the middle ages. See also E. Driault, *Vue générale de l'histoire de la civilisation*, 2 vols., Paris, 1909 (Bibliothèque de l'histoire contemporaine).

734. Henne-am-Rhyn, O. Allgemeine Kulturgeschichte von der Urzeit bis auf die Gegenwart. 9 vols. Leipzig, 1877–1908.

735. Social England: a record of the progress of the people in religion, laws, learning, arts, industry, commerce, science, literature, and manners. Edited by H. D. Traill and written by various specialists. 6 vols. London, 1894–97. Illustrated and revised edition, 6 vols., 1901–04.

736. Guizot, F. Histoire de la civilisation en Europe depuis la chute de l'empire romain. Paris, 1828. Translated by C. S. Henry, History of civilization from the fall of the Roman empire to the French revolution, as vol. I of History of civilization. 4 vols. New York, 1846.

See no. **763.**

737. Milyoukov, P. Skizzen russischer Kulturgeschichte. German edition by E. Davidson. 2 vols. Leipzig, 1898–1901.

738. Baudrillart, H. Histoire du luxe privé et public, depuis l'antiquité jusqu'à nos jours. 2nd edition. 4 vols. Paris, 1880–81. Vol. III, Le moyen âge et la renaissance.

(*b*) History of Freedom of Thought

See also no. **817.**

739. White, A. D. A history of the warfare of science with theology in Christendom. 2 vols. New York, 1896.

740. Bury, J. B. A history of freedom of thought. New York [1913] (Home university library).

740a. Lord Acton. "The history of freedom in Christianity" in his The history of freedom and other essays. London, 1909.

740b. Bury, J. B. The idea of progress. London, 1920.

741. Lecky, W. E. H. History of the rise and influence of the spirit of rationalism in Europe. 2 vols. 1865. Revised edition. London, 1870.

742. Robertson, J. M. A short history of free-thought, ancient and modern. 2 vols. 3rd edition, revised, London, 1915.

743. Santayana, G. The life of reason: or, The phases of human progress. 5 vols. New York, 1905–06.

See especially vol. III, *Reason in religion.*

744. Ruffini, F. Religious liberty. Translated from the Italian by J. P. Heyes, with a preface by J. B. Bury. London, 1912.

745. Whetham, W. C. D., and Whetham, Catherine D. Science and the human mind: a critical and historical account of the development of natural knowledge. London, 1912.

746. Draper, J. W. History of the intellectual development of Europe. 2 vols. Revised edition, New York, 1876.

747. Holland, F. M. The rise of intellectual liberty from Thales to Copernicus. New York, 1885.

748. Zöckler, O. Geschichte der Beziehungen zwischen Theologie und Naturwissenschaften mit besonderer Rücksicht auf die Schöpfungsgeschichte. 2 vols. Gütersloh, 1877–79.

(*c*) Medieval Civilization in General

749. Beiträge zur Kulturgeschichte des Mittelalters und der Renaissance. Edited by W. Goetz. Leipzig and Berlin, 1908ff.

750. Vom Mittelalter zur Reformation: Forschungen zur Geschichte der deutschen Bildung. Edited by K. Burdach. Berlin, 1912ff.

Very broad in scope. By no means strictly confined to Germany, e.g., publication began in 1912 with parts 3 and 4 of vol. II, *Briefwechsel des Cola di Rienzo*, edited by K. Burdach and P. Piur. Original sources are edited along with special studies.

750a. Bezold, F. v. Aus Mittelalter und Renaissance: Kulturgeschichtliche Studien. Munich and Berlin, 1918.

Twelve miscellaneous essays, written 1876–1914.

751. Grupp, G. Kulturgeschichte des Mittelalters. 2 vols. Stuttgart, 1894–95. 3rd edition, vols. 1–4, Paderborn, 1921–25; 2nd edition, vol. 5, 1925; vol. 6 appeared 1925.

752. Kurth, G. Les origines de la civilisation moderne. 2 vols. 7th edition, Brussels, 1923.

Extends to the time of Charlemagne.

753. Lecky, W. E. H. History of European morals from Augustus to Charlemagne. 2 vols. London and New York, 1870. New cheap impression, London, 1911.

754. Wright, T. Essays on archaeological subjects, and on various questions connected with the history of art, science, and literature in the middle ages. 2 vols. London, 1861.

755. Merryweather, F. S. Glimmerings in the dark: or lights and shadows of the olden time. London, 1850.

(*d*) Medieval Intellectual Life in General

756. Taylor, H. O. The mediaeval mind. 2 vols. New York, 1911. 4th edition, 1925.

756a. Crump, G. C., and Jacob, E. F. The legacy of the middle ages. Oxford, 1926.

756b. Hearnshaw, F. J. C. (editor). Medieval contributions to modern civilization. A series of lectures delivered at King's College, University of London. London, 1921.

756c. Randall, J. H. The making of the modern mind. Boston, 1927.

Book I deals with the middle ages.

756d. Rand, E. K. Founders of the middle ages. Cambridge, 1928.

756e. Haskins, C. H. The renaissance of the twelfth century. Cambridge, 1927.

756f. Haskins, C. H. Studies in mediaeval culture. Oxford, 1929.

756g. Vossler, K. Mediaeval culture; an introduction to Dante and his times. 2 vols. New York [1929]. A translation by W. C. Lawton of Die göttliche Komödie. 2nd edition. 2 vols. Heidelberg, 1925.

757. Workman, H. B. Christian thought to the reformation. New York, 1911.

757a. Bussell, F. W. Religious thought and heresy in the middle ages. London, 1918.

758. NOVATI, F. L'influsso del pensiero latino sopra la civiltà italiana del medio evo. 2nd edition, Milan, 1899.

759. HAURÉAU, B. Singularités historiques et littéraires. Paris, 1861.

Ten studies, among which are the following: Ecoles d'Irlande; Théodulfe, évêque d'Orléans; Odon de Cluny; Anselme le Peripatéticien; Guillaume de Conches.

759a. LAUNOY, J. DE. De scholis celebrioribus, seu a Carolo Magno, seu post eundum Carolum, per occidentem instauratis, liber. Paris, 1672.

760. MAITLAND, S. R. The dark ages: a series of essays intended to illustrate the state of religion and literature in the ninth, tenth, eleventh, and twelfth centuries. London, 1844. 5th edition with introduction by Stokes. 1890.

This is a curious old defence of the culture of the period. Probably its oldest prototype is J. MABILLON, *Traité des études monastiques*, 2 vols., Paris, 1691.

761. FIGUIER, L. Vies des savants illustrés avec l'appréciation sommaire de leurs travaux. 5 vols. Paris, 1866–70.

Vol. II, *Moyen âge;* vol. III, *Renaissance.*

(*e*) FRANCE

See also no. **781.**

762. RAMBAUD, A. Histoire de la civilisation française. 7th edition, 2 vols., Paris, 1898.

762a. LANGLOIS, C. V. La vie en France au moyen âge de la fin du XIIe au milieu du XIVe siècle. 4 vols. Paris, 1924–28.

762b. GIRAUD, V. La civilisation française. Paris, 1917.

Is also printed in *R.D.M.*, Dec. 15, 1916.

763. GUIZOT, F. Histoire de la civilisation en France. 5 vols. Paris, 1829–38. 6th edition, 4 vols., Paris, 1857. Translated by W. HAZLITT as vols. II–IV of History of civilization. New York, 1846.

Extends from the 5th to the 14th century.

764. ROSIÈRES, R. Histoire de la société française au moyen âge (987–1483). 2 vols. Paris, 1880. 3rd edition, 1884.

765. REYNAUD, L. Les origines de l'influence française en Allemagne: étude sur l'histoire comparée de la civilisation en France et en Allemagne pendant la période précourtoise (950–1150). Vol. I. Paris, 1913.

765a. REYNAUD, L. Histoire générale de l'influence française en Allemagne. 2nd edition. Paris, 1915.

766. VOSSLER, K. Frankreichs Kultur im Spiegel seiner Sprachentwicklung. Heidelberg, 1913.

767. CHALLAMEL, A. Mémoires du peuple français. 8 vols. Paris, 1873.

(*f*) Germany

(1) *Medieval and Modern Times*

768. Steinhausen, G. Geschichte der deutschen Kultur. Leipzig, 1904. 2nd edition, revised, 2 vols., 1913.

Popular, but reliable. The best general survey.

769. Freytag, G. Bilder aus der deutschen Vergangenheit. 4 vols. in 5. Leipzig, 1859–62. 27th to 32nd editions, 1908–09.

Vols. I–II, part 1, to 1500.

770. Henne-am-Rhyn, O. Kulturgeschichte des deutschen Volkes. 2 vols. Berlin, 1886. 3rd edition, 1898.

771. Richard, E. History of German civilization: a general survey. New York, 1911. 2nd, revised, edition, 1913.

772. Scheer, J. Deutsche Kultur- und Sittengeschichte. Leipzig, 1852–53. 12th edition, 3 vols., 1909.

773. Scheer, J. Germania: zwei Jahrtausende deutsches Lebens kulturgeschichtlich geschildert. 6th edition by H. Prutz. Stuttgart, 1905.

774. Biedermann, K. Deutsche Volks- und Kulturgeschichte. 4th edition. 3 vols. Wiesbaden, 1901.

775. Monographien zur deutschen Kulturgeschichte. Edited by G. Steinhausen. 12 vols. Leipzig, 1899–1905. Two supplementary volumes, Deutsches Leben der Vergangenheit in Bildern. 1907–08.

For a list of vols. see no. **28,** Dahlmann-Waitz, no. 1733.

(2) *The Middle Ages*

776. Herre, P. Deutsche Kultur im Mittelalter in Bild und Wort. Leipzig, 1912.

777. Steinhausen, G. Kulturgeschichte der Deutschen im Mittelalter. Leipzig, 1910 (Wissenschaft und Bildung, 88).

778. Löher, F. v. Kulturgeschichte der Deutschen im Mittelalter. 3 vols. Munich, 1891–94.

779. Michael, E. Culturzustände des deutschen Volkes während des dreizehnten Jahrhunderts. 6 vols. Freiburg, 1897–1915.

780. Steinhausen, G. Geschichte des deutschen Briefes. 2 parts. Berlin, 1889–91.

See also the source-book, *Deutsche Privatbriefe des Mittelalters*, edited by G. Steinhausen, 2 vols., Berlin, 1899–1907.

781. Chélard, R. La civilisation française dans le développement de l'Allemagne (moyen âge). Paris, 1900.

(g) Histories of Literature

(1) *General Histories of Literature*

782. Baumgartner, A. Geschichte der Weltliteratur. 7 vols. St. Louis, 1897–1912. Vol. IV. Die lateinische und griechische Literatur der christlichen Völker. 1900.

783. Saintsbury, G. A history of criticism and literary taste in Europe from the earliest texts to the present day. 3 vols. Edinburgh and London, 1900–04.

Vol. I, *Classical and mediaeval criticism.*

784. Sismondi, J. C. L. S. de. Historical view of the literature of the south of Europe. Translated from the Italian by T. Roscoe. 4 vols. London, 1823.

(2) *Ancient Classical Literature and Learning*

785. Sandys, J. E. A history of classical scholarship. 3 vols. Cambridge, 1903–08. Vol. I From the sixth century B.C. to the end of the middle ages, in a 3rd edition.

There is an abridged edition in one volume, *A short history of classical scholarship from the sixth century B.C. to the present day*, Cambridge, 1915. See also A. Gudeman, *Grundriss der Geschichte der klassischen Philologie*, 2nd edition, Leipzig, 1909; and H. T. Peck, *A history of classical philology, from the 7th century B.C. to the 20th century A.D.*, London and New York, 1911.

786. Norden, E. Die antike Kunst-prosa vom 6[ten] Jahrhundert vor Christus bis in die Zeit der Renaissance. 2 vols. Leipzig, 1898. New edition, 1909.

(3) *Literary History of the Middle Ages*

See also no. **170.**

787. Manitius, M. Geschichte der lateinischen Literatur des Mittelalters. 2 vols. Munich, 1911–23.

This is now the standard handbook for the history of medieval Latin literature. The second volume extends to about 1050. Until the work is carried into later centuries, we must be content with G. Gröber, "Übersicht über die lateinische Literatur von der Mitte des 6. Jahrhunderts bis 1350" in no. **305,** vol. II, part I, 97–432; and with Sandys, no. **785.**

788. Ebert, A. Allgemeine Geschichte der Literatur des Mittelalters im Abendlande. 3 vols. Leipzig, 1874–87. Vol. 1 in 2nd edition, 1889.

Extends to the beginning of the 11th century. There is a French translation by J. Aymeric and J. Condamin, 3 vols., Paris, 1883–89.

790. Hervieux, A. L. Les fabulistes latins depuis le siècle d'Auguste jusqu'à la fin du moyen âge. 5 vols. Paris, 1893–99.

791. Spence, L. A dictionary of medieval romance and romance writers. London, 1913.

792. Ludlow, J. M. Popular epics of the middle ages of the Norse-German and Carlovingian cycles. 2 vols. London, 1865.

793. Ker, W. P. Essays on medieval literature. London, 1905.

On Dante, Boccaccio, Chaucer, Gower, Froissart, and an estimate of the late Gaston Paris.

794. Lawrence, W. W. Mediaeval story. New York, 1912.

795. McLaughlin, E. T. Studies in mediaeval life and literature. New York, 1894.

796. Bulfinch, T. Mythology: the age of fable, the age of chivalry, and legends of Charlemagne. Complete in one volume, revised and enlarged. New York, 1913.

797. Delisle, L. Littérature latine et histoire du moyen âge. Paris, 1890.

798. Falke, J. v. Geschichte des Geschmacks im Mittelalter und andere Studien auf dem Gebiete der Kunst und Literatur. 2nd edition. Berlin, 1892.

799. [Marténe, E., and Durand, U.] Voyage littéraire de deux religieux Bénédictins de la Congrégation de St. Maur. Paris, 1717. Second voyage littéraire de deux religieux Bénédictins de la Congrégation de St. Maur. Paris, 1724.

(4) *Byzantine Literature*

800. Krumbacher, K. Geschichte der byzantinischen Literatur von Justinian bis zum Ende des oströmischen Reiches (527–1453 A.D.). Munich, 1890. 2nd edition, 1897. (In Handbuch der klassichen Altertumswissenschaft.)

Of fundamental importance. See his condensed, but more recent (1907) treatment, "Die griechische Literatur des Mittelalters," in *Die Kultur der Gegenwart*, no. **729,** I, 8. See especially no. **643.**

801. Dieterich, K. Geschichte der byzantinischen und neugriechischen Literatur. Leipzig, 1902 (Die Literaturen des Ostens, 4).

802. Montelatici, G. Storia della letteratura bizantina, 324–1453. Milan, 1916.

(5) *France*

803. Histoire littéraire de la France. Vols. I–XXXVI. Paris, 1733–1927. Begun by the Religieux Bénédictins de la Congrégation de Saint-Maur and continued by the Académie des inscriptions et belles-lettres.

The first 26 vols. are analyzed in A. Franklin, no. **23,** pp. 585–97. For a detailed bibliography of medieval French literature, see outline XXIV in part III.

(6) *Germany and Austria*

804. SCHERER, W. Geschichte der deutschen Literatur. 11th edition. Berlin, 1910. Translated from the 3rd German edition by Mrs. F. C. CONYBEARE, History of German literature. 2 vols. New York, 1901.

805. NAGL, J. W., and ZEIDLER, J. Deutsch-österreichische Literaturgeschichte. Vols. I–II. Vienna, 1899–1909.

806. VOGT, F., and KOCH, M. Geschichte der deutschen Literatur von den ältesten Zeiten bis zur Gegenwart. 2 vols. Leipzig and Vienna, 1897. 3rd edition 1910.

807. KELLE J. Geschichte der deutschen Literatur von den ältesten Zeiten bis zum 13 Jahrhundert. 2 vols. Berlin, 1892–96.

(7) *Italy*

808. GASPARY, A. Geschichte der italienischen Literatur. 2 vols. Strasburg, 1885–88. Translated by H. OELSNER, The history of Italian literature to the death of Dante. London, 1901.

809. GARNETT, R. A history of Italian literature. London, 1908.

810. D'ANCONA, A., and BACCI, O. Manuale della letteratura italiana. New, revised, edition, vols. I–VI, Florence, 1907–10.

Vols. I and II cover the middle ages.

811. TIRABOSCHI, G. Storia della letteratura italiana [to 1700]. Modena, 1772ff. 16 vols. Milan, 1822–26.

See especially vols. III–V [476–1400 A.D.] in 2nd edition, Modena, 1787–94.

811a. Storia letteraria d'Italia, scritta da una società di professori. 12 vols. Milan [1897?–1926]. 3rd revised edition, Milan, 1929ff.

(8) *England*

812. Cambridge history of English literature. Edited by A. W. WARD and A. R. WALLER. Vols. I–XV. Cambridge, 1907–27. Vol. XV. Index.

For additional references see GROSS, no. **36**.

(9) *Spain and Portugal*

813. FITZMAURICE-KELLY, J. A history of Spanish literature. London, 1898. Latest edition, 1917. A new history of Spanish literature. Oxford, 1926.

The second Spanish edition, *Historia de la literatura española*, Madrid, 1916, is especially valuable for its full bibliography. See also G. TICKNOR, *History of Spanish literature*, 3rd edition, 3 vols., London, 1863; the Spanish translation by P. DE GAYANGOS, 4 vols., Madrid, 1851–61, contains additions and corrections. For Portugal, see A. LOISEAU, *Histoire de la littérature portugaise*, Paris, 1885.

(10) *Russia and Scandinavia*

814. Brückner, A. Geschichte der russischen Literatur. Leipzig, 1905 (Die Literaturen des Ostens, 2).

See also K. Waliszewski, *Histoire de la littérature russe*, Paris, 1900; W. R. Morfill, *Slavonic literature*, London, 1883; and G. Krek, *Einleitung in die slavische Literaturgeschichte*, Graz, 1874; 2nd edition, 1887. For Scandinavia, See P. Schweitzer, *Geschichte der skandinavischen Literatur*, 3 vols., Leipzig, 1885–89; E. Mogk, "Nordische Literatur," in Paul's *Grundriss*, no. **307**, and F. Jónsson, *Den oldnorskislandske litteraturs historie*, 3 vols., Copenhagen, 1894–1902. New edition, 1920–24.

(*h*) History of Philosophy and "Weltanschauung"

(1) *Medieval "Weltanschauung"*

815. Poole, R. L. Illustrations of the history of mediaeval thought. London, 1884. Second edition, revised. Illustrations of the history of medieval thought and learning. London, 1920.

See also C. C. J. Webb, *Studies in the history of natural theology*, Oxford, 1915, on St. Anselm, Abelard, St. Thomas Aquinas, etc.

816. Eicken, H. v. Geschichte und System der mittelalterlichen Weltanschauung. Stuttgart, 1887.

E. Troeltsch, *Die Soziallehren der christlichen Kirchen und Gruppen*, vol. I of his *Gesammelte Schriften*, Tübingen, 1912, 178–426.

817. Reuter, H. Geschichte der religiösen Aufklärung im Mittelalter. 2 vols. in 1. Berlin, 1875–77.

The period covered is from the 8th to the 14th century.

818. Weltanschauung: Philosophie und Religion in Darstellungen. Edited by W. Dilthey and about twenty others. Berlin, 1911.

819. Eucken, R. Die Lebensanschauungen der grossen Denker. 8th edition. Leipzig, 1909. Translated by W. S. Hough and W. R. Boyce-Gibson, The problem of human life as viewed by the great thinkers. London, 1909.

820. Dilthey, W. Einleitung in die Geisteswissenschaften: Versuch einer Grundlegung für das Studium der Gesellschaft und der Geschichte. Vol. I. Leipzig, 1883.

821. Troels-Lund, T. F. Himmelsbild und Weltanschauung im Wandel der Zeiten. Authorized German translation by L. Bloch. 3rd edition, Leipzig, 1908.

(2) *General History of Philosophy*

822. Ueberweg, F. Grundriss der Geschichte der Philosophie. 10th edition, 4 vols. Berlin, 1905–09. Translated from the 4th German edition by G. S. Morris, A history of philosophy from Thales to the present time. 2 vols. New York, 1872–74, also 1892.

See also W. Turner, *History of philosophy*, Boston, 1903.

823. WINDELBAND, W. Lehrbuch der Geschichte der Philosophie. 5th edition. Tübingen, 1910. Translated by J. H. TUFTS, A history of philosophy. 2nd edition. New York, 1901.

824. FABRE, J. Histoire de la philosophie depuis l'antiquité jusqu'à la révolution française. 5 vols. Paris, 1902ff. Vol. II, La pensée chrétienne: des Evangiles à l'Imitation de Jésus-Christ.

825. WULF, M. DE. Histoire de la philosophie scholastique dans les Pays-Bas et la principauté de Liège jusqu'à la révolution française. Louvain, 1895. 2nd edition, 1910.

(3) *Medieval Philosophy*

826. Beiträge zur Geschichte der Philosophie des Mittelalters: Texte und Untersuchungen. Edited by C. BAEUMKER and G. v. HERTLING. Münster, 1891ff.

A collection as valuable for the original texts as for the scholarly expositions of the editors.

827. WULF, M. DE. Histoire de la philosophie médiévale. Louvain, 1900. 5th edition in French, enlarged and revised. 2 vols. Louvain, 1924–25. English translation of 5th edition by E. C. MESSENGER. 2 vols. London, 1925–26.

For Jewish philosophy in the middle ages see NEUMARK, no. **866**.

828. PICAVET, F. Esquisse d'une histoire générale et comparée des philosophies médiévales. Paris, 1905. 2nd edition, 1907.

829. HAURÉAU, B. Histoire de philosophie scolastique. 2nd edition, 3 vols., Paris, 1872–80.

830. GRABMANN, M. Die Geschichte der scholastischen Methode. Nach den gedruckten und ungedruckten Quellen dargestellt. Vols. I and II. Freiburg-i-B., 1909–11.

830a. HEIM, K. Das Gewissheitsproblem in der systematischen Theologie bis zur Schleiermacher. Leipzig, 1911.

831. BAEUMKER, C. "Die europäische Philosophie des Mittelalters." Berlin and Leipzig, 1909. In Kultur der Gegenwart, no. **729,** I, 5.

831a. BAEUMKER, C. Der Anteil des Elsass an den geistigen Bewegungen des Mittelalters. Strasburg, 1912.

832. ENDRES, J. A. Geschichte der mittelalterlichen Philosophie im Abendlande. Kempten, 1908.

833. PRANTL, K. v. Geschichte der Logik im Abendlande. 4 vols. Leipzig, 1855–70. Vol. II in 2nd edition, 1885. Manueldruck der Originel-Ausgabe, 1927.

Extends to the Renaissance.

834. STÖCKL, A. Geschichte der Philosophie des Mittelalters. 3 vols. Mainz, 1864–66.

835. RICKABY, J. Scholasticism. London, 1908.

A primer based largely on WULF, no. **827.**

(i) HISTORY OF EDUCATION

(1) *General Histories of Education*

836. Geschichte der Erziehung vom Anfang bis auf unsere Zeit. Edited by K. A. SCHMID. Continued by G. SCHMID. 5 vols. in 10 parts. Berlin, 1884–1902.

837. WILLMANN, O. Didaktik als Bildungslehre. 2 vols. Brunswick, 1882. 4th edition, in one vol., 1909.

838. BAUMEISTER, [K.] A. Handbuch der Erziehungs- und Unterrichtslehre für höhere Schulen. 4 vols. Munich, 1895–98.

839. ZIEGLER, T. Geschichte der Pädagogik mit besonderer Rücksicht auf das höhere Unterrichtswesen. 3rd edition. Munich, 1909.

840. SCHERER, H. Die Pädagogik in ihrer Entwickelung im Zusammenhange mit dem Kultur- und Geistesleben. Vols. I and II, 1–2. Leipzig, 1897–1907.

(2) *History of Medieval Education*

841. GRAVES, F. P. A history of education during the middle ages and the transition to modern times. New York, 1910.

842. ECKSTEIN, F. A. Lateinischer Unterricht. Leipzig, 1882.

Extract from no. **118,** IV, 1, 204–405.

843. ECKSTEIN, F. A. Lateinischer und griechischer Unterricht im Mittelalter. Edited by H. HEYDEN (part I, Geschichte). Leipzig, 1887.

844. MASIUS, H. "Die Erziehung im Mittelalter." Stuttgart, 1892. In no. **836,** II, part I, 94–333.

845. DRANE, AUGUSTA T. Christian schools and scholars. London, 1881. Reprint, New York, 1909.

846. SPECHT, F. A. Geschichte des Unterrichtswesens in Deutschland von den ältesten Zeiten bis zur Mitte des 13 Jahrhunderts. Stuttgart, 1885.

847. PAULSEN, F. Das deutsche Bildungswesen in seiner geschichtlichen Entwickelung. Leipzig, 1906 (Aus Natur und Geisteswelt, 100).

848. LEACH, A. F. Some results of research in the history of education in England with suggestions for its continuance and extension. British Academy publications. Oxford, 1915.

849. LEACH, A. F. Educational charters and documents, 598–1909. Cambridge, 1911.

§ 17. Medieval Political Theory

849a. CARLYLE, R. W. and CARLYLE, A. J. A history of medieval political theory in the west. 5 vols. Edinburgh and London, 1903–28.

§ 18. Jews

For a general bibliography see no. **62.** For Jews in England see GROSS, no. **36,** 69*d;* in Germany, DAHLMANN-WAITZ, no. **28,** pp. 150ff.

(*a*) GENERAL HISTORY OF THE JEWS

850. GRÄTZ, H. Geschichte der Juden von den ältesten Zeiten bis auf die Gegenwart. 13 vols. Partly in 2nd–4th editions. Leipzig, 1894–1908. Translated into English, History of the Jews from the earliest times to the present day. 6 vols. Philadelphia, 1891–98.

The English translation omits the notes, references, and appendixes which give the book its scientific character, but has an index volume not found in the original.

Popular edition of the above, entitled *Volkstümliche Geschichte der Juden*, 2nd edition, 3 vols., 1909.

S. M. DUBNOW, *History of the Jews in Russia and Poland from the earliest times until the present day*, translated from the Russian by I. FRIEDLÄNDER, vol. 1, Philadelphia, 1916.

850a. DUBNOW, S. Weltgeschichte des jüdischen Volkes von seinen Uranfängen bis zur Gegenwart. Band IV: Das frühere Mittelalter. 1926. Band V: Das späte Mittelalter. 1927.

To be completed in 10 vols.

851. HOSMER, J. K. The Jews, ancient, mediaeval, and modern. New York, 1891. Often reprinted (Story of nations).

852. ABBOTT, G. F. Israel in Europe. London, 1907.

853. HERRMANN, F. Geschichte des jüdischen Volkes seit der Zerstörung Jerusalems. Calw and Stuttgart, 1908.

854. CASSEL, SELIG (later PAULUS). "Judea" section II, vol. XXVII, 1–238 in no. **100,** still deserves high commendation.

855. LIEBE, G. H. T. Das Judentum in der deutschen Vergangenheit. Leipzig, 1903.

Part of no. **775.**

856. BÉDARRIDE, I. Les Juifs en France, en Italie, et en Espagne: recherches sur leur état depuis leur dispersion jusqu'à nos jours sous le rapport de la législation, de la littérature et du commerce. Paris, 1859. 3rd edition, revised, 1867.

(b) Jews in the Middle Ages

(1) *Social and Economic History*

857. Abrahams, I. Jewish life in the middle ages. London and Philadelphia, 1896.

See also D. S. Schaff, "The treatment of the Jews in the middle ages," *Bibliotheca sacra* (1903), 547–69; J. H. Bridges, "The Jews of Europe in the middle ages," *Living age*, LV, 769–88; and J. v. Döllinger, "The Jews in Europe," in his *Studies*, no. **913.**

857a. Cracroft, B. "The Jews of western Europe," Westminster review, LXXIX (1863), 428–70. Reprinted in B. Cracroft. Essays political and miscellaneous. 2 vols. Philadelphia, 1868. Vol. II, 1–70.

858. Caro, G. Sozial- und Wirtschaftsgeschichte der Juden im Mittelalter und der Neuzeit. 2 vols. Leipzig, 1908–20.

859. Hahn, B. Die wirtschaftliche Tätigkeit der Juden im fränkischen und deutschen Reich bis zum 2 Kreuzzug. Freiburg, 1911.

859a. Zimmels, H. J. Beiträge zur Geschichte der Juden in Deutschland im 13 Jahrhundert. Frankfurt, 1926.

860. Hoffmann, M. Der Geldhandel der deutschen Juden während des Mittelalters bis zum Jahre 1350. Leipzig, 1910.

861. Schipper, I. Anfänge des Kapitalismus bei den abendländischen Juden im früheren Mittelalter bis zum Ausgang des 12 Jahrhunderts. Vienna, 1907. 66 pp. (Reprint from Zeitschrift für Volkswirtschaft, XV.)

(2) *Intellectual Life of Medieval Jews*

862. Schleiden, M. J. Die Bedeutung der Juden für Erhaltung und Wiederbelebung der Wissenschaften im Mittelalter. 4th edition. Leipzig, 1879. 32 pp. Translated by M. Kleimenhagen. The importance of the Jews for the preservation and revival of learning during the middle ages. London, 1911.

863. Steinschneider, M. Die arabische Literatur der Juden. Frankfurt, 1902.

See also D. Karpeles, *Geschichte der jüdischen Literatur des Mittelalters*, 2nd edition, 2 vols., Berlin, 1898.

864. Steinschneider, M. Die hebräischen Übersetzungen des Mittelalters, und die Juden als Dolmetscher: ein Beitrag zur Literaturgeschichte des Mittelalters. 2 vols. Berlin, 1893.

865. Steinschneider, M. Die Geschichtsliteratur der Juden in Druckwerken und Handschriften. Frankfurt, 1905.

865a. Steinschneider, M. Jewish literature. London, 1857. Translated by W. Spottiswoode with an index of authors and persons. Frankfurt, 1893.

Is reliable, though brief and dry.

865b. WINTER, J., and WÜNSCHE, A. Die jüdicshe Literatur seit Abschluss des Kanons. 3 vols. Trier, 1896.

Is excellent in some parts.

866. NEUMARK, D. Geschichte der jüdischen Philosophie des Mittelalters. 2 vols. Berlin, 1907–10.

See also I. HUSIK, *A history of mediaeval Jewish philosophy*, New York, 1916; and A. BONILLA Y SAN MARTÍN, *Historia de la filosofia española*, 2 vols., Madrid, 1908–11, the second volume of which is on Jewish philosophy to the twelfth century.

867. GÜDEMANN, M. Geschichte des Erziehungswesens und der Cultur der abendländischen Juden während des Mittelalters und der neueren Zeit. 3 vols. Vienna, 1880–88.

See also his *Quellenschriften zur Geschichte des Unterrichts und der Erziehung bei den deutschen Juden von den ältesten Zeiten bis auf Mendelssohn*, Berlin, 1891.

868. GÜDEMANN, M. Das jüdische Unterrichtswesen während der spanisch-arabischen Periode. Vienna, 1873.

(3) *Medieval Jewries*

869. PHILIPSON, D. Old European jewries. Philadelphia, 1894.

870. RODOCANACHI, E. Le saint-siège et les juifs: le ghetto à Rome. Paris, 1891.

871. BERLINER, A. Geschichte der Juden in Rom von der ältesten Zeit bis zur Gegenwart. 2 vols., in one. Frankfurt, 1893.

871a. VOGELSTEIN, H., and RIEGER, P. Geschichte der Juden in Rom. 2 vols. Berlin, 1895–96.

Superseded Berliner.

872. ROBERT, U. Les signes d'infamie au moyen âge: Juifs, Sarasins, héretiques, lépreux, cagots, et filles publiques. Paris, 1891.

(4) *General Accounts and Miscellanea*

873. DEPPING, G. B. Les Juifs dans le moyen âge: essai historique sur leur état civil, commercial et littéraire. Paris, 1845.

874. BAER, F. Studien zur Geschichte der Juden im Königreich Aragonien während des 13 und 14 Jahrhunderts. Berlin, 1913.

875. STRAUSS, R. Die Juden im Königreich Sizilien unter Normannen und Staufern. Heidelberg, 1910 (Heidelberger Abhandlungen).

876. RÉGNÉ, J. Etude sur la condition des Juifs de Narbonne du Ve au XIVe siècle. Narbonne, 1912.

876a. SAIGE, G. Les Juifs de Languedoc. Paris, 1881.

876b. Gremieux, A. Les Juifs de Marseille au moyen-âge. Paris, 1903.

Is a record of probably the best treatment Jews met with anywhere.

876c. Gross, H. Gallia judaica. Paris, 1897.

A record of all the places in France which occur in Hebrew literature with an account of the men living there.

877. Steinberg, Augusta. Studien zur Geschichte der Juden in der Schweiz während des Mittelalters. Zürich, 1902.

878. Stobbe, O. Die Juden in Deutschland während des Mittelalters. Brunswick, 1866. Reprint, Leipzig, 1902.

879. Scherer, J. E. Die Rechtsverhältnisse der Juden in den deutsch-österreichischen Ländern; mit einer Einleitung über die Principien der Judengesetzgebung in Europa während des Mittelalters. Leipzig, 1901.

880. Stern, M. Urkundliche Beiträge über die Stellung der Päpste zu den Juden. Kiel, 1893. Vol. II, part I, 1895.

881. Maulde la Clavière, A. R. de. Les Juifs dans les états français de saint-siège au moyen âge: documents pour servir à l'histoire des Israélites et de la papauté. Paris, 1886.

K. Eubel, "Zu dem Verhalten der Päpste gegen die Juden in Rom," *Romische Quartalschrift*, XIII (1899), 29–42.

882. Adler, E. N. Auto da fé and Jew. London, 1908.

883. The itinerary of Benjamin of Tudela: critical text, translation and commentary by E. N. Adler. London, 1907.

See also Beazley, *Dawn of modern geography*, II, ch. iv, "Benjamin of Tudela and other Jewish travellers" to ca. 1250.

883a. Newman, L. I. Jewish influence on Christian reform movements. New York, 1925. (Columbia University Oriental Studies, XXIII.)

Valuable for the extensive bibliographical references in the footnotes on the relations of Jews and Christians in the middle ages.

883b. Revue des études juives. Paris, 1880ff.

§ 19. Economic and Social History

884. Thompson, J. W. Economic and social history of the middle ages (300–1300). New York, 1928.

884a. Knight, M. M. Economic history of Europe to the end of the middle ages. Boston, 1926.

884b. Dopsch, A. Wirtschaftliche und soziale Grundlagen der europäischen Kulturentwicklung aus der Zeit von Cäsar bis auf Karl den Grossen. 2 vols. Vienna, 1920–23.

§ 20. Collections

See more extended lists for France in MONOD, no. **22,** pp. 120–27; for Germany, DAHLMANN-WAITZ, no. **28,** pp. 19ff. STEIN no. **1,** on pp. 642–49, gives a list of indexes of the publications of academies and miscellaneous learned societies, and on pp. 697–708 a similar list of indexes of serial publications of historical societies. Fortunately we have in English the following articles by foreign scholars in the Annual report of the *A.H.A.*, 1909, 229–77: "Historical societies in Great Britain," by G. W. PROTHERO; "The work of Dutch historical societies," by H. T. COLENBRANDER; "The historical societies of France," by C. ENLART; "The work of historical societies in Spain," by R. ALTAMIRA.

See also the various issues of the *Bulletin of the International Committee of historical sciences.*

(a) IMPORTANT ACADEMIES AND LEARNED SOCIETIES

(1) *France and Belgium*

885. Académie des inscriptions et belles-lettres [of Paris]. Histoire et mémoires. 50 vols. Paris, 1717–1809. Mémoires, 1803ff. Mémoires présentés à l'Académie par divers savants étrangers; first series, Sujets divers, Paris, 1844ff.; second series, Antiquités de la France, 1843ff. Notices et extraits des manuscrits de la Bibliothèque nationale et autres bibliothèques, Paris, 1787ff. Monuments et mémoires (Fondation EUGÈNE PIOT), Paris, 1894ff.

See also nos. **460, 803,** and **975,** and the *Recueil des historiens des croisades,* under outline XXI in part II below.

886. Société de l'histoire de France. Paris.

Issues an *Annuaire-Bulletin,* 1837ff., in addition to the publications, for which see no. **966.** Also see **974.**

887. Bibliothèque des écoles françaises d'Athènes et de Rome. Paris, 1876ff.

For series II and III see no. **959.** See also the *Mélanges d'archéologie et d'histoire,* edited by the Ecole française de Rome.

888. Bibliothèque de l'Ecole pratique des hautes études [of Paris]. Section des sciences philologiques et historiques. Paris, 1869ff.

889. Bibliothèque de la Faculté des lettres, Université de Paris. Paris, 1896ff.

890. Ecole des chartes. Paris.

Mémoires de la Société de l'Ecole des chartes, Paris, 1896ff.
See nos. **164** and **231.**

891. Académie des sciences morales et politiques. Comptes rendus. Paris, 1840ff.

892. Académie royale des sciences, des lettres et des beaux-arts de Belgique. Bulletins. Brussels, 1836ff.

893. Recueil de travaux publiés par les membres de la conférence d'histoire, . . . Louvain. Louvain, 1890ff.

(2) *Germany and Austria*

For collections edited by individuals see DAHLMANN-WAITZ, nos. 1364–89.

894. Abhandlungen der königlichen Akademie der Wissenschaften in Berlin, 1815ff. Philosophisch-historische Klasse, 1908ff. Sitzungsberichte, 1882ff.

895. Abhandlungen der königlichen bayerischen Akademie der Wissenschaften zu München. Historische Klasse. Munich, 1833ff. Sitzungsberichte. Philosophisch-philologisch-historische Klasse. Munich, 1871ff.

896. Abhandlungen der königlichen sächsischen Gesellschaft der Wissenschaften zu Leipzig. Philologisch-historische Klasse. Leipzig, 1846ff.

897. Abhandlungen der königlichen Gesellschaft der Wissenschaften zu Göttingen, 1843ff. Historisch-philologische Klasse, 1893ff. Nachrichten, 1894ff.

898. Studien und Darstellungen aus dem Gebiete der Geschichte, im Auftrage der Görres-Gesellschaft und in Verbindung mit der Redaktion des historischen Jahrbuches herausgegeben von H. Grauert. Freiburg, 1900ff.

See no. **152.**

898a. Historische Studien. Edited by E. EBERING. Berlin, 1896ff.

899. Bibliothek des königlichen preussischen historischen Instituts in Rom. Rome, 1905ff.

See also nos. **41** and **993.**

900. Publikationen des österreichischen historischen Instituts in Rom. Vienna and Leipzig, 1910ff.

Both of these publications contain studies as well as texts.

900a. Litterarischer Verein, Stuttgart Bibliothek, Tübingen, 1839ff.

901. Sitzungsberichte der kaiserlichen Akademie der Wissenschaften zu Wien. Philosophisch-historische Klasse. Vienna, 1848ff.

See also no. **986.**

902. Sitzungsberichte der königlichen böhmischen Gesellschaft der Wissenschaften zu Prag. Prague, 1859ff. Philosophisch-historisch-philologische Klasse, 1885ff.

(3) *England*

903. Royal historical society. Transactions. London, 1872ff.

904. The British academy for the promotion of historical, philosophical and philological studies. London, 1903ff.

(4) *Italy*

905. Istituto storico italiano. Bulletino, no. **162,** and Fonti, no. **990.**

906. Reale accademia dei Lincei. Founded 1603.

Since 1875 divided into two classes, one of which is devoted to "scienze morali, storiche e filologiche."

(5) *Spain*

907. Real academia de la historia. Madrid, 1738ff. Boletin, 1877ff.

For a list of its publications see *Annual report, A.H.A.*, 1909, p. 271.

(6) *United States*

907a. Mediaeval academy of America. Founded 1925. Publishes Speculum, no. **164a.**

(b) Collections of Historical Essays

For similar collections, mostly German, see Dahlmann-Waitz, nos. 1304–38.

908. Fustel de Coulanges, N. D. Recherches sur quelques problèmes d'histoire. Paris, 1894.

909. Coulton, G. G. Mediaeval studies. London, 1905ff. First series, 2nd revised edition, with three appendixes. London, 1915.

910. Creighton, M. Historical lectures and addresses. London, 1903.

910a. Church, R. W. Miscellaneous essays. London, 1888.

911. Creighton, Louise (von Glehn) "Mrs. Mandell Creighton." Heroes of European history. London and New York, 1906.

912. Cutts, E. L. Scenes and characters of the middle ages. London, 1872. 3rd edition, 1911.

913. Döllinger, J. v. Akademische Vorträge. 3 vols. Nordlingen and Munich, 1888–91. Translated by Margaret Warre, Studies in European history. London, 1890.

914. Edélstand du Méril, M. Etudes sur quelques points d'archéologie et d'histoire littéraire. Paris, 1862.

915. Edelstand du Méril, M. Mélanges archéologiques et littéraires. Paris, 1850.

Especially pp. 243–89, "Des origines de la basse latinité et la nécessité de glossaires spéciaux."

916. Freeman, E. A. Historical essays. 4 series in 4 vols. London, 1871ff.

917. Froude, J. A. Short studies in great subjects. 2 vols. London, 1894. (Also Everyman's Library, New York, 1915.)

918. Gasquet, F. A. The last abbot of Glastonbury and other essays. London, 1908.

919. Gasquet, F. A. Old English Bible and other essays. London, 1897.

920. Graevenitz, G. v. Deutsche in Rom: Studien und Skizzen aus elf Jahrhunderten. Leipzig, 1902.

Ch. 1, Charlemagne; ch. 2, Otto III.

921. Harrison, F. The meaning of history. New York, 1908.

922. Jessopp, A. The coming of the friars and other historical essays. 5th edition. London, 1889. Reprinted, 1928.

923. Jessopp, A. Studies by a recluse. London, 1893. 3rd edition, 1895.

924. Jourdain, C. Excursions historiques et philosophiques à travers le moyen âge. Paris, 1888.

925. Langlois, C. V. Questions d'histoire et d'enseignement. Paris, 1902.

926. Luchaire, A. Mélanges d'histoire du moyen âge. Paris, 1908.

926a. Marvin, F. S. The living past. 4th edition Oxford, 1923.

926b. Marvin, F. S. The unity of western civilization. London, 1915.

926c. Marvin, F. S. Progress and history. London, 1916.

926d. Newton, A. P., editor. Travel and travellers in the middle ages. London, 1926.

927. Pattison, R. P. Dunn-. Leading figures in European history. New York, 1912.

927a. Power, Eileen E. Medieval people. Boston, 1924.

L. F. Salzmann, *English life in the middle ages*, Oxford, 1926.

927b. Prestage, E., editor. Chivalry: a series of studies to illustrate its historical significance and civilizing influence. London and New York, 1928.

927c. Quicherat, J. Mélanges d'archéologie et d'histoire. 2 vols. Paris, 1885–86.

928. Salzmann, L. F. Mediaeval byways. Boston, 1912.

929. Shahan, T. J. The middle ages: sketches and fragments. New York, 1904.

930. Stillé, C. J. Studies in mediaeval history. Philadelphia, 1882. 2nd edition, 1883.

931. STUBBS, W. Lectures on European history. Edited by A. HASSALL. London, 1904.

932. STUBBS, W. Seventeen lectures on the study of mediaeval and modern history and kindred subjects. Oxford, 1886. 3rd edition, 1900.

933. WRIGHT, T., and HALLIWELL, J. O. Reliquae antiquae. 2 vols. London, 1845.

933a. VINOGRADOFF, P. The collected papers of Paul Vinogradoff, with a memoir by H. A. L. FISHER. 2 vols. Oxford, 1928.

(*c*) COMMEMORATIVE ESSAYS

For other similar essays, mostly German, see DAHLMANN-WAITZ, nos. 1339–53.

934. Mélanges d'histoire offerts à M. CHARLES BÉMONT, par ses élèves à l'occasion de la vingt-cinquième année de son enseignement à l'Ecole pratique des hautes études. Paris, 1913.

935. Mélanges offerts à M. EMILE CHATELAIN. Paris, 1909.

936. Mélanges PAUL FABRE: étude d'histoire du moyen âge. Paris, 1902.

937. Mélanges FITTING (Soixante-quinzième anniversaire de M. le professeur HERMAN FITTING). 2 vols. Paris, 1908.

938. Recueil de travaux d'érudition dédiés à la mémoire de JULIEN HAVET. Paris, 1895.

939. Mélanges d'études d'histoire du moyen âge dédiées à GABRIEL MONOD. Paris, 1896.

939a. Forschungen und Versuche zur Geschichte des Mittelalters und der Neuzeit. Festschrift Dietrich Schäfer zum siebzigster Geburtstag dargebracht von seinen Schülern. Jena, 1915.

939b. Festgabe Friederich von Bezold dargebracht zum 70. Geburtstag von Schülern, Kollegen und Freunden. Bonn, 1921.

939c. Essays in mediaeval history presented to Thomas Frederick Tout. Edited by A. G. LITTLE and F. M. POWICKE. Manchester, 1925.

939d. Mélanges d'histoire du moyen âge offerts à M. Ferdinand Lot par ses amis et ses élèves. Paris, 1925.

939e. Mélanges d'histoire offerts à Henri Pirenne par ses anciens élèves et ses amis à l'occasion de sa quarantième année d'enseignement à l'Université de Gand, 1886–1926. 2 vols., Brussels, 1926.

939f. Festgabe der Historischen Zeitschrift zum 50. Jährigen Doktorjubiläum von Karl Wenck. (Historische Zeitschrift, Band 134, Heft 2, Munich, 1926.)

939g. Essays in history presented to Reginald Lane Poole. Oxford, 1927.

939h. The crusades and other historical essays presented to Dana C. Munro. Edited by L. J. PAETOW. New York, 1928.

939i. Mélanges Paul Fournier. Paris, 1929.

939j. Anniversary essays in mediaeval history by students of Charles Homer Haskins. Edited by C. H. TAYLOR. Boston and New York, 1929.

939k. Feierschrift Oswald Redlich. Ergänzungsband, 11, Mitteilungen des Oesterreichischen Instituts für Geschichtsforschung. Innsbruck, 1929.

(*d*) MISCELLANEOUS COLLECTIONS

940. Cambridge historical series. Edited by G. W. PROTHERO.

942. Cambridge manuals of science and literature. Cambridge University Press.

943. Continental legal history. Published under the auspices of the Association of American Law Schools. Boston, Little, Brown, and Company.

944. Everyman's library. London and New York.

945. Göschen Sammlung: geschichtliche Bibliothek aus der "Sammlung Göschen." Berlin and Leipzig.

946. Home university library. New York, 1911ff.

947. Aus Natur und Geisteswelt. Teubner, Leipzig.

948. Wissenschaft und Bildung. Quelle and Meyer. Leipzig.

948a. Helps for students of history. Edited by C. JOHNSON and J. P. WHITNEY. London, 1918ff. (S.P.C.K.)

CHAPTER V

LARGE COLLECTIONS OF ORIGINAL SOURCES

§ 1. General Collections

See also nos. **379–392.**

949. Records of civilization: sources and studies. Edited by A. P. Evans. (Formerly under the editorship of J. T. Shotwell.) New York, 1915ff.

A collection of translations from the sources, with introductions and bibliographies. The volumes thus far published which pertain to the middle ages are: *History of the Franks by Gregory, bishop of Tours*, selections, by E. Brehaut, New York, 1916; *The book of the popes* (*Liber pontificalis*), I, to the pontificate of Gregory I, by Louise R. Loomis, New York, 1916; *An introduction to the history of history*, by J. T. Shotwell, New York, 1922; *The see of Peter*, by J. T. Shotwell and Louise R. Loomis, New York, 1927; *The history of Yaballaha III*, by J. A. Montgomery, New York, 1927; *The two cities, by Otto, bishop of Freising*, by C. C. Mierow, New York, 1928; *An Arab-Syrian gentleman and warrior in the period of the Crusades, memoirs of Usāmah ibn-Munqidh*, by P. K. Hitti, New York, 1929; *The sources for the early history of Ireland: an introduction and guide. I. Ecclesiastical*, by J. F. Kenney, New York, 1929. See announcement (1930) of volumes in preparation.

A similar collection of translations into German, but on a humbler scale, is the *Quellensammlung für den geschichtlichen Unterricht an höheren Schulen*, Leipzig.

See also the *Temple classics* (Dutton and Dent); *King's classics* (Chatto); *Broadway translations* (Dutton); *Broadway travelers* (Harpers); *The medieval library* (Oxford); *Broadway medieval library* (Harcourt, Brace and Co.).

950. Bibliotheca scriptorum medii aevi Teubneriana. Leipzig.

Prints Latin texts.

951. Thesaurus novus anecdotorum seu collectio monumentorum, complectens regum ac principum aliorumque virorum illustrium epistolas et diplomata bene multa. 5 vols. Edited by E. Martène and U. Durand. Paris, 1717ff.

952. Veterum scriptorum et monumentorum amplissima collectio. Edited by E. Martène and U. Durand. 2nd edition. 9 vols. Paris, 1724–33.

The above are two typical older collections of miscellaneous material, most of which can now be found in critical newer editions.

§ 2. Medieval Church

(*a*) General Collections of Ecclesiastical Writings

953. Patrologiae cursus completus. Series latina, 221 vols. Paris, 1844–64. Vols. 218–21 are index vols., Paris, 1862–64. Series graeca, 161 vols., in 165 [no index], Paris, 1857–86. Edited by J. P. Migne.

This is still the most complete collection, but frequently the text is a mere reprint from an older and imperfect edition. An alphabetical list of the authors in each series is given in Potthast, no. **18.** A very full index of the *Series graeca* will soon be available in 2 volumes. The first fascicule was published by Guethner, Paris, 1929.

A well-selected collection of source material for school use is *Quellen zur Geschichte des Papsttums and des römischen Katholizismus*, edited by C. Mirbt, Freiburg, 1895; 4th edition, Tübingen, 1925.

954. Corpus scriptorum ecclesiasticorum latinorum. Vienna, 1866ff.

This is to comprise all the writings of church fathers to the seventh century. An attempt is made to establish the very best texts from the most important manuscripts. The contents of vols. I–XXXI are given in Potthast, *Wegweiser*, no. **18,** I, p. lviii.

The principal set of English translations of the writings of the church fathers since about 324 is *A select library of Nicene and post-Nicene fathers of the Christian church*, edited by P. Schaff and H. Wace, in two series: series I, 14 vols., New York, 1886–90; series II, 14 vols., New York, 1890–1900.

955. Collection de textes et documents pour l'étude historique du christianisme. Edited by H. Hemmer and P. Lejay. Paris.

Original texts, with translations into French. See also *Sammlung ausgewählter kirchen- und dogmengeschichtlicher Quellenschriften*, edited by G. Krüger, Tübingen, Leipzig and Freiburg, 1891–1911.

955a. Quellensammlung zur kirchlichen Rechtsgeschichte und zum Kirchenrecht. Edited by E. Eichmann. 3 vols. Paderborn, 1912–16.

(*b*) The Papacy

956. Regesta pontificum Romanorum ad annum 1198. Edited by P. Jaffé. 2 vols. Berlin, 1851; 2nd edition, Leipzig, 1885–88.

957. Regesta pontificum Romanorum, inde ab anno post Christum natum 1198 ad annum 1304. Edited by A. Potthast. 2 vols. Berlin, 1874–75.

958. Regesta pontificum Romanorum (to 1198). Edited by P. F. Kehr under the auspices of the Academy of sciences in Göttingen. 7 vols. Berlin, 1906–25.

Cf. *C.M.H.*, VI, 851 and P. Kehr, *Rom und Venedig ins 12 Jahrhundert*, Rome, 1927. *Liber diurnus, ou Recueil des formules usitées par la chancellerie pontificale du Ve au XIe siècle*, edited by E. de Rozière, Paris, 1869. This edition is not superseded by that of T. v. Sickel which appeared in 1889.

959. Bibliothèque des écoles françaises d'Athènes et de Rome. 2nd and 3rd series. Paris, 1884ff.

Contains the registers of popes of the 13th century and also the best complete edition of the *Liber pontificalis*, edited by L. DUCHESNE, 2 vols., Paris, 1886, 1892, translated in part in no. **949.** (A new edition of the *Liber pontificalis* in the *Monumenta Germaniae historica, Gesta pontificum*, I, was begun by T. MOMMSEN in 1898, but it is still incomplete.) In the 3rd series the publication of letters of the popes of the 14th century has been begun. For the 1st series, see no. **887.** See also BERNHEIM, no. **64,** p. 561, and BRESSLAU, no. **240,** I, 72–85, 104–24, for references to papal documents.

For information concerning papal registers see *Catholic encyclopedia*, IV, 544 (*Crusades*); *C.M.H.*, VI, 852; and P. FOURNIER, "La publication des registres des papes" in *B.E.C.*, LXXXIX (1928), 448–453.

960. Acta pontificum Romanorum inedita (97–1198). Edited by J. v. PFLUGK-HARTTUNG. 3 vols. Tübingen and Stuttgart, 1881–88.

For documents concerning the papal states see the *Codex diplomaticus dominii temporalis S. Sedis*, edited by A. THEINER, 3 vols., Rome, 1861–62; and the old collection, *Monumenta dominationis pontificae*, edited by CENNI, Rome, 1760–61.

961. Epistolae pontificum Romanorum ineditae. Edited by S. LOEWENFELD. Leipzig, 1885.

Pontificum Romanorum qui fuerunt inde ab ex. saecula IX usque ad finem saeculi XIII vitae, edited by J. M. WATTERICH, 2 vols., Leipzig, 1862.

(*c*) CHURCH COUNCILS

962. Sacrorum conciliorum nova et amplissima collectio. Edited by J. D. MANSI and others. 31 vols. Florence and Venice, 1759–98 [to 1590 A.D.]. New edition and continuation, vols. 32–53. Paris, 1901ff.

There is a conspectus for vols. I–XLVI and an alphabetical index in vol. XXXVI*a*. See HEFELE, *Conciliengeschichte*, no. **469.** Note the important volume *Jean-Dominique Mansi et les grandes collections conciliaires*, by H. QUENTIN, Paris, 1900, which gives a critical estimate of MANSI and previous collections.

962a. Sacrosancta concilia . . . edited by P. LABBÉ and G. COSSART. 23 vols. Venice, 1728–33.

962b. Conciliorum collectio regia maxima . . . edited by J. HARDOUIN. 12 vols., Paris, 1714–15.

(*d*) LIVES OF SAINTS

963. Acta sanctorum. Begun by J. BOLLANDUS. Vol. 1. Antwerp, 1643. (In progress.)

This vast collection of biographies of saints is arranged according to saints' days, and now extends well into November. For editions and dates see *C.M.H.*, VI, 850, and H. DELEHAYE, *The work of the Bollandists through three centuries*, Princeton, 1922, ch. ix.

The more recent volumes have been edited under the able supervision of the late C. DE SMEDT. See the description of the set in POTTHAST, no. **18,** **I,** p. xxxii. There is an index to the volumes for January to October in vol. 62. For guides to the various biographies contained in the collection, see also POTTHAST, section "Vita"; and the *Bibliotheca hagiographica*, no. **53.** The *Analecta Bollandiana*, no. **177,** form a periodical supplement to the *Acta sanctorum*. See also C. NARBEY, *Supplément aux Acta sanctorum pour les vies de saints de l'époque mérovingienne*, vols. I and II, Paris, 1899, 1912; and S. BARING-GOULD, *Lives of the saints*, 16 vols., Edinburgh, 1914.

(*e*) MONASTIC RULES

964. Codex regularum monasticarum. Edited by L. HOLSTEN. 3 parts. Rome, 1661. 2nd edition, 6 vols. Vienna, 1759.

Still the largest collection of monastic rules.

§ 3. France and Belgium

965. Collection de documents inédits sur l'histoire de France. Publié par les soins du ministre de l'instruction publique. Paris, 1835ff.

I: Chroniques, mémoires, journaux, récits et compositions historiques; II: Cartulaires et recueils de chartes; III: Correspondances et documents politiques et administratives, IV: Documents de la période révolutionnaire; V: Documents philologiques, philosophiques, juridiques, etc.; VI: Publications archéologiques.

The first 177 vols. are analyzed in A. FRANKLIN, no. **23,** 107–83. POTTHAST, no. **18,** I, p. liv, gives an alphabetical list of the contents of the first 212 vols.

966. Publications de la Société de l'histoire de France. Paris, 1835ff.

Contents of the first 130 vols. are analyzed in A. FRANKLIN, no. **23,** 207–51; and the contents of the first 203 vols. in POTTHAST, no. **18,** I, p. cxl. See also no. **886.** The *Publications de la Société de l'histoire de Normandie*, Rouen, 1870ff., contain valuable additional material.

967. Rerum Gallicarum et Francicarum scriptores. (Recueil des historiens des Gaules et de la France.) Edited by M. BOUQUET and others. 24 vols. Paris, 1738–1904. Extends to 1328. New impression of first 19 vols. by L. DELISLE. Paris, 1868–80; vols. XX–XXIII, 1893–94. Vol. XXIV, Paris, 1904. Nouvelle série in quarto, Paris, 1899ff. (Documents financiers, obituaires, pouillés.)

There is an index in vol. XXIII. The contents of the first 22 vols. are analyzed in FRANKLIN, no. **23,** 82–94. POTTHAST, no. **18,** I, p. xlii, has a short analysis. This collection is commonly referred to as "Bouquet."

968. Collection de textes pour servir à l'étude et à l'enseignement de l'histoire. 1er série. Des origines au XVIIIe siècle. Paris, 1886ff.

Similar to the German *Scriptores rerum Germanicarum in usum scholarum*, no. **979,** but more comprehensive. Includes sources for modern history. The texts are accompanied by notes and introductions.

Beginners will find much help in the following guides to the study of medieval chronicles of France: G. MASSON, *Early chroniclers of Europe: France*, London, 1879; L. CONSTANS, *Les grands historiens du moyen âge*, Paris, 1891; and A. DEBIDOUR and E. ETIENNE, *Les chroniquers français au moyen âge*, Paris, 1895.

968a. Les classiques de l'histoire de France au moyen âge publiés sous la direction de L. HALPHEN. Paris, 1923ff.

A convenient collection of texts fundamental for French history. Page for page translations of Latin texts are given in French.

968b. Les classiques français du moyen âge, publiés sous la direction de M. ROQUES. Paris, 1910ff.

969. Collection complète des mémoires relatifs à l'histoire de France depuis la règne de Philippe-Auguste jusqu'en 1763. Edited by C. B. PETITOT [and M. MONMERQUÉ]. Series I, 52 vols.; series II, 79 vols. Paris, 1819–29.

Dissertations are interspersed here and there. The first 15 vols. of series I extend to almost 1500. Their contents are analyzed in FRANKLIN, no. **23,** 288–302.

970. Nouvelle collection des mémoires sur l'histoire de France depuis le 13e siècle jusqu'à la fin du 18e siècle. Edited by J. MICHAUD and P. POUJOULAT. 32 vols. Paris, 1836–39.

A new edition of the previous set, with additions. A publishers' venture rather than a serious historical work. Vols. I–IV treat the period up to 1500. The contents are analyzed in FRANKLIN, no. **23,** 303–15. In this edition there are no dissertations.

971. Collection des mémoires relatifs à l'histoire de France, depuis la fondation de la monarchie française jusqu'à XIIIe siècle. Edited by F. P. G. GUIZOT. 31 vols in 17. Paris, 1824–35.

French translations without the original texts. Not a scholarly piece of work. Contents are analyzed in FRANKLIN, no. **23,** 270–78; also in POTTHAST, no. **18,** I, p. lxxx.

972. Collection des chroniques nationales françaises écrites en langue vulgaire du XIIIe au XVIe siècle. Edited by J. A. BUCHON. 47 vols. Paris, 1824–29.

Contents analyzed in FRANKLIN, no. **23,** 279–87.

973. Choix de chroniques et mémoires sur l'histoire de France. Edited by J. A. BUCHON. 17 vols. Paris, 1836–38.

This and the above collection are analyzed in POTTHAST, no. **18, I,** pp. xliv–xlvi.

974. Les grandes chroniques de France. Paris, 1910ff.

A new edition begun by the Société de l'histoire de France.

975. Chartes et diplômes relatifs à l'histoire de France publiés par les soins de l'Académie des inscriptions et belles-lettres. Paris, 1908ff.

For contents up to 1917, see *R.H.*, CXXI, 321, note 2, and *A.H.R.*, XXII (1917), 463. See also *Table chronologique des diplômes, chartes, titres et actes imprimés concernant l'histoire de France*, edited by L. G. O. DE BRÉQUIGNY; vols. I–III, Paris, 1736–76; continued, vols. IV–VIII (to 1314), Paris, 1836–76. Likewise *Recueil général des anciennes lois françaises de 420 à 1789*, edited by ISAMBERT and others, 29 vols., Paris, 1822–33. For the later middle ages we have a better collection, *Ordonnances des rois de France de la IIIe race jusqu'en 1514*, 22 vols., Paris, 1723–1849 (often called Ordonnances du Louvre).

976. L'histoire de France racontée par les contemporains. Extraits des chroniques et des mémoires. Edited by B. ZELLER. 65 vols. Paris, 1881–90.

An older, similar venture is DUSSIEUX, *L'histoire de France racontée par les contemporains*.

977. Collection de chroniques belges inédites. 111 vols. Brussels, 1836ff.

The first 44 vols. are analyzed in FRANKLIN, no. **23,** 184–206; and the contents of the first 86 vols. are indicated in POTTHAST, no. **18,** I, p. liii. See also the *Collection des chroniquers et trouvères belges*, Brussels, 1863ff.; the *Recueil de chroniques, chartes et autres documents concernant l'histoire et les antiquités de la Flandre occidentale*, publié par la Société d'émulation de Bruges, 56 vols., Bruges, 1839–64. For Holland we have *Werken uitgegeven door het Historisch Genootschap te Utrecht*, 1863ff., which is devoted largely to the history of the seventeenth century; the contents of the few volumes relating to the middle ages is indicated in POTTHAST, I, p. cxlvi. The same society also published a *Codex diplomaticus neerlandicus*, 8 vols., Utrecht, 1848–63.

§ 4. Germany, Austria, and Switzerland

978. Monumenta Germaniae historica (500–1500). Edited by G. H. PERTZ, T. MOMMSEN, et al. Folio series, Berlin, 1826–96; quarto series, 1876ff.

This is the most famous nineteenth-century collection of medieval sources. Brief analyses of its contents will be found in DAHLMANN-WAITZ, no. **28,** no. 892; HERRE, no. **14,** no. 1020; POTTHAST, no. **18,** I, p. cxii; *C.M.H.*, no. **340,** V, 840–841; VI, 852. FRANKLIN, no **23,** 95–106, analyzes the folio series published before 1874. A great deal has been written about this remarkable achievement of German scholarship; POTTHAST listed all that had appeared before 1895. *N.A.*, no. **167,** keeps the world of scholars informed regarding the progress of work on the *Monumenta*. WATTENBACH, no. **29,** is the best introduction to the main contents of the set.

979. Scriptores rerum Germanicarum in usum scholarum, ex Monumentis Germaniae historicis recusi. Hanover, 1840ff.

This octavo collection for pedagogical use is a selection from the chronicles which appear in no. **978.** In some cases, however, the octavo edition contains the more recent and more trustworthy text of a medieval author. The contents of the set are analyzed briefly in DAHLMANN-WAITZ, no. **28,** no. 1001.

980. Quellensammlung zur deutschen Geschichte. Edited by E. BRANDENBURG and G. SEELIGER. Leipzig, 1907ff.

Intended primarily for seminar use in German universities, but also makes a wider appeal to scholars. The works which appeared before 1912 are listed in DAHLMANN-WAITZ, no. **28,** no. 895.

981. Die Geschichtschreiber der deutschen Vorzeit. Edited by G. H. PERTZ, et al. Berlin and Leipzig, 1849ff. 2nd edition, 90 vols., by W. WATTENBACH, *ibid.*, 1884ff. 3rd edition and continuation by O. HOLDER-EGGER and M. TANGL, 1909ff.

The contents are given in POTTHAST, no. **18,** I, p. lxxiv. This very convenient set contains good German translations of the most interesting parts of the section "Scriptores" in no. **978.**

982. Die Chroniken der deutschen Städte von 14 bis ins 16 Jahrhundert. Herausgegeben durch die historische Kommission bei der Akademie der Wissenschaften zu München, unter Leitung VON K. HEGEL und G. v. BELOW. Leipzig, 1862ff.

The contents are briefly indicated in DAHLMANN-WAITZ, no. **28,** no. 1003.

983. Bibliotheca rerum Germanicarum. Edited by P. JAFFÉ. 6 vols. Berlin, 1864–73.

Contents in POTTHAST, no. **18,** I, p. lxxxv. See also *Monumenta Germaniae selecta ab anno 768 usque ad annum 1250*, edited by M. DOEBERL, III, IV, and V, Munich, 1889–94. Vols. I and II never appeared.

984. Fontes rerum Germanicarum. Edited by J. F. BÖHMER. 4 vols. Stuttgart, 1843–68.

This collection contains sources, mostly chronicles, from the later middle ages, whereas JAFFÉ, no. **983,** is devoted to the early middle ages. These two collections contain important sources which had not been edited in no. **978.** Even now both are still useful.

985. Regesta imperii. Edited by J. F. BÖHMER. Frankfurt, 1831ff. New edition in several parts by various authors. Innsbruck, 1877ff.

For titles of the various parts of the new edition, see HERRE, no. **14,** no. 1024, or BERNHEIM, no. **64,** p. 560. Detailed information about the archives and archive material for Germany is in BRESSLAU, no. **240,** *passim.* For pedagogical purposes J. F. BÖHMER, *Acta imperii selecta,* Innsbruck,

1870; and E. WINKELMANN, *Acta imperii inedita saeculi XIII et XIV*, 2 vols., Innsbruck, 1880–85, are valuable; but the best book for that purpose is the *Quellensammlung zur Geschichte der deutschen Reichsverfassung in Mittelalter und Neuzeit*, edited by K. ZEUMER, Leipzig, 1904; new edition, 1913.

985a. Deutsche Texte des Mittelalters herausgegeben von der königlich preussischen Akademie der Wissenschaften. Berlin, 1904ff.

986. Fontes rerum Austriacarum: österreichische Geschichtsquellen. By the Vienna Academy. Part 1, Scriptores, vols. I–IX, 1. Part 2, Diplomataria et acta, vols. I–LXII. Vienna, 1849ff.

Contents of vols. published up to 1896 in POTTHAST, no. **18,** I, p. lxix. See also *Monumenta historiae Bohemica*, edited by A. GINDELY, 5 vols., Prague, 1864–90.

987. Quellen zur Schweizer Geschichte. Herausgegeben von der allgemeinen geschichtsforschenden Gessellschaft der Schweiz. Vols. I–XXV. Basel, 1877–1907. New series,. 1908ff.

Contents in DAHLMANN-WAITZ, no. **28,** no. 918. See also *Mittheilungen zur vaterländischen Geschichte* issued by the Historischer Verein in St. Gallen, 20 vols., St. Gall, 1862–85, contents in POTTHAST, no. **18,** p. cx.

§ 5. Italy

988. Rerum Italicarum scriptores ab anno aerae christianae 500 ad 1500. Edited by L. A. MURATORI [died 1750]. 25 vols. in 28. Milan, 1723–51. Indexes, Turin, 1885. New edition by G. CARDUCCI and V. FIORINI. Città di Castello, 1900ff.

The new edition is now in the hands of the Istituto storico italiano (PIETRO FEDELE is chief editor). About 21 volumes were ready in 1927. See *Archivio storico italiano*, LXXXV (1927), 116–21.

This renowned collection was the first great attempt to collect all the medieval sources of one country. Work on the new edition, together with additions, is reported in the *Archivio muratoriano*, no. **168.** See also the additions in the *Archivio storico italiano*, no. **160.**

A serviceable introduction to the sources of medieval Italy is U. BALZANI, *Le cronache italiane nel medio evo*, Milan, 1884; 3rd edition, Milan, 1909; English edition, *Early chroniclers of Italy*, London, 1883.

989. Antiquitates Italicae medii aevi. 6 vols. Edited by L. A. MURATORI. Milan, 1738–42. Index, Turin, 1885.

990. Fonti per la storia d'Italia. Published by the Istituto storico italiano. Rome, 1887ff.

In the following divisions: Scrittori; Epistolari e Regesti; Diplomi; Statuti; Leggi; Antichità (Necrologi). This is supplemented by the *Bollettino dell' Istituto storico italiano*, no. **162.**

990a. Archivio della Società romana di storia patria. Rome, 1877ff.

991. Monumenta historiae patriae edita iussu Caroli Alberti regis. First series in folio, vols. I–XX; second series in quarto, vols. XXIff. Turin, 1836ff.

992. Documenti di storia italiana. Publicati a cura della R. Deputazione di Toscana, dell' Umbria e delle Marche. 9 vols. Florence, 1867–89.

For contents see POTTHAST, no. **18,** I, p. lxiii. Especially devoted to the middle ages.

992a. Biblioteca della Società storica subalpina. Pinerolo, 1899ff.

993. Regesta chartarum Italiae. Edited by Kgl. Preuss. historisches Institut and the Istituto storico italiano. Rome, 1907ff.

Interrupted by war, but continued in 1927.
Contents in DAHLMANN-WAITZ, no. **28,** no. 1274.

994. La storia d'Italia, narrata da scrittori contemporanei agli avvenimenti. Edited by P. ORSI. 3 vols. Turin, 1896–1905. Vol. I (473–1313) in 2nd edition, 1905.

A collection of extracts from the sources, translated into Italian with explanatory remarks and bibliographies.

§ 6. England

995. Rerum Britannicarum medii aevi scriptores: or Chronicles and memorials of Great Britain and Ireland during the middle ages, published by the authority of her Majesty's treasury under the direction of the Master of the Rolls. 99 works in 244 vols. London, 1858–96.

This collection is commonly called the "Rolls Series." For the contents in alphabetical arrangement according to titles of works, see GROSS, no. **36,** pp. 704–11. POTTHAST, no. **18,** I, pp. cxxviiff., lists the separate works according to their order in the set.

996. Foedera, conventiones, litterae, et cujuscunque generis acta publica inter reges Angliae et alios quosvis imperatores, reges, pontifices, principes, vel communitates [1101–1654]. Edited by T. RYMER.

For various editions and aids see GROSS, no. **36,** no. 2097. Also see GROSS in general for source material relating to English history.

§ 7. Spain and Portugal

997. Colección de documentos inéditos para la historia de España. 112 vols. Madrid, 1842–95. Index to vols. I–CII, Madrid, 1891. Nueva colección de documentos inéditos para la historia de España y de sus Indias. Vols. I–VI. Madrid, 1892–96.

These important collections are supplemented by a great mass of source material in the *España sagrada*, no. **467.** For a guide to the narrative sources of medieval Spain see R. BALLESTER Y CASTELL, *Las fuentes naratívas de la historia de España durante la edad media* (417–1474), Palma de Mallorca, 1908. On pp. 203–07 he prints an analysis of the contents of the old collection, *Hispaniae illustratae*, edited by A. SCHOTT, 4 vols., Frankfurt, 1603–08. See also C. CIROT, *Etudes sur l'historiographie espagnole: les histoires générales d'Espagne entre Alphonse X et Philippe II* (*1284–1556*), Bordeaux, 1904 (Bibliothèque des universités du Midi, 9).

997a. Collección de fueros municipales, etc. Edited by T. MUÑOZ Y ROMERO. Madrid, 1847.

Incomplete, but still invaluable. Cf. also his "Del estado de personas," etc., reprinted in *Revista de archivos*, 2nd series, IX (1883), 3–17; 51–60; 86–99; 119–25.

997b. España sagrada. 51 vols. Madrid, 1747–1879.

A vast mine of information for the history of the Spanish church, corresponding to the *Gallia Christiana* for France. All the minor monastic chronicles will be found in it. A key to it will be found in vol. XXII of the *Documentos inéditos* (**977**), and a table of contents of the first 47 volumes in *El bibliógrafo español*, año III, 106–12, 115–17.

998. Colección de las crónicas y memorias de los reyes de Castilla. 7 vols. Madrid, 1779–87.

An important special collection, the contents of which are given in POTTHAST, no. **18**, I, p. lii.

999. Colección de documentos inéditos del Archivo general de la Corona de Aragón. 41 vols. Barcelona, 1847–76, 1910.

See also *Colección de documentos para el estudio de la historia de Aragón*, edited by E. IBARRA Y RODRIGUEZ, etc., vols. I–X, Saragossa, 1904–15; and *Colección de documentos inéditos para la historia de Navarra*, vol. I, Pamplona, 1900.

1000. Cortes de los antiguos reinos de León y de Castilla. Vols I–V (to 1559). Madrid, 1861–1906. With an introduction by M. COLMEIRO. 2 vols. Madrid, 1883–84.

See also *Cortes de los antiguos reinos de Aragón y de Valencia y Principado de Cataluña*, Barcelona, 1896ff.

1001. Portugaliae monumenta historica a saeculo VIII post Christum usque ad XV. Edited by A. HERCULANO. Lisbon, 1856ff.

Other collections consisting chiefly of chronicles are: *Collecção de livros ineditos da historia Portugueza*, edited by J. CORREA DA SERRA, 5 vols., Lisbon, 1790–93; *Collecção dos principaes auctores da historia Portugueza*, 8 vols., Lisbon, 1806–09; and *Collecção dos documentas e memorias da Academia real da historia Portugueza*, 15 vols., Lisbon, 1722–36. Archive material is collected in *Quadro elementar das relacões politicas e diplomaticas dc Portugal*, edited by the Viscount of SANTAREM, 18 vols., Paris, 1842–60, continued as *Corpo diplomatico Portuguez* [to 1640], edited by REBELLO DA SILVA, 36 vols., 1856–78.

§ 8. Byzantine Empire

1002. Byzantinae historiae scriptores. 39 (or 47, or 23, or 27, according to arrangement) vols. Paris, 1645–1711.

Contains excellent translations from Greek into Latin along with the Greek texts. Begun under the auspices of Louis XIV. Contents listed in POTTHAST, no. **18,** I, p. xlvi. Extracts in French translation by L. COUSIN, *Histoire de Constantinople depuis le règne de Justin jusqu'à la fin de l'empire,* 8 vols., Paris, 1672–74. Another edition (more valuable) printed in Holland, 11 vols., 1685. In large part reprinted in *Patrologiae graecae,* edited by MIGNE, no. **953.** See also *Fragmenta historicorum Graecorum,* edited by C. MÜLLER, 5 vols., Paris, 1841–83.

1003. Corpus scriptorum historiae Byzantinae. 50 vols. Bonn, 1828–97.

Very poorly edited. Contents in POTTHAST, no. **18,** I, p. lix. See also *Fontes rerum Byzantinarum,* St. Petersburg, 1892; and *Analecta Byzantino-russica, ibid.,* 1891, both edited by W. REGEL.

1003a. Corpus der griechischen Urkunden des Mittelalters und der neueren Zeit herausgegehen von den Akademieen der Wissenschaften in München und Wien. Munich and Berlin, 1924ff.

The first two volumes appeared in 1924 and 1925, F. DÖLGER, *Regesten der Kaiserurkunden des oströmischen Reiches,* I, 565–1025; II, 1025–1204.

§ 9. Eastern Europe

1004. Monumenta medii aevi historica res gestas Poloniae illustrantia. 18 vols. in 15. Crakow, 1874–1908.

See also *Scriptores rerum Polonicarum,* vols. I–XX, Crakow, 1872–1907; and *Monumenta Poloniae historica,* edited by A. BIELOWSKI and others, 6 vols., Lemberg and Crakow, 1864–93.

1005. Codex diplomaticus Poloniae (to 1506). 4 vols. Warsaw, 1847–87.

See also *Codex diplomaticus maioris Poloniae* (to 1444), vols. I–V, Posen, 1877–1908; and *Codex diplomaticus Poloniae minoris,* vols. I–IV, Crakow, 1876–1905.

1006. Monumenta Hungariae historica. Part 1, Diplomataria. Part 2, Scriptores. Part 3, Monumenta comitialia. Part 4, Acta extera. Budapest, 1857ff.

See also *Codex diplomaticus Hungariae,* edited by G. FEJER, 43 vols., Budapest, 1829–44, with a chronological table, 1862, and an index, 1866; and *Codex diplomaticus regni Croatiae, Dalmatiae, et Slavoniae,* edited by T. SMICIKLAS, vols. I–V (1101–1272), Agram, 1904–07. Vol. I is vol. VII of the older collection, *Monumenta spectantia historiam Slavorum meridionalium,* 11 vols., Agram, 1868–93. See also, *Acta et diplomata res Albaniae mediae aetatis illustrantia,* edited by L. DE THALLÓCZY and others, vol. I (344–1343), Vienna, 1913.

§ 10. Northern Europe

1007. Scriptores rerum Danicarum medii aevi. Edited by J. LANGEBEK, et al., 8 vols. Copenhagen, 1772–1834. Index, 1878.

1007a. Danmarks Gilde- og Lavsskraaer fra Middelalderen. Edited by C. Nyrop. 2 vols. (elaborately indexed). Copenhagen, 1899–1904.

1007b. Monumenta historiae Danicae. Edited by H. RÖRDAM. 4 vols. Copenhagen, 1873–87.

1007c. Scriptores minores historiae Danicae medii aevi. Edited by M. CL. GERTZ. 2 vols. (index), Copenhagen, 1917–20.

1008. Repertorium diplomaticum regni Danici mediaevalis. Edited by K. ERSLEV and others. Copenhagen, 1894ff.

Regesta diplomatica historiae Danicae [to 1660], series I, vols. I–II, Copenhagen, 1847–70; series II, vols. I–II, 1889–1907.

1008a. Acta pontificum Danica, 1316–1536. 5 vols. Copenhagen, 1904–13.

Vol. I, edited by L. MOLTESEN, Copenhagen, 1904; vols. II–V, edited by A. KRARUP and J. LINDBÆK, Copenhagen, 1907–13.

1009. Diplomatarium Norvegicum. Edited by C. C. A. LANGE and others. Christiania, 1847ff.

1010. Scriptores rerum Suecicarum medii aevi. 3 vols. Uppsala and Lund, 1818–76.

1011. Diplomatarium Suecanum (Svenskt diplomatarium), 817–1350. 6 vols. Stockholm, 1829–78. Continuations, 1351–1414, Stockholm, 1866–87.

1011a. Bidrag till Skandinaviens historia (1314–1520), ur utländska arkiver. Edited by C. G. STYFFE. 5 vols. Stockholm, 1859–84.

1011b. Corpus juris Sveo-Gotorum antiqui. Edited by C. J. SCHLYTER. 13 vols. Stockholm and Lund, 1827–77.

1011c. Handlingar rörande Skandinaviens. 40 vols. plus index vol. 41, Stockholm, 1816–65.

The medieval portions are found in parts 3, 9, 13–17, 19, 21, 29, 32.

1011d. MAGNUS, J. Historia Ioannis Magni Gothi Sedis Apostolicae Legati Svetiae et Gotiae Primatis ac Archiepiscopi Vpsalensis De Omnibvs Gothorvm Sveonvmqve Regibvs qui vnqvam ab initio nationis extitere. Rome, 1554.

The second known edition of this work was published in Basel, 1558, under title, Gothorvm Sveonvm'qve Historia, Ex Probatis Antiqvorvm Monvmentis Collecta, & in xxiiij libros redacta. Avtore Io. Magno Gotho, Archiepiscopo Vpsalensi.

Note: This is the first printed history of Sweden. It covers the period from earliest times to Gustavus Vasa. It is generally very authentic and at times quotes documents in full.

1011e. Sveriges Traktater med främande makter jemte andra dithörande handlingar. Edited by O. S. RYDBERG and others. Stockholm, 1877–1903.

Vols. I–V cover the period 822–1630.

1011f. Diplomatarium Islandicum. Edited by J. SIGURDSSON and J. THORKELSSON. Copenhagen, 1857ff.

§ 11. Education and Learning

1012. Monumenta Germaniae paedagogica. Schulordnungen, Schulbücher und paedagogische Miscellaneen aus den Landen deutscher Zunge. Edited by K. KEHRBACH. Berlin, 1886ff.

List of contents in DAHLMANN-WAITZ, no. **28**, no. 2932. Includes many secondary accounts. See also the *Beiträge* edited by BAEUMKER, no. **826**, which contain many original texts.

§ 12. Jews

1013. Regesten zur Geschichte der Juden im fränkischen und deutschen Reiche bis zum Jahre 1273. Edited by J. ARONIUS and others. Berlin, 1887–1902.

See also nos. **863, 864, 865, 880, 883.**

1013a. WIENER, M. Regesten zur Geschichte der Juden in Deutschland während des Mittelalters.

Vol. I, Hanover, 1862, covers mainly the later period not treated by Aronius.

1013b. Quellen zur Geschichte der Juden in Deutschland. Vols. I–III. Berlin, 1888–98.

1013c. Zeitschrift für Geschichte der Juden in Deutschland, Vols. I–V. Berlin, 1887–92.

1013d. BONDY, G., and DWORSKY, F. Zur Geschichte der Juden in Böhmen, Mähren und Schlesien von 906 bis 1620. 2 vols. Vol. I, 906–1576 A.D. Prague, 1906, contains 552 pp. of Regesten.

1013e. Quellen und Forschungen zur Geschichte der Juden in Deutsch-Österreich. Vols. I–VI. Vienna, 1908ff.

1013f. SAGUMINA, B. and G. Codice diplomatico dei Giudei di Sicilia Vols. I–III, 2. Palermo, 1884–1909.

PART II

GENERAL HISTORY OF THE MIDDLE AGES

PERIOD I. 500–1100

I. INTRODUCTION

A. OUTLINE

1. The period usually designated as the "middle ages." Various limits:—1 A.D., 313, 325, 378, 395, 410, 476, pontificate of Gregory the Great 590–604, 800, as the beginning; and as the close, "the revival of learning" (ca. 1350), 1453, 1492, 1517 or 1520, 1648, 1789. Attempts to eliminate the period altogether.

2. History of the rise and spread of the term "middle ages." The conceptions of the humanists. The part played by the idea of a "revival of learning" and of a "renaissance." Importance of the history of the Latin language in developing the idea of a middle period. DU CANGE, *Glossarium mediae et infimae latinitatis.* The great influence of the hand-books of CHRISTOPHER KELLER (CELLARIUS, 1634–1707), who divided history: (1) *Historia antiqua*, to Constantine the Great; (2) *Historia medii aevi*, to the fall of Constantinople in 1453; and (3) *Historia nova.*

3. Ideas which medieval scholars had about the time in which they lived.

4. Futility of basing divisions of history upon any other ground except that of convenience. Convenience and simplicity of calling the thousand years from about 500 to about 1500 the middle ages, now that the peculiar phrase is so deeply rooted in the modern languages and in books on history. Reasons for the division which has been adopted in this *Guide:* period I, 500–1100; period II, 1100–1500. The continuity of history.

5. Danger of investing the "middle ages" with attributes which make the period appear to have an individuality all its own. Curious modern connotations of "medieval" and "middle ages." "The dark ages." "The thousand years of gloom."

6. The geographical area concerned in medieval history. Its main physical features. Importance of the two great basins, the Mediterranean and the North and Baltic seas, and the routes which connected them.

7. Broad classification of the people who lived in this area in 500 A.D.

8. The main tools available for studying the political geography of the middle ages.

9. The relationship of geography and history.

10. Geographical knowledge in the middle ages. Dante's conception of the world in which he lived.

B. Special Recommendations for Reading

Meaning of middle ages. The most suggestive survey is J. T. Shotwell's article "Middle Ages" in the eleventh edition of the *Ency. Brit.* The fourteenth edition, has an article "Middle Ages" by F. M. Powicke. An important contribution to our knowledge of the origin of the conception of "middle ages" is P. Lehmann, "Vom Mittelalter und von der lateinischen Philologie des Mittelalters," *Quellen und Untersuchungen zur lateinischen Philologie des Mittelalters*, V (1914), 1–25; also printed separately, Munich, 1914. This article is summarized briefly by G. L. Burr, "How the middle ages got their name," *A.H.R.*, XX (1915), 813–14. See also Burr's article "Anent the middle ages," *A.H.R.*, XVIII (1913), 710–26; and F. Keutgen, "On the necessity in America of the study of the early history of modern European nations," *Annual report, A.H.A.*, 1904, 91–106. G. S. Gordon, *Medium aevum and the Middle Age* (*Society for pure English, Tract no. XIX*, 1925, 1–28). A summary and criticism of most of the literature mentioned below may be found in Bernheim, *Lehrbuch der historischen Methode*, 70–84. There are some good suggestions in G. B. Adams, *Civilization during the middle ages*, ch. i; H. O. Taylor, *Mediaeval mind*, I, ch. i; J. H. Robinson, *History of western Europe*, ch. i; and in his *Readings*, I, ch. i.

Geography. As an introduction to the study of geography for medieval history, Shepherd, *Atlas*, 2–3, 42–3; E. A. Freeman, *The historical geography of Europe;* and the standard historical atlases, nos. **121–29a.** For Dante's geography, see E. Moore, *Studies in Dante*, 3rd series, Oxford, 1903, 109–43.

C. Bibliography

The middle ages as a period of history. M. Büdinger, "Ueber Darstellungen der allgemeinen Geschichte, insbesonders des Mittelalters," in *H.Z.*, VII (1862), 108–32. O. Lorenz, *Die Geschichtswissenschaft*, Berlin, 1886, 228–60. W. Stubbs, *Seventeen lectures*, chs. ix–x, "Characteristic differences between mediaeval and modern history." On the date 476 a.d. see J. H. Robinson, *The new history*, New York, 1912, 155–94. F. X. v. Wegele, *Geschichte der deutschen Historiographie*, Munich and Leipzig, 1885, 473–89. E. Emerton, "The periodization of history," in *Massachusetts Historical Society*, *Proceedings*, Oct.–Dec., 1918. Brown, *Achievement*, no. **353,** 9–45. R. M. Meyer, "Mittelalter," in *Feuilleton der Nationalzeitung*, 1907, no. 277. H. Günter, "Das Mittelalter in der späteren Geschichtsbetrachtung," *Hist. Jahrbuch*, XXIV (1903), 1–14. E. A. Freeman, *The methods of historical study*, 20–40, 191–225. P. Lehmann, "Mittelalter und Küchenlatein," *H.Z.*, CXXXVII (1927), 197–213 (sums up much of the recent research on the name "Middle Ages"); see also H. Spangenberg, "Die Perioden der Weltgeschichte," *ibid.*, CXXVII (1923), 1–49. O. de Halecki, "Moyen âge et temps modernes: une nouvelle défense des divisions traditionelles de l'histoire," *R.S.H.*, XLIII (1927), 69–82. See Dahlmann-Waitz, no. 27, for a bibliography on the division of history into periods.

Characteristics of the middle ages. G. KURTH, *Qu'est-ce que le moyen âge?*, Brussels, 1898; 5th edition, Paris, 1907; translated by V. DAY, *What are the Middle Ages?*, 1924 (privately printed). A. EHRHARD, *Das Mittelalter und seine kirchliche Entwickelung*, Munich and Mainz, 1908, combats the idea of "dark ages." H. GRISAR, *Das Mittelalter einst und jetzt: zwei Beiträge über Erhard's "Der Katholicismus und das 20 Jahrhundert,"* 2nd edition, Munich, 1902. F. PICAVET, "Le moyen âge: caractéristique théologique et philosophico-scientifique, limites chronologiques," *Académie des sciences morales et politiques*, CLV (1901), 630–54. F. J. C. HEARNSHAW, *Mediaeval contributions to modern civilisation*, 11–41. N. JORGA, *Les bases nécessaires d'une nouvelle histoire du moyen âge*, Paris, 1913. S. R. MAITLAND, *The dark ages.* F GUIZOT, *History of civilization in Europe*, lecture I. L. GAUTIER, *Comment faut-il juger le moyen âge?*, Paris, 1876.

Geography and history. E. C. SEMPLE, *The influences of geographical environment*, New York, 1911. This is based on F. RATZEL, *Anthropogeographie*, 2 vols., Stuttgart, 1882–91; 2nd edition, 1891–99, I, *Grundzüge der Anwendung der Erdkunde auf die Geschichte.* H. B. GEORGE, *The relation of geography and history*, Oxford, 1901; 3rd edition, 1907; 4th edition, 1910. E. HUNTINGTON, *Civilization and climate*, Yale University Press, 1915. Sir R. L. PLAYFAIR, "The Mediterranean, physical and historical," in *Smithsonian report* (1890), 259–76 (see also nos. **359–61**). W. Z. RIPLEY, *The races of Europe*, London and New York, 1899. J. FAIRGRIEVE, *Geography and world power*, London, 1915. E. BABELON, *Le Rhin dans l'histoire: l'antiquité, Gaulois et Germains*, vol. I, Paris, 1916, vol. II, 1917.

Historical atlases. See nos. **121–29a.**

Dictionaries of geographical names. See nos. **130–38a.**

Historical geographies. See nos. **139–46.**

II. THE LATIN WEST IN THE SIXTH CENTURY

A. OUTLINE

1. Fundamental differences in civilization between the Roman (Latin) West and the Hellenic (Greek) East, destined to become more and more pronounced, in spite of the essential unity of the Mediterranean world, even at the end of the fifth century, illustrated especially by the universality of the Christian religion and the Roman law.

2. The constant weakening of Roman government and the steady decline of Graeco-Roman culture in the Latin West. The events of the year 476 in Italy. Romulus (Augustulus), nominal boy emperor, son of Orestes, deposed by Odovacar (Odoacer), who now ruled in Italy.

3. The infiltration of "Gothonic" peoples into the Roman Empire. Location of the more important "Gothons" about 475 A.D. Visigoths in Spain and southern Gaul, with capital at Toulouse (battle of Adrianople, 378; sack of Rome by Alaric, 410). Vandals in Africa (sack of Rome by

Gaiseric, or Genseric, 455). Burgundians in the Rhone valley (*Nibelungenlied*). Angles, Saxons, and Jutes in England since about 449. Franks in northern Gaul. Ostrogoths in the Danube valley.

4. The Visigothic kingdom in Spain, 415–711. King Euric, 466–84. Alaric II and the Franks under Clovis. Battle of Vouglé, 507. The *Breviarium Alarici*, 506. Conversion of the Arian Visigoths to orthodox Christianity. Isidore of Seville (ca. 570–636). Arab conquest, 711.

5. The nomad Huns (not "Gothons"), dispersed before 475 A.D. Attila, their king (died 453). "Battle of Châlons," 451. Huns in Italy, 452. Pope Leo the Great and Attila.

6. Italy was still the center of the western world about 475. Its attractiveness to "Gothonic" barbarians.

7. The rise of Theodoric the Ostrogoth. Born about 455, son of King Theodemir. At the age of seven he was sent to Constantinople as a hostage. Befriended by Aspar. When about eighteen he returned to his people living in old Pannonia (modern Hungary). King of Ostrogoths, 471. In 488 he set out for Italy with the consent of Zeno, the eastern emperor.

8. Conquest of Italy by Theodoric. Siege of Ravenna. Murder of Odovacar in 493. Theodoric proclaimed king in Italy by his troops. This established the kingdom of the Ostrogoths in Italy which lasted from 493 to 555, with capital at Ravenna.

9. Theodoric's attempt to establish an Ostrogothic hegemony in the west. Marriage alliances. Diplomatic relations with the Vandals, Visigoths, and the Franks under Clovis.

10. Theodoric's attempt to establish a dualism in Italy. The *Edictum Theodorici*, about 500.

11. The "golden age" of Italy, about 511–22. The glory of Ravenna, and the great public works in Rome (for the last time "felix Roma") and Verona. Famous men of letters: Boëthius, Symmachus, Cassiodorus.

12. The Arianism of the Ostrogoths. Theodoric's relations with the orthodox bishops of Italy and with the pope in Rome. Comparative weakness of the papacy during Theodoric's reign, as shown by the mission of Pope John I in Constantinople, and his imprisonment and death in 526.

13. Theodoric's relations with the Byzantine empire. He never thought of setting up a rule in Italy independent of the Byzantine emperor. His growing suspicions that intrigues against him were hatching in Constantinople. Execution of Boëthius and Symmachus, 525.

14. Last bitter years of Theodoric. He had no son. Death of his son-in-law Eutharic, whom he had chosen as his successor, about 522. Death of Theodoric in 526. Succeeded by his grandson Athalaric. Rapid decline of the Ostrogothic kingdom (see next outline).

15. The failure of Theodoric's attempt to unite the Latin West, under "Gothonic" leadership—a task not attempted again until the time of Charlemagne.

16. The legends of Theodoric (Dietrich von Bern).

17. Ostrogothic kings of Italy, 493–553.

Theodoric, 493–526	Hildibad, 540–41
Athalaric, 526–34	Eraric, 541
Theodohad, 534–36	Totila (Baduila), 541–52
Witigis, 536–40	Teias, 552–53

18. Visigothic kings in Spain.

Atawulf, 415	Agila, 549–54
Sigeric, 415	Athanagild, 554–67
Wallia, 415–20	Leova I, 567–72
Theodoric (Theodored), 420–51	Leovigild, 570–86
Thorismund, 451–52	Reccared I, 586–601
Theodoric, 452–66	Leova II, 601–03
Euric, 466–83	Witeric, 603–10
Alaric II, 483–506	Gundimar, 610–12
Theodoric and Amalric, 506–22	Sisibut, 612–20
Amalric, sole ruler, 522–31	Reccared II, 620–21
Theudis, 531–48	....
Theudigisel, 548–49	Roderic, 710–11

B. Special Recommendations for Reading

Brief general accounts which establish a connection with Roman history. Emerton, *Introduction to the study of the middle ages*, 1–59. Adams, *Civilization during the middle ages*, chs. i–v. Bryce, *Holy Roman empire*, chs. i–iii. W. S. Davis, *An outline history of the Roman empire* (44 B.C. to 378 A.D.), New York, 1909. A. E. R. Boak, *A history of Rome to 565 A. D.*, New York, 1922; rev. ed. 1929; chs. xxiii, xxiv. T. Frank, *History of Rome*, New York, 1923, ch. xxxi. Thorndike, *Medieval Europe*, chs. ii–vii. Hulme, *Middle ages*, 1–40, 110–213. Sellery and Krey, *Medieval foundations*, 1–32. Thompson, *Economic and social history*, chs. i, iii, iv. Munro and Sontag, *Middle ages*, chs. i, iii–v.

Longer accounts with special emphasis on the Ostrogoths. Lavisse et Rambaud, *Histoire générale*, I, chs. i and ii. *C.M.H.*, I, especially chs. xiv and xv. Villari, *The barbarian invasions of Italy*, book II. Oman, *The dark ages*, chs. i–ii. Bury, *History of the later Roman empire*, I, books II–III. H. Bradley, *The story of the Goths to the end of the Gothic dominion in Spain*, New York, 1888. E. A. Freeman, *Historical essays*, 3rd series, 121–72, "The Goths at Ravenna."

Biographies of Theodoric. T. Hodgkin, *Theodoric the Goth*, New York, 1891; new edition, London, 1923. G. Pfeilschifter, *Die Germanen im römischen Reich: Theodorich der Grosse*, Mainz, 1911 (pictures in the latter and in C. Diehl, *Ravenne*, Paris, 1907). J. v. Pflugk-Harttung, "Der erste König von Italien," in *Deutsche Revue*, XI (1886), 235–42.

Visigothic Spain. *C.M.H.*, II, ch. vi. Oman, *The dark ages*, 128–44. T. Hodgkin, "Visigothic Spain," in *E.H.R.*, II (1887), 209–34. Hume, *The*

Spanish people, 41–70. Longer and more authoritative accounts, U. R. BURKE, *History of Spain*, I, chs. IV–XI; and R. ALTAMIRA, *Historia de España* (1913 edition), I, 165–223.

Detailed general accounts. HODGKIN, *Italy and her invaders*, III. GIBBON, *Decline and fall of the Roman empire*, chs. XXVIff. GREGOROVIUS, *Rome in the middle ages*, I. J. V. PFLUGK-HARTTUNG, *The great migrations*, translated from *Allgemeine Weltgeschichte* as vol. VI of no. **314.** LOT, *La fin du monde antique.* J. B. BURY, *The invasion of Europe by the barbarians*, edited by F. J. C. HEARNSHAW, London, 1928.

Original sources. *Germania* of Tacitus, in Latin with a parallel translation by M. HUTTON in the Loeb Classical Library or translated in *Translations and reprints* (no. **391**), VI, no. 3. The *Letters of Cassiodorus*, translated in part by T. HODGKIN, London, 1886. JORDANES, *Origin and deeds of the Goths*, translated by C. C. MIEROW, Princeton, 1908; new edition, 1915.

Maps. SHEPHERD, *Atlas*, 42, 43, 45, 50. E. NIEPMANN (editor), *Eduard Rotherts Karten und Skizzen aus der Geschichte des Altertums*, Düsseldorf, 1928, important for later Roman Empire and especially for invasions.

C. BIBLIOGRAPHY

General books. Most of the subjects in this outline are touched upon in many of the general histories of Germany, nos. **560–87** and of Italy, **599–621,** see especially **614.** See also E. A. FREEMAN, *Western Europe in the fifth century: an aftermath*, London, 1904; C. KINGSLEY, *The Roman and the Teuton*, London, 1875; A. THIERRY, *Récits de l'histoire romaine au Ve siècle*, Paris, 1860; and E. STEIN, *Geschichte des spätrömischen Reiches*, 2 vols., Vienna, 1928–29, vol. I.

General accounts of the German invasions. L. SCHMIDT, *Geschichte der deutschen Stämme bis zum Ausgang der Völkerwanderung*, vols. I–II, Berlin, 1904–11; a shorter account is *Allgemeine Geschichte der germanischen Völker bis zur Mitte des sechsten Jahrhunderts*, Munich, 1909, part of no. **330;** summarized in brief and popular form in *Die germanische Reiche der Völkerwanderung*, Leipzig, 1913 (Wissenschaft und Bildung). F. DAHN, *Urgeschichte der germanischen und romanischen Völker*, 3 vols., Berlin, 1880–89, part of no. **313,** and *Die Könige der Germanen*, 13 vols., Munich, 1861–1911, vols. I, II, VI in second edition. R. VON ERKERT, *Wanderungen und Siedelungen der germanischen Stämme in Mittel-Europa von der ältesten Zeit bis auf Karl den Grossen*, Berlin, 1900. W. M. F. PETRIE, *Migrations*, London, 1906, has an interesting series of maps. See also the slight sketch by A. C. HADDON, *The wanderings of peoples*, Cambridge, 1911, ch. III. F. MARTROYE, *L'occident à l'époque byzantine: Goths et Vandales*, Paris, 1904. L. WILSER, *Die Germanen*, new edition, vol. I, Leipzig, 1913. G. KAUFMANN, *Deutsche Geschichte bis auf Karl den Grossen*, 2 vols., Leipzig, 1880–81. O. GUTSCHE and W. SCHULTZE, *Deutsche Geschichte von der Urzeit bis zu den Karolingern*, 2 vols., Stuttgart, 1894–96. E. V. WIETERSHEIM, *Geschichte der Völkerwanderung*, 4 vols., Leipzig, 1859–64; 2nd edition, by F. DAHN, 2 vols., 1880–81. F. LOT, "Les migrations saxonnes en Gaule et en Grande-Bretagne du IIIe au Ve siècle," *R.H.*, CXIX (1915), 1–40. G. Waitz, *Deutsche Verfassungsgeschichte*, vol. I, is our main source of information for early German institutions, but see also F. B. Gummere, *Germanic origins*, New York, 1892; new edition, *Founders of England*, with notes by F. P. Magoun, Jr., New York, 1930. T. Arldt, *Germanische Völkerwellen und ihre Bedeutung in der Bevölkerungsgeschichte von Europa*, Leipzig, 1917. J. Bühler, *Die Germanen in der Völkerwanderung: nach zeitgenössichen Quellen*, Leipzig, 1922. N. Åberg, *Die Franken und die Westgoten in der Völkerwanderungszeit*, Uppsala, 1922; *Die Goten und Langobarden in Italien*, Uppsala, 1923; *Ostpreussen in der Völkerwanderungszeit*, Stockholm, 1919. L. Halphen, *Les barbares, des grandes invasions aux conquêtes turques du XIe siècle*, Paris, 1926; 2d revised edition, 1930.

Ostrogoths. L. M. Hartmann, *Geschichte Italiens im Mittelalter*, vol. I, best general survey of the Ostrogoths in Italy. E. Loncao, *Fondazione del regno di Odoacre e suoi rapporti con l'Oriente*, Scansano, 1908. M. Dumoulin, "Le gouvernement de Théodoric et la domination des Ostrogoths en Italie d'après les oeuvres d'Ennodius," *R.H.*, LXXVIII (1902), 1–7, 241–65, LXXIX (1902), 1–22. L. Schmidt, "Die letzten Ostgoten," *Zeitschrift für schweizerische Geschichte*, III (1923), 443–65. T. Mommsen, "Ostgotische Studien," *N.A.*, XIV (1889), 223–49, 451–544, XV (1890), 181–86 (also in his *Gesammelte Schriften*, VI), are fundamental studies on Ostrogothic law and institutions; see also, P. del Giudice, *Sulla questione dell' unità o dualità del diritto in Italia sotto la dominazione ostrogota*, Milan, 1913. G. Salvioli, *Sullo stato e la popolazione d'Italia primo e dopo le invasioni barbariche*, Palermo, 1900. A. Ponchielli, *Commento all' editto di Teodorico*, Milan, 1923.

Visigoths. H. von Eicken, *Der Kampf der Westgothen und Römer unter Alaric*, Leipzig, 1876. A. F. Guerra, *Historia de España desde la invasión de los pueblos germánicos hasta la ruina de la monarquía visigoda*, 2 vols., Madrid, 1890, part of no. **622**. H. Leclercq, *L'Espagne chrétienne* [to 711], Paris, 1905; 2nd edition, 1906. J. Ortega y Rubio, *Los visigodos en España*, Madrid, 1903. E. Pérez Pujol, *Historia de las instituciones sociales de la España goda*, 4 vols., Valencia, 1896. F. Dahn, *Die Verfassung der Westgothen*, 2nd edition, Leipzig, 1885; and *Die äussere Geschichte der Westgothen*, Würzburg, 1870. J. Aschbach, *Geschichte der Westgoten*, Frankfurt, 1827. R. D. Shaw, "The fall of the Visigothic power in Spain," *E.H.R.*, XXI (1906), 209–28. R. de Ureña y Smenjaud, *La legislación gotico-hispana*, Madrid, 1905.

Burgundians. C. Binding, *Das burgundisch-romanische Königreich von 433 bis 532*, Leipzig, 1868. A. Jahn, *Geschichte der Burgundionen und Burgundiens bis zum Ende der I Dynastie*, 2 vols., Halle, 1874. J. Havet, "Des partages des terres entre les Romains et les barbares chez les Burgondes et les Visigoths," in *R.H.*, VI (1878), 87–99. H. de Claparède, *Les Burgondes jusqu'en 443: contribution à l'histoire externe du droit germanique*, Geneva, 1909.

Vandals. F. Martroye, *Genséric: la conquête vandale en Afrique et la* *destruction de l'empire d'occident*, Paris, 1907. L. SCHMIDT, *Geschichte der Wandalen*, Leipzig, 1901. S. LA ROCCA, *Le incursioni vandaliche in Sicilia*, Girgenti, 1917. See also Bouchier, *Roman Africa*, 105–11.

Huns. E. HUTTON, *Attila and his Huns*, New York, 1915. *C.M.H.*, I, ch. XII. HELMOLT, *History of the world*, V, 319–26. J. J. M. DE GROOT, *Die Hunnen der vorchristlichen Zeit: 'Chinesische Urkunden zur Geschichte Asiens, übersetzt und erläutert,'* parts 1–2, Berlin, 1921–26. G. KAUFMANN, "Über die Hunnenschlacht des Jahres 451," *F.D.G.*, VIII (1868), 115–46.

Original sources. An examination of the general nature and trustworthiness of the sources in C. J. H. HAYES, *An introduction to the sources relating to the Germanic invasions*, New York, 1909. Most of the important sources are edited in *M.G.H.*, no. **978,** *Auctores antiquissimi*, vols. I–XIV, Berlin, 1877–1904. Some of these are translated into German in *Geschichtschreiber*, no. **981,** such as vol. X, *Isidors Geschichte der Goten, Vandalen, Sueven, nebst Auszügen aus der Kirchengeschichte des Beda Venerabilis*, revised edition by D. COSTE, Leipzig, 1910. O. SEECK, *Regesten der Kaiser und Päpste für die Jahre 311–476*, Stuttgart, 1918–19. M. G. CLARK, *Sidelights on Teutonic history during the migration period: being studies from Beowulf and other old English poems*, Cambridge, 1911.

Bibliographies. The best systematic bibliography is in DAHLMANN-WAITZ, nos. 3506–4090. The sources are best described by WATTENBACH, no. **29.** See also the elaborate lists of books in *C.M.H.*, I, especially those for chs. VII–XV, and II, ch. VI; also the other general bibliographies for the history of Germany, nos. **31–34,** and Italy, nos. **37–41.**

III. THE GREEK EAST IN THE SIXTH CENTURY

A. OUTLINE

1. Recent change of attitude towards the eastern or Byzantine empire on the part of historians. GIBBON's misconceptions. The *Byzantinische Zeitschrift*, and other periodicals, see no. **174**ff. The foreshadowing of the "Eastern Question" in Europe.

2. The stability of the Byzantine empire and its services to western civilization. No enemy ever entered Constantinople until 1204 and the empire did not fall before the Mohammedan Turks until 1453.

3. Description of the city of Constantinople in the time of Justinian.

4. The reigns of Justin I (518–27) and Justinian I (527–65). Both born in Macedonia. The empress Theodora. The Hippodrome. Greens and Blues. The Nika riot (532).

5. The codification of the Roman law. Previous codifications, especially the Theodosian code, 438. The *Corpus iuris civilis*, 529ff. (Code, Pandects or Digest, Institutes, Novels. Most of the Novels in Greek.) Tribonian was editor-in-chief. Significance of the fact that it was written and promulgated in Latin, although it was compiled in the Greek East.

6. Justinian's administration of the empire. The Byzantine army. The Persian wars against Chosroes. Disastrous financial policy. Relations with

the church. The great plague of 542. Justinian's interest in building and in theology. The controversy about "The Three Chapters." Imprisonment of Pope Vigilius. Humiliation of the papacy.

7. The plan of Justinian to reconquer the west and to re-establish the empire as it was in the time of Constantine.

8. The fall of the Vandal kingdom in Africa, 533–34. Belisarius versus Gelimer. Rise of the Berber tribes, 534–39; 546–48. Imperial Africa after the fall of the Vandal kingdom.

9. The reconquest of Italy and the fall of the Ostrogothic kingdom. Two stages, 535–40; and 540–55. Murder of Amalasuntha, 535. Belisarius and Narses against Theodahad, Witigis, Totila, and Teias. The desolation of Rome and of all Italy. The reconstruction of Italy under imperial administration. The Pragmatic Sanction of 554.

10. Justinian's foothold in Spain, 554. The rivalry between king Agila and Athanagild gave the Greeks the opportunity to intervene. Capture of Cartagena, Malaga, and Cordova. Visigothic resistance under Athanagild, 554–67.

11. The Lombard invasion of Italy, 568, under Alboin.

12. The fate of Italy: divided between the Byzantine empire (exarchate of Ravenna), the Lombards, and the rising papacy.

13. Failure of Justinian's attempt to reunite the Mediterranean world. His feeble old age and death in 565 at the age of 83. Rapid decline of the Greek East in the generation after Justinian. Persistence of the idea of a united Roman empire.

14. The eastern emperors, 395–565.

Arcadius, 395–408
Theodosius II, 408–50
Marcian, 450–57
Leo I, the Thracian, 457–74
Zeno, the Isaurian, 475–91
Anastasius I, 491–518
Justin I, 518–27
Justinian I, 527–65

15. Lombard kings in Italy, 568–774.

Alboin, 568–72
Clepho, 572–73
Authari, 584–90
Agilulf, 590–615
Adaloald, 615–25
Arioald, 625–36
Rothari, 636–52
Rodoald, 652–53
Aribert, 653–62
Godebert, 662
Grimoald, 662–71
Berthari, 672–88
Cunibert, 688–700
Liutbert, 700–01
Aribert II, 701–11
Ansprand, 712
Liutprand, 712–43
Hildebrand, 743–44
Ratchis, 744–49
Aistulf, 749–56
Desiderius, 756–74

B. Special Recommendations for Reading

General surveys. Vasiliev, *History of the Byzantine empire*, chs. II–III. Bémont and Monod, *Medieval Europe*, ch. VIII. *C.M.H.*, II, 1–52 and 222–35 (see also I, ch. I); BURY, *Later Roman empire*, book IV, part I; LAVISSE et RAMBAUD, *Histoire générale*, I, ch. IV; OMAN, *Dark ages*, chs. III, V, VI, XI; OMAN, *Byzantine empire*, chs. I–VIII, XI. DIEHL, *History of the Byzantine empire*, 3–39. F. LOT, *La fin du monde antique*, 277–470. THORNDIKE, *Medieval Europe*, ch. VIII. SELLERY and KREY, *Medieval foundations*, 32–37, 46–48. THOMPSON, *Economic and social history*, ch. VI. F. SCHEVILL, *History of the Balkan peninsula from the earliest times to the present day*, ch. IV.

Justinian. E. GRUPE, *Kaiser Justinian*, Leipzig, 1923. C. DIEHL, *Justinien et la civilisation byzantine au VIe siècle*, Paris, 1901. W. G. HOLMES, *The age of Justinian and Theodora*, 2 vols., London, 1905–07. A. GFRÖRER, "Kaiser Justinian I," in *Byzantinische Geschichten*, II, 315–401. K. KRUMBACHER, "Kaiser Justinian" (1901), in *Populäre Aufsätze*, 153–68. N. H. BAYNES, "Justinian and Amalasuntha," *E.H.R.*, XL (1925), 71–73. The article "Justinian" in the *Ency. Brit.* is by J. BRYCE.

Constantinople. *Cambridge medieval history*, I, ch. I, has a brief description of the city as founded by Constantine. C. DIEHL, "Constantinople Byzantine," essay V in *Dans l'Orient byzantin*, pp. 45–82. VAN MILLINGEN, *Byzantine Constantinople, the walls of the city and adjoining historical sites*, London, 1899. For Justinian's city see BURY, *Later Roman empire*, book I, ch. V, and HOLMES, *The age of Justinian*, I, ch. I. MUNRO and SELLERY, *Medieval civilization*, 87–113, "The Hippodrome," is a translation of a very interesting extract from DIEHL, *Justinien*. *Preliminary report upon the excavations carried out in the Hippodrome of Constantinople in 1927*, London, 1928. F. HARRISON, *The meaning of history*, 309–67, "Constantinople." See also the general works on Constantinople, nos. **661–69.**

Roman law. The article " Roman law " in the *Ency. Brit.* will serve as an introduction to the codification of the Roman law. BURY, *Later Roman empire*, book IV, ch. III. *C.M.H.*, II, ch. III. GIBBON, *Decline and fall*, ch. XLIV. MILMAN, *History of Latin Christianity*, book III, ch. V, 1–34.

Modern attitude towards Byzantine history. F. HARRISON, *Byzantine history in the early middle ages*, London, 1900; the same author's "Constantinople as an historic city," *Fortnightly review*, LXI (1894), 438–58; and E. A. FREEMAN, "The Byzantine empire," in his *Historical essays*, 3rd series, 231–37.

Lombards. OMAN, *Dark ages*, ch. XI; and a more detailed account in *C.M.H.*, II, ch. VII.

Detailed general accounts. HODGKIN, *Italy and her invaders*, vols. IV and VI. GIBBON, *Decline and fall*, chs. XXX–XLIII.

Original sources. Extracts illustrating the church in the Eastern Empire in J. C. AYER, *A source book for ancient church history*, 538–64.

Maps. SHEPHERD, *Atlas*, 50, 52.

C. BIBLIOGRAPHY

General books. For general works on the Byzantine empire see nos. **643–79; 800–02.** Many of the general works under "Eastern Europe," nos. **680–716,** touch upon the subject of this outline.

Byzantine administration. C. DIEHL, *Etudes sur l'administration byzantine dans l'Exarchat de Ravenne (568–751)*, Paris, 1888. L. M. HARTMANN, *Untersuchungen zur Geschichte der byzantinischen Verwaltung in Italien (540–750)*, Leipzig, 1889. A. GAUDENZI, *Sui rapporti tra l'Italia e l'impero d'Oriente (476–554)*, Bologna, 1888. H. E. MIEROW, "The Roman provincial governor as he appears in the Digest and Code of Justinian," in *Colorado college publications*, vol. III, no. 1, 1926. M. GELZER, *Studien zur byzantinishen Verwaltung Aegyptens*, Leipzig, 1909. Y. MASPERO, *L'organisation militaire de l'Egypte byzantine*, Paris, 1912. E. STEIN, *Studien zur Geschichte des byzantinischen Reiches vornehmlich unter den Kaisern Justinus II und Tiberius Constantinus*, Stuttgart, 1919. G. ROUILLARD, *L'administration civile de l'Egypte byzantine*, 2nd edition, Paris, 1928. A. BOAK, "Byzantine imperialism in Egypt," *A.H.R.*, XXXIV (1928), 1–8.

Byzantine Africa. C. DIEHL, *L'Afrique byzantine, histoire de la domination byzantine en Afrique (553–709)*, Paris, 1896. P. MONCEAUX, *Histoire littéraire de l'Afrique chrétienne depuis les origines jusqu'à l'invasion arabe*, 7 vols., Paris, 1901–23, vol. V.

Byzantine warfare. H. DELBRÜCK, *Geschichte der Kriegskunst*, II, Berlin, 1902, sometimes corrects and supplements C. W. C. OMAN, *A history of the art of war*, London, 1898; 2nd edition, London, 1924. J. PRESLAND, *Belisarius: general of the east*, London, 1913.

The Empress Theodora. C. DIEHL, *Théodora: impératrice de Byzance*, Paris, 1904. A. DEBIDOUR, *L'impératrice Théodora*, Paris, 1885. C. E. MALLET, "The empress Theodora," *E.H.R.*, II (1887), 1–20. H. STADELMANN, *Theodora von Byzanz*, 2 vols., Dresden, 1926. C. DIEHL, *Byzantine portraits*, ch. III (see also *Athenais*, ch. II). L. DUCHESNE, "Les protégés de Théodora," Paris, 1915, *Mélanges d'archéologie et d'histoire de l'école française de Rome*, XXXV (1915), 57–79.

Greek Church under Justinian. W. H. HUTTON, *The church in the sixth century*, London, 1897. H. S. ALIVISATOS, *Die kirchliche Gesetzgebung des Kaisers Justinian*, I, Berlin, 1913. J. PARGOIRE, *L'église byzantine de 527 à 847*, Paris, 1905. E. L. WOODWARD, *Christianity and nationalism in the later Roman empire*, London, 1916, has chapters on Justinian, on Egypt and Syria, and on Africa.

Roman law. P. COLLINET, *Etudes historiques sur le droit de Justinien*, Paris, 1912. J. DECLAREUIL, *Rome, the law-giver*, trans. by E. A. PARKER, New York, 1927. For other works on Roman law see outline XX, part III below.

Byzantine studies in Germany. K. DIETRICH, "Die Byzantinische Zeitschrift und die byzantinischen Studien in Deutschland," *Internationale Monatsschrift*, VI, no. 3 (1912), 345–76.

Lombards. K. BLASEL, *Die Wanderzüge der Langobarden*, Breslau, 1909.

Original sources. For collections of sources for Byzantine history see nos. **1002–03a**. For the time of Justinian the works of PROCOPIUS have attracted most attention, especially the *De Bellis*, 2 vols., Leipzig, 1905; and the *Historia arcana*, Leipzig, 1906, both edited by J. HAURY who has written an authoritative estimate of PROCOPIUS, *Zur Beurteilung des Geschichtschreibers Procopius von Cäsarea*, Munich, 1896. Compare also BURY's appendix to his edition of GIBBON, vol. IV, 513–18. The *De Bellis* is translated by H. B. DEWING, *Procopius, History of the wars, books I–IV*, 4 vols., London and New York, 1914–28 (Loeb Library), the *Historia arcana* by the Athenian Society, Athens, 1906. The *De aedificiis* of PROCOPIUS also edited by HAURY is translated by A. STEWART and others, *Of the buildings of Justinian*, Palestine pilgrims text society, London, 1896. PROCOPIUS OF CAESAREA, *Secret history of Procopius*, newly translated from the Greek with an introduction by R. ATWATER, Chicago, 1927.

The standard edition of the Roman law of Justinian is the *Corpus iuris civilis*, 3 vols., Berlin, 1884ff.: vol. I, *Institutiones*, edited by P. KRÜGER, *Digesta*, edited by T. MOMMSEN, 11th edition, 1908; vol. II, *Codex*, edited by T. KRÜGER, 8th edition, 1906; vol. III, *Novellae*, edited by R. SCHOELL and W. KROLL, 1895. For other editions of the Roman law see *C.M.H.*, II, 726, and outline XX, part III below.

PAULUS DIACONUS, *Historia Langobardorum*, translated by W. D. FOULKE, *History of the Langobards, by Paul the Deacon: with explanatory and critical notes, a biography of the author, and an account of the sources of the history*, University of Pennsylvania, Philadelphia, 1907.

Bibliographies. A good bibliography is in C. DIEHL, *Justinien*, 667–70; see also the classified lists of books in the *C.M.H.*, II, for chs. I, II, III, VII, VIII (A), pp. 720–27, 739–42. A. A. VASILIEV, *History of the Byzantine empire*, vol. I, ch. III. Works in Greek, Russian, and other Slavic languages are omitted in this book although frequently they are the best. The most important titles can be found in VASILIEV's excellent bibliographies.

IV. MONASTICISM IN THE SIXTH CENTURY

A. OUTLINE

1. Since the church, as organized by the papacy, was still in its infancy in the first half of the sixth century, the nature and importance of universal Christianity in that period can be appreciated best by a study of monasticism. Hagiography. The *Acta sanctorum*, no. **963**.

2. Monasticism originated in asceticism and mysticism. It is by no means peculiar to Christianity.

3. Evolution of monasticism in northern Egypt. Hermits or anchorites and coenobites. St. Anthony (born about 250 A.D. in middle Egypt). Semi-eremitical life in the deserts of Nitria and Scete. The *Life of St. Anthony* by Athanasius. The reports of Palladius, Cassian, St. Jerome, and Rufinus on monastic life in Egypt in the fourth century. The legend of Paul of Thebes.

4. Evolution of monastic life in southern Egypt. Pachomius (born about 290, died 346), the founder of the coenobitical monastic life.

5. The anchorites of Syria and Mesopotamia. "The Sons of the Covenant" early in the fourth century. The stylites, or pillar saints, especially

St. Simeon Stylites near Antioch about the middle of the fifth century. Excessive austerities practiced by these eastern saints. The monastery of Jerome and the convent of Paula in Bethlehem towards the end of the fourth century.

6. Monasticism in the Greek world. St. Basil, near Neocaesarea in the Pontus region during the second half of the fourth century. Well organized community life. Moderate asceticism. His two rules, the longer and the shorter, taught moderation in the ascetic life. Basilian monasticism in Constantinople. Its spread into the Slavonic world. Mount Athos.

7. Introduction of monasticism into the west. St. Athanasius brought two Egyptian monks to Rome in 339. Spread of the monastic ideal in Rome, especially among the women of the higher classes, such as Paula and Melania. St. Jerome (died 420). Rufinus. Ambrose in Milan (died 397). Eusebius, bishop of Vercelli (died 371). St. Augustine, bishop of Hippo (died 430). Paulinus of Nola near Rome (died 431). Holy islands in the Tyrrhenian sea, such as Capraria.

8. Monasticism in Gaul. St. Martin, bishop of Tours in 372. Founded a monastery near Poitiers about 362. Marmoutier. John Cassian in Marseilles. Honoratus on the island of Lerins. The monastery of Condat in the Jura mountains. Decline of monasticism in Gaul in the late fifth and early sixth century.

9. Irish monasticism (see outline VI).

10. St. Benedict of Nursia (ca. 480–ca. 550). His cave at Subiaco. Founded Monte Cassino about the third decade of the sixth century. Here he wrote his *Rule*. Visit of Totila in 543.

11. The famous *Rule* of St. Benedict. Its moderation. Lack of stress on learning. Although little known in the sixth century its influence became vast after 600.

12. Cassiodorus (died between 575–85) founded the monastery called Vivarium at Squillace in Calabria. His great services in encouraging monastic learning.

13. Contrast between eastern and western monasticism. The importance of monasticism in early medieval civilization.

14. The evolution of a difference between regular and secular clergy.

15. Women under monasticism.

B. Special Recommendations for Reading

Short general surveys. *C.M.H.*, I, 521–42, written by E. C. Butler, an authority on monasticism, who also wrote the articles "Monasticism, Benedictines, Benedict" in *Ency. Brit.*, xi ed. Flick, *Medieval church*, ch. xi. Hulme, *Middle ages*, ch. iv. Thompson, *Economic and social history*, ch. v. Munro and Sontag, *Middle ages*, ch. vi.

Various estimates of monasticism. A. Harnack, *Das Mönchtum: seine Ideale und seine Geschichte*, Giessen, 1895, translated by E. E. Kellett and F. H. Marseille, *Monasticism: its ideals and history, and the Confessions of St. Augustine*, London, 1901. D. O. Zöckler, *Askese und Mönchtum*,

Frankfurt, a. M., 1897. E. C. BUTLER, *Benedictine monachism*, London, 2nd edition, 1924, is a collection of studies. Cardinal Gasquet, *Monastic life in the middle ages: with a note on Great Britain and the Holy See, 1792–1806*, London, 1922. J. B. O'CONNOR, *Monasticism and civilization*, New York, 1927. H. O. TAYLOR, *The classical heritage of the middle ages*, New York, 1903; 3rd edition, 1911, 136–97. J. O. HANNAY, *The spirit and origin of Christian monasticism*, London, 1903. WORKMAN, *The evolution of the monastic ideal*. L. GOUGAUD, "La 'Theoria' dans la spiritualité médiévale," and "Anciens traditions ascétiques," *Revue d'ascétique et de mystique*, III (1922), 381–94; IV (1923), 1–17. MONTALEMBERT, *Monks of the west*, introduction. GIBBON, *Decline and fall*, ch. XXXVII. TENNYSON'S poem, *St. Simeon Stylites*.

St. Benedict. Excellent sketch of his life and work in F. H. DUDDEN, *Gregory the Great: his place in history and thought*, 2 vols., London, 1905, I, 109–15; II, 161–69. J. B. CARTER, *The religious life of ancient Rome*, Boston, 1911, ch. VII. Longer account in MONTALEMBERT, *Monks of the west*, I, book IV; and in MILMAN, *History of Latin Christianity*, book III, ch. VI.

The legends about St. Benedict as told by pope GREGORY THE GREAT can be read in English, in E. G. GARDNER, *The Dialogues of St. Gregory*, London, 1911; E. J. LUCK, *The life and miracles of St. Benedict by St. Gregory the Great* (from an old version), London, 1880; *The little flowers of St. Benedict, gathered from the Dialogues of St. Gregory the Great*, London, 1901.

Monte Cassino. LOEW, *The Beneventan script*, 1–21, gives a short sketch of the rôle of Monte Cassino in the history of medieval culture.

Women under monasticism. LINA ECKENSTEIN, *Women under monasticism*. H. WILMS, *Aus mittelalterlichen Frauenklöstern*, 2nd and 3rd edition, Freiburg, 1918. EILEEN E. POWER, *Medieval English nunneries, c. 1275–1535*, Cambridge, 1922.

Original sources. The famous *Life of St. Anthony* by ATHANASIUS is translated in *Nicene and post-Nicene fathers*, 2nd series, IV, 195–221; also in E. A. T. W. BUDGE, *The paradise or garden of the fathers*, 2 vols., London, 1907, 1, 3–76. For the works of St. Basil see *Nicene and post-Nicene fathers*, 2nd series, VII.

The all-important *Rule* of ST. BENEDICT is translated in large part in HENDERSON, *Select documents*, 274–313, and in THATCHER and MCNEAL, *Source book*, 432–84; Selections in OGG, *Source-book*, 83–90, and a short selection in WEBSTER, *Historical selections*, 439–42. A good translation has been made by F. A. GASQUET, *Rule of St. Benedict*, London, 1908.

Maps. SHEPHERD, *Atlas*, 46–7, 94–5.

C. BIBLIOGRAPHY

General books. For general works on monasticism see nos. **479–87,** especially **483.** Naturally all general books on the church, nos. **393–498,** treat of monasticism. See also encyclopaedias and dictionaries of church history, nos. **104–14,** e.g., the article, "Cénobitisme" by H. LECLERCQ in **111.** For Greek monasticism see also **800.**

General surveys. L. S. de Le Nain de Tillemont, *Mémoires pour servir à l'histoire ecclésiastique des six premiers siècles*, 15 vols., Brussels, 1693–1707; 2nd edition, 16 vols., Paris, 1701–12. T. W. Allies, *The monastic life: from the fathers of the desert to Charlemagne*, London, 1896. I. G. Smith, *Christian monasticism from the fourth to the ninth centuries*, London, 1892. J. Mabillon, *Annales ordinis sancti Benedicti*, 6 vols., Paris, 1703–39. L. Gougaud, *Ermites et reclus, études sur d'anciennes formes de vie religieuse*, Abbaye de Saint-Martin de Ligugé, 1928 (Moines et monastères, 5).

Egyptian monasticism. A good general sketch of Egyptian monasticism is in L. Duchesne, *Histoire ancienne de l'église*, 3 vols., Paris, 1905ff. (various later editions), translated into English, *Early history of the Christian church*, New York, 1909ff., II, ch. xiv. A supplementary volume to Duchesne's work, *L'église au VIe siècle*, Paris, 1926, edited from his nearly completed manuscript by Dom H. Quentin. E. C. Butler, *The Lausiac history of Palladius* (in *Texts and studies*, vol. VI), 2 vols., Cambridge, 1898–1904. H. Delehaye, *Les martyrs d'Egypte*, Brussels, 1923. P. Van Cauwenbergh, *Etude sur les moines d'Egypte, depuis le concile de Chalcédoine (451) jusqu'à l'invasion arabe (640)*, Paris, 1914. C. Kingsley, *The hermits: their lives and works*, London, 1885. G. K. Grützmacher, *Pachomius und das älteste Klosterleben*, Freiburg, 1896. W. H. Mackean, *Christian monasticism in Egypt to the close of the fourth century*, London and New York, 1920. P. Ladeuze, *Etude sur le cénobitisme pakhomien pendant le IVe siècle et la première moitié du Ve*, Louvain, 1898.

Eastern monasticism. The best general book is J. M. Besse, *Les moines d'Orient antérieure au concile de Chalcédoine (451)*, Paris, 1900. S. Schiwietz, *Das morgenländische Mönchtum*, Mainz, 1904, a series of collected articles. H. Delehaye, "Les Stylites, Saint Syméon et ses imitateurs," *R.Q.H.*, LVII (1895), 52–103 (also printed separately, Brussels, 1895), is full of curious details about this most striking example of excessive asceticism in the East. E. Marin, *Les moines de Constantinople depuis la fondation de la ville jusqu'à la mort de Photius (330–898)*, Paris, 1897. A. R. von Pessic (tr. from Russian of N. Milasch), *Das Kirchenrecht der Morgenländischen Kirche*, 2nd edition, Mostar, 1905. E. C. Butler, "Basilian monks," in *Encyc. Brit.*, 11th edition, 1910. L. Oeconomos, *La vie religieuse dans l'empire byzantin au temps des Comnènes et des Anges*, Paris, 1918. *Oriens christianus: Halbjahrheft für die Kunde des christlichen Orients*, edited by A. Baumstark, new series, XXIII, Leipzig, 1926. H. Delehaye, *Les saints stylites*, Brussels, 1923.

St. Basil. W. K. L. Clarke, *St. Basil the Great: a study in monasticism*, Cambridge, 1913. E. F. Morison, *Basil and his rule: a study in early monasticism*, London, 1912. E. F. Morison, "St. Basil and Monasticism," *Church quarterly review*, October, 1912. R. J. Deferrari, *St. Basil: letters*, vol. I, London, 1926.

Mount Athos. K. Lake, *The early days of monasticism on Mount Athos*, Oxford, 1909. A. Riley, *Athos: or, The mountain of the monks*, London, 1887. F. W. Hasluck, *Athos and its monasteries*, London, 1924. P. Meyer,

Die Haupturkunden für die Geschichte der Athoskloster, Leipzig, 1894. R. CURZON, *Visits to monasteries of the Levant*, New York, 1849. P. DE MEESTER, *Voyage de deux bénédictins au monastère du Mont-Athos*, Paris, 1908.

African monasticism. J. M. BESSE, *Le monachisme africain*, Ligugé, 1900; and H. LECLERCQ, *L'Afrique chrétienne*, Paris, 1904. E. BUONAIUTI, *Il cristianesimo nell' Africa romana*, Bari, 1928. E. A. W. BUDGE (translator), *The book of the saints of the Ethiopian church*, 4 vols., Cambridge, 1928.

Early monasticism in Gaul. J. M. BESSE, *Les moines de l'ancienne France: période gallo-romaine et mérovingienne*, Paris, 1906. E. C. BABUT, *Saint Martin de Tours*, Paris, 1912. A. LECOY DE LA MARCHE, *Vie de saint Martin, évêque de Tours*, Tours, 1895. H. BAS, *Saint Martin*, Tours, 1898. P. MONCEAUX, *Saint Martin: récits de Sulpice Sevère, mis en français avec une introduction*, Paris, 1926. E. K. RAND, "St. Martin of Tours," *Bulletin of John Rylands library*, Manchester, XI (1927), 101–9. J. C. CAZENOVE, *St. Hilary of Poitiers and St. Martin of Tours*, London, 1883. L. LAUNOY, *Histoire de l'église gaulois depuis les origines jusqu'à la conquête franque (511)*, vols. I–II, Paris, 1906. A. C. COOPER-MARSDEN, *The history of the Island of Lerins: monastery, saints and theologians of St. Honorat*, Cambridge, 1913. F. BONNARD, *Saint Honorat de Lérins*, Tours, 1914. *Gallia Christiana (vetus)*, 4 vols., Paris, 1656. *Gallia Christiana (nova)*, 16 vols., Paris, 1715–1865. J. M. CLARK, *The abbey of St. Gall*, Cambridge, 1926. R. AIGRAIN, *Sainte Radegonde, vers 520–587*, Paris, 1918 (Les saints).

St. Benedict of Nursia. P. P. LECHNER, *St. Benedict and his times*, London, 1900. D. B. MARÉCHAUX, *Saint Benoît: sa vie, sa règle, sa doctrine spirituelle*, Paris, 1911. L. TOSTI, *San Benedetto*, Monte Cassino, 1892, translated into English by W. R. WOODS, London, 1896. ABBOT HERWEGEN, *Der heilige Benedict*, 3rd edition, Düsseldorf, 1926. A. STAUB, *Leben des heiligen Benedikts*, Einsiedeln, 1920. G. GRÜTZMACHER, *Die Bedeutung Benedikts von Nursia und seine Regel in der Geschichte des Mönchtums*, Berlin, 1892. A. l'HUILLIER, *Explication de la règle de S. Benoît*, 2 vols., Paris, 1901; and *Le patriarche S. Benoît*, Paris, 1905.

Serial publications. *Studien und Mitteilungen zur Geschichte des Benediktinerordens und seiner Zweige* (since 1911, vol. XXXII, this is a new title for *Studien und Mitteilungen aus den Benediktiner und Cistercienserorden*, vols. I–XXXI, Brünn, Würzburg, and Vienna, 1880ff.). *Beiträge zur Geschichte des alten Mönchtums und des Benediktinerordens* (edited by Father Herwegen of the abbey of Maria-Laach) was begun 1912. *Archives de la France monastique. Revue Mabillon*, Paris, 1899ff. *Revue bénédictine*, Abbaye de Moredsous, 1884–85ff.

Original sources. Much of the original material for early monasticism may be found in nos. **953–55a, 963, 978.** The most complete collection of monastic rules is no. **964.** See also *Patrologia orientalis*, edited by R. GRAFFIN and F. NAU, Paris, 1903ff.; *Corpus scriptorum christianorum orientalium*, edited by J. B. CHABOT and others, Paris, 1903ff.; *Lausiac history of Palladius*, translated into English by W. K. L. CLARKE, London, 1918, and

Codice diplomatico del monastero di S. Colombano di Bobbio fino all'anno MCVIII, edited by C. CIPOLLA and G. BUZZI. 3 vols., Rome, 1918.

The original *Rule* of ST. BENEDICT can best be studied in the edition of E. C. BUTLER, *Sancti Benedicti regula monachorum: editio critico-practica*, Freiburg-i-B., 1911. B. LINDERBAUER, *S. Benedicti Regula philologisch erklärt*, Metten, 1922. Valuable for the philological commentary on the vocabulary and latinity of the *Rule*. Documents for the history of early Benedictine monks have been edited by B. ALBERS, *Consuetudines monasticae*, 5 vols., Monte Cassino, 1900–12. For lives of Benedictine saints we have the old collection, *Acta sanctorum ordinis sancti Benedicti in saeculorum classes distributa* [to 1100 A.D.], edited by J. MABILLON, 9 vols., Paris, 1668–1702.

Bibliographies. See the bibliography for ch. XVIII, on monasticism, in the *C.M.H.*, I, 683–87, and the bibliographies there referred to. Also consult the general bibliographies of church history, nos. **49–55.**

V. THE RISE OF THE PAPACY IN THE SIXTH CENTURY

A. OUTLINE

1. Retrospect: the rise of Rome and the papacy to headship in western Christendom. The Petrine theory.

2. The position of the bishops of Rome in the time of Theodoric and the Ostrogothic wars. Relations with other prelates, with Arian and heathen barbarians, and with Justinian and Theodora.

3. Emergence of the papacy from the chaos in Italy produced by the fall of the Ostrogoths, 555, and the invasion of the Lombards, 568.

4. Pope Gregory I, the Great (590–604). The real founder of the papacy. *Servus servorum dei.*

5. Early career of Gregory. Born about 540 in Rome. Desolation of the city in his youth. Received a good education. Prefect of the city in 573.

6. Gregory as a monk. Established six monasteries in Sicily and turned his father's house in Rome into the monastery of St. Andrew. Interest in missionary work in the island of Britain.

7. His active church work. He became one of the seven deacons of Rome ca. 578. In 579 Pope Pelagius II sent him to Constantinople as *apocrisiarius*, where he stayed about six years. Met Leander of Seville there. Gregory did not learn Greek. About 585 he returned to his monastery in Rome and was abbot there until 590.

8. Election of Gregory to the papacy. Pope Pelagius died of a plague which swept Rome in 590. With remarkable unanimity the clergy and people of Rome chose Gregory as their new pope. The septiform litany to stay the plague. The legend of the archangel Michael on the Mausoleum of Hadrian. Maurice, the eastern emperor, sanctioned the election, and Gregory, although reluctant, was consecrated September 3, 590. "Monasticism ascended the papal throne in the person of Gregory the Great."—Milman.

9. The politics of Gregory the Great. He was lord of the city of Rome. Transformation of imperial Rome into the capital of western Christendom (see outline III, part III). He was likewise the lord of Italy and took the neglected place of the eastern emperor in protecting Rome and Italy against the "unspeakable" Lombards. His careful administration of papal lands. More and more he became arbiter of all western Christendom.

10. Relations with Constantinople. His disputes with the emperor on account of the Lombards. His quarrel with the patriarch, John the Faster, over the phrase, *sacerdos universalis.* Gregory supported the emperor Phocas, the murderer of his predecessor, Maurice, in 602.

11. Gregory's attempts to stamp out Arianism, especially among the Visigoths and the Lombards. Conversion of the Visigothic king Reccared to orthodox Christianity, 587 (see next outline).

12. Missionary work under Gregory (see next outline).

13. Enhancement of the Christian cult by Gregory. Gregorian music.

14. His interesting *Letters* and influential books: *Pastoral care, Dialogues,* and *Moralia.*

15. Gregory's real greatness contrasted with his inability to foresee the glorious future of the remarkable papal monarchy which he had founded.

16. Popes, 440–604.

Leo, I 440–61	Boniface II, 530–32
Hilary, 461–67	John II, 532–35
Simplicius, 467–83	Agapetus I, 535–36
Felix III, 483–92	Silverius, 536–37
Gelasius, 492–96	Vigilius, 537–55
Anastasius II, 496–98	Pelagius I, 555–60
Symmachus, 498–514	John III, 560–73
Hormisdas, 514–23	Benedict I, 574–78
John I, 523–26	Pelagius II, 578–90
Felix IV, 526–30	Gregory I, 590–604

B. Special Recommendations for Reading

Sketch of the rise of the church and the papacy. No attempt is made in this *Guide* to include the vast literature on the history of the early church and the rise of the papacy to about 500. Adams, *Civilization during the middle ages,* 39–64, 107–36 will serve as a brief review. Hulme, *Middle ages,* 40–75. Thompson, *Economic and social history,* ch. ii. Munro and Sontag, *Middle ages,* ch. ii. Thorndike, *Medieval Europe,* revised edition, chs. vi, ix.

The papacy in the sixth century up to 590. For the papacy in the time of Theodoric see the literature under outline II above. L. Duchesne, *L'église au VIe siècle,* Paris, 1925. H. Grisar, *History of Rome and the popes in the middle ages,* vol. III, London, 1912. The conditions after 555 are described briefly in Dudden, *Gregory the Great,* I, 58–68, 80–98, 158–86.

Short general accounts of the pontificate of Gregory. Lavisse et Rambaud, *Histoire générale,* I, 237–64; *C.M.H.,* II, 235–62. For summaries and tabulations of most of the subjects mentioned in the outline read Flick,

The rise of the medieval church, chs. v, ix, x; or BARRY, *Papal monarchy*, ch. iii. See also CARTER, *The religious life of ancient Rome*, ch. viii, and O. BARDENHEWER, *Patrologie*, Freiburg, 1894; 3rd edition, 1910, translated by T. J. SHAHAN, St. Louis, 1908, § 123. A spirited article on the importance of this pontificate is E. LAVISSE, "L'éntrée en scène de la papauté," *R.D.M.*, 3rd period, LXXVIII (1886), 842–80.

Longer accounts. MANN, *Lives oj the popes*, I, part I, 1–250; MILMAN, *History of Latin Christianity*, II, ch. vii; HODGKIN, *Italy and her invaders*, V, chs. vii–x; MONTALEMBERT, *Monks of the west*, book V; GREGOROVIUS, *Rome in the middle ages*, II, 16–103.

Biographies of Gregory the Great. The standard biography of Gregory is by F. H. DUDDEN, *Gregory the Great: his place in history and in thought*, 2 vols., London, 1905. J. BARMBY, *Gregory the Great*, London, 1892 (The fathers for English readers) called forth a long article by R. W. CHURCH, "The letters of Pope Gregory I," in his *Miscellaneous essays*, New York, 1904, 205–79. H. H. HOWORTH, *St. Gregory the Great*, London, 1912, and P. BATIFFOL, *Saint Grégoire le Grand*, Paris, 1928 [Les saints], are shorter biographies.

Original sources. GREGORY'S *Pastoral rule* and select *Letters* are translated in the *Select library of Nicene and post-Nicene fathers*, 2nd series, XII and XIII. His *Dialogues* can be read in English in E. G. GARDNER, *The Dialogues of St. Gregory*, London, 1911. The biographies of the popes in the *Liber pontificalis* to the pontificate of Gregory, are translated into English by L. R. LOOMIS, *The book of the popes*, see no. **949,** note. See also POOLE, *Papal chancery*, 166–70. Extracts from Gregory's works are translated in ROBINSON, *Readings*, I, 73–82; OGG, *Source Book*, 90–6; WEBSTER, *Historical selections*, 341–87, 453–56; AYER, *Source book*, 590–602.

Maps. SHEPHERD, *Atlas*, 46–7, 94–5.

C. BIBLIOGRAPHY

General books. For general works on the church see nos. **439–54a** in particular and nos. **393–498** in general. Many books on Italy deal with the papacy in some detail, see nos. **599–621,** especially **611.** See also the encyclopaedias for the history of the church and religion, nos. **104–14**, e.g., the article "Gregory the Great," by G. R. HUDLESTON, in **104,** and the periodicals for church history, nos. **176–80d.**

Biographies of Gregory the Great. Probably the oldest life of Gregory was written by an anonymous monk of Whitby, about 713, and is edited by F. A. GASQUET, *A life of Pope St. Gregory, the Great*, Westminster, 1904. G. CAPPELLO, *Gregorio I e il suo pontificato*, Saluzzo, 1905. J. CARDUCCI, *Storia di San Gregorio Magno e del suo tempo*, Rome, 1909. E. CLAUSIER, *St. Grégoire le Grand: pape et docteur de l'église*, Paris, 1886–91. H. GRISAR, *San Gregorio Magno*, Rome, 1904. T. TARDUCCI, *Storia di Gregorio Magno e del suo tempo*, Rome, 1909. W. WISBAUM, *Die wichtigsten Richtungen und Ziele der Thätigkeit des Papstes Gregors des Grossen*, Cologne, 1884. C. WOLFSGRUBER, *Gregor der Grosse*, Saulgau, 1890; 2nd edition, Ratisbon, 1897.

F. and P. BÖHRINGER, *Die Väter des Papsttums: Leo I und Gregor I*, Stuttgart, 1879. T. BONSMANN, *Gregor der Grosse: ein Lebensbild*, Paderborn, 1890.

Gregory before his elevation to the papacy. W. STUHLFATH, *Gregor I, der Grosse: sein Leben bis zu seiner Wahl zum Papste nebst einer Untersuchung der ältesten Viten*, Heidelberg, 1914. C. WOLFSGRUBER, *Die vorpäpstliche Lebensperiode Gregors des Grossen nach seinen Briefen dargestellt*, Vienna, 1886.

Politics of Pope Gregory. E. CASPAR, "Gregor der Grosse" in *Meister des Politik*, Stuttgart, 1923, III, 117ff. E. SPEARING, *The patrimony of the Roman church in the time of Gregory the Great*, Cambridge, 1918. J. DOIZE, *Deux études sur l'administration temporelle du pape Grégoire le Grand*, Paris, 1904. F. NOBILI-VITELLESCHI (POMPONIO LETO), *Della storia civile e politica del papato dall' imperatore Teodosio a Carlomagno*, Bologna, 1902. F. W. KELLETT, *Pope Gregory the Great and his relations with Gaul*, Cambridge, 1888. L. PINGAUD, *La politique de Saint Grégoire le Grand*, Paris, 1872. T. WOLLSCHACK, *Die Verhältnisse Italiens, insbesondere des Langobardenreichs, nach dem Briefwechsel Gregors I*, Horn, 1888. R. BAXMANN, *Die Politik der Päpste von Gregor I bis auf Gregor VII*, 2 vols., Elberfeld, 1868–69. Gregory's relations with the eastern empire are described by BURY, *The later Roman Empire*, II, 145–58. D. E. BENEDETTI, *S. Gregorio Magno e la schiavitù*, Rome, 1904.

Gregorian music. *The Oxford history of music*, edited by W. H. HADOW, 6 vols., Oxford, 1901ff., vol. I. G. MORIN, *Les véritables origines du chant grégorien*, Rome and Tournai, 1904 (à propos du livre de F. A. GEVAERT, *Les origines du chant liturgique de l'église latine*, Ghent, 1890). A. GATARD, *La musique grégorienne: étude descriptive et historique, illustrée de douze planches*, Paris [1913]. C. VIVELL, *Der gregorianische Gesang*, Graz, 1904.

Original sources. For general collections of source material on the papacy see nos. **956–61;** for the church in general, nos. **953–64.** See also H. DELEHAYE, "S. Grégoire le Grand dans l'hagiographie grecque," *Analecta Bollandiana*, XXIII (1904), 440–54.

The most convenient collection of the works of Gregory is in MIGNE, no. **953,** *Series latina*, vols. LXXV–LXXIX, which includes in vol. LXXV the *Vita Gregorii* of JOHN THE DEACON and PAUL THE DEACON. His letters are edited in a more critical edition by P. EWALD and L. M. HARTMANN, *Gregorii I papae registrum epistolarum*, 2 vols., Berlin, 1891–99 (*M.G.H., Epistolae*, I–II). Cf. PEITZ, *Das Register Gregor's I.*

Bibliographies. In addition to the general bibliographies of the church, nos. **49–55,** classified list of books in the *C.M.H.*, II, 743–46.

VI. EXPANSION OF ORTHODOX LATIN CHRISTENDOM FROM ABOUT 590 TO ABOUT 755

A. OUTLINE

1. The importance of the spread of Mohammedanism as a factor determining the direction of expansion.

2. Importance of the missionary work of the Christian church. The

two problems: (1) conversion of the Arians to orthodoxy, (2) conversion of the heathen; the two main factors: (1) the monks, (2) the papacy; the two main centers from which the work was carried on: (1) British Isles, especially Ireland, (2) Rome.

3. Conversion of western Arians to the orthodox faith. Burgundians had been converted about 517. Before 570, the Sueves in Spain had been converted by St. Martin of Braga. Strength of Arianism among the Visigoths in Spain. Conversion of Leovigild's rebel son Hermenegild by his Frankish wife Ingundis in Seville about 580. Conversion of king Reccared in 587 at the beginning of his reign. Orthodox Latin culture represented by Leander, archbishop of Seville, who died in 601, and by Isidore, bishop of Seville, who died in 636. The Arian Lombards in Italy were converted before the end of the seventh century.

4. Conversion of the Franks from heathendom to orthodox Christianity. Baptism of Clovis and 3000 warriors in 496 (see the next outline).

5. Christianity in Ireland. Pre-Patrician Christianity in Ireland. St. Patrick, the "Apostle of the Irish," labored in Ireland 432–61. St. Bridget, the "Mary of Ireland," died 525. Ireland became the "Isle of Saints."

6. Irish missionaries in Scotland. [Legend of St. Ninian (ca. 353–ca. 432), a Briton.] St. Columba occupied the island of Iona in 563. Soon after he went among the northern Picts. Died 597. St. Kentigern (died 612) in Strathclyde. The Culdees.

7. Irish missionaries on the continent. Columban, a monk of Bangor, with twelve companions, went to France about 585. Near the Vosges mountains he founded the monasteries of Luxeuil ("the monastic capital of France"—Montalembert), Anegray, and Fontaines. Banished from the Burgundian kingdom by Brunhild. Went to Switzerland and then to Italy where he was granted land by the Lombard king Agilulf for the foundation of a monastery at Bobbio, and where he died in 615. The rule of Columban contrasted with that of Benedict. St. Gall (died 645) the most famous disciple of Columban, founded the monastery of St. Gall in Switzerland. St. Wandrille and Eustasius, abbot of Luxeuil, were other disciples. Other Irish monks in Germany were Fridolin, Trudbert in the Black Forest, and Kylian, the "Apostle of Franconia."

8. Conversion of the English by monks from Rome. In 596 Pope Gregory sent Augustine with forty monks to England where they landed in 597. Conversion of King Ethelbert of Kent who had married Bertha, a Christian princess from Paris. St. Augustine was consecrated first archbishop of Canterbury. Augustine's methods of spreading the faith among the heathen.

9. Celtic and Roman Christianity in England. Conflict between St. Augustine (died 604) and the British bishops. Aidan (died 651), at the call of king Oswald of Northumbria, came from Iona in 635 and established himself on Lindisfarne (called "Holy Isle" since the eleventh century). St. Cuthbert. Differences between the two churches (date of Easter, tonsure, celibacy, Vulgate, etc.); not settled until the Council of Whitby in

Northumbria in 664. Theodore of Tarsus in Cilicia, archbishop of Canterbury in 668; died in 690. Benedict Biscop founded a monastery at Wearmouth in 674, dedicated to St. Peter, and another at Jarrow in 680, dedicated to St. Paul. Although seven miles apart, these two monasteries were practically one, called the monastery of the Apostles Peter and Paul. Bede (or Baeda), "the Venerable," 673–735, entered Jarrow when seven years of age and spent his whole life there.

10. Early English missionaries on the continent. Wilfrith I (St. Wilfrid), bishop of York from 665–709, among the heathen Frisians. In 690 he was followed by Willibrord (658–ca. 739), a Northumbrian, who was made archbishop of the Frisians (with his seat at Utrecht) at the request of Pepin. The two Hewalds, or Ewalds (Black and White Hewald) among the Saxons.

11. St. Boniface (ca. 680–755), the "Apostle of Germany," the most important English missionary. His name was Winfrith and he was born of noble parents near Crediton about 680. Entered a monastery at Exeter when he was seven years old. About 716 he sailed to Frisia. In 719 Pope Gregory II formally made him missionary to German tribes. Later worked among the Thuringians and Hessians. In 723 he went to Rome and was consecrated "regionary" bishop by Pope Gregory II. Destruction of the sacred oak of Thor at Geismar. In 732 Pope Gregory III made him missionary archbishop and papal legate (in 743 he fixed his see in Mainz). The alliance of Boniface with the see in Rome was of far-reaching importance. Boniface was the friend of Charles Martel and of Pepin, whom he crowned king of the Franks at Soissons in 751. Monastery of Fulda founded 744, its first abbot, Sturm. Boniface resigned his see at Mainz to Lul and met a martyr's death among the wild Frisians in 755. Buried in Fulda. The work of Boniface in Frisia was continued by St. Willehad who went there in 770.

12. Means and methods of spreading the Christian faith.

13. Popes, 604–816.

Sabinianus, 604–06
Boniface III, 607
Boniface IV, 608–15
Deusdedit, 615–18
Boniface V, 619–25
Honorius I, 625–38
Severinus, 638–40
John IV, 640–42
Theodorus I, 642–49
Martin I, 649–54
Eugenius I, 654–57
Vitalianus, 657–72
Adeodatus, 672–76
Donus I, 676–78
Agatho, 678–81
Leo II, 682–83
Benedict II, 684–85
John V, 685–86
Conon, 686–87
Sergius I, 687–701
John VI, 701–05
John VII, 705–07
Sisinnius, 708
Constantine, 708–15
Gregory II, 715–31
Gregory III, 731–41
Zachary, 741–52
Stephen II, 752–57
Paul I, 757–67
Stephen III, 768–72
Hadrian I, 772–95
Leo III, 795–816

B. Special Recommendations for Reading

General accounts. *C.M.H.*, II, ch. xvi. Lavisse et Rambaud, *Histoire générale*, I, 255–64, 285–96 (portions of this are translated in Munro and Sellery, *Medieval civilization*, 114–28, see also 60–86, 129–36). Taylor, *The mediaeval mind*, I, 169–204. Milman, *History of Latin Christianity*, book IV, chs. iii–v. Montalembert, *Monks of the west*, especially book VII. Flick, *Rise of the mediaeval church*, ch. xii. C. H. Robinson, *The conversion of Europe*, London, 1917. Sellery and Krey, *Medieval foundations*, 49–61.

Pope Gregory's missionary labors. Dudden, *Gregory the Great*, II, 99–159.

St. Patrick and the Irish element. The standard biographies are J. B. Bury, *The life of St. Patrick*, London, 1905; and J. Healy, *The life and writings of St. Patrick*, Dublin, 1905. See also F. R. M. Hitchcock, *St. Patrick and his Gallic friends*, London, 1916; and L'abbé Riguet, *Saint Patrice (vers 389–461)*, Paris, 1911 (Les saints). If you heed the hint that H. Zimmer, "Über die Bedeutung des irischen Elements für die mittelalterliche Kultur," *Preussische Jahrbücher*, LIX (1887), 26ff., translated by J. L. Edmonds, *The Irish element in mediaeval culture*, New York, 1891, reprint, London, 1913, tends to paint too bright a picture, the sketch is safe and agreeable reading.

The Christian church in the British Isles. W. Hunt, *The English church (597–1066)*, London, 1901, chs. i–xii, *passim*. W. Bright, *Chapters on early English church history* [to 709], Oxford, 1878; 3rd edition, 1897. A. Plummer, *The churches in Britain before A.D. 1000*, vols. I and II, London, 1911–12 (Library of historical theology, edited by W. C. Piercy). T. A. Tidball, *The making of the Church of England (A.D. 597–1087)*, Boston, 1919. J. C. Wall, *The first Christians of Britain*, London, 1927.

Biographies of Boniface. The best biography in English is G. F. Browne, *Boniface of Crediton*, London, 1910; in French, G. Kurth, *Saint Boniface*, Paris, 1902; 4th edition, 1913 (Les saints).

English monastic life. F. A. Gasquet, *English monastic life*, London, 1904; 3rd edition, 1905, draws an ideal but trustworthy picture of life in a monastery, which applies to all periods of the middle ages; see especially ch. vi.

Original sources. The *Life of St. Columban* by the monk Jonas is translated in *Translations and reprints*, no. **391,** II, no. 7. The most important primary source is Bede, *Historia ecclesiastica gentis Anglorum*, edited by C. Plummer, 2 vols., Oxford, 1896, and translated, with notes, by A. M. Sellar, *Bede's ecclesiastical history of England*, London, 1912 (also translated in Everyman's library). For the conversion of the English, the salient portions of it are extracted in *The mission of St. Augustine to England according to original documents*, edited by A. J. Mason, Cambridge, 1897. See also *Documents illustrative of English church history*, edited by H. Gee and W. J. Hardy, London, 1896. Webster, *Historical selections*, 388–420.

The *English letters of St. Boniface* are edited by E. KYLIE, London, 1911 (King's classics). There is a German translation of his letters by M. TANGL, *Die Briefe des hl. Bonifatius*, in *Die Geschichtschreiber der deutschen Vorzeit*, XCII, Leipzig, 1912. *The life of Saint Boniface by Willibald* in translation by G. W. ROBINSON, Cambridge, 1916 (Harvard translations).

Maps. SHEPHERD, *Atlas*, 46–7, contains a very important map on the "Development of Christianity to 1300"; see also 94–5, 97 and 101 (ground plan of St. Gall in Switzerland).

C. BIBLIOGRAPHY

General books. General histories of the church are listed above, nos. **393–498,** of which no. **461** is especially valuable; periodicals on church history, nos. **176–80,** and encyclopaedias for the history of the church and religion, nos. **104–14.**

Visigothic church. M. E. MAGNIN, *L'église wisigothique au VIIe siècle*, vol. I, Paris, 1912.

Celtic Christianity. L. GOUGAUD, *Les chrêtientês celtiques*, Paris, 1911. H. WILLIAMS, *Christianity in early Britain*, Oxford, 1912. H. ZIMMER, *The Celtic church in Britain and Ireland*, London, 1912, translated by MISS A. MEYER from the *Realencyklopädie für protestantische Theologie*, X (1901), 204–43. MRS. J. R. GREEN, *The old Irish world*, Dublin, 1912. G. F. BROWNE, *The Christian Church in these islands before Augustine*, 2nd edition, London, 1895. G. T. STOKES, *Ireland and the Celtic church*, 2nd edition, London, 1888. J. MACNAUGHT, *The Celtic church and the See of Peter*, London, 1927.

St. Columba. E. A. COOKE, *The Life and work of St. Columba*, London, 1888. V. BRANFORD, *St. Columba: a study of social inheritance and spiritual development*, Edinburgh, 1913. LUCY MENZIES, *Saint Columba of Iona*, London, 1920. W. D. SIMPSON, *The historical Saint Columba*, Aberdeen, 1927.

Irish missionaries on the continent. MARGARET STOKES, *Three months in the forests of France: a pilgrimage in search of vestiges of the Irish saints in France*, London, 1895; *Six months in the Apennines*, London, 1892, an account of her visit to the region where St. Columban died. W. LEVISON, "Die Iren und die fränkische Kirche," *H.Z.*, CIX (1912), 1–22. L. GOUGAUD, "L'oeuvre des Scotti dans l'Europe continentale (fin VIe–fin XIe siècles)," *R.H.E.*, IX (1908), 21–46; 255–77. J. v. PFLUGK-HARTTUNG, "The old Irish on the continent," *Trans. R.H.S.*, new series, V (1891), 75–102 (translated from the German). T. S. HOLMES, *The origin and development of the Christian church in Gaul during the first six centuries of the Christian era*, London, 1911, ch. XVII. HODGKIN, *Italy and her invaders*, VI, book VII, ch. III. J. H. A. EBRARD, *Die iroschottische Missionskirche des 6, 7 und 8 Jahrhunderts*, Gütersloh, 1873; *Bonifatius, der Zerstörer des columbanischen Kirchenthums auf dem Festlande: ein Nachtrag zu dem Werke "Die iroschottische Missionskirche,"* Gütersloh, 1882. E. MARTIN, *Saint Columban*, Paris, 1905. L. DEDIEU, *Colomban, législateur de la vie monastique*, Cahors, 1901

(Diss.). O. SEEBASS, *Über Columba von Luxeuil Klosterregel*, Dresden, 1883 (Diss.). W. WATTENBACH, "Irish monasteries in Germany," *Ulster Journal of Archaeology*, VII (1860), 227ff., 295ff. A. W. HADDON, "Irish missions on the continent," *Remains*, Manchester, 1876, 258ff. "Scottish religious houses abroad," *Edinburgh review*, CXIX, 162. C. R. BEAZELEY, *Dawn of modern geography*, I, ch. v. H. O. TAYLOR, *Mediaeval mind*, I, ch. IX, sec. I; ch. VII. P. LUGANO, *S. Colombana monaco e scrittore*, 542–615, Perugia, 1917 (Extract from *Rivista storica benedettina*). G. B. MAURY, "Saint Columban et la fondation des monastères irlandais en Brie au VIIe siècle," *R.H.*, LXXXIII (1903), 277–99. HELENA CONCANNON, *The life of Saint Columban*, St. Louis, 1916.

St. Augustine and the conversion of the English. *C.M.H.*, II, 515–32. T. S. HOLMES, "The conversion of Wessex," *E.H.R.*, VII (1892), 437f. A. PLUMMER, *The churches in Britain before 1000 A.D.*, 2 vols., London, 1911–12 (Library of historical theology). H. H. HOWORTH, *Saint Augustine of Canterbury*, London, 1913 (Birth of the English church, vol. II). E. L. CUTTS, *St. Augustine of Canterbury*, London, 1895. G. F. BROWNE, *Augustine and his companions*, London, 1895; 2nd edition, 1897, continued by *The conversion of the heptarchy*, London, 1906. F. E. BASSENGE, *Die Sendung Augustins zur Bekehrung der Angelsachsen*, Leipzig, 1890. H. H. HOWORTH, *The golden days of the early English church, from the arrival of Theodore to the death of Bede*, 3 vols., London, 1917. J. T. MILLS, *The great days of Northumbria*, New York, 1911. ELIZABETH W. GRIERSON, *The story of the Northumbrian saints: S. Oswald, S. Aidan, S. Cuthbert*, London, 1913. F. CABROL, *L'Angleterre chrêtienne avant les Normands*, Paris, 1908; 2nd edition, 1909 (bibliography, pp. ix–xxxiii). W. H. HUTTON, *The influence of Christianity upon national character illustrated by the lives and legends of the English saints*, London, 1903.

Boniface and the conversion of Germany. G. SCHNÜRER, *Bonifatius: die Bekehrung der Deutschen zum Christentum*, Mainz, 1909. F. ZEHETBAUER, *Das Kirchenrecht bei Bonifatius dem Apostel der Deutschen*, Vienna, 1910. *Festgabe zum Bonifatius-Jubiläum*, Fulda, 1905, a collection of studies. B. KUHLMANN, *Der heilige Bonifatius, Apostel der Deutschen*, Paderborn, 1895. O. FISCHER, *Bonifatius, der Apostel der Deutschen*, Leipzig, 1881. F. J. v. BUSS, *Winifrid-Bonifacius*, Graz, 1880. A. WERNER, *Bonifacius der Apostel der Deutschen und die Romanisierung von Mitteleuropa*, Leipzig, 1875. P. PFAHLER, *S. Bonifacius und seine Zeit*, Ratisbon, 1880. J. J. LAUX, *Der heilige Bonifatius, Apostel der Deutschen*, Freiburg, 1922. On the friends of Boniface see H. HAHN, *Bonifaz und Lul: ihre angelsächsischen Korrespondenten*, Leipzig, 1883. E. LAVISSE, "La conquête de la Germanie par l'église romaine," *R.D.M.*, 3e période, LXXX (1887), 878. F. W. RETTBERG, *Kirchengeschichte Deutschlands*, vols. I and II, Göttingen, 1846–48; and J. FRIEDRICH, *Kirchengeschichte Deutschlands*, vols. I–II, Bamberg, 1867–69. H. NOTTURP, *Die Bistumserrichtung in Deutschland im VIII. Jahrhundert*, Stuttgart, 1920. A. GRIEVE, *Willibrord*, London, 1923. W. LAMPEN, *Saint Willibrord*, Utrecht, 1916. H. HAHN, *Jahrbücher des fränk. Reichs (741–52)*,

Berlin, 1863, especially Exkursus XIV, XV, XVI, XXVI. A. HAUCK, *Kirchengeschichte Deutschlands*, I, 580ff. W. KÖHLER, "Bonifatius in Hessen," *Zeitschrift für Kirchengeschichte*, XXV (1904), 197–232.

Methods of early missionaries. H. LAU, *Die angelsächsische Missionsweise im Zeitalter des Bonifaz*, Kiel, 1909 (Diss.). W. KONEN, *Die Heidenpredigt in der Germanenbekehrung*, Düsseldorf, 1910 (Diss.). E. KYLIE, "The conditions of the German provinces as illustrating the methods of Boniface," *Journal of theological studies*, London, VII (1905–06), 29ff. W. FLASKAMP, "Die Missionsmethode des hl. Bonifatius," in *Zeitschrift für Missionswissenschaft*, XV (1925), 18–49, 85–100. See also VACANDARD, "L'idolatrie en Gaule," *R.Q.H.*, LXV (1899), 424–54.

Original sources. The main sources are found in such general collections as nos. **953, 963,** and **978,** but for classified lists of them see the bibliographies noted below. *The life of Saint Columba by Adamnan* is edited with a translation by W. REEVES, Edinburgh, 1874; new edition by J. T. FOWLER, Oxford, 1894, and a translation has appeared also in the New universal library published by Dutton. P. H. KÜHL (translator), *Sämmtliche Schriften des hl. Bonifacius*, 2 vols., Ratisbon, 1859. M. TANGL (translator), *Die Briefe des heiligen Bonifatius, nach der Ausgabe in der Monumenta Germaniae historica, in Auswahl übersetzt und erläutert*, Leipzig, 1912. *The calendar of St. Willibrord*, edited by H. A. WILSON, Oxford, 1918 (Henry Bradshaw Society). *The life of Ceolfrid, abbot of the monastery of Wearmouth and Jarrow by an unknown author of the eighth century*, edited and translated by D. S. BOUTFLOWER, London, 1912. T. HÄNLEIN, *Die Bekehrung der Germanen zum Christentum*, I, *Die Bekehrung der Franken und Angelsachsen*, Leipzig, 1914 (Voigländers Quellenbücher, 78).

Bibliographies. For additional books on this subject, both original sources and secondary works, it is sufficient to consult GROSS, no. **36,** especially nos. 1423–71, 1591–1663; DAHLMANN-WAITZ, no. **28,** nos. 4151–4219; and the *C.M.H.*, II, 793–97.

VII. THE RISE OF THE FRANKS TO THE TIME OF CHARLEMAGNE

A. OUTLINE

1. The Franks were destined to succeed in founding a strong, well-nigh universal, state in western Europe. The Teutonic versus the Romanic elements in European civilization.

2. The origin of the Franks and their coming into Roman Gaul. The *Pranci* of Peutinger's chart. Salian and Ripuarian Franks. Salian Franks were in Toxandria about 400. Tournai became the capital. Clodion, the first recorded Frankish king. Merovech (= sea-born; the word "Merovingians" is derived from his name). His son Childeric died 481. The Salian Franks aided Aëtius against the Huns at the so-called battle of Châlons in 451. Ripuarian Franks in the region of Aix-la-Chapelle, Cologne and Bonn. The *Lex Salica*, written down about 510, reflects the primitive civilization of the Franks.

3. Various peoples on the soil which is now France about 500 A.D., Gallo-Romans, Visigoths, Burgundians, Alemans, Salian and Ripuarian Franks, Thuringians, etc.

4. Clovis, king of the Salian Franks from 481 to 511. Defeated Syagrius, the Roman official, at his capital, Soissons, in 486. In 491 he overcame the Thuringians. In 496 he attacked the Alemans in a battle near Strasburg. Clovis married Clotilda, daughter of Chilperic, the king of the Burgundians. Theodoric, king of the Ostrogoths, married Audeflade, the sister of Clovis. Conversion of Clovis to orthodox Christianity, baptized in Rheims on Christmas day, 496. War with the Burgundians under their king Gundobad, 500ff. Renewed wars with the Alemans (505–07), who were rescued by Theodoric the Ostrogoth. Visigoths defeated at Vouglé, near Poitiers, in 507; Alaric II, their king, was slain. Burning of Toulouse. Theodoric again intervened, took Provence for himself and gave Septimania to the Visigoths, thus shutting the Franks off from the Mediterranean. Clovis made Paris his capital where he died in 511 and was buried in the church which afterward became Sainte-Geneviève.

5. The sons of Clovis.

(1) Theodoric (Capital, Rheims) died 534. His son was Theudibert, the best king of the period, who died 548, leaving Theodebald, who died of debauchery in 555.

(2) Clodimir (Capital, Orleans) died 524. His children were murdered by (3) and (4).

(3) Childebert (Capital, Paris) died 558.

(4) Chlotar I (Capital, Soissons). Sole ruler in 558. Burned his rebellious son Chramnus, together with his wife and children, in a hut, and died of remorse in 561.

6. Frankland in the time of the sons of Clovis. Burgundy taken in 534, Provence in 536. Thuringians were crushed. In 542 Childebert marched against Saragossa in Spain (foundation of the monastery of St. Vincent, later St. Germain-des-Près, to house the tunic of St. Vincent which he brought from Spain). But Armorica (= Brittany) and the Basques remained independent, and Septimania remained in the hands of the Visigoths, from whom it passed to the Arabs and was not won by the Franks until the time of king Pepin.

7. Grandsons of Clovis. His son Chlotar I (died 561) left four sons:

(1) Charibert (Capital, Paris) died 567.

(2) Sigebert (Capital, Metz), was the husband of Brunhild (Brunehaut), the daughter of Athanagild, king of the Visigoths. Sigebert assassinated 575, by henchmen of Fredegund.

(3) Chilperic (Capital, Soissons), married Galswintha, sister of Brunhild. When Galswintha was strangled, he married Fredegund, a serving-woman. Chilperic murdered in 584. His son was Chlotar II, sole king, 613–29, and his son Dagobert, sole king, 629–39.

(4) Guntram (Capital, Orleans), tried to hold balance of power between (2) and (3), died 593.

8. Frankland in the time of the grandsons of Clovis. Chilperic (died 584) was a good type of the Merovingian despot. Fierce rivalry between Brunhild (in Austrasia) and Fredegund (in Neustria). Brunhild became regent for her son Childebert (575–96), and later for her grandsons, Theodoric (died 613) and Theodebert. Fredegund died 597. Brutal execution of Brunhild at Lake Neuchâtel in 613. Gregory, bishop of Tours, (ca. 538–94) the historian of this period. His *Historiae Francorum libri X*.

9. Reigns of Chlotar II (613–29) and Dagobert (629–39), sole rulers of Frankland, but even they were obliged to recognize the essential division of Gaul into Neustria, Austrasia, and Burgundy.

10. *Rois fainéants* (Do-nothing kings), 639–751. In this period the Merovingian kings were mere puppets in the hands of the mayors of the palace in the three kingdoms.

11. The mayors of the palace in Austrasia were most important. Arnulf, bishop of Metz, and Pepin, "of Landen," were founders of the office in Austrasia. When Pepin died 640, he was soon succeeded by his son Grimoald (643–56) who tried to oust the Merovingian puppet king and to put his own son Childebert on the throne but did not succeed. About 680 Pepin of Heristal, grandson of Arnulf and Pepin of Landen, became mayor of the palace in Austrasia. In 687 he defeated Berthar, the mayor of Neustria, at Testry, near St. Quentin. This event marked the real beginning of the Carolingian line.

12. Charles Martel, illegitimate son of Pepin, mayor of the palace, 714–41. Defeated the Arabs in the battle of Tours, in 732. In 739 Pope Gregory III appealed to Charles against Liutprand, king of the Lombards, but Charles refused to march against Liutprand who had been his ally against the Arabs.

13. Pepin, first Carolingian king. Charles, who died in 741, divided the kingdom between his sons Carloman and Pepin. In 747 Carloman entered a monastery on Mount Soracte in Italy. In 751 Pope Zachary sanctioned the crowning of Pepin as king of the Franks. In all probability Boniface consecrated him. The last Merovingian puppet, Childeric III, was sent to a monastery. In 752 Pepin got control of Septimania (except Narbonne which fell in 758). In 753 he invaded Saxony and extracted tribute.

14. The alliance of the Franks with the papacy. Lombards were threatening the pope in Rome. The Mohammedan menace in the south. The Eastern emperor failed to protect Italy and the papacy. In 753 Pope Stephen II visited Pepin in Frankland. The "Donation of Constantine." The "Donation of Pepin." The "Roman Question." In 754 or 755 and again in 756 Pepin sent armies against Aistulf, the Lombard. In 756 Desiderius became king of the Lombards and continued to threaten the pope who appealed to Pepin in vain.

15. Last deeds and death of Pepin. Subdued Aquitaine in 768 when Waifar died. Aquitainians were given right to live under their own laws. Pepin himself died in Paris in 768 and was buried in St. Denis.

16. Frankish institutions in the time of the Merovingians.

B. Special Recommendations for Reading

Brief general accounts. Emerton, *Introduction*, chs. vii, x, xii. Bémont and Monod, *Medieval Europe*, chs. v, vi, xii. Adams, *The growth of the French nation*, chs. ii–iv. Hulme, *Middle ages*, ch. xi. Funck-Brentano, *Earliest times*, ch. iv. Munro and Sontag, *Middle ages*, chs. vii–viii. Sellery and Krey, *Medieval foundations*, 62–5. Bryce, *Holy Roman empire*, ch. iv. Adams, *Civilization*, 137–54. Munro and Sellery, *Medieval civilization*, 60–86.

Longer general accounts. The most satisfactory account in English is in *C.M.H.*, I, 292–303, II, 109–58, 575–94. K. Schumacher, *Siedelungs- und Kulturgeschichte des Rheinlands von der Urzeit bis in das Mittelalter*, 3 vols., Mainz, 1921–25. The standard survey in French is in Lavisse, *Histoire de France*, II, part I, 67–279; a similar but shorter account is in Lavisse et Rambaud, *Histoire générale*, I, 114–58, 274–308. See also C. Jullian, *De la Gaule à la France, nos origines historiques*, Paris, 1922.

Detailed accounts in English. Hodgkin, *Italy and her invaders*, VII. Sergeant, *The Franks*, chs. vi–xv. Oman, *The dark ages*, chs. iv, vii, x, xv, xvii, xix. S. Dill, *Roman society in Gaul in the Merovingian age*, London, 1926.

Original sources. Gregory of Tours, *Historiae Francorum libri X* translated into English by O. M. Dalton, *The history of the Franks by Gregory of Tours*, 2 vols., Oxford, 1927. Selections in E. Brehaut, *History of the Franks by Gregory, bishop of Tours*, New York, 1916, in no. **949.** Short extracts are translated in Ogg, *Source book*, 47–59; Robinson, *Readings*, I, 51–55; and Thatcher and McNeal, *Source book*, 26–37. The "Donation of Constantine" is translated in C. B. Coleman, *The treatise of Lorenzo Valla on the Donation of Constantine*, New Haven, 1922, and in Henderson, *Select documents*, 319–29; and the Salic law, *ibid.*, 176–89.

Maps. Shepherd, *Atlas*, 53, and especially Longnon, *Atlas historique de la France*, plates II–IV. Peutinger's chart is edited by K. Miller, *Tabula Peutingeriana: die Weltkarte des Castorius, genannt die Peutingerische Tafel*, Ravensburg, 1888.

C. Bibliography

General books. General histories of France, Belgium, and the Netherlands, nos. **508–59,** and of Germany, nos. **560–98,** are almost equally valuable for this early history of the soil of modern France. Many books listed under outline II above are valuable for this subject.

General accounts. M. Prou, *La Gaule mérovingienne*, Paris, 1897. G. Richter, *Annalen des fränkischen Reiches im Zeitalter der Merovinger*, Halle, 1873. O. Gutsche and W. Schultze, *Deutsche Geschichte von der Urzeit bis zu den Karolingern*, 2 vols., Stuttgart, 1894–96. G. Kaufmann, *Deutsche Geschichte bis auf Karl den Grossen*, 2 vols., Leipzig, 1880–81. J. Schmaus, *Geschichte und Herkunft der alten Franken*, Bamberg, 1912. G. Kurth, *Etudes franques*, 2 vols., Paris, 1919.

Clovis. The best biography is G. KURTH, *Clovis*, Tours, 1896; 3rd ed., 2 vols., Brussels, 1923. H. VON SCHUBERT, *Staat und Kirche in den arianischen Königreichen und im Reiche Chlodwigs*, Munich and Berlin, 1912 (Historische Bibliotek, 26). A. LECOY DE LA MARCHE, *La fondation de la France du 4e au 6e siècle*, Lille, 1893. C. PFISTER, "Le baptême de Clovis," *Revue hebdomadaire*, October 21, 1916.

Dagobert. J. H. ALBERS, *König Dagobert in Geschichte, Legende und Sage*, Worms, 1884.

Mayors of the Palace. G. EITEN, *Das Unterkönigtum im Reiche der Merovinger und Karolinger*, Heidelberg, 1907 (in Heidelberger Abhandlungen zur mittleren und neueren Geschichte, 18). E. HERRMANN, *Das Hausmeieramt, ein echt germanisches Amt*, Breslau, 1880. H. VON SYBEL, *Die Entstehung des deutschen Königthums*, 3rd edition, Frankfurt, 1884. H. E. BONNEL, *Die Anfänge des karolingischen Hauses*, Berlin, 1866. P. A. F. GERARD, *Histoire des Francs d'Austrasie*, 2 vols., Brussels, 1864. G. H. PERTZ, *Geschichte der merovingischen Hausmeier*, Hanover, 1819.

Charles Martel. J. VAN DEN GHEYN, *Histoire de Charles Martel*, Paris, 1910. T. BREYSIG, *Jahrbücher des fränkischen Reichs, 714–41*, Leipzig, 1869, part of **570.**

Pepin. H. HAHN, *Jahrbücher*. L. OELSNER, *Jahrbücher des fränkischen Reichs unter König Pippin*, Leipzig, 1871. Part of no. **570.**

Church and state to the time of Charlemagne. A very authoritative study on the relations between church and state in the time of Pepin is E. CASPAR, *Pippin und die römische Kirche: kritische Untersuchungen zum fränkish-päpstlichen Bunde im 8 Jahrhundert*, Berlin, 1914. T. SOMMERLAD, *Die wirtschaftliche Tätigkeit der Kirche in Deutschland*, II, ch. 2. A. CRIVELLUCCI, *Storia delle relazioni tra lo stato e la chiesa*, vols. I–III (to Hadrian I, 772–95) and Appendix to vol. I, Bologna, 1886, Leghorn, 1888, Pisa, 1909. F. NOBILI-VITELLESCHI (POMPONIO LETO), *Della storia civile e politica del papato*, 3 vols., Bologna, 1900–06, extends to the renaissance; vol. II on Charlemagne. L. ARMBRUST, *Die Territorialpolitik der Päpste, 500–800*, Göttingen, 1885. J. FEHR, *Staat und Kirche im fränkischen Reiche bis auf Karl den Grossen*, Vienna, 1869. H. v. SCHUBERT, *Staat und Kirche von Constantin bis Karl den Grossen*, Kiel, 1906.

Donation of Constantine. C. B. COLEMAN, *Constantine the Great and Christianity: three phases: the historical, the legendary, and the spurious*, New York, 1914 (Columbia University Studies), 175–242, also 99–172 for the legend of Constantine, 217–42 contain the texts which are essential, and 243–54 a comprehensive bibliography. This should be supplemented by his edition of *The treatise of Lorenzo Valla on the Donation of Constantine* noted in B above. See also the bibliography of the most important critical studies in *C.M.H.*, II, 805, and G. LAEHR, *Die Konstantinische Schenkung in der abendländischen Literatur des Mittelalters bis zur Mitte des XIV Jahrhunderts*, Berlin, 1926.

Constitutional history. By far the most important books are those by N. D. FUSTEL DE COULANGES, *Histoire des institutions politiques de l'ancienne*

France, 6 vols., Paris, 1888–91; re-edited, revised, and completed from the author's notes by C. JULLIAN: I, *La Gaule romaine*, 4th edition, 1914; II, *L'invasion germanique et la fin de l'empire*, 3rd edition, 1911; III, *La monarchie franque*, 3rd edition, 1905; IV, *L'alleu et le domaine rural pendant l'époque mérovingienne*, 1914; V, *Les origines du système féodal: le bénéfice et le patronat pendant l'époque mérovingienne*, 4th edition, 1914; VI, *Les transformations de la royauté pendant l'époque carolingienne*, 3rd edition, 1914. See also his *Recherches sur quelques problèmes d'histoire*, Paris, 1885; 2nd edition, 1894, and *Nouvelles recherches*, published by C. JULLIAN, Paris, 1891. JULLIAN, *Histoire de la Gaule*. E. LESNE, *La propriété ecclésiastique en France aux époques romaine et mérovingienne*, Paris, 1910. J. TARDIF, *Etudes sur les institutions politiques et administratives de la France: époque mérovingienne*, Paris, 1881. S. HOFBAUER. *Die Ausbildung der grossen Grundherrschaften im Reiche der Merowinger*, Vienna, 1927. See also the general books on German, nos. **578–87,** and French constitutional history, nos. **527–36.**

Faith, morals, and learning of the Franks. See outline VI in part III.

Miscellaneous. J. HAVET, *Questions mérovingiennes*, in *Oeuvres complètes* vol. I, Paris, 1896. J. DEPOIN, "Questions mérovingiennes et carolingiennes," *Revue des études historiques* (1904); also "Etudes mérovingiennes," *ibid.* (1909). E. A. FREEMAN, *Western Europe in the eighth century and onward: an aftermath*, London, 1904. G. LAFONT, *Les origines de la nationalité française: essais sur les Celtes, les Kymris, les Gaulois, les Francs, et les Ibères*, Tours, 1901. G. REVERDY, *Les relations de Childebert II et de Byzance*, Paris, 1913 [*R.H.*, CXIV (1913), 61–86]. K. PLATH, *Die Königspfalzen der Merovinger und Karolinger*, Leipzig, 1892. G. ROLOFF, "Die Umwandlung des fränkischen Heeres von Chlodwig bis Karl den Grossen," *Neue Jahrbücher für das klassische Altertum*, IX (1902). C. PFISTER, *Le duché mérovingien d'Alsace et la légende de sainte Odile*, Paris, 1892. G. DE MAREZ, *Le problème de la colonisation franque et du régime agraire en Belgique*, Brussels, 1926. H. PIRENNE, "Un contraste économique: mérovingiens et carolingiens," *Revue belge de philologie et d'histoire*, II (1923), 223–35.

Original sources. Most of the sources for this period are edited in *M.G.H.*, no. **978,** and in BOUQUET, no. **967.** The best edition of the *Historiae Francorum libri X* of GREGORY OF TOURS is in vols. II and XVI of no. **968,** Paris, 1886–93; new edition by R. POUPARDIN, 1 vol., Paris, 1913. The chroniclers are described by G. MASSON, *Early chroniclers of Europe: France*, and by W. WATTENBACH, *Deutschlands Geschichtsquellen.* The Merovingian charters are edited and described by P. LAUER and C. SAMARAN, *Les diplômes originaux des Mérovingiens, fac-similes phototypiques, avec notices et transcriptions*, with a preface by M. PROU, 2 fasc., Paris, 1908; and *Les diplômes mérovingiens des Archives nationales*, Paris, 1915.

Bibliographies. DAHLMANN-WAITZ, book II, *passim;* and *C.M.H.*, I, 657; II, 728–32, 801–08, especially the excellent portions on pp. 801–08 drawn up by G. L. BURR. See also the important bibliographies in THOMPSON, *Economic and social history*, 821–23, and the footnotes of LAVISSE,

Histoire de France, II, part I. Besides, all the bibliographies for France and Germany, nos. **21–34**, especially MOLINIER, no. **21**, for Belgium, no. **45**, and for the church, nos. **49–55**, are serviceable.

VIII. CHARLEMAGNE

A. OUTLINE

1. The importance of the idea of universal empire in medieval thought.

2. Charlemagne's personality. Einhard's *Vita Caroli magni*.

3. Fairly abundant sources of information for the reign of Charlemagne. Famous annals. Capitularies. *Monumenta Germaniae historica*, no. **978.**

4. Charlemagne's accession. Pepin divided his kingdom between his two sons, Charles (the elder, born ca. 742) and Carloman. Bertrada, their mother, tried to keep them at peace. She married Charles to a daughter of Desiderius in spite of the violent protests of pope Stephen III, but the union was broken within a year. Carloman died in 771 and Charles made himself sole ruler.

5. Completion of the military work of his predecessors; the farthest extension of Frankland. (1) Major conquests: (*a*) The overthrow of the Lombard kingdom in Italy. Desiderius threatened pope Hadrian I who appealed to Charles. Desiderius was captured by Charles in Pavia in 774. Charles made his second son, Pepin, king of Italy. (*b*) Saxon wars lasted over thirty years. The Saxon hero Widukind. Execution of about 4500 Saxons in one day at Verden on the Aller in 782. The Capitulary concerning Saxony. (2) Frontier wars: (*a*) In Spain, 778–811. Roncesvalles. Roland. The Spanish March. Balearic Islands a Frankish protectorate in 799. (*b*) In Bavaria against Duke Tassilo. (*c*) With the Danish king Godfred who sent a fleet in 810 hoping to attack Aix-la-Chapelle. (*d*) With the Slavs to the east, especially the Wiltzi and Sorbs. (*e*) With the Avars. The "rings" of the Avars. They were defeated and dispersed in 795 and 796 by Charles and his son Pepin.

6. Relations of Charles with the papacy before 800. His visit to Rome in 774 to see pope Hadrian I. The famous scene in St. Peter's when Charles confirmed the "Donation of Pepin." The "Roman Question." The beginnings of the Papal States. Precarious position of the pope in Rome, especially of Leo III (795–816).

7. Relations of Charles with the Byzantine empire. Intrigues of the Byzantine empire in Benevento with the dispossessed Lombards in Italy, against Charles. Echoes of the iconoclastic controversy. In 780 the empress Irene had her young son Constantine VI betrothed to Rotrud, a daughter of Charlemagne, but the engagement was broken. In 797 Constantine was blinded by Irene and died. Irene declared herself empress.

8. Revival of the empire in the west in 800. World politics in the year 800: Irene in Constantinople, pope Leo III in Rome, Haroun-al-Raschid in Bagdad. Charles was crowned emperor of the Romans by pope Leo III

in St. Peter's, Rome, on Christmas day, 800. Foundations of, and theories about, the revival of the empire. The nature of the empire in the time of Charlemagne.

9. Imperial government of Charlemagne. The general assemblies. The capitularies. Charlemagne's court (*palatium*) whose members were called palatines (*ministri* and *ministeriales*). Local government—dukes, counts, *missi dominici*. Central and local courts (*scabini*). His army (the group system of military service). Primitive financial system.

10. Carolingian learning and art. The palace school. Charlemagne's interest in learning. His edict concerning monastic and cathedral schools. Charlemagne imported scholars, Alcuin, Paul the Deacon, Paul of Pisa. The reform in writing, the "Caroline minuscule." New interest in architecture and literature, especially history writing.

11. The succession to Charlemagne. The partition of 806 between his three sons, Charles, Louis, and Pepin. Pepin died in 810 and Charles in 811, leaving Louis sole successor of Charlemagne. Charlemagne died in Aix-la-Chapelle, in 814, at the age of about 72 years. He was buried there in an ancient sarcophagus which may still be seen.

12. The legend of Charlemagne.

B. Special Recommendations for Reading

Brief general accounts. Emerton, *Introduction*, chs. xiii-xiv. Kitchin, *History of France*, I, 118–53. Dunn-Pattison, *Leading figures*, 15–38. Hulme, *Middle ages*, ch. xii. Funck-Brentano, *Earliest times*, ch. v. Sellery and Krey, *Medieval foundations*, 65–76. Munro and Sontag, *Middle ages*, ch. x. Thompson, *Economic and social history*, ch. viii. A comparatively brief account of great excellence is in *Handbuch der deutschen Geschichte*, edited by Gebhardt, I, chs. vi-vii.

Longer general accounts. A scholarly summary of the period in English is *C.M.H.*, II, chs. xviii, xix, xxi, xxii; which is better than Oman, *The dark ages*, chs. xx, xxi, xxii; or Sergeant, *The Franks*, chs. xvi–xx. The standard general accounts in French are Lavisse, *Histoire de France*, II, part I, 280–357; and a shorter survey in Lavisse et Rambaud, *Histoire générale*, I, ch. vii. A survey of the times of Charlemagne from the standpoint of Italy and the Byzantine empire is in Hodgkin, *Italy and her invaders*, VIII (see also VII, chs. xiii–xiv); a similar account, but shorter, Villari, *The barbarian invasions of Italy*, II, book IV. Gregorovius, *Rome in the middle ages*, II, 462–512; III, 1–21. Gibbon, *Decline and fall*, ch. xlix. C. L. Wells, *The age of Charlemagne*, New York, 1898 (Ten epochs of church history).

Revival of the empire. Bryce, *Holy Roman empire*, chs. iv, v. Fisher, *Mediaeval empire*, I, ch. i.

Biographies of Charlemagne. T. Hodgkin, *Charles the Great*, London, 1897 (Foreign statesmen). H. W. C. Davis, *Charlemagne (Charles the Great): the hero of two nations*, London and New York, 1899 (Heroes of the nations).

J. I. MOMBERT, *A history of Charles the Great*, New York, 1888. F. KAMPERS, *Karl der Grosse*, Mainz, 1910, popular sketch with excellent pictures.

Original sources. The best introduction to the study of Charlemagne is the biography by his friend EINHARD (sometimes spelled EGINHARD), translated by S. E. TURNER, *Life of Charlemagne by Eginhard*, New York, 1880; and by A. J. GRANT, *Early lives of Charlemagne*, London, 1907. DUNCALF and KREY, *Parallel source problems*, 3–26, translated contemporary accounts of the coronation of Charlemagne in 800. See also *Translations and reprints*, VI, no. 5, "Laws of Charles the Great," and III, no. 2, for the capitulary "De villis." All the source books listed above, nos. **379–92**, give considerable space to the time of Charlemagne.

Maps. SHEPHERD, *Atlas*, 54, 55; and especially, LONGNON, *Atlas historique de la France*, plates v, and vii–x.

C. BIBLIOGRAPHY

General books. A large number of general books touch upon the history of Charlemagne, chief among them are those on France, Belgium, the Netherlands, Germany and Italy, nos. **508–621.** See also those on the church, nos. **393–498,** and especially those on the medieval empire in the west, nos. **499–507.**

General surveys. E. MÜHLBACHER, *Deutsche Geschichte unter den Karolingern*, Stuttgart, 1896. S. ABEL and B. v. SIMSON, *Jahrbücher des fränkischen Reichs unter Karl dem Grossen*, vol. I, 2nd edition, Leipzig, 1888, vol. II, Leipzig, 1883, part of no. **570.** G. RICHTER and H. KOHL, *Annalen des fränkischen Reichs in Zeitalter der Karolinger*, 2 vols., Halle, 1885–87, part of no. **571.** F. DAHN, *Die Könige der Germanen*, vol. VIII. W. STUBBS, *Germany in the early middle ages 476–1250*, chs. ii–iii.

The Empire of Charlemagne. A. KLEINCLAUSZ, *L'empire carolingien: ses origines et ses transformations*, Paris, 1902. W. OHR, *Der karolingische Gottesstaat in Theorie und Praxis*, Leipzig, 1902. W. OHR, *Die Kaiserkronung Karls des Grossen*, Tübingen, 1904. E. LAVISSE, "La fondation du Saint Empire," *R.D.M.*, LXXXVII (1888), 357–92. L. HIMMELREICH, *Papst Leo III und die Kaiserkrönung Karls des Grossen im Jahre 800*, Munich, 1919.

Charlemagne's relations with the church and the papacy, H. LILIENFEIN, *Die Anschauungen von Staat und Kirche im Reich der Karolinger*, Heidelberg, 1902 (Heidelberger Abh., 1). J. DE LA SERVIÈRE, *Charlemagne et l'église*, Paris, 1904. J. A. KETTERER, *Karl der Grosse und die Kirche*, Munich and Berlin, 1898. B. MALFATTI, *Imperatori e papi ai tempi della signoria dei Franchi in Italia*, 2 vols., Milan, 1876. L. M. HARTMANN, *Geschichte Italiens im Mittelalter*, vols. II–III. R. BAXMANN, *Die Politik der Päpste von Gregor I bis auf Gregor VII.* See also the bibliography of the previous outline under "Relations between the church and state to the time of Charlemagne."

Donations to the papacy. The "Roman Question." Beginnings of the Papal States. For comprehensive bibliographies see *C.M.H.*, II, 805–06, and DAHLMANN-WAITZ, *Quellenkunde*, no. 4372. The following will serve as an introduction: L. DUCHESNE, *Les premiers temps de l'état pontifical*, Paris, 1898; 2nd edition, 1904, translated by A. H. MATHEW, *The beginnings of the temporal sovereignty of the popes, 754–1073*, London, 1908. A. CRIVELLUCCI, *Le origini dello stato della chiesa: storia documentata*, Pisa, 1909. G. SCHNÜRER, *Die Entstehung des Kirchenstaates*, Cologne, 1894. W. GUNDLACH, *Die Entstehung des Kirchenstaates und der kuriale Begriff der "respublica Romanorum,"* Breslau, 1899 (Heft 59 of Gierke's Untersuchungen). P. PINTON, *Le donazioni barbariche ai papi*, Rome, 1890. H. C. LEA, "Rise of the temporal power," in *Studies in church history*. J. HALLER, "Die Karolinger und das Papsttum," *H.Z.*, CVIII (1911), 38–76.

Relations with the Eastern Empire. J. B. BURY, *Later Roman empire, 395–800*, especially II, book VI, ch. XI; and *A history of the eastern Roman empire (802–67)*, ch. X. L. BRÉHIER, *La querelle des images*, Paris, 1904. A. GASQUET, *Etudes byzantines: l'empire byzantin et la monarchie franque*, Paris, 1888. O. HARNACK, *Das karolingische und das byzantinische Reich in ihren politischen Beziehungen*, Göttingen, 1880. R. L. POOLE, "The seal and monogram of Charles the Great," in *E.H.R.*, XXXIV (1919), 198–200.

Charlemagne. B. HAURÉAU, *Charlemagne et sa cour, 742–814*, Paris, 1888. H. MARTIN, *Charlemagne et l'empire carlovingien*, Paris, 1893. H. BROSIEN, *Karl der Grosse*, Leipzig, 1885. A. VÉTAULT, *Charlemagne*, with an introduction by LÉON GAUTIER, 4th edition, Tours, 1908. P. MACHERL, *Karl der Grosse: ein Lebensbild*, Graz, 1912. P. CLEMEN, *Die Portraitdarstellungen Karls des Grossen*, part I, Aachen, 1889. C. PFISTER, *Le personage et l'oeuvre de Charlemagne*, Metz, 1914. A. HUYSKENS, *Karl der Grosse und seine Lieblingspfalz Aachen*, Aachen, 1914.

Administration. N. D. FUSTEL DE COULANGES, *Les transformations de la royauté pendant l'époque carolingienne*, Paris, 1892; 3rd edition, 1914 (this is vol. II of his *Histoire*). G. WAITZ, *Deutsche Verfassungsgeschichte*, vols. III–IV. E. SEYFARTH, *Fränkische Reichsversammlungen unter Karl d. Grossen und Ludwig d. Frommen*, Leipzig, 1910. G. SEELIGER, *Die Kapitularien der Karolinger*, Munich, 1893. H. BRUNNER, *Die Entstehung der Schwurgerichte*, Berlin, 1872, proves the Frankish origin of the jury. T. QUOIDBACH, *Esquisse du régime politique de la nation franque sous Charlemagne*, Louvain, 1914 (extract from *l'Annuaire de l'Université catholique de Louvain.*). G. BAIST, "Zur Interpretation der Brevium exempla und des Capitulare de villis," *Vierteljahrschrift für Sozial- und Wirtschaftsgeschichte*, XII (1914). See also the general constitutional histories of France, nos. **527–36**, and of Germany, nos. **578–87**.

Economic conditions. THOMPSON, *Economic and social history*, ch. VIII. A. DOPSCH, *Die Wirtschaftsentwickelung der Karolingerzeit, vornehmlich in Deutschland*, 2 vols., Weimar, 1912–13; 2nd edition, 1921–22. This is supplemented by P. SANDER, *Über die Wirtschaftsentwicklung der Karolingerzeit*, in SCHMOLLER'S *Jahrbuch für Gesetzgebung*, XXXVII (1913), 1. S. LOISEL, *Essai sur la législation économique des Carolingiens d'après les capitulaires*, Caen, 1904 (Diss.). K. T. v. INAMA-STERNEGG, *Deutsche Wirtschaftsgeschichte*, I, *Bis zum Schluss der Karolingerperiode*, 2nd edition, Leipzig, 1909.

A. Dopsch, *Wirtschaftliche und soziale Grundlagen der europäischen Kulturentwicklung aus der Zeit von Cäsar bis auf Karl den Grossen*, Vienna, 1918, part 2, 1920. K. Voigt, *Die karolingische Klosterpolitik und der Niedergang des westfränkischen Königtums*, Stuttgart, 1917. C. Barrière-Flavy, *Les arts industriels des peuples barbares de la Gaule du VIe au VIIIe siècle*, 3 vols., Paris, 1901.

Legend of Charlemagne. A. Kleinclausz, *L'empire carolingien*, 491ff. T. Bulfinch, *Mythology . . . legends of Charlemagne*, revised and enlarged edition, New York, 1913. A. J. Church, *Stories of Charlemagne and the twelve peers of France, from the old romances*, New York, 1902. The *Song of Roland* is translated by O'Hagen, 2nd edition, London, 1883; by Isabel Butler, Boston, 1904; by L. Bacon, New Haven, 1919; and by C. K. Scott-Moncrieff, New York, 1920. G. Rauschen, *Die Legende Karl des Grossen im 11 und 12 Jahrhundert*, Leipzig, 1890. E. Müntz, *La légende de Charlemagne dans l'art du moyen-âge*, Paris, 1885 (reprint from *Romania*, XIV (1885), 321–42). Jesse Weston, *The romance cycle of Charlemagne and his peers*, 2nd edition, London, 1905. Anna J. Cooper, *Le pêlerinage de Charlemagne*, Paris, 1925. H. Hoffmann, *Karl der Grosse im Bilde der Geschichtschreibung des frühen Mittelalters*, Berlin, 1919.

Carolingian learning and art. See outline VIII of part III.

Original sources. Almost everything of prime importance is edited in *M.G.H.*, no. **978**, see also Bouquet, no. **967**. The archive material for the whole Carolingian period is available in the edition of *Die Regesten des Kaisserreichs unter den Karolingern, 751–918*, edited by E. Mühlbacher, 2nd edition, completed by J. Lechner, Innsbruck, 1908, which is a recast of part I of Böhmer, *Regesta imperii*, no. **985**. A convenient source book for the origin of the papal states is, *Die Quellen zur Geschichte der Entstehung des Kirchenstaates*, edited by J. Haller, Leipzig and Berlin, 1907. The Latin text of the *Life of Charlemagne* by Einhard is edited by H. W. Garrod and R. B. Mowat, with introduction and notes, Oxford University Press, 1915; by O. Holder-Egger, in *M.G.H.*, and published separately, 6th edition, Hanover and Leipzig, 1911, part of no. **979**; by L. Halphen (with translation into French), *Eginhard, Vie de Charlemagne* (Classiques de l'histoire de France au moyen âge), Paris, 1923. See G. Monod, *Etudes critiques sur les sources de l'histoire carolingienne*, Paris, 1898, vol. CXIX of no. **888**; G. Masson, *Early chronicles of Europe: France*. L. Halphen, *Etudes critiques sur l'histoire de Charlemagne*, Paris, 1921, and F. Kurze, *Die karolingischen Annalen bis zum Tode Einhards*, Berlin, 1913 (Prog.).

Bibliographies. The best general bibliography is Dahlmann-Waitz, *Quellenkunde*, 289–324. For administration and economic condition Thompson, *Economic and social history*, ch. viii, bibliography, especially pp. 821–23. For the relations with the church see especially the *C.M.H.*, II, 814–17 (see also 801–09, 813 for general bibliographies). The bibliographies in the footnotes of Lavisse, *Histoire de France*, II, part I are of great value. The sources are best described in Molinier, *Les sources de l'histoire de France*,

I, 181–227. Almost all the general bibliographies for France, Germany, and Italy, nos. **21–41**, and those for the church, nos. **49–55**, are useful.

IX. FOES OF WESTERN CHRISTENDOM, FROM THE EIGHTH TO THE ELEVENTH CENTURY. FROM THE SOUTH. MUSLIMS

A. Outline

1. Recent progress made in the historical study of Islam. Contrast with the interesting chapters on the subject in Gibbon, *Decline and fall of the Roman empire.* In this outline no attempt is made to treat in detail the rise and spread of Islam in the east. The subject is treated from the standpoint of the Latin west.

2. The rise and spread of Islam in Arabia. The physical and political geography of the peninsula before 600 A.D. The civilization, and especially the religion, of the Arabs before that date. The Kaaba in Mecca. Muhammad (often also spelled Mahomet or Mohammed), 570–632. The Emigration (Hegira) in 622 from Mecca to Medina, which is the beginning of the Muslim era. Military exploits of Muhammad. The fall of Mecca in 630. The *Qur'ân.*

3. Meaning of the terms: Muslims (or Moslems), Sabians, Islam, Moors, Saracens.

4. The spread of Islam in the east after the death of the prophet in 632. The successors of Muhammad, soon called Caliphs (successors [to the prophet]), Abu Bekr, 632–34; Omar, 634–44; Othman, 644–55; Ali, 655–61. Conquest of Arabia, war of the apostates. Conquest of Syria, fall of Damascus in 634, the terrible defeat of the Byzantines on the Yarmuk in 636, fall of Jerusalem in 638. Conquest of Persia by 652. Conquest of Egypt, evacuation of Alexandria, 642.

5. Attacks upon Constantinople. Muslims took Chalcedon in 668 and from thence threatened the capital. Sea-fights, ca. 674–80. Great siege of Constantinople, 716–17.

6. Later history of Islam in the east. Divisions between Sunnites and Shi'ites. Omayyads with capital at Damascus in 661–750. Abbassides with capital at Bagdad, 750–1258. Ultimate division into three caliphates, with capitals at Bagdad, Cairo, and Cordova.

7. Conquest of northern Africa west of Egypt. Occupation of Barka, in the Pentapolis, in 642. The importance of the conversion of the Berbers to Islam. Weak hold of the Byzantine government in northern Africa. Foundation of Kairawan in 670. Conquest of Carthage in 697. Supremacy of the Muslim fleet in the Mediterranean. Disappearance of Latin civilization in northern Africa about 700.

8. Conquest of Spain. Weakness of the Visigothic state in Spain. Legend of the overtures made to the Muslims by count Julian (Urban) to avenge himself on the last Visigothic king, Roderic. Landing of Tarik near Gibraltar

(= Gebel Tarik, the Mount Tarik), in 711. Easy conquest of Spain. Fall of Cordova and Toledo. Jealousy of Tarik's superior, Musa, who came over and subdued Seville.

9. Invasion of Gaul. Hurr crossed the Pyrenees in 717 or 718. Narbonne occupied in 720. Defense of Toulouse by duke Eudo of Aquitaine. Internal dissensions among the Muslims due largely to quarrels between Arabs and Berbers. Their defeat by Charles Martel in the battle of Tours or Poitiers in 732. In 759 they gave up Narbonne to Pepin and disappeared behind the Pyrenees. Charlemagne's invasion of northern Spain and the establishment of the Spanish march.

10. Occupation of Sicily. Sporadic attacks on the Byzantines in Sicily as early as 664. Derivation of the word corsair from *κοῦρσον*, a summer campaign. Renewed raids upon many islands of the Mediterranean towards the end of the reign of Charlemagne. Crete occupied in 826. Conquest of Sicily by the Aghlabids from Kairawan, 827–902. (For the reconquest of Sicily by the Normans in 1061, see outline XX.)

11. Invasion of Italy. Appeal of duke Andrea of Naples to the Saracens in Sicily against duke Sikard of Benevento in 837. Saracens conquered Bari about 841. Attack on Rome in 846. Naval battle off Ostia in 849. Ineffective assistance given by the Carolingians. Co-operation with the Byzantines. Pillage and destruction of Monte Cassino. Final expulsion of the Saracens from Italy about 915. The "Saracen towers" near Naples.

12. Peaceful relations between Muslims and Christians in the west. Muslim civilization in the ninth and tenth centuries especially in Spain and Sicily. Lasting effects on the culture of western Christendom. (See outline X of part III.)

13. In the eleventh century Latin Christians took the offensive against the Muslims from Spain to Palestine.

B. Special Recommendations for Reading

General surveys. The best general survey is now in *C.M.H.*, II, chs. x–xii. Another good account is in Lavisse et Rambaud, *Histoire générale*, I, chs. ix, xv. Bémont and Monod, *Medieval Europe*, chs. x-xi, is a more elementary sketch. Gibbon, *Decline and fall*, chs. l-li, although out of date in many respects, will always remain interesting reading. Thorndike, *Medieval Europe*, ch. x; Davis, *Short history of the near east*, 100–66; Hulme, *Middle ages*, 214–36, 439–54; Sellery and Krey, *Medieval foundations*, 38–46; Thompson, *Economic and social history*, chs. vii and xv. Munro and Sontag, *Middle ages*, chs. ix and xix. See also the articles "Mahomet" (by Margoliouth), "Mahommedan Institutions," "Mahommedan Law," "Mahommedan Religion," "Caliphate," and "Berbers," in the *Ency. Brit.*, XI, XII and XIII editions.

Muhammad. The best biography is W. Muir, *The Life of Mohammed from original sources*, London, 1861, 3 vols.; 3rd edition, 1894, abridged to 1 vol.; a new and revised edition by T. H. Weir, Edinburgh, 1912. D. S. Margoliouth, *Mohammed and the rise of Islam*, New York and London,

1905 (Heroes of the nations) is very good. G. M. DRAYCOTT, *Mahomet: founder of Islam*, New York, 1916. H. GRIMME, *Mohammed, die weltgeschichtliche Bedeutung Arabiens*, Mainz, 1904 (Weltgeschichte in Charakterbildern), is particularly valuable for its pictures.

Moors in Spain. MERRIMAN, *Spanish empire*, I, introduction. *C.M.H.*, III, ch. XVI. U. R. BURKE, *History of Spain*, I, chs. XII, XIV, XVI. R. ALTAMIRA, *Historia de España* (1913 edition), I, 224–300. S. LANE-POOLE, *Moors in Spain*, New York, 1903 (Story of the nations). See the pages from DOZY on "Moslem civilization in Spain," in MUNRO and SELLERY, *Medieval civilization*, 224–39. HELMOLT, *History of the world*, IV, 494–510. HUME, *The Spanish people*, 71–111. A. G. PALENCIA, *Historia de la España musulmana; Historia de la literatura arábigo-española*, Barcelona, 1925, 1928 (in Colección Labor).

Saracens and the Byzantine empire. J. B. BURY, *Later Roman empire*, II, 258–73, 401–07; and, *A history of the eastern Roman empire (802–867)*, ch. VIII.

Saracens in Sicily, Italy, and Crete. J. B. BURY, *A history of eastern Roman empire (802–67)*, ch. IX. R. LANCIANI, *Destruction of ancient Rome*, New York, 1899, ch. XI. GREGOROVIUS, *History of the city of Rome*, III, 65–8, 87–100, 178–87, 259–70. E. W. BROOKS, "The Arab occupation of Crete," *E.H.R.*, XXVIII (1913), 431–43.

Maps. SHEPHERD, *Atlas*, 53, 54–5, 58–9, 64, 66–7. *C.M.H.*, II, maps 23, 24. K. SPRUNER-MENKE, *Hand-atlas für die Geschichte des Mittelalters und der neueren Zeit*, 3rd edition, edited by TH. MENKE, Gotha, 1880.

C. BIBLIOGRAPHY

General books. For an encyclopaedia and a dictionary of Islam see no. **120.** Many of the general books on Spain and Portugal, nos. **622–42,** Italy, nos. **599–621,** and the Byzantine empire, nos. **643–79,** give much space to the Muslims. See also the general histories of the Mediterranean, nos. **359–61.**

General accounts. AMEER ALI SYED, *A short history of the Saracens*, London, 1899; reprinted with corrections, 1900. T. W. ARNOLD, *The Caliphate*, Oxford, 1924. L. C. CAETANI, *Annali dell'Islam*, vols. I–VII, Milan, 1905–14. R. DOZY, *Essai sur l'histoire de l'Islamisme*, translated from the Dutch by V. CHAUVIN, Leyden and Paris, 1879. GAUDEFROY-DEMOMBYNES, *La Syrie à l'époque des Mamelouks d'après les auteurs arabes*, Paris, 1923. D. G. HOGARTH, *Arabia*, Oxford, 1922. C. HUART, *Histoire des Arabes*, Paris, 1912–13. C. S. HURGRONJE, *Geschriften betreffende den Islam en zijne Geschiednis* (Verspreide Geschriften, deel I, Bonn, 1923). S. LANE-POOLE, *The Mohammedan dynasties*, Westminster, 1894; reprint, 1925. D. B. MACDONALD, *The development of Muslim theology, jurisprudence, and constitutional theory*, New York, 1903. A. MÜLLER, *Der Islam im Morgen- und Abendland*, 2 vols., Berlin, 1885–87. W. MUIR, *The Caliphate, its rise, decline, and fall, from original sources*, London, 1883; a new and revised edition, edited by T. H. WEIR, Edinburgh, 1915. (This book was first published under the title: *Annals of the early Caliphate.*) TH. NÖLDEKE, *Sketches from eastern history*, London, 1892. E. SACHAU, *Ein Verzeichnis muhammedanischer Dynastien*, Berlin, 1923. (Designed as a supplement to LANE-POOLE, *The Mohammedan dynasties.*) G. WEIL, *Geschichte der Chalifen*, 5 vols., Mannheim, 1846–62. J. WELLHAUSEN, *Das arabische Reich und sein Sturz*, Berlin, 1902; English translation by M. G. WEIR, under the title *The Arab kingdom and its fall*, Calcutta, 1927. E. WÜSTENFELD, *Geschichte der arabischen Ärzte und Naturförscher*, Göttingen, 1840, and "Die Geschichtschreiber der Araber und ihre Werke" in *Abhandlungen der K. Gesellschaft zu Göttingen*, XXVIII (1881); XXIX (1882). E. DE ZAMBOUR, *Manuel de gênéalogie et de chronologie pour l'histoire de l'Islam*, Hannover, 1927.

Muhammad. AMEER ALI SYED, *The spirit of Islam: or the life and teachings of Mohammed*, Calcutta, 1902; amplified and revised edition, London, 1922. L. CAETANI, *Studi di storia orientale*, vol. III. *La biografia di Maometto profeta ed uomo di stato; il principio del califato, la conquista d'Arabia*, Milan, 1914. R. F. DIBBLE, *Mohammed*, New York, 1926. G. M. DRAYCOTT, *Mahomet: founder of Islam*, New York, 1916. A. GEIGER, *Was hat Mohammed aus dem Judentum aufgenommen?*, 2nd edition, Leipzig, 1902. H. GRIMME, *Mohammed*, 2 vols., Münster, 1892–95, and *Mohammed: die weltgeschichtliche Bedeutung Arabiens.* (Weltgeschichte in Charakterbilden.) P. DE LACY JOHNSTONE, *Muhammad and his power*, Edinburgh, 1901. (The world's epoch-makers.) H. LAMMENS, *Fatima et les filles de Mahomet*, Rome, 1912. D. S. MARGOLIOUTH, *Mohammed and the rise of Islam*, New York and London, 1905. (Heroes of the nations.) T. NÖLDEKE, *Das Leben Muhammeds, nach den Quellen populär dargestellt*, Hannover, 1863. H. RECHENDORF *Muhammed und die Seinen*, Leipzig, 1907. (Wissenschaft und Bildung.) A. SPRENGER, *Das Leben und die Lehre des Mohammed: nach bisher grösstentheils unbenutzten Quellen*, 2nd edition, 3 vols., Berlin, 1869.

Conquest of north Africa. M. CAUDEL, *Les premiers invasions arabes dans l'Afrique du Nord*, Paris, 1900. E. MERCIER, *Histoire de l'Afrique septentrionale (Berbêrie) depuis les temps les plus reculês jusqu'à la conquête française*, 3 vols., Paris, 1888–90. S. L. POOLE, *The history of Egypt in the middle ages*, London, 1901. E. AMÉLINEAU, "La conquête de l'Egypte par les Arabes, I," *R.H.*, CXIX (1915), 273–310. H. FOURNEL, *Les Berbers: étude sur la conquête de l'Afrique par les Arabes*, 2 vols., Paris, 1875–81. C. H. BECKER, *Beiträge zur Geschichte Aegyptens unter dem Islam*, 2 parts, Strasburg, 1902–03. G. FAURE-BIGUET, *Histoire de l'Afrique septentrionale sous la domination musulmane*, Paris, 1905. IBN KHALDUN, *Histoire des Berbères et des dynasties musulmanes de l'Afrique septentrionale*, translated from the Arabic by W. MACGUCKIN, BARON DE SLANE, 4 vols., Algiers, 1852–56. IBN KHALDUN lived 1322–1406. E. F. GAUTIER, *Les siècles obscurs du Moghreb*, Paris, 1927. A. BEL, *Les Almoravides et les Almohades*, Oran, 1910. R. MILLET, *Les Almohades, histoire d'une dynastie berbère*, Paris, 1923. M. VANDERHEYDEN, *La Berbêrie orientale sous la dynastie des Benou 'l-Arlab*, Paris, 1927

Moors in Spain and the Balearic islands. R. P. A. DOZY, *Histoire des Musulmans d'Espagne*, 4 vols., Leyden, 1861, translated by F. G. STOKES, with a biographical introduction and additional notes, *Spanish Islam: a history of the Moslems in Spain*, London, 1913. AL MAKKARI, *The history of the Mohammedan dynasties in Spain*, translated from the Arabic by P. DE GAYANGOS, 2 vols., London, 1840–43. The author was born in Tlemcen in the latter part of the 16th century. S. P. SCOTT, *History of the Moorish empire in Europe*, 3 vols., Philadelphia, 1904. F. CODERA, *Estudios críticos de historia árabe española*, Saragossa, 1903. J. A. CONDÉ, *History of the dominion of the Arabs in Spain*, translated by Mrs. J. FOSTER from the Spanish (*Historia de la dominación de los Arabes en España*, new edition, 3 vols., Barcelona, 1844). 3 vols., London, 1854–55. H. COPPÉE, *History of the conquest of Spain by the Arab Moors*, 2 vols., Boston, 1881. L. SCHWENKOW, *Die lateinische geschriebenen Quellen zur Geschichte der Eroberung Spaniens durch die Araber*, Göttingen, 1894. A. FERNANDEZ GUERRA, *Caida y ruina del imperio visigótico-español*, Madrid, 1883. E. SAAVEDRA, *Estudio sobre la invasión de los Arabes en España*, Madrid, 1892. CAMPANER, *Reseña histórico-crítica de la dominación de los Arabes y de los Moros en las islas Baleares* [to 1286], Madrid, 1888. A. GONZÁLEZ, *Historia de la España musulmana*, 2nd edition, Barcelona, 1928. S. LANE-POOLE, *Moors in Spain*, New York, 1903 (Story of nations). A. PRIETO Y VIVES, *Los reyes de Taijas*, Madrid, 1926. J. RIBERO, *Historia de la conquistá de España de Abenalcofia el Cordobes*, Madrid, 1926.

Muslim invasion of Gaul. G. LOKYS, *Die Kämpfe der Araber mit den Karolingern bis zum Tode Ludwigs II*, Heidelberg, 1906 (Heidelberger Abh.). M. H. ZOTENBERG, *Invasions des Visigoths et des Arabes en France*, Toulouse, 1876, extract from no. **540.** M. REINAUD, *Invasions des Sarrazins en France*, Paris, 1836.

Saracens in Italy and Sicily. M. AMARI, *Storia dei Musulmani di Sicilia*, 4 vols., Florence, 1854–68. J. GAY, *L'Italie méridionale et l'empire byzantin depuis l'avênement de Basile I jusqu'à la prise de Bari par les Normands*, Paris, 1904; translated into Italian, Florence, 1917. G. B. MOSCATO, *Cronica dei Musulmani in Calabria*, San Lucido, 1902. C. WAERN, *Medieval Sicily*, New York, 1911, chs. I–II.

Arab conquests in central Asia. H. A. R. GIBB, *The Arab conquests in central Asia*, London, 1923. F. SKRINE and E. D. ROSS, *The heart of Asia*, London, 1899.

Arabian commerce in the north of Europe. G. JACOB, *Der nordisch-baltische Handel der Araber im Mittelalter*, Leipzig, 1887; and *Welche Handelsartikel bezogen die Araber des Mittelalters aus den nordisch-baltischen Ländern?* 2nd edition, Berlin, 1891. E. BABELON, *Du commerce des Arabes dans le nord de l'Europe avant les croisades*, Paris, 1882.

Periodical on Islam. *Der Islam: Zeitschrift für Geschichte und Kultur des islamischen Orients*, edited by C. H. BECKER, Strasburg, 1910ff.

Original sources. EL-BOKHÂRI (died 870 A.D.), *Les traditions islamiques*, translated from the Arabic with notes and an index by O. HOUDAS and

W. Marcais, 3 vols., Paris, 1903–08. *The origins of the Islamic state:* being a translation from the Arabic accompanied with annotations, geographic and historical notes of the *Kitâb Futûh al-Buldân* of al-Imâm abu-l 'Abbâs Ahmâd ibn Jâbir al-Balâdhuri, vol. I, by P. K. Hitti, New York, 1916. *Traités de paix et de commerce et documents divers contenant les relations des chrétiens avec les Arabs d'Afrique septentrionale au moyen âge*, edited by De Mas-Latrie, Paris, 1866, supplement, 1872. (See the introduction to this, reprinted as *Relations et commerce de l'Afrique septentrionale avec les nations chrétiennes au moyen âge*, Paris, 1866.) *Biblioteca arabo-sicula, versione italiana*, 2 vols. and a supplement, edited by M. Amari, Turin and Rome, 1880–89. J. Wellhausen, *Muhammed in Medina: das ist Vakidī's Kitāb al Maghāzī in verkürzter Wiedergabe*, Berlin, 1882. *Bibliotheca arabico-hispana*, edited by F. Codera y Zaidin, 10 vols., Madrid, 1882–95.

Bibliographies. *C.M.H.*, II, 758–65, and the special bibliographies indicated there. G. Gabrieli, *Manuele di bibliografia musulmana*, Rome, 1916. G. Pfannmüller, *Handbuch der Islam-Literatur*, Berlin, 1923. B. Heller, *Bibliographie des oeuvres de Ignace Goldziher*, Paris, 1927. See also no. **42.**

D. B. Macdonald.
W. M. Randall.

X. FOES OF WESTERN CHRISTENDOM, FROM THE EIGHTH TO THE ELEVENTH CENTURY. FROM THE NORTH. NORTHMEN

A. Outline

1. The fury of the Northmen. "From the fury of the Northmen, good Lord, deliver us" (*a furore Normannorum libera nos*). This phrase, so common in litanies of the middle ages, was not in use in Carolingian times, but the following prayer, dating ca. 900, is an interesting prototype: "*Summa pia gratia nostra conservando corpora et custodita, de gente fera Normannica nos libera, quae nostra vastat, deus, regna*, etc." (See L. Delisle, *Littérature latine et histoire du moyen âge*, p. 17.)

2. The civilization of the Teutonic people of the north, Danes, Norwegians, and Swedes. The *scalds*. The *sagas*. The Gokstad and Oseberg ships. The *vikings* (= warriors).

3. Causes and character of their migrations. Often women and even children accompanied the men on their ships. The chief raids of the Northmen occurred between 800 and 1000.

4. The Northmen in the British and northern islands. Mentioned in the *Anglo-Saxon chronicle* under the year 787. Monastery of Lindisfarne raided in 793. In 795 they were in Ireland. Iona was raided about 800. Faroe Islands, Orkneys, Shetland Islands and Hebrides were occupied in the time of Charlemagne. Towards the middle of the ninth century the Northmen were numerous in England. King Alfred (871–901) and the Danes. The Danelaw. Iceland occupied about 874. Greenland touched upon about 900 and North America about 1000.

5. Raids on the continent in the west and in the Mediterranean. In 810, in Charlemagne's time, king Godfred of Denmark plundered the coast of Frisia. About the time of the death of Charlemagne (814) Vikings visited the mouth of the Loire and in 843 made a settlement on the island of Noirmoutier and also occupied the Ile de Rhé near the mouth of the Charente. Antwerp was destroyed about 836, and the island of Walcheren was occupied in 837. In 841 they appeared on the Seine and destroyed Rouen. Nantes was plundered in 843. They were on the Garonne in 844, when Toulouse was attacked. In 845 they appeared before Paris and in the same year destroyed Hamburg. In 856 Paris was plundered. The next year they sailed down to Spain, appeared before Lisbon, sacked Cadiz and ascended the Guadalquivir to Seville. Under Hasting a band sailed into the Mediterranean to sack Rome in 859 but got no further than Luna. Some sailed up the Rhone river and occupied the island of Camargue. Charles the Bold treated with Hasting and his followers, some of whom became Christians and accepted feudal holdings. Orleans was reached in 865. Northmen were defeated at Saucourt in 881 but they plundered Aachen, Cologne, etc. Paris was besieged 885. Charles the Fat paid tribute and allowed the raiders to plunder Burgundy. Decisive defeat of the Northmen by the German king Arnulf near Louvain in 891.

6. Expeditions to the East. Rurik and his followers, the Varangians, came from Sweden and settled at Novgorod about 862. Varangians in the service of the emperor in Constantinople.

7. The important settlement of Northmen in northern France, in and about Rouen, about 911. Charles III, the Simple, offered Normandy as a fief to Rollo, or Rolf, and gave him his daughter Gisela in marriage. Rolf was baptized soon after.

8. Conversion of Northmen to Christianity in the tenth century and the political reorganization of the North. The beginnings of modern Norway.

9. The sudden and short-lived burst of Danish imperialism under Canute the Great, 1014–35.

10. The important part the Normans were destined to play in medieval history (see outline XX).

B. Special Recommendations for Reading

Introductory surveys. C. H. Haskins, *The Normans in European history*, Boston and New York, 1915, ch. ii. Lavisse et Rambaud, *Histoire générale*, II, ch. xiii. Oman, *The dark ages* (see "vikings" in the index). Thorndike, *Medieval Europe*, ch. xii; Thompson, *Economic and social history*, ch. x; *C.M.H.*, III, ch. xiii.

Longer general accounts. The best general survey is Gjerset, *History of the Norwegian people*, I, especially pp. 45–280. C. F. Keary, *The Vikings in western Christendom* A.D. *789 to* A.D. *888*, London, 1891. A. Mawer, *The Vikings*, Cambridge University Press, 1913 (Cambridge manuals), is a popular sketch. Beazley, *Dawn of modern geography*, II, 17–111. Mary W. Williams, *Social Scandinavia in the viking age*, New York, 1920.

Danes and Norsemen in Great Britain. C. OMAN, *England before the Norman conquest*, London, 1910, 382–491. C. PLUMMER, *The life and times of Alfred the Great*, Oxford, 1902, lecture IV. For Canute and Danish imperialism the best book is L. M. LARSON, *Canute the Great, 995 (circ.)–1035, and the rise of Danish imperialism during the Viking age*, New York, 1912 (Heroes of the nations). *Old-lore miscellany of Orkney, Shetland, Caithness and Sutherland*, published by the Viking society for Northern research, London, 1907ff., contains much interesting material. G. HENDERSON, *The Norse influence on Celtic Scotland*, Glasgow, 1910. E. EKWALL, *Scandinavians and Celts in north-west of England*, Lund, 1918. J. GRAY, *Sutherland and Caithness in saga-time*, Edinburgh, 1922. R. L. BRENNER, *The Norsemen in Alban*, Glasgow, 1923. P. W. BRÖGGER, *Ancient emigrants. A history of the Norse settlements in Scotland*, New York, 1929. F. M. STENTON, "The Danes in England," in *History*, V (1920), 173–77.

Northmen in Russia. RAMBAUD, *History of Russia*, ch. IV. KLUCHEVSKY, *A history of Russia*, I, ch. V.

Original sources. The *sagas* are the best introduction to a study of life in the Viking age. See original sources under C, pp. 184–85. For interesting extracts concerning the raids of Northmen, OGG, *Source book*, 157–73. See A. BUGGE, "The origin and credibility of the Icelandic saga," in *A.H.R.*, XIV (1908–09), 249–61.

Maps. The best map for the raids and settlements of the Northmen is in MEYER's *Historischer Handatlas*, 25. See also SHEPHERD, *Atlas*, 46–7, 57, 58–9, 64. VOGEL, *Die Normannen*, has an excellent map showing the territory overrun by Northmen in France, Germany, the Netherlands, and northern Spain. W. A. CRAIGIE's map of *Scandinavia in the 13th century*, in POOLE's *Historical atlas of modern Europe*, Oxford, 1902.

C. BIBLIOGRAPHY

General books. For general works on the Scandinavian countries see nos. **717–28c.** Due to the wide range of the viking raids, many of the general works on all the countries of Europe, nos. **508–716,** touch upon their history.

General accounts. J. STEENSTRUP, *Normannerne*, 4 vols., Copenhagen, 1876–82, vol. I, translated by E. de BEAUREPAIRE, *Etudes prêliminaires pour servir à l'histoire de Normands et de leur invasions*, Caen, 1880. SARAH O. JEWETT, *The story of the Normans told chiefly in relation to their conquest of England*, London and New York, 1886 (Story of nations), chs. I and II. A. H. JOHNSON, *The Normans in Europe*, London, 1877, chs. I–III (part of no. **335**). W. ROOS, "The Swedish part in the viking expeditions," *E.H.R.*, VII (1892), 209–23. G. B. DEPPING, *Histoire des expêditions maritimes des Normands*, Paris, 1843. R. NORDENSTRENG, *Die Züge der Vikinger*, Leipzig, 1925. ELEANOR HULL, *The Northmen in Britain*, London, 1913. T. CARLYLE, *Early kings of Norway*, New York, 1875.

Civilization of the Northmen. P. B. DU CHAILLU, *Viking age: the early history, manners, and customs of the ancestors of the English-speaking nations*,

2 vols., New York, 1889. A. BUGGE, *Vikingerne*, 2 series, Copenhagen, 1904–06, translated from the Norwegian by H. HUNGERLAND, *Die Wikinger: Bilder aus der nordischen Vergangenheit*, Halle, 1906. O. MONTELIUS, *Kulturgeschichte Schwedens von den ältesten Zeiten bis zum elften Jahrhundert nach Christi*, Leipzig, 1906. S. MÜLLER, *Nordische Altertumskunde*, German edition by O. L. JIRICZEK, 2 vols., Strasburg, 1879–98. C. MÜLLER, *Altgermanische Meeresherrschaft*, Gotha, 1914, treats the period up to 1200. A. OLRIK, *Nordisches Geistesleben in heidnischer und frühchristlicher Zeit*, translated by W. RANISCH, Heidelberg, 1908. J. J. A. WORSAAE, *The prehistory of the north, based on contemporary memorials*, translated by M. F. MORLAND SIMPSON, London, 1886. F. NIEDNER, *Islands Kultur zur Wikingerzeit*, Jena, 1913, in *Thule: altnordische Dichtung und Prosa*, I, 1. Reprinted 1920. Numerous articles on the civilization and the history of the Northmen are to be found in the *Saga book of the Viking club, society for northern research*, London, 1895ff. A. BUGGE, *Vesterlandenes Indflydelse paa Nordboernes og saerlig Nordmaendenes ydre Kultur, levesaet og somfundsforhold Vikingetiden*, Christiania, 1905. C. WEIBULL, *Sverge och dess nordiska Granmakter under den tidigare Medeltiden*, Lund, 1921.

Northmen in France. W. VOGEL, *Die Normannen und das fränkische Reich bis zur Gründung der Normandie 799–911*, with a very important map, Heidelberg, 1906 (in Heidelberger Abhandlungen zur mittleren und neueren Geschichte, 14). This work of fundamental importance is supplemented by F. LOT, "La grande invasion normande, 856–862," *B.E.C.*, LXIX (1908), 5–62; and by the same author's *Etudes critiques sur l'abbaye de Saint-Wandrille*, Paris, 1913, ch. III, (part of no. **888**). E. FREEMAN, "The early sieges of Paris," in his *Historical essays*, series I, 207–51. H. H. HOWORTH, "The early intercourse of the Danes and Franks," *Trans.*, *R.H.S.*, VI (1877), 147–82; VII (1878), 1–29. E. THUBERT, "Les Northmen en France," *Revue d'histoire diplomatique*, XX (1906), 511–36. LINDEN, "Les Normands à Louvain (884–92)," *R.H.*, CXXIV (1917), 64–81. F. LOT, "Les tributs aux Normands et l'église de France au IXe siècle," *B.E.C.*, LXXXV, (1924), 58–78. J. CALMETTE, "Le siège de Toulouse par les Normands en 864," *Annales du midi*, XXIX–XXX (1917–18), 153–74. G. STORM, *Kritiske Bidrag til Vikingetidens Historie*, Christiania, 1876. E. JORANSON, *The Danegeld in France*, Rock Island, Ill., 1923. J. De VRIES, *De Wikingen in de Lage Landen bij de Zee*, Haarlem, 1923. J. STEENSTRUP, *Normandiets Historie under de syv forste Hertuger 911–1066. Avec un résumé en français*, Copenhagen, 1925.

Vikings in Spain. A. K. FABRICIUS, *La première invasion des Normands dans l'Espagne musulmane en 814*, Lisbon, 1892; and, *La connaissance de la péninsule espagnole par les hommes du Nord*, Lisbon, 1892. R. DOZY, *Recherches sur l'histoire et la littérature de l'Espagne pendant le moyen âge*, 3rd edition, 2 vols., Paris, 1881, II, 252–332.

Eastward expeditions of Northmen. *Antiquités russes d'après les monuments historiques des Islandais et des anciens Scandinaves*, 2 vols., Copenhagen, 1850–52. T. J. ARNE, *La Suède et l'orient: études archéologiques sur* *les relations de la Suède et l'orient pendant l'âge des Vikings*, Uppsala, 1914ff. V. Thompson, *The relations between ancient Russia and Scandinavia, and the origin of the Russian state*, Oxford, 1878. S. Rožniecki, *Varsegiske Minder i den russiske Heltedigtning*, Copenhagen, 1914. S. H. Cross, "Yaroslav the Wise in Norse tradition," *Speculum*, VI (1929), 177–97.

Northmen in America. W. Hovgaard, *The voyages of the Norsemen to America*, New York, 1914. G. M. Gathorne-Hardy, *The Norse discoveries of America*, Oxford, 1921. F. Nansen, *In northern mists: arctic explorations in early times*, translated by G. Chater, 2 vols., London and New York, 1911 (bibliography, II, 384–96). W. H. Babcock, *Early Norse visits to North America*, Smithsonian Institution (no. 2138), 1913 (bibliography, pp. 179–89). A. Schalck de la Faverie, *Les Normands et la découverte de l'Amérique au Xᵉ siècle*, Paris, 1912. J. Fischer, *Die Entdeckungen der Normannen in America*, Freiburg, 1902, translated into English by B. H. Soulsby, London, 1903. G. B. de Lagrèze, *Les Normands dans les deux mondes*, Paris, 1890. H. P. Steensby, *The Norsemen's route from Greenland to Wineland*, Copenhagen, 1917. H. Hermannsson, "The Wineland voyage," *The geographical review*, XVII (1927), 107–14. P. Nörlund, *Buried Norsemen at Herjolfsnes. An archæological and historical study*, Copenhagen, 1924.

Original sources. The old Norse-Icelandic literature is of the greatest importance. There are now critical editions of most of the sagas, many of these published by the Samfund tri udgivelse af gammel nordisk Litteratur and the Royal Society of Northern Antiquaries (Copenhagen). Of collections may especially be mentioned *Fornmanna Sögur*, 12 vols., Copenhagen, 1825–37, also in Latin translation: *Scripta historica Islandorum*, 12 vols., 1828–47; *Íslendinga Sögur*, 38 vols., Reykjavík, 1891–1902; *Altnordische Sagabibliothek*, 18 vols., Halle, 1892–1929; *Fornaldarsögur Norðrlanda*, 3 vols., Copenhagen, 1829–30 (new edition, Reykjavík, 1885–89). The largest collection of translations is the German *Thule, Altnordische Dichtung und Prosa*, 24 vols., Jena, 1911ff. The Icelandic text and English translation are to be found in G. Vigfússon and F. Y. Powell's *Origines islandicæ, a collection of the more important sagas and other narrative writings relating to the settlement and early history of Iceland*, 2 vols., Oxford, 1905, and in Vigfússon and Dasent's *Icelandic sagas and other historical documents relating to the settlement of the Northmen in the British Isles* (Rolls Series), 4 vols., London, 1887–94. An English translation of five Icelandic sagas and Snorri Sturlason's *Heimskrîngla* is to be found in W. Morris and E. Magnússon's *Saga library*, 6 vols., London, 1891–1905; *Volsunga Saga*, published separately, London, 1888; (the *Heimskrîngla* also translated by S. Laing, London, 1844; reprint, 1889); they also translated *Three Northern love stories and other tales*, London, 1875 (and later editions). Among English translations of individual sagas the following may especially be mentioned: *The story of Burnt Njal* by Sir G. W. Dasent, 2 vols., Edinburgh, 1861 (and often reprinted, e.g., Everyman's Library); *The story of Gisli the Outlaw*, by Dasent, Edinburgh, 1866; *The story of Egili Skakagrimsson*, by

W. C. GREEN, London, 1893; *The story of Grettir the Strong*, by MORRIS and MAGNÚSSON, London, 1869 (and later editions); *The Laxdœlasaga*, by MRS. MURIEL PRESS, London, 1899, and by T. VEBLEN, New York, 1925; *The life and death of Cormak the Skald*, by W. G. COLLINGWOOD and J. STEFÁNNSON, Ulverston, 1902; *The Fereyinga saga* by F. Y. POWELL, London, 1896; *The saga of King Olaf Tryggwason*, by J. SEPHTON, London, 1895, and *The saga of King Sverri*, by the same, London, 1899.—The poetry is to be found in VIGFÚSSON and POWELL'S *Corpus poeticum boreale: a poetry of the old Northern tongue from the earliest times to the thirteenth century*, 2 vols., Oxford, 1883, which has now been largely superseded by F. JÓNSSON'S *Den norsk-islandske Skjaldedigtning*, 4 vols., Copenhagen, 1912–15. The most important edition of the Poetic Edda is the facsimile edition of the *Codex regius* (Gl. kgl. Sml. 2364,4°) by F. JÓNSSON and L. F. A. WIMMER, Copenhagen, 1890; English translations by H. A. BELLOWS, *The Poetic Edda*, New York, 1923, and by L. M. HOLLANDER, *The Poetic Edda*, Austin, Texas, 1928. The most important editions of the *Edda* by SNORRI STURLUSON are those of Copenhagen, 1848–87 (3 vols.) and of 1900; an English translation by A. G. BRODEUR, *The Prose Edda*, New York, 1916. A convenient short introduction to the sagas is W. A. CRAIGIE, *The Icelandic sagas*, Cambridge University Press, 1913 (Cambridge manuals).

A very sumptuous work on the Oseberg burial ship, to consist of five volumes, is being published by the Norwegian government, *Osebergfundet*, edited by A. W. BROGGER and others, 1916ff. The ship, which was found in 1904 and dates from the ninth century, is now exhibited in a special building in Oslo; the objects found in it are on exhibition in the Historical Museum. The well-known Gokstad ship is described briefly by I. UNDSET, *A short guide for the use of visitors to the viking ship from Gokstad*, Oslo, 1925.

The sources for the Norsemen in America were collected in *Antiquitates americanæ* by C. C. RAFN, Copenhagen, 1837, and a facsimile edition of the principal sagas with English translation is to be found in A. M. REEVES' *The finding of Wineland the Good*, London, 1890, the translation reprinted in the *Original narratives of early American history, Columbus and Cabot 985–1503*, New York, 1906 (edited by J. E. OLSON).

Bibliographies. For the old Norse *Sagas*, see GROSS, no. **36**, §35, and for modern books on the Northmen, especially in their relation to England, *ibid.*, §42. For the sources on the Northmen in France, see A. MOLINIER, *Les sources*, I, 264–71. H. HERMANNSSON, *Catalogue of the Icelandic collection bequeathed by Willard Fiske to the Cornell University Library*, Ithaca, New York, 1914, and the *Supplement*, 1927, contain the greatest number of titles on the subject to be found in any American library. In the *Islandica: an annual relating to Icelandic and the Fiske Icelandic Collection in Cornell University Library*, Ithaca, 1908ff., are the following bibliographies by H. HERMANNSSON: *of the Icelandic sagas and minor tales* (vol. I, 1908), *of the Northmen in America* (vol. II, 1909), *of the sagas of the kings of Norway and related sagas and tales* (vol. III, 1910), *of the ancient laws of Norway and Iceland* (vol. IV, 1911), *of the mythical heroic sagas* (vol. V, 1912), and *of* *the Eddas* (vol. XIII, 1920), *Icelandic manuscripts* (vol. XIX, 1929). See also the first part of P. Riant's library, 2641 items on Scandinavia, acquired by Yale University.

XI. FOES OF WESTERN CHRISTENDOM FROM THE EIGHTH TO THE ELEVENTH CENTURY. FROM THE EAST. SLAVS AND ASIATIC NOMADS

A. Outline

1. The grand divisions of European peoples in the middle ages; Romanic, Teutonic, Slavic, and the eastern background formed by the Asiatic nomads.

2. The rôle of the Slavs in medieval history. They served as a buffer between the Teutonic west and the Asiatic nomads. Lack of organization among the Slavs. Enslavement of the Slavs by Teutons and Asiatic nomads.

3. The civilization and extent of the Slavs about 700 A.D. Wends, Serbs, Slavs. Western Slavs: Polabians (Sorbs, Abodrites, Wilzians, Pomeranians), Poles, Czechs, Moravians, Slovaks; eastern and northern Slavs: Russians (White, Little, and Great Russians); southern Slavs: Serbs, Croats, Slovenes and Bulgarians. The Lithuanians (Letts and Prussians).

4. Relations of Merovingians and Carolingians with the Slavs. Samo, a Frank adventurer, became king of the Czechs of Bohemia, 623–68.

5. The evanescent empire of Moravia. Struggles of the Moravians with the Franks after Charlemagne. Svatopluk II acknowledged by Charles III, the Fat (881–87). The conversion of these Slavs. The eastern emperor Michel III (842–67) sent as apostles of the Slavs two brothers, born in Salonica, Constantine [later Cyrillus, (died 869)] and Methodius (died 885). Their relations with the pope in Rome.

6. Decline of the Slavs in the region between the Elbe and the Oder where the Polabians were practically wiped out by the Germans in the tenth and eleventh centuries.

7. Rise and decline of Poland. Boleslav the Valiant (992–1025) conquered far and wide but did not gain a permanent hold on the Baltic. Poland declined after his death. Close relations with the Latin church. The archbishopric of Gnesen founded about 1000 A.D. Quasi-parliamentary government under Boleslav.

8. Bohemia. Amalgamation of the Czechs. Latin Christianity prevailed. Vratislav II, the first king (1086), practically a vassal of the emperor Henry IV.

9. The glorious era of Bulgarian history. The Bulgars, a Finnish tribe, organized the Slavs of old Moesia in the seventh century. Converted to Byzantine Christianity in the ninth century. Simeon (892–927), the first czar of the Bulgarians. Preslav the capital. Golden era of literature. The Bogomils (Manichaean heretics). Subjugation of Bulgarians by the eastern emperors, especially by Basil II, "Slayer of the Bulgarians."

10. The beginnings of Russia. Rurik and his Swedes, the Varangians, settled around Novgorod about 962. Oleg, Rurik's successor, made Kiev

his capital. Attacked Constantinople in 907. Sviatoslav (964–72) seriously threatened Constantinople, but was checked in 971 by John Zimisces. Vladimir (972–1015), the Clovis of Russia, was baptized about 990. A flood of Byzantine civilization came into Russia with eastern Christianity. Yaroslav the Great (1015–54), the Charlemagne of Russia. Close relations of Russia with the west during this early period.

11. The Asiatic nomads. The peculiar geographic influences which shaped their destinies. Finns, Huns, Avars, (Bulgars), Khazars, Petchenegs, Cumans, Magyars, etc.

12. Avars occupied old Pannonia and Dacia when the Lombards forsook that region. Their "rings." Charlemagne's campaigns against them 795–96. Shortly after his death they were dispersed as the Huns had been in the fifth century.

13. Hungarians or Magyars. About 900 they dispossessed the Moravians in modern Hungary. Their low state of civilization. Their dread invasions of Europe in the tenth century, penetrating even into Provence and Lorraine. Crushed by Otto I in 955 in the battle of the Lechfeld. Stephen I (955–1038), the founder of modern Hungary, accepted Latin Christianity. The great archbishopric of Gran was established about 1000 A.D.

14. The state of eastern Europe just before the crusades.

B. Special Recommendations for Reading

General accounts. The best short survey is in LAVISSE et RAMBAUD, *Histoire générale*, I, ch. XIV. *C.M.H.*, II, ch. XIV, is authoritative and important, but rather confusing; vol. IV, chs. VII, VIII. A fairly comprehensive account may be pieced together from J. B. BURY'S books, *History of the later Roman empire*, II, 11–24, 274–80, 331–38, 470–76; *A history of the eastern Roman empire*, chs. XI–XIII. See also HELMOLT, *History of the world*, vol. V, 222–23, 227–42, 271–88, 326–38, 347–48, 353–55, 374–79, 425–61, 469–76 and GIBBON, *Decline and fall*, ch. LV.

Nomads. The general character of nomadic life is well described in *C.M.H.*, I, ch. XII; and by ELLEN C. SEMPLE, *Influences of geographic environment*, ch. XIV.

Histories of various countries of eastern Europe. General books on eastern Europe, nos. **680–716.** See also KERNER, *Slavic Europe.*

Maps. *C.M.H.*, I, map 3; II, maps 25, 26a, 26b; IV, maps 40, 41. SHEPHERD, *Atlas*, 2–3, 46–7, 52–9. Use FREEMAN, *The historical geography of Europe*, especially pp. 113–17, 155–58, as a guide to these maps; and see also RIPLEY, *The races of Europe*, chs. XIII, XV.

C. Bibliography

General books. For books on eastern Europe see nos. **680–716, 588–96, 311–12;** but for the contact of Slavs and nomads with western civilization a large number of general books on other European countries are also of value; see e.g., nos. **313–61, 499–598, 643–79, 717–27b.** For histories of Slavic literature see no. **814.** See also KERNER, *Slavic Europe.*

Early Slavic history in general. L. LEGER, *Le monde slave: études politiques et littéraires*, series 1 and 2, 2 vols., Paris, 1897–1902; *Etudes slaves: voyages et littérature*, Paris, 1875; *Nouvelle études slaves: histoire et littérature*, Paris, 1880; *La mythologie slave*, Paris, 1901. C. HÖFLER, *Epochen der slavischen Geschichte bis zum Jahre 1526*, Vienna, 1881 (vol. 97 of *S. B., Vienna Acad.*). A. BRÜCKNER, *Eintritt der Slaven in die Weltgeschichte*, Berlin, 1909. L. HAUPTMANN, "Politische Umwälzungen unter den Slovenen vom Ende des sechsten Jahrhunderts bis zur mitte des neunten," *M.I.O.G.*, XXXV (1915), 229–87. L. MEDERLE, *Manuel de l'antiquité slave*, 2 vols., Paris, 1923–26. S. RAPOPORT, "Mohammedan writers on Slavs and Russians," *Slavonic review*, VIII (1929), 80–98, 331–41. H. MERBACH, *Die Slawenkriege des deutschen Volkes*, Leipzig, 1914. W. OHNESORGE, *Ausbreitung und Ende der Slawen zwischen Nieder-Elbe und Oder*, Lübeck, 1911. A. MEITZEN, *Siedelung und Agrarwesen der West- und Ostgermanen, der Kelten, Römer, Finnen und Slaven*, 3 vols. and an atlas, Berlin, 1895. M. MURKO, *Geschichte der älteren südslawischen Literaturen*, Leipzig, 1908. A. LÉFÈVRE, *Germains et Slaves: origines et croyances*, Paris, 1903. W. R. S. RALSTON, *Early Russian history*, London, 1874. R. W. SETON-WATSON, *Racial problems in Hungary: a history of the Slovaks*, London, 1909. O. HÖTZSCH, "Staatenbildung und Verfassungsentwickelung in der Geschichte des germanisch-slavischen Ostens," *Zeitschrift für osteuropäische Geschichte*, I (1911), 363–412. M. WEHRMANN, *Geschichte von Pommern*, I. Bd., 2nd edition, Gotha, 1919. E. MISSALEK, "Die Forschung auf dem Gebiete der ältesten polnischen Geschichte," *H.Z.*, CXIII (1914), 62–9. E. ZHARSKI, *Die Slavenkriege zur Zeit Ottos III und dessen Pilgerfahrt nach Gnesen*, Lemberg, 1882 (Prog.).

Samo. O. NEMECEK, *Das Reich des Slawenfürsten Samo*, Mährisch-Ostrau, 1906 (Prog.).

Rumania. N. JORGA, *Les éléments originaux de l'ancienne civilisation roumaine*, Jassy, 1911. E. FISCHER, *Die Herkunft der Rumänen*, Bamberg, 1904. N. JORGA, *Geschichte des rumänischen Volkes im Rahmen seiner Staatsbildungen*, 2 vols., Gotha, 1905; *Histoire des Roumains de Transylvanie et de Hongrie*. For bibliography see KERNER, *Slavic Europe*, 259ff.

Poland. H. GRAPPIN, *Histoire de la Pologne des origines à 1922*, Paris, 1923. E. MESSALEK, *Geschichte Polens*, 3rd edition, Breslau, 1921.

Bulgaria. W. N. SLATARSKI, *Geschichte der Bulgaren*, I Teil (679–1396), Leipzig, 1918. J. A. ILIĆ, *Die Bogomillen in ihrer geschichtlichen Entwicklung*, Sv. Karlovci, 1923.

Conversion of Slavs to Christianity. Chief interest centers in the work of Constantine and Methodius. A. BRÜCKNER, *Die Wahrheit über die Slavenapostel*, Tübingen, 1913. F. SNOPEK, *Konstantinus-Cyrillus und Methodius: die Slavenapostel*, Kremsier, 1911. L. K. GOETZ, *Geschichte der Slavenapostel Konstantinus (Kyrillus) und Methodius*, Gotha, 1897. L. LEGER, *Cyrille et Méthode: étude historique sur la conversion des Slaves au christianisme*, Paris, 1868 (see also A. NAEGLE, *Kirchengeschichte Böhmens*, under no. **461**). L. K. GOETZ, *Staat und Kirche in Altrussland: Kiever Periode, 998–1240*,

Berlin, 1908. L. K. GOETZ, *Das Kiever Höhlenkloster als Kulturzentrum des vormongolischen Russlands*, Passau, 1904. M. USPENSKI, *La Russie et Byzance au Xe siècle*, Odessa, 1888. F. DVORNIK, *Les Slaves, Byzance et Rome au IXe siècle*, Paris, 1926.

The home of the Asiatic nomads. E. HUNTINGTON, *The pulse of Asia: a journey in central Asia illustrating the geographical basis of history*, New York, 1907. F. H. SKRINE and E. D. ROSS, *The heart of Asia*, London, 1899. SVEN HEDIN, *Central Asia and Tibet*, 2 vols., New York, 1903. G. F. WRIGHT, *Asiatic Russia*, 2 vols., New York, 1902. A. VÁMBÉRY, *Travels in central Asia*, New York, 1865. L. BONVAT, *L'empire Mongol.* (Histoire du Monde, edited by CAVAIGNAC, tome VIII), Paris, 1927. H. LAMB, *Genghis Khan*, New York, 1927, and *Tamerlane*, New York, 1928.

Asiatic nomads. F. RATZEL, *The history of mankind*, translated from the 2nd German edition by A. J. BUTLER, 3 vols., London, 1896–98, III, 313–533. H. v. KUTSCHERA, *Die Chasaren: historische Studie*, Vienna, 1909. E. H. PARKER, *Thousand years of the Tartars*, London, 1895. A. THIERRY, *Histoire d'Attila et de ses successeurs jusqu'à l'établissement des Hongrois en Europe, suivis des légendes et traditions*, 2 vols., Paris, 1856. H. T. CHESHIRE, "The great Tatar invasion of Europe," *Slavonic review*, V (1926), 89–105. G. VERNADSKY, *A history of Russia*, New Haven, 1929.

Avars. K. GROH, *Kämpfe der Avaren und Langobarden*, Halle, 1889 (Diss.).

Hungarians in Europe. R. LÜTTICH, *Ungarnzüge in Europa im 10 Jahrhundert*, Berlin, 1910 (Historische Studien, edited by E. EBERING, 84). E. DANIËLS, *De Invallen der Hongaren: hun Groote Inval in Lotharingen ten Jare 954*, Antwerp, 1927. For literature on the battle of the Lechfeld in 955 see DAHLMANN-WAITZ, *Quellenkunde*, no. 4816. J. B. BURY, "The coming of the Hungarians: their origin and early homes," *Scottish review*, XX (1892), 29–52. A. VÁMBÉRY, *Der Ursprung der Magyaren*, Leipzig, 1882. L. DUSSIEUX, *Essai sur les invasions des Hongrois en Europe et en France*, Paris, 1839.

Original sources. See the large collections, nos. **1002–06** and *Enchiridion fontium historiae Hungarorum*, edited by H. MARCZALI and others, Budapest, 1901.

Bibliographies. *C.M.H.*, I, 660–65; II, 770–84. LAVISSE et RAMBAUD, *Histoire générale*, I, 741–42. KERNER, *Slavic Europe*, 202–03; 222. See also nos. **46–7.**

XII. EARLY MEDIEVAL INSTITUTIONS

A. OUTLINE

1. Danger of massing together almost all medieval institutions, and studying them under the caption "Feudalism." Meaning and application of this term in the history of medieval Europe and in other times and places. In this outline chief attention is given to the institutions of the area which is now France.

2. The intermingling of ancient institutions, Graeco-Roman, Jewish, Celtic, Teutonic, and Slavic. Impossibility of disentangling the various elements.

3. Germanic ideas of law and their application. Personality of law. Peculiar ideas about legal evidence. Compurgation. Ordeals. Wager of battle. Wergeld. The *Leges barbarorum*, especially the *Lex Salica*, the *Lex Ripuariorum*, the *Leges Visigothorum*, *Leges Burgundionum*, *Lex Saxonum*, *Lex Frisionum*, *Lex Alamannorum*, and the *Leges Langobardorum*. The *Leges Romanae*, epitomes of Roman law.

4. The survival of a very narrow stream of Roman law (*Lex Romana*) in the early middle ages. Its chief hold was in the church which also fostered Jewish ideas of law. Until about 1100 A.D. the Justinian code was little known in the west. The *Edictum Theodorici* about 500, the *Breviarium Alarici*, 506 (also known as the *Breviarium Alaricianum* or *Lex Romana Visigothorum*), and the *Lex Romana Burgundionum* promulgated by king Gundobad.

5. The dreams of a universal empire and a universal Christian brotherhood contrasted with the actual political and social state of Europe after Charlemagne.

6. Political disorganization caused by the inroads of the foes of western Christendom and by internal disorder. Consequent lack of improvement of economic conditions. Failure of the empire to guard life and property and the consequent rise of other agents which performed this service. Unusual importance of the strongly armed and mounted man and the fortified house and walled town. Petty feudal warfare.

7. Older institutions which may have had some influence in shaping feudal institutions: Germanic *comitatus:* Roman *patrocinium* and *precarium*.

8. Fundamental elements in feudalism: (1) the personal element; (2) the economic element; and (3) the governmental element. The very gradual fusion of all these elements. Endless confusion resulting from this commingling which made feudalism anything but a system.

9. The personal element. Need of the weaker and poorer man to bind himself to a stronger and richer man in times of disorder when the state did not give adequate protection. Commendation. Homage and fealty. Lord and vassal. Capitulary of Kiersey, 877 A.D. Duties of lord to his vassal: protection and justice. Duties of vassal to his lord: aid and counsel. Aid consisted largely of military service, which was honorable, noble service (castleward); but in time the vassal was bound to aid his lord in many other ways, e.g., relief, fines on alienation, the technical "aids," three ordinary and two extraordinary, entertainment (droit de gîte, coshering). The lord had many special rights, escheat, forfeiture, coinage. Counsel consisted largely of service in the lord's court, but might also be merely advice and helpfulness when the lord was in difficulties.

10. The economic element. The infeudation of land and other sources of income. The benefice. The fief (*feudum*). Rarity of allodial holdings. Peculiar ideas about tenure (ridiculous customs). Development of primogeniture.

11. The governmental element. The localization of governmental functions by usurpation, long undisputed exercise, and the granting of immunities. Special importance of the legal rights of land holders. Feudal courts and feudal law. Justice as a source of income.

12. Sharp division of classes of people. Drastic distinction between nobles and non-nobles. Slavery in the middle ages. Feudal relations existed only among the nobles. The non-nobles were not concerned in feudalism except that they formed the economic basis upon which it was reared. A serf was not the vassal of his lord. Lay nobles and ecclesiastical nobles. For the life of nobles in the middle ages, see outline XXVII; for the life of non-nobles, see outline XXVI.

13. Monarchy in the midst of feudalism. Theoretically the king was the apex of an imaginary feudal pyramid, but actually monarchy was fundamentally at variance with feudal conditions.

14. The church in the midst of feudalism. Especially by bequests the church acquired much land and wealth which became infeudated as did almost all property in the middle ages. Mortmain. Lay investiture. Efforts of the church to serve as peacemaker in the endless feudal warfare. The "Truce of God" and the "Peace of God."

B. Special Recommendations for Reading

Short general accounts. Most of the subjects in this outline are treated briefly in Emerton, *Introduction*, chs. viii and xv; and in *Mediaeval Europe*, ch. xiv. Adams, *Civilization during the middle ages*, ch. ix (see also the same author's article "Feudalism" in the fourteenth edition of the *Ency. Brit.*). Robinson, *History of western Europe*, ch. ix, or *Medieval and modern times*, ch. vi. Evans, *Life in mediaeval France*, ch. ii. Crump and Jacob, *Legacy*, 287–319. Munro and Sontag, *Middle ages*, ch. xii. Thorndike, *Medieval Europe*, ch. xiii. Hulme, *Middle ages*, ch. xiv. Brown, *The achievement of the middle ages*, 46–120. Thompson, *Economic and social history*, ch. xxvi. Munro and Sellery, *Medieval civilization*, 159–211.

More extended accounts. The best survey of moderate compass is by Seignobos, in Lavisse et Rambaud, *Histoire générale*, II, ch. i, translated by E. W. Dow, *The feudal régime*, New York, 1902. A similar treatment with more particular reference to France is in Lavisse, *Histoire de France*, II, part I, 194–215, 414–39; part II, 1–38. *C.M.H.*, III, chs. xviii, xx. J. Calmette, *La société féodale*, 2nd edition, Paris, 1927. J. Declareuil, *Histoire générale du droit français*, 171–388. The article "Féodalité" by Mortet in *La grande encyclopédie*, XVII, 191–229, is authoritative.

Germanic ideas of law. Emerton, *Introduction*, ch. viii. H. C. Lea, *Superstition and force*, Philadelphia, 1878; 4th edition, 1892. J. B. Thayer, *A preliminary treatise on evidence at the common law*, Boston, 1898, chs. i and ii. G. Neilson, *Trial by combat*, London, 1890, 1–74. J. W. Jeudwine, *Tort, crime, and police in medieval Britain, a review of some early law and custom*, London, 1917.

Roman law in the early middle ages. P. VINOGRADOFF, *Roman law in mediaeval Europe*, New York, 1909; new edition, 1929.

The church and feudalism. H. C. LEA, *Studies in church history*, 342–91 (see also pp. 524–74 on slavery). THOMPSON, *Economic and social history*, ch. XXV.

Peace of God and Truce of God. LAVISSE, *Histoire de France*, II, part II, 133–38. Article "Truce of God" in *Ency. Brit.*

Original sources. For illustrative documents in English translation see *Translations and reprints*, IV, no. 3, "Documents illustrative of feudalism," and no. 4, "Ordeals, compurgation, etc."; OGG, *Source book*, 196–232; THATCHER and MCNEAL, *Source book*, 341–87; WEBSTER, *Historical selections*, 467–70, 483–500; and ROBINSON, *Readings*, I, 171–91.

Maps. SHEPHERD, *Atlas*, 69. LONGNON, *Atlas historique de la France*, plates VII–XI.

C. BIBLIOGRAPHY

General books. Feudal conditions are touched upon in a large number of general books on the middle ages, but see especially the manuals on the history of institutions of France, Germany and Italy, nos. **527–36, 552, 578–87, 605–09.** See also the important books of FUSTEL DE COULANGES, pp. 168–69.

Feudalism in general. V. MENZEL, *Die Entstehung des Lehnswesens*, Berlin, 1890. F. LOT, *Fidèles ou vassaux: étude sur la nature juridique du lien qui unissait les grands vassaux à la royauté depuis le milieu du IXe siècle jusqu'à la fin du XIIe siècle*, Paris, 1904 (Diss.). J. T. ABDY, *Feudalism: its rise, progress, and consequences*, London, 1890. R. WIART, *Essai sur la precaria*, Paris, 1894. A. PROST, *L'immunité: études sur l'histoire et la développement de cette institution*, Paris, 1882, extract from *Nouvelle revue historique du droit français*. E. BOUTARIC, "Le régime féodal, son origine et son établissement, et particulièrement de l'immunité," *R.Q.H.*, XVIII (1875), 325–80. P. ROTH, *Feudalität und Unterthanenverband*, Weimar, 1863 [see the important review of this book by G. WAITZ, "Die Anfänge des Lehnwesens," *H.Z.*, XIII (1865), 90–111]. P. ROTH, *Geschichte des Benefizialwesens von den ältesten Zeiten bis ins zehnte Jahrhundert*, Erlangen, 1850. E. BEAUDOIN, *Etudes sur les origines du régime féodal: la recommandation et la justice seigneuriale* (Annales de l'enseignement supérieur de Grenoble, 1889). A. GENGEL, *Die Geschichte des fränkischen Reichs im besonderen Hinblick auf die Entstehung des Feudalismus*, Frauenfeld, 1908. G. WAITZ, *Über die Anfänge der Vassalität*, Göttingen, 1856 (from vol. VII of no. **897**). H. P. FANGERON, *Les bénéfices et la vassalité au IXe siècle*, Rennes, 1868. F. LOT, *L'impôt foncier et la capitation personelle sous le bas empire et à l'époque franque*, Paris, 1928. DU CANGE, *Glossarium*, no. **309** note, contains much valuable information about feudal terms.

Feudalism in France. P. GUILHIERMOZ, *Essai sur l'origine de la noblesse en France au moyen âge*, Paris, 1902. H. SÉE, *Les classes rurales et le régime domanial en France au moyen âge*, Paris, 1901, has an excellent bibliography, pp. vi–xxxvii. M. KRÖLL, *L'immunité franque*, Paris, 1911. E. BOURGEOIS, *Le capitulaire de Kiersy-sur-Oise (877)*, Paris, 1885 (Diss.). C. SEIGNOBOS, *Le régime féodal en Bourgogne jusqu'en 1360*, Paris, 1882. A. MOLINIER, "Géographie féodale du Languedoc," *Histoire générale de Languedoc*, XII, 225–312; and "Etude sur l'administration féodale dans le Languedoc, 900–1250," *ibid.*, VII, 132–213. SOULGÉ [pseudonym], *Essai d'introduction à la publication de terriers foréziens: le régime féodal et la propriété paysanne*, Paris, 1923. C. STEPHENSON, "The origin and nature of the 'Taille,'" in *Revue belge de philologie et d'histoire*, V (1926), 801–70.

Feudalism in Germany and the Low Countries. THOMPSON, *Feudal Germany*, chs. IX–X. S. E. TURNER, *A sketch of the Germanic constitution from early times to the dissolution of the empire*, New York and London, 1888. V. ERNST, *Die Entstehung des niederen Adels*, Stuttgart, 1916. G. L. v. MAURER, *Geschichte der Frohnhöfe, Bauernhöfe und Hofverfassung in Deutschland*, 4 vols., Erlangen, 1862. V. ERNST, *Die Entstehung des deutschen Grundeigentums*, Stuttgart, 1926. W. BLOMMAERT, *Les châtelains de Flandre: étude d'histoire constitutionelle*, Ghent, 1915. F. L. GANSHOF, *Etude sur les ministeriales en Flandre et en Lotharingie*, Brussels, 1926.

Slavery and serfdom. P. ALLARD, *Les esclaves chrétiens*, Paris, 1914; and *Les origines du servage en France*, Paris, 1913. AGNES M. WERGELAND, *Slavery in Germanic society during the middle ages*, Chicago, 1916. F. SCHAUB, *Studien zur Geschichte der Sklaverei im Frühmittelalter*, Berlin, 1913 (Abhandlungen zur mittleren und neueren Geschichte, 44). F. PIJPER, "The Christian church and slavery in the middle ages," *A.H.R.*, XIV (1909), 675–95. M. BLOCH, *Rois et serfs, un chapitre d'histoire capétienne*, Paris, 1920.

Church and feudalism. E. LESNE, *Histoire de la propriété ecclésiastique en France aux époques romaine el mérovingienne*, Paris, 1910. G. A. PRÉVOST, *L'église et les campagnes au moyen âge*, Paris, 1892. U. STUTZ, *Geschichte des kirchlichen Benefizialwesens von seinen Anfängen bis auf die Zeit Alexanders III*, Berlin, 1896.

Peace of God and Truce of God. L. HUBERTI, *Studien zur Rechtsgeschichte der Gottesfrieden und Landfrieden*, vol. I, *Die Friedens-Ordnungen in Frankreich*, Ansbach, 1892. K. W. NITZSCH, *Heinrich IV und die Gottes- und Landfrieden* [in *F.D.G.*, XXI (1881), 269–97]. S. HERZBERG-FRÄNKEL, *Die ältesten Land- und Gottesfrieden in Deutschland* (*ibid.*, III). E. SÉMICHON, *La paix et la trève de dieu*, Paris, 1857; 2nd edition, 1869. F. KÜCH, *Die Landfriedensbestrebungen Kaiser Friedrichs I*, Marburg, 1887 (Diss.). J. FEHR, *Der Gottesfriede und die katholische Kirche des Mittelalters*, Augsburg, 1861. A. KLUCKHOLM, *Geschichte des Gottesfriedens*, Leipzig, 1857.

Germanic law. K. VON AMIRA, *Grundriss des germanischen Rechts*, 3rd edition, Strasburg, 1913 (vol. V of the 3rd edition of no. **307**). E. H. MACNEAL, *The minores and mediocres in the Germanic tribal laws*, Chicago, 1905 (Diss.). E. JENKS, *Law and politics in the middle ages with a synoptic table of sources*, London, 1913 (see especially ch. I). F. POLLOCK and F. W. MAITLAND, *The history of English law before the time of Edward I*, 2 vols., Cambridge, 1895; 2nd edition, 1898. W. STACH, "Lex Salica und Codex

Euricianus," *H.V.J.S.*, XXI (1923), 385–422. O. DECLAREUIL, *Les épreuves judiciaires dans le droit franc du Ve au VIIIe siècle*, Paris, 1899. F. PATETTA, *Le ordalie*, Turin, 1890. S. BIDAULT DES CHAUMES, *Etude sur le Mallum*, Paris, 1906. J. J. H. DAGASSAN, *Du relèvement de l'autorité publique sous Charlemagne, étude sur le droit public aux VIIIe et IXe siècles d'après les capitulaires*, Bordeaux, 1895. H. BRUNNER, *Die Entstehung der Schwurgerichte*, Berlin, 1872; to be supplemented by C. H. HASKINS, "The early Norman jury," *A.H.R.*, VIII (1902–03), 613–40. R. HUEBNER, *A history of Germanic private law*, translated by FRANCIS S. PHILBRICK, Boston, 1918. R. HIS, *Geschichte des deutschen Strafrechts bis zur Karolina*, Munich and Berlin, 1928, part of no. **330.** F. KERN, "Recht und Verfassung in Mittelalter," *H.Z.*, CXX (1919), 1–79.

Roman law in the early middle ages. A. v. HALBAN-BLUMENSTOCK, *Das römische Recht in den germanischen Volksstaaten*, Breslau, 1899–1907 (parts 56, 65, and 89 of Untersuchungen zur deutschen Staats und Rechtsgeschichte, edited by O. GIERKE, Breslau, 1878ff.).

Original sources. Much miscellaneous matter may be found in such general collections as nos. **967, 978,** and **988.** The important *Formulae Merovingici et Karolini aevi*, edited by K. ZEUMER in no. **978,** *Leges*, vol. V, Hannover, 1882–86, had been edited by E. DE ROZIÈRE entitled, *Recueil général des formules usités dans l'empire des Francs du Ve au Xe siècle*, 3 vols., Paris, 1859–71. *Textes relatifs aux institutions privées et publiques aux époques mérovingienne et carolingienne*, edited by M. THÉVENIN, Paris, 1887, part of no. **968.** *Layettes du trésor des chartes*, edited by A. TEULET and DE LABORDE, 3 vols., Paris, 1863–75. *Livre des vassaux du comté de Champagne et de Brie, 1172–1222*, edited by A. LONGNON, Paris, 1869. *Documents relatifs au comté de Champagne et de Brie, 1172–1361*, edited by A. LONGNON, 3 vols., Paris, 1901–14. A very interesting picture of the way in which the most famous abbey of Paris was involved in feudalism is furnished by the *Polyptique de l'abbé Irminon ou dénombrement des manses, des serfs et des revenus de l'abbaye de St. Germain de Prés sous le règne de Charlemagne*, edited with prolegomena by B. GUÉRARD, 2 vols., Paris, 1844; new edition by A. LONGNON, 2 vols., Paris, 1886–95.

Bibliographies. The best bibliography is in DAHLMANN-WAITZ, nos. 4383–4614. See also *C.M.H.*, II, 810–12.

XIII. THE BEGINNINGS OF THE GREATER MEDIEVAL MONARCHIES

A. OUTLINE

1. The inevitable conflict between the various political factors in the middle ages: (1) papacy, (2) empire, (3) kingdoms, (4) local feudal principalities, (5) cities. The ultimate victory of the kingdoms. The nature and importance of kingship in the middle ages.

2. Louis the Pious, the successor of Charlemagne, 814–40. His relations with the church and the papacy. Various divisions of his empire during

his reign. The birth of Charles (the Bald), in 822. Wars with his sons. The "Field of Lies," 833.

3. The break-up of the empire of Charlemagne. The fatal principle of division, the attacks of foes from all sides, and other causes. Civil strife between the sons of Louis the Pious: Lothair, Louis the German, and Charles (Pepin had died in 838). The battle of Fontenay, 841. The Strasburg oaths, 842. The important Treaty of Verdun, 843. The shoe-strong portion of Lothair, *Lotharii regnum* (later Lotharingia), a permanent source of trouble. Well-defined East-Frankish and West-Frankish regions. Partition of Mersen, 870. Charles II, the Bald, 875–81. Charles the Fat (881–87), sole ruler of the Franks in 885. His weakness was illustrated by the siege of Paris by the Northmen in 885, and he was deposed in 887.

4. The grand divisions of the Carolingian empire: (1) West-Frankish kingdom, (2) East-Frankish kingdom, (3) Italy, (4) Burgundy, (5) Provence, (6) Lorraine.

5. Germany, the East-Frankish kingdom. The great stem duchies: (1) Saxony, (2) Franconia, (3) Bavaria, (4) Swabia. The intermediate position of Lotharingia, or Lorraine. The early kings of Germany: Arnulf of Carinthia (887–99), Louis the Child, (899–911), Conrad I of Franconia (911–18), Henry I, the Fowler (919–36). The importance of the last reign. Battle near Merseburg on the Unstrut against the Hungarians in 933.

6. France, the West-Frankish kingdom. Odo, count of Paris, hero of the siege of Paris, king of West Frankland 888–98, soon after became the vassal of Arnulf, king of Germany. For a whole century it was doubtful whether France would be independent or subject to Germany. The successors of Odo: Charles the Simple, 898–923; Robert I, 923; Rudolf of Burgundy, 923–36. Reinstatement of the Carolingian line in the person of Louis IV, d'Outre-mer, 936–54, (son of Charles the Simple). His successors, Lothaire, 954–86, and Louis V, le Débonnair, 986–87, were the last of the Carolingians in the West. The change of dynasty in 987 when Hugh Capet (987–96), founder of the Capetian line) was chosen king. Paris became the capital. Painfully slow growth of kingly power under his successors, Robert II, the Pious, 996–1031; Henry I, 1031–60; Philip I, 1060–1108. During this last reign, William of Normandy won England, 1066, and the crusades began in 1095.

7. Italy. Rivalry between Berengar of Friuli and Guy of Spoleto. Invasions of the Saracens (see outline IX) and Hungarians (see outline XI). Alberic's domination in Rome, 928–41. The degradation of the papacy (Marozia; pope John XI, 931–36).

8. England, from Alfred the Great (871–901) to William the Conqueror (1066–87).

9. The importance of the middle region, Lorraine and Burgundy.

10. The rising kingdoms of Spain (see outline XXXIV).

B. Special Recommendations for Reading

Short general sketches. Emerton, *Medieval Europe*, chs. i and iii. Davis, *Medieval Europe*, chs. iii–iv. Thompson, *Economic and social his-*

tory, ch. IX. THORNDIKE, *Medieval Europe*, ch. XIV. HULME, *Middle ages*, ch. XIII. MUNRO and SONTAG, *Middle ages*, chs. XI, XIV, and XVI. SELLERY and KREY, *Medieval foundations*, 77–99.

Longer general accounts. *C.M.H.*, III, chs. I–VII. OMAN, *The dark ages*, chs. XXIII–XXIX, together with TOUT, *Empire and papacy*, chs. II (in part) and IV. LAVISSE et RAMBAUD, *Histoire générale*, I, chs. VIII, X, XI.

France. Short sketches in English may be found in ADAMS, *Growth of the French nation*, chs. V–VI. FUNCK-BRENTANO, *Middle ages*, chs. I–V. THOMPSON, *Economic and social history*, ch. XII. MACDONALD, *A history of France*, I, chs. VI–VII. The best account is in LAVISSE, *Histoire de France*, II, part I, 358–413; part II, 39–77, 144–78.

Germany. THOMPSON, *Feudal Germany*, ch. I. E. F. HENDERSON, *A history of Germany in the middle ages*, chs. VI–VIII. W. STUBBS, *Germany in the early middle ages*, chs. III–V. *Handbuch der deutschen Geschichte*, edited by GEBHARDT, I, portions of chs. VI and VIII.

Italy. THOMPSON, *Economic and social history*, ch. XIII. P. VILLARI, *Mediaeval Italy from Charlemagne to Henry VII*, 1–75. H. B. COTTERILL, *Mediaeval Italy*, 385–98. H. D. SEDGWICK, *Short history of Italy*, chs. VII–VIII.

Maps. SHEPHERD, *Atlas*, 56, 58–65. (Read FREEMAN, *Historical geography of Europe*, in connection with it.) TILLEY, *Medieval France*, ch. I. LONGNON, *Atlas historique de la France*, plates VI–XI, and explanatory text.

C. BIBLIOGRAPHY

General books. The general books on France, Belgium, and the Netherlands, Germany, and Italy, nos. **508–621**, are especially useful. Some of the books mentioned in the outline on "Charlemagne," above, such as MÜHLBACHER and KLEINCLAUSZ, pertain to this period. The same is true of many books in the previous outline on "Early medieval institutions," such as GENGEL and BOURGEOIS.

Decline of the Carolingians. J. CALMETTE, *La diplomatie carolingienne du traité de Verdun à la morte de Charles le Chauve, 843–77*, Paris, 1901, part of no. **888.** J. W. THOMPSON, *The decline of the missi dominici in Frankish Gaul*, Chicago, 1903. G. MONOD, *Du rôle de l'opposition des races et des nationalités dans la dissolution de l'empire carolingien* (in Annuaire de l'Ecole pratique des hautes études, 1896). T. POUZET, *La succession de Charlemagne et le traité de Verdun*, Paris, 1890. F. LOT and L. HALPHEN, *Annales de l'histoire de France à l'époque carolingienne: le règne de Charles le Chauve (840–877)*, part I, 840–51, Paris, 1909, part of no. **888.** K. VOIGT, *Die karolingische Klosterpolitik.* F. LOT, *La Loire, l'Aquitaine et la Seine, de 862 à 866: Robert le Fort*, Nogent-le-Rotrou, 1916. W. VOGEL, *Die Normannen und das fränkische Reich*, Heidelberg, 1906. F. LOT, "La grande invasion (856–62)," *B.E.C.*, LXIX (1908), 1–62. E. JORANSON, *The Danegeld in France.*

Oaths of Strasburg. A. GASTÉ, *Les serments de Strasbourg: étude historique, critique et philologique*, 2nd edition, Paris, 1888. A. KRAFFET, *Les serments carolingiens de 842 à Strasbourg en roman et tudesque: avec nouvelles interpré-*

tations linguistiques et considérations ethnographiques, Paris, 1901. J. W. THOMPSON, "The romance text of the Strassburg Oaths: was it written in the ninth century?", *Speculum*, I, 410–38. For replies to this see F. L. GANSHOF, "Une nouvelle théorie sur les serments de Strasbourg," *Studi medievali* (N. S.), II:1 (1929), 9–25 and L. F. H. LOWE and B. EDWARDS, "The language of the Strassburg oaths," *Speculum*, II (July, 1927), 316ff.

Beginnings of France. J. FLACH, *Les origines de l'ancienne France: Xe et XIe siècles*, 4 vols., Paris, 1886–1917. F. FUNCK-BRENTANO, *L'ancienne France: le roi.* H. SCHREUER, *Die rechtlichen Grundgedanken der französischen Königskrönung.* A. LONGNON, *Origines et formation de la nationalité française, éléments ethniques, unité territoriale*, Paris, 1912; *La formation de l'unité française*, Paris, 1922. R. LATOUCHE, *Histoire du comté du Maine pendant le Xe et le XIe siècle*, Paris, 1910. L. HALPHEN, *Le comté d'Anjou au XIe siècle*, Paris, 1906. F. LOT, *Mélanges d'histoire bretonne* [6–11 century], Paris, 1907. J. FLACH, "Le comté de Flandre et ses rapports avec la couronne de France du IXe au XIIe siècle,'' *R.H.*, CXV (1914), 1–33, 241–71. F. FUNCK-BRENTANO, *The earliest times.* J. CALMETTE, *La société féodale.*

Early kings of France, 888–987. E. FAVRE, *Eudes, comte de Paris et roi de France, 882–898*, Paris, 1893, part of no. **888.** A. ECKEL, *Charles le Simple*, Paris, 1899, part of no. **888.** P. LAUER, *Robert Ier et Raoul de Bourgogne, rois de France, 923–936*, Paris, 1910, part of no. **888.** W. LIPPERT, *König Rudolf von Frankreich*, Leipzig, 1886 (Diss.). P. LAUER, *Le règne de Louis IV, d'Outre-mer*, Paris, 1900, part of no. **888.** A. HEIL, *Die politischen Beziehungen zwischen Otto dem Grossen und Ludwig IV von Frankreich (936–954)*, Berlin, 1904 (Historische Studien, 46). C. SCHOENE, *Die politischen Beziehungen zwischen Deutschland und Frankreich 953–980*, Berlin, 1910. F. LOT, *Les derniers Carolingiens: Lothaire, Louis V, Charles de Lorraine (954–991)*, Paris, 1891, part of no. **888.** A. HIMLY, *Wala et Louis le Débonnaire*, Paris, 1849.

Hugh Capet and the Capetian kings, 987–1108. A. LUCHAIRE, *Histoire des institutions monarchiques de la France (987–1180)*, 2 vols., 2nd edition, Paris, 1891ff. F. LOT, *Etudes sur le règne de Hugues Capet et la fin du Xe siècle*, Paris, 1903, part of no. **888.** C. PFISTER, *Etudes sur le règne de Robert le Pieux, 996–1031*, Paris, 1885, part of no. **888.** A. FLICHE, *Le règne de Philippe Ier, roi de France (1060–1108)*, Paris, 1912.

Germany. B. SIMSON, *Jahrbücher des fränkischen Reiches unter Ludwig dem Frommen*, 2 vols., Leipzig, 1874–76; E. DÜMMLER, *Geschichte des ostfränkischen Reiches* [to 918], 2nd edition, 3 vols., Leipzig, 1887–88; G. WAITZ, *Jahrbücher des deutschen Reiches unter Heinrich I*, 3rd edition, Leipzig, 1885; all part of no. **570.**

Italy. G. ROMANO, *Le dominazioni barbariche in Italia, 395–1024*, Milan, 1909ff., part of no. **599.** C. W. PREVITÉ-ORTON, *The early history of the House of Savoy, 1000–1233*, Cambridge, 1912. G. MENGOZZI, *La città italiana nell' alto medio evo: il periodo longobardo-franco*, Rome, 1914. S. HELLMANN, *Die Grafen von Savoyen und das Reich bis zum Ende der staufischen Periode*, Innsbruck, 1900. A. HOFMEISTER, *Markgrafen und*

Markgrafschaften im italischen Königreich in der Zeit von Karl dem Grossen bis auf Otto den Grossen, Ergänzungsband, VII (1906) of no. **166.**

Lorraine. R. PARISOT, *Le royaume de Lorraine sous les Carolingiens, 843–923*, Paris, 1899 (Diss.); and *Les origines de la Haute-Lorraine et sa première maison ducale, 959–1033*, Paris, 1909. H. WELSCHINGER, *Strasbourg*, Paris, 1908. See also nos. **597–98.**

Burgundy. A. HOFMEISTER, *Deutschland und Burgund im früheren Mittelalter: eine Studie über die Entstehung des arelatischen Reiches und seine politische Bedeutung*, Leipzig, 1914. E. PETIT, *Histoire des ducs de Bourgogne de la race capétienne* [to 1363], 9 vols., Paris, 1885–1905. R. POUPARDIN, *La royaume de Bourgogne (888–1038)*, Paris, 1907. L. JACOB, *Le royaume de Bourgogne sous les empereurs franconiens, 1038–1125*, Paris, 1906. M. CHAUME, *Les origines du duché de Bourgogne*, vol. I: *Histoire politique*, Dijon, 1925. A. J. KLEINCLAUSZ, *Dijon et Beaune*, Paris, 1907, and A. HALLAYS, *Nancy*, Paris, 1908.

Provence. G. DE MANTEYER, *La Provence du premier au douzième siècle*, Paris, 1908, in Mémoires et documents of the Société de l'École des chartes, vol. VIII. R. POUPARDIN, *Le royaume de Provence sous les Carolingiens (855–933)*, Paris, 1901, part of no. **888.** F. KIENER, *Verfassungsgeschichte der Provence seit der Ostgothenherrschaft bis zur Errichtung der Konsulate (510–1200)*, Leipzig, 1900. C. W. PREVITÉ-ORTON, "Italy and Provence, 900–50," in *E.H.R.*, XXXII (1917), 335–47. E. DUPRAT, *La Provence dans le haut moyen âge (406–1113)*, Marseilles, 1923. E. CAMAN, *La Provence à travers les siècles*, II. *Invasions barbares; au pouvoir des rois francs; les rois de province; l'église du VIe au XIIe siècle*, Paris, 1920. V. L. BOURILLY and R. BUSQUET, *La Provence au moyen âge*, Marseilles, 1924. R. POUPARDIN, *Recueil des actes des rois de Provence, 855–928*, Paris, 1920.

Original sources. Practically all of the important sources have been published in nos. **965–94.** NITHARD, *Histoire des fils de Louis le Pieux, avec un fac-simile des serments de Strasbourg*, is edited and translated by P. LAUER, Paris, 1926. *Die Regesten des Kaiserreichs unter den Karolingern, 751–918*, 2nd edition, completed by J. LECHNER, Innsbruck, 1908, are continued by *Die Regesten des Kaiserreichs unter den Herrschern aus dem sächsischen Hause, 919–1024*, new edition by E. v. OTTENTHAL, part I (to 973), Innsbruck, 1893, parts of no. **985.** For documentary material on early France, see especially no. **975.**

Bibliographies. DAHLMANN-WAITZ, pp. 289–95 *passim*, 298–301, 324–33. The sources, especially for France, are best described in A. MOLINIER, *Les sources*, I, pp. 227–86; II, 1–18. See also the general bibliographies, nos. **21–41** and THOMPSON, *Economic and social history*, 824.

XIV. REVIVAL OF THE MEDIEVAL EMPIRE IN THE WEST IN GERMANY

A. OUTLINE

1. The manifold transformations of the medieval empire make it a difficult and elusive subject to study. Glaring contrasts between theory and actuality.

2. The early years of the reign of Otto I, 936–62. Splendid coronation at Aachen. Local German affairs with feudal nobles and the church. Wars with Slavs and Hungarians (Lechfeld, 955). Relations with Italy. The political state of Italy and the papacy in the tenth century. Alberic II. Saracens and Byzantines in the south. Adelaide of Burgundy, widow of Lothair, was imprisoned by Berengar of Ivrea. Otto intervened in Italy in 951, married Adelaide, and became king of Italy.

3. The creation of the German-Roman empire. Fearful degradation of the papacy and the church in Italy. In 961 Otto crossed the Alps to restore order. In 962 he was crowned emperor by pope John XII. Otto's empire compared with that of Charlemagne. Results of the revival of the imperial dignity for Germany and Italy, especially the papacy. Otto I relations with the Byzantine empire. His son (later Otto II), who had been crowned king of the Germans in 961 and emperor on Christmas day 967, was married in 972 to Theophano, daughter of the eastern emperor Romanus II.

4. Otto II, 973–83. He ascended the throne at the age of eighteen. Laid more stress on his position as emperor than on his position as German king. Crescentius, duke of the Romans, ca. 980. Wars with the Greeks in south Italy. Diet of Verona in 983 to plan a campaign against the Saracens. Otto II died at the age of twenty-eight and was buried in St. Peter's in Rome.

5. Otto III, 983–1002, the "Wonder of the world." Only three years old at his accession. His Greek mother Theophano (died 991) became regent. Coronation of Otto in 996. Revolt of the second Crescentius. Influence of the clergy on Otto III. His dream of a real Roman empire with Rome as its capital. Gerbert of Aurillac (pope Sylvester II, 999–1003). Learning at the Ottonian court. Otto's loss of hold in Germany and failure in Italy. He died in 1002 at the age of twenty-two, and was buried in Aachen.

6. Henry II (the Saint), 1002–24, son of Henry the Quarrelsome of Bavaria. Wars with the king of Poland, Boleslav, and extension of German influence and the Roman church eastward. Crowned emperor in Rome in 1014 by pope Benedict VIII. Close relations of Henry with the Cluniac reforming monks in Germany.

7. The empire at its height; Conrad II (1024–39), and Henry III (1039–56). With Conrad the Saxon line of kings and emperors (911–1024) ended, and the Franconian or Salian line (1024–1125) began. Conrad's wars with the Poles. Union of Burgundy with the empire in 1032. Henry III's successful foreign policy. Comparative order within his empire. His control of the German church and his ardor for church reform. The synod at Sutri, 1046, and the deposition of three rival popes (Sylvester III, Benedict IX, Gregory VI). Henry appointed as pope the German Clement II, who crowned him emperor December 25, 1046.

8. The impending irrepressible conflict between the empire and the papacy.

9. The origin of the name "Holy Roman Empire of the German People."

10. Kings of Germany, 887–1056.

Arnulf, 887–96	Otto II, 973–83
Louis, the Child, 899–11	Otto III, 983–1002
Conrad I, 911–19	Henry II, the Saint, 1002–24
Henry I, the Fowler, 919–36	Conrad II, 1024–39
Otto I, the Great, 936–73	Henry III, the Black, 1039–56

B. Special Recommendations for Reading

General accounts. Best of all is J. Bryce, *Holy Roman Empire*, chs. vii-ix. *C.M.H.*, III, chs. viii-xii. Emerton, *Medieval Europe*, chs. iii-vi. Tout, *The empire and the papacy*, chs. i-iii. Munro and Sontag, *Middle ages*, chs. xiv-xv. Hulme, *Middle ages*, 325–60. Lavisse et Rambaud, *Histoire générale*, I, 542–69. Henderson, *A history of Germany in the middle ages*, chs. viii-xii (or a shorter sketch in *A short history of Germany*, ch. iii). Fisher, *The medieval empire*, I, chs. i-ii, *passim*. Thompson, *Economic and social history*, ch. xi. *Handbuch der deutschen Geschichte*, edited by B. Gebhardt, I, ch. viii. Thompson, *Feudal Germany*. E. H. Zeydel, *The Holy Roman Empire in German literature*, New York, 1918 (Diss.).

Italy in this period. Villari, *Medieval Italy from Charlemagne to Henry VII*, part I, chs. v-vi. Gregorovius, *Rome in the middle ages*, II, book VI. L. M. Hartmann, *Geschichte Italiens im Mittelalter*, vol. IV, part I. *Die ottonische Herrschaft*, Gotha, 1915. H. K. Mann, *Lives of the popes in the early middle ages*, vols. IV–VI, London, 1902ff. L. Duchesne, *Beginnings of the temporal sovereignty of the popes*, chs. xv-xix (English translation), Chicago, 1908.

Nature of the German empire. A. Kleinclausz, *L'empire carolingien*, pp. 541–85. J. Janssen, "International conception of the Holy Roman empire," in *History of the German people*, translated from the German by M. A. Mitchell, St. Louis, 1896ff., II, 105–17. A. J. Carlyle, *History of political theories*, vol. IV, Edinburgh and London, 1922.

Origin of name, " Holy Roman Empire of the German People." K. Zeumer, *Heiliges römisches Reich deutscher Nation*, Weimar, 1910.

Original sources. Among the interesting sources of the period is *Der Hrotsuitha Gedicht über Gandersheims Gründung und die Thaten Kaiser Oddo I*, translated into German by T. G. Pfund, 2nd edition, Leipzig, 1891, part of no. **981.** For short extracts from the sources see Robinson, *Readings*, I, 245–65; and Thatcher and McNeal, *Source book*, 72–81.

Maps. Shepherd, *Atlas*, 58–9, 62–3. F. Philippi, *Atlas zur westlichen Altertumskunde des deutschen Mittelalters*, part I, Bonn, 1923.

C. Bibliography

General books. See works on the medieval empire in the west, nos. **499–507**, and general books on Germany and Italy, nos. **560–621.** See also no. **538.**

General accounts. M. Manitius, *Deutsche Geschichte unter den sächsischen und salischen Kaisern, 911–1125*, Stuttgart, 1889, part of no. **560.**

J. Bühler, *Die sächsischen und salischen Kaiser*, Leipzig, 1924. K. Hampe, *Deutsche Kaisergeschichte in der Zeit der Salier und Staufer*, Leipzig, 1909; 3rd edition, 1916, part of no. **320.** J. Zeller, *Fondation de l'empire germanique: Otton le Grand et les Ottonides*, Paris, 1873. E. Rosenstock, *Könighaus und Stämme in Deutschland zwischen 911 und 1250*, Leipzig, 1914. Gerda Bäseler, *Die Kaiserkrönungen in Rom und die Römer von Karl dem Grossen bis Friederich II (800–1250)*, Freiburg, 1919. A. Kroener, *Wahl und Krönung der deutschen Kaiser und Könige in Italien (Lombardei)*, Freiburg, 1901. T. Lindner, *Die deutschen Königswahlen, und die Entstehung des Kurfürstenthums*, Leipzig, 1893. B. Schmeidler, *Hamburg-Bremen und Nordost-Europa vom 9. bis 11. Jahrhundert*, Leipzig, 1918.

Otto I. R. Köpke and E. Dümmler, *Jahrbücher Kaiser Otto der Grosse*, Leipzig, 1876, part of no. **570.** The life of the empress Adelaide is told in the two doctoral dissertations: E. P. Wimmer, *Kaiserin Adelheid, Gemahlin Ottos I der Grosse, in ihrem Leben und Wirken von 931–73*, Erlangen, 1897; and J. Bentzinger, *Das Leben der Kaiserin Adelheid, Gemahlin Ottos I, während der Reigierung Ottos III*, Breslau, 1883. For wars with Slavs and especially Hungarians, see outline XI, above.

Otto II. K. Uhlirz, *Jahrbücher des deutschen Reiches unter Otto II und Otto III*, vol. 1, *Otto II*, Leipzig, 1902, part of no. **570.** G. Müller-Mann, *Die auswärtige Politik Kaiser Ottos II*, Lörrach, 1898 (Göttingen Diss.). For the Greek Theophano, wife of Otto II, see J. Moltmann, *Theophano, die Gemahlin Ottos II, in ihrer Bedeutung für die Politik Ottos I und Ottos II*, Göttingen, 1878 (Diss.).

Otto III. R. Wilmans, *Jahrbücher des deutschen Reiches unter Otto III*, Berlin, 1840. P. Kehr, "Zur Geschichte Ottos III," *H.Z.*, LXVI (1891), 385–443. L. Halphen, "La cour d'Otto III à Rome (998–1001)," *Mélanges d'archéologie et d'histoire*, XXV. C. Lux, *Papst Silvester II Einfluss auf die Politik Kaiser Ottos III*, Breslau, 1898. W. Norden, *Erzbischof Friedrich von Mainz und Otto der Grosse*, Berlin, 1912.

Henry II. S. Hirsch, *Jahrbücher des deutschen Reiches unter Heinrich II*, 3 vols., Leipzig, 1862–74, part of no. **570.**

Conrad II. H. Bresslau, *Jahrbücher des deutschen Reichs unter Konrad II*, 2 vols., Leipzig, 1879–84, part of no. **570.** J. v. Pflugk-Harttung, *Untersuchungen zur Geschichte Kaiser Konrads II*, Stuttgart, 1890. L. Jacob, *Le royaume de Bourgonde sous les empereurs franconiens*, Paris, 1906.

Henry III. E. Steindorf, *Jahrbücher des deutschen Reichs unter Heinrich III*, 2 vols., Leipzig, 1874–81, is part of no. **570.**

Original sources. All the essential sources are printed in nos. **978–87.**

Bibliographies. Dahlmann-Waitz, *Quellenkunde*, pp. 324–37, 344–45. See also nos. **29–35.** R. Bemmann, *Bibliographie der sächsischen Geschichte*, Leipzig, 1918.

XV. THE CHURCH FROM THE EIGHTH TO THE ELEVENTH CENTURY

A. Outline

1. Relation of the church and state in Carolingian times. Contrast between the reigns of Charlemagne and Louis the Pious. Beginnings of the struggle between empire and papacy for pre-eminence. The question of the crowning of emperors by popes and the recognition of popes by emperors.

2. The papacy in the ninth century. The donations to the papacy. The states of the church ("Patrimony of St. Peter"). Attacks of Saracens on Rome before and during the pontificate of Leo IV, 847–55. The "Leonine City." The pseudo-Isidorian Decretals ("False Decretals"). The very real power of pope Nicholas I (858–67), illustrated by his action in the Photian schism in Constantinople, in the divorce of king Lothair II of Lorraine, and by his victory over Hincmar, the defiant archbishop of Rheims.

3. The widening gulf between the Latin and Greek churches. The iconoclastic controversy began early in the eighth century, when the emperor Leo III, the Isaurian (717–40), declared against images. In 754 the Synod of Constantinople condemned images. The position of Charlemagne and the empress Irene on this question. Other differences between the eastern and western churches. In 863, pope Nicholas I deposed the patriarch Photius in Constantinople, who in turn deposed the pope in a synod at Constantinople in 867. In 1054, pope Leo IX had a bull of excommunication against the patriarch Michael Cerularius and his church laid upon the high altar of St. Sophia. This marks the practical separation of the two churches.

4. Period of utter degradation of the papacy: last quarter of the ninth and first half of the tenth century. Practical disappearance of the empire in the west during this same period. The trial of the corpse of pope Formosus, by pope Stephen VI (896–97). Local factions in Rome in control of the papacy. Theodora and her two daughters, Marozia and Theodora. Alberic and the papacy, 932–54. The interference of Otto I in Rome.

5. The monastic (Cluniac) reform movement in the church in the ninth and tenth centuries. Foundation of the monastery of Cluny in 910. The great abbot Odo of Cluny, 927–48. "The Congregation of Cluny."

6. The papacy and the new German empire. Otto I and pope John XII, 955–64, who crowned him emperor in 962. In his time the empire was supreme over the papacy. Bruno, cousin of Otto III, was the first German pope, with the title Gregory V, 996–99. Dependence of Otto III upon the great French scholar Gerbert, whom he made pope Sylvester II, 999–1003. Absolute control of Henry II over appointment to bishoprics in Germany and Italy. Independence of the German clergy and their zeal for reform. Pope Benedict VIII, 1012–24, and his sympathy with the Cluniac reform movement. Degradation of the papacy in the reign of Conrad II. The young pope, Benedict IX, 1033–48. Reforming zeal of Henry III. Synod at Sutri, 1046. Henry's German popes. Gradual rise of power and dignity of the papacy. The strength of pope Leo IX, 1048–54. Importance given

to creation of the college of cardinals by the Lateran council held in 1059. Impending struggle between the papacy and empire. Peter Damian, 1007–72. Romuald.

7. The expansion of the Latin church, 800–1100. Ansgar, the "Apostle of the North," archbishop of Hamburg in 846, effectually introduced Christianity in Denmark and Sweden, 827ff. Sweden was not completely christianized until the middle of the twelfth century. Christianity found entrance in Norway in the tenth century. Olaf (died 1000) established it firmly, and the famous Olaf the Saint (1014–30) completed the work. Christianity in Greenland about 1000. As a missionary center in the Slav region of the Elbe, the archbishopric of Magdeburg was established in 968. Adalbert was the first archbishop. For the conversion of Moravia by Cyrillus and Methodius see outline XI, above. In Bohemia the archbishopric of Prague was established in 973. In Poland, Posen became an important ecclesiastical center. King Stephen of Hungary made Latin Christianity the legal religion about 1000, and the great archbishopric of Gran was established.

8. The church and society. Increasing wealth of the church and the machinery created to take care of it. Mortmain. Tithes. The church and feudal conditions. The "Truce of God" and the "Peace of God." The life and morals of the clergy. The extensive social and educational work of the church. The church and slavery. The church as a civilizing force in an age of disorganization.

9. The growth of church institutions and practices. The church service; preaching, hymns, the mass, the sacraments. Saints and relics.

10. The growth of ecclesiastical jurisdiction and church discipline. The beginnings of canon law. Conflicts with secular law. Attitude of the church towards ordeals. Ecclesiastical courts. "Benefit of clergy." Means of enforcing church discipline; spiritual suasion and threat, penance, excommunication and interdict. Co-operation on the part of the state.

11. The development of the ecclesiastical hierarchy among the secular clergy; pope, archbishop (primate, or metropolitan), bishop, priest. The cardinals. Ranks and grades among the regular clergy or monks. The election of the clergy. Investiture. Simony.

12. Popes, 816–1054.

Stephen IV, 816–17
Paschal I, 817–24
Eugenius II, 824–27
Valentinus, 827
Gregory IV, 827–44
Sergius II, 844–47
Leo IV, 847–55
Benedict III, 855–58
Nicholas I, 858–67
Hadrian II, 867–72
John VIII, 872–82
Marinus I, 882–84
Hadrian III, 884–85
Stephen V, 885–91
Formosus, 891–96
Boniface VI, 896
Stephen VI, 896–97
Romanus, 897
Theodore II, 897–98
John IX, 898–900
Benedict IV, 900–03
Leo V, 903
Christopher, 903–04
Sergius III, 904–11

Anastasius III, 911–13
Lando, 913–14
John X, 914–28
Leo VI, 928–29
Stephen VII, 929–31
John XI, 931–36
Leo VII, 936–39
Stephen VIII, 939–42
Marinus II, 942–46
Agapitus II, 946–55
John XII, 955–64
Leo VIII, 963–65
Benedict V, 964
John XIII, 965–72
Benedict VI, 972–74
Benedict VII, 974–83
John XIV, 983–84
Boniface VII (antipope, 974–84), 984–85
John XV, 985–96
Gregory V, 996–99
Sylvester II, 999–1003
John XVII, 1003
John XVIII, 1003–09
Sergius IV, 1009–12
Benedict VIII, 1012–24
John XIX, 1024–33
* Benedict IX, 1033–48
* [Sylvester III, 1045–46 antipope]
* Gregory VI, 1045–46
Clement II, 1046–47
Damasus II, 1048
Leo IX, 1048–54
* *Deposed in* 1046.

B. Special Recommendations for Reading

Brief general accounts. Hulme, *Middle ages*, ch. xvi. Munro and Sontag, *Middle ages*, ch. xiii. Thorndike, *Medieval Europe*, ch. xv. Flick, *The rise of the mediaeval church*, chs. xv-xviii. Emerton, *Mediaeval Europe*, 41–88, 115–209. W. H. Hutton, *The church and the barbarians*, London, 1906, chs. xi, xiv-xvii. Barry, *The papal monarchy*, chs. viii-xii. Wells, *The age of Charlemagne*, chs. xxiii-xxiv, xxxii-xxxiv. Bartlet and Carlyle, *Christianity and history*, part III.

Longer account. *C.M.H.*, III, ch. xvii; and V, ch. i. A large portion of this outline is treated authoritatively in H. C. Lea, *Studies in church history*. Gregorovius, *City of Rome*, III and IV. Hartmann, *Geschichte Italiens*, III.

Cluny. Lavisse, *Histoire de France*, II, part II, 123–32 (translated in Munro and Sellery, *Medieval civilization*, 137–52). Tout, *The empire and the papacy*, ch. v. See also the introduction to the book by Duckett, under "Original sources." L. M. Smith, *The early history of the monastery of Cluny*, Oxford, 1920.

Pope Nicholas I. J. Roy, *St. Nicholas Ier*, Paris, 1899 (Les saints), translated by Margaret Maitland, London, 1901.

Gerbert (Pope Sylvester II). Munro and Sellery, *Medieval civilization*, 376–405. R. Allen, "Pope Sylvester II," in *E.H.R.*, VII (1892), 625–68. The best biography of Gerbert is F. J. Picavet, *Gerbert, un pape philosophe*, Paris, 1897.

Interdict. E. B. Krehbiel, *The interdict, its history and its operation, with especial attention to the time of pope Innocent III*, Washington, 1909, 1–85.

Original sources. The foundation charter of the order of Cluny is translated in Ogg, *Source book*, 245–49, and also in Henderson, *Select documents*, 329–33. Henderson, 361–65, has a translation of the Decree of 1059 concerning papal elections, which may also be found in THATCHER and McNEAL, *Source book*, 126–31 (see also 109–26 for other interesting documents). There are examples of excommunication and interdict in *Translations and reprints*, vol. IV, no. 4, "Ordeals, compurgation, excommunication and interdict," pp. 22–32.

Maps. SHEPHERD, *Atlas*, 94–5, 97.

C. BIBLIOGRAPHY

General books. The general histories of the medieval church are listed above, nos. **393–498.** See also the encyclopaedias for the history of the church and religion, nos. **104–14,** and the periodicals for church history, nos. **176–80.**

General accounts. MILMAN, *Latin Christianity*, vol. III, book V. R. H. WRIGHT, *The "Sancta Respublica Romana," A.D. 395–888*, 2nd edition, London, 1891.

The papacy in this period. MANN, *Lives of the popes*, vols. II–VI. L. DUCHESNE, *Les premiers temps de l'état pontifical*, 3rd edition, Paris, 1912, translated by A. H. MATHEW, *The beginnings of the temporal sovereignty of the Popes*, London, 1908. R. BAXMANN, *Die Politik der Päpste von Gregor I bis auf Gregor VII.* H. DOPFFEL, *Kaisertum und Papstweschsel unter den Karolingern*, Freiburg, 1889. M. HEIMBUCHER, *Die Papstwahlen unter den Karolingern*, Augsburg, 1889. J. GAY, *Les papes du XIe siècle et la chrétienté*, Paris, 1926. W. SICKEL, "Die Verträge der Päpste mit den Karolingern," *Deutsche Zeitschrift für Geschichtswissenschaft*, XI (1894), 301–91; XII (1895), 1–43; "Kirchenstaat und Karolinger," *H.Z.*, XLVIII (1900), 389–409. A. LAPÔTRE, *L'Europe et la Saint-Siége à l'époque carolingienne*, vol. I, *Le pape Jean VIII (872–82)*, Paris, 1895. L. HALPHEN, *Etude sur l'administration de Rome au moyen âge (757–1282)*, Paris, 1907. J. HAVET, *Lettres de Gerbert*, Paris, 1889, (part of no. **968**), introduction.

Pope Nicholas I. A. GREINACHER, *Die Anschauungen des Papstes Nikolaus I über das Verhältnis von Staat und Kirche*, Berlin, 1909. J. RICHTERICH, *Papst Nikolaus I*, Bern, 1903 (Diss.). F. ROCQUAIN, *La papauté au moyen âge: Nicolas Ier, Grégoire VII, Innocent III, Boniface VIII*, Paris, 1881. J. ROY, "Principes du pape Nicholas Ier sur les rapports des deux puissances" in no. **939,** 95–105. A. FLICHE, *La chrétienté médiévale, 395–1254*, Paris, 1929. (Vol. VII, Histoire du monde, edited by E. CAVAIGNAC.)

Pseudo-Isidorian Decretals. DÖLLINGER, *Fables respecting the popes in the middle ages;* and *The pope and the council.* E. H. DAVENPORT, *The False Decretals*, Oxford, 1916. P. FOURNIER, *Etudes sur les fausses Décrétales*, Louvain, 1907. F. LOT, "La question des Fausses Décrétales," *R.H.*, XCIV (1907), 290–99. P. FEDELE, "Richerche per la storia da Roma e del papato nel secolo X," *Archivi della R. Società romana di storia patria*, XXXIIIff. R. L. POOLE, *Benedict IX and Gregory VI*, New York, 1918. (From Proceedings of the British Academy VIII.) HEFELE, *Histoire des conciles*, translated by LECLERCQ, Vols. III and IV with full bibliographical notes.

The schism between the Greek and Latin churches. The iconoclastic controversy. *C.M.H.*, IV, ch. IX. VASILIEV, *Byzantine empire*, I, 401–12. BURY, *History of eastern Roman empire.* A very convenient summary of the split between the churches is in W. NORDEN, *Das Papsttum und Byzanz*, 1–31. L. DUCHESNE, *The churches separated from Rome*, translated by A. H. MATHEW, London, 1907. G. B. HOWARD, *The schism between the oriental and western churches*, London, 1892. L. BRÉHIER, *Le schisme oriental du XIe siècle*, Paris, 1899. A. PICHLER, *Geschichte der kirchlichen Trennung zwischen Orient und Okzident*, vols. I and II, Munich, 1864–65. NEUMANN, *Weltstellung*.

L. BRÉHIER, *La querelle des images*, Paris, 1904. K. SCHWARZLOSE, *Der Bilderstreit*, Gotha, 1890. J. HERGENRÖTHER, *Photius: Patriarch von Constantinopel*, 3 vols., Regensburg, 1867–69. For the interesting monks of the *Studium* in Constantinople, who braved persecution in their resistance to the iconoclasts, see E. MARIN, *De studio coenobio constantinopolitano*, Paris, 1897; and *Les moines de Constantinople depuis la fondation de la ville jusqu'à la mort de Photius (300–898)*, Paris, 1897. Their leader in the eighth century was Theodore, whose biography has been written by A. GARDNER, *Theodore of Studium: his life and times*, London, 1905, and G. A. SCHNEIDER, *Der hl. Theodor von Studion: sein Leben und Wirken*, Münster, 1900, part V of **492.** A. MICHEL, *Humbert und Kerullarios*, part I, Paderborn, 1925.

Hincmar. G. C. LEE, *Hincmar: an introduction to the study of the revolution in the organization of the church in the ninth century*, Baltimore, 1897 (Diss.) printed in *American society of church history*, VIII. H. SCHRÖRS *Hincmar Erzbischof von Rheims: sein Leben und seine Schriften*, Freiburg, 1884. C. v. NOORDEN, *Hincmar, Erzbischof von Rheims*, Bonn. 1863. E. LESNE, "Hincmar et l'empereur Lothaire," *R.Q.H.*, LXXVIII (1905), 5–58. G. LETONNELIER, *L'abbaye exempte de Cluny et le Saint-Siége*, Paris, 1923 (Archives de la France monastique, vol. XIII).

Cluniac reform. The standard work on this subject is E. SACKUR, *Die Cluniacenser in ihrer kirchlichen und allgemeingeschichtlichen Wirksamkeit bis zur Mitte des elften Jahrhunderts*, 2 vols., Halle, 1892–94. THOMPSON, *Feudal Germany*, ch. II. LUCY M. SMITH, "Cluny and Gregory VII," in *E.H.R.*, XXVI (1911), 20–33. L. CHAUMONT, *Histoire de Cluny depuis les origines jusqu'à la ruine de l'abbaye*, 2nd edition, enlarged, Paris, 1911. For Saint Odo, the famous abbot of Cluny (927–48), see A. DU BOURG, *Saint Odon (879–942)*, Paris, 1905 (Les saints). Of Saint Odilo, who soon followed Odo, we have two biographies: P. JARDET, *Saint Odilon, abbé de Cluny: sa vie, son temps, ses oeuvres, 962–1049*, Lyons, 1898; O. RINGHOLZ, *Der heilige Abt Odilo von Cluny*, Brünn, 1885. A. HESSEL, "Odo von Cluni und das französische Kulturproblem im früheren Mittelalter," *H.Z.*, CXXVIII (1923), 1–25. J. VIREY, *L'abbaye de Cluny*, Paris, 1921. See THOMPSON, *Reference studies*, 106–09.

The spread of Christianity. G. F. MACLEAR, *A history of christian missions during the middle ages*, Cambridge, 1863, chs. XI–XIV; *Apostles of mediaeval Europe*, London, 1869; *Conversion of the Slavs*, London, 1879; *Conversion of the northern nations*, London, 1865. C. MERIVALE, *The con-*

version of the northern nations, London, 1865. T. SMITH, *Mediaeval missions*, Edinburgh, 1880. K. MAURER, *Bekehrung des norwegischen Stammes zum Christentum*, 2 vols., Munich, 1855–56.

Ecclesiastical elections. Simony. G. WEISE, *Königtum und Bischofswahl im fränkischen und deutschen Reich vor dem Investiturstreit*, Berlin, 1912. A. FLICHE, "Le cardinal Humbert de Moyenmoutier: étude sur les origines de la réforme grégorienne," in *R.H.*, CXIX (1915), 41–76. H. LÉVY-BRUHL, *Etudes sur les élections abbatiales en France jusqu'à la fin du règne de Charles le Chauve*, Paris, 1913 (Diss.). P. IMBART DE LA TOUR, *Les élections épiscopales dans l'église de France, du IXe au XIIe siècles (814–1150)*, Paris, 1890. H. PAHNCKE, *Geschichte der Bischöfe Italiens deutscher Nation von 951–1264*, I: *Geschichte der Bischöfe Italiens deutscher Nation von 951–1004, nebst eine Beilage zur Kritik von P. B. Gams Series episcoporum*, Berlin, 1913. U. BERLIÈRE, *Les élections abbatiales au moyen-âge*, Brussels, 1927. N. A. WEBER, *History of simony* (to A.D. 804), Baltimore, 1909 (Diss.).

Leo IX. W. BRÖCKING, *Die französische Politik Papst Leos IX*, Stuttgart, 1891. J. DREHMANN, *Papst Leo IX und die Simonie*, Leipzig and Berlin, 1908. (Beiträge zur Kulturgeschichte, II). O. DELARC, *Un pape alsacien Léon IX et son temps*, Paris, 1876.

College of Cardinals. G. SCHOBER, *Das Wahldekret vom Jahre 1059*, Breslau, 1914 (Diss.). For additional special literature on this subject see DAHLMANN-WAITZ, no. 4954; and see **453.**

The church and feudalism. A. BERR, *Die Kirche gegenüber Gewalttaten von Laien (Merovinger- Karolinger- und Ottonenzeit)*, Berlin, 1913 (Historische Studien, 111). P. IMBART DE LA TOUR, "Des immunités commerciales accordées aux églises du VIIe au IXe siècle," in **939.** T. SOMMERLAD, *Die wirthschaftliche Thätigkeit der Kirche in Deutschland*, vols. I–II, Leipzig, 1900–05.

Evolution of church institutions. H. C. LEA, *A history of auricular confession and indulgences in the Latin church*, 3 vols., Philadelphia, 1896. E. HATCH, *The growth of church institutions*, 4th edition, London, 1895. L. DUCHESNE, *Les origines du culte chrétien*, Paris, 1890; 4th edition, 1910, translated from the 4th edition, *Christian worship: its origin and evolution*, London, 1910. P. IMBART DE LA TOUR, *Les origines religieuses de la France, les paroisses rurales du 4e au 11e siècle*, Paris, 1900. W. SCHMITZ, *S. Chrodegangi Metensis episcopi (742–66) Regula canonicorum*, Hannover, 1889.

The church and society. G. KURTH, *Notger de Liège et la civilization au Xe siècle*, 2 vols., Paris, 1905. M. DMITREWSKI, *Die christliche freiwillige Armut vom Ursprung bis zum 12 Jahrhundert*, Berlin, 1913 (*Abh.m.n.G.*, 53). S. R. MAITLAND, *The Dark Ages*.

Life of the clergy. H. C. LEA, *An historical sketch of sacerdotal celibacy in the Christian church*, 2 vols., 3rd and enlarged edition, New York, 1907, chs. I–XII. A. DRESDNER, *Kultur- und Sittengeschichte der italienischen Geistlichkeit*, Breslau, 1890. W. E. H. LECKY, *History of European morals*. L. ZÖPF, *Das Heiligenleben im 10 Jahrhundert*, Leipzig, 1908 (Beiträge zur Kulturgeschichte, I).

Romuald. W. Franke, *Romuald v. Camaldoli und seine Reformtätigkeit zur Zeit Ottos III*, Berlin, 1913.

Peter Damian. R. Biron, *Saint Pierre Damien (1007–1072)*, 2nd edition, Paris, 1908. Eckenstein, *Women under monasticism*, chs. 4–5. G. G. Coulton, *Five centuries of religion.* J. Kleinermanns, *Der heilige Petrus Damiani*, Steyl, 1882. L. Kuhn, *Petrus Damiani und seine Anschauungen über Staat und Kirche*, Karlsruhe, 1913. F. Neukirch, *Das Leben des Petrus Damiani*, Göttingen, 1875 (Diss.). J. P. Whitney, "Peter Damiani and Humbert," *Cambridge historical journal*, I (1925), 225–48.

Original sources. The great collections of material are listed above, nos. **953–64.** See especially the *Liber pontificalis*, no. **959** note. The best edition of the famous False Decretals is that by P. Hinschius, *Decretales pseudo-Isidorianae et capitula Angilramni*, Leipzig, 1863. *Charters and records of the ancient Abbey of Cluni, 1077–1534*, edited by G. Duckett, 2 vols., London, 1888, has a good historical introduction. *Bibliotheca symbolica ecclesiae universalis: the creeds of Christendom*, with a history and critical notes, edited by P. Schaff, 3 vols., 4th edition, revised and enlarged, New York, 1905, contains the original texts with translations into English. *Bibliothek der Symbole und Glaubensregeln der alten Kirche*, edited by A. Hahn, 3rd edition, Breslau, 1897. M. Marrier, *Bibliotheca Cluniacensis*, Mâcon, 1915.

Bibliographies. The general bibliographies for church history are listed above, nos. **49–55.** Also *C.M.H.*, III and V.

XVI. THE INVESTITURE STRIFE

A. Outline

1. This first phase of the conflict between the empire and papacy grew out of a movement to reform the papacy and the church. As soon as the papacy became powerful and dignified, its high claims to power clashed with those of the emperor as well as of other temporal rulers. The importance of this dramatic duel between an emperor and a pope has been unduly exaggerated in modern books.

2. The grand period of the papal monarchy lay between 1073, the accession of Gregory VII, and 1303, the death of Boniface VIII.

3. The minority of the emperor Henry IV, 1056–72. Weakness of the regent, the empress Agnes, 1056–62. Strength of the nobles, especially the ecclesiastical lords, Anno, archbishop of Cologne, and Adalbert, archbishop of Bremen.

4. The youth of Hildebrand. Born between 1020 and 1025 in the village of Rovaco near Soana in Tuscany. He was of humble origin, probably the son of a peasant. Educated in Rome at the time when the papacy was utterly degraded. Became the chaplain of pope Gregory VI, who was deposed in 1046. Hildebrand never was a monk of Cluny.

5. Hildebrand the power behind the papal chair. He was a cardinal-subdeacon in Rome under pope Leo IX, 1048–54. In 1054 he was in France as a papal legate. Victor II, Stephen IX, and Nicholas II, were practically nominated by him. The alliance with the Normans, by the treaty of Melfi, 1059, and the decree of 1059 which placed the election of the popes in the

hands of a college of cardinals, were largely his work. In 1059 Hildebrand was made archdeacon of the Roman church, and Alexander II made him chancellor of the apostolic see. The *Patarini* in Lombardy, and Matilda, countess of Tuscany, strengthened the papacy in the north of Italy as did the Normans in the south.

6. The chief evils in the church which confronted Hildebrand: simony, marriage of the clergy, lay investiture.

7. Hildebrand became pope Gregory VII in 1073. His uncanonical election. His character and his ideal of papal power. The *Dictatus papae*. Troubles at the beginning of his pontificate.

8. The duel between Gregory VII and Henry IV. The general decree against simony and lay investiture in the synod of Rome, 1075. Henry IV and his German bishops deposed the pope at the council at Worms in 1076. Thereupon the pope excommunicated and deposed the emperor at the Vatican synod of 1076. The famous scene at Canossa, 1077, where Henry IV was absolved by Gregory VII. Duke Rudolf of Swabia was elected anti-king. Henry's excommunication and deposition renewed in 1080. Clement III was elected anti-pope in 1080 and crowned Henry IV emperor in Rome in 1084. Upon the death of Rudolf of Swabia, Herman of Luxemburg succeeded him as anti-king. Henry IV besieged Gregory VII in Rome. The pope was rescued by Robert Guiscard and his Normans, who sacked Rome in 1084. Gregory left Rome with the Normans and died in exile at Salerno in 1085.

9. The relations of Gregory VII with other princes of western Europe. His relations with the Eastern emperor who feared the Turks and addressed Gregory VII for help in 1074.

10. The continuance of the struggle between Henry IV and popes Victor III and Urban II. The preaching of the first crusade by Urban II at Clermont, in 1095, diverted interest from the investiture contest. Paschal II renewed Henry's excommunication. Revolt of the Saxons led by his rebel son, also named Henry. Sad end of the excommunicated Henry IV, who died in Liége, 1106.

11. Echoes of the investiture strife outside of Germany and Italy. Anselm of Canterbury.

12. Henry V, 1106–25, and his contests with the papacy. The compromise of 1111. Pope Paschal II renounced the temporalities of the church and crowned Henry V emperor in St. Peter's, but soon after repudiated these rash concessions. Finally when Calixtus II was pope, the great difficulty was compromised by the concordat of Worms in 1122.

13. The inevitable sequel of strife between the empire and the papacy.

14. Popes, 1054–1124.

Victor II, 1054–57
Stephen IX, 1057–58
Benedict X, 1058
Nicholas II, 1059–61
Alexander II, 1061–73
Gregory VII, 1073–85
Victor III, 1086–87
Urban II, 1088–99
Paschal II, 1099–1118
Gelasius II, 1118–19
Calixtus II, 1119–24.

B. Special Recommendations for Reading

Brief general accounts. Adams, *Civilization*, ch. x. Emerton, *Mediaeval Europe*, ch. viii. Tout, *Empire and papacy*, ch. vi. Bryce, *Holy Roman empire*, ch. x. Barry, *Papal monarchy*, chs. xiii–xiv. Villari, *Mediaeval Italy*, 169–203. Flick, *Rise of the mediaeval church*, chs. xviii–xix. W. Miller, *Mediaeval Rome*, New York, 1902, ch. i. Lea, *History of sacerdotal celibacy*, I, ch. xiv, treats the subject of celibacy in the time of Hildebrand. Sellery and Krey, *Medieval foundations*, ch. vii. Hulme, *Middle ages*, ch. xvii. Thorndike. *Medieval Europe*, ch. xv. Munro and Sontag, *Middle ages*, ch. xv.

Longer general accounts. *C.M.H.*, V, ch. ii. D. J. Medley, *The church and the empire 1003–1304*, New York, 1910, chs. i–iii. Lavisse et Rambaud, *Histoire gênérale*, ii, ch. ii. Milman, *Latin Christianity*, IV, chs. i–iii. Gregorovius, *History of Rome in the middle ages*, IV, part I, chs. iii–vi. Henderson, *A History of Germany in the middle ages*, chs. xii–xiv. Stubbs, *Germany in the early middle ages*, chs. ix–x.

Biographies of Hildebrand. A. H. Mathew, *The life and times of Hildebrand, pope Gregory VII*, London, 1910. W. Stephens, *Hildebrand and his times*, New York, 1888. M. R. Vincent, *Age of Hildebrand*, New York, 1896. Mann, *Lives of the popes*, VII. Dunn-Pattison, *Leading figures*, 58–86, "Hildebrand," J. P. Whitney, "Gregory VII," *E.H.R.*, XXXIV (1919), 129–151, has full bibliographical notes.

Original sources. All the " source books " contain illustrative material. Dunclaf and Krey, *Parallel source problems in medieval history*, 29–91, have translated contemporary accounts of the famous scene at Canossa. The violent letters which passed between pope Gregory VII and the emperor Henry IV, along with much additional material, may be found in Henderson, *Select documents*, 351–409; Robinson, *Readings*, I, 266–95; Thatcher and McNeal, *Source book*, 121–66; and Ogg, *Source book*, 261–81.

Maps. Shepherd, *Atlas*, 62–63, 64, 66–67.

C. Bibliography

General books. The general histories of the church are listed above, nos. **395–498.** The books on the medieval empire, nos. **499–507**, especially **501,** and those on Germany, nos. **560–98**, and Italy, nos. **599–621**, are especially useful.

General accounts. Thompson, *Feudal Germany*, ch. iii with bibliographical references in notes. M. Manitius, *Deutsche Geschichte, 911–1125.* A. Hauck, *Kirchengeschichte Deutschlands*, III. Baxmann, *Die Politik der Päpste*, II. T. Greenwood, *Cathedra Petri*, IV, 139–678. J. Hergenröther, *Katholische Kirche und christlicher Staat in ihrer geschichtlichen Entwickelung und in Beziehung auf die Fragen der Gegenwart*, 2nd edition, Freiburg, 1876, translated into English, *Catholic church and Christian state*, I, 380ff. J. v. Pflugk-Harttung, *Die Papstwahlen und Kaisertum, 1046–1328*, Gotha, 1908. Hefele, *Histoire des conciles*, trans. Leclercq, vols. IV and V.

A. FLICHE, *La chrétienté médiévale*, Paris, 1929 (Histoire du monde, VII). G. FICKER and H. HERMELINK, *Das Mittelalter* (Handbuch der Kirchengeschichte für Studierende, hrsg. von G. Krüger, II Teil, 2nd edition) 1929.

Nicholas II. O. DELARC, "Le pontificat de Nicolas II," *R.Q.H.*, XL (1886), 341–402.

Gregory VII. W. MARTENS, *Gregor VII: sein Leben und Werken,* 2 vols., Leipzig, 1894. O. DELARC, *Saint Grégoire VII et la réforme de l'église au XIe siècle*, 3 vols., and an index, Paris, 1889–90. A. F. GFRÖRER, *Papst Gregorius VII und sein Zeitalter*, 7 vols., and index, Schaffhausen, 1859–64, is distinctly Roman catholic in tone and very polemical. J. BRUGERETTE, *Grégoire VII et la réforme du XIe siècle*, Paris, 1906. A. F. VILLEMAIN, *Histoire de Grégoire VII*, 2 vols., Paris, 1873; translated into English, *The life of Gregory VII*, 2 vols., London, 1874. E. LANGERON, *L'église au moyen âge: Grégoire VII et les origines de la doctrine ultramontaine*, 2nd edition, Paris, 1874. The first seriously critical work on Gregory VII was J. VOIGT, *Hildebrand als Papst Gregorius VII und sein Zeitalter*, Weimar, 1815; 2nd edition, 1846, translated into French with additions by l'abbé JAGER, *Histoire du pape Grégoire VII et de son siècle*, 4th edition, 2 vols., Paris, 1854. C. MIRBT, *Die Wahl Gregors VII*, Marburg, 1892. W. v. GIESEBRECHT, "Die Gesetzgebung der römischen Kirche zur Zeit Gregors VII," *Münchner historisches Jahrbuch für 1866*, Munich, 1866, 91–193. E. VOOSEN, *Papauté et pouvoir civil à l'époque de Grégoire VII*, Gembloux, 1927. E. CASPAR, "Gregor VII in seinen Briefen," *H.Z.*, CXXX (1924), 1–30. A. FLICHE, *Saint Grégoire VII*, 2nd edition, Paris, 1920 (Les saints).

Dictatus papae. R. L. POOLE, *Lectures on the papal chancery*, ch. VI. See the literature quoted in Poole's footnotes and in DAHLMANN-WAITZ, no. 4928. See also *C.M.H.*, V, 57, note 2.

Canossa. W. SACHSE, *Canossa: historische Untersuchung*, Leipzig, 1896. R. FRIEDRICH, *Studien zur Vorgeschichte von Canossa*, 2 parts, Hamburg, 1905–08. For other special works on the famous scene at Canossa see DAHLMANN-WAITZ, *Quellenkunde*, no. 5007.

Gregory VII and the Byzantine empire. W. NORDEN, *Das Papsttum und Byzanz*, 38–46.

Henry IV. G. MEYER v. KNONAU, *Jahrbücher des deutschen Reichs unter Heinrich IV und Heinrich V*, 7 vols., Leipzig, 1890–1909, part of no. **570.** E. HÖHNE, *Kaiser Heinrich IV: sein Leben und seine Kämpfe 1050–1106, nach dem Urteile seiner deutschen Zeitgenossen*, Gütersloh, 1906. T. LINDNER, *Kaiser Heinrich IV*, Berlin, 1881. H. FLOTO, *Kaiser Heinrich der Vierte und sein Zeitalter*, 2 vols., Stuttgart, 1855–56, defends Henry IV against the accusations of pope Gregory VII. O. SCHUMANN, *Die päpstlichen Legaten in Deutschland zur Zeit Heinrichs IV und Heinrichs V (1056–1125)*, Marburg, 1912 (Diss.).

Henry V. G. PEISER, *Der deutsche Investiturstreit unter Kaiser Heinrich V bis zu dem päpstlichen Privileg vom 13 April, 1111*, Berlin, 1883.

Investiture. G. WEISE, *Königtum und Bischofswahl im fränkischen und deutschen Reich vor dem Investiturstreit*, Berlin, 1912. F. X. BARTH, *Hildebert* *von Lavardin (1056–1133) und das Recht der kirchlichen Stellenbesetzung*, Stuttgart, 1906, parts 34–6 of no. **491.** H. FEIERABEND, *Die politische Stellung der deutschen Reichsabteien während des Investiturstreites*, Breslau, 1913 (Historische Untersuchungen, III).

Investiture strife in France. B. MONOD, *Essai sur les rapports de Pascal II avec Philippe I, 1099–1108*, Paris, 1907, part 164 of no. **888.** P. IMBART DE LA TOUR, *Les élections épiscopales dans l'église de France du IXᵉ au XIIᵉ siècle*, Paris, 1891. A. GIRY, *Grégoire VII et les évêques de Térouanne*, *R.H.*, I (1876), 387–409. A. CAUCHIE, *La querelle des investitures dans les diocèses de Liége et de Cambrai*, I, Louvain, 1890.

Urban II. A. FLICHE, "L'élection d'Urbain II," *M. A.*, *XIX* (1916), 356–94.

Polemical literature concerning investiture. J. DE GHELLINCK, "La littérature polémique durant la querelle des investitures,"*R.Q.H.*, XCIII (1913), 71–89. The fundamental work on the subject is C. MIRBT, *Die Publizistik im Zeitalter Gregors VII*, Leipzig, 1894. It should be supplemented by L. SALTET, *Les réordinations: étude sur le sacrement de l'ordre*, Paris, 1907. A. FLICHE, *Etudes sur la polémique religieuse à l'époque de Grégoire VII: les prégrégoriens*, Paris, 1916. See review *E.H.R.*, XXXII (1917), 593. For the vast mass of controversial pamphlet literature which has come down to us see DAHLMANN-WAITZ, no. 4925. See also M. T. STEAD, "Manegold of Lautenbach," in *E.H.R.*, XXIX (1914), 1–15, and A. SCHARNAGL, *Der Begriff der Investitur in den Quellen und der Literatur des Investiturstreits*, Stuttgart, 1908, part 56 of no. **490.**

Concordat of Worms, 1122. E. BERNHEIM, *Das Wormser Konkordat und seine Vorurkunden*, Breslau, 1906 (part 81 of Untersuchungen zur deutschen Staats- und Rechtsgeschichte, edited by O. GIERKE). A. HOFMEISTER, "Das Wormser Konkordat," *Festschift Dietrich Schäfer*, Jena, 1915. For special literature on the Concordat of Worms of 1122 see DAHLMANN-WAITZ, no. 5039.

Matilda of Tuscany. NORA DUFF, *Matilda of Tuscany: la Gran Donna d'Italia*, London, 1909. E. HUDDY, *Mathilda, countess of Tuscany*, London, 1906. A. OVERMANN, *Gräfin Mathilde von Tuscien, ihre Besitzungen, Geschichte ihres Guts, 1115-1230 und ihre Regesten*, Innsbruck, 1895. N. ZUCCHELLI, *La contessa Matilde nei documenti pisani MLXXVII–MCXII*, Pisa, 1916. L. TONDELLI, *Matilde di Canossa: profilo storico*, 2nd edition, Rome, 1926. N. GRIMALDI, *La contessa Matilde e la sua stirpe feudale*, Florence, (1928).

Original sources. A very convenient collection of extracts has been edited by E. BERNHEIM, *Quellen zur Geschichte des Investiturstreites*, vol. I, 2nd edition, Leipzig, 1913, vol. II, 1907, part of no. **980.** *A selection of the letters of Hildebrand*, edited by G. FINCH, London, 1853.

Bibliographies. By far the best bibliography for both original sources and secondary works is in DAHLMANN-WAITZ, nos. 4872–5039, but the general bibliographies for Germany, nos. **29–34,** Italy, nos. **37–41**, and the church, nos. **49–55** are all useful. Also *C.M.H.*, V.

XVII. THE BYZANTINE EMPIRE FROM THE DEATH OF JUSTINIAN, 565, TO THE FIRST CRUSADE, 1095

A. Outline

1. The place of Constantinople and the Byzantine empire in European history, see outline III.

2. The work of Justinian was ruined by his immediate successors. The Avars established themselves in Pannonia. The Lombards invaded Italy in 568. The Slavs crossed the Danube and moved into the Balkan peninsula. The Persian wars dragged on until 591, and were resumed again in 603. The rebellion of the uncultured cut-throat Phocas in 602 illustrated the degradation of the empire. He was recognized, however, by pope Gregory the Great.

3. Heraclius, 610–41, and the Persians. Under Chosroes they captured Jerusalem in 614 and in 616 overran Egypt. In 617 Chalcedon fell. The church and the emperor now declared a crusade against the Persian fire-worshippers. Persians, Avars, and Slavs made a combined but unsuccessful attack on Constantinople in 626. By the peace of 628 with Persia the boundaries of the empire were restored.

4. The Heraclian dynasty and the Mohammedans, 610–717. In this period the Persian menace gave way to a still greater one, namely, Islam. In 637 Jerusalem was taken by the Muslims. Not only Syria but Egypt and all northern Africa soon fell into the hands of the Mohammedans. Relations of Constans II and Constantine IV with Italy and Sicily. The two great sieges of Constantinople, in 673–77 and in 717–18, which formed a turning point in the relations between Christians and Mohammedans.

5. Byzantine civilization and administration under the Heraclian dynasty. Latin practically disappeared in the east and the empire became virtually Greek. Decline of Greek learning co-eval with the decline of Latin learning in the west in Merovingian times. The new provinces, called "themes," of military origin. Greek diplomacy. Poor fiscal administration. Reorganization of the army. Main stress now laid on the cavalry. Remarkable advance of military tactics and theory. Development of a strong fleet under Constans II, 642–68. Liquid or marine fire, which we call "Greek fire."

6. The iconoclastic period, 717–867. Image worship among Greek Christians was made the mark of taunts of the Mohammedans. In 726, the emperor Leo III issued his first edict against images. Opposition in both the Latin and Greek churches. Iconoclasm sanctioned by the council of Constantinople in 753. Reaction in favor of images under Constantine and Irene, 780–802. Leo V, 813–20, again denounced image worship, but those who favored images won a final victory in 843 under Theodora and Michael III, 842–67. Echoes in the west of the iconoclastic controversy.

7. Political history in the iconoclastic period, 717–867. The internal reforms of Leo III, 717–40. Increasing oriental influence. Desultory warfare

with the Saracens. The Lombards ended the exarchate of Ravenna in 750. Shortly after, the eastern emperors definitely lost Rome at the hands of the Franks. Relations of Charlemagne with the Byzantine empire in the time of Constantine and Irene. Early in the ninth century the rising power of the Bulgarians became a menace. In 826 a band of Muslim adventurers from Spain took Crete.

8. The Byzantine empire at its height under the Macedonian dynasty, 867–1057. Basil I and his successor reconquered southern Italy, 875–94, but in 878 Syracuse fell into the hands of the Moors. A revival of learning began in the ninth century and Cyrillus and Methodius converted the Slavs (outline XI above). In the east, Crete was won back in 961, Antioch in 968, and Cyprus about the same time. The reign of Basil II, 963–1025, marks the culmination of the power and glory of the Byzantine empire. He subdued the Bulgarians, hence he is usually called Bulgaroctonus, "Slayer of Bulgarians." The Russians, who under Sviatoslav had seriously threatened Constantinople, were checked in 971 by John Zimisces and when Vladimir, the Clovis of Russia, was baptized about 990, Russia was opened to a flood of Byzantine influence. In 1054 came the practical separation between the Greek and Latin churches.

9. The rise of the Seljuk Turks. With the end of the Macedonian dynasty in 1057 there came a period of decline and turmoil such as that after the death of Justinian. This gave an opportunity for conquest to the nomad Seljuk Turks who had become Mohammedans and in 1055 occupied Bagdad and in 1076 entered Jerusalem. In 1071 the Turks under Alp Arslan defeated and took prisoner the emperor Romanus at the famous battle of Manzikert. In the same year the Normans took Bari from the Byzantines. In 1074 Michael VII appealed to pope Gregory VII for help against the Turks. The Turks captured Nicaea in 1080. Constantinople seemed to be doomed.

10. Alexius Comnenus, 1081–1118, saved the empire by his statesmanship. He kept at bay the Seljuk Turks, the Petchenegs, and the Normans who, under Robert Guiscard, attacked him, 1081–85, but were beaten back with the help of Venice. Venice was granted exceptional commercial privileges in the Levant. In 1095 Alexius appealed to pope Urban II for aid and that ushered in the crusades which completely transformed the Byzantine empire.

11. Byzantine emperors, 565–1118.

Justinian dynasty

(1) Justin II, 565–78
(2) Tiberius II, 578–82
(3) Maurice, 582–602
(4) Phocas, 602–10

Heraclian dynasty, 610–711

(1) Heraclius, 610–41
(2) Constantine III, 641
(3) Heracleonas, 641–42

(4) Constans II, 642–68
(5) Constantine IV, 668–85
(6) Justinian II, 685–95
[Leontius, 695–98
Tiberius II, 698–705]
(6) Justinian II (restored), 705–11
Philip Bardanes, 711–13
Anastasius II, 713–16
Theodosius III, 716–17

Isaurian (Syrian) dynasty, 717–802

(1) Leo III, 717–41
(2) Constantine V, 741–75
(3) Leo IV, 775–80
(4) Constantine VI, 780–97
(5) Irene, 797–802
Nicephorus I, 802–11
Stauracius, 811
Michael I, 811–13
Leo V (Armenian), 813–20

Phrygian or Armorian dynasty, 820–67

(1) Michael II, 820–29
(2) Theophilus, 829–42
(3) Michael III, 842–67

Macedonian dynasty, 867–1057

(1) Basil I, 867–86
(2) Leo VI and Alexander, 886–913
(3) Constantine VII (Porphyrogenitus), 913–59.
(4) Romanus I, 919–44
(5) Romanus II, 959–63
(6) Basil II (Bulgaroctonus) and Constantine VIII, 963–1025
Nicephorus II (Phocas), 963–69
John Zimisces, 969–76
(7) Constantine VIII (sole ruler), 1025–28
(8) Romanus III, 1028–34
(9) Michael IV, 1034–41
(10) Michael V, 1041–42
(11) Constantine IX, 1042–55
(12) Theodora, 1055–56
(13) Michael VI, 1056–57
Isaac I (Comnenus), 1057–59
Constantine X, 1059–67
Romanus IV, 1067–71
Michael VII, 1071–78
Nicephorus III, 1078–81

Comnenian dynasty, 1081–1204

(1) Alexius I (nephew of Isaac I), 1081–1118

B. Special Recommendations for Reading

General surveys. Vasiliev, *History of the Byzantine empire*, chs. iv–vi. Munro and Sontag, *Middle ages*, ch. xx. F. Schevill, *History of the Balkan peninsula*, chs. v–ix. Hulme, *Middle ages*, 430–39. Thompson, *Economic and social history*, ch. xiv. Oman, *Dark ages*, chs. ix, xii, xiv, xviii, xxviii, together with Tout, *Empire and papacy*, ch. vii. Lavisse et Rambaud, *Histoire générale*, I, 193–203, 625–87 (pp. 672–82 of this selection have been translated by Munro and Sellery, *Medieval civilization*, 212–23, under the title "Byzantine civilization" [9th to 11th centuries]). Bryce, *Holy Roman empire*, 4th edition, ch. xvii. Oman, *The Byzantine empire*, chs. ix–xx. N. H. Baynes, *Byzantine empire*, London and New York, 1925. C. Diehl, *A history of the Byzantine empire*, 40–137. The period to 717 is treated in the *C.M.H.*, II, ch. ix, and xiii. The article "Roman empire, later" in the *Ency. Brit.*, is written by J. B. Bury, the greatest English authority in this field.

Standard accounts in English. The best and most authoritative account of the period to 867 is J. B. Bury, *A history of the later Roman empire*, vol. II, together with *A history of the eastern Roman empire, 802–867*. Vasiliev, *History of the Byzantine empire*, in two volumes, vol. I, *From Constantine the Great to the epoch of the crusades (A.D. 1081)*. *C.M.H.*, IV, chs. i–xi. The first comprehensive history in English which met the requirement of modern scholarship was written by G. Finlay, *History of Greece*, vol. II (see nos. **645** and **656**). Until the time of Finlay the English-speaking world drew its information about this period of Byzantine history largely from Gibbon, *Decline and fall*, chs. xlv, xlvi, xlviii, lii, liii, who was chiefly responsible for a general misunderstanding of the true nature of the history of the eastern empire during these centuries when it did much service for western civilization; see Bury's introduction to his edition of Gibbon.

Italy and the Byzantine empire after Justinian. P. Villari, *The barbarian invasions of Italy*, II, 274–374. Dudden, *Gregory the Great*, I, ch. vi, contains a good description of Constantinople at the end of the sixth century; see also, II, ch. x, for Gregory's relations with the churches of the east. L. Bréhier, "Normal relations between Rome and the church of the east before the schism of the eleventh century," in *Constructive quarterly*, IV, (1916), 645–72.

Byzantine warfare. Oman, *Art of war*, 169–226, and H. Delbrück, *Geschichte der Kriegskunst*, III, 194–209; Delbrück differs from Oman in some important points. The great siege of Constantinople in 717 is told in a popular way by E. A. Foord, "The repulse of the Saracens from Europe," *Contemporary review*, XCVI (1909), 327–41.

The Byzantine empire at its height. The glorious period about the year 1000 is described in a spirited way by J. B. Bury, "Roman emperors from Basil II to Isaac Komnênos," *E.H.R.*, IV (1889), 41–64, 251–85. G. Schlumberger, *L'épopée byzantine à la fin du dixième siècle. Seconde partie. Basil II le tueur des Bulgares*, Paris, 1900.

Constitutional history. J. B. Bury, *The constitution of the later Roman empire*, Cambridge, 1910.

Byzantine scholarship. SANDYS, *History of classical scholarship*, I, chs. XXII, XXIII.

Original sources. HENDERSON, *Select documents*, 441–77, "Liutprand's report of his mission to Constantinople, 968 A.D." C. H. HASKINS, "A Canterbury monk at Constantinople, c. 1090," *Studies in mediaeval culture*, 160–63. E. W. BROOKS, "Byzantines and Arabs in the time of the early Abbasids," *E.H.R.*, XV (1900), 728–47.

Maps. SHEPHERD, *Atlas*, 54–55, 58–59, 66–67. *C.M.H.*, II, maps 18 and 25.

C. BIBLIOGRAPHY

General books. See nos. **643–79**, and also the periodicals for Byzantine history, nos. **174–75**, as well as the books on Byzantine literature, nos. **800–02**. For important works in Greek, Russian and other Slavic languages see VASILIEV, *History of the Byzantine empire*, vol. I, ch. I and bibliographies.

General survey. The best handbook on things Byzantine is K. KRUMBACHER, *Geschichte der byzantinischen Literatur*, second edition, 1897. On pp. 911ff. there is a general survey of Byzantine history by H. GELZER.

Sicily and southern Italy and the Byzantine empire. M. AMARI, *Storia dei musulmani di Sicilia*, vols. I–III, Florence, 1854–72. B. PACE, *I barbari e i Bizantini in Sicilia: studi sulla storia dell' isola dal sec. V al IX*, Palermo, 1911. J. GAY, *L'Italie mèridionale et l'empire byzantin*, 867–1071, Paris, 1904, part 90 of no. **887**. DIANE DE GULDENCRONE, *L'Italie byzantine. Etude sur le haut moyen-âge, 400–1050*, Paris, 1914.

Relations between the Greek East and the Latin West. N. JORGA, "Der lateinische Westen und der byzantinische Osten in ihren Wechselbeziehungen während des Mittelalters: einige Gesichtspunkte," p. 89–99 in *Lipsiense: Ehrengabe Karl Lamprecht dargebracht*, Berlin, 1909. G. REVERDY, *Les relations de Childebert II et de Byzance, R.H.*, CXIV (1913), 61–86. L. HARTMANN, *Ein Kapitel vom spätantiken und frühmittelalterlichen Staate*, Stuttgart, 1913, is a sketch of 24 pages which contrasts the Byzantine empire with the Lombard and Frankish kingdoms. C. TIEDE, *Quellenmässige Darstellung der Beziehungen Carls des Grossen zu Ost-Rom*, Rostock, 1892. A. GASQUET, *Etudes byzantines: l'empire byzantin et la monarchie franque*, Paris, 1888. O. HARNACK, *Die Beziehungen des fränkisch-italischen zum byzantinischen Reiche unter der Regierung Karls des Grossen und der späteren Kaiser karolingischen Stammes*, Göttingen, 1880. B. MYSTAKIDIS, *Byzantinisch-deutsch Beziehungen zur Zeit der Ottonen*, Stuttgart, 1891. A. OSTERMANN, *Karl der Grosse und das byzantinische Reich*, Luckau, 1895. P. E. SCHRAMM, "Neun Briefe des byzantinischen Gesandten Leo von seiner Reise zu Otto III aus den Jahren 997–998," in *B.Z.*, XXV (1925), 89–105.

The Greek church. For books on the schism between the Greek and Latin churches and the iconoclastic controversy, see p. 206. A. FORTESCUE, *The orthodox eastern church*, London, 1907; 3rd edition, 1911. A. H. HORE, *Eighteen centuries of the orthodox Greek church*, New York, 1899. J. PARGOIRE, *L'église byzantine de 527–847*, Paris, 1905. H. F. TOZER, *The church and the* *eastern empire*, new impression, London, New York, 1904. L. Bréhier, "L'hagiographie byzantine des VIIIe et IXe siècles à Constantinople et dans les provinces," *Journal des savants*, August, October, 1916. A. P. Stanley, *History of the eastern church*, 5th edition, London, 1883. L. Oeconomos, *La vie religieuse dans l'empire byzantin*, Paris, 1918.

Administration. J. B. Bury, *The imperial administrative system in the ninth century, with a revised text of the Kletorologion of Philotheos*, London, 1911, II, part of no. **904,** *Supplementary papers*, 1. A. E. R. Boak, *The master of the offices in the later Roman and Byzantine empires*, New York, 1919. J. E. Dunlap, *The office of the grand chamberlain in the later Roman and Byzantine empires*, New York, 1924. C. M. Macri, *L'organisation de l'économie urbaine dans Byzance sous la dynastie de Macédonie*, 867–1057, Paris, 1925. F. Dölger, *Beiträge zur Geschichte der byzantinischen Finanzverwaltung besonders des 10 und 11 Jahrhunderts*, Leipzig-Berlin, 1927. A. Stöckle, *Spätrömische und byzantinische Zünfte*, Leipzig, 1911. G. Ostrogorsky, "Die ländliche Steuergemeinde des byzantinischen Reiches im X Jahrhundert," in *Vierteljahrschrift für Sozial-und Wirtschaftsgeschichte*, XX (1927), 347ff.

Byzantine warfare. J. B. Bury, *The naval policy of the Roman empire in relation to the western provinces from the seventh to the ninth centuries*, Palermo, 1910. J. Maspero, *Organisation militaire*, Paris, 1912. F. Aussaresses, *L'armée byzantine à la fin du VI siècle, d'après le Strategicon de l'empereur Maurice*, Bordeaux, 1909.

Byzantine scholarship. L. Laborde, *Les écoles de droit dans l'empire d'Orient*, Bordeaux, 1912. F. Schemmel, *Die Hochschule von Konstantinopel vom 5 bis 11 Jahrhundert*, Berlin, ca. 1912. F. Fuchs, *Die höheren Schulen von Konstantinopel im Mittelalter*, Leipzig, 1926.

Histories of various emperors arranged chronologically. K. Groh, *Geschichte des oströmischen Kaisers Justin II, nebst den Quellen*, Leipzig, 1889. E. Stein, *Studien zur Geschichte des byzantinischen Reiches vornehmlich unter den Kaisern Justinus II und Tiberius Constantinus*, Stuttgart, 1919. L. Drapeyron, *L'empereur Héraclius et l'empire byzantin au VIIe siècle*, Paris, 1869. O. Adamek, *Beiträge zur Geschichte des byzantinischen Kaisers Maurikios*, Graz, 1890. R. Spintler, *De Phoca imperatore Romanorum*, Jena, 1905. A. Pernice, *L'imperatore Eraclio: saggio di storia bizantina*, Florence, 1905. T. Kaestner, *De imperio Constantini III, 641–648*, Leipzig, 1907. K. Schenk, *Kaiser Leo III*, Halle, 1880. A. Lombard, *Etudes d'histoire byzantine: Constantin V, empereur des Romains (740–775)*, with a preface by C. Diehl, Paris, 1902, part of no. **889.** A. Vogt, *Basile Ier empereur de Byzance et la civilisation byzantine à la fin du IXe siècle*, Paris, 1908. A. Rambaud, *L'empire grec au Xe siècle: Constantin Porphyrogénète*, Paris, 1870. G. Schlumberger, *Un empereur byzantin au 10e siècle: Nicéphore Phocas*, Paris, 1890; new edition, 1923; and *L'épopée byzantine*, 1–11. F. Chalandon, *Alexis Comnène (1081–1118)*, Paris, 1900.

The Byzantine empire at its height. G. Schlumberger, *L'épopée byzantine à la fin du dixième siècle*, 3 parts, Paris, 1890–1905, covers the period 960–1057 and has excellent illustrations. New edition of vol. I, 1925.

Byzantine history just before the crusades. C. Neumann, *Die Weltstellung des byzantinischen Reiches vor den Kreuzzügen*, Leipzig, 1894 (Diss.); French translation in *Revue de l'Orient latin*, X, Paris, 1905. W. Fischer, *Studien zur byzantinischen Geschichte des elften Jahrhunderts*, Plauen, 1883.

Seljuk Turks. M. T. Houtsma, *Histoire des Seljoukides d'Asie Mineure d'après Ibn Bibi*, Leyden, 1903. N. Jorga, *Geschichte des osmanischen Reiches*, vol. I, Gotha, 1908. J. Laurent, *L'Arménie entre Byzance et l'Islam depuis la conquête arabe jusqu 'en 886*, Paris, 1919.

Original sources. The large collections of sources for Byzantine history are listed above, nos. **1002–03.** The important collection of Byzantine coins in the British Museum is described and illustrated in W. Wroth, *Catalogue of the imperial Byzantine coins in the British Museum*, 2 vols., London, 1908.

Bibliographies. *C.M.H.*, II, 747–57, 766–69; IV, 782–840. Valuable notes in appendix to Bury's edition of Gibbon, frequently with bibliography. Vasiliev, *History of the Byzantine empire*, I, 232–34, 284–85, 363–65, 452–57. Bury, *History of the eastern Roman empire*, 493–510. Krumbacher, *Geschichte der byzantinischen Literatur*, 2nd edition, 1068ff. Diehl, *History of the Byzantine empire*, 189–92.

XVIII. CULTURE OF THE EARLY MIDDLE AGES

A. Outline

1. The gradual change from ancient to medieval modes of thought and learning. Christianity and the barbarian invaders as factors in this change.
2. The universality of the Latin language in western Europe. The decadence of Greek.
3. "The classical heritage" of the early middle ages.
4. The Christian ideal of life.
5. Books that were studied and written during this period.
6. Medieval schools before the rise of universities.
7. The illustrious part played by the British Isles in the history of learning from the fifth to the eighth centuries.
8. The age of Charlemagne.
9. Slow advancement of culture in Christian Europe from the ninth to the eleventh century. Contrast with the Muslim world.
10. The beginning of a new era towards the end of the eleventh century.

B. Special Recommendations for Reading

The best book on the transition from ancient to medieval conditions is S. Dill, *Roman society in the last century of the western empire*, London, 1898; 2nd edition, revised, 1910, supplemented by his less satisfactory *Roman society in Gaul in the Merovingian age*. After these the best general guides in English are the two books by H. O. Taylor, *The mediaeval mind*, and *The classical heritage of the middle ages*, New York, 1901; 3rd edition, 1911. Munro and Sellery, *Medieval civilization*, is a collection of valuable miscellaneous extracts. For the period before Charlemagne, M. Roger, *L'enseigne-*

ment des lettres classiques d'Ausone à Alcuin, Paris, 1905, is extremely useful. *C.M.H.*, III, chs. XIX–XXI. Much can be gleaned from LAVISSE, *Histoire de France* (see table of contents of each volume). Essential books for reference are SANDYS, *A history of classical scholarship;* and MANITIUS, *Geschichte der lateinischen Literatur des Mittelalters*.

C. BIBLIOGRAPHY

For detailed outlines and bibliographies see part III, period I.

PERIOD II. 1100–1500

XIX. BEGINNING OF A NEW ERA IN THE HISTORY OF WESTERN EUROPE ABOUT 1100

A. Outline

Introduction. Current misconceptions concerning the middle ages.

"The twelfth century renaissance." The following were the main features of the new era:

1. Political: (1) The struggle for empire. (2) Losing struggle of the great feudal nobles with the rising kingdoms. Parliamentary machinery.

2. Religious: (1) Conflict between church and state. (2) New monastic movement, especially the mendicants. (3) Heresies. (4) Crusades. (5) The conciliar movement.

3. Social and economic: (1) Emancipation of the lower rural classes. (2) Growth of cities and commerce. (3) Geographical explorations and discoveries. (4) Crusades.

4. Intellectual and artistic: (1) Spirit of inquiry. (2) Better Latin literature. (3) New interest in classical Latin. (4) Some interest in Greek and other languages. (5) Revival of Roman law. (6) Revival of medicine. (7) Some interest in natural sciences. (8) Systematization of theology and philosophy. (9) Growth of universities. (10) Development of vernacular languages and literatures. (11) Gothic architecture.

B. Special Recommendations for Reading

The article "Middle ages" by Professor Shotwell, in the eleventh ed. of *Ency. Brit.* Lavisse, *Histoire de France*, II, part II, 203. F. Harrison, *The meaning of history*, New York, 1908, ch. v, "A survey of the 13th century," first printed in the *Fortnightly review*, LVI (1891), 325–45. Hearnshaw, *Mediaeval contributions*, 42–81, 109–211, 212–31. Crump and Jacob, *Legacy*, 23–57. M. de Wulf, "The society of nations in the thirteenth century," in *International journal of ethics*, XXIX (1919), 210–29.

XX. THE NORMANS

A. Outline

1. The transformation of the Northmen in northern France into Normans in the tenth and eleventh centuries. The nature of the land which Rollo won as a dukedom about 911. Its history under the first six dukes. The

influence of Frankish customs and institutions. The work of the Roman church and schools in Normandy. Mont St. Michel. The monastic school of Bec established in 1042 by Lanfranc who was followed by Anselm. Striking Norman characteristics.

2. The expansion of the duchy of Normandy into a Norman empire. Marriage of duke William with Matilda, daughter of the count of Flanders. Conquest of Maine, 1063. Conquest of England by William in 1066. Battle of Hastings. The Bayeux tapestry. Separation of England and Normandy at the death of William in 1087. They were reunited in 1106 under Henry I. His daughter, Matilda, married count Geoffrey of Anjou, who wrested Normandy from Stephen of Blois. Origin of the name "Angevin empire." Plantagenets. Geoffrey's son Henry became duke of Normandy in 1150, count of Anjou in 1151. In 1152 he married Eleanor, duchess of Aquitaine, divorced wife of king Louis VII of France, and thus became lord of Poitou, Aquitaine, and Gascony. In 1154 he became king of England and was thus ruler of a large empire which straddled the English channel. "Occupying this international position, Henry must not be viewed, as he generally is, merely as an English king."—Haskins.

3. Norman administration in England and the continent, especially the fiscal and judicial system. *The Dialogue on the Exchequer*, written by Richard, the treasurer of Henry II, in 1178–79. The Norman jury.

4. Break-up of the Norman empire. Wars of Henry II with king Philip of France and with his own faithless sons. His tragic death at Chinon in 1189. Richard the Lion-Hearted, 1189–99. In spite of the fact that he and king Philip of France went on the third crusade together, they soon came to blows on account of Richard's possessions on the continent which Philip coveted. Château Gaillard, Richard's strong castle on the Seine. King John's quarrel with his suzerain, king Philip of France. The murder of Arthur, 1203. Capture of Château Gaillard in 1204. In 1204 John lost Normandy and all his lands north of the Loire, which were attached directly to the French crown. That marked the end of the Norman empire.

5. The Normans in southern Italy. The roaming spirit of the Normans. Norman pilgrims to the Holy Land and other famous shrines. The shrine of St. Michael on Monte Gargano in Italy. There is a record of Normans at this spot as early as 1016. Their dealings with Greeks and Saracens and Latins in southern Italy. Aversa founded in 1030. The sons of Tancred of Hauteville in Italy, especially Roger and Robert Guiscard (died 1085). Their relations with the papacy. The defeat of the papal army at Civitate, in 1053. The treaty of Melfi between Robert Guiscard and pope Nicholas II in 1059. Robert was acknowledged as a duke by the papacy. Monte Cassino and the Normans. Gregory VII and the Normans. The sack of Rome by the Normans in 1084. Death of Gregory VII among the Normans in Salerno in 1085.

6. Conquest of Sicily by the Normans, 1061–91. The island under the rule of the Saracens. Count Roger captured Messina in 1061, Palermo in 1072. In 1091 Noto, the last Saracen fastness fell to Roger. Relations of Roger with the papacy.

7. The Normans as a Mediterranean power. The development of a strong fleet. Robert Guiscard and the Byzantine empire. His conquests in the Balkan peninsula. The opposition of Venice. The Normans on the first crusade, Bohemond (lord of Antioch), and Tancred. Normans in Spain and in northern Africa.

8. The Norman Kingdom of the Two Sicilies. In 1130 Roger II had united all the Norman possessions in Italy and Sicily and was crowned king by the pope. Palermo became the capital of the new kingdom. The Norman power and civilization was at its height in the reign of Roger, who died in 1154. Decline under his successors, William I, 1154–66, and William II, 1166–89. Wars of the latter with Frederick Barbarossa. Marriage of the heiress of the Norman kingdom, Constance, daughter of Roger II, with Henry VI. For the history of the kingdom under the Hohenstaufen, see outline XXII.

9. Norman administration and culture in Sicily and southern Italy. Mingling of Byzantine, Mohammedan, Jewish, and Latin civilization in Sicily. The study of Greek, and translations from the Greek into Latin. The adaptability of the Norman conquerors. Their tolerance. The splendor of Palermo. Relations of the Norman kingdom in the Mediterranean with the Norman empire in the north. Consequent close touch of England with Mediterranean civilization. Similarity of institutions in Sicily and England.

10. The ultimate absorption of the Normans by the native population in all the lands where they ruled in the middle ages.

11. Dukes of Normandy.

Rolf (Rollo), 911–27.
William (Longsword), 927–43.
Richard I (The Fearless), 943–96
Richard II (The Good), 996–1027
Richard III, 1027
Robert I (The Magnificent or the Devil), 1027–35
William (The Bastard, The Conqueror), 1035–87
Robert II, 1087–1106
  William (Rufus), regent, 1096–1100
Henry I, 1106–35
Stephen of Blois, 1135–44
Geoffrey, Count of Anjou and Maine, 1144–50
Henry II, 1150–89
Richard (The Lion-Hearted), 1189–99
John, 1199–1204, when Normandy was conquered by the king of France.

12. Sons of Tancred of Hauteville of Normandy.

(1) William of the Iron Arm, lord of Apulia, died 1046
(2) Drogo, Count of Apulia, died 1051
(3) Humphrey, Count of Apulia, died 1057
(4) Robert Guiscard, Duke of Apulia, died 1085
(5) Roger I, Count of Sicily, died 1101.

13. Norman kings of the Kingdom of the Two Sicilies.
    Roger II, son of Roger I, first king of Sicily, 1130, died 1154
    William I, 1154–66
    William II, 1166–89
    Tancred, 1190–94
    William III, 1194
    Henry VI, the Hohenstaufen, married Constance, daughter of Roger II, 1194–97
    Frederick II, 1197–1250.

B. Special Recommendations for Reading

General surveys. By far the best account is C. H. Haskins, *The Normans in European history*, Boston and New York, 1915. The best brief sketch is in Lavisse, *Histoire de France*, II, part II, 53–7, 87–106. Tout, *Empire and papacy*, 83–6, 103–09, 114–19, 135, 174–75. *Ency. Brit.*, article on "Normandy" by R. Latouche and F. M. Stenton; that on the "Normans" by E. A. Freeman. Dunn-Pattison, *Leading figures*, 39–57, "Richard the Fearless." Hulme, *Middle ages*, 412–28. Munro and Sontag, *Middle ages*, chs. xvii–xviii. The history of the Normans in England is not treated in this *Guide*, but attention may be called to two general books which treat the subject chiefly from that aspect: A. H. Johnson, *The Normans in Europe*, chs. vi–xvii; and Sarah O. Jewett, *The Normans: told chiefly in relation to their conquest of England*. A short popular account in German is H. Dondorff, "Die Normannen und ihre Bedeutung für das europäische Kulturleben im Mittelalter," *Sammlung gemienverständlicher wissenschaftlicher Vorträge*, edited by R. Virchow and F. v. Holtzendorff, Berlin, 1866–1901, X (1875), 259–98. R. L. Poole, "Henry II, duke of Normandy," *E.H.R.*, XLII (1927), 569–71.

Normans in Sicily and southern Italy. P. Villari, *Mediaeval Italy*, 126–33, 150–61, 179–203, 241–52. *C.M.H.*, V. ch. iv. C. H. Haskins, "England and Sicily in the twelfth century," *E.H.R.*, XXVI (1911), 433–47. E. A. Freeman, "The Normans at Palermo," in *Historical essays*, third series, 437–76. E. Curtis, *Roger of Sicily and the Normans in lower Italy, 1016–1154*, New York, 1912. F. M. Crawford, *The rulers of the south, Sicily, Calabria, Malta*, 2 vols., New York, 1901, II, 124–333. Cotterill, *Medieval Italy*, 399–412. Gibbon, *Decline and fall*, ch. lvi.

Mont St. Michel. H. Adams, *Mont-Saint-Michel and Chartres*, Boston, 1913. Olga Rojdestrensky, *Le culte de Saint Michel et le moyen âge latin*, Paris, 1922. The shrine of Saint Michael on Monte Gargano in Italy is described by E. Gothein, *Die Culturentwickelung Süd-Italiens*, Breslau, 1886, pp. 41–111.

Normans in Spain. R. Dozy, *Recherches sur l'histoire et la littérature de l'Espagne*, II, 332–71.

Original sources. For reproductions of the famous Bayeux tapestry see no. **202** above. The well-known *Dialogue of the Exchequer* is translated in Henderson, *Select documents*, 20–134. R. Davies, *Civilization in medieval*

England, New York, 1927, 19–26. CECILIA WAERN, *Mediaeval Sicily*, New York, 1911, is largely devoted to Norman Sicily. It is included under this heading because ch. IV contains translations from contemporary sources.

Maps. The only satisfactory map is in MEYERS *Historischer Handatlas*, 25. See also SHEPHERD, *Atlas*, 61, 65, 66–67, 69; and DOW, *Atlas*, 13 (inset).

C. BIBLIOGRAPHY

General books. J. REVEL, *Histoire des Normands*, 2 vols. Paris, 1918–19. Information concerning the Normans is scattered in the general books on medieval history. The general histories of France, nos. **508–48** and Italy, nos. **599–621** are especially useful. See also nos. **360–61**.

Normandy. H. PRENTOUT, *Essai sur les origines et la fondation du duché de Normandie*, Paris, 1911; *La Normandie*, Paris, 1910 (Les régions de la France, VII, Publications de la Revue de synthèse historique); *Etude critique sur Dudon de Saint-Quentin et son histoire des premiers ducs normands*, Paris, 1916; *Les états provinciaux de Normandie*, 2 vols., Caen, 1925–26; *Etudes sur quelques points d'histoire de Normandie*, Caen, 1926; *Guillaume le Conquérant, le chef d'armée et l'organisateur*, Caen, 1927. A. ALBERT-PETIT, *Histoire de Normandie*, 6th edition, Paris, 1912. VICOMTE DU MOTEY, *Origines de la Normandie et du duché d'Alençon*, Paris, 1921. J. STEENSTRUP, *Normandiets Historie*. G. MONOD, *Le rôle de la Normandie dans l'histoire de France*, Paris, 1911. F. M. POWICKE, *The loss of Normandy*, Manchester, 1913. There is an important introduction in L. DELISLE, *Recueil des actes de Henri II, roi d'Angleterre et duc de Normandie, concernant les provinces françaises et les affaires de France*, vol. I Paris, 1916, part of no. **975**. DELISLE'S *Etude sur la condition des classes agricoles en Normandie*, Evreux, 1851, reprinted 1906, is still our most thorough study of life in Normandy. A. LABUTTE, *Histoire des ducs de Normandie jusqu'à la mort de Guillaume le Conquérant*, 2nd edition, Paris, 1866. F. PALGRAVE, *The history of Normandy and of England*, 2 vols., London, 1851–57; new edition, 1919, for a long time was the standard work in English on Normandy. It was superseded by the works of Freeman and others whose books are not listed in this *Guide* and should be sought for in GROSS' *Sources and literature of English history*. H. BÖHMER, *Kirche und Staat in England und in der Normandie im 11 und 12 Jahrhundert*, Leipzig, 1899, extends to 1154. HASKINS called attention to R. N. SAUVAGE, *L'abbaye de Saint-Martin de Troarn au diocèse de Bayeux des origines au seizième siècle*, Caen, 1911, as the best study of a Norman monastery. See also JEAN BIRDSALL, "The English manors of La Trinité at Caen," *Anniversary essays in medieval history by students of Charles Homer Haskins*, 25–44. T. A. COOK, *The story of Rouen*, London, 1905. C. ENLART, *Rouen*, Paris, 1910. H. PRENTOUT, *Caen et Bayeux*, Paris, 1909. *C.M.H.*, V, ch. XV. VICOMTE DE GIBON, *Un archipel normand. Les îles Chausey et leur histoire*, Coutances, 1918. C. W. DAVID, *Robert Curthose, duke of Normandy*, Cambridge, Mass., 1920. VICOMTE DU MOTEY, *Le champion de Normandie. Robert II de Bellême, lieutenant du duc Robert Courteheuse seigneur d'Alençon, etc., comte de Ponthieu et de Shrewsbury, et son temps, 1056–112?*, Paris, 1923.

Chateau Gaillard. DIEULAFOY, "Le château Gaillard," *Mémoires de l'Académie des inscriptions*, XXXVI, part I (1898), 325–86 (good illustrations).

Norman institutions. C. H. HASKINS, *Studies in Norman institutions*, Cambridge, 1918, incorporates studies on Norman matters which appeared in *E.H.R.* and *A.H.R.* On Norman law see especially chs. VII–IX of H. BRUNNER, *Die Entstehung der Schwurgerichte*, Berlin, 1872; book I, ch. III of F. POLLOCK and F. W. MAITLAND, *The history of English law*, 2 vols., Cambridge, 1895; 2nd edition, 1899; and L. VALIN, *Le duc de Normandie et sa cour (912-1204): étude d'histoire juridique*, Paris, 1910, to be supplemented by R. DE FRÉVILLE, "Etude sur l'organisation judiciaire en Normandie au XIIe et XIIIe siècles," *Nouvelle revue historique de droit*, 1912, pp. 681–736. E. MAYER, *Geschworengericht und Inquisitionsprozess*, Munich, 1916. SUZANNE DECK, *Une commune normande au moyen âge. La ville d'Eu; son histoire, ses institutions (1151-1475)*, Paris, 1925, part of **888.** On Norman institutions in Sicily and Italy: H. NIESE, *Die Gesetzgebung der normannischen Dynastie im Regnum Siciliae*, Halle, 1910. EVELYN JAMISON, *The Norman administration of Apulia and Capua, more especially under Roger I and William I, 1127-1166* (Papers of the British school at Rome, 1913, VI, no. 6). M. HOFMANN, *Die Stellung des Königs von Sizilien nach den Assisen von Ariano (1140)*, Münster, 1915. C. A. GARUFI, "Sull' ordinamento amministrativo normanno in Sicilia: exhiquier o diwan?", *Archivio storico italiano*, 5th series, XXVII (1901), 225–63.

Bayeux tapestry. For literature on the Bayeux tapestry see C. GROSS, *Sources and literature*, no. 2139, and no. **202.** P. LAUER, "Le poème de Baudri de Bourgueil adressé à Adèle, fille de Guillaume le Conquérant, et la date de la tapisserie de Bayeux," *Mélanges d'histoire offerts à Charles Bémont*, 43–58. J. B. BERTRAND, *Notice historique sur la tapisserie brodée de la reine Mathilde, épouse de Guillaume le Conquérant, exposée dans la galerie de la bibliothèque de Bayeux*, Bayeux, 1914. C. GARNIER, *La tapisserie de la reine Mathilde: notice historique et descriptive, textes français et anglais*, Bayeux, 1914. A. LEVÉ, *La tapisserie de la reine Mathilde dite la tapisserie de Bayeux*, Paris, 1919. CTE. LEFEBVRE DES NOETTES, "La tapisserie de Bayeux, datée par l'examen technique de sa cavalerie," in *Larousse Mensuel*, VII, 358–60, illustrated, 1927.

Normans in Sicily and southern Italy. Important general surveys of large portions of the field: F. CHALANDON, *Histoire de la domination normande en Italie et en Sicile, 1009-1194*, 2 vols., Paris, 1907; L. v. HEINEMANN, *Geschichte der Normannen in Unteritalien und Sicilien bis zum Aussterben des normannischen Königshauses*, vol. I, to 1085, Leipzig, 1894; O. DELARC, *Les Normands en Italie, depuis les premières invasions jusqu'à l'avènement de S. Grégoire VII (859–862, 1016–1073)*, Paris, 1883; J. W. BARLOW, *Short history of the Normans in southern Europe*, London, 1886; A. F. VON SCHACK, *Geschichte der Normannen in Sicilien*, 2 vols., Stuttgart, 1889; A. PALOMES, *La storia di li Nurmanni 'n Sicilia*, 4 vols., Palermo, 1882–87; H. OTTENDORFF, *Die Regierung der beiden letzten Normannenkönige Tancreds und*

Wilhelms III von Sizilien und ihre Kämpfe gegen Kaiser Heinrich VI, Bonn, 1899; G. B. SIRAGUSA, *Il regno di Guglielmo I in Sicilia*, 2 vols., Palermo, 1885–86. G. LA MANTIA, *La Sicilia ed il suo dominio nell' Africa settentrionale dal secolo XI al XVI*, Palermo, 1922. W. COHN, *Das Zeitalter der Normannen in Sizilien*, Bonn, 1920.

The standard work on the first Norman king in the south is E. CASPAR, *Roger II (1101–1154) und die Gründung der normannisch-sicilianischen Monarchie*, Innsbruck, 1904. R. STRAUS, *Die Juden im Königreich Sizilien unter Normannen und Staufern*, Heidelberg, 1910. On Norman art see E. BERTAUX, *L'art dans l'Italie méridionale*, vol. I, Paris, 1904; C. DIEHL, *L'art byzantin dans l'Italie méridionale*, Paris, 1894; and *Palerme et Syracuse*, Paris, 1907. DI GIOVANNI, *La topografia antica di Palermo dal secolo 10 al 15*, 2 vols., Palermo, 1889–90. G. LA MANTIA, *Sugli studi di topografia palermitana del medio evo*, Palermo, 1919. N. MACCARRONE, *La vita del latino in Sicilia fino all' età normanna*, Florence, 1915. Popular books which attempt to revive interest in Norman Sicily and Italy are numerous; e.g., M. S. BRIGGS, *In the heel of Italy: a study of an unknown city* [Lecce], London, 1910; and N. DOUGLAS, *Old Calabria*, London, 1915.

Monte Cassino and the Normans. R. PALMAROCCHI, *L'abbazia di Montecassino et la conquista normanna*, Rome, 1913. See also the short but valuable introduction to E. A. LOEW, *The Beneventan script*.

The Normans and the papacy. A. WINCKLER, "Gregor VII und die Normannen," in vol. X (1875), 605–43, of *Sammlung gemeinverständlicher wissenschaftlicher Vorträge*. A. WAGNER, *Die unteritalischen Normannen und das Papstthum, von Victor III bis Hadrian IV (1086–1156)*, Breslau, 1887.

The Normans and the Byzantine empire. J. GAY, *L'Italie méridionale et l'empire byzantin*, Paris, 1904. G. L. F. TAFEL, *Komnenen und Normannen: Beiträge zur Erforschung ihrer Geschichte im verdeutschten und erläuterten Urkunden des zwölften und dreizehnten Jahrhunderts aus dem Griechischen*, Ulm, 1852; 2nd edition, part II, Stuttgart, 1870. C. SCHWARTZ, *Die Feldzüge Robert Guiscard's gegen das byzantinische Reich*, Fulda, 1854 (Prog.). W. COHN, *Die Geschichte der normannisch-sicilischen Flotte*, 3 vols., Breslau, 1910–26. G. SCHLUMBERGER, "Deux chefs normands des armées byzantines," in *R.H.*, XVI (1881), 289–303. See also outline XVIII above.

Normans in Syria. B. KUGLER, *Boemund und Tankred*, Tübingen, 1862. G. REY, in *Revue de l'Orient latin*, IV (1896), 321–407; VIII (1900), 116–57. E. KÜHNE, *Geschichte des Fürstentums Antiochia unter normannischen Heerschaft (1098-1130)*, Berlin, 1897 (Prog.). O. VON SYDOW, *Tancred: ein Lebensbild aus den Zeiten der Kreuzzüge*, Leipzig, 1880. R. B. YEWDALE, *Bohemond I, prince of Antioch*, Princeton, 1924.

Original sources. The general collections for France and Belgium, nos. **965–77** and for Italy, nos. **988–94**, especially no. **988**, contain much material for a study of the Normans. *Historiae normannorum scriptores antiqui . . . 838–1220*, edited by A. DUCHESNE, Paris, 1619. The publications of the Société de l'histoire de Normandie, Rouen, 1870ff., contain source materials; e.g., L. MARX, *Gesta normannorum ducum* of WILLIAM OF JUMIÈGES, Paris,

1914; and L. HALPHEN and R. POUPARDIN, *Chroniques des comtes d'Anjou et des seigneurs d'Amboise*, Paris, 1914. An important source for the Normans in the south is AMATUS (AIMÉ) OF MONTE CASSINO, *L'ystoire de li Normant* [to 1078], edited by O. DELARC, Rouen, 1892. K. A. KEHR, *Die Urkunden der normannisch-sicilischen Könige: eine diplomatische Untersuchung*, Innsbruck, 1902, is a careful study of the archive material for the Normans in Sicily.

Bibliographies. The most serviceable bibliography is that at the end of chapters in HASKINS, *The Normans in European history*. GROSS, *Sources and literature*, part IV. *Catalogue des ouvrages normands de la Bibliothèque municipale de Caen*, Caen, 1910–12. A. MOLINIER, *Les sources de l'histoire de France*, II, chs. XXV, XXXIII. U. CHEVALIER, *Répertoire: Topo-bibliographie*, II, 2140.

XXI. THE CRUSADES

A. OUTLINE

1. After having been more or less on the defensive against its foes from the eighth to the eleventh centuries, western Christendom was ready to take the offensive towards the end of the eleventh century. Compare the ousting of the Mohammedans from Sicily by the Normans, 1061–91.

2. Nature and causes of the crusades. Contact between Europe and Asia in the early middle ages. The "Syrians" in the west. Pilgrimages to Jerusalem and other holy places.

3. Syria and Asia Minor in the eleventh century. The Christian state of Armenia. Treatment of Christian pilgrims in Jerusalem before and after the capture of the holy city by the Seljuk Turks in 1076.

4. The preaching of the first crusade by pope Urban II at the council of Clermont, 1095. The legend of Peter the Hermit. Persecutions of the Jews. In the spring of 1096 several unorganized bands, mostly peasants, set out under Peter the Hermit, Walter the Penniless, and others. Most of them perished miserably.

5. The first crusading army set out in the fall of 1096. The following were some of the prominent leaders: Godfrey of Lorraine (of Bouillon) and his brother Baldwin; Raymond of Saint-Gilles, count of Toulouse; Robert, duke of Normandy; Hugh, count of Vermandois; Stephen, count of Blois; Bohemond, son of Robert Guiscard, and his nephew Tancred; Adhemar, bishop of Puy, the legate of the pope.

6. The crusading hosts in Constantinople. Their relations with the emperor Alexius Comnenus. The anomalous position of the Norman leaders. The *Alexiad* of Anna Comnena, daughter of Alexius.

7. March through Asia Minor and conquest of the Holy Land. Siege of Nicaea. Battle of Dorylaeum. Capture of Edessa and Antioch in 1098. The legend of the holy lance. Fall of Jerusalem in 1099.

8. The organization of the conquests. The Latin kingdom of Jerusalem. The *Assizes of Jerusalem*. Feudalism in Palestine. The county of Tripoli, the principality of Antioch, and the county of Edessa.

9. The religious military orders; Hospitallers, Templars, Teutonic knights. The Teutonic knights in Prussia in the first half of the thirteenth century under their grand master, Hermann of Salza.

10. The management of the constant flow of population and goods to and from the Holy Land. *Passagia.* Importance of the sea routes. The rapid rise of Italian towns and merchants.

11. Results of the fall of Edessa in 1144. The preaching of St. Bernard of Clairvaux. Conrad III of Germany and Louis VII of France led armies to Palestine.

12. The capture of Jerusalem in 1187 by Saladin led to the crusade of the three kings, Frederick I (Barbarossa) of Germany, Richard the Lion-Hearted of England, and Philip II of France. The death of Frederick Barbarossa by drowning in the river Saleph, 1190. Capture of Acre by the Christians in 1191. Truce with Saladin, 1192. The failure of this crusade marked the end of the heroic crusading era.

13. The crusading plans of the emperor Henry VI.

14. The ambition of pope Innocent III to launch an overwhelming crusade. The capture of Constantinople by so-called crusaders in 1204 and the establishment of the Latin empire of Constantinople, 1204–61. The children's crusade, 1212. Innocent preached a "crusade" against the Albigensian heretics in southern France, and aided the Christians against the Mohammedans in Spain (Battle of Tolosa, 1212).

15. The capture of Damietta by the Christians in 1219. Ultimate loss of the city and failure of this expedition into Egypt. St. Francis of Assisi in Egypt.

16. The emperor Frederick II in the Holy Land. His treaty with El-Kamil, the sultan of Egypt, in 1229, by which he got possession of Jerusalem, Bethlehem, and Nazareth. Frederick assumed the crown of Jerusalem. Capture of Jerusalem by the fierce Charismian Turks in 1244.

17. The crusading fervor of king Louis IX of France. The *Life of St. Louis* by his friend Joinville. Capture of Damietta in Egypt in 1249. Louis did not follow up his first successes and was taken prisoner. When released he went as a pilgrim to Palestine. Fall of Jaffa and Antioch, 1268, into the hands of the sultan Bibars. The second crusade of St. Louis to Tunis where he died in 1270.

18. The fall of Acre in 1291 and the end of the Latin kingdom of Jerusalem.

19. Crusading movements after 1291. The *De recuperatione Terrae Sanctae* of Pierre Dubois (1309). Missionary activities set in motion largely by the crusades. Raymund Lull.

20. Changes in Europe in the twelfth and thirteenth centuries which can in a measure be attributed to the crusades.

21. Latin emperors in Constantinople.

Baldwin I, 1204–05
Henry of Flanders, 1206–16
Peter of Courtenay, 1216–17
Robert, 1221–28
John of Brienne, 1228–37
Baldwin II, 1237–61

22. Kings of Jerusalem.

Godfrey of Bouillon, 1099–1100 (without the title of king)	Baldwin V, 1185–86
Baldwin I, 1100–18	Guy of Lusignan, 1186–92
Baldwin II, 1118–31	[Conrad of Montferrat, 1192]
Fulk of Anjou, 1131–43	[Henry of Champagne, 1192–97]
Baldwin III, 1143–62	Amalric II of Lusignan, 1197–1205
Amalric I, 1162–74	John of Brienne, 1210–25
Baldwin IV, 1174–85	Frederick II, 1229–50

B. Special Recommendations for Reading

Brief surveys. C. Oman, "East and west," *Trans., R.H.S.*, IV series, III, London, 1920, 1–24. Bémont and Monod, *Medieval Europe*, 336–74. Emerton, *Mediaeval Europe*, 357–97. Adams, *Civilization*, 258–78. Flick, *Mediaeval church*, ch. xx. Munro and Sontag, *Middle ages*, chs. xxi and xxv. Thompson, *Economic and social history*, ch. xvi. Hulme, *Middle ages*, 456–99. Sellery and Krey, *Medieval foundations*, 107–23, 170–78. C. Diehl, *History of the Byzantine empire*, 138–50. Evans, *Life in mediaeval France*, ch. v. R. A. Newhall, *The crusades* (Berkshire studies), New York, 1927. The article "Crusades" in the *Ency. Brit.*, was written by E. Barker, that in *The Catholic encyclopedia* by L. Bréhier; both are excellent and contain good bibliographical notes. Langlois, *Lectures historiques*, ch. ix, reprints several passages from modern authors on the crusades. *C.M.H.*, IV, chs. xii–xiv; V, chs. vi–ix. Tout, *The empire and the papacy*, chs. viii, xiii, xv, xix. Lavisse et Rambaud, *Histoire générale*, II, ch. vi (translated in part by Munro and Sellery, *Medieval civilization*, 248–56). Lavisse, *Histoire de France*, II, part, II, 227–50. Gibbon, *Decline and fall*, chs. lvii–lx.

Books on the crusades in English. E. Barker, *Crusades*, London, 1923; reprint of article in *Ency. Brit.* T. A. Archer and C. L. Kingsford, *The crusades: the story of the Latin Kingdom of Jerusalem*, New York, 1895 (Stories of nations). W. B. Stevenson, *The crusaders in the east: a brief history of the wars of Islam with the Latins in Syria during the twelfth and thirteenth centuries*, Cambridge, 1907, presents the subject from the eastern point of view. W. Miller, *The Latin Orient*, London, 1920 (Helps for students of history, 37).

Speech of Pope Urban II. This speech has been analyzed by D. C. Munro, *A.H.R.*, XI (1905–06), 231–42.

Pilgrimages. Beazley, *Dawn of modern geography*, I, 125–75; II, 112–217. Lacroix, *Military and religious life in the middle ages*, 262–393. E. Joranson, "The great German pilgrimage of 1064–1065," in *The crusades, etc., presented to Dana C. Munro*, New York, 1928, 3–43.

Original sources. *Translations and reprints*, vol. I, no. 2, " Urban and the crusaders"; vol. I, no. 4, "Letters of the crusaders"; vol. III, no. 1, "The fourth crusade." For translations of several accounts of the capture of Jerusalem in 1099 see DUNCALF and KREY, *Parallel source problems*, 95–133. MUNRO and SELLERY, *Medieval civilization*, 257–68, "Ibn Jubair's account of his journey through Syria (1184)." ROBINSON, *Readings*, I, 312–45. THATCHER and McNEAL, *Source book*, 510–44. OGG, *Source book*, 282–96. HENDERSON, *Documents*, 337–44. DAVIES, *Civilization in medieval England*, 149–95.

The following are the most available longer accounts in English: A. C. KREY, *The first crusade: the accounts of eyewitnesses and participants*, Princeton, 1921. ELIZABETH A. S. DAWES, *The Alexiad*, London, 1928. HITTI, *An Arab-Syrian gentleman and warrior in the period of the crusades. Chronicles of the crusades: being contemporary narratives of the crusade of Richard Coeur de Lion by Richard of Devizes and Geoffrey de Vinsauf and of the crusade of St. Louis, by Lord John de Joinville*, London, 1848. T. A. ARCHER, *The crusade of Richard I, 1189–1192*, New York, 1889 (English history by contemporary writers). VILLEHARDOUIN'S *Chronicle of the fourth crusade and the conquest of Constantinople*, and JOINVILLE'S *Chronicle of the crusade of St. Lewis*, are translated by Sir F. MARZIALS, *Memoirs of the crusades*, London [1908] (Everyman's Library). The second of these is also translated conveniently in *The memoirs of the Lord of Joinville: a new English version*, by ETHEL WEDGEWOOD, London, 1906.

Maps. SHEPHERD, *Atlas*, 66–7, 68, 70–1, 73.

C. BIBLIOGRAPHY

General books. Information on the crusades is widely scattered in the general books on medieval history. Those on the church, nos. **393–498**, France, Germany, and Italy, nos. **508–621**, and the Byzantine empire, nos. **643–79**, are especially useful. See also W. HEYD, *Histoire du commerce du Levant au moyen âge*, and A. SCHAUBE, *Handelsgeschichte*. S. L. POOLE, *A history of Egypt in the middle ages*, New York, 1901.

General accounts. B. KUGLER, *Geschichte der Kreuzzüge*, Berlin, 1880; 2nd edition, 1891, part of no. **313**. L. BRÉHIER, *L'eglise et l'Orient au moyen âge: les croisades*, 5th edition, Paris, 1928. E. HEYCK, *Die Kreuzzüge und das heilige Land*, Bielefeld and Leipzig, 1900. R. RÖHRICHT, *Geschichte der Kreuzzüge im Umriss*, Innsbruck, 1899. N. JORGA, *Brève histoire des croisades et de leurs fondations en Terre Sainte*, Paris, 1924.

The two most comprehensive histories of the crusades are antiquated, having been written early in the nineteenth century under the influence of the romantic movement: J. F. MICHAUD, *Histoire des croisades*, 3 vols., Paris, 1812–17; in 7 vols., 1824–29, translated into English by W. ROBSON, *History of the crusades*, 3 vols., [1852] (often reprinted); F. WILKEN, *Geschichte der Kreuzzüge nach morgenländischen und abendländischen Berichten*, 7 vols. in 8, Leipzig, 1807–32.

Pilgrimages to the Holy Land. A. BAUMSTARK, *Abendländische Palästinerpilger des ersten Jahrtausends und ihre Berichte*, Cologne, 1906. P. RIANT, *Expéditions et pélerinages des Scandinaves en Terre Sainte au temps des croisades*, Paris, 1865. E. JORANSON, "The great German pilgrimage of 1064–1065," in *The crusades, etc., presented to Dana C. Munro*, 3–43.

First crusade. T. WOLFF, *Die Bauernkreuzzüge des Jahres 1096. Ein Beitrag zur Geschichte des ersten Kreuzzugs*, Tübingen, 1891. H. VON SYBEL, *Geschichte des ersten Kreuzzuges*, Leipzig, 1841; 2nd edition, 1881. R. RÖHRICHT, *Geschichte des ersten Kreuzzuges*, Innsbruck, 1901. H. HAGENMEYER, *Chronologie de la première croisade, 1094–1100*, Paris, 1902, is taken from *Revue de l'Orient latin*, VI–VIII. F. DUNCALF, "The peasants' crusade," in *A.H.R.*, XXVI (1921), 440–53. W. HOLTZMANN, "Studien zur Orientpolitik des Reformpapsttums und zur Entstehung des ersten Kreuzzuges," *H.V.J.S.*, XXII (1924), 167–99. YEWDALE, *Bohemond I*. F. CHALANDON, *Histoire de la première croisade jusqu'à l'élection de Godefroi de Bouillon*, Paris, 1925. DAVID, *Robert Curthose*. F. DUNCALF, "The Pope's plan for the first crusade," in *The crusades, etc., presented to Dana C. Munro*, 44–56; A. C. KREY, "A neglected passage in the *Gesta* and its bearing on the literature of the first crusade," *ibid.*, 57–78; M. M. KNAPPEN, "Robert II of Flanders in the first crusade," *ibid.*, 79–100; A. A. BEAUMONT, "Albert of Aachen and the county of Edessa," *ibid.*, 101–38.

Historiography of the first crusades. H. VON SYBEL, translated by Lady DUFF GORDON, *The history and literature of the crusades*, London, 1861, reprint (n.d.) by Routledge. O. J. THATCHER, "Latin sources of the first crusade," *Annual report, A.H.A.*, (1900) I, 499–509. T. A. ARCHER, "The Council of Clermont and the first crusade," *Scottish review*, XXVI (1895), 274–95. C. NEUMANN, *Griechische Geschichtschreiber und Geschichtsquellen im 12 Jahrhundert: Studien zu Anna Comnena, Theod. Prodromus, Joh. Cinnamus*, Leipzig, 1888. See also MOLINIER, *Les sources de l'histoire de France*, V, pp. xcvff.

The Latin Kingdom of Jerusalem and other Latin states in Syria. C. R. CONDER, *The Latin kingdom of Jerusalem, 1099–1291*, London, 1897. R. RÖHRICHT, *Geschichte des Königreichs Jerusalem* (*1100–1291*), Innsbruck, 1898. G. DODU, *Histoire des institutions monarchiques dans le royaume latin de Jérusalem* (*1099–1291*), Paris, 1894; and *Le royaume latin de Jérusalem*, Paris, 1914. HELEN G. PRESTON, *Rural conditions in the kingdom of Jerusalem during the twelfth and thirteenth centuries*, Philadelphia, 1903 (Diss.). E. REY, *Les colonies franques de Syrie aux XIIe et XIIIe siècles*, Paris, 1884. E. G. REY, *Essai sur la domination française en Syrie durant le moyen âge*, Paris, 1866, and *Recherches géographiques et historiques sur la domination des Latins en Orient*, Paris, 1877. G. SCHLUMBERGER, *Les principautés franques dans le Levant*, Paris, 1879; *Campagnes du roi Amaury I de Jérusalem en Egypte, au XIIe siècle*, Paris, 1906; *Fin de la domination franque en Syrie après les dernières croisades: prise de Saint-Jean d'Acre en l'an 1291 par l'armée du Soudan d'Egypte*, Paris, 1914, is an extract from the *R.D.M.*, July 15, 1913. C. DUCANGE, *Familles d'outre mer*, publiées par E. G. Rey, Paris, 1869, part of **965.** R. NICOLAS, *Geschichte der Vorrechte und des Einflusses Frankreichs in Syrien und in der Levante, vom Beginn des Mittelalters bis zum Friedensvertrag von Paris 1802*, Bern, 1917.

Second crusade. B. KUGLER, *Analekten zur Geschichte des zweiten Kreuzzuges*, Tübingen, 1878, 1885; *Neue Analekten*, 1885. C. NEUMANN, *Bernhard* *von Clairvaux und die Anfänge des zweiten Kreuzzuges*, Heidelberg, 1882. H. COSACK, "Konrads III Entschluss zum Kreuzzug," *M.I.O.G.*, XXXV (1914), 278–96. J. B. CHABOT, "Un épisode inédit de l'histoire des croisades: le siège de Birta, 1145," *Comptes rendus de l'Académie des inscriptions et belles-lettres*, March, 1917.

Third crusade. S. LANE POOLE, *Saladin and the fall of the kingdom of Jerusalem*, New York, 1898; new edition, London, 1926. KATE NORGATE, *Richard the Lion Heart*, London and New York, 1924. A. CARTELLIERI, "Richard Löwenherz im heiligen Lande," *H.Z.*, CI (1908), 1–25. G. SCHLUMBERGER, *Renaud de Châtillon, prince d'Antioche*, Paris, 1898. A. GRUHN, *Der Kreuzzug Richards I*, Berlin, [1892]. K. FISCHER, *Geschichte des Kreuzzuges Kaiser Friedrichs I*, Leipzig, 1870.

Henry VI, plan for a crusade. W. LEONHARDT, *Der Kreuzzugsplan Kaiser Heinrichs VI* (Diss. Giessen, ca. 1914). E. TRAUB, *Der Kreuzzugsplan Kaiser Heinrichs VI im Zusammenhang mit der Politik der Jahre 1195–1197*, Jena, 1910.

Capture of Constantinople in 1204 and the Latin Empire 1204–1261. A. LUCHAIRE, *Innocent III*, 6 vols., Paris, 1905–08, vol. IV, *La question d'Orient.* E. PEARS, *The fall of Constantinople: being the story of the fourth crusade*, New York, 1886. C. DIEHL, "L'empire latin de Constantinople," essay IX, in *Dans l'Orient byzantin*, pp. 167–202. M. R. GUTSCH, "A twelfth century preacher—Fulk of Neuilly," in *The crusades, etc., presented to Dana C. Munro*, 183–206. E. GERLAND, *Geschichte des lateinischen Kaiserreiches von Konstantinopel*, part I, *Geschichte der Kaiser Balduin I und Heinrich, 1204-1216*, Homburg, 1905. W. NORDEN, *Der vierte Kreuzzug im Rahmen der Beziehungen des Abendlandes zu Byzanz*, Berlin, 1898. H. MOESER, *Gottfried von Villehardouin und der Lateinerzug gegen Byzanz*, 1899. E. GERLAND, "Der vierte Kreuzzug und seine Probleme," in *Neue Jahrbücher für das klassische Altertum, Geschichte und deutsche Literatur*, XIII (1904), 505–14. J. TESSIER, *La quatrième croisade: la diversion sur Zara et Constantinople*, Paris, 1884. L. STREIT, *Beiträge zur Geschichte des vierten Kreuzzuges*, Anklam, 1877. Count RIANT, *Le changement de direction de la quatrième croisade*, Paris, 1878. C. DU CANGE, *Histoire de l'empire de Constantinople sous les empereurs françois*, Paris, 1657; new edition by J. A. BUCHON, 2 vols., Paris, 1826. K. HOPF, *Geschichte Griechenlands* in Ersch-Gruber, vols. LXXXV–LXXXVI, Leipzig, 1867–68. VASILIEV, *History of the Byzantine empire*, II, 109ff., with bibliographical references. OMAN, *Story of the Byzantine empire*, 274–306, gives a brief summary.

The Byzantine empire and the crusades. W. NORDEN, *Das Papsttum und Byzanz*, Berlin, 1903. F. CHALANDON, *Essai sur le règne d'Alexis Comnène (1081–1118);* and *Jean II Comnène (1118–1143)*, Paris, 1912. ALICE GARDNER, *The Lascarids of Nicaea: the story of an empire in exile*, London, 1912. W. MILLER, *The Latins in the Levant; Essays on the Latin Orient*, Cambridge, 1921. L. DE MAS LATRIE, *Les princes de Morée ou d'Achaïe, 1203–1461*, Venice, 1882. FINLAY, *History of Greece*, II–IV. R. RODD, *The princes of Achaia and the chronicles of Morea, a study of Greece in the middle ages*, London,

1907. J. K. Fotheringham, *Marco Sanudo, conqueror of the Archipelago*, Oxford, 1915. G. Schlumberger, *Récits de Byzance et des croisades*, 2 vols., Paris, 1916, 1922. A. Gruhn, *Die byzantinische Politik zur Zeit der Kreuzzüge*, Berlin, 1904. E. de Muralt, *Essai de chronographie byzantine (1057–1453)*, 2 vols., Basel and Geneva, 1871–73. J. Dräseke, "Bischof Anselm von Havelberg und seine Gesandtschaftsreisen nach Byzanz," *Zeitschrift für Kirchengeschichte*, XXI (1901), 160–85. For a summary see Lavisse et Rambaud, *Histoire générale*, II, ch. xv.

The children's crusade. D. C. Munro, "The children's crusade," *A.H.R.*, XIX (1914), 516–24. R. Röhricht, "Der Kinderkreuzzug, 1212," in *H.Z.*, XXXVI (1876), 1–8. G. de Janssens, *Etienne de Cloyes et les croisades d'enfants au XIIIe siècle*, Paris, 1890.

Fifth crusade. R. Röhricht, *Studien zur Geschichte des fünften Kreuzzuges*, Innsbruck, 1891.

Frederick II and the crusades. W. Jacobs, *Patriarch Gerold von Jerusalem: ein Beitrag zur Kreuzzugsgeschichte Friedrichs II*, Aachen, 1905 (Diss., Bonn). R. Röhricht, *Die Kreuzfahrt Friedrich II*, Berlin, 1872. Reinaud, "Histoire de la sixième croisade (1228–1229)," *Journal asiatique*, VIII (1826), 18–40, 88–110, 149–69. Blochet, "Relations diplomatiques des Hohenstaufens avec les sultans d'Egypte," in *R.H.*, LXXX (1902), 51–64. E. Kestner, *Der Kreuzzug Friedrichs II*, Göttingen, 1873.

Crusades of King Louis IX. F. Perry, *Saint Louis*, New York and London, 1901 (Heroes of the nations). E. J. Davis, *The invasion of Egypt in A.D. 1249 by Louis 9th of France*, London, 1898. R. Sternfeld, *Ludwigs des Heiligen Kreuzzug nach Tunis 1270 and die Politik Karls I von Sizilien*, Berlin, 1896. Le Nain de Tillemont, *Vie de St. Louis*, 6 vols., Paris, 1847–51, part of **966.** H. F. Delaborde, *Jean de Joinville et les seigneurs de Joinville*, Paris, 1894.

Religious military orders. H. Prutz, *Die geistlichen Ritterorden: ihre Stellung zur kirchlichen, politischen, gesellschaftlichen und wirtschaftlichen Entwicklung des Mittelalters*, Berlin, 1908; *Der Anteil der geistlichen Ritterorden an dem geistigen Leben ihrer Zeit*, Munich, 1908. F. C. Woodhouse, *The military religious orders*, London, 1879.

A. Rastoul, *Les Templiers 1118–1312*, 2nd edition, Paris, 1905. H. C. Lea, *History of inquisition*, III, ch. 5. H. Prutz, *Entwicklung und Untergang des Templerherrenordens*, Berlin, 1888. J. Gmelin, *Schuld oder Unschuld des Templerordens: kritscher Versuch zur Lösung der Frage*, Stuttgart, 1893. K. Schottmüller, *Der Untergang des Templer-Ordens*, 2 vols., Berlin, 1887. L. Delisle, "Operations financières des Templiers," *Mémoires de l'Académie des Inscriptions*, XXXIII (1889). G. Lizerand, "Les dépositions du Grand Maître Jacques de Molay au procès des Templiers, 1307–14," *M.A.*, XXVI (1913), 81–106. M. Schüpferling, *Der Templerherren Orden in Deutschland*, Bamberg, 1915. F. Lundgreen, *Wilhelm von Tyrus und der Templerorden*, part I, Berlin, 1911 (Diss.). V. Carrière, *Histoire et cartulaire des Templiers de Provins avec une introduction sur les débuts du Temple en France*, Paris, 1919. E. J. Martin, *The trial of the Templars*, London, 1928.

Baron DE DELABRE, *Rhodes of the Knights*, Oxford, 1909. J. DELAVILLE LE ROULX, *Les Hospitaliers en Terre Sainte et à Chypre, 1100–1310*, Paris, 1904; *Les Hospitaliers à Rhodes jusqu'à la mort de Philibert de Nailhac, 1310–1421*, Paris, 1913. *Mélanges sur l'Ordre de S. Jean de Jérusalem*, Paris, 1910. W. K. R. BEDFORD and R. HOLBECHE, *The order of the hospital of St. John of Jerusalem*, London, 1902. W. PORTER, *Knights of Malta or the Order of St. John of Jerusalem*, 2 vols., London, 1858; 3rd edition of vol. I, 1884. J. F. SYMONS-JEUNE, *Eight hundred years of the order of the hospital of St. John of Jerusalem*, London, 1922. ROSE G. KINGSLEY, *The order of St. John of Jerusalem, past and present*, London, 1919. R. PÉTIET, *Contribution à l'histoire de l'Ordre de Saint-Lazare de Jérusalem en France*, Paris, 1914.

Crusading movements after 1291. F. HEIDELBERGER, *Kreuzzugsversuche um die Wende des 13 Jahrhunderts*, Berlin and Leipzig, 1911 (*Abh.m.n.G.*, 31). A. GOTTRON, *Ramon Lulls Kreuzzungsideen*, Berlin, 1912. J. DELAVILLE LE ROULX, *La France en Orient au XIVe siècle: expéditions du maréchal Boucicaut*, 2 vols., Paris, 1886, part of no. **887.** U. CHEVALIER, *La croisade du dauphin Humbert II (1345–1347)*, Paris, 1920. N. JORGA, *Notes et extraits pour servir à l'histoire des croisades au XVe siècle*, 5 vols., Paris, 1899–1915.

Preaching of crusades. A. LECOY DE LA MARCHE, "La prédication de la croisade au XIIIe siècle," *R.Q.H.*, XLVIII (1890), 5–28. R. RÖHRICHT, "Die Kreuzpredigten gegen den Islam," *Zeitschrift für Kirchengeschichte*, VI (1884), 550–72.

Privileges of the crusaders. E. BRIDREY, *La condition juridique des croisés, et le privilège de la croix*, Paris, 1900. EDITH BRAMHALL, "The privileges of the crusaders," *American journal of theology*, V (1902), 279ff. A. GOTTLOB, *Kreuzablass und Almosenablass*, Stuttgart, 1906.

Archaeological evidences of the crusades. G. REY, *Etudes sur les monuments de l'architecture militaire des croisades en Syrie et dans l'île de Chypre*, Paris, 1871. C. ENLART, *L'art gothique et la renaissance en Chypre*, 2 vols., Paris, 1899. A. GABRIEL, *La cité de Rhodes*, Vol. I, *Topographie, Architecture militaire*, Vol II, *Architecture civile et religieuse*, Paris, 1921. C. ENLART, *Les monuments des croisés dans le royaume de Jérusalem: architecture religieuse et civile*, 2 vols., and 2 atlases, Paris, 1925–28. G. SCHLUMBERGER, *Numismatique de l'Orient latin*, Paris, 1878.

Cyprus. L. DE MAS LATRIE, *Histoire de l'île de Chypre sous le règne des princes de la maison de Lusignan*, 3 vols., Paris, 1855–61. *Documents nouveaux servant de preuves à l'histoire de l'île de Chypre*, Paris, 1882. B. STEWART, *Cyprus: the people, mediaeval cities, castles, antiquities, and history of the island*, London, 1908. W. STUBBS, "The mediaeval kingdoms of Cyprus and Armenia," in his *Seventeen lectures*, ch. VIII.

Culture and the crusades. H. PRUTZ, *Kulturgeschichte der Kreuzzüge*, Berlin, 1883. O. HENNE AM RHYN, *Kulturgeschichte der Kreuzzüge*, Leipzig, 1894. O. HENNE AM RHYN, *Die Kreuzzüge und die Kultur ihrer Zeit*, Leipzig, 1886. A. v. KREMER, *Culturgeschichtliche Beziehungen zwischen Europa und dem Oriente*, Vienna, 1876, is a short lecture. E. H. BYRNE, "The Genoese colonies in Syria," in *The crusades, etc., presented to Dana C. Munro*, 139–82;

"Commercial contracts of the Genoese in the Syrian trade," *Quarterly journal of economics*, XXXI (1916–17), 128–70; "Genoese trade with Syria in twelfth century," *A.H.R.*, XXV (1919–20), 191–219; and "Easterners in Genoa," *Journal American Oriental society*, XXXVIII (1918), 176–87.

Legends of the crusades. The classic refutation of the legend of Peter the Hermit is H. Hagenmeyer, *Peter der Eremite*, Leipzig, 1879; French translation, Paris, 1883. The famous legend of the finding of the holy lance in Antioch is treated in full by J. Straubinger, *Die Kreuzauffindungslegende*, Paderborn, 1912 (part of no. **489**). B. Kugler, *Albert von Aachen*, Stuttgart, 1885; *Analekten zur Kritik Alberts von Aachen*, Tübingen, 1888 (Albert was the author of a "saga" of the first crusade c. 1120). G. Paris, in the introduction of his edition of *L'estoire de la guerre sainte*, Paris, 1897 (part of **965**), discussed the legend of the third crusade. H. Pigeonneau, *Le cycle de la croisade et de la famille de Bouillon*, Paris, 1877. Munro and Sellery, *Medieval civilization*, 269–76.

Art of war of the crusaders. O. Heermann, *Die Gefechtsführung abendländischer Heere im Orient in der Epoche des ersten Kreuzzugs*, Marburg, 1888. See also Oman, *The art of war*, 229–350; and H. Delbrück, *Geschichte der Kriegskunst*, III, 226–31.

Miscellaneous books. D. C. Munro, H. Prutz, and C. Diehl, *Essays on the crusades*, Burlington, Vermont, 1903. R. Röhricht, *Beiträge zur Geschichte der Kreuzzüge*, 2 vols., Berlin, 1874–78; *Kleine Studien zur Geschichte der Kreuzzüge*, Berlin, 1890. O. Volk, *Die abendländischhierarchische Kreuzzugsidee*, Halle, 1911. G. Marcais, *Les Arabes en Berbérie du XIe au XIVe siècle*, Paris, 1913. *Oriens christianus, römische Halbjahrhefte für Kunde des christlichen Orients*, Leipzig, 1901ff. C. M. Watson, *The story of Jerusalem*, London, 1912 (Mediaeval towns). Estelle Blythe, *Jerusalem and the crusades*, New York, 1914. G. Le Strange, *Palestine under the Moslems: a description of Syria and the Holy Land from A.D. 650 to 1500*, London, 1890. L. J. Paetow, "The crusading ardor of John of Garland," in *The crusades, etc., presented to Dana C. Munro*, 207–22. M. Gaudefroy-Demombynes, *La Syrie à l'époque des Mamélouks d'après les auteurs arabes*. R. Dussaud, *Topographie historique de la Syrie, antique et médiévale*, Paris, 1927.

Original sources. The most comprehensive collection of sources for the crusades is the *Recueil des historiens des croisades*, publié par les soins de l'Académie des inscriptions et belles-lettres, in 16 huge folio vols., Paris, 1841–1906. (H. Dehérain, "Les origines du Recueil des Historiens des croisades," *Journal des Savants*, Sept.–Oct., 1919, 260–66.) This almost entirely supersedes the old collection by J. Bongars, *Gesta dei per Francos sive orientalium expeditionum et regni Francorum hierosolimitani historia*, vols. I and II, Hanau, 1611. The Société de l'Orient Latin, founded in 1875 by Count Riant, published much source material for a history of the crusades in its *Publications*, 1879ff., in a série géographique, and a série historique, the contents of which are listed in Potthast, *Wegweiser*, I, cxxiii; its *Archives*, 2 vols., 1881 and 1884; and its *Revue*, 1893–11, which, besides articles, book-reviews, and bibliographies, contains many texts. A. Chroust,

Quellen zur Geschichte des Kreuzzugs Friedrichs I. Scriptores rerum Germanicarum, new series, vol. 5, Berlin, 1928.

English translations of pilgrimages to the Holy Land are given in *Palestine pilgrims text society*, 13 vols., London, 1897 (the contents of which are analyzed in J. W. THOMPSON, *Reference studies in medieval history*, revised and enlarged edition, 3 vols, Chicago, 1923–24, pp. 121–122); and in *Early travels in Palestine, comprising the narratives of Arculf*, etc., edited by T. WRIGHT, London, 1848. See also *Deutsche Pilgerreisen nach dem Heiligen Lande*, edited by R. RÖHRICHT and H. MEISNER, Berlin, 1880; new edition, abridged and edited by R. RÖHRICHT, Innsbruck, 1900.

French translations of extracts from the sources of the crusades were issued by J. MICHAUD, *Bibliothèque des croisades*, 2nd edition, 4 vols., Paris, 1829–30. See especially vol. IV for Arabic authors. GUIZOT's *Collection des mémoires*, no. **971**, also contains translations of accounts of the crusades. H. MICHELANT et G. RAYNAUD, *Itinéraires à Jérusalem et descriptions de la Terre Sainte, redigés en français aux XIe, XIIe, et XIIIe siècles*, Geneva, 1882.

It would carry us too far afield to try to enumerate separate editions of original sources of the crusades. It will be serviceable, however, to mention the following works edited by H. HAGENMEYER, *Historia Hierosolymitana, 1095–1127*, of FOULCHER OF CHARTRES, Heidelberg, 1913; *Anonymi gesta Francorum et aliorum Hierosolymitanorum*, Heidelberg, 1890; (Better edition by L. BRÉHIER, editor and translator, *Histoire anonyme de la première croisade*, Paris, 1924. See also BEATRICE A. LEES, *Anonymi Gesta Francorum et aliorum Hierosolymitanorum*, Oxford, 1924); *Ekkehardi Uraugiensis abbatis Hierosolymita nach der Waitzschen Recension*, Tübingen, 1877; *Die Kreuzzugsbriefe aus dem Jahren 1098–1100, mit Erlaüterungen*, Innsbruck, 1901 (RIANT has an *Inventaire critique* of these letters in the *Archives de l'Orient latin*, I). See also the documentary material for the kingdom of Jerusalem, edited by R. RÖHRICHT, *Regesta regni Hierosolymitani* (*1098–1291*), Innsbruck, 1893, with an *Additamentum, ibid.*, 1904. Important material has been edited by P. RIANT, *Exuviae sacrae constantinopolitanae*, 2 vols., Geneva, 1877–78; and an additional volume by F. DE MELY, Paris, 1904. PIERRE DUBOIS, *De recuperatione Terrae Sanctae*, edited by C. V. LANGLOIS, Paris, 1891 (part of no. **968**), written in 1309, is the best source of information concerning crusading ideas in the fourteenth century. *Cartulaire général de l'ordre du Temple, 1119–1150*, edited by MARQUIS D'ALBON, Paris, 1913; H. DE CURZON, *Règle du Temple*, Paris, 1886; G. LIZERAND, *Le dossier de l'affaire des Templiers*, Paris, 1923. *Cartulaire générale de l'ordre des Hospitaliers de S. Jean de Jerusalem, 1100–1310*, edited by J. DELAVILLE LE ROULX, 4 vols., Paris, 1894–1906, are important collections of source material for the study of the military religious orders. E. DE ROZIÈRE, *Cartulaire de l'Eglise du Saint Sépulcre de Jérusalem*, Paris, 1849. *Chronicle of Morea*, edited by J. SCHMITT, London, 1904. Naturally much material on the crusades is also found in many of the great national collections, such as nos. **965–71, 978, 986, 988,** and **995.**

Bibliographies. The best bibliography of the sources of the crusades, especially the first, is in MOLINIER, *Les sources de l'histoire de France*, II, 266–304, III, 25–54, 104–13, 237–44. See also BARKER, *Crusades*. R. RÖHRICHT, *Bibliotheca geographica Palestinae: chronologisches Verzeichniss der an die Geographie des Heiligen Landes bezüglichen Literatur, von 333 bis 1878, und Versuch einer Cartographie*, Berlin, 1890. G. GOLUBOVICH, *Biblioteca bio-bibliografica della Terra Santa e dell 'Oriente francescano*, 4 vols., Quarrachi, 1906–23. P. MASSON, *Elêments d'une bibliographie française de la Syrie*, Paris, 1919 (Congrès français de la Syrie, III). *C.M.H.*, V, 867–71, IV, 857–66. M. DESSUBRÉ, *Bibliographie de l'ordre des Templiers, imprimês et manuscrits*, Paris, 1928. A great amount of bibliographical information may be found in the various publications of the Société de l'Orient latin (see above). The large library of Count RIANT was acquired by Harvard University in 1899. The catalogue is printed under the title *Catalogue de la bibliothèque de feu M. le Comte Riant: redigê par L. de Germon et L. Polain*, 2nd part, 2 vols., Paris, 1899 (for crusades see especially nos. 2958–3433); and the collection is described by A. C. POTTER, *The library of Harvard University*, 3rd edition, Harvard University Press, 1915.

XXII. THE POPES AND THE HOHENSTAUFEN

A. OUTLINE

1. A new phase of the irrepressible conflict between the empire and the papacy. The struggle was now almost a purely political one, and the immediate bone of contention was the possession of Italy.

2. The truce, 1123–57. Origin of the quarrel between the Hohenstaufen (Waiblingen, Ghibellines) and the Welfs (Guelfs). The schism of popes Innocent II and Anaclete in 1130. Harmony between Lothar II, 1125–37, and pope Innocent II. Conrad III (1138–52), the first Hohenstaufen emperor, on the second crusade in 1147. The political influence of St. Bernard of Clairvaux. Arnold of Brescia in Rome in 1147.

3. The emperor Frederick I (Barbarossa), of Hohenstaufen, 1152–90. His remarkable personality. His exalted position as a German king. Striking advance in German civilization during his reign. His reliance on the Roman law. Henry the Lion and the Slavs.

4. Frederick's imperial policy in Italy renewed the strife between empire and papacy. His Roncaglian diets in Italy. The astounding rise of Italian cities in Lombardy and Tuscany and their resistance to the encroachment of the emperor. Execution of Arnold of Brescia and the end of the commune in Rome in 1155. In that year Frederick was crowned emperor in St. Peter's by pope Hadrian IV (an Englishman). Strength of the papacy; its alliance with the Normans and its sympathy with the Italian cities. The Besançon episode in 1158. Destruction of Milan in 1158. Accession of pope Alexander III (Roland Bandinelli) in 1159. The founding of Alessandria. The Lombard League, 1167. Battle of Legnano, 1176. Peace of Venice, 1177. Peace of Constance, 1183. The treachery of Henry the Lion.

5. The last years of Frederick Barbarossa. The fateful marriage of his son Henry (Henry VI) to Constance, heiress of the kingdom of the Two Sicilies, in 1186. Frederick went on the third crusade and was drowned in the river Saleph in Asia Minor in 1190. The legend of Frederick Barbarossa (Kyffhaüser).

6. The reign of Henry VI, 1190–97. His difficulty in maintaining a hold on his kingdom of the Two Sicilies. His plans to conquer the whole orient. Capture and ransom of Richard the Lion-Hearted.

7. The renewed Guelf-Ghibelline struggle in Germany, 1198–1215. Disputed election between Philip of Swabia (a Hohenstaufen) and Otto IV of Brunswick (a Guelf), the son of Henry the Lion. The rôle of pope Innocent III as king-maker. In 1212 he put forth his ward, Frederick II, son of Henry VI, as emperor. Battle of Bouvines in 1214.

8. The political power of pope Innocent III, 1198–1216. He became pope at the age of 38 years. Educated at the universities of Bologna and Paris. The *Liber censuum ecclesiae romanae*, 1192. Innocent's political supremacy in Rome and in Italy. His power in Germany has been indicated above. The kings of the Two Sicilies, of Sweden, Denmark, Portugal, Aragon, and Poland became his vassals. He humbled king Philip Augustus of France. England was laid under an interdict in 1208 and in 1213 king John became the vassal of the pope. Innocent III condemned the Great Charter of 1215. His plans for a vast crusade. The Albigensian crusade. The great victory of the Christians in Spain at Tolosa, 1212. The Fourth Lateran Council in 1215.

9. The death-struggle between the emperor Frederick II (*Stupor mundi*), the last great Hohenstaufen, and the papacy. His peculiar character and his education in the Norman kingdom of Sicily. His colony of Saracen soldiers at Lucera in Italy. Excommunication of Frederick II by pope Gregory IX (Cardinal Ugolino) in 1227. Frederick's crusade, 1228–29. Acquisition of Jerusalem by treaty with El-Kamil, the sultan of Egypt in 1229. Frederick's trouble with the Lombard towns, supported by the papacy. Renewed excommunication of the emperor in 1239. Capture of a general council, 1241. Deposition of Frederick II at the council of Lyons in 1245, in the pontificate of Innocent IV. Henry Raspe, landgrave of Thuringia, and after his death, William, count of Holland, were set up as anti-kings. Death of Frederick II in 1250 near Lucera.

10. The last of the Hohenstaufen. Conrad IV, 1250–54, son of Frederick II. In 1254 Conrad died leaving an infant son, Conradin. Manfred, illegitimate son of Frederick II, became king of the Two Sicilies in 1258. In 1266 pope Clement IV made Charles of Anjou, brother of king Louis IX, king of Sicily. Manfred was killed in the battle of Grandella in 1267 and the boy Conradin was beheaded in Naples in 1268.

11. The Great Interregnum in Germany, 1254–73. The period of "fist-law" (*Faustrecht*).

12. Eastward expansion of Germany, especially in the times of the Hohenstaufen. Recent emphasis on the importance of this expansion of the

German people, which had been obscured by the undue prominence given to the struggle between empire and papacy. (Compare with the recent appreciation of the importance of the "Westward Movement" in American history.) Possible avenues of German expansion. The pioneers: missionaries (especially Cistercians), adventurous knights, traders, cultivators of the soil. The zone of the Elbe: margraves of Brandenburg, ruthless extermination of the Slavs, Czechs of Bohemia. The zone of the Oder: Pomerania, Poland, and Silesia. The zone of the Vistula and Niemen: Lithuanians, Letts, and Prussians; Knights of the Sword (1200) and the Teutonic Knights, 1220. Herman of Salza, grand master of the order. The beginnings of the Hanseatic League. The nomad Tartars in Russia ca. 1240. Beginnings of Prussia and Austria.

13. Emperors, 1125–1272.
Lothar II, 1125–37
Conrad III, 1138–52
Frederick I (Barbarossa), 1152–90
Henry VI, 1190–97
Otto IV, 1197–1212 } rivals
Philip II, 1197–1208 } rivals
Frederick II, 1212–50
[Henry Raspe, 1246–47; and William of Holland, 1247–56] anti-kings.
Conrad IV, 1250–54
The Great Interregnum, 1254–73, during which Richard, earl of Cornwall, and Alfonso X, king of Castile, were non-resident rivals.

14. Popes, 1124–76.
Honorius II, 1124–30
Innocent II, 1130–43
[Anacletus, 1130–38, and Victor, 1138, anti-popes]
Celestine II, 1143–44
Lucius II, 1144–45
Eugenius III, 1145–53
Anastasius IV, 1153–54
Hadrian IV, 1154–59
Alexander III, 1159–81
[Victor, 1159–64; Paschal III, 1164–68; Calixtus III, 1168–78; and Lando, 1178–80, anti-popes.]
Lucius III, 1181–85
Urban III, 1185–87
Gregory VIII, 1187
Clement III, 1187–91
Celestine III, 1191–98
Innocent III, 1198–1216
Honorius III, 1216–27
Gregory IX, 1227–41
Celestine IV, 1241
Innocent IV, 1243–54
Alexander IV, 1254—61
Urban IV, 1261–64
Clement IV, 1265–68
Gregory X, 1271–76

B. Special Recommendations for Reading

Short general accounts. Emerton, *Mediaeval Europe*, chs. ix–x. Bryce, *Holy Roman empire*, chs. xi–xiii. Henderson, *A short history of Germany*, ch. iv. Adams, *Civilization*, ch. x. Hulme, *Middle ages*, 501–37. Sellery and Krey, *Medieval foundations*, 155–60, 178–85, 188–200. Munro and Sontag, *Middle ages*, chs. xxiv and xxxii. Thompson, *Economic and social history*, chs. xvii–xix.

Longer surveys. *C.M.H.*, V, chs. x–xiv; VI, chs. i–vi. Thompson, *Feudal Germany*, chs. viii and xi. Tout, *Empire and papacy*, chs. x–xiv, xvi, xxi. Lavisse et Rambaud, *Histoire générale*, II, chs. iii–iv. Villari, *Mediaeval Italy*, 197–286. Henderson, *A history of Germany in the middle ages*, chs. xv–xxviii. H. D. Sedgwick, *Italy in the thirteenth century*, 2 vols., Boston, 1912, I, chs. vi, ix, x, xiii, xxii–xxiii. E. A. Freeman has two interesting essays on Frederick I and Frederick II in *Historical essays*, first series, 257–322. The best summary in German is in *Handbuch der deutschen Geschichte*, edited by Gebhardt, I, chs. ix–x.

Short books in English on the subject. U. Balzani, *The popes and the Hohenstaufen*, London, 1888. The subject is approached from the standpoint of the papacy in D. J. Medley, *The church and the empire, 1003–1304*, chs. vi–x, xv; and in Barry, *The papal monarchy*, chs. xvi–xviii, xxi–xxii.

Lombard communes. W. F. Butler, *The Lombard communes*, New York, 1906, chs. v–x. H. Fisher, *The medieval empire*, II, ch. xiii.

Henry the Lion. A. L. Poole, *Henry the Lion*, London, 1912.

Innocent III. The standard work is A. Luchaire, *Innocent III*, 6 vols., Paris, 1905–08 (vol. I, *Rome et l'Italie*, 1904, 2nd edition, 1905; II, *La croisade des Albigeois*, 1905, 2nd edition, 1906; III, *La papauté et l'empire*, 1906; IV, *La question d'Orient*, 1907; V, *Les royautés vassales du Saint-Siège*, 1908; VI, *Le concile de Latran et la réforme de l'église*, with an index of the six vols., 1908). For a short sketch of the pontificate of Innocent III, see Flick, *Rise of the mediaeval church*, ch. xxii. Thorndike, *Medieval Europe*, ch. xxiv. G. B. Adams, "Innocent III and the Great Charter," no. 2 in *Magna Carta: commemorative essays*, edited by H. E. Malden, London, 1917.

Frederick II. Dunn–Pattison, *Leading figures*, 114–43. E. Emerton, *Beginnings of modern Europe*, 1–27. L. Allshorn, *Stupor mundi: the life and times of Frederick II*, London, 1912. T. L. Kington, *History of Frederick II*, 2 vols., London, 1862. The most thorough examination of the life and times of Frederick II, is in the introduction of J. L. A. Huillard-Bréholles, *Historia diplomatica Friderici Secundi*, 7 vols. in 12, Paris 1852–61 (the introduction is in the last volume). The capture of the council which was to meet in Rome in 1241 is told by G. C. Macaulay, "The capture of a general council, 1241," *E.H.R.*, VI (1891), 1–17.

Eastward expansion of Germany. Thompson, *Feudal Germany*, 387–658; *Economic and social history*, ch. xx. A remarkably pithy survey was written by the Nestor of French historians, E. Lavisse, *Political history of Europe*, 45–57. Other short accounts in English are H. Fisher, *The medieval empire*, II, 1–54; Henderson, *A history of Germany in the middle ages*, ch. xxvii; Lodge, *The close of the middle ages*, chs. v and xix, *passim.* A short sketch in German with a good bibliography is J. Loserth, *Geschichte des späteren Mittelalters*, 130–36. K. Lamprecht, *Deutsche Geschichte*, III, 330–420; E. Michael, *Geschichte des deutschen Volkes*, I, 3rd edition, Freiburg, 1897, 86–128; H. Gerdes, *Geschichte des deutschen Volkes*, III, 413–40.

Original sources. A large amount of miscellaneous matter relating to this period is translated in Thatcher and McNeal, *Source book*, 166–259.

See also ROBINSON, *Readings*, I, 296–311; OGG, *Source book*, 398–409; and HENDERSON, *Select documents*, 211–18, 410–32; WEBSTER, *Historical selections*, 461–63.

The most engaging historian of the twelfth century was OTTO OF FREISING, whose *Gesta Friderici I* was edited by G. WAITZ in 1884, and translated into German, *Die Taten Friedrichs*, 2nd edition, Leipzig, 1894, part of no. **981.** His chronicle is translated by MIEROW, *The two cities.* For the time of the last Hohenstaufen, the most entertaining work is the *Cronica* of SALIMBENE DE ADAM (1221–88), edited by O. HOLDER-EGGER in no. **978,** and translated into German in no. **981.** This chronicle has been translated in part into English by G. G. COULTON, *From Francis to Dante: translations from the chronicle of the Franciscan Salimbene* (*1221–1288*), 2nd edition, London, 1907. Another important and interesting source of information for the time of Frederick is MATTHEW PARIS, *Chronica majora*, translated by J. A. GILES, 4 vols., London, 1852.

Sources on the eastward expansion of Germany have been collected by R. KÖTZSCHKE, *Quellen zur Geschichte der ostdeutschen Kolonisation im 12 bis 14 Jahrhundert*, Leipzig, 1912.

Maps. SHEPHERD, *Atlas*, 70–73. For the eastward expansion of Germany see also 46–47, 57, 62–63, 94–95.

C. BIBLIOGRAPHY

General books. The general histories of Germany and Italy, nos. **560–621,** and of the church, nos. **393–498,** are most useful.

General accounts. K. HAMPE, *Deutsche Kaisergeschichte in der Zeit der Salier und Staufer*, Leipzig, 1909; 2nd edition, 1912. I. JASTROW and G. WINTER, *Deutsche Geschichte im Zeitalter der Hohenstaufen, 1125–1273*, 2 vols., Berlin, 1893–1901, part of no. **560.** F. v. RAUMER, *Geschichte der Hohenstaufen und ihrer Zeit*, 6 vols., Leipzig, 1823–25; 5th edition, 1878. J. LOSERTH, *Geschichte des späteren Mittelalters, 1197–1492*, pp. 1–148 (contains excellent bibliographies). MILMAN, *History of Latin Christianity*, books VIII–X (vols. IV–V). J. LANGEN, *Geschichte der römischen Kirche von Gregor VII bis Innocenz III*, Bonn, 1893. GREGOROVIUS, *History of the city of Rome in the middle ages*, books VIII, IX. E. ROSENSTOCK, *Könighaus und Stämme in Deutschland zwischen 911 und 1250*, Leipzig, 1914. H. BLOCH, *Die staufischen Kaiserwahlen und die Entstehung des Kurfürstentums*, Leipzig, 1911. J. v. PFLUGK-HARTTUNG, *Die Papstwahlen und das Kaisertum, 1046–1328*, Gotha, 1908. J. ZELLER, *L'empire germanique sous les Hohenstaufen*, Paris, 1881. P. SCHEFFER-BOICHORST, *Zur Geschichte des 12 und 13 Jahrhunderts: diplomatische Studien*, Berlin, 1877 (Historische Studien, edited by E. EBERING, 8). J. BÜHLER, *Die Hohenstaufen. Nach zeitgenossischen Quellen*, Leipzig, 1925. P. E. SCHRAMM, *Die deutschen Kaiser und Könige in Bildern ihrer Zeit 751–1152*, Leipzig, 1928.

Conrad III. W. BERNHARDI, *Konrad III*, 2 vols., Leipzig, 1883, part of no. **570.**

Frederick I (Barbarossa). H. SIMONSFELD, *Jahrbücher des deutschen Reichs unter Friedrich I*, vol. I (1152–58), Leipzig, 1908, part of no. **570.** W. v. GIESEBRECHT, *Geschichte der deutschen Kaiserzeit*, V and VI. A. KÜHNE, *Das Herrscherideal des Mittelalters und Kaiser Friedrich I*, Leipzig, 1898, part 5:2 of Leipziger Studien. H. PRUTZ, *Kaiser Friedrich I*, 3 vols., Danzig, 1871–74. G. v. BELOW, *Die italienische Kaiserpolitik des deutschen Mittelalters, mit besonderer Hinblick auf die Politik Friedrich Barbarossas*, in Beiheft 10 of the *H.Z.*, Munich, 1927.

Frederick Barbarossa's relations with the papacy can be studied in detail in the following books: H. K. MANN, *Nicholas Breakspear (Hadrian IV), the only English pope (1154–1159)*, London, 1914. J. D. MACKIE, *Pope Adrian IV*, Oxford, 1907. O. J. THATCHER, *Studies concerning Adrian IV*, Chicago, 1903 (in the decennial publications of the University of Chicago, first series, vol. IV). H. SCHRÖRS, *Untersuchungen zu dem Streite Kaiser Friedrichs I mit Papst Hadrian IV, 1157–1158*, Berlin, 1916. EDITH ALMEDINGEN, *The English pope (Adrian IV)*, London, 1925. J. BÄSELER, *Die Kaiserkrönungen in Rom.* H. REUTER, *Geschichte Alexanders des Dritten und der Kirche seiner Zeit*, 3 vols., vols. I and II in 2nd edition, Leipzig, 1860–64. F. DE LAFORGE, *Alexander III ou rapports de ce pape avec la France aux débuts de la lutte du sacerdoce et de l'empire*, 2nd edition, Sens, 1905. G. KLEEMANN, *Papst Gregor VIII, 1187*, Bonn, 1912. The legends concerning Frederick Barbarossa are collected in J. GRIMM, *Gedichte des Mittelalters auf König Friedrich I, den Staufer*, Berlin, 1843; and in W. GUNDLACH, *Barbarossalieder*, Innsbruck, 1899.

Lombard communes. G. B. TESTA, *History of the war of Frederick I against the communes of Lombardy*, translated from the Italian, revised by author, London, 1877. G. VOLPE, *Questioni fondamentali sull' origine e svolgimento dei comuni italiani (sec. 10–14)*, Pisa, 1905. L. v. HEINEMANN, *Zur Entstehung der Stadtverfassung in Italien*, Leipzig, 1896. F. LANZANI, *Storia dei comuni italiani dalle origini al 1313*, Milan, 1882. C. VIGNATI, *Storia diplomatica della lega lombarda*, Milan, 1866. F. GÜTERBOCK, *Der Friede von Montebello und die Weiterentwicklung des Lombardenbundes*, Berlin, 1895 (Diss.). M. A. v. BETHMANN-HOLLWEG, *Ursprung der lombardischen Städtefreiheit*, Bonn, 1846. F. GRÄF, *Die Gründung von Alessandria: ein Beitrag zur Geschichte des Lombardenbundes*, Berlin, 1887 (Diss.). A. VICINELLI, *Bologna nelle sue relazioni col papato e l'impero dal 774 al 1278*, Bologna, 1922. W. LENEL, "Der Konstanzer Friede von 1183 und die italienische Politik Friedrichs I," *H.Z.*, CXXVIII (1923), 189–261. Although largely devoted to description and travel the following books have historical notices: E. HUTTON, *The cities of Lombardy*, New York and London, 1912. E. R. WILLIAM, *Lombard towns of Italy: or the cities of ancient Lombardy*, New York and London, 1914. W. HEYWOOD, *A history of Pisa, 11th and 12th centuries*, Cambridge, 1921.

Arnold of Brescia. A. HAUSRATH, *Arnold von Brescia*, Liepzig, 1891 (also in his *Weltverbesserer*, vol. II, Leipzig, 1895). E. VACANDARD, "Arnauld de Brescia," *R.Q.H.*, XXXV (1884), 52–114. R. BREYER, "Arnold von

Brescia," in MAURENBRECHER, *Historisches Taschenbuch*, 1889, pp. 123ff. G. GAGGIA, *Arnaldo da Brescia*, Brescia, 1881. G. GUERZONI, *Arnaldo da Brescia*, Milan, 1882. W. v. GIESEBRECHT, "Über Arnold von Brescia," Munich, 1873, part of no. **895**. G. DE CASTRO, *Arnaldo da Brescia e la rivoluzione romana del XII secolo*, Leghorn, 1875. R. L. POOLE, *Ioannis Saresberiensis Historiae Pontificalis*, Oxford, 1927, LVIII–LXX. G. GUIBAL, *Arnauld de Brescia et les Hohenstauffen*, Paris, 1868. V. CLAVEL, *Arnauld de Brescia et les Romains du XIIe siècle* (avec une carte de Rome), Paris, 1868, is of little value, but the map will be found useful. A. DE STEFANO, *Arnaldo da Brescia e i suoi tempi*, Rome, 1921. K. HAMPE, "Zur Geschichte Arnolds von Brescia," *H.Z.*, CXXX (1924), 58–69.

Henry the Lion. J. HALLER, *Der Sturz Heinrichs des Löwen*, Leipzig, 1911 [see the review of it by H. NIESE, *H.Z.*, CXII (1914), 548–61]. F. GÜTERBOCK, *Der Prozess Heinrichs des Löwen: kritische Untersuchungen*, Berlin, 1909. M. PHILIPPSON, *Geschichte Heinrichs des Löwen*, 2 vols., Leipzig, 1867. H. PRUTZ, *Heinrich der Löwe, Herzog von Baiern und Sachsen*, Leipzig, 1865. M. PHILIPPSON, *Heinrich der Löwe, Herzog von Bayern und Sachsen. Sein Leben und seine Zeit*, 2nd edition, Leipzig, 1922. EDITHA GRONEN, *Die Machtpolitik Heinrichs des Löwen und sein Gegensatz gegen das Kaisertum*, Berlin, 1919. F. PHILIPPI, "Heinrich der Löwe als Beförderer von Kunst und Wissenschaft," *H.Z.*, CXXVII (1923), 50–65 and 376. P. BARTELS, *Heinrich der Löwe, der letzte Sachsenherzog*, Hermannsburg, 1925.

Henry VI. A. CARTELLIERI, *Heinrich VI und der Höhepunkt der staufischen Kaiserpolitik*, Leipzig, 1914, lecture of 20 pages. J. HALLER, "Kaiser Heinrich VI," *H.Z.*, CXIII (1914), 473–504. V. PFAFF, *Kaiser Heinrichs VI, höchstes Angebot an die römische Kurie (1196)*, Heidelberg, 1927 (part 55, Heidelberg. Abh.). H. BLOCH, *Forschungen zur Politik Kaiser Heinrichs VI in den Jahren 1191–1194*, Berlin, 1892. T. TOECHE, *Kaiser Heinrich VI*, Leipzig, 1867, part of no. **570**.

Philipp and Otto IV. E. WINKELMANN, *Philipp von Schwaben und Otto IV von Braunschweig*, 2 vols., Leipzig, 1873–78, part of no. **570**.

Innocent III. F. HURTER, *Geschichte Papst Innocenz III und seiner Zeitgenossen*, 4 vols., Hamburg, 1834–42 (vol. I in 3rd edition, 1841; II–IV in 2nd edition, 1842–44), translated by A. DE SAINT-CHÉRON and J. B. HAIBER, *Histoire du Pape Innocent III*, 3 vols., Paris, 1838; 2nd edition, 1855. F. BAETHGEN, *Die Regentschaft Papst Innocenz III im Königreich Sizilien*, Heidelberg, 1914 (Heidelberg. Abh. 44). J. N. BRISCHAR, *Papst Innozenz III und seine Zeit*, Freiburg, 1883. E. ENGELMANN, *Philipp von Schwaben und Papst Innocenz III während des deutschen Thronstreites, 1198–1208*, Berlin, 1896 (Prog.). R. SCHWEMER, *Innocenz III und die deutsche Kirke während des Thronstreites von 1198–1208*, Strasburg, 1882. A. SERAFINI, *Innocenzo III e la riforma religiosa agli inizi del secolo XIII*, Rome, 1917. J. HALLER, "Innozenz III und Otto IV," A. BRACKMAN (editor), *Papsttum und Kaisertum*, Munich, 1926, 473–507.

Frederick II. E. WINKELMANN, *Kaiser Friedrich II*, 2 vols. (to 1233), Leipzig, 1889–97, part of no. **570.** F. J. BIEHRINGER, *Kaiser Friedrich II*, Berlin, 1912 (*Historische Studien*, 102). F. SCHNEIDER, *Beiträge zur Geschichte Friedrichs II und Manfreds*, Rome, 1912. K. HAMPE, "Kaiser Friedrich II," *H.Z.*, LXXXIII (1899), 1–42. *Kaiser Friderich II. in der Auffasung der Nachwelt*, Berlin and Leipzig, 1925. F. SCHIRMER, *Beiträge zur Geschichte Kaiser Friedrichs II*, Friedland, 1904 (Diss.). G. BLONDEL, *Etude sur la politiqne de l'empereur Frédéric II en Allemagne*, Paris, 1892. A. DE STEFANO, *L'idea imperiale di Federico II*, Florence, 1927. J. ZELLER, *L'empereur Frédéric II, et la chute de l'empire germanique au moyen âge*, Paris, 1885. F. W. SCHIRRMACHER, *Kaiser Friedrich der Zweite*, 4 vols., Göttingen, 1859–65. J. L. A. HUILLARD-BRÉHOLLES, *Vie et correspondence de Pierre de la Vigne, ministre de l'empereur Frédéric II*, Paris, 1865. W. COHN, *Das Zeitalter der Hohenstaufen in Sizilien*, '*Ein Beitrag zur Entstehung des modernen Beamtenstaates*,' Breslau, 1925. E. KANTOROWICZ, *Kaiser Friedrich der Zweite*, Berlin, 1927. F. STIEVE, *Ezzelino von Romano*, Leipzig, 1909. C. CANTÙ, *Ezelino da Romano*, Milan, 1901. P. REINHOLD, *Die Empörung König Heinrichs (VII) gegen seinen Vater*, Leipzig, 1911 (part 25 of Leipziger historische Abhandlungen). M. STIMMING, "Kaiser Friedrich II. und der Abfall der deutschen Fürsten," *H.Z.*, CXX (1920), 210–49. R. MALSCH, *Heinrich Raspe, Landgraf von Thüringen und deutscher König* (†*1247*), Halle, 1911. F. KNÖPP, *Die Stellung Friedrichs II. und seiner beiden Söhne zu den deutschen Städten*, Berlin, 1928 (part 181 of Historische Studien, edited by Ebering). F. GRAEFE, *Die Publizistik in der letzten Epoche Kaiser Friedrichs II, 1239–1250*, Heidelberg, 1909 (part 24 of Heidelberg. Abh). E. STHAMER, *Die Verwaltung der Kastelle im Königreich Sizilien unter Kaiser Friedrich II. und Karl I. von Anjou*, Leipzig, 1914. O. VEHSE, *Die amtliche Propaganda in der Staatskunst Kaiser Friedrichs II*, Munich, 1929. For Frederick's interesting colony of Saracen soldiers at Lucera in Italy, see P. EGIDI, *La colonia saracena di Lucera e la sua distruzione*, Naples, 1915. H. CHONE, *Die Handelsbeziehungen Kaiser Friedrichs II zu den Seestädten Venedig, Pisa, Genua*, Berlin, 1902. A. DE STEFANO, *Federico II e le correnti spirituali del suo tempo*, Rome, 1922. W. VON DEN STEINEN, *Das Kaisertum Friedrichs II.* '*Nach den Anschauungen seiner Staatsbriefe*,' Berlin and Leipzig, 1922. C. H. HASKINS, "The 'de arte venandi cum avibus' of the emperor Frederick II," *E.H.R.*, XXXVI (1921), 334–55.

Frederick's relations with the papacy can be studied in detail in the following books: C. KÖHLER, *Das Verhältnis Kaiser Friedrichs II zu den Päpsten seiner Zeit*, Breslau, 1888 (part 24 of Gierke's Untersuchungen). M. HALBE, *Friedrich II und der päpstliche Stuhl*, Berlin, 1888. F. FEHLING, *Kaiser Friedrich II und die römischen Cardinäle in den Jahren 1227 bis 1239*, Berlin, 1901 (part 21 of Historische Studien, edited by EBERING). B. SÜTTERLIN, *Die Politik Kaiser Friedrichs II. und die römischen Kardinäle in den Jahren 1239–1250*, Heidelberg, 1929 (part 58 Heidelberg. Abh.). J. CLAUSEN, *Papst Honorius III*, Bonn, 1895. E. BREM, *Papst Gregor IX bis zum Beginn seines Pontifikats*, Heidelberg, 1911 (part 32 of Heidelberg.

Abh.). J. Felten, *Papst Gregor IX*, Freiburg, 1886. K. Hampe, "Zu der von Friedrich II. 1235 eingesetzten sizilischen Regentschaft," *H.V.J.S.*, XXI (1922), 76–79. P. Deslandres, *Innocent IV et la chute des Hohenstaufen*, Paris, 1907. A. Folz, *Kaiser Friedrich II und Papst Innocenz IV: ihr Kampf in den Jahren 1244 und 1245*, Strasburg, 1905. W. E. Lunt, "The sources for the first council of Lyons, 1245," *E.H.R.*, XXXIII (1918), 72–78. T. Frantz, *Der grosse Kampf zwischen Kaisertum und Papstum zur Zeit des Hohenstaufen Friedrich II*, Berlin, 1903. C. Rodenberg, *Innocenz IV und das Königreich Sizilien 1245–1254*, Halle, 1892.

The last Hohenstaufen. F. W. Schirrmacher, *Die letzten Hohenstaufen*, Göttingen, 1871. A. Karst, *Geschichte Manfreds vom Tode Friedrichs II bis zu seiner Krönung* (*1250–1258*), Berlin, 1897 (part 6 of Historische Studien, edited by Ebering). K. Hampe, *Urban IV und Manfred* (*1261–1264*), Heidelberg, 1905 (part 11 of Heidelberg. Abh.). A. Bergmann, *König Manfred von Sizilien, 1264–1266*, Heidelberg, 1909 (part 23 of Heidelberg. Abh.). K. Hampe, *Geschichte Konradins von Hohenstaufen*, Innsbruck, 1894. E. Jordan, *Les origines de la domination angevine en Italie*, Paris, 1909. K. G. Hugelmann, *Die Wahl Konrads IV zu Wien im Jahre 1237*, Weimar, 1914. E. Tuccio, *I moti sicialini in favore di Corradino di Svevia*, Palermo, 1922.

The Great Interregnum. J. Kempf, *Geschichte des deutschen Reiches während des grossen Interregnums, 1254–1273*, Würzburg, 1893. E. Müller, *Peter von Prezza: ein Publizist der Zeit des Interregnums*, Heidelberg, 1914. J. J. Bappert, *Richard von Cornwallis 1257–1272*, Bonn, 1905. G. Lemcke, *Beiträge zur Geschichte Königs Richard von Cornwall*, Berlin, 1909.

Eastward expansion of Germany. R. Kötzschke, *Staat und Kultur im Zeitalter der ostdeutschen Kolonisation*, Leipzig, 1910. R. Sebicht, *Unsere mittelalterliche Ostmarkenpolitik eine Geschichte der Besiedelung und Wiedereindeutschung Ostdeutschlands*, Breslau, 1910. R. Kotzschke, "Neuere Forschungen zur Geschichte der ostdeutschen Kolonisation," *Deutsche Geschichtsblätter*, 11. H. Witte, "Zur Erforschung der Germanisation unseres Ostens," *Hansische Geschichtsblätter*, 1908. H. Ernst, *Die Kolonisation von Ostdeutschland: Übersicht und Literatur*, erste Hälfte, 1888 (Prog.). G. Wendt, *Die Germanisierung der Länder östlich der Elbe*, Liegnitz, 1884–89 (Prog.). E. O. Schulze, *Die Kolonisierung der Gebiete zwischen Saale und Elbe*, Leipzig, 1896. A. Püschel, *Das Anwachsen der deutschen Städte in der Zeit der mittelalterlichen Kolonialbewegung*, Berlin, 1910. F. Schmidt, *Kolonisation und Besiedelung Mährens im 12 und 13 Jahrhunderts*, Nentitschein, 1905 (Prog.). W. Uhlemann, "Zur Frage nach dem Ursprung und der Herkunft der Deutschen in Böhmen und Mähren," *H.V.J.S.*, XXII (1925), 541–49. G. Blumschein, *Über die Germanisierung der Länder zwischen Elbe und Oder*, Cologne, 1895 (Prog.). B. Heil, *Gründung der norddeutschen Kolonialstädte und ihre Entwicklung bis zum Ende des 13 Jahrhunderts*, Wiesbaden, 1896 (Prog.). V. Hasenöhrl, *Deutschlands südöstliche Marken im 10, 11, und 12 Jahrhundert*, Vienna, 1895 (also in *Archiv für österreichische Geschichte*, 82). G. v. Ropp, *Deutsche Kolonien im 12 und 13*

Jahrhundert, Giessen, 1886. A. MEITZEN, *Die Ausbreitung der Deutschen in Deutschland und ihre Besiedelung der Slawengebiete*, Jena, 1879. W. WATTENBACH, "Die Germanisierung der östlichen Grenzmarken des deutschen Reichs," *H.Z.*, IX (1863), 386–417. L. LEGER, *Les luttes séculaires des Germains et des Slaves*, Paris, 1916. V. SEIDEL, *Der Beginn der deutschen Besiedlung Schlesiens*, Breslau, 1913. H. REUTTER, *Das Siedlungswesen der Deutschen in Mähren und Schlesien bis zum 14 Jahrhundert*, Leipzig, 1918.

Missionaries in eastern Germany. J. W. THOMPSON, "The German church and the conversion of the Baltic Slavs, I," *American journal of theology*, April (1916). H. GRÖSSLER, *Die Begründung der christlichen Kirche in dem Lande zwischen Saale und Elbe*, Eisleben, 1907. L. NOTTROTT, *Aus der Wendenmission*, Halle, 1897. W. WIESENER, *Die Geschichte der christlichen Kirche in Pommern zur Wendenzeit*, Berlin, 1889. SIENIAWSKI, *Die Missionsreisen des Bischofs Otto v. Bamberg nach dem Lande der heidnischen Pommern 1125–1127 (1128)*, Glatz, 1908. G. JURITSCH, *Geschichte des Bischofs Otto I von Bamberg, des Pommern-apostels (1102–1139)*, Gotha, 1889. C. MASKUS, *Bischof Otto I von Bamberg als Bischof, Reichsfürst und Missionär*, Breslau, 1889. (Diss.). M. WEHRMANN, "Die Lehr- und Predigttätigkeit des Bischofs Otto von Bamberg in Pommern," *Baltische Studien*, N. S. XXVI (1924), 157–89. H. C. VOIGT, *Brun von Querfurt: Mönch, Eremit, Erzbischof, Märtyrer*, Stuttgart, 1907. H. C. VOIGT, *Adalbert von Prag*, Berlin, 1898.

The Teutonic knights in Prussia. M. ÖHLER, *Geschichte des deutschen Ritterordens*, vol. I, Elbing, 1908. A. WERMINGHOFF, *Der deutsche Orden und die Stände in Preussen bis zum 2 Thorner Frieden im Jahre 1466*, Munich, 1912. W. v. KETRZYNSKI, *Die deutschen Orden und Konrad v. Masovien (1225–1235)*, enlarged German edition, Lemberg, 1904. A. KOCH, *Hermann von Salza, Meister des deutschen Ordens*, Leipzig, 1885. K. LOHMEYER, *Geschichte von Ost- und Westpreussen*, vol. I (to 1411), Gotha, 1880; 3rd edition, 1908. A. L. EWALT, *Die Eroberung Preussens durch die Deutschen*, 4 vols., [to 1283], Halle, 1872–86. M. PERLBACH, *Die Statuten des deutschen Ordens*, Halle, 1890. P. NIEBOROWSKI, *Peter von Wormdith, ein Beitrag zur Geschichte des Deutschen-Ordens*, Breslau, 1915. M. DE DUKSZTA, *Le royaume de Lithuanie au XIIIe siècle et l'ordre teutonique*, Geneva, 1917. E. CASPAR, *Hermann von Salza und die Gründung des Deutschordensstaats in Preussen*, Tübingen, 1924. G. E. MÜLLER, "Die Ursachen der Vertreibung des deutschen Ordens aus dem Burzenlande und Rumanien im Jahre 1225," *Korrespondenzblatt des Vereins für siebenbürgische Landeskunde*, XLVIII (1925), 41–68. P. OSTWALD, *Das Werk des deutschen Ritterordens in Preussen*, Berlin, 1926.

Original sources. *Regesta imperii V: Die Regesten des Kaiserreichs unter Philipp, Otto IV, Friedrich II, Heinrich (VII), Konrad IV, Heinrich Raspe, Wilhelm und Richard, 1198–1272*, edited by J. F. BOEHMER, new edition by J. FICKER and E. WINKELMANN, 5 parts, with an index, Innsbruck, 1881–1901. *Historia diplomatica Friderici Secundi*. *Le liber censuum de l'église romaine publié avec une introduction et un commentaire*, edited by P. FABRE and L. DUCHESNE, vol. I, Paris, 1889–1910 (no. **959**). Almost all of the important sources are printed in nos. **978** and **988.** For the registers of the popes of the thirteenth century century see no. **959.**

Bibliographies. The most useful bibliography is in DAHLMANN-WAITZ, *Quellenkunde*, pp. 351–413. See also the general bibliographies for Germany, nos. **29–35,** Italy, nos. **37–41,** and the church, nos. **49–55;** and *C.M.H.*, V and VI.

XXIII. THE NEW MONASTIC MOVEMENT

A. OUTLINE

1. The constant succession of revival and decline in monastic history. The decline of the Cluniacs in the eleventh century. A marked religious revival in the eleventh century was one of the manifestations of the new era which ushered in the crusades. Much religious ferment preceded and was augmented by the investiture strife.

2. The new monastic orders founded in the eleventh century appear mostly as reforms of the Benedictine rule with a strong tendency toward extreme ascetic practices. In these orders the old principle of the autonomy of each monastery is discarded and all the monasteries of the same "congregation" remain under the jurisdiction of the abbot of the "mother-house," following the system initiated by the congregation of Cluny. Camaldolites, founded by St. Romuald at Camaldoli in the Apennines, about 1018. Vallombrosians founded by St. John Gualbert, a Tuscan lord, about 1036. The monastery of Hirschau in the Black Forest under the reform régime of its abbot William of Bavaria about 1070. Order of Grammont founded by St. Stephen of Tigerno about 1075 near Limoges (removed later to a place nearby called Grandmont). Carthusians founded by Bruno of Cologne about 1085 at Grande Chartreuse, in a desolate valley near Grenoble. Charterhouses. Order of Fontevrault founded by the Breton Robert of Abrissel about 1095 between Anjou and Poitou.

3. The Cistercians. Founded by Robert of Molême, in northern Burgundy, about 1100. He soon removed to a place called Cîteaux (=pools of standing water). The great Bernard of Fontaines established a daughter house at Clairvaux in 1115. The *Carta Caritatis*, "Charter of Charity." The asceticism of the Cistercians. The monastic reform and ideals of Joachim of Fiore (died 1202). Relations of the military orders of Spain, Calatrava, 1158, Alcantara, 1152, with the Cistercians.

4. The Canons Regular or Austin Canons. The Victorines of Paris, 1113. The Premonstratensians founded near Laon in 1120 by Norbert of Xanten, who had been a secular canon at Cologne and Xanten. The relations of the crusading religious military orders with the Austin Canons.

5. Forerunners of the mendicant orders. Arnoldists. The Humiliati. "Brotherhoods and sisterhoods of penance."

6. The attempted check, by the fourth Lateran council, 1215, upon the formation of new orders.

7. The mendicant orders of the thirteenth century. Franciscans (*Fratres Minores*, Grey Friars); Dominicans (*Fratres Praedicatores*, Black Friars, also called Jacobins in France); Carmelites (White Friars); and Augustinians (Austin Friars or Hermits of St. Augustine). The mendicant ideal. The great needs which called the mendicants into being and their great services. The distinction between a monk and a friar.

8. St. Francis, the founder of the Franciscans. He was the son of a merchant and was born in 1182 in Assisi. His conversion about 1209. The first Franciscan group at Santa Maria della Portiuncola. In 1210 Francis went to Rome to interview pope Innocent III. In 1217 was held the first general chapter of Franciscans. Cardinal Ugolino (afterwards pope Gregory IX). St. Francis in Egypt in 1219. The *Rules* of St. Francis, 1221 and 1223. The stress laid upon poverty. The "stigmata" of St. Francis. His death in 1226. He was canonized in 1228. His body was buried in 1230 in the great basilica of San Francesco in Assisi. The wonderful character and personal influence of St. Francis. Sources of information concerning St. Francis. His own writings. The *Vita prima* (before 1229) and *Vita secunda* (1244–47) of Thomas of Celano. The *Legenda major*, "New legend," of St. Bonaventura, written about 1263. *Legenda trium sociorum* (Legend of the three companions, Angelus, Leo, and Rufinus). *Speculum perfectionis* (Mirror of perfection). *Sacrum commercium*. The *Fioretti*, or in Latin, *Floretum S. Francisci Assisiensis* (The Little Flowers of St. Francis).

9. The Franciscans in the thirteenth century. St. Clare and the Poor Clares. The Tertiaries of St. Francis. Brother Elias of Cortona. St. Bonaventura. The bitter conflict between the Spiritual Franciscans and the Conventual Franciscans. Fraticelli. The great influence of the life and legend of St. Francis on Italian literature and art.

10. The Dominicans. Dominic, the founder of the order, was born in 1170 in Calahorra in Spain. He was trained for the priesthood in the university of Valencia. Combated Albigensian heresy in Toulouse. He went to Rome in 1215. In 1216 Honorius III recognized the "Preaching Brothers of Toulouse." Dominic's interview with Francis. Dominic died in Bologna 1221 and was canonized in 1234.

11. The important part played by the mendicants in the history of the thirteenth century. Their rapid spread, especially in the cities of all Europe. Their great influence in the rising universities. Alexander of Hales, Bonaventura, Roger Bacon, and Duns Scotus were Franciscans. Albert the Great and Thomas Aquinas were Dominicans. The mendicants and the inquisition. Their revival of popular preaching. The missionary activity of the mendicants in the thirteenth century. Their decline in the fourteenth century.

B. Special Recommendations for Reading

Brief general surveys. Emerton, *Mediaeval Europe*, 555–81. *C.M.H.*, V, ch. xx; VI, ch. xxi. Lavisse et Rambaud, *Histoire générale*, II, 243–51. Taylor, *Mediaeval mind*, I, Book III. Hulme, *Middle ages*, 712–54. Munro and Sontag, *Middle ages*, chs. xxvii and xxx. Article "Monasticism" by

D. CABROL in Hastings, *Encyclopaedia of religion and ethics*, VIII, 792–97. Articles "Monasticism, Franciscans, Dominicans, etc., in *Catholic encyclopaedia.*

St. Bernard and the Cistercians. The best account in English of the Cistercians is by J. S. BREWER in the preface to vol. IV of the *Opera* of Giraldus Cambrensis (no. 21 of Rolls Series). See also W. A. P. MASON, "Beginnings of the Cistercian order," *Trans. R.H.S.*, XIX (1905), 169–207. The best short sketch of Bernard of Clairvaux is in MUNRO and SELLERY, *Medieval civilization*, new edition, 406–31, which is a translation from LAVISSE, *Histoire de France*, II, part II, 266–82. For other literature on St. Bernard see outline XIV of part III.

The mendicants in general. JESSOPP, *The coming of the friars*, ch. I. LEA, *A history of the inquisition*, I, ch. VI. The preface by J. S. BREWER in vol. I of *Monumenta franciscana* (no. 4 of Rolls Series). MILMAN, *Latin Christianity*, book IX, chs. IX–X. P. SABATIER and others, *Franciscan essays*, Aberdeen, 1912 (British society of Franciscan studies, extra series, I). JACKSON, *Introduction to the history of Christianity*, ch. X.

St. Francis of Assisi. The most famous biography is by P. SABATIER, *Vie de S. François d'Assise*, Paris, 1894, translated by LOUISE S. HOUGHTON, *Life of St. Francis of Assisi*, London, 1894. Both the original and the English translation have been reprinted again and again. The book has been translated into almost all the European languages. CUTHBERT, *Life of St. Francis of Assisi*, London and New York, 1912; 2nd edition, 1913. J. JÖRGENSEN, *Den hellige Frans af Assisi*, Copenhagen, 1907, authorized translation from the Danish by T. O'CONNOR SLOANE, New York, 1912. L. SALVATORELLI, *The life of Saint Francis of Assisi*, translated from the Italian by E. Sutton, New York and London, 1928.

St. Dominic. B. JARRETT, *Life of Saint Dominic*, London, 1924. J. GUIRAUD, *Saint Dominique (1170–1221)*, Paris, 1901 (Les saints), translated by KATHERINE DE MATTOS, *Saint Dominic*, London, 1901.

Original sources. Most of the sources concerning St. Francis and the early history of his order can now be read in English translation. For translations of his own works, well edited by P. ROBINSON, *The writings of St. Francis of Assisi*, Philadelphia, 1906, also *The writings of St. Francis of Assisi*, newly translated into English by CONSTANCE DE LA WARR, London, [1907]; and, *The words of Saint Francis: from his works and the early legends*, translated by ANNE MACDONELL, London, 1904.

The biographies by CELANO may be read in, *The lives of St. Francis of Assisi by Brother Thomas of Celano*, translated into English by A. G. FERRERS HOWELL from the new edition of the original by D'ALENÇON, Rome, 1906, London, 1908. For BONAVENTURA'S official biography, see *The Life of St. Francis by St. Bonaventure*, translated by E. G. SALTER, London, 1904.

The *Legenda trium sociorum* under the title, *The legend of Saint Francis by the three companions*, now first translated into English by E. G. SALTER, London, 1905 (The temple classics). For the hotly debated *Speculum perfectionis*, see, *The mirror of perfection*, translated from the Cottonian manuscript by R. STEELE, London, 1903 (The temple classics). *Sacrum commercium: the converse of Francis and his sons with holy poverty*, translated by Canon RAWNSLEY, London, 1904 (The temple classics). An earlier translation of the *Sacrum commercium* was made by M. CARMICHAEL, *The Lady Poverty*, London, 1901.

Naturally the *Fioretti*, so very popular in Italy in the fourteenth century, have attracted most attention. The best Italian text is that of CESARI, Verona, 1822 (often reprinted). The Latin text was edited by P. SABATIER, *Floretum S. Francisci*, Paris, 1902. The following are some of the most available translations: *The little flowers, and the life of St. Francis, with the mirror of perfection*, London, 1910 (Everyman's library); *The little flowers of the glorious Messer St. Francis and of his friars*, done into English with notes by W. HEYWOOD, with an introduction by A. G. FERRERS HOWELL, London [1906]; *The little flowers of St. Francis*, translated by T. W. ARNOLD, London, 1898 (The temple classics).

Anthologies: *Franciscan days: being selections for every day in the year from ancient Franciscan writings*, translated and arranged by A. G. FERRERS HOWELL, London [1906]. M. BEAUFRETON, *Anthologie franciscaine du moyen-âge*, Paris, 1921. L. VINCENT, *The little brown company: an anthology of Franciscan poetry and prose*, London, 1925.

The earliest biography of St. Clare may be read in two English versions: *The life of Saint Clare ascribed to Fr. Thomas of Celano of the order of Friars minor* [1225–1261], translated and edited from the earliest MSS. by P. ROBINSON, with an appendix containing the *Rule* of Saint Clare, Philadelphia, 1910; and, *The life and legend of Lady Saint Clare*, translated from the French version (1563) of Brother FRANCIS DU PUIS, by CHARLOTTE BALFOUR, with an introduction by Father CUTHBERT, London, 1910.

The famous chronicle of THOMAS OF ECCLESTON is translated under the title, *The friars and how they came to England: being a translation of Thomas of Eccleston's "De adventu FF. Minorum in Angliam,"* with an introduction by Father CUTHBERT, St. Louis, 1903. The translator revised his work for the critical student under the title, *The chronicle of Thomas of Eccleston "De adventu Fratrum minorum in Angliam"* newly done into English with preface and notes by Father CUTHBERT, St. Louis, 1909. THOMAS OF ECCLESTON and JORDAN OF GIANO, *The coming of the Friars Minor to England and Germany: the chronicles*, translated from the critical editions of A. G. LITTLE and H. BOCHNER by E. G. SALTER, London, 1926.

For translations from the interesting chronicle of the gossipy thirteenth century Franciscan, SALIMBENE, see G. G. COULTON, *From St. Francis to Dante*. Read in connection with it, E. EMERTON, "Fra Salimbene and the Franciscan ideal," *Harvard theological review* (1915). W. W. SETON, *Blessed Giles of Assisi* (British Franciscan Studies, VIII), Manchester, 1918, edits the text of the Short Life of St. Giles (attributed to Brother LEO) with a translation and an introduction.

The rule and the will of Francis may also be found in HENDERSON, *Select documents*, 344–49; OGG, *Source book*, 362–79; ROBINSON, *Readings*, 387–95;

and THATCHER and MCNEAL, *Source book*, 497–507. WEBSTER, *Historical selections*, 442–53.

Monastic conditions in England in the twelfth century are well depicted in *The Chronicle of Jocelin of Brakelonde*, translated by L. C. JANE, London, 1907 (Kings classics). CLARA KÖNIG, *Englisches Klosterleben im 12 Jahrhundert*, Jena, 1927, is based almost entirely on this chronicle.

Maps. SHEPHERD, *Atlas*, 94–5, 97.

C. BIBLIOGRAPHY

General books. See the general histories of the church, nos. **393–498,** especially those on monasticism, nos. **479–87.** The encyclopaedias of the history of the church and religion, nos. **104–14,** will be found particularly useful.

Monastic orders in general. The ideals of medieval monastic life as described by PETER DAMIANI in his *Opuscula* (Migne, *P.L.*, CXLV) are well summarized by A. FLICHE, *Les Pré-Grégoriens*, Paris, 1916, 65ff. BUTLER, *Benedictine monachism.* Several volumes of the French collection *Les grand ordres monastiques*, Paris, 1925ff., English translation, *The great monastic orders*, London, deal with orders established in this period. HEIMBUCHER, *Die Orden und Congregationen der katholischen Kirche*, 2 vols., Paderborn, 1896–97. U. BERLIÈRE, *L'ordre monastique des origines au XIIe siècle*, 2nd edition, Paris, 1921. GASQUET, *Monastic life in the middle ages*. F. CHAMARD, "Les abbés au moyen âge," *R.Q.H.*, XXXVIII (1885), 71–108. U. BERLIÈRE, *Le recruitement dans les monastères bénédictines au XIIIe et au XIVe siècles*, Brussels, 1924. COULTON, *Five centuries of religion*, vol. II, chs. I–VII. The history of the orders in England is enshrined in the following old, but famous, works: *Monasticon Anglicanum: sive, Pandectae Coenobiorum, Benedictinorum, Cluniacensium, Cisterciensium, Carthusianorum a primordiis ad eorum usque dissolutionem*, edited by R. DODSWORTH and Sir W. DUGDALE, 3 vols., London, 1655–77; new edition by J. CALEY, etc., 6 vols. in 8, London, 1817–30; and T. TANNER, *Notitia monastica: or, An account of all the abbies, priories, and houses of friers, formerly in England and Wales, and also of all the colleges and hospitals founded before* A.D. *1560*, London, 1744; reprinted by J. NASMITH, Cambridge, 1787. The former contains many original sources. F. A. GASQUET, *English monastic life*, 3rd edition, London, 1905 (The antiquary's books); and A. H. THOMPSON, *English monasteries*, Cambridge, 1913 (The Cambridge manuals). R. H. SNAPE, *English monastic finances in the later middle ages*, Cambridge, 1926. A. H. SWEET, "The English Benedictines and their bishops in the XIII century," *A.H.R.*, XXIV (1919), 565–77. D. H. S. CRANAGE, *The home of the monk: English monastic life and buildings in the middle ages*, 2nd edition, Cambridge, 1926. R. GRAHAM, "A papal visitation of Bury St. Edmunds in 1234," *E.H.R.*, XXVII (1912), 728–40. M. DEMIMUID, *Pierre le Vénérable: ou la vie et l'influence monastique au XIIe siècle*, Paris, 1876. P. OPLADEN, *Die Stellung der deutschen Könige zu den Orden im dreizehnten Jahrhundert*, Bonn, 1908 (Diss.). G. SCHREIBER, *Kurie und Kloster im 12*

Jahrhundert, vol. 1, Stuttgart, 1910, parts 65–6 of no. **491.** O. WOLFF, *Mein Meister Rupertus, ein Mönchsleben aus dem 12 Jahrhundert*, Freiburg, 1920. J. SCHUMACHER, *Deutsche Klöster*, Bonn, 1928; *Benediktinisches Klösterleben in Deutschland*, Berlin, 1929. J. BÜHLER, *Klosterleben im deutschen Mittelalter*, Leipzig, 1921. The monastic history of the various countries is well represented by many monographs for which see the *Bulletin d'histoire bênédictine* in appendix to the *Revue bênédictine*, and other monastic reviews.

Hirschau. *Codex Hirsaugiensis*, by R. SCHNEIDER, Stuttgart, 1887. M. FISCHER, *Studien zur Entstehung der Hirsauer Konstitutionen*, Stuttgart, 1910. E. TOMEK, *Studien zur Reform der deutschen Klöster im XI Jahrhundert: I, Frühreformation*, Vienna, 1910. P. GISEKE, *Die Hirschauer während des Investiturstreites*, Gotha, 1883.

Carthusians. C. LE COUTEULX, *Annales ordinis Cartusiensis ab anno 1084 ad annum 1429*, 8 vols., Monstrolii, 1887–91. H. LÖBBEL, *Der Stifter des Carthäuser-Ordens: der heilige Bruno aus Köln*, Münster, 1899, part V, 1 of no. **492.** F. A. LEFEBVRE, *Saint Bruno et l'ordre des Chartreux*, 2 vols., Paris, 1884. E. M. THOMPSON, *A history of the Somerset Carthusians*, London, 1895.

Order of Fontevrault. *Histoire de l'Ordre de Fontevrault, 1100–1908*, by the Religieuses de Sainte-Marie de Fontevrault de Boulaur, now located in Vera in Navarre, 3 vols., Auch, 1911–15. J. v. WALTER, *Die ersten Wanderprediger Frankreichs: Studien zur Geschichte des Mönchtums;* part I, *Robert von Abrissel*, Leipzig, 1903, part IX, 3 of no. **495.** E. MALIFAUD, *L'abbaye de Fontevrault*, Angers, 1866.

Cistercians. A good general survey of the history of the Cistercians to 1335 in *Cisterzienser Chronik*, Bregenz, XXXVII (1925); XXXVIII (1926). *Exordium ordinis Cisterciensis* auctore CONRADO EBERSBACENS., Migne, *P.L.*, CLXVI, 1501ff. and CLXXXV, 995ff. C. HENRIQUEZ, *Regula, constitutiones et privilegia ord. cister.*, Antwerp, 1630. D. Julien Paris, *Monasticon cisterciense*, Paris, 1664. New edition with the fullest collection of Cistercian statutes, Solesmes, 1892 (edited by H. P. SÉJALON). J. T. FOWLER, "Cistercian Statutes," *Yorkshire arch. and topograph. ass. Journal*, IX (1886), 223–40, 338–61; X (1889), 51–62, 217–33, 388–406, 502–22; XI (1891), 95–127. A. MANRIQUE, *Annales cistercienses*, Lyons, 1642–59. H. D'ARBOIS DE JUBAINVILLE, *Etat intérieur des abbayes cisterciennes et en particulier de Clairvaux au XIIe et XIIIe siècles*, Paris, 1868. L. JANAUSCHEK, *Origines cistercienses*, vol. I, Vienna, 1877. Partial histories of the Cistercian abbeys of various countries: F. WINTER, *Die Cistercienser der nordöstlichen Deutschland*, 3 v. Gotha, 1868–71; 2nd edition, 1913. R. LEHMANN, *Die ältere Geschichte des Cisterzienserklosters Dobribergk in der Lausitz*, Heidelberg, 1916. J. S. FLETCHER, *The Cistercians in Yorkshire*, London, 1919. J. W. THOMPSON, " The Cisterian order and colonization in mediaeval Germany," *American journal of theology* (1920), 67–93. H. ROSE, *Die Baukunst der Cistercienser*, Munich, 1916. G. HODGES, *Fountains abbey: the story of a mediaeval monastery*, London, 1904. F. SCHEVILL, "San Galgano: a Cistercian abbey of the middle ages," *A.H.R.*, XIV (1908), 22–37. La Trappe, the cradle of the modern Trappists, is described at length by H. C. CHARENCEY (Comte de), *Histoire de l'abbaye de la Grande-Trappe*, 2 vols., Mortagne, 1896–1911; he also edited the *Cartulaire de l'Abbaye de Notre-Dame de la Trappe*, Alençon, 1889.

Canons Regular. P. SCHROEDER, "Die Augustinerchorherrenregel," *Archiv f. Urkundenforschung*, IX (1926), 271–306. H. E. SALTER, "Chapters of the Augustinian Canons," *Canterbury and York Soc.*, LXX (1922). *Annales Praemonstratensium*, 2 vols., Nancy, 1734–36. *Vita S. Norberti*, ed. by WILMANS, *M.G.H.*, Script., XII. P. F. PETIT, *L'ordre de Prêmontrê*, 2nd edition, Paris, 1927. Important studies in *Analecta praemonstratensia*, Tongerloo, 1925ff. B. WOZASEK, *Der hl. Norbert: Stifter des Prämonstratenser-Ordens und Erzbischof von Magdeburg*, Vienna, 1914. R. ROSENMUND, *Die ältesten Biographien des heiligen Norbert*, Berlin, 1874. F. WINTER, *Die Prämonstratenser des 12 Jahrhunderts und ihre Bedeutung für das nordöstliche Deutschland*, Berlin, 1865.

Other religious orders and houses. *Vita S. Romualdi*, by PETER DAMIANI, Migne, *P.L.*, CXLIV, 953ff. J. B. MITTARELLI et A. COSTADONI, *Annales Camaldulenses*, 9 vols., Venice, 1755–73. *Vita S. Ioannis Gualberti* by ALTO PACENSIS, Migne, *P. L.*, CXLVI, 268ff. A. FERRANTE, *S. Giovanni Gualberto*, Monza, 1883. R. GRAHAM and A. W. CLAPHAM, *The order of Grammont and its houses in England.* (Archaeologia, LXXV), Oxford, 1926. J. C. ROMAN, *Les chartes de l'Ordre de Chalais*, (1101–1400), 3 vols., Paris, 1923. A. SIMON, *L'ordre des Pénitentes de Ste. Marie Madeleine en Allemagne au XIIIe siècle*, Freiburg, 1918. E. BARNIKOL, *Studien zur Geschichte der Brüder von gemeinsamen Leben*, Tübingen, 1917. E. EMERTON, "Altopascio, a forgotten order," *A.H.R.*, 1925, 1–23. *Monumenta historica carmelitana*, I, ed. by B. ZIMMERMAN, Lerin, 1907. VILLIERS DE ST. ETIENNE, *Bibliotheca carmelitana* (1752), new edition with additions and supplements, Rome, 1927. *Etudes carmélitaines*, Paris, 1911ff. F. EHRLE, "Joachim von Flore," in *Kirchenlexicon* of Wetzer and Welte, 2nd edition, 1889. E. TOCCO, *L'eresia nel medio evo*, Florence, 1884; *Studi francescani*, Naples, 1909, 191–223. P. FOURNIER, *Etudes sur Joachim de Flore*, Paris, 1909. H. GRUNDMANN, *Studien über Ioachim von Floris*, Leipzig, 1927. E. AEGERTER, *Joachim de Flore*, 2 vols., Paris, 1928. E. BUONAIUTI, *Tractatus super quatuor Evangelia di Gioacchino da Fiore*, Istituto storico italiano, Fonti per la storia d'Italia, Rome, 1930, first volume of a critical edition of the unedited writings of Joachim. See also various essays of the same author in *Ricerche religiose*, Rome, Sept., Nov., 1928, May, Sept., 1929. The best brief survey in English of Joachim's life and thought is G. COULTON, *Five centuries of religion*, II, 114ff.

Forerunners of the mendicants. E. S. DAVISON, *The forerunners of St. Francis*, Boston and New York, 1927. G. TIRABOSCHI, *Vetera humiliatorum monumenta*, 3 vols., Milan, 1766–67. L. ZANONI, *Gli umiliati*, Milan, 1911. DE STEFANO, *Arnaldo da Brescia.* A. HAUSRATH, *Arnold v. Brescia* (III. *Die Arnoldisten*), Leipzig, 1895. R. BREYER, "Die Arnoldisten,"

Zeitschrift für Kirchengeschichte, XII (1890–91), 387–413. ROSE GRAHAM, *S. Gilbert of Sempringham and the Gilbertines: a history of the order*, London, 1901; reprinted; 1904.

The mendicants in general. J. HERKLESS, *Francis and Dominic and the mendicant orders*, New York, 1901 (The world's epochmakers, IX). H. HEFELE, *Die Bettelorden und das religiöse Volksleben Ober- und Mittelitaliens im 13 Jahrhundert*, Leipzig and Berlin, 1910, part 9 of no. **749**. COULTON, *Five centuries of religion*, II, chs. VII–XIII. M. BIERBAUM, *Bettellorden und Weltgeistlichkeit an der Universität Paris, Texte und Untersuchungen zum literarischen Armuts-und Exemtionsstreit des 13 Jahrhunderts, 1255–1272*, Münster, 1920. ZÖCKLER, *Askese und Mönchtum*, 470ff. A series of biographies of famous friars has been published under the general title, *Lives of the friar saints*, New York, 1911ff. A. OTT, *Thomas von Aquin und das Mendikantentum*, Freiburg, 1908. J. WIESCHOFF, *Stellung der Bettelorden in den deutschen freien Reichsstädten im Mittelalter*, Münster, 1905 (Diss.). R. P. GRATIEN, "Ordres mendiants et clergé séculier à la fin du XIIe siècle," *Etudes franciscaines*, XXVI (1924). A. G. LITTLE, "Measures taken against the Friars in A.D. 1289–90," *Misc. Ehrle*, III, Rome, 1924; "Educational organization of the Mendicant Orders in England," *Trans. R.H.S.*, VIII (1895). L. GILLET, *Histoire artistique des ordres mendiants*, Paris, 1912.

Franciscans in general. L. WADDING, *Annales Minorum seu trium ordinum a S. Francisco institutorum* [1208–1540], 8 vols., Lyons, 1625–54; 2nd edition, with a syllabus, 16 vols., Rome, 1731–41, Tom. XVII–XIX by J. DE LUCA, Rome, 1740ff., Tom. XX by MICALESI, Rome, 1794, Tom. XXI–XXVI by the FRANCISCANS OF QUARACCHI, 1886ff.; *Scriptores ordinis minorum*, Rome, 1650; new edition with supplements by J. H. SBARALEA, 2 vols., Rome, 1806; other supplements 1906–08. K. MÜLLER, *Die Anfänge des Minoriten-ordens und der Bussbruderschaften*, Freiburg, 1885. H. HOLZAPFEL, *Handbuch der Geschichte des Franziskanerordens*, Freiburg, 1909. E. GEBHART, *L'Italie mystique: histoire de la renaissance religieuse au moyen âge*, Paris, 1890; English translation by HULME, 1922. P. GRATIEN, *Histoire de la fondation et de l'évolution de l'ordre des frères mineurs au XIIIe siècle*, Paris, 1928. E. JORDAN, *Le premier siècle franciscain*, Paris, 1927. A. LÉON, *St. François d'Assise et son oeuvre, histoire de l'ordre des frères mineurs*, Paris, 1928. V. KYBAL, *Die Ordensregeln des hl. Franz v. Assisi und die ursprüngliche Verfassung des Minoritenordens*, Leipzig, 1915. E. LEMPP, *Frère Elie de Cortone*, Paris, 1902. A. G. LITTLE, *Studies in English Franciscan history*, Manchester, 1917; *Introduction of the Observant friars into England*, Proc. Brit. Acad., XI (1923); *The Grey Friars in Oxford*, Oxford Hist. Soc., XX (1892); "Franciscan School at Oxford in the XIIIth century," *A.F.H.*, XIX (1926). E. HUTTON, *The Franciscans in England, 1224–1538*, London, 1926. C. COTTON, *The Grey Friars of Canterbury, 1224–1538*, Brit. Soc. Franc. Stud., 1924. C. S. KINGSFORD, *The Grey Friars of London*, Manchester, 1915. J. SEVER, *The English Franciscans under Henry III*, Oxford, 1915. W. M. BRYCE, *The Scottish Grey Friars*, 2 vols., London, 1909.

A. G. LITTLE and E. B. FITZMAURICE, *Materials for the history of the Franciscan province of Ireland*, Manchester, 1920. Father CUTHBERT, *The romanticism of St. Francis and other studies in the genius of the Franciscans*, London, 2nd edition, 1924. P. MINGES, *Geschichte der Franziskaner in Bayern*, Munich, 1896. C. EUBEL, *Geschichte der oberdeutschen Minoritenprovinz*, Würzburg, 1886. L. LEMMENS, *Niedersächsisiche Franziskanerklöster im Mittelalter*, Hildesheim, 1896. S. DIRKS, *Histoire littéraire et bibliographies des frères mineurs en France, en Belgique et dans le Pays-Bas*, Antwerp, 1885. A. SCHÄFER, *Der Orden des hl. Franz von Assisi i. Württemberg*, Blätter für Württemberger Kirchengeschichte, XXIII (1920). A. BÜRGLER, *Die Franziskaner-Orden in der Schweiz*, Schwyz, 1926. A. LOPEZ, *La provincia de España de los fratres menores*, Santiago, 1915. J. M. LENHART, *Science in the Franciscan Order*, New York, 1924. B. VOGT, *The origin and development of the Franciscan school*, New York, 1925. H. FELDER, *Geschichte der wissenschaftlichen Studien im Franziskanerorden*, Freiburg, 1904. A. ZAWART, *The history of Franciscan preaching and of Franciscan preachers: a bio-bibliographical study*, New York, 1928. H. DAUSEND, *Der Franziskanerorden und die Entwicklung der Liturgie*, Münster, 1924. N. PAULUS, "Ablässe der Franziskanerorden im Mittelalters," *Franziskanische Studien*, X.

St. Francis. It is beyond the scope of this Guide to indicate all the biographies and studies concerning St. Francis which have appeared during these last years, especially in connection with the seventh centennial of his death. Only a few among the most important are listed below. For the biographies by SABATIER, CUTHBERT, JÖRGENSEN and SALVATORELLI, see above.

In English. W. J. KNOX LITTLE, *St. Francis of Assisi: his times, life, and work*, lectures delivered in 1896, London, 1897; new edition, 1904. E. W. GRIERSON, *The story of St. Francis of Assisi*, London, 1912. G. K. CHESTERTON, *St. Francis of Assisi*, New York, 1924. W. H. LEATHEM, *Life of St. Francis of Assisi*, New York, 1926. E. M. WILMOT-BUXTON, *St. Francis of Assisi*, New York, 1926. W. W. SETON, *St. Francis of Assisi, Essays in commemoration* with a preface by P. SABATIER, London, 1926. (Valuable essays by BURKITT, GARDNER, LITTLE, and others on various aspects of Franciscan history.) D. H. S. NICHOLSON, *The mysticism of St. Francis of Assisi*, London, 1923.

In French. L. LE MONNIER, *Histoire de St. François d'Assise*, 2 vols., Paris, 1889; 6th edition, 1907, English translation by a Tertiary, London, 1894. P. HENRY, *S. François d'Assise et son école, d'après les documents originaux*, Paris, 1903. A. BARINE, *St. François d'Assise et la légende des trois compagnons*, 6th edition, Paris, 1910. L. DE CHÉRANCÉ, *Saint François d'Assise*, 7th edition, Paris, 1900, translated into English by R. F. O'CONNOR, 3rd edition, London, 1901. F. MORIN, *Saint François et les Franciscains*, Paris, 1858. M. BEAUFRETON, *Saint François d'Assisi*, Paris, 1925. A. BONNARD, *Saint François d'Assisi*, Paris, 1929. R. BOUTT DE MONVEL, *Saint François d'Assisi*, Paris, 1921. H. LEMAÎTRE ET A. MASSERON, *Saint*

François d'Assise, son oeuvre, son influence, Paris, 1927. A group of essays. P. GRATIEN, *Saint François d'Assise, sa personnalité, sa spiritualité*, 2nd edition, Paris, 1928.

In German. J. v. WALTER, *Franz von Assisi und die Nachahmung Christi*, Gross-Lichterfelde, 1910. B. CHRISTEN, *Leben des heiligen Franciscus von Assisi*, Innsbruck, 1899; 3rd edition, 1922. K. WENCK, *Franz von Assisi*, Leipzig, 1908. H. TILEMANN, *Studien zur Individualität des Franziskus von Assisi*, Leipzig, 1914, part of **749.** U. PETERS, *Franz von Assisi*, Tübingen, 1912. E. DIMMLER, *Franz v. Assisi*, Münich, 1913. R. SAITSCHICK, *Franziskus v. Assisi*, Munich, 1916. H. FELDER, *Die Ideale des hl. Franz v. Assisi*, Paderborn, 1923; English translation by B. BITTLE, *The ideals of St. Francis of Assisi*, New York, 1925.

In Italian. F. TARDUCCI, *Vita di S. Francesco d'Assisi*, Mantua, 1904. PANFILO DA MAGLIANO, *Storia compendiosa di S. Francesco e dei Francescani*, 2 vols., Rome, 1874–76, was left incomplete due to the death of the author. L. PALOMES, *Storia di S. Francesco*, 2 vols., Palermo, 1873–74. S. MINOCCHI, *La leggenda antica: nuova fonte biografica di San Francesco d'Assisi*, Florence, 1905. N. TAMASSIA, *S. Francesco d'Assisi e la sua leggenda* (English translation by L. RAGG, London, 1910). A. FORTINI, *Nuova Vita di S. Francesco d'Assisi*, Milan, 1926. E. BUONAIUTI, *S. Francesco d'Assisi, Profilo*, Rome, 1925. V. FACCHINETTI, *S. Francesco d'Assisi nella storia, nella leggenda e nell'arte*, Rome, 1926.

In Spanish. P. BAZÁN, *San Francisco de Assis*, new edition, Madrid, 1903.

The social work of St. Francis. L. L. DUBOIS, *St. Francis of Assisi: social reformer*, Washington, D. C., 1904 (Diss.). F. GLASER, *Die franziskanische Bewegung: ein Beitrag zur Geschichte sozialer Reformideen im Mittelalter*, Stuttgart and Berlin, 1903 (in Münchener volkswirtschaftliche Studien, 59, pp. 11–45). J. GAPP, *Der heilige Franciscus von Assisi und die soziale Frage*, 2nd edition, Trier, 1898, 16 pages. G. RATZINGER, "Die soziale Bedeutung des heiligen Franziskus," in *Forschungen zur bayrischen Geschichte*, Kempten, 1898.

Stigmata of St. Francis. K. HAMPE, "Altes und Neues über die Stigmatisation des hl. Franz von Assisi," *Archiv für Kulturgeschichte*, VIII (1910), 257–90. F. X. SEPPELT, "Die Wundmale des hl. Franz von Assisi," Vortrag vor der *Generalversammlung der Görresgesellschaft zu Metz*, Cologne, 1910, pp. 110–20. J. MERKT, *Die Wundmale des heiligen Franziskus von Assisi*, Leipzig, 1910, part V of no. **749**; see the review by M. BIHL, in *A.F.H.*, III (1910), 393–432. K. HASE, *Franz von Assisi: ein Heiligenbild*, Leipzig, 1856; new edition, 1892, devotes a large part of his book to the stigmata. J. WEBER, "The stigmata of Francis of Assisi," *Papers of the American society of church history*, second series, III (1912). C. H. LYTTLE, "The stigmata of St. Francis considered in the light of possible Joachimite influence upon Thomas of Celano," *ibid.*, second series, IV (1914). E. B. KRUMBHAAR, "The stigmata of St. Francis of Assisi," *Annals of medical history*, IX (1927), 111–19.

Tertiaries of St. Francis. E. Descloux, *Le tiers ordre de Saint-François*, Fribourg, 1913. P. Mandonnet, *Origines de l'Ordo de Poenitentia*, Freiburg, 1898. F. van den Borne, *Die Anfänge des franziskanischen Drittenordens. Vorgeschichte, Entwicklung der Regel*, Münster, 1925. (Franzisk. Stud. 8.) W. W. Seton, *Two Franciscan rules. E.E.T.S.* (1914). G. J. Reinmann, *The third order secular of St. Francis*, Washington, 1928 (Diss.).

Saint Clare. E. Gilliat-Smith, *Saint Clare of Assisi: her life and legislation*, London, 1914. M. Beaufreton, *Sainte Claire d'Assise, 1194–1253*, Paris, 1916 (Les saints). L. Moisson, *Une fille de Saint François: Sainte Claire d'Assise, sa vie et son oeuvre*, Paris, 1912. P. Robinson, *The Rule of St. Clare and its observance in the light of early documents*, Philadelphia, 1912. L. de Chérancé, *Saint Clare of Assisi*, New York, 1910. E. Wauer, *Entstehung und Ausbreitung des Klarissenordens*, Leipzig, 1906. C. Mauclair, *La vie de Sainte Claire d'Assise d'après les anciens textes*, Paris, 1924. "A brief history of Franciscan nuns," by L. Oliger, *A.F.H.*, V (1912). Anne F. C. Bourdillon, *The order of Minoresses in England*, Manchester, 1926 (British society of Franciscan studies, 12).

Assisi and the home of the early Franciscans. Lina Duff Gordon, *The story of Assisi*, London, 1900. Beryl D. De Selincourt, *Homes of the first Franciscans in Umbria, the borders of Tuscany, and the northern Marches*, London and New York, 1905. E. Hutton, *The cities of Umbria*, London, 1906. J. Jörgensen, *Pilgrim walks in Franciscan Italy*, London, 1908. H. E. Goad, *Franciscan Italy*, London, 1926. E. Schneider, *Sur les traces de Saint François au pays d'Assise*, Paris, 1926. F. Hermanin, *Assise, la ville de Saint François*, Paris, 1927. G. Faure, *The land of St. Francis, Assisi and Perugia*, London, 1924. C. Ricci, *Umbria santa*, English transl. by H. C. Stewart, Oxford, 1927. B. Kleinschmidt, *Die Basilika San Francesco in Assisi*, 2 vols., Berlin, 1915–26.

Spiritual Franciscans. D. S. Muzzey, *The spiritual Franciscans*, New York, 1907. F. Ehrle, "Die Spiritualen, ihr Verhältniss zum Franziskanerorden und zu den Fraticellen," *Archiv für Literatur- und Kirchengeschichte*, I, 509–69; II, 106–64; III, 553–623; IV, 1–190. This fundamental study contains many original sources. "Petrus Olivi, sein Leben und seine Schriften," *ibid.*, 1887, 409ff. K. Balthaser, *Geschichte des Armutsstreites im Franziskanerorden bis zum Konzil von Vienne*, Münster, 1911 (Vorreformationsgeschichtliche Forschungen, 6). J. C. Huck, *Ubertinus von Casale und dessen Ideenkreis*, Freiburg, 1903.

Franciscan influence on art and literature. H. Thode, *Franz von Assisi und die Anfänge der Kunst der Renaissance in Italien*, Berlin, 1885; 3rd edition, 1926, is a work of fundamental importance. Emma G. Salter, *Franciscan legends in Italian art: pictures in Italian churches and galleries*, London and New York, 1905. Clarissa C. Goff, *Assisi of Saint Francis: together with the influence of the Franciscan legend on Italian art*, London, 1908. B. Berenson, *A Sienese painter of the Franciscan legend* [Sassetta], New York, 1909. N. H. J. Westlake, *On the authentic portraiture of St. Francis of Assisi*, London, 1897. B. Kleinschmidt, *Maria und Franziskus* *von Assisi in Kunst und Geschichte*, Düsseldorf, 1926. F. J. SANCHEZ CANTON, *San Francisco de Asis en la escultura española*, Madrid, 1926.

A. F. OZANAM, *Les poètes franciscains en Italie*, 6th edition, Paris, 1882, translated and annotated by A. E. NELLEN and W. C. CRAIG, *The Franciscan poets in Italy of the thirteenth century*, London, 1914. C. MARIOTTI, *S. Francesco, i Francescani e Dante Alighieri*, Quaracchi, 1912. H. HESSE, *Franz von Assisi*, Berlin [1904] (Die Dichtung, 13). P. SABATIER, *L'influence de Saint François d'Assise sur la culture italienne*, Paris, 1927.

Periodicals devoted to Franciscan studies. *Archivum Franciscanum historicum: periodica publicatio trimestris*, begun in 1908 by the Franciscans of Quaracchi near Florence. *Etudes franciscaines*, Paris, 1899ff. *Collection d'études et de documents sur l'histoire religieuse et littéraire du moyen âge*, edited by P. SABATIER, 5 vols., Paris, 1898–1904, is devoted almost entirely to Franciscan studies and texts. *Société internationale d'études franciscaines à Assise*, 1902ff. *La France franciscaine: mélanges d'archéologie, d'histoire et de littérature relatifs aux ordres de Saint François en France du XIIIe siècle*, Lille, 1912ff. *Franziskanische Studien: Quartalschrift*, Münster, 1914ff. *Bolletino critico di cose francescane*, Florence, 1905ff. *Miscellanea francescana di storia, di lettere, di arte*, Foligno, 1886ff. *Estudis franciscans*, Sarria.

Dominicans in general. T. M. MAMACHI, *Annales ordinis Praedicatorum*, I, Rome, 1756. D. A. MORTIER, *Histoire des maîtres généraux de l'ordre des Frères Prêcheurs*, 8 vols., 1913ff. *Lives of the brethren of the Order of Preachers (1206–1259)*, translated by P. CONWAY and with notes of B. JARRET, London, 1924. M. GANAY, *Les bienheureuses Dominicaines (1190–1577)*, Paris, 1913. J. QUETIF et J. ECHARD, *Scriptores ord. Praed.*, 2 vols., Paris, 1719–21; new revised edition by R. COULON, I–VI, Paris, 1910–13. C. ZELLER, *La vie dominicaine*, Paris, 1927. J. ANCELET-HUSTACHE, *La vie mystique d'un monastère des Dominicains au moyen âge*, Paris, 1928. G. R. GALBRAITH, *The constitution of the Dominican order* (1216–1360), Manchester, 1925. *Dominikanischen Geistleben*, by the FATHERS OF ST. JOSEPH COLLEGE, Oldenburg, I, 1923. P. G. TAURISANO, *Hierarchia ordinis Praedicatorum*, I, Rome, 1916. C. DOUAIS, *Essai sur l'organisation des études dans l'ordre des Frères Prêcheurs au XIIIe et au XIVe siècles*, Paris, 1884. A. DANZAS, *Etudes sur les temps primitifs de l'ordre de Saint-Dominique: le bienheureux Jourdain de Saxe*, 6 vols., 1874–88. AUGUSTA T. DRANE, *The spirit of the Dominican order*, London, 1896. W. D. G. FLETCHER, *The Black Friars of Oxford*, Oxford, 1882. E. BARKER, *The Dominican order and convocation: a study of the growth of representation in the church during the thirteenth century*, Oxford, 1913. B. E. K. FORMOY, *The Dominican order in England before the Reformation*, London, 1925. B. JARRETT, *The English Dominicans*, London, 1921. M. MCINERNY, *A history of the Irish Dominicans*, I (1224–1307), London, 1916. R. P. MORTIER, *Histoire abrégée de l'ordre de Saint Dominique en France*, Paris, 1920. G. ROAAULT DE FLEURY, *Gallia dominicana; les couvents de St. Dominique au moyen âge*, 2 vols., Paris, 1903. C. DOUAIS, *Les Frères Prêcheurs en Gascogne au XIIIe et au XIVe siècle*, Paris, 1886. M. D. CHAPOTIN, *Etudes historiques sur la province dominicaine de France*,

4 vols., Rouen, 1890–93. M. D. SCHOMBURG, *Die Dominikaner im Erzbistum Bremen während des dreizehnten Jahrhunderts, mit einer einleitenden Übersicht über die Ausbreitung des Ordens in Deutschland bis 1250*, 1910 (Diss. Jena). P. v. LOË and B. M. REICHERT, *Quellen und Forschungen zur Geschichte des Dominikanerordens in Deutschland*, Leipzig, 1907ff. F. BANGEMANN, *Mittelhochdeutsche Dominikuslegenden und ihre Quellen*, Halle, 1919. H. FINKE, "Zur Geschichte der deutschen Dominikaner im 13 u. 14 Jahr.," *Römische Quartalscrift*, VIII (1894), 367–92. R. MARTÍNEZ VIGIL, *La orden de Predicadores: sus glorias en santidad, apostolado, ciencias, artes y gobierno de los pueblos, seguidos de una biblioteca de Dominicos españoles*, Madrid, 1884. *Les congrégations dominicaines du Tiers Ordre regulier*, Paris, 1924. *Miscellanea Dominicana*, Rome, 1924.

St. Dominic. AUGUSTA T. DRANE, *History of St. Dominic, founder of the Friars Preachers*, London, 1891. H. D. DE LACORDAIRE, *Vie de saint Dominique*, Paris, 1840; new edition, Paris [1912], translated into English by HAZELAND, London, 1883. P. MANDONNET, *Saint Dominique, l'idée, l'homme et l'oeuvre*, Ghent, 1921. L. RAMBAUD, *Saint Dominique, sa vie, son âme, son ordre*, Paris, 1926. H. SCHEEBEN, *Der hl. Dominikus*, Freiburg, 1928. *A new life of Saint Dominic by Blessed Jordan of Saxony* annotated by Fr. G. VERGARA and translated from Spanish by E. C. MCENIRY, Columbus, 1926. W. LESCHER, *St. Dominic and the rosary*, London, 1902. C. M. ANTONY, *In St. Dominic's country*, New York, 1912.

Original sources. Only the most important large collections of sources on the mendicants are listed below. See the bibliographical guides below for details. Much material can also be found scattered in the large collections for church history, nos. **953–64.** *Bullarium franciscanum*, edited by J. H. SBARALEA, 4 vols., Rome, 1759–68, supplement, 1780, vols. V–VII by C. EUBEL, Rome, 1898–1904; Epitome and supplement to vols. I–IV by C. EUBEL, Rome, 1908. A new series of the *Bullarium* has been started by U. HUNTEMANN, *Bullarium franciscanum*, nova series, I, (1431–55), Quaracchi, 1929. *Analecta franciscana*, Quaracchi, 1885ff. *Documenta antiqua franciscana*, edited by L. LEMMENS, Quaracchi, 1901–02. *Opuscules de critique historique*, edited by P. SABATIER, Paris, 1901–19. *Speculum perfectionis*, ed. by Sabatier, Manchester, 1928. L. LEMMENS, *Testimonia minora saeculi XIII de S. Francisco Assissiensi*, Quaracchi, 1926. MADELAINE HAVARD DE LA MONTAGNE, *Sainte Claire d'Assise: sa vie et ses miracles, racontés par Thomas de Celano*, translated with introduction and notes, Paris, 1917. *British society of Franciscan studies*, Aberdeen, 1909ff. *Monumenta franciscana*, edited by J. S. BREWER, 2 vols., London, 1858 (Rolls Series, no. 4), for the Franciscans in England. F. EHRLE, *Die ältesten Redaktionen der Generalkonstitutionen des Franziskanerordens*, 1891, part of no. **170**, "Zur Quellenkunde der alteren Franziskanergeschichte," *Zeitschr. f. kath. Theol.*, VII (1883). W. GOETZ, *Die Quellen zur Geschichte des hl. Franz v. Assisi*, Gotha, 1904.

The chief collections for the Dominicans are the following: *Monumenta ordinis Fratrum Praedicatorum historica*, edited by B. M. REICHERT, vols.

I–XIV, Louvain and Stuttgart, 1896–1904. T. RIPOLL et A. BRÉMOND, *Bullarium ordinis Praedicatorum*, 8 vols., Rome, 1737ff. P. T. MASETTI, *Documenta et antiquitates veteris disciplinae ord. Praed.* (1218–1348), Rome, 1864. *Analecta fratrum Praedicatorum*, 13 vols., Rome, 1893–1918. B. ALTANER, *Die Briefe Jordans von Sachsen, des zweiten Dominikanergenerals* (1222–37): Texte und Untersuchungen, Leipzig, 1925. H. DENIFLE, "*Die Constitutionen des Prediger-Ordens vom Jahre 1228*," no. **170,** I (1885), 165–227; "*Die Constitutionen des Prediger-Ordens in der Redaction Raimundus v. Peñafort*," no. **170,** V, (1889), 530–564; "*Quellen zur Gelehrtengeschichte des Predigerordens im 13 und 14 Jahrh.*," no. **170,** II (1886), 165–248.

Bibliographies. In general consult the bibliographies for the history of the church, nos. **49–55.** Many excellent bibliographies are appended to articles in the encyclopaedias listed above, nos. **104–44.** On the mendicants in general there is a valuable bibliography in J. LOSERTH, *Geschichte des späteren Mittelalters*, 15–17; also *C.M.H.*, V and VI.

For Saint Francis see P. ROBINSON, *A short introduction to Franciscan literature*, New York, 1907 and A. G. LITTLE, *A guide to Franciscan studies*, London and New York, 1920. CUTHBERT, *Life of St. Francis*, in four appendixes, 393–446, has a full discussion and bibliography of the original sources on St. Francis. ROBINSON, in his bibliography just mentioned, pp. 28–29, calls attention to summaries of the scholarly work on the history of St. Francis. Add to his references, R. SEEBERG, "Zur Charakteristik des hl. Franz von Assisi," *Deutsche Literaturzeitung*, XXXII (1911), 1989–94; 2053–58.

XXIV. ORGANIZATION AND WORK OF THE CHRISTIAN CHURCH IN THE TWELFTH AND THIRTEENTH CENTURIES

A. OUTLINE

1. The character of the church as a state, and the most important state of Europe in these two centuries. It was a splendidly organized absolute monarchy. Its executive, legislative, and judicial powers. Its territorial extent. Conflicts with temporal princes. Spiritual and temporal powers. Regular and secular clergy. This outline deals with the secular clergy.

2. The ecclesiastical hierarchy. Influence of the old Roman officialism in the development of grades among churchmen. Distinctions among the secular clergy, emphasized by titles, dress, residence, ceremonial of investment into office, and order of precedence, as well as by differences of duties and incomes. The higher ranks of the clergy were classed with the nobles in medieval society; its lower ranks, such as the parish priests, were classed with the common people. Difficulty of fitting the clergy of all ranks into feudal society. Differences between laymen and the clergy. The morals of the clergy; the nature of the evidence. Records of episcopal visitations.

3. The pope in Rome. The growth of the theory of papal absolutism and infallibility. The Lateran. Disputes about his election even after the erection of the college of cardinals in 1059. Institution of the two-thirds vote in

1179. The conclave (*cum clave*) of the council of Lyons in 1274. Growth of the dignity of cardinals (the red hat bestowed in 1245, and the purple robe in 1297). Their political influence. The Roman curia. The papal chancery. Papal bulls. The decretals of the popes. Legates of the popes. Papal legations and papal visitations.

4. Archbishops and bishops. Provinces and dioceses. Unsuccessful efforts to make the rank of an archbishop a very distinct grade above that of a bishop. The pallium. Primates or metropolitans. The exalted power of a bishop in his diocese. Episcopal elections. The Lateran council of 1215 placed the election in the hands of the cathedral chapters. Spiritual and temporal duties of a bishop. Episcopal visitations.

5. The intermediate clergy. Archdeacons. Canons of the cathedral chapter. Officers of the cathedral chapter, such as the dean (or provost), chancellor, and chanter. Prebends. Conflict between the chapters and archdeacons on the one hand, and the bishops on the other. Vicars general and "officials."

6. The parish priests. The right of presentation or advowson. Patrons. *Cura animarum* (French *curé*). Elaborate parish churches. Social duties of the parish priests. Their work as teachers. Rectors. Vicars. Archpriests.

7. The legislative bodies of the church. The great universal or oecumenical councils, especially the Lateran council of 1215. Provincial and diocesan councils. The tendency to hold "national" councils, and to limit the absolute power of the pope by conciliar action. Mansi, *Concilia*.

8. The financial system of the church. The papal exchequer (*camera*) in Rome. Some of the sources of papal income were: the revenues from the Papal States, feudal dues from vassal states, pious gifts and bequests, fees of all kinds, benefice taxes especially annates, Peter's pence, special levies on the clergy all over Christendom, crusading taxes. The income of a bishop. The wealth of some cathedral chapters. The income of a parish. Tithes. The endless complexity of the expenditures of the church. Abuses due to the wealth of the church. Misappropriations by greedy priests.

9. The law and the jurisdiction of the church. The growth of canon law. Gratian's *Decretum* (1140–50). The *Corpus iuris canonici*. (For details on canon law see outline XX, part III.) The legal status of the clergy. Legal status of university students. Ecclesiastical jurisdiction over non-clerical persons. Multiplicity of cases judicable in church courts. Ceaseless conflicts with secular courts and jurisdiction. The papal curia. The papal penitentiary. Appelate jurisdiction of the pope's courts. Delay of justice and other abuses in the papal judiciary system. The judicial functions of bishops. The judicial work of archdeacons, archpriests, and cathedral chapters. The episcopal courts. The episcopal "officials," and their assistants. Lawyers and notaries.

10. Church discipline and control. Confession and penances, especially pilgrimages. Excommunication and interdict.

11. Heresies. Conditions which gave rise to heresies. Waldensians and Albigensians. The inquisition. (For details see outline XVI, part III.)

12. The Christian cult. The evolution of doctrines and practices. In the thirteenth century most of the doctrines and practices of the medieval church were crystallized. Use of Latin in the church service. The sacramental system. The eucharist. The revival of preaching. The great hymns. Organs and church music. The ecclesiastical calendar. Saints' days. Patron saints. Canonization of saints. Festivals. Feast of Fools (*Festum stultorum*). Miracle plays. Relics.

13. Ecclesiastical buildings, furnishings, vestment and plate. Romanesque and Gothic cathedrals. Chapter houses. Baptisteries. The papal palaces. Episcopal residences. Cemeteries. Dedication of sacred buildings and places.

14. The social and educational work of the secular church. Charitable work of the clergy, especially of the parish priests. The alms of the church. The care of the sick by the secular clergy. The Beguines and Beguins (Beghards). Elementary education in the parishes. Cathedral schools.

15. The missionary work of the church in the East. "Prester John." Influence of the crusades, and of the rise of universities. The College of Constantinople (or Oriental College), established in the time of Innocent III, in Paris. The missionary activity of the Franciscans and Dominicans. John of Plano Carpini. William Rubruck (Rubruquis). Raymund Lull.

16. Sources of weakness and decay within the church.

B. Special Recommendations for Reading

Short general surveys. Emerton, *Mediaeval Europe*, 541–55, 582–92. Flick, *The rise of the mediaeval church*, ch. xxiii. Bémont and Monod, *Medieval Europe*, 488–514. Hulme, *Middle ages*, 362–86. Thorndike, *Medieval Europe*, ch. xxiii. Sellery and Krey, *Medieval foundations*, 124–35.

Longer general accounts. *C.M.H.*, VI, chs. xvi and xix. Lavisse et Rambaud, *Histoire générale*, II, 253–91. Medley, *The church and the empire*, chs. iv, x–xii, xiv. Milman, *Latin Christianity*, vol. IX, book XIV, chs. i–ii. A. Luchaire, *Manuel des institutions françaises*, 1–144. E. Michael, *Culturzustände des deutschen Volkes während des dreizehnten Jahrhunderts*, II, 1–265. E. L. Cutts, *Scenes and characters of the middle ages*, 157–265.

Financial system of the papacy. W. E. Lunt, "The financial system of the mediaeval papacy," *Quarterly journal of economics*, XXIII (1909), 251–95; *The valuation of Norwich*, Oxford, 1926. A. Blumenstock, *Der päpstliche Schutz im Mittelalter*, Innsbruck, 1890. P. Fabre, *Etude sur le Liber Censuum de l'église romaine*, Paris, 1892. C. Bauer, "Die Epochen der Papstfinanz," *H.Z.*, CXXXVIII, 3 [1928], 457–504.

Interdict. E. B. Krehbiel, *Interdict*. A. C. Howland, "The origin of the local interdict," *Annual report, A.H.A.*, 1899, vol. I, 431–48.

Parish life. F. A. Gasquet, *Parish life in mediaeval England*, London and New York, 1906; 2nd edition, 1907. E. L. Cutts, *Parish priests and* *their people in the middle ages in England*, London, 1891. A. H. Thompson, *The historical growth of the English parish church*, Cambridge, 1911.

The Christian cult. Y. Hirn, *The sacred shrine: a study of the poetry and art of the Christian church*, London, 1912 (important bibliography, pp. 555–70). On the Feast of Fools see G. V. Hemming, "Festum stultorum," *Nineteenth century*, LVII (1905), 1000–08.

Eastern missions. C. R. Beazley, *The dawn of modern geography*, 3 vols., London, 1897–1906, especially II, ch. v; III, chs. ii–iii. L. Bréhier, *L'église et l'orient au moyen âge*, chs. x–xi.

Inquisition. The standard work is H. C. Lea, *History of the inquisition of the middle ages*, 3 vols. E. Vacandard, *The inquisition*, translated from the 2nd French edition, by B. L. Conway, New York, 1908. A. L. Maycock, *The inquisition from its establishment to the great schism*, London, 1926.

Original sources. Robinson, *Readings*, I, 346–87. *Translations and reprints*, II, no. 4, "Medieval sermon stories"; III, no. 6, "Pre-reformation period." G. G. Coulton, *A medieval garner* (no. **380**), *passim*.

Maps. Shepherd, *Atlas*, 46–47, 94–95, 97.

C. Bibliography

General books. The general works on the medieval church are listed above, nos. **393–498.** See also the periodicals for church history, nos. **176–80d,** and especially the encyclopaedias, nos. **104–44,** which are indispensable in studying this outline.

The pope and the papal curia. R. L. Poole, *Lectures on the history of the papal chancery down to the time of Innocent III*, Cambridge, 1915. P. M. Baumgarten, *Aus Kanzlei und Kammer: Erörterungen zur kurialen Hof- und Verwaltungsgeschichte im XII, XIV, und XV Jahrhundert*, Freiburg, 1907. R. Zoepffel, *Die Papstwahlen und die mit ihnen im nächsten Zusammenhange stehenden Ceremonien in ihrer Entwickelung vom 11 bis 14 Jahrhundert; nebst einer Beilage: die Doppelwahl des Jahres 1130*, Göttingen, 1871. E. Jungfer, *Die Unterschiede zwischen der Papstwahl und den Bischofswahlen nach dem gemeinen Kirchenrecht*, Borna, 1909 (Diss.). F. Rocquain, *La cour de Rome et l'esprit de réforme avant Luther*, vol. I, *La théocratie*, Paris, 1893. R. W. Carlyle and A. J. Carlyle, *A history of mediaeval political theory*, V, 152ff.

Cardinals. J. Maubach, *Die Kardinäle und ihre Politik um die Mitte des XIII Jahrhunderts*, Bonn, 1902 (Diss.). D. Sägmüller, *Thätigkeit und Stellung der Cardinäle bis Papst Bonifaz VIII*, Freiburg, 1896.

Papal legates. H. Zimmermann, *Die päpstliche Legation in der ersten Hälfte des 13 Jahrhunderts, 1198–1241*, Paderborn, 1913. K. Ruess, *Die rechtliche Stellung der päpstlichen Legaten bis Bonifaz VIII*, Paderborn, 1912 (Görresgesellschaft; Sektion für Rechts-und Sozialwissenschaft, 13). J. Bachmann, *Die päpstlichen Legaten in Deutschland und Skandinavien (1125–1159)*, Berlin, 1913 (Historische Studien, 115).

Papal provisions. The situation in Germany may be studied in H. Baier, *Päpstliche Provisionen für niedere Pfründen bis zum Jahre 1304*, Münster,

1911. H. Krabbo, *Die Besetzung der deutschen Bistümer unter der Regierung Friedrichs II*, part I (to 1227), Berlin, 1901 (Historische Studien, 25). W. Fuchs, *Die Besetzung der deutschen Bistümer unter Papst Gregor IX (1227–1241) und bis zum Regierungsantritt Papst Innocenz IV (1243)*, Berlin, 1911. P. Aldinger, *Die Neubesetzung der deutschen Bistümer unter Papst Innocenz IV, 1243–1254*, Leipzig, 1901. For England the same conditions are described by A. L. Smith, *Church and state in the middle ages*, Oxford, 1913; and F. A. Gasquet, *Henry the Third and the church: a study of his ecclesiastical policy and of the relations between England and Rome*, London, 1905. U. Stutz, *Geschichte des kirchlichen Benefizialwesens bis auf Alexander III*, part I, Berlin, 1895.

The bishop and his diocese. Edith K. Lyle, *The office of an English bishop in the first half of the fourteenth century*, Philadelphia, 1903 (Diss.). J. Krieg, *Der Kampf der Bischöfe gegen die Archidiakone im Bistum Würzburg unter Benutzung ungedruckter Urkunden und Akten dargestellt*, Stuttgart, 1914 (Kirchengeschichtliche Abhandlungen, 82). J. Müller, *Die bischöflischen Diözesanbehörden*, Stuttgart, 1905. A. Pöschl, *Bischofsgut und Mensa episcopalis*, 2 vols., Bonn, 1908–09. J. B. Sägmüller, *Die Bischofswahl bei Gratien*, Cologne, 1908. A. Desprairies, *L'élection des évêques par les chapitres au XIIIe siècle*, Paris, 1922. P. Imbart de la Tour, *Les élections épiscopales dans l'église de France du IXe au XIIe siècle (814–1150)*, Paris, 1891. Mortet, *Maurice de Sully (1160–1196): étude sur l'administration épiscopale pendant la deuxième moitié du XIIe siècle*, Paris, 1890. A. Gréa, "Essai historique sur les archidiacres," *B.E.C.*, XII (1851), 39–67, 215–47. A. Meyer, *Der politische Einfluss Deutschlands und Frankreichs auf den metzer Bischofswahlen in Mittelalter*, Metz, 1916. Amadazzi, "Dissertazione canonico-filologico sopra il titolo dell' istituzioni canoniche 'de officio archidiaconi,'" Calogera, *Nuovo raccolto d'opuscoli*, XVII, Venice, 1768. F. X. Glasschröder, "Zur Geschichte des Archidiakonates," *Festschrift z. elfhundert-jährigen Jubiläum des deutschen Campo Santo in Rom*, Freiburg, 1897.

Parish life. Olga Dobiache-Rojdestvensky, *La vie paroissiale en France au XIIIe siècle d'après les actes épiscopaux*, Paris, 1911. G. A. Prévost, *L'église et les campagnes au moyen âge*, Paris, 1892. A. Jessopp, *Before the great pillage*, London, 1901. A. H. Thompson, *Parish history and records*, London, 1919 (S. P. C. K. Helps, no. 15).

Church councils. The great authority is Hefele, *Conciliengeschichte*, no. **469.** A. N. Blatchford, *Church councils and their decrees*, London, 1909. J. v. Döllinger, *The pope and the council.*

Financial system of the church. M. Tangl, "Das Taxenwesen der päpstlichen Kanzlei vom 13ten bis zur Mitte des 15ten Jahrhunderts," *M.I.O.G.*, XIII, 1–106. W. E. Lunt, "Papal taxation in England in the reign of Edward I," in *E.H.R.*, XXX (1915), 398–417; and "The first levy of papal annates," *A.H.R.*, XVIII (1912), 48–64. P. Viard, *Histoire de la dîme ecclésiastique dans le royaume de France aux XIIe et XIIIe siècles*, Paris, 1912. W. Easterby, *The history of the law of tithes in England*, Cambridge, 1888. O. A. MARTI, " Popular protest and revolt against papal finance in England from 1226 to 1258," *Princeton theological review*, XXV (1927), 610–29. A. GOTTLOB, *Die päpstlichen Kreuzzugssteuern des 13ten Jahrhunderts: ihre rechtliche Grundlage, politische Geschichte und technische Verwaltung*, Heiligenstadt, 1892. G. SCHNEIDER, *Die finanziellen Beziehungen des florentiner Bankiers zur Kirche von 1285–1304*, Leipzig, 1899 (Staats- und sozialwissenschaftliche Forschungen, 17). E. GÖLLER, *Die Einnahmen der apostolischen Kammer unter Benedikt XII*, Paderborn, 1920.

Ecclesiastical jurisdiction. E. GÖLLER, *Die päpstliche Pönitentiarie von ihrem Ursprung bis zu ihrer Umgestaltung unter Pius V*, 2 vols., Rome, 1907–11. H. C. LEA, *Formulary of the papal penitentiary in the thirteenth century*, Philadelphia, 1892; "The taxes of the papal penitentiary," *E.H.R.*, VIII (1893), 424–38. L. BEAUCHET, "Origine de la jurisdiction ecclésiastique et son développement en France jusqu'au XIIe siècle," *Nouvelle revue historique de droit français et étranger*, VII (1883), 387–477, 503–36. P. FOURNIER, *Les officialités au moyen âge*, Paris, 1880. A. LUCIDI, *De visitatione sacrorum liminum*, Rome, 1878. J. C. AYER, "The development of the appellate jurisdiction of the Roman see," *Papers of the Amer. society of church history*, O. S. VIII (1897). F. CHAMARD, "De l'immunité ecclésiastique et monastique," *R.Q.H.*, XXII (1877), 428–64.

Preaching. L'abbé BOURGAIN, *La chaire française au XIIe siècle, d'après les manuscrits*, Paris, 1879. A. LECOY DE LA MARCHE, *La chaire française au moyen âge, spécialement au XIIIe siècle: d'après les manuscrits contemporains*, Paris, 1868; 2nd edition, 1886. F. R. ALBERT, *Die Geschichte der Predigt in Deutschland bis Luther*, 3 parts, Gütersloh, 1892–96. A. LINSENMAYER, *Geschichte der Predigt in Deutschland von Karl dem Grossen bis zum Ausgang des 14 Jahrhunderts*, Munich, 1886. R. CRUEL, *Geschichte der deutschen Predigt im Mittelalter*, Detmold, 1879. G. R. OWST, *Preaching in medieval England*, Cambridge, 1926.

Pilgrim life. E. L. GUILFORD, *Travellers and travelling in the middle ages*, New York and London, 1924. S. HEATH, *Pilgrim life in the middle ages*, Boston, 1912. J. J. JUSSERAND, *Les Anglais au moyen âge: la vie nomade et les routes d'Angleterre au XIVe siècle*, Paris, 1884, translated by L. T. Smith, *English wayfaring life in the middle ages*, 8th edition, London, 1905; revised edition, part III, New York, 1925. J. JÖRGENSEN, *Pélerinages franciscains*, translated from the Danish by T. DE WYZEWA, Paris, 1910. A. MÜLLER, *Das heilige Deutschland: Geschichte und Beschreibung sämtlicher im deutschen Reiche bestehender Wallfahrtsorte*, 2nd edition, 2 vols., Cologne, 1897.

Life and morals of the secular clergy. H. C. LEA, *An historical sketch of sacerdotal celibacy*. E. E. SPERRY, *An outline of the history of clerical celibacy in western Europe to the council of Trent*, New York, 1905 (Diss.). S. SCHELER, *Sitten und Bildung der französischen Geistlichkeit nach den Briefen Stephans von Tournai* [died 1203], Berlin, 1915 (Historische Studien, 130).

Christian cult. A. J. DORNER, *Die Entstehung der christlichen Glaubenslehren*, Munich, 1906. M. HÉBERT, *L'évolution de la foi catholique*, Paris,

1905. F. E. von Hurter, *Tableau des institutions et des moeurs de l'église au moyen âge*, translated from the German by J. Cohen, 3 vols., Paris, 1843. H. Dausend, *Der Franziskanerorden und die Entwicklung der Liturgie.*

On confession the standard work is H. C. Lea, *A history of auricular confession.* G. Gromer, *Die Laienbeichte im Mittelalter*, Munich, 1909. H. Teetaert, *La confession aux laïques dans l'église latine depuis le VIIIe jusqu'au XIVe siècle*, Paris, 1926. A. M. Koeniger, *Die Beicht nach Cäsarius von Heisterbach*, Munich, 1906. F. Gandert, *Das Buss- und Beichtwesen gegen Mitte des 13 Jahrhunderts*, Leipzig, 1894. H. J. Schmitz, *Die Bussbücher und das kanonische Bussverfahren (nach Quellen)*, 2 vols., Düsseldorf, 1898. O. D. Watkins, *A history of penance to A. D. 1215*, 2 vols., London, 1920.

E. Lucius, *Die Anfänge des Heiligenkults in der christlichen Kirche*, Tübingen, 1904. T. F. Macken, *The canonisation of saints*, London, 1910. H. P. Brewster, *Saints and festivals of the Christian church*, New York [1904]. See also Kellner, *Heortologie*, no. **258.** C. J. Cox, *The sanctuaries and sanctuary seekers in mediaeval England*, London, 1911. F. Bond, *Dedications and patron saints of English churches*, Oxford University Press, 1915. D. H. Kerler, *Die Patronate der Heiligen*, Ulm, 1905. M. Benzerath, *Die Kirchenpatrone der alten Diözese Lausanne im Mittelalter*, Freiburg, 1914. S. Beissel, *Geschichte der Verehrung Marias in Deutschland während des Mittelalters*, Freiburg, 1809. G. Herzog, *La sainte Vierge dans l'histoire*, Paris, 1908. A. D. Severance, "Beatification and canonization, with special reference to historic proof and the proof of miracles," *Papers of the American society of church history*, 2nd series, III (1912).

A. Franz, *Die Messe im deutschen Mittelalter*, Freiburg, 1902. P. J. Wagner, *Geschichte der Messe* [to 1600], Leipzig, 1913 (Kleine Handbücher der Musikgeschichte, XI, 1). A. Franz, *Die kirchlichen Benediktionen im Mittelalter*, 2 vols., Freiburg, 1909. A. Meyer, *Das Weihnachtsfest: seine Entstehung und Entwicklung*, Tübingen, 1913. J. Braun, *Die liturgische Gewandung im Occident und Orient nach Ursprung*, Freiburg, 1907. L. Duchesne, *Christian worship*, London, 1910. A. Fortescue, *The mass: a study of the Roman liturgy*, London, 1914, is the best account of the origin and history of the mass. J. Walsh, *The mass and vestments of the Catholic church: liturgical, doctrinal, historical, and archeological*, New York, 1916. H. Laboureau, *La messe au cours des âges*, Paris, 1914. E. Bishop, *The genius of the Roman rite*, London, 1902. I. Schuster, *The sacramentary (Liber sacramentorum): historical and liturgical notes on the Roman missal*, London, 1925.

Social work of the church. F. Schaub, *Die katholische Caritas und deren Gegner*, Freiburg, 1909. L. Lallemand, *Histoire de la charité*, 3 vols., Paris, 1902–06. G. Uhlhorn, *Die christliche Liebestätigkeit*, 3 vols., Stuttgart, 1882–1890; 2nd edition, 1895. E. v. Moeller, *Die Elendenbrüderschaften: ein Beitrag zur Geschichte der Fremdenfürsorge im Mittelalter*, Leipzig, 1906. J. Greven, *Die Anfänge der Beginen*, Münster, 1912 (Vorreformatische Forschungen, 8). R. Hoornaert, *Les Béguines de Bruges, leur histoire, leur règle, leur vie*, Rome, 1925.

Missions. *Biblioteca bio-bibliografia*, compiled by G. GOLUBOVICH. P. SCHLAGER, *Mongolenfahrten der Franziskaner*, Trier, 1911. R. P. MARCELLIN DE CIVEZZA, *Histoire universelle des missions franciscaines*, translated from the Italian by R. P. BERNARDIN, Paris, 1898. BROU. "L'évangélisation de l'Inde au moyen âge," *Etudes des PP. de la Compagnie de Jésus*, LXXXVII (1901). EUBEL, "Die während des XIV Jahrhunderts im Missionsgebiet der Dominikaner und Franziskaner errichteten Bisthümer," *Festschrift zum Jubiläum des deutschen Campo Santo in Rom*, Freiburg, 1897. P. H. KÜLB, *Geschichte der Missionsreisen nach der Mongolei während des 13 und 14 Jahrhunderts*, Regensburg, 1860. A. BATTON, *Wilhelm von Rubruk*, Münster, 1921. H. MATROD, *Le voyage de Fr. Guillaume de Rubrouck*, Couvin, 1909; *Notes sur le voyage de Fr. Jean de Plan-Carpin (1245–1247)*, Paris, 1912. F. M. SCHMIDT, "Über Rubrucks Reise von 1253 bis 1255," *Zeitschrift der Gesellschaft für Erdkunde zu Berlin*, XX (1885), 161–253. L. TINTI, *Vita . . . del beato Odorico*, Rome, 1901. F. ZARNCKE, "Der Priester Johannes," *Abh. Leipzig Acad.*, VII (1879), 627–1030; VIII (1883), 1–186. H. CORDIER, *Le Christianisme en Chine et en Asie centrale sous les Mongols*, T'Oung Pao, 1917.

W. T. A. BARBER, *Raymond Lull, the illuminated doctor: a study in mediaeval missions*, London, 1903. S. M. ZWEMER, *Raymund Lull, first missionary to the Moslems*, New York, 1902. J. H. PROBST, *Caractère et origines des idées du bienheureux Raymond Lulle*, Toulouse, 1912. M. ANDRÉ, *Le bienheureux Raymond Lulle*, 3rd edition, Paris, 1900. P. JOSÉ CASADESUS, *El arte magna de Raimundo Lulio, doctor iluminado y mártir*, Barcelona, 1917.

J. A. GINDRAUX, *Histoire du christianisme dans le monde paien: les missions en Asie*, Geneva, 1909. M. R. A. HENRION, *Histoire générale des missions catholiques depuis le XIIIe siècle*, 2 vols., Paris, 1844–47. H. HAHN, *Geschichte der katholischen Missionen*, 5 vols., Cologne, 1857–73. T. SMITH, *Mediaeval missions*. G. F. MACLEAR, *A history of Christian missions during the middle ages*. *The encyclopedia of missions: descriptive, historical, biographical, statistical*, 2nd edition, New York and London, 1904.

Original sources. Pictures of the life of the church in the thirteenth century are furnished by bishops who recorded their experiences gained in visitations in their dioceses. The most complete account is by the archbishop of Rouen, EUDE RIGAUD, *Registrum visitationum archiepiscopi Rothomagensis* [1248–1269], edited by T. BONNIN, Rouen, 1852, analyzed by L. DELISLE, in *B.E.C.*, VIII (1846), 479–99. See also G. G. COULTON, *Five centuries of religion*, Cambridge, 1927, II, ch. XIV. Next in importance is *Le livre de Guillaume le Maire, évêque d'Angers, 1291* (part of no. **965**, *Mélanges historiques*, II), analyzed in LAVISSE, *Histoire de France*, III, part II, 355–61. Similar information from England may be gleaned from the letters of ROBERT GROSSETESTE, bishop of Lincoln, 1235–54, *Roberti Grosseteste episcopi Lincolnienesis Epistolae*, edited by H. R. LUARD, London, 1861 (Rolls series, no. 25).

For sources on the missionary work in Asia see *Cathay and the way thither: being a collection of medieval notices of China*, edited by H. YULE, 2 vols.,

London, 1866; new edition, revised by H. CORDIER, 3 vols., London, 1913–15 (Hakluyt society, series 2, vols. XXX, XXXVII–XXXVIII); *Texts and versions of John de Plano Carpini and William de Rubruquis* [Latin and English texts], edited by C. R. BEAZLEY, London, 1903 (Hakluyt society, extra series); and *The journey of William Rubruk to eastern parts of the world, 1253–1255, as narrated by himself, with two accounts of the earlier journey of John of Pian de Carpine*, translated and edited, with introductory notices, by W. W. ROCKHILL, London, 1900 (Hakluyt society). The accounts of Rubruquis and Pordenone are also translated in an appendix to the *Travels* of Sir JOHN MANDEVILLE, edited by POLLARD, New York, 1900, which in itself is worthless.

Enchiridion symbolorum et definitionum et declarationum de rebus fidei et morum, edited by H. DENZINGER, Freiburg, 1908. *Liturgische Bibliothek: Sammlung gottesdienstlicher Bücher aus dem deutschen Mittelalter*, edited by A. SCHÖNFELDER, vols. I and II, *Ritualbücher*, Paderborn, 1904–06.

For large collections of the sources of church history see nos. **953–64.**

Bibliographies. See the general bibliographies for church history, nos. **49–55.**

XXV. POLITICAL HISTORY OF FRANCE, 1108–1328

A. OUTLINE

1. The undisputed leadership of France in western Europe during this period. The Ile de France. The importance of Paris. Contrast between French and German political history. The strength and importance of the Capetian line of kings. Their difficulties: feudalism, lack of geographical unity, diversity of peoples, languages, and laws.

2. The real beginning of the French monarchy is the reign of Louis VI (*le Gros*, the Fat), 1108–37. He had been made king designate in 1100. His feudal wars. His popularity due largely to his liberal economic policy. A protector of the church. His relations with England. Etienne de Garlande. Suger, abbot of Saint-Denis, the famous minister of Louis VI.

3. Retrogression under Louis VII (1137–80). Weak character of the king. The disastrous second crusade. Louis and St. Bernard of Clairvaux. The divorce of Louis VII from Eleanor of Aquitaine in 1152, and the extension of the Angevin (Norman) empire through marriage of Eleanor with Henry (later Henry II) of England.

4. Rapid advance under Philip II, Augustus, 1180–1223. His supremacy over the great feudal lords. Dismemberment of the Norman empire; wars with Henry II, Richard I, and John; fall of Château Gaillard and the loss of Normandy by John in 1204. The coalition of 1214 and the battle of Bouvines. Philip and pope Innocent III. Beginnings of the Albigensian crusade. Creation of central machinery of government; *baillis* and *sénéchaux;* improvement of finances, justice, and the army. The communes, industry, and commerce. The great wall of Philip Augustus around Paris.

The real beginnings of a university of Paris in this reign. The short reign of Louis VIII, 1223–26, witnessed no great changes. Continuance of the Albigensian wars. Appanages.

5. The minority of Louis IX, 1226–34. Regency of his mother, Blanche of Castille. Failure of a serious feudal reaction. The migration of the university of Paris in 1229.

6. France at the height of her medieval glory under Saint Louis (Louis IX), 1226–70. His character and popularity. His foreign policy. Development of central machinery of government. *Enquêteurs.* Beginnings of the differentiation of the *curia regis* into a *grand conseil*, a *parlement*, and a *chambre des comptes*. The king's interest in justice. His relations with the mendicants. His charitable institutions in Paris. His friends, Joinville and Robert de Sorbon. The Sainte Chapelle. The disastrous crusades of Louis in Egypt, 1248–54, and Tunis, 1270. Death of St. Louis in Carthage, 1270.

7. Philip III (*le Hardi*, the Bold), 1270–85. The county of Toulouse was annexed to the French crown. His relations with the Spanish kingdoms, especially after the Sicilian Vespers in 1282.

8. Consolidation of the French absolute monarchy under Philip IV (*le Bel*, the Fair), 1285–1314. Foreign relations with Flanders, England, and the empire. Reliance on the Roman law. Relations with pope Boniface VIII. The papal bulls *Clericis laicos* and *Unam sanctam.* The burning question of taxation. Financial and other administrative reforms. Meeting of the Estates General in 1302 and other internal reforms. The beginning of the "Babylonish Captivity" of the papacy. Anagni. The suppression of the Templars, 1309–14.

9. Louis X, 1314–16, Philip V, 1316–22, Charles IV, 1322–28. Charles was the last male descendant of Philip IV and with his death the direct line of Capetians came to an end. The antecedents of the Hundred Years' War with England.

B. Special Recommendations for Reading

Short general accounts. *C.M.H.*, V, ch. xviii; VI, chs. ix–x. G. B. Adams, *The growth of the French nation*, 73–107; *Civilization during the middle ages*, ch. xiii. Mackinnon, *Growth of the French monarchy*, ch. i. Thorndike, *Medieval Europe*, ch. xxvi; Hulme, *Middle ages*, 630–49; Sellery and Krey, *Medieval foundations*, 167–69, 201–15, 278–94; Munro and Sontag, *Middle ages*, ch. xxiii. Crump and Jacob, *Legacy*, 465–503. Tilley, *Medieval France*, 30–103. Thompson, *Economic and social history*, ch. xviii. See also the first pages in C. V. Langlois, *The historic rôle of France among the nations.* Mary Duclaux, *A short history of France.*

Longer general accounts. Lavisse et Rambaud, *Histoire générale*, II, ch. vii; III. ch. v. Masson, *The story of mediaeval France*, chs. iii–viii. Tout, *Empire and papacy*, chs. xii, xvii, together with Lodge, *The close of the middle ages*, ch. iii. Funck-Brentano, *Middle ages*, chs. vi–xviii.

KITCHIN, *History of France*, 4th edition, I, 255–413. MACDONALD, *A history of France*, I, 112–218. J. LOSERTH, *Geschichte des späteren Mittelalters*, 44–52, 149–59, 217–46.

Standard work. LAVISSE, *Histoire de France*, II, part II, 311–31, and both parts of vol. III.

The Ile de France. M. BLOCH, *L'Ile-de-France (les pays autour de Paris)*, Paris, 1913 (vol. IX of Les régions de la France), assembles articles which appeared in the *R.S.H.*

Philip Augustus. DUNN-PATTISON, *Leading figures*, 87–113. W. H. HUTTON, *Philip Augustus*, London, 1896 (Foreign statesmen). A. LUCHAIRE, *La société française au temps de Philippe-Auguste*, 2nd edition, Paris, 1909, authorized translation by E. B. KREHBIEL, *Social France at the time of Philip Augustus*, New York, 1912.

Saint Louis. F. PERRY, *Saint Louis (Louis IX of France), the most Christian king*, New York, 1901 (Heroes of nations). E. EMERTON, *Beginnings of modern Europe*, 28–46. MUNRO and SELLERY, *Medieval civilization*, new edition, 366–75; 491–523 (the latter pages being a translation from LAVISSE, *Histoire de France*, III, part II, 18–40).

Templars. The best general account of the suppression of the Templars in 1309 is H. C. LEA, *History of the inquisition*, III, 238–334. The pertinent documents are gathered in G. LIZERAND (editor), *Le dossier de l'affaire des Templiers*. For other literature see under the outline "Crusades" above.

Original sources. Translations of JOINVILLE'S *Life of St. Louis*, see outline on the crusades. Extracts from it may be read in ROBINSON, *Readings*, I, 198–221; OGG, *Source book*, 311–24; and WEBSTER, *Historical selections*, 519–22.

Maps. SHEPHERD, *Atlas*, 69, 70–71, 76. For excellent detailed maps see A. LONGNON, *Atlas historique de la France.*

C. BIBLIOGRAPHY

General books. The general histories of France are listed above, nos. **508–48.**

Louis VI. A. LUCHAIRE, *Louis VI le Gros: annales de sa vie et de son règne, 1081–1137, avec une introduction historique*, Paris, 1890. J. W. THOMPSON, *The development of the French monarchy under Louis VI le Gros*, Chicago, 1895.

Louis VII. A. LUCHAIRE, *Etudes sur les actes de Louis VII*, Paris, 1885. R. HIRSCH, *Studien zur Geschichte König Ludwigs VII von Frankreich (1119–1160)*, Leipzig, 1892. O. CARTELLIERI, *Abt Suger von Saint-Denis, 1081–1115*, Berlin, 1898 (Historische Studien, 11). A. HUGUENIN, *Suger et la monarchie française au XIIe siècle (1108–1152)*, Paris, 1857. A. LUCHAIRE, *Histoire des institutions monarchiques de la France sous les premiers Capétiens, 987–1180.* E. VACANDARD, "Le divorce de Louis le Jeune [Louis VII]," *R.Q.H.*, XLVII (1890), 408–32. E. VACANDARD, "Saint Bernard et la royauté française," *R.Q.H.*, XLIX (1891), 353–409. E. DUVERNOY, *Le duc de Lorraine, Mathieu Ier, 1139–1176*, Paris, 1904. In his *Catalogue des* *actes des ducs de Lorraine de 1048 à 1139 et de 1176 à 1220*, Nancy, 1915, the author has supplemented and completed the work begun in the Appendix of the earlier work.

Louis VIII. C. PETIT-DUTAILLIS, *Etude sur la vie et le règne de Louis VIII (1187–1226)*, Paris, 1894, no. 101 of no. **888**.

Philip Augustus. A. CARTELLIERI, *Philipp II August, König von Frankreich*, 4 vols., Leipzig, 1899–1922, is the standard work; his *Philipp II August und der Zusammenbruch des angevinischen Reiches*, Leipzig, 1913, is a sketch of sixteen pages. F. M. POWICKE, *The loss of Normandy.* W. WALKER, *On the increase of royal power in France under Philip Augustus*, Leipzig, 1888 (Diss.). L. DELISLE, *Catalogue des actes de Philippe Auguste, avec une introduction sur les sources, les caractères et l'importance historique de ces documents*, Paris, 1856. L. L. BORRELLI DE SERRES, *La réunion des provinces septentrionales à la couronne par Philippe Auguste: Amiénois, Artois, Vermandois, Valois*, Paris, 1899. R. DAVIDSOHN, *Philipp II August von Frankreich und Ingeborg*, Stuttgart, 1888 (Diss.). P. SCHEFFER-BOICHORST, *Deutschland und Philipp II August von Frankreich 1180–1214*, 1868, *F.D.G.*, VIII (1868), 465–562. C. BÉMONT, *De la condemnation de Jean-Sans-Terre par la cour des pairs de France en 1202*, Paris, 1886. C. PETIT-DUTAILLIS, "Le déhéritement de Jean-Sans-Terre et le meurtre d'Arthur de Bretagne," in *R.H.*, CXLVII (1924), 161–203.

For the battle of Bouvines see E. AUDOUIN, *Essai sur l'armée royale au temps de Philippe-Auguste*, Paris, 1913; C. BALLHAUSEN, *Die Schlacht bei Bouvines 27 VII 1214*, Jena, 1907; A. HORTZSCHANSKY, *Die Schlacht an der Brücke von Bouvines*, 1883 (Diss., Halle); and H. MALO, *Un grand feudataire, Renaud de Dammartin et la coalition de Bouvines: contribution à l'étude du règne de Philippe-Auguste*, Paris, 1898.

Saint Louis. C. V. LANGLOIS, *Saint Louis*, Paris, 1886. A. LECOY DE LA MARCHE, *France sous St. Louis et sous Philippe le Hardi*, Paris, 1894. L. S. LE NAIN DE TILLEMONT, *Vie de Saint Louis*, 6 vols., Paris, 1847–51. H. WALLON, *Saint Louis et son temps*, 2 vols., 4th edition, Paris, 1895. M. SEPET, *Saint Louis*, 7th edition, Paris, 1905 (Les saints), translated by G. TYRRELL, London, 1899. WINIFRED F. KNOX, *The court of a saint*, London [1909]. E. BERGER, *Les dernières années de Saint Louis*, Paris, 1902; *Saint Louis et Innocent IV*, Paris, 1893; *Histoire de Blanche de Castille, reine de France*, Paris, 1895. J. S. DOINEL, *Histoire de Blanche de Castille*, Tours, 1908. M. GAVRILOVITCH, *Etude sur le traité de Paris de 1259 entre Louis IX, roi de France, et Henri III, roi d'Angleterre*, Paris, 1899, part of **888**. E. BOUTARIC, *Saint Louis et Alphonse de Poitiers*, Paris, 1870. A. MOLINIER, "Etude sur l'administration de Louis IX et d'Alphonse de Poitiers (1226–71)," *Histoire générale de Languedoc*, VII, 462ff. C. E. NORTON, *St. Louis and Joinville*, Boston, 1864. A. D. SERTILLANGES, *Saint-Louis*, Paris, 1918 (L'art et les saints).

Philip III. C. V. LANGLOIS, *Le règne de Philippe III le Hardi*, Paris, 1887. L. LECLÈRE, *Les rapports de la papauté et de la France sous Philippe III, 1270–1285*, Paris, 1889.

Philip the Fair. E. BOUTARIC, *La France sous Philippe le Bel*, Paris, 1861. F. KERN, *Die Anfänge der französischen Ausdehnungspolitik bis zum Jahr 1308*, Tübingen, 1910; *Grundlagen der französischen Ausdehnungspolitik*, Leipzig, 1910. J. JOLLY, *Philippe le Bel: ses dessins, ses actes, son influence*, Paris, 1869. E. RENAN, *Politique religieuse du règne de Philippe le Bel*, Paris, 1899. F. FUNCK-BRENTANO, *Les origines de la guerre de cent ans: Philippe le Bel en Flandre*, Paris, 1897. P. FOURNIER, *Le royaume d'Arles*, Paris, 1892. R. HOLTZMANN, *Wilhelm von Nogaret: Rat und Grossiegelbewahrer Philipps des Schönen von Frankreich*, Freiburg, 1898 (Diss.).

Finances in the time of Philip the Fair. L. L. BORRELLI DE SERRES, *Recherches sur divers services publics du XIIIe au XVIIe siècles*, 3 vols., Paris, 1895–1909; *Les variations monétaires sous Philippe le Bel et les sources de leur histoire*, Paris, 1902. A. VUITRY, *Etudes sur le régime financier de la France avant la révolution de 1789*, 2 vols., Paris, 1877–83. C. V. LANGLOIS, *Registres perdus des archives de la chambre des comptes de Paris*, Paris, 1917, reprinted from vol. XL of no. **885.** L. LAZARD, *Essai sur la condition des Juifs dans le domaine royal au XIIIe siècle*, Paris, 1887. For the preceding centuries see M. PROU, *Esquisse de la politique monétaire des rois de France du Xe au XIIe siècle*, Paris, 1901.

Estates General. G PICOT, *Histoire des états généraux*, 6 vols , 2nd edition, Paris, 1889. A. CALLERY, *Histoire de l'origine des états généraux*, Brussels, 1881. G. PICOT, *Documents relatifs aux états généraux et assemblées réunis sous Philippe le Bel*, Paris, 1901. H. HERVIEU, *Recherches sur les premiers états généraux et les assemblées représentatives pendant la première moitié du XIVe siècle*, Paris, 1879.

The Parlement of Paris. F. AUBERT, *Histoire du Parlement de Paris de l'origine à François 1er, 1250–1515*, 2 vols., Paris, 1894. E. MAUGIS, *Histoire du Parlement de Paris, de l'avènement des rois Valois à la mort d'Henri IV*, 3 vols., Paris, 1913–16. C. V. LANGLOIS, "Les origines du Parlement de Paris," *R.H.*, XLII (1890), 74–114. F. AUBERT, *Le Parlement de Paris de Philippe le Bel à Charles VII, 1314-1422*, 2 vols., Paris, 1886–90. E. PERROT, *Les cas royaux: origine et développement de la théorie aux XIIIe et XIVe siècles*, Paris, 1910. F. AUBERT, "Nouvelles recherches sur le Parlement de Paris," *Nouvelle revue historique de droit*, XXXIX (1916), 62–109. J. VIARD, "La cour (*curia*) au commencement du XIVe siècle," *B.E.C.*, LXXVII (1916), 74–87.

The feudal reaction of 1314–15. M. ARTONNE, *Le mouvement de 1314 et les chartes provinciales de 1315*, Paris, 1913.

Philip V. P. LEHUGEUR, *Histoire de Philippe le Long*, Paris, 1896.

Original sources. The large collections of sources for the history of France are listed above, nos. **965–77.** Much material of value is in the Rolls Series, no. **995.** MOLINIER, no. **21,** is the best guide for sources on French history.

Special mention may be made of the *Oeuvres complètes de Suger*, edited by LECOY DE LA MARCHE, Paris, 1867; the separate edition of his book on Louis the Fat, *Gesta Ludovici regis cognomento Grossi, ou Vie de Louis le*

Gros, edited by A. Molinier, Paris, 1887; and of Suger, *Vie de Louis VI le Gros*, edited and translated into French by H. Waquet, Paris, 1929 (Les classiques de l'histoire de France au moyen âge). *Acta imperii Angliae et Franciae ab a. 1267 ad a. 1313*, edited by F. Kern, Tübingen, 1910. *Etablissements de Saint Louis*, edited by P. Viollet, 4 vols., Paris, 1881–86, part of no. **966.** H. F. Delaborde, "Le texte primitif des Enseignements de Saint-Louis à son fils," *B.E.C.*, LXXIII (1912), 73–100, 237–62; *Etude sur la constitution du trésor des chartres*, Paris, 1909; *Recueil des actes de Philippe-Auguste, roi de France*, vol. I [1179–94], Paris, 1916, part of no. **975.** C. Bémont, *Recueil d'actes relatifs à l'administration des rois d'Angleterre en Guyenne au XIIIe siècle*, Paris, 1914, part of no. **965.**

Bibliographies. See the general bibliographies for the history of France, nos. **21–27a.** There are excellent bibliographical notes for this period in the footnotes of Lavisse, *Histoire de France*, vol. III. For the Angevin (Norman) Empire, see Gross, no. **36.**

XXVI. ECONOMIC CONDITIONS

A. Outline

1. Importance of economic history. Until recently, this was unduly neglected; now it has gained such prominence that there is danger of giving it too much emphasis.

2. Prominent features of medieval economic life. Predominance of rural life. Importance of corporations. Comparatively stable conditions. The barter system.

3. Rural life. The manor. The lord of the manor and his free and servile tenants. The duties which tenants owed their lord. Gradual emancipation of the servile population. Chief features of the agricultural system: the demesne land, open fields, the strip system, the three-field system. Crude methods of agriculture. Difficulty of keeping animals during the winter. Housing and labor conditions, and amusements of the masses. Peasants' revolts; the Jacquerie in France, 1358, and the Peasants' Revolt in England, 1381.

4. Urban life. Origin of medieval towns; their relations with feudal lords. Enfranchisement of towns. Town charters. Communes, boroughs. Differences of town life in different countries. The inhabitants of towns and their occupations. Aliens, especially Jews. Regulation of manufacture and trade. Merchant gilds and craft gilds. Social and religious gilds. Mystery plays. City walls, streets, churches, town halls, and markets. Remarkable growth and improvement of cities in the thirteenth century. The wealthy class in cities. Towns which have preserved their medieval character, such as Bruges and Nürnberg.

5. Sufferings from cold, famine, and pestilences. The Black Death of 1348–49.

6. Money and banking in the middle ages. Disadvantages of the barter system. Relatively poor system of coinage. Widespread privileges of coinage

and prevalence of debasement of coin. Italian standard coins, banks, and bills of exchange. Money-lending Jews and Lombards. Medieval ideas about interest.

7. Commerce. Hindrances to commerce in the middle ages. Just price. Forestalling. Sudden increase of business in the twelfth century. The chief Asiatic and European routes. The importance of the Mediterranean and the Baltic and North Seas. Luxuries from the east and raw materials from the north. Markets and fairs. Commercial associations and leagues, especially the Hanseatic League. Importance of the Italian cities. Intermunicipal trade. Captains of industry and trade. Jews. Influence of the rise of the Ottoman Turks on commerce.

8. The extension of geographical knowledge through commerce and other causes, such as missionary endeavor. Marco Polo. The compass. Medieval geographical knowledge and cartography (the *portolani*).

B. Special Recommendations for Reading

Brief general accounts. Emerton, *Mediaeval Europe*, ch. xv. Adams, *Civilization*, ch. xii. Luchaire, *Social France*, ch. xiii. Tilley, *Medieval France*, ch. v. *C.M.H.*, V, ch. xix; VI, chs. xiv–xv. Crump and Jacob, *Legacy*, introduction. Munro and Sontag, *Middle ages*, chs. xxviii, xxix, xxxiii, xxxix. Sellery and Krey, *Medieval foundations*, 145–54, 216–39, 327–54. Thorndike, *Medieval Europe*, chs. xvii–xix. Hulme, *Middle ages*, 566–627. See the pictures in nos. **187, 188,** and **207.** For particular terms, Palgrave's *Dictionary*, no. **115**, is helpful.

Longer general accounts. J. W. Thompson, *Economic and social history.* Lavisse et Rambaud, *Histoire générale*, II, chs. i, viii, and ix; ch. i, by C. Seignobos, translated by E. W. Dow, *The feudal régime*, New York, 1906; ch. viii, by A. Giry, translated by F. G. Bates, *Emancipation of mediaeval towns*, New York, 1908. Knight, *Economic history of Europe.* P. Boissonade, *Life and work in medieval Europe (fifth to fifteenth centuries)*, translated by Eileen Power, New York, 1927. W. Cunningham, *Western civilization in its economic aspects: medieval and modern*, Cambridge, 1900, book IV. Helmolt, *History of the world*, VII, 1–62. Lavisse, *Histoire de France*, II, part II, 332–57; III, part I, 390–414. Luchaire, *Manuel des institutions françaises*, part III. E. Michael, *Culturzustände des deutschen Volkes während des dreizehnten Jahrhunderts*, I, 1–85, 129–204. Hearnshaw, *Mediaeval contributions to modern civilisation*, 232–54.

Medieval commerce. E. P. Cheyney, *European background to American history*, New York, 1904 (The American nation series), chs. i–iii. C. Day, *A history of commerce*, New York, 1907, part II.

The following are interesting studies. L. Hutchinson, "Oriental trade and the rise of the Lombard communes," *Quarterly journal of economics*, XVI (1901–02), 413–32. H. C. Lea, "Ecclesiastical treatment of usury," in *Yale review*, II (1893–94), 356–85. Alice Law, "The English nouveaux-riches in the fourteenth century," *R.H.S.*, *Transactions*, new series, IX

(1895), 49–73; and "Notes on English medieval shipping," in *Economic review*, VIII (1898), 349–85. On medieval ships and shipping see also LA RONCIÈRE, *Histoire de la marine française*, I, 244–98; and ENLART, *Manuel d'archéologie*, II, 568–620.

Hanseatic League. EMERTON, *Beginnings of modern Europe*, 187–99. LODGE, *Close of the middle ages*, ch. XVIII. HENDERSON, *Short history of Germany*, 181–202. HELMOLT, *History of the world*, VII, 10–62. Article by E. F. GAY in the *Ency. Brit.* HELEN ZIMMERN, *The Hansa towns*, New York, 1889. D. SCHÄFER, *Die deutsche Hanse*, Leipzig, 1903; 2nd edition, revised, 1915, part 19 of no. **326.**

The Black Death. J. E. T. ROGERS, *English agriculture*, I, ch. XXVIII; *Work and Wages*, chs. VIII–IX. JESSOPP, *Coming of the friars*, chs. IV–V. CHEYNEY, *Industrial history of England*, 96–134; "Disappearance of English serfdom," *E.H.R.*, XV (1900), 20ff. TOUT, *History of England (1216–1377)*, 870–921. VINOGRADOFF, *Oxford studies in social and legal history*, V. A. E. LEVETT, *Black Death.* J. W. THOMPSON, "The aftermath of the Black Death and the aftermath of the Great War," *American journal of sociology*, XXVI (1920–21), 565–72. F. A. GASQUET, *The Black Death of 1348 and 1349*, London, 1908; 2nd edition of *Great Pestilence of 1348–49*, London, 1893. J. F. PALMER, "Pestilences: their influence in the destiny of nations, as shown in the history of the plague," *Trans. R.H.S.*, new series, I (1884), 242–59. EILEEN POWER, "The effects of the Black Death on rural organisation in England," *History*, III (1918), 109–16.

Geographical discovery. C. R. BEAZLEY, *The dawn of modern geography*, II, ch. VI; III, chs. IV–V. S. RUGE, *Geschichte des Zeitalters der Entdeckungen*, 35–81. J. B. BROWN, "The last great dreamer of the crusades," *Nineteenth century*, X (1881), 701–22. *The Renaissance* (Mary Tuttle Bourdon Lectures, Mount Holyoke College, 1929), Lecture I. J. W. THOMPSON, "Exploration and discovery during the renaissance." ABBOTT, *Expansion of Europe*, I, ch. III.

Original sources. E. L. STEVENSON, *Portolan charts, their origin and characteristics, with a description of those belonging to the Hispanic Society of America*, New York, 1911; *Facsimiles of Portolan charts belonging to the Hispanic Society*, New York, 1917; *Portolan Atlas, Egerton MS. 2803, in British Museum*, New York, 1911. Selections in ROBINSON, *Readings*, I, ch. XVIII; THATCHER and MCNEAL, *Source book*, 545–612; OGG, *Source book*, ch. XX; and *Translations and reprints*, II, no. 1, "English towns and gilds," III, no. 2, "Statistical documents," III, no. 5, "English manorial documents." WEBSTER, *Historical selections*, 525–72, 611–23. DAVIES, *Civilization in medieval England*, 106–40; 268–310.

On geographic discovery most important is *The book of Ser Marco Polo, the Venetian, concerning the kingdoms and marvels of the east*, translated and edited by Sir H. YULE, 2 vols., London, 1871; 3rd edition, revised by H. CORDIER, London, 1903. See also H. CORDIER, *Ser Marco Polo: notes and addenda to Sir Henry Yule's edition, containing the results of recent research and discovery*, New York, 1920. Translation of MARCO POLO in *Everyman's library.* M. KOMROFF (editor), *The travels of Marco Polo (the Venetian)*, New York, 1926. The best edition of the original is *Marco Polo, Il Milione: prima edizione integrale*, edited by L. F. BENEDETTO, Florence, 1928. Next in importance is *Cathay and the way thither*, edited by H. YULE. *Book of the knowledge of all the kingdoms, lands, and lordships that are in the world, and the arms and devices of each land and lordship*, edited by Sir C. MARKHAM, London, 1912 (Hakluyt society, 2nd series, XXIX), account by a fourteenth century Spanish Franciscan. CHAN JU-KUA, *His work on the Chinese and Arab trade in the 12th and 13th centuries, entitled Chufanchi*, translated from the Chinese and annotated by F. HIRTH and W. W. ROCKHILL, Leipzig, 1912. H. CORDIER, *Histoire générale de la Chine et de ses relations avec les pays étrangers depuis les temps les plus anciens jusqu'à la chute de la dynastie Mandchoue*, 4 vols., Paris, 1920.

For a contemporary account of the Black Death BOCCACCIO's introduction to *Decameron*, the essentials of which are printed in *Source book of the renaissance*, edited by M. WHITCOMB, revised edition, 21–24.

Maps. SHEPHERD, *Atlas*, 44, 76, 98–99, 102–103, 104B–C, 107–110.

C. BIBLIOGRAPHY

General books. The general histories of civilization, nos. **729–38, 751,** and **762–81,** are especially valuable. Almost all the books on the Jews, nos. **850–84b,** lay stress on their place in economic history, but see especially nos. **857–61.** In addition, read H. C. LEA, *Inquisition in Spain*, I, 81–144.

General economic history. M. KOVALEWSKY, *Die ökonomische Entwicklung Europas bis zum Beginn der kapitalistischen Wirtschaftsform*, translated into German from the Russian by L. MOTZKIN and others, 7 vols., Berlin, 1901–14. G. D'AVENEL, *Histoire économique de la propriété, des salaires, des denrées, et de tous les prix en général, depuis l'an 1200 jusqu'en l'an 1800*, 6 vols., Paris, 1894–1912, abridged and altered under the titles, *Paysans et ouvriers depuis sept cents ans*, Paris, 1899; *Les riches depuis sept cents ans: revenus et bénéfices, appointements et honoraires*, Paris, 1909; *La fortune privée à travers sept siècles*, 3rd edition, Paris, 1895; *Histoire de la fortune française: la fortune privée à travers sept siècles*, Paris, 1927, is practically a revised edition of his 1895 book; also *L'évolution des moyens de transport*, Paris, 1919. J. STRIEDER, *Studien zur Geschichte kapitalistischer Organisationsformen: Monopole, Kartelle und Aktiengesellschaften im Mittelalter und zu Beginn der Neuzeit*, Munich, 1914; 2nd edition, 1925. H. BIKEL, *Die Wirtschaftsverhältnisse des Klosters St. Gallen von der Gründung bis zum Ende des dreizehnten Jahrhunderts*, Freiburg-i-B., 1914. W. T. ASHLEY, *Surveys, historic and economic*, London and New York, 1900, deals with the middle ages in the first chapters. DOPSCH, *Wirtschaftliche und soziale Grundlagen der europäischen Kulturentwicklung.* V. BRANTS, *Les théories économiques aux XIIIe et XIVe siècle*, Louvain, 1895. R. KÖTZSCHKE, *Allgemeine Wirtschaftsgeschichte des Mittelalters*, Jena, 1924.

Economic history of France. E. LEVASSEUR, *Histoire des classes ouvrières et de l'industrie en France avant 1789*, 2 vols., Paris, 1859; 2nd edition, 1900–01. AGNES M. WERGELAND, *History of the working classes in France: a review of Levasseur's "Histoire des classes ouvrières et de l'industrie en France avant 1789,"* Chicago, 1916.

Economic history of Germany. K. T. v. INAMA-STERNEGG, *Deutsche-Wirtschaftsgeschichte*, 3 vols. in 4, Leipzig, 1879–1901, vol. 1 in 2nd edition, 1909. K. LAMPRECHT, *Deutsches Wirtschaftsleben im Mittelalter*, 3 vols. in 4, Leipzig, 1885–86. R. KÖTZSCHKE, *Deutsche Wirtschaftsgeschichte bis zum 17 Jahrhundert*, Leipzig, 1908, part 2, 1, of no. **331.**

Economic History of England. W. J. ASHLEY, *An introduction to English economic history and theory*, 2 vols., London, 1888–93, 3rd edition of vol. I, 1894. W. CUNNINGHAM, *Growth of English industry and commerce*, 2 vols., 5th edition, Cambridge, 1910–12. J. E. T. ROGERS, *A history of agriculture and prices in England, 1259–1793*, 7 vols., Oxford, 1866–1902; *Six centuries of work and wages: the history of English labour*, 2 vols., London, 1884; 11th edition in 1 vol., 1912, is based on the above; see also *The economic interpretation of history*, London, 1888; 7th edition, 1909. F. SEEBOHM, *The English village community: an essay on economic history*, London, 1883; 4th edition, 1890. E. LIPSON, *The economic history of England, I, The middle ages*, New York, 1915. L. BRENTANO, *Eine Geschichte der wirtschaftlichen Entwicklung Englands*, vol. I to the end of the fifteenth century, Jena, 1927. E. P. CHEYNEY, *An introduction to the industrial and social history of England*, New York, 1901; revised edition, New York, 1921; new edition, Oxford, 1923. L. F. SALZMANN, *English industries of the middle ages*, London, 1913, see also no. **735.**

Agricultural conditions and life of the peasants. L. DELISLE, *Etudes sur la condition de la classe agricole et sur l'état de l'agriculture en Normandie pendant le moyen âge*, Paris, 1851. H. SÉE, *Les classes rurales et le régime domanial en France au moyen âge*, Paris, 1901. R. FAGE, *La propriété rurale en Bas-Limousin pendant le moyen âge*, Paris, 1917. J. M. RICHARD, "Thierri d'Hireçon, agriculteur artésian," *B.E.C.*, LIII (1892), 383–416, 571–604. M. FOURNIER, "Les affranchissements du Ve au XIIIe siècle," *R.H.*, XXI (1883), 1–58. J. BRAND, *Observations on popular antiquities, chiefly illustrating the origin of our vulgar customs*, etc., revised by H. ELLIS, 2 vols., London, 1813; new edition by W. C. HAZLITT, 2 vols., London, 1905. P. BERNARD, *Etude sur les esclaves et les serfs d'église en France, du VIe au XIIIe siècle*, Paris, 1919. D. CHADWICK, *Social life in the days of Piers Plowman*, Cambridge, 1922. G. G. COULTON, *The medieval village*, Cambridge, 1925. R. MIELKE, *Das deutsche Dorf*, Leipzig, 1913.

Popular insurrections. G. DES MAREZ, *Les luttes sociales en Flandre au moyen âge*, Brussels, 1900. L. MIROT, *Les insurrections urbaines au début du règne de Charles VI (1380–83)*, Paris, 1905. G. v. D. ROPP, *Sozialpolitische Bewegungen im Bauernstande vor dem Bauernkriege*, Marburg, 1899.

Medieval towns. CRUMP and JACOB, *Legacy*, ch. VIII. See the following series: *Mediaeval towns*, London, Dent, 1898ff.; *Historic towns*, edited by

E. A. Freeman and W. Hunt, 9 vols., London, 1887–93; and *Ancient cities*, edited by B. C. A. Windle, 8 vols., London, 1903–08. For London see also the profusely illustrated books by Sir W. Besant, *Early London, prehistoric, Roman, Saxon, and Norman*, London, 1908; *Mediaeval London*, 2 vols., vol. I, *Historical and social*, vol. II, *Ecclesiastical*, London, 1906. John Stow, *Survey of London* (containing Fitzstephen's description), various editions, e.g., conveniently in no. **944**, London, 1912. J. M. Vincent, *Municipal problems in mediaeval Switzerland*, Baltimore, 1905 (Johns Hopkins University studies, series XXIII, nos. 11–12). H. Pirenne, "L'origine des constitutions urbaines au moyen âge," *R.H.*, LIII (1893), 52–83; LVII (1895), 57–98, 293–327; *Medieval cities: their origins and the revival of trade*, Princeton, 1925 (published, with corrections, as *Les villes du moyen âge*, Brussels, 1927). C. Enlart, *Villes mortes du moyen âge*, Paris, 1920. T. F. Tout, *Mediaeval town-planning*, Manchester, 1917 (Bulletin of the John Rylands Library, IV, 1). Brown, *Achievement of the middle ages*, 121–60.

French cities. Joan Evans, *Life in mediaeval France*, ch. iii. A. Luchaire, *Les communes françaises à l'époque des Capétiens directs*, Paris, 1890; new edition by L. Halphen, 1911. G. Espinas, *La vie urbaine de Douai au moyen-âge*, 4 vols., Paris, 1913 (vols. III–IV contain "pièces justificatives"). Geneviève Acloque, *Les corporations, l'industrie, et le commerce à Chartres du XIe siècle à la révolution*, Paris, 1917. G. Bourgin, *La commune de Soissons, et le groupe communal soissonais*, Paris, 1908, part 167 of no. **888.** A. Giry, *Les établissements de Rouen*, 2 vols., Paris, 1883–85, parts 55 and 59 of no. **888.** C. Bémont, "Les institutions municipales de Bordeaux au moyen âge: la mairie et la jurade," *R.H.*, CXXIII (1916), 253–93. F. B. Marsh, *English rule in Gascony, 1199–1259, with special reference to the towns*, Ann Arbor, 1912 (University of Michigan studies). Mary Bateson, "The laws of Breteuil," *E.H.R.*, XV (1900), 73–78, 302–18, 496–523, 754–7; XVI (1901), 92–110, 332–45.

See Thompson, *Economic and social history*, pp. 849–50 for works on France and Flanders. For a detailed bibliography on medieval Paris see outline XIII in part III below.

German cities. K. Hegel, *Städte und Gilden der germanischen Völker im Mittelalter*, 2 vols., Leipzig, 1891; *Die Entstehung des deutschen Städtewesens*, Leipzig, 1898. G. v. Below, *Das älteste deutsche Städtewesen und Bürgertum*, Bielefeld and Leipzig, 1898, part of no. **326;** *Der Ursprung der deutschen Städteverfassung*, Düsseldorf, 1892. R. Sohm, *Die Entstehung des deutschen Städtewesens*, Leipzig, 1890. G. L. v. Maurer, *Geschichte der Städteverfassung in Deutschland*, 4 vols., Erlangen, 1869–71. F. W. Barthold, *Geschichte der deutschen Städte und des deutschen Bürgertums*, 4 vols., Leipzig, 1850–54. B. Heil, *Die deutschen Städte und Bürger im Mittelalter*, Leipzig, 1903 (Aus Natur und Geisteswelt, 43). R. Koebner, *Die Anfänge des Gemeinwesens der Stadt Köln. 'Zur Entstehung und ältesten Geschichte des deutschen Städtewesens,'* Bonn, 1922. G. Schmoller, *Deutsches Städtewesen in älterer Zeit*, Bonn, 1922. C. Koehne, "Burgen, Burgmannen und Städte. Ein Beitrag zur Frage der Bedeutung der ländlichen Grundrenten für die mittelalterliche Städtentwicklung," *H.Z.*, CXXXIII (1925), 1–19. J. FRITZ, *Deutsche Stadtanlagen*, Strasburg, 1894 (Prog.).

The following are interesting studies on cities: W. KING, *Chronicles of three free cities, Hamburg, Bremen, Lübeck*, London, 1914. W. REISNER, *Die Einwohnerzahl deutscher Städte in früheren Jahrhunderten, mit besonderer Berücksichtigung Lübecks*, Jena, 1903. H. KEUSSEN, *Topographie der Stadt Köln im Mittelalter, nebst Karten und Beigaben*, 2 vols., Bonn, 1910. W. BEHAGHEL, *Die gewerbliche Stellung der Frau im mittelalterlichen Köln*, Berlin and Leipzig, 1910. K. BÜCHER, *Die Berufe der Stadt Frankfurt am Main im Mittelalter*, Leipzig, 1914. F. BOTHE, *Geschichte der Stadt Frankfurt a. M.*, vol. I, Frankfurt a. M., 1913. I. KRACAUER, *Geschichte der Frankfurter Juden im Mittelalter, aus der inneren; Geschichte der Juden Frankfurts im 14 Jahrhundert* (*Judengasse, Handel und sonstige Berufe*), Frankfurt, 1913. See also his important source book, *Urkundenbuch zur Geschichte der Juden in Frankfurt am Main von 1150–1400*, vol. I, Frankfurt, 1914. G. SCHMOLLER, *Strasburgs Blüte*, Strasburg, 1875, eulogizes the growth in the twelfth and thirteenth centuries. P. SANDER, *Die Reichsstädtische Haushaltung Nürnbergs, auf Grund ihres Zustandes von 1431–1440 dargestellt*, Leipzig, 1902. R. WACKERNAGEL, *Geschichte der Stadt Basel*, 3 vols., Basel, 1907–24. H. KEUSSEN, *Köln im Mittelalter*, Bonn, 1918. J. GEBAUER, *Geschichte der Stadt Hildesheim*, 2 vols., Hildesheim and Leipzig, 1922–24. E. KEYSER, *Die Bevölkerung Danzigs und ihre Herkunft im XIII und XIV Jahrhundert*, Lübeck, 1924.

See also the literature on the "Eastward expansion of Germany," under outline XXII above, and THOMPSON, *Feudal Germany*, ch. XX; *Economic and social history*, p. 837.

Cities of the Netherlands. H. PIRENNE, *Les anciennes démocraties des Pays-Bas*, Paris, 1910; English translation by J. V. SAUNDERS, *Belgian democracy, its early history*, Manchester and London, 1915.

Italian cities. J. LUCHAIRE, *Les démocraties italiennes*, Paris, 1915. *C.M.H.*, V, ch. v. F. SCHEVILL, *Siena: the story of a mediaeval commune*, New York, 1909. For other literature on Italian cities see outline XXII above and outline XXXII below.

Gilds. C. GROSS, *The gild merchant: a contribution to British municipal history*, 2 vols., Oxford, 1890. E. R. A. SELIGMAN, *Two chapters on the mediaeval guilds of England*, Baltimore, 1887 (American economic association monographs, vol. II, no. 5). A. H. JOHNSON, *The history of the worshipful company of drapers of London: preceded by an introduction on London and her gilds up to the close of the XVth century*, 2 vols., Oxford, 1914. G. UNWIN, *The gilds and companies of London*, London, 1908. A. F. JACK, *An introduction to the history of life insurance*, London and New York, 1912, "The gild-system," 15–149. R. EBERSTADT, *Der Ursprung des Zunftwesens und die älteren Handwerkerverbände des Mittelalters*, Leipzig, 1900; 2nd ed., Munich, 1915; *Das französische Gewerberecht in Frankreich vom XIII^ten Jahrhundert bis 1581*, Leipzig, 1899 (in Staats- und sozialwissenschaftliche Forschungen, XVII, 2). A. DOREN, *Untersuchungen zur Geschichte der*

Kaufmannsgilden im Mittelalter, Leipzig, 1893 (Forschungen, edited by Schmoller, 12). M. SAINT-LÉON, *Histoire des corporations des métiers*, Paris, 1897; 3rd edition, 1923. G. RENARD, *Guilds in the middle ages*, translated, with an introduction by G. H. D. COLE, London, 1919.

Mystery plays. E. K. CHAMBERS, *The mediaeval stage*, 2 vols., Oxford, 1903. S. TUNISON, *Dramatic traditions of the dark ages*, Chicago, 1907. D. C. STUART, *Stage decoration in France in the middle ages*, New York, 1910. G. COHEN, *Histoire de la mise en scène dans le théâtre religieux français du moyen âge*, Paris, 1906; 2nd edition, 1926, translated into German in an enlarged and improved edition by C. BAUER, *Geschicte der Inszenierung im geistlichen Schauspiele des Mittelalters in Frankreich*, Leipzig, 1907; see also his "Le théâtre à Paris et aux environs à la fin du XIVe siècle," *Romania*, XXXVIII (1909), 587–95. M. HERMANN, *Forschungen zur deutschen Theatergeschichte des Mittelalters und der Renaissance*, Berlin, 1914. K. YOUNG, "Observations on the medieval passion play," *P.M.L.A.*, XXV (1910), 309–54. F. J. MONE, *Schauspiele des Mittelalters*, Carlsruhe, 1846. See outlines XXIII and XXIV, Part III, below.

Epidemics and famines. J. F. K. HECKER, *Der schwarze Tod im vierzehnten Jahrhundert*, Berlin, 1832; new edition by A. HIRSCH, with the title, *Die grossen Volkskrankheiten des Mittelalters*, 1865, translated by B. C. BABINGTON, *The epidemics of the middle ages*, London, 1844; 3rd edition, 1859; see also his *The Black Death and the dancing mania*, translated by B. G. BABINGTON, New York [1888] (Cassell's national library). R. CRAWFORD, *Plague and pestilence in literature and art*, Oxford University Press, 1914, has interesting illustrations. G. STICKER, *Abhandlungen aus der Seuchengeschichte und Seuchenlehre*, vol. I, *Die Pest*, erster Theil: *Die Geschichte der Pest*, Giesen, 1908; zweiter Theil: *Die Pest als Seuche und als Plage*, 1910. C. CREIGHTON, *A history of epidemics in Britain* [A.D. 664–1866], 2 vols., Cambridge, 1891–94. E. BASCOME, *A history of epidemic pestilences from the earliest ages, 1495 years before the birth of Our Savior to 1848*, London, 1851. K. LECHNER, *Das grosse Sterben in Deutschland in der Jahren 1348 bis 1351 und die folgenden Pestepidemien bis zum Schlusse des 14 Jahrhunderts*, Innsbruck, 1884; "Die grosse Geisselfahrt des Jahres 1349," *Historisches Jahrbuch*, V (1884), 437–62. R. HOENIGER, *Der schwarze Tod in Deutschland*, Berlin, 1882. W. SEELMANN, *Die Totentänze des Mittelalters*, Norden, 1893 (extract from *Jahrbuch des Vereins für niederdeutsche Sprachforschung*). F. CURSCHMANN, *Hungersnöte des Mittelalters (8–13 Jahrhundert)*, Leipzig, 1900 (Leipziger Studien, 6, 1). J. NOHL, *The black death, a chronicle of the plague*, translated by C. H. CLARKE, London, [1926].

Money and banking. W. W. CARLILE, *Evolution of modern money*, London, 1901. W. A. SHAW, *The history of currency, 1252 to 1894*, New York, 1896. J. SCHOENHOF, *History of money and prices: an inquiry into their relations from the 13th century to the present time*, 2nd edition, New York, 1897. A. DEL MAR, *History of monetary systems*, London, 1895; *Money and civilization*, London, 1886. J. LUBBOCK (Lord Avebury), *Short history of coins and currency*, New York, 1902. A. DIEUDONNÉ, "Histoire monétaire du denier parisis jusqu'à Saint Louis," *Mémoires de la Société nationale des antiquaires de France*, 1911, pp. 111–47; "La monnaie royale depuis la réforme de Charles V," *B.E.C.*, LXXII (1911), 473–99; LXXIII (1912), 263–82. L. CIANI, *Monnaies royales françaises de Hugues Capet à Louis XVI, avec indication de leur valeur actuelle*, Paris, 1926. F. SCHAUB, *Der Kampf gegen den Zinswucher, ungerechten Preis und unlauteren Handel im Mittelalter*, Freiburg, 1905. R. J. WHITWELL, "Italian bankers and the English crown," *R.H.S., Transactions*, New series, XVII (1903), 173–233. O. MELTZING, *Das Bankhaus der Medici und seine Vorläufer*, Jena, 1907. S. L. PERUZZI, *Storia del commercio e dei banchieri di Firenze, 1200–1345*, Florence, 1868. A. v. KOSTANECKI, *Das öffentliche Kreditwesen im Mittelalter*, Leipzig, 1889 (Schmollers Staat- und sozialwissenschaftliche Forschungen, 9, 1). W. JESSE, *Quellenbuch zur Münz- und Geldgeschichte des Mittelalters*, Halle, 1924. A. DIEUDONNÉ, *Manuel des poids monétaires*, Lahure, 1925. A. VON EBENGREUTH, *Allgemeine Münzkunde und Geldgeschichte des Mittelalters und der neuren Zeit*, Munich and Berlin, 1926. See also nos. **292–98**, and THOMPSON, *Reference studies in medieval history*, Pt. III, pp. 292–93, for other literature.

General history of commerce. O. NOËL, *Histoire du commerce du monde depuis les temps les plus reculés*, 3 vols., Paris, 1891–1906. G. LUZZATTO, *Storia del commercio*, vol. I, *Dall' antichità al rinascimento*, Florence, 1914. A. SEGRE, *Manuale di storia del commercio*, vol. I, *Dalle origini alla rivoluzione francese*, Turin, 1913; second edition, 1923. A. SCHAUBE, *Handelsgeschichte der romanischen Völker des Mittelmeergebiets bis zum Ende der Kreuzzüge*, Munich, 1906. M. WEBER, *Zur Geschichte der Handelsgesellschaften im Mittelalter nach südeuropäischen Quellen*, Stuttgart, 1889. H. PIRENNE, "Villes, marchés, et marchands au moyen âge," *R.H.*, LXVII (1898), 59–70. K. JIREČEK, "Die Bedeutung von Ragusa in die Handelsgeschichte des Mittelalters," *S.B. Vienna Acad.*, 1899. F. LUDWIG, *Untersuchungen über die Reise- und Marschgeschwindigkeit im XII und XIII Jahrhundert*, Berlin, 1897 (Diss.). B. HAGENDORN, *Die Entwicklung der wichtigsten Schiffstypen bis ins 19 Jahrhundert*, Berlin, 1914. P. GUILHIERMOZ, "Remarques diverses sur les poids et mesures du moyen âge," *B.E.C.*, LXXX (1919), 1–100. G. LEGARET, *Histoire du développement du commerce depuis la chute de l'Empire romain jusqu'à nos jours*, Paris, 1927. J. VALERY, *Contrat d'assurance maritime du XIIIe siècle*, Paris, 1916.

Levant trade. W. HEYD, *Geschichte des Levantehandels im Mittelalter*, 2 vols., Stuttgart, 1879, translated into French, with additions by the author, by F. RAYNAUD, *Histoire du commerce du Levant au moyen âge*, 2 vols., Leipzig, 1885–86. See the review of HEYD'S book by F. HIRSCH, "Die Eröffnung des inneren Asiens für den europäischen Handelsverkehr im 13 und 14 Jahrhundert," *H.Z.*, XLIV (1880), 385–408; and A. H. LYBYER, "The Ottoman Turks and the routes of oriental trade," *E.H.R.*, XXX (1915), 577–88. See THOMPSON, *Economic and social history*, pp. 831, 832, 833, 834, on Venice and Genoa.

Commerce in France. THOMPSON, *Economic and social history*, ch. XXIII.

E. Levasseur, *Histoire du commerce de la France*, 2 vols., Paris, 1911–12. H. Pigeonneau, *Histoire du commerce de la France*, 2 vols., Paris, 1887–89. *Mémoires et documents pour servir à l'histoire du commerce et de l'industrie en France*, edited by J. Hayem, vols. I–IV, Paris, 1911–16. C. Piton, *Les Lombards en France et à Paris*, 2 vols., Paris, 1891–92. H. D. Imbart de la Tour, *La liberté commerciale en France aux XIIe et XIIIe siècles*, Paris, 1890. C. D. de Freville de Lorme, *Mémoire sur le commerce maritime de Rouen*, Rouen, 1857. P. Mantellier, *Histoire de la communauté des marchands fréquentant la rivière de Loire*, 3 vols., Orleans, 1867–69. C. Alengry, *Les foires de Champagne*, Paris, 1915. F. Bourquelot, *Etudes sur les foires de Champagne et de Brie, sur la nature, l'étendue et les règles du commerce qui s'y faisait aux XIIe–XIVe siècles*, 2 vols., Paris, 1865–66 (Mémoires, Académie des Inscriptions). J. W. Thompson, "The commerce of France in the ninth century," *Journal of political economy*, XXIII (1915), 857–87. A. P. Usher, *The history of the grain trade in France, 1400–1710*, Cambridge, 1913. H. Hauser, *Travailleurs et marchands dans l'ancienne France*, Paris, 1920. J. Mathorez, *Les étrangers en France sous l'ancien régime*, 2 vols., Paris, 1919–21. Thompson, *Economic and social history*, chs. xii, xviii, xx, and pp. 826–27, 835–36 for bibliography on Champagne fairs.

Commerce in the Netherlands. R. Häpke, *Brügges Entwickelung zum mittelalterlichen Weltmarkt*, Berlin, 1908; *Der deutsche Kaufmann in den Niederlanden*, Leipzig, 1911. W. Stein, *Die Genossenschaft der deutschen Kaufleute zu Brügge in Flandern*, Berlin, 1890. M. Rooseboom, *The Scottish staple in the Netherlands*, The Hague, 1910. J. Finot, *Etude historique sur les relations commerciales entre la Flandre et la république de Gênes au moyen âge*, Paris, 1906; *Etude historique sur les relations commerciales entre la Flandre et la France au moyen âge*, Paris, 1894; *Etude historique sur les relations commerciales entre la Flandre et l'Espagne au moyen âge*, Paris, 1899. T. Wilkins, "Zur Geschichte des niederländischen Handels im Mittelalter," *Hansische Geschichtsblätter*, 1908, 1909. H. S. Lucas, *The Low Countries and the Hundred Years' War*, Ann Arbor, 1929; valuable bibliography.

Commerce in Italy. G. Yver, *Le commerce et les marchands dans l'Italie méridionale au 13e et au 14e siècle*, Paris, 1903, part II of no. **887.** See the Introduction, by R. Brown, to the *Calendar of State Papers, Venetian*, I (1864), for a sketch of Venetian commerce. W. Stieda, *Hansisch-venezianische Handelsbeziehungen im 15 Jahrhundert*, Halle, 1894. A. Schaube, "Die Anfänge der venezianischen Galeerenfahrten nach der Nordsee (seit 1314)," *H.Z.*, CI (1908), 28–89. P. H. Scheffel, *Verkehrsgeschichte der Alpen*, vol. II, Berlin, 1914. O. Meltzing, *Das Bankhaus der Medici und seine Vorläufer*, Jena, 1907. E. Friedmann, *Der mittelalterliche Welthandel von Florenz in seiner geographischen Ausdehnung*, Vienna, 1912. G. Toniolo, *Dei remoti fattori della potenza economica di Firenze nel medio evo*, Milan, 1882. E. Dixon, "The Florentine wool trades in the middle ages," in *R.H.S., Transactions*, new series, XII (1898), 151–79. A. Doren, *Studien aus der florentiner Wirthschaftsgeschichte*, vols. I–II, Stuttgart and Berlin, 1901–08. E. H. Byrne, "Genoese trade with Syria in the twelfth century,"

A.H.R., XXV (1920), 191–219; see also his other works, p. 235–6. L. CHIAPELLI, "Una lettera mercantile del 1330, e la crisi del commercio italiano nella prima metà del Trecento," *Archivio storico italiano*, LXXXII (1924), 229–56. M. CHIAUDANO, *Contratti commerciali genovesi del sec. XII, contributo alla storia dell' accomandatio e della societas*, Turin, 1925. A. SAPORI, *Delle compagnie mercantili dei Bardi e dei Peruzzi*, Florence, 1926. THOMPSON, *Economic and social history*, chs. XIII, XVII, and bibliography, 827, 833.

Commerce in Germany. E. VOLKMANN, *Germanischer Handel und Verkehr: synoptische Handelsgeschichte der germanischen Völker (von der Urzeit bis 1600)*, Würzburg, 1925. W. VOGEL, *Geschichte der deutschen Seeschiffahrt*, I, *Von der Urzeit bis zum Ende des XV Jahrhunderts*, Berlin, 1915. R. HENNIG, "Zur Verkehrgeschichte Ost-und Nordeuropas im 8 bis 12 Jahrhundert," *H.Z.*, CXV (1915), 1–30. H. BÄCHTOLD, *Der norddeutsche Handel im 12 und beginnenden 13 Jahrhundert*, Berlin and Leipzig, 1910 (Abh.m.n.G., 21). A. SCHULTE, *Geschichte des mittelalterlichen Handels und Verkehrs zwischen Westdeutschland und Italien mit Ausschluss von Venedig*, 2 vols., Leipzig, 1900. H. SIMONSFELD, *Der Fondaco dei Tedeschi in Venedig und die deutsch-venetianischen Handelsbeziehungen*, 2 vols., Stuttgart, 1887. E. NÜBLING, *Ulm's Handel im Mittelalter*, Ulm, 1900. F. RAUERS, *Zur Geschichte der alten Handelsstrassen in Deutschland*, Gotha, 1906. G. STEINHAUSEN, *Der Kaufmann in der deutschen Vergangenheit*, Leipzig, 1899. T. HAMPE, *Die fahrenden Leute in der deutschen Vergangenheit*, Leipzig, 1902. H. ECKERT, *Die Krämer in süddeutschen Städten bis zum Ausgang des Mittelalters*, Berlin, 1910 (Abh.m.n.G., 4). M. SCHELLER, *Zoll und Markt im 12 und 13 Jahrhundert*, Blankenheim, 1903 (Diss.). J. FALKE, *Die Geschichte des deutschen Handels*, Leipzig, 1859. L. K. GOETZ, *Deutsch-russische Handelsverträge des Mittelalters*, Hamburg, 1917. F. RÖRIG, *Der Markt von Lübeck*, Leipzig, 1922. A. DOPSCH and others, *Nordwesteuropas Verkehr, Handel, und Gewerbe im frühen Mittelalter*, Vienna, 1924. P. KLETLER, *Nordwesteuropas Verkehr, Handel, und Gewerbe im frühen Mittelalter*, Vienna, 1924. HANS-JOACHIM SEEGER, *Westfalen Handel und Gewerbe vom 9 bis zum Beginn des 14 Jahrhunderts*, Berlin, 1926.

Hanseatic League. E. DAENELL, *Die Blütezeit der deutschen Hanse: hansische Geschichte von der zweiten Hälfte des 14 bis zum letzten Viertel des 15 Jahrhunderts*, 2 vols., Berlin, 1905–06; *Geschichte der deutschen Hanse in der zweiten Hälfte des 14 Jahrhunderts*, Leipzig, 1896. T. LINDNER, *Die deutsche Hanse: ihre Geschichte und Bedeutung*, Leipzig, 1898; 4th edition, 1911. W. STEIN, *Beiträge zur Geschichte der deutschen Hanse bis um die Mitte des 15 Jahrhunderts*, Giessen, 1900. A. KIESSELBACH, *Die wirtschaftlichen Grundlagen der deutschen Hanse und die Handelstellung Hamburgs bis in die 2 Halfte des 14 Jahrhunderts*, Berlin, 1907. A. HOLM, *Lübeck, die freie und Hansestadt*, Bielefeld and Leipzig, 1900. F. SCHULZ, *Die Hanse und England von Edwards III bis auf Heinrichs VIII Zeit*, Berlin, 1911 (Abhandlungen zur Verkehrs- und Seegeschichte, vol. V). F. KEUTGEN, *Die Beziehungen der Hanse zu England im letzten Drittel des 14 Jahrhunderts*, Giessen, 1890. K. BAHR, *Handel und Verkehr der deutschen Hanse in Flandern während des*

14 Jahrhunderts, Leipzig, 1911. W. BUCK, *Der deutsche Kaufmann in Novgorod bis zur Mitte des 14 Jahrhunderts*, Berlin, 1891. A. WINKLER, *Die deutsche Hanse in Russland*, Berlin, 1886. A. AGATS, *Der hansische Baienhandel*, Heidelberg, 1904, describes the activities of the League in Spain and Portugal. H. HARTMEYER, *Der Weinhandel im Gebiete der Hanse im Mittelalter*, Jena, 1905. F. RÖRIG, "Aussenpolitische und innerpolitische Wandlungen in der Hanse nach dem Stralsunder Frieden (1370)," in *H.Z.*, CXXXI (1925), 1–18. B. SCHMEIDLER, *Hamburg-Bremen und Nordost-Europa.* See last edition of DAHLMANN-WAITZ, *Quellenkunde*.

Geographical discoveries in the middle ages. BEAZLEY, *Dawn of modern geography*. J. LELEWEL, *Géographie du moyen âge*, 4 vols., Brussels, 1850–52, with an *Epilogue*, 1857. L. VIVIEN DE SAINT-MARTIN, *Histoire de la géographie*, Paris, 1873. J. BENSAUDE, *L'astronomie nautique en Portugal à l'époque des grandes découvertes*, Bern, 1912, in an appendix gives a chronological list of geographical discoveries from 1290 to 1529. A. BLÁZQUEZ, *Estudio acerca de la cartografía española en la edad media*, Madrid, 1906. E. L. STEVENSON, *Terrestrial and celestial globes: their history and construction*, 2 vols., New Haven, 1921. C. J. BÜNDGENS, *Was verdankt die Länder- und Völkerkunde den mittelalterlichen Mönchen und Missionären*, Frankfurt, 1889. T. FISCHER, *Über italienische Seekarten und Kartographen des Mittelalters*, Berlin, 1882. O. PESCHEL, *Geschichte des Zeitalters der Entdeckungen*, Stuttgart, 1858. C. ERRERA, *L'epoca delle grandi scoperte geografiche*, Milan, 1910. S. GÜNTHER, *Geschichte der Erdkunde*, Leipzig, 1904 (vol. I of *Die Erdkunde*, edited by M. KLAR), chs. III–IV. F. VICOMTE DE SANTAREM, *Essai sur l'histoire de la cosmographie pendant le moyen âge*, 3 vols., 1849–52. C. DE LA RONCIÈRE, *La découverte de l'Afrique au moyen âge, cartographes et explorateurs*, 3 vols., Cairo, 1925–27. L. SALEMBIER, "Pierre d'Ailly and the discovery of America," *Historical records and studies of the United States catholic historical society*, VII (1914). S. P. THOMPSON, "The rose of the winds: the origin and development of the compass-card," *Proceedings of the British academy*, vol. VI (also printed separately by Oxford University Press, 1916). MARGARET B. SYNGE, *A book of discovery: the history of the world's exploration from the earliest times to the finding of the south pole*, London, 1912. S. RUGE, "Die Literatur zur Geschichte der Erdkunde vom Mittelalter an 1900–03," *Geographisches Jahrbuch*, XXVI (1903).

Travel. W. C. FIREBAUGH, *The inns of the middle ages*, Chicago, 1924. JEAN J. JUSSERAND, *English wayfaring life.* NEWTON, *Travel and travellers.*

Medieval industries. R. BENNETT and J. ELTON, *History of cornmilling*, 4 vols., London, 1898–1904. L. BECK, *Die Geschichte des Eisens*, 5 vols., Brunswick, 1884–1903; 2nd edition of vol. I [to 1500], 1891.

Original sources. *Documents relatifs à l'histoire de l'industrie et du commerce en France*, edited by G. FAGNIEZ, 2 vols., Paris, 1898–1900, parts of no. **968.** *Réglemens sur les arts et métiers de Paris, rédigés au 13 siècle et connus sous le nom du livre des métiers d'*ETIENNE BOILEAU, edited by G. B. DEPPING, Paris, 1837, part 31 of no. **965** (see also part 34), also edited by R. DE LESPINASSE and F. BONNARDOT, Paris, 1879, in *Histoire générale de Paris*

(Portions of this interesting document are translated in *Studies in European history*, edited by F. M. FLING, II, no. 8). A. GIRY, *Choix de documents sur les relations de la royauté avec les villes en France, 1180–1314*, Paris, 1895. *Cartulaire de l'ancienne estaple de Bruges* [*862–1492*], edited by L. GILLIODTS VAN SEVEREN, for the *Société d'émulation de Bruges, Recueil de chroniques*, etc., 4 vols., Bruges, 1904–06. WALTER OF HENLEY'S *Husbandry*, together with an anonymous *Husbandry, Seneschaucie*, and ROBERT GROSSETESTE'S *Rules* [with a translation], edited by ELIZABETH LAMOND, with an introduction by W. CUNNINGHAM, London, 1890. *Recueil des monuments inédits de l'histoire du tiers état*, edited by A. THIERRY, 4 vols., Paris, 1850–70, part of no. **965.** For a large collection of medieval chronicles of German cities see no. **982.**

The chief sources for the Hanseatic League are the following. *Die Recesse und andere Akten der Hansetage von 1256–1430*, 8 vols., Leipzig, 1870–97; *Hanserecesse, 1431–1524*, 15 vols., Leipzig, 1876–1910. *Hansisches Urkundenbuch*, vols. I–X [to 1485], Halle, 1876–1907. *Hansische Geschichtsquellen*, 7 vols., Halle, 1875–94, neue Folge, Berlin, 1899ff. *Hansische Geschichtsblätter*, 16 vol., Leipzig, 1871–1900.

The following materials will serve as an introduction to the history of geographical discovery in the middle ages. *Recueil de voyages et mémoires publié par la Société de géographie*, Paris, 1824–66. *Recueil de voyages et de documents pour servir à la géographie*, Paris, 1890ff. G. FERRAND, *Relations de voyages et textes géographiques arabes, persans et turks relatifs à l'extrème orient, du VII au XVIII siècles, traduits, revus et annotés*, 2 vols., Paris, 1913–14. A. E. NORDENSKIOLD, *Facsimile atlas to the early history of cartography*, translated from the Swedish by J. A. EKELÖF and C. R. MARKHAM, Stockholm, 1889; *Periplus: an essay on the early history of charts and sailing directions*, with an atlas, translated from the Swedish, by F. A. BATHER, Stockholm, 1897, is practically a second volume of the *Facsimile atlas*. K. MILLER, *Mappae mundi: die ältesten Weltkarten herausgegeben und erläutert*, 6 parts, Stuttgart, 1895–98. E. L. STEVENSON, *Genoese world map, 1457*, with facsimile and critical text, New York, 1912; *Marine world chart of Nicolo de Conerio Januensis 1502* (*circa*), New York, 1908. *Sammlung mittelalterlichen Welt- und Seekarten italienischen Ursprungs*, edited and elucidated by T. FISCHER, Venice, 1886 (in his Beiträge zur Geschichte der Erdkunde und der Kartographie im Mittelalter). *Eine Geographie aus dem dreizehnten Jahrhundert*, edited by J. V. ZINGERLE [aus RUDOLF VON EMS *Weltkronik*], Vienna, 1865. *Die Ebstorfkarte: eine Weltkarte aus dem dreizehnten Jahrhundert*, edited by K. MILLER, 3rd edition, Stuttgart, 1900.

Bibliographies. G. ESPINAS, *Une bibliographie de l'histoire économique de France au moyen âge*, Paris, 1907. C. GROSS, *Bibliography of British municipal history, including gilds and parliamentary representation*, New York, 1897. H. HALL, *A select bibliography for the study, sources, and literature of English economic history*, London, 1914. W. STIEDA, *Ueber die Quellen der Handelsstatistik im Mittelalter*, Berlin, 1903 (*Abh. Berlin Acad.*, 1902). THOMPSON, *Economic and social history*. *Bibliographie der Volkswirtschaftslehre und*

Rechtswissenschaft appears since 1906 as a Supplement to *Blätter für vergleichende Rechtswissenschaft und Volkswirtschaftslehre. Jahrbücher fur Nationalökonomie und Statistik*, Jena, 1863ff.

XXVII. LIFE OF THE NOBLES IN THE MIDDLE AGES

A. Outline

1. Essential characteristics of nobility and aristocracy. Chief classes in the middle ages: (1) clergy (some noble, others not), (2) lay nobles, (3) common people (rise of the rich burghers within this class).

2. Origin of a distinct class of nobles in the middle ages. Importance of cavalry service or knight's service (*caballarius—chevalerio—chivalry—Ritter*).

3. Privileges and insignia of nobility. Degrees of nobility. The study of genealogy. *Almanach de Gotha.* The crusades and the origin of heraldry. Orders of knighthood.

4. Sanctification by the church of many of the customs and practices of the nobles. Peace movements in the middle ages. For the "Peace of God" and "Truce of God" see p. 193.

5. The education of the nobles. Stress on athletics, the use of arms, the practice of courtesy, and the "gay sciences." Pages and squires. The lettered nobility.

6. Position of women in feudal society. Their free, athletic, and often warlike life. Women and chivalry.

7. Life of the nobles in times of peace. Their luxuries and amusements. Importation of spices, rugs, hangings, silks, and other luxuries from the east. Furniture and dress. Their amusements: jousts and tournaments, feasting, hunting (falconry), minstrelsy and games, especially chess, jongleurs and jesters. Knight-errantry. Attitude of nobles toward business and learning.

8. Homes of the nobles. Manor houses and fortified houses in the towns. Strong wooden towers and palisades in the open country. The gradual evolution of the stone castle, the stone wall and the moat in the twelfth and thirteenth centuries. Donjons. Keeps. Wonderful castles such as Château Gaillard.

9. Feudal warfare. Importance of defence; the armored man and the fortified house. Arms, armor, and siegecraft. Influence of the crusades on medieval warfare. Changes brought about by the rise of the foot-soldier and the use of gunpowder.

10. The decline of chivalry. The influence of the rise of centralized monarchies, the gradual disappearance of serfdom, the rise of a rich merchant and comfortable artisan class in the cities, and of a distinct intellectual class in the universities. Ridicule and satire directed against the nobles, especially in the rising vernacular languages.

B. Special Recommendations for Reading

Brief general accounts. Seignobos, *The feudal régime*, 27–38, 64–65. Crump and Jacob, *Legacy*, 401–33. Munro and Sontag, *Middle ages*, ch. xxvi. Hulme, *Middle ages*, 539–64. Sellery and Krey, *Medieval foundations*, 136–44. J. Flach, *Les origines de l'ancienne France*, II, 561–79. Bémont and Monod, *Medieval Europe*, 257–67. Henderson, *A short history of Germany*, I, ch. v. See also articles "Knighthood and chivalry," "Castle," and "Fortification and siegecraft," in the *Ency. Brit.*

Longer general accounts. A. Luchaire, *Social France*, chs. viii–xii. E. L. Cutts, *Scenes and characters of the middle ages*, 311–460. Lavisse, *Histoire de France*, II, part II, 14–22; IV, part II, 152–76. Prestage (editor), *Chivalry*. W. C. Meller, *A knight's life in the days of chivalry*, London, 1924. W. S. Davis, *Life on a mediaeval barony, a picture of a typical feudal community in the thirteenth century*, New York, 1923.

Chivalry. L. Gautier, *La chevalerie*, 3rd edition, Paris, 1895, translated by H. Frith, *Chivalry*, London, 1891. F. Cornish, *Chivalry*, New York, 1901. A. Schultz, *Das höfische Leben zur Zeit der Minnesinger*, 2 vols., 2nd edition, Leipzig, 1889. *C.M.H.*, VI, ch. xxiv. B. C. Waeyf, *La tradition chevaleresque des Arabes*, Paris, 1919. Taylor, *The mediaeval mind*, 4th edition, I, 537–603, attempts to describe the spirit of chivalry. See also Munro and Sellery, *Medieval civilization*, 240–47.

Feudal warfare. C. W. C. Oman, *A history of the art of war*, especially book VI. H. Delbrück, *Geschichte der Kriegskunst*, vol. III, especially 235ff. E. Viollet-le-Duc, *Annals of a fortress*, translated from the French by B. Buckwall, Boston, 1875. Several books listed in this bibliography contain illustrations; see in addition, nos. **187, 188, 200, 202.** Also see "Development of the castle in England and Wales," *History teachers' magazine*, III (1912), 191–200. R. G. Albion, *Introduction to military history*, New York, 1929, Part I. *C.M.H.*, VI, ch. xxiii.

Original sources. *Studies in European history*, edited by F. M. Fling, II, no. 4. Webster, *Historical selections*, 470–83. The best picture of chivalry during the Hundred Years' War is in Froissart's *Chronicles*. Joinville, *Chronicle of the crusade of St. Lewis*, reveals the spirit of crusading knights. See in general the literature under "Crusades," outline XXI above, and under "Vernacular literatures," outline XXIV in part III below, for the life of nobles in the middle ages.

C. Bibliography

General books. Histories of civilization, nos. **729–38, 749–55, 762–81.** See also books on genealogy and heraldry, nos. **268–91e.**

Origin and nature of medieval nobility. P. Guilhiermoz, *L'origine de la noblesse en France au moyen âge*, Paris, 1902. O. Henne-am-Rhyn, *Geschichte des Rittertums*, Leipzig, 1893. K. H. Roth von Schreckenstein, *Die Ritterwürde und der Ritterstand*, Freiburg, 1886. W. Vedel, *Mittelalterliche Kulturideale*, I, *Heldenleben*, Leipzig, 1910 (Aus Natur und Geisteswelt, 292).

A. Schulte, *Der Adel und die deutsche Kirche im Mittelalter: Studien zur Social-, Rechts- und Kirchengeschichte*, Stuttgart, 1910 (Kirchenrechtliche Abhandlungen, edited by U. Stutz, 63–64). N. Paulus, "Die Wertung der weltlichen Berufe im Mittelalter," *Hist. Jahrbuch*, XXXII (1911), 725–55.

Medieval warfare. G. T. Denison, *A history of cavalry from the earliest times: with lessons for the future*, London, 1877; 2nd edition, 1913, pp. 97–184. G. F. Laking, *A record of European armour and arms through seven centuries*, 5 vols., London, 1920–22. G. Köhler, *Die Entwicklung des Kreigswesens und der Kriegführung in der Ritterzeit von der Mitte des 11 Jahrhunderts bis zu den Hussitenkriegen*, 3 vols., Breslau, 1886–90. M. Jähns, *Geschichte der Kriegswissenschaften vornehmlich in Deutschland*, 3 vols., Munich, 1889–91; *Handbuch einer Geschichte des Kriegswesens von der Urzeit zur Renaissance*, 2 vols., Leipzig, 1880. In *L'armée à travers les âges: conférences faites en 1898 à l'Ecole spéciale militaire de Saint-Cyr*, 2nd edition, Paris, 1899, articles by C. V. Langlois, "Le service militaire en vertu de l'obligation féodale"; and "Le service militaire soldé"; and E. Gebhart, "Les armées mercenaires de l'Italie, du 14ᵉ siècle à 1527." O. v. Dungern, *Der Heerenstand im Mittelalter*, Papiermühle, 1908. H. Delpech, *Le tactique au XIIIᵉ siècle*, 2 vols., Paris, 1886, gives particular attention to the battles of Bouvines and Muret. E. Boutaric, *Les institutions militaires de la France avant les armées permanentes*, Paris, 1863. H. Belloc, *Warfare in England*, London, 1912 (Home university library). C. Ffoulkes, *Armour and weapons*, Oxford, 1909. R. Payne-Gallwey, *The crossbow*, London, 1903, appendix, 1907. J. Schwietering, *Zur Geschichte von Speer und Schwert im 12 Jahrhundert*, Hamburg, 1912. C. H. Ashdown, *Armour and weapons in the middle ages*, London, 1925. W. Giese, *Waffen nach der spanischen Literatur des XII. und XIII. Jahrhunderts*, Hamburg, 1925.

Medieval castles. The following pertain especially to France. C. Enlart, *Manuel d'archéologie française*, vol. II, "Architecture civile et militaire." E. E. Viollet-le-Duc, *L'architecture militaire au moyen âge*, Paris, 1854, translated by M. Macdermott, *Military architecture*, 2nd edition, Oxford, 1879; see also his *Cité de Carcassonne (Aude)*, Paris, 1888. A. Deville, *Histoire du Chtâeau-Gaillard*, Rouen, 1829; *Histoire du château d'Argues*, Rouen, 1839. M. F. Mansfield, *Castles and châteaux of old Burgundy*, Boston, 1909. T. A. Cook, *Twenty-five great houses of France: the story of the noblest French châteaux*, with an introduction by W. H. Ward, New York, 1916.

For Great Britain there are several good books with excellent illustrations. A. H. Thompson, *Military architecture in England during the middle ages*, London, 1912. A. Harvey, *The castles and walled towns of England*, London, 1911 (The antiquary's books). Ella S. Armitage, *The early Norman castles of the British Isles*, New York, 1912. H. A. Evans, *Castles of England and Wales*, London, 1912. G. T. Clark, *Mediaeval military architecture in England*, 2 vols., London, 1884. E. B. D'Auvergne, *The castles of England*, London [1907]. J. D. Mackenzie, *The castles of England*, London, 1897. C. Oman, *Castles*, London, 1926. W. M. Mackenzie, *The medieval castle in Scotland*, London, 1927.

For Germany the following works of O. PIPER are authoritative, *Burgenkunde: Forschungen über gesammtes Bauwesen und Geschichte der Burgen innerhalb des deutschen Sprachgebietes*, Munich, 1895; 3rd edition, revised, 1914; *Österreichische Burgen*, 1902; and *Abriss der Burgenkunde*, 2nd edition, Munich and Leipzig, 1904 (Sammlung Göschen). P. SALVISBERG, *Die deutsche Kriegsarchitektur von der Urzeit bis auf die Renaissance*, Stuttgart, 1887. H. ZELLER-WERDMÜLLER, *Mittelalterliche Burganlagen der Ostschweiz*, Leipzig, 1893 (extract from *Mittheilungen der antiquarischen Gesellschaft in Zürich*).

Origin of fire-arms. H. W. L. HIME, *The origin of artillery*, New York, 1915, is a revised edition of a book published in 1904 under the title, *Gunpowder and ammunition*. Here as in his essay, "Roger Bacon and gunpowder," pp. 321–35 in *Roger Bacon essays*, Oxford, 1914, he gives Bacon credit for the invention of gunpowder; but see L. THORNDIKE, "Roger Bacon and gunpowder," *Science*, XLII (1915), 799–800. T. F. TOUT, "Firearms in England in the fourteenth century," *E.H.R.*, XXVI (1911), 666–702. F. R. SCHNEIDER, *Die Artillerie des Mittelalters*, Berlin, 1910. L. FOIN, *Artillerie lourde en Bourgogne au XVe siècle*, Auxerre, 1917. E. O. v. LIPPMANN, *Zur Geschichte des Schiesspulvers und der älteren Feuerwaffen*, Stuttgart, 1899. J. F. v. REITZENSTEIN, "Die Sage von der Erfindung des Schiesspulvers und der deutsche Ursprung des abendländischen Geschützwesens," *Allgemeine Militärzeitung*, 1896, no. 36. L. LACABANE, "De la poudre à canon et de son introduction en France," *B.E.C.*, 2nd series, I (1844), 28–57.

Chivalry. LA CURNE DE SAINTE-PALAYE, *Mémoires sur l'ancienne chevalerie: avec une introduction et des notes historiques* par C. NODIER, new edition, 2 vols., Paris, 1826. P. LACROIX, *L'ancienne France: chevalerie et les croisades, féodalité, blason, ordres militaires*, Paris, 1886. S. LUCE, *Histoire de Bertrand du Guesclin et de son époque*, 2nd edition, Paris, 1882. HURD's *Letters on chivalry and romance*, edited by EDITH J. MORLEY, London, 1911 (the text of the letters reprinted from the first edition, 1762). A. T. B. BYLES (editor), *The Book of the Ordre of Chyvalry, translated and printed by William Caxton from a French version of Ramón Lull's "Le libre del orde de cavayleria," together with Adam Lontfut's Scottish Transcript* (*Harleian MS. 6149*), London, 1926 (Early English text society). JOAN EVANS (translator), *The unconquered knight: a chronicle of the deeds of Don Pero Niño, Count of Buelna, by his standard-bearer Gutierre Diaz de Gamez* (*1431–1449*), with introduction and notes by JOAN EVANS, London, 1928.

Women of chivalry. T. KRABBES, *Die Frau im altfranzösischen Karls-epos*, Marburg, 1884. K. WEINHOLD, *Die deutschen Frauen in dem Mittelalter*, 2 vols., Vienna, 1851; 3rd edition, 1897. E. L. LINTON, "The women of chivalry," *Fortnightly review*, XLVIII (1887), 559–79. E. WECHSSLER, "Frauendienst und Vassalität," *Zeitschrift für französische Sprache und Literatur*, XXIV (1902), 159–90. MYRRHA BORODINE, *La femme et l'amour au XIIe siècle*, Paris, 1909. ALICE HENTSCH, *De la littérature didactique du moyen âge s'adressant spécialement aux femmes*, Cahors, 1903. T. L. NEFF,

La satire des femmes dans la poésie lyrique du moyen âge, Paris, 1900. R. Briffault, *The mothers*, 3 vols., New York, 1928, especially chs. xxvii–xxix. Eunice R. Goddard, *Women's costume in French texts of the XIth and XIIth centuries*, Baltimore, 1927 (Johns Hopkins studies in romance literatures and languages, 7).

Romances of chivalry. J. Ashton, *Romances of chivalry*, New York, 1887. J. B. Bury, *Romances of chivalry on Greek soil*, Oxford, 1911. H. Thomas, *Spanish and Portuguese romances of chivalry: the revival of the romance of chivalry in the Spanish peninsula and its extension and influence abroad*, Cambridge, 1923. See also Pt. III, Outline XXIV.

Sports and pastimes of the nobles. J. J. Jusserand, *Les sports et jeux d'exercise dans l'ancienne France*, Paris, 1901. J. Strutt, *Glig-gamena Angel-ðeod: the sports and pastimes of the people of England*, London, 1801; often reprinted, new edition, enlarged by J. C. Cox [1903]. H. J. R. Murray, *A history of chess*, Oxford University Press, 1914. F. Niedner, *Das deutsche Turnier im 12 and 13 Juhrhundert*, Berlin, 1881. F. H. Cripps-Day, *The history of the tournament in England and in France*, London, 1918. R. C. Clephan, *The tournament: its periods and phases*, with a preface by C. J. Ffoulkes, London, 1919. E. L. Guilford, *Select extracts illustrating sports and pastimes in the middle ages*, London, 1920 (S.P.C.K., Texts for students, 23).

Life of nobles in the middle ages. C. V. Langlois, *La vie en France*, no. **762a,** Pt. I. E. M. Tappan, *In feudal times: social life in the middle ages*, London, 1913. H. Oschinsky, *Der Ritter unterwegs und die Pflege der Gastfreundschaft im alten Frankreich*, Halle, 1900 (Diss.). G. Raynaud, "La société et la vie en France au moyen âge," *Journal des savants*, new series, 7th year, 1909, pp. 214–23. N. De Pauw, *La vie intime en Flandre au moyen âge, d'après des documents inédits*, Brussels, 1913 (extract from Bulletin de la Commission royale d'histoire de Belgique, LXXXII, 1913). L. Garreau, *L'état social de la France au temps des croisades*, Paris, 1899. J. Falke, *Die ritterliche Gesellschaft im Zeitalter des Frauencultus*, new edition, Berlin [1862]. L. Delisle, *De l'instruction littéraire de la noblesse française au moyen âge*, Paris, 1855 (extract of 8 pp. from *Journal de l'instruction publique*, XXIV, no. 46, June, 1855). T. Wright, *A history of domestic manners and sentiments in England*, London, 1862; new edition, *The homes of other days, a history of domestic manners, etc.*, London, 1871. M. Boehn, *Die Mode: Menschen und Moden im Mittelalter, nach Bildern und Kunstwerken der Zeit*, I, *Mittelalter: vom Untergang der Altenwelt bis zur Renaissance*, Munich, 1925. E. E. Viollet-le-Duc, *Dictionnaire du mobilier*, 2nd edition, Paris, 1868–75. W. Münch, *Gedanken über Fürstenerziehung aus alter und neuer Zeit*, Munich, 1909. P. Hemmerle, *Das Kind im Mittelalter*, part I, *Mutter und Kind*, Breslau, 1915. O. Cartellieri, *Am Hofe der Herzöge von Burgund, 'Kulturhistorische Bilder,'* Basel, 1926.

Bibliography. C. V. Langlois, "Les travaux sur l'histoire de la société française au moyen âge, d'après les sources littéraires," *R.H.*, LXIII (1897), 241–65.

XXVIII. CULTURE IN THE TWELFTH AND THIRTEENTH CENTURIES

A. Outline

1. France was the center of culture during these two centuries. The great importance of this era in the history of the culture of western Europe has been overshadowed by the subsequent intense interest in ancient Greek and Roman literature and art.

2. Sudden increase in learning and education towards the beginning of the twelfth century.

3. Rise of a spirit of inquiry, based on logic (dialectic). Abelard and Bernard of Clairvaux.

4. The "New Aristotle." Systematization of scholastic theology and philosophy. Albertus Magnus and Thomas Aquinas.

5. Rise and decline of interest in the ancient classics. The schools of Chartres. John of Salisbury. The schools of Orleans. John Garland of Paris. The *Battle of the seven arts*.

6. The *ars dictaminis*, the "business course" in medieval universities. Boncompagno.

7. Revival of Roman law. Irnerius at Bologna. The systematic study of canon law. The *Decretum* of Gratian, ca. 1140–50. The *Corpus iuris canonici*.

8. Rise and decline of interest in the natural sciences, including medicine. Robert Grosseteste and Roger Bacon.

9. Rise of medieval universities, especially Bologna, Paris, and Oxford. Studies and life of medieval students.

10. The literature of this period: (1) Latin (Goliardic literature, sermon stories, etc.); (2) Vernacular literature.

11. The art of the period, especially Gothic architecture.

B. Special Recommendations for Reading

General accounts. The standard account is C. H. Haskins, *Renaissance of the twelfth century*, which is supplemented by his *Studies in mediaeval culture*. Emerton, *Mediaeval Europe*, ch. xiii. Thorndike, *Medieval Europe*, chs. xx–xxii. Munro and Sontag, *Middle ages*, ch. xxxi. Hulme, *Middle ages*, 682–709, 778–837. Sellery and Krey, *Medieval foundations*, 240–77. Crump and Jacob, *Legacy*, 59–285. Brown, *Achievement*, 161–240. J. H. Randall, *The making of the modern mind*, Bk. I. Lavisse et Rambaud, *Histoire générale*, II, ch. x. Lavisse, *Histoire de France*, II, part II, 384–411; III, part I, 323–45; part II, 380–429. Portions of the latter, along with other material translated into English, will be found in Munro and Sellery, *Medieval civilization*, enlarged edition, 277–357, 458–90, 524–46. Taylor, *Mediaeval mind*, is devoted in large part to the period covered by this outline. Sandys, *A history of classical scholarship*, I, is valuable as a work for reference.

Medieval universities. C. H. HASKINS, *The rise of universities*, New York, 1923, serves as an excellent introduction. H. RASHDALL, *The universities of Europe in the middle ages*, 2 vols., in 3, Oxford, 1895, the standard work; read especially I, chs. I and II, and II, ch. XIV. A. S. RAIT, *Life in the mediaeval university*, Cambridge, 1912. HASKINS, "Life of medieval students as seen in their letters," *A.H.R.*, III (1897–98), 203–29, and "The University of Paris in the sermons of the thirteenth century," *ibid.*, X (1904), 1–27, both now published in *Studies in mediaeval culture*, 1–72. LUCHAIRE, *Social France*, ch. III. J. MCCABE, *Peter Abelard*, New York, 1901. *Translations and reprints*, II, no. 3, "The medieval student." Many additional translations from documents are printed with introductions in A. O. NORTON, *Readings in the history of education: mediaeval universities*, Cambridge, 1909.

Medieval art. For a very brief sketch of the art of the period, read S. REINACH, *Apollo: an illustrated manual of the history of art*, New York, 1907; new edition, translated by F. SIMMONDS, New York, 1917, chs. XII–XIII. W. R. LETHABY, *Medieval art*, London, 1904; new and revised edition, 1912. C. ENLART, *Manuel d'archéologie française.*

Original sources. Short extracts, in English translation, of the literature of the period are gathered in G. G. COULTON, *A medieval garner*, London, 1910. Translations of some medieval students' songs are in J. A. SYMONDS, *Wine, women, and song*, and in HELEN WADELL, *The wandering scholars*, London, 1907. Possibly the most interesting French tale of the twelfth century is *Aucassin and Nicolette*, of which the best translation is by A. LANG, London and New York, 1899 (often reprinted).

C. BIBLIOGRAPHY

For detailed bibliographies on all the subjects touched upon in the above outline, see part III, Medieval Culture, period II, 1100–1300.

XXIX. THE CHURCH FROM ABOUT 1300 TO ABOUT 1450

A. OUTLINE

1. Importance of this period in the constitutional history of the church and in the history of medieval political thought.

2. The relations of pope Boniface VIII, 1294–1303, with the rising monarchical states, especially England under Edward I and France under Philip IV, the Fair. Importance of the question of finances. The Papal Jubilee, 1300. The papal bulls, *Clericis laicos*, issued in 1296, *Ausculta fili*, 1301, and *Unam sanctam*, 1302. Action of the Estates General of France in 1302. The scene at Anagni, where Boniface VIII, 86 years of age, was insulted by Nogaret and Sciarra Colonna, 1303.

3. The "Babylonish Captivity" of the papacy, 1305–77. Election of pope Clement V, archbishop of Bordeaux, 1305–14, a creature of king Philip IV of France. Removal of the papacy to Avignon. The suppression

of the Templars, 1312. Evils of the "Babylonish Captivity." The Flagellants. Conflict of the Avignon popes with the empire and their peculiar position at the outbreak of the Hundred Years' War (see the next two outlines). The Statutes of Provisors and Praemunire in England, 1351, 1353.

4. Return of the papacy to Rome. Temporary stay of pope Urban V in Rome, 1367–70. St. Catherine of Siena, 1347–80. The return of pope Gregory XI to Rome in 1377 where he died in 1378.

5. The great western schism, 1378–1417. Double election in 1378: pope Urban VI at Rome, in April, and pope Clement VII at Fondi, in September, elected by cardinals with French sympathies. Political as well as religious division of Europe during the schism.

6. The conciliar movement. Proposals to heal the schism and reform the church. The part played by the university of Paris. Jean Gerson, Pierre d'Ailly, and Conrad of Gelnhausen. The constitutional crisis in the history of the church.

7. The council of Pisa, 1409. Attempted deposition of the two rival popes and the election of a new pope, Alexander V (succeeded by John XXIII in 1410). Now there were three rival popes.

8. The council of Constance, 1414–18, summoned by the emperor Sigismund and pope John XXIII. Division of the council into "nations." Its chief work: (1) it healed the schism by disposing of the rival popes, John XXIII, Gregory XII, and Benedict XIII, and by electing Martin V; (2) it tried to stem the tide of heresy, which had set in strong since the time of Wiclif, especially in Bohemia, by burning John Huss and Jerome of Prague, which resulted in the Hussite wars, 1419ff. (John Ziska, Utraquists, Taborites); (3) it made futile efforts to reform the church in "head and members." The decree *Sacrosancta*, 1415. The decree *Frequens*, 1417.

9. The council of Basel, 1431–49. Conflict between the council and pope Eugenius IV (1431–47), who summoned a rival council at Ferrara (later at Florence), 1438–39, which brought about an ineffective union between the Greek and Latin churches. Deposition of Eugenius IV by the council of Basel in 1439 and the election of an anti-pope, Felix V. Cardinal Cesarini, Nicholas Cusa, and Aeneas Sylvius at the council of Basel. Its dissolution, 1449.

10. Failure of the conciliar movement. Sporadic efforts to emphasize the idea of national churches by the Pragmatic Sanction of Bourges, 1438, and the Pragmatic Sanction of Mainz, 1439. The Concordat of Vienna, 1448. The bull *Execrabilis*, issued by pope Pius II, in 1460. The reaction in favor of the papacy during the second half of the fifteenth century.

11. The church and the people. Popular preachers and religious movements. St. Bernardino of Siena. The spread of mysticism in the Low Countries, and Germany. Meister Eckart, John Tauler, Henry Suso, Thomas à Kempis.

12. Popes, 1276–1503.
    - Innocent V, 1276
    - Hadrian V, 1276
    - John XX or XXI, 1276–77
    - Nicholas III, 1277–80
    - Martin IV, 1281–85
    - Honorius IV, 1285–87
    - Nicholas IV, 1288–92
    - (vacancy, 1292–94)
    - Celestine V, 1294
    - Boniface VIII, 1294–1303
    - Benedict XI, 1303–04
    - Clement V, 1305–14
    - (vacancy, 1314–16)
    - John XXII, 1316–34
    - (Nicholas V, anti-pope, 1328–30)
    - Benedict XII, 1334–42
    - Clement VI, 1342–52
    - Innocent VI, 1352–62
    - Urban V, 1362–70
    - Gregory XI, 1370–78
    - Urban VI, 1378–89
    - (Clement VII, anti-pope, 1378–94)
    - Boniface IX, 1389–1404
    - (Benedict XIII, anti-pope, 1394–1415)
    - Innocent VII, 1404–06
    - Gregory XII, 1406–09
    - Alexander V, 1409–10
    - John XXIII, 1410–15
    - (Gregory XII, rival pope to 1415)
    - (vacancy, 1415–17)
    - Martin V, 1417–31
    - Eugenius IV, 1431–47
    - (Felix V, anti-pope, 1439–49)
    - Nicholas V, 1447–55
    - Calixtus III, 1455–58
    - Pius II, 1458–64
    - Paul II, 1464–71
    - Sixtus IV, 1471–84
    - Innocent VIII, 1484–92
    - Alexander VI, 1492–1503

B. Special Recommendations for Reading

Short general accounts. Adams, *Civilization*, 392–415. Henderson, *Short history of Germany*, I, ch. ix, 203–27. W. Barry, *The papacy and modern times: a political sketch, 1303–1870*, New York, 1911 (Home university library), 1–78. R. L. Poole, *Wycliffe and movements for reform*, London, 1889, chs. vii–xii. Munro and Sontag, *Middle ages*, chs. xxxiv, xxxviii. E. Emerton, *Beginnings of modern Europe*, chs. iii, vii. Thorndike, *Medieval Europe*, ch. xxx. Bartlet and Carlyle, *Christianity in history*, part IV, ch. i. Sellery and Krey, *Medieval foundations*, 301–26.

Longer general accounts. E. Hulme, *Renaissance and reformation*, ch. viii. T. Burckhardt, *The civilization of the renaissance in Italy*, London, 1892, Pt. VI. C. Beard, *The reformation of the sixteenth century in its relation to modern thought and knowledge*, new edition, New York, 1927. H. Bruce, *The age of schism: being an outline of the history of the church from* A.D. *1304 to* A.D. *1503*, London, 1907, chs. i–viii. Lodge, *Close of the middle ages*, chs. ii, ix, x, xi. Lavisse et Rambaud, *Histoire générale*, III, ch. vi, and ch. xiii for the Hussite wars. P. van Dyke, *The age of the renascence: an outline sketch of the history of the papacy from the return from Avignon to the sack of Rome* (*1377–1527*), New York, 1897, chs. i–xi. H. C. Lea, *History of auricular confession and indulgences in the Latin church*, vol. III, Philadelphia,

1896. LAVISSE, *Histoire de France*, III, part II, 127–200; IV, part II, 260–74. J. LOSERTH, *Geschichte des späteren Mittelalters*, 206–43, 309–12, 385–529 (contains excellent bibliographies).

Standard surveys of the period. M. CREIGHTON, *A history of the papacy during the period of the reformation*, 5 vols., London, 1882–94; new edition, *A history of the papacy from the great schism to the sack of Rome*, 6 vols., London, 1897, vols. I–II. L. PASTOR, *Geschichte der Päpste seit dem Ausgang des Mittelalters*, vols. I–V (to 1549), Leipzig, 1884–1910, translated by F. I. ANTROBUS and R. F. KERR, *The history of the popes from the close of the middle ages*, vols. I–XII, St. Louis, 1898–1912, vols. I–II (1305–1458). The standard work on the councils of this period is HEFELE, *Conciliengeschichte*, VI, 266–1042, and all of vol. VII; French edition by H. LECLERCQ, *Histoire des conciles*, vol. VII, Paris, 1916. GREGOROVIUS, *Rome in the middle ages*, VI, and VII, part I, 1–185.

The religion of the people. P. MONNIER, *Le quattrocento*, Paris, 1924, II, 168–218. J. A. SYMONDS, *Age of the despots*, London, 1913, Appendix IV, "Religious revivals in mediaeval Italy." D. MUZZEY, *The Spiritual Franciscans*, New York, 1907. B. MANNING, *The people's faith in the time of Wyclif*, Cambridge, 1919. On the character and influence of popular preachers see the accounts in church histories and A. FERRES-HOWELL, *S. Bernardino of Siena*, London, 1913. W. HEYWOOD, *The ensamples of Fra Filippo: a study of mediaeval Siena*, Siena, 1901. V. FITZGERALD, *St. John Capistran* (Lives of the friar saints), New York, 1911. G. OWST, *Preaching in medieval England*, and F. GASQUET, *Parish life in medieval England* (Antiquary's book), London, 1909. The mystical and reforming movements in the North are described in A. HYMA, *The christian renaissance*, Grand Rapids, 1924; C. ULLMANN, *Reformers before the reformation*, 2 vols., Edinburgh, 1860; R. JONES, *Studies in mystical religion*, 3rd edition, New York, 1909; K. FRANCKE, "Medieval German mysticism," *Harvard theological review*, V (1912), 110–120. E. UNDERHILL, *The mystics of the church*, New York, 1926; W. R. INGE, *Christian mysticism*, 2nd edition, London, 1912; F. BEVAN, *Three friends of God: John Tauler, Nicholas of Basle, Henry Suso*, New York, 1887; E. UNDERHILL, *Ruysbroeck*, London, 1915; T. MONTMORENCY, *Thomas à Kempis, his age and his book*, New York, 1906; C. HORSTMAN, *Richard Rolle of Hampole and his followers*, 2 vols., London, 1895.

Council of Constance. J. H. WYLIE, *The council of Constance to the death of John Hus*, London, 1900. E. J. KITTS, *Pope John XXII and Master John Hus of Bohemia*, London, 1910. A very stimulating short story of the conciliar idea is by J. N. FIGGIS, *Studies of political thought from Gerson to Grotius, 1414–1625*, 2nd edition, Cambridge, 1916, essay II; *ibid*, *Politics at the council of Constance* (*R.H.S.*, *Trans.*, new series, XIII, 105ff.). W. A. DUNNING, *A history of political theories: ancient and medieval*, New York, 1902, ch. X. E. EMERTON, "The first European congress," *Harvard theological review*, XII (1919), 275–93.

John Huss. LEA, *History of the inquisition*, II, 427–567. D. S. SCHAFF, *John Huss: his life, teachings, and death, after five hundred years*, New York,

1915. Count LÜTZOW, *The life and times of Master John Hus*, London, 1909. W. N. SCHWARZE, *John Hus, the martyr of Bohemia: a study of the dawn of protestantism*, New York, 1915. J. HERBERN, *Huss and his followers*, London, 1926.

Original sources. The papal bulls, *Clericis laicos* and *Unam sanctam*, or various other materials, are translated in THATCHER and MCNEAL, *Source book*, 309–32; ROBINSON, *Readings*, I, 488–515 (contains the decree *Sacrosancta* and the decree *Frequens*); HENDERSON, *Historical documents*, 432–39, 349–50 (Jubilee of 1300); OGG, *Source book*, 383–97 (includes the Pragmatic Sanction of Bourges); *Translations and reprints*, III, no. 6, "The pre-reformation period," 19–33; II, no. 5, "England in the time of Wycliffe," 5–9 (Statutes of Provisors and Praemunire). E. EMERTON, *Humanism and tyranny*, Cambridge (Mass.), 1925, chs. IV, V contains important selections from the constitutions of Albornoz and other material on the condition of the papal states. Some of the writings of SAINT CATHERINE are translated in V. SCUDDER'S *St. Catherine of Siena as seen in her letters*, New York, 1926, and A. THOROLD'S *The dialogue of the Seraphic Virgin Catherine of Siena*, London, 1907. A biography by a close friend is RAYMOND OF CAPUA, *Life of St. Catherine of Siena*, New York, n.d. PLATINA'S *Lives of the popes*, edited by BENHAM, 2 vols., London, n.d. begin to be valuable during this period and the *Memoirs of the Florentine bookseller, Vespasiano da Bisticci*, translated by W. and E. WATERS, New York, 1926, contain lives of Eugene IV and many prominent cardinals and bishops. WEBSTER, *Historical selections*, 435–39, 463–66.

The important work of JAN HUS, *De ecclesia: the church*, has been translated, with introduction and notes, by D. S. SCHAFF, New York, 1915, and a selection from his letters is in H. WORKMAN and R. POPE, *The letter of John Huss*, London, 1904. The account of POGGIO, who witnessed the trial and death of Jerome, is translated in *A literary source-book of the renaissance*, by M. WHITCOMB, 2nd edition, Philadelphia, 1903, 44–51.

Extracts from the vivid sermons of ST. BERNARDINO are translated in the *Sermons of St. Bernardino*, edited by N. ORLANDI, Siena, 1920, and *The examples of St. Bernardino*, translation by A. HOWE, London, 1926. Another illustration of popular preaching is JOHANNES HEROLT, *Miracles of the Virgin Mary* (Broadway Medieval Library), 1928. For the northern mystics see W. R. INGE, *Light, life and love*, New York, 1904, selections from ECKHART, TAULER, SUSO, et al.; *Meister Eckhart*, translation by C. DE B. EVANS, London, 1924; *John Tauler, Twenty five sermons*, translation by S. WINKWORTH, new edition, London, 1906; *ibid.*, *The inner way*, translation by A. HULTON, 3rd edition, London, 1909; *ibid.*, *Meditations on the life and passion of our Lord Jesus Christ*, translation by A. CRUIKSHANCK, New York, 1925; *Suso, life*, translation by T. F. KNOX, London, 1913; *ibid.*, *The little book of eternal wisdom*, London, 1910; RUYSBROECK, *The XII Béguines*, translation by J. FRANCIS, London, 1913; *Theologia Germanica*, translation by S. WINKWORTH, new edition, London, 1907; RICHARD ROLLE, *The form of perfect living*, edited by G. HODGSON, London, 1910; *ibid.*: *The fire of love and the mending of life*, edited by F. Comper, London, 1914; Julian of Norwich, *Revelations of divine love*, edited by G. Warrack, London, 1901; *Comfortable words for Christ's lovers*, edited by D. Harford, London, 1911; *The cell of self knowledge: seven old English mystical works*, edited by E. Gardner (Medieval Library) London, 1910. *The Imitation of Christ* may be read in any one of many versions and the *Complete works* of Thomas à Kempis have recently been published in translation in London, edited by Duthoit, Arthur and Scully, 1905ff.

Maps. Shepherd, *Atlas*, 81, has a map showing the division of Europe during the great schism, 1378–1417.

C. Bibliography

General books. The general histories of the church, nos. **393–498,** are most useful, although many histories of the Empire, of France, Germany, and Italy, nos. **499–621,** are of almost equal value. See also the encyclopaedias for the history of the church, nos. **104–14.** For the Hussite movement the general histories of Bohemia, nos. **699–703.**

Church reform in the later middle ages. J. Guiraud, *L'église romaine et les origines de la renaissance*, 3rd edition, Paris, 1904, begins with the pontificate of Boniface VIII. F. Thudichum, *Papsttum und Reformation im Mittelalter, 1143–1517*, Leipzig, 1903. G. Ficker, *Das ausgehende Mittelalter und sein Verhältniss zur Reformation*, Leipzig, 1903. F. Rocquain, *La cour de Rome et l'esprit de rêforme avant Luther*, vols. I–III, Paris, 1893–97. J. Haller, *Papsttum und Kirchenreform: vier Kapitel zur Geschichte des ausgehenden Mittelalters*, vol. I, Berlin, 1903. L. Celier, "L'idée de réforme à la cour pontificale du concile de Bâle au concile de Latran," *R.Q.H.*, LXXXVI (1909), 418–35. A. L. Smith, *Church and state in the middle ages. Vorreformationsgeschichtliche Forschungen*, edited by H. Finke, Münster, 1900ff.

Boniface VIII and Europe. H. Finke, *Aus den Tagen Bonifaz VIII: Funde und Forschungen*, Münster, 1902 (Vorreformationsgeschichtliche Forschungen, 2). J. del Lungo, *Da Bonifazio VIII ad Arrigo VII*, Milan, 1899. L. Tosti, *Storia di Bonifazio VIII*, 2nd edition, Cassino, 1886. K. Wenck, "War Bonifaz VIII ein Ketzer?", *H.Z.*, XCIV (1905), 1–66. R. Scholz, "Zur Beurteilung Bonifaz' VIII und seines sittlich-religiösen Charakters," *H.V.J.S.*, IX (1906), 470–515. W. Drumann, *Geschichte Bonifacius* VIII, 2 vols., Königsberg, 1852. P. Dupuy, *Histoire du differend d'entre le pape Boniface VIII et Philippes le Bel roy de France*, Paris, 1655, contains the most important documents from French archives. L. Mohler, *Die Kardinäle Jacob und Peter Calonna: ein Beitrag zur Geschichte des Zeitalters Bonifaz VIII*, Paderborn, 1914 (Quellen und Forschungen aus dem Gebiete der Geschichte, XVII). R. Scholz, *Die Publizistik zur Zeit Philipps des Schönen und Bonifaz' VIII*, Stuttgart, 1903 (Kirchenrechtliche Abhandlungen, 6–8). F. Ehrmann, *Die Bulle "Unam sanctam" des Papstes Bonifacius VIII nach ihrem authentischen Wortlaut erklärt*, Munich, 1896. J. Berchtold, *Die Bulle Unam sanctam: ihre wahre Bedeutung und Tragweite für Staat und Kirche*, Munich, 1887. C. Sommer, *Die Anklage der*

Idolatrie gegen Papst Bonifaz VIII und seine Porträtstatuen, Freiburg, 1920. R. W. and A. J. CARLYLE, *A history of medieval political theory*. J. RIVIÈRE, *Le problème de l'église et de l'état au temps de Philippe le Bel: étude de théologie positive*, Paris, 1926.

For a short contemporary account of the scene at Anagni see KERVYN DE LETTENHOVE, "Une relation inédite de l'attentat d'Anagni," *R.Q.H.*, XI (1872), 511–20. The subject is treated in detail by R. HOLTZMANN, *Wilhelm von Nogaret, Rat und Grossiegelbewahrer Philipps des Schönen von Frankreich*, Freiburg, 1898 (Diss.). C. V. LANGLOIS, *Les papiers de Guillaume de Nogaret et de Guillaume de Plaisians au Trésor des Chartes*, Paris, 1908. P. FEDELE, "Rassegna delle publicazioni su Bonifazio VIII e sull' età sua, degli anni 1914–1921," *Archivio della r. società romana di storia patria*, 1921, 311–32.

" Babylonish Captivity " of the papacy. G. MOLLAT, *Les papes d'Avignon* (*1305–78*), Paris, 1912; *Etudes critiques sur les vitae paparum avenionensium d'Etienne Baluze*, Paris, 1917. S. BALUZIUS, *Vitae paparum avenionensium, hoc est Historia pontificum Romanorum qui in Gallia sederunt ab anno Christi MCCCV usque ad annum MCCCXCIV*, new edition, edited by G. MOLLAT, vols. I–IV, Paris, 1914–22. T. OKEY, *The story of Avignon*, New York, 1911 (Mediaeval towns). M. SOUCHON, *Die Papstwahlen von Bonifaz VIII bis auf Urban VI und die Entstehung des Schismas 1378*, Braunschweig, 1888. H. FINKE, *Papsttum und Untergang des Templerordens*, 2 vols. in one, Münster, 1907 (Vorreformationsgeschichtliche Forschungen, edited by H. FINKE, IV–V). H. C. LEA, *History of the inquisition in the middle ages*, III, chs. I, V. A. EITEL, *Der Kirchenstaat unter Klemens V* [1305–14], Berlin, 1906 (part 1 of Abhandlungen zur mittleren und neueren Geschichte). K. JACOB, *Studien über Papst Benedikt XII* (*1334–42*), Berlin, 1910. C. BOUVIER, *Vienne au temps du concile, 1311–1312*, Paris, 1912. E. MÜNTZ, "L'argent et le luxe à la cour pontificale d'Avignon," *R.Q.H.*, LXVI (1899), 5–44, 378–406. J. MONTERO Y VIDAL, *Benoît XII* (*1334–1342*), 2 vols., Paris, 1919. L. H. LABANDE, *Avignon au XVe siècle. Légation de Charles de Bourbon et du Cardinal Julien de la Rovère*, Monaco and Paris, 1920. G. MOLLAT, *La collation des bénéfices ecclésiastiques sous les papes d'Avignon* (*1305–1378*), Paris, 1921. A. DEELEY, "Papal provision and royal rights of patronage in the early fourteenth century," *E.H.R.*, XLIII (1928), 497–527. C. TIHON, "Les expectatives in forma pauperum particulièrement au XIVe siècle," *Bulletin de l'Institut historique belge de Rome*, Liége, 1925. L. H. LABANDE, *Le palais des papes et les monuments d'Avignon au XIVe siècle*, 2 vols., Marseilles, 1925. R. BRUN, *Avignon au temps des papes*, Paris, 1928. S. PUIG Y PUIG, *Pedro di Luna, ultimo papa de Aviñon, 1387–1430*, Barcelona, 1920. H. WURM, *Cardinal Albornoz, der zweite Begründer des Kirchenstaats*, Paderborn, 1892.

Saint Catherine of Siena and pope Gregory IX. E. G. GARDNER, *Saint Catherine of Siena: a study in the religion, literature, and history of the fourteenth century in Italy*, London, 1907. JERUSHA D. RICHARDSON, *The mystic bride: a study of the life-story of Catherine of Siena*, London [1911]. [MAR-

GARET ROBERTS], *Saint Catherine of Siena and her times*, London, 1906. P. GAUTHIEZ, *Sainte Catherine de Sienne, 1347–1380*, Paris, 1916. K. WENCK, *Die Heilige Elizabeth und Pabst Gregor IX*, Munich, 1908 (extract from the review *Hochland*, November, 1907). F. BLIETMETZRIEDER, "Raimund von Capua und Caterina von Siena zu Beginn des grossen abendländischen Schismas," *Hist. Jahrbuch*, XXX (1909), 231–73. C. M. WOODROCK, *Saint Catherine of Siena, her life and times*, London, 1916. N. ZUCCHELLI and E. LAZZARESCHI, *S. Caterina de Siena ed i Pisani*, Florence, 1917. ELEONORE VON SECKENDORFF, *Die kirchenpolitische Tätigkeit der Heiligen Katharina von Siena unter Papst Gregor XI, 1371–1378*, Berlin, 1917. J. JÖRGENSEN, *Santa Catalina de Siena*, Madrid, 1925.

The great western schism, 1378–1417. N. VALOIS, *La France et le grand schisme d'Occident*, 4 vols., Paris, 1896–1902. L. SALEMBIER, *Le grand schisme d'Occident*, Paris, 1900; 4th edition, 1902, translated, *The great western schism*, London, 1907. L. GAYET, *Le grand schisme d'Occident*, vols. I and II, Paris, 1889–90 (see review by E. ALLAIN, *R.Q.H.*, XLVII (1890), 582–96). A. RASTOUL, *L'unité religieuse pendant le grand schisme d'Occident (1378–1417)*, Paris, 1904. C. LOCKE, *The age of the great western schism*, Edinburgh, 1897.

L. SALEMBIER, *Deux conciles inconnus au temps du grand schisme*, Lille, 1902. M. SOUCHON, *Die Papstwahlen in der Zeit des grossen Schismas (1378–1417)*, 2 vols., Braunschweig, 1898–1900. F. J. SCHEUFFGEN, *Beiträge zur Geschichte des grossen Schismas*, Freiburg, 1887. L. MIROT, *La politique pontificale et le retour du Saint-Siège à Rome en 1376*, Paris, 1899. J. P. KIRSCH, *Die Rückkehr der Päpste Urban V und Gregor XI von Avignon nach Rom*, Paderborn, 1898. E. RODOCANACHI, *Histoire de Rome de 1354 à 1471: l'antagonisme entre les Romains et le Saint-Siège*, Paris, 1922. F. EHRLE, *Der Sentenzenkommentar Peters von Candia, des Pisaner Papstes Alexanders V*, Münster, 1925. (See *E.H.R.*, XLIII, 111–13.) O. HÜTTEBRÄUKER, *Der Minoritenorden zur Zeit des grossen Schismas*, Berlin, 1893 (Diss.). R. P. FAGES, *Histoire de Saint Vincent Ferrier*, Paris, 1894; 2nd edition, revised, 2 vols., 1901. J. GUIRAUD, *L'état pontifical après le grand schisme: étude de géographie politique*, Paris, 1896, part of no. **887**. A. BAYOT, "Un traité inconnu sur le grand schisme dans la bibliothèque des ducs de Bourgogne," *Revue d'histoire ecclésiastique*, Oct., 1908.

The conciliar movement. N. VALOIS, *La crise religieuse du XVe siècle: le pape et le concile (1418–50)*, 2 vols., Paris, 1909. F. BLIETMETZRIEDER, *Das Generalkonzil im grossen abendländischen Schisma*, Paderborn, 1904. A. KNEER, *Die Entstehung der Konziliaren Theorie*, Rome, 1893 (Römische Quartalschrift, supplement 1). W. THÉREMIN, *Beiträge zur öffentlichen Meinung über Kirche und Staat in der städtischen Geschichtsschreibung Deutschlands von 1399–1415*, Berlin, 1909 (part 68 of Historische Studien, edited by E. EBERING). J. HASGHAGEN, "Papsttum und Laiengewalten im Verhältnis zu Schisma und Konzilien," *H.V.J.S.*, XXIII (1926), 325–37. J. H. VON WESSENBERG, *Die grossen Kirchenversammlungen des 15 und 16 Jahrhunderts*, 4 vols., Constance, 1840.

Following is some biographical material on men who took a prominent part in the movement. A. LAFONTAINE, *Jehan Gerson (1363–1429)*, Paris, 1906. A. J. MASSON, *Jean Gerson*, Lyons, 1894. J. B. SCHWAB, *Johannes Gerson*, Würzberg, 1858. J. L. CONNOLLY, *John Gerson, reformer and mystic*, Louvain, 1928. (*Université de Louvain, Recueil de travaux publiês par les membres des conférences d'histoire et de philologie*, 2nd series, 12th fasc.). L. SALEMBIER, *Petrus de Alliaco*, Lille, 1886. P. TSCHACKERT, *Peter von Ailli*, Gotha, 1877. C. SCHMIDT, *Kard. Nikolaus Cusanus*, Coblenz, 1907. E. VANSTEENBERGHE, *Le cardinal Nicolas de Cues (1401–1464), l'action, la pensée*, Paris, 1920 (Bibliothèque du XVe siècle, XXIV). P. ROTTA, *Il cardinale Nicolò di Cusa: la vita e il pensiero*, Milan, 1928. (For additional literature see DAHLMANN-WAITZ, *Quellenkunde*, no. 7024). E. KÖNIG, *Kardinal Giordano Orsini: ein Lebensbild aus der Zeit der grossen Konzilien und des Humanismus*, Freiburg, 1906. A. RÖSLER, *Kardinal Johannes Dominici 1357–1419: ein Reformatorenbild aus der Zeit des grossen Schismas*, Freiburg, 1893. H. V. SAUERLAND, "Cardinal Johannes Dominici und sein Verhalten zu den kirchlichen Unionsbestrebungen während der Jahre 1406–1415," *Zeitschift für Kirchengeschichte*, IX (1888), 240–92; X (1889), 345–98. P. MANDONNET, "Beiträge zur Geschichte des Kardinals Dominici," *Hist. Jahrbuch*, XXI (1900), 388–402. K. WENCK, "Konrad von Gelnhausen und die Quellen der konziliaren Theorie," *H.Z.*, LXXVII (1896), 6–61. W. HASENOHR, *Der Patriarch Johannes Maurosii von Antiochien: ein Charakterbild aus der Zeit der Reformkonzilien*, Berlin, 1909.

Council of Pisa. J. LENFANT, *Histoire du concile de Pise*, 2 vols., Amsterdam, 1724–27. E. J. KITTS, *In the days of the councils: a sketch of the life and time of Baldassare Cossa, afterwards pope John XXIII*, London, 1908.

Council of Constance. H. FINKE, *Forschungen und Quellen zur Geschichte des Konstanzer Konzils*, Paderborn, 1889; *Bilder vom Konstanzer Konzil*, Heidelberg, 1903 (Neujahrblatt der badischen historischen Kommission). H. BLUMENTHAL, *Die Vorgeschichte des Konstanzer Konzils bis zur Berufung*, Halle, 1897 (Diss.). A. LENNÉ, *Der erste literarische Kampf auf dem Konstanzer Konzil im Nov. und Dez. 1414*, Rome, 1913. J. KEPPLER, *Die Politik des Kardinalkollegiums in Konstanz, Jan.–März 1418*, Münster, 1899. H. DENIFLE, "Les délégués des universités françaises au concile de Constance," in *Revue des bibliothèques* (1892). B. HÜBLER, *Die Konstanzer Reformation und die Konkordate von 1418*, Leipzig, 1867. L. TOSTI, *Storia del concilio di Constanza . . . con documenti*, 2 vols., Naples, 1853, translated into German by B. ARNOLD, *Geschichte des Konzilium's von Konstanz*, Schaffhausen, 1860. J. LENFANT, *Histoire du concile de Constance*, 2 vols., Amsterdam, 1714. H. G. PETER, *Die Informationen Papst Johanns XXIII und dessen Flucht von Konstanz bis Schaffhausen*, Freiburg, 1926. G. C. POWERS, *Nationalism at the council of Constance*, Washington, 1928 (Diss.).

Wyclif. G. M. TREVELYAN, *England in the age of Wycliffe*, London, 1899; 4th edition, 1909. H. B. WORKMAN, *John Wyclif*, 2 vols., Oxford, 1926. For other literature on Wyclif and his movement see GROSS, no. **36.**

John Huss. H. B. WORKMAN, *The dawn of the reformation*, vol. II, *The age of Hus*, London, 1902. G. VON LECHLER, *Johannes Hus*, Halle, 1889. J. LOSERTH, *Huss und Wiclif: zur Genesis der husitischen Lehre*, Prague and Leipzig, 1884; 2nd edition, Munich, 1925; translated by M. J. EVANS, *Wiclif and Hus*, London, 1884. E. H. GILLETT, *The life and time of John Huss: or the Bohemian reformation of the fifteenth century*, 2 vols., Boston, 1863. W. BERGER, *Johannes Hus und König Sigmund*, Augsburg, 1871. C. HÖFLER, *Magister Johannes Hus und der Ausgang der deutschen Professoren und Studenten aus Prag 1409*, Prague, 1864. J. MARTINU, *Die Waldesier und die husitische Reformation in Böhmen*, Vienna, 1910. E. AMANN, "Jacobel et les débuts de la controverse utraquiste," *Miscellanea Francesco Ehrle*, I, 375–87, Rome, 1924. POGGIO-BRACCIOLINI, *Todesgeschichte des Johannes Huss und des Hieronymus von Prag: beide um ihres Glaubens Willen verbrannt zu Konstanz am 6 Juli 1415 und am 30 Mai 1416 geschildert in Sendbriefen des Poggius Florentinus*, Constance, 1926.

Hussite wars. Count LÜTZOW, *The Hussite wars*, London and New York, 1914. E. DENIS, *Huss et la guerre des Hussites*, Paris, 1878; *Fin de l'indépendance de la Bohême*, 2 vols., Paris, 1890, has a full bibliography. J. LENFANT, *Histoire de la guerre des Hussites et du concile de Basle*, 2 vols., Utrecht, 1731, supplements by J. DE BEAUSOBRE, 1745. F. v. BEZOLD, *Zur Geschichte des Husitentums*, Munich, 1874. F. PALACKY, *Urkundliche Beiträge zur Geschichte des Husitenkrieges*, Prague, 1872. W. W. TOMEK, *Johann Zizka*, translated into German by V. PROCHASKA, Prague, 1882.

Council of Basel. P. LAZARUS, *Das Basler Konzil*, Berlin, 1912. G. PÉROUSE, *Le cardinal Louis Aleman, président du concile de Bâle, et la fin du grand schisme*, Paris, 1905. E. PREISWERK, *Der Einfluss Aragons auf den Prozess des Basler Konzils gegen Papst Eugen IV*, Basle, 1902 (Diss.). O. RICHTER, *Die Organisation und Geschäftsordnung des Basler Konzils*, Leipzig, 1877. F. SCHNEIDER, *Der europäische Friedenskongress von Arras (1435) und die Friedenspolitik Papst Eugens IV und des Basler Konzils*, Greiz, 1919. E. BURSCHE, *Die Reformarbeiten des Basler Konzils*, Lodz, 1921. R. WITTRAM, *Die französische Politik auf dem Basler Konzil während der Zeit seiner Blüte*, Riga, 1927.

Council of Ferrara-Florence. E. VACANDARD, "An attempt at union between Greeks and Latins at the council of Ferrara-Florence, 1438-1439," *Constructive quarterly*, June, 1917.

Pragmatic Sanction of Bourges. N. VALOIS, *Histoire de la Pragmatique Sanction de Bourges sous Charles VII*, Paris, 1906; see review by J. HALLER, "Die Pragmatische Sanktion von Bourges," *H.Z.*, CIII (1909), 1–51. J. SALVINI, *L'application de la Pragmatique Sanction sous Charles VII et sous Louis XI au chapitre cathédral de Paris*, Paris, 1912. A. WERMINGHOFF, *Nationalkirchliche Bestrebungen im deutschen Mittelalter*, Stuttgart, 1910, part of no. **491.**

The bull Execrabilis. G. B. PICOTTI, *La pubblicazione e i primi effetti della Execrabilis di Pio II*, Perugia, 1914 (extract from Archivio della r. Società romana di storia patria).

Papal finances in the 14th and 15th centuries. G. MOLLAT and C. SAMARAN, *La fiscalité pontificale en France au XIVe siècle*, Paris, 1905, part of no. **887**. E. HENNIG, *Die päpstlichen Zehnten aus Deutschland im Zeitalter des avignonesischen Papsttums und während des grossen Schismas*, Halle, 1909. J. P. KIRSCH, *Die päpstlichen Annaten in Deutschland während des 14 Jahrhunderts*, vol. I, Paderborn, 1903 (part 9 of Quellen und Forschungen, Görresgesellschaft). *Die Einnahmen der apostolischen Kammer unter Johann XXII* [*1316–1334*], edited by E. GÖLLER, 2 vols., Paderborn, 1910. A. ECKSTEIN, *Zur Finanzlage Felix V und des Basler Konzils*, Berlin, 1912. A. GOTTLOB, *Aus der Camera apostolica des 15 Jahrhunderts*, Innsbruck, 1889. M. TANGL, *Die päpstlichen Kanzleiordnungen, 1200–1500*, Innsbruck, 1894. See also under outline XXIV.

Religion of the people. G. BARZELOTTI, *Italia mistica e Italia pagana*, Rome, 1891. E. WALSER, "Der Sinn des Lebens im Zeitalter der Renaissance," *Archiv für Kulturgeschichte*, XVI (1926), 300–16. P. THUREAU-DANGIN, *Un prédicateur populaire dans l'Italie de la renaissance*, Paris, 1896. R. CRUEL, *Geschichte der deutschen Predigt im Mittelalter*, Detmold, 1879. J. T. WELTER, *L'Exemplum dans la littérature religieuse et didactique du moyen âge*, Paris, 1927. A. AUGER, *Etude sur les mystiques des Pays-Bas au moyen âge*, Brussels, 1902. W. PREGER, *Geschichte der deutschen Mystik im Mittelalter*, 3 vols., Leipzig, 1874–93; "Beiträge zur Geschichte der religiösen Bewegung in den Niederlanden in der 2. Hälfte des 14. Jahrhunderts," *Abh. Munich Acad.*, vol. XXI (1894), 1–64. H. DELACROIX, *Le mysticisme spéculatif en Allemagne au XIVe siècle*, Paris, 1900. T. ALTMEYER, *Les précurseurs de la réforme aux Pays-Bas*, 2 vols., Paris, 1886. H. DENIFLE, *M. Eckeharts lateinische Schriften und die Grundanschauung seiner Lehre* (Archiv für Literatur- und Sprachgeschichte, II, 416–652). G. SIEDEL, *Die Mystik Taulers*, Leipzig, 1913. W. WINDSTOSSER, *Etude sur la 'Théologie germanique,'* Paris, 1912. P. PUYOL, *L'auteur du livre de Imitatione Christi*, 2 vols., Paris, 1899, 1900.

Original sources. H. X. ARQUILLIÈRE, *Le plus ancien traité de l'église: Jacques de Viterbe, De regimine christiano*, Paris, 1926. This is the first printed edition of an important tract which throws contemporary light on the conflict between Boniface VIII and Philip the Fair. G. LIZERAND, *Le dossier de l'affaire des Templiers*. E. DÉPREZ, *Clément VI, 1342–1352, lettres closes, patentes et curiales*, fasc. 1 and 2, 1921–25. A. AUER, "Eine verschollene Denkschrift über das grosse Interdikt des 14 Jahrhunderts," *Hist. Jahrbuch*, XLVI (1926), 532–49, report on the hitherto lost *Exhortatio ad Carolum IV* written by the Dominican friar JOHANN VON DAMBACH in 1347–48, in which Charles is urged to undertake the reform of the church; the article includes a complete reprint of the *exhortatio*. *Costituzioni Egidianae dell' anno MCCCLVII*, edited by P. SELLA, Rome, 1912. *Les registres d'Urbain V* (*1362–1363*), *d'après les manuscrits originaux du Vatican*, publiés par M. Dubrulle, Paris, 1927 (Bib. de l'école française de Rome). A. FIERENS and C. TIBON (editors), *Lettres d'Urbain V*, vol. I (1362–66), Brussels, 1928 (Analecta Vaticana, Belgica, vol. IX). K. HANQUET, *Docu-*

ments relatifs au grand schisme, vol. I: *Suppliques de Clément VII, 1378–79*, Paris, 1924. (Analecta Vaticana, Belgica, vol. VIII). *Literarische Polemik zu Beginn des grossen abendländischen Schismas (Kard. Petrus Flandrin, Kard. Petrus Amelii, Konrad von Gelnhausen): ungedruckte Texte und Untersuchungen*, edited by F. J. P. BLIEMETZRIEDER, Vienna, 1910, vol. 1 of no. **900.** THEODORICUS DE NIEM, *De schismate libri tres*, edited by G. ERLER, Leipzig, 1890. PLATINA, *Vitae pontificum*, in Muratori, Rerum Italicarum Scriptores, vol. III, part I, 1913. LEONARDO ARETINO, secretary to John XXIII, *Commentarius rerum suo tempore gestarum*, Muratori, *op. cit.*, vol. XIX, part III, 1914–26, 423–58. ADAM OF USK, *Chronicon*, edited and translated by E. M. THOMPSON, 2nd edition, London, 1904, a lively description of Rome and the papal court at the beginning of the fifteenth century. N. TOMMASEO, *Le lettere di S^a^ Caterina da Siena*, 4 vols., Florence, 1860. For the works of such men as PIERRE D'AILLY and JEAN GERSON, see POTTHAST, *Wegweiser*, no. **18,** and MOLINIER, *Les sources*, no. **21.** D. H. CARNAHAN, *The Ad deum vadit of Jean Gerson*, University of Illinois studies, Urbana, 1918. See also the great collections of source material for the history of the church, nos. **953–64,** and for the history of Bohemia, no. **986,** note.

The great collection of sources for the council of Constance is *Magnum oecumenicum Constantiense concilium*, edited by H. VAN DER HARDT, 6 vols., Frankfort, 1700, with an index vol. by G. C. BOHNSTEDT, Berlin, 1742 (now also reprinted in MANSI, no. **962,** vols. XXVII–XXVIII). This must be supplemented by *Acta concilii Constantiensis*, edited by H. FINKE, 4 vols., Münster, 1896–1928 and ULRICH VON RICHENTAL, *Das Conciliumbuch zu Constanz*, edited by N. A. and M. R. BUCK, in *Bibliothek des literarischen Vereins*, vol. CLVIII, Stuttgart, 1882. A reprint of the original Augsburg edition of 1483 with its quaint illustrations was published at Potsdam in 1922. For the letters of a delegate to the council from the University of Vienna, see PETER OF PULKA, *Epistolae*, in the Archiv für Kunde österreichischer Geschichtsquellen, vol. XV, Vienna, 1856, 3–70.

For the Council of Basel we have *Concilium Basiliense: Studien und Quellen zur Geschichte des Konzils von Basel*, 7 vols., edited by J. HALLER, and others, Basel, 1896–1926. *Monumenta conciliorum generalium seculi XV: Scriptorum I, II, III*, edited by O. RICHTER, Vienna, 1857–95; and AENEAS SYLVIUS PICCOLOMINI, *De rebus Basileae gestis*, edited by M. CATALANI, Firmi, 1803, by C. FEA, Rome, 1823.

For the Council of Ferrara-Florence there should be added to the documents in Mansi, no. **962,** E. CECCONI, *Studi storici sul concilio de Firenze*, part I (all published), Florence, 1869, an indispensable collection of materials for the preliminary stages of the council, and SGUROPOULOS, *Vera historia unionis non verae inter Graecos et Latinos*, edited by CREYGHTON, The Hague, 1660, the report of a Greek hostile to the union. See also VESPASIANO DA BISTICCI, *Vite de uomini illustri del secolo XV*, edited by A. BARTOLI, Florence, 1859. A famous attack on the temporal authority of the pope was LORENZO VALLA's treatise on the Donation of Constantine, produced in 1440 and edited with translation by C. Coleman, New Haven, 1922. Lorenzo Valla, *Opera*, Basel, 1540. W. Schwahn, *Laurentii Vallae de Falso credita et ementita Constantini Donatione Declamatio*, Leipzig, 1928.

Joannis Hus, *Opera omnia*, edited by W. Flajshans, 3 vols., Prague, 1903–[08]. *Beiträge zur Geschichte der husitischen Bewegung*, edited by J. Loserth, 5 parts, Vienna, 1877–95 (Archiv für österreichische Geschichte, 55, 57, 60, 75, 82). F. Palacky, *Documenta M. Joannis Hus*, Prague, 1869. S. H. Thomson, *Mag. J. Hus, Tractatus responsivus*, Princeton, 1927.

Preachers and mystics. *Predighe volgari di S. Bernardino da Siena*, Ed. Bianchi, 1880. Meister Eckhart, *Werke*, edited by F. Pfeiffer, Göttingen, 1924. *Meister Eckeharts Schriften und Predigten aus dem Mittelhochdeutschen übersetzt*, H. Büttner, 2 vols., Jena, 1921–23. H. Seuse's, *Deutsche Schriften*, edited by W. Lehmann, 2 vols., Jena, 1911. *Theologia deutsche mit einer neudeutschen Uebersetzung*, edited by F. Pfeiffer, 4th edition, Gütersloh, 1900. Thomas à Kempis, *Opera omnia*, edited by J. Pohl, 7 vols., Freiburg, 1902–21. *De imitatione Christi*, edited by A. Hyma, New York, 1927. Gerard Groat, *Epistolae*, edited by Acquoy, Amsterdam, 1857.

Bibliographies. Dahlmann-Waitz, *Quellenkunde*, is the most serviceable bibliography; see pp. 420–23, 429–32, 450–52, 456–60, and especially 503–24. The elaborate bibliographies at the head of chapters in Loserth, *Geschichte des späteren Mittelalters*, are valuable. See also the bibliographies for church history, nos. **49–55.**

XXX. FRANCE DURING THE HUNDRED YEARS' WAR

A. Outline

1. France at the end of the direct line of Capetian kings, 1328. The strength of the monarchy. Weakness of the feudal nobility. Large extent of the kingdom of France, and the brilliancy of its capital, Paris. Effective monarchial institutions. Dominance of the French kings over the papacy at Avignon. Loyalty and self-effacement of the people. The question of nationality in the middle ages.

2. France under the Valois kings, 1328–1498. A period of retrogression from the glorious position of France under the Capetians. Weakness of the royal line. Trials and mistakes of the period of the Hundred Years' War. Awakening of the bourgeoisie. Renewed strength of the feudal nobility leading to civil war and almost wrecking the monarchy. The decline and desolation of the city of Paris an index of the times.

3. The causes of the war: (1) territorial: the standing menace to France of the remnants of the old Norman empire on the continent; (2) dynastic: the claim of king Edward III of France to the French crown; (3) economic: the English wool-trade with Flanders, Jacob van Artevelde of Ghent. Relations of France with Scotland.

4. The succession to the French throne in 1328:

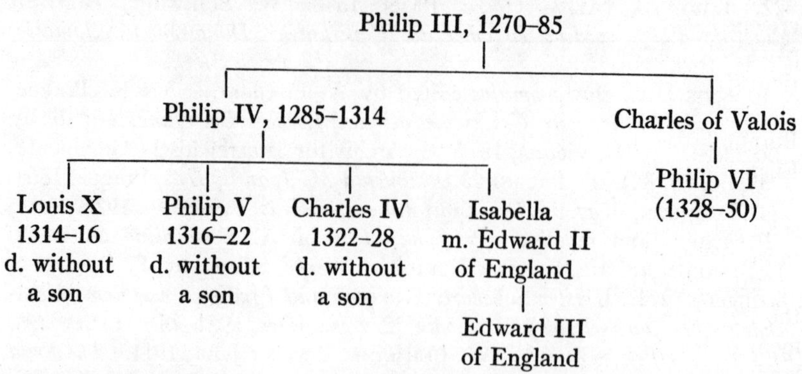

5. The periods of the war: (1) 1338–80, first forty-year period of active war ending favorably for France; (2) 1380–1415, thirty-five year period of disastrous comparative peace; (3) 1415–53, second forty-year period of active war, ending with the expulsion of the English from France.

6. The war to 1360. English naval victory at Sluys, 1340. The war in Brittany. Defeat of the French at Crécy, August, 1346. Calais captured by the English in 1347. Overwhelming defeat of the French at Poitiers, 1356, where the French king, John II, was captured. For the Black Death and the *Jacquerie* see outline XXVI. The treaty of Brétigny, 1360.

7. Constitutional upheaval in France 1355–58. The question of taxation and mismanagement of funds before the Estates General. Etienne Marcel, provost of the merchants of Paris, and Robert le Coq, bishop of Laon. The "Great Ordinance" of 1357. Complications caused by the *Jacquerie.* Failure of the constitutional movement and the murder of Etienne Marcel in 1358.

8. French successes, 1360–78. The "Great Company" of freebooters in France. Bertrand du Guesclin and the Black Prince. Renewal of the war in 1369. Gradual recovery of territory by the French until in 1378 the English held only Bayonne, Bourdeaux, Brest, Cherbourg, and Calais.

9. France during the great western schism, 1378–1417. Weakness of Charles VI, 1380–1422, who became insane in 1392. The defeat of the Flemish under Philip van Artevelde at the battle of Roosebek, 1382, was an index of the rise of the feudal nobility to old-time power. Riots in Paris. The *Marmousets.* The *Tuchins.* The struggle for the regency led to civil war between the Burgundians and Orleanists (Armagnacs). Reign of terror in Paris (*Cabochiens*).

10. The English invasion of France under king Henry V, 1415, aided by the Burgundian party. His claim to the French crown. Victory of the English at Agincourt, 1415. Treaty of Troyes, 1420. When Henry V of England and Charles VI of France died in 1422, Henry VI, son of Henry V, was proclaimed at Paris king of France and England, according to the terms of this treaty. Weakness of the French king, Charles VII (1422–61).

11. Joan of Arc. A peasant girl born in Domrémy in Lorraine. Her "voices." In 1429 she raised the siege of Orleans and had Charles VII crowned at Rheims. Her capture, trial, and death at the stake, in the market place of Rouen, May 30, 1431, at about nineteen years of age. Her rehabilitation. Joan of Arc and French patriotism. Her canonization, in 1919.

12. The expulsion of the English from France. The *Ecorcheurs*. Philip of Burgundy became reconciled with Charles VII by the treaty of Arras. The English lost Normandy in 1450, Guienne in 1453, and retained only Calais.

13. Results of the Hundred Years' War. Reaction in favor of absolutism. Low state of civilization in France at the end of the war. The projected crusade against the Turks in 1454.

14. Louis XI, 1461–83, and Charles the Bold of Burgundy. Leagues of the Public Weal. Death of Charles at Nancy in 1477 and the dismemberment of the Burgundian possessions. The House of Austria in the Netherlands. Autocratic rule of Louis XI. Decline of the feudal nobility.

15. The invasion of Italy by Charles VIII in 1494 began a new era in the history of France.

16. Civilization, learning, and art in France during the fourteenth and fifteenth centuries.

17. The Valois kings of France, 1328–1498:
Philip VI, 1328–50.
John II, 1350–64.
Charles V, 1364–80.
Charles VI, 1380–1422.
Charles VII, 1422–61.
Louis XI, 1461–83.
Charles VIII, 1483–98.

18. Kings of England, 1327–1485:
Edward III, 1327–77.
Richard II, 1377–99.
Henry IV, 1399–1413.
Henry V, 1413–22.
Henry VI, 1422–61.
Edward IV, 1461–83.
Edward V, 1483.
Richard III, 1483–85.

B. Special Recommendations for Reading

Brief general accounts. Adams, *Growth of the French nation*, 108–46. Hassall, *The French people*, chs. viii–ix. Headlam, *France*, chs. x–xiii. T. F. Tout, *France and England: their relations in the middle ages and now*, Manchester, 1922. Munro and Sontag, *Middle ages*, chs. xxv and xxvi. Tilley, *Medieval France*, 103–52; see also chs. iii and iv. E. Emerton, *Beginning of modern Europe*, ch. vi. Thorndike, *Medieval Europe*, ch. xxvii. Funck-Brentano, *Middle ages*, chs. xix–xx. Sellery and Krey, *Medieval foundations*, 294–300.

For military history, see Oman, *Art of war*, book VIII; and Munro and Sellery, *Medieval civilization*, 547–74.

Longer general accounts. Kitchin, *History of France*, I, book IV; II, book I. Masson, *Mediaeval France*, chs. ix–xvi. Lodge, *Close of the middle ages*, chs. iv, xv–xvi. Lavisse et Rambaud, *Histoire générale*, III, chs. ii–iv. Loserth, *Geschichte des späteren Mittelalters*, 324–42, 541–62, 670–83. The standard account in French is Lavisse, *Histoire de France*, IV, both parts.

Etienne Marcel. E. EMERTON, *Beginning of modern Europe*, 207–14.

The Black Prince and Bertrand du Guesclin. R. P. DUNN-PATTISON, *The Black Prince*, London, 1910. E. V. STODDARD, *Bertrand du Guesclin, constable of France: his life and times*, New York, 1897.

Joan of Arc. There is an immense amount of literature on the Maid of Orleans; unfortunately, much of it marred by bitter polemics. A safe course for the English reader is to approach the subject through the pages of two American writers, LEA, *The inquisition of the middle ages*, III, 338–78; and F. C. LOWELL, *Joan of Arc*, Boston, 1896. Following are some of the biographies. A. FRANCE, *Vie de Jeanne d'Arc*, 2 vols., Paris, 1908, translated by WINIFRED STEPHENS, *Life of Joan of Arc*, London, 1909. A. LANG, *The Maid of France: being the story of the life and death of Jeanne d'Arc*, London and New York, 1908, is in large measure a review of the book by A. France. G. HANOTAUX, *Jeanne d'Arc*, Paris, 1911. MARY R. BANGS, *Jeanne d'Arc, the Maid of France*, Boston, 1910. GRACE JAMES, *Joan of Arc*, New York, 1910.

Flanders. E. EMERTON, *Beginning of modern Europe*, 199–207.

Louis XI and Charles the Bold. A. C. S. HAGGARD, *Louis XI and Charles the Bold*, London, 1913. C. HARE (pseudonym), *The life of Louis XI, the rebel dauphin and the statesman king, from his original letters and other documents*, London and New York, 1907. E. A. FREEMAN, "Charles the Bold," *Historical essays*, first series, 314–72. RUTH PUTNAM, *Charles the Bold: last duke of Burgundy, 1433–1477*, New York, 1908.

Civilization, learning, and art. The best account is in LAVISSE, *Histoire de France*, IV, part II, 115–227, 436–52, where an abundance of literature is cited, much of which appears in part III below.

Original sources. The inimitable contemporary narrator of the first part of the Hundred Years' War is Sir JOHN FROISSART, *The chronicles of England, France, and the adjoining countries, from the latter part of the reign of Edward II to the coronation of Henry IV*, translated from the French by T. JOHNES, 4 vols., London, 1803–10 (often reprinted); also translated by LORD BERNERS in the Tudor translations, 6 vols., London, 1901–03. For a rapid survey, such condensations as the volume in *Everyman's library*, London and New York, 1906; and the Globe edition of *The chronicles of Froissart*, edited by G. C. MACAULAY, London and New York, 1899, do very well. FROISSART'S *Chronicles* were continued by ENGUERRAND DE MONSTRELET, *The chronicles of Monstrelet, containing the cruel wars between the houses of Orleans and Burgundy, 1400ff.*, translated by T. JOHNES, 2 vols., London, 1867. For the times of Louis XI and Charles VIII, we have *The mêmoires of* PHILIP DE COMMINES, to which is added the *Scandalous chronicle, or secret history of Louis XI*, by JEAN DE TROYES, 2 vols., London, 1900.

The chief contemporary materials for Joan of Arc are translated in *Jeanne d'Arc, Maid of Orleans, deliverer of France: being the story of her life, her achievements, and her death, as attested on oath and set forth in original documents*, edited by T. D. MURRAY, new and revised edition, New York, 1907.

Interesting extracts from these works, together with some other material, will be found in ROBINSON, *Readings*, I, 466–87; OGG, *Source book*, 418–43; E. P. CHEYNEY, *Readings in English history*, New York, 1908, 225–305; W. J. ASHLEY, *The wars of Edward III*, London, 1887; and DAVIES, *Civilization in medieval England*, 230–67.

A description of the most important writings of this period is by G. MASSON, *Early chroniclers of Europe: France*, chs. XI–XVI.

Maps. SHEPHERD, *Atlas*, 76–79, 81, 84. There is an excellent map of "the Low Countries and adjacent parts at the opening of the Hundred Years' War" appended to H. S. LUCAS, *The Low Countries and the Hundred Years' War, 1326–1347*.

C. BIBLIOGRAPHY

General books. The general histories of France, Belgium, and the Netherlands are listed, nos. **508–59.** See also nos. **338, 89, 92–93.**

The Hundred Years' War in general. S. LUCE, *La France pendant la guerre de cent ans*, 2 vols., Paris, 1890–94. J. LACHAUVELAYE, *Guerres des Français et des Anglais du XIe au XVe siècle*, Paris, 1875. A. JOUBERT, *Les invasions anglaises en Anjou au XIVe et XVe siècle*, Paris, 1872. The military history of the war is treated in E. HARDY, *La guerre de cent ans, 1346–1453*, Paris, 1879 (extract from "Histoire de la tactique"). HANOTAUX, *Histoire de la nation française*, vol. VIIe is *Histoire militaire et navale, des origines à la révolution*, Part II. "Le declin des armées féodales," Part III. "L'avènement de l'infanterie et des armes à feu." See also the literature on the art of war, p. 289, and for naval battles, LA RONCIÈRE, no. **546.** G. GUIBAL, *Histoire du sentiment national en France pendant la guerre de cent ans*, Paris, 1875. E. LEVASSEUR, *La population française*, 3 vols., Paris, 1889–92, in vol. I touches upon the depopulation in France and especially in Paris during the war. S. B. TERRY, *The financing of the Hundred Years' War, 1337–1360*, London, 1914. E. RUSSEL, "Societies of the Bardi and the Peruzzi and their dealings with Edward III, 1327–1345," *Finance and trade under Edward III* by members of the History School (pp. 93–135), Manchester, 1918. The other studies in this book are also important. R. DOUCET, "Les finances anglaises en France à la fin de la guerre de cent ans 1413–1435," *M.A.*, XXXVI (1926), 265–332. ELEANOR C. LODGE, *The estates of the archbishop and chapter of Saint-André of Bordeaux under English rule*, Oxford, 1912. P. FOURNIER, *Le royaume d'Arles et de Vienne.*

Great battles of the war. H. B. GEORGE, "The archers at Crécy," *E.H.R.*, X (1895), 733–38. J. E. MORRIS, "The archers at Crécy," *ibid.*, XII (1897), 427–36. H. BELLOC, *Crécy*, London, 1912; *Poitiers*, London, 1913 (British battles). G. WROTTLESLEY, *Crécy and Calais*, London, 1898. R. CZEPPAN, *Die Schlacht bei Crécy*, Berlin, 1906 (Diss.). N. H. NICOLAS, *History of the battle of Agincourt and of the expedition of Henry V*, London, 1827; 3rd edition, 1833. R. DE BELLEVAL, *Azincourt*, Paris, 1865. F. NIETHE, *Die Schlacht bei Azincourt, 1415*, Berlin, 1906. A. DE LOISNE, *La bataille d'Azincourt*, Paris, 1898. L. MANYON, "An examination of the historical reliability of Froissart's account of the battle and campaign of Crécy," *Papers of the Michigan Academy of science, arts, and letters*, VII (1926), 207–24.

First period, 1338–80. H. DENIFLE, *La désolation des églises, monastères et hôpitaux en France pendant la guerre de cent ans* [to 1380], 2 vols., Paris, 1897–99. E. DÉPREZ, *Les préliminaires de la guerre de cent ans: la papauté, la France et l'Angleterre (1328–42)*, Paris, 1902, part of no. **887.** J. CORDEY, *Les comtes de Savoie et les rois de France pendant la guerre de cent ans (1329–1391)*, Paris, 1911, part of no. **888.** C. PETIT DUTAILLIS and P. COLLIER, "La diplomatie française et le traité de Brétigny," *M.A.*, X (1897), 1–35. J. VIARD, "La France sous Philippe de Valois," in *R.Q.H.*, LIX (1896), 337–402. A. LÉROUX, *Recherches critiques sur les relations politiques de l'Allemagne et de la France, 1292–1378*, Paris, 1882, part of no. **888.** F. MICHEL, *Les Ecossais en France, les Français en Ecosse*, 2 vols., London, 1862.

Flanders. W. J. ASHLEY, *James and Philip van Artevelde*, London, 1883. H. PIRENNE, *Le soulèvement de la Flandre maritime de 1323–1328: documents inédits publiés avec une introduction*, Brussels, 1900. F. FUNCK-BRENTANO, *Les origines de la guerre de cent ans: Philippe le Bel en Flandre*, Paris, 1897. L. VANDERKINDERE, *Le siècle des Arteveldes*, Brussels, 1879; 2nd edition, 1907. Baron KERVYN DE LETTENHOVE, *Histoire de Flandre*, 7 vols., Brussels, 1846–50; 2nd edition, 5 vols., 1853–54; *Jacques d'Artevelde*, Ghent, 1863. J. VIARD, "La guerre de Flandre (1328)," *B.E.C.*, LXXXIII (1922), 362–82. H. S. LUCAS, *The Low Countries and the Hundred Years' War, 1326–1347*.

Etienne Marcel. F. T. PERRENS, *Etienne Marcel, prévôt des marchands (1354–1358)*, Paris, 1874 (Histoire générale de Paris); *Etienne Marcel et le gouvernement de la bourgeoisie au quatorzième siècle (1356–58)*, Paris, 1860; *La démocratie en France au moyen âge, histoire des tendances démocratiques dans les populations urbaines au XIVe et au XVe siècle*, 2 vols., Paris, 1875. L. LAZARD, *Un bourgeois de Paris: Etienne Marcel*, Paris, 1890. J. TESSIER, *La mort d'Etienne Marcel*, Paris, 1886. S. LUCE, *Histoire de la Jacquerie, d'après des documents inédits*, 2nd edition, Paris, 1894. N. VALOIS, *Le conseil du roi aux XIVe, XVe et XVIe siècles*, Paris, 1888. A. DESJARDINS, *Les Etats Généraux, 1350–1614*, Paris, 1873. YVES LE FEBVRE, *Etienne Marcel et le Paris des marchands au XIVe siècle*, Paris, 1927. See also the literature on the Estates General and the Parlement, outline XXV.

The Black Prince and Bertrand du Guesclin. J. MOISANT, *Le Prince Noir en Aquitaine, 1355–70*, Paris, 1894. A. DEBIDOUR, *Histoire de Du Guesclin*, Paris, 1880. D. F. JAMISON, *The life and times of Bertrand du Guesclin: a history of the fourteenth century*, London, 1864. S. LUCE, *La jeunesse de Bertrand du Guesclin*, Paris, 1876. C. BÉMONT, *La Guyenne pendant la domination anglaise, 1152–1453, esquisse d'une bibliographie méthodique*, New York, 1920. E. C. LODGE, *Gascony under English rule*, London, 1926. V. L. BOURRILLY, "Duguesclin et le duc d'Anjou en Provence, 1368," *R. H.*, CLII (1926), 161–80. M. BOUDET, *La Jacquerie des Tuchins (1363–1384)*, Paris, 1895.

Charles V, 1364–1380. R. DELACHENAL, *Histoire de Charles V*, 4 vols., Paris, 1909–28. M. PROU, *Etude sur les relations politiques d'Urbain V avec les rois de France Jean II et Charles V*, Paris, 1888, part of no. **888**. E. LAVISSE, "Etude sur le pouvoir royal au temps de Charles V," *R.H.*, XXVI (1884), 233–80. E. PERROY, "Charles V et le traité de Brétigny," *M. A.*, 2 série, XXIX (1928) 255–81.

Hundred Years War, 1380–1424. N. VALOIS, *La France et le grand schisme*, is the best general history of France during this period. L. JARRY, *La vie politique de Louis de France, duc d'Orléans (1372–1408)*, Paris, 1889. L. MIROT, "Une tentative d'invasion en Angleterre pendant la guerre de cent ans, 1385–86," *Revue des études historiques*, 1915. A. COVILLE, *Les Cabochiens et l'ordonnance de 1413*, Paris, 1888. R. A. NEWHALL, *The English conquest of Normandy (1416–1424). A study in fifteenth century warfare*, New Haven, 1924. W. T. WAUGH, "The administration of Normandy, 1420–1422," *Essays in medieval history presented to Thomas Frederick Tout*, Manchester, 1925, 349–60. R. A. NEWHALL, "Henry V's policy of conciliation in Normandy, 1417–1422," *Anniversary essays in mediaeval history by students of Charles Homer Haskins*, 205–30. J. H. WYLIE, *The reign of Henry the Fifth*, 2 vols., Cambridge, 1914, and W. T. WAUGH's continuation of the same, Cambridge, 1929.

Charles VII, 1422–61. G. DU FRESNE DE BEAUCOURT, *Histoire de Charles VII et de son époque*, 6 vols., Paris, 1881–91. A. VALLET DE VIRIVILLE, *Histoire de Charles VII et son époque*, 3 vols., Paris, 1862–65. E. GLASSON, *Le parlement de Paris: son rôle politique depuis le règne de Charles VII jusqu'à la révolution*, 2 vols., Paris, 1901. A. LEROUX, *Nouvelles recherches critiques sur les relations politiques de la France avec l'Allemagne de 1378 à 1461*, Paris, 1882. A. TUETEY, *Les Ecorcheurs sous Charles VII*, 2 vols., Paris, 1874. H. PRUTZ, *Jacques Coeur von Bourges: Geschichte eines patriotischen Kaufmanns aus dem 15 Jahrhundert*, Berlin, 1911 (Historische Studien, 93). P. CLÉMENT, *Jacques Coeur et Charles VII, ou la France au XVᵉ siècle*, 2 vols., Paris, 1853; 4th edition, 1874. A. B. KERR, *Jacques Coeur*, New York, 1927. R. BOUVIER, *Un financier colonial au XVᵉ siècle. Jacques Coeur*, Paris, 1928. E. COSNEAU, *Le connétable de Richemont (Arthur de Bretagne, 1393–1458)*, Paris, 1886. J. QUICHERAT, *Rodrique de Villandrando, l'un des combattants pour l'indépendance française au quinzième siècle*, Paris, 1879. F. BARBEY, *Louis de Châlon, prince d'Orange, (1390–1463)*, Lausanne, 1926. P. CHAMPION, *François Villon, sa vie et son temps*, 2 vols., Paris, 1913. H. DE VERE STACPOOLE, *François Villon, his life and times, 1431–1463*, London, 1916. FRANÇOIS VILLON, *Oeuvres complètes, publiées avec une étude sur Villon, des notes, la liste des personnages historiques et la bibliographie*, by L. MOLAND, Paris, 1914. G. DODU, "Le roi de Bourges, ou dix-neuf ans de la vie de Charles VII," *R.H.*, CLIX (1928), 38–78.

Joan of Arc. The bibliography by P. LANÉRY D'ARC, *Le livre d'or de Jeanne d'Arc: bibliographie raisonnée et analytique des ouvrages relatifs à Jeanne d'Arc*, Paris, 1894, has 2102 numbers U. CHEVALIER, *Répertoire: bio-bibliographie*, II, 2513–2546, furnished a long alphabetical list which brought the bibliography up to the year 1907. Only specialists can use such stupendous lists with profit. Helpful criticism of the literature is furnished by M. SEPET, "Jeanne d'Arc et ses plus récents historiens," *R.Q.H.*, LXXXVIII (1910), 107–34, who writes from the Roman catholic point of view.

The following are some of the most important works by Roman catholics. P. H. DUNAND, *Etudes critiques*, 5 vols., Paris, 1903–09; and *Histoire complète de Jeanne d'Arc*, 3 vols., Paris, 1898–99. J. B. J. AYROLES, *La vraie Jeanne d'Arc*, 5 vols, and two supplements, Paris, 1890–1902 (one of the supplements treats *L'université de Paris au temps de Jeanne d'Arc, et la cause de sa haine contre la libératrice*). H. DEBOUT, *La Jeanne d'Arc, grande histoire illustrée*, 2 vols., Paris, 1905–06. H. WALLON, *Jeanne d'Arc*, Paris, 1860; 7th edition, Paris, 1901, is illustrated beautifully. J. QUICHERAT, *Aperçus nouveaux sur l'histoire de Jeanne d'Arc*, Paris, 1850. J. DUPONT, *Jeanne d'Arc, d'après ses propres déclarations, les dépositions juridiques des témoins de sa vie, les écrits de ses contemporains*, Paris, 1916.

Following is a selection of a few of the more popular or more recent biographies. L. PETIT DE JULLEVILLE, *La vénérable Jeanne d'Arc*, Paris, 1900 (Les saints), translated into English, London, 1907. M. SEPET, *Jeanne d'Arc*, Tours, 1885, often reprinted; *La bienheureuse Jeanne d'Arc: son vrai caractère*, Paris, 1909. A. MARTY, *L'histoire de Jeanne d'Arc d'après les documents originaux et les oeuvres d'art du XVe au XIXe siècle*, Paris, 1907, introduction by M. SEPET. F. DE RICHEMONT, *Jeanne d'Arc d'après les documents contemporains*, Paris, 1913. S. LUCE, *Jeanne d'Arc à Domrêmy*, Paris, 1886; 2nd edition, 1887. J. FABRE, *Jeanne d'Arc libératrice de la France*, Paris, 1884. A. FABRE, *Etude sur Jeanne d'Arc*, Paris, 1912. MARGARET OLIPHANT, *Jeanne d'Arc: her life and death*, London, 1896 (Heroes of nations). R. GOWER, *Joan of Arc*, London, 1893. J. MICHELET, *Jeanne d'Arc, 1412–32*, Paris, 1890, is practically a reprint from his *Histoire de France*, vol. V. G. RUDLER, *Michelet, historien de Jeanne d'Arc*, vol. I, *La méthode*, Paris, 1925. RUDLER has also edited, *Jeanne d'Arc*, par J. MICHELET, édition critique, 2 vols., Paris, 1925 (Société des textes français modernes). A. M. TONNA-BARTHET, *Los dos procesos de la Ven^ble^ Juana de Arco*, Barcelona, 1904. CHARLOTTE BLENNERHASSETT, *Die Jungfrau von Orleans*, Bielefeld, 1906 (Frauenleben, vol. IX). R. MAHRENHOLTZ, *Jeanne Darc in Geschichte, Legende, Dichtung, auf Grund neuerer Forschung*, Leipzig, 1890. K. HASE, *Die Jungfrau von Orléans*, Leipzig, 1893. A. B. PAINE, *Joan of Arc, Maid of France*, 2 vols., New York, 1925.

On the military career of Joan of Arc: P. MARIN, *Jeanne d'Arc: tacticien et stratégiste*, 4 vols., Paris, 1889–90. H. BARANDE, *Orléans, et Jeanne d'Arc: étude critique et stratégique du siège d'Orléans*, Paris, 1910. F. CANONGE, *Jeanne d'Arc guerrière*, Paris, 1908. L. JARRY, *Compte de l'armée anglaise au siège d'Orléans*, Paris, 1892. BOUCHER DE MOLANDON and A. DE BEAUCORPS, *L'armée anglaise vaincue par Jeanne d'Arc*, Orleans, 1892. P. CHAMPION, *Guillaume de Flavy, capitaine de Compiègne: contribution à l'histoire de Jeanne d'Arc*, Paris, 1906. A. SOREL, *La prise de Jeanne d'Arc devant Compiègne*, Paris, 1889.

Some special studies on Joan of Arc. C. DE MALEYSSIE, *Les lettres de Jehanne d'Arc et la prétendue abjuration de Saint-Ouen*, with a preface by G. HANOTAUX, Paris, 1911. IRENE M. ROPE, "The letters of Jeanne d'Arc: an epitome," *Dublin review*, CLVI (1915), 57–72. H. JADART, *Jeanne d'Arc à Reims, ses relations avec Reims, ses lettres aux Rémois. Notes additionnelles*, 2 vols., Paris, 1887–1910. E. PRUTZ, "Die Briefe Jeanne d'Arcs," *S.B., Munich Acad.*, 1914, I; "Die falsche Jungfrau von Orléans (1436–57)," *ibid.*, 1911; "Studien zur Geschichte der Jungfrau von Orleans," *ibid.*, 1913, 2. H. DENIFLE, and E. CHATELAIN, "Le procès de Jeanne d'Arc et l'université de Paris," *Mémoires de la Société de l'histoire de Paris*, XXIV (1897), 1–32. G. GOYAU, *Jeanne d'Arc devant l'opinion allemande*, Paris, 1907. G. GOYAU, *Les étapes d'une gloire religieuse: Sainte Jeanne d'Arc*, Laurens, 1920. M. SEPET, "Observations critiques sur l'histoire de Jeanne d'Arc, la relation officielle du procès de condamnation et la diplomatie de l'Angleterre," *R.Q.H.*, XCVI (1914), 420–39. P. A. PIDOUX, *Un précurseur de la bienheureuse Jehanne d'Arc, le bienheureux Jehan de Gand: sa vie et son culte*, Lille, 1912. A. BOULÉ, *Jeans sans Peur et Jeanne d'Arc: ou, dernière période de la guerre de cent ans*, 2 vols., Paris, 1901. A. SARRAZIN, *Jeanne d'Arc et la Normandie au XIVe siècle*, Paris, 1896; *Pierre Cauchon*, Paris, 1901. R. BERGOT, *Jeanne d'Arc et l'histoire moderne*, Paris, 1914. *Charles VII et Jeanne d'Arc*, edited by B. ZELLER and A. LUCHAIRE, Paris, 1886, is part of no. **976.** J. FABRE, *Les bourreaux de Jeanne d'Arc et sa fête nationale; notices sur les personnages du procès de condamnation; documents sur la fête du patriotisme*, Paris, 1915.

Louis XI, 1461–83. P. F. WILLERT, *The reign of Louis XI*, London, 1876 (Historical handbooks). A. DESJARDINS, *Louis XI, sa politique extérieure, ses rapports avec l'Italie*, Paris, 1874. M. THIBAULT, *La jeunesse de Louis XI (1423–44)*, Paris, 1906. R. REY, *Louis XI et les états pontificaux de France au XVe siècle, d'après des documents inédits*, Grenoble, 1899. H. SÉE, *Louis XI et les villes*, Paris, 1891. J. COMBET, *Louis XI et le Saint-Siège (1461–1483)*, Paris, 1903. A. GANDILHON, *Contribution à l'histoire de la vie privée et la cour de Louis XI (1423–1481)*, Bourges, 1906. H. STEIN, *Charles de France frère de Louis XI*, Paris, 1921 (Mémoires et documents publiés par la Société de l'Ecole des chartes). P. CHAMPION, *Vie de Louis XI*, vol. I, *Le dauphin*, vol. II, *Le roi*, Paris, 1927; also an English translation by WINIFRED S. WHALE, *Louis XI*, London, [1929]. O. CRAMER, *Die innere Politik Ludwigs XI von Frankreich, Anh: Uebersicht über die Briefe Ludwigs XI zur Innenpolitik*, Cologne, 1927. C. SAMARAN, *La maison d'Armagnac au XVe siècle et les dernières luttes de la féodalité dans le midi de la France*, Paris, 1907.

Burgundy and Charles the Bold. E. PETIT, *Ducs de Bourgogne de la maison Valois, d'après des documents inédits*, vol. I, *Philippe le Hardi*, Part I, 1363–80, Paris, 1909, continues his great work, *Histoire des ducs de Bourgogne de la race capétienne.* O. CARTELLIERI, *Geschichte der Herzöge von Burgund, 1363–1477*, vol. I, *Philipp der Kühne*, Leipzig, 1910. A. G. P. B. DE BARANTE, *Histoire des ducs de Bourgogne, 1364–1477*, 13 vols., Paris, 1824ff.; 8th edition, 1858. J. F. KIRK, *History of Charles the Bold*, 3 vols., London, 1863–68.

P. Frédéricq, *Le rôle politique et social des ducs de Bourgogne dans les Pays-Bas*, Ghent, 1875. E. Toutey, *Charles le Téméraire et la ligue de Constance*, Paris, 1902. R. J. Casey, *The lost kingdom of Burgundy*, London, 1924. The brilliant life at the ducal court is discussed in two recent works: J. Huizinga, *The waning of the middle ages*, London, 1924, which is a translation and adaptation of a Dutch work first published in 1919; O. Cartellieri, *Am Hofe der Herzöge von Burgund;* English translation in the History of Civilization series, London, 1929.

Charles VIII, 1483–98. H. F. Delaborde, *L'expédition de Charles VIII*, Paris, 1888. E. Herbst, *Der Zug Karl's VIII nach Italien im Urteil der italienischen Zeitgenossen*, Berlin, 1911 (part 28 of *Abh.m.n.G.*). J. S. C. Bridge, *A history of France from the death of Louis XI*, vol. I, *Regency of Anne of Beaujeu, 1483–1493*, vol. II, *Reign of Charles VIII, 1493–1498*, Oxford, 1921, 1924.

Original sources. Practically all the essential contemporary sources may be found in the large collections on French history, nos. **965–77.** Much may also be found in the Rolls Series, no. **995,** such as nos. 22 and 32, *Letters and papers illustrative of the wars of the English in France during the reign of Henry VI, king of England*, 2 vols., London, 1861–64; and *Narratives of the expulsion of the English from Normandy, 1449–50*, London, 1863, both edited by J. Stevenson. F. J. Tanquerey, *Recueil de lettres anglo-françaises (1265–1399)*, Paris, 1916. The treaties of the war are printed in Rymer, *Foedera*, no. **996,** but we have a better collection by E. Cosneau, *Les grandes traités de la guerre de cent ans*, Paris, 1889, vol. 7 of no. **968.**

Almost everything of importance concerning Joan of Arc is in *Procès de condamnation et de rêhabilitation de Jeanne d'Arc . . . suivis de tous les documents historiques qu'on a pu rêunir et accompagnés de notes*, edited by J. Quicherat, 5 vols., Paris, 1841–49, part of no. **966.** The extracts from it, translated into English by Murray, have been mentioned above. Similar translations of extracts into French have been made by J. Fabre, *Procès de condemnation de Jeanne d'Arc, d'après les textes authentiques des procès-verbaux officiels*, traduction avec éclaircissements, Paris, 1884; *Procès de rêhabilitation de Jeanne d'Arc, raconté et traduit d'après les textes latins officiels*, 2 vols. Paris, 1888; new edition, Paris, 1913. P. Champion (editor), *Procès de condemnation de Jeanne d'Arc: texte, traduction, et notes*, 2 vols., Paris, 1920–21. C. Samaran, "La chronique latine inédite de Jean Chartier, 1422–1450 et les derniers livres du religieux de Saint-Denis," *B.E.C.*, LXXXVII (1926), 140–63.

Bibliographies. Molinier, *Les sources*, IV–V, dissects the original sources for this period in great detail. The best practical guide for both sources and secondary works is Lavisse, *Histoire de France*, IV (bibliographies in footnotes). For the general bibliographies on France, see nos. **21–27a,** and for Belgium, no. **45,** which is particularly useful for this period. H. S. Lucas, *The Low Countries*, 593–624, is excellent for recent material.

XXXI. GERMANY FROM THE GREAT INTERREGNUM TO MAXIMILIAN I, 1273–1493

A. Outline

1. Contrast between decentralization in Germany and centralization in France during this period. Persistence of the bond between Germany and Italy based on the idea of universal empire. Importance of the great feudal princes in Germany. The great houses of Ascania, Welf, Wittelsbach, Wettin, and the rising houses of Luxemburg, Hapsburg, and Hohenzollern. The important ecclesiastical princes, especially the archbishops of Mainz, Cologne, and Trier (Trèves). The independent imperial cities such as Lübeck, Bremen, and Rostock in the north, and Nuremberg and Augsburg in the south.

2. The new empire after the Great Interregnum. Rudolf, count of Hapsburg, elected emperor in 1273, chiefly with the aid of his cousin, Frederick III of Hohenzollern, burggraf of Nuremberg. The *Habichtsburg* in Switzerland. Rudolf's German policy. War with Ottokar of Bohemia. His failure to have his son succeed him. Adolf of Nassau, 1292–98, intervened between Rudolf and his son, Albert I, 1298–1308.

3. Henry VII of Luxemburg, 1308–13, and the sporadic revival of old imperial claims in Italy. John of Luxemburg, king of Bohemia in 1310. Henry's descent into Italy where he died in Siena, 1313. Dante's *De monarchia*.

4. Origin of the Swiss Confederacy. The league of 1291 between the cantons Uri, Schwyz, and Unterwalden. Recognized by Henry VII in 1309. The legend of William Tell and the imperial bailiff Gessler. Victory of the Swiss confederates at Morgarten in 1315 over Leopold of Austria. Gradual expulsion of Austria from Switzerland. Battle of Sempach, 1386. Practical independence of Switzerland, which was finally recognized in the Peace of Westphalia, 1648.

5. Disputed election in 1314 and civil war between Louis of Bavaria and Frederick of Austria, son of Albert. The trouble with the pope at Avignon, John XXII. Louis was crowned emperor in Rome, by the anti-pope Nicholas V. The war of pamphlets. Marsiglio of Padua's *Defensor pacis* and the writings of other supporters of Louis against the papacy such as William of Ockam, John of Jandun, and Michael Cesena, the general of the Franciscan order. The Declaration of Rense, 1338.

6. The development of the electoral college. Gradual emergence of the seven electors, three ecclesiastical lords: (1) archbishop of Mainz, (2) archbishop of Trier, (3) archbishop of Cologne; and four lay princes: (4) king of Bohemia, (5) count palatine of the Rhine, (6) duke of Saxony, and the (7) margrave of Brandenburg.

7. Charles IV of Bohemia, 1347–78, and the Golden Bull of 1356. The establishment of the university of Prague in 1348. The Black Death in Germany. The Flagellants.

8. Decline of imperial power in the period of the great western schism and the conciliar movement. The emperor Sigismund, 1410–37, at the council of Constance. The Hussite wars, 1419–36.

9. Private leagues strove to preserve order. The Hanseatic League and the Swiss Confederation have been treated elsewhere. League of Rhenish cities. The Swabian League of cities. Associations of lesser nobles.

10. The Hapsburgs in the fifteenth century, beginning with Albert II in 1438. Frederick III, 1440–93, and his advisor, Aeneas Sylvius Piccolomini (pope Pius II). Marriage of Frederick's son, archduke Maximilian, with Mary, the daughter and heiress of Charles the Bold, duke of Burgundy, who died in 1477. The Turkish menace. Futile efforts at constitutional reform.

11. German civilization in the fifteenth century. Conditions which prepared for the protestant revolt in the sixteenth century.

12. German emperors, 1273–1519.

Rudolf I (of Hapsburg), 1273–92.
Adolf (of Nassau), 1292–98.
Albert I (of Hapsburg), 1298–1308.
Henry VII (of Luxemburg), 1308–13.
Louis IV (of Bavaria), 1314–47.
(Frederick of Austria, rival.)
Charles IV (of Luxemburg), 1347–78.
(Günther of Schwarzburg, rival.)
Wenzel (of Luxemburg), 1378–1400.
Rupert (of the Palatinate), 1400–10.
Sigismund (of Luxemburg), 1410–37.
(Jobst of Moravia, rival.)
Albert II (of Hapsburg), 1438–39.
Frederick III (of Hapsburg), 1440–93.
Maximilian I (of Hapsburg), 1493–1519.

B. Special Recommendations for Reading

Brief general accounts. Bryce, *Holy Roman empire*, chs. xiii–xv, xvii. Henderson, *A short history of Germany*, I, chs. vi–x. E. Lavisse, *Political history of Europe*, 45–57. Munro and Sontag, *Middle ages*, ch. xxxvii. Dunn-Pattison, *Leading figures*, 144–64, "Charles IV." E. Emerton, *Beginnings of modern Europe*, ch. ii and 187–99. Thorndike, *Medieval Europe*, ch. xxviii. Hulme, *Middle ages*, 656–65.

Longer general accounts. Lodge, *The close of the middle ages*, chs. i, v–vii, xvii. Lavisse et Rambaud, *Histoire générale*, III, ch. xii. Loserth, *Geschichte des späteren Mittelalters*, 177–203, 246–324, 416–52, 643–70. Gebhardt, *Handbuch der deutschen Geschichte*, I, chs. xii–xiv. K. Lamprecht, *Deutsche Geschichte*, Abt. I, Vol. 5, 4th edition, Berlin, 1911. W. Stubbs, *Germany in the later middle ages, 1200–1500*. See especially Outline XXV of Part III.

Switzerland. E. EMERTON, *Beginnings of modern Europe*, 170–87. W. D. McCRACKEN, *The rise of the Swiss republic*, Boston, 1892; 2nd edition, revised and enlarged, New York, 1901 (see 92–104 for the legend of William Tell). K. DÄNDLIKER, *A short history of Switzerland*, translated by E. SALISBURY from the 2nd edition of his *Lehrbuch*, revised, New York, 1899, second period, pp. 37–125; cf. books listed in C. below. LINA HUG and R. STEAD, *Switzerland*, New York, 1890 (Story of nations), chs. IX–XV. A. SCHULTE, "Über Staatenbildung in der Alpenwelt," *Hist. Jahrbuch* (1901), 1–22.

Original sources. The Golden Bull is translated in HENDERSON, *Select documents*, 220–61, and in THATCHER and McNEAL, *Source book*, with other material pertaining to this outline, pp. 260–308. A portion of the Golden Bull, showing the seal, is reproduced in facsimile in *Weltgeschichte*, edited by J. v. PFLUGK-HARTTUNG, II, 464.

Maps. SHEPHERD, *Atlas*, 77–79, 85–88, 91, 104D. *Historisch-geographischer Atlas der Schweiz*, edited by J. C. VÖGELIN and others, Zurich; and OECHSLI-BALDAMUS, *Wandkarte zur Schweizergeschichte*, 2nd edition, Leipzig 1902.

C. BIBLIOGRAPHY

General books. The general histories of Germany are listed above, nos. **560–98.** See also those of Bohemia, nos. **699–703.**

General surveys. T. LINDNER, *Deutsche Geschichte unter den Habsburgern und Luxemburgern, 1273–1437*, 2 vols., Stuttgart, 1888–93, is continued by V. v. KRAUS, *Deutsche Geschichte im Ausgange des Mittelalters, 1438–1517*, vol. I (1438–93), Stuttgart, 1888–1905, both parts of no. **560**. W. COXE, *History of the house of Austria, 1278–1792*, 3 vols., London, 1882. O. LORENZ, *Deutsche Geschichte im 13 und 14 Jahrhundert*, 2 vols., Vienna, 1863–67. A. SCHULTZ, *Deutsches Leben im 14 und 15 Jahrhundert*, Leipzig, 1892. E. MICHAEL, *Geschichte des deutschen Völkes vom dreizehnten Jahrhundert bis zum Ausgang des Mittelalters*, 6 vols., Freiburg, 1897–1915. G. GRUPP, *Kulturgeschichte des Mittelalters*, Vol. VI. HOFMANN, *Politische Geschichte des Deutschen*, Vol. III. K. ZEUMER, *Heiliges Römisches Reich deutscher Nation*, discusses the titles applied to the empire during this and earlier periods. W. SCHEFFLER, *Die Porträts der deutschen Kaiser und Könige im späteren Mittelalter von Adolf von Nassau bis Maximilian I, 1292–1519* (in Repertorium für Kunstwissenschaft, 33). W. MÜLLER, "Deutsches Volk und Deutsches Land im späteren Mittelalter," *H.Z.*, CXXXII (1925), 450–71.

Rudolf I, 1273–92. O. REDLICH, *Rudolf von Habsburg: das deutsche Reich nach dem Untergange des alten Kaisertums*, Innsbruck, 1903. H. OTTO, *Die Beziehungen Rudolfs von Habsburg zu Papst Gregor X*, Innsbruck, 1894. J. HELLER, *Deutschland und Frankreich in ihren politischen Beziehungen vom Ende des Interregnums bis zum Tode Rudolfs von Habsburg*, Göttingen, 1874.

Adolf, 1292–98, and Albert I, 1298–1308. F. W. E. ROTH, *Geschichte des römischen Königs Adolf I von Nassau*, Wiesbaden, 1879. A. BERGENGRÜN, *Die politischen Beziehungen Deutschlands zu Frankreich während der Regierung*

Adolfs von Nassau, Strasburg, 1884. H. HENNEBERG, *Die politischen Beziehungen zwischen Deutschland und Frankreich unter König Albrecht I, 1298–1308*, Strasburg, 1891 (Diss.). M. VANCSA, *Die Anfänge des Hauses Habsburg in Österreich*, Leipzig, 1917.

Henry VII, 1308–14. K. GRÄFE, *Die Persönlichkeit Kaiser Heinrichs VII*, Leipzig, 1911. M. KRAUSSOLD, *Die politischen Beziehungen zwischen Deutschland und Frankreich während der Regierung Heinrichs VII*, Munich, 1900 (Diss.). G. SOMMERFELDT, *Die Romfahrt Kaiser Heinrichs VII (1310–1313)*, Königsberg, 1888. K. WENCK, *Clemens V und Heinrich VII*, Halle, 1882. F. SCHNEIDER, *Kaiser Heinrich VII*, vol. I (to 1310), Greiz, 1924; vol. II. *Der Romzug, 1310–1313*, 1926.

Louis of Bavaria, 1314–47. R. MOELLER, *Ludwig der Bayer und die Kurie im Kampf um das Reich: Forschungen*, Berlin, 1914. J. V. DÖLLINGER, "Deutschlands Kampf mit dem Papstthum unter Kaiser Ludwig dem Bayer" (*Akademische Vorträge*, I), translated into English, "The struggle of Germany with the papacy under the emperor Ludwig of Bavaria," in *Studies in European history*, London, 1890. K. MÜLLER, *Der Kampf Ludwigs des Bayern mit der römischen Kurie*, 2 vols., Tübingen, 1879–80. G. SIEVERS, *Die politischen Beziehungen Kaiser Ludwigs des Bayern zu Frankreich, 1314–1347*, Berlin, 1896 (part 2 of Historische Studien). W. ALTMANN, *Der Römerzug Ludwigs des Baiern*, Berlin, 1886. K. HÖHLBAUM, "Der Kurverein zu Rense, 1338," *Abh. Göttingen Acad.*, VII, 1903.

Switzerland. K. DÄNDLIKER, *Geschichte der Schweiz*, 3 vols., Zürich, 1884–87, vol. I, 4th edition, 1901, vols. II and III, 3rd edition, 1902–03. There is an abridgment of this work under the title, *Auszug aus der Schweizergeschichte*, Zürich, 1910. The same author's *Schweizerische Geschichte*, Leipzig, 1904 (Sammlung Göschen), is an earlier abridgment. See also translation, edited by E. J. BENTON, in *History of nations*, vol. XIII, New York, 1928. J. DIERAUER, *Geschichte der schweizerischen Eidgenossenschaft*, 5 vols., Gotha, 1887–1917, part of no. **332**, translated into French by A. REYMOND, *Histoire de la confédération suisse*, 4 vols., Paris, 1918. E. GAGLIARDI, *Geschichte der Schweiz von den Anfängen bis auf die Gegenwart*, Zürich, 1920. W. MARTIN, *Histoire de la Suisse: essai sur la formation d'une confédération d'états*, Paris, 1926. H. VULLIÉTY, *La Suisse à travers les âges: histoire de la civilisation depuis les temps préhistoriques jusqu'à la fin du XVIIIe siècle*, Paris, 1902, has many illustrations. J. V. MÜLLER, *Geschichte schweizerischer Eidgenossenschaft mit allen Fortsetzungen*, 26 vols., Leipzig, 1806–55, translated by C. MONNARD and L. VULLIEMIN, *Histoire de la confédération suisse*, 18 vols., Paris, 1837–51. *Archiv für Schweizergeschichte*, 20 vols., extends to 1875; followed by *Jahrbuch für Schweizergeschichte*, 1876ff. W. ÖCHSLI, *Die Anfänge der schweizerischen Eidgenossenschaft*, Bern, 1891, and *Bausteine zur Schweizergeschichte*, Zürich, 1891. W. PLATTNER, *Die Entstehung des Freistaats der drei Bünde und sein Verhältnis zur alten Eidgenossenschaft*, Davos, 1895. J. HÜRBIN, *Handbuch der Schweizergeschichte*, 2 vols., Stans, 1901–09. M. DE LA RIVE, *Histoire abrégée de la confédération suisse*, 2 vols., 2nd edition, Geneva, 1907. B. VAN MUYDEN, *Histoire de la nation suisse*, 3 vols.,

Lausanne, 1899–1901. A. DAQUET, *Histoire de la confédération suisse*, 7th edition, revised, 2 vols., Geneva and Paris, 1879. A. HUBER, *Die Waldstätte Uri, Schwyz, Unterwalden bis zur ersten Begründung ihrer Eidgenossenschaft*, Innsbruck, 1861. A. RILLIET, *Les origines de la confédération suisse: histoire et légende*, Geneva, 1868; 2nd edition, 1869. L. VULLIEMIN, *Histoire de la confédération suisse*, 2 vols., revised edition, Lausanne, 1879. O. HENNE-AM-RHYN, *Geschichte des Schweizervolkes und seiner Kultur*, 3 vols., Leipzig, 1865–66.

Special books on the Tell legend are: A. BERNOULLI, *Die Sagen von Tell und Stauffacher: eine kritische Untersuchung*, Basel, 1899; and E. L. ROCHOLZ, *Tell und Gessler in Sage und Geschichte*, Heilbronn, 1877.

Charles IV, 1347–78, and the Golden Bull. E. WERUNSKY, *Geschichte Kaiser Karls IV und seiner Zeit*, vols. I–III (1316–68), Innsbruck, 1880–92. K. ZEUMER, *Die Goldene Bulle Kaiser Karls IV*, 2 vols., Weimar, 1908. O. HALM, *Ursprung und Bedeutung der Goldenen Bulle Karls IV*, Breslau, 1902 (Diss.). W. SCHEFFLER, *Karl IV und Innocenz VI: Beiträge zur Geschichte ihrer Beziehungen (1355–1360)*, Berlin, 1912 (part 101 of Historische Studien). S. GROTEFEND, *Die Erwerbungspolitik Kaiser Karls IV*, Berlin, 1909. A. GOTTLOB, *Karls IV private und politische Beziehungen zu Frankreich*, Innsbruck, 1883. E. HEINZE, "Das kursächsische Reichsvirkariatsrecht vor der Goldenen Bulle," *H.V.J.S.*, XXII (1924), 1–27. U. KÜHNE, "Geschichte des böhmischen Kur in dem Jahrhundert des Goldenen Bulle," *Archiv für Urkundenwesen*, X (1926), 1–110. H. REINCKE, *Machtpolitik und Weltwirtschaftspläne Kaiser Karls IV*, Lübeck, 1924.

Wenzel, 1378–1400, and Rupert, 1400–10. T. LINDNER, *Geschichte des deutschen Reichs unter König Wenzel*, 2 vols., Braunschweig, 1875–80. C. HOEFLER, *Ruprecht von der Pfalz, genannt Clem, römischer König, 1400–1410*, Freiburg, 1861.

Sigismund. J. ASCHBACH, *Geschichte Kaiser Sigmunds*, 4 vols., Hamburg, 1838–45. O. SCHIFF, *König Sigmunds italienische Politik bis zur Romfahrt (1410–1431)*, Frankfurt, 1909. E. GÖLLER, *König Sigismunds Kirchenpolitik vom Tode Bonifaz' IX bis zur Berufung des Konstanzer Konzils (1404–1413)*, Freiburg, 1901. A. DOREN, "Zur Reformation Sigismundi," *H.V.J.S.*, XXI (1922), 1–59.

Hapsburgs in the fifteenth century. W. WOSTRY, *König Albrecht II (1437–1439)*, 2 parts, Prague, 1906–07. A. BACHMANN, *Deutsche Reichsgeschichte im Zeitalter Friedrichs III und Maximilian I*, vol. I (1461–68), vol. II, parts I and II (1467–86), Leipzig, 1884–94. K. KASER, *Deutsche Geschichte zur Zeit Maximilians I, 1486–1519*, Berlin, 1912, part of no. **560**. C. HARE, *Maximilian the dreamer, holy Roman emperor, 1459–1519*, London, 1913. K. SCHALK, *Aus der Zeit des österreichischen Faustrechts, 1440–1463*, Vienna, 1919.

Constitutional history of Germany. O. EBERBACH, *Die deutsche Reichsritterschaft in ihrer staatsrechtlich-politischen Entwicklung von den Anfängen bis zum Jahre 1495*, Leipzig, 1913 (Beiträge zur Kulturgeschichte des Mittelalters und der Renaissance). M. KRAMMER, *Das Kurfürstenkolleg von seinen*

Anfängen bis zum Zusammenschluss im Renser Kurverein des Jahres 1338, Weimar, 1913 (Quellen und Studien). T. LINDNER, *Die deutschen Königswahlen und die Entstehung des Kurfürstenthums*, Leipzig, 1893. O. HARNACK, *Das Kurfürstencollegium bis zur Mitte des vierzehnten Jahrhunderts*, Giessen, 1883. F. SCHÖNHERR, *Die Lehre vom Reichsfürtenstande des Mittelalters*, Leipzig, 1914 (Diss.). H. SPANGENBERG, *Vom Lehnstaat zum Standstaat*, Munich, 1912. G. SEELIGER, *Das deutsche Hofmeisteramt im späteren Mittelalter*, Innsbruck, 1885. T. LINDNER, *Die Veme*, Münster and Paderborn, 1888; and *Der angebliche Ursprung der Vemgerichte aus der Inquisition*, Paderborn, 1890. R. HIS, *Das Strafrecht des deutschen Mittelalters*, I., Leipzig, 1920. E. MOLITOR, *Die Reichsreform Bestrebungen des 15. Jahrhunderts bis zum Tode Kaiser Friederichs III* (Untersuchungen zur deutschen Staats- und Rechtsgeschichte, Heft 132, Breslau, 1921). A. MEISTER, *Deutsche Verfassungsgeschichte*, 3rd edition, Leipzig and Berlin, 1922 (Part of **331**). E. BOCK, *Der schwäbische Bund und seine Verfassungen, 1488–1534.* (Untersuchungen zur deutschen Staats- und Rechtsgeschichte, Heft 137, Breslau, 1927.) E. USTERI, *Das öffentlich-rechtliche Schiedsgericht in der Schweizerischen Eidgenossenschaft des 13. bis 15. Jahrhunderts*, Zürich and Leipzig, 1925.

Original sources. The general collections of source materials for this period are listed above, nos. **980–87**. To these should be added, *Deutsche Reichstagsakten*, herausgegeben durch die historische Kommission bei der kgl. Akademie der Wissenschaften, vols. I–XIII, Munich, 1867ff.; and *Acta imperii Angliae et Franciae ab anno 1267 ad annum 1313: Dokumente vornehmlich zur Geschichte der auswärtigen Beziehungen Deutschlands*, edited by F. KERN, Tübingen, 1911. W. ALTMANN and E. BERNHEIM, *Auesgewählte Urkunden zur Erläuterung der Verfassungsgeschichte Deutschlands im Mittelalter*, 5th edition, Berlin, 1920. H. SAUERLAND, *Vatikanische Urkunden und Regesten zur Geschichte Lothringens vom Anfange des Pontifikats Bonifaz VIII bis zum Ende des Pontifikats Urbans V* (*24 Dec. 1294–24 Dec. 1370*), 2 vols., Metz, 1901–05. E. WINKELMANN, *Acta imperii inedita saeculi XIII et XIV*, 2 vols., Innsbruck, 1880–85. O. REDLICH, *Die Regesten der Herzöge von Österreich sowie Friedrich des Schönen als deutschen Königs*, Innsbruck, 1922–24. (Part III of *Regesta Habsburgica.*)

Extracts from the sources for the study of Switzerland may be found in *Quellenbuch zur Schweizergeschichte*, edited by W. OECHSLI, 2 vols., 1893, vol. I, in 2nd edition, 1902; and E. GAGLIARDI, *Geschichte der schweizerischen Eidgenossenschaft bis zum Abschluss der mailändischen Kriege* (*1516*): *Darstellung und Quellenberichte*, Leipzig, 1914 (Voigtländer's Quellenbücher, 67). For large collections see no. **987**, and *Amtliche Sammlung der älteren eidgenössischen Abschiede 1245 bis 1798*, 8 vols., Luzern, Basel, and Zürich, 1839–84.

Bibliographies. The standard bibliography for this subject is DAHLMANN-WAITZ, pp. 413–542. The other bibliographies for German history are listed above, nos. **29–35.** For Bohemia see no. **47** note, and for Switzerland, see nos. **43–44.** For the Tell legend there is a special bibliography by F. HEINEMANN, *Tell-Bibliographie*, Bern, 1907. J. L. BRANDSTETTER, *Reperto-*

rium über die in Zeit- und Sammelschriften der Jahre 1813–1890 enthaltenen Aufsätze . . . schweizergeschichtlichen Inhaltes, Basel, 1892, continued 1891–1900) by H. Barth, 1906. H. WILD, *Bibliographie der Schweizergeschichte*, 1925, *Beilage zur Zeitschrift für schweizerische Geschichte*, 1926; also published separately, Zürich, 1927. HAMPE, *Mittelalterliche Geschichte.*

XXXII. ITALY IN THE FOURTEENTH AND FIFTEENTH CENTURIES

A. OUTLINE

1. Italy a "geographical expression," not a political entity, in this period. Importance of the papacy and the empire in Italian history. Guelphs and Ghibellines. Predominance of Italian cities which developed a culture as marvellous as the world has ever seen. In this period Italy was the center of European civilization, whereas in the twelfth and thirteenth centuries that center was in France. Italy became the preceptress of modern Europe in politics. "Europe would certainly have learned political knavery without a master, but she profited by the lessons which she received from Italy. She fervently meditated the gospel according to Machiavelli."—E. LAVISSE, *General view*, 82–83.

2. The great states of Italy were the republics of Venice and Florence, the duchy of Milan, the kingdom of Naples, and the Papal States, but there were also many important minor states such as Genoa, Ferrara, Verona, Mantua, Urbino, and Rimini.

3. The Sicilian Vespers, 1282. The misrule of Charles of Anjou in Sicily. The massacre of over 4000 French men, women, and children in Sicily on Easter Monday, 1282. Peter III of Aragon, who had married Constance, a daughter of Manfred, became king of Sicily. Sicily and Naples had separate rulers until 1435, when they were united under the king of Aragon, Alfonso V, who was formally recognized as Alfonso I of Naples in 1442.

4. Rome during the "Babylonish Captivity" of the papacy. The Roman nobility, especially the Orsini and the Colonna. Cola di Rienzo and his *buono stato*, 1347. His exile and his return and execution in 1354. Cardinal Albornoz saved the Papal States for the papacy, 1353–60.

5. The age of the despots in Italy. The peculiar political conditions which created the *podestà*, the captain of the people, and the *condottiere*, also gave rise to the tyrant. The condottiere Sir John Hawkwood. Characteristics of typical tyrants. Their rôle as patrons of scholars and artists. Ezzelino da Romano (died 1259).

6. Milan. Its struggles with the Hohenstaufen. The rise of the Visconti family. Matteo Visconti, a vicar of the emperor, usurped authority in 1311. Gian Galeazzo, 1378–1402, duke of Milan. Filippo Maria, 1412–47, the last of the Visconti. Attempt to establish a republic, 1447. In 1450, the successful condottiere, Francesco Sforza, became duke of Milan. War with Venice.

His relations with France. Galeazzo Maria Sforza, 1466–78. Ludovico il Moro called in the French king, Charles VIII, against Naples. This led finally to the expulsion of the Sforzas from Milan by Louis of Orleans.

7. The remarkable growth of Venice in the time of the crusades. Her influence and her possessions in the Levant. The coming of the Ottoman Turks. Wars with Genoa (war of Chioggia, 1378–81), Padua and Milan. The constitution of Venice. Gradual development of an oligarchy. The doge and the Great Council. The Council of Ten in 1310. Rivalry between Venice and Milan in the fifteenth century (execution of Carmagnola, 1432). Wars with the Turks, 1463–79, and the subsequent decline of Venice.

8. Florence. Her rise in the time of Matilda of Tuscany (died 1115). Rivalry between the feudal nobles or *grandi* (Ghibellines), and the prosperous burghers (Guelfs). The burghers organized in gilds (*arti*). Later a distinction between greater and lesser gilds (*arti maggiori* and *arti minori*). The clash of the Buondelmonte and the Amidei families in 1215. The first commonwealth (*il primo popolo*) in 1251. The Captain of the People. The *Parte Guelfa*, 1267. The glory of the Trecento (about 1266–1378). Ordinances of Justice, 1293. Rivalry between two Guelf factions, the Whites and the Blacks (*Bianchi* and *Neri*). Exile of Dante (a White) in 1302. The tyrant, Walter of Brienne, duke of Athens, 1342–1343. The Black Death in Florence, 1348. Strife between the old *Parte Guelfa* and the Signory of Priors, 1378. The rising of the Ciompi, 1378. Oligarchial tendency in Florence which prepared for the rise of the rich Medici family (Giovanni de' Medici), which favored the lesser gilds. Cosimo de' Medici, 1434–1464. Piero de' Medici, 1464–69. Lorenzo de' Medici, "The Magnificent," 1464–92.

9. Naples. Endless dynastic rivalries in the southern kingdom which did much to retard its development. In the fourteenth century, the rivalry between Angevins and Aragonese finally made Alfonso V of Aragon king of Naples and Sicily. Lorenzo Valla at the court of Alfonso. Naples under the rule of Ferrante, 1458–94. The claims of the second house of Anjou on the crown of Aragon became a prime factor in the invasion of Italy by Charles VIII in 1494.

10. The papal states in the fifteenth century. In this period the history of the papacy is largely that of a petty Italian principality. Martin V, 1417–31, the pope elected at Constance, regained control in Rome and over the Papal States. The unsuccessful plot of Stefano Porcaro in 1453. Nicholas V, 1447–55, the humanist pope. Pius II, 1458–64, the famous Aeneas Sylvius Piccolomini, who issued the bull *Execrabilis* in 1460, was another typical humanist pope. Sixtus IV, 1471–84, was hardly more than a secular prince. His attempt to overthrow the Medici in Florence. The papacy in the hands of the Borgias with the accession of Rodrigo Borgia, pope Alexander VI, 1492.

11. Savonarola (burned, 1498) in Florence, and the beginning of foreign domination in Italy, with the invasion of Charles VIII of France in 1494.

B. Special Recommendations for Reading

General introductory accounts. E. Emerton, *Beginnings of modern Europe*, chs. v, viii. Hulme, *Middle ages*, 665–70. J. A. Symonds, *A short history of the renaissance in Italy*, New York, [1893], chs. ii–vi. H. D. Sedgwick, *A short history of Italy*, chs. xvii, xx, xxii–xxiii. For the period up to the second decade of the fourteenth century, see P. Villari, *Mediaeval Italy*, book III; and H. B. Cotterill, *Medieval Italy*, part V. Cotterill, *Italy from Dante to Tasso*. A survey of Italy in the fifteenth century may be found in P. Villari, *Niccolò Machiavelli e i suoi tempi*, 3 vols., Florence, 1877–82, translated by Linda Villari, *The life and times of Niccolò Machiavelli*, 2 vols., London, 1898, 1–62. H. D. Sedgwick, *Italy in the thirteenth century*, I, chs. xiii, xiv, xv; xviii; vol. II, chs. ii–iv, ix–xi. E. A. Freeman, "Ancient Greece and mediaeval Italy," *Historical essays*, series II, 1–52.

More advanced general accounts. Lodge, *The close of the middle ages*, chs. ii, viii, xii–xiv. Lavisse et Rambaud, *Histoire générale*, III, ch. x. Burckhardt, *The civilization of the renaissance in Italy*, part I. Loserth, *Geschichte des späteren Mittelalters*, 203–06, 250–55, 306–17. E. Emerton, *Humanism and tyranny*. Maude V. Clarke, *The medieval city state. An essay on tyranny and federation in the later middle ages*, London, 1926.

Standard works. Symonds, *Renaissance in Italy*, vol. I, *The age of the despots*. Simonde de Sismondi, *History of the Italian republics in the middle ages*, entirely recast and supplemented by W. Boulting, London, 1905, see no. **613.**

Cola di Rienzo. M. E. Cosenza, *Francesco Petrarca and the revolution of Cola di Rienzo: a study in the history of Rome during the middle ages*, Chicago, 1913.

Rome, the Papal States, and the Papacy. W. Miller, *Mediaeval Rome*, chs. v–viii. P. van Dyke, *The age of the renascence*, 90–261. Gregorovius, *History of the city of Rome*, VII, part I. H. C. Lea, "The eve of the reformation," in *Cambridge modern history*, I, ch. xix. Bryce, *Holy Roman empire*, ch. xvi.

The standard works on the humanist popes are Creighton, *A history of the papacy*, III–IV; and Pastor, *History of the popes*, III–V.

Pope Pius II (Aeneas Sylvius). W. Boulting, *Aeneas Sylvius (Enea Silvio de' Piccolomini—Pius II) orator, man of letters, statesman, and pope*, London, 1908. Cecilia M. Ady, *Pius II (Aeneas Silvius Piccolomini) the humanist pope*, London, 1913. G. Voigt, *Enea Silvio de' Piccolomini, als Papst Pius II, und sein Zeitalter*, 3 vols., Berlin, 1856–63. A. Weiss, *Aeneas Sylvius Piccolomini als Papst Pius II*, Graz, 1897.

Florence. P. Villari, *I primi due secoli della storia di Firenze*, Florence, 1893, translated by Linda Villari, *The two first centuries of Florentine history: the republic and parties at the time of Dante*, 2 vols., London, 1894–95. E. G. Gardner, *The story of Florence*, London, 1901. A satisfactory book on the most brilliant rule of Florence is E. Armstrong, *Lorenzo de' Medici and*

Florence in the fifteenth century, New York, 1896 (Heroes of nations). DUNN-PATTISON, *Leading figures*, 165–89, "Lorenzo de' Medici." GENEVRA NICCOLINI DI CAMIGLIANO, "A medieval Florentine, his family and his possessions," in *A.H.R.*, XXXI (1925), 1–19.

Venice. For a short general survey see the *Cambridge modern history*, I, 253–87. W. C. HAZLITT, *The Venetian republic: its rise, its growth, and its fall, 409–1797*, 2 vols., 4th edition, London, 1915. W. R. THAYER, *A short history of Venice*, London and New York, 1905. H. BROWN, *Venice: an historical sketch of the republic*, London, 1893; 2nd, revised, edition, 1895; *The Venetian republic*, New York, 1902 (Temple primers). ALETHEA WIEL, *The navy of Venice*, London, 1910.

Savonarola. For short sketches see the *Cambridge modern history*, I, 144–89; or LEA, *Inquisition of the middle ages*, III, 209–37. The standard work is P. VILLARI, *La storia di G. Savonarola e de' suoi tempi*, 2 vols., Florence, 1859–61; 2nd edition, 1887–88, translated by LINDA VILLARI, *Life and times of Girolamo Savonarola*, 2 vols., London, 1888.

Invasion of Charles VIII. *Cambridge modern history*, I, 104–17, has a good summary of this event so momentous in the history of Italy.

Original sources. For the coronation of Cola di Rienzo, see DUNCALF and KREY, *Parallel source problems*, 177–237.

For the history of Florence we have the following in English: *Selections from the first nine books of the Chroniche Fiorentine of* GIOVANNI VILLANI, edited by P. H. WICKSTEED and translated by ROSE E. SELFE, London, 1906. *The Chronicle of* DINO COMPAGNI [about 1260–1324], translated by ELSE C. M. BENECKE and A. G. FERRERS HOWELL, London, 1906 (Temple classics). NICOLO MACHIAVELLI, *History of Florence together with The Prince*, London, Bohn Library (many editions). Another convenient translation of his *Florentine history* is in Everyman's library, London [1909]. *Lives of the early Medici as told in their correspondence*, translated and edited by JANET ROSS, Boston, 1911. T. LANDUCCI, *A Florentine diary from 1450 to 1516*, London, 1927.

For an insight into the thought of SAVONAROLA, see his *Triumph of the cross*, translated from the Italian, with an introduction, by J. PROCTOR, London, 1901. M. WHITCOMB, *A Literary source-book of the renaissance*, 66–92, prints various excerpts. AENEAS SYLVIUS (PIUS II), "How I became pope," translated in *Nineteenth century*, XLI (1897), 538–46, is extracted from this pope's autobiographical commentaries.

Maps. SHEPHERD, *Atlas*, 90, 96, 104D.

C. BIBLIOGRAPHY

General books. The general books on Italy are listed above, nos. **599–621.** See also the literature on the Normans in Sicily and southern Italy, outline XX, on the Lombard communes, outline XXII, and on Italian cities and commerce in Italy, outline XXVI.

General surveys. LUCHAIRE, *Les démocraties italiennes*. C. CIPOLLA, *Storia delle signorie italiane dal 1313 al 1530*, Milan, 1881, vol. IV of no. **599.**

P. ORSI, *Signorie e principati (1300–1530)*, Milan, 1901. E. SALZER, *Über die Anfänge der Signorie in Oberitalien*, Berlin, 1900. A. FRANCHETTI, *I primordi delle signorie e delle compagne di ventura: la vita italiana nel Trecento*, Milan, 1892. G. ARIAS, *Il sistema della constituzione economica e sociale italiana nell' età dei comuni*, Turin, 1905. G. B. FANUCCI, *Storia dei tre celebri popoli marittimi dell' Italia, Veneziani, Genovesi e Pisani*, 4 vols., Leghorn, 1853–55. E. MELILLO, *Le poste italiane nel medio evo, alta e media Italia (476–1600)*, Rome, 1904. L. GENUARDI, *Il comune nel medio evo in Sicilia*, Palermo, 1922.

Cola di Rienzo and Rome. E. RODOCANACHI, *Cola di Rienzo: histoire de Rome de 1342 à 1354*, Paris, 1888. E. RODOCANACHI, *Histoire de Rome de 1354 à 1471; Histoire de Rome: une cour princière au Vatican pendant la renaisance, 1471–1503*, Paris, 1925; "L'organisation municipale de Rome au XIVe siècle," *M.A.*, VIII (1895), 73–82. F. KÜHN, *Die Entwicklung der Bündnisspläne Cola di Rienzos im Jahre 1347*, Berlin, 1905 (Diss.). F. HERMANNI, *Die Stadt Rom im 15 und 16 Jahrhundert*, Leipzig, 1911. H. J. WURM, *Kardinal Albornoz, der zweite Begründer des Kirchenstaates*, Paderborn, 1892. A. EITEL, *Der Kirchenstaat unter Klemens V*, Berlin, 1907 (*Abh.m.n.G.*). A. DE BOÜARD, *Le régime politique et les institutions de Rome au moyen âge, 1252–1347*, Paris, 1920.

Condottieri. W. BLOCK, *Die Condottieri: Studien über die sogemannten unblutigen Schlachten*, Berlin, 1913. A. SEMERAN, *Die Condottieri*, Jena, 1909. F. H. JACKSON, *True stories of the condottieri*, London, 1904 (for Sir John Hawkwood see ch. IV). G. TEMPLE-LEADER, and G. MARCOTTI, *Giovanni Acuto (Sir John Hawkwood): storia d'un condottiere*, Florence, 1889.

Milan. CECILIA M. ADY, *A history of Milan under the Sforza*, London, 1907. ELLA NOYES, *The story of Milan*, London, 1908 (Mediaeval towns). W. P. URQUHART, *Life and times of Francisco Sforza, duke of Milan*, 2 vols., Edinburgh and London, 1852. JULIA CARTWRIGHT, *Beatrice d'Este, duchess of Milan, 1475–1497: a study of the renaissance*, London, 1912.

Among the Italian works G. GIULINI, *Memorie spettanti alla storia di Milano*, 12 vols., Milan, 1760–75; new edition, 7 vols., 1854–57, is still the most important. F. CUSANI, *Storia di Milano*, 8 vols., Milan, 1862–84. M. FORMENTINI, *Il ducato di Milano*, Milan, 1877. P. VERRI, *Storia di Milano*, Florence, 1851ff. C. MANARESI, *Gli atti del comune di Milano fino all' anno 1216*, Milan, 1919.

Venice. P. G. MOLMENTI, *La storia di Venezia nella vita privata*, 3rd edition, 3 vols., Bergamo, 1903–08, translated by H. F. BROWN, *Venice: its individual growth from the earliest beginnings to the fall of the republic*, 6 vols., London and Chicago, 1906–08. C. DIEHL, *Une république patricienne: Venise*, Paris, 1915. F. C. HODGSON, *The early history of Venice from the foundation to the conquest of Constantinople*, London, 1901; *Venice in the 13th and 14th centuries (1204–1400)*, London, 1910. F. M. CRAWFORD, *Salve Venetia: gleanings from Venetian history*, 2 vols., New York, 1906. J. K. FOTHERINGHAM, *Marco Sanudo, conqueror of the Archipelago*, Oxford, 1915. T. OKEY, *Venice and its story*, revised edition, New York, 1910. H. F.

BROWN, *Studies in the history of Venice*, 2 vols., New York, 1907. H. KRETSCHMAYR, *Geschichte von Venedig*, vols. I–II (to 1516), Gotha, 1905–20, part of no. **332.** H. v. ZWIEDINECK-SÜDENHORST, *Venedig als Weltmacht und Weltstadt*, Leipzig, 1899. E. MUSATTI, *La storia politica di Venezia secondo le ultimi ricerche*, Padua, 1897. MARGARET OLIPHANT, *Makers of Venice: doges, conquerors, painters, and men of letters*, London, 1889. AUBREY RICHARDSON, *The doges of Venice*, London [1914]. G. B. McCLELLAN, *The oligarchy of Venice: an essay*, Boston, 1904. A. BATTISTELLA, *La repubblica di Venezia*, Bologna, 1897.

Of the old monumental works the following still have value. S. ROMANIN, *Storia documentata di Venezia*, 10 vols., Venice, 1853–61. P. DARU, *Histoire de la rêpublique de Venise*, 9 vols., 4th edition, Paris, 1853.

Following is a selection of special studies: W. LENEL, *Die Entstehung der Vorherrschaft Venedigs an der Adria*, Strasburg, 1897. B. SCHMEIDLER, *Der Dux und die Commune Venetiarum von 1141–1229*, Berlin, 1902. P. M. PERRET, *Histoire des relations de France avec Venise du XIIIe siècle à Charles VIII*, 2 vols., Paris, 1896. M. CLAAR, *Die Entwickelung der venetianischen Verfassung von der Einsetzung bis zur Schliessung des grossen Rats (1172–1297)*, Munich, 1895 (Historische Abhandlungen). A. SORESINA, *Il Banco Giro di Venezia*, Venice, 1889. E. LATTES, *La libertà delle banche a Venezia dal secolo XIII a XVII*, Milan, 1869. A. BASCHET, *Les archives de Venise: histoire de la chancellerie secrète*, Paris, 1870. W. ANDREAS, *Die venezianischen Relazionen und ihr Verhältnis zu Kultur der Renaissance*, Leipzig, 1908 (Diss.).

Genoa. M. G. CANALE, *Nuova istoria della repubblica di Genova*, vols. I–IV (to 1528), Florence, 1858–64. C. VARESE, *Storia della repubblica di Genova*, 7 vols., Genoa, 1835–37. F. DONOWER, *Storia di Genova*, Genoa, 1890. J. T. BENT, *Genoa: how the republic rose and fell*, London, 1881. R. W. CARDEN, *The city of Genoa*, London, 1908. G. CARO, *Studien zur Geschichte von Genua 1190–1257*, Strasburg, 1891; *Genua und die Mächte am Mittelmeer, 1257–1311*, 2 vols., Halle, 1895–99. E. JARRY, *Les origines de la domination française à Gênes (1392–1402)*, Paris, 1896. E. HEYCK, *Genua und seine Marine im Zeitalter der Kreuzzüge*, Innsbruck, 1886.

Florence. The most important book is by R. DAVIDSOHN, *Geschichte von Florenz*, 4 vols., Berlin, 1896–1927, translated into Italian, with many fine illustrations, *Storia di Firenze*, Florence, 1907ff. (see especially the plan of Florence in the thirteenth century, near the end of vol. II, which is also in vol. I of the original German edition). This great work is supplemented by his *Forschungen zur Geschichte von Florenz*, vols. I–IV, Berlin, 1896–1908; and "Florenz zur Zeit Dantes," *Deutsche Rundschau*, July, 1912. In French the best work is by F. T. PERRENS, *Histoire de Florence jusqu'à la domination des Médicis*, 6 vols., Paris, 1877–84; continued by *Histoire de Florence depuis la domination des Médicis jusqu'à la chute de la rêpublique, 1434–1531*, 2 vols., Paris, 1888, translated by HANNAH LYNCH, *The history of Florence under the domination of Cosimo, Piero, Lorenzo di Medicis, 1434–1492*, London, 1892. G. CAPPONI, *Storia della repubblica di Firenze*, 3 vols., Florence, 1875–88.

G. Thomas, *Les révolutions politiques de Florence 1177–1530*, Paris, 1887. T. A. Trollope, *History of the commonwealth of Florence*, 4 vols., London, 1865. H. E. Napier, *Florentine history*, 6 vols., London, 1846–47.

Shorter books. F. A. Hyett, *Florence: her history and art to the fall of the republic*, London and New York, 1903. J. W. Brown, *The builders of Florence*, New York, 1907; *Florence, past and present*, New York, 1911. C. E. Yriarte, *Florence*, 3rd edition, Paris, 1881, translated by C. B. Pitman, *Florence: its history, the Medici, the humanists, letters, arts*, New York, 1882; new edition, Philadelphia, 1897. Margaret Oliphant, *Makers of Florence: Dante, Giotto, Savonarola and their city*, 3rd edition, London, 1889. Bella Duffy, *The Tuscan republics (Florence, Siena, Pisa, Lucca) with Genoa*, London, 1893.

Special studies. E. Staley, *The guilds of Florence*, London, 1906. A. Doren, *Entwickelung und Organisation der florentiner Zünfte im 13 und 14 Jahrhundert*, Leipzig, 1897. F. Smith, *Beiträge zur florentinischen Verfassungs- und Heeresgeschichte*, Leipzig, 1914. R. Gaggese, *Firenze dalla decadenza di Roma al risorgimento d'Italia*, Florence, 1913. G. Salvemini, *La dignità cavelleresca nel comune di Firenze*, Florence, 1896; *Magnati e popolani in Firenze dal 1280 al 1295*, Florence, 1899. C. Falletti-Fossati, *Il tumulto dei Ciompi*, Florence, 1882.

The Medici. G. F. Young, *The Medici*, London, 1909. W. H. O. Smeaton, *The Medici and the Italian renaissance*, New York, 1901 (World's epoch-makers). E. Heyck, *Florenz und die Mediceer*, Bielefeld and Leipzig, 1897 (Monographien zur Weltgeschichte). A. Castelnau, *Les Médicis*, 2 vols., Paris, 1879. K. Dorothea Ewart, (Mrs. H. M. Vernon), *Cosimo de' Medici*, New York, 1899 (Foreign statesmen). F. Knapp, *Piero di Cosimo*, Halle, 1899. Cecily Booth, *Cosimo I, duke of Florence*, Cambridge, 1921.

Lorenzo the Magnificent. E. L. S. Horsburgh, *Lorenzo the Magnificent and Florence in her golden age*, London, 1908. W. Roscoe, *Life of Lorenzo de' Medici*, 2 vols., Liverpool, 1795; 10th edition, London, 1851; new edition by Hazlitt, 2 vols., London, 1890. A. v. Reumont, *Lorenzo de'Medici und seine Zeit*, 2 vols., 2nd, revised, edition, Leipzig, 1883, translated by R. Harrison, *Lorenzo the Magnificent*, 1883. B. Buser, *Lorenzo de Medici als italianischer Staatsmann*, Leipzig, 1879; *Die Beziehungen der Mediceer zu Frankreich 1434–1494*, Leipzig, 1879.

Savonarola. E. L. S. Horsburgh, *Girolamo Savonarola*, London, 1901; 4th edition, revised and enlarged [1911]. H. Lucas, *Fra Girolamo Savonarola: a biographical study based on contemporary documents*, London, 1899; 2nd edition, 1906. G. McHardy, *Savonarola*, New York, 1901 (World's epoch-makers). J. Schnitzer, *Quellen und Forschungen zur Geschichte Savonarolas*, 4 vols., Munich and Leipzig, 1902–10; *Savonarola*, 2 vols., Munich, 1924. J. A. Gobineau, *The renaissance: Savonarola, Cesare Borgia, Julius II, Leo X, Michael Angelo*, English edition by O. Levy, London, 1913. F. T. Perrens, *Jérome Savonarole, sa vie, ses prédications, ses écrits*, 2 vols., Paris, 1856. L. v. Ranke, *Savonarola und die florentinische Republik gegen Ende des 15 Jahrhunderts*, Leipzig, 1877 (Collected works, 40–41).

Sicilian Vespers. M. Amari, *La guerre del Vespro Siciliano*, 3 vols., 9th edition, Milan, 1886, translated by the Earl of ELLESMERE, *History of the war of the Sicilian Vespers*, 3 vols., London, 1850; *Altre narrazioni del Vespro Siciliano*, Milan, 1887; *Racconte popolare del Vespro Siciliano*, Rome, 1882. O. CARTELLIERI, *Peter von Aragon und die Sizilianische Vesper*, Heidelberg, 1904 (Heidelberg. Abh., 7).

Naples and Sicily. The following old works are still valuable: P. GIANNONE, *Storia civile del regno di Napoli*, Naples, 4 vols., 1723; new edition, 5 vols., Milan, 1844–47; translated in part by J. OGILVIE, *Civil history of the kingdom of Naples*, 2 vols., London, 1729–31. A. DI MEO, *Annali critico-diplomatichi del regno di Napoli*, 13 vols., Naples, 1785–1819. E. DI BLASI, *Storia civile del regno di Sicilia*, 16 vols., Palermo, 1811; new edition, 22 vols., 1830; *Storia del regno di Sicilia*, 3 vols., Palermo, 1844–47. SAN FILIPPO, *Compendio della storia di Sicilia*, 7th edition, Palermo, 1859.

Special works. E. JORDAN, *Les origines de la domination angevine en Italie*, Paris, 1909. H. E. ROHDE, *Der Kampf um Sizilien in den Jahren 1291–1302*, vol. I, Berlin, 1913 (in Abhandlungen zur mittleren und neueren Geschichte, 42). E. HABERKERN, *Der Kampf um Sizilien in den Jahren 1302–1337*, Berlin and Leipzig, 1921. D. SCARPETTA, *Giovanna I di Napoli*, Naples, 1903. W. ST. CLAIR BADDELEY, *Queen Joanna I of Naples, Sicily, and Jerusalem*, London, 1893; *Robert the Wise and his heirs 1278–1352*, London, 1897. A. D. MESSER, *Le codice aragonese, étude générale, publication du manuscrit de Paris: contribution à l'histoire des Aragonais de Naples*, Paris, 1912 (in Bibliothèque du XVe siècle, vol. XVII). M. SCHIPA, *Contese sociali napoletane nel medio evo*, Naples, 1908. P. DURRIEU, *Les archives angevines de Naples: étude sur les registres du roi Charles Ier (1265–1285)*, 2 vols., Paris, 1886–87, part of no. **887.** L. CADIER, *Essai sur l'administration du royaume de Naples sous Charles Ier et Charles II d'Anjou*, Paris, 1891, part of no. **887.** W. ISRAEL, *König Robert von Neapel und Kaiser Heinrich VII*, Hersfeld, 1903. D. J. AMETLLER Y VINYAS, *Alfonso V de Aragon en Italia y la crisi religiosa del siglo 15*, vol. I, Gerona, 1903. F. SCADUTO, *Stato e chiesa nelle due Sicilie dai Normanni ai tempi nostri*, Palermo, 1886. S. V. BOZZO, *Note storiche siciliane del secolo XIV*, Palermo, 1882, throws light on the Catalan Grand Company. A. LECOY DE LA MARCHE, *Le roi René*, 2 vols., Paris, 1875. I. LA LUMIA, *Storie siciliane*, 4 vols., Palermo, 1881–83; *Studi di storia siciliana*, 2 vols., Palermo, 1870. R. CAGGESE, *Roberto d'Angiô e i suoi tempi*, vol. I, Florence, 1922. C. CALISSE, *Storia del parlamento in Sicilia*, Turin, 1887.

Other states of Italy. E. G. GARDNER, *The story of Siena and San Gimignano*, London, 1902. E. HUTTON, *Siena and southern Tuscany*, New York, 1910. C. CHLEDOWSKI, *Siena*, third edition, 2 vols., Berlin, 1918. ELLA NOYES, *The story of Ferrara*, London, 1904 (Mediaeval towns). M. ALLEN, *A history of Verona*, New York, 1910. ALETHEA WIEL, *The story of Verona*, 2nd edition, London, 1904. C. CIPOLLO, *Compendio di storia politica di Verona*, 1900. JANET A. ROSS and NELLY BRICHSEN, *The story of Pisa*, London, 1909 (Mediaeval towns). W. HEYWOOD, *A history of Pisa*. KATHERINE JAMES, *The city of contrasts: a story of old Perugia*, London, 1915. MARGARET SYMONDS and LINA D. GORDON, *The story of Perugia*, London, 1900

(Mediaeval towns). E. P. VICINI, *I podestà di Modena*, part I (1156–1336), Rome, 1914. E. HUTTON, *Sigismundo Pandolfo Malatesta, lord of Rimini: a story of a XV century Italian despot*, New York, 1906. JULIA CARTWRIGHT, *Isabella d'Este, marchioness of Mantua, 1474–1539*, New York, 1903. H. SPANGENBERG, *Can Grande della Scala*, 2 vols., Berlin, 1892–95. J. DENNISTOUN, *Memoirs of the dukes of Urbino, illustrating the arms, arts, and literature of Italy, 1440–1639*, 3 vols., London, 1853–54; new edition, 1909. ALETHEA WIEL, *The romance of the house of Savoy 1003–1519*, 2 vols., New York, 1898. J. ORSIER, *Pierre II, de Savoie, dit le Petit Charlemagne, 1202–1268*, Paris, 1918. D. LOCATELLI, *Ravenna nella storia, nei monumenti e nella vita attuale*, Ravenna, 1917. W. HEYWOOD, *A history of Pisa*.

Corsica. A. AMBROSI, *Histoire des Corses et de leur civilisation*, Bastia, 1914. L. CAIRD, *The history of Corsica*, London, 1899.

Original sources. The large collections of sources for Italian history are listed above, nos. **988–94;** see also vols. XII–XIV of no. **986.** For Italy, the collections for individual states are especially important, but no attempt can be made here to list even the most important ones. See also *Nuovo archivio veneto*, Venice, 1891–1921. *Archivio storico per le provincie napoletane*, Naples, 1876ff. For details, see the special bibliographies listed below.

The letters of COLA DI RIENZO have been edited and studied anew by K. and P. PIUR, *Briefwechsel des Cola di Rienzo*, Berlin, 1912 (vol. II of no. **750**). *Epistolario di Cola di Rienzo*, edited by A. GABRIELLI, Rome, 1890, is an older collection.

For Venice, special mention may be made of *Calendar of State Papers: Venetian*, vol. I, 1202–1607, edited by R. BROWN, London, 1864.

G. LA MANTIA, *Codice diplomatico dei re aragonesi di Sicilia dalla revoluzione siciliana del 1282 ino al 1355*, Palermo, 1917.

For SAVONAROLA, see *Scelta di prediche e scritta di Fra Girolamo Savonarola con nuovi documenti intorno alla sua vita*, edited by P. VILLARI and E. CASANOVA, Florence, 1898.

C. A. MILLS (editor), *Ye solace of pilgrims. A description of Rome, circa 1450, by John Capgrave, an Austin friar of King's Lynn*, Oxford, 1911.

Bibliographies. The general bibliographies for Italy are listed above, nos. **37–41.** See also no. **19,** 447–49 (a very convenient summary of the most essential source material), and 479–503.

Special bibliographies. P. LAURIEL, *Bibliografia del 6 centenario del Vespro Siciliano*, Palermo, 1882; see also C. CIPOLLA, "Les Vêpres Siciliennes: compte-rendu des principales publications historiques parues à propos du septième centenaire célébré à Palerme le 31 mars 1882," *R.H.*, XXI (1883), 135–47. G. SORANZO, *Bibliografia veneziana*, Venice, 1885 (see also the bibliography for ch. VIII of the *Cambridge modern history*, I). L. S. OLSCHKI, *Bibliotheca Savonaroliana*, Florence and Venice, about 1902 (see also the bibliography for ch. V of the *Cambridge modern history*, I). L. FONTANA, *Bibliografia degli statuti dei comuni dell' Italia superiore*, 3 vols., Turin, 1907. C. W. PREVITÉ-ORTON, "Recent work in Italian medieval history," *Cambridge historical journal*, I (1923–25), 10–22.

XXXIII. THE REMARKABLE INTEREST IN ANCIENT CLASSICAL LITERATURE, ART, AND ARCHAEOLOGY IN ITALY DURING THE FOURTEENTH AND FIFTEENTH CENTURIES

A. Outline

1. The meaning of "Renaissance" and "Revival of learning." As general historical terms these expressions are rapidly losing the definiteness and color which was given to them by such writers as Burckhardt, Voigt, and Symonds, however useful they may still be in the history of certain branches of literature and art in western Europe. Humanism. *Litterae humaniores.* The "discovery of man" and the "discovery of the world." Controversies between "ancients and moderns." "Battles of books."

2. Retrospect: interest in these subjects during the twelfth and thirteenth centuries. For details see outline XVIII in part III.

3. Dante, 1265–1321, and the ancient world. For details concerning Dante scholarship see outline XXVIII in part III.

4. The place of Petrarch, 1304–76, in the history of culture. The growth of his interest in the Latin classics. Means by which he interested others in them. His slight knowledge of Greek. His search for manuscripts. The retreat at Vaucluse. His popularity as a poet. His famous *Letters* and other writings, especially the *Africa.* The influence of the Latin revival on Italian.

5. The feverish search in medieval libraries for the manuscripts of ancient classical belles-lettres. Poggio Bracciolini, 1380–1459, at the council of Constance and his subsequent travels. The collection of Greek books by Aurispa (died 1459) and Filelfo, 1398–1481.

6. Interest in classical epigraphy and archaeology. Ciriaco, about 1391–1450, "the Schliemann of his time." Flavio Biondo, 1388–1463, and his four great works on the antiquities and history of Rome and Italy.

7. Interest in Greek. The share of Petrarch and Boccaccio, 1313–75, in creating this interest. Greek scholars from Constantinople in Italy. Manuel Chrysoloras (about 1350–1415) in Florence, 1396. Gemistos Plethon, about 1356–1450, and Bessarion, 1395 or 1403–72, at the council of Ferrara-Florence, 1438–39. Theodorus Gaza, about 1400–75. Controversies over the merits of Plato and Aristotle. The fall of Constantinople in 1453 did little or nothing to encourage the study of Greek in the west.

8. Florence was the center of humanism. The monastery of Santo Spirito and Luigi de' Marsigli (died 1394). Coluccio Salutati, 1330–1406. The Medici as patrons of literature. Niccolo de' Niccoli, 1363–1437, Leonardo Bruni, 1369–1444, in the time of Cosimo de' Medici. The brilliant circle of Lorenzo de' Medici. The Platonic Academy of Florence. Ficino, 1433–99. Pico della Mirandola, 1463–94. Politian, 1454–94.

9. Humanism in Rome. Its effect upon the papacy and on the Christian religion. Popularity of pagan ideas and rites. The humanist popes Nicolas V, 1447–55, and Pius II (Æneas Sylvius), 1458–64. The Academy of Rome and Pomponius Laetus, 1425–98.

10. The Academy of Naples in the time of Alfonso of Aragon, 1442–58. Laurentius Valla, 1407–57, and his criticism of the Donation of Constantine. His famous book *On the elegancies of Latin language*. Beccadelli, 1394–1471. Pontano, 1426–1503. Sannazaro, 1458–1530.

11. Aldus Manutius, 1449–1515, the printer of Greek texts in Venice. In 1500 he founded the New Academy of Hellenists in Venice.

12. Other centers of humanism. The Visconti and Sforza as patrons of letters in Milan. Can Grande della Scala of Verona. Federigo, count of Montefeltro, and his famous library at Urbino. The humanism of the fierce Sigismondo Malatesta of Rimini.

13. In the schools, humanism brought about a revolution, the effects of which have lasted down to this day. Vittorino da Feltre, 1378–1446, in Mantua. Guarino da Verona, 1370–1460, in Ferrara. The *De ordine docendi et studendi* (1459) of his son, Battista Guarino. Comparative lack of interest in humanism in universities.

14. Renaissance art contrasted with medieval art. The wonderful development of painting which culminated in the first half of the sixteenth century. Important painters: Cimabue, 1240–about 1302; Giotto, 1276–1336; Masaccio, 1402–29; Fra Angelico, 1387–1455; Filippo Lippi, 1406–69; Botticelli, 1447–1510; Ghirlandajo, 1449–98; Leonardo da Vinci, 1452–1519; Raphael, 1483–1520; Titian, about 1477–1576; Correggio, 1494–1534. Important architects: Brunelleschi, 1377–1446; Leo Battista Alberti, 1404–72; Bramante, about 1444–1514. Important sculptors: Orcagna, 1308–68; Ghiberti, 1378–1455; Donatello, 1386–1466; Luca della Robbia, 1400–82. The genius of Michael Angelo Buonarroti, 1475–1564.

15. The invention of printing, about 1450. The Gutenberg controversy.

16. The spread and influence of the Italian culture of this period.

B. Special Recommendations for Reading

Brief general surveys. Adams, *Civilization*, ch. xv. Lodge, *The close of the middle ages*, ch. xxii. Abbott, *Expansion of Europe*, I, ch. ii. Emerton, *Beginnings of modern Europe*, ch. ix. Munro and Sontag, *Middle Ages*, ch. xl. Sellery and Krey, *Medieval foundation*, 355–73. Thorndike, *Medieval Europe*, 586–95, 597–607.

Longer accounts. Villari, *The life and times of Niccolò Machiavelli*, I, 63–167. *Cambridge modern history*, I, chs. xvi–xvii. Lavisse et Rambaud, *Histoire générale*, III, ch. xi. Loserth, *Geschichte des späteren Mittelalters*, 613–43. J. H. Randall, *Making of the modern mind*, Bk. II. H. O. Taylor, *Thought and expression in the sixteenth century*, New York, 1920, 2 vols., I (largely on the 14th and 15th centuries, so far as Italy is concerned).

Short books on the subject. J. E. Sandys, *Harvard lectures on the revival of learning*, Cambridge, 1905. Edith Sichel, *The renaissance*, New York, 1914 (Home university library). W. H. Hudson, *The story of the renaissance*, New York, 1912. J. B. Oldham, *The renaissance*, New York, 1912 (Temple primers). Sandys, *Classical scholarship*, II, is a handy volume for reference. W. Pater, *The renaissance*. R. A. Taylor, *Aspects of the Italian renaissance*,

Boston, 1923. F. CLEMENT, editor, *The civilization of the renaissance*, Chicago, 1929 (lectures by J. W. THOMPSON, F. SCHEVILL, G. SARTON, and G. ROWLEY).

Meaning of "Renaissance." The easiest introduction to the present controversy concerning the "Renaissance" may be got by reading in juxtaposition two articles in the *Ency. Brit.*, XI edition, "Renaissance" by J. A. SYMONDS, and "Middle ages" by Professor SHOTWELL.

Standard works. The popular conceptions of "Renaissance" and "Revival of Learning" were stereotyped chiefly by the following books. J. BURCKHARDT, *Die Kultur der Renaissance in Italien*, 1860; 10th edition, 2 vols., Leipzig, 1908, translated by S. G. C. MIDDLEMORE, *The civilization of the renaissance in Italy*, 2 vols., London, 1878; 7th edition in one volume, 1914. G. VOIGT, *Die Wiederbelebung des classischen Alterthums*, Berlin, 1859; 3rd edition, edited by M. LEHNERDT, 2 vols., 1893. J. A. SYMONDS, *The renaissance in Italy*, 5 parts in 7 vols., London, 1875–81; new edition, 1897–8, vol. I, *The age of the despots;* vol. II, *The revival of learning;* vol. III, *The fine arts;* vols. IV and V, *Italian literature;* vols. VI and VII, *The catholic reaction.* L. GEIGER, *Renaissance und Humanismus in Italien und Deutschland*, Berlin, 1882, part of no. **313**.

Dante. C. H. GRANDGENT, *Dante*, New York, 1916. P. J. TOYNBEE, *Dante*, New York, 1910. C. A. DINSMORE, editor, *Aids to the study of Dante*, Boston, 1903. For details about the literature on Dante see outline XXVIII of part III.

Petrarch. The best introduction is J. H. ROBINSON and H. W. ROLFE, *Petrarch: the first modern scholar and man of letters*, New York, 1898; new edition, 1914, which contains many of his letters in translation. E. TATHAM, *Francesco Petrarca; the first modern man of letters: a study of the early fourteenth century*, 2 vols., London, 1925–26. H. C. HOLLWAY-CALTHROP, *Petrarch: his life and times*, New York, 1907. MAUD F. JERROLD, *Francesco Petrarca: poet and humanist*, New York, 1909.

P. DE NOLHAC, *Petrarch and the ancient world*, Boston, 1908, is a translation of an interesting portion of his French work listed below. G. B. ADAMS, "Petrarch and the beginning of modern science," in *Yale review*, I (1892), 146–61, is a study of Petrarch's historical criticism; the author, indeed, thinks it possible that the renaissance acted as a check on the natural sciences.

Greek. LOUISE R. LOOMIS, "The Greek renaissance in Italy," *A.H.R.*, XIII (1908), 246–58.

Humanism and education. For a general survey, F. P. GRAVES, *A history of education during the middle ages*, 106–39. W. H. WOODWARD, *Vittorino da Feltre and other humanist educators*, Cambridge, 1897; *Studies in education during the age of the renaissance, 1400–1600*, Cambridge, 1907. R. C. JEBB, *Humanism in education*, London and New York, 1899.

Renaissance art. J. BURCKHARDT, *Der Cicerone: eine Einleitung zum Genuss der Kunstwerke Italiens*, 9th edition in 2 parts in 4 volumes, Leipzig, 1904, translated by Mrs. A. H. CLOUGH, *The cicerone: or, Art guide to painting in Italy*, London, 1873; new and illustrated impression, New York, 1908.

F. J. MATHER, JR., *A history of Italian painting*, New York, 1923.

W. J. ANDERSON, *The architecture of the renaissance in Italy*, 5th edition, London, 1927. G. SCOTT, *The architecture of humanism*, 2nd edition, London, 1924. G. H. CHASE and C. P. POST, *A history of sculpture*, New York, 1925.

J. A. SYMONDS, *The fine arts* (vol. III of his *Renaissance in Italy*) gives details.

Invention of printing. J. H. HESSELS, *The Gutenberg fiction*, London, 1912; and his article "Typography," *Ency. Brit.*, XI edition, furnish a good bibliography. Excellent work in this field was done by the American scholar T. L. DE VINNE, *Invention of printing*, 2nd edition, New York, 1878; *Notable printers of Italy during the fifteenth century*, New York, 1910. C. MORTET, *Les origines et les débuts de l'imprimerie d'après les recherches les plus récentes*, Paris, 1923.

Original sources. M. WHITCOMB, *A literary source book of the renaissance*, 2nd edition, Philadelphia, 1903, part I, *The Italian renaissance*, translates many extracts. See also ROBINSON, *Readings*, I, ch. XXII; and OGG, *Source book*, ch. XXVI.

Petrarch's letters to classical authors, translated from the Latin by M. E. COSENZA, Chicago, 1910. *Petrarch's secret: or the soul's conflict with passion*, translated from the Latin by W. H. DRAPER, London, 1911. *The Triumph of Francesco Petrarch, Florentine poet laureate*, translated by H. BOYD, London, 1906. *Some love songs of Petrarch*, translated and annotated, with a biographical introduction, by W. D. FOULKE, Oxford, 1915. BOCCACCIO'S *Decam ron.* F. SCHEVILL, *First century of Italian humanism*, New York, 1928. E. EMERTON, *Humanism and tyranny.* N. E. GRIFFIN and A. B. MYRICK, *The Filostrato of Giovanni Boccaccio, a translation with parallel text*, introduction by N. E. GRIFFIN, Philadelphia, 1929. J. M. RIGG, editor, *Giovanni Pico della Mirandola: his life by his nephew*, etc., trans. from the Latin by SIR THOMAS MORE, London, 1890. J. ZEITTEN, *The life of solitude, by Francis Petrarch*, translated with notes, Urbana, Ill., 1924.

G. VASARI (1512–74), *Vite de' più eccellenti pittori, scultori e architettori*, new edition with a summary of the latest researches in the notes, by K. FREY, vol. I, Munich, 1911ff., translated by Mrs. J. FOSTER, *Lives of seventy of the most eminent painters, sculptors and architects*, complete in 5 vols., London, 1850–64 (Bohn library); new trans. by G. DE VERE, published in 10 vols. with five hundred illustrations by the Medici Society, 1912–15; another edition of selected lives, by E. W. BLASHFIELD and A. A. HOPKINS, 4 vols., New York, 1902 (Temple classics). VITRUVIUS (first century A.D.), *The ten books on architecture*, translated by M. H. MORGAN, Cambridge, 1914, had such a profound influence on the artists of the renaissance period that it must be read in order to understand their art. BALDASSARE CASTIGLIONE, *The book of the courtier*, translated by L. E. OPDYCKE, New York, 1929; translated by T. HOBY, Everyman's Library. *The life of Benvenuto Cellini*, written by himself, translated out of the Italian by J. A. SYMONDS, various editions; a version by R. H. H. CUST, 2 vols., London, 1910, also translated by ANNE MACDONNEL in Everyman's Library.

C. Bibliography

General books. Among the books on the history of civilization listed above see especially nos. **729–50a.** Of the general histories of literature, see especially nos. **782–86, 808–11a.** Many of the histories of education, nos. **836–43**, are useful. See also the literature mentioned under the preceding outline on Italy, especially that on Florence.

Meaning of renaissance. At least as early as 1885, with the appearance of the first edition of H. Thode, *Franz von Assisi und die Anfänge der Kunst der Renaissance in Italien*, 2nd edition, revised, Berlin, 1904, a reaction set in against the conception of the renaissance which was popularized especially by Burckhardt. The controversy may be pursued in the following booklets and articles, arranged according to date of publication: C. Neumann, "Byzantinische Kultur and Renaissancekultur," *H.Z.*, XCI (1903), 215–32 (translated in part by Munro and Sellery, *Medieval civilization*, 524–46). W. Goetz, "Mittelalter und Renaissance," *ibid.*, XCVIII (1907), 30–54. K. Brandi, *Das Werden des Renaissance*, Göttingen, 1908. K. Burdach, "Sinn und Ursprung der Worte 'Renaissance' und 'Reformation,'" *S.B.*, Berlin Acad., 1910, I, 595ff. P. Wernle, *Renaissance und Reformation: sechs Vorträge*, Tübingen, 1912. A. Philippi, *Der Begriff der Renaissance: Daten zu seiner Geschichte*, Leipzig, 1912. E. Heyfelder, "Die Ausdrücke 'Renaissance' und 'Humanismus,'" *Deutsche Literaturzeitung*, September 6, 1913. E. Troeltsch, "Renaissance und Reformation," *H.Z.*, CX (1913), 519–56. K. Burdach, "Über den Ursprung des Humanismus," *Deutsche Rundschau*, CLVIII, CLIX, 1914. K. Francke, *Personality in German literature before Luther*, Cambridge, 1916. See also the *Literaturbericht* of P. Funk, "Geschichte der geistigen Kultur: Renaissance," *Archiv für Kulturgeschichte*, XI (1913–14), 377–88. H. Hefele, "Zum Begriff der Renaissance," *Hist. Jahrbuch*, XLIX (1929), 444–59.

Renaissance in general. J. D. Symon and S. L. Bensusan, *The renaissance and its makers*, London, 1913, say in their preface, "this book is intended for the general reader." J. P. Hervás, *Historia del renacimiento*, 2 vols., Barcelona, 1916. P. van Dyke, *Renascence portraits*, New York, 1905. J. Cartwright, *Baldassare Castiglione*, 2 vols., London, 1908. R. Saitschick, *Menschen und Kunst der italienischen Renaissance*, 2 vols., Berlin, 1903–04. E. Rodocanachi, *La femme italienne à l'époque de la renaissance*, Paris, 1907. G. Mazzoni, *Vita italiana nel rinascimento*, Milan, 1899. H. Janitschek, *Die Gesellschaft der Renaissance in Italien und die Kunst: vier Vorträge*, Stuttgart, 1879. E. Gebhart, *Les origines de la renaissance en Italie*, Paris, 1879; *La renaissance italienne et la philosophie de l'histoire*, Paris, 1887. O. Schütz, *Der grosse Mensch der Renaissance*, Bonn, 1906 (Diss.). H. Hettner, *Geschichte der Renaissance: Italienische Studien*, Braunschweig, 1879. W. Dilthey, "Über die Auffassung und Analyse des Menschen im 15 und 16 Jahrhundert," *Archiv für Geschichte der Philosophie*, IV (1891), 604–51; V (1892), 337–400 (also reprinted in *Gesammelte Schriften*, I, Leipzig, 1913). E. Gothein, "Die Weltanschauung der Renaissance," *Jahrbuch des freien deutschen Hochstifts in Frankfurt*, 1904, 95–131.

Renaissance and Reformation. E. M. HULME, *The renaissance, the protestant revolution, and the catholic reformation in continental Europe*, New York, 1914; revised edition, New York, 1923. JEAN M. STONE, *Reformation and renaissance (circa 1377–1610)*, London, 1904. MARY A. HOLLINGS, *Europe in renaissance and reformation, 1453–1659*, London, 1909.

Humanism in general. R. SABBADINI, *Le scoperte dei codici latini e greci ne' secoli XIV e XV*, Florence, 1905; *Storia del ciceronianismo e di altre questione letterarie nell' età della rinascenza*, Turin, 1885. G. FIORETTO, *Gli umanisti o lo studio del latino e del greco nel secolo XV in Italia*, Verona, 1881. A. ROERSCH, *L'humanisme belge à l'époque de la renaissance*, Brussels, 1910. T. ZIELINSKI, *Die Antike und wir*, translated by E. SCHÖLER, 2nd edition, Leipzig, 1909; *Cicero im Wandel der Jahrhunderte*, 3rd edition, Leipzig, 1912. G. TOFFANIN, *Che cosa fu l'umanesimo?*, Florence, 1929.

Renaissance literature in general. J. E. SPINGARN, *A history of literary criticism in the renaissance*, New York, 1899; 2nd edition, 1908. M. MONNIER, *La renaissance de Dante à Luther*, Paris, 1884; *Le quattrocento: essai sur l'histoire littéraire du XVe siècle italien*, new edition, 2 vols., Paris, 1908. O. KUHNS, *The great poets of Italy*, Boston, 1904. F. J. SNELL, *The fourteenth century*, New York, 1899 (Periods of European literature). G. G. SMITH, *The transition period* [15th and 16th centuries], New York, 1900 (Periods of European literature). *The renaissance library*, New York, Dutton. F. DE SANCTIS, *Storia della letteratura italiana*, I (an English translation is announced).

Petrarch. P. DE NOLHAC, *Pétrarque et l'humanisme*, Paris, 1892; new edition, 2 vols., 1907. G. KÖRTING, *Petrarca's Leben und Werke* (vol. I of *Geschichte der Literatur Italiens im Zeitalter der Renaissance*), Leipzig, 1878. G. BOLOGNA, *Note e studi sul Petrarca*, Berlin, 1913 (Die Religion der Klassiker, 3). G. FINZI, *Petrarca*, Florence, 1900. A. MÉZIÈRES, *Pétrarque: étude d'après de nouveaux documents*, Paris, 1868; new edition, 1895. B. ZUMBINI, *Studi sul Petrarca*, Naples, 1878; new edition, Florence, 1895. F. DE SANCTIS, *Saggio critico sul Petrarca* (introduction by B. Croce), Naples, 1924. H. HEFELE, *Francesco Petrarca*, Berlin, 1913.

Boccaccio. H. HAUVETTE, *Boccace*, Paris, 1914. E. HUTTON, *Giovanni Boccaccio: a biographical study*, London, 1910. E. RODOCANACHI, *Boccace: poëte, conteur, moraliste, homme politique*, Paris, 1908. J. A. SYMONDS, *Giovanni Boccaccio as man and author*, London, 1895. G. KÖRTING, *Boccaccio's Leben und Werke* (vol. II of his *Geschichte der Literatur Italiens im Zeitalter der Renaissance*), Leipzig, 1880. A. HORTIS, *Studi sulle opere latine del Boccaccio*, Trieste, 1879.

Poggio. W. SHEPHERD, *The life of Poggio Bracciolini*, Liverpool, 1802; 2nd edition, 1837. E. WALSER, *Poggius Florentinus: Leben und Werke*, Leipzig, 1914.

Greek. T. KLETTE, *Beiträge zur Geschichte und Literatur der italienischen Gelehrtenrenaissance*, 3 vols., Greifswald, 1888–90, important for its studies on Greek scholars; also contains documentary material. H. VAST, *Le cardinal Bessarion*, Paris, 1878. E. LEGRAND, *Bibliographie hellénique, XVe et XVIe siècles*, 3 vols., Paris, 1884–5.

Florence. C. Hare (pseudonym), *Life and letters in the Italian renaissance*, London, 1915. G. S. Godkin, *Monastery of San Marco*, London, 1901. K. Brandi, *Die Renaissance in Florenz und Rom*, 4th edition, Leipzig, 1913. F. T. Perrens, *La civilisation florentine du 13 au 16 siècle*, Paris, 1893. W. B. Scaife, *Florentine life during the renaissance*, Baltimore, 1893. A. della Torre, *Storia dell' Accademia platonica di Firenze*, Florence, 1902. P. Villari, *Life and times of Savonarola*, London, 1918; *Life and Times of Machiavelli*, 2 vols. in 1, New York, n.d.

Coluccio. A. Martin, *Mittelalterliche Welt- und Lebensanschauung im Spiegel der Schriften Coluccio Salutatis*, Munich and Berlin, 1913 (Historische Bibliothek, XXXIII); *Coluccio Salutatis Traktat "Vom Tyrannen": eine kulturgeschichtliche Untersuchung nebst Textedition, mit einer Einleitung über Salutatis Leben und Schriften und einem Exkurs über seine philologisch-historische Methode*, Berlin and Leipzig, 1913 (*Abh.m.n.G.*, 47).

Marsigli of Florence (died 1394). S. Bellandi, *Luigi Marsili degli Agostiniani, apostolo ed anima del rinascimento letterario in Firenze, 1342–1394*, Florence, 1911.

Rome. Gregorovius, *Rome in the middle ages*, book XII, ch. vii; book XIII, *passim.* J. Strzygowski, *Cimabue und Rom: Funde und Forschungen zur Kunstgeschichte und zur Topographie der Stadt Rom*, Vienna, 1888. C. v. Chledowski, *Rom: die Menschen der Renaissance*, translated from the Polish by Rosa Schapiro, Munich, 1912. E. Steinmann, *Rom in der Renaissance von Nicolaus V bis Leo X*, 3rd edition, Leipzig, 1908. J. Klaszko, *Rome and the renaissance: The pontificate of Julius II*, translated from the French by J. Dennie, New York, 1903. E. Rodocanachi, *Une cour princière au Vatican pendant la renaissance: Sixte IV, Innocent VIII, Alexandre VI Borgia (1471–1503)*, Paris, 1925. R. Lanciani, *The golden days of the renaissance in Rome: from the pontificate of Julius II to that of Paul III*, Boston and New York, 1906.

Naples. W. Goetz, *Konig Robert von Neapel (1309–1343): seine Persönlichkeit und sein Verhältnis zum Humanismus*, Tübingen, 1910.

Laurentius Valla. L. Barozzi and R. Sabbadini, *Studi sul Panormita e sul Valla*, Florence, 1891 (the portion on Laurentius Valla is by Sabbadini). G. Mancini, *Vita di Lorenzo Valla*, Florence, 1891. M. v. Wolff, *Lorenzo Valla: sein Leben und seine Werke*, Leipzig, 1893. W. Schwahn, *Lorenzo Valla: ein Beitrag zur Geschichte des Humanismus*, Berlin, 1896 (Diss.). Laehr, *Die Konstantinische Schenkung in der abendländischen Literatur des Mittelalters bis zur Mitte des XIV Jahrhunderts.*

Aldus Manutius. A. F. Didot, *Alde Manuce et l'hellênisme à Venise*, Paris, 1875. W. D. Orcutt, editor, *The book in Italy during the 15th and 16th centuries* (facsimile reproduction), London, 1928.

Religion and humanism. J. Owen, *The skeptics of the Italian renaissance*, 2nd edition, London, 1893. E. Walser, "Christentum und Antike in der Auffassung der italienischen Frührenaissance," *Archiv für Kulturgeschichte*, XI (1913), 273–88. C. Dejob, *La foi religieuse en Italie au XIVe siècle*, Paris, 1905.

Education. R. SABBADINI, *La scuola e gli studî di Guarini*, Catania, 1896; edition of *Letters of Guarino of Verona*, vol. I, Venice, 1915.

Renaissance art in general. E. MÜNTZ, *Histoire de l'art pendant la renaissance*, 3 vols., Paris, 1889–95 (contains good bibliographies); *Les précurseurs de la renaissance*, Paris, 1882; *Les arts à la cour des papes pendant le XVe et le XVIe siècle*, 3 vols., Paris, 1878–82, parts 4 and 9 of no. **887**; *La renaissance en Italie et en France à l'époque de Charles VIII*, Paris, 1885. A. VENTURI, *Storia dell' arte italiana*, vols. I–VII, Milan, 1901–15 (vols. IV–VII treat the art of the fourteenth and fifteenth centuries). A. PHILIPPI, *Die Kunst der Renaissance in Italien*, 2 vols., Leipzig, 1905. H. WÖLFFLIN, *Die klassische Kunst: Einführung in die italienische Renaissance*, Munich, 1901, translated by W. ARMSTRONG, *The art of the Italian renaissance: a handbook for students and travellers*, New York, 1903.

Many books listed under outline XXVII in part III, on medieval art, also treat renaissance art.

Criticism of renaissance art. J. RUSKIN, *Mornings in Florence*, New York, 1876; *Modern painters*, 4 vols., New York, 1858–9; *Stones of Venice*, 3 vols., New York, 1860. H. TAINE, *Philosophie de l'art en Italie*, Paris, 1866; 3rd edition, 1880. VIOLET PAGET (VERNON LEE, pseudonym), *Euphorion: studies of the antique and the mediaeval in the renaissance*, 2nd edition, revised, London, 1885; *Renaissance fancies and studies*, 1895; 2nd edition, London, 1909. M. CARRIERE, *Die Kunst im Zusammenhang der Culturentwicklung*, 3rd, revised, edition, 5 vols., Leipzig, 1877–86, vol. IV, *Renaissance und Reformation*.

Renaissance painting. B. BERENSON, *The Florentine painters of the renaissance*, New York, 1896; 3rd edition, revised, 1909; *The Venetian painters of the renaissance*, New York, 1895; 3rd edition, 1897; *The north Italian painters of the renaissance*, New York [1907]; *The central Italian painters of the renaissance*, 2nd edition, revised, New York, 1909. J. A. CROWE and G. B. CAVALCASELLE, *A history of painting in north Italy from the fourteenth to the sixteenth century*, edited by T. BORENIUS, 3 vols., London, 1912; *A new history of painting in Italy*, 3 vols., London and New York, 1908–9. R. VAN MARLE, *The development of the Italian schools of painting*, 11 vols., The Hague, 1923–29, particularly useful because of illustrations. L. VENTURI, *Le origini della pittura veneziana, 1300–1500*, Venice, 1907.

Renaissance architecture. A. SCHUETZ, *Die Renaissance in Italien: eine Sammlung der werthvollsten Monumente*, 4 vols., Hamburg, 1893–96. L. PALUSTRE, *L'architecture de la renaissance*, Paris, 1892. H. WÖLFFLIN, *Renaissance und Barock*, 4th edition, Munich, 1926.

Renaissance sculpture. D. A. E. L. BALCARRES, *The evolution of Italian sculpture*, London, 1909. W. BODE, *Florentine sculptors of the renaissance*, New York, 1909, translation of *Die italienischen Bildhauer der Renaissance*, Berlin, 1887. M. REYMOND, *La sculpture florentine*, 4 vols., Florence, 1897–1900.

Leonardo da Vinci. O. SIRÉN, *Leonardo da Vinci: the artist and the man*, Yale University Press, 1915. O. SIRÉN wrote this book originally in Swedish

(Stockholm, 1911), a new edition in French in three volumes, *Léonard de Vinci: l'artiste et l'homme*, Paris, 1928. P. DUHEM, *Etudes sur Léonardo de Vinci, ceux qu'il a lus et ceux qui l' ont lu*, 3 vols., Paris, 1906–13. E. MÜNTZ, *Leonardo da Vinci*, 2 vols., London, 1898. E. McCURDY, *The mind of Leonardo da Vinci*, New York, 1928. R. A. TAYLOR, *Leonardo the Florentine*, New York, 1928.

Michael Angelo. R. ROLLAND, *Michaelangelo*, translated from the French by F. STREET, New York, 1915; another translation by F. LEES, *The life of Michael Angelo*, London, 1912. H. THODE, *Michelangelo und das Ende der Renaissance*, 3 vols. in 4, Berlin, 1902–12. J. A. SYMONDS, *The life of Michelangelo Buonarroti*, London, 1893. E. STEINMANN and R. WITHKOWER, editors, *Michaelangelo Bibliographie*, 1510–1926, Leipzig, 1929. Individual biographies of other artists may be found in such series as: *Great artists series; Great masters in painting and sculpture*, edited by G. C. WILLIAMSON; *Masters in art*, Boston, Bates, 1900ff.

Original sources. *Das Zeitalter der Renaissance: ausgewählte Quellen zur Geschichte der italienischen Kultur*, edited by MARIE HERZFELD, Jena, 1911ff. *Die Renaissance in Briefen von Dichtern, Künstlern, Staatsmänner, Gelehrten und Frauen*, edited by L. SCHMIDT, vol. I, Leipzig, 1908, an uncritical collection for the general public. VESPASIANO DA BISTICCI [died 1498], *Vite di uomini illustri del secolo XV*, Florence, 1849; new edition in 3 vols., Bologna, 1892. MATTEO VILLANI, *Cronica*, 6 vols., Florence, 1825–26.

F. PETRARCH, *Epistolae de rebus familiaribus et variae*, 3 vols., edited by G. FRACASSETTI, Florence, 1859–63. These famous letters were also translated into Italian by the same editor, with notes, *Lettere di Francesco Petrarca delle cose familiari libri ventiquattro, lettere varie libro unico*, 5 vols., Florence, 1892; and *Lettere senile*, 2 vols., Florence, 1892. A. F. JOHNSON (editor), *Francisci Petrarchae epistolae selectae*, Oxford, 1923. L. VALLA, *Treatise on the Donation of Constantine*, text and introduction by C. B. COLEMAN. For a general survey of this question of historical criticism, see C. B. COLEMAN, *Constantine the Great and Christianity*, New York, 1914.

E. McCURDY (editor), *Leonardo da Vinci's Note book*, New York, 1923. J. P. RICHTER, editor, *The literary works of Leonardo da Vinci*, London, 1883. *Epistolario di* COLUCCIO SALUTATI, edited by F. NOVATI, vols. I–III, Rome, 1891–6, vols. XV–XVII of no. **990.** *Briefwechsel des* ÆNEAS SILVIUS PICCOLOMINI, edited by R. WOLKAN, Vienna, 1909. *Ausgewählte Schriften* von GIOVANNI PICO DELLA MIRANDOLA, edited, with an introduction, by A. LIEBERT, Jena and Leipzig, 1905.

Large collections of sources for the history of Italy in general are listed above, nos. **988–94.**

Bibliographies. There are general bibliographies in VOIGT, *Wiederbelebung*, II, 511–25, which is especially valuable for original sources; SANDYS, *Classical scholarship*, II, xv–xix; and *Cambridge modern history*, I, 779–83. E. CALVI, *Bibliografia analitica Petrarchese, 1877–1904*, Rome, 1904. See also the *Catalogue of the Petrarch collection bequeathed by Willard Fiske to the Cornell university library*, compiled by MARY FOWLER, Oxford university press, 1916.

XXXIV. CHRISTIAN SPAIN IN THE LATER MIDDLE AGES

A. Outline

1. The protracted crusade against the Moors was the chief factor which molded the life of Christian Spain in the middle ages. Its effect upon political and social institutions and upon the character of the people.

2. The nuclei of Christian states in northern Spain: (1) Asturias (capital Oviedo), with Cantabria, developed into Leon and Castile (Alfonso III, the Great, 866–910); (2) Navarre (Basques); (3) Aragon; (4) Barcelona (Spanish mark of Charlemagne) developed into the kingdom Catalonia; (5) Galicia (St. James of Compostella) gave rise to Portugal, but was itself won by Castile.

3. The breakup of the Omayyad caliphate of Cordova. Death of the great minister and general Almansor in 1002. The division of the caliphate into several small states between 1002 and 1031.

4. Union of Castile and Aragon under Ferdinand I of Castile, 1033–65. The reconquest of Spain. In 1085 Alfonso VI, 1065–1109, captured Toledo. His famous condottiere, Ruy Diaz, *el Cid Campeador* (died 1099). The Moors invited the Almoravides from Africa, who, under Yussuf, defeated Alfonso at the battle of Zallaca, 1086. Rivalry between the Almoravides and the Almohades during the twelfth century.

5. The rise of Aragon. Alfonso I, *el Batallador*, 1104–34, took Saragossa in 1118. Union of Aragon with Catalonia or Barcelona, thus giving Aragon access to the Mediterranean and wresting Catalonia from French influence. In 1283 Aragon took Valencia and soon developed a Mediterranean policy under James I, 1213–76, the first step being the conquest of the Balearic Islands.

6. The papacy and the Roman church in Spain. Influence of the crusades in drawing the attention of the papacy to Spain. The Cistercians in Spain. The Cistercian military monastic orders of Calatrava and Alcantara. The order of St. James (Santiago). The great interest of pope Innocent III in Spain. In his pontificate was fought the decisive battle of Las Navas de Tolosa, 1212, which finally gave the Christians the upper hand in the peninsula.

7. The constitutional history of Spain. Importance of the burgher class in the struggle against the Moors. The cortes in the twelfth century. The *hermandades*, or brotherhoods of cities, and the nobles. The peculiar office of the *justicia* in Aragon. Strength of royalty in Spain. The *Siete Partidas* of Alfonso X of Castile.

8. The predominance of Castile under Saint Ferdinand III, 1214–52 (a contemporary of Saint Louis IX of France). Final union between Leon and Castile in 1230. The winning of Andalusia. Capture of Cordova in 1236, of Seville in 1244, and of Xeres and Cadiz in 1250. The Moors were now confined to Granada, but there they were allowed to remain until 1492. The castles of Alhambra and Generalife.

9. After 1250 interest centers in the balance of power between the Christian states in the peninsula and in their relations with the states of Europe.

10 Castile, 1252–1469. Alfonso X, the Wise, 1252–84, and Richard of Cornwall became rival Holy Roman emperors during the Great Interregnum. Anarchy after his death. Under Alfonso XI, the Moors laid siege to Tarifa in 1340, but they were badly defeated in the battle of Salado. Alfonso took Algeciras in 1344. The rivalry between Peter I, the Cruel, 1350–69, and his half-brother Henry of Trastamara led to the battle between du Guesclin and the Black Prince on Spanish soil, at Najara, in 1367 Castile had a very troublous century under the rule of the house of Trastamara, 1369–1468. Marriage of Isabella, with Ferdinand, the heir of Aragon, in 1469.

11. Aragon, 1276–1469. Peter III, 1276–85, secured Sicily after the Sicilian Vespers, 1282. The Catalan Grand Company. In the reign of James III, 1327–36, Sardinia was taken from Genoa and Pisa and annexed to Aragon. Alfonso V, 1416–58, wrested Naples from the second house of Anjou. The union with Castile, 1469.

12. Union of Aragon and Castile under Ferdinand II, 1479–1516, and Isabella, 1474–1504, "the Catholic kings," and the foundation of united Spain. The fall of Granada, the expulsion of the Jews, and the discovery of America in 1492.

13. Spanish culture in the later middle ages, especially in Catalonia. Heresy and the inquisition. The Jews in Spain.

14. Portugal. Early growth of Portugal around Oporto (Porto Calle) and Coimbra, included in 1064. Establishment of the county of Portugal, 1095. In 1140 count Alfonso became king of Portugal and in 1147, with the help of German and Dutch adventurers, took Lisbon from the Moors. Thus by 1250 Portugal had reached its present limits. Development of a navy in the twelfth century. Internal organization of Portugal under king Diniz (Dionysius, 1279–1325), "Denis the Laborer." Prince Henry the Navigator, 1394–1460, and the beginnings of Portugal's heroic age. In 1486 Vasco da Gama rounded the Cape of Good Hope, and in 1498 he reached Calicut, India. In 1500 the Portuguese discovered Brazil.

15. Kings of Castile, 1214–1504.
- Saint Ferdinand III, 1214–52.
- Alfonso X, 1252–84.
- Sancho IV, 1284–95.
- Ferdinand IV, 1295–1312.
- Alfonso XI, 1312–50.
- Peter I (the Cruel), 1350–69.
- Henry II, of Trastamara, 1369–79.
- John I, 1379–90.
- Henry III, 1390–1406.
- John II, 1406–54.
- Henry IV, 1454–74.
- Isabella, 1474–1504.

16. Kings of Aragon, 1213–1516.
- James I, 1213–76.
- Peter III, 1276–85.
- Alfonso III, 1285–91.
- James II, 1291–1327.
- Alfonso IV, 1327–36.
- Peter IV, 1336–87.
- John I, 1387–95.
- Martin, 1395–1410.
- Ferdinand I, 1412–16.
- Alfonso V, 1416–58.
- John II, 1458–79.
- Ferdinand II, 1479–1516.

B. SPECIAL RECOMMENDATIONS FOR READING

Brief general accounts. ABBOTT, *Expansion of Europe*, I, ch. VI. HELMOLT, *History of the world*, IV, 510–40. TOUT, *Empire and papacy*, 464–77; together with LODGE, *Close of the middle ages*, 468–93. *History of all nations*, X, 336–57. CLARA C. PERKINS, *Builders of Spain*, 118–51. LEES, *The central period of the middle ages*, 239–44, together with ELEANOR C. LODGE, *The end of the middle age*, 240–54. LOSERTH, *Geschichte des späteren Mittelalters*, 52–57, 345–59, 693–707.

Longer accounts. HUME, *The Spanish people*, 103–305. LAVISSE et RAMBAUD, *Histoire générale*, II, ch. XII, and III, ch. IX. *C.M.H.*, VI, ch. XII.

Standard works. U. R. BURKE, *A history of Spain*, I, 133–41, 152–62, 178–388, and all of vol. II. ALTAMIRA, *Historia de España*, I, 351–646, and all of vol. II; founded on this, CHAPMAN, *A history of Spain*. R. B. MERRIMAN, *Rise of the Spanish empire*, vol. I.

The Cid. H. B. CLARK, *The Cid Campeador and the waning of the crescent in the west*, New York, 1897 (Heroes of nations). J. ORMSBY, *The poem of the Cid*, London, 1879.

The Cortes. R. B. MERRIMAN, "The Cortes of the Spanish kingdoms in the later middle ages," in *A.H.R.*, XVI (1910–1911), 476–95, contains important bibliographical notes.

James the First of Aragon, 1213–1270. F. D. SWIFT, *The life and times of James the First the conqueror, king of Aragon, Valencia, and Majorca*, Oxford, 1894. C. R. BEAZLEY, *James I of Aragon*, Oxford, 1890.

Heresy and inquisition in Spain. H. C. LEA, *A history of the inquisition of Spain*, 4 vols., New York, 1906–07, I, 1–288; *The Moriscos of Spain: their conversion and expulsion*, Philadelphia, 1901, chs. I–II; see also *History of the inquisition of the middle ages*, II, ch. III.

Portugal and Spain in the age of discovery. CHEYNEY, *European background*, 60–103. *Cambridge modern history*, I, ch. I. J. KLEIN, *The mesta: a study in Spanish economic history, 1273–1836*, Cambridge, Mass., 1920.

Portugal. H. M. STEPHENS, *Portugal*, New York, 1891 (Story of nations), chs. I–VIII, is the best account. V. DE BRAGANÇA CUNHA, *Eight centuries of Portuguese monarchy: a political study*, London, 1911, has a very slight sketch on medieval Portugal in ch. I, but appends a long list of books, pp. 255–65. H. DE GAMA BARROS, *Historia da administração publico em Portugal*, a standard work; useful for Castile also.

Henry the Navigator. E. G. BOURNE, *Essays in historical criticism*, New York, 1901, 173–89, is a good sketch. J. P. OLIVEIRA MARTINS, *Os filhos de Dom João I*, Lisbon, 1891, translated from the 1901 edition by J. J. ABRAHAM and W. E. REYNOLDS, *The golden age of Prince Henry the Navigator*, London, 1914. C. R. BEAZLEY, *Prince Henry the Navigator*, London, 1895.

Ferdinand and Isabella. R. B. MERRIMAN, *Rise of the Spanish empire*, vol. II, *The catholic kings*. *Cambridge modern history*, I, ch. XI. IERNE L. PLUNKET, *Isabel of Castile and the making of the Spanish nation, 1451–1504*, New York, 1915 (Heroes of nations). D. CLEMENCIN, *Elogio de la Reina*

Católica Doña Isabel, Madrid, 1821; it has a useful appendix of documents. W. H. PRESCOTT, *History of the reign of Ferdinand and Isabella the Catholic*, 3 vols., London, 1838 (often reprinted).

Original sources. *The chronicle of James I, king of Aragon* [1213–76], translated, with an historical introduction, by P. DE GAYANGOS, London, 1883. *The chronicle of the Cid*, translated from the Spanish by R. SOUTHEY, London, 1883 (Morley's universal library), is "based partly upon an Arab contemporary original now lost"—BURKE. *The unconquered knight*, translated by Joan Evans. BERNAT ESCLOT, *Chronicle of the reign of King Pedro III of Aragon*, A.D. *1276–1285*, translated from the original Catalan text, by F. L. CRITCHLOW, Princeton, 1928.

Maps. SHEPHERD, *Atlas*, 82–83.

C. BIBLIOGRAPHY

General books. The general histories of Spain and Portugal are listed above, nos. **622–42.** See the books on the church in Spain, nos. **467–68.** See also nos. **813** and **103.** For the publications of the *Real Academia de la Historia* of Madrid, see no. **907.**

General and miscellaneous accounts. M. COLMEIRO, *Reyes cristianos desde Alfonso VI hasta Alfonso XI en Castilla, Aragón, Navarra y Portugal* (*1072–1312*), vol. I, Madrid, 1891, part of no. **622.** J. DE DIOS DE LA RADA Y DELGADO, *La España cristiana* (*970–1072*), Madrid, 1890, part of no. **622,** is incomplete. L. DOLLFUS, *Les Espagnes au XIe siècle*, Paris, 1903. A. SALCEDO Y RUIZ, *Historia de España: resumen crítico*, Madrid, [1914], is illustrated profusely. A. PAZ Y MELIA, *España de la edad media*, Madrid, 1898. CONDE DE TORREÁNAZ, *Los consejos del rey durante la edad media*, 2 vols., Madrid, 1884–92. DEL CASTILLO, *Gran diccionario geográfico, estadístico e histórico de España*, Barcelona, 1890ff. P. N. PÉREZ, *San Pedro Nolasco, fundador de la orden de la Merced* (*siglo XIII*), Barcelona, 1915. R. ALTAMIRA, "Magna Carta and Spanish mediaeval jurisprudence," in *Magna Carta commemorative essays*, 225–43. G. CARO, "Aus der spanischen Geschichte im Mittelalter," in *H.V.J.S.*, XVI (1913), 161–80. H. FINKE, "Das Aufblühen der Geschichtsforschung in Spanien," in *H.Z.*, CXIII (1914), 70–82. E. MAYER, *Historia de las instituciones sociales y políticas de España y Portugal durante los siglos V á XIV*, 2 vols., Madrid, 1925–26.

The Cid. A. WILLEMAERS, *Le Cid: son histoire, ses légendes, ses poètes*, Brussels, 1873. R. P. A. DOZY, *Le Cid d'après de nouveaux documents*, new edition, Leyden, 1860. R. MENÉNDEZ PIDAL, *De la vida del Cid*, Madrid, 1926.

Castile. J. CATALINA Y GARCIA, *Castilla y León durante los reinados de Pedro I, Enrique II, Juan I y Enrique III*, vols. I–II, Madrid, 1891–1901, part of no. **622.** G. DAUMET, *Mémoire sur les relations de la France et de la Castille de 1255 à 1320*, Paris, 1914; *Etude sur l'alliance de la France et de la Castille au xive et xve siècles*, Paris, 1898, contains important original sources. C. FERNÁNDEZ DURO, *La marina de Castilla*, Madrid, 1894, part of no. **622.** J. LAURENTIE, *Saint Ferdinand III* (*1198?–1252*), Paris, 1910 (Les saints).

W. HERRMANN, *Alfons X von Castilien als römischer König*, Berlin [1897] (Diss.). L. DE CORRAL, *Don Alvaro de Luna según testimonios inéditos de la época*, Valladolid, 1915. J. GOROSTERRATZU, *Don Rodrigo Jiménez de Rada*, Pamplona, 1923. A notable study, crowned by the Royal Academy of History, of a noted Primate of Spain in the early thirteenth century. A. NAVARRETE, *Historia marítima militar de España*, vol. I, Madrid, 1901.

Peter I, the Cruel, 1350–69, has attracted considerable attention and some attempts have been made to vindicate him, e.g., J. GUICHOT, *D. Pedro Primero de Castilla: ensayo de vindicación crítico-histórico de su reinado*, Seville, 1878. FERNÁNDEZ GUERRA, *El rey D. Pedro de Castilla*, Madrid, 1868. P. MÉRIMÉE, *Histoire de Don Pèdre Ier roi de Castille*, Paris, 1848; new edition, 1865. A. FERRER DEL RÍO, *Examen histórico-crítico del reinado de Don Pedro de Castilla*, Madrid, 1851. J. CALMETTE, *Louis XI, Jean II, et la révolution catalane (1461–1473)*, Toulouse, 1903, is indispensable. J. B. SITGES, *Las mujeres del rey Don Pedro I de Castilla*, Madrid, 1910; *Enrique IV y la Excelente Señora*, Madrid, 1912. A scientific study with an excellent critical bibliography.

Aragon and Catalonia. V. BALAGUER, *Historia de Cataluña y de la corona de Aragón*, 2nd edition, 11 vols., Madrid, 1885–87. J. RIBERA, *Orígenes del Justicia Mayor de Aragón*, Saragossa, 1897; on this cf. A. GIMÉNEZ SOLER, *Revista de Archivos*, 3rd series V, 201–06, 454–65, 625–32; also I, 337–48; III, 385–91; X, 119–26. E. DE HINOJOSA, *El regimen señorial y la cuestión agraria en Cataluña durante la edad media*, Madrid, 1905 (Biblioteca de derecho). J. BALARI Y JOVANY, *Orígenes históricos de Cataluña*, Barcelona, 1899. L. KLÜPFEL, *Die äussere Politik Alfonsos III von Aragonien (1285–1291)*, Berlin and Leipzig, 1911–12 (*Abh.m.n.G.*, 35); *Verwaltungsgeschichte des Königreichs Aragon zu Ende des 13 Jahrhunderts*, Stuttgart, 1915 (posthumous work, edited by H. E. ROHDE). K. SCHWARZ, *Aragonische Hofordnungen im 13 und 14 Jahrhundert*, Berlin and Leipzig, 1914. G. DESDEVISES DU DEZERT, *Don Carlos d'Aragón, Prince de Viane: étude sur l'Espagne du nord au XVe siècle*, Paris, 1889. P. KEHR, *Das Papsttum und der katalanische Prinzipat bis zur Vereinigung mit Aragon*, Berlin, 1926. A. GIMÉNEZ SOLER, *La corona de Aragón y Granada*, Barcelona, 1908. C. PARPAL Y MARQUÉS, *La conquista de Menorca en 1287 por Alfonso III de Aragón*, Barcelona, 1901. M. DANVILA Y COLLADO, *Las libertades de Aragón*, Madrid, 1881. S. SANPERE Y MIQUEL, *Minoría de Jaime I*, Barcelona, 1910. A. LECOY DE LA MARCHE, *Les relations politiques de la France avec le royaume de Majorque*, 2 vols., Paris, 1892. C. BAUDON DE MONY, *Relations politiques des comtes de Foix avec la Catalogne*, 2 vols., Paris, 1896 (excellent). A DE CAPMANY Y DE MONTPALAU, *Memorias históricas sobre la marina, comercio y artes de Barcelona*, 4 vols., Madrid, 1779–92. Two volumes of invaluable documents, and two of introduction; cf. PRESCOTT, *Ferdinand and Isabella*, appendix to section II of the Introduction. CAPMANY also published the *Libre del Consolat*, or *Maritime code of Barcelona* (Madrid, 1791). A. HUICI (editor), *Colección diplomática de Jaime I, el Conquistador, 1217 á 1253*, vol. I, Valencia, 1916. A. DE BOFARULL Y BROCÁ, *Historia crítica de Cataluña*,

9 vols., Barcelona, 1876–78; elaborate, and very useful, but without references or footnotes. J. AMETTLER Y VINYAS, *Alfonso V de Aragón en Italia*, 2 vols., Gerona, 1903; mostly narrative history and very exhaustive, but totally lacking in footnotes and references. H. FINKE, *Acta Aragonensia*, 3 vols., Berlin, 1908, 1922; an invaluable collection of documents, mostly from the archives in Barcelona, on the reign of James II of Aragon (1291–1327). FINKE'S seminary at Freiburg in Breisgau has furnished the inspiration for a number of admirable monographs on the medieval history of Aragon and the Aragonese Empire in the Mediterranean, of which O. CARTELLIERI, *Peter von Aragon und die Sizilianische Vesper*, Heidelberg, 1904; L. KLÜPFEL, *Die aüssere Politik Alfonso's III von Aragonien 1285–1291*, Berlin, 1911–12; and *Verwaltungsgeschichte des Königreichs Aragonien zu Ende des 13 Jahrhunderts*, Berlin, 1915; H. E. ROHDE, *Der Kampf um Sizilien, 1291–1302*, Berlin, 1913; F. BAER, *Studien zur Geschichte der Juden in Königreich Aragonien, während des 13 und 14 Jahrhunderts*, Berlin, 1913; K. SCHWARZ, *Aragonische Hofordnungen im 13 und 14 Jahrhundert*, Berlin, 1914; and HABERKERN, *Der Kampf um Sizilien in den Jahren 1302–1337*, are the most notable. H. FINKE (editor), *Gesammelte Aufsätze zur Kulturgeschichte Spaniens*, Erste Reihe, Vol. I, Münster, 1928. F. DURÁN, *La escultura medieval catalana*, Madrid, 1927. I. EPSTEIN, *The "Responsa" of Rabbi Solomon Ben Ardreth of Barcelona (1235–1310) as a source of the history of Spain*, London, 1925.

Navarre. J. DE JAURGAIN, *La Vasconie: étude historique et critique sur les origines du royaume de Navarre*, etc., 2 vols., Pau, 1898–1902.

Cortes of Spain. V. BOIX, *Historia de la ciudad y reino de Valencia*, 3 vols., Valencia, 1845–47. V. DE LA FUENTE, *Estudios críticos sobre la historia y el derecho de Aragón*, 3 vols., Madrid, 1884–86, is especially important for the early cortes in Aragon. J. COROLEU and D. J. PELLA Y FORGAS, *Las Cortes catalanas*, Barcelona, 1876, contains important original sources; his *Los Fueros de Cataluña*, Barcelona, 1878 is prolix, but gives some useful information.

Hermandades. J. PUYOL Y ALONSO, *Las hermandades de Castilla y León*, Madrid, 1913. K. HAEBLER, "Über die älteren Hermandades in Kastilien," *H.Z.*, LIII (1885), 385–401; "Die kastilischen Hermandades zur Zeit Heinrich's IV (1454–1474)," *ibid.*, LVI (1886), 40–50. A. SACRISTÁN Y MARTINEZ, *Municipalidades de Castilla y León*, Madrid, 1878. F. R. DE UHAGON, *Órdenes militares*, Madrid, 1898. H. KENISTON (editor), *Fuero de Guadalajara (1219)*, Princeton, 1924.

Spanish church. M. MENÉNDEZ Y PELAYO, *Historia de los heterodoxos españoles*, 3 vols., Madrid, 1880–81; new edition, 1912ff. M. VAN HENCKELUM, *Spiritualistische Strömungen an den Höfen von Aragon und Anjou während der Höhe des Armustsstreites*, Berlin, 1912, a study on the spiritual Franciscans. Q. MORALEDA, *El rito mozárabe, su antigüedad, vicisitudes, costumbres mozárabes*, Toledo, 1904. K. J. v. HEFELE, *Der Cardinal Ximenes*, Tübingen, 1851, translated into English, *The life of cardinal Ximenez*, London, 1860. J. B. KISSLING, *Kardinal Francisco Ximenez de Cisneros, 1436–1517; Erzbischof von Toledo, Spaniens katholischer Reformator*, Münster, 1917.

Jews in Spain. J. AMADOR DE LOS RÍOS, *Historia social, política y religiosa de los judíos de España y Portugal*, 3 vols., Madrid, 1875–76. M. KAYSERLING, *Geschichte der Juden in Spanien und Portugal*, 2 vols., Berlin, 1861–67. J. JACOBS, *An inquiry into the sources of the history of the Jews in Spain*, New York, 1894. F. DE BOFARULL Y SANS, *Los Judíos en el territorio de Barcelona*, Barcelona, 1911. F. FITA, *La España hebrea*, 2 vols., Madrid, 1889–98. M. DOS REMEDIOS, *Os Judeus em Portugal*, I, Coimbra, 1895. J. RÉGNÉ, *Catalogues des actes de Jaime I, Pedro III et Alfonso III, rois d'Aragon, concernant les Juifs, I: 2, Jaime I*, Paris, 1911; II:1, *Pedro III*, Paris, 1914. See also the general histories of the Jews, nos. **850–883b**, especially **874** and **876.**

Culture in Spain in the later middle ages. R. P. A. DOZY, *Recherches sur l'histoire et la littérature de l'Espagne pendant le moyen âge*, 2 vols., 3rd edition, Leyden, 1881. J. P. OLIVEIRA MARTINS, *Historia de la civilización ibérica*, Madrid, 1894. *Estado de la cultura española y principalmente catalana en el siglo XV*, by various authors, Barcelona, 1893. H. FINKE, "Die Beziehungen der aragonesischen Könige zur Literatur, Wissenschaft, und Kunst im 13 und 14 Jahrhundert," *Archiv für Kulturgeschichte*, VIII (1910), 20–42. L. COMENGE, *La medicina en el reinado de Alfonso V de Aragón*, Barcelona, 1903. M. MENÉNDEZ Y PELAYO, *Antología de poetas líricos castellanos*, Madrid, 1890, contains introductions which constitute a general history of learning and society in Spain in the later middle ages. See also no. **813.** J. M. ANTEQUERA, *Historia de la legislación española*, 4th edition, Madrid, 1895: valuable, though somewhat out of date. M. F. LADREDA, *Estudios sobre los códigos de Castilla*, Corunna, 1896, is a most convenient little book. J. CEJADOR Y FRAUCA, *Historia de la lengua y literatura castellana: desde los orígines hasta Carlo V*, Madrid, 1915. V. DE LA FUENTE, *Historia de las universidades, colegios y demás establecimientos de enseñanza en España*, 4 vols., Madrid, 1884–89. CONDE DE CLONARD, *Historia orgánica de las armas españolas*, 16 vols. J. M. PIERNAS Y HURTADO, *Tratado de hacienda pública y examen de la Española*, 2 vols., 5th ed., Madrid, 1900–01. COLMEIRO, *Historia de la economía política en España*. COMTE DE PUYMAIGRE, *La cour littéraire de Don Juan II, roi de Castille*, 2 vols., Paris, 1873. E. LAMBERT, *Tolède*, Paris, 1925. M. SALZMAN (translator), *The chronicle of Ahimaaz*, New York, 1924 (Columbia university oriental studies, XVIII). F. ANTON, *Monasterios medievales de la provincia de Valladolid*, Madrid, 1923.

Portugal. C. R. PEPPER, *Le Portugal: ses origines, son histoire*, Paris, 1879. F. KURTH, "Der Anteil Niederdeutscher Kreuzfahrer an den Kämpfen der Portugiesen gegen die Mauren," in *M.I.O.G.*, VIII, Ergänzungsband, I, 1909.

Prince Henry the Navigator. M. BARRADAS, *O Infante Dom Henrique*, Lisbon, 1894. A. ALVES, *Dom Henrique o Infante*, Oporto, 1894. R. H. MAJOR, *Life of Prince Henry of Portugal surnamed the Navigator*, London, 1868; condensed edition, 1874.

Expulsion of the Moors. F. CODERA, *Decadencia y desaparición de los Almoravides en España*, Saragossa, 1899 (Collección de estudios árabes, 3); *Estudios críticos de historia árabe española*, Saragossa, 1903; second series,

Madrid, 1917 (Collección de estudios, 8). L. EGUILAZ Y YANGUAS, *Reseña histórica de la conquista del reino de Granada*, 2nd edition, Granada, 1894. M. GASPAR, *Granada en poder de los Reyes Católicos*, Granada, 1912. V. BALAGUER, *Las guerras de Granada*, Madrid, 1898. A. HUICI, *Estudio sobre la campaña de Las Navas de Tolosa*, Valencia, 1916. M. G. REMIRO, *Ultimos pactos y correspondencia íntima entre los Reyes Católicos y Boabdil*, Granada, 1910.

Ferdinand and Isabella. V. BALAGUER, *Los Reyes Católicos*, 2 vols., Madrid, 1891–98, part of no. **622.** P. BOISSONNADE, *Histoire de la rêunion de la Navarre à la Castille, 1479–1521*, Paris, 1893. D. F. RUANO–PRIETO, *Anexión del reino de Navarra en tiempo del Rey Católico*, Madrid, 1899. J. H. MARIÉJOL, *L'Espagne sous Ferdinand et Isabelle: le gouvernement, les institutions, les moeurs*, Paris [1892]. G. SELA, *Política internacional de los Reyes Católicos*, Madrid, 1905. K. HÄBLER, *Geschichte Spaniens unter den Habsburgern*, vol. I, Hamburg, 1907, part of no. **332**. See also H. C. LEA, *Moriscos of Spain; History of the inquisition of Spain.*

Original sources. General collections of sources for the history of Spain and Portugal are listed above, nos. **997–1001.** *Acta Aragonensia: Quellen zur deutschen, italienischen, französischen, spanischen, zur Kirchen- und Kulturgeschichte, aus der diplomatischen Korrespondenz Jaymes II, 1291–1327*, edited by H. FINKE, Berlin and Leipzig, 3 vols., 1908–22 is a well-edited collection of documents from the time of Dante which bear some resemblances to the famous *Venetian relations*. *Documents per l'historia de le cultura catalana mig-eval*, edited by A. RUBIÓ Y LLUCH for the Institut d'Estudis Catalans, vol. I, Barcelona, 1908, throws much new light on the important Catalan culture of the middle ages, vol. II, Barcelona, 1921. See H. FINKE, "Die katalanische Renaissance," in *Internationale Wochenschrift* (1910), 209ff. See also the article on Catalan language and literature in the *Ency. Brit.*

ZURITA, *Anales de la corona de Aragón*. For other important sources see MERRIMAN, *Spanish empire*, II, 44 and 76. *Primera crónica general: Estoria de España que mandó componer Alfonso el Sabio y se continuaba bajo Sancho IV en 1289*, edited by R. MENÉNDEZ PIDAL, vol. I, text, Madrid 1906. *Códigos de España: colección completa desde el Fuero Juzgo hasta la novísima recopilación*, edited by M. MARTINEZ ALCUBILLA, 2 vols., Madrid, 1885–86, is the most convenient collection in a single volume of the laws of Spain from the *Fuero Juzgo* to the *Novísima Recopilación*. *Fuentes para la historia de Castilla*, edited by L. SERRANO, vol. I, Valladolid, 1906, contains archive material, 1068–1500. *Histoire de l'Afrique et de l'Espagne intitulée Al Baguano 'l Mogrib* [of IBNAL IDHÂRÎ], translated and annotated by E. FAGNAN, Algiers, 1901. GOMES EANNES DE AZURARA, *Chronicle of the discovery and conquest of Guinea*, 2 vols., 1896–99 (Hakluyt society), is an important source for early Portuguese explorations. *Privilegis i ordinacions de les valls Pirenneques*, vol. I, *Vall d'Aran (1265–1496)*, edited by F. V. TABERNER, Barcelona, 1915. F. TRINCHERA, *Codice Aragonese*, 3 vols., Naples, 1866–74. A. A. MESSER, *Codice aragonese*, Paris, 1912.

For general bibliographies see no. **42,** MERRIMAN, *Spanish empire* and *C.M.H.* VI, 912–922.

XXXV. EASTERN AND NORTHERN EUROPE IN THE LATER MIDDLE AGES

A. Outline

1. The crusades widened the sphere of action of Latin Christendom which began to develop world interests and policies in the twelfth and thirteenth centuries. The chief factors with which it had to deal in the later middle ages were the Slavs belonging to the Greek church, the Asiatic nomads, the Byzantine Greeks, the Ottoman Turks in the east and the Moors in Spain and northern Africa.

2. The invasion of Russia, Poland, and Hungary by Asiatic nomads in the thirteenth century. A new wave of "Mongols, Tartars or Tatars" from the steppes of Asia. Rise of these nomads in Asia under Temujin, 1162–1227, better known as Jenghiz Khan (Genghis Khan), or great Khan, which title he obtained in 1206. He penetrated beyond the great wall of China. His son turned westward and defeated the Russian princes in 1223. His grandson, Batu, took Kiev in 1240, and devastated Hungary and Poland frightfully. Some bands of nomads came into the neighborhood of Vienna. Batu's realm was called the realm of the "Golden Horde" (from *ordu*, the camp of the leader, who had a "golden" tent). Most of the nomads returned to Asia, but southern Russia remained in their clutch until 1480, when Ivan III, the Great, overthrew them and united the Russian monarchy. Isolation of Russia from both the Latin West and the Greek East, due to this invasion. Growth of Moscow.

3. The greatness of Poland. Conflict between the Teutonic Order and Poland. Dominance of the order during the grand-mastership of Winzig of Kniprode, 1351–82. End of the rule of the Piasts in Poland, 1370. Union of Poland and Lithuania under the house of Jagello, 1386–1572. Now there arose a strong anti-German movement in Poland, similar to that in Bohemia (Hussites). Defeat of the Teutonic Order by Poland at the battle of Tannenberg, 1410. Peace of Thorn, 1411. The treaty of Thorn, 1466, marked the triumph of Poland over the Teutonic Order. Under Casimir IV, Jagello, 1477–92, Poland reached the height of her glory. His younger son Ladislas was elected king of Bohemia in 1471 and king of Hungary in 1490. Fatal weakness of the Polish constitution, due to excessive power of the great nobles.

4. The rise and decline of Hungary. The Golden Bull of 1222, the "Magna Carta" of Hungary. Devastation of Hungary by the nomads, 1241–42. End of the Arpád dynasty, 1301. Dominance of turbulent nobles. Regeneration under the house of Anjou (Charles I, 1310–42, and Louis I, 1342–82). The coming of the Ottoman Turks. Sigismund, of the house of Luxemburg, king of Hungary, 1387–1437. His successful warfare with the Turks, after his defeat by Bayezid at Nicopolis in 1396. John Hunyadi (ca. 1387–1456), the hero in the struggle against the Turks. The succession of his house to the throne in the person of his son Matthias I (Corvinus), 1458–90, in whose reign Hungary reached the pinnacle of her power. Union of Hungary with Bohemia in 1490 under Ladislas II of the house of Jagello. Sudden decline of Hungary.

5. The Greek empire under the Palaeologi, 1261–1453. Restoration of the Byzantine rule with the accession of Michael Palaeologus, 1261, a prince who had ruled at Nicaea. Weakness of his empire. Its diminished territories. Inroads made upon them by the Latins of the west in the Balkan peninsula and the Aegean. The "Grand Company of the Catalans." In 1333, Stephen Dushan, king of Serbia, 1331–55, was on the point of taking Constantinople. Dependence of the empire on the west. Continuous negotiations with the papacy concerning the union of the two churches. Council of Ferrara-Florence, 1438–39. The Turkish menace. The coming of the gipsies into Europe.

6. The Ottoman Turks in Europe. The rise of the Ottoman Turks or Osmanlis under Othman, 1307–26. Nicaea was in their hands in 1330. The Janissaries. In 1354 the Turks took Gallipoli, their first foothold on European soil. In 1361 Murad I took Adrianople. Emperor John V went to Rome to appeal to pope Urban V for help in 1369. Bayezid, I, 1389–1403, actually besieged Constantinople but he was diverted by the great nomad hero Timur, or Tamerlane, who defeated him and made him captive in the battle of Angora in 1402.

7. The fall of Constantinople, 1453. Weakness of the Palaeologi and gradual recovery of the Ottoman Turks. They were checked temporarily by the genius of the Hungarian John Hunyadi and by the guerilla warfare of the Albanians under their famous leader, George Castriot, or Scanderbeg (Iskander Bey, Prince Alexander, a complimentary name given him by the Turks in reference to Alexander the Great). Negotiations between the Greek and Latin churches due to the pressure of the Turks. In 1453, Mohammed II captured Constantinople. Importance of this event in the history of Europe. The "Eastern Question." The fall of Constantinople had little or nothing to do with the revival of the study of Greek in Italy. Did the advance of the Turks lead to the discovery of America and of a new route to India? Decline of the importance of the Mediterranean at the close of the fifteenth century.

8. Palaeologian dynasty in Constantinople, 1259–1453.

Michael VIII, 1259–82 (in Constantinople, 1261ff.).
Andronicus II (Elder), 1282–1328.
Andronicus III (Younger), 1328–41.
John V, 1341–91.
John (Cantacuzenus), 1347–55 (non-dynastic).
Manuel II, 1391–1425.
John VI, 1425–48.
Constantine XI or XII (Dragases), 1449–53.

9. Denmark, Norway, and Sweden. Denmark was the leading state during this period. Its expansion and prosperity under Waldemar I, the Great, 1137–82, Knut VI, 1182–1202, and Waldemar II, the Conqueror, 1202–41. Importance of Norway under Hakon IV, 1217–62. The *Speculum regale*, "The king's mirror," written about 1250–60, gives a splendid picture of civilization in the north. Conquest of Iceland (1260) and the submission of Greenland. Relations of the Teutonic Knights, the Sword Bearers, and

the Hanseatic League with the northern states. Waldemar III of Denmark, 1340–75. Treaty of Stralsund, 1370. The Union of Kalmar, 1397, which united the three Scandinavian kingdoms, and lasted formally till 1524, although actually it was dissolved with the election of Christian I of Oldenburg in 1448. Decline of the importance of the Baltic in the fifteenth century.

B. Special Recommendations for Reading

Brief general surveys. Lodge, *The close of the middle ages*, 430–51, 457–67, 494–514. Eleanor Lodge, *The end of the middle age*, chs. xi, xiii. W. S. Davis, *A short history of the near East, 330 A.D.–1922*, New York, 1922. Thorndike, *Medieval Europe*, ch. xxix. Hulme, *Middle ages*, 670–80. Thompson, *Economic and social history*, ch. xxi.

Longer general accounts. Lavisse et Rambaud, *Histoire générale*, II, chs. xiv, xvi; III, chs. xiv–xviii. Helmolt, *History of the world*, II, *passim;* III, 363–76; V, 106–47, 224–26, 243–68, 288–302, 338–48, 355–59, 363–67, 380–87, 409–12, 415–24, 461–518; VI, 446–52, 466–71, 478–84. Loserth, *Geschichte des späteren Mittelalters*, 57–67, 359–65, 563–67, 107–12, 575–81, 199–203, 369–75, 581–612. *C.M.H.*, IV, chs. xvi–xxiv; VI, chs. xi and xiii. F. Schevill, *History of the Balkan peninsula*, chs. x–xiii.

Europe and Asia. Beazley, *Dawn of modern geography*, III, ch. ii, "The great Asiatic travellers, 1260–1420."

Russia and the nomad Mongols. A. Rambaud, *History of Russia*, I, chs. x–xiii; or V. O. Kluchevsky, *History of Russia*, I, chs. xii–xx, furnish a general survey. W. F. Reddaway, *Introduction to the study of Russian history*, London, 1920. S. Platonov, *History of Russia*, New York, 1925. Pares, *History of Russia*. J. Curtin, *The Mongols in Russia*, London, 1908, a companion volume to *The Mongols: a history*, with a foreword by T. Roosevelt, Boston, 1908. Lamb, *Genghis Khan*. See also Gibbon, *Decline and fall*, ch. lxiv. L. v. Ranke, *Weltgeschichte*, 9 vols., Leipzig, 1883ff., VIII, 417–54, "Überfluthung der asiatischen und osteuropäischen Welt durch die Mongolen." C. R. Beazley, "Russian expansion toward Asia and the Arctic in the middle ages (to 1500)," *A.H.R.*, XIII (1907–08), 731–41.

Hungary. A. Vámbéry, *The story of Hungary*, chs. vii–xi. C. M. Knatchbull-Hugessen, *The political evolution of the Hungarian nation*, 2 vols., London, 1908. G. G. Zerffi, "Hungary under Mathias Hunyady, surnamed Corvinus, 1458–1490," *Trans., R. H. S.*, new series, I (1884), 260–72. J. Szinnyei, *Die Herkunft der Ungarn*, Berlin and Leipzig, 1923. P. Teleki, *The evolution of Hungary and its place in European history*, New York, 1923.

A confirmation of the Golden Bull of 1222, the "magna carta" of Hungary, is reproduced in facsimile in Helmolt, *History of the world*, V, 380; compare this with the *Articles of the Barons* of England, the original draft of the *Magna Carta*, 1215, reproduced in facsimile in *Weltgeschichte*, edited by J. v. Pflugk-Harttung, II, 208.

Balkans. W. Miller, *The Balkans*, 35–61, 167–93, 272–98, 353–82. N. Forbes, *The Balkans*, 41–46, 89–101, 175–81, 256–63, 319–32. Šišić,

Geschichte der Kroaten, vol. I (to 1102). N. JORGA, *Histoire des états balkaniques jusqu'à 1924*, Paris, 1925; *Histoire des Roumains de Transylvanie et de Hongrie*, 2 vols., Bucharest, 1915–16. O. G. LECA, *Formation et développement du pays et des états roumains. La Valachie au XIIIe siècle. La Moldavie au XIVe*, Paris, 1922. J. MOTHERSOLE, *Czechoslovakia: the land of an unconquerable ideal*, London, 1926. J. PROKEŠ, *Histoire tchécoslovaque*, Prague, 1927.

Bulgaria. S. S. BOBCHEV, "Bulgaria under Tsar Simeon," *Slavonic review*, VII (1928–29), 621–33; VIII (1929–30), 99–119. J. C. JIREČEK, *Geschichte der Bulgaren*, Prague, 1876.

Serbia. W. MILLER, "The mediaeval Serbian empire," *Quarterly review*, CCXXVI (1916), 488–507. TEMPERLEY, *History of Serbia*.

Latins in the Levant. W. MILLER, *The Latins in the Levant*. J. B. BURY, "The Lombards and Venetians in Euboia, 1205–1470," *Journal of Hellenic studies*, VII (1886), 309–52; VIII (1887), 194–213; IX (1888), 91–117. W. MILLER, *Essays on the Latin Orient; Trebizond, 'The last Greek empire,'* London, 1926. E. A. FREEMAN, "Mediaeval and modern Greece," *Historical essays*, third series, 303–78. H. F. TOZER, "The Franks in the Peloponnesus," *Journal of Hellenic studies*, IV (1883), 165–236. J. T. BENT, "The lords of Chios," *E.H.R.*, IV (1889), 467–80. See also the literature under "The Byzantine empire and the crusades," in outline XXI, especially MILLER, FINLAY, and RODD.

Byzantine Empire, 1261–1453. VASILIEV, *History of the Byzantine empire*, II. OMAN, *Story of the Byzantine empire*, 307–50. DIEHL, *History of the Byzantine empire*, 151–76. GIBBON, *Decline and fall*, chs. LXI–LXVIII, with BURY'S additional notes. W. H. HUTTON, *Constantinople*, 119–53. W. NORDEN, *Das Papsttum und Byzanz*, books III and IV, the best authority on the attempts made in this period to unite the Greek and Latin churches. A. WÄCHTER, *Der Verfall des Griechentums in Kleinasien im 14 Jahrhundert*, Leipzig, 1903. DIEHL, *Byzance, grandeur et décadence*, Paris, 1919. L. OECONOMAS, *La vie religieuse dans l'empire byzantin*. A. GARDNER, *The Lascarids of Nicaea: the story of an empire in exile*, London, 1912. C. CHAPMAN, *Michael Paléologue restaurateur de l'empire byzantin* (*1261–1282*), Paris, 1926. B. DE XIVREY, *Mémoire sur la vie et les ouvrages de l'empereur Manuel Paléologue.* (Mémoires de l'Institut de France. Académie des inscriptions et belles-lettres, XIX, 2e partie, Paris, 1853.) C. DIEHL, *Andronic Comnène. Figures byzantines*, sec. série, Paris, 1908, 86–133.

Ottoman Turks. S. POOLE, *The story of Turkey*, London, 1888 (Story of the nations), 1–139.

Gipsies. See the article "Gipsies" in the *Ency. Brit.;* and HELMOLT, *History of the world*, V, 415–24.

Fall of Constantinople, 1453. J. B. BURY, "The fall of Constantinople," *Yale review*, new series, III (1913–14), 56–77, is a good short summary. The standard work with criticism of sources is E. PEARS, *The destruction of the Greek empire and the story of the capture of Constantinople by the Turks*, London and New York, 1903. H. VAST, "Le siège et la prise de Constantinople par les Turcs," *R.H.*, XIII (1880), 1–40. G. SCHLUMBERGER, *Le siège, la prise et le sac de Constantinople par les Turcs en 1453*, Paris, 1915 (on the basis of PEARS' work). *Cambridge modern history*, I, ch. III, describes the Ottoman conquests after the fall of Constantinople. See also BURY's Appendix to his edition of GIBBON, *Decline and fall*.

Ottoman Turks and oriental trade routes. A. H. LYBYER, "The Ottoman Turks and the routes of oriental trade," *E.H.R.*, XXX (1915), 577–88. See also W. HEYD, *Geschichte des Levantehandels*.

Scandinavia. GJERSET, *History of the Norwegian people*, I, 410–92; II, 1–103 (in I, 448–51, there is a good description of the *Speculum regale* or *King's mirror*). BOYESON, *The story of Norway*, 400–80. L. M. LARSON, "Household of the Norwegian kings in the thirteenth century," *A.H.R.*, XIII (1907–08), 459–79. C. HALLENDORFF and A. SCHÜCK, *A history of Sweden*, Stockholm, 1929. GJERSET, *History of Iceland*.

Original sources. *The chronicle of Novgorod, 1016–1471*, translated from the Russian by R. MICHELL and N. FORBES, London, 1914 (Camden Soc., 3d series, XXV). L. M. LARSON, *The king's mirror*, New York, 1917. *Mediaeval researches from eastern Asiatic sources* (*13th to 17th century*), 2 vols., with a map of middle Asia, edited by E. BRETSCHNEIDER, London, 1910 (the work was completed in 1887, and incorporates the material in three or four of his older works). *A history of the Moghuls of central Asia: being the Tarikh-i-Rashidi of* MIRZA MUHAMMAD HAIDAR, Dughlát, an English version by N. ELIAS, London, 1895. *Life and acts of the great Tamerlane: narrative of the Castilian embassy to the court of Timur at Samarcand*, by ROY GONSALES DE CLAVIJO, 1403–06, translated, with notes, by C. R. MARKHAM, London, 1859 (Hakluyt Society). R. GONZALES DE CLAVIJO, *Embassy to Tamerlane 1403–1406*, translated from the Spanish by G. LE STRANGE, London, 1928. *The Mulfuz al Timury: or Autobiographical memoirs of the Moghul emperor Timur*, translated into English by C. STEWART, London, 1830. MATTHEW PARIS' *English history from the year 1235 to 1273*, translated from the Latin by J. A. GILES, 3 vols., London, 1852, vol. I, 467–73, "A shocking letter about the cruelty of the Tartars." "An eastern embassy to Europe, 1287–1288," translated by N. MCLEAN, *E.H.R.*, XIV (1899), 299–318. The first nine books of the *Danish history* of SAXO GRAMMATICUS, translated and edited by O. ELTON and F. Y. POWELL, London, 1894 (The history was written about 1208). A section from the *King's mirror* is given in WEBSTER, *Historical selections*, 522–24. J. A. MONTGOMERY, *History of Yaballaha III*.

Maps. SHEPHERD, *Atlas*, 2–3, 77, 87, 88, 89, 92, 93, 104B-C-D, 107–110.

C. BIBLIOGRAPHY

General books. The general works on the Byzantine empire and on eastern and northern Europe are listed, nos. **643–728c.** See also periodicals for the history of the Byzantine empire, nos. **174–75b,** and the *Encyclopaedia of Islam*, no. **120.** For histories of literature see nos. **800–802,** and **814.**

Mongol nomads from Asia. L. CAHUN, *Introduction à l'histoire de l'Asie: Turcs et Mongols, des origines à 1405*, Paris, 1896. R. GROUSSET, *Histoire de l'Asie:* I, *L'ancien Orient hellénistique, l'Islam, l'Orient latin et les croisades;* II, *L'Inde ancienne, la Chine ancienne et médiévale, les civilisations de l'Indo-Chine;* III, *Les empires mongols, la Perse, l'Inde et la Chine modernes, histoire du Japon;* 3 vols., Paris, 1921–22. G. STRAKOSCH-GRASSMANN, *Der Einfall der Mongolen in Mitteleuropa in den Jahren 1241 und 1242*, Innsbruck, 1893. H. H. HOWORTH, *History of the Mongols from the 9th to the 19th century*, 2 vols. in 3, London, 1876–80, Pt. IV, 1928, with indexes. *The northern frontages of China*, 4 vols., London, 1875–77 (Journal of the royal Asiatic society of Great Britain, new series, VII–IX). N. ELIAS, *A history of the Moghuls of central Asia*, London, 1898. R. STÜBE, "Tschinghizchan: seine Staatsbildung und seine Persöhnlichkeit," in *Neue Jahrbücher für das klassische Altertum*, 1908. O. WOLFF, *Geschichte der Mongolen oder Tataren*, Breslau, 1872. G. BACHFELD, *Die Mongolen in Polen*, Innsbruck, 1889. J. v. HAMMER-PURGSTALL, *Geschichte der Goldenen Horde in Kiptschack, das ist: der Mongolen in Russland*, Budapest, 1840. M. DE GUIGNES, *Histoire générale des Huns, des Turcs, des Mongols*, 5 vols., Paris, 1756–58. KOUNIK, *Renseignements sur les sources et recherches relatives à la première invasion des Tatars en Russie*, Petersburg, 1856 (in Mélanges asiatiques). F. PÉTIS DE LA CROIX, *Histoire du grand Genghizcan*, Paris, 1710, translated into English, *The history of Genghizcan the Great*, London, 1722. See also the literature on the early history of the Asiatic nomads, outline XI.

Poland and Bohemia. See nos. **693–703**, and A. NAEGLE, *Kirchengeschichte Böhmens*, vol. I, *Einführung des Christentums in Böhmen*, Vienna and Leipzig, 1915–18. A. SAPORI, "Gl' Italiani in Polonia nel medioevo," in *Archivo storico italiano*, LXXXIII (1923), 125–55. K. SCHNEIDER, *Die Geschichte des deutschen Ostböhmens*, Bd. I, *Von der ältesten Zeit bis zum Beginn der Hussitenstürme*, Reichenberg, 1924. C. E. MAURICE, *The story of Bohemia from the earliest times to the fall of national independence, 1620*, 2nd edition, New York, 1926.

Hungary. J. ANDRÁSSY, *The development of Hungarian constitutional liberty*, translated by C. ARTHUR and ILNOA GINEVER, London, 1908, extends to 1619. G. BECHMANN, *Der Kampf König Sigmunds gegen die werdende Weltmacht der Osmanen, 1392–1437*, Gotha, 1902. L. KUPELWIESER, *Die Kämpfe Ungarns mit den Osmanen bis zur Schlacht bei Mohács*, Vienna, 1895. W. FRAKNÓI, *Mathias Corvinus, König von Ungarn, 1458–1490*, a German translation, Freiburg, 1891.

Serbia. Prince and Princess LAZAROVICH-HREBELIANOVICH, *The Servian people: their past glory and their destiny*, 2 vols., New York, 1910. K. JIREČEK, *Geschichte der Serben*, 2 vols., Gotha, 1911–13; and his *Staat und Gesellschaft im mittelalterlichen Serbien: Studien zur Kulturgeschichte des 13–15 Jahrhundert*, Part I, Vienna, 1912 (Denkschriften Vienna Acad., 56, vols., II–III).

Latins in the Levant. G. SCHLUMBERGER, *Expéditions des Almugavares ou routiers catalans en Orient de l'an 1302–1311*, Paris, 1902. C. BUCHON,

Histoire des conquêtes et de l'établissement des Français dans les provinces de l'ancienne Grèce au moyen âge, Paris, 1846. A. RUBIÓ Y LLUCH, *La expedición y dominación de los Catalanes en Oriente*, Barcelona, 1883; *Los Navarros en Grecia y el Ducado Catalán de Atenas*, Barcelona, 1886. E. GERLAND, "Der vierte Kreuzzug und seine Probleme," in *Neue Jahrbücher für das klassische Altertum*, XIII (1904), 504–14. DIANE DE GULDENCRONE, *L'Achaie féodale. Etude sur le moyen âge en Grèce (1205–1456)*, Paris, 1886. L. NICOLAU D'OLIVER, *L'expansió de Catalunya en la Mediterránia oriental*, Barcelona, [1926?]. C. A. CHEKREZI, *Albania past and present*, New York, 1919.

Scanderbeg. J. PISKO, *Scander-beg*, Vienna, 1894. G. T. PETROVITCH, *Scander-beg (Georges Castriota)*, Paris, 1881. C. PAGANEL, *Histoire de Scanderbeg: ou Turcs et Chrétiens au XVe siècle*, Paris, 1855 [see review of this and other books on Albania and Scanderbeg, *Edinburgh review*, CLIV (1881), 325–56].

Ottoman Turks. N. JORGA, *Geschi hte des osmanischen Reiches nach den Quellen dargestellt*, 5 vols., Gotha, 1908–13, part of no. **332**, is now the standard work. It supersedes J. v. HAMMER-PURGSTALL, *Geschichte des osmanischen Reiches*, 2nd edition, 4 vols., Pesth, 1834–36, translated into French by J. J. HELLERT, 18 vols., and an atlas, Paris, 1835–43; see the long review of the French edition of this book by R. W. CHURCH, "The early Ottomans," in his *Miscellaneous essays*, 281–435; and J. W. ZINKEISEN, *Geschichte des osmanischen Reichs in Europa*, 7 vols., Hamburg and Gotha, 1840–63, part of no. **332**.

H. A. GIBBONS, *The foundation of the Ottoman empire: a history of the Osmanlis up to the death of Bayezid I (1300–1403)*, New York, 1916. O. TAFRALI, *Thessalonique, des origines au quatorzième siècle*, Paris, 1918. E. A. FREEMAN, *The Ottoman power in Europe: its nature, its growth, and its decline*, London, 1877. E. S. CREASY, *History of the Ottoman Turks*, new and revised edition, London, 1878. C. ELIOT, *Turkey in Europe*, London, 1907; new edition, 1908. Sir M. SYKES, *The caliphs' last heritage: a short history of the Turkish empire*, London, 1915. *Journal of the Royal Asiatic society*, London, 1834ff.

A. DE LA JONQUIÈRE, *Histoire de l'empire ottoman depuis les origines jusqu'à nos jours*, Paris, 1881; new edition, revised, 2 vols., Paris, 1914. H. GANEM, *Les sultans ottomans*, 2 vols. in one, Paris, 1901–02. T. G. DJUVARA, *Cent projets de partage de la Turquie (1281–1913)*, Paris, 1914. Y. FEHMI, *Histoire de la Turquie*, with a preface by A. BAUMANN, Paris, 1909. T. LAVALLÉE, *Histoire de la Turquie*, 2nd edition, 2 vols., Paris, 1859. A. VÁMBÉRY, *Das Türkenvolk in seinen ethnologischen und ethnographischen Beziehungen geschildert*, Leipzig, 1885.

Fall of Constantinople, 1453. C. MIJATOVICH, *Constantine, the last emperor of the Greeks: or the conquest of Constantinople by the Turks (A.D. 1453) after the latest historical researches*, London, 1892. E. A. VLASTO, *Les derniers jours de Constantinople*, Paris, 1883. J. H. KRAUSE, *Die Eroberungen von Konstantinopel im 13 und 15 Jahrhundert*, Halle, 1870. A. D. MORDTMANN, *Belagerung und Eroberung von Konstantinopel durch die Türken im Jahre 1453*, Stuttgart, 1858.

Scandinavia. Y. Brilioth, *Svensk kyrka, konungadöme och pavemakt 1363–1414*, Uppsala, 1925. G. Dehio, *Geschichte des erzbistums Hamburg-Bremen bis zum Ausgang der Mission*, 2 vols., Berlin, 1877. A. D. Jörgensen, *Den nordiske kirkes grundlaeggelse og förste udvikling* [til 1314], I–II, Copenhagen, 1874–78. L. J. Moltesen, *De avignonske pavers forhold til Danmark*, Copenhagen, 1896. J. Lindbaek, *Pavernes forhold til Danmark under kongerne Kristiern og Hans*, Copenhagen, 1907 (Diss.). L. Delevaud, "Les Français dans le nord," *Bulletin de la Société normande de géographie*, Rouen, 1911. Hildebrand, *Sveriges medeltid*. K. Erslev, *Dronning Margrethe og Kalmarunionens grundlaeggelse*, Copenhagen, 1882; *Erik af Pommern, hans kamp for Sönderjylland og Kalmarunionens oplösning*, Copenhagen, 1901. H. Schück, *Forntiden och den äldre medeltiden* (Afd. 1); *Folkungatiden och unionstiden* (Afd. 2), in *Svenska Folkets Historia*, Lund, 1914–15. A. Åkerhlom, *Sveriges förhållande till norge under Medelstidsunionen* (från 1389), Lund, 1888. M. Mackeprang, *Dansk Köbstadstyrelse fra Valdemar Sejr til Kristian IV*, Copenhagen, 1900. W. Christensen, *Dansk statsforvaltning i det 15 aarhundrede*, Copenhagen, 1903. C. Weibull, *Sverige och dess nordiska grammakter under den tidigare medeltiden.* "Om det Svenska och det Danska rekets uppkomst," *Historisk Tidskrift för Skåneland*, VII (1921), 301–60. E. Arup, *Danmarks historie, I. Land og folk til 1282*, Copenhagen, 1925. J. Paul, *Nordische Geschichte*, Breslau, 1925; "Engelbrecht Engelbrechtsson und sein Kampf gegen die Kalmarer Union," *Nordische Studien* herausgegeben vom Nordischen Institut der Universität Greifswald, Greifswald, 1921. P. Girgensohn, *Die skandinavische Politik der Hanse 1375–1395*, Uppsala, 1899. A. Sach, *Das Herzogtum Schleswig in seiner ethnographischen und nationalen Entwickelung*, I–III Abt., Halle, 1896–1907. H. Denicke, *Die Hansestädte, Dänemark und Norwegen 1369–1376*, Halle, 1880. D. Schäfer, *Dänische Annalen und Chroniken von der Mitte des XIII bis zum XV Jahrhundert*, Hannover, 1872; *Die Hansestädte und König Waldemar von Dänemark: Hansische Geschichte bis 1376*, Jena, 1879. M. Oehler, *Die Beziehungen Deutschlands zu Dänemark von der Kölner Konföderation bis zum Tode Karls IV*, Halle, 1892. D. Schäfer, *Das Buch des lübeckischen Vogts auf Schonen*, 2nd edition, Lübeck, 1927. J. C. H. R. Steenstrup, *Danmarks sydgraense og herredömmet over Holsten ved den historiske tids begyndelse (800–1100)*, Copenhagen, 1900. W. Christensen, *Unionskongerne og Hansestaederne 1439–1466*, Copenhagen, 1895. R. Usinger, *Deutsch-dänische Geschichte 1189–1227*, Berlin, 1863. P. Zorn, *Staat und Kirche in Norwegen bis zum Schluss des XIII Jahrhunderts*, Munich, 1873. C. Weibull, *Lübech och Skånemarknaden*, Lund, 1922. C. E. Hill, *The Danish Sound dues and the command of the Baltic*, Durham, N. C., 1926. K. Höhlbaum, "Zur deutsch-dänischen Geschichte der Jahre, 1332–1346," *Hansische Geschichtsblätter*, 1878.

Original sources. The general collections of sources for the east and north of Europe in the middle ages are listed above, nos. **1002–1011f.** See also no. **986.**

Documents inédits relativs à l'histoire de la Grèce au moyen âge, edited by

C. N. SATHAS, first series, 9 vols., Paris, 1880–90. *Acta et diplomata graeca medii aevi sacra et profana*, edited by F. MIKLOSICH and J. MÜLLER, 6 vols., Vienna, 1860–90. *Urkunden zur Geschichte der veneto-byzantinischen Beziehungen*, edited by G. L. TAFEL and G. M. THOMAS, Vienna, 1858, in *Fontes rerum Austriacarum*, 2, XII–XIV. *Monumenta spectanta ad unionum ecclesiarum Graecae et Romanae*, Vienna, 1872, edited by A. THEINER and F. MIKLOSICH, contains documents from 1124–1582. *Chroniques gréco-romanes inédites*, edited by K. HOPF, Berlin, 1873. *Recueil de documents sur l'Asie centrale d'après les écrivains chinois*, Paris, 1881, edited by C. IMBAULT-HUART, in *Bibliothèque de l'Ecole des langues orientales*, XVI. *The tale of the armament of* IGOR, *A.D. 1185; a Russian historical epic*, edited and translated by L. A. MAGNUS, London, 1915.

The main manuscript of Konungs Skuggsjá [king's mirror] in phototype reproduction with diplomatic text, edited for the university of Illinois by G. T. FLOM, Urbana, Ill., 1915. ELLEN JÖRGENSEN (editor), *Annales danici medii aevi*, Copenhagen. 1920.

Bibliography. The general bibliographies for eastern and northern Europe are listed above, nos. **46–48h.** For the Byzantine empire K. KRUMBACHER, *Geschichte der byzantinischen Literatur*, no. **800,** is our great store house of learning, including historical bibliography. Note especially KERNER, *Slavic Europe*, and VASILIEV, *History of the Byzantine Empire.*

Good general bibliographies are also to be found at the end of chapters in LAVISSE et RAMBAUD, *Histoire générale*, and the head of the paragraphs indicated above in LOSERTH, *Geschichte des späteren Mittelalters.* There is a very good bibliography on the early Ottoman empire in H. A. GIBBONS, *The foundation of the Ottoman empire*, 319–68. W. RECKE and A. M. WAGNER, *Bücherkunde zur Geschichte und Literatur Königreichs Polen*, Warsaw, 1918. M. S. STANOYEVICH, *Early Jugoslav literature*, New York, 1922. B. HOLLANDER, *Bibliographie der baltischen Heimatkunde*, Riga, 1924. L. BRÉHIER, "Histoire byzantine: publications des années 1922–1926," *R.H.*, CLIII (1926), 193–224. F. BABINGER, *Die Geschichtsschreiber der Osmanen und ihre Werke*, Leipzig, 1927. WARMHOLTZ, *Bibliotheca historica sueo-gothica.* See also the bibliographies under outlines XI, XVII, XXI, XXII (eastward expansion of Germany), XXIV (missions), XXVI (Levant trade and Hanseatic League).

PART III

MEDIEVAL CULTURE

PERIOD I. 500–1100

I. TRANSITION FROM ANCIENT TO MEDIEVAL CULTURE

A. Outline

1. Meaning of "history of culture." How it differs from the German conception of *Kulturgeschichte*. Current notions about the culture of the middle ages.

2. The transformation of the ancient Graeco-Roman World into the Greek Christian East and the Latin Christian West. On the difficulty of finding definite lines of division in history see outline I, part II. Importance of dwelling long on the stability of the Roman empire and on its permanent contributions to civilization. Relative importance of the various factors which produced change from the fourth to the sixth century. Pagan and Christian moralists of the time, especially the pagan Ammianus Marcellinus (ca. 320–ca. 395), and the Christians St. Jerome (331–420) and Salvian (died ca. 484), a presbyter of Marseilles, who wrote the *De gubernatione Dei*. Danger of resorting to sweeping explanations of the decline of the Roman empire.

3. The victory of the Latin language in the west. Its introduction and spread in the provinces by soldiers, colons, slaves, officials, teachers and priests. Difference between spoken and written Latin. The *Vulgate* of St. Jerome. The relation of Latin to the romanic languages.

4. The decline of the study of Greek in the west and of Latin in the east. Neither of these interesting phenomena has been investigated thoroughly. Gradual evolution of two clear-cut spheres of Christian culture, the Greek East and the Latin West. Waning interest in the Greek and the Latin classics and in learning in general about 500 A.D. The closing of the School of Athens in 529.

5. The changing Roman civilization is illustrated best in southern Gaul, in the fourth and fifth centuries. Famous schools in Bordeaux, Toulouse, Narbonne, Poitiers, and Angoulême (Imperial Trèves.) The program of studies. The study of oratory. Influence of the *Institutes* of Quintilian (ca. 35–95 A.D.). Increase of formalism in education. State support of schools. Ausonius (ca. 310–ca. 393) and his circle. His acquaintance with the Latin classics. His famous poem, *Mosella*. The coming of the barbarians into this region.

6. Prominent Roman nobles in this time of change. Q. Aurelius Symmachus (ca. 345–ca. 405); praefect of Rome in 384–385, and consul in 391. His literary learning. Apollinaris Sidonius (ca. 431–ca. 484), a provincial noble of Lyons, bishop of Clermont-Ferrand. His enthusiasm for classical learning in a land overrun by the Visigoths.

7. The conflict of religions. Conflict between Christianity and the worship of Isis, Mithraism (*Taurobolium*), Manichaeism, and Neo-platonism. Heresies within the church. Arianism and Donatism. The lingering death of paganism. Christian proscription of paganism; edicts concerning it in the Theodosian Code, 438. The emperor Julian, "the Apostate," 361–363. The appeal of Symmachus in 384 for the restoration of the Altar of Victory in Rome. Pagan revivals, especially that after the sack of Rome in 410.

8. Christianity and Graeco-Roman culture. Attitude of the church fathers towards the ancient classics. The fundamental difference of ideals in ancient classical and Christian life and literature. The conversion of Ausonius' pupil Paulinus (353–431), who became bishop of Nola in 409.

9. The barbarians and Graeco-Roman culture. Comparatively small number of invading barbarians. Exaggerated notion of the destruction which they wrought. Their respect for the culture of the Graeco-Roman world. Evidence concerning the sacks of Rome in 410 and 455. For the behavior of Theodoric and his Ostrogoths see outline II, part II, above. The *Life of Saint Severinus* (died ca. 482 in Noricum) by Eugippius.

B. Special Recommendations for Reading

Short general surveys. H. O. Taylor, *The classical heritage of the middle ages*, New York, 1901; 3rd edition, 1911; 1–43. Bury, *Later Roman empire*, I, 1–36. *C.M.H.*, I, 452–597. W. L. Westermann, "The economic basis of the decline of ancient culture," *A.H.R.*, XX (1915), 723–43.

Longer general accounts. H. O. Taylor, *The mediaeval mind*, I, 1–123. Rand, *Founders of the middle ages*. F. Guizot, *History of civilization in Europe*, lectures I–III. See also nos. **753** and **763**. C. Jullian, *Histoire de la Gaule;* V and VI, *La civilisation gallo-romaine*, Paris, 1920; VII and VIII, *Les empereurs de Trèves*, Paris, 1928. G. Rauschen, *Grundriss der Patrologie: die Schriften der Kirchenväter und ihr Lehrgehalt*, 8th–9th edition, Freiburg, i. B., 1926. L. Friedlaender, *Darstellungen aus der Sittengeschichte Roms*, vol. I, Leipzig, 1919. J. B. Bury, *History of the later Roman empire from the death of Theodosius I to the death of Justinian* (*A.D. 395 to A.D. 565*), 2 vols., London, 1923. L. Thorndike, *A history of magic and experimental science*, 2 vols., New York, 1923, especially vol. II, 337–550. F. Lot, *La fin du monde antique*. C. Foligno, *Latin thought during the middle ages*, Oxford, 1929. E. Albertini, *L'empire romain*, Paris, 1929. (Peuples et civilisations, vol. IV). F. Lot, C. Pfister, F. L. Ganshof, *Histoire du moyen âge:* t. I: *Les destinées de l'empire en occident de 395 à 888*, fasc. 1ᵉ, Paris, 1928. (Section II of no. **313a.**) L. Halphen, *Les barbares*. M. Rostovtzeff, *The social and economic history of the Roman empire*, Oxford, 1926, esp. 344–487.

Standard book. By far the best treatment of the subject of this outline is S. Dill, *Roman society in the last century of the western empire*, London, 1898; second, revised, edition, 1899 (often reprinted).

Latin language and literature. Munro and Sellery, *Medieval civilization*, 3–17, translation of Lavisse, *Histoire de France*, I, part II, 385–423. Sandys, *Classical scholarship*, I, ch. xiii. E. Norden, "Die lateinische

Literatur im Übergang vom Alterthum zum Mittelalter," *Kultur der Gegenwart*, 1905, 1:8, 374–411; 3rd edition (1912), 483–522. M. ROGER, *L'enseignement des lettres classiques d'Ausone à Alcuin*, Paris, 1905, 1–88. D. COMPARETTI, *Virgilio nel medio evo*, 2 vols., Leghorn, 1872; 2nd edition, Florence, 1896; translated from the first edition by E. F. M. BENECKE, *Vergil in the middle ages*, London, 1895, chs. IV–V. GRISAR, *History of Rome*, III, 239–49, "Vulgar Latin." F. J. E. ROBY, *A history of Christian Latin poetry from the beginnings to the close of the middle ages*, Oxford, 1927. P. MONCEAUX, *Histoire de la littérature latine chrétienne*, Paris, 1924. P. WENDLAND, *Die christliche Literatur* (Gercke-Norden, Einleitung, vol. I, Heft 5), neu bearbeitet v. H. Lietzmann, Leipzig, 1923. P. DE LABRIOLLE, *History and literature of Christianity from Tertullian to Boethius*, translated by HERBERT WILSON, New York, 1925 (poor translation of the original French title, *Histoire de la littérature latine chrétienne*).

The triumph of Christianity. *C.M.H.*, I, ch. IV. E. EMERTON, "The religious environment of early Christianity," *Harvard theological review*, III (1910), 181–208. J. B. CARTER, *The religious life of ancient Rome*, Boston, 1911, 95–158. GIBBON, *Decline and fall*, chs. XX–XXI, XXIII, XXVIII. R. M. POPE, *Early church history: the relations of Christianity and paganism in the Roman empire*, London, 1918. G. FERRERO, *The ruin of ancient civilization and the triumph of christianity*, translated by HON. LADY WHITEHEAD, New York, 1921.

Original sources. Short extracts, J. C. AYER, *Source book for ancient church history*, 297–429. *The life of Saint Severinus* by EUGIPPIUS, translated by G. W. ROBINSON, Cambridge, 1914. *The letters of Sidonius*, translated by O. M. DALTON, Oxford, 1915. Some of his letters are also translated in HODGKIN, *Italy and her invaders*, II, 314–71. The more interesting writings of St. Jerome are translated in *Nicene and post-Nicene fathers*, 2nd series, vol. VI. *Fathers of the church: a selection from the writings of the Latin Fathers*, translated, with an introduction and biographical notices, by F. A. WRIGHT. Extracts from the *Institutes of* QUINTILIAN may be read in English translation in P. MONROE, *Source book of the history of education for the Greek and Roman period*, New York, 1901, 445–509. H. P. EVELYN-WHITE, *Ausonius*, with English translation, 2 vols., London and New York, 1920 (vol. II includes the *Eucharisticus* of Paulinus of Pella). F. S. FLINT, *The Mosella of Ausonius*, translated by F. S. FLINT, London, 1916 (Poets translation series). *The works of Julian* (the Apostate) translated by WRIGHT in Loeb Classical Library, 3 vols., London and New York, 1923. *The works of Quintilian*, translated by H. E. BUTLER, 4 vols., London and New York, 1921–22. M. PLATNAUER, *Claudian*, with an English translation, London and New York, 1922. KIDD, *Documents illustrative of the history of the church*, vol. II, 313–461 A.D. French series of texts and translations corresponding to the Loeb Classical Library, undertaken by the Association Guillaume Budé, published at Paris, Soc. d'édition "les belles lettres," (especially good is the translation of JULIAN, *Epistolae, leges, poematia, fragmenta varia*, by J. BIDEZ, 1922).

Maps. SHEPHERD, *Atlas*, 38–39, 42–43.

C. Bibliography

General books. See the bibliographies under outlines I and II of part II. Many histories of the church, nos. **393–478**, are useful.

Intellectual history. H. O. Taylor, *Freedom of the mind in history*, London, 1923. J. H. Robinson, "Some reflections on intellectual history," *The new history*, 101–31.

General accounts. T. R. Glover, *Life and letters in the fourth century*, Cambridge, 1901. A. F. Ozanam, *La civilisation au cinquième siècle*, vols. I and II of *Oeuvres complètes*, Paris, 1855; 5th edition, 1894; translated by A. C. Glyn, *History of civilization in the fifth century*, 2 vols., London, 1868. O. Seeck, *Geschichte des Untergangs der antiken Welt*, 6 vols., Berlin, 1895–1920 (see especially V, 217–59, "Die letzte Erhebung des Heidentums"). T. Whittaker, *Macrobius, or philosophy, science and letters in the year 400*, Cambridge, 1923. E. Kornemann, "Das Problem des Untergangs der antiken Welt," *Vergangenheit und Gegenwart*, XII (1922), 193–202, 241–54. M. Schuster, *Altertum und deutsche Kultur*, Vienna, 1926. Stein, *Geschichte des spätrömischen Reiches*. J. Kulischer, *Allgemeine Wirtschaftsgeschichte des Mittelalters und der Neuzeit;* Bd. I, *Das Mittelalter* (From Caesar to the XIth century), Munich and Berlin, 1928. A. Dopsch, *Wirtschaftliche und soziale Grundlagen der europäischen Kulturentwicklung von Caesar bis auf Karl den Grossen*, 2te Aufl., Vienna, 1923–24. M. P. Charlesworth, *Trade-routes and commerce of the Roman empire*, Cambridge, 1924. G. B. Picotti, *Il "patricius" nell' ultima età imperiale e nei primi regni barbarici d'Italia*, Florence, 1928. G. Volpe, *Il medioevo*, Florence, 1927. E. G. Sihler, *From Augustus to Augustine*, Cambridge, 1923.

Latin language and literature. W. S. Teuffel, *Geschichte der römischen Literatur*, 6th edition, 3 vols., Leipzig and Berlin, 1910–13, translated from the 5th German edition by G. C. W. Warr, 2 vols., London, 1900. M. Schanz, *Geschichte der römischen Literatur bis zum Gesetzgebungswerk des Kaisers Justinian*, 4 vols., Munich, 3rd edition, 1923 (I. Müller, *Handbuch der klassischen Altertumswissenschaft*, VIII). A. Baumgartner, *Geschichte der Weltliteratur*, IV, 84–203, 229–41. A. Ebert, *Allgemeine Geschichte der Literatur des Mittelalters*, I, book II. E. Norden, *Die antike Kunstprosa*, II, 573–656. F. Cumont, "Pourquoi le latin fut la seule langue liturgique de l'Occident?", *Mélanges Paul Frédéricq*, Brussels, 1904, 63ff. L. Hahn, "Zum Gebrauch der lateinischen Sprache in Konstantinopel," *Festgabe für Martin von Schanz*, Würzburg, 1912, 173–83. F. A. Belin, *Histoire de la latinité de Constantinople*, 2nd edition, Paris, 1894. L. Valentin, *Saint Prosper d'Aquitaine: étude sur la littérature latine au 5e siècle en Gaule*, Paris, 1900. H. Goelzer, *Etude lexicographique et grammaticale de la latinité de Saint Jérôme*, Paris, 1884; *Le latin de S. Avit, évêque de Vienne (450–526)*, Paris, 1909. A. Dubois, *La latinité d'Ennodius*, Paris, 1903. L. Bergmüller, *Bemerkungen zur Latinität des Jordanes*, Augsburg, 1903 (Prog.). C. H. Grandgent, *An introduction to vulgar Latin*, Boston, 1907; *From Latin to Italian*, Cambridge, 1927. F. G. Mohl, *Introduction à la chronologie du latin vulgaire*, Paris, 1899. C. Weyman, *Beiträge zur Geschichte der christlich-*

lateinischen Poesie, Munich, 1926. R. KENT, "The Latin language in the fourth century," *Trans. American philological association*, XL (1919), 91–100. A. H. SALONIUS, *Kritische Untersuchungen über Text, Syntax und Wortschatz der spätlateinischen Vitae Patrum*, Lund, 1920. T. FRANK, "Latin quantitative speech as affected by immigration," *American journal of philology*, XLV (1924), 161–75. U. MORICCA, *Storia della letteratura latina christiana*, 2 vols., Turin, 1924–28. O. BARDENHEWER, *Geschichte der altkirchlichen Literatur*, Freiburg, i. B., 1924. (The 4th vol. deals with Greek literature of the 5th century, Syrian of the 4th and 5th, Latin of the 5th.)

Greek. K. KRUMBACHER, "Die griechische Literatur des Mittelalters (324–1453 A.D.)," *Kultur der Gegenwart*, 1:8 (1905), 237–85; 2nd edition (1907), 239–90 (see also pp. 200–38). SANDYS, *Classical scholarship*, I, chs. XX–XXI. A. and M. CROISET, *Histoire de la littérature grecque*, 5 vols., Paris, 1887–1900; 2nd and 3rd editions, 1899–1914, V, last two chapters. See also ch. XXIX of their, *An abridged history of Greek literature*, translated by G. F. HEFFELBOWER, New York, 1904. H. STEINACHER, "Die römische Kirche und die griechischen Sprachkenntnisse des Frühmittelalters," *Festschrift für Theodor Gomperz*, Vienna, 1902, 324–41.

Saint Jerome. G. GRÜTZMACHER, *Hieronymus: eine biographische Studie zur alten Kirchengeschichte*, 3 vols., Leipzig, 1901–08. E. L. CUTTS, *Saint Jerome*, 4th edition, London, 1897 (The fathers for English readers). Mrs. C. MARTIN, *The life of St. Jerome*, London, 1888. J. DE SIGÜENZA, *The life of Saint Jerome, the great doctor of the church, in six books, from the original Spanish . . . 1595*, by M. MONTERIO, London, 1907. A. LARGENT, *Saint Jérôme*, 6th edition, Paris, 1907 (Les saints). J. BROCHET, *S. Jérôme et ses ennemis*, Paris, 1906. J. TURMEL, *St. Jérôme*, Paris, 1906. L. SANDERS, *Etudes sur St. Jérôme*, Paris, 1903. A. S. PEASE, "The attitude of St. Jerome toward pagan literature," *Trans., American philological assoc.*, L (1919), 150–67. F. CAVALLERA, *Saint Jérôme, sa vie et son oeuvre*, 2 vols., Paris, 1922. A. BAUER, *Vom Griechentum zum Christentum*, 2nd edition, Leipzig, 1923. W. VON CHRIST, *Geschichte der griechischen Literatur*, 6th edition, Munich, 1924. K. R. NELZ, *Die theologischen Schulen der morgenländischen Kirchen während der sieben ersten christlichen Jahrhunderte*, Bonn, 1916. A. PUECH, *Histoire de la littérature grecque chrétienne depuis les origines jusqu' à la fin du IVe siècle*, 2 vols., Paris, 1928. A. and M. CROISET, *Histoire de la littérature grecque*, new edition, vol. V, Paris, 1928. G. BARDY, *Littérature grecque chrétienne*, Paris, 1928 (Bibliothèque catholique des sciences religieuses). L. TRAUBE, *Einleitung in die lateinische Philologie des Mittelalters*, Munich, 1911 (vol. II of his *Vorlesungen*), 41–42. St. JEROME, *Dem Heiligen Hieronymus, Festschrift zur fünfzehnhundertsten Wiederkehr seines Todestages* [reprinted from *Benedikt Monatschrift*, II (1920), nos. 9–12], Beuron, 1920. *Miscellanea Geronimiana. Scritti varii pubblicati nel XV centenario della morte di San Girolamo*, Rome, 1920. A. P. VACCARI, *Girolamo. Studi e schizzi in occasione del XV centenario della sua morte*, Rome, 1921. E. BUONAIUTI, *San Girolamo*, 2nd edition, Rome, 1923. U. MORICCA, *San Girolamo: Il pensiero christiano*, 2 vols., Milan, 1923.

Later Roman education. P. R. COLE, *Later Roman education in Ausonius, Capella and the Theodosian Code*, New York, 1909. G. RAUSCHEN, *Das griechisch-römische Schulwesen zur Zeit des ausgehenden Heidentums*, Bonn, 1901. O. DENK, *Geschichte des gallofränkischen Unterrichts- und Bildungswesens*, Mainz, 1892, chs. I–V. G. KAUFMAN, *Rhetorenschulen und Klosterschulen oder heidnische und christliche Cultur in Gallien während des 5 und 6 Jahrhunderts*, Leipzig, 1869 (Historisches Taschenbuch). T. HAARHOFF, *Schools of Gaul: a study of pagan and Christian education in the last century of the western empire*, Oxford, 1920. L. HAHN, "Ueber das Verhältnis von Staat und Schule in der römischen Kaiserzeit," *Philologus*, LXXVI (N.F. XXX) (1920), 176–91. H. v. SCHUBERT, *Bildung und Erziehung in frühchristlichen Zeit.* Gothein-Festgabe, Munich and Leipzig, 1923, 75ff.

Ausonius. MARIE J. BYRNE, *Prolegomena to an edition of the works of Decimus Magnus Ausonius*, New York, 1917. R. PICHON, *Les derniers écrivains profanes: les panégyristes; Ausone; le Querolus; Rutilius Namatianus*, Paris, 1906 (Etudes sur l'histoire de la littérature latine dans les Gaules); see also book IV of his *Histoire de la littérature latine*, 3rd edition, Paris, 1903. P. DE LABRIOLLE, *Une épisode de la fin du paganisme: la correspondance d'Ausone et de Paulin de Nola*, Paris, 1910, contains translations into French together with studies. C. JULLIAN, *Ausone et Bordeaux: études sur les derniers temps de la Gaule romaine*, Paris, 1893. M. J. PATTIST, *Ausonius als Christen*, Amsterdam, 1925. E. K. RAND, "Decimus Magnus Ausonius, the first French Poet," *Proceedings, Classical association (British)*, XXIV (1927), 28–41. "Ausonius und das Christentum," *C. Weyman, Beiträge*, 90ff.

Apollinaris Sidonius. P. ALLARD, *Saint Sidoine Apollinaris (413–489)*, Paris, 1909 (Les saints). T. MOMMSEN, "Apollinaris Sidonius und seine Zeit," *Reden und Aufsätze*, Berlin, 1905, 132–43.

Conflict of religions in the Roman empire. The fundamental books are those by F. CUMONT, *Les religions orientales dans le paganism romain*, Paris, 1906; 2nd edition, 1909, translated by G. SHOWERMAN, *Oriental religions in Roman paganism*, Chicago, 1911; and *Les mystères de Mithra*, Paris, 1900; 3rd edition, 1913; translated from second edition by J. M. McCORMACK, *The mysteries of Mithra*, Chicago, 1910. F. LEGGE, *Forerunners and rivals of Christianity: being studies in religious history from 330* B.C. *to 330* A.D., 2 vols., Cambridge, 1915, II, chs. XII, XIII. T. R. GLOVER, *The conflict of religions in the early Roman empire*, London, 1910. C. ELSEE, *Neoplatonism in relation to christianity: an essay*, Cambridge, 1908. C. BIGG, *Neoplatonism*, London, 1895. W. R. HALLIDAY, *The pagan background of early christianity*, Liverpool, 1925. P. ALFARIC, *Les écritures manichéennes, leur constitution, leur histoire: étude analytique*, 2 vols., Paris, 1918–19. E. L. WOODWARD, *Christianity and nationalism in the late Roman empire*, London, 1916. J. GEFFCKEN, *Das Christentum im Kampf und Ausgleich mit der griechisch-römischen Welt.* (*Natur und Geisteswelt*, Bd. LIV, 3rd edition, Leipzig, 1920). K. CLEMEN, *Die Reste der primitiven Religionen in ältesten Christentum*, Giessen, 1916. T. WHITAKER, *The Neo-Platonists*, 2nd edition, Cambridge, 1918. U. FRACCASSINI, *Il misticismo greco e il* *cristianesimo*, Città di Castella, 1922. E. BEVAN, *Hellenism and Christianity*, London, 1921. A. LOISY, *Les mystères paiens et le mystère chrêtien*, Paris, 1919. R. EISLER, *Orpheus the Fisher. Comparative studies in Orphic and early Christian cult symbolism*, London, 1921. L. PATTERSON, *Mithraism and Christianity*, Cambridge, 1921. P. MONCEAUX, "Le manichéisme," *Journal des savants*, XIX (1921), 287–374. J. BERNHART, *Die philosophische Mystik des Mittelalters von ihren antiken Ursprungen bis zur Renaissance*, Munich, 1922, 33–47. W. SCHUBART, "Hellenismus und Weltreligion," *Neue Jahrbücher für Wissenschaft und Jugendbildung*, II (1926), 505–20. G. MESSINA, "La dottrina manichea e le origini del cristianesimo," *Biblica*, X (1929), 313–31. J. BEHM, *Die mandäische Religion und das Christentum*, Leipzig, 1927. L. DUCHESNE, *Origines du culte chrêtien: étude sur la liturgie latine avant Charlemagne*, 5e edition, Paris, 1920. F. C. BURKITT, *The religion of the Manichees*, Cambridge, 1925. R. EISLER, *Orphisch-dionysische Mysteriengedanken in der christlichen Antike*, Leipzig, 1925.

The end of paganism. G. BOISSIER, *La fin du paganisme*, 2 vols., Paris, 1891; 5th edition, 1907. MAUDE A. HUTTMANN, *The establishment of Christianity and the proscription of paganism*, New York, 1914 (Columbia university studies). W. K. BOYD, *The ecclesiastical edicts of the Theodosian Code*, New York, 1905 (*Ibid.*). G. UHLHORN, *Der Kampf des Christentums mit dem Heidentum*, Stuttgart, 1875, translated from the 3rd German edition by E. C. SMYTH and C. J. ROPES, *The conflict of Christianity with heathenism*, New York, 1879; revised edition, 1908. P. D. SCOTT-MONCRIEFF, *Paganism and Christianity in Egypt*, Cambridge, 1913. V. SCHULTZE, *Geschichte des Untergangs des griechisch-römischen Heidentums*, Jena, 1887. G. E. A. GRINDLE, *The destruction of paganism in the Roman empire*, Oxford, 1892. C. BIGG, *The church's task in the Roman empire*, Oxford, 1905. C. H. MOORE, "The pagan reaction in the late IV century," *Trans., American philological assoc.*, L (1919), 122–34. M. I. ROSTOVTZEFF, *Mystic Italy*, New York, 1928, depicts the religious and spiritual agitation of the Roman world, and interprets some of the most important archaeological evidence regarding the Greek mystery religions of the first three centuries A.D. in Pompeii and Rome. J. GEFFCKEN, *Der Ausgang des griechisch-römischen Heidentums*, Heidelberg, 1929. G. BLOCH, *L'empire romain, évolution et décadence*, Paris, 1922. G. GRUPP, *Kulturgeschichte der römischen Kaiserzeit*, 1ste Teil: *Die untergehende heidnische Kultur*, 3rd edition, Regensburg, 1921. V. MACCHIORO, *Zagreus, studi sull' Orfismo*, Bari, 1920. J. CARCOPINO, *Etudes romaines: la basilique pythagoricienne de la Porte Majeure*, Paris, 1927. F. J. DÖLGER, *Antike und Christentum: Kultur-und religionsgeschichtliche Studien*, Münster, i. W., 1929. C. CORBIÈRE, *Le christianisme et la fin de la philosophie antique: essai sur la polémique du néoplatonisme avec le christianisme*, Paris, 1921.

Julian the Apostate. P. ALLARD, *Julien l'Apostat*, 2 vols., Paris, 1900–03. ALICE GARDNER, *Julian, philosopher and emperor, and the last struggle of paganism against Christianity*, London, 1901. G. MAU, *Die Religionsphilosophie Kaiser Julians in seinen Reden auf König Helios und die Götter-Mutter*,

Leipzig, 1907, contains translations of the two speeches. G. NEGRI, *L'imperatore Giuliano l'Apostata*, Florence, 1902, translated by the Duchess LITTA-VISCONTI-ARESE, 2 vols., London, 1905. E. J. MARTIN, *The Emperor Julian*, London, 1919. P. ALLARD, *Le christianisme et l'empire romain de Néron à Théodose*, 9th edition, Paris, 1925. A. ROSTAGNI, *Giuliano l'Apostata: saggio critico con le operette politiche e satiriche, tradotte e commentate*, Turin, 1920. F. SCHEMMEL, "Die Schulzeit Kaiser Julians," *Philologus*, LXXXII (1927), 454–66. W. KOCH, *Comment l'empereur Julien tâcha de fonder une église paienne*, Brussels, 1928, reprinted from *Revue belge de philologie et d'histoire*, VII (1927–28), 3–26, 49–82, 511–50, 1363–85. H. GOLLANCZ, *Julian the Apostate* (an English rendering of the Syrian version of his life), Oxford, 1928. F. BOULENGER, "L'empereur Julian et la rhétorique," *Mélanges de philologie et d'histoire publiés à l'occasion du cinquantenaire de la Faculté des lettres de l'université catholique de Lille*, Lille, 1927.

Arianism. H. M. GWATKIN, *Studies of Arianism*, 2nd edition, Cambridge, 1900; *Arian controversy*, London, 1889 (Epochs of church history); *The knowledge of God*, 2 vols., Edinburgh, 1906. E. L. WOODWARD, *Christianity and nationalism in the later Roman empire*, London and New York, 1916.

Paulinus of Nola and Paulinus of Pella. J. S. PHILLIMORE, "St. Paulinus of Nola," *Dublin review*, CXLVII (1910), 288–305. J. BROCHET, *La correspondance de Saint Paulin de Nole et de Sulpice Sévère*, Paris, 1906. P. REINELT, *Studien über die Briefe des hl. Paulinus von Nola*, Breslau, 1903 (Diss.). J. ROCAFORT, *Un type gallo-romain, Paulin de Pella: sa vie, son poème*, Paris, 1896. L. VILLANI, "Sur l'ordre des lettres échangées par Ausone et Paulin de Nole," *Revue des études anciennes*, XXIX (1927), 35–44. H. WADDELL, *The wandering scholars*, London, 1927, 1–22. R. DE GOURMOND, *Le latin mystique*, 61–69.

The church and ancient culture. E. HATCH, *The influence of Greek ideas and usages upon the Christian church*, edited by A. M. FAIRBAIRN, 4th edition, London, 1892. G. HODGES, *The early church from Ignatius to Augustine*, Boston, 1915. A. H. LEWIS, *Paganism surviving in christianity*, New York, 1892. H. v. EICKEN, *Geschichte und System der mittelalterlichen Weltanschauung*, 109–47. J. A. LALANNE, *Influence des pères de l'église sur l'éducation publique pendant les cinq premiers siècles de l'ère chrétienne*, Paris, 1850. A. HARNACK, *History of dogma*, vol. I. G. LOESCHCKE, *Jüdisches und Heidnisches im christlichen Kult*, Bonn, 1910. P. WENDLAND, *Die hellenistisch-römische Kultur in ihren Beziehungen zu Judentum und Christentum*, Tübingen, 1907 (Handbuch zum neuen Testament, vol. I, part II). E. RENAN, *Lectures on the influence of the institutions, thought and culture of Rome on christianity and on the development of the catholic church*, translated by C. BEARD, London, 1880. U. BENIGNI, *Storia sociale della chiesa*, 2 vols., Milan, 1912–15. B. HERMANN, "Kirchenväter und altklassische Bildung," *Benedikt. Monatschrift*, I (1919), 51–56, 168–74, 345–51. E. T. MERRIL, "The church in the fourth century," *Trans., American philological association*, I (1919), 101–21. E. STEMPLINGER, "Hellenisches im Christentum," *Neue Jahrbücher* *für d. klass. Altertum und für Pädagogik*, XXI (1918), 81–89. B. J. KIDD, *A history of the church to A. D. 461*, 3 vols., Oxford, 1922. MOURRET, *Histoire générale de l'église*. E. G. SIHLER, *From Augustus to Augustine*. J. P. STEFFES, *Das Wesen des Gnostizismus und sein Verhältnis zum katholischen Dogma*, Paderborn, 1922. F. ANWANDER, "Die literarische Bekampfung des Christentums in der Antike," *Benedict. Monatschrift*, VI (1924), 297–320. O. STAHLIN, *Christentum und Antike*, Wurzburg, 1921. J. ZEILLER, *L'empire romain et l'église*, Paris, 1928. H. FUCHS, "Die frühe christliche Kirche unde die antike Bildung," *Die Antike*, V (1929), 107–19.

The barbarians and ancient culture. F. LAURENT, *Les barbares et le catholicisme*, Ghent, 1857; 2nd edition, Brussels, 1864 (Etudes sur l'histoire de l'humanité, 5). FUSTEL DE COULANGES, *Les institutions de l'ancienne France*, vols. I–II. M. ROSTOVTZEFF, *Iranians and Greeks in South Russia*, Oxford, 1922. A. v. MARTIN, "Antike, Germanentum, Christentum und Orient als Aufbaufactoren der geistigen Welt des Mittelalters," *Archiv für Kulturgeschichte*, XIX (1929), 301–345. L. SALVATORELLI, "From Locke to Reitsenstein: the historical investigation of the origins of Christianity," *Harvard theological review*, XXII (1929), 263–67; also in *Rivista storica italiana*, XLV–XLVI (1928), 5–66.

Saint Severinus. A. BAUDRILLART, *Saint Séverin*, Paris, 1908 (Les saints). T. SOMMERLAD, *Die Lebensbeschreibung Severins als kulturgeschichtliche Quelle*, Leipzig, 1903. C. C. MIEROW, "St. Severinus and the closing years of the province of Noricum," *Colorado college publications*, Language series, vol. II, no. 3 (1917).

Bibliographies. *C.M.H.*, I, 624–41, 691–95. M. ROGER, *L'enseignement*, pp. IX–XVIII. Bibliographical notes in DILL, *Roman society;* TAYLOR, *Mediaeval mind*, I, 1–123; SANDYS, *Classical scholarship*, I, ch. XIII; BAUMGARTNER, *Geschichte der Weltliteratur*, IV, 84–203; W. S. TEUFFEL, *Geschichte der römischen Literatur*, III, 210–472; and M. SCHANZ, *Römische Literaturgeschichte*, IV. The vast literature on the early church is beyond the scope of the above outline. EGIDI, *La storia medioevale*. (Guide bibliographiche, fasc. 8.) HAMPE, *Mittelalterliche Geschichte*. J. W. THOMPSON, *Reference studies in medieval history*.

II. TYPES OF THE TRANSITION PERIOD, ABOUT 400–600

A. OUTLINE

1. Necessity of choosing a few guiding threads in a maze of change. The value of biography.

2. St. Augustine (354–430). Born in Tagaste, in Numidia. The Africa of Augustine's youth. His mother Monica. His *Confessions*. His search for the true religion (Neo-platonism, Mithraism, Manichaeism). Influenced by St. Ambrose in Milan. The "conversion," in 386. Bishop of Hippo and religious arbiter of the west. His *City of God* (*De civitate Dei*). OROSIUS' *Seven books of history against the pagans* (*Historiarum adversum paganos libri VII*, sometimes called *Ormista* or *Ormesta*, the meaning of which is un-

known). Augustine's attitude toward classical learning, especially Greek. His attitude toward the barbarians and his *Weltanschauung* in his old age. He died in Hippo in 430 when the Vandals were before its gates.

3. Boethius (ca. 475–524). A type of the old Roman nobility, more or less unwillingly in the court of a barbarian king (Theodoric), and scarcely touched by christianity. His great contribution to the cause of learning. Translations from the Greek. His *Consolation of philosophy* (*Philosophiae consolatio*), composed in prison. His execution by Theodoric.

4. Cassiodorus (ca. 480–90—ca. 575–85). Contrast with Boethius. Also of old Roman noble stock, but a willing servant of Theororic, and, in old age, a pious monk, in Vivarium at Squillace in Calabria, his birthplace. His *Variae* and *Institutiones*, especially part II, *De artibus ac disciplinis liberalium litterarum*. His great services for monastic learning.

5. Pope Gregory I, the Great (ca. 540–604). Also a Roman noble; the lord of western Europe as pope. He foresaw the future of the barbarians as faithful sons of the church. His discouragement of secular learning. His very popular works. Gregory's *Weltanschauung* indicative of a great change in the world since the birth of Augustine.

B. Special Recommendations for Reading

St. Augustine. The following are short biographies in English. L. Bertrand, *Saint Augustin*, Paris, 1913, translated by V. O'Sullivan, *The life of St. Augustin*, New York, 1914. J. McCabe, *St. Augustine and his age*, New York, 1903. E. L. Cutts, *Saint Augustine*, London, 1909 (The fathers for English readers). Harnack, *History of dogma*, V, 1–240.

For surveys see Farrar, *Lives of the Fathers*, II, ch. xvii; Carter, *The religious life of ancient Rome*, ch. vi; R. Eucken, *Die Lebensanschauungen der grossen Denker*, translated by W. S. Hough, *The problem of human life as viewed by the great thinkers*, London, 1909; new edition, 1912, 172–248; W. Dilthey, *Einleitung in die Geisteswissenschaften*, Leipzig, 1883, I, 315–37; and M. Grabmann, *Die Geschichte der scholastischen Methode*, I, 125–43. For his *City of God* read Boissier, *Fin du paganisme*, II, 339–90; and A. Robertson, *Regnum Dei*, London, 1901. A short appreciation of his *Confessions* is in F. Drake, *Masters of the spiritual life*, London, 1916, ch. i. C. Douais, *Les Confessions de St. Augustin*, Paris, 1893. J. N. Figgis, *The political aspect of St. Augustine's City of God*, London, 1921. R. Deferrari and M. J. Keeler, "St. Augustine's 'City of God': its plan and development," *American journal of philology*, I (1929), 109–37. E. K. Rand, *Founders*, ch. viii.

Boethius. Hodgkin, *Italy and her invaders*, III, ch. xii; *Theodoric the Goth*, ch. xiii. Sandys, *Classical scholarship*, I, 2nd edition, 251–58. Manitius, *Geschichte der lateinischen Literatur des Mittelalters*, I, 22–36. M. Grabmann, *Geschichte der scholastischen Methode*, I, 148–77. L. M. Hartmann, *Geschichte Italiens im Mittelalter*, Leipzig, 1897, vol. I, ch. iv. Rand, *Founders*, ch. v.

Cassiodorus. R. W. CHURCH, "Cassiodorus," in his *Miscellaneous essays*, London, 1888, 155–204. SANDYS, *Classical scholarship*, I, 2nd edition, 258–70. HODGKIN, *The letters of Cassiodorus*, introduction. ROGER, *L'enseignement des lettres classiques*, 175–87. MANITIUS, *Geschichte der lateinischen Literatur*, I, 36–52. O. BARDENHEWER, *Patrologie*, 3rd edition, § 120. T. HODGKIN, *Theodoric the Goth*, ch. IX. G. PFEILSCHIFTER, *Theodorich der Grosse*, ch. VI. RAND, *Founders*, ch. VII.

Gregory the Great. DUDDEN, *Gregory the Great*, II, 285–443. ROGER, *L'enseignement*, 187–95. MANITIUS, *Geschichte der lateinischen Literatur*, I, 92–106. For general literature on Gregory the Great see outline V in part II above. H. H. HOWORTH, *Saint Gregory the Great*, London, 1912. RAND, *Founders*, ch. I.

Original sources. All the important works of St. Augustine are translated into English. For our purposes the most essential work is his *Confessions*, of which there is a good translation in the *Nicene and post-Nicene fathers*, first series, vol. I. The original Latin of the *Confessions*, together with the English translation by W. WATTS (1631), Loeb library, 2 vols., London, 1912. The *Confessions* are also translated, Everyman's library, 1907.

The famous *City of God* (*De civitate Dei*) is best read in the English translation of J. HEALEY (1610), 2 vols., Edinburgh, 1909. It may also be found in the *Nicene and post-Nicene fathers*, first series, vol. II; and is also translated by M. DODS, 2 vols., London, 1871. The translation in the Temple Classics is not so satisfactory. It omits much and is not well arranged.

Other works of St. Augustine are translated in *Nicene and post-Nicene fathers*, first series, vols. I–VIII; and in his *Works*, by M. DODS, 15 vols. Edinburgh, 1872–82. J. P. CHRISTOPHER (editor), *S. Aureli Augustini Hipponiensis episcopi De catechizandis rudibus liber unus*, translated with an introduction and commentary, Washington, 1926 (The Catholic university of America patristic studies, vol. VIII). See also the translation of his *Soliloquies*, by ROSE E. CLEVELAND, Boston, 1910; and AYER, *Source book*, 429–463.

King Alfred's Anglo-Saxon version of OROSIUS' *Seven books of history against the pagans* is translated into English in G. R. PAULI, *The Life of Alfred the Great*, 1853, 238–582. The best edition of the Latin original is edited by C. ZANGEMEISTER, 1882, in no. **954,** vol. V. A translation of OROSIUS will appear in no. **949.**

BOETHIUS, *The theological tractates*, with an English translation by H. F. STEWART and E. K. RAND; The *Consolations of philosophy* with the English translation of "I. T." (1609), revised by H. F. STEWART, London, 1918 (Loeb Library). The *Consolations of philosophy* have also been translated by H. R. JAMES, London, 1897; and by W. V. COOPER, London, 1902 (Temple classics).

For translations of some works of pope GREGORY see *Nicene and post-Nicene fathers*, second series, vols. XII–XIII.

C. Bibliography

General books. See the bibliographies under outlines II and V of part II.

Saint Augustine. W. Thimme, *Augustin; ein Lebens- und Charakterbild auf Grund seiner Briefe*, Göttingen, 1910; *Augustins geistige Entwickelung in den ersten Jahren nach seiner "Bekehrung," 386–391*, Berlin, 1908 (Neue Studien edited by N. Bonwetsch, 3). P. Gerosa, *Sant' Agostino e la decadenza dell' impero romano*, Turin, 1916. G. v. Hertling, *Der Untergang der antiken Kultur: Augustin*, Mainz, 1902 (Weltgeschichte in Karakterbildern). E. F. Humphrey, *Politics and religion in the days of Augustine*, New York, 1912 (Diss.). A. Dorner, *Augustinus*, Leipzig, 1908. A. Hatzfeld, *Saint Augustin*, 6th edition, Paris, 1902. J. Martin, *Saint Augustin*, Paris, 1901 (Grands philosophes). C. Wolfsgruber, *Augustinus*, Paderborn, 1898. A. v. Harnack, *Augustin: Reflexionen und Maximen, aus seinen Werken gesammelt und übersetzt*, Tübingen, 1922. H. Eibl, *Augustin und die Patristik*, Munich, 1923. P. v. Sokolwski, *Der heilige Augustin und die christliche Civilisation*, Halle, 1927.

Among the many books which treat of the spiritual development of Augustine are the following: H. Becker, *Augustin: Studien zu seiner geistigen Entwicklung*, Leipzig, 1908. J. Mausbach, *Die Ethik des heiligen Augustinus*, 2 vols., Freiburg, 1909. M. L. Burton, *The problem of evil: a criticism of the Augustinian point of view*, Chicago, 1909. W. Cunningham, *S. Austin and his place in the history of christian thought*, London, 1886. W. Montgomery, *St. Augustine: aspects of his life and thought*, London, 1914. L. Grandgeorge, *Saint Augustin et le néo-platonisme*, Paris, 1896, part of no. **888.** Ella H. Stokes, *The conception of a kingdom of ends in Augustine, Aquinas, and Leibniz*, Chicago, 1912 (Diss.). H. Reuter, *Augustinische Studien*, Gotha, 1887. W. J. S. Simpson, *St. Augustine and African church divisions*, London and New York, 1910. K. Holl, *Augustins innere Entwicklung*, Berlin, 1923 (Abhandlungen preuss. Akad. Wissensch., 1922, 4). P. Alfaric, *L'évolution intellectuelle de Saint Augustin; du manichéisme au néoplatonisme*, Paris, 1918; *Les écritures manichéennes*. C. Butler, *Western mysticism. The teaching of St. Augustine, Gregory, and Bernard on contemplation and the contemplative life*, London, 1922. C. Boyer, *Christianisme et néo-platonisme dans la formation de Saint Augustin*, Paris, 1920 (Diss.). A. Reul, *Die sittlichen Ideale des heiligen Augustinus*, Paderborn, 1928. H. Fuchs, *Augustin und der antike Friedensgedanke*, Berlin, 1926 (Neue philologische Untersuchungen, 3te Heft). A. Schultze, "Augustin und der Seelteil der germanischen Erbrechts," Leipzig, 1928 (*Abh. Leipzig Acad.*, XXXVIII, 4). E. Gilson, *Introduction à l'étude de Saint Augustin*, Paris, 1929. B. Roland-Gosselin, *La morale de Saint Augustin*, Paris, 1925. R. Reitzenstein, "Augustin als antiker und als mittelalterlicher Mensch," *Vorträge Bibl. Warburg*, 1922–23, I, 28–65. E. Buonaiuti, *San Agostino*, 2nd edition, Rome, 1923. H. Dörries, "Fünfzehn Jahre Augustins-Forschung," *Theologische Rundschau*, N.F.I. (1929), 217–45. M. Zepf, *Augustins Confessiones*, Tübingen, 1926 (Heidelberger Abhandlungen zur Philosophie und ihrer Geschichte, fasc. 9). G. Beyerhaus, "Neuere Augustin Probleme," *H.Z.*, CXXVII (1923), 189–209.

Augustine's De civitate Dei. E. TROELTSCH, *Augustin: die christliche Antike und das Mittelalter im Anschluss an die Schrift "De civitate Dei,"* Munich and Berlin, 1915 (Historische Bibliothek, 36). H. SCHOLZ, *Glaube und Unglaube in der Weltgeschichte: ein Kommentar zu Augustins De civitate Dei*, Leipzig, 1911. B. SEIDEL, *Die Lehre des heiligen Augustinus vom Staate*, Breslau, 1909 (Kirchengeschichtliche Abhandlungen, 9, 1). O. SCHILLING, *Die Staats- und Soziallehre des hl. Augustinus*, Freiburg, 1910. S. ANGUS, *The sources of the first ten books of Augustine's De civitate Dei*, Princeton, 1906. T. KOLDE, *Das Staatsideal des Mittelalters: I. Seine Begründung durch Augustin*, wissenschaftliche Beilage zum Jahresbericht der ersten städtischen Realschule zu Berlin, Ostern, 1902. A. NIEMANN, *Augustins Geschichtsphilosophie*, Greifswald, 1895. H. FUCHS, *Augustin und der antike Friedensgedanke: Untersuchungen zum 19 Buch der Civitas Dei*, Berlin, 1926 (Neue philologische Untersuchungen, 3).

Africa in the time of St. Augustine. J. MESNAGE, *Le christianisme en Afrique*, 3 vols., Paris, 1915; *L'Afrique chrétienne*, Paris, 1912. L. R. HOLME, *The extinction of the Christian churches in north Africa*, London, 1898. H. LECLERCQ, *L'Afrique chrétienne*, 2 vols., Paris, 1904. F. FERRÈRE, *La situation religieuse de l'Afrique romaine, depuis la fin du IV siècle jusqu'à l'invasion des Vandales, 429*, Paris, 1897. P. MONCEAUX, *Histoire littéraire de l'Afrique chrétienne*, vol. VII, *Saint Augustin et le donatisme.* E. ALBERTIN, *L'Afrique romaine*, Algiers, 1922. E. BUONAIUTI, *Il christianesimo nell' Africa romana.*

Boethius. H. F. STEWART, *Boethius*, Edinburgh and London, 1891. E. K. RAND, "On the composition of Boethius' Consolatio philosophiae," *Harvard studies in classical philology*, XV (1904), 1–28. V. DI GIOVANNI, *Boezio filosofo ed i suoi imitatori*, Palermo, 1880. J. G. SUTTERER, *Der letzte Römer*, Eichstädt, 1852. G. A. L. BAUR, *Boetius und Dante*, Leipzig, 1873. F. KLINGER, "De Boethii Consolatione philosophiae," *Philologische Untersuchungen herausgegeben von Kiessling*, Berlin, 1921. L. COOPER, *A concordance of Boethius*, Cambridge, 1928. See also *Speculum*, IV (1929), 62–72, 198–213.

On the question of Boethius' attitude towards Christianity, see G. SEMERIA, *Il christianesimo di Severino Boezio rivendicato*, Rome, 1900; G. BOISSIER, "Le christianisme de Boèce," in *Journal des savants* (1889), 449–62; and A. HILDEBRAND, *Boethius und seine Stellung zum Christentum*, Regensburg, 1885.

Cassiodorus. H. USENER, *Anecdoton Holderi: ein Beitrag zur Geschichte Roms in ostgothischer Zeit*, Bonn, 1877, a short but fundamental study on Cassiodorus, Boethius, and Symmachus. V. MORTET, *Notes sur la texte des Institutiones de Cassiodore, d'après divers manuscrits: recherches critiques sur la tradition des arts liberaux de l'antiquité au moyen âge*, Paris, 1904 (in part, a reprint from *Revue de philologie*, 1900–04). A. OLLERIS, *Cassiodore: conservateur des livres de l'antiquité latine*, Paris, 1841. G. MINASI, *M. A. Cassiodoro . . . ricerche storico-critiche*, Naples, 1895. A. M. FRANZ, *Aurelius Cassiodorus Senator*, Breslau, 1872. I. CIAMPI, *I Cassiodori nel V e nel VI secolo*, Rome, 1877. A. THORBECKE, *Cassiodorus Senator*, Heidelberg, 1867.

P. LEHMANN, "Cassiodorstudien," *Philologus*, LXXI (1912), 278–99; LXXII (1913), 505–17; LXXIII (1914), 253–73; LXXIV (1915), 351–83.

Original sources. Almost all the works of these men may be found in nos. **953, 954** and **978.** Ample directions for the works of Augustine may be found in TEUFFEL, *Geschichte der römischen Literatur*, 6th edition, III, 361ff., and for Boethius, Cassiodorus and Gregory in MANITIUS, *Geschichte der lateinischen Literatur*, I, and in SANDYS, *Classical scholarship*, I.

See also *Augustin's Enchiridion*, edited by O. SCHEEL, Tübingen and Leipzig, 1903 (Sammlung ausgewählter kirchen- und dogmen-geschichtlicher Quellenschriften, 2nd series, vol. IV).

Bibliographies. CHEVALIER, no. **16,** will be found useful. For classified lists of the best recent literature see TEUFFEL, MANITIUS and SANDYS just mentioned. For Gregory the Great the best bibliographical guide is DUDDEN, *Gregory the Great.*

III. TRANSFORMATION OF ANCIENT ROME INTO A MEDIEVAL CITY

A. OUTLINE

1. The enchantment of Rome in the middle ages and in modern times.

> "O Roma nobilis, orbis et domina,
> Cunctarum urbium excellentissima,
> Roseo martyrum sanguine rubea,
> Albis et virginum liliis candida:
> Salutem dicimus tibi per omnia,
> Te benedicimus: salve per secula."

(This is the first stanza of a poem written between the ninth and eleventh centuries, probably in Verona. See under TRAUBE below.) The sentiments which Rome aroused in Poggio Bracciolini, Petrarch, and Rienzo. GIBBON, author of *The decline and fall of the Roman empire*, wrote in his *Autobiography:* "I must not forget the day, the hour, the most interesting in my literary life. It was on the fifteenth of October [1764], in the gloom of evening, as I sat musing on the Capitol, while the barefooted fryers were chanting their litanies in the temple of Jupiter, that I conceived the first thought of my history."

2. The transformation of pagan into Christian Rome. Gradual disuse of pagan temples and other buildings, especially libraries. The rapid decline of the city in the later days of the empire, after it had ceased to be the capital of the world. Causes of the decay of Rome. Lord Byron's line, "The Goth, the Christian, Time, War, Flood, and Fire." The following saying of St. Benedict was reported by Gregory the Great in his *Dialogues*, II, 15: "Rome shall never be destroyed by the gentiles, but it shall be shaken by tempests, lightnings, and earthquakes, and shall decay of itself."

3. Rome and the barbarian invaders. The sack of Rome in 410 by Alaric the Visigoth, in 455 by the Vandal Gaiseric, and in 472 by Ricimer. Comparatively little injury done to buildings and statuary.

4. The rejuvenescence of the city in the "golden days" of Theodoric the Great. Archaeological evidence from the works of Cassiodorus. His plan to make Rome a great seat of Christian learning.

5. Her desolation in the period of the Gothic wars, 535–55. Rome was taken by force of arms in 536, 546, 547, 549, and 552. Depopulation of the city. The threat of Totila to destroy her utterly. The destruction of aqueducts. In this dread period Gregory the Great spent his childhood in Rome.

6. Consequences of the Byzantine restoration in 553. Although there was close connection between Rome and Constantinople, the study of Greek in the former city declined very rapidly.

7. The terror of the Lombards who came in 568. Rome now began to look for succor across the Alps. Weakness of the Byzantine hold upon the city. Gradual rise of the pope as real lord of Rome.

8. Topography of Rome at the accession of pope Gregory the Great in 590. Pagan buildings, especially the forums, temples, arches, baths, theatres, the Circus Maximus, Colosseum, Pantheon, the tombs of Hadrian and Augustus, the buildings of the Capitol, the aqueducts, and bridges. Christian buildings, especially the five patriarchal churches; the basilicas of St. John Lateran, of St. Peter, of St. Paul outside the wall, of S. Maria Maggiore, and of St. Lawrence. These, together with the basilicas of St. Sebastian and S. Croce in Gerusalemme, were the famous "seven churches of Rome." The "regions" of the city. The *Notitia* and *Curiosum urbis regionum XIV* of the fourth century. The *Itinerary* of the Anonymous of Einsiedeln, the *Mirabilia Romae*, and the *Graphia aureae urbis Romae*.

9. Restoration of Rome in the pontificate of Gregory the Great, 590–604. At his death it was "The Rome of the church, of the popes, of the middle ages"—Dudden.

B. Special Recommendations for Reading

The fame of Rome. J. Bryce, *Holy Roman empire*, ch. xvi. Gibbon, *Decline and fall*, ch. lxxi. F. Harrison, "Rome revisited," *The meaning of history*, 252–83. C. Diehl, "Rome reliquaire d'histoire," essay XIV, *Dans l'Orient byzantin*, 303–29.

Surveys of medieval Rome. N. Young, *The story of Rome*, London, 1905 (Mediaeval towns), especially chs. iii–v. See also the article "Rome" in the *Catholic encyclopedia*, and the *Ency. Brit.*

Rome in the sixth century. The best brief introductory sketch, Dudden, *Gregory the Great*, I, ch. ii. R. Lanciani, *Destruction of ancient Rome: a sketch of the history of the monuments*, New York, 1899, especially chs. i, iv–x; *Pagan and Christian Rome*, Boston, 1893; *Wanderings in the Roman Campagna*, New York, 1909, ch. iv. On the disappearance of the great libraries, his *Ancient Rome in the light of recent discoveries*, Boston, 1899, ch. vii; also the article "Bibliothèques" in *Dictionnaire d'archéologie chrétienne et de liturgie*, II, 1. W. G. Holmes, *Age of Justinian and Theodora*, II, ch. x.

Standard works on medieval Rome. GREGOROVIUS, *Rome in the middle ages*, especially I (entire), II, 1–69. This work is being superseded by H. GRISAR, *History of Rome and the popes in the middle ages*, see especially I, chs. IV–V.

Original sources. There are practically no contemporary archaeological writings concerning Rome about the time of Gregory the Great. We must content ourselves with written evidence before and after his time, and with the present-day archaeological finds which have revealed a good deal of indisputable evidence concerning the Rome of the popes.

The *Notitia* and *Curiosum* of the fourth century, the *Itinerary* of the ANONYMOUS OF EINSIEDELN (ninth century), and the *Mirabilia Romae* (twelfth century), are edited by H. JORDAN, *Topographie der Stadt Rom im Alterthum*, 2 vols., Berlin, 1871, II, 539–670. *Mirabilia urbis Romae, the marvels of Rome: or, A picture of the golden city, an English version of the medieval guide-book*, with a supplement, by F. M. NICHOLS, London, 1889. The *Mirabilia* were drawn from an older guide book, probably of the tenth century. The same book probably furnished material for the *Graphia aureae urbis Romae* (thirteenth century?), which is published by A. OZANAM, *Documents inédits pour servir à l'histoire littéraire de l'Italie*, Paris, 1850, 155ff. M. R. JAMES, "Magister Gregorius de mirabilibus urbis Romae," *E.H.R.*, XXXII (1917), 531–54, edits this document which he considers to be a work of the 12th century; also edited by G. McN. RUSHFORTH, in *Journal of Roman studies*, IX (1919), 14–58.

All of these old descriptions are very difficult for the ordinary student of history. For elucidations see GREGOROVIUS, *Rome in the middle ages*, III, 516–62; JORDAN, *Topographie*, II, 313–536 (see also I, 37–104); and R. LANCIANI, *Pagan and christian Rome*, ch. XIII; *L'itineraria di Einsiedeln e l'ordine di Benedetto: memoria*, Milan, 1891. On the regions of Rome see R. L. POOLE, *Papal chancery*, 6–12, 170–77. R. VAN MARLE has a survey of the chief descriptions of Rome in the middle ages, in *Medeleelingen van het nederlandsch Historisch Instituut te Rome*, III, The Hague, 1923.

For the poem of which the first few verses are printed at the head of this outline, see L. TRAUBE, "O Roma nobilis: philologische Untersuchungen aus dem Mittelalter," *Abh. Munich Acad.*, XIX (1892), 299–395.

Some evidence concerning pontifical Rome may be found in the *Liber pontificalis*, no. **949** note.

Maps. H. KIEPERT and C. HUELSEN, *Formae urbis Romae antiquae*, Berlin, 1912, chart III. See also the fine plan of Rome in GRISAR, *History of Rome*, I. For the interpretation of these plans some help will be derived from the panoramic restoration of Rome in the time of Constantine, by J. BÜHLMANN and A. WAGNER, *Das alte Rom mit dem Triumphzuge Kaiser Constantins im Jahre 312 nach Christo*, Munich, 1903. See also SHEPHERD, *Atlas*, 22–23, 24, and 96. For a detailed study the famous *Forma urbis Romae*, edited by R. LANCIANI in 46 sheets and published by the Academy of the Lincei, Milan, 1893–1902, is essential for all periods of old Rome.

C. Bibliography

General books. See especially the books on the history of the papacy, nos. **439–54a.** In the bibliography no attempt has been made to include either travellers' guide-books or special treatises on the topography of ancient Rome, some of which are valuable for our purposes, especially for their illustrations. It may be well, however, to call attention to the following guide-book: J. W. and A. M. Cruickshank, *Christian Rome,* 2nd edition, revised, New York, 1911. Note also G. Showerman, *Eternal Rome, the city and its people from the earliest times to the present day,* 2 vols., New Haven, 1924.

General works on medieval Rome. O. Rössler, *Grundriss einer Geschichte Roms im Mittelalter,* vol. I, Berlin, 1909. P. Adinolfi, *Roma nell' età di mezzo,* 2 vols., Rome, 1881–82. A. v. Reumont, *Geschichte der Stadt Rom.* F. Papencordt, *Geschichte der Stadt Rom,* Paderborn, 1857. A. Paravicini, *Il senato romano dal 6 al 12 secolo,* Rome, 1901. L. Pompili-Olivieri, *Il senato romano, 1143–1870,* Rome, 1886. O. Tommasini, "Della storia medievale della città di Roma e dei più recenti raccontatori di essa," in *Archivio della Società romana di storia patria,* I (1877). G. Buzzi, *Ricerche per la storia di Ravenna e di Roma dall' 850 al 1118,* Rome, 1915; extract from *l'Archivio delle r. Società romana di storia patria,* XXXVIII. L. Halphen, *Etude sur l'administration de Rome au moyen âge (757–1282),* Paris, 1907. F. Schneider, *Rom und Romgedanke im Mittelalter; Die geistigen Grundlagen der Renaissance,* Munich, 1926.

Catacombs and early Christians. M. Besnier, *Les catacombes de Rome,* Paris, 1909. Article "Catacombes" in *Dictionnaire d'archéologie chrétienne et de liturgie,* II, 2, coll. 2376–2466. A. Kuhn, *Roma: ancient, subterranean, and modern Rome, in word and picture,* New York, 1916, is especially valuable for its pictures of the catacombs, pp. 203–310. J. S. Northcote and W. R. B. Browlow, *Roma sotterranea: or, An account of the Roman catacombs,* compiled from the works of Commendatore de Rossi, 2nd edition, 2 vols., London, 1879. H. D. M. Spence-Jones, *The early Christians in Rome,* London, 1910. Ethel R. Barker, *Rome of the pilgrims and martyrs: a study in the martyrologies, itineraries, syllogae, and other contemporary documents,* London, 1913.

Churches of Rome. M. Armellini, *Le chiese di Roma dal secolo IV al XIX,* 2nd edition, Rome, 1891. C. Huelsen, *Le chiese di Roma nel medio evo: cataloghi ed appunti,* Florence, 1927.

The Lateran. P. Lauer, *Le palais de Latran: étude historique et archéologique,* Paris, 1911, and especially the long and invaluable article "Latran" by Leclerq in *Dictionnaire d'archéologie chrétienne et de liturgie,* VIII, 2, coll. 1529–1887, with full bibliography.

Monuments of Christian Rome. E. Rodocanachi, *Les monuments de Rome après la chute de l'empire,* Paris, 1914; *The Roman capitol in ancient and modern times,* translated from the French by F. Lawton, New York, 1906. A. L. Frothingham, *The monuments of Christian Rome from Constantine to the renaissance,* New York and London, 1908. E. Bertaux, *Rome: de l'ère des catacombes à l'avènement de Jules II,* 2nd edition, Paris, 1908 (Les villes d'art célèbres). H. BERGNER, *Rom im Mittelalter*, Leipzig, 1913 (Berühmte Kunststädtten, 39).

Roman Campagna. G. TOMASSETTI, *La Campagna romana antica, medioevale e moderna*, 4 vols., Rome, 1910–26. O. KAEMMEL, *Rom und die Campagna*, Leipzig, 1902 (Land und Leute: Monographien zur Erdkunde, XII). T. ASHBY, *The Roman Campagna in classical times*, London, 1927.

Periodicals for Christian archaeology of Rome. *Bullettino di archeologia cristiana*, edited by G. B. DE ROSSI, 13 vols., Rome, 1863–95; followed by the *Nuovo bullettino*, 1895ff. *Bullettino della Commissione archeologica comunale di Roma*, Rome, 1873ff. *Römische Quartalschrift für christliche Altertumskunde*, Rome, 1887ff.

Original sources. *Inscriptiones christianae urbis Romae VII° saeculo antiquiores*, edited by G. B. DE ROSSI, 2 vols., Rome, 1857–88. *Iscrizione delle chiese e di altri edifici di Roma dal secolo XI ai nostri giorni*, edited by V. FORCELLA, 14 vols., Rome, 1869–80. E. DIEHL, *Inscriptiones latinae christianae veteres*, I–III (1924–29) with full indexes of proper and place names, etc.

Bibliographies. E. CALVI, *Bibliografia di Roma nel medio evo (476–1499)*, Rome, 1906, with an appendix, 1908. F. CERROTI and E. CELANI, *Bibliografia di Roma medievale e moderna*, vol. I, Rome, 1893.

IV. CLASSICAL HERITAGE OF THE EARLY MIDDLE AGES

A. OUTLINE

1. The three great waves in the continuous flow of classical influences during the middle ages: (1) early middle ages, chiefly language and political and social institutions; (2) twelfth and thirteenth centuries, chiefly Roman law and Greek philosophy; (3) fourteenth and fifteenth centuries, chiefly Roman and Greek literature and art.

2. Survival of classical forms and ideas of government and social order in church and state.

3. Graeco-Roman influence in art and the crafts of the early middle ages. The importance of medieval archaeology.

4. The seven liberal arts (*artes liberales*): *trivium*—grammar, rhetoric, and dialectic; *quadrivium*—arithmetic, geometry, astronomy, and music. The Greek origin and the Roman elaboration of the idea of liberal arts. The *Disciplinarium libri novem* (not extant now) of Varro, 116–27 B.C. The *De nuptiis Philologiae et Mercurii* of Martianus Capella who wrote in Africa between 410 and 439 A.D. Cassiodorus, in his *Institutiones saecularium lectionum*, was the first Christian who used the expression "seven liberal arts." Changing conception of liberal arts, and differences of meaning and content of each of the arts from age to age. Variation in the popularity of the various arts, e.g., dialectic or logic.

5. The study and use of classical language and literature. Almost total neglect of Greek in the west. Decline of interest in the Latin classics of pagan times. Popularity of the works of Christian poets and of theologians.

The text books of Latin grammar. The *Ars grammatica minor* and *Ars grammatica major* of Donatus who lived about 350 A.D., and was the teacher of St. Jerome. The *Barbarismus*. The *Institutionum grammaticorum libri XVIII* of Priscian who flourished in Constantinople about 500 A.D. The first sixteen of these books were known as the *Priscianus major* and the last two as the *Priscianus minor*. Elementary Latin readers such as *Cato* (*Disticha*), *Aesopus*, and *Avianus*.

6. Transmission of ancient knowledge of natural sciences, medicine, and mathematics. Pliny's *Natural history*. Solinus. The *Physiologus*. Bestiaries and lapidaries.

7. The tiny stream of Roman law in the early middle ages. Neglect of the *Corpus iuris civilis* in the west. Roman influence in the law of the church.

8. Transmission of ancient philosophy. The services of Boethius as a translator of Aristotle. Predominance of theological learning, based largely on Jewish thought, but modified decidedly by Greek speculation and Latin practical sense.

9. The encyclopaedia of Isidore of Seville (ca. 570–636), known as the *Etymologiae* or *Origines*, in 20 books which were frequently abridged. Isidore's attitude towards the Latin classics.

10. Monastery and cathedral schools in the early middle ages. Contrast with the Roman schools in the time of Ausonius. The monastic *scriptorium* and the transmission of classical texts. Elementary instruction by parish priests.

11. Early medieval libraries. The *armarium*.

B. Special Recommendations for Reading

Short general surveys. TAYLOR, *Classical heritage*, especially 44–70, and portions of chs. VIII–X; *Mediaeval mind*, I, ch. V. E. NORDEN, "Die lateinische Literatur im Übergang vom Altertum zum Mittelalter," *Die Kultur der Gegenwart*, I, part 8 (1905), 374–411; 3rd edition (1912), 483–522. M. MANITIUS, *Geschichte*, I, 3–21; II, 3–17.

For details concerning Donatus, Priscian, Martianus Capella, Cato, etc., see the index of TEUFFEL, *Geschichte der römischen Literatur*, III; SCHANZ, *Geschichte der römischen Literatur*, IV; SANDYS, *Classical scholarship*, I.

The seven liberal arts. P. ABELSON, *The seven liberal arts*, New York, 1906 (Diss.). H. PARKER, "The seven liberal arts," in *E.H.R.*, V (1890), 417–61. A. F. WEST, *Alcuin and the rise of the Christian schools*, New York, 1892, ch. I. The article "Arts, the seven liberal," by O. WILLMANN, in *Catholic encyclopedia*.

Attitude towards the Latin classics. D. C. MUNRO, "The attitude of the western church towards the study of the Latin classics in the early middle ages," *American society of church history*, VIII, 1897, 181–94. D. COMPARETTI, *Vergil in the middle ages*, especially chs. V and VI.

Isidore of Seville. E. BREHAUT, *An encyclopedist of the dark ages: Isidore of Seville*, New York, 1912 (Diss.), translates freely from the *Etymologiae* and has bibliography. For details concerning his life and work, MANITIUS, I, 52–70. See also M. ROGER, *L'enseignement des lettres classiques d'Ausone à Alcuin*, 195–201.

Natural sciences and mathematics. F. LAUCHERT, *Geschichte des Physiologus*, Strasburg, 1889, edited this famous book in the Greek version, with a paraphrase in German, but most of his book consists of introduction and elucidations. M. GOLDSTAUB, "Der Physiologus," in *Philologus*, Supplementband VIII, 3, Leipzig, 1901. On mathematics see W. R. BALL, *A short account of the history of mathematics*, 4th edition, London, 1908, ch. VIII; or M. CANTOR, *Vorlesungen über Geschichte der Mathematik*, 4 vols., 3rd edition, Leipzig, 1898–1908, ch. XXXVIII. For details concerning natural sciences and mathematics see outline XXI. For law see outline XX.

Original sources. The *Natural history* of PLINY, 6 vols., London, 1855–57. SAN ISIDORO DE SEVILLA, *Mapa mundi*, translated into Spanish by A. BLÁZQUEZ Y DELGADO AGUILERA, Madrid, 1908. W. J. CHASE, *The Distichs of Cato*, Madison, 1922, and *The Ars minor of Donatus*, Madison, 1926. (University of Wisconsin Studies, Nos. 7 and 11.) But cf. on the former work M. BOAS in *Philologische Wochenschrift*, 47 (1927), 524–33.

C. BIBLIOGRAPHY

General books. See especially the general books on literature, nos. **782–814.** Much general literature will also be found under outlines XVIII and XXIII.

General surveys. L. FRIEDLÄNDER, "Das Nachleben der Antike im Mittelalter," *Erinnerungen, Reden, und Schriften*, 2 vols., Strasburg, 1905, I, 272–391, is the best systematic account we have; but see also G. KÖRTING, *Anfänge der Renaissance-literatur in Italien* (vol. III of *Geschichte der Literatur Italiens*), Leipzig, 1884, 1–75. A. GRAF, *Roma nella memoria e nelle immaginazioni del medio evo*, 2 vols., Turin, 1882–83.

Seven liberal arts. A. APPUHN, *Das Trivium und Quadrivium in Theorie und Praxis*, part I, *Das Trivium*, Erlangen, 1900. G. MEIER, *Die sieben freien Künste im Mittelalter*, Einsiedeln, 1886. F. FERRÈRE, "De la division des sept arts libéraux," in *Annales de philosophie chrétienne*, n. s., XLII (1900), 280–95. P. RAJNA, "Le denominazioni Trivium e Quadrivium" in *Studi medievali*, nuova serie I (1928), 4–36.

Heritage of classics. K. BORINSKI, *Die Antike in Poetik und Kunsttheorie*, I, *Mittelalter, Renaissance, Barock*, Leipzig, 1914. J. STIGLMAYR, *Kirchenväter und Klassizismus*, Freiburg, 1913. H. J. LEBLANC, *Essai historique et critique sur l'étude et l'enseignement des lettres profanes dans les premiers siècles de l'église*, Paris, 1852. P. WENDLAND, *Christentum und Hellenismus in ihren litterarischen Beziehungen; Vortrag gehalten auf der Strassburger Philologenversammlung am 1. Oktober 1901*, Leipzig, 1902, part 1, 2. J. W. THOMPSON, "Vergil in mediaeval culture," in *American journal of theology*, X (1906), 648–62. T. ZIEKINSKI, *Cicero im Wandel der Jahrhunderte*, 3rd edition, Berlin, 1912, chs. VII–VIII. G. ZAPPERT, *Virgil's Fortleben im Mittelalter*, Vienna, 1851 (reprinted from *Denkschriften* of

Vienna academy). For QUINTILIAN in the Middle Ages see the valuable introduction in F. H. COLSON's edition of *Institutio oratoria*, I, Cambridge, 1924. For medieval imitations of OVID see P. LEHMANN, *Pseudo-antike Literatur des Mittelalters*, Leipzig, 1927. E. K. RAND, *Ovid and his influence*, Boston, 1925, ch. II.

Natural science. M. P. E. BERTHELOT, "Essai sur la transmission de la science antique au moyen âge," in vol. I of *Histoire des sciences: La chimie au moyen âge*, 3 vols., Paris, 1893. F. STRUNZ, *Geschichte der Naturwissenschaften im Mittelalter*, Stuttgart, 1910, ch. II. F. DANNEMANN, *Die Naturwissenschaften*, vol. I, Leipzig, 1910, 213–22. K. RÜCK, "Die Naturalis Historia des Plinius im Mittelalter," in *S.B., Munich Acad.*, 1898, 203–318. F. MÉLY et C. E. RUELLE, *Les lapidaires de l'antiquité et du moyen âge*, 3 vols., Paris, 1896–1902.

Isidore of Seville. C. H. BEESON, *Isidor-Studien*, Munich, 1913 (Quellen und Untersuchungen zur lateinischen Philologie des Mittelalters, IV, 2). C. CAÑAL, *San Isidoro: exposición de sus obras e indicaciones acerca de la influencia que han ejercido en la civilización española*, Seville, 1897. M. MICHEL, "La livre des *Origines* d'Isidore de Séville," in *Revue internationale de l'enseignement*, 1891, 198. H. PHILIPP, *Die historisch-geographischen Quellen in den Etymologiae des Isidorus von Sevilla*, 2 vols., Berlin, 1912–13 (Quellen und Forschungen zur alten Geschichte und Geographie, edited by SIEGLIN, 25, 26).

Heritage of classical art. H. SEMPER, *Das Fortleben der Antike in der Kunst des Abendlandes*, Essling, 1908. A. SPRINGER, *Das Nachleben der Antike im Mittelalter: Bilder aus der neueren Kunstgeschichte*, 2nd edition, Bonn, 1886. A. GOLDSCHMIDT, "Das Nachleben der antiken Formen im Mittelalter," *Vorträge der Bibliothek Warburg, 1921–22;* Leipzig, 1923. See also in general nos. **299–302.**

Original sources. MARTIANUS CAPELLA, *De nuptiis Philologiae et Mercurii*, is edited by A. DICK, Leipzig, 1925. Cf. also M. L. W. LAISTNER, "Martianus Capella and his ninth-century commentators," *Bulletin of John Rylands library*, Manchester, XI (1925), 130–38. The grammatical works of Donatus and Priscian may be found in *Grammatici latini*, edited by H. KEIL, 7 vols., Leipzig, 1855–80; Donatus in vol. IV, 355–403; and Priscian in vols. II–III. The best edition of the *Etymologiae* is ISIDORI HISPALENSIS EPISCOPI *Etymologiarum sive originum libri XX*, edited by W. M. LINDSAY, 2 vols., Oxford, 1911.

Bibliographies. TAYLOR, *Classical heritage*, 358–92. ROGER, *L'enseignement*, IX–XVIII. The bibliographical notes in TEUFFEL, *Geschichte der römischen Literatur*, III; SCHANZ, *Geschichte der römischen Literatur*, IV.

V. MEDIEVAL "WELTANSCHAUUNG"

A. OUTLINE

1. Contrast between ancient (pagan) and medieval (Christian) views of life and the universe.

2. Medieval "otherworldliness" was the dominant factor in the intellectual and spiritual life of the time. The preoccupation of the medieval mind

with eschatology. Man's pilgrimage from the cradle to the grave was conceived of as merely a fateful period of probation, which terminated in eternal bliss or everlasting woe.

3. Medieval assurance of definite and detailed knowledge about essential temporal and eternal things. Reliance upon written evidence, especially the Old Testament. Reliance upon authority in general.

4. "The Christian epic." Conception of the universe, with the earth, the home of man, God's creature, at the center. The elaboration of lore concerning heaven and its denizens. Ideas of the beginning of all things and the creation of man. His first home. The chronology of man's existence upon earth. The expectation of a not far distant day of doom and of the rolling up of the heavens. Medieval ideas of the purpose of learning. Dominance of theology.

5. The medieval solution of the problem of evil. Man's state of innocence. His temptation and fall. His redemption and reconciliation with God. The Prince of Darkness, and his Kingdom of Darkness and its denizens. Elaboration of the idea of evil personified in the devil. Antichrist. The "powers of the air." Purgatory.

6. Belief in the speedy triumph of Christianity throughout the whole world. Consequent development of the idea of the brotherhood of all men. The writing of universal histories. Remarkable importance of ancient Hebrew history.

7. Asceticism and mysticism flourished in the midst of such ideas. Their embodiment in monasticism. Religious ecstasy.

8. Love of allegory and symbolism. Allegorical interpretation of the Bible and other books. The *Moralia* of Gregory the Great. Symbolism in the sacraments of the church. Miracles. Saints. Relics. Witchcraft.

9. The church and the world. The notions of temporal and spiritual things. The Church Militant and the Church Triumphant. The church versus the state. The organization of the powers of the church and the definition of its sphere of action. The important political and social consequences of a marked distinction between clergy and laymen.

10. The Christian cult and Christian iconography as sources for the study of medieval ideas. Pagan survivals in the Christian cult.

11. The writings of the so-called "Dionysius the Areopagite" (composed about 500 A.D. and spread in western Europe in the ninth century in the Latin translation of John Scotus), as a source of early medieval ideas about the celestial realms. See also outlines XVII and XXVIII.

B. Special Recommendations for Reading

General surveys. Milman, *History of Latin Christianity*, IX, 53–97. Harnack, *History of dogma*, especially I, 150–221; II, 247–318; III, 241–315; IV, 268–330 (corresponding pages in the 4th German edition). The beginnings of all chapters in A. D. White, *A history of the warfare of science with theology in Christendom.* Taylor, *Classical heritage*, especially chs. v–vii. R. Eucken, *The problem of human life as viewed by the great thinkers*,

131–252. V. RYDBERG, *The magic of the middle ages*, translated from the Swedish by A. H. EDGREN, New York, 1879, see especially ch. I, "The cosmic philosophy of the middle ages, and its historical development." LAVISSE, *Histoire de France*, II, part I, 237–42. H. v. EICKEN, *Geschichte und System der mittelalterlichen Weltanschauung*, is not so good for our purposes as its title would indicate; see especially 63–147, 311–25, 589–671. See the note under no. **816.** There is much material in VOSSLER, *Mediaeval culture.* P. T. HOFFMAN, *Der mittelalterliche Mensch gesehen aus Welt und Unwelt Notkers des Deutschen*, Gotha, 1922. H. GÜNTER, "Der mittelalterliche Mensch," *Hist. Jahrbuch*, XLIV (1924), 1–18. A. DEMPF, *Die Hauptform mittelalterlicher Weltanschauung*, Munich, 1925. K. BRANDI, *Mittelalterliche Weltanschauung, Humanismus und nationale Bildung*, Berlin, 1925. E. BERGMANN and H. LEISEGANG, *Weltanschauung:* Theil I, *Antike, Mittelalter, und Neuzeit bis zur Aufklärung*, Breslau, 1926. W. GÖTZMANN, *Die Unsterblichkeitsbeweise in der Väterzeit und Scholastik bis zum Ende des 13. Jahrhunderts*, Karlsruhe, 1927. BARTLET and CARLYLE, *Christianity in history.*

Asceticism. W. JAMES, *The varieties of rêligious experiences*, New York, 1902, 296ff., on saintliness. For literature on monasticism see outline IV in part II.

The Christian epic. G. SANTAYANA, *Reason in religion*, New York, 1905, ch. VI; *Interpretations of poetry and religion*, New York, 1905, chs. III–IV.

The legends of the saints. H. DELEHAYE, *Les lêgendes hagiographiques*, 3rd edition, Brussels, 1927, translated from the 2nd edition by Mrs. V. M. CRAWFORD, *The legends of the saints: an introduction to hagiography*, London and New York, 1907.

Medieval ideas reflected in art and poetry. Y. HIRN, *The sacred shrine: a study of the poetry and art of the catholic church*, London, 1912 (the bibliography on pp. 555–570 is very valuable).

Dionysius the Areopagite. R. F. WESTCOTT, "Dionysius the Areopagite," *Contemporary review*, V (1867), 1–28. See also the articles on Dionysius in nos. **104, 106, 108** and **112,** and MANITIUS, *Geschichte*, I, 325–28.

Original sources. Practically all the writings of the middle ages are of value in this study. The writings of the church fathers which are translated in the *Nicene and post-Nicene fathers*, will be found most useful. Add to these especially BEDE'S famous *Ecclesiastical history of England*, revised translation by A. M. SELLAR, London, 1912 (see especially the account of Drythelm's visit to the underworld with its graphic picture of hell and purgatory).

The celestial and ecclesiastical hierarchy of DIONYSIUS THE AREOPAGITE is translated by J. PARKER, London, 1894; his remaining *Works*, by the same translator, London, 1897–99.

The revelations to the monk of Evesham Abbey in the year of our Lord eleven hundred ninety-six concerning the places of purgatory and paradise, are rendered into English by V. PAGET, New York, 1909. C. S. BOSWELL,

Irish precursor of Dante: study on the vision of heaven and hell ascribed to the 8th century Irish S. Adamnan, with translation, London, 1908. G. G. COULTON, *Life in the middle ages*, vol. I. *The history of the translation of the blessed martyrs of Christ, Marcellinus and Peter*, translated by B. WENDELL, Cambridge (Mass.), 1926. CAESARIUS OF HEISTERBACH, *The dialogue on miracles*, translated by H. v. E. SCOTT and C. C. SWINTON BLAND with an introduction by G. G. COULTON, 2 vols., London, 1929.

C. BIBLIOGRAPHY

General books. See especially the books on the "History of freedom of thought," nos. **739–48,** and those on "Medieval *Weltanschauung*," nos. **815–21;** but almost all general books on the church, nos. **393–498,** and on the history of culture and civilization, nos. **729–849,** bear upon the subject of this outline more or less directly. The encyclopaedias for the history of the church, nos. **104–14,** are indispensable, and even the general encyclopaedias, nos. **96–103b,** will be found useful. See also the periodicals for church history, philosophy, and education, nos. **176–82** (also nos. **169–70**).

For additional general books on the church see outlines IV–VI, XV, and XXIV of part II. For medieval science in general see outline XXI. See also outline XXVIII on Dante.

Demonology, devil-lore, hell, and purgatory. G. ROSKOFF, *Geschichte des Teufels*, 2 vols., Leipzig, 1869. A. RÉVILLE, *Histoire du diable*, Strasburg, 1870, translated by A. R., *The devil: his greatness and decadence*, London, 1871. H. KERNOT, *Bibliotheca diabolica; being a choice selection of the most valuable works relating to the devil, etc.*, New York, 1874. J. BAISSAC, *Histoire de la diablerie*, I, *Le diable*, Paris, 1882. A. GRAF, *Il diavolo*, 4th edition, Milan, 1890, German translation by R. TEUSCHER, 2nd edition, 1893. M. J. RUDWIN, *Der Teufel in den deutschen geistlichen Spielen des Mittelalters und der Reformationszeit: ein Beitrag zur Literatur-, Kultur-, und Kirchengeschichte Deutschlands*, Göttingen and Baltimore, 1915. H. WIECK, *Die Teufel auf der mittelalterlichen Mysterienbühne Frankreichs*, Leipzig, 1887 (Diss.). W. MICHEL, *Das Teuflische und Groteske in der Kunst*, Munich, 1911. M. D. CONWAY, *Demonology and devil lore*, 2 vols., 3rd edition, New York, 1889. A. JAULMES, *Essai sur le satanisme et la superstition au moyen âge, précédé d'une introduction sur leurs origines: étude historique*, Paris, 1901. J. BOIS, *Le satanisme et la magie*, 4th edition, Paris, 1895. M. LANDAU, *Hölle und Fegefeuer im Volksglauben, Dichtung und Kirchenlehre*, Heidelberg, 1909. J. BAUTZ, *Die Hölle*, Mainz, 1882; *Das Fegefeuer*, Mainz, 1883. P. SCHMIDT, *Der Teufels- und Daemonenglaube in den Erzählungen des Caesarius von Heisterbach*, Basel, 1926. E. DÖRING-HIRSCH, *Tod und Jenseits im Spätmittelalter*, Berlin, 1927.

Antichrist. H. PREUSS, *Die Vorstellungen vom Antichrist im späteren Mittalelter bis Luther*, Leipzig, 1906. W. BOUSSET, *The Antichrist legend: chapter in Christian and Jewish folklore*, translated from the German, London, 1896. W. MEYER, "Ludus de Antichristo," *S.B., Munich Acad.*, 1882, no. 1. The Ludus is most fully studied by W. MEYER in *Gesammelte Abhandlungen*,

I, 136–339; edited conveniently in Münchener Texte I (1912); and translated by W. H. HULME, *Western Reserve university, Bulletin*, XXVIII (1925), no. 8. E. WADSTEIN, *Die eschatologische Ideengruppe: Antichrist, Weltsabbat, Weltende und Weltgericht*, Leipzig, 1896.

Asceticism. H. STRATHMAN, *Geschichte der frühchristlichen Askese bis zur Entstehung des Mönchtums im religionsgeschichtlichen Zusammenhange*, vol. I, Leipzig, 1914. F. MARTINEZ, *L'ascéticisme chrétien pendant les trois premiers siècles de l'église*, Paris, 1913 (Etudes de théologie historique publiées sous la direction des professeurs de théologie à l'Institut catholique, no. 6). H. JOLY, *The psychology of the saints*, translated by G. TYRELL, London, 1898. Note nos. **479–87.** I. FEUSI, *Das Institut der gottgeweihten Jungfrauen. Sein Fortleben im Mittelalter*, Fribourg, 1917. B. B. WARFIELD, *Counterfeit miracles*, ch. II, "Patristic and medieval marvels," New York, 1918. L. GOUGAUD, *Dévotions et pratiques ascetiques du moyen âge*, Paris, 1925; translated by G. C. BATEMAN, *Devotional and ascetic practices in the middle ages*, London, 1927.

Mysteries, miracles, and relics. G. ANRICH, *Das antike Mysterienwesen in seinem Einfluss auf das Christentum*, Göttingen, 1894. A. R. HABERSHON, *The study of the miracles*, London, 1910. P. SAINTYVES, *Le miracle et la critique historique*, Paris, 1907; *Les reliques et les images légendaires*, Paris, 1912.

Myths, legends, and superstitions. H. A. GUERBER, *Myths and legends of the middle ages: their origin and influence on literature and art*, London, 1909. L. F. A. MAURY, *Croyances et légendes du moyen âge*, new edition, Paris, 1896. C. MEYER, *Der Aberglaube des Mittelalters und der nächstfolgenden Jahrhunderte*, Basle, 1884. A. GRAF, *Miti, leggende e superstizioni del medio evo*, 2 vols., Turin, 1892; in one vol., 1925. F. W. HACKWOOD, *Christlore: legends, traditions, myths, symbols, customs, superstitions of the Christian church*, London, 1902. P. TUFFRAU, *Le merveilleux voyage de Saint Brandan à la recherche du Paradis: légende latine du IXe siècle renouvelée*, Paris, 1925. B. E. KÖNIG, *Ausgeburten des Menschenwahns im Spiegel der Hexenprozesse und der Auto-da-fés: eine Geschichte des After- und Aberglaubens bis auf die Gegenwart: ein Volksbuch*, Berlin, 1926 (Freidenker-Bücher, III). J. D. COOKE, "Euhemerism: a mediaeval interpretation of classical paganism," *Speculum*, II (1927), 396–410.

Saints. M. and W. DRAKE, *Saints and their emblems*, London, 1916. H. GÜNTER, *Die christliche Legende des Abendlandes*, Heidelberg, 1910. H. DELEHAYE, *Les origines du culte des martyrs*, Brussels, 1912. E. LUCIUS, *Die Anfänge des Heiligenkults in der christlichen Kirche*, Tübingen, 1904. H. QUENTIN, *Les martyrologes historiques du moyen âge: étude sur la formation du martyrologe romain*, Paris, 1908. P. SAINTYVES, *Les saints successeurs des dieux*, Paris, 1907. J. P. KIRSCH, *The doctrine of the communion of saints in the ancient church*, English translation, Edinburgh, 1910. See also no. **258.** M. S. TAVAGNUTTI, *Hagiographia, Verzeichniss der über Jesus Christus, die Jungfrau Maria, Heilige-, Selige Päpste und sonstige ehrwürdige und fromme Personen von 1830 bis 1890 erschienenen Lebensbeschrei-*

bungen, Predigten, Andachtsbücher und Legenden-Sammlungen, 2nd edition, Vienna, 1891. F. G. HOLWECK, *A biographical dictionary of the saints*, St. Louis, 1924. *Hagiographischer Jahresbericht für das Jahr 1900—Zusammenstellung aller im Jahre 1900—in deutscher Sprache erschienenen Werke, Übersetzungen und grösserer oder wichtigerer Artikel über Heilige, Selige und Ehrwürdige. Im Vereine mit mehreren Freunden der Hagiologie hrsg. von L. Helmling* . . ., Mainz, 1901.

Christian iconography. A. BELL, *Saints in Christian art*, 3 vols., London, 1901–04. S. HEATH, *The romance of symbolism and its relation to church ornament and architecture*, London, 1909. J. M. NEALE and B. WEBB, *The symbolism of churches and church ornaments*, translation of first book of *Rationale divinorum officiorum* of WILLIAM DURANDUS, 3rd edition, London, 1906. C. E. CLEMENT, *A handbook of Christian symbols and stories of the saints, as illustrated in art*, 5th edition, Boston, 1895. H. v. D. GABELENTZ, *Die kirchliche Kunst im italienischen Mittelalter: ihre Beziehungen zu Kultur und Glaubenslehre*, Strasburg, 1907. A. MUÑOZ, *Iconografia della Madonna*, Rome, 1905. R. PFLEIDERER, *Die Attribute der Heiligen: ein alphabetisches Nachschlagebuch zum Verständnis kirchlicher Kunstwerke*, Ulm, 1898; 2nd edition, 1920. J. E. WESSELY, *Ikonographie Gottes und der Heiligen*, Leipzig, 1874. See also the literature under outline XXVII. K. KÜNSTLE, *Ikonographie der Heiligen* (284 illustrations), Freiburg, 1926. ELIZABETH E. GOLDSMITH, *Sacred symbols in art*, 2nd edition, New York, 1912.

" Dionysius the Areopagite." J. STIGLMAYR, *Das Aufkommen der pseudo-dionysischen Schriften und ihr Eindringen in die christliche Literatur bis zum Lateranconzil*, Feldkirch, 1895; "Die Eschatologie des Pseudo-Dionysius," *Zeitschrift für katholische Theologie*, Innsbruck (1899), 1–21. H. KOCH, *Pseudo-Dionysius Areopagita in seinen Beziehungen zum Neuplatonismus und Mysterienwesen*, Mainz, 1900, vol. I, 2–3 of no. **489.** H. F. MÜLLER, *Dionysios, Proklos, Plotinos. Beiträge zur Geschichte der Philosophie des Mittelalters*, Texte und Untersuchungen hrsg. Clemens Baeumker, Bd. XX, Heft 3–4, Münster, 1918.

Original sources. For large general collections of sources for church history see nos. **953–64.** When no. **949** is completed as planned it will be a most valuable collection for the study of the subjects of this outline.

VI. FAITH, MORALS AND LEARNING OF THE MEROVINGIAN FRANKS AND OF THE VISIGOTHS IN SPAIN

A. OUTLINE

1. The phenomenal decline of learning and civilization especially in southern Gaul. The fate of the famous Roman schools in the fifth and sixth centuries. The problem of weighing the importance of Germanic influences in the civilization of Spain and Gaul. The religious differences: the Visigoths were Arians until about the accession of pope Gregory the Great, 590, whereas the Franks were converted directly to orthodox Christianity in 496.

2. The comparatively advanced civilization of Visigothic Spain. The Byzantine influences due to Justinian's conquest in the south. The legal turn of mind of the inhabitants of Spain. Church and state. The faith and the learning of Isidore of Seville who wrote his *Etymologiae* about 622. Scant archaeological remains of Visigothic civilization. The transformation wrought in Spain by the Mohammedans.

3. Merovingian Gaul and the Roman church and Italian culture from the time of Clovis to the death of Gregory the Great. The pope's correspondence with Brunhild. The "Syrians" in Gaul.

4. The learning of Gregory of Tours (ca. 538–94), bishop of Tours, 573–94. The Latin style of his famous *History of the Franks*. His attitude toward classical learning. His attitude toward the barbarians and the church. His poet friend Venantius Fortunatus (ca. 535–ca. 600).

5. Low state of faith, morals and learning among the clergy as well as laymen in the time of Gregory of Tours. Persistence of pagan practices. The superstition and violence depicted in the pages of the *History of the Franks*.

6. The reforms by Irish missionaries, especially Columban (see next outline).

7. The nadir of culture in Gaul was reached in the seventh century. Almost total lack of communication between the Franks and the papacy in that century. The laments of the so-called Fredegarius Scholasticus about the learning of his time. The ignorance of the grammarian "Virgilius Maro." The deplorable Merovingian script. Very scanty sources of information for the history of the seventh century. The lack of schools. The utter decline of art.

8. The Merovingian saints. Hagiography was the only species of literature which flourished in the sixth and seventh centuries in Gaul.

9. The Mohammedan menace in the eighth century.

10. The renewed relations of Gaul with Italy in the eighth century ushered in a new era. Light from the British Isles. Chrodegang, archbishop of Metz, 742–66.

B. Special Recommendations for Reading

Brief general surveys. MUNRO and SELLERY, *Medieval civilization*, 60–86, adapted from E. LAVISSE, "Etudes sur l'histoire d'Allemagne," *R.D.M.*, 3rd series, LXXIV (1886), 366–96; also "La décadence mérovingienne," *ibid.*, LXXII (1885), 796–820. E. K. RAND, "The brighter aspects of the merovingian age," *Proceedings of the classical association*, XVIII (1922), 165–82.

Longer standard accounts. ROGER, *L'enseignement des lettres classiques*, 89–169. LAVISSE, *Histoire de France*, II, part I, 216–55. F. GUIZOT, *Lectures on the history of civilization in France*, first course, lectures XII–XIII, XVI–XVIII. S. DILL, *Roman society in Gaul*. M. PROU, *La Gaule mérovingienne*, Paris, 1897. R. GOETTE, *Kulturgeschichte der Urzeit Germaniens, des Frankreichs und Deutschlands im frühen Mittelalter*, Bonn and Leipzig, 1920. SCHUMACHER, *Siedelungs- und Kulturgeschichte des Rheinlands.*

Culture of Visigothic Spain. U. R. BURKE, *A history of Spain*, I, 85–107. R. ALTAMIRA, *Historia de España*, 3rd edition, I, 213–23. For Isidore of Seville see outline IV.

Merovingian learning. A. S. WILDE, "The decline of learning in Gaul in the seventh and eighth centuries based on the lives of the saints," *American journal of theology*, VII (1903). E. VACANDARD, "La scola du palais mérovingien," *R.Q.H.*, LXI (1897), 490–502; LXII (1897), 546–51; LXXVI (1904), 549–53. A. S. WILDE, "Les écoles du palais aux temps mérovingiens," *ibid.*, LXXIV (1903), 553–56.

" Syrians " in Gaul. L. BRÉHIER, "Les colonies d'orientaux en occident au commencement du moyen âge," *B.Z.*, XII (1903), 1–39.

Idolatry in Gaul. E. VACANDARD, "L'idolatrie en Gaule au VIe et au VIIe siècle," *R.Q.H.*, LXV (1899), 424–54.

Original sources. The all important work is GREGORY OF TOURS, *Historiae Francorum libri X*, for translations see outline VII of part II.

Maps and geography. A. LONGNON, *Géographie de la Gaule au VIe siècle* Paris, 1878, is indispensable to a student of Gregory of Tours; see also his *Atlas historique de la France*, plates III–IV.

C. BIBLIOGRAPHY

General books. See the literature under outlines VII and VI in part II and the cross-references given there to still more general books. See also especially nos. **29, 461** and **788.**

Visigothic civilization. R. P. A. DOZY, *Recherches sur l'histoire et la littérature de l'Espagne pendant le moyen âge.* L. WIENER, *Contributions toward a history of Arabico-Gothic culture*, vol. I, New York, 1917. A. BONILLA Y SAN MARTÍN, *Historia de la filosofía española*, I, 207–68. E. BOURRET, *L'école chrétienne de Séville sous la monarchie des Visigoths*, Paris, 1855. J. AMADOR DE LOS RIOS, *El arte latino-bizantino y las coronas visigóticas de Guarrazar*, Madrid, 1861. J. TARDIF, *Extraits et abrégés juridiques des Etymologies d'Isidore de Séville*, Paris, 1896. K. ZEUMER, "Geschichte der westgothischen Gesetzgebung," in *N.A.*, XXIII (1898), 419–516; XXIV (1899), 39–122, 571–630. See also literature on Isidore of Seville in outline IV, and for Visigothic Spain in general, see outline II in part II.

Gregory of Tours. J. W. LOEBELL, *Gregor von Tours und seine Zeit*, Leipzig, 1839; 2nd edition, with additions by F. BERNHARDT, Leipzig, 1869. MANITIUS, *Geschichte*, I, 216–23. MOLINIER, *Les sources*, I, 55–63. S. HELLMAN, "Studien zur mittelalterlichen Geschichtschreibung: Gregor von Tours," *H.Z.*, CVII (1911), 1–43. M. BONNET, *Le latin de Grégoire de Tours*, Paris, 1890. PAULINE TAYLOR, *The latinity of the Liber Historiae Francorum*, New York, 1924. B. KRUSCH, "Zu M. Bonnet's Untersuchungen über Gregor von Tours," *N.A.*, XVI (1891), 432–34. R. URBAT, *Beiträge zu einer Darstellung der romanischen Elemente im Latein der Historia Francorum des Gregor von Tours*, Königsberg, 1890. G. KURTH, "Saint Grégoire de Tours et les études classiques au VIe siècle," *R.Q.H.*, XXIV (1878), 586–93. L. HALPHEN, "Grégoire de Tours, historien de Clovis," *Mélanges Ferdinand Lot*, Paris, 1925, 235–44.

Venantius Fortunatus. R. KOEBNER, *Venantius Fortunatus*, Leipzig, 1915. See also MANITIUS, *Geschichte*, I, 170–81.

Merovingian Latin. H. D'ARBOIS DE JUBAINVILLE, *Etudes sur la langue des Francs à l'époque mérovingienne*, Paris, 1900; *La déclinaison latine en Gaule à l'époque mérovingienne*, Paris, 1872. E. ERNAULT, *De Virgilio Marone: grammatico tolosano*, Paris, 1886. O. HAAG, "Die Latinität Fredegars," *Romanische Forschungen*, X (1899), 835ff. B. KRUSCH, "Die Sprache Fredegars," *N.A.*, VII (1882), 486–94. J. PIRSON, "Le latin de formules mérovingiennes et carolingiennes," *Romanische Forschungen*, XXVI (1909), 837–944.

Merovingian civilization. A. MARIGNAN, *Etudes sur la civilisation française*, vol. I, *La société mérovingienne*, vol. II, *Le culte des saints sous les mérovingiens*, Paris, 1899. A. F. OZANAM, *La civilisation chrétienne chez les Francs: recherches sur l'histoire ecclésiastique, politique et littéraire des temps mérovingiens et sur le règne de Charlemagne*, vol. IV of his *Oeuvres complètes*, 11 vols., Paris, 1872–81. C. GALY, *La famille à l'époque mérovingienne*, Paris, 1901. K. WEIMANN, *Die sittliche Begriffe in Gregors von Tours "Historica Francorum,"* Duisburg, 1900 (Diss.). H. RÜCKERT, *Kulturgeschichte des deutschen Volks in der Zeit des Übergangs aus dem Heidentum in das Christentum*, 2 vols., Leipzig, 1853–54. L. LINDENSCHMIT, *Die Alterthümer der merovingischen Zeit*, Braunschweig, 1880. B. ZELLER (editor), *L'histoire de France racontée par les contemporains*, Paris, 1880–87, vol. I, *Les invasions barbares*, vol. II, *Les Francs mérovengiens*. A. COVILLE, *Recherches sur l'histoire de Lyon du Ve au IXe siècle*, Paris, 1928. For Merovingian archaeology see nos. **299–301**.

Learning in Merovingian Gaul. O. DENK, *Geschichte des gallo-fränkischen Unterrichts- und Bildungswesens*, chs. VI–VIII. G. KURTH, *Histoire poétique des mérovingiens*, Paris, 1893. J. J. AMPÈRE, *Histoire littéraire de la France avant Charlemagne*, 3 vols., Paris, 1870. P. LAHARGOU, *De scholis Lerinensi aetate merovingiaca*, Paris, 1892. E. VACANDARD, "La scola du palais mérovingien," *R.Q.H.*, LXI (1897), 490–502. See also especially vol. III of no. **803**.

Merovingian saints and churchmen. J. M. BESSE, *Les moines de l'ancienne France; période gallo-romaine et mérovingienne*, Paris, 1906. L. DUCHESNE, "L'église dans la gaule franque au VIe siècle," *R.D.M.*, XXIV (1924), 273–306. C. A. BERNOUILLI, *Die Heiligen der Merowinger*, Tübingen, 1900. L. VAN DER ESSEN, *Etude critique et littéraire sur les Vitae des saints mérovingiens de l'ancienne Belgique*, Louvain, 1907. E. VACANDARD, *Vie de Saint Ouen, évêque de Rouen (641–684): étude d'histoire mérovingienne*, Paris, 1902. G. KURTH, *Sainte Clotilde*, Paris, 1897; 8th edition, 1905 (Les saints), translated by V. M. CRAWFORD, London, 1906. P. PARSY, *Saint Eloi (590–659)*, Paris, 1907. R. P. CAMERLINCK, *Saint Léger, évêque d'Autun, 616–678*, Paris, 1910. A. HAUDECOEUR, *Saint Rémi, évêque de Reims*, Rheims, 1896. A. MALNORY, *St. Césaire, évêque d'Arles, 503–543*, Paris, 1894, vol. CIII of no. **888**. F. ARNOLD, *Cäsarius von Arelate und die gallische Kirche seiner Zeit*, Leipzig, 1894. E. R. VAUCELLE, *La collégiale de saint Martin de Tours (397–1328)*, Paris, 1908. H. v. SCHUBERT, *Staat und*

Kirche in den arianischen Königreichen und im Reiche Chlodwigs, mit Exkursen über das älteste Eigenkirchenwesen, Munich and Berlin, 1912. E. DE MOREAUD, *Saint Amand, Apôtre de la Belgique et du nord de la France*, Louvain, 1927.

Original sources. *Inscriptions chrétiennes de la Gaule antérieures au VIIIe siècle*, edited by E. LE BLANT, 2 vols., Paris, 1856–65, supplemented by a *Nouveau recueil des inscriptions chrétiennes*, Paris, 1892.

Bibliography. MOLINIER, *Sources*, I, 1–180.

VII. LEARNING IN THE BRITISH ISLES FROM THE FIFTH TO THE EIGHTH CENTURY

A. OUTLINE

1. The peculiar place of the British isles, especially Ireland, in the history of medieval culture. Relations of the islands with the Mediterranean world, especially southern Gaul, before the Anglo-Saxon invasion. The introduction of Christianity. Relations of the western fringe of England with Ireland before and after the Anglo-Saxon conquest. Brittany and the British isles. Celtic versus Roman Christianity.

2. Nature of the remarkable Irish learning after the Anglo-Saxon conquest of England. The knowledge of Greek. Irish handwriting and illumination of manuscripts. The *Hisperica famina*. Foreign scholars in Ireland.

3. The spread of this culture on the continent largely through Irish missionaries like St. Columban. Its effect upon the ignorance in Gaul and Germany during Merovingian times. The libraries of the monasteries of Bobbio and St. Gall.

4. Mingling of the Irish and Roman streams of culture in England. Theodore of Tarsus, archbishop of Canterbury, 668–690, and his friend Hadrian established schools for the study of Latin and Greek at Canterbury and elsewhere. Benedict Biscop, died ca. 690. The Greek and Latin learning of Aldhelm, abbot of Malmesbury, ca. 650–709.

5. Bede, the Venerable, 672–735, the first English savant. "Semper aut discere aut docere aut scribere dulce habui." A product of both Irish and Roman training. All his life spent in the monastery of Jarrow. His voluminous writings of which the most remarkable is the *Historia ecclesiastica*.

6. The early spread of English culture on the continent. Winifred (Boniface), ca. 680–755, the "Apostle of Germany." His classical learning.

7. The school of York. Egbert, archbishop of York, 732–66, a disciple of Bede, was a patron of learning. His successor Aelbert was the master of Alcuin. The famous library of York.

8. Alcuin, ca. 735–804, born in Northumbria about the time when Bede died, was the most distinguished product of the school of York. He became the connecting link between the culture of the British isles and the continent in the time of Charlemagne (see next outline).

B. SPECIAL RECOMMENDATIONS FOR READING

Brief general accounts. POOLE, *Illustrations of the history of medieval thought*, 1–26. DRANE, *Christian schools and scholars*, chs. II–IV. *Cambridge history of English literature*, I, ch. V. A. BAUMGARTNER, *Geschichte der Weltliteratur*, IV, 268–91. F. A. SPECHT, *Geschichte des Unterrichtswesens in Deutschland*, Stuttgart, 1885, 1–14.

For literary details, see MANITIUS, *Geschichte*, I, 70–87 (Bede), 134–52 (Aldhelm and Boniface), 156–60 (*Hisperica famina*), 181–87, 236–39 (Adamnan of Hy); and SANDYS, *Classical scholarship*, I, 451–70. A. EBERT, *Geschichte der Litteratur des Mittelalters in Abendland*, 3 vols., Leipzig, 1874–87; 2nd edition of vols. I and II, 1889.

Standard account. ROGER, *L'enseignement*, chs. VI–XII.

Irish learning. For surveys see P. W. JOYCE, *The story of ancient Irish civilization*, London, 1907, chs. I–XIII; H. ZIMMER, *The Irish element in mediaeval culture;* and K. MEYER, *Learning in Ireland in the fifth century, and the transmission of letters: a lecture*, Dublin, 1913. C. H. SLOVER, "Early literary channels between Britain and Ireland," *University of Texas studies in English*, no. 6 (1926).

Standard works on the subject are: J. HEALY, *Insula sanctorum et doctorum: or Ireland's ancient schools and scholars*, Dublin, 1890; 5th edition, 1908; P. W. JOYCE, *A social history of ancient Ireland*, 2 vols., London, 1903; 2nd edition, 1914, vol. I, part II. MARY HAYDEN and G. A. MOONAN, *A short history of the Irish people from the earliest times to 1920*, London and New York, 1921.

Learning in England. MARGARETE RÖSLER, "Erziehung in England vor der normannischen Eroberung," *Englische Studien*, XLVIII (1914), 1–114. H. H. HOWORTH, *The golden days of the early English church from the arrival of Theodore to the death of Bede*, 3 vols., New York, 1917. P. F. JONES, "The Gregorian mission and English education," *Speculum*, III (1928), 335–48.

Greek learning in the British isles. G. T. STOKES, "The knowledge of Greek in Ireland between A.D. 500 and 900," *Proceedings of the royal Irish academy*, third series, II (1891–1893), 187–202. T. E. DOWLING and E. W. FLETCHER, *Hellenism in England*, London, 1915. J. R. LUMBY, *Greek learning in the western church during the seventh and eighth centuries*, Cambridge, 1878.

Original sources. *Texte und Forschungen zur englischen Kulturgeschichte; Festgabe für Felix Liebermann*, Halle, 1921. *Complete works of Bede*, with a translation, edited by J. A. GILES, 12 vols., London, 1843–44; the best edition of the *Historia ecclesiastica* is in vol. I of VENERABILIS BAEDAE *Opera historica*, edited by C. PLUMMER, 2 vols., Oxford, 1896; the best translation is by A. M. SELLAR, London, 1912. *Adamnani Vita S. Columbae*, edited from DR. REEVE'S Text, with an introduction on early Irish church history, notes and a glossary, by J. T. FOWLER; new edition, revised, Oxford, 1920. KENNEY, *The sources for the early history of Ireland.*

C. Bibliography

General books. See outline VI of part II. See also nos. **89, 94, 735** and **788.**

Irish element in medieval culture. J. Pokorny, "Beiträge zur ältesten Geschichte Irlands, I–II," *Zeitschrift für celtische Philologie*, XI (1917), 189–204; XII (1918), 308. H. Zimmer, "Über direkte Handelsverbindungen Westgalliens mit Irland im Altertum und frühen Mittelalter," *S.B., Berlin Acad.* (1909), 365ff. (answered by F. Haverfield, "Ancient Rome and Ireland," *E.H.R.*, XXVIII (1913), 1–12. H. Zimmer, *Der kulturgeschichtliche Hintergrund in den Erzählungen der alten irischen Heldensage*, Berlin, 1911; *Keltische Studien*, 2 vols., Berlin, 1881–84; "Über die frühesten Berührungen der Iren mit den Nordgermanen," *S.B., Berlin Acad.* (1891), 279–317. W. Schultze, "Die Bedeutung der iroschottischen Mönche für die Erhaltung und Fortpflanzung der mittelalterlichen Wissenschaft," *Centralblatt für Bibliothekswesen*, VI (1884), 185, 233, 281. J. v. Pflugk-Harttung, "The old Irish on the Continent," *Trans., R.H.S.* (n. s.), V, 75. W. Wattenbach, "Irish monasteries in Germany," *Ulster journal of archaeology*, VIII (1861). L. Traube, "Peronna Scottorum: ein Beitrag zur Ueberlieferungsgeschichte und zur Palaeographie des Mittelalters," *S.B., Munich Acad.* (1900), 469; see also his *O Roma nobilis*. H. d'Arbois de Jubainville, *Introduction à l'étude de la littérature celtique*, Paris, 1883, book II, ch. ix. A. B. Scott, *The Pictish nation: its people and its church*, Edinburgh, 1918. E. Sullivan, *The book of Kells*, London, 1914. C. Plummer (editor), *Vitae sanctorum Hiberniae partim hactenus ineditae*, 2 vols., Oxford, 1910. W. M. Lindsay, *Early Irish minuscule script*, Oxford, 1910. H. Graham, *The early Irish monastic schools; a study of Ireland's contribution to early medieval culture*, Dublin, 1923. L. Gougaud, *Gaelic pioneers of Christianity*, translated by V. Collins, Dublin, 1923. J. P. Fuhrmann, *Irish mediaeval monasteries on the continent*, Washington, 1927 (Diss.).

Brittany and the British isles. B. Plaine, *La colonisation de l'Armorique par les Bretons insulaires*, Paris, 1899. J. Loth, *L'émigration bretonne en Armorique du Ve au VIIe siècle de notre ère*, Rennes, 1883.

Theodore of Tarsus. G. F. Browne, *Theodore and Wilfrith*, London, 1897. W. Bright, *Chapters of early English church history*, Oxford, 1878; 3rd edition, 1897, *passim*.

Aldhelm. G. F. Browne, *Aldhelm: his life and times*, London, 1903. L. Bönhoff, *Aldhelm von Malmesbury: ein Beitrag zur Kirchengeschichte*, Dresden, 1894. A. S. Cook, "Aldhelm's legal studies," *Journal Engl. and Germ. philol.*, XXIII (1924), 107–13; "Sources of the biography of Aldhelm," *Trans. Connecticut Acad. arts and sciences*, XXVIII (1927), 273–93.

Bede. G. F. Browne, *The Venerable Bede*, London, 1887, a book for the general reader. K. Werner, *Beda der Ehrwürdige und seine Zeit*, Vienna, 1875; 2nd edition, 1881. M. Manitius, "Zu Aldhelm und Beda," *S.B., Vienna Acad.*, CXII (1886), 535ff. P. Lehmann, *Wert und Echtheit einer Beda abgesprochenen Schrift*, Munich, 1919. G. F. Browne, *The Venerable*

Bede, his life and writings, London, 1919. W. C. ABBOTT, "An uncanonized saint: the Venerable Bede," in *Conflicts with oblivion*, New Haven, 1924, 241–78.

Boniface and learning. H. KOCH, *Die Stellung des heiligen Bonifatius zur Bildung und Wissenschaft*, Braunsberg, 1905. E. KYLIE, *The English correspondence of St. Boniface*, London, 1911.

Original sources. *Councils and ecclesiastical documents relating to Great Britain and Ireland*, edited by A. W. HADDAN and W. STUBBS, 3 vols., Oxford, 1869–78. *The Hisperica famina*, edited by F. J. H. JENKINSON, with three facsimile plates, Cambridge, 1908. E. G. MILLAR, *The Lindisfarne Gospels*, three plates in color and thirty-six in monochrome, London, 1923. B. COLGRAVE (editor and translator), *The life of Bishop Wilfrid by Eddius Stephanus*, Latin text, translation and notes, Cambridge, 1927.

Bibliographies. ROGER, *L'enseignement*, IX–XVIII. *Cambridge history of English literature*, bibliography for ch. V. MANITIUS, *Geschichte*, use index. See also no. **36.**

VIII. AGE OF CHARLEMAGNE

A. OUTLINE

1. The medieval tendency to look back with admiration to the glorious period of imperial Rome found striking expression in the reign of Charlemagne. Contrast between the culture of the Merovingian and Carolingian periods.

2. Learning at the court of Charlemagne. His own intellectual accomplishments and limitations. His patronage of learning and art. Importation of scholars to grace his court: most important of all, Alcuin from York, England; Paul the Deacon (died ca. 800), Peter of Pisa (died before 799) from Italy, and probably Paulinus of Aquileia (died 802); Theodulf (died 821), bishop of Orleans, from Spain. Two famous native scholars were Angilbert (died 814) and Einhard (died 840). Three periods in the intellectual life at the court of Charlemagne: (1) 773–86, when the Italian scholars were most influential; (2) 786–800, the period of Alcuin, the high-water mark of Frankish learning; (3) 800–14, a period of gradual decline when Theodulf, Angilbert, and Einhard were the chief figures.

3. The palace school at Aix-la-Chapelle. In no sense a university, but rather an informal and heterogeneous academy. Puerility of much of the learning in this school. Its importance lies not in its achievements but in the promise which it held.

4. Alcuin as head of the palace school and as abbot of St. Martin's of Tours, where he died in 804. The wide scope of his literary efforts. His pedagogical genius. Limitations of his scholarship. His *scriptorium* in Tours. Disciples of Alcuin, especially Rabanus Maurus.

5. Educational reform. The letter to Baugulf, abbot of Fulda, written in 787, probably by Alcuin. Charlemagne's capitularies concerning education. Reorganization of monastery and cathedral schools. The elevation of the clergy to the position of a learned class.

6. Enthusiasm for the ancient Latin classics. Its connection with the revival of the empire. The classical learning of Alcuin. Classicism in Carolingian poetry, especially that of Theodulf, and in history writing, especially in that of Einhard. Interest in classical archaeology. The Einsiedeln *Itinerary*, ca. 900.

7. Revival of historiography. The *Vita Karoli* of Einhard and the *Historia Langobardorum* of Paul the Deacon. The famous Carolingian annals, especially the *Annales royales*.

8. The reform in calligraphy. The evolution of the Caroline minuscule which eventually became the pattern for our modern "Roman" letters. The importance of the *scriptorium* of Tours in this development.

9. The revival in art, especially architecture and the illumination of manuscripts. The royal chapel at Aix-la-Chapelle, and the royal palaces at Nimwegen, Ingelheim, and Aix-la-Chapelle. Byzantine influences.

10. Interest in native Teutonic song and story.

11. The apparent sudden decline of Carolingian culture.

B. Special Recommendations for Reading

Brief general surveys. Lavisse, *Histoire de France,* II, part I, 342–57. Taylor, *Mediaeval mind,* I, ch. x. Drane, *Christian schools and scholars,* ch. v. Townsend, *The great schoolmen,* ch. ii. W. P. Ker, *The dark ages,* New York, 1904 (Periods of European literature), ch. iii. Baumgartner, *Geschichte der Weltliteratur,* IV, 292–306. Specht, *Geschichte des Unterrichtswesens,* 15–30.

Authoritative general surveys. J. B. Mullinger, *The schools of Charles the Great,* London, 1877, anastatic reprints, New York, 1904 and 1911. *C.M.H.*, V, ch. xxii. G. Monod, *Etudes critiques sur les sources de l'histoire carolingienne,* Paris, 1898, part of no. **888**, 37–67 ["La renaissance carolingienne," *Séances et travaux de l'Académie des sciences morales et politiques,* CLII (1899), 137–66, corresponds almost word for word with pp. 37–59 of the publication just mentioned]. Manitius, *Geschichte,* I, 243–88; see also 368–70 (Paulinus of Aquileia), 452–56 (Peter of Pisa), 537–47 (Theodulf of Orleans and Angilbert), 639–46 (Einhard). Molinier, *Sources,* I, 181–227; V, Introduction, xxx–xli.

Alcuin. A. F. West, *Alcuin.* C. J. B. Gaskoin, *Alcuin: his life and his work,* London, 1904. G. F. Browne, *Alcuin of York,* London, 1908. Roger, *L'enseignement,* 313–28, 440–48.

Latin classics. L. Havet, "Que doivent à Charlemagne les classiques latins?", *Revue bleue,* fifth series, V (1906), 129–33. Sandys, *Classical scholarship,* I, 471–82.

Carolingian calligraphy. Putnam, *Books and their makers,* I, 106–17. A. Molinier, *Les manuscrits et les miniatures,* Paris, 1892, 107–39 (an extract from these pages may be found in C. V. Langlois, *Lectures historiques,* 5th edition, 171–80). E. M. Thompson, *An introduction to Greek and Latin palaeography,* 367–70, 403ff. M. Prou, *Manuel de paléographie,* 4th edition, 166–84. F. Delisle, "Mémoire sur l'école calligraphique de Tours au IXe

siècle," *Mémoires de l'Académie des inscriptions*, XXXII (1885), part I, 29–56. See also in general outline XXVI.

Original sources. *History of the Langobards*, by PAUL, THE DEACON, translated by FOULKE. For Einhard see outline VIII of part II. "The letters of Einhard," translated by H. PREBLE, annotated by J. C. AYER, *Papers of the American society of church history*, second series, I (1913), 109–58. B. WENDELL, *Eginhard's History of the translation of the blessed martyrs of Christ.*

C. BIBLIOGRAPHY

General books. See outline VIII of part II. See also especially nos. **29, 788** and **803.**

General and miscellaneous accounts. G. KURTH, *Les origines de la civilisation moderne*, 2 vols., 5th edition, Brussels, 1903. HAUCK, *Kirchengeschichte Deutschlands*, vol. II, *Die Karolingerzeit.* H. BASTGEN, "Alkuin und Karl der Grosse in ihren wissenschaftlichen und kirchenpolitischen Anschauungen," *Hist. Jahrbuch*, XXXII (1911), 809–25. W. TURNER, "Irish teachers in the Carolingian revival," *The Catholic university bulletin*, XIII (1907), 382, 567. G. PARIS, *Histoire poëtique de Charlemagne*, Paris, 1865; new edition by P. MEYER, 1905. L. MAÎTRE, *Les écoles épiscopales et monastiques de l'occident depuis Charlemagne jusqu'à Philippe-Auguste*, Paris, 1865; 2nd revised edition, 1924. G. BRUNHES, *La foi chrétienne et la philosophie au temps de la renaissance carolingienne*, Paris, 1903. H. BLOCK, *Geistesleben im Elsass zur Karolingerzeit*, Strasburg, 1901. J. PHILIPPE, *Lucrèce dans la théologie chrétienne du 3ᵉ au 13ᵉ siècle et spécialement dans les écoles carolingiennes*, I, Paris, 1895. K. STRECKER, "Studien zur karolingischen Dichtern," *N.A.*, XLIII, 3, and XLIV, 2, 3 (1922). A. SOLMI, *Sul capitolare di Lotarro dell' anno 825 relativo all' ordinamento scolastico in Italia*, Milan, 1923. R. STACHNIK, *Die Bildung des Weltklerus im Frankenreiche von Karl Martell bis auf Ludwig den Frommen*, Paderborn, 1926.

Alcuin. F. MONNIER, *Alcuin et son influence chez les Francs*, Paris, 1853; 2nd edition, *Alcuin et Charlemagne*, Paris, 1864. K. WERNER, *Alcuin und sein Jahrhundert*, Paderborn, 1876; 2nd edition, Vienna, 1881. F. LORENZ, *Alcuin's Leben*, Halle, 1829, translated by JANE M. SLEE, *The life of Alcuin*, London, 1837. R. B. PAGE, *The letters of Alcuin*, New York, 1909 (Diss.). E. DÜMMLER, "Zur Lebensgeschichte Alchvins," *N.A.*, XVIII (1893), 51–70. W. SCHMITZ, *Alcuins ars grammatica, die lateinische Schulgrammatik der karolingischen Renaissance*, Ratingen, 1908 (Diss.). J. B. LAFORÊT, *Histoire d'Alcuin*, Paris, 1898. F. HAMELIN, *Essai sur les oeuvres d'Alcuin*, Paris, 1873. A. DUPUY, *Alcuin et l'école de St. Martin de Tours*, Tours, 1876. RAND, *Script of Tours*, I.

Theodulf. C. CUISSARD, *Théodulfe, évêque d'Orléans*, Orleans, 1892.

Einhard. F. KURZE, *Einhard*, Berlin, 1899. A. SCHMIDT, *Die Sprache Einhards*, Greifswald, 1904 (Diss.). M. BUCHNER, "Zum Briefwechsel Einhards und des hl. Ansegis von Fontanelle (St. Wandrille)," *H.V.J.S.*, XVIII (1916–18), 353–85; *Einhard als Künstler. Forschungen zur karolingischen*

Kunstgeschichte und zum Lebengang Einhards, Stuttgart, 1919; *Einhards Künstler- und Gelehrtenleben*, Bonn and Leipzig, 1922. HALPHEN, *Etudes critiques*, III, 60–103.

Carolingian art. In general see no. **299,** I, ch. II. F. v. REBER, *Der karolingische Palastbau*, 2 parts, Munich, 1892 (*Abh. Munich Acad.*). G. HUMANN, *Zur Geschichte der karolingischen Baukunst*, Strasburg, 1909. C. RHOEN, *Die karolingische Pfalz zu Aachen*, Aachen, 1889. K. PLATH, *Nimwegen: ein Kaiserpalast Karl's des Grossen in den Niederlanden*, Berlin, 1895; *Die Königspfalzen der Merovinger und Karolinger*, Leipzig, 1892. W. EFFMANN, *Centula—St. Riguier: eine Untersuchung zur Geschichte der kirchlichen Baukunst in der Karolingerzeit*, Münster, 1912. G. WEISE, *Zwei fränkische Königspfalzen* (Quierzy and Samoussy), Tübingen, 1923. F. LEITSCHUH, *Geschichte der karolingischen Malerei*, Berlin, 1894. P. CLEMEN, *Merovingische und karolingische Plastik*, Bonn, 1892. J. R. RAHN, *Das Psalterium Aureum von Sanct-Gallen: ein Beitrag zur Geschichte der karolingischen Miniaturmalerei*, St. Gall, 1878, contains reproductions and text. P. E. SCHRAMM, *Die zeitgenössischen Bildnisse Karl des Grossen*, Leipzig, 1927.

Original sources. Almost all the writings of Alcuin and his contemporaries are found in nos. **978, 983** and **953.** For detailed references to individual authors and works consult the bibliographies listed below. For a discussion of the editions of the works of Alcuin see also A. F. WEST, *Alcuin*, 183–91. *Ausgewählte Schriften von Columban, Alcuin, Hrabanus Maurus* etc., edited by P. G. MEIER, in vol. III of *Bibliothek der katholischen Pädagogik*, Freiburg, 1890. *Historians of the church of York and its archbishops*, edited by J. RAINE, 3 vols., London, 1879–94, part of no. **995** (for Alcuin). *Schriftquellen zur Geschichte der karolingischen Kunst*, edited by J. v. SCHLOSSER, Vienna, 1896; *Materialen zur Quellenkunde der Kunstgeschichte*, Heft, 1–3, *S.B.*, *Vienna Acad.*, vols. 177, 179, 180, 1914–16.

Bibliographies. MOLINIER, *Les sources*, I, 181–227; and MANITIUS, *Geschichte*, I (use table of contents, index, and the chronological table at the end of the volume). See also SARTON, *Introduction*, 511, 529.

IX. LEARNING IN AND ABOUT THE IMPERIAL COURT DURING THE NINTH AND TENTH CENTURIES

A. OUTLINE

1. A period of disorder and very slow advancement of culture, due largely to foes from without and political disorganization within western Christendom.

2. Perpetuation of learning in the larger monastery and cathedral schools. In France: Tours, Ferrières, Cluny, Bec, Fleury, Auxerre, Paris (St. Germain, Ste. Geneviève, and the cathedral school), Chartres, Laon, Rheims, and Lyons. In Germany: Fulda, St. Gall, and Reichenau. In the Netherlands: Liége and Tournai. In England: York and Canterbury.

3. The generation after Charlemagne and Alcuin. Rabanus Maurus, 784–856, the pupil of Alcuin and abbot of Fulda, and later archbishop of

Mainz, called *primus praeceptor Germaniae.* His encyclopaedia *De rerum naturis*, and his popular book *De institutione clericorum.* His position as a thinker. Walafrid Strabo, ca. 809–49. The famous *Letters* of Servatus Lupus of Ferrières, 805–62, and his knowledge of the classics. Gottschalk (Godescale), ca. 805–ca. 869. Hincmar of Rheims, ca. 806–82. Remi of Auxerre, ca. 841–ca. 908.

4. A Carolingian aftermath at the court of Charles the Bald. About 845 John Scotus Eriugena came to this court, probably from Ireland. He was the *enfant terrible* of his time. His knowledge of Greek. About 858 he completed a Latin translation of the *Caelestis hierarchia* of the so-called Greek Dionysius the Areopagite. His daring *De divisione naturae*, which marked a turning point in the history of medieval thought.

5. Comparatively low state of culture on the continent about 900, when there was a somewhat brighter period in England, under king Alfred the Great (died 901). Translations into Anglo-Saxon connected with the name of Alfred: Bede's *Ecclesiastical history*, Boethius' *Consolations of philosophy*, Pope Gregory the Great's *Dialogues* and *Pastoral care*, Orosius' *Seven books of history against the pagans*, and probably Augustine's *Soliloquies.* Asser's *Life of Alfred.*

6. The court of the Ottos. Bruno, archbishop of Cologne (died 965), a brother of Otto the Great. The plays of the nun Roswitha of Gandersheim (born about 935). Hedwig, daughter of Henry of Bavaria, the brother of Otto I. Ekkehard I and Ekkehard II of St. Gall.

7. Gerbert, pope Silvester II (999–1003), and Otto III. Gerbert's visit to Barcelona. Muslim influences (see next outline). His interest in mathematics and the natural sciences, and in the Latin classics.

8. Renewed interest in Greek due to the close relations of the Ottonian court with the Byzantine empire.

9. The pursuit of learning in the great monasteries such as St. Gall (Notger the Stammerer, ca. 840–912), Cluny (Odo of Cluny, died 942), St. Germain des Prés of Paris (Abbo, flourished about 900, wrote a poem on *Bella Parisiacae urbis* describing the wars with the Northmen), and Monte Cassino before and after the ravages of the Saracens in south Italy.

10. The legend of the year 1000.

B. Special Recommendations for Reading

Short general surveys. Taylor, *Mediaeval mind*, I, 221–43. West, *Alcuin*, chs. vii–viii. Ker, *The dark ages*, 159–227. Sandys, *Classical scholarship*, I, 483–514. M. de Wulf, *A history of medieval philosophy*, 149–62, 167–73. Grabmann, *Die Geschichte der scholastischen Methode*, I, 192–214.

Longer accounts. A. T. Drane, *Christian schools and scholars*, chs. vi–x. Guizot, *History of civilization in France*, first course, lectures 28–29. For accurate details see Manitius, *Geschichte*, I, 288–314 (Rabanus Maurus and Walafrid Strabo), 323–67 (John Scotus, Hincmar, and Notger), 483–90 (Lupus), 504–19 (Remi), 568–74 (Gottschalk), 585–88 (Abbo), 609–14 (Ekkehard I), 619–32 (Roswitha). BAUMGARTNER, *Geschichte der Weltliteratur*, IV, 306–53. EBERT, *Geschichte der Literatur des Mittelalters*, II, 120–69 (Rabanus Maurus, Walafrid Strabo, Gottschalk), 203–09 (Servatus Lupus), III, 314–29 (Roswitha). For historical works see also WATTENBACH, *Deutschlands Geschichtsquellen*, I, 256ff. G. KURTH, *Notger de Liège et la civilisation au Xe siècle*, especially I, ch. XIV. M. MANITIUS, *Bildung, Wissenschaft, und Literatur im Abendlande von 800 bis 1100*, Crimmitschau, 1925.

John Scotus Eriugena. POOLE, *Illustrations of the history of medieval thought*, ch. II (see also the beginning of ch. III). W. TURNER, "John the Scot," *Catholic university bulletin*, Feb., 1912; or his article in *Catholic encyclopedia*. W. J. TOWNSEND, *The great schoolmen*, ch. III. ALICE GARDNER, *Studies in John the Scot (Erigena): a philosopher of the dark ages*, London, 1900. PICAVET, *Esquisse d'une histoire générale et comparée des philosophies médiévales*, ch. VI.

King Alfred the Great. *Cambridge history of English literature*, I, ch. VI. C. PLUMMER, *The life and times of Alfred the Great*, Oxford, 1902. BEATRICE A. LEES, *Alfred the Great, the Truth Teller, maker of England (848–899)*, London, 1919 (Heroes of nations). J. A. GILES (editor), *The whole works of king Alfred the Great*, 3 vols., Oxford, 1858. S. A. BROOKS, *King Alfred as educator of his people and man of letters*, London, 1901. G. F. BROWNE, *King Alfred's books*, London, 1920.

Roswitha. W. H. JUDSON, "Hrosvitha of Gandersheim," *E.H.R.*, III (1888), 431–57. ALICE K. WELCH, *Of six mediaeval women*, London, 1913, ch. I, "Roswitha." See also no. **482.** J. S. TUNISON, *Dramatic traditions of the dark ages*, 137ff. EVANGELINE W. BLASHFIELD, *Portraits and backgrounds*, New York, 1917. English translation of plays by H. J. W. TILLYARD, London, 1923, and by CHRISTOPHER ST. JOHN, i.e., CRISTABEL MARSHALL, London, 1923.

Gerbert. C. PFISTER, *Etudes sur le règne de Robert le Pieux*, 1–40. For additional reading on Gerbert see under outline XV, part II, to which may be added TOWNSEND, *Great schoolmen*, ch. IV.

Legend of the year 1000. G. L. BURR, "The year 1000 and the antecedents of the crusades," *A.H.R.*, VI (1900–01), 429–39. P. ORSI, *L'anno mille: saggio di critica storica*, Turin, 1887 (reprinted from the *Rivista storica italiana*, IV, 1887); *Le paure del finimondo nell' anno 1000*, Turin, 1891, 31 pp., is the same argument in a popular form. J. ROY, *L'an mille: formation de la légende de l'an mille, état de la France de l'an 950 à l'an 1050*, Paris, 1885, contains a bibliography. H. v. EICKEN, "Die Legende von der Erwartung des Weltunterganges und der Wiederkehr Christi im Jahre 1000," *F.D.G.*, XXIII (1883), 303–18. R. ROSIÈRES, "Etudes nouvelles sur l'ancienne France: la légende de l'an mille," *Revue politique et littéraire*, 2nd series, XIV (1878), 919–24. F. PLAINE, "Les prétendues terreurs de l'an mille," *R.Q.H.*, XIII (1873), 145–64. The famous passage of Ralph Glaber (died ca. 1044) on the year 1000, is translated by G. G. COULTON, *A medieval garner*, 4–11. F. DUVAL, *Les terreurs de l'an mille*, Paris, 1908.

Original sources. J. HAVET, *Lettres de Gerbert*, Paris, 1889, part of no. **968,** contains a very valuable introduction on the life and work of Gerbert. ASSER'S *Life of Alfred* is translated in *Six English chronicles*, new edition by W. H. STEVENSON, Oxford, 1904. *Der Hrotsuitha Gedicht über Gandersheims Gründung und die Thaten Kaiser Oddo I*, translated by T. G. PFUND, 2nd edition, Leipzig, 1891, part of no. **981.** "The school life of Walafrid Strabo," translated by J. D. BUTLER, in *Bibliotheca sacra*, XL (1883), 152–72, is a translation of a portion of Strabo's own works.

C. BIBLIOGRAPHY

Famous cathedral and monastery schools. L. MAÎTRE, *Les écoles épiscopales et monastiques de l'Occident depuis Charlemagne jusqu'à Philippe Auguste*, Paris, 1866. A. CLERVAL, *Les écoles de Chartres au moyen âge du Ve au XVIe siècle*, Chartres, 1895. W. B. ASPINWALL, *Les écoles épiscopales et monastiques de l'ancienne province ecclésiastique de Sens du VIe au XIIe siècle*, Paris, 1904 (Diss.). G. SALVIOLI, *L'istruzione pubblica in Italia nei secoli VIII, IX, X*, Florence, 1898. A. OZANAM, "Des écoles et de l'instruction publique en Italie aux temps barbares," *Documents inédits*, 1850. W. GIESEBRECHT, *De litterarum studiis apud Italos*, 1845, translated into Italian by C. PASCAL, *L'istruzione pubblica in Italia nei primi secoli del medio evo*, Florence, 1895. SPECHT, *Geschichte des Unterrichtswesens in Deutschland*. R. GRAHAM, "The intellectual influences of English monasteries between the tenth and twelfth centuries," *Trans. R.H.S.*, new series, XVII (1903), 23–64. E. A. LOEW, *Beneventan script*, introduction, for learning in Monte Cassino. R. VAN DOREN, *Etude sur l'influence musicale de l'abbaye de Saint-Gall (VIIIe au XIe siècle)*, Louvain, 1925. C. SANZÉ DE LHOUMEAU, *L'abbaye de Saint-Léonard de Ferrières, ordre de Saint-Benoît, diocèse de Poitiers*, Paris, 1926. CLARK, *The abbey of St. Gall*. MAUD JOYNT, *The life of St. Gall*, a translation of the work of WALAFRID STRABO with an introduction on the history of the abbey of St. Gaul and its library, London, 1927.

Rabanus Maurus. D. TÜRNAU, *Rabanus Maurus, der Praeceptor Germaniae: ein Beitrag zur Geschichte der Pädagogik des Mittelalters*, Munich, 1900. J. B. HABLITZEL, "Hrabanus Maurus und Claudius von Turin," *Hist. Jahrbuch*, XXVII (1906), 74–85. E. DÜMMLER, "Hrabanstudien," *S.B., Berlin Acad.*, 1898, 24–42. F. KUNSTMANN, *Rhabanus Magnentius Maurus*, Mainz, 1841. P. LEHMANN, "Fuldaer Studien," *S.B., Munich Acad.*, 1927, 2 Abh., 13–47. F. ÜBERWEG, *Grundriss der Geschichte der Philosophie*, vol. II, Berlin, 1928 (bibliography).

Lupus of Ferrières. L. LEVILLAIN, "Etude sur les lettres de Loup de Ferrières," *B.E.C.*, LXII (1901), 445–509; LXIII (1902), 69–118, 289–330, 537-86; "Une nouvelle édition des lettres de Loup de Ferrières," *ibid.*, LXIV (1903), 259–83 (the article refers to the new edition of the letters edited by E. DÜMMLER in 1902 as part of no. **978**). S. M. JACKSON, "Servatus Lupus, a humanist of the ninth century," *Papers of the American society of church history*, 2nd series, IV (1914). L. LEVILLAIN (editor and translator), *Loup de Ferrières, correspondance*, Paris, 1927 (Classiques de l'histoire de France au moyen âge). U. Berlière, "Un bibliophile du IXe siècle: Loup de Ferrières," Mons, 1912, 14 pp. (extract of the Bulletin des Bibliophiles belges séant à Mons, 1912). E. Norden, *Die antike Kunstprosa*, II, 698–705. W. Levison, "Eine Predigt des Lupus von Ferrières," *Kultur- und Universalgeschichte, Walter Goetz dargebracht*, Leipzig (1927), 3–14.

John Scotus Eriugena. E. K. Rand, *Johannes Scotus*, Munich, 1906 (Quellen und Untersuchungen zur lateinischen Philologie des Mittelalters, I, 2). C. C. J. Webb, "Scotus Erigena De divisione naturae," *Proceedings of the Aristotelian society*, II (1892–94), 121–37. J. Dräseke, *Johannes Scotus Erigena*, Leipzig, 1902 (Studien zur Geschichte der Theologie und der Kirche, IX, 2). L. Noack, *Johannes Scotus Erigena*, Leipzig, 1876. Saint-René Taillandier, *Scot Erigène et le philosophie scholastique*, Paris, 1843. N. Möller, *Johannes Scotus Erigena und seine Irrtümer*, Mainz, 1844. F. Staudenmaier, *Johannes Scotus Erigena und die Wissenschaft seiner Zeit*, Frankfurt, 1834. H. Bett, *Johannes Scotus Erigena: a study in medieval philosophy*, Cambridge, 1925. Marguerite Techert, "Le Plotinisme dans le système de Jean Scot Erigène," *Revue néo-scolastique*, XXVIII (1927), 28–68. A. Schneider, *Die Erkenntnisslehre des Johannes Scotus Eriugena*, 2 vols., Berlin, 1921–23.

Walafrid Strabo. L. Eigl, *Walahfried Strabo*, Vienna, 1908. A. Jundt, *Walafrid Strabon: l'homme et le théologien*, Cahors, 1900 (Diss.). F. von Bezold, "Kaiserin Judith und ihr Dichter Walahfrid Strabo," *H.Z.*, CXXX (1924), 377–439.

Roswitha. J. Schneiderhan, *Roswitha von Gandersheim die erste deutsche Dichterin*, Paderborn, 1912. P. v. Winterfeld, "Hrotsvits literarische Stellung," *Archiv. für das Studium der neueren Sprachen*, CXIV (1905), 25–75. K. Brandi, "Hrotsvit von Gandersheim," *Deutsche Rundschau* (1926), 247–60. F. Ermini, "Le opere di Hrosvitha," *Nuova antologia* (1927), 453–58.

Gerbert. F. J. Picavet, *Gerbert*, Paris, 1897. K. Werner, *Gerbert von Aurillac: die Kirche und Wissenschaft seiner Zeit*, Vienna, 1878. A. Franck, *Gerbert: état de la philosophie et des sciences au Xe siècle*, Paris, 1872. K. T. Schlockwerder, *Das Konzil zu St. Basle: ein Beitrag zur Lebensgeschichte Gerberts von Aurillac*, Madgeburg, 1907 (Prog.). K. Schultess, *Papst Silvester II (Gerbert) als Lehrer und Staatsmann*, Hamburg, 1891 (Prog.). On Gerbert's place in the history of mathematics see A. Nagl, "Gerbert und die Rechenkunst des 10ten Jahrhundert," *S.B., Vienna Acad.*, CXVI (1888), 861–922, with four plates. F. Weissenborn, *Gerbert: Beiträge zur Kenntniss der Mathematik des Mittelalters*, Berlin, 1888; *Zur Geschichte der Einführung der jetzigen Ziffern in Europa durch Gerbert*, Berlin, 1892. M. Cantor, *Vorlesungen über Geschichte der Mathematik*, ch. xxxviii. P. E. Schramm, "Die Briefe Kaiser Ottos III und Gerberts von Reims aus dem Jahre 997," *Archiv für Urkundenforschung*, IX (1926), 87–122.

Original sources. Most of the works of writers mentioned in this outline are printed in nos. **953** and **978,** to which the works mentioned under "Bibliographies" below will serve as guides. Special mention may be made of the following: *Oeuvres de Gerbert, pape sous le nom de Sylvestre II*, edited by A. OLLERIS, Paris, 1867. *Gerberti postea Silvestri II papae opera mathematica 972–1003*, edited by N. BUBNOV, Berlin, 1900. *Hrotsvithae opera*, edited by P. v. WINTERFELD, Berlin, 1902, part of no. **979**; another edition by K. STRECKER, Leipzig, 1906.

Bibliographies. Scattered references will be found in MANITIUS, *Geschichte*, I; SANDYS, *Classical scholarship*, I; and WATTENBACH, *Deutschlands Geschichtsquellen*, I.

X. MUSLIM CULTURE IN THE WEST

A. OUTLINE

1. The necessity of studying Mediterranean culture as a whole in medieval as well as in ancient times. Mingling of oriental, Byzantine, Muslim, and Latin Christian civilization. Relations between Christians and Muslims throughout the length of southern Europe.

2. The intellectual and artistic development of the Muslims. Influence of Hellenic civilization largely through the Syrian Nestorian Christians and the Persians, with some influence also from India. Comparatively small part played by Arabs in Muslim culture. The influence of Aristotle. Interest in theology, philosophy, philology, history, law, mathematics, medicine and natural sciences. Predilection for literature, especially poetry. Beginning with the ninth century there was remarkable activity in translating ancient books into Arabic. The height of cultured life in Damascus and Bagdad. The *Thousand and one nights* (*Alf Laila wa Laila*).

3. The binding force of Muslim culture kept Islam united even after the political disruption of the Caliphate. This is evident especially in Sicily and Spain.

4. The Jews as intermediaries between Muslims and Christians especially in Spain. Activity of the Jews as translators and commentators. Parallelism of Islamic and Jewish philosophy in the middle ages. Avicebron or Avicebrol (Solomon Ibn Gabirol), 1020–70, born in Malaga. The great Moses Maimonides, born in Cordova in 1135. He died in Egypt in 1204.

5. Centers of Muslim culture in Spain. Cordova was the Bagdad of the west. The ninth and tenth centuries were the periods of its greatest bloom. The famous library of Al Hakam in Cordova in the tenth century. Seville became the center of luxurious life especially after the decline of Cordova. Toledo was a famous seat of learning. Even before its capture by the Christians in 1085 it had been a center of intellectual influence upon Latin Christendom. The higher schools in these centers.

6. The natural sciences and medicine among the Muslims. The experimental method. Achievements in astronomy, chemistry, physics (especially optics), geography. Inventions and discoveries. See outline XXI.

7. Mathematics. The vexed question of the so-called Arabic numerals and their introduction into Latin Christendom. The zero. Algebra and geometry.

8. The great Aristotelians among the Muslims. Alfarabi (died 950) of Bagdad. Avicenna, 980–1036, born in the district of Bokhara. Averroes, born in Cordova in 1126; died in 1198. Muslim respect for the teaching of Aristotle. Efforts to reconcile the dogma of Islam with Muslim philosophy based on Aristotle and on Neo-Platonic sources.

9. The question of freedom of thought and the warfare between theology and science in Islam. Orthodox theologians and mystics among the Muslims. Gazali (Algazel), 1058–1111.

10. Muslim literature and art in Sicily and Spain. Princely patrons. Decorative art and architecture. The great Mosque (Mesquita) at Cordova (begun in the eighth century); the Giralda (twelfth century) and Alcazar (thirteenth century) of Seville; and the Alhambra of Granada (fourteenth century). The old palace in Palermo.

11. Influence of Muslim culture in Latin Christendom. Early Christian scholars in close touch with Muslim learning: Gerbert (pope Sylvester II, 999–1003); Constantinus Africanus (eleventh century), and Adelard of Bath and Daniel Morley from England (twelfth century). Danger of ascribing too much to Muslim influence in the Latin west and of minimizing the Byzantine influence. See outline XV.

12. Rather sudden decline of Muslim culture in the eleventh and twelfth centuries when Latin Christendom witnessed a remarkable outburst of intellectual activity which laid the basis of modern civilization.

B. Special Recommendations for Reading

Brief general surveys. There is very little satisfactory literature on this subject. An immense amount of research work must still be done, especially in the Arabic sources, before the true character of Muslim culture in the middle ages can be stated. R. Altamira, *Historia de España*, 3rd edition, 1, 261–300. Lavisse et Rambaud, *Histoire générale*, I, 773–93. J. W. Draper, *Intellectual development of Europe*, ch. xiii. Helmolt, *History of the world*, III, 332–42, 347–49. E. Renan, *L'Islamisme et la science*, Paris, 1893. G. F. Moore, *History of religions*, II, 386–521. (See bibliography.) G. Diercks, *Die arabische Cultur in mittelalterlichen Spaniens*, Hamburg, 1887.

Longer accounts. C. Huart, *Histoire des Arabes*, II, chs. xxxv–xxxvi. G. Le Bon, *La civilisation des Arabes*, Paris, 1884, especially 465–632. S. P. Scott, *History of the Moorish empire in Europe*, especially vol. III. H. Suter, *Die Araber als Vermittler der Wissenschaften in ihrem Übergang vom Orient in den Occident*, 2nd edition, Aarau, 1897.

Geography. H. Lammens, *Le berceau de l'Islam*, Rome, 1914. G. Le Strange, *The lands of the eastern caliphate*, Cambridge, 1905.

Muslim philosophy. T. de Boer, *Geschichte der Philosophie im Islam*, Stuttgart, 1901; English translation by E. Jones, *The history of philosophy in Islam*, London, 1903. M. de Wulf, *History of medieval philosophy*, 226–39. I. Goldziher, "Die islamische und die jüdische Philosophie," *Kultur der Gegenwart*, I, ch. v (1909), 45–77.

Medieval Jewish philosophy. I. HUSIK, *A history of medieval Jewish philosophy*, New York, 1916. See also nos. **850, 862–868.** A good book on Jewish philosophy is no. **105,** by MALTER, vol. IX. H. A. WOLFSON, *Crescas' critique of Aristotle*, Cambridge, 1929.

Muslim art in Spain. A. F. CALVERT, *The Alhambra: being a brief record of the Arabian conquest of the Peninsula with a particular account of the Mohammedan architecture and decoration*, London, 1907; *Moorish remains in Spain: being a brief record of the Arabian conquest of the Peninsula with a particular account of the Mohammedan architecture and decoration in Cordova, Seville, and Toledo*, London, 1906 (contain remarkable illustrations). C. G. HARTLEY (Mrs. W. GALLICHAN), *Moorish cities in Spain*, London, 1906, is a brief readable sketch with illustrations.

C. BIBLIOGRAPHY

General books. See outlines IX and XXXIV in part II. See also literature on the Normans in Sicily under outline XX in part II. For all that concerns the natural sciences see outline XXI.

General surveys. A. BEBEL, *Die mohammedanisch-arabische Kulturperiode*, 2nd edition, Stuttgart, 1889. C. H. BECKER, *Vom Werden und Wesen der islamischen Welt*, Leipzig, 1924. C. M. DOUGHTY, *Travels in Arabia Deserta*, 2 vols., London, Cambridge, 1921. (A reprint of the London edition of 1888, which is now unobtainable.) J. W. DRAPER, *Intellectual development of Europe*, ch. XIII. F. DIERKS, *Die Araber im Mittelalter und ihr Einfluss auf die Cultur Europas*, 2nd edition, Leipzig, 1882. S. GUYARD, *La civilisation musulmane*, Paris, 1884. (Léçon d'ouverture au Collège de France.) J. HELL, *Die Kultur der Araber*, Leipzig, 1909; new edition, 1919. (Wissenschaft und Bildung, 64.) English translation by S. KHUDA BUKHSH, Cambridge, 1926. E. HUNGERFORD, "The rise of Arab learning," *Atlantic monthly*, LVIII (1886), 539–55, 817–29. A. v. KREMER, *Culturgeschichtliche Streifzüge auf dem Gebiete des Islams*, Leipzig, 1873; English translation by S. KHUDA BUKHSH, *Contributions to the history of Islamic civilisation*, Calcutta, 1905; *Culturgeschichte des Orients unter den Chalifen*, 2 vols., Vienna, 1875–77; partial English translation by S. KHUDA BUKHSH, *The Orient under the Caliphs*, Calcutta, 1920. H. LAMMENS, *L'Islame, croyances et institutions*, Beirut, 1926. E. W. LANE, *Arabian society in the middle ages*, edited by S. LANE-POOLE, London, 1883 (in reality the notes to his translation of *The Arabian nights*). G. LE BON, *La civilisation des Arabes*, Paris, 1884 (especially pages 465–632). J. MANN, *The Jews in Egypt and Palestine under the Fatimid Caliphs*, vol. Iff. Oxford, 1920ff. J. RIBERO Y TARRAGÓ, *Disertaciones y opuscúlos*, Madrid, 1928. W. R. SMITH, *Kinship and marriage in early Arabia*, revised edition, London, 1903. *The thousand and one nights* (*Alf Laila wa Laila*), the translations of either LANE, or PAYNE.

Geography. IBN BATŪTAH, *Voyages d'ibn Batoutah, texte, accompagné d'une traduction par G. Defrêmery et le Dr. B. R. Sanguinetti*, 4 vols., Paris, 1874–79. G. FERRAND, *Voyage du marchand arabe Sulayman en Inde et en Chine*, Paris, 1922 (written in 851). H. LAMMENS, *La Mecque à la veille* *de l'Hégire*, Beirut, 1924. G. LE STRANGE, *Bagdad under the Abbasid Caliphate*, Cambridge, 1900; *Palestine under the Moslems*, London, 1890. K. MILLER, *Mappae arabicae: arabische Welt- und Länderkarten des 9–13 Jahrhunderts in arabischer Ürschrift, lateinischer Transkription und Übertragung, in neuzeitliche Kartenskizzen, mit einleitenden Texten*, Stuttgart, 1926ff.

The Qur'ân. The best translations of the *Qur'ân* are by E. H. PALMER, *Koran*, 2 vols., Oxford, 1880 (MÜLLER'S *Sacred books of the East*, vols. VI and IX); *El-kor'ân: or Korân, translated from the Arabic, the suras arranged in chronological order*, with notes and index, by J. M. RODWELL, 2nd edition, London, 1876 (also reprinted in Everyman's library, New York, 1909); *Koran, commonly called the Alkoran of Mohammed*, translated by G. SALE. 2 vols., London, 1825; latest edition by E. M. WHERRY, *A comprehensive commentary on the Qur'ân: comprising Sale's translation and preliminary discourse*, with additional notes and emendations, 4 vols., London, 1896 (Trübner's oriental series). There is also a small edition of the translation of PALMER, published in the World's Classics series, 1928, with a useful introduction by R. A. NICHOLSON. Extracts from the *Qur'ân* have been edited with a very good introduction by S. LANE-POOLE, under the title, *The Speeches and table talk of the prophet Mohammed*, New York, 1882, reprinted 1905, 1915. See also *Selections from the Kurân*, edited by E. W. LANE, London, 1879; and the article "Qurân" in the XI and XII edition of the *Ency. Brit.*

Commentaries on the Qur'ân. BENATTAR, CÉSAR, and others, *L'esprit liberal du Coran*, Paris, 1905. W. EICKMANN, *Die Angelologie und Dämonologie des Korans im Vergleich zu der Engel- und Geisterlehre der Heiligen Schrift*, New York and Leipzig, 1908. J. HOROVITZ, *Jewish proper names and derivatives in the Koran* (Hebrew union college Annual, vol. II, 145–227); *Koranische Untersuchungen*, Berlin and Leipzig, 1926 (Studien zur Geschichte und Kultur des islamischen Orients, Heft IV). D. S. MARGOLIOUTH, *The early development of Mohammedanism*, London, 1914 (Hibbert lectures). W. MUIR, *The Coran: its composition and teachings*, London, 1878. T. NÖLDEKE, *Geschichte des Qorâns*, Göttingen, 1860; new edition, revised by. F. SCHWALLY, vol. I, Leipzig, 1909. E. SELL, *The historical development of the Qurân*, London, 1905. I. SCHAPIRO, *Die haggadischen Elemente im erzählenden Teil des Korans*, Leipzig, 1907.

Muslim law. I. GOLDZIHER, *Muhammedanische Studien*, Halle, 2 vols., 1889–90; vol. II. *Vorlesungen über den Islam*, Heidelberg, 1910; French translation by F. ARIN, *Le dogme et la loi de l'Islam*, Paris, 1920; *Die Zahiriten*, Leipzig, 1884. A. G. GUILLAUME, *The traditions of Islam. An introduction to the study of Hadith literature*, Oxford, 1924. C. S. HURGRONJE, *Geschriften betreffende het mohammedaansche recht* (Verspreide geschriften, deel II). D. B. MACDONALD, *The development of Muslim theology, jurisprudence, and constitutional theory.* M. VAN BERCHEM, *La propiêtê territoriale et l'impôt foncier sous les premiers califes*, Geneva, 1886. R. ROBERTS, *Social laws of the Qurân*, London, 1925. A. L. KISMET, *A study in tolerance as practiced by Mohammed and his immediate successors*, New York, 1927.

Nestorius. E. LOOFS, *Nestorius and his place in the history of Christian doctrine*, New York, 1914, will serve as an introduction to the history of the Nestorian Christians, who did much to introduce western civilization into the Muslim world.

Muslim theology and philosophy (Note: It is impossible to separate these two subjects). T. W. ARNOLD, *The preaching of Islam: A history of the propagation of the Muslim faith*, Westminster, 1896; 2nd edition, revised and enlarged, London, 1913. M. ASÍN PALACIOS, *La escatologia musulmana en la Divina Comedia*, Madrid, 1919; English translation by Sunderland, London, 1926. C. H. BECKER, *Christentum und Islam*, Tübingen, 1907; English translation by H. J. CHAYTOR, *Christianity and Islam*, New York, 1909. R. BELL, *The origin of Islam in its Christian environment*, London, 1926. T. J. DE BOER, *Geschichte der Philosophie im Islam*, English translation by E. R. JONES, *The history of philosophy in Islam*. CARRA DE VAUX, *Le Mahométisme, le génie sémitique et le génie aryen dans l'Islam*, Paris, 1898, *Les penseurs de l'Islam*, Paris, 1921–26. F. DIETERICI, *Die Philosophie der Araber im X Jahrhundert*, Berlin, 1861. GAUDEFROY-DEMOMBYNES, *Le pêlerinage à la Mekke*, Paris, 1923. I. GOLDZIHER, *Muhammedanische Studien; Vorlesungen über den Islam;* French translation by F. ARIN, *Le dogme et la loi de l'Islam;* an article on "Muslim Theology" in *Kultur der Gegenwart*, I, III, 1. C. GÜTERBOCK, *Der Islam im Lichte der byzantinischen Polemik*, Berlin, 1912. M. HARTMANN, *Fünf Vorträge über den Islam*, Leipzig, 1912. J. HELL, *Von Mohammed bis Ghazali: Quellentexte aus dem Arabischen übersetzt und eingeleitet*, Jena, 1915; 2nd edition, 1923. M. J. HORTEN, *Die Philosophie des Islams*, Munich, 1924 (Geschichte der Philosophie in Einzeldarstellungen); *Die philosophischen Systeme der speculativen Theologen in Islam*, Bonn, 1912. A. v. KREMER, *Geschichte der herrschenden Ideen des Islams*, Leipzig, 1868. H. LAMMENS, *L'Islam: croyances et institutions.* D. B. MACDONALD, *Aspects of Islam*, New York, 1916; *The development of Muslim theology, jurisprudence, and constitutional theory*, New York, 1902; *The religious attitude and life in Islam*, Chicago, 1909. D. S. MARGOLIOUTH, *Early development of Mohammedanism*, London, 1911 (Home university library). A. MEZ, *Die Renaissance des Islams*, Heidelberg, 1922. MOHAMMAD ABDOU, *Rissalat al-tawhid. Exposé de la religion musulmane, tr. par B. Michel et Moustapha abdel Razik*, Paris, 1925. A. MÜLLER, *Die griechischen Philosophen in der arabischen Überlieferung*, Halle, 1873. D. O'LEARY, *Arabic thought and its place in history*, London, 1922. A. PERIER, *Yahyā ben Adī: un philosophe arabe chrétien du XIe siècle*, Paris, 1920. J. POLLAK, "Entwicklung der arabischen und jüdischen Philosophie im Mittelalter," *Archiv für Geschichte der Philosophie*, XVII (1903–04), 196–236, 433–59. J. B. RÜLING, *Beiträge zur Eschatologie des Islams*, Leipzig, 1895. C. SAUTER, "Die peripatetische Philosophie bei den Syrern und Arabern," *Archiv für Geschichte der Philosophie*, XVII (1903–04), 516–33. M. DE WULF, *Histoire de la philosophie médiévale.*

Mystics and fraternities. A. LE CHATELIER, *Confréries musulmanes du Hedjaz*, Paris, 1887. R. A. NICHOLSON, *Studies in Islamic mysticism*, Cambridge, 1921; *Mystics of Islam*, London, 1914. L'ABBÉ ROUQUETTE, *Les* *sociétés secrètes chez les Musulmans*, Paris, 1899. T. H. WEIR, *Shaikhs of Morocco*, London, 1904.

Magic, superstition, folk-lore. E. DOUTTÉ, *Magie et religion dans l'Afrique du nord*, Algiers, 1909. D. B. MACDONALD, *The religious attitude and life in Islam.* M. REINAUD, *Description des monumens musulmans du cabinet de M. le duc de Blacas*, 2 vols., Paris, 1828. S. M. ZWEMER, *Influence of animism on Islam*, New York, 1920. See also Article *Sihr*, by D. B. MACDONALD in **120.**

Philosophy in Spain. M. ASÍN PALACIOS, *Abenházam de Córdoba y su historia de las ideas religiosas*, 3 vols., Madrid, 1927–29; *Abenmassara y su escuela*, Madrid, 1914.

Jewish philosophy. I. GOLDZIHER, "Die islamische und die jüdische Philosophie," *Kultur der Gegenwart*, I (1909), ch. v, 45–77. I. HUSIK, *A history of medieval Jewish philosophy*, New York, 1916. S. MUNK, *Mélanges de philosophie juive et arabe*, Paris, 1857–59; 2nd edition, 1927.

Special philosophers. *1. AVEMPACE:* M. ASÍN PALACIOS, *El filósofo zaragozano Avempace.* (Rev. de Arágon, 1901). *2. AVERROES:* AVERROES, *Philosophie und Theologie von Averroes*, translated by M. J. MÜLLER, Munich, 1875. L. GAUTHIER, *La théorie d'ibn Rochd (Averroes) sur les rapports de la religion et la philosophie*, Paris, 1909. M. HORTEN, *Die Hauptlehren des Averroes nach seiner Schrift: Die Wiederlegung des Gazali*, Bonn, 1913; *Texte zu dem Streite zwischen Glauben und Wissen im Islam: die Lehre vom Propheten und der Offenbarung bei den islamitischen Philosophen Farabi, Avicenna und Averroes*, Bonn, 1913. *3. AVICEBRON:* C. BÄUMKER, *Avencebrolis fons vitae ex arabico in latinum translatus ab Johanne Hispano et Domenico Gundissalio*, Münster, 1895, part I, nos. 2–4, of no. **826.** IBN GABIROL (AVICEBRON): *Improvement of moral qualities*, translated by Stephen Wise, New York, 1902. M. WITTMANN, *Die Stellung Avencebrol's (ibn Gebirol's) im Entwicklungsgang der arabischen Philosophie*, Münster, 1905, part V, no. 1 of no. **826**. *4. AVICENNA:* L. CARRA DE VAUX, *Avicenne*, Paris, 1900. *5. GHAZALI:* M. ASÍN PALACIOS, *Algazel: dogmatica, moral, ascetica*, Saragossa, 1901. (Collección de estudios árabes, VI). L. CARRA DE VAUX, *Gazali*, Paris, 1902. AL-GHAZZALI, *Worship in Islam, being a translation with commentary and introduction of al-Ghazzali's Book of the Ihya on the worship*, by E. E. Calverly, MADEAS, ALLAHABAD, etc., 1925. *6. IBN ARABI:* M. ASÍN PALACIOS, *El mistico murciano Abenarabi*, 4 vols., Madrid, 1925–28, *La psicología según Mohidín Abenarabi*, Paris, 1906. *7. IBN TUFAIL:* L. GAUTHIER, *Ibn Thofail, sa vie, ses oeuvres*, Paris, 1909. *8. MAIMONIDES:* W. BACHER, and others, *Moses ben Maimon: sein Leben, seine Werke und sein Einfluss*, 2 vols., Leipzig, 1908–14. L. G. LÉVY, *Maimonide*, Paris, 1911. MAIMONIDES, *Le guide des égarés: traité de théologie et de philosophie, par Moïse ben Maimoun, dit Maëmonide, publié pour la première fois dans l'originale arabe et accompagné d'une traduction française* by S. Munk, 3 vols., Paris, 1856–66; *Guide to the perplexed, by Moses ben Maimon, called Maimonides*, translated by M. Friedländer, 3 vols., London, 1885; 2nd ed., 1 vol., London, 1928. J. MÜNZ, *Moses ben Maimon (Maimonides), sein Leben und* *seine Werke*, Frankfort, 1912. **9**. *AL–FARABI:* AL-FARABI, *Alfarabi's philosophische Abhandlungen aus Londener, Leidener und Berliner Handschriften*, edited by DIETERICI, Leyden, 1890 (German translation, 1892). M. STEINSCHNEIDER, *Al-Farabi, des arabischen Philosophen, Leben und Schriften* (in Mémoires de l'Académie impériale des sciences de St. Petersbourg, series VII, vol. XIII (1869), 4).

Arabic literature. C. BROCKELMANN, *Geschichte der arabischen Literatur*, 2 vols. and index, Berlin, 1898–1902; *Geschichte der arabischen Literatur*, Leipzig, 1901 (Die Literaturen des Ostens, v. VI, part 2). E. G. BROWNE, *Literary history of Persia*, 4 vols., New York, 1902–24. H. A. R. GIBB, *Arabic literature, an introduction*, London, Oxford, 1926. E. J. W. GIBB, *History of Ottoman poetry*, 6 vols., London, 1900–09. M. J. DE GOEJE, "Geschichte der arabischen Literatur," *Kultur der Gegenwart, I, VII*, 5. C. HUART, *Littérature arabe*, Paris, 1902; 2nd edition, 1912; English translation by LADY MARY LOYD, *A history of Arabic literature*, London, 1903. C. LYALL, *Ancient Arabic poetry*, London, 1885. MASUDI (ALI IBN HUSAIN, AL-MAS'UDI), *Les prairies d'or. Texte et traduction par C. Barbier de Meynarde et Pavet de Courteille*, Paris, 1859–77. R. A. NICHOLSON, *Eastern poetry and prose*, Cambridge, 1922; *Studies in Islamic poetry*, Cambridge, 1921; *A literary history of the Arabs*, London, 1907; 2nd edition, 1930. I. RIZZI, *Letteratura araba*, Milan, 1903 (Manuels Hoepli). S. SINGER, *Arabische und europäische Poesie im Mittelalter*, Berlin, 1918. *Thousand and one nights* (*Alf Laila wa Laila*) in the translation of PAYNE OR LANE.

Spanish Arabic literature. R. DOZY, and W. ENGELMANN, *Glossaire des mots espagnols dérivés de l'arabe*, 2nd. edition, Leyden, 1869. A. GONZÁLEZ PALENCIA, *Historia de la literatura arábigo-española*, Barcelona, 1928. J. HURTADO and A. GONZÁLEZ PALENCIA, *Historia de la literatura española*, 2nd edition, Madrid, 1925. MUHAMMED SOULAH, *Ibrahim ibn Sahl, poète musulman d'Espagne*, Algiers, 1914–17. A. F. v. SCHACK, *Poesie und Kunst der Araber in Spanien und Sizilien*, 2 vols., 2nd edition, Stuttgart, 1877, Spanish translation by J. VALERA, 3 vols., Madrid, 1893. J. C. L. S. DE SISMONDI, *Literature of the south of Europe*.

Muslim science. *1. GENERAL:* DANNEMANN, *Die Naturwissenschaften*. E. RENAN, *L'Islamisme et la science*, Paris, 1893. G. SARTON, *Introduction to the history of science*, vol. I, Baltimore, 1927. E. STRUNZ, *Geschichte der Naturwissenschaften*. H. SUTER, *Die Araber als Vermittler der Wissenschaften in ihrem Übergang vom Orient in den Occident*. E. WIEDEMANN, "Ueber die Naturwissenschaften bei den Arabern," *Sammlung gemeinverständlicher wissenschaftlichen Vorträge*, series II, vol. V, Hamburg, 1890. *2. ASTRONOMY:* O. SCHIRMER, *Studien zur Astronomie der Araber*, Erlangen, 1926. J. J. SEDILLOT, *Mémoires sur les instruments astronomiques des Arabes*, Paris, 1841–45. E. WIEDEMANN, "Zur Geschichte des Kompasses bei den Arabern," *Verhandlungen der deutschen physikalischen Gesellschaft zu Berlin*, IX (1907), 764–73. *3. CHEMISTRY:* AVICENNA, *Avicennae De congelatione et conglutinationis lapidum, being sections of the Kitab al-Shifa. The Latin and Arabic texts edited with an English translation of the latter, with* *critical notes*, Paris, 1927. M. BERTHELOT and M. HOUDAS, *La chimie au moyen âge*, vol. IV, *L'alchimie arabe*, Paris, 1893. E. DARMSTAEDTER, *Die Alchemie des Geber*, Berlin, 1922. MUHAMMAD B. AHMAD AL-'IRAQI, *Kitab al 'ilm al-muktasab fi zira'at adh-dhahab*, translated by E. J. HOLMYARD, Paris, 1923. J. RUSKA, *Arabische Alchimisten*, Heidelberg, 1924. E. WIEDEMANN, "Zur Chemie bei den Arabern," *S.B. der physikalische-medizinischen Societät in Erlangen*, XLIII (1911); "Die Alchemie bei den Arabern," *Journal für praktische Chemie*, *LXXVI* (1907) 85–87; 105–23.

Mathematics. W. W. R. BALL, *A short account of the history of mathematics*, 4th edition, London, 1908, 144–63; translated by L. FREUND, *Histoire des mathématiques*, 2 vols., Paris, 1906, I, 152–71. M. CANTOR, *Vorlesungen über Geschichte der Mathematik*, 4 vols., 3rd edition, Leipzig, 1898–1908, I, chs. XXXII–XXXVII. S. GÜNTHER, *Geschichte der Mathematik*, I, Leipzig, 1908, chs. XII–XIII. F. CAJORI, *A history of mathematics*, New York, 1895 (2nd edition, 1919), 100–17. H. SUTER, "Die Mathematiker und Astronomen der Araber und ihre Werke," *Abhandlungen zur Geschichte der mathematischen Wissenschaften*, Leipzig, X (1900), also XIV (1902), 155–85. L. JORDAN, "Materialien zur Geschichte der arabischen Zahlzeichen in Frankreich," *Archiv zur Kulturgeschichte*, III (1905), 155–95, contends that the so-called Arabic numerals are of Egyptian origin. A. HUEMER, "Die Einführung des dt.-arab. Zahlensystems in Frankreich und Deutschland," *Zeitschrift für die österreichischen Gymnasien*, 1904. M. SÉDILLOT, *Matériaux pour servir à l'histoire des sciences mathématiques chez les Grecs et les Orientaux*, 2 vols., Paris, 1845–49. J. RUSKA, *Zur ältesten arabischen Algebra und Rechenkunst*, Heidelberg, 1917. J. A. SÁNCHEZ PÉREZ, *Biografías de matemáticos árabes que florecieron en España*, Madrid, 1921. M. STEINSCHNEIDER, "Mathematik bei den Juden," *Bibliotheca mathematica*, 1893ff.

Muslim education. J. RIBERA, *La enseñanza entre los Musulmanes españoles*, Saragossa, 1893; *Bibliófilos y bibliotecas en la España musulmana*, 2nd edition, Saragossa, 1896. K. A. SCHMID, in *Geschichte der Erziehung*, II, part I, pp. 549–611. F. WÜSTENFELD, *Die Academien der Araber und ihre Lehrer*, Göttingen, 1837. D. HANEBERG, *Abhandlungen über das Schul- und Lehrwesen der Muhamedaner im Mittelalter*, Munich, 1850. G. FLÜGEL, *Die grammatischen Schulen der Araber, nach den Quellen bearbeitet*, part I, Leipzig, 1862 (Abhandlungen für die Kunde des Morgenlandes, vol. II, 4).

Muslim historiography. F. WÜSTENFELD, "Die Geschichtschreiber der Araber und ihre Werke," *Abh. Göttingen Acad.*, XXVIII (1881); XXIX (1882). F. PONS BOIGUES, *Ensayo bio-bibliográfico sobre los historiadores y geógrafos arábigo-españoles*, Madrid, 1898. DE GOEJE'S article, *Tabari*, in Ency. Brit.

Muslim art. *Monumentos arquitectónicos de España*, Madrid, 1877. H. SALADIN and G. MIGEON, *Manuel d'art musulman*, 2 vols., Paris, 1907. M. JUNGHÄNDEL, *Die Baukunst Spaniens in ihren hervorragenden Werken*, Dresden, 1889–93. W. and G. MARCAIS, *Les monuments arabes de Tlemçen*, Paris, 1903. B. and ELLEN M. WHISHAW, *Arabic Spain: sidelights on her history and art*, London, 1912. A. GAYET, *L'art arabe*, Paris [n. d.]. C.

UHDE, *Baudenkmäler in Spanien und Portugal*, Berlin, 1889–93. J. FRANZ-PASCHA, *Die Baukunst des Islam*, Darmstadt, 1896. R. BORRMANN and J. NEUWIRTH, *Geschichte der Baukunst*, I, 319–75. See also other general histories of art under outline XXVII. H. GLÜCK et E. DIEZ, *Die Kunst des Islam*, Berlin, 1925. G. MIGEON, *Les arts musulmanes*, Brussels, 1926.

Bibliographies. Short serviceable bibliographies will be found in MACDONALD, *Muslim theology*, 358–67; NICHOLSON, *A literary history of the Arabs*, 471–80; G. LE BON, *La civilisation des Arabes*, 679–86. ALTAMIRA, *Historia de España*, IV, 3rd edition, 600–08. For detailed information consult V. C. CHAUVIN, *Bibliographie des ouvrages arabes ou relatifs aux Arabes, publiés dans l'Europe chrétienne de 1810 à 1885*, Liége and Leipzig, 1892–1922; and *Orientalische Bibliographie*, edited by A. MÜLLER and others, Berlin, 1887ff. The catalogs of Arabic manuscripts in the British Museum; and in the State Library at Berlin—particularly the latter—are most useful sources for bibliographical and biographical materials.

D. B. MACDONALD.
W. M. RANDALL.

XI. EVE OF A NEW ERA IN MEDIEVAL CULTURE. THE ELEVENTH CENTURY

A. OUTLINE

1. The very sharp contrast usually drawn between the tenth and the eleventh centuries due largely to the legend of the year 1000.

2. Rapid growth of cathedral and monastery schools, especially in France. The rise of the famous schools of Chartres. Bishop Fulbert of Chartres (died 1028). Bishop Ivo of Chartres, the famous canonist (died 1115). The importance of the monastery of Bec, where both Lanfranc and Anselm lived before they became archbishops of Canterbury. Odo of Tournai (died 1113).

3. The conflict between faith and learning, authority and reason, because of the religious revival and the quickening intellectual life. Lanfranc, born ca. 1005 in Pavia, and died in 1089 as archbishop of Canterbury. Peter Damian (c. 1007–72), the hermit of Ravenna. Othloh of St. Emmeran, of Regensburg (died about 1073). Manegold of Lautenbach (died after 1103).

4. Anselm of Canterbury, the "Father of scholasticism." Born in 1033 in Aosta in Piedmont, abbot of Bec, 1078–93, and archbishop of Canterbury, 1093–1109. The meaning of Anselm's motto, "Nequo enim quaero intelligere, ut credam; sed *credo, ut intelligam.* Nam et hoc credo, quia nisi credidero non intelligam."—*Proslogium*, prooemium, c. 1, MIGNE, CLVIII, 227.

5. Champions of rationalism in the eleventh century. Berengar of Tours (999–1088), a product of the schools of Chartres, and his position on transubstantiation. Roscelin of Compiègne (died 1106). His trial at the council of Soissons in 1093 on a charge of tritheism.

6. Byzantine influences in the west in the eleventh century. Michael Psellos, 1018–79, the famous savant of Constantinople. Interest in Greek in the west.

7. The end of the eleventh century is the most important turning point in the intellectual history of the middle ages.

B. Special Recommendations for Reading

General surveys. Taylor, *Mediaeval mind*, I, chs. xi–xiii. Sandys, *Classical scholarship*, I, ch. xxvii. Lavisse, *Histoire de France*, II, part II, 184–98. Grabmann, *Geschichte der scholastischen Methode*, I, 215–339. Reuter, *Geschichte der religiösen Aufklärung im Mittelalter*, I, 85–136. Harnack, *Lehrbuch der Dogmengeschichte*, 4th edition, III, 363–67, 379–410 (vol. VI, 32–36, 45–83 in the English translation, *A history of dogma*). *C.M.H.*, V, chs. xxii–xxiii.

Schools of Chartres. Clerval, *Les écoles de Chartres*, 30–142. R. L. Poole, "The masters of the schools at Paris and Chartres in John of Salisbury's time," *E.H.R.*, XXXV (1920), 321–42.

Anselm. The best short account is in C. C. J. Webb, *Studies in the history of natural religion*, part III, no. 2. Grabmann, *Geschichte*, I, 258–339. R. W. Church, *Life of St. Anselm*, New York, 1905. A. C. Welch, *Anselm and his work*, New York, 1901. J. M. Rigg, *S. Anselm of Canterbury*, London, 1896. M. Rule, *Life and times of St. Anselm of Canterbury*, London, 1883.

Michael Psellos. Krumbacher, *Geschichte der byzantinischen Literatur*, 2nd edition, 433–44 (see also 79–80). Sandys, *Classical scholarship*, I, ch. xxiii. C. Zervos, *Un philosophe néoplatonicien du XIe siècle, Michel Psellos: sa vie, son oeuvre, ses luttes philosophiques, son influence*, Paris, 1920 (Diss.).

Original sources. St. Anselm, *Proslogium*, etc., translated by S. N. Deane, Chicago, 1903. French translation of *Monologium* and *Proslogium*, by L. F. H. Bouchitté, *Le rationalisme chrétien à la fin du XIe siècle*, Paris, 1842.

C. Bibliography

General books. The general histories of philosophy, nos. **822–35,** are especially useful. Among the books on the church, the encyclopaedias, nos. **104–14,** and the histories of dogma, nos. **472–78,** are the most serviceable. See also outline XV, of part II.

General accounts. Pfister, *Etudes sur le règne de Robert le Pieux*, 300–50, to be followed by Fliche, *Le règne de Philippe Ier roi de France (1060–1108)*. A. Dresdner, *Kultur- und Sittengeschichte der italienischen Geistlichkeit.* J. A. Endres, "Ueber den Ursprung und die Entwickelung der scholastischen Lehrmethode," *Philosophisches Jahrbuch*, II, 1. Schmid, *Geschichte der Erziehung*, I, part I, 232–58. U. Berlière, "Ecoles claustrales au moyen âge," *Bulletin de la classe des lettres, Académie royale de Belgique*, 1921, 12.

Ivo of Chartres. P. Fournier, "Les collections canoniques attribuées à Yves de Chartres," *B.E.C.*, LVII (1896), 645–98; LVIII (1897), 26–77,

293–326, 410–44, 624–76 (also printed separately, Paris, 1897). See also his "Yves de Chartres et le droit canonique," *R.Q.H.*, LXIII (1898), 51–98, 384–405. A. FOUCAULT, *Essai sur Yves de Chartres d'après sa correspondance*, Chartres, 1883. These letters have been translated into French, *Lettres de saint Ives, évêque de Chartres*, traduites et annotées, by L. MERLET, Chartres, 1885. L. SCHMIDT, *Der heilige Ivo, Bischof von Chartres*, Vienna, 1911.

Bec. A. PORÉE, *L'abbaye du Bec et ses écoles (1045–1790)*, Paris, 1892; "L'école du Bec et Saint Anselme," *Revue de philosophie*, XV(1909), 618–38.

Reason versus faith. J. A. ENDRES, "Die Dialektiker und ihre Gegner in 11 Jahrhundert," *Philosophiches Jahrbuch*, XIX (1906), 20–33. E. BEURLIER, "Les rapports de la raison et de la foi dans la philosophie de Saint Anselme," *Revue de philosophie*, XV (1909), 692–723. C. MOLINIER, "L'hérésie et la persécution au XIe siècle," *Revue des Pyrénées*, IV (1894).

Peter Damian. BIRON, *St. Pierre Damien.* J. A. ENDRES, *Petrus Damiani und die weltliche Wissenschaft*, Beiträge zur Geschichte der Philosophie des Mittelalters, VIII (1910), no. 3. L. KUHN, *Petrus Damiani und seine Anschauungen über Staat und Kirche*, Karlsruhe, 1913 (Diss.). J. P. WHITNEY, "Peter Damiani and Humbert," *The Cambridge historical journal*, I (1923–25), 225–48.

Othloh of St. Emmeran. J. A. ENDRES, "Otloh's von St. Emmeran Verhältniss zu den freien Künsten, insbesondere zur Dialektik," *Philosophisches Jahrbuch*, XVII (1904), 44–52.

Manegold of Lautenbach. J. A. ENDRES, "Manegold von Lautenbach *modernorum magister magistrorum*," *Hist. Jahrbuch*, XXV (1904), 168–76. See also STEAD on p. 212.

Lanfranc. J. DE CROZALS, *Lanfranc archévêque de Cantorbéry: sa vie, son enseignement, sa politique*, Paris, 1877. N. TAMASSIA, "Lanfranc arcivescovo di Canterbury e la scuola pavese," *Mélanges Fitting*, vol. II. P. MOIRAGHI, *Lanfranco da Pavia*, Padua, 1889. A. J. MACDONALD, *Lanfranc, a study of his life, work, and writing*, Oxford, 1926.

Anselm. E. C. E. DOMET DE VORGES, *Saint Anselme*, Paris, 1901; "Le milieu philosophique à l'époque de Saint Anselme," *Revue de philosophie*, XV (1909), 605–17. A. DUFOURCQ, "Saint Anselme: son temps, son rôle," *ibid.*, 593–604. L. VIGNA, *San Anselmo filosofo*, Milan, 1899. P. RAGEY, *Histoire de St. Anselme*, 2 vols., Paris, 1890. A. VAN WEDDINGEN, *Essai critique sur la philosophie de St. Anselme de Cantorbéry*, Brussels, 1875. E. DÜMMLER, *Anselm der Peripatetiker*, Halle, 1872. C. DE RÉMUSAT, *Saint Anselme de Cantorbéry*, Paris, 1853. The issue of December, 1909, of the *Revue de philosophie* was devoted entirely to Anselm on the occasion of the eighth centenary of his death.

Roscelin. F. PICAVET, *Roscelin philosophe et théologien d'après la légende et d'après l'histoire*, Paris, 1896; 2nd edition, 1911. ALDHOCH, "Roscelin und St. Anselme," *Philosophisches Jahrbuch* (1907), 422–56.

Berengar. R. HEURTEVENT, *Durand de Troarn et les origines de l'hérésie bérengarienne*, Paris, 1912. J. EBERSOLT, *Essai sur Bérenger de Tours et la* *controverse sacramentaire au XIe siècle*, Paris, 1903 (extract from the *Revue de l'histoire des religions*, XLVIII). J. SCHNITZER, *Berengar von Tours*, Munich, 1891. W. BROECKING, "Bischof Eusebius Bruno von Angers und Berengar von Tours," *Deutsche Zeitschrift für Geschichtswissenschaft*, XII (1895), 344.

Original sources. Most of the works of authors mentioned in this outline are to be found in no. **953.** *Berengarius Turonensis, oder eine Sammlung ihn betreffender Briefe*, edited by H. SUDENDORF, Gotha, 1850.

Bibliographies. The best bibliography will be found in the footnotes of GRABMANN, *Geschichte* I, 215–339.

PERIOD II. 1100–1300

XII. THE TWELFTH AND THIRTEENTH CENTURIES IN THE HISTORY OF CULTURE

A. Outline

1. The recent appreciation of the sudden advancement of civilization in western Europe beginning with the close of the eleventh century. Unfortunately this movement is now quite generally called "The twelfth century renaissance."

2. Relations of the culture of the twelfth and thirteenth centuries to that of the "renaissance" of the fourteenth and fifteenth centuries. See outline XXXIII in part II.

3. In the twelfth century the chief movements which mark the beginning of a new era in European history were well under way. See outline XIX of part II.

4. The importance of the thirteenth century in the history of culture. Recent glorification of that century. Comparison with the nineteenth century.

5. Importance of the medieval university as the embodiment of a new intellectual era.

6. France, especially northern France, was the center of this progressive movement which laid the basis of modern European civilization. In this era Paris was beginning to be the metropolis of Europe.

B. Special Recommendations for Reading

"The twelfth century renaissance." Haskins, *Renaissance of the twelfth century*. H. Rashdall, *The universities of Europe in the middle ages*, 2 vols., Oxford, 1895, I, ch. ii. Crump and Jacob, *Legacy*. Brown, *Achievement*, 121–240. Randall, *Making of the modern mind*, Bk. I. Munro and Sellery, *Medieval civilization*, 474–90. C. V. Langlois, *Questions d'histoire et d'enseignement*, Paris, 1902, 13–17. Norton, *Readings in the history of education: mediaeval universities*, 4–12. Grabmann, *Geschichte*, vol. II, Einleitung. G. Robert, *Les écoles et l'enseignement de la théologie pendant la première moitié du XIIe siècle*, Paris, 1909, 1–7. B. Groche, *Beiträge zur Geschichte einer Renaissancebewegung bei den deutschen Schriftstellern im 12 Jahrhundert*, Halle, 1910. Similar conditions in the Byzantine empire are described by K. Krumbacher, *Geschichte der byzantinischen Literatur*, 2nd edition, 15ff.

The thirteenth century. F. Harrison, *The meaning of history*, ch. v. Munro and Sellery, *Medieval civilization*, 458–73, "The intellectual movement of the thirteenth century," adapted from Lavisse, *Histoire de France*,

III, part II, 387–416. Lecoy de la Marche, *La chaire française au moyen âge, spécialement au XIIIe siècle*, Paris, 1886, 467–92. P. Mandonnet, "La crise scolaire au début du XIIIe siècle," *Revue d'histoire ecclésiastique*, XV (1914), 34–49. J. J. Walsh, *The thirteenth, greatest of centuries*, New York, 1907; 4th edition, reprinted with additions, 1912, is addressed to Roman Catholics and not to the world of scholarship as a whole.

XIII. THE CITY OF PARIS IN THE MIDDLE AGES

A. Outline

1. *Sacerdotium, Imperium, Studium.* During the twelfth and thirteenth centuries Paris was *par excellence* the seat of the *Studium.* Recent transformations in Paris which have almost entirely obliterated the monuments of the medieval city.

2. The site of Paris. Physical geography of the region. The Seine and its islands. St. Denis.

3. The development of Paris into the capital of France. Ancient Roman Lutetia. Caesar's presence there in 53 B.C. The revolt of the *Parisii.* Julian, "the Apostate," spent the winters 357–58 and 359–60 in Lutetia. Remains of Roman buildings, especially the *Thermae* (Hôtel de Cluny). Clovis made Paris his capital. During Merovingian times Paris remained the chief city in Neustria, and maintained its importance even under Charles Martel and Pepin. Charlemagne made Aix-la-Chapelle his capital. With the Norman siege in 885, and the elevation of Odo as king, Paris again became important. Since the accession of Hugh Capet in 987 Paris has been the capital of France.

4. Topography of medieval Paris. The grand divisions: Ville, Cité, Université. The Petit Pont and the Grand Pont. The wall of Philip Augustus begun about 1190.

5. The Cité. The cathedral Notre Dame de Paris. Parvis Notre Dame. Palais Episcopal. Hôtel-Dieu. Palais Royal. Sainte Chapelle. The Jewry.

6. The right bank of the Seine. Louvre. Grand Châtelet. St. Germain l'Auxerrois. St. Jacques. St. Martin des Champs. The Temple. St. Antoine. Place de Grêve.

7. The left bank. The Latin Quarter. St. Geneviève ("the hill"). Saint-Germain-des Prés. Pré-aux-Clercs. St. Victor. Les Bernardins. Houses of the Jacobins (Dominicans) and the Franciscans. St. Séverin. St. Julien le Pauvre. Petit Châtelet. Rue du Fouarre. The Sorbonne.

8. The business and social life of Paris in the middle ages.

9. Aspect of Paris in the time of Abelard and William of Champeaux, at the beginning of the twelfth century.

B. Special Recommendations for Reading

Paris as an historic city. Harrison, *The meaning of history*, 368–436. G. Monod, "Le rôle de Paris dans la France du moyen âge," *R.H.*, CXIX (1915), 77–85.

The site of Paris. LAVISSE, *Histoire de France*, I, part I, 124–43. L. GALLOIS, "The origin and growth of Paris," *Geographical review*, XIII (1923), 345–67.

General accounts. M. POËTE, *L'enfance de Paris*, Paris, 1908, chs. IX–XIII; "Les sources de l'histoire de Paris et les historiens de Paris," *Revue bleue*, 5th series, IV (1905), 657–60, 693–95, which are superseded by M. POËTE, *Une vie de cité: Paris de sa naissance à nos jours*, vol. I, *La jeunesse, des origines aux temps modernes*, Paris, 1924, vol. II, *La cité de la renaissance, du milieu du XVe à la fin du XVIe siècle*, Paris, 1927, *Album*, 1925. T. OKEY, *The story of Paris*, London, 1906 (Mediaeval towns). P. CORNU, *Histoire de Paris*, I, *Paris depuis la période gallo-romaine jusqu'à la fin du XIVe siècle*, Paris, 1901, is a series of 24 lantern slides with descriptive text. H. LEMOINE, *Manuel d'histoire de Paris*, Paris, 1924, 1–115. See also the articles on Paris in nos. **96, 98** and **104.** H. BELLOC, *Paris*, London, 1907.

Pictorial history of Paris. T. J. H. HOFFBAUER, *Paris à travers les âges*, 2 vols., 2nd edition, Paris, 1885. Interesting restoration of scenes in old Paris by T. HOFFBAUER are in *Histoire de France illustrée*, vol. I.

Paris in the twelfth and thirteenth centuries. L. HALPHEN, *Paris sous les premiers Capétiens (987–1223): étude de topographie historique*, Paris, 1909, with an *Album de planches*, in which see especially plate II, "Plan de Paris, sous Philippe Auguste." L. BOUTIÉ, *Paris au temps de Saint Louis*, Paris, 1911. L. OLSCHKI, *Paris nach den altfranzösischen nationalen Epen: Topographie, Stadtgeschichte und lokale Sagen*, Heidelberg, 1913, with 4 plans; *Der ideale Mittelpunkt Frankreichs im Mittelalter in Wirklichkeit und Dichtung*, Heidelberg, 1913. A. SPRINGER, *Paris im 13 Jahrhundert*, Leipzig, 1856 (contains a plan), translated freely into French by V. FOUCHER, *Paris au XIIIe siècle*, Paris, 1860. See also the few pages of description in J. McCABE, *Peter Abelard*, New York, 1901, 20–25. JOAN EVANS, *Life in mediaeval France*, ch. I.

Guide-books for Paris. K. BAEDEKER, *Paris and environs: handbook for travellers*, 18th revised edition, Leipzig and New York, 1913. Marquis de ROCHEGUDE et M. DUMOLIN, *Guide pratique à travers le vieux Paris*, Paris, 1923. A. J. C. HARE, *Paris*, 2 vols., London [n. d.]. MARIA H. LANDSALE, *Paris: its sites, monuments and history, compiled from the principal secondary authorities*, Philadelphia, 1898. MABELL S. C. SMITH, *Twenty centuries of Paris*, New York, 1913. M. MONMARCHÉ, *Paris et ses environs*, Paris, (Les guides bleus); English edition, *Paris and its environs*, edited, by F. MUIRHEAD and M. MONMARCHÉ, London.

Original sources. " Deux éloges de la ville de Paris," composed in 1323 by JEAN DE JANDUN and an anonymous called "DICTATOR," Latin text with a French translation on opposite pages, in *Paris et ses historiens aux XIVe et XVe siècles*, edited by A. J. V. LE ROUX DE LINCY and L. M. TISSERAND, Paris, 1867 (Histoire générale de Paris), pp. 1–79.

Plans. SHEPHERD, *Atlas*, 149. P. VIDAL DE LA BLACHE, *Atlas générale*, new edition, 46*b*. More detailed maps and plans are indicated in the bibliography.

C. Bibliography

General books. See the bibliography under outline XXV in part II. The special literature on the university of Paris, under outline XXII, is essential for a knowledge of Paris in the middle ages.

General histories of Paris. *Histoire générale de Paris*, published by authority of the municipality, Paris, 1866ff., is the fundamental work on the history of Paris. Next in importance are the publications of the Société de l'histoire de Paris et de l'Ile de France, namely, the *Bulletin*, Paris, 1874ff.; the *Mémoires*, Paris, 1874ff.; and the *Documents*, Paris, 1874ff. Abbé Lebeuf, *Histoire de la ville et de tout le diocèse de Paris*, 15 vols., Paris, 1754–58; new edition in 3 vols. by H. Cocheris, Paris, 1865–67 (incomplete, but valuable for its notes); another edition by A. Augier, 6 vols., Paris, 1883; to be supplemented by *Rectifications et additions* by F. Bournou, Paris, 1890–1901, and by Dom Beaunier, *La France monastique*, vol. I, Paris, 1905. J. B. M. Jaillot, *Recherches critiques, historiques et topographiques sur la ville de Paris*, 5 vols., Paris, 1772–75; new edition, 1782. H. Sauval, *Histoire et recherches des antiquités de la ville de Paris*, 3 vols., Paris, 1724. M. Félibien and G. A. Lobineau, *Histoire de la ville de Paris*, 5 vols., Paris, 1725. A. Christian, *Etudes sur le Paris d'autrefois*, 6 vols., Paris, 1904–07, are interesting popular volumes. H. Ramin, *Notre très vieux Paris*, Paris, 1909. E. de Ménorval, *Paris* [des origines à 1715], 3 vols., Paris, 1889–97. E. Fournier, *Paris-capitale*, Paris, 1881. E. Clouzot, "Les inondations à Paris du VIe au XXe siècle," *La géographie*, XXIII (1911), 81–100. G. Pessard, *Nouveau dictionnaire historique de Paris*, Paris, 1904, is not as accurate as it should be. L. Dubech and P. d'Espezel, *Histoire de Paris*, Paris, 1926.

Topography and archaeology of medieval Paris. A. Berty, H. Legrand, and others, *Topographie historique du vieux Paris*, 6 vols., Paris, 1866–97, in *Histoire générale de Paris*. *Statistique monumentale de Paris*, edited by A. Lenoir, 2 folio vols., and 1 quarto volume containing explanation of plates, Paris, 1867, part of no. **965**. C. Normand, *Nouvel itinéraire, guide artistique et archéologique de Paris*, published by the Société des amis des monuments parisiens, 2 vols., Paris, 1889–94. F. de Guilhermy, *Description archéologique des monuments de Paris*, 2nd edition, Paris, 1856. J. Du Breul, *Le théâtre des antiquitéz de Paris*, Paris, 1612. A. Bonnardot, "Iconographie du vieux Paris," *Revue universelle des arts*, vols. II–XII and XIX, Paris, 1855–60 and 1864. G. Riat, *Paris*, Paris, 1907 (Les villes d'art célèbres). G. Schmidt and G. Riat, *Paris: eine Geschichte seiner Kunstdenkmäler, vom Altertum bis auf unsere Tage*, Leipzig, 1912 (Berühmte Kunststädten, 6). E. Hessling, *Le vieux Paris: recueil de vues de ses monuments*, vol. I, *Moyen âge*, Berlin, [1906]. See also no. **299**. F. Boucher, *Le Pont Neuf*, 2 vols., Paris, 1925. H. Cordier, *Annales de l'Hôtel de Nesle*, Paris, 1916, is extracted from *Mémoires de l'Académie des inscriptions et belles-lettres*, XLI.

Plans of old Paris. The essential publication is the *Atlas des anciens plans de Paris*, Paris, 1880; 3rd edition, 3 vols., 1900, in *Histoire générale de*

Paris. A. FRANKLIN, *Les anciennes plans de Paris: notices historiques et topographiques*, 2 vols., Paris, 1878–80. A. BONNARDOT, *Etudes archéologiques sur les anciens plans de Paris des XVIe, XVIIe et XVIIIe siècles*, Paris, 1851; *Dissertations archéologiques sur les anciennes enceintes de Paris*, 3 vols., Paris, 1852–77. There is a facsimile of the important plan of *Paris in the XVI century* now in the Musée Carnevalet appended to M. POËTE, *Vie d'une cité: Paris*, I.

Streets of Paris. E. FOURNIER, *Promenade historique dans les rues de Paris*, new edition, Paris, 1894; *Chroniques et légendes des rues de Paris*, new edition, Paris, 1893; *Enigmes des rues de Paris*, new edition, Paris, 1892; *Histoire des enseignes de Paris*, Paris, 1884. E. BEAUREPAIRE, *Paris d'hier et d'aujourd'hui: la chronique des rues de Paris*, Paris, 1900. E. DE MÉNORVAL, *Promenades à travers Paris*, Paris [1897]. J. J. DUFOUR, *Les enseignes de Paris*, Paris, 1924.

Notre Dame. A. MARTY, *L'histoire de Notre-Dame de Paris d'après les estampes*, Paris, 1907, contains 100 plates together with an introduction and bibliographical notes. M. AUBERT, *La cathédrale Notre-Dame-de-Paris*, Paris, 1909. C. HIATT, *Notre Dame de Paris: a short history and description of the cathedral, with some account of the churches which preceded it*, London, 1902. V. MORTET, *Etude historique et archéologique sur la cathédrale et le palais épiscopal de Paris du VIe au XIIe siècle*, Paris, 1888; *Notes historiques et archéologiques sur la cathédrale et le palais épiscopal de Paris*, Paris, 1903–05 (three pamphlets). F. L. CHARTIER, *L'ancien chapitre de Notre-Dame-de-Paris et sa maîtrise, d'après des documents capitulaires (1326–1790)*, Paris, 1897. G. D'AVENEL, *Les évêques et archevêques de Paris, depuis Saint Denis jusqu'à nos jours, avec des documents inédits*, 2 vols., Paris, 1876, is untrustworthy. M. AUBERT, *Notre Dame de Paris, sa place dans l'architecture du XIIe au XIVe siècle*, Paris, 1920.

Other ecclesiastical establishments. W. LOUERGAN, *Historic churches of Paris*, London, 1896. S. SOPHIA BEALE, *The churches of Paris from Clovis to Charles X*, London, 1893. G. DUBOIS, *Historia ecclesiae parisiensis*, 2 vols., Paris, 1690–1710. H. L. BORDIER (editor), *Les églises et monastères de Paris: pièces en prose et en vers des IXe, XIIIe et XIVe siècles*, Paris, 1856. S. J. MORAND, *Histoire de la Sainte Chapelle royale du Palais*, Paris, 1790. A. LE BRUN, *L'église Saint-Julien le Pauvre: d'après les historiens et des documents inédits*, Paris, 1889. P. FERET, *L'abbaye de Sainte-Geneviève et la congrégation de France*, 2 vols., Paris, 1883. GIARD, "Etude sur l'histoire de l'abbaye de Saint-Geneviève de Paris jusqu'à la fin du XIII siècle," *Mémoires de la Société de l'histoire de Paris*, XXX (1903), 41–126. J. BOUILLART, *Histoire de l'abbaye royale de Saint-Germain-des-Prés*, Paris, 1724. FOURIER-BONNARD, *Histoire de l'abbaye royale et de l'ordre des chanoines réguliers de Saint-Victor de Paris*, first period (1113–1500), Paris [1904]. J. MEURGEY, *Histoire de la paroisse de Saint-Jacques-la-Boucherie*, Paris, 1926. See also no. **460**.

Hospitals. Hôtel Dieu. E. COYECQUE, *L'Hôtel-Dieu et Paris au moyen âge: histoire et documents*, Paris, 1889–91 (Documents de la Société de l'histoire de Paris). *Archives de l'Hôtel-Dieu de Paris (1157–1300)*, edited by

L. BRIÈLE and E. COYECQUE, Paris, 1894, part of no. **965.** A. CHEVALIER, *L'Hôtel-Dieu de Paris et les soeurs augustines (650–1810)*, Paris, 1901. L. BRIÈLE, *Notes pour servir à l'histoire de l'Hôtel-Dieu de Paris*, Paris, 1870 (extract from l'Union médicale); *l'Hôpital de Sainte-Catherine en la rue Saint-Denis (1184–1790)*, Paris, 1890. DOROTHY L. MACKAY, *Les hôpitaux et la charité à Paris au XIIIe siècle*, Paris, 1923.

Châtelet. L. BATIFFOL, "Le Châtelet de Paris vers 1400," *R.H.*, LXI (1896), 225–64; LXII (1896), 225–35; LXIII (1897), 42–55, 266–83, treats of the period from the eleventh to the fifteenth century. A. DE BOÜARD, *Etudes de diplomatique sur les actes des notaires du Châtelet de Paris*, Paris, 1911, part of no. **888.** L. BIZARD and JANE CHAPON, *Histoire de la prison de Saint-Lazare du moyen âge à nos jours*, Paris, 1925.

Economic and social life in Paris. A. FRANKLIN, *La vie privée au temps des premiers Capétiens*, 2 vols., 2nd edition., Paris, 1911, in particular; and in general, *La vie privée d'autrefois: arts et métiers, modes, moeurs, usages des Parisiens du XIIe au XVIIIe siècle*, 27 vols., Paris, 1887–1902. A. FRANKLIN, *Dictionnaire historique des arts, métiers et professions exercés dans Paris depuis le treizième siècle*, with a preface by E. LEVASSEUR, Paris, 1906. G. HUISMAN, *La jurisdiction de la municipalité parisienne de Saint Louis à Charles VII*, Paris, 1912 (Bibliothèque d'histoire de Paris), see the bibliography, pp. VII–XIII. A. FRANKLIN, *Les corporations ouvrières de Paris du XIIe au XVIIIe siècle*, Paris, 1885. W. GALLION, *Der Ursprung der Zünfte in Paris*, Berlin and Leipzig, 1910 (*Abh.m.n.G.*, 24). E. PICARDA, *Les marchands de l'eau: Hanse parisienne et compagnie française*, Paris, 1901, part of no. **888.** G. GUILMOTO, *Etudes sur les droits de navigation de la Seine de Paris à la Roche-Guyon du XIe au XVIIIe siècle*, Paris, 1889. O. MARTIN, *Histoire de la coutume de la prévôté et vicomté de Paris*, Paris, 2 vols., 1922–26; "La coutume de la prévôté et vicomté de Paris," *Mémoires de la Société de l'histoire de Paris et de l'Ile de France*, XLVIII (1925), 174–89, and, especially his Utrecht lectures, *La coutume de Paris: trait d'union entre le droit romain et les législations modernes*, Paris, 1925. See also the literature which pertains to France under outline XXVI in part II, where the editions of the *Livre des métiers* of ETIENNE BOILEAU are indicated under "Original sources." L. MIROT, "Etudes lucquoises: la colonie lucquoise à Paris du XIIIe siècle," *B.E.C.*, LXXXVIII (1927), 50–86. L. LEVILLAIN, "Essai sur les origines du Lendit," *R.H.*, CLV (1927), 241–76. *The goodman of Paris (Le ménagier de Paris)*, translated with introduction and notes by EILEEN POWER, New York, 1928 (Broadway medieval library).

Jews in Paris. L. KAHN, *Les Juifs à Paris depuis le VIe siècle*, Paris, 1889. For general histories on the Jews see nos. **850–83b.**

Original sources. Most of the printed source material is to be found in the *Histoire générale de Paris*, the *Publications* of the Société de l'histoire de Paris, and in nos. **965** and **966.** The following collections deserve particular mention. *Cartulaire générale de Paris, 528–1180*, edited by R. DE LASTEYRIE, vol. I (528–1180), Paris, 1887, in *Histoire générale de Paris. Documents inédits sur l'histoire de France—Paris sous Philippe le Bel*, edited by H. GÉ-

RAUD, Paris, 1837, contains a good plan by the architect LENOIR, part of no. **965.** *Cartulaire de Notre-Dame de Paris*, 4 vols., edited by B. GUÉRARD, Paris, 1850, part of no. **965.** *Recueil des chartes de l'abbaye de Saint-Germain-des-Prés, des origines au début du XIIIe siècle*, edited by R. POUPARDIN, vol. I, Paris, 1909, vol. XVI, part I of *Documents* of the Société de l'histoire de Paris. *Recueil de chartes et documents de Saint-Martin-les-Champs: monastère parisien*, edited by J. DEPOIN, 2 vols., Paris, 1912–13 (Archives de la France monastique, XIII–XIV). *Recueil des chartes de l'abbaye royale de Montmartre*, edited by E. DE BARTHÉLEMY, Paris, 1883. *Inscriptions de la France du Ve siècle au XVIIIe—ancien diocèse de Paris*, edited by F. DE GUILHERMY and R. DE LASTEYRIE, 5 vols., Paris, 1873–83. For the important *Chartularium universitatis parisiensis* see outline XXII.

Bibliographies. M. BARROUX, *Essai de bibliographie critique des généralités de l'histoire de Paris*, Paris, 1908, is the most essential bibliography, to be supplemented by the "Bibliographie" published since 1898 in the *Bulletin* of the Société de l'histoire de Paris. Bibliothèque historique de la ville de Paris, at no. 29 Rue de Sévigné, is a large public library exclusively for books and materials on the history of Paris. The activity of the municipality of Paris in furthering the study of the history of the city is reported in *Bulletin de la bibliothèque et des travaux historiques*, published by the Ville de Paris under the direction of M. POËTE, Paris, 1906ff. See especially G. HENRIOT and J. DE LA MONNERAYE, *Répertoire des travaux publiés par les sociétés d'histoire de Paris depuis leur fondation jusqu'au 31 décembre 1911*, Paris, 1914, in vols. VIII–IX of this bulletin. E. CLOUZOT, *Dépouillement d'inventaires et de catalogues*, 3 vols., Paris, 1916, prepared for the *Répertoire des sources manuscrits de l'histoire de Paris*, edited by M. POËTE. See also nos. **17, 21** and **26,** and the *Subject-index* by FORTESCUE under no. **3.** M. DUMOLIN, "Notes sur les vieux guides de Paris" in *Mémoires de la Société de l'histoire de Paris et de l'Ile de France*, XLVII (1924), 209–85. M. POËTE, *Une vie de cité: Paris*, Paris, 1925, I, *Introduction* has a splendid bibliographical essay which evaluates much of the material that has been published on the history of this most important city.

XIV. GROWTH OF A SPIRIT OF INQUIRY BASED ON LOGIC. ABELARD AND BERNARD OF CLAIRVAUX

A. OUTLINE

1. Remarkable interest in the twelfth century in logic or dialectic, which had been comparatively unimportant in the schools of the early middle ages. It served as a stimulus to investigation and to independent thinking.

2. Abelard and Bernard are types respectively of radical and conservative thought in the twelfth century.

3. Peter Abelard was born at Pallet in Brittany in 1079. His quest for knowledge led him to the school of Roscelin and then to Paris about 1100.

4. His checkered scholastic career. The encounter with William of Champeaux (1070–1120) in the cathedral school of Paris. The question of

universals. Nominalism and realism. Abelard at Melun and Corbeil. His teaching on the hill of St. Geneviève. He studied theology under Anselm of Laon. His love affair with Heloise, about 1118. He became a monk at St. Denis. Popularity of his teaching in his hermitage near Rheims. His trial for heresy at the councils of Soissons, 1121. His hermitage near Troyes (Paraclete). He aroused the antagonism of St. Norbert and St. Bernard of Clairvaux. Abelard as abbot of St. Gildas in Brittany. Back to Paris about 1136. Second trial for heresy at the council of Sens, 1141. Befriended by Peter the Venerable (died 1156), abbot of Cluny. Abelard died at St. Marcel lez Châlons, 1142.

5. Abelard's works. His famous *Sic et non. Scito te ipsum seu Ethica. Dialogus inter philosophum, judaeum et christianum.* Theological and dialectical works. *Historia calamitatum.*

6. Abelard's method and the degree of his rationalism. The question of the originality and influence of his *sic-et-non* method. "By doubting we are led to inquire; by inquiry we perceive the truth"—*Sic et non*, preface.

7. The life and work of St. Bernard of Clairvaux, ca. 1090–1153, who embodied the ascetic spirit of the new monastic movement, and at the same time was a practical active statesman. His book *On Consideration*, and his *Letters*. His attitude toward secular learning, and his reliance on faith.

8. The clash between Abelard and Bernard of Clairvaux. Bernard combated heresy in all its forms. His visit to Aquitaine. His denunciation of Gilbert de la Porrée and Arnold of Brescia as well as of Abelard. His diplomacy in connection with the trial of Abelard at Sens in 1141. The greatness of Bernard in his day contrasted with the ultimate failure of his ideals.

9. Mysticism in this age of reason. The school of St. Victor. The mystic strain in Bernard of Clairvaux and his influence upon Hugh (1096–1141) and Richard of St. Victor (prior, 1162–73).

10. Conflicting opinions concerning the character and influence of Abelard who is popularly renowned as the founder of the university of Paris. The need of a new critical edition of his works.

B. Special Recommendations for Reading

Short general surveys. Taylor, *Mediaeval mind*, 2nd edition, I, ch. xvii; II, ch. xxxvii. Lavisse, *Histoire de France*, II, part II, 366–83. S. Sweetser, "Church theology and free inquiry in the twelfth century," *Bibliotheca sacra*, XVII (1860), 43–64. Mary M. Wood, *The spirit of protest in old French literature*, New York, 1917 (Columbia university studies in Romance philology and literature) covers the period 1150–1350. F. D. Bancel, *Histoire des révolutions de l'esprit français, de la langue et de la littérature françaises au moyen âge*, Paris, 1878.

Standard accounts. Robert, *Les écoles et l'enseignement de la théologie pendant la première moitié du XIIe siècle*, Paris, 1909 (ch. vii on Abelard). Grabmann, *Geschichte*, vol. II (168–229 on Abelard). C. Prantl, *Geschichte der Logik im Abendlande*, Leipzig, 1927, II, 162–205.

Abelard. Excellent short sketches of Abelard are in POOLE, *Illustrations*, ch. v; R. L. POOLE, "Abailard as a theological teacher," *Church quarterly review*, XLI (1895), 116–45; also 314–17 (Note on Abelard's Masters); and C. C. J. WEBB, *Studies in the history of natural religion*, part III, no. 3, "Abelard." J. MCCABE, *Peter Abelard*, New York, 1901, is the most stimulating biography. A. HOFMEISTER, "Studien über Otto von Freising," *N.A.*, XXXVII (1912), 635–40, is a valuable contribution to our knowledge about Abelard.

Is the Abelard-Heloise correspondence genuine? B. SCHMEIDLER," Der Briefwechsel zwischen Abälard und Heloise eine Fälschung?", *Archiv für Kulturgeschichte*, XI (1913), 1–30 (see the references to the opinions of ORELLI, COUSIN, LALANNE, and PETRELLA in his notes).

Bernard of Clairvaux. G. G. COULTON, *St. Bernard, his predecessors and successors*, vol. I of *Five centuries of religion*. The best short sketch is in LAVISSE, *Histoire de France*, II, part II, 266–82 (translated in MUNRO and SELLERY, *Medieval civilization*, new edition, 406–31). The best authority on Bernard is E. VACANDARD, *Vie de St. Bernard, abbé de Clairvaux*, Paris, 1895; 4th edition, 2 vols., 1910; see also *Saint Bernard*, Paris, 1904; 2nd edition, 1905 (La pensée chrétienne). R. S. STORRS, *Bernard of Clairvaux*, New York, 1892. J. C. MORISON, *The life and times of St. Bernard, abbot of Clairvaux*, London, 1884; 2nd edition, 1901. A. MARTIN, *Saint Bernard*, Paris, 1925. W. WILLIAMS, *Studies in Saint Bernard of Clairvaux*, London, 1926.

Original sources. For brief extracts from Abelard's works see ROBINSON, *Readings*, I, 446–52. PETER ABELARD, Translation of introduction of *Glosses of Peter Abailard on Porphyry*, in *Selections from medieval philosophers*, by R. MCKEON, 2 vols., New York, 1929–30, vol. I, 202–58. PETER ABELARD, *Historia calamitatum*, translated into English by H. A. BELLOWS, St. Paul, Minn., 1922. C. K. SCOTT-MONCRIEFF (translator), *The letters of Abelard and Heloise*, New York, 1926. The Abelard-Heloise correspondence is analyzed and translated in part by TAYLOR, *Mediaeval mind*, II, ch. XXV; see also *Love letters of Abelard and Heloise* in the Temple classics series.

Some letters of St. Bernard, from the translation of Dr. EALES, selected, with a preface, by F. A. GASQUET, London, 1904, furnish a convenient introduction to the thought of Bernard and the reasons for his antagonism to Abelard. *The complete works of S. Bernard, abbot of Clairvaux*, translated into English from the edition of Dom JOANNES MABILLON (Paris, 1690), by S. J. EALES, 5 vols., London, 1889–96. Saint BERNARD's work *On Consideration* has been translated by G. LEWIS, Oxford, 1908. *The Book of Saint Bernard on the Love of God*, translated by E. G. GARDNER, London, 1915.

C. BIBLIOGRAPHY

General books. The general histories of philosophy, nos. **822–35,** are most useful. See especially nos. **822, 829** and **833**. The encyclopaedias for church history, nos. **104–14,** are very helpful. See also no. **472.**

Abelard. E. KAISER, *Pierre Abélard critique*, Fribourg, 1901. S. M. DEUTSCH, *Peter Abälard: ein kritischer Theologe des 12 Jahrhunderts*, Leipzig, 1883. A. HAUSRATH, *Peter Abälard*, Leipzig, 1895 (Weltverbesserer, vol. I). C. F. M. DE RÉMUSAT, *Abélard*, 2 vols., Paris, 1845 (do not confuse with his drama, *Abélard*, 1877). The article by E. PORTALIÉ, "Abélard," in I, 36–55, of no. **109**, is noteworthy.

Among the special studies the following deserve mention. R. DAHMEN, *Darstellung der Abälardschen Ethik*, Münster, 1906 (Diss.). J. SCHILLER, *Abälards Ethik in Vergleich zur Ethik seiner Zeit*, Munich, 1906 (Diss.). F. THANER, *Abälard und das canonische Recht*, Graz, 1900. B. HILLER, *Abälard als Ethiker*, Erlangen, 1900 (Diss.). H. DENIFLE, "Die Sentenzen Abälards und die Bearbeitungen seiner Theologia vor Mitte des 12 Jahrhunderts," *Archiv für Literatur- und Kirchengeschichte des Mittelalters*, I (1885), 402–69, 584–624. J. BACH, *Die Dogmengeschichte des Mittelalters*, II, 41–88. R. SEEBERG, *Lehrbuch der Dogmengeschichte*, III, 156–70, 226–33, 241–43. F. PICAVET, *Abélard et Alexandre de Hales: créateurs de la méthode scolastique*, Paris, 1896 (Bibliothèque de l'Ecole des hautes études, sciences religieuses, vol. VII, 1). G. ROBERT, "Abélard créateur de la méthode de la théologie scolastique," in *Revue des sciences philosophiques et théologiques*, III (1909), 60–83. F. PICAVET, *Roscelin, philosophe et théologien*, Paris, 1911. F. v. BEZOLD, *Über die Anfänge der Selbstbiographie im Mittelalter*, Erlangen, 1893. J. REINERS, *Der Nominalismus in der Frühscholastik. Ein Beitrag zur Geschichte der Universalienfrage im Mittelalter*, Münster, 1910, 41–59. B. GEYER, "Die Stellung Abaelards in der Universalienfrage," *Supplementband*, I (1913), 101–27, of no. **826**. P. FÉRET, *La faculté de théologie de Paris*, 4 vols., Paris, 1894–97, I, 100–03, 131–53. L. THORNDIKE, *A history of magic*, II, 3–8. P. GUILLOUX, "Abélard et le couvent du Paraclet," *Revue d'histoire ecclésiastique*, XXI (1925), 455–78.

Anselm of Laon. F. J. BLIEMETZRIEDER (editor), *Anselm's von Laon systematische Sentenzen*, Münster, 1919.

Bernard of Clairvaux. S. J. EALES, *St. Bernard, abbot of Clairvaux*, London, 1890 (Fathers for English readers). A. STEIGER, *Der hl. Bernhard von Clairvaux: sein Urteil über die Zeitzustände, seine geschichtsphilosophische und kirchenpolitische Anschauung*, Brünn, 1908. Comte D'HASSONVILLE, *Saint Bernard*, Paris, 1906. A. NEANDER, *Der heilige Bernhard und seine Zeitalter*, new edition, Gotha, 1889–90, translated by M. WRENCH, *The life and times of St. Bernard*, London, 1843. G. HÜFFER, *Der heilige Bernhard von Clairvaux: eine Darstellung seines Lebens und Wirkens*, vol. I, Münster, 1886. G. SALVAYRE, *Saint Bernard: maître de vie spirituelle*, Avignon, 1910. G. CHEVALIER, *Histoire de Saint Bernard*, 2 vols., Lille, 1888. G. HOFMEISTER, *Bernhard von Clairvaux*, Berlin, 1889–90 (Prog.). A. HOFMEISTER, "Studien über Otto von Freising," *N.A.*, XXXVII (1912), 747–67. R. SEEBERG, *Lehrbuch der Dogmengeschichte*, III, 118–35. J. RIES, "Die Gotteslehre des hl. Bernhard," *Jahrbuch für Philosophie und speculative Theologie*, XX (1906), 450–62. J. RIES, *Das geistliche Leben in seinen Entwicklungsstufen nach der Lehre des hl. Bernhard*, Freiburg, 1906. C. NEUMANN,

Bernhard von Clairvaux und die Anfänge des zweiten Kreuzzuges, Heidelberg, 1882 (Diss.). J. THIEL, *Die politische Thätigkeit des Bernhard von Clairvaux*, Königsberg, 1885 (Diss.). P. RASSOW, *Die Kanzlei Bernhards von Clairvaux*, Salzburg, 1913 (Diss.). J. SCHUCK, *Das religiöse Erlebnis beim hl. Bernhard von Clairvaux; ein Beitrag zur Geschichte der christlichen Gotteserfahrung*, Würzburg, 1922. R. LINHARDT, *Die Mystik des hl. Bernhard von Clairvaux*, Munich, 1924. R. LINHARDT, *Bernhard von Clairvaux 1090–1153, Ein Charakter- und Lebensbild nebst Auswahl von Stücken aus seinen Schriften*. Regensburg, 1925. W. VON DEN STEINEN, *Vom hl. Geist des Mittelalters. Anselm von Canterbury. Bernhard von Clairvaux*, Breslau, 1926.

Abelard and Bernard. E. VACANDARD, *Pierre Abélard et sa lutte avec saint Bernard, sa doctrine, sa méthode*, Paris, 1881. RAGNISCO, "P. Abelardo e S. Bernardo di Chiaravalle: la cattedra ed il pulpito, esame di alcuni guidizi su Abelardo, come logico, moralista e teologo," *Atti. di r. istit. Veneto di scienze*, VIII, Venice, 1905. W. MEYER, "Die Anklagesätze des heiligen Bernhard gegen Abälard," *Nachrichten, Göttingen Acad.*, 1898, 397–468. S. M. DEUTSCH, *Die Synode von Sens 1141, und die Verurteilung Abälards*, Berlin, 1880.

Faith and reason. T. HEITZ, *Essai historique sur les rapports entre la philosophie et la foi de Bérenger de Tours à S. Thomas d'Aquin*, Paris, 1909. REUTER, *Geschichte der religiösen Aufklärung*, 1, 183–259. F. PICAVET, *Esquisse d'une histoire générale et comparée des philosophies médiévales*, ch. IV, "Les écoles et les rapports de la philosophie et de la théologie au moyen âge," 71–94. J. M. VERWEYEN, *Philosophie und Theologie im Mittelalter*, Bonn, 1911. E. KREBS, *Theologie und Wissenschaft nach der Lehre der Hochscholastik. An der Hand der bisher ungedruckten Defensa doctrinae D. Thomae des Hervaeus Natalis* (Beiträge, XI, 3–4), Münster, 1912.

William of Champeaux. G. LEFÈVRE, *Les variations de Guillaume de Champeaux et la question des universaux: étude suivie de documents originaux*, Lille, 1898. E. MICHAUD, *Guillaume de Champeaux et les écoles de Paris au XIIe siècle*, 1st edition, Paris, 1867; 2nd edition 1868. F. PICAVET, "Note sur l'enseignement de G. de Champeaux d'après l'Historia calamitatum d'Abélard," *Revue internationale de l'enseignement*, October, 1910. B. HAURÉAU, *Histoire de la philosophie scolastique*, I, 320–61. GRABMANN, *Geschichte*, II, 136–68.

Peter the Venerable. M. DEMIMUID, *Pierre le Vénérable*, Paris, 1876; 2nd edition, 1895. B. DUPARAY, *Pierre le Vénérable, abbé de Cluny, sa vie, ses oeuvres, et la société monastique au douzième siècle*, Châlons-sur-Saône, 1862.

Hugo of St. Victor. B. HAURÉAU, *Les oeuvres de Hugues de St.-Victor: essai critique*, 2nd edition, Paris, 1886. A. MIGNON, *Les origines de la scolastique et Hugues de Saint-Victor*, 2 vols., Paris, 1895. J. KILGENSTEIN, *Die Gotteslehre des Hugo von Saint-Victor*, Würzburg, 1897 (Diss.). H. OSTLER, *Die Psychologie des Hugo von St. Viktor*, Münster, 1906, Beiträge Band VI, heft 1, of no. **826.** O. SCHMIDT, *Hugo von St.-Victor als Pädagog*, Meissen, 1893. A. STÖCKL, *Geschichte der Philosophie des Mittelalters*, II, 309–67. J. BACH, *Die Dogmengeschichte des Mittelalters*, II, 309–67. E.

KULESZA, *La doctrine mystique de Richard de Saint-Victor*, Saint-Maximin, 1925. Mgr. HUGONIN, *Essai sur la fondation de l'école de St. Victor de Paris*, Paris, 1879; also in MIGNE, *P. L.*, CLXXV. See also TAYLOR, *Mediaeval mind*, 2nd edition, II, ch. XXIX.

Original sources. The works of Abelard are printed in MIGNE, no. **953**, *P. L.*, CLXXVIII (a reprint of *Petri Abelardi opera*, edited by F. AMBOESIUS, Paris, 1616). *Petri Abelardi opera*, 2 vols., Paris, 1849–59; and *Ouvrages inédits d'Abélard*, Paris, 1836, part of no. **965**, both edited by V. COUSIN, whose introduction to the latter is valuable. *Abaelards 1121 zu Soissons verurtheilter Tractatus de unitate et trinitate divina: mit einer Einleitung*, edited by R. STÖLZLE, Freiburg, 1891. ABELARD'S *Sic et non* is edited separately by E. L. T. HENKE and G. S. LINDENKOHL, Marburg, 1851. B. GEYER, *Abaelards unedierte philosophische Werke*, Baümker-Beiträge, Bd. XXI, H. 1, Münster, 1919; *Peter Abaelards philosophische Schriften I, Die Logica "Ingredientibus. I. Die glossen zu Porphyrius*, Zum ersten Male herausgegeben, Münster, 1919. Portion of I. has been translated in McKeon, *Selections from medieval philosophers*, I, 202–58. The works of Bernard are in vols. CLXXXII–CLXXXV of MIGNE, *P. L.*, no. **953.** New critical edition of *Sermones de tempore, de sanctis, de diversis*, edited by B. GSELL and L. JANAUSCHEK in Xenia Bernardina, 1. ST. BERNARD OF CLAIRVAUX, *Select treatises: De diligendo Dei*, edited by W. W. WILLIAMS; *De gradibus humilitatis et superbiae*, edited by B. R. V. MILLS, Cambridge, 1926 (Cambridge patristic texts).

Bibliographies. Sufficient bibliographical guidance will be found in nos. **822, 827, 830,** and in HEITZ, *Essai historique*, 169–74; and ROBERT, *Les écoles*, IX–XVI. L. JANAUSCHEK, *Bibliographia Bernardina*, Vienna, 1891 (in Xenia Bernardina, 4).

XV. THE NEW ARISTOTLE

A. OUTLINE

1. A momentous intellectual revolution was caused by the introduction of all the works of Aristotle into western Europe in the twelfth and thirteenth centuries. Compare with Darwinism in the nineteenth century.

2. The transmission of Aristotle's works to the twelfth century. The life and work of Aristotle (born at Stageirus in 384 B.C., and died at Chalcis in 322). History of the Aristotelian books to the time of Boëthius. The translations and commentaries of Boëthius. Knowledge of Aristotle in the Latin west during the early middle ages. Works of Aristotle known to Abelard. A good history of Aristotle "à travers les âges" unfortunately is still a *desideratum.*

3. Mohammedans and Jews as transmitters of Greek philosophy to the west (see outline X). Their famous commentaries. Byzantine influences (Michael Psellos and John Italos).

4. Schools of translators in the west, especially in Sicily and Spain (Toledo). Relative importance of translations from the Greek and Arabic. Value of these Latin translations. Decline of interest in Plato as Aristotle became more popular.

5. The "New Logic." In the thirteenth century the curricula of universities distinguished between the "New" and "Old Logic." The "Old Logic" comprised the texts on logic which were in use in the schools before ca. 1128, namely, the *Categories* and *On interpretation* of Aristotle, the *Isagoge* of Porphyry and sometimes the *Divisions* and *Topics* of Boëthius (the *Six principles* of Gilbert de la Porrée are sometimes included). About 1128 the whole *Organon* of Aristotle became known in Latin translations. The "New Logic" comprised his *Prior* and *Posterior analytics*, the *Topics* and the *Sophistical refutations*. Even these new logical books of Aristotle created a great stir in the schools. James of Venice. Henricus Aristippus of Catania (died 1162).

6. The New Aristotle *par excellence* was introduced towards the close of the twelfth and in the beginning of the thirteenth century and consisted of Aristotle's books on moral and natural philosophy and metaphysics, namely, the *Ethics*, *Physics*, *Meteorics*, *On the heavens and the earth*, *On generation and destruction*, *On animals*, the "*Parva naturalia*," and the *Metaphysics*.

7. Famous translators of the New Aristotle. From the Arabic: Gerard of Cremona (died 1187), Michael Scot (died before 1235), Hermann the German (ca. 1250). From the Greek: William of Moerbeke (ca. 1215–86), archbishop of Corinth, 1278–86, translated for St. Thomas Aquinas.

8. Reception of the New Aristotle in the universities, especially the university of Paris. The prohibitions of 1210 and 1215. In 1231 pope Gregory IX appointed a committee of three to purge the condemned books of Aristotle. Evidence that the books were read quite openly in Paris, 1230–55, in spite of the ban. In 1255 the faculty of arts in Paris prescribed the forbidden books.

9. Various ways in which Aristotle was regarded in the thirteenth century. Mental ferment caused by his writings. Tendency toward heresies. Averroism.

10. Unconditional acceptance of Aristotle as presented to the scholastic world by Albert the Great and Thomas Aquinas (see outline XVII). Aristotle became "The Philosopher" among the Christians as he was among the Mohammedans. To Dante, "il maestro di color che sanno." Ineffective protests of the "Oxford school" (see outline XXI).

B. Special Recommendations for Reading

Life and works of Aristotle. For brief sketches see nos. **96, 98, 104.** Ueberweg, no. **822,** and Croisset, *Histoire de la littérature grècque*, IV, ch. xi (or the *Abridged history*, 335–49), furnish details.

W. D. Ross, *Aristotle*, London, 1923. E. Zeller, *Aristotle and the earlier Peripatetics*, translated from the German, 2 vols., London, 1897. G. Grote, *Aristotle*, 2 vols., London, 1872; 3rd ed., 1883. T. Gomperz, *Griechische Denker*, vol. III, Leipzig, 1902; English translation, vol. IV, London, 1912. F. Brentano, *Aristoteles und seine Weltanschauung*, Leipzig, 1911. O. Hamelin, *Le système d'Aristote*, Paris, 1920. A. Lalo, *Aristote*, Paris, 1922.

W. Jaeger, *Aristoteles*, Berlin, 1923. R. Shute, *On the history of the process by which the Aristotelian writings arrived at their present form: an essay*, Oxford, 1888, is a posthumous work. C. Piat, *Aristote*, Paris, 1903; 2nd edition, 1912 (Les grands philosophes). H. Siebeck, *Aristoteles*, Stuttgart, 1899; 4th edition, Stuttgart, 1922 (Frommanns Klassiker der Philosophie, 8). A. E. Taylor, *Aristotle*, London [n. d.]; 2nd edition 1919 (The people's books). E. Wallace, *Outlines of the philosophy of Aristotle*, 3rd edition, Cambridge, 1887.

Short surveys of Aristotle in the middle ages. Haskins, *Renaissance*, ch. ix. Rashdall, *Universities*, I, 351–68. Taylor, *Mediaeval mind*, II, ch. xxxviii. Sandys, *Classical scholarship*, I, ch. xxx. De Wulf, *History of medieval philosophy*, vol. I. Norton, *Readings in the history of education*, 40–49. G. H. Luquet, *Aristote et l'université de Paris pendant le XIIIe siècle*, Paris, 1904 (also in Bibliothèque de l'Ecole des hautes études, Sciences religieuses, XVI, 2). Brother Azarias, *Aristotle and the Christian church: an essay*, London, 1888. Féret, *La faculté de théologie de Paris: moyen âge*, II, 107–29. Traube, *Einleitung in die lateinische Philologie des Mittelalters*, 85–88. T. Heitz, *Essai historique sur les rapports entre la philosophie et la foi*, especially, 87–91. W. Turner, "Aristotle in relation to mediaeval christianity," *The Catholic university bulletin*, XVII (1911), 519–39. A. Schneider, *Die abendländische Spekulation des XII Jahrhunderts in ihrem Verhältnis zur aristotelischen und jüdischarabischen Philosophie. Eine Untersuchung über die historischen Voraussetzungen des Eindringens des Aristotelismus in die christliche Philosophie des Mittelalters* (Beiträge, XVI, 4), Münster, 1915.

Standard accounts on the New Aristotle. The best treatment is in P. Mandonnet, *Siger de Brabant et l'Averroïsme latin au XIIIe siècle*, Fribourg, 1899; second edition, Louvain, vol. I (1911), vol. II (1908), I, chs. i–ii. Mandonnet must be supplemented by M. Grabmann, *Neu aufgefundene Werke des Siger von Brabant und Boetius von Dacien*, Munich, 1924 (*S.B., Munich Acad.*, 1924, no. 2); and Haskins, "A list of text-books from the close of the twelfth century," in *Harvard studies in classical philology*, XX (1909), 75–94; now in *Studies in the history of mediaeval science*, Cambridge, 1924, ch. xviii, 356–76 [on this article see J. L. Heiberg, "Noch einmal die mittelalterliche Ptolemäusübersetzung," *Hermes*, XLVI (1911), 207–16]; C. H. Haskins and D. P. Lockwood, "The Sicilian translators of the twelfth century and the first Latin versions of Ptolemy's Almagest," ch. ix, 155–193; C. H. Haskins, "Further notes on Sicilian translators of the twelfth century," *ibid.*, ch. ix, 155–193; and his "Mediaeval versions of the Posterior analytics," *ibid.*, ch. x, 223–241. P. M. Bouyges, "Notes sur les philosophes arabes connus des Latins au moyen âge," *Mélanges de l'Université de St. Joseph*, VII–IX, Beirut, 1914–24. C. H. Haskins, "Pascalis Romanus: Petrus Chrysolanus," *Byzantion*, II (1925), 231–36. P. Duhem, "Du temps où la scolastic latine a connu la physique d'Aristote," *Revue de philosophie*, XV (1909), 163–78. R. McKeon, "The empiricist and experimentalist temper in the middle ages," *Essays in honor of John*

Dewey, New York, 1929, 216–34. For the "New Logic," GRABMANN, *Geschichte*, I, 64–81, also II, 54–94. F. BLIEMETZRIEDER, "Noch einmal die alte lateinische Übersetzung der Analytica Posteriora des Aristoteles," *Philosophisches Jahrbuch*, XXXVIII (1925), 230–49. HOFMEISTER, "Studien über Otto von Freising," *N.A.*, XXXVII (1912), 654–81; and CLERVAL, *Les écoles de Chartres*, 222, 244ff., and see his index under "Aristote." C. BAEUMKER, *Zur Rezeption des Aristoteles im lateinischen Mittelalter*, Munich, 1914, discusses Haskins, "A list of text-books."

Michael Scot. J. W. BROWN, *An enquiry into the life and legend of Michael Scot*, Edinburgh, 1897. A. G. RUDBERG, *Zum sogenannten 10. Buch der aristotelischen Tiergeschichte*, Uppsala, 1911. A. H. QUERFELD, *Michael Scot und seine Schrift De secretis naturae*, Leipzig, 1919 (Diss.). L. THORNDIKE, *History of magic and experimental science*, II, 307–37. HASKINS, *Mediaeval science*, 272–98. F. BOLL, *Sphaera*, Leipzig, 1903, 439ff.

Original sources. *Aristotle's Works*, translated into English under the editorship of J. A. SMITH and W. D. ROSS, London, 1910ff., deserve particular mention among the numerous translations of Aristotle. For translation of BOËTHIUS, *Commentary on the Isagoge of Porphyry* and Abailard's *Gloss on Porphyry*, see *Selections from medieval philosophers*, translated by R. McKEON.

C. BIBLIOGRAPHY

General books. See the histories of philosophy, nos. **822–35,** and the literature under outline XVII.

Aristotle in scholasticism. CHOLLET'S article on "L'aristotélisme de la scolastique," in no. **109,** I, 1869–87. A. SCHNEIDER, *Die abendländische Spekulation des 12 Jahrhunderts in ihrem Verhältnis zur aristotelischen und jüdischarabischen Philosophie*, Münster, 1915, vol. XVII, 4, of no. **826.** S. TALAMO, *L'aristotelismo nella storia della filosofia*, Naples, 1873; 3rd edition, Siena, 1900; translated into French, Paris, 1876. F. EHRLE, "Der Augustinismus und der Aristotelismus in der Scholastik gegen Ende des 13 Jahrhunderts," *Archiv für Literatur und Kirchengeschichte*, V (1889), 603–35; "John Peckham über den Kampf des Augustinismus und Aristotelismus in der zweiten Hälfte des 13 Jahrhunderts," *Zeitschrift für katholische Theologie*, XIII (1889), 172–193. J. H. LÖWE, *Der Kampf zwischen Realismus und Nominalismus im Mittelalter*, Prague, 1876. J. HESSEN, "Augustinismus und Aristotelismus in Mittelalter," *Franziskanische Studien*, VII (1920), 456–81. H. SPETTMANN," Der Ethikkommentar des Johannes Pecham," *Zweite Baeumker-Festschrift* (Beiträge, Suppl. II), Münster, 1923, 222. M. SCHNEID, *Aristoteles in der Scholastik*, Eichstädt, 1875. F. NITSCH, "Über die Ursachen des Umschwungs und Aufschwungs der Scholastik im 13 Jahrhundert," *Jahrbücher für protestantische Theologie*, II (1876), 532ff.

Latin translations of Aristotle. A. JOURDAIN, *Recherches critiques sur l'âge et l'origine des traductions latines d'Aristote, et sur les commentaires grecs ou arabes employés par les docteurs scolastiques*, Paris, 1819; 2nd edition, 1843, was the pioneer work in this interesting but difficult field of research.

M. GRABMANN, *Forschungen über die lateinischen Aristotelesübersetzungen des XIII Jahrhundert*, Münster, 1916 (Beiträge XVII, 5–6). V. ROSE, "Die Lücke im Diogenes Laertius und der alte Übersetzer," *Hermes*, I (1866), 367–97; "Ptolomäus und die Übersetzer-Schule von Toledo," *ibid.*, VIII (1874), 327–49. O. HARTWIG, "Die Übersetzungsliteratur Unteritaliens in der normannisch-staufischen Epoche," *Zentralblatt für Bibliothekswesen*, III (1886), 161–90, 223–25, 505. E. MOORE, *Studies in Dante*, first series, Oxford, 1896, 305–18. G. H. LUQUET, "Hermann l'Allemand," *Revue de l'histoire des religions*, XLIV (1901), 407–22. C. MARCHESI, *L'Etica nicomachea nella tradizione latina medievale*, Messina, 1904. A. VACANT, *Les versions latines de la morale à Nicomaque*, Paris, 1885. A. MÜLLER, *Die griechischen Philosophen in der arabischen Überlieferung*, Halle, 1873. B. BONCOMPAGNI, *Dalla vita e delle opere de Gherardo Cremonese*, Rome, 1851. A. PELZER, "Les versions latines des ouvrages de moral conservés sous le nom d'Aristote en usage au XIIIe siècle," *Revue néo-scolastique*, XXIII (1912), 316–41, 378–412. P. MINGES, "Zur Textgeschichte der sogenannte Logica nova der Scholastiker," *Philosophisches Jahrbuch*, XXIX (1916), 250–63; and "Robert Grosseteste Übersetzer der Ethica nichomachea," *ibid.*, XXXII (1919), 230–43. F. PELSTER, "Die griechisch-lateinische Metaphysikübersetzungen des Mittelalters," *Zweite Baeumker-Festschrift*, 89–118; *Kritische Studien zum Leben und zu den Schriften Alberts des Grossen*, 1920, 147ff. (on translations of metaphysics). For translation from the Arabic see outline X.

Aristotle's natural science. T. E. LONES, *Aristotle's researches in natural science*, London, 1912. D'ARCY W. THOMPSON, *On Aristotle as a biologist*, Oxford, 1913. C. HUIT, *La philosophie de la nature chez les anciens*, Paris, 1901. C. B. JOURDAIN, *Influence d'Aristote et de ses interprètes sur la découverte du nouveau-monde*, Paris, 1861. J. B. MEYER, *Aristoteles Thierkunde*, Berlin, 1855. A. E. CHAIGNET, *Essai sur la psychologie d'Aristote*, Paris, 1883. O. GILBERT, *Die meteorlogischen Theorien des griechischen Altertums*, Leipzig, 1907. F. RAVAISSON, *Essai sur la metaphysique d'Aristote*, 2nd edition, Paris, 1913. A. MANSION, *Introduction à la physique aristotélicienne*, Louvain and Paris, 1913. P. DUHEM, *Le système du monde: histoire des doctrines cosmologiques de Platon à Copernic*, 5 vols., Paris, 1913–17, vol. I, ch. IV., 130–241. F. H. FORBES, "Mediaeval versions of Aristotle's meteorology," *Classical review*, X (1915), 297–314. G. FURLANI, " Le antiche versioni araba latina ed ebraica del De partibus animalium di Aristotele," *Rivista degli studi orientali*, IX (1922), 237–57. W. L. LORIMER, "The text tradition of pseudo-Aristotle 'De mundo' together with an appendix containing the text of the mediaeval Latin versions," *St. Andrews university publications*, XVIII, Oxford, 1924, 42–96.

Study of logic. G. WALLERAND, *Les oeuvres de Siger de Courtrai*, Louvain, 1913 (Les philosophes belges, VIII), in his introduction treats on the literature of the "Sophismata."

Bibliographies. Bibliography in the notes of MANDONNET, *Siger de Brabant;* bibliographical notes in articles by HASKINS, HOFMEISTER, and in GRABMANN, *Geschichte.* M. SCHWAB, *Bibliographie d'Aristote*, Paris, 1896.

XVI. HERESIES AND THE INQUISITION

A. Outline

1. The connection between heresy and the pronounced intellectual activity and religious revival in the twelfth and thirteenth centuries.

2. Purely speculative novelties of the intellectual class. Notions about the Trinity and transubstantiation which disturbed the church. The trials of Abelard in 1121 and 1141. The trials at Paris in 1147 of Gilbert de la Porrée, 1076–1154, *scholasticus* in Paris in 1141, bishop of Poitiers in 1142, author of the *Liber sex principiorum*. The pantheism of Chartres. Amalric (Amaury) of Bène and David of Dinant whose doctrines were condemned at Paris in 1210. Roger Bacon. The trial of Siger de Brabant in Paris in 1277. Siger de Brabant and Averroism. The censorship of books. The degree of intellectual freedom in the twelfth and thirteenth centuries.

3. Demented innovators such as Tanchelm in Belgium and Eon de l'Etoile (Eudes de Stella) in Brittany in the first half of the twelfth century.

4. Antisacerdotal heresies in southern France in the twelfth century. Criticism of the practices of the church and of the lives of the clergy. Peter of Bruys (burned 1126) and the Petrobrusians. Henry of Lausanne (died in prison about 1149), and the Henricians. St. Bernard of Clairvaux in southern France to stem the tide of heresy. Peter Waldo of Lyons (died in Bohemia in 1197) and the Poor Men of Lyons or Waldensians, who were excommunicated by the pope in 1184, and driven from Aragon by Alphonse II in 1194.

5. Manicheans (Cathari or Albigensians, from Albi, near Toulouse). Theories about the origin of this sect. Possible connection with Paulicians and the Bogomiles of Bulgaria (*Bougre*). Their dualistic beliefs and ascetic practices. Spread of the heresy in the eleventh, twelfth, and thirteenth centuries. The Albigensian crusades (see outline XXV in part II).

6. The suppression of heresy. The theory and practice of persecution in the early middle ages. The canon law and heresy. Gradual development of inquisitorial machinery and punishments and the gradual growth of intolerance. Desultory efforts of bishops to stem the tide of heresy. Special papal legates sent into Languedoc by Innocent III. Gregory IX, 1227–41, organized the inquisition as a definite and permanent piece of machinery for the suppression of heresy (*inquisitio hereticae pravitatis*). The mendicants, especially the Dominicans, and the inquisition.

7. The inquisition. Co-operation of the state with the church. Legislation of Frederick II against heretics. The use of torture and secret and questionable legal procedure. Punishments: public recantation, fines, confiscation, penance, imprisonment, and abandonment of the prisoner to the secular arm. *Auto-da-fé* (act of faith). Attitude of canonists and theologians, especially St. Thomas Aquinas, towards the death penalty. Burning at the stake. Comparison of the medieval inquisition with the Spanish inquisition in the sixteenth century. The Jews and the inquisition.

8. The beginnings of persecutions for witchcraft by the papal inquisition

in the second half of the thirteenth century. The great days of witch persecution did not come until the fifteenth and sixteenth centuries.

9. Influence of the inquisition on the intellectual life of the thirteenth century.

B. Special Recommendations for Reading

Short general surveys. Lavisse et Rambaud, *Histoire générale*, II, 265–79. Milman, *History of Latin Christianity*, vol. V, book IX, ch. viii. C. V. Langlois, *L'inquisition d'après des travaux récents*, Paris, 1902. Trench, *Lectures in church history*, ch. xv. Holland, *Rise of intellectual liberty*, chs. v–vii. *C.M.H.*, VI, ch. xx. D. Schaff, *History of the christian church*, New York, 1907, V, ch. x. Hulme, *Middle ages*, 737–75. A. S. Turberville, *Mediaeval heresy and the inquisition*, London, 1920. C. T. Gorham, *The medieval inquisition*, London, 1919. Maycock, *The inquisition, from its establishment to the great schism*, introduction by P. R. Knox. A criticism of books on the inquisition by G. G. Coulton in *Edinburgh review*, CCXLV–CCXLVI (1927), 75–90, 242–58. See nos. **739–48**.

Standard works. "The most extensive, the most profound, and the most thorough history of the inquisition which we possess" (Frédéricq) was written by H. C. Lea, *A history of the inquisition of the middle ages*, 3 vols., New York, 1888, translated into French by S. Reinach, *Histoire de l'inquisition au moyen âge*, with a valuable introduction, entitled "Historiographie de l'inquisition," by P. Frédéricq, 3 vols., Paris, 1900–02, also translated into German, edited by J. Hansen, *Geschichte der Inquisition im Mittelalter*, Bonn, 1905ff. Lea's work is supplemented by C. H. Haskins, "Robert le Bougre and the beginnings of the inquisition in northern France," revised from the *A.H.R.*, VII (1902), 437–57, 631–52, in his *Studies in mediaeval culture*. In the first six chapters of vol. I, Lea gives a good account of the heresies and the general conditions which gave rise to the inquisition. Much has been written about Lea's books, especially by Roman Catholics; see e.g., P. M. Baumgarten, *Die Werke von Henry Charles Lea und verwandte Bücher*, Münster, 1908, translated into English, *Henry Charles Lea's historical writings*, New York, 1909; Lord Acton in *E.H.R.*, III (1888) or in his *History of freedom*, London, 1907, ch. xv; Blötzer in the *Hist. Jahrbuch* of the Görresgesellschaft, XI (1890), 302–23; P. Fournier in *Revue d'histoire ecclésiastique*, III (1902), 709; C. Moeller, *ibid.*, XIV (1913), 721. The best introduction to the position of modern Roman Catholic scholars on the question of medieval heresies and the inquisition is E. Vacandard, *L'inquisition: étude historique et critique sur le pouvoir coercitif de l'église*, Paris, 1906; 5th edition, 1909; translated by B. L. Conway, from the 2nd French edition, *The inquisition: a critical and historical study of the coercive power of the church*, New York, 1908. See also article "Inquisition," in *Catholic encyclopedia*.

Albigensian crusade. Lavisse, *Histoire de France*, III, part I, 259–68. The standard work is by A. Luchaire, *Innocent III*, vol. II, *La croisade des Albigeois*, the first pages of which have been translated in Munro and

SELLERY, *Medieval civilization*, 432–57. H. NICKERSON, *The inquisition*, New York, 1923.

Gilbert de la Porrée. POOLE, *Illustrations*, ch. VI, see also ch. IV. For opposition to the doctrines of the church in the beginning of the thirteenth century see LAVISSE, *Histoire de France*, III, part I, 313–18.

Averroism. MANDONNET, *Siger de Brabant et l'Averroïsme.* RENAN, *Averroès et Averroïsme.* C. V. LANGLOIS, *Questions d'histoire et d'enseignement*, 51–103.

Original sources. *Translations and reprints*, vol. III, no. 6, pp. 8–19. ROBINSON, *Readings*, I, ch. XVII. WEBSTER, *Historical selections*, 430–35.

C. BIBLIOGRAPHY

General books. All general histories of the church, nos. **393–498,** and the encyclopaedias and periodicals for church history, nos. **104–14,** and **176–80d,** are useful; but see especially the general histories of freedom of thought, nos. **739–48.** See also **540.**

General surveys. REUTER, *Geschichte der religiösen Aufklärung im Mittelalter*, vol. II, books V–VIII. THUDICHUM, *Papsttum und Reformation im Mittelalter.* BUSSELL, *Religious thought and heresy.*

Heresies. An important study of heretical repression in the Roman empire after Constantine is that of E. LOENING in his *Geschichte der deutschen Kirchenrecht*, Strasburg, 1878, ch. I, 20–102. G. ARNOLD, *Unpartheyischen Kirchen und Ketzer-Historie*, Frankfurt, 1729. J. v. DÖLLINGER, *Beiträge zur Sectengeschichte des Mittelalters*, Munich, 2 vols., 1890 (vol. II contains source material). J. FICKER, "Die gesetzliche Einführung der Todesstrafe für Ketzerei," *M.I.O.G.* (1880), 177–226, 430–31. J. HAVET, "L'hérésie et le bras séculier au moyen âge jusqu'au XIIIe siècle," *B.E.C.*, XLI (1880), 488–517, 570–607, 670 (or *Oeuvres complètes*, Paris, 1896, II, 117–80). G. G. COULTON, *The death penalty for heresy from 1184 to 1921*, London, 1924. E. JORDAN, *La responsabilité de l'église dans la répression de l'hérésie au moyen âge*, Paris, 1907–15. F. W. MAITLAND, "The deacon and the Jewess," in his *Roman canon law in the church of England*, London, 1898, 158–79. F. TOCCO, *L'eresia nel medio evo*, Florence, 1884. HAUCK, *Kirchengeschichte Deutschlands*, V, Bk. IX, 397ff. P. BEUZART, *Les hérésies pendant le moyen âge et le réforme jusqu'à la mort de Philippe II, 1598, dans le région de Douais, d'Arras, et au pays de l'Alleu*, Le Puy, 1912. P. FRÉDÉRICQ, "L'hérésie à l'Université de Louvain vers 1470," *Bull. de l'Académie royale de Belgique*, Classe des lettres et des sciences morales et politiques, 1905, 11–16. P. ALPHANDÉRY, *Les idées morales chez les hétérodoxes latins au début du XIIIe siècle*, Paris, 1903; *Notes sur le messianisme médiéval latin, XIe–XIIe siècles*, Paris, 1912. ZANONI, *Gli Umiliati.* L. FUMI, "Eretici e ribelli nell' Umbria," *Bollettino storico umbro*, III–V (1897–99); 2nd edition, Todi, 1917. G. VOLPE, *Movimenti religiosi e sette ereticali nella società medioevale italiana, secoli XI–XIV*, Florence, 1922. A. SERENA, "Fra gli eretici trevigiani," *Archivio veneto-tridentino*, III (1923), 169–202. HINSCHIUS, *Kirchenrecht*, V, 449–92. E. CONYBEARE, *Key of truth*, London, 1898. C. U. HAHN,

Geschichte der Ketzer im Mittelalter, 3 vols., Stuttgart, 1845–50. A. H. NEWMAN, "Recent researches concerning medieval sects," *Proc. American society church history*, IV (1892), 167–221. Article "Heresy" in *The Catholic encyclopedia*, VII (1910).

Gilbert de la Porrée. Abbé BERTHAUD, *Gilbert de la Porrée, évêque de Poitiers et sa philosophie*, Poitiers, 1892. CLERVAL, *Les écoles de Chartres*, 163ff. GRABMANN, *Geschichte*, II, 407–38.

Almaric, and David of Dinant. C. JOURDAIN, "Mémoire sur les sources philosophiques des hérésies d'Amaury de Chartres et de David de Dinan," in his *Excursions historiques*, 101–28. B. HAURÉAU, "Mémoire sur la vraie source des erreurs attribuées à David de Dinan," *Mémoires de l'Académie des inscriptions*, XXIX, part II (1879), 319–30. G. THÉRY, *Autour du décret de 1210;* I: *David de Dinant*, Kain, 1925. C. BAEUMKER, "Ein Tractat gegen die Amalricaner aus dem Anfange des XIII Jahrhundert," *Jahrbuch für Philosophie und spekulative Theologie*, 1893, 346ff.

Waldensians. T. DE CAUZONS, *Les Vaudois et l'inquisition*, 3rd edition, Paris, 1908. E. COMBA, *Histoire des Vaudois*, new edition, Lausanne, 1901. K. MÜLLER, *Die Waldenser und ihre einzelnen Gruppen bis zum Anfang des 14 Jahrhunderts*, Gotha, 1886. W. PREGER, "Beiträge zur Geschichte der Waldensier im Mittelalter," *Abh. Munich Acad.*, XIII (1877), 181–250; "Über die Verfassung der französischen Waldensier in der ältesten Zeit," *ibid.*, XIX (1891), 639–711. H. HAUPT, "Neue Beiträge zur Geschichte des mittelalterlichen Waldenserthums," in *H.Z.*, LXI (1889), 45ff.; *Waldensertum und Inquisition im südöstlichen Deutschland*, Freiburg, 1890; "Deutsche-böhmische Waldenser um 1340," in *Zeitschrift für Kirchengeschichte*, XIV (1894), 1ff. HERZOG (II.), *Die romanische Waldenser*, Halle, 1853. A. DIECKHOFF, *Die Waldenser im Mittelalter*, Göttingen, 1851. E. ARNAUD, "Histoire des persécutions endurées par les Vaudois du Dauphiné aux XIIIe, XIVe et XVe siècles," *Bull. de la soc. d'histoire vaudoise*, XII (1895), 17–140. H. C. VEDDER, "Origin and early teachings of the Waldenses, according to the Roman Catholic writers of the thirteenth century," *American journal of theology*, IV (1900), 465–89. H. BÖHMER, article "Waldenser" in the HERZOG-HAUCK, *Realencyclopädie*, 3rd edition, XX (1908), 812. C. H. HASKINS, "The heresy of Echard the Baker of Rheims," *Studies*, 245–55. See *Bulletin de la société d'histoire vaudoise.*

Albigensians. T. DE CAUZONS, *Les Albigeois et l'inquisition*, 2nd edition, Paris, 1908. C. SCHMIDT, *Histoire et doctrine de la secte des Cathares ou Albigeois*, 2 vols., Paris, 1849. C. DOUAIS, *L'Albigéisme et les Frères prêcheurs à Narbonne au XIIIe siècle*, Paris, 1894. N. PEYRAT, *Histoire des Albigeois*, 3 vols., Paris, 1870–72. C. DOUAIS, *Les Albigeois*, Paris, 1879. E. DULAURIER, *Les Albigeois ou les Cathares du Midi de la France*, in *Le cabinet historique*, XXVI (1880). A. MOLINIER, "L'église et la société cathare," *R.H.*, XCIV, 225–48; XCV (1907), 1–22, 263–91. E. BROECKX, *Le Catharisme; étude sur les doctrines, la vie religieuse et morale, l'activité littéraire et les vicissitudes de la secte cathare avant la croisade*, Hoogstraten, 1916 (Diss.). J. GUIRAUD, *Questions d'histoire et d'archéologie chrétienne*, Paris, 1906. KRAMP, *Gregori-*

anum, 1921. V. SHARENKOFF, *A study of Manichaeism in Bulgaria with special reference to the Bogomils*, New York, 1925. H. J. WARNER, *The Albigensian heresy*, 2 vols., London, 1922–28. BURKITT, *Religion of the Manichees*. E. G. A. HOLMES, *The Albigensian or Catharist heresy*, London, 1925. VERNET's article "Cathares," in no. **109**, is important. A. VILLEMAGNE, *Bullaire du bienheureux Pierre de Castelnau, martyr de la foi* (*16 février 1208*), Montpellier, 1917.

Inquisition. T. DE CAUZONS, *Histoire de l'inquisition en France*, 2 vols., Paris, 1909–12. C. DOUAIS, *L'inquisition: ses origines, sa procédure*, Paris, 1906. L. TANON, *Histoire des tribunaux de l'inquisition en France*, Paris, 1893. A. ESMEIN, *Histoire de la procédure criminelle en France et spécialement de la procédure inquisitoire depuis le XIIIe siècle jusqu'à nos jours*, Paris, 1882. P. HINSCHIUS, "Die päpstlichen Ketzer (Inquisitions) Gerichte," in his *Kirchenrecht*, Berlin, 1895, V, 449–92. E. CHÉNON, "L'hérésie à La Charité-sur-Loire et les débuts de l'inquisition monastique dans la France du nord au XIIIe siècle," *Nouvelle revue historique de droit*, XLI (1917), 299–345. R. GÉNESTAL, *La "Privilegium fori" en France du décret de Gratien à la fin du XIVe siècle*, 2 vols., Paris, 1921–24, vols. XXXV and XXXIX of no. **888**. C. HENNER, *Beiträge zur Organisation und Kompetenz des päpstlichen Ketzergericht*, Leipzig, 1890. C. MOLINIER, *L'inquisition dans le Midi de la France au XIIIe et au XIVe siècle: étude sur les sources de son histoire*, Toulouse, 1880. B. HAUREAU, *Bernard Délicieux et l'inquisition albigeoise*, Paris, 1887. M. DMITREWSKI, "Fr. Bernard Délicieux, O. F. M. Sa lutte contre l'inquisition de Carcassonne et d'Albi; son procès 1297–1319," *A.F.H.*, XVII (1924), 183–218, 313–33, 457–88 and XVIII (1925), 3–32. J. M. VIDAL, *Bullaire de l'inquisition française au XIVe siècle et jusqu'à la fin du Grand Schisme*, Paris, 1913; *Un inquisiteur jugé par ses victimes: Jean Galland et les Carcassonnais*, Paris, 1903. L. HERNANDEZ, *Le procès inquisitorial de Gilles de Rais, maréchal de France*, Paris, 1921. J. M. VIDAL, *Le tribunal d'inquisition de Pamiers*, Toulouse, 1906. R. BAUER, *Der Strafprozess der Inquisition in Südfrankreich*, Marburg, 1917 (Diss.). M. DMITREVSKI, "Notes sur le catharisme et l'inquisition dans le midi de France," *Annales du midi*, XXXV–XXXVI (1923–1924), 294–311; XXXVII–XXXVIII (1925–1926), 190–213. H. THELOE, *Die Ketzerverfolgungen im 11 und 12 Jahrhundert: em Beitrag zur Geschichte der Entstehung des päpstlichen Ketzerinquisitionsgericht*, Berlin, 1913 (*Abh.m.n.G.*, 48). H. MAILLET, *L'église et la répression sanglante de l'hérésie*, Liége and Paris, 1909 (Bibliothèque de la Faculté de philosophie et lettres de Liége, XVI). C. MOELLER, "Les bûchers et les autos-da-fé de l'inquisition depuis le moyen âge," *Revue d'histoire ecclésiastique*, XIV (1913), 720–51; XV (1914), 50–69. P. FRÉDÉRICQ, *Geschiedenis der inquisitie in de Nederlanden, 1025–1520*, 2 vols., Ghent, 1892–97. J. MARX, *L'inquisition en Dauphiné: étude sur le développement et la répression de l'hérésie et de la sorcellerie du XIVe siècle au début du règne de François Ier*, Paris, 1914, part of no. **888**. H. KÖHLER, *Die Ketzerpolitik der deutschen Kaiser und Könige in den Jahren 1152–1254*, Bonn, 1913 (Jenaer historische Arbeiten, VI). C. MOLINIER, "Etudes sur quelques manuscrits des bibliothèques d'Italie concernant l'inquisition et les croyances hérétiques," Paris, 1888; reprinted from *Archives des missions scientifiques et littéraires*, 3rd series, XIV. G. BISCARO, "Inquisitori ed eretici lombardi (1292–1318), *Miscellanea di storia italiana*, 3ª s., XIX (1921), 445–558. F. ZECHBAUER, *Über Herkunft und Wesen des sizilischen Inquisitionsverfahrens*, Berlin, 1908 (Diss.). R. SCHMIDT, *Die Herkunft des Inquisitionsprozesses*, Freiburg, 1902. P. FLADE, *Das römische Inquisitionsverfahren in Deutschland bis zu den Hexenprozessen*, Leipzig, 1902. A. HERCULANO, *History of the origin and establishment of the inquisition in Portugal*, translated by J. C. BRANNER, 1926. G. BRUNNER, *Ketzer und Inquisition in der Mark Brandenburg*, Berlin, 1904 (Diss.). J. GUIRAUD, "Inquisition," in A. d'Alès, *Dictionnaire apologêtique*, 4th edition, Paris, 1915, II, 823–90. E. VACANDARD, "Inquisition," in A. Vacant and E. Mangenot, *Dictionnaire de théologie catholique*, 1922, VII, 2016–68. J. GUIRAUD, *The mediaeval inquisition*, translated by E. C. MESSENGER, London, 1929.

Witch persecutions. J. HANSEN, *Quellen und Untersuchungen zur Geschichte des Hexenwahns und der Hexenverfolgung im Mittelalter: mit einer Untersuchung der Geschichte des Wortes "Hexe,"* von J. FRANCK, Bonn, 1901; *Zauberwahn, Inquisition und Hexenprozess im Mittelalter und die Entstehung der grossen Hexenverfolgung*, Munich and Leipzig, 1900. P. HINSCHIUS, "Die Verfolgung der Hexerei und der Hexenprozess," in his *System des katholischen Kirchenrechts*, 1897, VI, 397–425. G. P. v. HOENSBROECH, *Das Papstthum in seiner sozial-kulturellen Wirksamkeit*, Bd. I: *Inquisition, Aberglaube, Teufelsspuk und Hexenwahn*, Leipzig, 1901. L. WAHRMUND, *Inquisition und Hexenprozess*, Reichenberg, 1925. J. BAISSAC, *Les grands jours de la sorcellerie*, Paris, 1890. T. DE CAUZONS, *La magie en France*, 4 vols., Paris, 1909. O. CARTELLIERI, "La vauderie d'Arras," ch. X of *The court of Burgundy*, London and New York, 1929, 181–206. W. G. SOLDAN, *Geschichte der Hexenprozesse*, Stuttgart, 1843; new edition by H. HEPPE, 2 vols., 1880; there is also an illustrated edition by M. BAUER.

Original sources. *Corpus documentorum inquisitionis haereticae pravitatis Neerlandicae (1035–1528)*, edited by P. FRÉDÉRICQ, 5 vols., Ghent, 1889–1902. *Documents pour servir à l'histoire de l'inquisition dans le Languedoc*, Paris, 1900, edited by C. DOUAIS, part of no. **966.** Du Plessis d'Argentré, *Collectio judiciorum de novis erroribus*, 3 vols. in fol., Paris, 1728. BERNARD GUI (d. 1331), *Practica inquisitionis heretice pravitatis*, edited by C. DOUAIS, Paris, 1886. B. GUI, *Manuel de l'inquisiteur*. Edité et traduit par G. Mollat, 2 vols., Paris, 1926–27; (Vols. VIII–IX of *Les classiques de l'histoire de France au moyen âge*.) N. EYMERICUS, *Directorium inquisitorum* (1356–1358), edited by F. PEGNA, Rome 1578. P. LIMBORCH, *Historia Inquisitionis . . . , cui subjungitur Liber Sententiarum Inquisitionis Tholosanae, ab anno 1307 ad annum 1323*, Amsterdam, 1692. *Malleus maleficarum* of JACOB SPRENGER and HEINRICH INSTITORIS; German translation by J. W. R. SCHMIDT, Berlin, 1906; 3rd edition, 1922–23; English translation by M. SUMMERS, London, 1928; cf. *A.H.R.*, XXXIV (1929), 321–25. EICHMANN, *Quellensammlung zur kirchlichen Rechtsgeschichte und zum Kirchenrecht*. C. MIRBT, *Quellen zur Geschichte des Papsttums und des römischen Katholizismus*, 4th edition, Tübingen, 1924.

Bibliographies. Albigensian War and the Inquisition see MOLINIER, *Les sources*, III, pp. 54–82. H. HAUPT, "Literaturberichte über Inquisition, Aberglauben, Ketzerei und Sekten im Mittelalter," *Zeitschrift für Kirchengeschichte*, XVI (1896), 512–36; XVII (1897), 270–87. C. DOUAIS, "Les sources de l'histoire de l'inquisition dans le midi de la France aux XIII et XIVe siècles," in *R.H.Q.*, XXX (1881), 383–459. D. SCHAFF, *History of the christian church*, V, pt. I, 458–61, bibliography on "Heresy and its suppression." P. FRÉDÉRICQ, "Les récents historiens catholiques de l'inquisition en France," *R.H.*, CIX (1912), 307–34. G. L. BURR, "The literature of witchcraft," *Papers of the American historical association*, IV (1890), 237–66. Professor BURR has announced that a special catalogue of the collection in Cornell University on the inquisition, torture, and witch-persecution is in preparation. The collection in Cornell University of books on witchcraft is said to be the most complete in the world. The library of the University of Pennsylvania now houses the rich collection of materials relating to the inquisition and witchcraft made by H. C. LEA.

XVII. SYSTEMATIZATION OF MEDIEVAL PHILOSOPHY AND THEOLOGY

A. OUTLINE

1. The word "scholasticism" in intellectual history. Strange definitions of this word. Intimate relations between philosophy and theology in the middle ages. The dependence of both upon logic. The so-called scholastic method.

2. Old and new books which served as a basis for instruction in these subjects. The Bible and patristic writings. Graeco-Roman, Hebrew, Arabic, and Byzantine literature. Importance of reputed authoritative texts. Lack of a critical attitude towards these texts, many of which were current only in faulty Latin translations.

3. Peter Lombard, born in Novara in Lombardy, master in Paris from about 1140, died as bishop of Paris in 1160, the "Master of the Sentences." His *Libri quattuor sententiarum*. Their place and influence in the development of the scholastic method.

4. Alexander of Hales, an Englishman who became a Franciscan in Paris about 1231 and died there in 1245. His great fame as a Franciscan master of theology. His voluminous *Summa theologica* which was the first successful attempt to utilize the New Aristotle for theology.

5. Albert the Great, born about 1193 in Swabia, a Dominican in 1223, master of theology in Paris, 1245–48, died in Cologne in 1280. His paraphrase of the works of Aristotle for the use of the Latins. His acquaintance with Jewish and Arabic books.

6. Thomas Aquinas, born about 1225 near Monte Cassino, in the vicinity of ancient Aquinum, became a Dominican in 1243, the pupil of Albert in Cologne, whom he followed to Paris in 1245, died in 1274. His voluminous works, especially the great *Summa theologica* and his commentary on the

literal Latin text of Aristotle, procured directly from the Greek with the help of William of Moerbeke. His skill in welding Aristotelianism with Christian doctrine. The exalted place of Thomas Aquinas in the history of thought.

7. Attacks upon the apparently perfect philosophical and theological system of Thomas by scholars from the British Isles. John Duns Scotus, a Franciscan master of theology in Oxford and Paris, died 1308 at the early age of about thirty-four. William of Ockam, renowned as a master of theology in Paris about 1320, died about 1347.

8. Scholastic mysticism. The influence of the writings of the so-called Dionysius the Areopagite, and of the *Introductorius ad evangelium aeternum* falsely attributed to Joachim of Flora, died 1202. St. Bonaventura of Tuscany, 1221–74, and Franciscan mysticism. Mechthild of Magdeburg, died 1277. The phenomenal development of mysticism in the fourteenth century, especially in Germany.

9. The organization of instruction in philosophy and theology in the rising universities (see outline XXII).

10. Neo-scholasticism. The Encyclical *Aeterni Patris* of pope Leo XIII, 1879. Its influence in drawing attention to the intellectual history of the thirteenth century.

B. Special Recommendations for Reading

Short general surveys. The article " Scholasticism " in nos. **96** and **104.** J. Rickaby, *Scholasticism*, London, 1911. W. Turner, *History of philosophy*, 237–420. R. Eucken, *The problem of human life*, 248–69. H. B. Workman, *Christian thought to the reformation*, 188–243. See also M. R. James, "The Christian renaissance," in *Cambridge modern history*, I, 585–93. Crump and Jacob, *Legacy*, 227–53. M. de Wulf, "Western philosophy and theology in the thirteenth century," *Harvard theological review*, XI (1918), 409–32. Bartlet and Carlyle, *Christianity in history*, part III, ch. vi. Haskins, *Renaissance of the twelfth century*, ch. xi. Hearnshaw, *Mediaeval contributions*, 82–105. *C.M.H.*, V, ch. xxiii.

Longer accounts. E. Gilson, *La philosophie au moyen- âge*, 2 vols., Paris, 1922. M. de Wulf, *Philosophy and civilization in the middle ages*, Princeton, 1922; *Histoire de la philosophie médiévale*, 5th edition, 2 vols., Louvain, 1924–25; translated by E. C. Messenger, *History of mediaeval philosophy*, 2 vols., London, 1925–26. Taylor, *Mediaeval mind*, 2nd edition, II, chs. xxxv–xxxvi, xxxix–xli, xliii. W. J. Townsend, *The great schoolmen*, chs. viii–xvi. I. Husik, *History of mediaeval Jewish philosophy*, London, 1918. E. Michael, *Culturzustände des deutschen Volkes*, III, 63–211. H. Reuter, *Geschichte der religiösen Aufklärung*, vol. II. E. Bréhier, *Histoire de la philosophie*, vol. I, *L'antiquité et le moyen-âge*, I, *Introduction: période hellénique*, II, *Période hellénistique et romaine*, III, *Moyen âge et renaissance*, Paris, 1926–28. M. Grabmann, *Die Philosophie des Mittelalters*, Berlin, 1921. J. Hessen, *Patristische und scholastische Philosophie*, Breslau, 1922. A. Messer, *Geschichte der Philosophie im Altertum und Mittelalter*,

2nd edition, Leipzig, 1916. A. SETH, "Scholasticism," *Ency. Brit.*, 9th edition, 1886. O. WICHMANN, *Die Scholastiker*, Munich, 1921.

Peter Lombard. J. DE GHELLINCK, "The Liber sententiarum," in *Dublin review*, CXLVI (1910), 139–66. M. GRABMANN, *Geschichte*, II, 359–407.

Alexander of Hales. H. FELDER, *Geschichte der wissenschaftlichen Studien im Franziskanerorden*, Freiburg, 1904, 177–211; translated into French by T. R. P. EUSÈBE DE BAR-LE-DUC, *Histoire des études dans l'Ordre de Saint François depuis sa fondation vers la moitié du XIIIe siècle*, Paris, 1908. J. A. ENDRES, "Des Alexander von Hales Leben und psychologische Lehre," *Philosophisches Jahrbuch*, 1888. E. LONGPRÉ, "Guillaume d'Auvergne et Alexandre d'Halès," *A.F.H.* XVI (1923), 249–50. See also the biographical article on Alexander of Hales in no. **89**.

Thomas Aquinas. E. H. GILSON, *Le Thomisme; introduction au système de saint Thomas d'Aquin*, 3rd edition, Paris, 1923; English translation by E. BULLOUGH, Cambridge, 1924. E. GILSON, *Saint Thomas d'Aquin*, Paris, 1925 (Les moralistes chrétiens). C. C. J. WEBB, *Studies in the history of natural religion*, part III, no. 4. P. H. WICKSTEAD, *The reactions between dogma and philosophy illustrated from the works of S. Thomas Aquinas*, London, 1920. E. PEILLAUBE, *Initiation à la philosophie de saint Thomas*, Paris, 1926. R. MCKEON, "Thomas Aquinas' doctrine of knowledge and its historical setting," *Speculum*, III (1928), 425–44. SEDGWICK, *Italy in the thirteenth century*, II, ch. VI. R. W. B. VAUGHAN, *The life and labours of Saint Thomas of Aquin*, 2 vols., London, 1871–72; abridged edition with the same title, London, 1872; 2nd edition, 1890. D. J. KENNEDY, *St. Thomas Aquinas and medieval philosophy*, New York, 1919. PLACID CONWAY, *Saint Thomas Aquinas, of the Order of Preachers (1225–1274): a biographical study of the Angelic Doctor*, New York, 1911. F. OLGIATI, *The key to the study of St. Thomas*, translated by J. S. ZYBURA, St. Louis and London, 1925. *St. Thomas Aquinas:* being papers read at the sixth centenary of the canonization of Saint Thomas Aquinas, held at Manchester, 1924, St. Louis, 1925.

Bonaventura. E. H. GILSON, *La philosophie de St. Bonaventura*, Paris, 1924. L. COSTELLOE, *Saint Bonaventure.* SEDGWICK, *Italy in the thirteenth century*, II, ch. VII.

Neo-scholasticism. M. DE WULF, *Introduction à la philosophie néo-scolastique*, Paris, 1904, translated by P. COFFEY, *Scholasticism old and new*, London, 1907 (see ch. I for definitions of scholasticism). For a short sketch, see his article "Neo-scholasticism," in the *Catholic encyclopedia*. J. L. PERRIER, *The revival of scholastic philosophy in the nineteenth century*, New York, 1909. F. PICAVET, *Esquisse*, ch. IX. M. W. SHALLO, *Lessons in scholastic philosophy*, Philadelphia, 1916. J. S. ZYBURA, *Present-day thinkers and the new scholasticism: an international symposium*, St. Louis and London, 1926.

Original sources. *Selections from medieval philosophers* (translated by R. MCKEON), contains translations from BOËTHIUS, ERIUGENA, ANSELM, LOMBARD, ABAILARD, ROBERT GROSSETESTE, THE PSEUDO-GROSSETESTE, ALBERT THE GREAT (vol. I): ROGER BACON, BONAVENTURA, THOMAS AQUI-

NAS, MATTHEW OF AQUASPARTA, DUNS SCOTUS, WILLIAM OF OCKHAM. THOMAS AQUINAS, *Of God and his creatures*, a translation of *Summa contra gentiles*, by J. RICKABY, St. Louis, 1905. THOMAS AQUINAS, *The Summa theologica*, literally translated by Fathers of the English Dominican Province, vols. I–XVIII, London, 1911–22.

C. BIBLIOGRAPHY

General books. Almost all church histories, nos. **393–498,** especially nos. **472–78,** touch upon the subjects of this outline. The general histories of philosophy, nos. **822–35,** are most useful, particularly nos. **827–35.** See also nos. **104–16,** and **176–81a**. The general literature on the church in the twelfth and thirteenth centuries is listed under outline XXIV in part II.

Scholasticism in general. J. DE GHELLINCK, *Le mouvement théologique du XIIe siècle*, Paris, 1914. F. PICAVET, *Esquisse d'une histoire générale et comparée des philosophies médiévales*, Paris, 1905; 2nd edition, 1907; *Essais sur l'histoire générale et comparée des théologies et des philosophies médiévales*, Paris, 1913, contains essays previously published in various places. G. SORTAIS, *Histoire de la philosophie ancienne*, Paris, 1912, 156–252, is a good summary with excellent bibliographies. F. OVERBECK, *Vorgeschichte und Jugend der mittelalterlichen Scholastik: eine kirchenhistorische Vorlesung*, Basel, 1917. C. BAEUMKER, *Der Platonismus im Mittelalter*, Munich, 1916; "Mittelalterliche und Renaissance-Platonismus," in *Beiträge zur Geschichte der Renaissance und Reformation*, Festgabe für S. Schlecht, 1917, 1–13; and *Die chrisiliche Philosophie des Mittelalters*, Leipzig, 1913. E. HOFFMANN, "Platonismus und Mittelalter," *Vorträge der Bibliothek Warburg*, 1923–24; Leipzig, 1926, 17–82. M. DE WULF, "Civilisation et philosophie au XIIe et XIIIe siècles," in *Revue de metaphysique et de morale*, XXV (1918), 273–83; "Peut-il une philosophie scolastique au moyen âge?," *Revue néo-scolastique*, XXVIII (1927), 5–27. E. KREBS, *Theologie und Wissenschaft nach der Lehre der Hochscholastik*, Münster, 1913, part of no. **826.** T. HEITZ, *Essai historique sur les rapports entre la philosophie et la foi.* FÉRET, *La faculté de théologie de Paris.* A. DEMPF-BONN, *Die Ethik des Mittelalters*, Munich, 1927. P. DEUSSEN, *Die Philosophie des Mittelalters*, 2nd edition, Leipzig, 1919. J. A. ENDRES, *Forschungen zur Geschichte der frühmittelalterlichen Philosophie*, Münster, 1915. E. GILSON, *Etudes de philosophie médiévale*, Strasburg, 1921. M. GRABMANN, *Der Gegenwartswert der geschichtlichen Erforschung der mittelalterlichen Philosophie*, Vienna, 1913; *Die Philosophia Pauperum und ihr Verfasser Albert von Orlamünde*, Münster, 1918; "Studien zu Johannes Quidort von Paris," *S.B., Munich Acad., 1922, Abh. 3: Abhandlungen zur Geschichte der Philosophie des Mittelalters, Festgabe Clemens Baeumker zum 70. Geburtstag;* "Die logischen Schriften des Nikolaus von Paris (clm. 14460 und vat. lat. 3011) und ihre Stellung in der aristotelischen Bewegung des 13. Jahrhunderts," in *Beiträge*, Supplementband II, 119–146, Münster, 1923. *Mittelalterliches Geistesleben. 'Abhandlungen zur Geschichte der Scholastik und Mystik,'* Munich, 1926; *Des Ulrich Engelberti von Strasburg* († 1277) *Abhandlung 'De pulchro,'* Munich, 1926. A. SCHNEIDER, *Die Erkenntnislehre bei*

Beginn der Scholastik, Fulda, 1921. G. v. HERTLING, *Wissenschaftliche Richtungen und philosophische Probleme. im XIII Jahrhundert*, Munich, 1910 (Festrede). R. v. LILIENCRON, *Über den Inhalt der allgemeinen Bildung in der Zeit der Scholastik*, Munich, 1876 (Festrede). J. MARIÉTAN, *Le problème de la classification des sciences d'Aristote à Saint Thomas*, Paris, 1901. S. REINSTADLER, *Elementa philosophiae scholasticae*, 2 vols., Freiburg, 1901; 5th and 6th editions, 1911. G. M. MANSER, "Ueber Umfang und Charakter der mittelalterlichen Scholastik," *Historische-politische Blätter*, CXXXIX (1907), also printed separately. R. SEEBERG, "Neuere Arbeiten zur Geschichte der scholastischen Theologie und Philosophie," *Theologisches Literaturblatt*, XLVIII (1927), 57–64, 73–79, 89–95. H. DELACROIX, "La philosophie médiévale latine jusqu'au XIVe siècle," *R.S.H.*, V (1902), 96–124. J. M. VERWEGEN, *Die Philosophie des Mittelalters*, Berlin and Leipzig, 1921; 2nd edition, 1926. C. HOLZHEY, *Die Inspiration der Heiligen Schrift in der Anschauung des Mittelalters von Karl dem Grossen bis zum Konzil von Trient*, Munich, 1895. M. MAYWALD, *Die Lehre von der zweifachen Wahrheit: ein Versuch der Trennung von Theologie und Philosophie im Mittelalter*, Berlin, 1871. F. EHRLE, "Die Ehrentitel der scholastischen Lehrer im Mittelalter," in *S.B., Munich Acad.*, 1919, IX Abhandlung; *Grundsätzliches zur Charakteristik der neuren und neuesten Scholastik*, Freiburg, 1918; "Nikolaus Trivet, sein Leben, seine quodlibet und quaestiones ordinariae," *Festgabe Baeumker*. P. GLORIEUX, *La littérature quodlibétique de 1260 à 1320*, Le Saulchoir, 1925 (Bibliothèque thomiste, V). H. HEIMSOETH, *Die sechs grossen Themen der abendländischen Metaphysik und der Ausgang des Mittelalters*, Berlin, 1922. E. F. JACOB, "Scholasticism and personality in the thirteenth century," *Church quarterly review*, XCVII (1923–24), 274–94. J. GUTTMANN, *Die Scholastik des XIII Jahrhunderts in ihren Beziehungen zu Judentum und zur jüdischen Literatur*, Breslau, 1902. F. X. PFEIFER, *Harmonische Beziehungen zwischen Scholastik und moderner Naturwissenschaft*, Augsburg, 1881. H. LIEBESCHÜTZ, "Kosmologische Motive in der Bildungswelt der Frühscholastik," *Vorträge* (1923–24) *der Bibliothek Warburg*, Leipzig, 1926, 83–148. P. MINGES, *Über Väterzitate bei den Scholastikern*, Regensburg, 1923. S. REINSTADLER, *Elemenia philosophiae scholasticae*, 12th edition, 2 vols., Freiburg, 1923. G. TRUC, *Le retour à la scolastique*, Paris, 1919. A. TRIBBECHOVIUS, *De doctoribus scolasticis et corrupta per eos divinarum humanarumque rerum scientia*, Jena, 1719. F. SARTIAUX, *Foi et science au moyen âge*, Paris, 1926.

Peter Lombard. O. BALTZER, *Die Sentenzen des Petrus Lombardus: ihre Quellen und ihre dogmengeschichtliche Bedeutung*, Leipzig, 1902, part of no. **495.** J. DE GHELLINCK, *Le traité de Pierre Lombard sur les sept ordres ecclésiastiques*, Louvain, 1910 (extract from the *Revue d'histoire ecclésiastique*, X–XI). J. N. ESPENBERGER, *Die Philosophie des Petrus Lombardus und ihre Stellung im XII Jahrhundert*, Münster, 1901, part of no. **826.** F. PROTOIS, *Pierre Lombard, évêque de Paris, dit le Maître des Sentences: son époque, sa vie, ses écrits, son influence*, Paris, 1881. J. LECHNER, *Die Sakramentenlehre des Richard von Mediavilla*, Munich, 1925. ELIZABETH F. ROGERS, *Peter Lombard and the sacramental system*, New York, 1917 (Diss.).

Albert the Great. P. MANDONNET, "Albert le Grand," in no. **109.** F. PELSTER, *Kritische Studien zum Leben und zu den Schriften Alberts des Grossen*, Freiburg, 1920. N. THOEMES, *Albertus Magnus in Geschichte und Sage*, Cologne, 1880. J. BACH, *Des Albertus Magnus Verhältniss zu der Erkenntnisslehre der Griechen, Lateiner, Araber, und Juden*, Vienna, 1881. L. GAUL, *Alberts des Grossen Verhältniss zu Plato*, Münster, 1913, part of no. **826.** A. SCHNEIDER, *Die Psychologie Alberts des Grossen*, Münster, 1903, part of no. **826.** M. WEISS, *Primordia novae bibliographiae B. Alberti Magni*, 2nd edition, Paris, 1905. G. v. HERTLING, *Albert Magnus: Beiträge zu seiner Würdigung*, revised edition with help of BAEUMKER and ENDRES, Münster, 1914. F. PELSTER, "Alberts des Grossen Jugendaufenthalt in Italien," *Hist. Jahrbuck*, XLII (1922), 102–06. G. THÉRY, "Essai sur David de Dinant, d'après Albert le Grand et saint Thomas d'Aquin," *Mélanges thomistes*, 361–408. A. BIRKENMAJER, *Krakowskie wydania tak zwany "Philosophia pauperum," Alberto Wielkigo*, Crakow, 1924. F. STRUNTZ, *Albertus Magnus: Weisheit und Naturforschung im Mittelalter*, Vienna, 1926. A. SCHNEIDER, *Albertus Magnus, sein Leben und seine wissenschaftliche Bedeutung*, Rektoratsrede, Cologne, 1927. P. HARTIG, "Albert der Grosse und Thomas von Aquino," *Deutsche Vierteljahrschrift für Literaturwissenschaft und Geistesgeschichte*, V (1927), 25–36. For literature on Albert's interest in natural science see outline XXI.

Thomas Aquinas. M. GRABMANN, *Thomas von Aquin: eine Einführung in seine Persönlichkeit und Gedankenwelt*, Munich, 1912; 5th edition, 1926; English translation by MICHEL, *Thomas Aquinas: his personality and thought*, New York, 1928; *Das Seelenleben des heiligen Thomas*, Munich, 1924; *Einführung in die Summa theologiae des hl. Thomas von Aquin*, Freiburg, 1919; *Die Kulturphilosophie des hl. Thomas von Aquin*, Augsburg, 1925. A. D. SERTILLANGES, *Saint Thomas d'Aquin*, 2 vols., Paris, 1910. E. DE BRUYNE, *Saint Thomas d'Aquin, le milieu, l'homme, la vision du monde*, Paris, 1928. R. P. J. BERTHIER, *L'étude de la Somme théologique de Saint Thomas d'Aquin*, new edition, Paris, 1905. F. EHRLE, "Der Kampf um die Lehre des hl. Thomas von Aquin in den ersten fünfzig Jahren nach seinem Tode," *Zeitschrift für katholischer Theologie*, XXXVII (1913), 266–318. J. A. ENDRES, *Die Zeit des Hochscholastik: Thomas von Aquin*, Mainz, 1910; "Die Bedeutung des hl. Thomas für das wissenschaftliche Leben seiner Zeit," in *Historische-politische Blätter*, CXLVII (1911), 801–24. P. MANDONNET, *Des écrits authentiques de S. Thomas d'Aquin*, 2nd edition, Fribourg, 1910. E. TROELTSCH, *Die Soziallehren der christlichen Kirchen*, Tübingen, 1912, 286–358. P. ROUSSELOT, *L'intellectualisme de Saint-Thomas*, Paris, 1908; 2nd edition, 1924. M. GRABMANN, *Die echten Schriften des hl. Thomas von Aquin*, Münster, 1920. P. MANDONNET, "Chronologie sommaire de la vie et des écrits de St. Thomas," *Revue des sciences philosophiques et théologiques*, 1920, 142–53; "La canonisation de Saint Thomas d'Aquin, 1317–1323," *Mélanges thomistes*, 1–48. *Mélanges thomistes publiées par les Dominicains de la province de France à l'occasion du VI*[e] *centenaire de la canonisation de saint Thomas d'Aquin* (*18 juillet, 1323*), Kain, 1923 (Bibliothèque thomiste, III). E.

ROLFES, *Die Philosophie von Thomas von Aquin*, Leipzig, 1920. J. B. KORS, *La justice primitive et le péché originel d'après S. Thomas*, Kain, 1922 (Bibliothèque thomiste, II). F. PELSTER, "La famiglia di S. Tommaso d'Aquino, studio sulle fonti," *Civiltà catholica*, LXXIV (1923), 401–10; "I parenti prossimi di S. Tommaso," *ibid.*, 299–313. O. SCHILLING, *Die Staats- und Soziallehre des hl. Thomas von Aquino*, Paderborn, 1923. *Xenia thomistica: doctori angelico et communi a plurimis orbis catholici viris eruditissimis anno ab ejus canonizatione sescentesimo oblata*, curavit P. Sadoc Szabò, 3 vols., Paris, 1925. L. ROUGIER, *La scolastique et le thomisme*, Paris, 1925. T. PÈGUES and L'ABBÉ MAGNART, *Saint Thomas d'Aquin. Sa vie par Guillaume de Tocco et les têmoins au procès canonisation*, Paris, 1925. J. HESSEN, *Die Weltanschauung des Thomas von Aquinas*, Stuttgart, 1926. G. MATTIUSSI, *Les points fondamentaux de la philosophie thomiste, commentaire des vingt quatre thèses approuvêes par la S. congrêgation des êtudes, traduit et adaptê de l'italien avec l'autorisation de l'auteur par l'abbê Jean Levellain*, Turin, 1926. A. ROHNER, *Das Schöpfungsproblem bei Moses Maimonides, Albertus Magnus und Thomas von Aquin*, Münster, 1913. M. WITTMANN, *Die Stellung des hl. Thomas von Aquin zu Avencebrol*, Münster, 1900, part of no. **826.** M. CHOSSAT, "Saint Thomas d'Aquin et Siger de Brabant," *Revue de philosophie*, XXIV (1914) 553–75; XXV (1914), 25–52. M. ASÍN PALACIOS, "El averroismo de Santo Tomás de Aquino," *Homenaje á D. Francisco Codera*, Saragossa, 1904, 271–331, also printed separately. M. DE WULF, *Mediaeval philosophy, illustrated from the system of Thomas Aquinas*, Cambridge, 1922. A. MICHELITSCH, *Kommentatoren zur 'Summa theologiae' des hl. Thomas von Aquin*, Graz and Vienna, 1924.

Bonaventura. L. LEMMENS, *Der hl. Bonaventura, Kardinal und Kirchenlehrer aus dem Franziskanerorden*, Kempten, 1909; Italian translation, 1921. G. PALHORIÈS, *Saint Bonaventure*, Paris, 1913. D. SPARACIO, *Vita di S. Bonaventure*, Rome, 1921.

John Duns Scotus. C. R. S. HARRIS, *Duns Scotus:* I. *The place of Duns Scotus in medieval thought:* II. *The philosophical doctrines of Duns Scotus*, Oxford, 1927. R. SEEBERG, *Die Thcologie des Johannes Duns Scotus, Leipzig*, 1900; *Verhältniss zwischen Glauben und Wissen, Theologie und Philosophie, nach Duns Scotus*, Paderborn, 1908. K. WERNER, *J. Duns Scotus*, Vienna, 1881. M. HEIDEGGER, *Die Kategorien- und Bedeutungslehre des Duns Scotus*, Tübingen, 1916. P. MINGES, "Skotisches bei Richard von Mediavilla," *Theologische Quartalschrift*, XCIX (1917–18), 60–79. B. LANDRY, *Duns Scot*, Paris, 1922. A. PELZER, "Le premier livre des Reportata Parisiensia de Jean Duns Scot," *Annales de l'Institut supérieur de philosophie*, V (Louvain, 1924), 447–92. C. BALIC, *Les commentaires de Jean Duns Scot sur les quatre livres des Sentences*, Louvain, 1927 (Bibliothèque de la Revue de l'histoire ecclésiastique, I). A. CALLEBAUT, "L'Ecosse, la patrie du B. Jean Duns Scot," *A.F.H.*, XIII (1919), 78–88; "Le B. Jean Duns Scot étudiant à Paris vers 1293–1296," *ibid.*, XVII (1924), 3–12; "La mâitrise . . . 1305," *ibid.*, XXI (1928), 206–39; and P. E. LONGPRÉ, "L'ordination sacerdotale du B. Jean Duns Scot," *ibid.*, XXII (1929), 54–62. See also the article on John Duns Scotus in no. **89.**

William of Ockham. G. Ritter, *Marsilius von Inghen und die okkamistische Schule in Deutschland*, Heidelberg, 1921; *Via antiqua und via moderna auf den deutschen Universitäten des 15. Jahrhunderts*, Heidelberg, 1922. Ehrle, *Der Sentenzenkommentar Peters von Candia, des Pisanerpapstes Alexanders V*. C. K. Brampton (editor), *The De imperatorum et pontificum potestate of William of Ockham*, Oxford, 1927. A. Pelzer, "Les 51 articles de Guillaume Occam censurés en Avignon en 1362," *Revue de l'histoire des religions*, XVIII (1922), 240–70. A. Hofer, "Biographische Studien über Wilhelm von Ockham," *A.F.H.*, VI (1913), 209–33, 439–65. K. Michalski, "Les courants philosophiques à Oxford et à Paris pendant le XIVe siècle," *Bulletin international de l'Académie polonaise des sciences et des lettres*, Crakow, 1922, 63–68. F. Federhofer, "Ein Beitrag zur Bibliographie und Biographie des Wilhelm von Ockham," *Philosophisches Jahrbuch*, XXXVIII (1925), 26–48. E. Hochstetter, *Studien zur Metaphysik und Erkenntnisslehre Wilhelms von Ockham*, Berlin and Leipzig, 1927. *Guilelmi de Ockhami epistola ad fratres minores*, edited by C. K. Brampton, Oxford, 1929.

Mysticism. W. K. Fleming, *Mysticism in christianity*, London, 1913. W. R. Inge, *Christian mysticism*, London, 1899. Thérèse Labande-Jeanroy, *Les mystiques italiens: Saint François d'Assise, Sainte Catherine de Sienne, Jacapone da Todi*, Paris, 1918. A. B. Sharpe, *Mysticism: its true nature and value*, London, 1910. J. Bernhart, *Die philosophische Mystik des Mittelalters*. R. M. Jones, *Studies in mystical religion*, New York, 1909. E. Lehmann, *Mysticism in heathendom and christendom*, translated by G. M. G. Hunt, London, 1910. Evelyn Underhill, *Mysticism: a study in the nature and development of man's spiritual consciousness*, 4th edition, New York, 1912. R. A. Vaughan, *Hours with the mystics*, 2 vols., 5th edition, London, 1888. W. W. Stewart, Jr., "The mystical movement in the middle ages," *Anglican theological review*, 11 (2) (1928), 147–58. E. Gebhardt, *L'Italie mystique*. C. Oulmont, *Le verger, le temple et la cellule: essai sur la sensualité dans les oeuvres de mystique religieuse*, Paris, 1912. A. Leclère, *Le mysticisme catholique et l'âme de Dante*, Paris, 1906. W. Preger, *Geschichte der deutschen Mystik im Mittelalter*, 3 vols., Leipzig, 1874–93. J. v. Görres, *Die christliche Mystik*, new edition, 5 vols., Regensburg [1879–80]. M. Grabmann, *Neu aufgefundene lateinische Werke deutscher Mystiker*, Munich, 1922 (*S.B., Munich Acad.*, 1921, 3 Abh.). H. Dörries, *Zur Geschichte der Mystik. Erigena und der Neo-platonismus*, Tübingen, 1925. W. Öhl, *Deutsche Mystiker*, vol. I, Munich, 1910. R. Langenberg, *Quellen und Forschungen zur Geschichte der deutschen Mystik*, Bonn, 1901. P. Fournier, *Etudes sur Joachim de Flore et ses doctrines*, Paris, 1909. H. Grundmann, *Studien über Joachim von Floris*, Leipzig, 1927; *Dictionnaire de théologie catholique*, VIII (1925), 1420ff., and *Zeitschrift für Kirchengeschichte*, XLVIII (1929), 137–65. For a short sketch of Joachim see Sedgwick, *Italy in the thirteenth century*, I, ch. iv. M. de Wulf, "Mystic life and mystic speculation in the heart of the middle ages," *Catholic historical review*, n.s., III (1923–24), 175–89. Francesca M. Steele, *The life and *visions of St. Hildegarde*, London, 1914. L. ZOEPF, *Die Mystikerin Margaretha Ebner (c. 1291–1351)*, Leipzig, 1914, part of no. **749.** L. FERRETTI, *Vita di D. Caterina da Siena, terziaria domenicana*, Rome, 1925. V. SCULLY, *A medieval mystic: a short account of the life and writings of blessed John Ruysbroeck, canon regular of Grenendael, A.D. 1293–1381*, London, 1910. G. DOLEZICH, *Die Mystik Jan van Ruysbroecks des Wunderbaren 1293–1381*, Habelschwerdt, 1926 (Breslauer Studien zur historischen Theologie, t. IV). GERALDINE E. HODGSON, *The sanity of mysticism: a study of Richard Rolle*, London, 1928. E. D'ASCOLI, *Il misticismo nei canti spirituali di Frate Jacapone da Todi con prefazione di Alfredo Galletti*, Recanati, libr. ed. San Francesco d'Assisi, 1925. R. ZELLER, *Les mystères du rosaire d'après l'école mystique dominicaine du XIVe siècle*, Vienna, 1925. See also the literature on the Spiritual Franciscans under outline XXIII in part II above, and for books on the German mystics in the fourteenth century and the *De imitatione Christi* of THOMAS À KEMPIS see DAHLMANN-WAITZ, *Quellenkunde*, nos. 6973–82, 7099–7107.

Special reviews of scholasticism and neo-scholasticism. *Revue néo-scolastique de philosophie*, Louvain, 1894ff. *Revue thomiste*, Paris, 1893ff. *Revista italiana di filosofia neo-scolastica*, Florence, 1909ff. *Archives d'histoire doctrinale et littéraire du moyen âge*, edited by E. GILSON and G. THÉRY, Paris, 1926ff. *Scholastik: Vierteljahrschrift für Theologie und Philosophie, herausgegeben von den Professoren des Ignatiuskollegs in Valkenburg*, Freiburg, 1926ff. *Revue des sciences philosophiques et théologiques*, Kain, 1907ff. *Recherches de théologie ancienne et médiévale*, Louvain, 1929ff. *The new scholasticism*, Washington, 1927ff.

Original sources. THOMAS AQUINAS, *Opera omnia*, iussu impensaque Leonis XIII, 12 vols., Rome, 1882–1906, sometimes referred to as the "Vatican edition." The Libraria Marietti of Turin has published the following works: *Summa theologica*, 1925; *Summa contra gentiles*, 1926; *Catena aurea in quatuor evangelia*, 1925; *In evangelia S. Matthaei et S. Joannis*, 1925; *In omnes S. Pauli apostoli epistolas*, 1924; *Quaestiones disputatae, et quaestiones duodecim quodlibetales*, 1924; *De regimine principum et De regimine Judaeorum*, 1924; *Opusculum de ente et essentia*, 1926; *Theologicae summae compendium*, 1905; *In Aristotelis librum de anima commentarium*, 1924. ALBERT THE GREAT, *Opera omnia*, edited by A. BORGNET, 38 vols., Paris, 1890. H. STADLER (editor), *Albert Magnus: De animalibus libri XXVI*, 2 vols., Münster, 1916–21. F. PICAVET, "Un projet de publication d'oeuvres philosophiques du moyen âge," *Journal des savants*, March-April, 1919, 96–99. PETRUS LOMBARDUS, *Libri IV Sententiarum, studio et cura PP. collegii S. Bonaventurae in lucem editi*, 2nd edition, Quaracchi, 2 vols., 1916. ALEXANDER OF HALES, *Summa theologica*, vol. I, Quaracchi, 1924; vol. II, *Prima pars secundi libri*, 1928. SAINT BONAVENTURA, *Opera omnia*, 11 vols., Quaracchi, 1882–1902. JOHN DUNS SCOTUS, *Opera*, new edition, 26 vols., Paris, 1891–95. PETER LOMBARD, *Libri quatuor sententiarum*, a critical edition in vols. I–IV of the *Opera of St. Bonaventura*, Quaracchi, 1882ff. See also no. **826.** H. SPETTMANN (editor), *Johanni*

Pechami Quaestiones tractantes de anima, Münster, 1918. M. D. Roland-Gosselin, *Le 'De ente et essentia' de Thomas d'Aquin*, Kain, 1926. M. Grabmann and F. Pelster (editors), *Opuscula et textus historiam ecclesiae eiusque vitam atque doctrinam illustrantia*, 'Series scholastica et mystica,' Münster, 1926–29.

Bibliographies. For general bibliographies on church history and history of philosophy see nos. **49–57.** Chevalier, no. **16,** is particularly useful for this outline. The fifth French edition of M. de Wulf, *Histoire de la philosophie*, and G. Sortais, *Histoire de la philosophie ancienne*, furnish the best practical bibliographies. For Albert the Great see P. Mandonnet, *Siger de Brabant*, I (1911), 37, note. P. Mandonnet and J. Destrez, *Bibliographie thomiste*, Kain, 1921. A. Noyen, *Inventaire des écrits théologiques du XIIe siècle non insérés dans la Patrologie latine de Migne*, fascicule I, Paris, 1912 (extract from the *Revue des bibliothèques*).

XVIII. RISE AND DECLINE OF INTEREST IN THE ANCIENT CLASSICS

A. Outline

1. Current misconceptions about the so-called "revival of learning" and the neglect of the ancient classics in the middle ages (see outline XXXIII of part II). Résumé: the ancient classics in the early middle ages (see especially outlines IV, VII–IX).

2. The increasing interest in the Latin classics, taught as a part of grammar, in the beginning of the twelfth century. Northern France was the center of this growing interest. Hildebert of Lavardin.

3. The schools of Chartres. Bernard of Chartres, chancellor there from 1119 to 1126. William of Conches (died ca. 1154). Gilbert de la Porrée. Theoderic of Chartres, chancellor from 1141 to about 1150. The famous *Eptateuchon*, or manual of the seven arts, of Theoderic. His stress on the Latin classics. The English colony of students in Chartres. Decline of the schools of Chartres in the latter half of the twelfth and in the thirteenth century.

4. John of Salisbury, 1110–80, and humanistic studies. In 1136 he heard Abelard in Paris, but in 1138 went to Chartres to study "grammar." His denunciation of the narrow-minded students of logic (*Cornificians*). His *Entheticus*, *Policraticus* and *Metalogicus*. His enthusiasm for classical studies as taught in Chartres. He was bishop of Chartres when he died in 1180.

5. Classical studies in the schools of Orleans towards the beginning of the thirteenth century, before it became a famous seat for the study of law. The evidence of Matthew of Vendôme (died ca. 1200), Geoffrey of Vinsauf, and the monk Helinand.

6. The decline of the study of the classics in Paris about 1200–50. Evidence from Peter of Blois, ca. 1140–1212, Alexander Neckam, 1157–1217, Giraldus Cambrensis (Gerald of Barri), 1147–ca. 1222, and from an anony-

mous list of text-books. Vincent of Beauvais, died 1264, and his *Speculum mundi*, divided into three parts: *naturale, doctrinale, historiale.* Unavailing efforts made by John Garland to check the decline (see outline XXIII). The "Oxford school" of scholars, especially Robert Grosseteste and Roger Bacon (see outline XXI).

7. Neglect of the ancient classics in the universities, especially the university of Paris. There is no mention of them in the statutes of this university. Causes of this neglect.

8. The *Battle of the seven arts*, a French poem written by the trouvère Henri d'Andeli in the second quarter of the thirteenth century.

9. Interest in Greek, Hebrew, and Arabic, in the twelfth and thirteenth centuries (Robert Grosseteste, Roger Bacon, William of Moerbeke, and Thomas Aquinas). Greek in southern Italy and Sicily (see outline XV). Importance of Byzantine influences. The oriental college of Paris in the time of pope Innocent III, 1198–1216. The study of languages for missionary purposes. Raymund Lull, 1235–1315, a Franciscan, born in Majorca. The legislation of the council of Vienne, 1311, on the compulsory teaching of languages.

10. Textual criticism in the thirteenth century, concerned chiefly with the *Vulgate.* The efforts of Roger Bacon.

11. Sporadic interest in the ancient classics during the century preceding Petrarch. For Dante see outline XXVIII. Petrarch, called the "morning star of the renaissance," shone forth so brightly in his advocacy of the Latin classics because it happened to be darkest just before the dawn.

B. Special Recommendations for Reading

Brief general surveys. Taylor, *Mediaeval mind*, 4th edition, II, ch. xxxi. See also his "Antecedents of the quattrocento," *Annual report A.H.A.*, 1912, 89–94. C. H. Haskins, *Renaissance*, chs. iv–vi. Sandys, *Classical scholarship*, I, chs. xxviii–xxxii, *passim.* Munro and Sellery, *Medieval civilization*, 285–309. H. Felder, *Geschichte der wissenschaftlichen Studien im Franziskanerorden*, 402–17. Norden, *Die antike Kunstprosa*, II, 688–731. E. Michael, *Culturzustände des deutschen Volkes*, III, 279–319. Robert, *Les écoles*, ch. iv. Grabmann, *Geschichte*, II, 59–64. B. Hauréau, "De l'enseignement des langues anciennes," *Journal des savants*, 1891, 502–08.

Classics in European culture. E. K. Rand, "The classics in European education," pp. 260–82 in *Latin and Greek in American education: with symposia on the value of humanistic studies*, edited by F. W. Kelsey, New York, 1911.

Hildebert of Lavardin. H. O. Taylor, "A mediaeval humanist: some letters of Hildebert of Lavardin," *Annual report A.H.A.*, 1906, vol. I, 51–60; *Mediaeval mind*, II, 162–175.

Schools of Chartres. A. Clerval, "L'enseignement des arts libéraux à Chartres et à Paris dans la première moitié du XIIe siècle d'après l'Heptateuchon de Thierry de Chartres," in *Congrès scientifique internationale des* *catholiques tenu à Paris*, 1888, II, 277–96; *Les écoles de Chartres*, 144–272. POOLE, *Illustrations*, ch. IV. GRABMANN, *Geschichte*, II, 407–76, "Die Schule von Chartres," lays special stress on its influence in philosophy and theology rather than humanistic studies.

John of Salisbury. POOLE, *Illustrations*, ch. VII; see also his article in no. **89.** A. C. KREY, "John of Salisbury's knowledge of the classics," *Transactions of the Wisconsin academy of sciences, arts and letters*, XVI, 2 (1909–10), 948–87. C. C. J. WEBB, "John of Salisbury," *Proceedings of the Aristotelian society*, II, no. 2 (1893), 91–107. R. L. POOLE, "John of Salisbury at the papal court," *E.H.R.*, XXXVIII (1923), 321–30; "Masters of the schools at Paris and Chartres in John of Salisbury's time," *E.H.R.*, XXXV (1920), 321–42; "The early correspondence of John of Salisbury," *Proceedings of the British Academy*, XI (1924).

Schools of Orleans. L. DELISLE, "Les écoles d'Orléans au XIIe et au XIIIe siècle," *Annuaire-bulletin de la Société de l'histoire de France*, VII (1869), 139–54. Mlle. A. DE FOULQUES DE VILLARET, *L'enseignement des lettres et des sciences dans l'Orléanais depuis les premiers siècles du christianisme jusqu'à la fondation de l'université d'Orléans*, Orleans, 1875.

Vincent of Beauvais. E. BOUTARIC, *Vincent de Beauvais et la connaissance de l'antiquité classique au treizième siècle*, Paris, 1875 (also in *R.Q.H.*, XVII [1875], 5–57). BAUMGARTNER, *Geschichte der Weltliteratur*, IV, 468–75.

Neglect of classics in universities. L. J. PAETOW, *The arts course at medieval universities with special reference to grammar and rhetoric*, Urbana, Ill., 1910 (University of Illinois Studies, III, no. 7), ch. I. E. K. RAND, "The classics in the thirteenth century," *Speculum*, IV (19 [illegible]), 249ff.

Study of languages, especially Greek. A. LEFRANC, *Histoire du Collège de France*, Paris, 1893, ch. I. LOUISE R. LOOMIS, *Medieval hellenism*, Lancaster, Pa., 1906 (Diss.). C. JOURDAIN, "Un collège oriental à Paris au XIIIe siècle," in *Excursions historiques*, 221–29. K. KRUMBACHER, "Die griechische Literatur des Mittelalters," *Die Kultur der Gegenwart*, 1:8 (1905), 237–88; 3rd edition (1924), 319–70.

Textual criticism. F. A. GASQUET, "Roger Bacon and the Latin Vulgate," in *Roger Bacon essays*, edited by A. G. LITTLE, Oxford, 1914, 89–99; and in his *The last abbot of Glastonbury and other essays*, London, 1908, pp. 113–40, "English biblical criticism in the thirteenth century," first published in *Dublin review*, 1898. S. A. HIRSCH, "Roger Bacon and philology," *Roger Bacon essays*, 101–51. B. JARRETT, "A thirteenth century revision committee of the Bible," *Irish theological quarterly*, IV (1910), 56ff. For a description of the present revision committee of the Vulgate see the article "Vulgate, revision of," in the *Catholic encyclopedia*. E. FLÜGEL, "Roger Bacon's Stellung in der Geschichte der Philologie," *Philosophische Studien*, XIX (1902), 164–91.

Original sources. *The battle of the seven arts*, by Henri d'Andeli and the *Morale scolarium* of John of Garland, edited and translated, with introduction and notes and facsimilies of manuscripts, by L. J. PAETOW, Berkeley, 1914 and 1927 (Memoirs of the University of California, IV, nos. 1 and 2).

C. H. Haskins, "A list of text-books from the close of the twelfth century," in *Harvard studies in classical philology* (1909), 75–94; also in his *Studies in the history of mediaeval science*, 2nd edition, ch. xviii. Norton, *Readings*, 25–35, translates some extracts from the works of John of Salisbury, and pp. 60–75 translates the section from Gratian's *Decretum* entitled "Shall priests be acquainted with profane literature or no?" J. Dickinson, *The statesman's book of John of Salisbury*. The *Opus majus* of Roger Bacon, translated by Burke.

C. Bibliography

General books. Some of the general histories of literature, nos. **782–814** will be found useful, see e.g., no. **790.**

General accounts. A. Marigo, "Cultura letteraria e preumanistica nelle maggiori enciclopedie del dugento, lo '*Speculum*' ed il '*Tresors*,'" *Giornale storico della letteratura italiana*, LXVIII (1916), 1–42, 289–326. B. Groche, *Beiträge zur Geschichte einer Renaissancebewegung bei den deutschen Schriftstellern im 12 Jahrhundert*. F. Novati, *L'influsso del pensiero latino sopra la civiltà italiana del medio evo*, 2nd edition, Milan, 1899. J. L. Heiberg, "Et mislykket Renaissancetillφb," *Studier fra Sprog- og Oltidsforskning*, Copenhagen, 1892. G. Körting, *Geschichte der Literatur Italiens im Zeitalter der Renaissance*, III, 1–75. A. Graf, *Roma nella memoria e nelle immaginazioni del medio evo*. A. Bartoli, *I precursori del rinascimento*, Florence, 1877. C. Daniel, *Des études classiques dans la société chrétienne*, Paris, 1853, lays special stress on conditions in France in the twelfth and thirteenth centuries. W. Giesebrecht, *De litterarum studiis apud Italos*, Berlin, 1845, translated into Italian by C. Pascal, Florence, 1895. A. H. L. Heeren, *Geschichte der classischen Literatur im Mittelalter* [to 1400], 2 vols., Göttingen, 1822. O. Gruppe, *Geschichte der klassischen Mythologie und Reliogionsgeschichte während des Mittelalters im Abendland und während der Neuzeit*, Leipzig, 1921. Eva M. Sanford, "The use of classical Latin authors in *Libri manuales*," *Transactions of the American philological association*, LV (1924), 190–248.

Individual Latin classical authors in the middle ages. D. Comparetti, *Vergil*. G. Zappert, *Virgils Fortleben im Mittelalter*. N. Creizenach, *Die Aeneis, die vierte Ecloge und die Pharsalia im Mittelalter*, Frankfurt, 1864 (Prog.). T. Zielinski, *Cicero im Wandel der Jahrhunderten*, is very poor for the middle ages. G. Curcio, *Q. Orazio Flacco studiato in Italia dal secolo XIII al XVIII*, Catania, 1913. C. Pascal, *Letteratura latina medievale*, Catania, 1909, 117–74, on Seneca, Lucretius, and Ovid in the middle ages. L. Sudre, *Publii Ovidii Nasonis Metamorphoseon libros quomodo nostrates medii aevi poetae imitati interpretatique sint*, Paris, 1893 (Diss.). H. Unger, *De ovidiana in carminibus buranis quae dicuntur imitatione*, Berlin, 1914 (Diss.). M. Manitius, *Analekten zur Geschichte des Horaz im Mittelalter* [to 1300], Göttingen, 1893; "Beiträge zur Geschichte römischer Dichter im Mittelalter," *Philologus*, XLVII (1889), 710–20; XLIX (1890), 554–64; L (1891), 354–72; LI (1892), 156–71, 530–35, 704–19; LII (1894), 536–52; LVI (1897),

535–41; "Beiträge zur Geschichte römischer Prosaiker im Mittelalter," *ibid.*, XLVII (1889), 562–68; XLVIII (1889). 564–73; XLIX (1890), 191–92, 380–84; *Philologisches aus alten Bibliothekskatalogen bis 1300*, Frankfurt, 1892 (extract from *Rheinisches Museum*, neue Folge, XLVIII, 1892, Ergänzungsheft). K. DZIATZKO, "Zu Terentius im Mittelalter," *Neue Jahrbücher für Philologie und Pädagogik*, CIL (1894), 465–77. A. COLLIGNON, *Pétrone au moyen âge et dans la littérature française*, Paris, 1893. C. LANDI, "Stazio nel medio evo," in *Atti* of the Padua academy, XXXVII (1921), 201–32. RAND, *Ovid*. B. L. ULLMAN, "Tibullus in the mediaeval florilegia," *Classical philology*, XXIII, (1928), 128f.

Hildebert of Lavardin. B. HAURÉAU, *Les mélanges poétiques d'Hildebert de Lavardin*, Paris, 1882. C. PASCAL, *Poesia latina medievale*, Catania, 1907, 1–68. A. DIEUDONNÉ, *Hildebert de Lavardin*, Paris, 1898. P. DE DÉSERVILLER, *Un évêque au douzième siècle, Hildebert et son temps*, Paris, 1876. V. HÉBERT-DUPERRON, *De venerabilis Hildeberti vita et scriptis*, Bayeux, 1860.

John of Salisbury. C. SCHAARSCHMIDT, *Johannes Saresberiensis nach Leben und Studien, Schriften und Philosophie*, Leipzig, 1862. P. GENNRICH, "Zur Chronologie des Lebens Johanns von Salisbury," *Zeitschrift für Kirchengeschichte*, XIII (1892), 544–51. M. DEMIMUID, *Jean de Salisbury*, Paris, 1873 (Diss.).

Vincent of Beauvais. J. B. BOURGEAT, *Etudes sur Vincent de Beauvais*, Paris, 1856. F. RICHARD, *Vincentius von Beauvais als Pädagog nach seiner Schrift "De eruditione filiorum regalium,"* Leipzig, 1883. G. BIENTINESI, "Vincenzo di Beauvais et Pietro Dubois considerati come pedagogisti," Turin, 1916, is an extract from *Atti della r. accademia delle scienze di Torino*, LI (1915–16), 1411–30.

Greek in the middle ages. L. TRAUBE, *O Roma nobilis;* and *Vorlesungen*, 83ff. J. J. v. DÖLLINGER, "Einfluss der griechischen Literatur und Cultur auf die abendländische Welt im Mittelalter," translated into English in no. **913.** M. L. W. LAISTNER, "The revival of Greek in western Europe in the Carolingian age," *History*, IX (1924), 177f. M. R. JAMES, "A Greek-Latin lexicon of the XIII century, perhaps by Grosseteste," *Mélanges offerts à M. Emile Chatelain*, Paris, 1909. J. L. HEIBERG, "Die grieschische Grammatik Roger Bacons," *B.Z.*, IX (1900), 479–91. L. SCHÜTZ, "Der hl. Thomas von Aquin und sein Verständniss des Griechischen," *Philosophisches Jahrbuch*, VIII (1895), 271–83. A. TOUGARD, *L'hellénisme dans les écrivains du moyen âge du septième au douzième siècle*, Paris, 1886. C. CUISSARD, *L'étude du grec à Orléans depuis le IXe siècle jusqu'au milieu du XVIII siècle*, Orleans, 1883. E. EGGER, *L'hellénisme en France*, 2 vols., Paris, 1869, is superficial in its treatment of the middle ages. M. VOGEL, and V. GARDTHAUSEN, *Die griechischen Schreiber des Mittelalters und der Renaissance*, Leipzig, 1909. D. BIKÉLAS, *Die Griechen des Mittelalters und ihr Einfluss auf die europäische Cultur*, translated from the Greek by W. WAGNER, Gütersloh, 1878. C. GIDEL, *Les études grecques en Europe* [fourth century to 1453], Paris, 1878; *Nouvelles études sur la littérature grecque moderne*, pp. 1–289. J. F. CRAMER, *De graecis medii aevi studiis*, Stralsund,

1849–53. C. H. HASKINS, "The Greek element in the renaissance of the twelfth century," in *A.H.R.* XXV (1920), 603–15; also in *Studies in mediaeval science*, ch. VIII; see also ch. X, "North Italian translators of the twelfth century." P. PENDZIG, "Die griechischen Studien im deutschen Mittelalter," *Neue Jahrbücher für das klassische Altertum*, XLII (1918), 213f. A. HOFMEISTER, "Zur griechisch-lateinischen Übersetzungsliteratur des früheren Mittelalters," *Münchener Museum f. Philol. des Mittelalters*, IV (1922), 129–53.

For Greek in Sicily and southern Italy see outline XV, and the following: GOTHEIN, *Die Kultur-Entwickelung Süd-Italiens.* H. F. TOZER, "The Greek-speaking population of southern Italy," *Journal of Hellenic studies*, X (1889), 11–42. P. BATIFFOL, *L'abbaye de Rossano*, Paris, 1891; "Inscriptions byzantines de St. George au Vélabre;" "Librairies byzantines à Rome," *Mélanges d'archéologie et d'histoire*, VII (1887), 419–31; VIII (1888), 297ff., are studies on Greek emigrants from Byzantium to Rome in the seventh and eighth centuries. J. L. HEIBERG, "Eine mittelalterliche Übersetzung der Syntaxis des Ptolemaios," *Hermes*, XLV (1910), 57–66; see also XLVI (1911), 207–16. C. H. HASKINS, "Sicilian translators of the twelfth century," *Studies in the history of mediaeval science*, ch. IX. GAY, *L'Italie méridionale.*

Hebrew. S. A. HIRSCH, "Early English Hebraists: Roger Bacon and his predecessors," *Jewish quarterly review*, XII (1899), 34–88, reprinted in his *Book of essays*, London, 1905, 1–72. S. BERGER, *Quam notitiam linguae hebraicae habuerint Christiani medii aevi temporibus in Gallia*, Paris, 1893. K. NEUMANN, *Über die orientalischen Sprachstudien seit dem 13 Jahrhundert, mit besonderer Rücksicht auf Wien*, Vienna, 1899.

Textual criticism in the thirteenth century. P. J. WITZEL, "De Fr. Rogero Bacon eiusque sententia de rebus biblicis," *A.F.H.*, III (1910), 1–22, 185–213, contains the best bibliography. H. DENIFLE, "Die Handschriften der Bibel-Correctorien des 13 Jahrhunderts," *Archiv für Literatur- und Kirchengeschichte des Mittelalters*, IV (1888), 263–311, 471–601. S. BERGER, *De l'histoire de la Vulgate en France*, Paris, 1887; "Les essais qui ont été faits à Paris au treizième siècle pour corriger le texte de la Vulgate," *Revue de théologie et de philosophie* (Lausanne), XVI (1883), 41–66; *Histoire de la Vulgate*, Paris, 1893. P. MARTIN, "La Vulgate latine au XIIIe siècle d'après Roger Bacon," *Museon*, VII (1888), 88–107, 169–96, 278–91, 381–93; "Le texte parisien et la Vulgate latine," *ibid.*, VIII (1889), 444–66; IX (1890), 301–16. SALEMBIER, *Une page inédite de l'histoire de la Vulgate*, Amiens, 1890. F. KAULEN, *Geschichte der Vulgata*, Mainz, 1868; *Handbuch der Vulgata*, Mainz, 1870; 2nd edition, Freiburg, 1904. H. A. A. KENNEDY, "The old Latin versions of the Bible," *Dictionary of the Bible*, III (1902), 47–62; and H. J. WHITE, "Vulgate," *ibid.*, IV, 872–90.

Biblical scholarship in the Middle Ages; exegesis, translation and dissemination. C. HOLZHEY, *Die Inspiration der Heiligen Schrift in der Anschauung des Mittelalters von Karl dem Grossen bis zum Konzil von Trient.* F. KROPATSCHECK, *Das Schriftprinzip der lutherischen Kirche*, Bd. 1. *Das Erbe* *des Mittelalters*, Leipzig, 1904. L. DIESTEL, *Geschichte des Alten Testaments in der christlichen Kirche*, Jena, 1869. MARGARET DEANESLEY, *The Lollard Bible and other medieval biblical versions*. Cambridge, 1920, with bibliography. H. B. WORKMAN, *John Wyclif*, vol. II, chap. v, "Wyclif and the Bible." W. WALTHER, *Die deutsche Bibelübersetzung des Mittelalters*, 3 vols. in 1, Braunschweig, 1889–92. S. BERGER, *La Bible française au moyen âge*, Paris, 1884. F. FALK, *Die Bibel am Ausgange des Mittelalters, ihre Kenntnis und ihre Verbreitung*, Cologne, 1905.

Original sources. BEAUGENDRE'S uncritical edition of the works of HILDEBERT OF LAVARDIN is reprinted in MIGNE, *P.L.*, CLXXI. A number of his poems were critically edited by HAURÉAU in *Mélanges poëtiques d'Hildebert*. Twenty-two of HILDEBERT'S letters were reprinted by Brial in no. **967,** vol. XV, 312–28. JOHANNIS SARESBERIENSIS, *Opera omnia*, edited by J. A. GILES, 5 vols., Oxford, 1848, reprinted in no. **953,** *P. L.*, vol. CXCIX. There is a good edition of the *Policraticus*, IOANNIS SARESBERIENSIS Episcopi Carnotensis *Policratici sive de nugis curialium*, 2 vols., Oxford, 1909, and of the *Metalogicus*, Ioannis Saresberiensis Episcopi Carnotensis *Metalogicon*, Oxford, 1929, edited by C. C. J. WEBB. The *Historia Pontificalis* has been edited by R. L. POOLE, *Ioannis Saresberiensis historiae pontificalis quae supersunt*, Oxford, 1927. GIRALDUS CAMBRENSIS, *Opera*, edited by J. S. BREWER, 8 vols., London, 1861 (Rolls series, 21). *De bibliorum sacrorum textibus originalibus, versionibus graeca et latina vulgata*, edited by H. HODY, Oxford, 1705, published the portions of the works of Roger Bacon referring to the revision of the *Vulgate;* note that his book dates before JEBB'S edition of the *Opus majus* of BACON. ROGER BACON, *Opus majus*, part III, on the study of language, is the best source of information on textual criticism in the thirteenth century. *The Greek grammar of Roger Bacon and a fragment of his Hebrew grammar*, edited by E. NOLAN and S. A. HIRSCH, Cambridge, 1902. For Roger Bacon and Robert Grosseteste in general see also outline XXI. CONRADI HIRSAUGENSIS, *Dialogus super auctores sive Didascalon*, edited by G. SCHEPSS, Würzburg, 1889. HUGO OF TRIMBERG, *Registrum multorum auctorum*, edited by J. H. HUEMER, Vienna, 1888. NICOLAI DE BIBERA, *Carmen satiricum*, edited by T. FISCHER, Halle, 1870, translated into German by A. REINÄCKER, Erfurt, 1871.

Bibliographies. There are no systematic bibliographies of this subject which has been sadly neglected until a short time ago. See bibliographies and bibliographical footnotes in the works mentioned.

XIX. ARS DICTAMINIS AND ARS NOTARIA

A. OUTLINE

1. The transformation of rhetoric in medieval universities. For the importance of rhetoric in the Roman schools see outline I, and Baldwin, *Medieval rhetoric*, ch. III. The comparative unimportance of rhetoric in the early middle ages, when the study of the elements of Roman law was often a part of it.

2. The art of writing formal letters and legal documents in the middle ages. This art, which had been a very subordinate part of rhetoric in the early middle ages, became an independent branch of learning in some universities, especially those which stressed the study of law. In its earliest form it was called *ars dictaminis* or *dictamen prosaicum.* In some places it usurped the whole field of rhetoric and was called *rhetorica.*

3. The *ars dictaminis* as a separate branch of instruction originated in Italy. The *Formularius tabellionum* of Irnerius. Alberich of Monte-Cassino (second half of the eleventh century) was the founder of the art. His *Rationes dictandi.* Manuals consisting of explanatory text and illustrative material. Formularies and letter-books. Collections of model letters for students and their parents. The *cursus.*

4. The *ars dictaminis* in Bologna. Close association with the study of law. Tendency to make the art more and more practical. The famous Boncompagno (ca. 1165–ca. 1240). His *Rhetorica antiqua, Novissima rhetorica, Mirrha, Oliva,* and *Cedrus.* The *Candelabrum* (1220–23). Guido Faba, who wrote about 1225, systematized the art in his *Summa dictaminis* and *Dictamen.*

5. The character of the *ars dictaminis* and its transformation into the *ars notaria* in Bologna. Raynerius, master of the *ars notaria* in 1219. Degrees in *notaria.* Rolandinus Passagerius (died 1300), the most famous doctor of the art. His *Summa artis notariae.* The faculty of *notaria* in Bologna in the thirteenth century. The art in other Italian universities.

6. The *ars dictaminis* and the *ars notaria* beyond the Alps. The *Parisiana* of John Garland of Paris. The "Lombard dame, Rhetoric," mentioned in the *Battle of the seven arts.* Laurentius of Aquileia in Paris towards the close of the thirteenth century. The important school of the *ars dictaminis* in Orleans. The *Summa dictaminum* of Bernard Silvester of Tours (ca. 1153). Itinerant *dictatores* such as Ponce of Provence who wrote his *Summa de dictamine* about 1250. The art in Chartres, Toulouse, Montpellier, and in England and Germany.

7. Changes brought about in the curricula of medieval schools and universities by the popularity of this short-lived "business course." Rivalry of the art with the ancient classics. Causes of its decline in the universities in the fourteenth century.

8. The business world of the graduates of the *ars dictaminis* and *ars notaria.* Secretaries and notaries in the chanceries of state and church, especially the papal chancery.

B. Special Recommendations for Reading

General survey. C. S. Baldwin, *Medieval rhetoric,* especially ch. viii where the *Candelabrum* is digested.

Fundamental works. L. Rockinger, *Briefsteller und Formelbücher des XI bis XIV Jahrhunderts, Q.E.,* IX, in 2 parts, Munich, 1863–64; "Ueber die ars dictandi und die summae dictaminis in Italien," in *S.B., Munich Acad.,* 1861, I, 98–151. C. V. Langlois, "Formulaires de lettres du

XIIe, du XIIIe et du XIVe siècle," six articles in *Notices et extraits*, XXXIV, part I (1891), 1–32, 305–22; part II (1895), 1–29; XXXV, part II (1897), 409–34, 793–830. Both of these authors have included many original sources which illustrate their introductions.

Model student letters. C. H. HASKINS, in "Life of medieval students as seen in their letters," *A.H.R.*, III (1897–98), 203–29 (reprinted in *Studies in mediaeval culture*, ch. II) has given a fine demonstration of the way in which these model student letters can be used as sources of history.

The cursus. R. L. POOLE, *Lectures on the history of the papal chancery*, ch. IV. A. C. CLARK, *The cursus in mediaeval and vulgar Latin*, Oxford, 1910. HASKINS, *Renaissance*, ch. V.

Boncompagno, Bene of Lucca, and Guido Faba. A. GAUDENZI, "Sulla cronologia delle opere dei dettatori bolognesi da Buoncompagno a Bene di Lucca," *Bullettino del' Istituto storico italiano*, XIV (1895), 85–174. C. SUTTER, *Aus Leben und Schriften des Magisters Buoncompagno*, Freiburg and Leipzig, 1894.

The business world of graduates of the art. L. B. DIBBEN, "Secretaries in the thirteenth and fourteenth centuries," *E.H.R.*, XXV (1910), 430–44. BRESSLAU, *Urkundenlehre;* and POOLE, *Papal chancery, passim.* A. GIRY, *Manuel de diplomatique*, especially book V, and book VI, ch. I. W. WATTENBACH, *Das Schriftwesen*, 456–66. P. FOURNIER, *Les officialités au moyen âge*, Paris, 1880. See also E. SECKEL, in *Zeitschrift der Savigny-Stiftung für Rechtsgeschichte*, XXI (1900), 212–338.

C. BIBLIOGRAPHY

General books. See the books on diplomatics, nos. **238–44.**

General surveys. H. BRESSLAU, *Urkundenlehre*, vol. II, part I, second edition, pp. 225–81. K. BURDACH, *Schlesisch-Böhmische Briefmuster aus der Wende des vierzehnten Jahrhunderts*, Berlin (1926), 7. A. BÜTOW, *Die Entwicklung der mittelalterlichen Briefsteller bis zur Mitte des 12 Jahrhunderts mit bes. Berücksichtigung . . . der ars dictandi*, Greifswald, 1908 (Diss.). F. NOVATI, *L'influsso del pensiero latino*, ch. VIII. L. ROCKINGER, *Ueber Briefsteller und Formelbücher in Deutschland während des Mittelalters*, Munich, 1861; *Ueber Formelbücher vom XIII bis zum XVI Jahrhundert als rechtsgeschichtliche Quelle*, Munich, 1855. W. WATTENBACH, "Ueber Briefsteller des Mittelalters," *Archiv für Kunde österreichischer Geschichtsquellen*, XIV, 29–94, an appendix to *Iter Austriacum*, Vienna, 1853. PALACKY, "Ueber Formelbücher," *Abh. der böhmischen Gesellschaft der Wissenschaften*, II (1842), 219–368; V (1847), 1–216. PESCHEK, "Ueber Formelbücher aus dem Mittelalter," *Archiv für sächsische Geschichte*, 1843. H. BAERWALD, *Für Characteristik und Kritik mittelalterliche Formelbücher*, Vienna, 1858. F. K. v. SAVIGNY, *Geschichte des romischen Rechts*, III, ch. XXI.

Cursus. N. VALOIS, "Etude sur le rythme des bulles pontificales," *B.E.C.*, XLII (1881), 161–98, 257–72, also published separately, Paris, 1881. E. NORDEN, *Die antike Kunstprosa*, II, 923–60. A. GIRY, *Manuel de diplomatique*, 454–62. L. COUTURE, "Le 'cursus' ou rythme prosaïque dans la liturgie et dans la littérature de l'église latine du IIIe siècle à la renaissance," *R.Q.H.*, LI (1892), 253–61. L. HAVET, *La prose métrique de Symmache et les origines métriques du cursus*, Paris, 1892. L. DUCHESNE, "Note sur l'origine du '*cursus*' ou rythme prosaïque," *B.E.C.*, L (1889), 161–63. BALDWIN, *Medieval rhetoric*, 223–27. E. VACANDARD, "Le cursus, son origine, son histoire, son emploi dans la liturgie," *R.Q.H.*, XXXIV (1905), 59–102. K. POLHEIM, *Die lateinische Reimprosa*, Berlin, 1925. M. W. CROLL, "The cadence of English oratorical prose," *Studies in philology*, XVI (1919), 1–55. A. DE BOÜARD, *Manuel de diplomatique française et pontificale*, Paris, 1929. P. TOYNBEE, *Dantis Alagherii epistolae;* the letters of Dante, emended text with intro-translation, notes and indices, etc, Oxford, 1920.

Ars notaria. G. POLETTI, *Il notariato a Bergamo nel seculo XIII: appunti*, Bergamo, 1912. V. ROSE, "Ars notaria, Tironische Noten und Stenographie im 12 Jahrhundert," *Hermes*, VIII (1874), 303–26.

Ars dictaminis in Italy. C. H. HASKINS, "The early artes dictandi in Italy," *Studies in mediaeval culture*, 170–92. BÜTOW, *Die Entwicklung der mittelalterlichen Briefsteller*. G. MANACORDA, *Storia della scuola in Italia*, Milan, 1915, I: 2, 255–79.

Ars dictaminis in France. N. VALOIS, *De arte scribendi epistolas apud gallicos medii aevi scriptores rhetoresve*, Paris, 1880 (Diss.). C. V. LANGLOIS, "Maître Bernard," *B.E.C.*, LIV (1893), 225–50, 792–95; see also SANDYS, *Classical scholarship*, I, 534. HASKINS, "An early Bolognese formulary," *Mélanges d'histoire offerts à Henri Pirenne*, Brussels, 1926, 201–10; "An Italian master Bernard," *Essays presented to Reginald Lane Poole*, Oxford, 1927, 211–26. W. HOLTZMANN, "Eine oberitalienische Ars dictandi und die Briefsammlung des Priors Peter von St. Jean in Sens," *N.A.*, XLVI (1926), 34–52.

Original sources. ROCKINGER, *Briefsteller*. The *Formularius tabellionum* of IRNERIUS and the *Rhetorica antiqua* of BONCOMPAGNO are published in vols. I and II of the *Bibliotheca iuridica* listed in the following outline under "Original sources." "Notice sur une 'Summa dictaminis' jadis conservée à Beauvais," *Notices et extraits*, XXXVI, part I (1899), 171–205; "Des recueils épistolaires de Bérard de Naples," *ibid.*, XXVII, part 2 (1879), 87–149; "Le Formulaire de Clairmarais," *Journal des savants*, 1899, 172–95; *Le Formulaire de Tréguier et les écoliers bretons des écoles d'Orléans au commencement du XIVe siècle*, Orleans, 1890 (Mémoires de la Société archéologique de l'Orléanais), all edited by L. DELISLE. L. AUVRAY, *Documents orléanais du XIIe et du XIIIe siècle extraits du Formulaire de Bernard de Meung*, Orleans, 1892 (also *ibid.*, XXIII). *Eine Bologneser Ars dictandi des 12 Jahrhunderts*, edited by H. KALBFUSS, Rome, 1914 (extract from *Quellen und Forschungen aus italienischen Archiven und Bibliotheken*). RANIERI DA PERUGIA, *Ars notaria*, edited by A. GAUDENZI, Bologna, 1890. *Ein Donaueschinger Briefsteller*, edited by A. CARTELLIERI, Innsbruck, 1898. L. WAHRMUND (editor), *Die Ars notariae des Rainerius Perusinus*, Innsbruck, 1917 (Quellen zur Geschichte des römischkanonischen Processes im Mittelalter, III). "Formelbücher und Briefsteller in englischen Hss," edited by K. HAMPE, *N.A.*,

XXII (1897), 609–28. JOHN GARLAND, *Parisiana*, edited by G. MARI, under the title, "Poetria magistri Johannis Anglici de arte prosayca, metrica et rithmica," *Romanische Forschungen*, XIII (1902), 883–965, except that portion on "Rithmica" which he has previously published in his *I trattati medievali di rithmica latina*, Milan, 1899, 35–80. E. HELLER, *Die Ars dictandi des Thomas von Capua* (*S.B.*, *Heidelberg Acad.*, 4 Abh., 1929).

Bibliographies. Most of the materials essential for a thorough study of this outline are still in manuscript form and those which have been published are scattered widely in miscellaneous publications. The best guide is BRESSLAU; see also BALDWIN, *Medieval rhetoric*, ch. VIII. Some help will be obtained from MOLINIER, *Les sources*, II, 204–06. See also the bibliographical footnotes in the literature mentioned, especially Haskins, *Studies in mediaeval culture*, chs. I and IX, and nos. **20**, **24**, **25**, and **41**.

XX. STUDY OF ROMAN AND CANON LAW

A. OUTLINE

1. The history of the study and the application of Roman law in the early middle ages (see outline XII of part II). Causes of the revival of interest in law towards the beginning of the twelfth century. The legend of the discovery of the *Digest* in Amalfi in 1135.

2. Chief centers of the study of jurisprudence in the second half of the eleventh century, (1) Provence, (2) Lombard cities, (3) Ravenna, (4) Bologna. The *Exceptiones Petri*. Pepo in Bologna.

3. Irnerius, a master of arts, began to lecture on law in Bologna about 1088. The beginnings of the university of Bologna. The intense study of the *Corpus iuris civilis*, especially the *Digest*. The glossators such as Placentinus, Azo and Accursius. "In many respects the work of the School of Bologna represents the most brilliant achievement of the intellect of medieval Europe"—Rashdall. Law in other Italian universities.

4. The study of Roman law beyond the Alps. The legal knowledge of Ivo of Chartres. *Lo Codi* in Provence (ca. 1150). Placentinus in Montpellier. The law school of Orleans. Influence of Roman law upon the law of the rising kingdom of France. Vacarius in England in the twelfth century. His *Liber pauperum*. The vexed question of the degree of influence of the Roman law in England. The remarkable "reception" of Roman law in Germany in the fifteenth century.

5. Influence of the revived interest in Roman law upon the civil and political life in the middle ages.

6. Growth of canon law in the early middle ages from customs, canons of church councils, and decretals of the popes. Influence of the Roman law upon the law of the church.

7. Early compilations of the law of the church. The elementary attempt by Dionysius Exiguus in the sixth century. The *Pseudo-Isidorian decretals* (see outline XV of part II). The *Decretum* of bishop Burchard of Worms and the *Decretum* and the shorter *Panormia* of Ivo of Chartres (both in the eleventh century).

8. The famous *Decretum* of Gratian, published most probably in 1140 in Bologna, when the study of law was very vigorous there. He called the book, *Concordia discordantium canonum*. Origin of its *sic-et-non* method. The three parts of Gratian's *Decretum*. Largely through this text-book, canon law now branched off from theology and became a special study in medieval universities.

9. Compilations after Gratian. The official collections of popes Alexander III and Honorius III were superseded by the *Decretales* of pope Gregory IX, issued in 1234. The *Sextus* collection of pope Boniface VIII, 1298. The *Clementinae*, 1313. The *Extravagantes*, added towards the close of the fifteenth century. All these with Gratian's *Decretum* were published as the *Corpus iuris canonici* in 1582. In 1904 pope Pius X authorized the codification of canon law. The Code of Canon Law became effective in 1918.

10. Relations between the Roman and the canon law in the universities and in the medieval legal world. The part played by the enthusiasm for law in shaping the curricula of medieval universities.

B. Special Recommendations for Reading

Brief general surveys. Rashdall, *Universities*, I, 89–143, 254–68. Taylor, *Mediaeval mind*, second edition, II, ch. xxxiv. For Roman and canon law in England, see Pollock and Maitland, *History of English law*, book I, ch. v. C. H. Haskins, *Renaissance*, ch. vii. Crump and Jacob, *Legacy*, Canon law, 321–61; Roman law, 363–99. G. Schnürer, *Kirche und Kultur im Mittelalter*, 3 vols., 2nd edition, Paderborn, 1927, II, 407–13, 425 sq., 438. *C.M.H.*, V, ch. xxi.

Introductory books on Roman law. R. Sohm, *Institutionen: ein Lehrbuch der Geschichte des römischen Privatrechts*, Sohm-Mitteis-Wenger 17th German edition, Leipzig, 1923. Translated into English from the 8th and 9th German edition, by J. C. Ledlie, *The Institutes*, 3rd edition, Oxford, 1907, see especially ch. iii. R. W. Leage, *Roman private law*, New York, 1906. P. F. Girard, *A short history of Roman law: being the first part of his Manuel élémentaire de droit romain*, translated by A. H. F. Lefroy, Toronto, 1906. J. Hadley, *Introduction to Roman law: in twelve academic lectures*, New York, 1873 (often reprinted). W. C. Morey, *Outlines of Roman law*, 2nd edition, New York, 1885. H. J. Robey, *An introduction to the study of Justinian's Digest*, Cambridge, 1884. C. P. Sherman, *Roman law in the modern world*, 3 vols., 2nd edition, New York, 1922. W. W. Buckland, *Textbook of Roman law, Augustus to Justinian*, Cambridge, 1921. W. A. Hunter, *Roman law*, 4th edition, London, 1903. P. Girard, *Traité élémentaire de droit romain*, 7th edition, Paris, 1924. W. W. Buckland, *A manual of Roman private law*, Cambridge, 1925. See also under outline III in part II.

Roman law in the middle ages. By far the best account is P. Vinogradoff, *Roman law in medieval Europe*, 2nd edition by F. de Zulueta, Oxford, 1929; decay, 11–41; revival, 43–69; select bibliography at end of chapters. *The Continental legal history series*, published under the auspices of the Association of American law schools, 11 vols., Boston, 1912, vol. I, especially, 87–147, 206–13, 334–78, 617–58, contains translations from several European books. TAYLOR, *Classical heritage*, 56–70. J. BRYCE, *The ancient Roman empire and the British empire in India; The diffusion of Roman and English law throughout the world: two historical essays, reprinted and revised from Studies in history and jurisprudence*, Oxford University Press, 1914. W. GOETZ, "Das Wiederaufleben des römischen Rechtes im 12 Jahrhundert," *Archiv für Kulturgeschichte*, X (1912), 25–39. HULME, *Middle ages*, 201–03, 635–37, 644–46, 685, 686, 698ff. F. P. GIRARD, "Les préliminaires de la renaissance du droit romain," *Revue historique de droit français et étranger*, 4 série, I (1922), 5–46. E. M. MEYERS, "De universiteit van Orleans in de XIIIe eeuw," *Tijdschrift voor Rechtsgeschiedenis*, 1918, 1919. G. DIGARD, "La papauté et l'étude du droit romain au XIIIe siècle à propos de la fausse bulle d'Innocent IV Dolentes," *B.E.C.*, LI (1890), 381–419. C. N. S. WOOLF, *Bartolus of Sasseferrato, his position in the history of medieval political thought*, Cambridge, 1913. A. C. JEMOLO, *Il "Liber minoritarium" e la povertà minoritica nei giuristi del XIII e del XIV secolo*, Sassari, 1921.

Standard work on the history of Roman law. F. C. v. SAVIGNY, *Geschichte des römischen Rechts im Mittelalter*, 6 vols., Heidelberg, 1815–31; 2nd edition, 7 vols., 1834–51; translated in part into French from the second edition, *Histoire du droit romain au moyen âge*, 4 vols., Paris, 1839. "Roman law in the universities of the middle ages," is an extract from this work translated in H. BARNARD, *An account of universities*, revised edition, Hartford, 1873, 273–330.

Canon law. EMERTON, *Mediaeval Europe*, 582–92. LAVISSE et RAMBAUD, *Histoire générale*, II, 262–65. The articles "Canon law" in the *Ency. Brit.*, and "Law, canon," in the *Catholic encyclopedia*. *The Continental legal history series*, I, 705–24. M. GRABMANN, *Geschichte*, see index in vol. II under "Kanonisches Recht." For the canon law in England, F. W. MAITLAND, *Roman canon law*. W. STUBBS, "History of canon law in England," in his *Seventeen lectures*, lectures XIII–XIV. Additional material in GROSS, *Sources*, no. 767.

Original sources. NORTON, *Readings*, 49–75. BARTOLUS, *On the conflict of laws*, translated into English by J. H. BEALE, Cambridge, 1914.

C. BIBLIOGRAPHY

General books. The constitutional histories of the various countries of western Europe are essential for a thorough study of this outline; see nos. **527–36, 578–84, 605–09,** and **633–35b.** For the canon law almost all general histories of the church, nos. **395–498,** are helpful, but see especially no. **462.** The encyclopaedias for church history, nos. **104–14,** are indispensable. See also the literature under outline XII in part II, and the books on the university of Bologna, under outline XXII, and nos. **183** and **937.** J. H. WIGMORE, *A panorama of the world's legal systems*, 3 vols., St. Paul, 1928; Roman law, vol. I, 373ff.; Romanesque law, vol. III, 981ff.; Canon law, vol. III, 935ff. H. HAZELTINE, *C.M.H.*, V, 921–33, bibliography on civil and canon law. R. W. CARLYLE and A. J. CARLYLE, *History of mediaeval political* *thought*, vol. V, *The political theory of the thirteenth century*. (Canonists of the later thirteenth century on the temporal authority of the papacy, 318–38.) H. FEHR, *Das Recht im Bilde* (a history of medieval and early modern law), Munich and Leipzig, 1923.

General works on Roman law. J. FLACH, *Etudes critiques sur l'histoire du droit romain au moyen âge, avec textes inédits*, Paris, 1890. M. A. v. BETHMANN-HOLLWEG, *Der Civilprozess des gemeinen Rechts in geschichtlicher Entwickelung*, 6 vols., Bonn, 1864–74, vols. IV–VI, traverse the same field covered by SAVIGNY's great work. H. FITTING, "Zur Geschichte der Rechtswissenschaft im Mittelalter," in no. **183**, Romanic division, VI (1885), 94–186. M. FOURNIER, "L'église et le droit romain au XIIIe siècle," *Nouvelle revue historique de droit français et étranger*, XIV (1890), 50ff.; XV (1891), 134ff. H. FITTING, *Zur Geschichte der Rechtswissenschaft am Anfange des Mittelalters: eine Rede*, Halle, 1875.

Sources and literature of Roman law. M. CONRAT (COHN), *Geschichte der Quellen und Literatur des römischen Rechts im früheren Mittelalter*, vol. I, Leipzig, 1891. P. KRÜGER, *Geschichte der Quellen und Literatur des römischen Rechts*, Leipzig, 1888; 2nd edition, 1912. SHERMAN, *Roman law*, III, 257–73. P. BONFANTE, *Storia del diritto romano*, 2 vols., Rome, 1923; le interpolazioni, vol. I, 126–46; bibliografia, vol. I, 126–28 footnote.

Roman law in Italy. H. FITTING, *Die Anfänge der Rechtsschule zu Bologna*, Berlin and Leipzig, 1888. B. BRUGI, *Per la storia della giurisprudenza e delle università italiane*, Turin, 1914. A. PROLOGO, *Due grandi giureconsulti del secolo XIII: Andrea de Barulo e Andrea d'Isernia*, Trani, 1914. E. BESTA, *L'opera d'Irnerio: contributo alla storia del diritto romano*, 2 vols., Turin, 1896. GAY, *L'Italie méridionale et l'empire byzantin*. SHERMAN, *Roman law*, bibliography, vol. III, 40–43; influence, vol. I, 195 sqq.

Roman law in France. M. FOURNIER, *Histoire de la science du droit en France*, 3 vols., Paris, 1892, especially vol. III, which treats of law in the medieval French universities. G. PÉRIES, *La faculté de droit dans l'ancienne université de Paris, 1160–1793*, Paris, 1890. H. FITTING, "Le scuole di diritto in Francia durante l'XI seculo," *Bullettino dell' Istituto di diritto romano*, IV (1891–92). VINOGRADOFF, *Roman law*, 71–96. SHERMAN, *Roman law*, bibliography, vol. III, 48–52; influence, vol. I, 224ff. G. GAVET, *Sources de l'histoire des institutions et du droit français*, Paris, 1899, 675–84.

Roman law in England. T. E. SCRUTTON, *The influence of the Roman law on the law of England*, Cambridge, 1885. VINOGRADOFF, *Roman law*, 97–118. W. H. HOLDSWORTH, *Sources and literature of English law*, Oxford, 1925, 6, 8, 23, 24, 29–32, 72, 203ff., 234, 235. SHERMAN, *Roman law*, bibliography, vol. III, 73ff.; influence, vol. I, 344ff. W. H. HOLDSWORTH, *A history of English law*, 9 vols., 3rd edition, 1926, vol. II, 133–49, 267–68; vol. IV, 217–93. W. G. DE BURGH, *The legacy of the ancient world*, London, 1924, 380–95. F. DE ZULUETA, "The 'Liber Pauperum' of Vacarius," *Selden Society publications*, London, 1927. *Anglo-American legal history, select essays*, Boston, 1907–09. For special works, see GROSS, *Sources*, p. 683.

Roman law in Germany. G. v. BELOW, *Die Ursachen der Rezeption des römischen Rechts in Deutschland*, Munich, 1906 (Historische Bibliothek, 19). W. MODDERMANN, *Die Rezeption des römischen Rechts*, translated from the Dutch into German by K. SCHULTZ, Jena, 1875. E. SECKEL, *Beiträge zur Geschichte beider Rechte im Mittelalter*, Tübingen, 1898. VINOGRADOFF, *Roman law*, 119–44, bibliography, 145ff. SHERMAN, *Roman law*, bibliography, vol. III, 66–71; influence, reception, etc., vol. I, 302ff.

Canon law in general. See U. STUTZ for History of Canon law in HOLTZENDORFFS, *Enzyklopädie der Rechtswissenschaft*, 2nd edition, Leipzig, 1914, V, 279–368. A. M. KOENIGER, *Grundriss einer Geschichte des katholischen Kirchenrechts*, Cologne, 1919. Abbé DUBALLET, *Cours complet de droit canonique et de jurisprudence canonico-civile*, Paris, 1896ff., will be even more comprehensive than no. **462.** J. DODD, *History of canon law*, London, 1884, ch. v. F. LAURIN, *Introductio in Corpus juris canonici*, Freiburg, 1889. R. GENESTAL, "L'enseignement du droit canonique et son importance pour l'histoire du droit," *Revue de l'histoire des religions*, LXIX 54–69. A. VAN HOVE, *Prolegomena ad codicem iuris canonici*, Mechlin, 1928. J. J. HERZOG, *Realencyclopädie*, 3rd edition (editor, A. HAUCK), Leipzig, 1896–1913. C. MIRBT, *Quellen zur Geschichte des Papsttums und des römischen Katholizismus.* A. AMANIEU, A. VILLIEN, and E. MAGNIN, *Dictionnaire de droit canonique*, Paris, 1924ff. C. F. ROSSHIRT, *Geschichte des Rechts im Mittelalter*. I, *Canonisches Recht*, Mainz, 1846.

Text-books of church law. E. FRIEDBERG, *Lehrbuch des katholischen und evangelischen Kirchenrechts*, 6th edition, Leipzig, 1909. R. v. SCHERER, *Handbuch des Kirchenrechts*, 2 vols., Graz, 1886–98. A. L. RICHTER, *Lehrbuch des katholischen und evangelischen Kirchenrechts*, Leipzig, 1842; 8th edition by R. W. DOVE and W. KAHL, Leipzig, 1886. J. B. SÄGMÜLLER, *Lehrbuch des katholischen Kirchenrechts*, Freiburg, 4th edition, 1925. U. STUTZ, *Die kirchliche Rechtsgeschichte*, Stuttgart, 1905. J. HERGENRÖTHER, *Lehrbuch des katholischen Kirchenrechts*, 2nd edition, Freiburg, 1905. R. SOHM, *Kirchenrecht*, 2nd edition (editors, E. JACOBI, O. MAYER), Leipzig, 1923. P. C. AUGUSTINE, *A commentary on the new code of canon law*, 8 vols., St. Louis, 1921–23. S. WAYWOOD, *A practical commentary on the code of canon law*, 2 vols., 2nd edition, New York, 1926.

Sources and literature of canon law. J. F. v. SCHULTE, *Die Geschichte der Quellen und Literatur des canonischen Rechts von Gratian bis auf die Gegenwart*, 3 vols., Stuttgart, 1875–80 (see the review of this fundamental work by P. VIOLLET, in *Bulletin critique de littérature, d'histoire et de philologie*, 1881, nos. 23 and 24). A. TARDIF, *Histoire des sources du droit canonique*, Paris, 1887. P. SCHNEIDER, *Die Lehre von den Kirchenrechtsquellen*, Regensburg, 1892. F. MAASSEN, *Geschichte der Quellen und der Literatur des canonischen Rechts im Abendlande*, Gratz, 1870. A. FRANTZ, *Die Literatur des Kirchenrechts, 1884–1894*, Leipzig, 1896. F. WALTER, *Fontes juris ecclesiastici antiqui et hodierni*, Bonn, 1861. C. G. MOR, "Le droit romain dans les collections canoniques des Xe et XIe siècles," *Revue historique de droit français et étranger*, 4 série VI (1927), 512–24. L. WAHRMUND, *Quellen zur*

Geschichte des römisch-kanonischen Processes im Mittelalter, Innsbruck, 1905. For works of P. FOURNIER, E. SECKEL, H. SINGER, F. GILLMANN, and others on sources and literature see VAN HOVE, *Prolegomena ad codicem iuris canonici*, in copious footnotes on canon law in the middle ages.

Decretum of Gratian. F. POMETTI, *Il Decretum di Graziano nei suoi precedenti storici e nelle sue consequence storico-ecclesiastiche*, Corigliano Calabro, 1910. F. FOURNIER, "La date du Décret de Gratien," *Revue d'histoire et de littérature religieuses*, III (1898). G. OESTERLE, "Graziano e l'opera sua giuridica," *Rivista camaldolese*, I (1926), 62–79.

Periodicals on church law. *Archiv für katholisches Kirchenrecht*, Innsbruck, 1857ff., Mainz, 1862ff. (several indexes). *Zeitschrift für Kirchenrecht*, Berlin and Tübingen, 1861–80, 2nd series, Freiburg, 1881–90, 3rd series with the title, *Deutsche Zeitschrift für Kirchenrecht*, Freiburg, 1891ff. See also nos. **183** and **491.** *Apollinaris*, Rome, 1928ff. *Ius pontificum* (editor, A. Toso), Rome, 1922ff. *Acta sanctae sedis*, Rome, 1865–1908. *Le canoniste contemporain*, Paris, 1878ff. *Il diritto ecclesiastico*, Rome, 1890ff. *Periodica de re canonica et morali* (editor, A. VERMEERSCH, S. J., and others), Bruges and Rome, 1907ff. *Ephemerides theologicae lovanienses*, Bruges, 1924ff. *Kirchenrechtliche Abhandlungen*, by U. STUTZ and J. HECKEL (since 1928), Stuttgart, 1902ff. *Zeitschrift der Savigny-Stiftung fuer Rechts-Geschichte*, Kanonistische Abteilung, I (32), Weimar, 1911ff.

Original sources. For pre-Justinian law see *Fontes iuris romani anteiustiniani* (editors, S. RICCOBONO, I. BAVIERA, C. FERRINI), Florence, 1909; *Fontes juris romani*, edited by C. G. BRUNS, 7th ed. by O. GRADENWITZ, Tübingen, 1909. *Collectio librorum iuris anteiustiniani*, 2nd edition (editors, P. KRÜGER, TH. MOMMSEN, G. STUDEMUND), Berlin, 1912; *Codex Theodosianus* (edition, P. KRÜGER), Berlin, 1923–26. For Justinian law see *Corpus iuris civilis* (editors, P. KRÜGER, Th. MOMMSEN, R. SCHOELL, G. KROLL) edition stereotypa, Berlin, 1922. *The Institutes of Justinian*, translated into English, by J. B. MOYLE, 5th edition, Oxford, 1913. *The Digest of Justinian*, translated by C. H. MONRO, 2 vols., Cambridge, 1904–09. R. POUND, *Readings in Roman law*, 2nd edition, Cambridge, 1914. IRNERIUS, *Summa codicis*, and *Quaestiones de iuris subtilitatibus*, both edited by H. FITTING, Berlin, 1894. *Bibliotheca iuridica medii aevi: scripta, anecdota glossatorum*, 3 vols., edited by A. GAUDENZI, Bologna, 1888–1901. *Juristische Schriften des früheren Mittelalters aus Handschriften meist zum ersten Mal herausgegeben und erörtert*, edited by H. FITTING, Halle, 1876. *Lo Codi*, edited by H. FITTING and H. SUCHIER, 1906. E. H. FRESHFIELD, *A manual of Roman law. The Ecloga*, English translation, Cambridge, 1926; *A manual of Roman law. The Procheiros Nomos*, English translation, Cambridge, 1928. C. E. ZACHARIAE V. LINGENTHAL, *Collectio librorum iuris graeco-romani ineditorum*, Leipzig, 1852. (For Epanagoge, see 53–217.) G. E. HEIMBACH, *Basilicorum libri LX*, 7 vols., Leipzig, 1833–97; last volume is by C. FERRINI and I. MERCATI, *Basilicorum libri LX editionis Heimbachianae supplementum*, Leipzig, 1897. E. H. FRESHFIELD, *A manual of Roman law. The Ecloga ad Procheiron mutata*, including the Rhodian maritime law (1166), English translation,

Cambridge, 1927. G. E. HEIMBACH, *Constantini Harmenopuli manuale legum sive Hexabiblos*, Leipzig, 1851 (Greek text, also Latin translation). B. BIONDO, *Istituzioni di diritto romano*, vol. I, Catania, 1929; important for research.

The best edition of the canon law is *Corpus juris canonici*, edited by E. FRIEDBERG, 2 vols., Leipzig, 1879–81 (reprint, 1922). *Fontes juris canonici selecti*, edited by A. GALANTE, Innsbruck, 1906. *Kirchliche Rechtsquellen: Urkundenbuch zur Vorlesungen über Kirchenrecht*, edited by B. HÜBLER, 2nd edition, Berlin, 1893. *Codex iuris canonici*, promulgated Rome, 1917. *Acta apostolicae sedis*, Rome, 1909ff. (official publication). P. GASPARRI, *Codicis iuris canonici fontes*, Rome, 1923ff. U. STUTZ, *Der Geist des codex iuris canonici*, Stuttgart, 1918. A. ORTSCHEID, *Essai concernant la nature de la codification et son influence sur la science juridique, d'après le concept du Code de droit canonique*, Paris, 1922. A. BERNAREGGI, *Metodi e sistemi delle antiche collezioni e del nuova Codice di diritto canonico*, Monza, 1919. For the Pseudo-Isidorian Decretals see under outline XV in part II.

Bibliographies. See the general bibliographies for church history, nos. **49–55.** For Roman law there is a short practical bibliography at the head of chapters in VINOGRADOFF, *Roman law*, and for canon law a similar bibliography in MATER, *L'église catholique*, 19–43. A. GRANDIN, *Bibliographie générale des sciences juridiques, politiques, économiques et sociales de 1800 à 1925–26*, 3 vols., Paris, 1926. For more detail see the books listed under the headings, "Sources and literature" and no. **60.**

XXI. RISE OF INTEREST IN THE NATURAL SCIENCES

A. OUTLINE

1. Neglect of this field of medieval intellectual life in modern books. Prevalence of misconceptions about it now as in the sixteenth and seventeenth centuries when the legend of friar Bacon and friar Bungay was current.

2. Résumé. The transmission of natural sciences from ancient to medieval times (see outline IV). Neglect of the *quadrivium* in western Christendom during the early middle ages. Natural sciences among the Muslims (see outline X).

3. The development of a feeling for nature in the middle ages.

4. Popular notions about nature and the world. Occult science and magic. The tendency to find religious and moral lessons in nature. Bestiaries and lapidaries. Hildegard of Bingen's (1098–1179) astronomical visions and folk medicine.

5. Interest of the intellectual class in the natural sciences in the twelfth and thirteenth centuries. The influence of the New Aristotle together with Ptolemy, Hippocrates, and Galen. The interplay of Muslim, Byzantine, and Jewish interests in natural science with those of Latin Christendom. Relations with Spain, southern Italy and Sicily, and with the Muslim world. Adelard of Bath (early twelfth century). Robert of Ketene or of Chester, about 1150. Hermann of Carinthia. John of Spain, flourished 1135–53.

Gerard of Cremona, died 1187. Daniel of Morley (late twelfth century). The school of Chartres and science: William of Conches, Bernard Silvester. Alexander Neckam, 1157–1217. Alfred of Sereshel (Alfredus Anglicus, died 1217), Michael Scot, died about 1235.

6. The "Oxford school" of scholars who reacted against the prevalent methods in logic, philosophy and theology by stressing the study of the natural sciences and the languages. (For languages see outline XVIII.) Robert Grosseteste, bishop of Lincoln, 1235–53, Roger Bacon, Adam Marsh. The experimental method.

7. Roger Bacon (ca. 1214–ca. 1292). His tributes to Robert Grosseteste. His *Opus maius*, *Opus minus*, and *Opus tertium*. Danger of overestimating Bacon and of treating him as an isolated phenomenon. The mooted question of his imprisonments. The legend of friar Bacon.

8. Other men of the thirteenth century interested in natural sciences. Thomas of Cantimpré, *De natura rerum*, is still unpublished. Bartholomew of England, *De proprietatibus rerum*, editor, Lingelbach, Heidelberg, 1488. Vincent of Beauvais (died 1264 or later), *Speculum naturale;* Anth. Koburger, Nürnberg, 1485, is the only trustworthy edition. Albert the Great, 1193–1280, and his interest in botany. Jordanus Nemorarius. Peter of Maricourt, praised by Roger Bacon. Witelo, born about 1230 in Silesia. Henry Bate of Malines, born about 1244. Theoderic of Freiburg, late in the thirteenth and early in the fourteenth century. Raymund Lull, 1235–1315. Dante (see outline XXVIII).

9. The natural sciences in the medieval universities. Considerable interest in them at the university of Paris in the first half of the thirteenth century due especially to the influx of ancient Greek and of Arabic learning. Aristotle's works of natural philosophy as textbooks in medieval universities. Arabic and Latin commentators. Combined Arts and Medicine course in Italian universities. The Paris school of astronomers in the second half of the thirteenth century. Merton College, Oxford, school of astronomy in the early fourteenth century. Criticism of the Aristotelian physics at Paris.

10. Geographical study and theory in the middle ages.

11. Mathematics in medieval universities. The introduction of the so-called Arabic numerals into western Europe.

12. Salerno and the beginnings of systematic higher instruction in medicine in the twelfth century. The study of medicine in other universities. Clinics and hospitals. Chirurgy. Dissections. The medical profession.

13. The forces which retarded or encouraged the progress of the natural sciences in the middle ages. Experimental standards. Medieval schoolmen more interested in discussing natural problems than were the Italian humanists.

B. Special Recommendations for Reading

Brief general surveys. E. S. Holden, "The renaissance of science," *Popular science monthly*, LXIV (1903), 5–25. L. Thorndike, "Natural science in the middle ages," *ibid.*, LXXXVII (1915), 271–91. Lavisse et Rambaud, *Histoire générale*, II, 566–68; III, 244–62. T. C. Allbutt, *Science* *and medieval thought*, London, 1901. L. M. LARSON, "Scientific knowledge in the north in the thirteenth century," *Publications of the society for the advancement of Scandinavian study*, I (1911–14), 139–46; see also his *King's mirror*. M. ESPOSITO, "On some unpublished poems attributed to Alexander Neckam," *E.H.R.*, XXX (1915), 450–71. F. SARTIAUX, *Foi et science au moyen âge*, Paris, 1926. J. L. HEIBERG, "Les sciences grecques et leur transmission, II. L'oeuvre de conservation et de transmission des Byzantins et des Arabes," *Scientia*, XXXI (1922), 97–104. HASKINS, *Renaissance*, ch. x. HEARNSHAW, *Mediaeval contributions*, 106–48. See also the introduction to ALEXANDER NECKHAM, *De naturis rerum*, edited by T. WRIGHT, London, 1863 (Rolls series). F. STRUNZ, *Geschichte der Naturwissenschaften im Mittelalter: im Grundriss dargestellt*, Stuttgart, 1910; *Die Vergangenheit der Naturforschung: ein Beitrag zur Geschichte des menschlichen Geistes*, Jena, 1913, 1–85. DANNEMANN, *Die Naturwissenschaften in ihrer Entwicklung und in ihren Zusammenhange dargestellt*, vol. I, Leipzig, 1910, 258–87; new edition, 1928. MICHAEL, *Culturzustände des deutschen Volkes*, III, 395–460.

Popular notions about nature and the world. C. V. LANGLOIS, *La connaissance de la nature et du monde au moyen âge d'après quelques écrits français à l'usage des laics*, Paris, 1911; new edition, 1927. P. CAZIN, *Le bestiaire des deux testaments*, Paris, 1928. T. PLASSMANN, "Bartholomaeus Anglicus," *A.F.H.*, XII (1919), 68–109. G. E. LEBOYER, "Bartholomaeus Anglicus and his Encyclopaedia," *Journal of English and Germanic philology*, XIX (1920), 168–89.

Hildegard of Bingen. For bibliography see L. THORNDIKE, *Magic and experimental science*, II, 125–26. There has since appeared, H. FISCHER, *Die heilige Hildegard von Bingen; die erste deutsche Naturforscherin und Aerztin*, Munich, 1927.

The reception of Arabic science. See especially HASKINS' *Mediaeval science*, and STEINSCHNEIDER'S *Arabische Uebersetzungen*. Also THORNDIKE, *Magic and experimental science*, chs. 28, 30, 32, 36, 38, etc. J. W. BROWN, *An enquiry into the life and legend of Michael Scot*, Edinburgh, 1897. C. BAEUMKER, "Die Stellung des Alfred von Sareschel (Alfredus Anglicus) und seiner Schrift *De motu cordis* in der Wissenschaft des beginnenden XIII Jahrhunderts," *S.B., Munich Acad.*, 1913, 9. H. GRAUERT, "Meister Johann von Toledo," *ibid.*, 1901, 111–325.

The "Oxford school." F. A. GASQUET, "English scholarship in the thirteenth century," in his *The last abbot of Glastonbury and other essays*, 141–65, reprinted from the *Dublin review*, CXXIII (1898), 356–75. FELDER, *Geschichte der wissenschaftlichen Studien*, 254–304. R. T. GUNTHER, *Early science at Oxford*, 4 vols., Oxford, 1921–25; *Early medical and biological science*, Oxford, 1926. T. C. ALLBUTT, *The rise of experimental method in Oxford*, London, 1902. A. G. LITTLE, "The Franciscan school at Oxford in the thirteenth century," *A.F.H.*, XIX (1926), 803–74.

Roger Bacon. L. THORNDIKE, "The true Roger Bacon," *A.H.R.*, XXI (1916), 237–57, 468–80; "Roger Bacon and experimental method in the middle ages," *Philosophical review* (1914), 271–98. TAYLOR, *Mediaeval mind*, second edition, II, ch. XLII. J. H. BRIDGES, *The life and works of Roger Bacon, an introduction to the Opus majus*, edited, with additional notes and tables, by H. G. JONES, London, 1914; "Roger Bacon," a lecture printed in *Essays and addresses*, London, 1907. W. R. NEWBOLD, *The cipher of Roger Bacon*, edited by R. C. KENT, Philadelphia, 1928; a posthumous volume which sufficiently demonstrates the author's failure to unravel the so-called Roger Bacon manuscript. J. M. MANLY, "The most mysterious manuscript in the world, did Roger Bacon write it and has the key been found?," *Harper's magazine*, CXLIII (1921), 186–97. R. STEELE, "Roger Bacon and the state of science in the thirteenth century," *Studies in history and methods of science*, II, 121–50, Oxford, 1921. A. G. LITTLE, "Roger Bacon," *Proceedings of the British Academy*, XIV, 1928. See also the articles "Roger Bacon," in nos. **89, 104,** and **109.**

The standard biography is still the dissertation of E. CHARLES, *Roger Bacon: sa vie, ses ouvrages, ses doctrines*, Bordeaux, 1861; but students should now begin a detailed study of the life and work of Bacon by reading the *Roger Bacon essays*, edited by A. G. LITTLE, Oxford University Press, 1914. The introductions to the various fascicles of *Opera hactenus inedita Rogeri Baconi*, edited by R. STEELE and others since 1905, contain much valuable information.

Geographical theory. C. R. BEAZLEY, *The dawn of modern geography*, II, ch. VII; III, ch. VI. J. K. WRIGHT, *Geographical lore of the time of the crusades*, New York, 1925. F.S. BETTEN, "An alleged champion of the sphericity of the earth in the eighth century," *Catholic historical review*, IV (1924), 187–201.

Mathematics. W. R. R. BALL, *A short account of the history of mathematics*, ch. VIII. See also "Arabic numerals" and "Mathematics" under outline X. D. E. SMITH, *History of mathematics*, vol. I, *General survey of the history of elementary mathematics*, Boston, 1923; and L. C. KARPINSKI, *The history of arithmetic*, Chicago, 1925; both devote some space to medieval mathematics. FLORENCE A. YELDHAM, *The story of reckoning in the middle ages*, with an introduction by CHARLES SINGER, London, 1926.

Medicine. RASHDALL, *Universities*, I, 75–86, 233–49, and see "medicine" in his index. T. C. ALLBUTT, *On the historical relations of medicine and surgery down to the sixteenth century*, New York, 1905. For a review of our knowledge of the history of medicine in the middle ages, see the "Literaturbericht" of P. DIEPGEN, "Geschichte der Medizin," *Archiv für Kulturgeschichte*, X (1913), 465–80. T. C. ALLBUTT, *Greek medicine in Rome*, London, 1921, 389–528, supplementary chapters dealing with medieval medicine. H. P. CHOLMELEY, *John of Gaddesden and the Rosa Medicinae*, Oxford, 1912. H. E. HANDERSON, *Gilbertus Anglicus*, Cleveland, 1918. *Essays on the history of medicine presented to Karl Sudhoff*, editors, C. SINGER and H. E. SIGERIST, Zurich, 1924; pp. 87–182 deal with the middle ages; especially may be mentioned P. DIEPGEN, "Die Bedeutung des Mittelalters für den Fortschritt in der Medizin," and C. and D. SINGER, "The origin of the medical school of Salerno." K. SUDHOFF, *Essays in the history of medicine*, translated by various hands and edited by F. H. GARRISON, New York, 1926.

Original sources. Our best source of information concerning natural science in the thirteenth century is the *Opus majus* of ROGER BACON, edited by J. H. BRIDGES, 2 vols., Oxford, 1897; new edition, with a supplementary volume containing a "revised text of the first three parts, corrections, emendations, and additional notes," 1900; English translation by R. B. BURKE, 2 vols., Philadelphia, 1928. BARTHOLOMEW ANGLICUS, *De proprietatibus rerum*, abridged in English under the title, *Medieval lore*, translated by R. STEELE, London, 1907; new edition, 1924 (medieval library, 20). G. W. CORNER, *Anatomical texts of the earlier middle ages*, Washington, 1927. J. ARDERNE, *Treatises of fistula in ano*, translated by D'ARCY POWER, London, 1910; *De arte phisicali et de cirurgia*, translated by D'ARCY POWER, London, 1922. J. HARRINGTON, *The school of Salerno*, an English translation of that famous medical poem, was reprinted, London, 1922, with introductory material by F. R. PACKARD and F. H. GARRISON. WEBSTER, *Historical selections*, 244–70, may serve as a useful introduction to the science of the ancients upon which so many medieval conceptions were formed, also 604–11.

C. BIBLIOGRAPHY

General books. See the general books on medieval culture, nos. **729–849**, especially those on the history of freedom of thought, nos. **739–48.** See also the literature on natural science and mathematics under outlines IV and X, and nos. **188** and **803.**

General accounts. G. SARTON, *Introduction to the history of science*, vol. I (to 1100 A.D.). C. H. HASKINS, *Studies in the history of mediaeval science.* L. THORNDIKE, *History of magic and experimental science; Science and thought in the fifteenth century*, New York, 1929. C. SINGER, *From magic to science*, London, 1928; *Studies in the history and method of science*, 2 vols., Oxford, 1917–21. W. CURRY, *Chaucer and the mediaeval sciences*, New York, 1926. L. DARMSTAEDTER, *Handbuch zur Geschichte der Naturwissenschaften und der Technik in chronologischer Darstellung*, 2nd edition, Berlin, 1908. C. JOURDAIN, *Dissertation sur l'état de la philosophie naturelle en occident et principalement en France pendant la première moitié du XIIe siècle*, Paris, 1838. L. CHOULANT, *Die Anfänge wissenschaftlichen Naturgeschichte und naturhistorischen Abbildung*, Dresden, 1856. A. DUFOURCQ, "Les origines de la science moderne d'après les découvertes récentes," *R.D.M.*, 6th series, XVI (1913), 349–78. W. WHEWELL, *History of the inductive sciences, from the earliest times to the present time*, 2 vols., 3rd edition, New York, 1875. E. DARMSTAEDTER (editor), *Münchener Beiträge zur Geschichte und Literatur der Naturwissenschaften und der Medizin*, Munich, 1926ff. J. J. WALSH, *Catholic churchmen in science*, 2nd series, Philadelphia, 1906–09; *The popes and science: the history of the papal relations to science during the middle ages and down to our own time*, New York, 1908; *The thirteenth, the greatest of centuries*, are popular books addressed primarily to Roman catholics.

Periodicals. *Isis:* editor, G. SARTON, Brussels, 1913–14 and 1919–29, has been since 1924 the official journal of The history of science society. *Archeion*, formerly *Archivio di storia della scienza*, edited by A. MIELI, Rome,

1919–29. *Scientia*, Bologna, 1907ff. *Archiv für die Geschichte der Naturwissenschaften und der Technik*, edited by K. v. Buchka, H. Stadle, and K. Sudhoff, Leipzig, 1908–22: revived 1927 by J. Schuster, Berlin, as *Archiv für Geschichte der Mathematik, der Naturwissenschaften und der Technik.* See Medicine for periodicals on the history of medicine.

Feeling for nature. A. Biese, *Die Entwickelung des Naturgefühls im Mittelalter*, Leipzig, 1892, translated, *The development of feeling for nature in the middle ages*, London, 1905. Gertrud Stockmayer, *Ueber Naturgefühl in Deutschland im 10 und 11 Jahrhundert*, Leipzig and Berlin, 1910. W. Ganzenmüller, "Die empfindsame Naturbetrachtung im Mittelalter," *Archiv für Kulturgeschichte*, XII (1914), 195–228; *Das Naturgefühl im Mittelalter*, Leipzig, 1914, vol. XVIII of no. **749.**

Popular natural science, occult science, and magic. L. Thorndike, "Some medieval conceptions of magic," *The monist*, XXV (1915), 107–39; *The place of magic in the intellectual history of Europe*, New York, 1905 (Diss. in Columbia university studies, XXIV, 1); *Magic and experimental science;* and "Magic and medicine," *Medical life*, 1929, 1–8. A. Maury, *La magie et l'astrologie dans l'antiquité et au moyen âge*, Paris, 1877. A. Lehmann, *Aberglaube und Zauberei, von den ältesten Zeiten*, German translation, 2nd edition, Stuttgart, 1908. C. Meyer, *Der Aberglaube des Mittelalters und der nächtsfolgenden Jahrhunderte*, Basle, 1884. P. Diepgen, *Traum und Traumdeutung als medizinisch-naturwissenschaftliches Problem im Mittelalter*, Berlin, 1912. L. Pannier, *Les lapidaires français du moyen âge des XIIe, XIIIe et XIVe siècles*, Paris, 1882. Agnes Arber, *Herbals: their origin and evolution*, Cambridge, 1912. G. W. Gessmann, *Die Pflanze im Zauberglauben*, Vienna, 1899. F. Unger, *Die Pflanze als Zaubermittel*, Vienna, 1859. C. Joret, *La rose dans l'antiquité et au moyen âge*, Paris, 1892; *Les plantes dans l'antiquité et au moyen âge*, 2 vols., Paris, 1897 and 1904; it seems not to have reached the Latin middle ages. Joan Evans, *Magical jewels of the middle ages and the renaissance particularly in England*, Oxford, 1922. P. Studer and Joan Evans, *Anglo-Norman lapidaries*, Paris, 1924. R. M. Garrett, *Precious stones in Old English literature*, Münchener Beiträge, 1909. V. Rose, "Aristoteles De lapidibus und Arnoldus Saxo," *Zeitschrift für deutsches Alterthum*, XVIII (1875), 321–447. J. Ruska, *Das Steinbuch des Aristoteles*, Heidelberg, 1912. See also the introduction in *Leechdoms, wortcunning and starcraft in early England*, edited by O. Cockayne, 3 vols., London, 1864–66 (Rolls series); and *Popular treatises on science written during the middle ages in Anglo-Saxon, Anglo-Norman and English*, edited by T. Wright, London, 1841. See also under outline V.

Albert the Great and natural sciences. F. A. Pouchet, *Histoire des sciences naturelles au moyen âge: ou, Albert le Grand et son époque considérés comme point de départ de l'école expérimentale*, Paris, 1853. H. Stadler, "Albertus Magnus als selbständiger Naturforscher," *Forschungen zur Geschichte Bayerns*, XIV (1905), 95ff.; "Vorbemerkungen zur neuen Ausgabe der Tiergeschichte des Albertus Magnus," *S.B., Munich Acad.* (1912), 1–58. S. Killermann, *Die Vogelkunde des Albertus Magnus*, Regensburg, 1910.

M. STEINSCHNEIDER, "Zum *Speculum astronomicum* des Albertus Magnus: über die darin angeführten Schriftsteller und Schriften," *Zeitschrift für Mathematik und Physik*, Leipzig, XVI (1871), 357–96. J. WIMMER, *Deutsches Pflanzenleben nach Albertus Magnus (1193–1280): ein Nachtrag zur Geschichte des deutschen Bodens*, Halle, 1908. A. FELLNER, *Albertus Magnus als Botaniker*, Vienna, 1881. For general books on Albert the Great see outline XVII.

Bonaventura. L. BAUR, "Die Lehre von der Natur und Naturrecht bei Bonaventura," *Baeumker Festgabe*, 217ff. L. DE CARVALHO E CASTRO, *Saint Bonaventure: l'idéal de Saint François et l'oeuvre de Saint Bonaventure à l'égarde de la science*, Paris, 1923.

Robert Grosseteste. F. S. STEVENSON, *Robert Grosseteste, bishop of Lincoln*, London, 1899, is the standard biography, but does not stress his career as a scholar. L. BAUR, *Das philosophische Lebenswerk des Robert Grosseteste, Bischofs von Lincoln*, Cologne, 1910; "Der Einfluss des Robert Grosseteste auf die wissenschaftliche Richtungen des Roger Bacon," *Roger Bacon essays*, 33–54. L. BAUR, "Das Licht in der Naturphilosophie des Robert Grossetête," *Festgabe von Hertling*, Freiburg, 1913.

Roger Bacon. In 1914 considerable interest was aroused in Bacon by the celebration at Oxford of the seventh centenary of his birth. The ceremonies in Oxford are described in *Nature*, XCIII (1914), 354–55, 405–06, where there is a photograph of a statue of Roger Bacon unveiled in the University Museum on June 10, 1914. Similar to the *Roger Bacon essays* noted above are the *Scritti vari pubblicati in occasione del VII centenario della nascita di Ruggero Bacone*, edited by A. GEMELLI, Florence, 1914 (*Rivista di filosofia neo-scolastica*, VI, 6), which contains the following articles: M. BRUSADELLI, "R. Bacone nella storia"; D. FLEMING, "R. Bacone e la scolastica"; M. BRUSADELLI, "Lo Speculum astronomiae di R. Bacone"; P. ROBINSON, "Alcune opere recenti su R. Bacone." J. I. VALENTI, "Roger Bacon," *Science catholique*, Paris, XVI (1902), 236–71. L. MARCHAL, "Roger Bacon: sa méthode et ses principes," Université catholique de Louvain, séminaire historique, *Rapport sur les travaux pendant l'année académique 1909–1910*, Louvain, 1911. A. G. LITTLE, *The Grey Friars in Oxford*, Oxford, 1892. C. NARBEY, "Le moine Roger Bacon et le mouvement scientifique au XIIIe siècle," *R.Q.H.*, XXXV (1884), 115–66. L. DOUBLIER, *Roger Bacon: eine culturgeschichtliche Studie*, Vienna, 1886. J. LANGEN, "Roger Baco," *H.Z.*, LI (1883), 434–50. H. T. ADAMSON, *Roger Bacon: the philosophy of science in the middle ages*, Manchester, 1876. L. SCHNEIDER, *Roger Bako*, Augsburg, 1873. H. SIEBERT, *Roger Bacon: sein Leben und seine Philosophie*, Marburg, 1861. P. ROBINSON, "The seventh centenary of Roger Bacon" (1214–1914), *Catholic university bulletin*, XX (1914), 3–9. R. CARTON, *L'expérience physique chez Roger Bacon; L'experience mystique de l'illumination intérieure chez Roger Bacon; la synthèse doctrinale de Roger Bacon*, 3 vols., Paris, 1924.

Following are important special studies: S. VOGL, *Die Physik Roger Bacos*, Erlangen, 1906 (Diss.). P. FERET, "Les imprisonnements de Roger Bacon," *R.Q.H.*, L (1891), 119–42. J. E. SANDYS, "Roger Bacon," *Proceedings of the British academy*, vol. VI (1914), also printed separately by the Oxford

University Press [no date]. E. DÜHRING, "The two Bacons," *Open court magazine*, XXVIII (1914), 468–85 (this whole August number of the *Open court* is devoted to Bacon). A. DÖRING, "Die beiden Bacon," *Archiv für Geschichte der Philosophie*, XVII (1904), 341–48. F. PICAVET, "Deux directions de la théologie catholique au XIIIe siècle: Saint Thomas d'Aquin et Roger Bacon," *Revue de l'histoire des religions* (1905), 172ff. C. BAEUMKER, "Roger Bacons Naturphilosophie, insbesondere seine Lehre von Materie und Form," *Franziskanische Studien*, III (1916), 1–40. A. VALDARNINI, *Esperienza e ragionamento in Rogero Bacone*, Rome, 1896, 20 pages. S. SCHINDELE, "Vorschläge zur Verbesserung des Studienbetriebs im 13ten Jahrhundert (Roger Bacon)," *Mitteilungen der Gesellschaft für deutsche Erziehungs- und Schulgeschichte* (1908). C. JOURDAIN, "Discussion de quelques points de la biographie de Roger Bacon," in his *Excursions historiques*, 129–71. K. WERNER, "Die Psychologie, Erkentniss- und Wissenschaftslehre des Roger Baco," *S.B., Vienna Acad.*, XCIII (1879), 467–576. O. KEICHER, "Der Intellectus agens bei Roger Baco," *Supplementband* (1913), 297–308, of no. **826.** A. SCHÜCK, *Der Kompass*, 3 vols., Hamburg, 1917–18. H. C. LONGWELL, *The theory of mind of Roger Bacon*, Strasburg, 1908. For books on Bacon's interest in textual criticism see outline XVIII.

On the works of Roger Bacon: F. PICAVET, "Pour une future édition des oeuvres de Roger Bacon," *Journal des savants*, 1912, 405–11, 456–63; "Les éditions de Roger Bacon," *ibid.*, 1905, 362–69. P. MANDONNET, "Roger Bacon et la composition des trois 'opus,'" *Revue néoscolastique*, 1913; "Roger Bacon et le *Speculum astronomiae*," *ibid.*, XVII (1910), 313–35, which, however, is controverted by L. THORNDIKE, *History of magic, etc.*, ch. LXII, "The *Speculum astronomiae.*" F. M. DELORME, "Un opuscule inédit de R. Bacon," *A.F.H.*, IV (1911), 209–12. V. COUSIN, "Roger Bacon: de l'Opus tertium, récemment trouvé dans la bibliothèque de Douai," in his *Fragmenst philosophiques*, II (1865), 218–310. R. CARTON, "Le chiffre de Roger Bacon," *Revue d'histoire de la philosophie*, III (1929), 31–66; 165–79. C. BOIROMÉE VANDEWALLE, "Roger Bacon dans l'histoire de la philologie," *La France franciscaine*, série II, XI (1928), 315–409; XII (1929), 45–90; 161–228.

For the legend of Roger Bacon, *The famous historie of fryer Bacon*, written about 1600, first edition, 1630, now in *Miscellanea antiqua anglicana*, London, 1816; the play written about 1585 by R. GREENE, *The honourable history of friar Bacon and friar Bungay;* and *A piece of friar Bacon's brazen heade's prophesie*, written 1604 and printed in the *Publications of the Percy society*, XV (1844). See also *Roger Bacon essays*, 359–72.

Peter of Maricourt. E. SCHLUND, "Petrus Peregrinus von Maricourt: sein Leben und seine Schriften (ein Beitrag zur Roger Baco-Forschung)," *A.F.H.*, IV (1911), 436–55, 633–43; V (1912), 22–40. F. PICAVET, "Nos vieux maîtres, Pierre de Maricourt, le Picard, et son influence sur Roger Bacon," *Revue internationale de l'enseignement*, LIV (1907), 289–315. See article by P. DUHEM in *Catholic encyclopaedia* for bibliography. The famous letter on the magnet is translated by S. P. THOMPSON, *Peter Peregrinus of Maricourt: Epistle to Sygerus of Fouconcourt, soldier, concerning the magnet,*

Chiswick Press [n.d.] extract from Proceedings of the British academy, 1905–06, 377–408; and also by BROTHER ARNOLD, *The letter of Petrus Peregrinus on the magnet, A.D. 1269*, with introductory note by BROTHER POTAMIAN, New York, 1904.

Witelo. C. BAEUMKER, *Witelo: ein Philosoph und Naturforscher des XIII Jahrhunderts*, Münster, 1908, vol. III of no **826.** A BIRKENMAJER, *Studja nad Witelonem*, Crakow, 1921; publishes and studies the *De natura demonum* and *De primaria causa poenitentiae*. C. BAEUMKER, "Sur la date et l'auteur du 'Liber de intelligentibus,' faussement attribué à Witelon," in *Miscellanea Francesco Ehrle*, I, 87–102, Rome, 1924.

Theoderic of Freiburg. E. KREBS, *Meister Dietrich (Theodericus Teutonicus de Vriberg): sein Leben, seine Werke, seine Wissenschaft*, in no. **826,** 1906, V, parts 5–6, Münster, 1906. DIETRICH VON FREIBERG, *Über den Regenbogen und die durch Strahlen erzeugten Eindrücke* (Theodoricus Teutonicus de Vriberg de iride et radialibus impresionibus), zum ersten Male nach den Handschriften herausgegeben und mit einer Einleitung versehen, by J. WÜRSCHMIDT, Münster, 1914, *ibid.*, vol. XII, parts 5–6.

Henry Bate of Malines. M. DE WULF, "Henri Bate de Malines" (*Bulletins de l'Academie royale de Belgique*, Classe de lettres, etc., 1909); see in connection with it the notes by C. BAEUMKER in *Philosophisches Jahrbuch*, edited by GUTBERLET, XXIII (1910), 208ff.

Physics. E. GERLAND, *Geschichte der Physik, von den ältesten Zeiten bis zum Ausgange des achtzehnten Jahrhunderts*, Munich, 1913 (Geschichte der Wissenschaften in Deutschland, XXIV), pp. 131–219 are on the middle ages. E. GERLAND and F. TRAUMÜLLER, *Geschichte der physikalischen Experimentierkunst*, Leipzig, 1899. A. LALANDE, "Histoire des sciences: la physique du moyen âge," *R.S.H.*, VII (1903), 191–218. A. HELLER, *Geschichte der Physik von Aristoteles bis auf die neueste Zeit*, 2 vols., Stuttgart, 1882–84. L. THORNDIKE, "Blasius of Parma (Biagio Pelacani)," *Archeion*, IX (1928), 177–90.

Chemistry and alchemy. M. BERTHELOT, *Introduction à l'étude de la chimie des anciens et du moyen âge*, Paris, 1890, translated into German by E. KALLIWODA with notes by F. STRUNZ, *Die Chemie in Altertum und Mittelalter*, Leipzig and Vienna, 1909. M. BERTHELOT, *Histoire des sciences: la chimie au moyen âge*, 3 vols., Paris, 1893; *Les origines de l'alchimie*, Paris, 1885. F. PICAVET, "La science experimentale au XIIIe siècle," *M.A.*, VII (1894), 241–48, is a review of Berthelot's books. L. MABILLEAU, *Histoire de la philosophie atomistique*, Paris, 1895. K. LASSWITZ, *Geschichte der Atomistik vom Mittelalter bis Newton*, 2 vols., Leipzig, 1890. J. C. BROWN, *A history of chemistry*, London, 1913. E. v. MEYER, *Geschichte der Chemie von den ältesten Zeiten bis zur Gegenwart*, 3rd edition, Leipzig, 1905. H. KOPP, *Die Alchemie in älterer und neuerer Zeit*, Heidelberg, 1886. E. O. v. LIPPMANN, *Entshehung und Ausbreitung der Alchemie*, Berlin, 1919. E. O. v. LIPPMANN, *Beiträge zur Geschichte der Naturwissenschaften und der Technik*, Berlin, 1923. J. E. MERCER, *Alchemy, its science and romance*, London, 1921. J. M. STILLMAN, *Story of early chemistry*, New York, 1924. A. MIELI, *Pagine di storia* *della chimica*, Rome, 1922. A. Poisson, *Histoire de l'alchemie, XIVe siècle*, Paris, 1893; *Théories et symboles des alchimistes*, Paris, 1891. J. R. de Luanco, *La alquimia en España*, Barcelona, 1889. G. W. Gessmann, *Die Geheimsymbole der Alchymie, Arzneikunde, und Astrologie des Mittelalters*, 2nd edition, Berlin, 1922. D. W. Singer, "The alchemical testament attributed to Raymund Lull," *Archeion*, IX (1928), 43–52.

Astronomy and astrology. P. Duhem, *Le système du monde*, is a work of fundamental importance of which vols. II, 393–501, III–IV, are on the middle ages; *Essai sur la notion de théorie physique de Platon à Galilée*, Paris, 1908 (extract from *Annales de philosophie chrétienne*); *Etudes sur Léonard de Vinci*. J. L. E. Dreyer, "Mediaeval astronomy," *Studies in the history and method of science*, II, 102–20, Oxford, 1921, is a review of the medieval portion of Duhem. J. L. E. Dreyer, *History of the planetary systems from Thales to Kepler*, Cambridge, 1906. K. Sudhoff, *Ein Beitrag zur Geschichte der Astronomie im Mittelalter* [9th to 15th centuries], Leipzig, 1908 (Studien zur Geschichte der Medizin, 4). R. Wolf, *Handbuch der Astronomie: ihre Geschichte und Literatur*, 2 vols., Zürich, 1890–93. J. P. J. Delambre, *Histoire de l'astronomie au moyen âge*, Paris, 1819. J. Sorlano Viguera, *La astronomía de Alfonso X el Sabio*, 1926. A. Birkenmajer, *Henri Bate de Malines, astronome et philosophe du XIIIe siècle*, Crakow, 1923: reprinted from *La Pologne au Congrès International de Bruxelles*. L. Thorndike, "Andalò di Negro, Profacius Judaeus, and the Alphonsine Tables," *Isis*, X (1928), 52–56; "The clocks of Jacopo and Giovanni de' Dondi," *Isis*, X (1928), 360–62. B. Boncompagni, "Della vita e delle opere di Guido Bonatti astrologo ed astronomo," *Giornale arcadico*, CXXIII–CXXIV, Rome, 1851. A. Favaro, "Intorno alla vita ed alle opere di Prosdocimo de' Beldomandi, matematico padovano del secolo XV," *Bullettino di bibliografia e di storia delle scienze matematiche e fisiche*, XII (1879), 1–74, 115–251. B. Hauréau, *Le Mathematicus de Bernard Silvestris*, Paris, 1895. T. O. Wedel, *The medieval attitude toward astrology, particularly in England*, New Haven, 1920. G. Hellmann, "Die Wettervorhersage im ausgehenden Mittelalter," *Beiträge zur Geschichte der Meteorologie*, Berlin, II (1917), 169–229. A. Marx, "The correspondence between the rabbis of southern France and Maimonides about astrology," *Hebrew union college annual*, III (1926), 311–58. R. Levy, *The astrological works of Abraham Ibn Ezra: a literary and linguistic study with special reference to the old French translation of Hagin*, Baltimore, 1927. Florence M. Grimm, *Astronomical lore in Chaucer*, Lincoln, Neb., 1919. J. S. P. Tatlock, "Astrology and magic in Chaucer's Franklin's tale," *Kittredge anniversary papers*, Boston, 1913, 339–50. D. M. Dalton, *The Byzantine astrolabe at Brescia*, Oxford, 1926. C. Vitanza, *Dante e l'astrologia*, Pavia, 1918.

Geographical theory. K. Kretschmer, *Die physische Erdkunde im christlichen Mittelalter*, Vienna, 1889 (IV, part I, of Geographische Abhandlungen). O. Peschel, *Geschichte der Erdkunde bis auf Alexander v. Humboldt und Karl Ritter*, 2nd edition, Munich, 1878 (Geschichte der Wissenschaften in Deutschland, neuere Zeit, IV). P. Mandonnet, "Les idées cosmographiques d'Albert le Grand et de S. Thomas d'Aquin et la découverte de l'Amérique," *Revue thomiste*, I (1893), 46–64, 200–21. C. GUIGNEBERT, *De imagine mundi ceterisque Petri de Alliaco geographicis opusculis*, Paris, 1902. M. SCHNEID, "Die Lehre von der Erdrundung und Erdbewegung im Mittelalter," *Historisch-politische Blätter*, LXXX (1877), II, 433–51. A. BLÁSQUEZ, *Estudio acerca de la cartografía española en la edad media*, Madrid, 1906. L. GALLOIS, "La cartographie du moyen âge et la carte attribuée à Christophe Colomb," *R.H.*, 153 (1926), 40–51. LA RONCIÈRE, *La découverte de l'Afrique*. See also "Geographical discoveries," under outline XXVI in part II.

Zoology. J. V. CARUS, *Geschichte der Zoologie*, Munich, 1872. R. BURCKHARDT, *Geschichte der Zoologie*, Leipzig, 1907 (Sammlung Göschen). G. LOISEL, *Histoire des ménageries de l'antiquité à nos jours*, 3 vols., Paris, 1912, vol. I covers the ancient, medieval and renaissance periods.

Botany. E. L. GREENE, *Landmarks of botanical history*, part I, prior to 1562, London, 1910. J. R. GREEN, *A history of botany in the United Kingdom, from the earliest times to the end of the nineteenth century*, London, 1914. J. SACHS, *Geschichte der Botanik*, Munich, 1875.

Medicine. The study of the history of medicine in the middle ages is still in its infancy. The work that must be done is outlined by K. SUDHOFF, "Aufgaben und Forschungswege der Medizingeschichte im Mittelalter im Abendland," Vortrag auf der historischen Abteilung der 84 Versammlung deutschen Naturforscher und Ärzte in Münster, i. W. 1912 (see "Bericht" in *Verhandlungen* der Gesellschaft).

General histories of medicine. M. NEUBURGER, *Geschichte der Medizin*, vols. I–II, Stuttgart, 1906, 1911, translated by E. PLAYFAIR, *History of medicine*, London, 1910, 1925. T. PUSCHMANN, *Handbuch der Geschichte der Medizin*, edited by M. NEUBURGER and J. PAGEL, 3 vols., Jena, 1901–05. *Studien zur Geschichte der Medizin*, edited by T. PUSCHMANN and K. SUDHOFF, Leipzig, 1907ff. J. PAGEL, *Grundriss eines Systems der medizinischen Kulturgeschichte*, Berlin, 1905. L. MEUNIER, *Histoire de la médecine, depuis ses origines jusqu'à nos jours*, Paris, 1911. E. WITHINGTON, *History of medicine*, London, 1894. T. PUSCHMANN, *A history of medical education*, English translation, London, 1891. H. HAESER, *Lehrbuch der Geschichte der Medicin und der Volkskrankheiten*, 3rd edition, 1875–82. F. H. GARRISON, *Introduction to the history of medicine*, 4th edition, Philadelphia, 1928. N. MOORE, *History of the study of medicine in the British Isles*, London, 1908. J. ASTRUC, *Mémoires pour servir à l'histoire de la Faculté de médecine de Montpellier*, Paris, 1767. K. SUDHOFF, *Geschichte der Zahnheilkunde*, 2nd edition, revised, Leipzig, 1926.

Periodicals for the history of medicine. *Archiv für Geschichte der Medizin*, edited by K. SUDHOFF, Leipzig, 1908ff. *Mitteilungen zur Geschichte der Medizin und der Naturwissenschaften*, edited by S. GÜNTHER and K. SUDHOFF, Hamburg and Leipzig, 1902ff. *Bulletin de la Société française de l'histoire de la médecine*. *Annals of medical history*, New York, 1917ff. *Medical life*, New York, vol. 36 was for 1929. *Janus*, Leyden, 1896ff.

Medicine in the middle ages. E. WICKERSHEIMER, *Les médecins de la nation anglaise (ou allemande) de l'université de Paris aux XIVe et XVe siècles*, Le Mans, 1913 (from the Bulletin de la Société française de l'histoire de la médicine). *Commentaires de la Faculté de médecine de l'université de Paris 1395–1516*, edited by E. WICKERSHEIMER, Paris, 1915, part of no. **965.** P. GIACOSA, *Magistri salernitani nondum editi*, Turin, 1901. S. DE RENZI, *Collectio salernitana*, 5 vols., Naples, 1852–59. P. CAPPARONI, *Magistri salernitani nondum cogniti*, Basel, 1923. P. PANSIER, "Les maîtres de la faculté de médecine de Montpellier au moyen âge," *Janus*, IX–X, 1903–04. F. LAUE, *Über Krankenbehandlung und Heilkunde in der Literatur des alten Frankreichs*, Arnstadt, 1904. P. DIEPGEN, "Medizinisches aus theologischen Schriften des Mittelalters," *Medizinische Klinik*, Berlin, 1913, nos. 3, 4. P. DIEPGEN, *Die Theologie und Medizin im Mittelalter*, Berlin, 1922; *Die Theologie und der ärztliche Stand*, Berlin, 1924. MILLOT-CARPENTIER, "La médecine au XIIIe siècle," *Annales internationales d'histoire*, Congrès de Paris, 1900, V^e section, histoire des sciences. A. RIEUNIER, *Quelques mots sur la médecine au moyen âge d'après le Speculum maius de Vincent de Beauvais*, Paris, 1892. L. REUTTER, *Des médicaments d'origine humaine et animale prescrits en Europe au moyen âge et au temps de la renaissance*, Paris, 1913 (Bibliothèque historique de la France médicale, 51). C. VIEILLARD, *Gilles de Corbeil*, Paris, 1909. H. QUENTIN, "Une correspondance médicale de Pierre le Vénérable avec 'Magister Bartholomaeus,'" *Miscellanea Francesco Ehrle*, I, 80–86, Rome, 1924. S. D'IRSAY, "Gilles de Corbeil," *Annals of medical history*, VII (1925), 362–78; "Teachers and textbooks of medicine in the medieval university of Paris," *ibid.*, VIII (1926), 234–39. L. KOTELMANN, *Gesundheitspflege im Mittelalter: kulturgeschichtliche Studien nach Predigten des 13, 14, und 15 Jahrhunderts*, Leipzig, 1890. J. J. WALSH, *Old time makers of medicine*, New York, 1911; *Education: how old the new*, New York, 1910; and *Medieval medicine*, London, 1920, are popular books written for Roman catholic readers. Chapters II–VI of THORNDIKE'S *Science and thought*, deal with medicine, surgery, and an autopsy. G. HENSLOW, *Medical works of the fourteenth century*, London, 1899.

Physicians and surgeons. H. BERTHAUD, *Les médicins et chirurgiens des rois capêtiens du XIe au XIIIe siècle*, Poitiers, 1907 (extract from the *Bulletin de la Société française de l'histoire de la médecine*). L. DUBREUIL-CHAMBARDEL, *Les médecins dans l'ouest de la France aux XIe et XIIe siècles*, Paris, *ibid.*, 1914. A. FRANKLIN, *La vie privée d'autrefois: les médecins*, Paris, 1892; *La vie privée d'autrefois: les chirurgiens*, Paris, 1893. J. H. BAAS, *Die geschichtliche Entwicklung des ärztlichen Standes und der medizinischen Wissenschaften*, Berlin, 1896. E. GURLT, *Geschichte der Chirurgie und ihrer Ausübung*, 2 vols., Berlin, 1898. MÉLANIE LIPINSKA, *Histoire des femmes médecins depuis l'antiquité jusqu'à nos jours*, Paris, 1900. SANTE FERRARI, "I tempi, la vita, le dottrine di Pietro d'Abano," *Atti dell' Università di Genova*, XIV (1900); "Per la biografia e per gli scritti di Pietro d'Abano," *Atti dell' Accademia dei Lincei; Memorie della classe di scienze morali*, Rome, XV (1918), 629–727. R. STAPPER, *Papst Johannes XXI*, Münster, 1898. M. GRABMANN,

"Ein ungedrucktes Lehrbuch der Psychologie des Petrus Hispanus," *Spanische Forschungen der Görresgesellschaft*, I (1928), 166–73, Münster, 1928. H. SCHÖPPLER, "Die Krankheiten Kaiser Heinrichs II und seine 'Josefsche,'" *Archiv für Gesch. der Medizin*, XI, 200–32. R. LIVI, *Guido da Bagnolo, medico del re di Cipro (con nuovi documenti)*, Modena, 1916. J. SCHUSTER, "Secreta salernitana und Gart der Gesundheit: eine Studie zur Geschichte der Naturwissenschaften und Medizin des Mittelalter," *Mittelalterliche Handschriften*, Leipzig, 1926. C. DAUMET, "Une femme-médecin au XIIIe siècle," *Revue des études historiques*, LXXXIV (1918), 69–71.

Anatomy. K. SUDHOFF, *Beiträge zur Geschichte der Anatomie im Mittelalter: speziel der anatomischen Graphite nach Handschriften des IX–XV Jahrhunderts*, Leipzig, 1908 (Studien zur Geschichte der Medizin, 4). R. v. TÖPLY, *Studien zur Geschichte der Anatomie im Mittelalter*, Leipzig, 1898. F. H. GARRISON, *The principles of anatomic illustration before Vesalius*, New York, 1926. J. L. CHOULANT, *History and bibliography of anatomic illustration*, Chicago [1920].

Pharmacy. General histories such as E. GILBERT, *La pharmacie à travers les siècles*, Toulouse, 1892, and H. SCHELENZ, *Geschichte der Pharmacie*, 1904, touch on the middle ages, as do local histories like A. BAUDOT, *Etudes historiques sur la pharmacie en Bourgogne avant 1803*, Paris, 1905, and P. RAMBAUD, *La pharmacie en Poitou*, 1907. I. SCHWARZ, *Geschichte der Wiener Apothekenwesens im Mittelalter*, Vienna, 1917. R. CIASCA, *Storia dell' arte dei medici e speziali de Firenze, dalle origine alla metà del secolo XV*, Melfi, 1924; *L'arte dei medici e speziali nella storia e nel commercio fiorentino dal secolo XII al XV*, Florence, 1927 (Biblioteca storica toscana, IV). P. BARTHÉLEMY, *Histoire des apothécaires marseillais, du XIIIe siècle à la révolution*, Toulouse, 1924.

Hospitals and leprosy. ROTHA M. CLAY, *The mediaeval hospitals of England*, London, 1909 (The antiquary's books). ELIZABETH SPEAKMAN, "Mediaeval hospitals," *Dublin review*, CXXXIII (1903), 283–96. C. MERCIER, *Leper houses and mediaeval hospitals*, London, 1915. L. LALLEMAND, *La lèpre et les lèproseries du Xe au XVIe siècle* (Compte rendu des séances de l'Académie des sciences morales et politiques, 1905). E. LESSER, *Die Aussatzhäuser des Mittelalters*, Zürich, 1896. N. MOORE, *The history of St. Bartholomew's hospital*, 2 vols., London, 1918. L. LE GRAND, *Statuts d'Hôtels-Dieu et de lèproseries: recueil de textes du XIIe siècle*, Paris, 1901, part 32 of no. **968**. J. M. HOBSON, *Some early and later houses of pity*, London, 1926. L. THORNDIKE, "Sanitation, baths, and street-cleaning in the middle ages and renaissance," *Speculum*, III (1928), 192–203. DOROTHY L. MACKAY, *Les hôpitaux et la charité à Paris au XIIIe siècle*. V. LEBLOND, *Cartulaire de l'Hôtel-Dieu de Beauvais*, Paris, 1919; *Cartulaire de la maladrerie de Saint-Lazare de Beauvais*, Paris, 1922. A. PÖSCHL, "Steierische Kirchenhospize im Mittelalter," *Zeitschrift des historischen Vereins für Steiermark*, XVIII (1923), 46–50. E. JEANSELME, "La lèpre en France au moyen-âge," *Revue de technique médicale* (1925), 985–93. See also "Epidemics" under outline XXVI in part II, and "Hospitals" under outline XIII.

Mathematics. M. CANTOR, *Vorlesungen über Geschichte der Mathematik* 4 vols., 3rd edition, Leipzig, 1899–1908. CANTOR has been corrected by G. ENESTRÖM in *Bibliotheca mathematica.* F. CAJORI, *A history of mathematics*, New York, 1895. S. GÜNTHER, *Geschichte des mathematischen Unterrichts im deutschen Mittelalter bis zum Jahre 1525*, Berlin, 1887, part of no. **1012**; *Geschichte der Mathematik*, I, *Von den ältesten Zeiten bis Cartesius*, Leipzig, 1908. H. SUTER, *Die Mathematik auf den Universitäten des Mittelalters*, Zürich, 1887. H. G. ZEUTHEN, *Die Mathematik im Altertum und im Mittelalter*, Leipzig, 1912, in no. **729**, III, 1, I. D. E. SMITH, *Rara arithmetica: a catalogue of the arithmetics written before MDCI*, 2 vols., Boston, 1908. R. L. POOLE, *The exchequer in the twelfth century*, London, 1912; see also the introduction to the *Dialogus de Scaccario*, by RICHARD [FITZNEALE], son of Nigel, edited by A. HUGHES and others, Oxford, Clarendon Press, 1902. C H. HASKINS, "The abacus and the king's curia," *E.H.R.*, XXVII (1912), 101–06, also H. RICHARDSON, "Richard fitz Neal and the Dialogus de Scaccario," *E.H.R.*, XLIII (1928), 161–71; 321–40. J. GIESING, *Leben und Schriften Leonardos da Pisa: ein Beitrag zur Geschichte der Arithmetik des 13 Jahrhunderts*, Döbeln, 1886. G. LIBRI, *Histoire des sciences mathématiques en Italie*, Paris, 1838; 2nd edition, 1865. A. BJÖRNBO, "Die mittelalterlichen Übersetzungen aus dem Griechischen auf dem Gebiete der mathematischen Wissenschaften," *Archiv für die Geschichte der Naturwissenschaften und Technik*, I (1909), 385–94. L. C. KARPINSKI, *Robert of Chester's Latin translation of the Algebra of al-Khowarizmi*, New York, 1915. F. P. BARNARD, *The casting-counter and the counting-board*, Oxford, 1916. G. LORIA, *Guida allo studio della storia delle matematiche*, Milan, 1916. N. BUBNOW, *Arithmetische Selbständigkeit der europäischen Kultur: ein Beitrag zur Kulturgeschichte*, Berlin, 1914. *Bibliotheca mathematica: Zeitschrift für Geschichte der mathematischen Wissenschaften*, Stockholm, 1884ff. *Abhandlungen zur Geschichte der mathematischen Wissenschaften*, Leipzig, 1877ff. BONCOMPAGNI'S *Bullettino di bibliografia e di storia delle scienze matematiche e fisiche*, Rome, 1868–87 (vols. I–XX).

Original sources. Works of the twelfth century and before. H. E. SIGERIST, *Studien und Texte zur frühmittelalterlichen Rezeptliteratur*, Leipzig, 1923. L. CHOULANT, editor, *Macer Floridus de viribus herbarum una cum Walafridi Strabonis, Othonis Cremonensis et Ioannis Folcz carminibus similis argumenti*, Leipzig, 1832. *Nemesii episcopi Premnon physicon sive περὶ φύσεως ἀνθρώπου liber a N. Alfano, archiepiscopo Salerni in latinum translatus*, recognovit CAROLUS BURKHARD, Leipzig, 1917: there was an earlier edition by Holzinger, Leipzig, 1887. *Gregorii Nysseni (Nemesii Emeseni) Peri phuseos anthropou liber a burgundione in latinum translatus;* nunc primum ex libris mss., editor, C. I. BURKHARD, Vienna, 1891–1902. *Dominicus Gundissalinus, De divisione philosophiae*, edited by L. BAUER, Münster, 1903, part VI, 2–3 of no. **826**, has a valuable introduction; see also C. BAEUMKER, *Dominicus Gundissalinus als philosophischer Schriftsteller*, Münster, 1899. *Hildegardis causae et curae*, editor, P. KAISER, Leipzig, 1903. R. STEELE, "Practical chemistry in the XIIth century; Rasis de aluminibus et de salibus, translated by GERARD OF CREMONA," *Isis*, XII (1929), 10–46. Daniel of Morley's *Philosophia*, edited by K. SUDHOFF, *Archiv f. Gesch. d. Naturwiss. u. Technik*, 1917. ALFREDUS ANGLICUS, *De motu cordis*, editor, C. BAEUMKER, *Beiträge z. Gesch. d. Philos.*, vol. 23, Münster, 1923. C. S BARACH, *Bibliotheca philosophorum mediae aetatis*, Innsbruck, vol. II, 1878, includes some science. ADELARD OF BATH, *Quaestiones naturales*, 1480, 1485, etc. *De eodem et diverso*, editor, H. WILLNER, Münster, 1903. C. J. FORDYCE, "A rhythmical version of Bede's De ratione temporum," in *Archivium latinitatis mediae aevi* (*ALMA*), 1927, 2, 59–73. J. H. PITNAM, *The riddles of Aldhelm:* text and translation, Yale studies in English, LXVII, New Haven, 1925.

Mathematics. ADELARD OF BATH, *Regula abaci*, Boncompagni's *Bullettino*, XIV (1881), 1–134. P. TREUTLEIN, *Jordanus Nemorarius "de numeris datis,"* Leipzig, 1879. C. HENRY, *Prologus Ocreati in Helceph ad Adelardum Batensem*, Leipzig, 1880. H. WEISSENBORN, *Die Uebersetzung des Euclid aus dem Arabischen in das Lateinische durch Adelard von Bath*, Leipzig, 1880. A. NAGL, *Das arithmetische Traktat des Radulph von Laon*, Leipzig, 1890. *Das Quadripartitum des Ioannes de Muris und das praktische Rechnen im vierzehnten Jahrhundert*, Leipzig, 1890. M. CURTZE, *Urkunden zur Geschichte der Mathematik im Mittelalter und der Renaissance*, Leipzig, 1902. A. A. BJÖRNBO and S. VOGL, *Alkindi, Tideus und Pseudo-Euclid*, Leipzig, 1911. D. E. SMITH, *Compotus manualis magistri Aniani*, Paris, 1928. *Scritti di Leonardo Pisano*, editor, B. BONCOMPAGNI, 2 vols., Rome, 1857, 1862. E. G. R. WATERS, "A thirteenth century Algorism in French verse," *Isis*, XI (1928), 45–84.

FRATRIS ROGERI BACON, ordinis minorum, *Opus majus ad Clementem quartum, pontificem romanum*, edited by S. JEBB, London, 1733, reprinted in Venice, 1750, was the first printed edition of this, the most famous work of Roger Bacon. It proved to be incomplete. The modern edition by BRIDGES has been noted above. The *Opus tertium*, the *Opus minus*, the *Compendium philosophiae*, and, as appendices, the *Epistola de secretis operibus artis et naturae, et de nullitate magiae*, are in FR. ROGERI BACON, *Opera quaedam hactenus inedita*, edited by J. S. BREWER, with a valuable introduction, London, 1859 (Rolls series, 15). *Part of the Opus tertium of Roger Bacon, including a fragment now printed for the first time*, edited by A. G. LITTLE, Aberdeen, 1912 (British society of Franciscan studies, IV); see also the editor's note, "The missing part of Roger Bacon's Opus tertium," *E.H.R.*, XXVII (1912), 318–21. *Un fragment inédit de l'Opus tertium de R. Bacon précédé d'une étude sur ce fragment*, edited by P. DUHEM, Quaracchi, 1909. *Opera hactenus inedita* ROGERI BACONI, edited by R. STEELE, London, 1905ff., thus far contains the *Metaphysica, Communia naturalium, Secretum secretorum cum glossis et notulis, Compotus*, and medical opuscula. FRATRIS ROGERI BACON *Compendium studii theologiae*, edited by H. RASHDALL, Aberdeen, 1911 (British society of Franciscan studies, III). "An unpublished fragment of a work by Roger Bacon," edited by F. A. GASQUET, in *E.H.R.*, XII (1897), 494–517. For Bacon's Greek grammar see outline XVIII.

Die philosophischen Werke des Grosseteste, Bischofs von Lincoln, edited by L. BAUR, Münster, 1912, part of no. **826.** C. FERCKEL, *Die Gynäkologie des Thomas von Brabant, ausgewählte Kapitel aus Buch I de naturis rerum*, Munich, 1912. For the scientific writings of Albertus Magnus see the edition of his *Opera* by E. BORGNET, Paris, 1890, vols. 3–12, and 37. H. STADLER has a critical edition of the *De animalibus* of Albert the Great, Münster, 1916–20. There is an old edition of the *De vegetabilibus*, with notes, by E. MEYER and C. JESSEN, Berlin, 1867. *Lapidario del rey D. Alfonso X, Codice original* (in color facsimile), Madrid, 1881. *La composizione del mondo di Ristoro d'Arezzo*, edited by E. NARDUCCI, Rome, 1859; Milan, 1864. BRUNETTO LATINI, *I libri naturali del "Tesoro,"* edited by G. BATTELLI, Florence, n.d. (ca. 1917). E. BURON (editor), *Ymago mundi* of Cardinal Pierre d'Ailly, chancellor of the University of Paris, Paris, 1928, Latin text with French translation; a chapter on Pierre d'Ailly and Columbus. *Recueil des plus célèbres astrologues . . . faict par Symon de Phares*, edited by E. WICKERSHEIMER, Paris, 1929. D. V. THOMPSON, "Liber de coloribus illuminatorum sive pictorum from Sloane MS., no. 1754," *Speculum*, I (1926), 280–307.

Medicine and surgery. K. SUDHOFF, "Pestschriften aus den ersten 150 Jahren nach der Epidemie des Schwarzen Todes, 1348," a series of articles in *Archiv. f. Gesch. d. Medizin*, IV–XVII, 1910–25. A. C. KLEBS and E. DROZ, *Remèdes contre la peste: fac-similés, notes et liste bibliographiques des incunables sur la peste*, Paris, 1925. JOANNES DE KETHAM ALEMANUS, *Fasciculus medicinae*, 1491 (introduction and notes by K. SUDHOFF, translated and adapted by C. SINGER), Milan, 1924. P. PANSIER, *Collectio ophthalmologica veterum auctorum*, Paris, 1903ff. J. L. PAGEL edited a number of medieval medical and surgical texts, such as *Die Chirurgie des Heinrich von Mondeville*, Berlin, 1892; *Die Concordanciae des Joannes de Sancto Amando*, Berlin, 1894 E. NICAISE edited *La grande chirurgie de Guy de Chauliac*, Paris, 1890; and published a French translation of HENRY OF MONDEVILLE, Paris, 1893.

Bibliographies. *Isis* contains frequent critical bibliographies for the history of science, classified chronologically by centuries, and also by subjects. Similar bibliographies will be found in *Archeion*, formerly *Archivio di storia della scienza.* A *List of books on the history of science in the John Crerar Library*, was edited by A. G. S. JOSEPHSON, Chicago, 1911, with a supplementary volume, 1917. G. SARTON, *Introduction to the history of science*, vol. I (to 1100 A.D.), has very full bibliographical apparatus.

The best bibliographies on Roger Bacon are by T. WITZEL, appended to his article on "Roger Bacon" in the *Catholic encyclopedia*, and especially in his article "De Fr. Rogero Bacon," *A.F.H.*, III (1910), 9–14. For Bacon's own works, both in printed and manuscript form, see A. G. LITTLE, "Roger Bacon's works," in *Roger Bacon essays*, 375–426. See also R. STEELE, "Roger Bacon," *Quarterly review*, CCXX (1914), 250–74, and A. G. LITTLE, "Roger Bacon," *Proceedings of the British Academy*, XIV (1928).

Manuscript catalogues. L. Thorndike, "Vatican Latin manuscripts in the history of science and medicine," *Isis*, XIII (1929), 53–102. D. W. Singer and Annie Anderson, *Catalogue of Latin and vernacular alchemical manuscripts in Great Britain and Ireland dating before the XVI century*, vol. I, Brussels, 1928. F. Saxl, *Verzeichnis astrologischer und mythologischer illustrierter Handschriften des lateinischen Mittelalters*, 2 vols., *S.B.*, *Heidelberg Acad.*, 1915, 1927. G. Carbonelli, *Sulle fonti storiche della chimica e dell' alchimia in Italia*, Rome, 1925. *Catalogue des manuscrits alchimiques grecs*, edited by J. Bidez, F. Cumont, J. L. Heiberg, and O. Lagercrantz, Brussels, 1924–28, vols. I–VI. *Catalogus codicum astrologorum graecorum*, edited by Boll, Cumont, Kroll, et al., Brussels, 1898–1924, 10 vols.; only a fraction of the material is medieval. K. Sudhoff, *Beiträge z. Geschichte d. Chirurgie im Mittelalter: graphische und textliche Untersuchungen in mittelalterlichen Handschriften*, 2 vols., Leipzig, 1914, 1918. A. de Poorter, "Catalogue des manuscrits de médicine de la bibliothèque de Bruges," *Revue des bibliothèques*, XXXIV (1924), 271–306.

XXII. MEDIEVAL UNIVERSITIES

A. Outline

1. The institutions of learning, now known as universities, originated in the twelfth and thirteenth centuries; hence such expressions as "the universities of ancient Greece" lead to confusion and should be avoided. This outline deals with the outward aspects of medieval universities, and the life of masters and students. Their intellectual activities and interests have been dealt with in preceding outlines.

2. How the medieval universities got their name. *Studium. Studium generale.* The derivation of the word "university" from such phrases in the early university charters as *Universitas magistrorum et scholarium parisiensium*, and *Universis presentes litteras inspecturis.* Foundation charters. *Jus ubique docendi.*

3. The university of Paris, the typical medieval university. Its legendary history. Gradual evolution from the cathedral school on the island in the Seine. The chancellor and the license to teach. Written statutes of the university. The four nations. Rector and proctors. The chancellor of Ste. Geneviève. Paris was the typical masters' university. The development of a Latin Quarter in Paris.

4. The mendicant friars in the university of Paris. Ecclesiastical control and influence in medieval universities. Growth of the influence of the mendicants during the great dispersion of 1229. The violent constitutional struggle towards the middle of the thirteenth century.

5. Organization of faculties and branches of study. The arts course and the higher faculties: theology, law, and medicine. "Graduate work."

6. University degrees. The license to teach (*licentia docendi*). The gild of masters. Inception and the mastership. The terms master, doctor, and professor were synonymous. Gradual evolution of the bachelorship in the

thirteenth century. Determinations and responsions. The B.A. degree. Examinations for degrees. The LL.D. degree. The Ph.D. degree was not invented in medieval universities. Academical dress.

7. The evolution of colleges in Paris. The problem of housing the numerous students in Paris. Hospicia and self-government of students. The comfortable houses of the mendicant friars in Paris. Robert de Sorbon, the founder of the famous Sorbonne. Multiplication of colleges in Paris in the fourteenth and fifteenth centuries. The colleges entirely transformed the life and work of medieval universities.

8. The enigmatical medical school at Salerno, famous as early as the eleventh century. Constantinus Africanus in Salerno, in the second half of the eleventh century. Frederick II and Salerno.

9. The university of Bologna was the typical law university and students' university. Large numbers of foreigners, especially Germans, in Bologna. The colleges.

10. Universities of Oxford and Cambridge. The bishop of Lincoln and his Oxford chancellor. The famous old colleges of Oxford, especially Balliol, Merton, and University College.

11. Other important medieval universities. Padua (1222), and Naples (1224) in Italy. Montpellier (twelfth century), Toulouse (1229), and Orleans (thirteenth century), in France. Salamanca, Valladolid, and Lisbon (Coimbra), all of the thirteenth century, in Spain and Portugal. The late rise of German universities. Prague (1348), Vienna (1365), Heidelberg (1385), Leipzig (1409), Louvain (1426).

12. Daily routine in a medieval university. Lectures, disputations, university meetings, festivals, holidays, vacations. Numbers of students.

13. Life of medieval students. Their average age and previous training. Their food and shelter before and after the growth of colleges. Athletic games and other amusements. Hazing. Privileges of students. Their clerical status. Town and gown riots. Migrations of medieval universities.

14. The influence of universities in medieval life and thought.

B. Special Recommendations for Reading

General surveys. C. H. Haskins, *Renaissance*, ch. xii; *C.M.H.*, VI, ch. xvii. C. V. Langlois, *Questions d'histoire et d'enseignement*, 3–50. Taylor, *Mediaeval mind*, fourth edition, II, ch. xxxviii. Lavisse, *Histoire de France*, III, part I, 332–45; part II, 380–87. The article "Universities" by J. B. Mullinger and C. Brereton, in the *Ency. Brit.* Tilley, *Medieval France*, ch. vi. Crump and Jacob, *Legacy*, 255–85. A. Gray, "The beginnings of colleges," *History*, VI (1921), 1–10.

Standard works. Haskins, *Rise of universities;* and the contribution of his student, G. Post, "Alexander III, the 'Licentia docendi,' and the rise of the universities" in *Anniversary essays in medieval history by students of Charles Homer Haskins*, Boston and New York, 1929, 255–78. H. Rashdall, *The universities of Europe in the middle ages*, 2 vols. in 3, Oxford, 1895. A new edition of this fundamental work is announced. H. Denifle, *Die Ent-*

stehung der Universitäten des Mittelalters bis 1400, vol. I, Berlin, 1885. This was the epoch-making modern book on the history of medieval universities. The author planned to complete the work in five volumes. He died in 1905.

University of Bologna. H. D. SEDGWICK, *Italy in the thirteenth century*, I, chs. XVI–XVII.

Life of medieval students. R. S. RAIT, *Life in the mediaeval university*, Cambridge, 1912, is based on the last chapter in RASHDALL, *Universities*, which see. C. H. HASKINS, "Life of mediaeval students as seen in their letters," *A.H.R.*, III (1897–98), 203–29; "The university of Paris in the sermons of the thirteenth century," *ibid.*, X (1904), 1–27. These two articles are now most satisfactorily available in his *Studies in mediaeval culture*, 1–71; note also his "Manuals for students," *ibid.*, 72–91. A. LUCHAIRE, *Social France*, ch. III. A. MOIREAU, *La journée d'un écolier au moyen âge*, Paris, 1889. P. FUCHS, "Student life in Paris during the middle ages," *Living age*, CCCXXIX (1926), 682–85. MUNRO and SELLERY, *Medieval civilization*, 348–57. J. B. MILBURN, "University life in mediaeval Oxford," *Dublin review*, CXXIX (1901), 72–97, is a review of *Epistolae academicae*, edited by H. ANSTEY, 2 vols., Oxford, 1901, and depicts university life in the fifteenth century. W. T. HEWETT, "University life in the middle ages," *Harper's magazine*, XCVI (1898), 945–55. P. MONROE, *Thomas Platter, 1499–1582, and the educational renaissance of the sixteenth century*, New York, 1904.

Original sources. WEBSTER, *Historical selections*, 579–604. A. O. NORTON, *Readings in the history of education: mediaeval universities*, Cambridge, 1909. DUNCALF and KREY, *Parallel source problems*, 137–74. "The departure of the university from Paris, 1229–1231." *Translations and reprints*, vol. II, no. 3. RUTEBEUF's [thirteenth century] satire on the Parisian student is freely translated under the title, "The song of the university of Paris," pp. 125–27 in *Legends and satires from mediaeval literature*, edited by MARTHA H. SHACKFORD, Boston [1913]. SYMONDS, *Wine, women and song*. DAVIES, *Civilization in medieval England*, 140–48. *Manuale scholarium*, edited by R. F. SEYBOLT, Cambridge, 1921. R. F. SEYBOLT, *Renaissance student life*, a translation of *Paedologia* of Petrus Mossellanus, Urbana, 1927. R. B. BURKE, *Compendium on the magnificence, dignity, and excellence of the university of Paris in the year of grace 1517* [by Robert Goulet], Philadelphia, 1928.

Maps. SHEPHERD, *Atlas*, 100, shows the location of the chief medieval universities. A better map is at the beginning of vol. II, part I of RASHDALL, *Universities*.

C. BIBLIOGRAPHY

General books. See especially the histories of education, nos. **836–49.** For literature on the intellectual interests in medieval universities see especially outlines XIV–XV, XVII, XIX–XX. For general works on medieval Paris, see outline XIII.

University of Paris. Following are the important older works. C. E. DU BOULAY (BULAEUS), *Historia universitatis parisiensis a Carolo Magno* *ad nostra tempora*, 6 vols., in folio, Paris, 1665–73, is analyzed in A. FRANKLIN, *Les sources de l'histoire de France*, 598–603. J. B. L. CREVIER, *Histoire de l'université de Paris depuis son origine jusqu'en l'année 1600*, 7 vols., Paris, 1761. E. DUBARLE, *Histoire de l'université de Paris*, 2 vols., Paris, 1844. C. RICHOMME, *Histoire de l'université de Paris*, Paris, 1840, is scarcely more than an abridgment of DUBARLE.

Among modern special books, the best is still C. THUROT, *De l'organisation de l'enseignement dans l'université de Paris au moyen âge*, Paris, 1850. A. BUDINSKY, *Die Universität Paris und die Fremden an derselben im Mittelalter*, Berlin, 1876. R. DELÈGUE, *L'université de Paris (1224–1244)*, Paris, 1902. A. LUCHAIRE, *L'université de Paris sous Philippe-Auguste*, Paris, 1889. E. ALLAIN, "L'université de Paris aux XIIIe et XIVe siècles," *Revue du clergé français*, IV (1895), 193–206, 308–22. C. JOURDAIN, *Excursions historiques et philosophiques à travers le moyen âge*, 247–63, "La taxe des logements dans l'université de Paris"; see also pp. 265, 309, and 337. C. GROSS, "The political influence of the university of Paris in the middle ages," *A.H.R.*, VI (1900–01), 440–45. A. CALLET, *Le vieux Paris universitaire*, Paris [1907], is a popular sketch. L. LIARD, "La vieille université de Paris," *Revue de Paris*, May, 1908, 85–110. N. VALOIS, *Guillaume d'Auvergne, évêque de Paris*, Paris, 1880. P. FERET, "Les origines de l'université de Paris et son organisation aux XIIe et XIIIe siècles," *R.Q.H.*, LII (1892), 337–90; this article now is the introduction to his large work entitled, *La faculté de théologie de Paris*. C. DESMAZE, *L'université de Paris, 1200–1875: La nation de Picardie; les collèges de Laon et de Presles; la loi sur l'enseignement supérieur*, Paris, 1876. Abbé PAGUELLE DE FOLLENAY, *Notice historique sur l'école épiscopale de Notre-Dame de Paris*, Paris, 1878. See also ASPINWALL, *Les écoles épiscopales*. F. M. POWICKE, *Stephen Langton*, Oxford, 1928. A. DOUARCHE, *L'université de Paris et les Jésuites (XVIe et XVIIe siècles)*, Paris, 1888, reaches back into the middle ages. P. LÉVY, "Histoire du collège de La Marche et de Winiville en l'université de Paris," *Thèse, École de Chartes*, 1921. DOROTHY L. MACKAY, "Le système d'examen du XIIIe siècle d'après le *De conscientia* de Robert de Sorbon," *Mélanges Ferdinand Lot*, Paris, 1925, 491–500. G. C. BOYCE, *The English-German nation in the university of Paris during the middle ages*, Bruges, 1927. J. BONNEROT, "L'ancienne université de Paris, centre international d'études," *Bulletin of the International committee of historical sciences*, I, Part V, no. 5 (1928), 661–82. G. LACOMBE, *Prepositini cancellarii parisiensis (1206–1210) opera omnia, I, La vie et les oeuvres de Prêvostin*, Kain, 1927. CONNOLLY, *John Gerson, reformer and mystic*. L. HALPHEN, "Les débuts de l'université de Paris," *Studi medievali*, VII (1929), 152ff.

Mendicants in the university of Paris. F. X. SEPPELT, "Der Kampf der Bettelorden an der Universität Paris in der Mitte des 13 Jahrhunderts," *Kirchengeschichtliche Abhandlungen*, III (1905); "Wissenschaft und Franziskanerorden," *ibid.*, IV (1906), 149–79; see also VI (1908), 73–139. FELDER, *Geschichte der wissenschaftlichen Studien im Franziskanerorden*. GRATIEN, "Les Franciscaines à l'université de Paris: notes et documents," *Etudes* *franciscaines*, January, 1912. P. MANDONNET, "De l'incorporation des Dominicains dans l'ancienne université de Paris," *Revue thomiste*, IV (1896), 156ff. H. DENIFLE, "Das erste Studienhaus der Benediktiner an der Universität Paris," *Archiv für Literatur und Kirchengeschichte*, I (1885), 570–83. M. PERROD, *Maître Guillaume de Saint-Amour: l'université de Paris et les ordres mendiants au 13 siècle*, Paris, 1895, was sharply criticised by Mandonnet and Felder. M. PERROD, *Etude sur la vie et sur les oeuvres de Guillaume de Saint Amour (1202–1272)*, Lons-le-Saunier, 1902, seems to be a new edition of his work printed in 1895. MARY M. WOOD, *The spirit of protest in old French literature*, ch. III, "The defense of Guillaume de Saint-Amour," 115–33. E. JALLONGHI, "La grande discordia tra l'università di Parigi e i mendicanti," *Scuola cattolica*, XIII (1917); XIV (1918). E. BERNARD, *Les Dominicains dans l'université de Paris*, Paris, 1883. A. VAN DEN WYNGAERT, "Querelles du clergé séculier et des ordres mendiants à l'université de Paris au XIIIe siècle," *La France franciscaine*, V (1922), 257–81, 369–97; VI (1923), 47–70. E. LONGPRÉ, "Maîtres franciscains de Paris: Guillaume de Ware, O. F. M.," *ibid.*, V (1922), 71–82; 289–306. A. CALLEBAUT, "Alexandre de Halès et ses confrères en face de condamnations parisiennes de 1241 et 1244," *ibid.*, sér. II, Vol. X (1927), 257–72; "Essai sur l'origine des mineurs à Paris et sur l'influence de frère Grégoire de Naples," *ibid.*, sér. II, Vol. XI (1928), 5–30, 179–209; "Les séjours du B. Jean Duns Scot à Paris," *ibid.*, sér. II, Vol. XII (1929), 353–73. BIERBAUM, *Bettelorden und Weltgeistlichkeit.* R. MARTIN, "Quelques premiers maîtres dominicains de Paris et d'Oxford et la soi-disant école dominicaine augustinienne," *Revue des sciences philosophiques et théologiques*, IX (1920), 556–80. F. EHRLE, *San Domenico, le origini del primo studio generale del suo ordine a Parigi e la Somma teologica del primo maestro Rolando de Cremona* (*Miscell' Dominicana in memoriam VII anni saecul. ab obitu S. Dominici*, Rome, 1923). See also the general literature on the mendicants in outline XXIII of part II above.

Sorbonne. Colleges in Paris. O. GRÉARD, *Nos adieux à la vieille Sorbonne*, 2nd edition, Paris, 1893; "Derniers souvenirs de la vieille Sorbonne," *Revue de Paris*, VI (1901), 270–304, 560–78. A. FRANKLIN, *La Sorbonne: ses origines, sa bibliothèque*, 2nd edition, Paris, 1875. E. MÉRIC, *La Sorbonne et son fondateur*, Paris, 1888. ROBERT DE SORBON, *De consciencia et de tribus dietis*, edited by F. CHAMBON, Paris, 1903 (fasc. 35 of **968**) contains a sketch of his life and a good bibliography. P. DE LONGUEMARE, *Notes sur quelques collèges parisiens de fondation normande aux XIIIe, XIVe et XVe siècles*, Rouen, 1911. R. THAMIN, "Nos grandes écoles: la Sorbonne," in *R.D.M.*, XXXIX (1927), 591–611, 855–75. L. BARRAU-DIRIGO and J. BONNEROT, *La Sorbonne: six siècles de son histoire par l'image*, Paris, 1928. J. BONNEROT, *La Sorbonne: sa vie, son rôle, son oeuvre à travers les siècles*, Paris, 1928. P. ANGER, *Le collège de Cluny, fondé à Paris dans le voisinage de la Sorbonne et le ressort de l'université*, Paris, 1916.

Other French universities. M. FOURNIER, *Histoire de la science du droit en France*, vol. III, Paris, 1892, *Les universités françaises et l'enseignement* *du droit en France au moyen âge.* A. MOLINIER, "Etude sur l'organisation de l'université de Toulouse, au quatorzième et au quinzième siècle (1309–1450)," in DEVIC and VAISSETTE, *Histoire générale de Languedoc*, VII, 570–608. L. SALTET, "L'ancienne université de Toulouse," *Bulletin littéraire ecclésiastique*, 1912ff. R. GADAVE, *Les documents sur l'histoire de l'université de Toulouse et spécialement de sa faculté de droit civil et canonique (1229–1789)*, Toulouse, 1910 (Diss.). E. J. BARBOT, *Les chroniques de la faculté de médecine de Toulouse du XIIIe au XXe siècles*, 2 vols., Toulouse, 1905. R. CAILLET, *L'université d'Avignon et sa faculté des droits au moyen âge (1303–1503)*, Paris, 1907. J. MARCHAND, *La faculté des arts de l'université d'Avignon*, Paris, 1897. F. BELIN, *Histoire de l'ancienne université de Provence (Aix) 1400–1793, d'après les manuscrits et les documents originaux*, Aix, 1892. J. E. BIMBENET, *Histoire de l'université de lois d'Orléans*, Paris, 1853. L. BAYER, "Documents inédits sur l'ancienne université et sur les écoles de Grenoble et de son diocèse au XVe siècle," *Annales de l'université de Grenoble*, III (1926), 1–12. J. C. RUSSELL, *Three short studies in mediaeval intellectual history: I. An ephemeral university at Angers (1229–1234)* (Colorado college publication, general series, no. 148, Colorado Springs, 1927).

University of Bologna. Among the older works the following still have value. M. SARTI and M. FATTORINI, *De claris archigymnasii bononiensis professoribus a saeculo XI usque ad saeculum XIV*, Bologna, 1769–72; new edition, 2 vols., 1888–96. C. GHIRARDACCI, *Della historia di Bologna*, 2 parts, Bologna, 1596, 1657. SAVIGNY, *Geschichte des römischen Rechts*, ch. XXI.

Much literature was called forth by the great centenary in 1888 described by J. KIRKPATRICK, *The octocentenary festival of the university of Bologna*, Edinburgh, 1888. See also *Catalogo del museo dell' ottavo centenario dello studio bolognese*, Bologna, 1892; and the reviews of the literature called forth by this celebration by A. DEL VECCHIO in *Archivio storico italiano*, 5th series, II (1888), 394–452; by C. CIPOLLA, in *Jahresberichte der Geschichtswissenschaft*, XI (1891), III, 5–7; and by LANDSBERG in *Zeitschrift der Savignystiftung für Rechtsgeschichte*, romanistische Abteilung, neue Folge, IX. Some of the best of those books are the following: H. FITTING, *Die Anfänge der Rechtsschule zu Bologna*, Leipzig, 1888. C. MALAGOLA, *Monografie storiche sullo studio bolognese*, Bologna, 1888; *I rettore delle università dello studio bolognese*, Bologna, 1887. C. RICCI, *I primordi dello studio bolognese: nota storica*, Bologna, 1887; 2nd edition, 1888. G. CASSANI, *Dell' antico studio di Bologna e sua origine*, Bologna, 1888. L. CHIAPPELLI, *Lo studio bolognese nelle sue origini e nei suoi rapporti colla scienza pre-irneriana*, Pistoia, 1888.

Following are some publications since that date: *Studi e memorie per la storia dell' università di Bologna*, Bologna, 1907ff. G. MANACORDA, *Storia della scuola in Italia*, vols. I–II [on middle ages]. F. CAVAZZA, *Le scuole dell' antico studio bolognese*, Milan, 1896. A. HESSEL, *Geschichte der Stadt Bologna von 1116 bis 1280*, Berlin, 1910.

Other Italian universities. E. COPPI, *Le università italiane nel medio evo*, 3rd edition, Florence, 1886. S. DE RENZI, *Storia documentata della scuola* *medica di Salerno*, 2nd edition, Naples, 1857. *L'école de Salerne*, translation of the *Regimen sanitatis*, in French verse, with the Latin text, by C. MEAUX SAINT-MARC, with an introduction by C. DAREMBERG, Paris, 1880. F. HARTMANN, *Die Literatur von Früh- und Hoch Salerno*, Leipzig, 1919. K. HAMPE, "Zur Gründungsgeschichte der Universität Neapel," *Mitteilungen aus der Capuaner Briefsammlung, V*, in *S.B., Heidelberg Acad.*, 1923, 10 Abh. F. TORRACA, GENNARO MARIA MONTI, RICCARDO FILANGERI DI CANDIDA et al., *Storia dell' università di Napoli*, Naples, 1924. L. C. BOLLEA, "Le pubblicazioni dell' undecimo centenario dell' università di Pavia," *Bolletino della società pavese di storia patria*, Pavia, XXV (1925), 141–81. G. MENGOZZI, *Ricerche sull' attività della scuola di Pavia nell' alto medio evo*, Paris, 1924. G. ZACCAGNINI, *La vita dei maestri e degli scolari nello studio di Bologna nei secoli XIII e XIV*, Geneva, 1926 (*Biblioteca dell' Archivum romanicum*, ser. I, vol. 5). M. SCHIPA, *La fondazione dell' università di Napoli e l'Italia del tempo*, Naples, 1924. See also for Naples, additional titles in *H.Z.*, 132 (1925), 488–92. F. LANDOGNA, "Maestri e scolari pisani nello studio di Bologna tra il secolo XII e la metà del XIV," *Archivio storico italiano*, serie VII, vol. V (1926), 173–231.

English universities. E. V. VAUGHAN, *The origin and early development of the English universities to the close of the thirteenth century*, University of Missouri, Studies, Social science series, II, no. 2, 1908. J. F. WILLARD, *The royal authority and the early English universities*, Philadelphia, 1902. H. FLETCHER [delineator], *Oxford and Cambridge*, with an introduction by J. W. CLARK, London, 1910. J. B. COISSAC, *Les universités d'Ecosse depuis la fondation de l'université de Saint-Andreux jusqu'au triomphe de la réforme*, Paris, 1915.

University of Oxford. A. À. WOOD, *The history and antiquities of the university of Oxford*, edited by J. GUTCH, 2 vols., Oxford, 1792–96. H. C. M. LYTE, *A history of the university of Oxford to 1530*, London, 1886. G. C. BRODRICK, *A history of the university of Oxford*, London, 1886; 3rd edition, 1894. T. E. HOLLAND, "The origin of the university of Oxford," in *E.H.R.*, VI (1891), 238–49. C. HEADLAM, *Oxford and its story*, 2nd edition, London, 1912. A. LANG, *Oxford: brief historical and descriptive notes*, London, 1890. C. W. BOASE, *Oxford*, London, 1887 (Historic towns). E. A. G. LAMBORN, *The story of architecture in Oxford stone*, London, 1913. C. E. MALLET, *A history of the university of Oxford*, vol. I, *The mediaeval university and the colleges founded in the middle ages*, London and New York, 1924. S. GIBSON, "The congregations of the university of Oxford," Oxford, 1926, reprinted from *Bodleian quarterly record*, IV (1926), 296–314. A. G. LITTLE, "The Franciscan school at Oxford in the thirteenth century," *A.F.H.*, XIX (1926), 803–74. H. E. SALTER, "The medieval university of Oxford," *History*, N. S. XIV (1929), 57–61.

Oxford colleges. *The colleges of Oxford, their history and traditions: twenty-one chapters contributed by members of the colleges*, edited by A. CLARK, London, 1891. A. VALLANCE, *The old colleges of Oxford: their architectural history*, London, 1912, has remarkable illustrations. G. C. BRODRICK,

Memorials of Merton college, Oxford, 1885 (O.H.S.). *Foundation statutes of Merton college, 1270, with subsequent ordinances*, from the Latin, translated by E. F. PERCIVAL, London, 1887. A. B. EMDEN, *An Oxford hall in mediaeval times, being the early history of St. Edmund Hall*, Oxford, 1927.

University of Cambridge. J. B. MULLINGER, *The university of Cambridge from the earliest times to 1535*, Cambridge, 1873, vol. II, to Charles the First, 1884, vol. III, to 1667, 1911; *History of the university of Cambridge*, London, 1888 (Epochs of church history), a popular abridgment. R. WILLIS and J. W. CLARK, *The architectural history of the university of Cambridge and of the colleges of Cambridge and Eton*, 4 vols., Cambridge, 1886. C. H. COOPER, *Annals of Cambridge*, 5 vols., Cambridge, 1842–1908; *Memorials of Cambridge*, 3 vols., new edition, Cambridge, 1884. A. GRAY, *Cambridge and its story*, London, 1912. J. W. CLARK, *Cambridge*, new edition, Philadelphia, 1908. W. W. ROUSE BALL, *The king's scholars and King's Hall*, printed privately, 1917; *Cambridge papers*, London, 1918. A. GRAY, *Cambridge university: an episodical history*, London, 1926.

Spanish universities. V. DE LA FUENTE, *Historia de las universidades, colegios y demás establecimientos de enseñanza en España*, 4 vols., Madrid, 1884–89. E. ESPERABÉ ARTEAGA, *Historia de la universidad de Salamanca*, vol. I, Salamanca, 1914. G. REYNIER, *La vie universitaire dans l'ancienne Espagne*, Paris, 1902, chiefly concerned with Salamanca. T. BRAGA, *Historia da universidade de Coimbra*, 4 vols., Lisbon, 1892–1902, vol. I, 1289–1555.

German universities. G. KAUFMANN, *Die Geschichte der deutschen Universitäten*, 2 vols., Stuttgart, 1888–96. F. v. BEZOLD, "Die ältesten deutschen Universitäten in ihrem Verhältnis zum Staat," *H.Z.*, LXXX (1898), 436–67. F. PAULSEN, "Die Gründung der deutschen Universitäten im Mittelalter," *ibid.*, XLV (1881), 251–311; "Organisation und Lebensordnungen der deutschen Universitäten im Mittelalter," *ibid.*, 385–440. J. v. DÖLLINGER, *Die Universitäten sonst und jetzt*, Munich, 1867, translated by APPLETON, *The universities new and old*, Oxford, 1867. A. THORBECKE, *Die älteste Zeit der Universität Heidelberg (1386–1449)*, Heidelberg, 1886. J. ASCHBACH, *Geschichte der Wiener Universität im ersten Jahrhundert ihres Bestehens*, 3 vols., Vienna, 1865–88. M. MEYHÖFER, "Die kaiserlichen Stiftungsprivilegien für Universitäten," *Archiv für Urkundenforschung*, IV (1912), 291–418. F. BENARY, *Zur Geschichte der Stadt und der Universität Erfurt am Ausgang des Mittelalters*, Gotha, 1919. G. RITTER, "Aus dem geistigen Leben der Heidelberger Universität im Ausgang des Mittelalters," *Zeitschrift für die Geschichte des Ober-Rheins*, LXXVI (1922), 1–32. J. F. ABERT, "Aus der Geschichte der ersten Würzburger Universität unter Bischof Johann von Efloffstein," in *Archiv des historischen Vereins von Unterfranken und Aschaffenburg*, LXIII (1923), 1–32. O. REDLICH, "Über die Geschichte der Universität Wien," *Wien, sein Boden und seine Geschichte*, Vienna, 1924, 179–96. EHRLE, *Der Sentenzenkommentar Peters von Candia des Pisaner Papstes Alexanders V*, Münster. G. M. LÖHR, *Die theologischen Disputationen und Promotionen an der Universität Köln im ausgehenden 15. Jahrhundert nach den Angaben des P. Servatius Franckel*, Leipzig, 1926. E. STÜBLER, *Geschichte der medizinischen*

Facultät der Universität Heidelberg, 1386–1920, Heidelberg, 1926. H. Schönebaum, "Die ungarischen Universitäten im Mittelalter," *Archiv für Kulturgeschichte*, XVI (1926), 41–59.

University of Louvain. P. Delannoy, *L'université de Louvain*, Paris, 1915. L. Noël, *Louvain: 891–1914*, Oxford, 1915. L. van der Essen, *Une institution d'enseignement supérieur sous l'ancien régime: l'université de Louvain (1425–1797)*, Brussels and Paris, 1921. L. van der Essen and others, *L'université de Louvain à travers cinq siècles: études historiques*, Brussels, 1927.

Original sources. *Chartularium universitatis parisiensis*, edited by H. Denifle and E. Chatelain, 4 vols., Paris, 1889–97; supplemented by the *Auctarium chartularium universitatis parisiensis*, by the same editors, 2 vols., Paris, 1894–97, containing documents which were excluded from the *Chartularium* on account of their length. See also H. Denifle, "Documents relatifs à la fondation et aux premiers temps de l'université de Paris," in *Mémoires de la Société de l'histoire de Paris*, X (1883), 243ff. See the review of the *Chartularium* in the *R.Q.H.*, XLVIII (1890), 577–86. H. Omont (editor) "Le 'livre' ou 'cartulaire' de la nation de Normandie de l'université de Paris," *Mélanges, Société de l'histoire de Normandie*, Rouen (1918), 1–10; "Le 'livre' ou 'cartulaire' de la nation de France, de l'université de Paris," *Mémoires de la Société de l'histoire de Paris*, XLI (1914), 1–124. *Les statuts et privilèges des universités françaises depuis leur fondation jusqu'en 1789*, edited by M. Fournier, 4 vols., Paris, 1890–94 (see in connection with it H. Denifle, *Les universités françaises au moyen âge: avis à M. Fournier*, Paris, 1892). *Cartulaire de l'université de Montpellier*, edited by A. Germain, Montpellier, vol. I, 1890, vol. II, 1912.

Chartularium studii bononiensis: documenti per la storia dell' università di Bologna dalle origini fino al secolo XV, edited by L. Nordi and E. Orioli, vols. I–VIII, Bologna and Imola, 1909–27. *Acta nationis germanicae universitatis bononiensis*, Berlin, 1887. *Atti della nazione germanica dei legisti allo studio di Padova*, edited by B. Brugi, Padua, 1912ff. *Atti della nazione germanica artistica nello studio di Padova*, Padua, 1912; *Atti della nazione germanica di Padova*, 2 vols., Venice, 1911, both edited by A. Favaro. P. U. González de la Calle and A. Huarte y Echenique, "Constituciones de la universidad de Salamanca (1422), edición paleográfica," *Revista de archivos, bibliotecas y museos*, XLVI (1925), 217–28, 345–59, 402–19; XLVII (1926), 348–71, 467–501.

Munimenta academica: or, documents illustrative of academical life and studies at Oxford, edited by H. Anstey, 2 vols., London, 1868 (Rolls series). *Statutes of the colleges of Oxford*, edited by H. Anstey, 3 vols., Oxford, 1853. *Collectanea*, edited by C. R. L. Fletcher and others, 4 vols., Oxford, 1885–1905 (O.H.S.); for contents see Gross, *Sources*, no. 2779. *Enactments in Parliament, specially concerning the universities of Oxford and Cambridge, the colleges and halls therein, and the colleges of Winchester, Eton and Westminster*, edited by L. L. Shadwell, 4 vols., Oxford, 1912 (O.H.S.), see especially, I, 1–74. H. E. Salter (editor), *The Oxford deeds of Balliol college*, Oxford (O.H.S.),

1913; *A cartulary of the hospital of St. John the Baptist*, 3 vols., Oxford (O.H.S.), 1914–17; *Mediaeval archives of the university of Oxford*, 2 vols., Oxford (O.H.S.), 1920–21; *Munimenta civitatis Oxonie*, Devizes (O.H.S.), 1920; *Registrum annalium collegii mertonensis;* Oxford (O.H.S.), 1923. G. C. RICHARDS and H. E. SALTER, *The dean's register of Oriel (1446–1661)*, Oxford (O.H.S.), 1926. C. L. SHADWELL and H. E. SALTER, *Oriel college records*, Oxford (O.H.S.), 1926. P. S. ALLEN and H. W. GARROD, editors, *Merton muniments*, Oxford (O.H.S.), 1928. *Documents relating to the university and colleges of Cambridge*, published by direction of the commissioners appointed to inquire into the state, etc., of the university and colleges, 3 vols., London, 1852. R. L. POOLE, *A lecture on the history of the university archives*, Oxford, 1912. *Early records of the university of St. Andrews*, transcribed and edited by J. M. ANDERSON, Edinburgh, 1926. (*Publications of the Scottish history society*, 3rd series, vol. VIII.)

Bibliographies. The best bibliographies of books which appeared before 1895 are at the head of chapters in RASHDALL, *Universities*. E. CHATELAIN, "Essai d'une bibliographie de l'ancienne université de Paris," *Revue des bibliothèques*, I (1891). L. FRATI, *Opere della bibliografia bolognese che si conservano nella biblioteca municipale di Bologna*, 2 vols., Bologna, 1888. L. MANZONI, *Saggio di una bibliografia storica bolognese*, part I, Bologna, 1888. W. ERMAN and E. HORN, *Bibliographie der deutschen Universitäten*, 3 parts, Leipzig, 1904. A convenient short bibliography is in HASKINS, *Rise of universities*, 127–30.

XXIII. LATIN LANGUAGE AND LITERATURE IN THE TWELFTH AND THIRTEENTH CENTURIES

A. OUTLINE

1. The deplorable neglect of these important subjects. Strange to say, there is scarcely anything even approaching a history of medieval Latin. During the last five centuries endless effort has been expended on classical Latin, to the almost utter neglect of the form of the language which was the medium of expression of all western scholars during the middle ages. The efforts of the late Ludwig Traube, and of his successor, Paul Lehmann, in Munich, to arouse interest in medieval Latin philology. The crying need of a modern dictionary of medieval Latin.

2. The nature and importance of medieval Latin in western Christendom. Definitions of: classical Latin; vulgar Latin; low, middle, barbarous or medieval Latin; new or modern Latin.

3. The revival of interest in the study of Latin in the twelfth century. The "new grammar." The new grammars, especially the *Doctrinale* (1199) of Alexander of Villedieu, and the *Graecismus* (1212) of Eberhard of Bethune. The unpublished grammatical works of John Garland, especially the *Clavis compendii*, the *Compendium grammatice*, and the *Accentarius*. His unavailing efforts to arouse interest in the reform of grammar. The popularity of versified grammars.

4. The teaching of grammar in medieval universities. The use of the new grammars. Special degrees in grammar in the university of Tolouse and elsewhere.

5. The decline of interest in the study of the Latin language during the thirteenth century. For the failing enthusiasm for the Latin classics and textual criticism see outline XVIII.

6. The bloom of medieval Latin belles-lettres in the twelfth century compared with the decay in the thirteenth century. Popularity of poetry. The use of rhyme. Popular poems of the day mentioned in the *Battle of the seven arts:* the *Alexandreis* of Gautier of Lille (written 1176–79); the *Tobias* of Matthew of Vendôme (died ca. 1200); the *Architrenius*, or "Arch-Weeper," of Jean of Hauteville (near the end of the twelfth century); the *Anti-Claudianus* of Alain of Lille (ca. 1128–1202); and the *Aurora*, or versified Bible, of Peter Riga, a canon of Reims (died 1209). The fate of this literature in medieval universities.

7. The *Carmina burana.* The Goliardi. Primat of Orleans (Hugh, canon of Orleans, ca. 1140). Primat of Cologne (the Archpoet, wrote ca. 1161–65) author of the *Confessio Goliae episcopi.* Walter Map (Mapes), archdeacon of Oxford, 1197. *Exempla*, or sermon stories.

8. The learned monumental prose works of the twelfth and thirteenth centuries (see outlines XVII, XX–XXI). Decline of Latin style in these writings and in official correspondence in the thirteenth century. The great Latin hymns. The *Legenda aurea* of Jacob of Voragine. For history writing see outline XXV.

9. The relation of Latin with the rising vernacular languages and literatures.

B. Special Recommendations for Reading

Short surveys of medieval Latin. A. Souter, *Hints on the study of Latin (A.D. 125–750)*, London, 1920 (*S.P.C.K., Helps*, no. 21), contains valuable bibliographical material. F. Palgrave, *The history of Normandy and of England*, 2 vols., London, 1851, I, ch. ii. The introduction to *Das Doctrinale des Alexander de Villa-Dei*, edited by D. Reichling, Berlin, 1893, vol. XII of no. **1012,** is the best account of the status of the Latin language at the beginning of the thirteenth century. V. S. Clark, *Studies in the Latin of the middle ages and the renaissance*, Lancaster, Pa., 1900 (Diss.). P. Lehmann, *Vom Mittelalter und von der lateinischen Philologie des Mittelalters*, Munich, 1914. L. J. Paetow, "Latin as a universal language," *Classical journal*, XV (1920), 340–49; see also *The classical weekly*, XIV (1920), 17–19. A. L. Guérard, *Short history of the international language movement*, London [1922]. Note also a plea for the thirteenth century by E. K. Rand, "The classics in the thirteenth century," *Speculum*, IV (1929), 249–69. Crump and Jacob (editors), *Legacy*, 147–72.

Latin grammar in medieval universities. Paetow, *The arts course*, ch. ii. Abelson, *The seven liberal arts*, *passim.*

Latin literature. TAYLOR, *Medieval mind*, 2nd edition, II, chs. XXXII–XXXIII. SANDYS, *Classical scholarship, passim;* "English scholars of Paris and Franciscans of Oxford: Latin literature of England from John of Salisbury to Richard of Bury," *Cambridge history of English literature*, I, ch. X. W. STUBBS, "Literature and learning at the court of Henry II," lectures VI and VII in his *Seventeen lectures*. E. MICHAEL, *Culturzustände des deutschen Volkes*, III, 296–319. BAUMGARTNER, *Geschichte der Weltliteratur*, IV, 378–405. SEDGWICK, *Italy in the thirteenth century*, II, ch. XVII. RABY, *History of Christian Latin poetry*. P. DE LABRIOLLE, *Histoire de la littérature latine chrétienne*, Paris, 1920; 2nd edition, enlarged, 1924. D. H. MADDEN, *Chapters of mediaeval history: the fathers of the literature of field sport and horses* (*Albertus Magnus to the emperor Frederick II*), London, 1926. K. YOUNG, "The home of the Easter play," *Speculum*, I (1926), 71–86. C. H. HASKINS, "The Latin literature of sport," *Speculum*, II (1927), 235–52 and reprinted in his *Studies in mediaeval culture* (1929), 105–23; note also *ibid.*, 124–47. P. H. ALLEN, *The romanesque lyric: studies in its background and development from Petronius to the Cambridge songs, 50–1050, with renderings into English verse*, by H. M. JONES, Chapel Hill, N. C., 1928. C. S. BALDWIN, *Medieval rhetoric and poetic*.

Original sources. COULTON, *A medieval garner. Translations and reprints*, II, no. 4. *Wine, women and song: mediaeval Latin students' songs now first translated into English verse*, with an essay, by J. A. SYMONDS, London, 1884. *Gesta romanorum*, translated by C. SWAN, London, 1899 (Bohn library); selections from the *Gesta* along with other material are translated in *Mediaeval tales*, with an introduction by H. MORLEY, London, 1884. *Gesta romanorum: das älteste Mährchen-und Legendenbuch des christlichen Mittelalters, zum ersten Male vollständig aus dem Lateinischen ins Deutsche übertragen*, by J. G. T. GRÄSSE, 2 vols., Leipzig, 1905. (SWAN is not a complete translation.) A. WESSELSKI, *Märchen des Mittelalters*, Berlin, 1925. *Exempla* in French translation are printed in A. LECOY DE LA MARCHE, *L'esprit de nos aieux*, Paris, 1888. Convenient translations of goliardic verse are in HELEN WADDELL, *The wandering scholars*, supplemented by her *Mediaeval Latin lyrics*, London, 1929, and in P. S. ALLEN, *The Romanesque lyric*. S. GASELEE, *An anthology of medieval Latin*, London, 1925. C. U. CLARK and J. B. GAME, *Medieval and late Latin selections*, Chicago, 1925. C. H. BEESON, *A primer of medieval Latin: an anthology of prose and verse*, Chicago, 1925. H. BACHMANN (editor), *Mittellateinische Gedichte: ausgewählt und erklärt*, Paderborn, 1926. S. GASELEE, *The Oxford book of medieval Latin verse*, Oxford, 1928. MARGARET SCHLAUCH, *Medieval narratives: a book of translations*, New York, 1928.

C. BIBLIOGRAPHY

General books. See the general histories of literature, nos. **782–814,** especially **785–99**; also nos. **170, 303, 309–10,** and **842–43.** See also outline XVIII.

Medieval Latin. L. TRAUBE, *Einleitung in die lateinische Philologie des Mittelalters*, especially pp. 31–103. *Quellen und Untersuchungen zur lateinischen Philologie des Mittelalters*, originally edited by L. TRAUBE, Munich,

1906ff. *Münchener Archiv für Philologie des Mittelalters und der Renaissance*, Munich, 1913ff. J. FELDER, *Die lateinische Kirchensprache nach ihrer geschichtlichen Entwickelung*, Feldkirch, 1905 (Prog.). R. DE GOURMONT, *Le latin mystique: les poètes de l'antiphonaire et la symbolique au moyen âge*, Paris, 1913. J. BRÜCH, *Der Einfluss der germanischen Sprachen auf das Vulgärlatein*, Heidelberg, 1913. For the Latin of medieval official documents, see BRESSLAU, *Handbuch der Urkundenlehre*, I, 555–608 (now see the first pages in vol. II, part I of the new edition); and A. GIRY, *Manuel de diplomatique*, 433–76. EDÉLSTAND DU MÉRIL, *Mélanges archéologiques et littéraires*, Paris, 1850, especially pp. 243–89, "Des origines de la basse latinité et la nécessité de glossaires spéciaux." U. PETERS, P. WETZEL and W. NEUMANN (editors), *Lateinische Quellen des deutschen Mittelalters*, Frankfurt, 1924–26. See also outline I. H. F. MULLER, "On the use of the expression Lingua romana from the first to the ninth century," *Zeitschrift für romanische Philologie*, XLIII (1923), 9–23. G. KOFFMANE, *Geschichte des Kirchenlateins*, Breslau, 1879–81. H. RÖNSCH, *Itala und Vulgata: das Sprachidiom der urchristlichen Itala und der katholischen Vulgate unter Berücksichtigung der römischen Volkssprache, durch Beispiele erläutert*, Marburg, 1868; new edition, 1874. ABBÉ DELFOUR, *La culture latine . . . l'identité du XIIIe et du XVIIe siècle français dans la continuité de la vie latine*, Paris, 1916. T. BENFEY, *Geschichte der Sprachwissenschaft*, Munich, 1869, 170–204. J. MARTIN, "Volkslatein, Schriftlatein, Kirchenlatein," *Hist. Jahrbuch*, XLI (1921), 201–14. H. P. V. NUNN, *An introduction to ecclesiastical Latin*, Cambridge, 1922. P. RUMPF, "L'étude de la latinité médiévale," *Archivum romanicum*, IX (1925), 218–89; *L'étude de la latinité médiévale*, Geneva, 1925 (Diss.). POLHEIM, *Die lateinische Reimprosa*. M. B. OGLE, "Some aspects of medieval Latin style," *Speculum*, I (1926), 171–89. W. E. PLATER and H. J. WHITE, *A grammar of the Vulgate*, Oxford, 1926. P. LEHMANN, "Mittelalter und Küchenlatein," *H.Z.*, CXXXVII (1927), 197–213. H. M. MARTIN, "A brief study of the latinity of the diplomata issued by the Merovingian kings," *Speculum*, II (1927), 258–67. W. B. SEDGWICK, "The style and vocabulary of the twelfth and thirteenth centuries," *Speculum*, III (1928), 349–381; "Notes and emendations on Faral's *Les arts poétiques du XIIe et du XIIIe siècle*," *ibid.*, II (1927), 331–43. K. STRECKER, *Einführung in das Mittellatein*, Berlin, 1928. JEANNE VIELLIARD, *Le latin des diplômes royaux et chartes privées de l'époque mérovingienne*, Paris, 1928, part of no. **888**.

Medieval Latin dictionaries and glossaries. C. D. DU CANGE, *Glossarium mediae et infimae latinitatis*, 3 vols., Paris, 1678; revised edition, 6 vols., Paris, 1733–36; another edition by G. A. L. HENSCHEL, 7 vols., Paris, 1840–50; newest edition by L. FAVRE, 10 vols., Niort, 1883–87. W. H. MAIGNE D'ARNIS, *Lexicon manuale ad scriptores mediae et infimae latinitatis*, Paris, 1858, reprinted 1866, 1890. L. DIEFENBACH, *Glossarium latino-germanicum mediae et infimae aetatis*, Frankfort, 1857; *Novum glossarium latino-germanicum mediae et infimae aetatis*, Frankfort, 1867. E. BRINKMEIER, *Glossarium diplomaticum*, 2 vols., Gotha, 1850–55. A. BARTAL, *Glossarium mediae et *infimae latinitatis regni Hungariae*, Leipzig, 1901. M. A. SCHELER, *Lexicographie latine du XIIe et du XIIIe siècle; trois traités de Jean de Garlande, Alexandre Neckam, et Adam de Petit-Pont*, Leipzig, 1867 (also in *Jahrbuch für romanische und englische Literatur*, VI, 43–59, 142–62, 287–320, 370–79; VII, 58–74, 155–73; VIII, 75–93). T. WRIGHT, *A volume of vocabularies, 10th–15th centuries*, 2 vols., London, 1857; 2nd edition by R. P. WÜLKER, *Anglo-Saxon and old English vocabularies* [*Latin-English*], 2 vols., London, 1884. E. LITTRÉ, "Glossaires [XIIIe siècle]," *Histoire littéraire de la France*, XXII (1852), 1–38. *Corpus glossarium latinorum*, vol. I, History of glosses, is by G. GOETZ, Leipzig, 1923, vols. II–VII, edited by G. LOEWE, Leipzig, 1888–1903. *Prodromus corporis glossariorum latinorum*, edited by G. LOEWE, Leipzig, 1876. C. SCHMIDT, *Petit supplément au dictionnaire de Du Cange*, Strasburg, 1906. Glossaries are often appended to individual editions of works in large collections of source material like nos. **965–66, 978** and **995.** *Corpus glossariorum latinorum, a Gustavo Loewe inchoatum, auspiciis Academiae litterarum saxonicae*, composuit, recensuit, edidit GEORGIUS GOETZ, Leipzig and Berlin, 1888–1922. I. LEVINE, *The language of the glossary Sangallensis 912 and its relationship to the language of other Latin glossaries*, Philadelphia, 1924 (Thesis). W. M. LINDSAY and H. J. THOMSON, *Ancient lore in medieval Latin glossaries*, Oxford, 1921. J. F. MOUNTFORD, *Quotations from classical authors in medieval Latin glossaries*, New York, 1925 (Cornell studies in classical philology, 21). C. H. BEESON, "The vocabulary of the *Annales Fuldenses*," *Speculum*, 1926, 31–37. J. WHATMOUGH (editor), "Scholia in Isidori Etymologias vallicelliana," *Archivum latinitatis mediae aevi*, 1926, (3–4), 134–69; and see *ibid.*, 1926, B (2). A. HOFFMAN, *Liturgical dictionary* (Popular liturgical library, series III, no. 1), Collegeville, Minn., 1928.

Medieval Latin grammar. C. THUROT, *Notices et extraits de divers mss. latins pour servir à l'histoire des doctrines grammaticales au moyen âge*, Paris, 1868, vol. XXII, part II of *Notices et extraits des manuscrits de la Bibliothèque nationale*. J. J. BÄBLER, *Beiträge zur Geschichte der lateinischen Grammatik im Mittelalter*, Halle, 1885. C. MARCHESI, *Due grammatici latini del medio evo*, Perugia, 1910. E. VOIGT, "Das erste Lesebuch des Triviums in den Kloster- und Stiftsschulen des Mittelalters," *Mitteilungen der Gesellschaft für deutsche Erziehungs- und Schulgeschichte*, I, Berlin, 1891, 42–53. G. MANACORDA, "Un testo scolastico di grammatica del seculo XII in uso nel basso Piemonte," *Giornale storico e letterario della Liguria*, VIII (1907), 241–82. H. BEESON, "The Ars grammatica of Julian of Toledo," *Miscellanea Ehrle*, 1924, I, 50ff.

Alexander of Villa Dei. D. REICHLING, *Das Doctrinale des Alexander de Villa-Dei*, Berlin, 1893, introduction. C. THUROT, *De Alexandri de Villa Dei Doctrinali eiusque fatis*, Paris, 1850. K. J. NEUDECKER, *Das Doctrinale des Alexanders de Villa Dei und der lateinische Unterricht während des späteren Mittelalters in Deutschland*, Pirma, 1885 (Prog.). L. DELISLE, "Alexandre de Villedieu et Guillaume le Moine de Villedieu," *B.E.C.*, LV (1894), 488–504, also LXII (1901), 158–59.

John Garland. L. J. PAETOW, *Morale scolarium of John of Garland (Johannes de Garlandia), a professor in the universities of Paris and Toulouse in the thirteenth century,* edited, with an introduction on the life and works of the author, together with facsimiles of four folios of the Bruges manuscript, Berkeley, 1927 (Memoirs of the university of California, vol. IV, no. 2). E. HABEL, "Johannes de Garlandia," in *Mitteilungen der Gesellschaft für deutsche Erziehungs- und Schulgeschichte,* XIX (1909), 1–34, 119–30. B. HAURÉAU, "Notices sur les oeuvres authentiques ou supposées de Jean de Garlande," in *Notices et extraits des manuscrits de la Bibliothèque nationale,* XXVII, part II (1879), 1–86. A. F. GATIEN-ARNOULT, "Jean de Garlande, docteur régent de grammaire à l'université de Toulouse de 1229 à 1232," *Revue de Toulouse* (1866), 117–37.

Medieval Latin literature in general. TRAUBE, *Einleitung in die lateinische Philologie des Mittelalters,* 121–76. A. G. LITTLE, *Initia operum latinorum quae saeculis XIII, XIV, XV attribuuntur,* Manchester, 1904. A. FRANKLIN, *Dictionnaire des noms, surnoms et pseudonymes latins de l'histoire littéraire du moyen âge (1100 à 1530),* Paris, 1875. J. A. FABRICIUS, *Bibliotheca latina mediae et infimae aetatis,* 6 vols., Hamburg, 1734–46; revised edition, by J. D. MANSI, 6 vols., Padua, 1754. P. LEHMANN, "Literaturgeschichte im Mittelalter," *Germanische-romanische Monatschrift,* IV (1912), 569–82, 617–30. NOVATI, "Rapports littéraires de l'Italie et de la France au XII siècle," *Académie des inscriptions, Comptes rendus,* 1910, 169ff. W. CLOETTA, *Beiträge zur Literaturgeschichte des Mittelalters und der Renaissance,* I, *Komödie und Tragödie im Mittelalter,* Halle, 1890. C. V. LANGLOIS, "Travaux de Ch. H. Haskins sur la littérature scientifique en latin du XIIe siècle," *Journals des savants,* 1919, 57–73. J. HUEMER, "Das Registrum multorum auctorum des Hugo von Trimberg: ein Quellenbuch zur lateinischen Literaturgeschichte des Mittelalters," *S.B. Vienna Acad.,* 116 (1888), 149–90. F. NOVATI, *Studi critici e letterari,* Turin, 1889. ELIZABETH SPEAKMAN, "Satire in the middle ages," *Dublin review,* series IV, XXVII (1904), 48ff. PASCAL, *Poesia latina medievale.* W. MEYER (editor), *Die Arundel Sammlung mittellateinischer Lieder* [*Abh.* der k. Gesellschaft der Wis. zu Göttingen, phil-hist. Klasse, N. F., XI (1908–09), No. 2]. C. PASCAL, *Letteratura latina medievale,* Catania, 1909. F. v. BEZOLD, *Das Fortleben der antiken Welt im mittelalterlichen Humanismus,* Bonn, 1922. W. CREIZENACH, *Geschichte des neuren Dramas,* vol. I, 2nd edition, Halle, 1911. G. R. COFFMAN, *A new theory concerning the origin of the miracle play,* Menasha, 1914; corrected by K. YOUNG in the *Manly anniversary studies,* Chicago, 1923, 254–68. See also COFFMAN'S "A new approach to medieval Latin drama," *Modern philology,* XXII (1925), 239–71. P. LEHMANN, *Aufgaben und Anregungen der lateinischen Philologie des Mittelalters,* Munich, 1918. (*S.B. Munich Acad.,* 1918, 8). F. PELSTER, "Der Heinrich von Gent zugeschriebene *Catalogus virorum illustrium* und sein wirklicher Verfasser," *Hist. Jahrbuch,* XXXIX (1919), 253–68. H. WALTHER, *Das Streitgedicht in der lateinischen Literatur des Mittelalters,* Munich, 1920. P. LEHMANN, "Mittellateinische Verse in Distinctiones monasticae et morales vom Anfang des 13. Jahrhunderts," Munich 1922, (*S.B. Munich Acad.*, 63, 2). E. FARAL, *Les arts poétiques du XIIe et du XIIIe siècle* (Recherches et documents sur la technique littéraire du moyen âge), Paris, 1923; see also W. B. SEDGWICK, "Notes and emendations on FARAL's *Les arts poétiques*," *Speculum*, II (1927), 331–43. M. VOIGT, *Beiträge zur Geschichte der Visionenliteratur im Mittelalter*, Leipzig, 1924. O. STANGE and P. DITTRICH (editors), *Vox latina III: Ausgewählte Proben lateinischen Schrifttums von 200 n. Chr. bis zur Gegenwart*, Leipzig, 1924. G. PANSA, *Ovidio nel medioevo e nella tradizione popolare*, Sulmona, 1924. H. BRINKMANN, *Geschichte der lateinischen Liebesdichtung im Mittelalter*, Halle, 1925. E. FARAL, *La littérature latine au moyen âge*, Paris, 1925. MORICCA, *Storia della letteratura latina cristiana*, vol. I, *Dalle origini fino al tempo di Constantino*. E. LEVI, "Troveri ed abbazie," *Archivio storico italiano*, LXXXIII (1925), 45–81. K. P. HARRINGTON, *Mediaeval Latin*, Boston, 1925. E. v. EHRHARDT-SIEBOLD, *Die lateinischen Rätzel der Angelsachsen*, Heidelberg, 1925 (Anglistische Forschungen, LXI). A. BRUN, *La littérature en langue latine en Provence au moyen âge*, Paris, 1926. E. v. FRAUENHOLZ, "Imperator Octavianus Augustus in der Geschichte und Sage des Mittelalters," *Hist. Jahrbuch*, XLVI (1926), 86–122. F. TUPPER, *Types of society in medieval literature*, New York, 1926. WEYMAN, *Beiträge zur Geschichte der christlichlateinischen Poesie*. E. K. RAND, "On the history of the De vita Caesarum of Suetonius in the early middle ages," *Harvard studies in classical philology*, XXXVII (1926), 1–48. L. BEHRENDT, *The ethical teaching of Hugo of Trimberg*, Washington, 1926 (The catholic university of America, Studies in German, I). HELEN WADDELL, *The wandering scholars*. H. R. PATCH, *The goddess Fortuna in mediaeval literature*, Cambridge, 1927. LEHMANN, *Pseudo-antike Literatur des Mittelalters*. J. C. RUSSELL, "Literature at Croyland abbey under Henry Longchamp (1191–1237)," *Colorado college publications*, general series, no. 148, 1927. G. BERTONI, *Poesie, leggende, costumanze del medio evo*, 2nd edition, Modena, 1927; *Poeti et poesie del medio evo e del renascimento*, Modena, 1922. L. THORNDIKE, "Some thirteenth-century classics," *Speculum*, II (1927), 374–84. J. C. RUSSELL, "Master Henry of Avranches as an international poet," *Speculum*, III (1928), 34–63.

Goliardic literature. C. V. LANGLOIS, "La littérature goliardique," *Revue bleue*, L (1892), 807–13; LI (1893), 174–80. A. GABRIELLI, *Su la poesia dei Goliardi: saggio critico*, Città di Castello, 1889. L. DELISLE, "Le poète Primat," *B.E.C.*, XXXI (1870), 302–11; B. HAURÉAU, in *Notices et extraits*, XXXII, part I (1886), 253–314. N. SPIEGEL, *Die Grundlagen der Vagantenpoesie*, Würzburg, 1908. S. JAFFE, *Die Vaganten und ihre Lieder*, Berlin, 1908. A. STRACCALI, *I Goliardi*, Florence, 1880. W. MEYER (aus Speyer), *Gesammelte Abhandlungen zur mittellateinischen Rythmik*, 2 vols., Berlin, 1905. K. FRANKE, *Zur Geschichte der lateinischen Schulpoesie des XII und XIII Jahrhunderts*, Munich, 1879. W. WATTENBACH, "Die Anfänge lateinischer profaner Rythmer des Mittelalters," *Zeitschrift für deutsches Alterthum*, neue Folge, III (1870), 469–506. B. E. LUNDIUS, *Deutsche Vagantenlieder in den Carmina burana*, Halle, 1907 (Diss.). A. HEINRICH, *Quatenus* *carminum buranorum auctores veterum Romanorum poetas imitati sint*, Cilli, 1882 (Prog.). O. Hubatsch, *Die lateinischen Vagantenlieder des Mittelalters*, Görlitz, 1870. J. M. Manly, "The 'Familia Goliae,'" *Modern philology*, V (1907), 201–09. J. H. Hanford, "The mediaeval debate between wine and water," *P.M.L.A.*, XXVIII (1913), 315–67. H. Unger, *De Ovidiana in carminibus buranis quae dicuntur imitatione*, Berlin, 1914 (Diss.). H. Süssmilch, *Die lateinische Vagantenpoesie des 12. und 13. Jahrhunderts als Kulturerscheinung*, Leipzig, 1917, vol. XXV of no. **749**. V. Crescini, "Appunti su l'etimologia di Goliardo," *Atti del reale istituto veneto*, LXXIX (1919–20), pt. II, 1097–1131. J. J. A. Frantzen, "Zur Vagantendichtung," in *Neophilologus*, V (1920), 58–79; "Die Gedichte des Archipoeta," *ibid.*, 170–79; also 180–81. G. Ermini, "Il Golia dei Goliardi," *La cultura*, I (1922), 169–73. J. W. Thompson, "The origin of the word Goliardi," *Studies in philology*, XX (1923), 83–98. W.H. Moll, *Ueber den Einfluss der lateinischen Vagantendichtung auf die Lyrik Walthers von der Vogelweide und seiner Epigonen im 13 Jahrhundert*, Amsterdam, 1925. J. H. Hanford, "The progenitors of Golias," *Speculum*, I (1926), 38–58. K. Strecker, *Die Cambridger Lieder*, Berlin, 1926. B. I. Jarcho, "Die Vorläufer des Golias," *Speculum*, IV (1928), 523–79.

Collections of Goliardic poems. *Carmina burana: lateinische und deutsche Lieder und Gedichte einer Handschrift des XIII Jahrhunderts*, edited by J. A. Schmeller, 3rd, unaltered, edition, Bresslau, 1894 (the first edition appeared in Bibliothek des literarischen Vereins in Stuttgart, XVI, 1847, 1–275). *Die Gedichte des Archipoeta*, edited by M. Manitius, Munich, 1913. "Fragmenta burana," edited by W. Meyer (aus Speyer), in *Festschrift* zum 150 jährigen Bestehen der Gesellschaft der Wissenschaften zu Göttingen, 1901, phil.-hist. Klasse; *Carmina burana*, Berlin, 1904; "Die Oxforder Gedichte des Primas (des Magisters Hugo von Orleans)," *Nachrichten* der Göttingen Ak., philos.-hist. Kl., 1907, 75–175, 231–34. *The Cambridge songs: a Goliard's song-book of the eleventh century*, edited by K. Breul, Cambridge university press, 1915. *The Latin poems commonly attributed to Walter Mapes*, edited by T. Wright, Camden society, 1841. *Carmina medii aevi*, edited by F. Novati, Florence, 1883. *Carmina burana selecta*, 1880, and *Ubi sunt qui ante nos?*, edited by A. P. v. Bärnstein, Würzburg, 1881.

Latin hymns and liturgy. G. M. Dreves, *Ein Jahrtausend lateinischer Hymnendichtung*, 2 vols., Leipzig, 1910; *Die Kirche der Lateiner in ihren Liedern*, Kempten, 1908. J. Pacheu, *Jacopone de Todi, frère mineur franciscain, 1230–1306, auteur présumé du Stabat Mater*, Paris, 1914. A. d'Ancona, *Jacopone da Todi, il giullare di Dio del seculo XIII*, Todi, 1914. C. Blume, *Hymnologie und Kulturgeschichte des Mittelalters*, Kempten, 1914, 14 pp. J. Julian, *A dictionary of hymnology*, London, 1907; revised edition, 1915. U. Chevalier, *Poésie liturgique du moyen âge*, Paris, 1893. L. Gautier, *Histoire de la poésie liturgique au moyen âge*, Paris, 1886. M. Esposito, "Thirteenth century rhythmus: De humana miseria tractatus," *E.H.R.*, XXXII (1917), 400–05. Alice K. MacGilton, *A study of Latin hymns*, Boston, 1918.

Latin sermons. L. Bourgain, *La chaire française au XIIe siècle, d'après les manuscrits*, Paris, 1879. A. Lecoy de la Marche, *La chaire française au moyen âge, spécialement au XIIIe siècle*, Paris, 1868; 2nd edition, 1886. C. V. Langlois, "Sermons parisiens de la première moitié du XIIIe siècle, contenus dans la manuscrit 691 de la bibliothèque d'Arras," *Journal des savants*, Nov., 1916, 488–94; Dec., 1916, 548–59; "L'éloquence sacrée au moyen âge," in *R.D.M.*, CXV (1893), 170–201. P. Funk, *Jacob von Vitry: Leben und Werke*, Leipzig, 1909 (part 3 of Beiträge zur Kulturgeschichte des Mittelalters). J. M. Neale, *Mediaeval preachers and mediaeval preaching: a series of extracts, translated from the sermons of the middle ages, chronologically arranged*, London, 1856. Owst, *Preaching in medieval England.* H. Caplan, "Rhetorical invention in some mediaeval tractates on preaching," *Speculum*, II (1927), 284–95; the earlier literature on the subject is cited in the notes.

Exempla, or sermon stories. *The Exempla or illustrative stories from the sermones vulgares of Jacques de Vitry*, edited by T. F. Crane, London, 1890 (Folk lore society). *Die Exempla des Jakob von Vitry: cin Beitrag zur Geschichte der Erzählungsliteratur des Mittelalters*, edited by G. Frenken, Munich, 1914, in Quellen und Untersuchungen zur lateinischen Philologie des Mittelalters, V, part I. Caesar of Heisterbach, *Dialogus miraculorum*, edited by J. Strange, 2 vols., Cologne, 1851; English translation, *A dialogue on miracles*, by H. v. E. Scott and C. C. S. Bland with introduction by G. G. Coulton, 2 vols., New York, 1929. O. Hellinghaus, *Hundert auserlesne, wunderbare, und merkwürdige Geschichten des Zisterziensers Cäsarius von Heisterbach*, Aachen, 1925. Etienne de Bourbon, *Anecdotes historiques*, edited by A. Lecoy de la Marche, Paris, 1877. J. A. Mosher, *The exemplum in the early religious and didactic literature of England*, New York, 1911. J. T. Welter, "Etude des recueils d'exempla du moyen âge" (*Positions*, présentées à la Faculté des lettres, Université de Paris, 1907, 259–65). J. T. Welter, *Le Speculum laicorum*, Paris, 1914. C. G. N. De Vooys, *Middelnederlandse Legenden en Exempelen: Bijdrage tot de kennis van de prozalitteratuur en het volksgeloof der Middeleeuwen*, 2nd edition, Groningen and The Hague, 1926. J. T. Welter, *L'exemplum dans la littérature religieuse et didactique du moyen âge; La tabula exemplorum*, Paris, 1928. See the bibliography on *Exempla* by C. H. Haskins, in *A.H.R.*, X (1904–05), 4, note 2; now in *Studies in mediaeval culture*, 40–41.

Original sources. Grammatical and rhetorical works. *Grammatici latini*, edited by H. Keil. *Une grammaire latine inédite du XIIIe siècle*, edited by C. Fierville, Paris, 1886. *Rhetores latini minores*, edited by C. F. Halm, Leipzig, 1863. A. de Poorter, "Catalogue des manuscrits de grammaire latine médiévale de la bibliothèque de Bruges," *Revue des bibliothèques* (1926), 1–35; "Catalogue des manuscrits de prédication médiévale de la bibliothèque de Bruges," *Revue d'histoire ecclésiastique*, XXIV (1928), 62–124.

Poetry. *Historia poetarum et poematum medii aevi*, edited by P. Leyser, Magdeburg, 1721; reprinted 1741. *Poésies inédites du moyen âge*, edited by

Edélstand du Méril, Paris, 1854; *Poésies populaires latines antérieures au douzième siècle*, Paris, 1843; *Poésies populaires latines du moyen âge*, Paris, 1847. *Anglo-Latin satirical poets and epigrammatists of the twelfth century*, edited by T. Wright, 2 vols., London, 1872 (Rolls series). John Garland, *De triumphis ecclesiae*, edited by T. Wright, Roxburghe club, 1856. *The complaint of nature*, by Alain de Lille, translated from the Latin by D. M. Moffat, New York, 1908. *Die zehn Gedichte von* Walther von Lille, edited by W. Müldener, Hanover, 1859. *The liturgical poetry of* Adam of St. Victor, from the text of Gauthier, translated by D. S. Wrangham, 3 vols., London, 1881, contains Latin text with English translation on opposite pages. C. de Boer, *Ovide moralisé, poème du commencement du quatorzième siècle*, 2 vols., Amsterdam, 1915–20 (Verhandelingen der koninklijke Akademie). Marya Kasterska, *Les poètes latins-polonais jusqu'à 1589*, Paris, 1918. F. Ermini, *Poeti epici latini del secolo X*, Rome, 1920. P. Lehmann, *Parodistische Texte. Beispiele zur lateinischen Parodie im Mittelalter*, Munich, 1923. C. Beck, *Mittellateinische Dichtung. Eine Auswahl mittellateinischen Gedichte aus d. 8 bis 13 Jh.*, Berlin, 1926. K. Strecker, *Carmina Cantabrigiensia*, edited by K. Strecker, in *M.G.H.*, octavo series, Berlin, 1926. J. Nève, *Catonis disticha: fac-similés, notes, listes des éditions du XVe siècle*, Liége, 1926. M. Manitius and R. Ulrich (translators), *Vagantenlieder aus der lateinischen Dichtung des 12 and 13 Jahrhunderts*, Jena, 1927. A. Kaiser, *Lateinische Dichtungen zur deutschen Geschichte des Mittelalters*, Munich and Berlin, 1927. K. Strecker, *Die Apokalypse des Golias* (Texte zur Kulturgeschichte des Mittelalters hrsg. von Fedov Schneider, 5, Hft), Rome, 1928.

Prose works. Walter Map, *De nugis curialium*, edited by M. R. James, Oxford, 1914 (Anecdota oxoniensia, medieval and modern series, XIV), supersedes the edition by T. Wright, Camden society, 1850. *Morceaux choisis de prosateurs latins du moyen âge*, edited by P. Thomas, Ghent, 1902. *A selection of Latin stories from mss. of the 13th and 14th centuries*, edited by T. Wright, London, 1842. C. Giordano, *Alexandreis, poema di Gautier da Châtillon*, Naples, 1917. K. Strecker (editor), *Die Gedichte Walters von Chatillon*, I, *Die Lieder der Handschrift 351 von St. Omer*, Berlin, 1925. A. Hilka (editor), *Sammlung mittellateinischer Texte*, parts 1–9, Heidelberg, 1911–14. P. Lehmann, *Die Parodie im Mittelalter*, Munich, 1922. Walter Map, *De nugis curialium*, translated by M. R. James, with historical notes by J. E. Lloyd, edited by E. S. Hartland, London, 1923. *Master Walter Map's book De nugis curialium* (*Courtier's trifles*), Englished by F. Tupper and M. B. Ogle, Oxford, 1924. The plan and composition of the De nugis curialium are discussed by J. Hinton, *P.M.L.A.*, XXXII (1917), 81–132.

Hymns. *Analecta hymnica medii aevi*, edited by C. Blume und G. M. Dreves, 23 vols., Leipzig, 1886–1911; see also *Hymnologische Beiträge* by G. M. Dreves, 2 vols., Leipzig, 1897–1901. *Lateinische Hymnen des Mittelalters*, edited by F. J. Mone, 3 vols., Freiburg, 1853–55. *Repertorium hymnologicum: catalogue des chants, hymnes, proses, séquences, tropes, en usage dans l'église latine depuis les origines jusqu'à nos jours*, edited by U. Cheva-

LIER, 6 vols., Louvain and Brussels, 1892–1921. *The source of "Jerusalem the golden," together with other pieces attributed to* BERNARD OF CLUNY, translated by H. PREBLE, with an introduction and notes by S. M. JACKSON, Chicago, 1910. *Latin hymns,* selected and annotated by W. A. MERRILL, Boston, 1904. Other brief collections like that of MERRILL, by R. C. TRENCH (1849), and F. A. MARCH (1874). E. W. BRAINERD (compiler), *Great hymns of the middle ages,* New York, 1909. S. W. DUFFIELD, *The Latin hymn writers and their hymns,* edited and completed by R. E. THOMPSON, New York, 1889. C. C. NOTT, *Seven great hymns of the mediaeval church,* New York, 1902. A. G. MCDOUGAL and A. FORTESCUE, *Pange Lingua, breviary hymns of old uses with an English rendering,* London, 1916. A. S. WALPOLE, *Early Latin hymns: with introduction and notes,* Cambridge, 1922. M. BRITT (editor), *The hymns of the breviary and missal,* New York, 1922. C. BROWN, *Religious lyrics of the XIVth century,* Oxford, 1924.

Bibliographies. For the Latin languages, see BERNHEIM, *Lehrbuch,* 286-88. L. TRAUBE, *Vorlesungen,* II, 47, 75–82. For Latin literature see footnotes in SANDYS, *Classical scholarship,* and his bibliography in *Cambridge history of English literature,* I, 452–57. Also MOLINIER, *Les sources,* I, 192–213. C. BLUME, *Repertorium repertorii,* Leipzig, 1901, and U. CHEVALIER'S *Repertorium* are our bibliographical guides to medieval hymns.

XXIV. VERNACULAR LANGUAGES AND LITERATURES

I. OLD FRENCH LANGUAGE AND LITERATURE

A. OUTLINE

1. Of the rising Romanic vernaculars, destined to compete with and eventually to outstrip Latin, French is a striking type. First old English (Anglo-Saxon), A.D. 700ff., then Old Norse (Icelandic), and Old Church Slavic had already developed flourishing vernacular literatures. About 1260–70, the Italian Brunetto Latini (died 1290) wrote in his *Tresor,* "Et se aucuns demandoit por quoi cist livres est escriz en romans, selonc le langage des François, puisque nos somes Ytaliens, je diroie que ce est por .ij. raisons: l'une, car nos somes en France; et l'autre, porce que la parleure est plus delitable et plus commune à toutes gens."

2. The origin of the French language. Its development from the spoken Latin in Gaul, the vulgar or popular Latin. The Celtic and Germanic influence. The earliest texts. Glossaries. The Oaths of Strasbourg, 842. Various dialects. Chief divisions: Langue d'Oc in the south (*oc* =Latin *hoc*); Langue d'Oïl in the north (*oïl* =Latin *hoc ille*). The ultimate predominance of the French spoken in Paris.

3. The influence of French in foreign countries before the end of the thirteenth century, especially in England, Germany, Italy, and the Orient, where it played an important rôle because France furnished the greatest number of crusaders.

4. The attitude of the learned class towards the vernacular. Evidence from the works of Roger Bacon. French was used rarely even in elementary instruction and it was probably seldom taught in the schools. Before the end of the thirteenth century there was no thought of a conflict between the "ancients and the moderns" such as inflamed France in the seventeenth century.

5. The beginnings of French literature in religious narrative poetry. Among the earliest known pieces of French literature is the *Vie de saint Alexis*, written in the middle of the eleventh century. Others lives of saints in French verse. Pious tales like the *Tumbler of Notre-Dame.*

6. The great national epics, "matter of France," which expressed the life and ideals of the warlike feudal class. The origin of the *chansons de geste* sung by *Jongleurs*. The *Chanson de Roland*. *Huon de Bordeaux*.

7. The matter of antiquity ("Rome"). Influence of classical history and literature. Romances of Alexander, Thebes, Aeneas, and Troy.

8. Romances of gallantry and courtly love. The Arthurian romances. The Holy Grail. Tristam and Iseult. Perceval. This literature was most original in the twelfth century when it reflected the new era of culture in western Christendom which had been ushered in by the crusades.

9. Lyric poetry. The songs of the troubadours in large measure reflect the aristocratic ideals in southern France before the Albigensian crusades in the thirteenth century. *Aucassin et Nicolette.* In Latin, the Goliardic poetry falls mainly under this heading (see the previous outline).

10. Literature of the middle class, especially satirical literature. The *Fabliaux* bear witness to the sudden rise of the burgher class in the twelfth and thirteenth centuries. *Renard the Fox*. *Rutebeuf* (middle of the thirteenth century).

11. Didactic and moral literature. Allegory. The *Romance of the rose*, in two parts, the first by William of Lorris (first half of the thirteenth century), and the second by John Clopinel, of Meun (about 1277).

12. Historical writing in the vernacular. Villehardouin and Joinville. See the next outline.

13. Vernacular literature as a source for the history of culture during the twelfth and thirteenth centuries.

B. Special Recommendations for Reading

Brief general surveys. Bémont and Monod, *Medieval Europe*, 527–36. Crump and Jacob, *Legacy*, 173–95. Lavisse et Rambaud, *Histoire générale*, II, 568–80; III, 212–18. Munro and Sellery, *Medieval civilization*, 310–25. Taylor, *Mediaeval mind*, I, ch. xxiv; II, ch. xxv. On French in England see F. W. Maitland, "The Anglo-French law language," *Cambridge history of English literature*, I (1908), ch. xx, and J. Vising, *Anglo-Norman language and literature*, Oxford, 1923 (for other literature on French in England see Gross, *Sources*, nos. 200–09).

Longer accounts. *C.M.H.*, VI, ch. xxv. Lavisse, *Histoire de France*, II, part II, 179–82, 389–99; III, part I, 371–82, 409–14, part II, 372–79,

404–12. C. H. C. WRIGHT, *A history of French literature*, New York, 1912, 1–110. W. A. NITZE and E. P. DARGAN, *A history of French literature from the earliest times to the Great War*, New York, 1923; new edition, 1927. TILLEY, *Medieval France*. HANOTAUX, *Histoire de la nation française*, XII, 177–355. F. BRUNETIÈRE, *Manual of the history of French literature*, authorized translation, New York, 1898, book I. G. LANSON, *Histoire de la littérature française*, 12th edition, Paris, 1912, part I.

Standard accounts. F. E. BRUNOT, *Histoire de la langue française des origines à 1900*, vols. I–VII, IX, Paris, 1905ff. vol. I on the middle ages. *Histoire de la langue et de la littérature française des origines à 1900*, edited by L. PETIT DE JULLEVILLE, 8 vols., Paris, 1896–99, vols. I–II. G. PARIS, *La littérature française au moyen âge (XI*[e]*–XIV*[e] *siècle)*, 5th edition, Paris, 1914, translated in Temple primers, *Medieval French literature; Esquisse historique de la littérature française au moyen âge*, Paris, 1907; 2nd edition, 1913. J. BÉDIER and P. HAZARD, *Histoire de la littérature française illustrée*, Paris, 1923, vol. I, 1–125.

Troubadours. LUCHAIRE, *Social France*, ch. XII. J. H. SMITH, *The troubadours at home*, 2 vols., New York and London, 1899. H. J. CHAYTOR, *The troubadours*, Cambridge, 1912 (Cambridge manuals).

French literature as a source for the history of medieval culture. C. V. LANGLOIS, *La société française au XIII*[e] *siècle d'après dix romans d'aventure*, 3rd edition, Paris, 1911; *La vie en France au moyen âge, de la fin du XII*[e] *au milieu du XIV*[e] *siècle d'après des moralistes du temps; La connaissance de la nature et du monde*, part of no. **762a.** K. VOSSLER, *Frankreichs Kultur im Spiegel seiner Sprachentwicklung*, Heidelberg, 1913. J. R. REINHARD, *The old French romance of Amadas et Ydoine: an historical study*, Durham, N. C., 1927. G. DOUTREPONT, *Les types populaires dans la littérature française*, vol. I, Brussels, 1927. G. B. FUNDENBURG, *Feudal France in the French epic*, Princeton, 1919.

Translated texts. English translations of old French classics: *The song of Roland*, translated into English verse by L. BACON, New Haven, 1914; translated into English verse by A. S. WAY, Cambridge, 1913; translated by C. K. SCOTT-MONCRIEFF, New York, 1920; translated into English prose by ISABEL BUTLER, Boston, 1904; translated into English verse by J. O'HAGEN, 2nd edition, London, 1883. *The romance of Tristam and Iseult*, translated from the French of J. BÉDIER by FLORENCE SIMMONDS, London, 1910, and by H. BELLOC, New York, 1927. W. W. COMFORT, *Eric and Enid by Chrêtien de Troyes* (contains also *Cligês, Yvain*, and *Lancelot*), Everyman's library. For note of several other recent translations of Old French texts see *Speculum*, III (1929), 129–30. *Aucassin et Nicolette*, translated by A. LANG, London, 1887; also in Everyman's library, New York, 1910. *The tumbler of our Lady and other miracles*, now translated from the middle French with introduction and notes by ALICE KEMP-WELCH in The new medieval library, which see for other translations of old French classics. W. LORRIS and J. CLOPINEL, *The romance of the rose*, translated by F. S. ELLIS, 3 vols., London, 1900 (Temple classics). *Huon of Bordeaux:* done into English by Sir J. BOURCHIER, lord BERNERS, and now retold by R. STEELE, London, 1895; see also R. STEELE's translation of *Renaud of Montauban,* London, 1897. For the *Battle of the seven arts* see outline XVIII. Also see translations by J. GEDDES, New York, 1906.

Old French romances, done into English by W. MORRIS, London, 1896. *Tales from the old French,* translated by ISABEL BUTLER, Boston, 1910. *French mediaeval romances from the lays of Marie de France,* translated by E. MASON, New York, 1911 (Everyman's library). *Legends and satires from mediaeval literature,* edited by MARTHA H. SHACKFORD, New York, 1913.

C. BIBLIOGRAPHY

General books. Many general histories of literature, nos. **782–814,** are useful. Naturally, the great *Histoire littéraire de la France,* no. **803,** is most essential. See also nos. **171–72** and **303–06,** especially GRÖBER's *Grundriss,* no. **305,** II, part II, 433–1247. Much of the literature under outline XXVII in part II is important. For the legend of Charlemagne see outline VIII in part II.

Grammars of old French. A. DARMESTETER, *Cours de grammaire historique de la langue française,* 7th to 9th edition, 4 vols., Paris [no date]. A. BRACHET, *Grammaire historique de la langue française,* Paris, 1915. K. NYROP, *Philologie française,* Paris, 1915. E. SCHWAN and D. BEHRENS, *Grammatik des Altfranzösischen,* 11th edition, Leipzig, 1919, translated into French by O. BLOCH, *Grammaire de l'ancien français,* 3d edition, Leipzig, 1923. K. NYROP, *Grammaire historique de la langue française,* vols. I–V, Copenhagen, 1899–1925, vol. I, *Histoire générale de la langue française,* 3rd edition, 1914. W. MEYER-LÜBKE, *Historische Grammatik der französischen Sprache,* 2nd and 3rd edition, Heidelberg, 1913ff. L. E. MENGER, *The Anglo-Norman dialect,* New York, 1904. C. VORETZSCH, *Einführung in das Studium der Altfranzösischen Sprache,* Halle, 1918; 3rd edition, 1925.

Dictionaries of old French. F. GODEFROY, *Dictionnaire de l'ancienne langue française,* 10 vols., Paris, 1881–1902; and his smaller *Lexique de l'ancien français,* Paris, 1901. G. KÖRTING, *Lateinisch-romanisches Wörterbuch,* 3rd edition, Paderborn, 1907. W. MEYER-LÜBKE, *Romanisches etymologisches Wörterbuch,* Heidelberg, 1911. E. GAMILLSCHEG, *Etymologisches Wörterbuch der französischen Sprache,* Heidelberg, 1928.

Histories of medieval French literature. H. SUCHIER and A. BIRCH-HIRSCHFELD, *Geschichte der französischen Literatur von den ältesten Zeiten bis zur Gegenwart,* 2nd edition, 2 vols., Leipzig, 1913. P. A. BECKER, *Grundriss der altfranzösischen Literatur,* Heidelberg, 1907. See also no. **305.**

Special works on medieval French literature. J. BÉDIER, *Les légendes épiques: recherches sur la formation des Chansons de geste,* 4 vols., 3rd edition, 1930. P. BOISSONNADE, *Du nouveau sur la Chanson de Roland, la genèse historique, le cadre géographique, le milieu, les personnages, la date et l'auteur* *du poème*, Paris, 1923. J. BÉDIER, *La chanson de Roland, commentée*, 3rd edition, Paris, 1927 (complete author's edition of the *chanson*, Paris, [1924]). T. A. JENKINS, *La chanson de Roland, Oxford version, edition, notes and glossary*, Boston, 1924. L. GAUTIER, *Les épopées françaises*, 2nd edition, 5 vols., Paris, 1878–97. G. PARIS, *Légendes du moyen âge*, 4th edition, Paris, 1912; *La poésie du moyen âge: leçons et lectures*, 2 vols., vol. I in 5th edition, vol. II in 3rd edition, Paris, 1903–06; *Mélanges de littérature française du moyen âge*, Paris, 1912. J. BÉDIER, *Les fabliaux*, Paris, 1893; 4th edition, 1925. L. FOULET, *Le roman de renard*, Paris, 1914 (part of no. **888**). E. FARAL, *Recherches sur les sources latines des contes et romans courtois du moyen âge*, Paris, 1913; *Les jongleurs en France au moyen âge*, Paris, 1910, part of no. **888**; and "Le fabliau latin au moyen âge," *Romania*, L (1924), 321–85. G. E. B. SAINTSBURY, *The flourishing of romance and the rise of allegory*, London, 1897 (Periods of European literature). E. LANGLOIS, *Origines et sources du Roman de la rose*, Paris, 1891. L. CLÉDAT, *La poésie lyrique et satirique en France au moyen âge*, Paris, 1893. G. COHEN, *Le théâtre en France au moyen âge*, Paris, 1928. A. JEANROY, *Le théâtre religieux en France du XIe au XIIIe siècle*, Paris, 1924. E. LANGLOIS, *Table des noms propres de toute nature compris dans les chansons de geste imprimées*, Paris, 1904. On the main cycles of romance see the following. In general, W. VON WURZBACH, *Geschichte des französischen Romans. I. Von den Anfängen bis zum Ende des XVII. Jahrhunderts*, Heidelberg, 1912, 1–128. ARTHURIAN: J. D. BRUCE, *The evolution of Arthurian romance from the beginnings down to the year 1300*, 2 vols., Göttingen, 1923; R. S. LOOMIS, *Celtic myth and Arthurian romance*, New York, 1927; "An index of abbreviations in Miss Alma Blount's unpublished Onomasticon Arthurian," *Speculum*, I (1926), 190–216; W. J. ENTWISTLER, *The Arthurian legend in the literatures of the Spanish peninsula*, London, 1925. CHARLEMAGNE, see **174**. THEBES: L. CONSTANS, *La légende d'Oedipe étudiée . . . dans le Roman de Thèbes*, Paris, 1880. TROY: R. K. ROOT, *The book of Troilus and Criseyde by Geoffrey Chaucer* (Introduction, pp. xxff.), Princeton, 1926; also GRIFFIN and MYRICK, *The Filostrato of Giovanni Boccaccio* (Introduction, especially pp. 24ff.). ALEXANDER THE GREAT: P. MEYER, *Alexandre le Grand dans la littérature française du moyen âge*, 2 vols., Paris, 1886, and F. P. MAGOUN, JR., *The Gests of King Alexander of Macedon* (Introduction, pp. 22ff.), Cambridge, 1929.

Troubadours. J. ANGLADE, *Les troubadours*, Paris, 1908; 3rd edition, 1922. A. JEANROY, *Les origines de la poésie lyrique en France au moyen âge*, 3rd edition, Paris, 1925. J. BECK, *La musique des troubadours*, Paris, 1910 (see his bibliography, 121–22); *Les chansonniers des troubadours et des trouvères*, etc., Philadelphia, 1927. K. BARTSCH, *Grundriss zur Geschichte der provenzalischen Literatur*, Elberfeld, 1872. F. DIEZ, *Leben und Werke der Troubadours*, 2nd edition, Leipzig, 1882. P. AUBRY, *Trouvères et troubadours*, Paris, 1909; 2nd edition, 1910, translated by C. AVELING, *Trouvères and troubadours: a popular treatise*, New York, 1914. IDA FARNELL, *The lives of the troubadours*, London, 1896. J. F. ROWBOTHAM, *The troubadours and courts* *of love*, London, 1895. F. Hueffer, *The troubadours: a history of Provençal life and literature in the middle ages*, London, 1878. J. Rutherford, *The troubadors*, London, 1873. J. Anglade, "Pour étudier les troubadours: notice bibliographique," Toulouse, 1916, an extract from *Bulletin de la société archéologique du midi de la France*, 1914–15. J. J. Salverda de Grave, *De troubadours*, Leyden, 1918. J. Audian, *Les troubadours et l'Angleterre: contribution à l'étude des poètes anglais de l'amour du moyen âge (XIII*[e] *et XIV*[e] *siècles)*, revised edition, Paris, 1927. H. J. Chaytor, *The troubadours of Dante*, Oxford, 1902. Haskell, *Provençal literature and language . . . history of southern France*. C. Dickinson, *Troubadour songs, with an historical introduction, biographical notes and English texts*, New York, 1920.

Periodicals. *Romania*, Paris, 1872ff. *Zeitschrift für französische Sprache und Literatur*, Leipzig, 1879ff. *Zeitschrift für romanische Philologie*, Halle, 1875ff. *The romanic review*, New York, 1910ff. *Archivum romanicum*, 1917ff. *Germanisch-romanische Monatschrift*, 1909ff. *Literaturblatt für german. u. roman. Philologie*, 1880ff. *Neophilologus*, 1915ff. *Modern language review*, 1905ff. *Modern language notes*, 1886ff. *Nuovi studi medievali*, 1924ff. *Casopis pro moderní filologi, a literatury*, Prague, 1911ff.

Original sources. No attempt can be made in this *Guide* to list even the most important special editions of the classics of medieval French literature. Most of them are edited in the following series: *Société des anciens textes français. Classiques français du moyen âge. Bibliothèque française du moyen âge. Bibliotheca normannica. Gesellschaft für romanische Literatur. Romanische Bibliothek. Altfranzösische Bibliothek. Les anciens poètes de la France.*

For short selections from old French see the following: *Chrestomathie du moyen âge: extraits publiés avec des traductions, des notes, une introduction grammaticale et des notices littéraires*, edited by G. Paris and E. Langlois, 8th edition, Paris, 1912. *Chrestomathie de l'ancien français (VIII*[e]*–XV*[e] *siècle)*, edited by K. Bartsch, Leipzig, 1866; 11th edition, 1913. *La poésie française du moyen âge (XI*[e]*–XV*[e] *siècle): recueil de textes accompagnés de traductions, de notices et précédé d'une étude littéraire*, edited by C. Oulmont, Paris, 1913.

Bibliographies. Lucien Foulet, *A bibliography of medieval French literature for college libraries*, edited by A. Schinz and G. E. Underwood, New Haven, 1915. G. Raynaud, *Bibliographie des chansonniers français des XIII*[e] *et XIV*[e] *siècles*, Paris, 1884. L. Spence, *A dictionary of mediaeval romance and romance writers*, New York, 1913, is unsatisfactory. R. Federn, *Répertoire bibliographique de la littérature française*, Paris, 1912. A. Jeanroy, *Bibliographie sommaire des chansonniers provençaux* (manuscrits et éditions), Paris, 1916 (Classiques français du moyen âge); *Les études sur la littérature française du moyen âge*, Paris, 1915. A. Långfors, *Les incipit des poèmes français antérieurs au XVI*[e] *siècle: répertoire bibliographique établi à l'aide de notes de M. Paul Meyer*, vol. I, Paris (1917).

II. OLD ENGLISH (ANGLO-SAXON) AND MIDDLE ENGLISH LANGUAGE AND LITERATURE

A. Language

General. Kennedy, *A bibliography of writings on the English language.* For current literature see *Annual bibliography of English language and literature*, 1921ff.

Old and Middle English grammars. H. C. Wyld, *A short history of English with a bibliography of recent books*, 3rd edition, New York, 1927. K. Luick, *Historische Grammatik der englischen Sprache*, Vienna, 1914ff. E. Sievers, translated by A. S. Cook, *An Old English grammar*, 3rd edition, Boston, 1903. J. and E. M. Wright, *Old English grammar*, 3rd edition, Oxford, 1925. R. Huchon, *Histoire de la langage anglaise.* Vol. I: *Des origines à la conquête normande (450–1066)*, Paris, 1923; vol. II, *De la conquête normande à l'introduction de l'imprimerie*, Paris, 1930. R. Jordan, *Handbuch der mittelenglischen Grammatik. 1. Teil: Lautlehre*, Heidelberg, 1925. J. and E. M. Wright, *An elementary Middle English grammar*, 2nd edition, Oxford, 1928. H. R. Patch, "A bibliography of Middle English dialects," *Studies in philology*, XX, 479–95. On Chaucer see especially, B. ten Brink, revised by E. Eckhardt, *Chaucers Sprache und Verskunst*, 3rd edition, Leipzig, 1920, and F. Wild, *Die sprachlichen Eigentümlichkeiten der wichtigeren Chaucer-Handschriften und die Sprache Chaucers* (Wiener Beiträge zur englischen Philologie, XLIV), Vienna, 1915.

Dictionaries. J. Bosworth and T. N. Toller, *An Anglo-Saxon dictionary*, Oxford, 1899, and *Supplement* to the same by T. N. Toller, Oxford, 1921. There are two smaller Old English-English dictionaries useful for rapid reading: H. Sweet, *The student's dictionary of Anglo-Saxon*, New York, 1897, and J. R. C. Hall, *A concise Anglo-Saxon dictionary for the use of students*, 2nd edition, Cambridge, 1916. F. Holthausen and J. J. Köhler, *Sprachschatz der angelsächsischen Dichter*, Heidelberg, 1921. A. L. Mayhew and W. W. Skeat, *A concise dictionary of Middle English from A. D. 1150 to 1580*, Oxford, 1888. A. L. Mayhew, *The Promptorium parvulorum: the first English-Latin dictionary, c. 1440 A. D.*, London, 1908 (E. E. T. S. CII). F. H. Stratmann and H. Bradley, *A Middle-English dictionary*, Oxford, 1891. Much use can be made of the *New English dictionary*, Oxford, 1928. The Modern Language Association of America has in hand the preparation of an adequate dictionary of Middle-English.

Palaeographic aids. In general see Kennedy, *Bibliography*, cited above, pp. 73–84. W. Keller, *Angelsächsische Palaeographie* (Palaestra, XLIII), Berlin, 1906; and *idem* under "Angelsächsische Schrift" in J. Hoops' *Reallexikon.* On runic writing: especially O. v. Friesen under "Runenschrift" in Hoops, *op. cit.; idem* under "Runes," *Ency. Brit.*, 14th edition. There is no comprehensive treatment of Middle-English palaeography. W. W. Skeat, *Twelve facsimiles of Old* (i.e. Middle) *English manuscripts with transcriptions* *and an introduction*, Oxford, 1892, and many plates in the volumes of the Palaeographical society (1st and 2nd series) and of the New palaeographical society are useful for the study of literary texts.

B. Literature

General. *The Cambridge history of English literature*, vols. I, II (to the end of the middle ages), New York, 1907–08. There are valuable bibliographies at the end of each volume. B. ten Brink, revised by A. Brandl, *Geschichte der englischen Literatur*, 2 vols. (to the Reformation), Strasburg, 1899–1912. V. Mathesius, *Dějiny literatury anglické v hlavních jejích- proudech a představitelích* (Old and Middle English literature), 2 vols., Prague, 1910–15. Current bibliographical information will be found in the *Jahresberichte über die Erscheinungen auf dem Gebiete der germanischen Philologie*, and in the *Annual bibliography of English language and literature*, 1921ff.

Old English (Anglo-Saxon) literature. There is no adequate modern bibliography of Old English literature. See under **General** above. For *Beowulf*, however, see F. Klaeber, *Beowulf*, 2nd edition, Boston, 1928, introduction. Almost the entire corpus of Old-English verse has been recently translated by R. K. Gordon, *Anglo-Saxon poetry* (Everyman's library); note also C. W. Kennedy's translations: *The Caedmon poems*, London, 1916; *The poems of Cynewulf*, London, 1910. A. S. Cook and C. B. Tinker, *Select translations from Old English poetry*, 2nd edition, Boston, 1927; *Select translations from Old English prose*, Boston, 1908. A. R. Benham, *English literature from Widsith to the death of Chaucer: a source-book*, New Haven, 1916. F. B. Gummere, *Founders of England*, with supplementary notes by F. P. Magoun, Jr., New York, 1930.

Middle-English literature. For Middle English it will suffice to cite J. E. Wells, *A manual of writings in Middle English, 1050–1400*, New Haven, 1916, and *Supplements* appearing at intervals. For the fifteenth century: L. L. Tucker and A. R. Benham, *A bibliography of fifteenth century literature* (Univ. of Washington publications in language and literature, Vol. II, No. 3), Seattle, 1928. E. P. Hammond, *English verse between Chaucer and Surrey*, Durham, N. C., 1927 (valuable introductory essay). For medieval Scottish writers: W. Geddie, *A bibliography of Middle Scots poets with an introduction on the history of their reputation* (Scottish text society), Edinburgh, 1912, and T. F. Henderson, *Scottish vernacular literature: a succinct history*, 3rd edition, Edinburgh, 1910.

Periodicals. Besides those periodicals cited under French literature, whose interest is obviously not restricted to Romance linguistics and literatures, note the following: *Anglia, Zeitschrift für englische Philologie*, 1877ff. *Englische Studien*, 1877ff. *Journal of English and Germanic philology*, 1903ff. *Review of English studies*, 1925ff. *Beiblatt zur Anglia*, 1890. *The year's work in English studies*, London, 1919ff. *Studia neophilologica*, Uppsala, 1928.

Francis P. Magoun, Jr.

III. OLD AND MIDDLE HIGH GERMAN LANGUAGE AND LITERATURE

A. Language

General. Paul, *Grundriss der germanischen Philologie*, no. **307.** R. Bethge, *Ergebnisse und Fortschritte der germanistischen Wissenschaft im letzten Vierteljahrhundert* (1878–1902), Leipzig, 1902. G. Baesecke, *Deutsche Philologie*, Gotha, 1919, covers the period 1914–18. *Jahresberichte über die Erscheinungen auf dem Gebiete der germanischen Philologie*, 1879ff., an annual bibliography covering the whole field of Germanic philology as well as medieval Latin. The earlier volumes treat German literature down to the year 1624; beginning with the bibliography for 1919 the report on German literature has been extended to the year 1770. *Indogermanisches Jahrbuch*, 1913ff.

Old and Middle High German grammars. J. Grimm, *Deutsche Grammatik*, new enlarged edition by Scherer, Schroeder and Roethe, 4 vols., Gütersloh 1893ff., important for the rich collection of materials. W. Braune, *Althochdeutsche Grammatik*, 3rd and 4th edition, Halle, 1911. G. Baesecke, *Einführung in das Althochdeutsche*, Munich, 1918. J. Schatz, *Althochdeutsche Grammatik*, Göttingen, 1927. J. Wright, *Historical German grammar*, Oxford, 1907. K. Weinhold, *Alemannische Grammatik*, Berlin, 1863; *Bairische Grammatik*, Berlin, 1867. J. Schatz, *Altbairische Grammatik*, Göttingen, 1907. J. Franck, *Altfränkische Grammatik*, Göttingen, 1909. K. Weinhold, *Mittelhochdeutsche Grammatik*, 2nd edition, Paderborn, 1883. Weinhold-Ehrismann, *Kleine mittelhochdeutsche Grammatik*, Vienna and Leipzig, 1919. H. Paul-E. Gierach, *Mittelhochdeutsche Grammatik*, 12th edition, Halle, 1929. V. Michels, *Mittelhochdeutsches Elementarbuch*, 3rd edition, Heidelberg, 1924. O. Behaghel, *Deutsche Syntax*, 3 vols., Heidelberg, 1923ff. Erdmann-Mensing, *Grundzüge der deutschen Syntax*, 2 vols., Stuttgart, 1886–98. H. Wunderlich, *Der deutsche Satzbau*, 3rd edition, Stuttgart, 1924. W. Wilmanns, *Deutsche Grammatik*, 2nd edition, 4 vols., Strasburg, 1897–1909.

Dictionaries. O. Schade, *Altdeutsches Wörterbuch*, 2 vols., Halle, 1872–82, includes Gothic as well as Old and Middle High German; an extremely handy and fairly reliable book. The only more or less complete Old High German dictionary is E. G. Graff, *Althochdeutscher Sprachschatz*, 6 vols., Berlin, 1834ff. As Graff arranged the words by roots which are no longer recognized today the word sought must first be looked up in H. F. Massmann, *Vollständiger alphabetischer Index zu dem althochdeutschen Sprachschatze von E. G. Graff*, Berlin, 1846. For elementary purposes it is preferable to use Schade, and the special glossaries: W. Braune in his *Althochdeutsches Lesebuch*, 9th edition, by K. Helm, Halle, 1928; E. Sievers in his edition of *Tatian*, 2nd edition, Paderborn, 1892; Sievers in *Die Murbacher Hymnen*, Halle, 1874; J. Kelle, *Glossar der Sprache Otfrids*, Regensburg, 1881; P. Piper, *Otfrids Evangelienbuch, II Teil, Glossar*, Freiburg, 1887; G. A.

HENCH, *Der althochdeutsche Isidor*, Strasburg, 1893; P. PIPER, *Die älteste deutsche Literatur bis um das Jahr 1050*, Stuttgart, n.d. A complete Old High German dictionary based upon the collections of E. STEINMEYER is in preparation under the direction of the Deutsche Akademie of Munich.

The most complete Middle High German dictionary is that by BENECKE, MÜLLER, and ZARNCKE, *Mittelhochdeutsches Handwörterbuch*, 4 vols., Leipzig, 1854ff. Containing more words but fewer citations, M. LEXER, *Mittelhochdeutsches Handwörterbuch*, Leipzig, 1872ff. The latter is also useful as an index to the inconveniently arranged older work. Supplementary to the above is F. JELINEK, *Mittelhochdeutsches Wörterbuch zu den deutschen Sprachdenkmälern Böhmens und der mährischen Städte Brünn, Iglau und Olmütz*, Heidelberg, 1911. For study purposes: M. LEXER, *Mittelhochdeutsches Taschenwörterbuch*, Leipzig, 1891 (all editions since 1891, the fourth, are mere reprints). The many special glossaries may be found listed in the literary histories. The latest volumes of GRIMM'S *Deutsches Wörterbuch*, Leipzig, 1854ff., may occasionally be found useful. F. KLUGE, *Etymologisches Wörterbuch der deutschen Sprache*, 9th edition, Berlin, 1921; the first installment of the 10th edition appeared early in 1930. Rapid completion is promised.

Palaeographic aids. W. ARNDT, *Schriftkunde. 2. Lateinische Schrift*, in Paul's *Grundriss*, 2nd edition, I, 263–82, and the literature there cited. The article "Deutsche Schrift" in HOOPS' *Reallexikon*. On runes see E. SIEVERS in Paul's *Grundriss*, I, 248–62, and O. v. FRIESEN under "*Runenschrift*" in HOOPS, *op. cit.* Of the many facsimiles we may cite: M. ENNECCERUS, *Die ältesten deutschen Sprachdenkmäler*, Frankfort, 1897; P. PIPER, *Otfrid und die übrigen Weissenburger Schreiber des 9. Jahrhunderts*, Frankfort, 1899; G. BAESECKE, *Lichtdrucke nach althochdeutschen Handschriften*, Halle, 1926; and the magnificent reproduction of the *Heidelberger Liederhandschrift*, Leipzig, 1924ff. Other literature in HOOPS' *Reallexikon, art. cit.*

B. LITERATURE

General. W. GOLTHER, *Die deutsche Dichtung im Mittelalter*, 2nd edition, Stuttgart, 1922. R. KÖGEL, *Geschichte der deutschen Literatur bis zum Ausgange des Mittelalters*, 2 vols., Strasburg, 1894–97. J. KELLE, *Geschichte der deutschen Literatur von der ältesten Zeit bis zur Mitte des elften Jahrhunderts*, 2 vols., Berlin, 1892ff. W. v. UNWERTH und T. SIEBS, *Geschichte der deutschen Literatur bis zur Mitte des elften Jahrhunderts* (Grundriss der deutschen Literaturgeschichte, vol. I), Berlin and Leipzig, 1920. F. VOGT, *Geschichte der mittelhochdeutschen Literatur*, I. Teil, 3rd edition (formerly in Paul's *Grundriss* now in *Grundriss der deutschen Literaturgeschichte*, vol. II), Berlin and Leipzig, 1922. G. EHRISMANN, *Geschichte der deutschen Literatur bis zum Ausgange des Mittelalters*, 3 vols. published, one more to follow, Munich, 1918ff. S. ASCHNER, *Geschichte der deutschen Literatur vom 9. Jahrhundert bis zu den Staufern*, vol. I, 1920. Some care is advisable in the use of the last book. H. SCHNEIDER, *Heldendichtung, Geistlichendichtung, Ritterdichtung* (Geschichte der deutschen Literatur, hrsg. VON A. KÖSTER und J. PETERSEN,

Vol. I), Heidelberg, 1925. Numerous special articles with excellent bibliographies may be found in P. Merker and W. Stammler, *Reallexikon der deutschen Literaturgeschichte*, 3 vols., Berlin, 1925ff. Current bibliographies in the *Jahresberichte*.

Old High German literature. The last edition of Braune, *Althochdeutsches Lesebuch*, above, contains the most complete bibliographies available for the monuments included in it. E. Steinmeyer, *Die kleineren althochdeutschen Sprachdenkmäler*, Berlin, 1916, contains full bibliographies and commentaries for the remaining minor monuments. For the more extensive works see Ehrismann.

Middle High German literature. The general works cited above list the literature in full. For Germanic and German metrics see vol. II, part 2, *Metrik*, in Paul's *Grundriss*, 2nd edition, Strasburg, 1905, and A. Huesler, *Deutsche Versgeschichte* (Paul's *Grundriss*, 3rd edition), 3 vols., Berlin, 1925–29.

Periodicals. To the periodicals cited under French and English literature which also publish articles on German literature and language add the following: *Zeitschrift für deutsches Altertum*, Berlin, 1841ff. *Zeitschrift für deutsche Philologie*, Stuttgart, 1869ff. *Beiträge zur Geschichte der deutschen Sprache und Literatur*, Halle, 1874ff. *Germania, Vierteljahresschrift für deutsche Altertumskunde*, Vienna, 1856–92. *Zeitschrift für deutsche Wortforschung*, Strasburg, 1900–14. *Revue germanique*, Paris, 1905ff. *Neuphilologische Mitteilungen*, Helsingfors, 1902ff. *Deutsche Vierteljahresschrift für Literaturwissenschaft und Geistesgeschichte*, Halle, 1923ff. *The Germanic review*, New York, 1926ff. C. Diesch, *Bibliographie der germanistischen Zeitschriften* (Bibliographical publications of the Germanic section of the Modern language association of America, vol. I), Leipzig, 1927.

Taylor Starck.

IV. OLD SAXON AND MIDDLE LOW GERMAN LANGUAGE AND LITERATURE

A. Language

Grammars. J. H. Gallée, *Altsächsische Grammatik*, 2nd edition by J. Lochner, Halle, 1910. F. Holthausen, *Altsächsisches Elementarbuch*, 2nd edition, Heidelberg, 1921. O. Behaghel, *Syntax des Heliand*, Vienna, 1897. A. Lasch, *Mittelniederdeutsche Grammatik*, Halle, 1914.

Dictionaries. E. H. Sehrt, *Vollständiges Wörterbuch zum Heliand und zur altsächsischen Genesis*, Göttingen, 1925. *Mittelniederdeutsches Wörterbuch* von K. Schiller und A. Lübben, Bremen, 1875. A. Lasch und C. Borchling, *Mittelniederdeutsches Handwörterbuch*, Hamburg, 1928ff.

B. Literature

General. The works cited under Old and Middle High German contain for the most part a section on Old Saxon. The articles "*Altsächsische*

Dichtung" and "*Niederdeutsche Literatur*" in MERKER-STAMMLER, *Reallexikon.* H. JELLINGHAUS, *Geschichte der mittelniederdeutschen Literatur* (PAUL'S *Grundriss*), 3rd edition, Berlin and Leipzig, 1925.

Periodicals. The periodicals cited under Old and Middle High German and the following: *Jahrbuch des Vereins für niederdeutsche Sprachforschung*, 1875ff. *Korrespondenzblatt des Vereins für niederdeutsche Sprachforschung*, 1877ff. *Zeitschrift für deutsche Mundarten*, Berlin, 1906ff. *Zeitschrift für die Wissenschaft der Sprache*, edited by A. HÖFER, 4 vols., Berlin, Greifswald, 1845–53.

V. OLD FRISIAN

T. SIEBS, *Geschichte der friesischen Sprache*, PAUL'S *Grundriss*, 2nd edition, I, 1152–1464. W. HEUSER, *Altfriesisches Lesebuch*, Heidelberg, 1903. W. STELLER, *Abriss der altfriesischen Grammatik*, Halle, 1928. Brief glossary and bibliography. K. FREIHERR V. RICHTHOFEN, *Altfriesisches Wörterbuch*, Göttingen, 1840. F. HOLTHAUSEN, *Altfriesisches Wörterbuch*, Heidelberg, 1925. T. SIEBS, *Friesische Literatur*, PAUL'S *Grundriss*, 2nd edition, II, 1, 521–54. The article "Friesische Literatur" in Merker-Stammler, *Reallexikon.*

VI. OLD AND MIDDLE DUTCH

JAN TE WINKEL, *Geschichte der niederländischen Sprache*, PAUL'S *Grundriss*, 2nd edition, I, 781–925. J. FRANCK, *Mittelniederländische Grammatik*, 2nd edition, Leipzig, 1910. M. J. VAN DER MEER, *Historische Grammatik der niederländischen Sprache*, Heidelberg, 1927ff. J. VERDAM, *Middelnederlandsch Woordenboek*, 8 vols. complete, 9th in progress, The Hague, 1885ff. *Woordenboek der Nederlandsche Taal*, bewerkt door M. DE VRIES en L. A. TE WINKEL, Leiden, 1864ff. J. FRANCK, *Etymologisch Woordenboek der Nederlandsche taal*, 2nd edition by N. v. WIJK, The Hague, 1912. JAN TE WINKEL, *Niederländische Literatur*, PAUL'S *Grundriss*, 2nd edition, II, 1, 419–520.

Periodicals. Those cited above and the following: *Tijdschrift voor Nederlandsche taal- en letterkunde*, Leiden, 1881ff. *Taal en Letteren*, 1891–1906. *Noord en Zuid*, 1877–1907. *De Nieuwe Taalgids*, 1907ff. *Tijdschrift voor Taal en Lettern*, 1913ff. From 1913 to February, 1918, the title reads *Bijblad voor Taal en Letteren zu Opvoeding en Onderwijs. Leuvensche Bijdragen*, 1896ff.

TAYLOR STARCK.

VII. OLD NORSE LANGUAGE AND LITERATURE

A. LANGUAGE

General. A. NOREEN, *Geschichte der nordischen Sprachen*, 3rd edition, Strasburg, 1913 (PAUL'S *Grundriss*).

Grammars. A. NOREEN, *Altisländische und altnorwegische Grammatik*, 4th edition, Halle, 1923; *Altschwedische Grammatik*, Halle, 1904. A. HEUSLER, *Altisländisches Elementarbuch*, 2nd edition, Heidelberg, 1921. H. McM. BUCKHURST, *An elementary grammar of Old Icelandic*, London, 1925. A "Short grammar of Old Norse" in E. V. GORDON, *An Introduction to Old Norse*, Oxford, 1927.

Dictionaries. CLEASBY-VIGFÚSSON, *An Icelandic-English dictionary*, Oxford, 1874. J. FRITZNER, *Ordbog over det gamle norske Sprog*, 2nd edition, Christiania, 1886–96. G. ZOËGA, *A concise dictionary of Old Icelandic*, Oxford, 1910. For the poetry: F. JÓNSSON, *Lexicon Poeticum Antiquae Linguae Septentrionalis* (*Ordbog over det norsk-islandske Skjaldesprog*), Copenhagen, 1913–16. H. GERING, *Vollständiges Wörterbuch zu den Liedern der Edda*, Halle, 1903. Danish: O. KALKAR, *Ordbog til det ældre danske Sprog* (*1300–1700*), 5 vols., Copenhagen, 1881–1918. Swedish: D. O. J. SCHLYTER, *Ordbok till Samlingen af Sveriges gamla Lagar*, Lund, 1877. K. F. SÖDERWALL, *Ordbok öfver svenska Medeltids-språket*, Lund, 1884ff.

B. LITERATURE

General. JÓNSSON, *Den oldnorske og oldislandske Litteraturs Historie*, 2nd edition, 3 vols., Copenhagen, 1920–24, is the best general treatment. E. MOGK, *Norwegisch-Isländische Literatur*, in PAUL'S *Grundriss*, 2nd edition, vol. II, pp. 555ff. H. SCHÜCK, *Schwedisch-Dänische Literatur*, in PAUL'S *Grundriss*, 2nd edition, II, 924ff. G. VIGFÚSSON, Prolegomena to *Sturlunga Saga*, Oxford, 1878, is antiquated, but still usable. W. A. CRAIGIE, *The Icelandic sagas*, Cambridge, 1913. A. HEUSLER, *Die Anfänge der isländischen Saga*, Berlin, 1914. W. P. KER, *Epic and romance*, London, 1908. Excellent bibliographies covering various fields of Icelandic literature by H. HERMANNSSON in the Cornell series *Islandica*. Similar information may also be found in *Arkiv för nordisk Filologi* and *Acta Philologica Scandinavica* (see Periodicals).

Translations. *The Poetic Edda*, by H. A. BELLOWS. *The Poetic Edda*, by L. M. HOLLANDER. *Edda*, by F. GENZMER (vol. I, *Heldendichtung*, 2nd edition, 1914; vol. II, *Götterdichtung und Spruchdichtung* 1920), in *Sammlung Thule*, Jena, 1914ff. *The Prose Edda*, by A. G. BRODEUR. A bibliography of English translations of the sagas in CRAIGIE, *The Icelandic sagas* (see above). See also HERMANNSSON, *Bibliography of the Icelandic sagas*. Good German versions in *Sammlung Thule* (see above) and *Bauern und Helden*, Hamburg, 1923ff.

Antiquities. J. HOOPS, *Reallexikon*. S. MÜLLER, *Vor Oldtid*, Copenhagen, 1897; German translation, *Nordische Altertumskunde*, 2 vols., Strasburg, 1897–98.

Paleography. *Paleografisk Atlas. Dansk Afdeling*, Copenhagen, 1903. *Oldnorsk-islandsk Afdeling*, 1905; *Ny Serie*, 1907. L. F. A. WIMMER and F. JÓNSSON, *Håndskriftet Nr. 2365 4*[to] *gl. kgl. Samling* (*Codex Regius af den ældre Edda*), Copenhagen, 1891. F. JÓNSSON, *Håndskriftet Nr. 748, 4*[to]*, bl. 1–6, i den Arnamagnæanske samling* (*Brudstykke af den ældre Edda*), Copenhagen, 1896.

Periodicals. *Arkiv för* (*for*) *nordisk Filologi*, Christiania, 1883–86; Lund, 1887ff. *Aarbøger for nordisk Oldkyndighed og Historie*, Copenhagen, 1866ff. *Acta Philologica Scandinavica*, Copenhagen, 1925ff. *The Saga-Book of the Viking Club*, London, 1895ff. *Publications of the Society for the Advancement of Scandinavian Study* (*Scandinavian studies and notes*), Urbana, 1911–13; Menasha, Wis., 1914ff.

F. S. CAWLEY

VIII. CELTIC LANGUAGES AND LITERATURES

A. Language

General. J. K. Zeuss, *Grammatica Celtica*, 1st edition, Leipzig, 1853, laid the foundations of Celtic philology. The 2nd edition, with valuable revision by H. Ebel, Berlin, 1871, is still very useful to consult. But the present state of grammatical knowledge is better represented by H. Pedersen's *Vergleichende Grammatik der keltischen Sprachen*, 2 vols., Göttingen, 1909–13, with its good reference lists on the different languages. On Celtic studies in general see G. Dottin, *Manuel pour servir à l'étude de l'antiquité celtique*, 2nd edition, Paris, 1915; H. Zimmer in "Die romanischen Literaturen und Sprachen, mit Einschluss des Keltischen," *Kultur der Gegenwart*, I, 11, i, Berlin, 1909, 16ff. "Die keltischen Sprachen"; and R. Thurneysen, *Die Kelten in ihrer Sprache und Literatur*, Bonn, 1914. A good, though by no means complete, bibliography of current works in Celtic scholarship has been published for many years in the *Revue celtique* under "Bibliographie" and "Chronique."

Periodicals. The principal learned journals relating to Celtic philology and archaeology and medieval Celtic literature are the following: *Revue celtique*, 1870ff.; *Zeitschrift für celtische Philologie*, 1896ff.; Royal Irish Academy, *Proceedings and transactions*, 1841ff.; *Proceedings and transactions of the Kilkenny (and south east of Ireland) archaeological society*, 1849ff., continued under the titles *Journal of the Royal historical and archaeological association of Ireland* and *Proceedings and papers of the Royal society of antiquaries of Ireland; Eriu* 1904ff.; *Archivium hibernicum*, 1912ff.; *Celtic magazine*, 1875–88; *Celtic review*, 1900–16; *Scottish Gaelic studies*, 1926ff.; *Archaeologia cambrensis*, 1846ff.; *Transactions of the honourable society of Cymmrodorion*, 1892ff.; *Y Cymmrodor*, published by the same society, 1877ff.; *Bulletin of the Board of Celtic studies*, Univ. of Wales, 1921ff.; *Annales de Bretagne*, 1886ff. Of the numerous literary journals in Welsh the following contain many articles of value relating to the mediaeval period: *Y Traethodydd*, 1845ff.; *Y Geninen*, 1883ff.; *Cymru*, 1891–1927; *Y Beirniad*, 1911–18; *Y Llenor*, 1922ff.

Gaulish. The most important collection of materials, both linguistic and historical, is A. Holder's *Altceltischer Sprachschatz*, Leipzig, 1896ff. References to inscriptions discovered or published since Holder will be found in the successive volumes of the *Revue archéologique*. For systematic grammar see G. Dottin, *La langue gauloise*, Paris, 1920.

Irish. An admirable general bibliography, compiled by R. I. Best, has been published by the National Library, Dublin: *A bibliography of Irish philology and printed Irish literature*, Dublin, 1913. For later publications see the periodic bibliographies in the *Revue celtique*. The authoritative grammar of Old Irish is R. Thurneysen's *Handbuch des Altirischen*, 2 pts., Heidelberg, 1909; a much shorter grammar in English by F. W. O'Connell, *A grammar of Old Irish*, Belfast, 1912, is based upon it. Other good treatments of the subject are the *Grammaire du vieil-irlandais by* J. Vendryès,

Paris, 1908, and J. POKORNY'S very brief *Altirische Grammatik* (Sammlung Göschen, Berlin, 1925). For Middle Irish the most convenient grammar and reader is G. DOTTIN'S *Manuel d'irlandais moyen*, 2 vols., Paris, 1913. There are numerous text-books on Modern-Irish grammar: J. O'DONOVAN'S *Grammar of the Irish language*, Dublin, 1845, which has long been a standard work, deals rather with the conventional literary language of early Modern Irish than with actual present speech. Two of the practical text-books most in use are E. O'GROWNEY'S *Simple lessons in Irish*, Dublin, 1901–11 and the *Graiméar na Gaedhilge* of the Christian Brothers, first printing, Dublin, 1901. Another convenient presentation of the subject is given in PÓL Ó COIGLIGH'S *Graimeur Riaghhlac na nuadh-Gaedhilge*, Dundalk, 1924. A more elaborate scientific treatment of Irish grammar is furnished by T. O'MAILLE'S *Urlabhraidheacht agus Graiméar na Gaedhilge*, Dublin, 1927, of which only the first part has been published. There is no adequate lexicon of the language of the Old-Irish and Middle-Irish periods. The most convenient working dictionary is the "Wörterbuch" in E. WINDISCH'S *Irische Texte*, Vol. I, Leipzig, 1881; now out of print and scarce. Hundreds of special glossaries have been published to accompany Irish texts, and a new dictionary, which will embody their contents, is now being prepared, under the supervision of PROFESSOR THURNEYSEN, by DR. RUDOLF HERTZ, DR. VERNAM HULL, and FATHER LEHMACHER. For the modern period the best Irish-English dictionary is that of P. J. DINNEEN, revised and enlarged edition, Dublin, 1927, and the best English-Irish that of T. O'NEILL LANE, enlarged edition, Dublin, 1915. E. O'REILLY'S *Irish-English dictionary*, revised edition, Dublin, an uncritical work, contains many words of the earlier period.

Scottish Gaelic. There is no adequate scientific grammar on historical principles. The best descriptive grammars are those of A. STEWART, *Elements of Gaelic grammar*, 5th edition, rev., 1901 and G. CALDER, *A Gaelic grammar*, Glasgow, 1923. The most comprehensive dictionaries are that of the Highland Society, *Dictionarium Scoto-Celticum*, 2 vols., Edinburgh, 1828, and the *Faclair Gaidhlig*, by DEALBHAN, 3 vols., Herne Bay, 1902ff. More concise works are N. MACLEOD and D. DEWAR'S *Dictionary of the Gaelic language*, Glasgow, 1853; M. MACLENNAN'S *Pronouncing and etymological dictionary of the Gaelic language: Gaelic-English and English-Gaelic*, Edinburgh, 1925; and A. MACBAIN'S *Etymological dictionary of the Gaelic language*, Stirling, 1911. The last is convenient and the treatment of etymologies is competent for the time of its publication.

Manx. H. JENNER, "The Manx language," London Philological Soc., *Trans.*, 1875, 172ff. J. RHYS, "The Outlines of the phonology of Manx Gaelic," in A. W. MOORE and J. RHYS, *The book of common prayer in Manx Gaelic*, London, 1895; J. KELLY, *A practical grammar of the Ancient Gaelic, or language of the Isle of Man, usually called Manks* (Manx soc. publ., II, 1870). There are two dictionaries: that of J. KELLY, *Fockleyr Manninagh as Baarlagh . . . currit magh fo chiarail Illiam Gill* (Manx soc. publ., vol. XIII, 1866) and A. CREGEEN, *A dictionary of the Manks language*, Douglas, 1835.

Welsh. The standard historical grammar is by J. M. JONES, *A Welsh grammar, historical and comparative*, Oxford, 1913, while the best introductory text-book on the modern language is the same author's *Elementary Welsh grammar*, Oxford, 1922. The best treatment of the earlier stages of the language is J. STRACHAN'S *Introduction to early Welsh*, Manchester, 1909. There is no adequate dictionary of early Welsh. W. O. PUGHE'S *A dictionary of the Welsh language*, 2nd edition, Denbigh, 1832, undertakes to include the vocabulary of older periods, but is a thoroughly uncritical work. D. S. EVANS'S *Dictionary of the Welsh language—Geiriadur Cymraeg*, Carmarthen, 1887ff., a more satisfactory work, stops with the letter *D*. The most convenient and trustworthy work for practical use is W. SPURRELL'S *Geiriadur Cymraeg a Saesneg*, as revised by J. BODVAN ANWYL, 7th edition, Carmarthen, 1916, which records archaic and obsolete words. A considerable number of special glossaries of early Welsh have been published, usually to accompany texts. Particular mention may be made of those in STRACHAN'S *Introduction* cited above, in K. MEYER'S edition of *Peredur ab Efrawc*, Leipzig, 1887, and L. MÜHLHAUSEN'S edition of *Die vier Zweige des Mabinogi*, Halle, 1925, and T. LEWIS'S *Glossary of mediaeval Welsh law*, Manchester, 1913.

Cornish. For the grammar, besides the Cornish material in ZEUSS and PEDERSEN, see E. NORRIS, "A sketch of Cornish grammar," *Ancient Cornish drama*, Oxford, 1859; H. JENNER, *Handbook of the Cornish language*, London, 1904. H. LEWIS, *Llawalyfr Cernyweg Canol*, Wrexham, 1923, gives a concise grammar of Middle Cornish in Welsh. There are two dictionaries: Cornish-English by R. WILLIAMS, *Lexicon Cornu-Britannicum*, London, 1865, and F. W. P. JAGO, *An English Cornish dictionary*, Plymouth, 1887.

Breton. For the grammar ZEUSS and PEDERSEN (cited under **General**) are again of primary importance. There is a very concise grammar of Middle Breton (in Welsh) by H. LEWIS, *Llawlyfr Llydaweg Canol*, Aberdeen, 1922. J. LOTH'S *Chrestomathie bretonne*, Paris, 1890, though it does not contain a formal grammar, is an invaluable source of information on early Breton. For the later period there are a number of grammars, of which the following are important: J. MAUNOIR, *Le sacré collège de Jésus*, Quimper-Corentin, 1659, translated in E. LUHYS' *Archaeologia britannica*, Oxford, 1707; G. DE ROSTRENEN, *Grammaire française-celtique ou française-bretonne*, Rennes, 1738; Guingamp, 1833; E. ERNAULT, *Petite grammaire bretonne*, St.-Brieuc, 1897; F. VALLÉE, *La langue bretonne en 40 leçons*, 6th edition, St.-Brieuc, 1918, a good introduction to the language. The vocabulary of the Old-Breton glosses is collected in J. LOTH'S *Vocabulaire vieux-breton*, Paris, 1884; for supplementary material from charters, etc., see his *Chrestomathie*, cited above. For the Middle-Breton period there are two useful glossaries by E. ERNAULT: the first, an etymological dictionary published with his *Le mystère de Sainte-Barbe*, Paris, 1888; the second, *Glossaire moyen-breton*, Paris, 1895. For Modern Breton there are a considerable number of dictionaries, some of which have appeared in many editions. Historically important are the glossaries of MAUNOIR in *Le sacré collège de Jésus*, cited above. Of the later dictionaries the following may be mentioned: G. DE ROSTRENEN, *Dictionnaire français-celtique, ou français-breton*, Rennes, 1732, Guingamp, 1834; L. LE PELLETIER, *Dictionnaire étymologique de la langue bretonne*, Paris, 1752; LE GONIDEC, *Dictionnaire breton-français*, Angoulême, 1821; re-edited by DE LA VILLEMARQUÉ, St.-Brieuc, 1847; E. ERNAULT, *Geiriadurig brezonek-gallek*, St.-Brieuc, 1927; and, for the dialect of Vannes, P. DE CHÂLONS, *Dictionnaire breton-français du diocèse de Vannes*, Vannes, 1723; new edition, J. LOTH, Rennes, 1895. V. HENRY, *Lexique étymologique des termes les plus usuels du breton moderne*, Rennes, 1900, though it deals with only a limited vocabulary, is useful to consult for etymologies.

Pictish. Some reference to Pictish should be included here, though opinions differ as to whether that language is related to British or Goidelic, or is not even Indo-European. On the general problem, see J. RHYS and D. B. JONES, *The Welsh people*, London, 1900, 36ff.; T. R. HOLMES, *Ancient Britain and the invasions of Julius Caesar*, Oxford, 1907, 409ff.; J. FRAZER, *History and etymology*, Oxford, 1923. The Pictish inscriptions have been edited and translated by RHYS (on the theory that they are non-Indo-European) in the *Proceedings of the Society of antiquaries of Scotland*, XXVI (1891–92), 263–351. E. W. NICHOLSON in *The vernacular inscriptions of the Ancient Kingdom of Alban*, London, 1896, argues for an interpretation on the theory that they are early Gaelic; see also his *Keltic researches*, London, 1904. Pictish materials from the early Irish chronicles were collected by W. STOKES in BEZZENBERGER'S *Beiträge z. Kunde d. indogerman. Sprachen*, XVIII (1892), 84–115.

Palaeography and epigraphy. Celtic palaeography is a branch of Latin, and the development of handwriting in the Celtic countries is included in F. STEFFENS'S *Lateinische Paläographie*, 2nd edition, Trier, 1909; also in French translation, Trier, 1910. For more detailed studies see LINDSAY, *Early Irish minuscule script*, Oxford, 1910, and *Early Welsh script*, Oxford, 1912. Many specimens of Irish writing are given by J. T. GILBERT, *Facsimiles of national manuscripts of Ireland*, Dublin, 1874–84. A considerable number of Irish manuscripts have also been published separately in facsimile. For a list see R. I. BEST'S *Bibliography* (cited under **Irish** above), pp. 64ff. Photographic reproductions of several of the most important Welsh manuscripts have appeared in the Oxford series of *Welsh texts*, edited by J. GWENOGVRYN EVANS. On the Ogham alphabet, in which many very early inscriptions, Irish and Pictish, are written, see THURNEYSEN'S *Handbuch* (cited above), pp. 10–12. For the Irish inscriptions themselves see R. A. S. MACALISTER, *Studies in Irish epigraphy*, 3 pts., London, 1897–1907. For the Pictish inscriptions see the references under **Pictish** above.

B. LITERATURE

Of the various Celtic literatures only Irish and Welsh include any large amount of medieval material. The monuments preserved in Gaulish and Pictish are not literary. Those in Scottish Gaelic, Manx, Cornish, and Breton are mostly of a date later than the Middle Ages, though the materials—especially in folk-lore, saints' legends, and ecclesiastical drama—are often of interest to medieval students. The early literature in Irish and Welsh is so voluminous that there is not room here for an adequate bibliography. For these literatures, as well as for those of the other Celtic countries, references are given only to the more important general treatises and collections.

Irish. BEST'S *Bibliography* (already cited) is very full and adequate. D. HYDE'S *Literary history of Ireland*, New York, 1899, ELEANOR HULL'S *Text book of Irish literature*, 2 vols., Dublin, 1906–08, and AODH DEBLÁCAM'S *Gaelic literature surveyed*, Dublin, 1929, give good general accounts of Irish literature. A concise sketch of its history, very well documented, was published by G. DOTTIN in the *R.S.H.*, III (1901), 60–97; this has been translated by J. DUNN as, *The Gaelic literature of Ireland*, Washington, D. C., privately printed, 1906. Other excellent short accounts are those of K. MEYER in *Kultur der Gegenwart*, I, 11, i, pp. 78–95 (already cited) and of QUIGGIN and HYDE in the *Ency. Brit.*, 14th edition, XII, 638ff. Of the numerous articles and treatises on special topics R. THURNEYSEN'S *Irische Königs- und Heldensage bis zum siebzehnten Jahrhundert*, pts. i and ii, Halle, 1921, on the elder saga-cycle, may be singled out as the most important investigation in the field. For a practically complete corpus of the literature preserved in manuscripts of the Old-Irish period, see W. STOKES and J. STRACHAN, *Thesaurus Palaeohibernicus*, 2 vols., Cambridge, 1901–03 and STOKE'S *Supplement* to the same, Halle, 1910.

There is no systematic history of the extensive medieval Latin literature written in Ireland, but a useful bibliography was published by G. DOTTIN in the *Revue d'histoire et de littérature religieuses*, V (1900), 162–67. See also C. PLUMMER, *Miscellanea hagiographica hibernica*, Brussels, 1925; M. ESPOSITO, "A bibliography of Latin writers of mediaeval Ireland," *Studies*, II (1913), no. 8; see also **36b.**

Welsh. Literary histories: T. STEPHENS, *Literature of the Kymry*, Llandovery, 1842; 2nd edition, D. S. EVANS, London, 1876, the first work of critical scholarship on the subject; GWEIRYDD AP RHYS (i.e. J. R. PRYSE), *Hanes Llenyddiaeth Gymreig, 1300–1650*, London, 1885; T. G. JONES, *Llenyddiaeth y Cymry*, Denbigh, 1915. For good short accounts of the history of the literature see G. DOTTIN in the *R.S.H.*, VI (1903), 317–62; L. C. STERN in *Kultur der Gegenwart*, I, 11, i, pp. 144ff.; W. J. GRUFFYDD in the *Ency. Brit.*, 14th edition, XXIII, 504ff. References to important special studies and to books on the literature of the modern period are given by GRUFFYDD. Of the older collections of early Welsh literature the most important are *The Myvyrian archaeology of Wales*, 3 vols., London, 1801; 2nd edition, in 1 vol., with additions, Denbigh, 1870; and *The four ancient books of Wales*, edited by W. F. SKENE, 2 vols., Edinburgh, 1868. Many of the texts in these collections have been superseded by the editions of J. G. EVANS in the Oxford series of Welsh Texts. The poems of Dafydd ap Gwlym, the principal poet of the later medieval period, were edited by OWEN JONES and W. OWEN [Pughs], London, 1789; 2nd edition by "Cyuddeler," Liverpool, 1873. The selections from Dafydd and his contemporaries (*Cywyddan*

Dafydd ap Gwilym a' i Gyfoeswyr), edited by I. WILLIAMS and T. ROBERTS, Bangor, 1914 (2nd edition containing poems of Dafydd alone, Bangor, 1921) have an important historical introduction. Valuable editions of medieval texts, as well as critical articles of importance, have appeared in the publications of the Honourable Society of Cymmrodorion and in the *Bulletin of the Board of Celtic Studies*. For accounts of unpublished ms. materials see J. G. EVANS, *Report on ms. in the Welsh language* (Hist. Ms. Comm.), London, 1908–1910.

Scottish Gaelic and Manx. There is a good brief outline of the history of these literatures by L. C. STERN in *Kultur der Gegenwart*, I, 11, i, pp. 98ff. On Scottish Gaelic see also QUIGGIN and HYDE in the *Ency Brit.*, 14th edition, XX, 185ff.; and for fuller treatment N. MACNEILL, *The literature of the Highlanders*, Inverness, 1892 and M. MACLEAN, *The literature of the Highlands*, London, 1904. On the Ossianic poetry, genuine and spurious, see L. C. STERN in the *Zeitschrift für vergleichende Literaturgeschichte*, New Ser., VIII (1895), 51–86, 143–74, and J. S. SMART, *James Macpherson*, London, 1905. The materials relating to Manx will be found in the Publications of the Manx Society, 1859ff.

Cornish. Brief sketches of the literary history, with references, are given by L. C. STERN in *Kultur der Gegenwart*, I, 11, i, pp. 131–32 and by H. LEWIS in the *Ency. Brit.*, 14th edition, VI, 446ff. Fuller treatment in JENNER, *Handbook of the Cornish language;* E. NORRIS, *The ancient Cornish drama*, 2 vols., Oxford, 1859; A. LE BRAZ, *Le théâtre celtique*, Paris, 1905.

Breton. For brief accounts, with references, see again STERN, *loc. cit.*, pp. 132–37, and H. LEWIS in the *Ency. Brit.*, 14th edition, IV, 96ff. Somewhat fuller is the sketch by G. DOTTIN, in the *R.S.H.*, VIII (1904), 93–104. See also A. LE BRAZ, already cited; P. LE GOFF, *Petite histoire littéraire du dialecte breton de Vannes*, Vannes, 1904. Many Breton texts have been published in the *Revue celtique* and the *Annales de Bretagne*.

FRED NORRIS ROBINSON.

IX. MEDIEVAL SLAVIC LANGUAGES AND LITERATURES

General. A. N. PYPIN and V. D. SPASOVICH, *Istorija Slavjanskich Literatur*, Leningrad, 1880. J. KARÁSEK, *Slavische Literaturgeschichte* I (ältere Literatur bis zur Wiedergeburt), Leipzig, 1906.

Church Slavic grammars. A. LESKIEN, *Handbuch der altbulgarischen Sprache*, 6th edition, Weimar, 1922; *Grammatik der altbulgarischen (altkirchenslavischen) Sprache*, Heidelberg, 1909. W. VONDRÁK, *Altkirchenslavische Grammatik*, Berlin, 1912. The only lexicons (though incomplete) are I. I. SREZNEVSKI, *Materialy dlja Slovarja Drevne-russkago Jazyka*, Leningrad, 1893ff., and Miklosich, *Lexicon Palaeoslovenico-graeco-latinum*, Vienna, 1862ff.

Comparative and historical grammars. W. VONDRÁK, *Vergleichende Grammatik der slavischen Sprachen*, Göttingen, 1906ff. N. DURNOVO, *Vvedenije v Istoriju Russkogo Jazyka*, Brno, 1927 (especially valuable for complete bibliography of early Slavic and Russian Texts). R. F. BRANDT, *Lekcii po Istorii Russkago Jazyka*, Moscow, 1913. A. A. SHAKHMATOV, *Vvedenije v Kurs Istorii Russkago Jazyka*, Leningrad, 1916. K. H. MEYER,

Historische Grammatik der russischen Sprache, I, Bonn, 1923. D. Daničić, *Istorija Oblika Srpskoga ili Hrvatskoga Jezika do Svršetka XVII Vijeka*, Belgrade, 1872. S. Mladenov, *Geschichte des bulgarischen Sprache*, Berlin, 1929. M. Kušar, *Povijest Razvitka Našega Jezika Hrvackoga ili Srpskoga od Najdavnijeh Vremena do Danas*, Ragusa, 1884. J. Gebauer, *Historická Mluvnice Jazyka Českého*, Prague, 1894ff. A. A. Shakhmatov, *Kratki Očerk Istorii Malorusskago (Ukrainskago) Jazyka*, Leningrad, 1916. Shakhmatov-Krimski, *Narisi z Istorii Ukrainskoi Movi ta Chrestomatija z Pamjatnikiv Pismenskoi Staroukrainščini*, 2nd edition, Kiev, 1924. A. Kalina, *Historya Języka Polskiego* I, Lwow, 1883; *Studya nad Historyą Języka Bulgarskiego*, Crakow, 1891.

Palaeographic aids. V. N. Ščepkin, *Učebnik Russkoi Paleografii*, Moscow, 1920. V. N. Jagić, *Vopros o Runach u Slavjan; Glagoličeskoje Pismo*, both in *Enciklopedija Slavjanskoi Filologii*, III, Leningrad, 1911. P. A. Lavrov, *Paleografičeskoje Obozrěnie Kirillovskago Pisma*, *Enciklopedija Slav. Fil.* IV, Leningrad, 1915. The two monographs of Jagić and Lavrov on the Glagolitic and Cyrillic alphabets respectively cover the whole field of Slavic palaeography, except for the languages using Latin characters.

Antiquities. P. J. Šafařík, *Slovanské Starozitnosti*, 2nd edition, Prague, 1862ff., German translation, *Slawische Althertümer*, Leipzig, 1843. L. Niederle, *Slovanské Starožitnosti* (the most authoritative modern work), Prague, 1906ff. Niederle, *Manuel de l'antiquité slave.* L. Léger, *Les anciennes civilisations slaves*, Paris, 1921. Dvorník, *Les Slaves, Byzance et Rome au IXe siècle.* S. H. Cross, "The Russian primary chronicle," in *Harvard studies and notes in philology and literature*, XII, Cambridge, 1930.

Literature. A. N. Pypin, *Istorija Russkoi Literatury*, I–III, 4th edition, Leningrad, 1911. P. V. Vladimirov, *Drevnjaja Russkaja Literatura Kievskago Perioda*, Kiev, 1900. V. M. Istrin, *Očerk Istorii Drevnerusskoi Literatury*, Leningrad, 1922. M. N. Speranski, *Istorija Drevnei Russkoi Literatury*, Moscow, 1920ff. E. Lo Gatto, *Storia della letteratura russa* I, Rome, 1928. A. Brückner, *Dzieje Literatury Polskiej w Zarysie*, I, Warsaw, 1907. J. Jakubec, *Dějiny Literatury České*, Prague, 1926ff. P. J. Šafařík, *Geschichte der südslawischen Literaturen*, Prague, 1864ff. M. Murko, *Geschichte der älteren südslawischen Literaturen*, Leipzig, 1908. V. N. Jagić, *Entstehungsgeschichte der altkirchenslavischen Sprache*, 2nd edition, Berlin, 1913.

Periodicals. *Archiv für slavische Philologie* 1876ff. *Revue des études slaves*, 1921ff. *Slavia*, 1922ff. *Slavonic review*, 1922ff. *Zeitschrift für slavische Philologie*, 1924ff.

S. H. Cross.

XXV. HISTORIOGRAPHY AND POLITICAL THOUGHT

A. Outline

1. Unfavorable conditions for good history writing in the middle ages. Almost total absence of historical critical sense and hence a lack of trustworthy texts and bibliographical tools. Comparatively little interest in the

history and historiography of the Greek and Roman world, to say nothing of Egypt or Babylonia. The history of the Jews formed the basis of all study of ancient history. Josephus was much more popular than Livy. There was no systematic study of history as a separate discipline in the schools and universities. Consequent insignificance of all medieval histories properly speaking, that is, those attempting to depict the past from records. On the other hand, the middle ages produced some remarkable chronicles, that is, accounts of contemporary events written largely from observation and hearsay.

2. Historiography in the early middle ages. For Orosius see outline II, for Gregory of Tours and Merovingian hagiography, outline VI, for Bede, outline VII, for the Carolingian revival of history writing, outline VIII, and for the ninth, tenth and eleventh centuries see the literature listed under outlines IX and XI.

3. The remarkable impulse given to history writing by the crusades and by the new intellectual interests of the twelfth century. For the historiography of the crusades see outline XXI in part II.

4. The twelfth century. Sigebert of Gembloux (died 1112), *Chronographia*, and its continuations, notably by Robert of Torigni (died 1186). Ordericus Vitalis (died ca. 1142), *Historia ecclesiastica* [1–1141 A.D.]. Suger, abbot of St. Denis (died 1151), *Vita Ludovici Grossi regis*. William of Malmesbury (died ca. 1142), *De gestis regum anglorum* [449–1127 A.D.], *Historiae novellae libri tres* [1125–42 A.D.]. Otto of Freising (died 1158), *Historia de duabus civitatibus*, or *Chronica*.

5. The thirteenth century. Rigord, a monk of St. Denis (died ca. 1209), *Gesta Philippi Augusti* [1179–1208 A.D.], continued by William of Armorica, or Guillaume le Breton, to 1223. Vincent of Beauvais (died 1264), *Speculum historiale*. Matthew Paris (died ca. 1259), *Chronica majora* [to 1259]. Roger of Wendover (died 1236), *Flores historiarum* [to 1235]. Salimbene (1221–88); *Chronica*.

6. The beginnings of history writing in the vernacular languages. The famous *Anglo-Saxon chronicle*. Historical elements in the *Chansons de geste*. The *Vie de Guillaume le Maréchal*, written about 1225, in French verse. Villehardouin (died 1213), *Conquête de Constantinople*. The *Grandes chroniques françaises de Saint-Denis*. Jean de Joinville (ca. 1224–ca. 1319), *Histoire de Saint Louis*. For Froissart and Commines see outline XXX in part II.

7. Historical criticism in the middle ages. For the textual criticism of Roger Bacon and other scholars of the thirteenth century see outline XVIII. Reasons for the decline, in the thirteenth century, of critical interest in the records of the past.

8. Political theory in the early middle ages. Its ideas derived from the New Testament and the writings of the church fathers. The chief topic of interest the relation of the ruler to God and to the divine law. The relation of church to state conceived in terms of this problem. The Carolingian "divine-state." Increasing tendency to view the church as the defender

and protector of the divine law against infractions by the temporal ruler. Sweeping claims made for the authority of the church during the investiture controversy (see outline XVI). Struggle between empire and papacy lays theoretical basis for wider conflict between temporal and spiritual power in general. Question whether temporal ruler derives his authority from God directly, or only indirectly through medium of church.

9. New influence introduced into political thought in twelfth century by systematic study of Roman law and development of canon law (see outline XX). The political thought of John of Salisbury stands at the beginning of this transition, and carries older ideas to fuller development. In the succeeding period there is closer examination of the concept of law, and beginning of divergence between older view that law is independent of the state and above it, and the newer view that law is the command of the human law-giver.

10. A still more profound transformation in political thought came in the thirteenth century with the recovery of the political writings of Aristotle (see outline XV). The chief contribution from this new source was the conception of the sovereignty of the community, rather than of the law or the ruler. This idea, the way for which had been prepared by earlier studies of the Roman law, made its influence felt within the organization of the church, as well as in the state. St. Thomas Aquinas, the great interpreter of Aristotle for the middle ages (see outline XV), succeeded in making satisfactory compromise with the older notions, but the democratic implications of the Aristotelian political theory come to a head in the fourteenth century in Marsiglio of Padua, and furnish the beginnings of the political theory of the eighteenth century. In the church this theory gave rise to the conciliar movement (see outline XXIX); in the state it was largely confined to the communes, and while it may have had some share in the widespread democratic movements at the end of the fourteenth century, the triumph of royal authority served to bring back in force the earlier theories of the relation between the ruler and God.

11. Medieval political theory conceived Christendom as a unity and had no distinct idea of separate nation-states. This conception fostered the claims of both the emperor and the pope to world supremacy. The imperial pretensions were permanently shattered by the fall of Frederick II (see outline XXII); but an effort was made to revive them by Dante in his *De monarchia*, a powerful argument for the necessity of a supreme world-government as a condition of world peace. The papal pretensions lasted much longer, and opposition to them by the growing spirit of nationalism was one of the causes of the Reformation.

B. Special Recommendations for Reading

Historiography—General surveys. Poole, *Chronicles and annals*. T. F. Tout, *The study of medieval chronicles*, London, 1922. M. Ritter, *Die*

Entwicklung der Geschichtswissenschaft an den führenden Werken betrachtend, Munich and Berlin, 1919. BAUMGARTNER, *Geschichte der Weltlitteratur*, IV, 353–78. H. v. EICKEN, *Mittelalterliche Weltanschauung*, 641–71, "Die Geschichtsschreibung." M. RITTER, "Die christlich-mittelalterliche Geschichtsschreibung," *H.Z.*, CVII (1911), 237–305. HASKINS, *Renaissance*, ch. VIII. B. CROCE, *Teoria e storia storiografia*, Bari, 1920, 183–205. English translation by D. AINSLIE, *History, its theory and practice*, New York, 1921, 200–23.

Historiography—Sources. The *Everyman's library* contains in cheap form translations of the *Anglo-Saxon chronicle*, and the chronicles of Villehardouin, de Joinville, and Froissart. For other translations, see Bibliography; Historiography, Original Sources. Selections from the German chronicles (in the original) in handy form are contained in *Geschichtsschreiber des frühen Mittelalters*, edited by F. KERN, Leipzig, 1915, *Deutsche Geschichtsschreiber der Kaiserzeit*, edited by F. VIGENER, Leipzig, 1915. Handy recent editions of two significant chronicles are C. JOHNSON, *Selections from the "Historia rerum anglicarum" of William of Newburgh*, London and New York, 1920; R. LANE POOLE, editor, *Historia pontificalis*, Oxford, 1927.

General surveys of medieval political thought. *C.M.H.*, VI, ch. XVIII. The standard work is R. W. and A. J. CARLYLE, *History of mediaeval political theory*, which, as so far published, comes down only to the end of the thirteenth century. Other full treatments are W. A. DUNNING, *A history of political theories, ancient and mediaeval*, New York, 1902; P. JANET, *Histoire de la science politique dans ses rapports avec la morale*, 2 vols., 3rd edition, Paris, 1887, I, 263–489. O. GIERKE, *Political theories of the middle age*, translated by F. W. MAITLAND, Cambridge, 1900, is a short closely reasoned analysis of the main tendencies of medieval political thought, with a full bibliography of the sources, and invaluable notes. Other general accounts are F. J. C. HEARNSHAW, editor, *The social and political ideas of some great mediaeval thinkers*, London and New York, 1923. L. GUMPLOWICZ, *Geschichte der Staatstheorien*, Innsbruck, 1905, 87–126. B. JARRETT, *Social theories of the middle ages, 1200–1500*, London, 1926. CRUMP and JACOB, *Legacy*, ch. X. M. DE WULF, "Les théories politiques du moyen âge," "*Revue néo-scolastique*, XXVI (1924), 249ff. A. J. CARLYLE, "The sources of mediaeval political theory and its connection with mediaeval politics," *A.H.R.*, XIX (1913), 1–12. Material of value is to be found in BRYCE, *Holy Roman empire, passim* (consult the index). FIGGIS, *From Gerson to Grotius*, 1–71, gives the best analysis and interpretation of political thought between the middle of the fourteenth century and the Reformation.

Political thought—Sources. See below under Bibliography; Political Thought, Original Sources, for translations of JOHN OF SALISBURY'S *Policraticus* and DANTE'S *De monarchia.* A useful collection is F. W. COKER, *Readings in political philosophy*, New York, 1914, which contains translations of brief selections from THOMAS AQUINAS, DANTE, and MARSIGLIO OF PADUA.

C. Bibliography

I

HISTORIOGRAPHY

General and miscellaneous works on medieval historiography. H. Scholz, *Glaube und Unglaube in der Weltgeschichte. Ein Kommentar zur Augustin's "De civitate Dei,"* Leipzig, 1911. M. Büdinger, *Die Universalhistorie im Mittelalter* (Denkschriften der kaiserlichen Akademie der Wissenschaften, philos.-hist. Klasse, XLVI, Abhandlungen 1 and 2), Vienna, 1900. D. Rinaudo, *Gli studi storici nel medio evo*, Turin, 1883. R. Jahncke, *Guilelmus Neubrigensis: ein pragmatischer Geschichtsschreiber des zwölften Jahrhunderts*, Bonn, 1912. F. Baethgen, "Franziskanische Studien," *H.Z.*, CXXXI (1925), 420–71, has special reference to Salimbene and Johann von Winterthur. R. Teuffel, *Individuelle Persöhnlichkeitsschilderung in dem deutschen Geschichtswesen des 10 und 11 Jahrhunderts*, Leipzig, 1914, part 12 of no. **749.** G. Misch, *Geschichte der Autobiographie*, vol. I, Leipzig, 1907. H. Bresslau, "Internationale Beziehungen in den Urkunden des Mittelalters," *Archiv für Urkundenforschung*, VI (1918), 19–76. M. Steinschneider, *Die Geschichtslitteratur der Jüden in Druckwerken und Handschriften*, Frankfurt, 1905. F. v. Bezold, "Astrologische Geschichtsconstruction im Mittelalter," *Zeitschrift für Geschichtswissenschaft*, VIII (1892), 29.

Historical criticism in the middle ages. B. Lasch, *Das Erwachen und die Entwickelung der historischen Kritik im Mittelalter* (*vom VI–XII Jahrhundert*), Breslau, 1887. Marie Schulz, *Die Lehre von der historischen Methode bei den Geschichtsschreibern des Mittelalters, VI–XIII Jahrhundert*, Berlin, 1909 (*Abh. m. n. G.*, 13). G. Ellinger, *Das Verhältniss der öffentlichen Meinung zu Wahrheit und Lüge im 10, 11, und 12 Jahrhundert*, Berlin, 1884, chs. I and V. A. Blasquez, *Estudios de historia y crítica medioevales*, Madrid, 1926. A. Lefranc, "Le traité des reliques de Guibert de Nogent et les commencements de la critique historique au moyen âge," *Etudes d'histoire du moyen âge dediées à G. Monod*, Paris, 1896, 285–307. B. Monod, *Le moine Guibert et son temps* (*1053–1124*), Paris, 1905.

Historiography by countries. England—W. L. Jones, "Latin chroniclers from the eleventh to the thirteenth centuries," *Cambridge history of English literature*, I (1908), ch. IX (see also the bibliography, 448–51). C. Jenkins, *The monastic chronicles and the early school of St. Albans*, London, 1922 L. F. Rushbrook Williams, *History of the abbey of St. Alban*, London, 1917.

Germany—W. Wattenbach, *Deutschlands Geschichtsquellen.* O. Lorenz, *Deutschlands Geschichtsquellen.* E. Michael, *Culturzustände*, III, 320–95, is confined to the thirteenth century. H. Bresslau, *Die ältere Salzburger Annalistik*, Berlin, 1923.

France—C. V. Langlois, "L'historiographie," *Histoire de la langue et de la littérature française*, edited by L. Petit de Julleville, II, ch. VI. A. Molinier, *Les sources de l'histoire de France*, vol. V, pp. i–clxxxvii, contains the introduction to the work in the form of a history of history writing in France in the middle ages.

Italy—B. SCHMEIDLER, *Italienische Geschichtsschreiber des XII und XIII Jahrhunderts: ein Beitrag zur Kulturgeschichte*, Leipzig, 1909 (Leipziger historische Abhandlungen, 11). U. BALZANI, *Early chronicles of Europe: Italy.*

For the Byzantine chroniclers see K. KRUMBACHER, *Geschichte der byzantinischen Literatur*, 219–40; and Vasiliev, no. **46b.**

Otto of Freising. J. HASHAGEN, *Otto von Freising als Geschichtsphilosoph und Kirchenpolitiker*, Leipzig, 1900. J. SCHMIDLIN, *Die geschichtsphilosophische und kirchenpolitische Weltanschauung Ottos von Freising*, Freiburg, 1906, part IV, 2–3, of no. **898**. A. HOFMEISTER, "Studien über Otto von Freising," *N.A.*, XXXVII (1911–12), 99–161, 635–768.

Salimbene and Joachim of Flora. E. MICHAEL, *Salimbene und seine Chronik: eine Studie zur Geschichtsschreibung des 13 Jahrhunderts*, Innsbruck, 1889. P. M. BICILLI, *Salimbene*, Odessa, 1916. O. HOLDER-EGGER, "Zur Lebensgeschichte des Bruders Salimbene de Adam," *N.A.*, XXXVII (1911–12), 165–218. COULTON, *From Saint Francis to Dante.* TAYLOR, *Mediaeval mind*, 4th edition, I, ch. XXII. GRUNDMANN, *Studien über Joachim von Floris.* FOURNIER, *Etudes sur Joachim de Flore.*

Original sources. For collected editions of the French chronicles, see nos. **965–67**; of the German, no. **978**; of the Italian, no. **988**; of the English, no. **995**; of the Spanish, nos. **997–98.** For separate editions of particular authors see index under name of author. See also B. SCHMEIDLER, "Neuere Ausgaben mittelalterlicher Geschichtsschreiber," *Die Geisteswissenschaften*, Nov. 26, 1914. A number of medieval chronicles are available in English translations. OTTO OF FREISING, *The two cities:* translated by MIEROW. The Bohn Antiquarian Library contains translations of a number of the English chronicles: *Henry of Huntingdon* (translated by T. FORESTER, London, 1853); *Ordericus Vitalis* (translated by T. FORESTER, 4 vols., London, 1853–56); *Giraldus Cambrensis* (translated by R. C. HOARE, London, 1863); *Roger of Hoveden* (translated by H. T. RILEY, 2 vols., London, 1853); *Roger of Wendover* (translated by J. A. GILES, 2 vols., London, 1849); *Matthew Paris* (translated by J. A. GILES, London, 3 vols., 1852–54); *Florence of Worcester* (translated by T. FORESTER, London, 1854); *William of Malmesbury* (translated by J. A. GILES, London, 1841); the so-called "Matthew of Westminster" (translated by C. D. YONGE, 2 vols., London, 1853). Recent translations are L. C. JANE, editor, *The chronicle of Jocelin of Brakelond, monk of St. Edmundsbury*, New York and Oxford, 1922, and *The autobiography of Guibert, abbot of Nogent-sous-Coucy*, translated by C. C. S. BLAND, New York, 1926.

II

POLITICAL THOUGHT

Conceptions of the nature of law and of the relation of law to the state. This is a central issue in medieval political thought. Many of its most characteristic contributions center round it. F. L. G. v. RAUMER, *Geschichtliche Entwicklung der Begriffe von Recht, Staat und Politik*, Leipzig, 1861. O. SCHILLING, *Naturrecht und Staat nach der Lehre der alten Kirche*, Paderborn, 1914 (Görresgesellschaft, Sektion für Rechts und Sozialwissenschaft,

24). F. KERN, "Über die mittelalterliche Anschauung vom Recht," *H.Z.*, CXV (1916), 496–515; "Recht und Verfassung im Mittelalter," *H.Z.*, CXX (1919), 1–79. J. PETRAU-GAY, *La notion de "Lex" dans la coutume salienne*, Grenoble, 1920. F. L. GANSHOF, "Note sur la compétence des cours féodales en France," *Mélanges Pirenne*, 161–70. A. SCHUBERT, *Augustin's "lex-aeterna" Lehre nach Inhalt und Quellen*, Münster, 1924, vol. XXIV, pt. 2 of no. **826**. M. GRABMANN, "Das Naturrecht der Scholastik von Gratian bis Thomas von Aquin" in his *Mittelalterliches Geistesleben*, Munich, 1926. L. BAUR, "Die Lehre vom Naturrecht bei Bonaventura," *Festschrift Baeumker*. P. ODON LOTTIN, "Le droit naturel chez S. Thomas et ses prédécesseurs," *Ephémérides lovanienses* (1924–25). B. C. KUHLMANN, O. P., *Der Gesetzesbegriff beim hl. Thomas von Aquin im Lichte des Rechtsstudiums seiner Zeit*, Bonn, 1912. W. STOCKUMS, *Die Unveränderlichkeit des natürlichen Sittengesetz in der scholastischen Ethik* (Freiburger theol. Studien, herausgegeben von G. HOBERG und G. PFEILSCHRIFTER, Heft 4, 1911). R. BEDEL, *La notion de la loi chez théologiens et canonistes du XIIIe siècle*, Paris, 1914.

Ideas of kingship, divine right and the right of resistance. J. DICKINSON, "The mediaeval conception of kingship and some of its limitations," *Speculum*, I (1926), 308–37. L. K. BORN, "The perfect prince," *Speculum*, IV (1928), 470–504. W. MUNCH, *Gedanken über Fürstenerziehung aus alter und neuer Zeit*, Munich, 1909. A. DE POORTER, *Le traité Eruditio regum et principum de Gilbert de Tournai* (Les philosophes belges, IX, 1914), contains the text and a study of this book, dating from 1259. It is based largely on the *Policraticus* of John of Salisbury. A. KUHNE, *Das Herrscherideal des Mittelalters und Kaiser Friedrich I*, Leipzig, 1898 (Leipziger Studien aus dem Gebiet der Geschichte, vol. V, pt. 2). J. N. FIGGIS, *The divine right of kings*, 2nd edition, Cambridge, 1914. M. BLOCH, *Les rois thaumaturges, études sur le charactère surnaturel attribué à la puissance royale, particulièrement en France et en Angleterre*, Paris and Strasburg, 1924. K. VON AMIRA, *Der Stab in der germanischen Rechtssymbolik*, Munich, 1909 (*Abh. Munich Acad.*, vol. 25, pt. 1). F. KERN, *Gottesgnadentum und Widerstandsrecht im früheren Mittelalter. Zur Entwicklungsgeschichte der Monarchie*, Leipzig, 1914. (Mittelalterliche Studien herausgegeben von FRITZ KERN, Vol. I, heft 2.) O. KELLNER, *Das Majestätsverbrechen im deutschen Reich bis zur Mitte des 14 Jahrhunderts*, Halle, 1911 (Diss.). A. ESMEIN, "La maxime 'princeps legibus solutus' dans l'ancien droit public français," *Oxford essays in legal history*, editor, P. VINOGRADOFF, Oxford, 1913. K. BRANDL, "Erbrecht und Wahlrecht," *H.Z.*, CXXIII (1921), 221–38. U. STUTZ, "Zur Geschichte der deutschen Königwahlrechts im Mittelalter," *Zeitschrift der Savigny Stiftung für Rechtsgeschichte, Germanistische Abteilung*, XLIV (1924), 263–315; "Neue Forschungen zur Geschichte des deutschen Königwahlrechts," *ibid.*, XLVII (1927), 646–85. E. HOYER, "Die Selbstwahl vor, in und nach der Goldenen Bulle," *ibid.*, XLII (1921), 1–109.

Medieval ideas of sovereignty. F. v. BEZOLD, "Die Lehre von der Volkssouveranität während des Mittelalters," *H.Z.*, XXXVI (1876), 313–67. E. CROSA, *Il principio della sovranità popolare dal medioevo alla rivoluzione* *francese*, Turin, 1914 (Biblioteca di scienze moderne, 70). J. RICKABY, "Contract as the origin of government," *American catholic quarterly*, XXXV (1910), 548–57, 624–32. A. FLICHE, "Les théories germaniques de la souveraineté à la fin du XIe siècle," *R.H.*, CXXV (1917), 1–67.

Ideas of the relation of temporal and spiritual power. O. GIERKE, "Die theokratische Idee des Mittelalters," in *Johannes Althusius und die Entwicklung der naturrechtlichen Staatstheorien*, 2nd edition, Breslau, 1902. W. OHR, *Der karolingische Gottesstaat in Theorie und Praxis*, Leipzig, 1902 (Diss.). R. LANE-POOLE, *Illustrations of the history of medieval thought*, 2nd ed., London, 1920, chs. VIII, IX. P. KIRN, "Der mittelalterliche Staat und das geistliche Gericht," *Zeitschrift der Savigny-Stiftung*, XLVI (1926), Kanonistische Abteilung 15, pp. 162–99. W. KISSLING, *Das Verhältnis zwischen Sacerdotium und Imperium*, Paderborn, 1921 (Görresgesellschaft, Veröffentlichungen der Sektion für Rechts-und Sozialwissenschaft, Heft 38). F. BAETHGEN, "Der Anspruch des Papsttums auf das Reichsvikariat," *Zeitschrift der Savigny-Stiftung*, XLI (1920), Kanonistische Abteilung 10, pp. 168–268. A. HAUCK, *Der Gedanke der päpstlichen Weltherrschaft bis auf Bonifaz VIII*, Leipzig, 1904. A. M. KOENIGER, "Prima sedes a nemine iudicatur," *Beiträge des christlichen Altertums, Festgabe für A. Ehrhard*, Bonn, 1922, 273–300. F. GILLMANN, "Romanus pontifex iura omnia in scrinio pectoris sui habere," *Archiv für katholisches Kirchenrecht*, CVI (1926), 156–74. A. J. CARLYLE, "Le développement de la théorie de l'autorité pontificale en matière temporelle chez les canonistes de la seconde moitié du XIII siècle," *Revue historique de droit français et étranger*, V (1926), 4th série, 591–612. F. MASERA, *La politica della chiesa di S. Tommaso di Dante*, part I, Chieri, 1912.

Ideas of a world-state. J. KARST, *Die antike Idee der Oekumene in ihrer politischen und kulturellen Bedeutung*, Leipzig (1903). J. N. FIGGIS, "Res publica christiana," *Trans. R.H.S.*, 3rd series, V (1911), 63–88. F. KERN, *Humana Civilitas. Eine Dante-Untersuchung*, Leipzig, 1913. R. WALLACH, *Das abendländische Gemeinschaftsbewusstsein im Mittelalter*, Leipzig, 1928, vol. 34 of no. **749.** A. C. KREY, "The international state of the middle ages," *A.H.R.*, XXVII (1922), 1–12. J HARTUNG, *Die Lehre von der Weltherrschaft im Mittelalter*, Halle, 1909. W. M. RAMSAY, *The imperial peace: an ideal in European history*, Oxford, 1913. F. KAMPERS, *Die deutsche Kaiseridee in Prophetie und Sage*, Munich, 1896 (2nd edition of *Kaiserprophetieen und Kaisersagen im Mittelalter*, Munich, 1895); *Alexander der Grosse und die Idee des Weltimperiums in Prophetie und Sage*, Freiburg, 1901. M. POMTOW, *Über den Einfluss der altrömischen Vorstellungen vom Staat auf die Politik Kaiser Friedrichs I*, Halle, 1885. H FINKE, *Weltimperialismus und nationale Regungen im späteren Mittelalter*, Freiburg, 1916. E. WILL, *Die Gutachten des Oldradus de Ponte zum Prozess Heinrichs VII gegen Robert von Neapel*, Berlin and Leipzig, 1917 (*Abh. m.n.G.*, Heft 65) contains an account of one of the early denials of the theory of world-empire. UBERTUS DE LAMPUGNANO, *Utrum omnes christiani subsunt romano imperio* (1380) is a brief tract reprinted and edited in *Zeitschrift für geschichtliche Rechtswissenschaft*, II (1816), 238–56. Also see below under ST. AUGUSTINE and DANTE.

Peace, war, and international relations. H. Prutz, "Die Friedensidee im Mittelalter," *S.B. Vienna Acad.*, 1915. E. Nys, *Les origines du droit international*, Brussels and Paris, 1894. C. L. Lange, *Histoire de l'internationalisme*, vol. I, New York and Christiania, 1919. A. Vanderpool, *Le droit de guerre d'après les théologiens et les canonistes du moyen âge*, Paris, 1911. G. Ermini, *I trattati della guerra et della pace di Giovanni da Legnano*, Imola, 1923. G. da Legnano, *De bello, de repraesaliis et de duello*, edited by T. E. Holland with a translation by J. L. Brierly, Oxford, 1917 (Carnegie Endowment for International Peace, Classics of international law, no. 8). M. Novacovitch, *Les compromis et les arbitrages internationaux du XII au XV siècle*, Paris, 1905 (Diss.). J. Dumont, *Corps universel diplomatique du droit des gens*, Amsterdam, 1726–31, contains medieval materials in the first three volumes.

Political theories of St. Augustine. Roland-Gosselin, *La morale de Saint Augustin*. O. Schilling, *Die Staats- und Soziallehre des hl. Augustin*, Freiburg, 1910. B. Seidel, *Die Lehre des hl. Augustinus vom Staate*, 1909, vol. IX, pt. 1 of no. **490.** E. Troeltsch, *Augustin, die christliche Antike und das Mittelalter im Anschlusz an die Schrift "De civitate Dei,"* Munich and Berlin, 1915. E. Salin, *Civitas Dei*, Tübingen, 1926. Figgis, *The political aspects of St. Augustine's City of God*. E. Bernheim, "Politische Begriffe des Mittelalters im Lichte der Anschauungen Augustins," *Deutsche Zeitschrift für Geschichtswissenschaft*, Neue Folge, I (1897), 1–23. C. Mirbt, *Die Stellung Augustins in der Publizistik der gregorianischen Kirchenstreits*, Leipzig, 1888.

Miscellaneous political writers before St. Thomas Aquinas. E. Troeltsch, *Die Soziallehren der christlichen Kirchen*, 178–358. F. Kolde, *Das Staatsideal des Mittelalters*, Berlin, 1902. F. P. Bliemetzrieder, *Zu den Schriften Ivos von Chartres* (*S. B. Vienna Akad.*, vol. 182, Abhandlung 6), 1917. M. T. Stead, "Manegold of Lautenbach," *E.H.R.*, XXIX (1914), 1–15. For more detailed references on the polemical literature of the investiture controversy, see above, outline XVI. Imbart de la Tour, "L'évolution des idées sociales du XIe au XIIe siècle," *Séances et travaux de l'Académie des sciences morales*, Paris, 1898. E. W. Meyer, *Staatstheorien Papst Innocent III* (Jenaer historische Arbeiten, Heft 9), Bonn, 1920.

John of Salisbury. P. Gennrich, *Die Staats- und Kirchenlehre Johannes von Salisbury*, Gotha, 1894. E. Schubert, *Die Staatslehre Johanns von Salisbury*, Berlin, 1897. H. Hublocher, *Helinand von Froidmont und sein Verhältnis zu Johannes von Salisbury*, Regensburg, 1913. For a translation of portions of the *Policraticus* see above under "Original Sources"; for other books on John of Salisbury and editions of his writings see outline XVIII.

Saint Thomas Aquinas. C. Jourdain, *La philosophie de Saint Thomas d'Aquin*, 2 vols., Paris, 1858. A. D. Sertillanges, *La philosophie morale de Saint Thomas d'Aquin*, 2nd edition, Paris, 1922. H. R. Feugueray, *Essai sur les doctrines politiques de Saint Thomas d'Aquin*, Paris, 1857. J. J.

BAUMANN, *Die Staatslehre des hl. Thomas von Aquino*, Leipzig, 1873. E. CRAHAY, *La politique de S. Thomas d'Aquin*, Louvain, 1896. A. MALAGOLA, *Le teorie politiche di S. Tommaso d'Aquino*, Bologna, 1912. J. ZEILLER, *L'idée de l'état dans Saint Thomas d'Aquin*, Paris, 1910. B. ROLAND-GOSSELIN, *La doctrine politique de Saint Thomas d'Aquin*, Paris, 1928. SCHILLING, *Die Staats- und Soziallehre des hl. Thomas von Aquin*. W. MÜLLER, *Der Staat in seinen Beziehungen zur sittlichen Ordnung bei Thomas von Aquin*, Münster, 1916, vol. XIX, pt. 1 of no. **826**. O. RENZ, *Die Synteresis nach dem hl. Thomas von Aquin*, 1911 (*ibid.*, vol. 10, pts. 1–2). E. MURPHY, *St. Thomas's political doctrine and democracy*, Catholic University of America, 1921. For translations from the political writings of St. Thomas see COKER, *Readings in political philosophy*, above. For editions and general literature see outline XVII.

Pierre Dubois. E. H. MEYER, *Die Staats- und völkerrechtlichen Ideen von Peter Dubois*, Leipzig, 1908 (Diss.). E. ZECK, *Der Publizist Pierre Dubois: seine Bedeutung im Rahmen der Politik Phillips IV des Schönen und seine litterarische Denk- und Arbeitsweise im Traktat*, "De recuperatione terre sancte," Berlin, 1911. RENAN, *Etudes sur la politique religieuse du règne de Philippe le Bel*, Paris, 1899. F. M. POWICKE, "Pierre Du Bois" in *Historical essays* (edited by TOUT and TAIT, London, 1902), pp. 169–91. For edition of *De recuperatione terrae sanctae* see under "Original Sources." For references on the controversy between Boniface VIII and Philip the Fair, see outlines XXV and XXIX.

Dante. H. KELSEN, *Die Staatslehre des Dante Alighieri*, Vienna and Leipzig, 1905. F. ERCOLE, *Il pensiero politico di Dante*, 2 vols., Milan, 1927–28. A. SOLMI, *Il pensiero politico di Dante*, Florence, 1922. E. FLORI, *Dell' idea imperiale di Dante*, Bologna, 1921. B. NARDI, "Il concetto dell' impero nello suolgimento del pensiero dantesco," *Giornale storico della lett. ital.*, LXXVIII, 1–52. L. PRIEUR, *Dante et l'ordre social: Le droit public dans la Divine Comédie*, Paris, 1923. S. VENTO, *Dante e il diritto pubblico italiano*, Palermo, 1920; *La filosofia politica di Dante nel De monarchia studiata in se stesse e in relazione alla pubblicistica medievale da S. Tommaso a Marsilio da Padova*, Torino, 1921. J. WILLIAMS, *Dante as a jurist*, Oxford, 1906. J. J. ROLBIECKI, *The political philosophy of Dante Alighieri*, Washington, 1921. A. H. GILBERT, *Dante's conception of justice*, Durham, N. C., 1925. L. PICECE, *La filosofia politica di Dante nel De monarchia*, Naples, 1921. P. FOURNIER, *La Monarchie de Dante et l'opinion française*, Abbéville, 1921. F. WIEGAND, *Dante und Kaiser Heinrich VII*, Griefswald, 1922. E. JORDAN, "Dante et la théorie romaine de l'empire," *Revue historique de droit français et étranger*, XLV (1921), 353–96; *ibid.*, 4th series, I (1922), 333–90. C. NEGRONI, *Dante Alighieri e Bartolo da Sassoferrato*, Lonigo, 1890. A. CAPPALAGORA, *La politica di Dante e di Marsilio da Padova*, Turin, 1906. W. H. V. READE, *Dante, De monarchia, the Oxford text with an introduction on the political theory of Dante*, Oxford, 1916. For other editions and translations of the *De monarchia*, see above under "Original Sources." For general literature on Dante see outline XXVIII.

Marsiglio of Padua and William of Ockam. W. A. SCHREIBER, *Die politischen und religiösen Doctrinen unter Ludwig dem Baier*, Landshut, 1858. G. VON LECHLER, *Der Kirchenstaat und die Opposition gegen den päpstlichen Absolutismus im Anfange des 14 Jahrhunderts*, Leipzig, 1870. S. RIEZLER, *Die literarischen Widersacher der Päpste zu Zeit Ludwig des Bayers*, Leipzig, 1874. R. SCHOLZ, *Studien über die politischen Streitschriften des 14 und 15 Jahrhunderts*, Rome, 1909 (Quellen und Forschungen aus italienischen Archiven und Bibliotheken, no. 12). A. BAUDRILLARD, "Les idées qu'on se faisait au XIVe siècle sur le droit d'intervention du souverain pontif dans les affaires politiques," *Revue d'histoire et de littérature religieuse* (1898). J. SULLIVAN, "Marsiglio of Padua and William of Ockam," *A.H.R.*, II (1896–97), 409–26, 593–610. C. K. BRAMPTON, "Marsiglio of Padua, life," *E.H.R.*, XXXVII (1922), 501ff. C. W. PREVITÉ-ORTON, "Marsiglio of Padua, doctrines," *E.H.R.*, XXXVIII (1923), 1–18. E. EMERTON, *The "Defensor pacis" of Marsiglio of Padua, a critical study*, Cambridge, 1920. E. RUFFINI AVONDO, "Il 'Defensor pacis' di Marsilio da Padova," *Rivista storica italiana*, XLI (1924), 127ff. N. VALOIS, "Jean de Jandun et Marsile de Padove, auteurs de 'Defensor pacis,'" *Histoire littéraire de France*, XXXIII (1906), 528–623. MARIAN J. TOOLEY, "The authorship of the Defensor pacis," *Trans.*, *R.H.S.*, 4th series, IX (1926), 85–106. J. A. SULLIVAN, "The manuscripts and date of Marsiglio of Padua's 'Defensor pacis,'" *E.H.R.*, XX (1905), 293ff. R. SCHOLZ, "Zur Datierung und Überlieferung des Defensor pacis von Marsilius von Padua," *N.A.*, XLVI (1926), 490ff. L. STIEGLITZ, *Die Staatstheorie des Marsilius von Padua*, Leipzig, 1914, vol. XIX of no. **749.** M. GUGGENHEIM, "Marsilius von Padua und die Staatslehre des Aristoteles," *H.V.J.S.*, VII (1904), 343–62. R. SCHOLZ, "Marsilius von Padua und die Idee der Demokratie," *Zeitschrift für Politik*, I (1908), 61–95. H. FINKE, "Zu Dietrich von Niem und Marsilius von Padua," *Römische Quartal-Schrift*, VII. A. FRANK, *Réformateurs et publicistes de l'Europe: moyen âge*, Paris, 1864. J. SILBERNAGE, "Wilhelms von Occam Ansichten über Kirche und Staat," *Hist. Jahrbuch*, VII (1886), 423–33. W. MULDER, "Gulielmi Ockham tractatus de imperatorum et pontificum potestate," *A.F.H.*, XVI (1923), 469–92, and XVII (1924), 72–97.

Miscellaneous works on medieval political thought after St. Thomas Aquinas. E. MÜLLER, *Peter von Prezza, ein Publizist der Zeit des Interregnums*, Heidelberg, 1913 (Heidelberg. Abh. 37). W. SCHRAUB, *Jordan von Osnabrück und Alexander von Roes*, Heidelberg, 1910 (*ibid.*, no. 26). A. POSCH, *Die Staats- und kirchenpolitische Stellung Engelberts von Admont*, Paderborn, 1920 (Görresgesellschaft, Veröffentlichungen der Sektion für Rechts-und Sozialwissenschaft, Heft 37). H. MEYER, *Lupold von Bebenburg, Studien zu seinen Schriften*, 1909, vol. VII, pts. 1–2 of no. **898.** WOOLF, *Bartolus of Sassoferrato*. G. SALVEMINI, "La teoria del Bartolo da Sassoferrato sulle constituzioni politiche," *Studi storici*, Florence, 1901. J. B. SCHWAB, *Johannes Gerson, Professor der Theologie und Kanzler der Universität Paris*, Wurzburg, 1858. T. STUMPF, *Die politische Ideen des Nicolaus* *von Cues*, Cologne, 1865. F. SCHARPFF, *Nicolaus v. Cusa als Reformator in Kirche, Reich und Philosophie*, Tübingen, 1871. L. THORNDIKE, "Lippus Brandolinus de Comparatione rei publicae et regni," *Political science quarterly*, XLI (1926), 413–35. V. BRANTS, *Esquisse des théories économiques professées par les écrivains des XIIIe et XIVe siècles*, Louvain, 1895.

Original sources. Most of the important political treatises written before 1200 are printed among the works of their respective authors in MIGNE, *Pat. lat.* (no. **953**). *M.G.H.* (no. **978**), *Libelli de lite*, 3 vols. contains the literature of the Investiture conflict, including Manegold of Lautenbach, Hugh of Fleury, Honorius of Augsburg, Petrus Crassus and Gerhoh of Reichersberg. For the controversies after the end of the thirteenth century see the great collection of MELCHIOR GOLDAST, *Monarchia sancti romani imperii: sive tractatus de jurisdictione imperiali et pontificia*, 3 vols., Frankfurt and Hanover, 1611–14, containing, among others, works of John of Paris, Marsiglio of Padua, William of Ockam, Gerson, and Aeneas Silvius. This collection is rare. Other collections which include important political works are SCHARD, *De iurisdictione auctoritate et praeeminentia imperiali ac potestate ecclesiastica*, Basel, 1566, which contains the treatise of Lupold of Bebenburg and the "De concordantia catholica" of Nicholas of Cues; LUC D'ACHERY, *Spicilegium*, 3 vols., 2nd edition, Paris, 1723. For editions of Augustine, John of Salisbury, Albertus Magnus, St. Thomas Aquinas, Gerson, etc., see index under name of author. Works printed in separate modern editions are: *De duodecim abusivis saeculi*, editor, S. HELLMANN, Leipzig, 1910 (Texte und Untersuchungen zur Geschichte der altchristlichen Literatur, editors, HARNACK and SCHMIDT); SEDULIUS SCOTUS, *Liber de rectoribus christianis*, editor, S. HELLMANN, Munich, 1920 (Quellen und Untersuchungen zur latein. Philol. des Mittelalters, editor, TRAUBE, I, 1); HINCMAR OF RHEIMS, *De ordine palatii*, editor, M. PROU, Paris, 1885, part 58 of no. **888**; *Li livres du gouvernement des rois; a 13th century French version of Egidio Colonna's treatise De regimine principum*, editor, S. P. MOLENAER, New York, 1899; PIERRE DUBOIS, *De recuperatione terrae sanctae*, in *Collection de textes pour servir à l'étude de l'histoire*, editor, LANGLOIS, Paris, 1891; DANTE, *De monarchia*, text edited by E. MOORE with an introduction on the political theory of Dante by W. H. V. READE, Oxford, 1916; *The defensor pacis of Marsilius of Padua*, edited by C. W. PREVITÉ-ORTON, Cambridge, 1928; *Marsilius of Padua, Defensor minor*, editor, C. K. BRAMPTON, Birmingham, 1922. The following works of Wyclif published by the Wyclif society have political importance: *De civili dominio* (editor, R. L. POOLE, 1885 and J. LOSERTH, 1900–04); *De dominio divino* (editor, R. L. POOLE, 1890); *De officio regis* (editors, POLLARD and SAYLE, 1887); *De potestate papae* (editor, LOSERTH, 1907). The list of translated works is practically exhausted by the following: ST. AUGUSTINE, *The city of God* (old translation, 1610, by J. HEALEY), 2 vols., Edinburgh, 1909; 3 vols., London, 1903 (The temple classics). A more recent translation is by M. DODS, 2 vols., Edinburgh, 1871. ST. BERNARD OF CLAIRVAUX, *On consideration*, translated by G. LEWIS, Oxford, 1908. JOHN OF SALISBURY, *The statesman's book of John of*

Salisbury, being the 4th, 5th, and 6th books, and selections from the 7th and 8th books, of the "Policraticus," translated and edited with an introduction and notes by J. Dickinson, New York, 1927. *The "De monarchia" of Dante Alighieri,* edited with translation by Aurelia Henry, and by P. H. Wicksteed, see p. 544. William of Ockam, *Dialogus,* translated by John Trevisa in *Trevisa's Dialogus,* edited by A. J. Perry for E. E. T. S. (London, 1925). Emerton, *Humanism and tyranny,* contains translations of works of Coluccio Salutati and Bartolus on tyranny.

John Dickinson.

XXVI. MEDIEVAL BOOKS AND LIBRARIES

A. Outline

1. The importance of the invention of printing in the history of culture. The intellectual life of ancient and medieval times was conditioned in large measure by the lack of a cheap and rapid method of multiplying books.

2. Materials for book-making. Papyrus. Parchment and vellum. Waxed tablets. Paper. The introduction of paper into western Europe.

3. Writing implements. Stilus for waxed tablets. Reed (*calamus*), and quill (*penna*). Black ink (*atramentum* or *incaustum*). Red ink (*minium* or *rubrica*). Gold and silver writing on purple vellum. Implements for ruling and erasing.

4. Forms of books. The roll (*liber, volumen, rotulus*). "Pipe roll." "Master of the Rolls." The codex was the ordinary style of book in the middle ages. Forms of public documents (diplomatics). Seals (sphragistics). Palimpsests.

5. Latin palaeography. Book-hand and cursive writing. Majuscule writing; capitals and uncials. Minuscule book-hands. The famous Caroline minuscule writing (see outline VIII). Distinct characteristics of writing in different countries. Elegance of the book-hand in the twelfth century. Compressed "Gothic" writing of the thirteenth century. Increase of abbreviations and contractions. Tironian notes or short-hand. Official and legal scripts. Degeneracy of writing in the fourteenth and fifteenth centuries. Reversion of the humanists to older forms of medieval writing, which they called "Roman" script. The effect of style and habits of handwriting upon the art of printing.

6. The ornamentation of books. Illuminated manuscripts. Ornamental titles and initials, usually in red ink. Rubrics. Ornate margins and miniature paintings. The use of gold and silver in this art. Costly bindings.

7. The making of books and the book trade. Medieval scribes or copyists, especially monks and nuns. The *scriptorium* in a monastery. Correction of copies. The commonest errors in manuscripts. The scribes of official documents (see outline XIX). Professional lay scribes under the jurisdiction of medieval universities. Beginnings of a book-trade in medieval university towns. The *stationarii* and *librarii.* The price of books.

8. The love of books in the middle ages. The collection of St. Louis (Louis IX of France) in the Sainte Chapelle. Richard of Bury (1287–1345), the typical bibliophile, author of the *Philobiblon*.

9. The censorship of books before the establishment of the Congregation of the Index in 1571. For the condemnation of books of Abelard and Aristotle see outlines XIV and XV.

10. The beginnings of medieval libraries. The almost complete disappearance of ancient classical books and libraries. Foundation and growth of monastic libraries. Some famous early libraries: Monte Cassino, Bobbio, Fleury, Cluny, St. Riquier, Corbie, Tours, St. Germain-des-Prés, Fulda, Reichenau, St. Gall, Canterbury, and York. Libraries attached to cathedrals.

11. Striking increase in the multiplication and collection of books in the twelfth and thirteenth centuries. Private collections by kings and princes. The beginnings of college libraries in universities. Founders and patrons of medieval libraries. The libraries of Paris.

12. Arrangements and rules in medieval libraries. The *armarium* or book-press. The *armarius*. Need of a special room set aside for books. The lectern system. The stall system. Chained books. Sources of income. Donors of books. Readers in a medieval library. Library hours. The loan of books, especially to university students. Catalogues of medieval libraries. Their value as sources for the history of culture. The destruction of medieval books and libraries. The dispersion of books which survived.

13. Medieval archives. The papal archives in the Lateran palace. Remarkable preservation of the contents of English archives.

B. Special Recommendations for Reading

Short general account. Michael, *Culturzustände des deutschen Volkes*, III, 1–62. L. Traube, *Zur Paläographie*, vol. I of his *Vorlesungen*, 83–127. Haskins, *Renaissance*, ch. III.

Books and their makers. G. H. Putnam, *Books and their makers during the middle ages*, 2 vols., New York, 1896–97, vol. I, part I, "Books in manuscript." C. Davenport, *The book: its history and development*, New York, 1908, chs. II–III. R. Pietschmann, "Das Buch," in *Die Kultur der Gegenwart*, I, part I, 2nd edition, Berlin, 1912, 556–80. R. K. Root, "Publication before printing," *P.M.L.A.*, XXVIII (1913), 417–31. K. Löffler, *Einführung in die Handschriftenkunde*, Leipzig, 1929. K. Haebler, *Handbuch der Inkunabulenkunde*, Leipzig, 1925.

Writing in the middle ages. E. M. Thompson, *Greek and Latin palaeography*, chs. II–V, XIII–XIX; *A companion to Latin studies*, 765–91. W. Wattenbach, *Das Schriftwesen im Mittelalter*, 3rd edition, Leipzig, 1896. E. A. Lowe, "Handwriting" (in Crump and Jacob, *Legacy*, 197–226).

Stationarii and librarii in Paris. P. Delalain, *Etude sur le libraire parisien du XIIIe au XVe siècle, d'après les documents publiés dans le Cartulaire de l'université de Paris*, Paris, 1891. See also Rashdall, *Universities*, I, 191, 415–18.

Censorship of books. G. H. Putnam, *The censorship of the church of Rome and its influence upon the production and distribution of literature*, 2 vols.,

New York and London, 1907, I, chs. I–III. For additional literature see his bibliography, pp. XVII–XXV of vol. I, and the books under outline XVI.

Short popular sketches of medieval libraries. F. A. GASQUET, *The old English Bible and other essays*, London, 1897; new edition, 1908, 1–53. J. W. CLARK, *Libraries in the medieval and renaissance periods*, Cambridge, 1894. E. C. RICHARDSON, *Beginnings of libraries*, Princeton, 1914. J. J. WALSH *The thirteenth, greatest of centuries*, ch. IX. E. A. SAVAGE, *The story of libraries and book-collecting*, London, 1909, especially chs. II and III. Article "Libraries," in *Ency. Brit. Cambridge history of English literature*, IV (1909), ch. XIX, "Foundation of libraries," by J. B. MULLINGER. F. MILKAU, "Die Bibliotheken," in *Die Kultur der Gegenwart*, I, part I, 2nd edition, Berlin, 1912, 580–629. J. LIPSIUS, *Brief outline of the history of libraries*, Chicago, 1907.

Standard works on medieval libraries. J. W. CLARK, *The care of books, an essay on the development of libraries from the earliest times*, Cambridge, 1901; 2nd edition, 1902; new and cheaper edition, 1909. E. EDWARDS, *Memoirs of libraries*, 2 vols., London, 1859; 2nd edition (partial), 1901, I, book II; *Libraries and founders of libraries*, London, 1864, chs. II–IV.

Original sources. The *Philobiblon* of RICHARD DE BURY, bishop of Durham, treasurer and chancellor of Edward III, edited and translated by E. C. THOMAS, London, 1888 (contains the Latin text also), the translation was issued separately under the title, *The love of books: the Philobiblon* of RICHARD DE BURY, London, 1902; 2nd edition, 1903 (The king's classics). RICHARD DE BURY, *Il Philobiblon: testo, note illustrative, traduzione e documenti*, edited by M. BESSO, Rome, 1914.

C. BIBLIOGRAPHY

General books. See the literature on the largest libraries in the world, nos. **3–6**; on palaeography, diplomatics, and sphragistics, nos. **212–49a**; also the pictorial works, nos. **187–207**, particularly **187**, **188**, and **207**. Many of the general histories of literature, nos. **782–814**, are useful; see especially **785**.

Books in the middle ages. A. CIM, *Le livre*, 5 vols., Paris, 1905–08. M. AUDIN, *Le livre*, 2 vols., Paris, 1924–26. E. EGGER, *Histoire du livre depuis ses origines jusqu'à nos jours*, 2nd edition, Paris, 1880. M. P. LOUISY, *Le livre et les arts qui s'y rattachent, depuis les origines jusqu'à la fin du XVIII*[e] *siècle*, Paris, 1886. G. MEIER, *Die Bücher im Mittelalter*, Einsiedeln, 1899 (extract from Pädagogische Blätter). V. GARDTHAUSEN, *Griechische Palaeographie*, I, *Das Buchwesen im Altertum und im byzantinischen Mittelalter*, 2nd edition, Leipzig, 1911. F. MADAN, *Books in manuscript: a short introduction to their study and use, with a chapter on records*, London, 1893; 2nd edition, 1920. *Mittelalterliche Handschriften: paläographische, kunsthistorische, literarische und bibliotheksgeschichtliche Untersuchungen*, Festgabe zum 60 Geburtstage von H. DEGERING, Leipzig, 1926.

I. TAYLOR, *A history of the transmission of ancient books to modern times*, Liverpool, 1889 (first written about 1828). CLARK, *The descent of manuscripts*. M. R. JAMES, *The wandering and homes of manuscripts*, London,

1919 (*S.P.C.K., Helps*, no. 17). John Rylands Library, Manchester, *Catalogue of an exhibition illustrating the transmission of the Bible*, Manchester, 1925. R. R. Steele, "What fifteenth-century books are about," *Library*, n.s. 4, 6, 8 (1903–07), *passim*. S. R. Maitland, *The dark ages*. F. W. Hall, *A companion to classical texts*, Oxford, 1913, ch. iv, "The history of Latin texts from the age of Charlemagne to the Italian renaissance," ch. ix, "The nomenclature of Greek and Latin manuscripts with the names of former possessors." C. I. and Mary A. Elton, *The great book-collectors*, London, 1893, chs. ii–v. W. Blades, *Books in chains and other bibliographical papers*, London, 1892 (Book lovers' library).

Book-making and book trade. A. A. Björnbo, "Ein Beitrag zum Werdegang der mittelalterlichen Pergamenthandschriften," *Zeitschrift für Bücherfreunde*, XI (1907–08). J. Loubier, "Die Herstellung der mittelalterlichen Bücher nach einer Miniatur des 12 Jahrhunderts," *ibid.*, XII (1908–09). A. Kirchhoff, *Die Handschriftenhändler des Mittelalters*, Leipzig, 1852; 2nd edition, 1853, with additions, in J. Petzholdt, *Anzeiger für Bibliographie und Bibliothekwissenschaft*, 1854. R. Focke and others, *Das Buchgewerbe und die Kultur*, six lectures, Leipzig, 1907. K. J. Benziger, *Geschichte des Buchgewerbes im fürstlichen Benediktinerstifte von Einsiedeln*, Einsiedeln, 1912. G. J. Gray, *The earlier Cambridge stationers and bookbinders and the first Cambridge printer*, Oxford, 1914, part I. H. P. Stokes, *Cambridge stationers, printers, bookbinders, etc.*, Cambridge, 1919. M. Spirgatis, *Personalverzeichniss der Pariser Universität von 1464 und die darin aufgeführten Handschriften- und Pergamenthändler*, Leipzig, 1888. E. Kirchner, *Das Papier*, Biberach, 1897. H. A. Maddox, *Paper: its history, sources, and manufacture*, London, 1917. H. Alibaux, *Les premières papeteries françaises*, Paris, 1926. T. F. Tout, *Mediaeval forgers and forgeries*, Manchester, 1920. H. Louhier, *Der Bucheinband von seinen Anfängen bis zum Ende des XVIII Jahrhunderts*, 2nd edition, Leipzig, 1926.

Illuminated manuscripts. J. A. Herbert, *Illuminated manuscripts*, New York, 1911. J. H. Middleton, *Illuminated manuscripts in classical and mediaeval times*, Cambridge, 1892. G. Vitzthum, *Die Pariser Miniaturmalerei von der Zeit des hl. Ludwig bis zu Philipp von Valois und ihr Verhältniss zur Malerei in Nordwesteuropa*, Leipzig, 1907. A. Molinier, *Les manuscrits et les miniatures*, Paris, 1892. H. M. R. Martin, *Les peintures de manuscrits et la miniature en France*, Paris, 1909. A. Labitte, *L'art de l'enluminure: métier, histoire, pratique*, Paris, 1914. J. Bradley, *Illuminated manuscripts*, Chicago, 1909; *Dictionary of miniaturists, illuminators, calligraphers and copyists*, 3 vols., London, 1887–89. W. de Gray Birch and H. Jenner, *Early drawings and illuminations: an introduction to the study of illustrated manuscripts*, London, 1897. E. M. Thompson, *English illuminated manuscripts*, London, 1895. H. Shaw, *A handbook of the art of illumination in the middle ages*, London, 1866. M. D. Wyatt, *The art of illuminating as practiced in Europe from the earliest times*, London, 1866. H. N. Humphreys, *Illuminated books of the middle aage*, London, 1848. A. Merten, *Die Buchmalerei in St. Gallen vom 9 bis zum 11 Jahrhundert*, Leipzig, 1912. A. Niedling,

Bücherornamentik in Miniaturen, Initialen usw., in historischer Darstellung vom 9–18 Jahrhundert, 2nd edition, Weimar, 1897. A. LECOY DE LA MARCHE, *Les manuscrits et la miniature*, new edition, Paris [1884]; in his *L'art d'enluminer*, Paris, 1890, he prints, with commentary, an ancient Latin tract entitled, *De arte illuminandi*, dating 1350–1400 A.D. S. FARNSWORTH, *Illumination and its development in the present day*, New York, 1922. D. V. THOMPSON, "Liber de coloribus illuminatorum sive pictorum from Sloane MS. no. 1754," *Speculum*, I (1926), 280–307. F. WICKHOFF, *Beschriebenes Verzeichniss der illuminierten Handschriften in Oesterreich*, 5 vols., Leipzig, 1905–10. H. FETT, *Miniatyrer fra islandske haandskrifter*, Bergen, 1911. English translation in *Sagabook of the Viking society*, VII, 111ff., 177ff. P. E. SCHRAMM, "Zur Geschichte der Buchmalerei in der Zeit der sächisschen Kaiser," *Jahrbuch für Kunstwissenschaft*, 1923, 54–82. *Beschriebende Verzeichniss der Miniaturen-Handschriften der preussischen Staatsbibliothek zu Berlin*, vols. 1–11, by J. KIRCHNER and H. WEGENER, Leipzig, 1926–28. R. CANTINELLI and E. DACIER, *Les trésors des bibliothèques de France*, 2 vols., Paris, 1927–29.

Facsimiles of illuminated manuscripts. *Reproductions de manuscrits et miniatures de la Bibliothèque nationale*, published under the direction of, and with notices by H. OMONT, Paris, 1901ff.; see also his *Listes des recueils de fac-similés et des reproductions de manuscrits conservés à la Bibliothèque nationale*, 2nd edition, Paris, 1912. *Société française pour la publication des livres à miniatures*, Paris, 1910ff. (interrupted in 1914). *Illuminated manuscripts in the British Museum. Miniatures, borders, and initials reproduced in gold and colours*, with descriptive text by G. F. WARNER, series 1–4, London, 1903. *Schools of illumination: reproductions from manuscripts in the British Museum*, part I, *Hiberno-Saxon and early English schools, A. D. 700–1000*, London, 1915; II, *English, 12th and 13th centuries*, 1915. *Reproductions from illuminated manuscripts in the British Museum*, by G. F. WARNER, series 1–4, London, 1910–28. F. G. KENYON, *Facsimiles of biblical manuscripts in the British Museum*, London, 1900. *Collection d'éditions photographiques de la Bibliothèque royale de Bruxelles. Le musée des enluminures*, Haarlem, 1904ff. L. v. KOBELL, *Kunstvolle Miniaturen mit Initialen aus Hss. des 4–16 Jahrhunderts*, 2nd edition, Munich, 1892 (from manuscripts in Munich). A. BOINET, *La miniature carolingienne*, Paris, 1913. A. DE BASTARD, *Peinture et ornements des manuscrits depuis le 14e siècle jusqu'au fin du 16e*, 2 vols., Paris, 1832ff. J. O. WESTWOOD, *Palaeographia sacra pictoria: being a series of 50 illustrations of the ancient versions of the Bible*, copied from illuminated manuscripts executed between the fourth and sixteenth centuries, London, 1843. J. P. MORGAN, *Catalogue of manuscripts of:* edited by M. R. JAMES with many plates, New York, 1906. *Illustrations from one hundred manuscripts in the library of Henry Yates Thompson*, consisting of 82 plates illustrating 16 manuscripts of English origin from the XIIth to the XVth centuries, 5 vols., London, 1907–18. L. DOREZ, *Les manuscrits à peintures de la bibliothèque de lord Leicester à Holhham Hall, Norfolk*, Paris, 1908. P. DURRIEU, *Les très riches heures de Jean de France, duc de Berry*,

Paris, 1914; *La miniature flamande au temps de la cour de Bourgogne (1415–1530)*, 2nd edition, Paris, 1926. J. EBERSOLT, *La miniature byzantine*, Paris, 1926. J. E. DARMON, *Dictionnaire des peintres-miniaturistes sur vélin, parchemin, ivoire et écaille*, Paris, 1927. H. MARTIN, *Les joyaux de l'enluminure à la Bibliothèque nationale*, Paris, 1928. H. FETT, *En islandsk tegnebog fra middelalderen*, Christiania, 1910. *Bulletin de la société française de reproductions de manuscrits à peintures*, Paris, 1911ff. G. LEIDINGER (editor), *Der Codex aureus der bayerischen Staatsbibliothek in München*, 6 vols., Munich, 1921–25. H. MARTIN, *La miniature française du XIIIe au XVe siècle*, Paris, 1923; 2nd edition, rev., 1927. P. D'ANCONA, *La miniature italienne du Xe au XVIe siècle*, Paris, 1925. K. LÖFFLER, *Der Landgrafenpsalter*, "*Eine Bilderhandschrift aus dem Anfang dies XIII Jahrhunderts in der württembergischen Landesbibliothek*," Leipzig, 1925. H. CORNELL, *Biblia pauperum*, Stockholm, 1925. E. BLOCHET, *Les enluminures des manuscrits orientaux de la Bibliothèque nationale*, Paris, 1926. PH. LAUER, *La miniature romane*, Paris, 1926; *La miniature gothique*, Paris, 1927. C. OURSEL, *La miniature du XIIe siècle à l'abbaye de Cîteaux, d'après les mss. de la Bib. de Dijon*, Dijon, 1926. E. G. MILLAR, *English illuminated manuscripts from the tenth to the thirteenth century*, Paris, 1926; *English illuminated manuscripts of the XIVth and XVth centuries*, Paris, 1928. *Manuscrits conservés en Belgique*, 1st series, fasc. A and B: *Bibliothèque publique de Bruges, miniatures des mss. 8 et 411*, edited by A. DE POORTER, Brussels, 1926ff. J. BOUISSOUNOUSE, *Jeux et travaux, d'après un livre d'heures du XVe siècle*, Paris, 1926. C. COUDERC, *Les enluminures des manuscrits du moyen âge (du VIe au XVe siècle): exposition de la Bibliothèque nationale*, Paris, 1926 (cf. *Speculum*, I, 217–18). A. W. BYVANCK and G. J. HOOGEWERFF, *La miniature hollandaise et les manuscrits illustrés du XIVe au XVIe siècle aux Pays-Bas septentrionaux*, The Hague, 1927. O. E. SAUNDERS, *English illumination*, 2 vols., Florence, 1928. A. GOLDSCHMIDT, *Die deutsche Buchmalerei*, Bd I. *Die karolingische Buchmalerei*, Bd II. *Die ottonische Buchmalerei*, Florence, 1928. J. D. BORDONI, *Spanish illumination*, 2 vols., Florence, 1929. For a bibliography of other reproductions of individual manuscripts containing miniatures, see J. A. HERBERT, *Illuminated manuscripts*, 333–7. Most of the general manuals on illuminated manuscripts also contain good facsimiles. See also nos. **230–37b.**

Waxed tablets in the middle ages. M. EDÉLSTAND DU MÉRIL, "De l'usage des tablettes en cire," in no **914.** L. SERBAT, *Tablettes à écrire du XIVe siècle*, Paris, 1914 (extract of Mémoires de la Société nationale des antiquaires de France, LXXIII). H. J. HUITFELDT-KAAS, *En notitsbog paa voxtavler fra Middelalderen*, Christiania, 1886.

Medieval libraries. F. S. MERRYWEATHER, *Bibliomania in the middle ages, with anecdotes illustrating the history of the monastic libraries of Great Britain*, London, 1849; reprinted with an introduction by C. ORR, New York, 1900. G. A. E. BOGENG, *Die grossen Bibliophilen*, 3 vols., Leipzig, 1922. E. A. SAVAGE, *Old English libraries: the making, collection, and use of books during the middle ages*, London and Chicago, 1912 (Antiquaries books).

S. GIBSON, *Some Oxford libraries*, Oxford, 1914. M. BEAZLEY, "History of the chapter library of Canterbury cathedral," *Transactions of the Bibliographical society*, London, VIII (1904–06), 113–85. M. R. JAMES, "On the abbey of S. Edmund at Bury," *Cambridge antiquarian society*, Cambridge, 1895. D. R. PHILLIPS, *The romantic history of the monastic libraries of Wales: from the fifth to the sixteenth centuries, Celtic and mediaeval periods*. London, 1912. E. BEGNI, *The Vatican*. M. MARRIER and A. DUCHESNE, *Bibliotheca cluniacensis*, Mâcon, 1915. E. G. VOGEL, *Literatur früherer und noch bestehender europäischer öffentlicher und Corporations-Bibliotheken*, Leipzig, 1840. F. EHRLE, *Historia bibliothecae romanorum pontificum*, Rome, 1890. E. MÜNTZ and P. FABRE, *La bibliothèque du Vatican au XVe siècle*, Paris, 1887, part of no. **887.** H. OMONT, *Recherches sur la bibliothèque de l'église cathédrale de Beauvais*, Paris, 1914 (extract from Mémoires de l'Académie des inscriptions et belles-lettres, XL). L. DELISLE, *Recherches sur l'ancienne bibliothèque de Corbie*, Paris, 1860. J. A. B. MORTREUIL, *L'ancienne bibliothèque de l'abbaye St. Victor* [of Marseilles], Marseilles, 1854, prints a list of books of this monastery, 1195–98 A.D., which includes several of the Latin classics. For the transmission of classical books see outline XVIII. E. OLMER, *Boksamlingar på Island 1179–1490 enligt diplom*, Gottenborg, 1902. ELLEN JÖRGENSEN, "Les bibliothèques danoises au moyen âge," *Nordisk Tidskrift för Bok- och Biblioteksväsen*, 1915. K. O. MEINSMA, *Middeleeuwsche Bibliotheken*, Zutphen, 1904. P. LEHMANN, "Johannes Sichardus und die von ihm benutsten Bibliotheken und Handschriften," *Quellen und Untersuchungen zur lateinischen Philologie des Mittelalters*, IV, part I. A. CZERNY, *Die Bibliothek des Chorherrenstiftes St. Florian: Geschichte und Beschreibung, ein Beitrag zur Kulturgeschichte Oesterreichs*, Linz, 1874. R. P. M. ZIEGELBAUER, *Historia rei literariae ordinis S. Benedicti*, 4 vols., 1754, vol. I, on Benedictine schools and libraries. C. SCHMIDT, "Livres et bibliothèques à Strasbourg au moyen-âge," *Annales de l'est*, Nancy, VII (1893), 538–93. L. TRAUBE, "Die Bibliotheken," in *Vorlesungen und Abhandlungen*, I, 103–27. E. G. VOGEL, "Einiges über Amt und Stellung des Armarius in den abendländischen Klöstern des Mittelalters," *Serapeum*, IV (1843), 17–29, 33–43, 49–55. A. BIRKENMAJER, *Bibljoteka Ryszarda de Furnival i jej pözniejszelosy*. [The library of Richard of Furnival (1201–60?) and its later fate.] Crakow. M. FLIEGEL, "Die Dombibliothek zu Breslau im ausgehenden Mittelalter," *Zeitschrift des Vereins für Geschichte Schlesiens*, LIII (1919), 84–133. J. DE GHELLINCK, "Un évêque bibliophile au XIVe siècle: Richard Aungerville de Bury (1345): contribution à l'histoire de la littérature et des bibliothèques médiévales," *Revue d'histoire ecclésiastique*, XVIII (1922), 271–312, 482–508; XIX (1923), 157–200. K. LÖFFLER, *Deutsche Klosterbibliotheken*, 2nd edition, Bonn and Leipzig, 1922. A. HESSEL, *Geschichte der Bibliotheken: ein Überblick von ihren Anfängen bis zur Gegenwart*, Göttingen, 1925. (Full bibliography, pp. 128–42.) R. BEER, "Handschriftenschätze Spaniens," *S.B., Vienna Acad.*, CXXIV–CXXVI, CXXVIII–CXXIX, CXXXI (1891–94); "Die Handschriften des Klosters Maria de Ripoll," *ibid.*, CLV, 3; CLVIII, 2 (1907–08). P. LEHMANN, *Cor-*

veyer Studien, Munich, 1919, *Abh. Munich Acad.*, XXX, 5 (1919). J. THEELE *Die Handschriften des Benediktinerklosters S. Petri zu Erfurt. Ein bibliotheksgeschichtlicher Rekonstruktionsversuch*, Leipzig, 1920. P. LEHMANN, "Quellen zur Feststellung und Geschichte mittelalterlicher Bibliotheken, Handschriften und Schriftsteller," *Hist. Jahrbuch*, XL (1920), 44–105; Fuldaer Studien, *S.B., Munich Acad.*, 3 (1925). H. SCHREIBER, *Die Bibliothek der ehemaligen Mainzer Kartause. Die Handschriften und ihre Geschichte*, Leipzig, 1927. G. MACON, *Chantilly: archives, le cabinet des titres*, vol. I, Paris, 1927.

Libraries in medieval Paris. A. FRANKLIN, *Les anciennes bibliothèques de Paris*, 3 vols., Paris, 1867–73 (Histoire générale de Paris); *La Sorbonne* is devoted in large part to the library. L. DELISLE, *Le cabinet des manuscrits de la Bibliothèque nationale: étude sur la formation de ce dépôt, comprenant les éléments d'une histoire de la calligraphie, de la miniature, de la reliure, et du commerce des livres à Paris avant l'invention de l'imprimerie*, 4 vols., Paris, 1868–81 (Histoire générale de Paris). H. MARCEL and others, *La Bibliothèque nationale*, 2 vols., Paris, 1907. T. MORTREUIL, *La Bibliothèque nationale*, Paris, 1878. A. FRANKLIN, *Histoire de la bibliothèque de l'abbaye de Saint-Victor à Paris*, Paris, 1865; *Recherches sur la bibliothèque de médecine de Paris*, Paris, 1864; *Recherches sur la bibliothèque publique de Notre-Dame de Paris au XIIIe siècle*, Paris, 1863. H. MEYER, "Mittelalterliche Bibliotheksordnungen für Paris und Erfurt," *Archiv für Kulturgeschichte*, XI (1913), 152–65. See also the general books on medieval Paris under outline XIII.

Catalogues of medieval libraries. T. GOTTLIEB, *Über mittelalterliche Bibliotheken*, Leipzig, 1890, additions by G. MEIER, *Centralblatt für Bibliothekswesen*, XX (1903), 16ff. T. GOTTLIEB, *Mittelalterliche Bibliothekskataloge Öesterreichs*, vol. I, Vienna, 1915. P. LEHMANN, *Mittelalterliche Bibliothekskataloge Österreichs*, vol. I, Vienna, 1915; *Mittelalterliche Bibliothekskataloge Deutschlands und der Schweiz*, 2 vols., Munich, 1918, 1928. G. BECKER, *Catalogi bibliothecarum antiqui*, Bonn, 1885, with additions by G. MEIER, *ibid.*, II (1885), 239–41. M. B. JAMES, *The ancient libraries of Canterbury and Dover: the catalogues of the libraries of Christ Church priory and St. Augustine's abbey at Canterbury and of St. Martin's priory at Dover*, Cambridge, 1903; "The catalogue of the library of the Augustinian friars at York," *Fasciculus Ioanni Willis Clark dicatus*, Cambridge, 1909, 2–96. F. EHRLE, "Un catalogo fin qui sconosciuto della biblioteca papale d'Avignone (1407)," *ibid.*, 97–114. H. DEGERING-BERLIN, "Der Katalog der Bibliothek des Klosters Marienfeld vom Jahre 1185," *Beiträge zum Bibliotheks- und Buchwesen Paul Schwenke gewidmet*, Berlin, 1913, 53–64. A. DANTIER, *Les monastères bénédictins d'Italie*, Paris, 1866, describes the contents of the library of Monte Cassino. For Cluny, see SACKUR, *Die Cluniacenser*. L. DELISLE, "Documents sur les livres et les bibliothèques au moyen âge," *B.E.C.*, 3rd series, I (1849), 216–31. *Catalogi veteres librorum, ecclesiae cathedralis Dunelm*, edited by B. BOTFIELD, *Surtees society*, VII (1840); *Notes on cathedral libraries of England*, London, 1849. For other catalogues see *Centralblatt für Bibliothekswesen;* E. EDWARDS, *Memoirs of libraries*, I, and nos. **951–52.**

Medieval archives. See the literature under outline XIX, especially BRESSLAU and GIRY, nos. **239–240.** For English archives see GROSS, no. **36,** pp. 77ff.

Bibliographies. A. HORTZSCHANSKY, *Bibliographie des Bibliotheks- und Buchwesens*, Leipzig, 1905ff., in *Beiheften* of *Centralblatt für Bibliothekswesen. Archiv für Bibliographie Buch- und Bibliothekswesen*, edited by M. GROLIG, Linz, 1926ff. E. M. THOMPSON, *Greek and Latin palaeography*, 571–83. PUTNAM, *Books and their makers*, I, XVII–XXVIII. J. A. HERBERT, *Illuminated manuscripts*, 331–40. E. A. SAVAGE, *Old English libraries*, 286–90.

XXVII. MEDIEVAL ART, ARCHITECTURE, AND MUSIC

A. OUTLINE

1. In the nineteenth century the prejudice against medieval art began to disappear. Today the word "Gothic," as applied in art, has lost all the connotations of barbarism which it suggested to the architects of the Italian renaissance. Importance of ecclesiastical and military architecture in medieval art.

2. The evolution of Christian art in the Greek East, especially in Constantinople. The influence of Byzantine art in the Latin West, especially in Rome and Ravenna. The basilica. For Rome see outline III, for Ravenna, outline II in part II, for Byzantine art, outline III in part II.

3. Merovingian and Carolingian art Paucity of remains from the Merovingian period. Byzantine influences in Carolingian art. For Charlemagne's chapel in Aix-la-Chapelle and his other buildings see outline VIII.

4. Romanesque art which culminated in the eleventh and early twelfth century. Compare with the evolution of Romanic languages. The finest specimens of romanesque ecclesiastical architecture are abbeys, not cathedrals. The French schools and the German and Lombard schools of romanesque art. The Norman genius exemplified in art. The abbey of Mont Saint-Michel.

5. Gothic art, the chief glory of the remarkable civilization of the twelfth and thirteenth centuries. The characteristic elements of the Gothic style are: the pointed arch, the flying buttress, and an original style of ornamentation, derived from nature and not from tradition. Northern France was the chief center of Gothic art.

6. Chief Gothic monuments in France. Notre Dame and the Sainte Chapelle of Paris. Amiens. Chartres. Rheims. Beauvais. For the churches of Paris see outline XIII.

7. Architects and workmen employed in building medieval cathedrals. Masters of masonry. Plans of medieval buildings. The cost of cathedrals and the methods of raising funds. It usually required many decades and sometimes several centuries to build the large cathedrals, and most of them were left incomplete.

8. Main features of a Gothic cathedral. Nave, aisle, transept, choir, apse, ambulatory, altar, chapel, ribbed vaulting, triforium, clerestory, façade, tower, porch, spire, flying buttress, rose-window, chapter house.

9. Symbolism in medieval art. Educative value of the elaborate medieval cathedrals, which served as important social as well as religious centers in medieval towns.

10. Civil and military architecture. For the latter see outline XXVII of part II.

11. Decorative arts. The sudden improvement of sculpture in the twelfth century employed chiefly in the internal and external decoration of cathedrals. The "beau Dieu d'Amiens." Gargoyles and grotesque figures on church buildings. Stained glass windows. The wonderful glass of Chartres cathedral and of the Saint Chapelle in Paris. Mural painting.

12. The minor arts and crafts in the middle ages: carving, metal-work, jewelry, enameling, tapestry-work, needle-work, etc. For the art of illuminating manuscripts see the previous outline.

13. Music. For Gregorian music see outline V in part II. Music as one of the seven liberal arts in the schools and universities. Musical theory and notation. The thirteenth and fourteenth centuries witnessed the highest development of medieval music, and its chief center was France. Musical instruments. For the music of the troubadours see outline XXIV.

I

General histories of art. See the pictorial and archaeological works, nos. **187–207, 299–302**; also nos. **108** and **111.** On military architecture, see outline XXVII in part II; on renaissance art, especially painting, outline XXXIII in part II. Some works on Christian iconography are listed under outline V. No attempt is made in the bibliography below to include works on early Christian art.

MILMAN, *History of Latin Christianity*, IX, 267–342. LAVISSE, *Histoire de France*, II, part I, 251–55, 349–56, part II, 399–411; III, part I, 323–27, part II, 413–29. LAVISSE et RAMBAUD, *Histoire générale*, II, 580–95. G. GRÖBER, *Grundriss*, vol. II, part III, 533–49. S. REINACH, *Apollo*, chs. XI–XIII. H. GARDNER, *Art through the ages; an introduction to its history and significance*, New York, 1926. L. HOURTICQ, *Encyclopédie des beaux-arts: architecture, sculpture, peinture, arts décoratifs*, 2 vols., Paris, 1925; *Ars una, histoire générale de l'art: France*, Paris, 1911; 2nd edition, 1914, has good bibliographies. H. TIETZE, *Methode der Kunstgeschichte, ein Versuch*, Leipzig, 1913.

A. MICHEL, *Histoire de l'art depuis les temps chrétiens jusqu'à nos jours*, 17 vols., Paris, 1905–28, vol. II, *L'art gothique*. W. LÜBKE, *Grundriss der Kuntsgeschichte*, 13th edition, 5 vols., Stuttgart, 1904–07; 14th edition, 1908ff.; translated by R. STURGIS, *Outlines of the history of art*, 2 vols., New York, 1904. A. SPRINGER, *Handbuch der Kunstgeschichte*, 5 vols., 8th edition, Leipzig, 1905–09, vol. II, *Das Mittelalter*. G. CAROTTI, *A history of art*, revised by Mrs. A. STRONG, vols. I, II, New York, 1908–09, vol. II, *The middle ages*. J. PIJOAN Y SOTERAS, *Historia del arte: el arte al traves de la historia*, 3 vols., Barcelona [1914ff.]; English translation by R. L. ROYS,

3 vols., New York, 1927. M. CARRIERE, *Die Kunst im Zusammenhang der Culturgeschichte*, 3rd edition, revised, 5 vols., Leipzig, 1877–86, vol. III, *Mittelalter*. C. WOERMANN, *Geschichte der Kunst aller Zeiten und Völker*, 3 vols., Leipzig, 1901–11, vol. II, *Die Kunst der christlichen Völker bis zum Ende des 15 Jahrhunderts*. H. KNACKFUSS and M. E. ZIMMERMANN, *Allgemeine Kuntsgeschichte*, 3 vols., Bielefeld, 1897–1903, vol. II, *Kunstgeschichte der Gotik und Renaissance*.

S. SPOONER, *A biographical dictionary of the fine arts*, 2 vols., New York, 1865. E. BÉNÉZIT, *Dictionnaire critique et documentaire des peintres, sculpteurs, dessinateurs et graveurs de tous les temps et de tous les pays*, Paris, 1911ff. U. THIEME and F. BECKER, *Allgemeines Lexikon der bildenden Künstler von der Antike bis zur Gegenwart*, Leipzig, 1907ff. (in process).

Early christian and Byzantine art. O. M. DALTON, *Byzantine art and archaeology*, Oxford, 1911. C. DIEHL, *Manuel d'art byzantin*, Paris, 1910; 2nd edition, 2 vols., 1926. J. STRZYGOWSKI, *Orient oder Rom: Beiträge zur Geschichte der spätantiken und frühchristlichen Kunst*, Leipzig, 1901. A. J. GAYET, *L'art byzantin d'après les monuments de l'Italie, de l'Istrie et de la Dalmatie*, 3 vols., Paris [1901–07]. C. BAYET, *L'art byzantin*, Paris, 1883; new edition, 1892.

Medieval art. A. VENTURI, *Storia dell' arte italiana*, vols. I–VII, Milan, 1901–15, vols. II–IV are especially valuable for the middle ages. F. X. KRAUS, *Geschichte der christlichen Kunst*, 3 vols., Freiburg, 1896–1908, vol. II, *Mittelalter*. C. SCHNAASE, *Geschichte der bildenden Künste im Mittelalter*, 7 vols., Düsseldorf, 1843–64; 2nd edition, 8 vols., 1865–79. R. BÜRKNER, *Geschichte der kirchlichen Kunst*, Freiburg, 1903; 3rd edition, Göttingen, 1907. H. V. D. GABELENTZ, *Die kirchliche Kunst im italienischen Mittelalter: ihre Beziehungen zu Kultur und Glaubenslehre*, Strasburg, 1907. A. N. DIDRON, *Iconographie chrétienne, histoire de Dieu*, Paris, 1843, part of no. **965**, translated by E. J. MILLINGTON, *Christian iconography: history of Christian art in the middle ages*, 2 vols., London, 1851. W. H. GOODYEAR, *Roman and mediaeval art*, New York, 1897, is a brief text-book.

C. ENLART, *Manuel d'archéologie française;* "The teaching of mediaeval archaeology," *Annual report A.H.A.* (1909), 105–14. The February, 1914, number of the *Revue de synthèse historique* is devoted entirely to the history of art. E. ANITCHKOF, "L'estétique au moyen-âge," *M.A.*, XX (1917–18), 221–58. W. R. LETHABY, *Mediaeval art from the peace of the church to the eve of the renaissance, 312–1350*, London, 1904; new edition, revised, 1912, is much inferior to the accurate volumes of ENLART. L. GONSE, *L'art gothique: l'architecture, la peinture, le décor, la sculpture*, Paris, no date, is better than LETHABY. L. BRÉHIER, *L'art byzantin*, Paris, 1924. O. M. DALTON, *Early Christian art*, London, 1925. J. STRZYGOWSKI, *Ursprung der christlichen Kirchenkunst*, Leipzig, 1920, translated by O. M. DALTON and H. J. BRAUNHOLTZ, *Origin of Christian art*, London, 1923. MARGUERITE VAN BERCHEM and E. CLOUZOT, *Mosaïques chrétiennes du IVe au Xe siècle*, Geneva, 1926. C. DIEHL, *L'art chrétien primitif et l'art byzantin*, Paris, 1928. M. LAURENT, *L'art chrétien primitif*, 2 vols., Brussels, 1919. O. WULFF,

Altchristliche und byzantinische Kunst, 2 vols., Berlin, 1914–18. J. WILBERT, *Die Malereien der Katakomben Roms*, 2 vols., Freiburg, 1903; *Die römischen Mosaiken und Malereien der kirchlichen Bauten vom IV bis XIII Jahrhundert*, 4 vols., Freiburg, 1916. E. B. SMITH, *Early Christian iconography and a school of ivory carvers in Provence*, Princeton, 1918. R. GARRUCCI, *Storia della arte cristiana nei primi otto secoli della chiesa*, 6 vols., Prate, 1873–81. H. KARLINGER, *Die Kunst der Gothik*, Berlin, 1927 (Propyläen Kunstgeschichte, fasc. 7). C. R. MOREY, *Sources of mediaeval style.* [In *Art bulletin* VII (1924), no. 2, also reprinted.] P. TOESCA, *Storia dell' arte italiana*, I, *Dalle origini cristiane alla fine del secolo XIII*, Turin, 1926. A. MAYER, *Gothik in Spanien*, Leipzig, 1928. J. PUIG Y CADAFALCH, *Le premier art roman*, Paris, 1928. G. DEHIO, *Geschichte der deutschen Kunst*, vol. I, Berlin, 1919.

Symbolism in medieval art. E. MÂLE, *L'art religieux du XIIIe siècle en France: étude sur l'iconographie du moyen âge et sur ses sources d'inspiration*, 3rd edition, revised, 1910, translated by DORA NUSSEY, *Religious art in France*, London and New York, 1913; and his *L'art religieux de la fin du moyen âge en France*, Paris, 1908 (see the review of this work in *R.S.H.*, XVIII, 1908, 311–30). E. MÂLE, *L'art religieux du XIIe siècle en France: étude sur les origines de l'iconographie du moyen âge*, Paris, 1922. Y. HIRN, *The sacred shrine.* J. RUSKIN, *The nature of Gothic: a chapter from The stones of Venice*, with a preface by W. MORRIS, Orpington, 1899. L. BRÉHIER, *L'art chrétien: son développement iconographique des origines à nos jours*, Paris, 1918. A. N. DIDRON, *Christian iconography*, translated by E. J. MILLINGTON. C. POHAULT DE FLEURY, *L'évangile: études iconographiques et archéologiques*, 2 vols., Tours, 1874; *La sainte vierge; études archéologiques et iconographiques*, Paris, 1878.

General histories of architecture. R. STURGIS and A. L. FROTHINGHAM, *A history of architecture*, vols. I–IV, 1906–15, vols. III–IV on Gothic architecture. F. M. SIMPSON, *A history of architectural development*, 3 vols., London, 1905–11; reprinted 1913, vol. II, *Medieval.* J. FERGUSSON, *A history of architecture in all countries*, 3rd edition, revised, 5 vols., London, 1891–93, vols. I–II, *Ancient and mediaeval architecture* (Porter says this work does not deserve its good reputation). C. O. HARTMANN, *Die Baukunst in ihrer Entwicklung von der Urzeit bis zur Gegenwart*, vols. I–III, Leipzig, 1910–11, vol. II, *Die Baukunst des Mittelalters und der Renaissance.* R. BORRMANN and J. NEUWIRTH, *Geschichte der Baukunst*, vol. II, *Die Baukunst des Mittelalters*, by J. NEUWIRTH, Leipzig, 1904. R. STURGIS, *A dictionary of architecture and building*, 3 vols., New York, 1901–02. F. BENOIT, *L'architecture*, 2 vols., Paris, 1911–12. A. M. BROOKS, *Architecture and the allied arts: Greek, Roman, Byzantine, Romanesque and Gothic*, London, 1926. F. KIMBALL, *A history of architecture*, New York, 1918.

R. STURGIS, *European architecture: an historical study*, New York, 1896; new edition under the title, A *short history of architecture*, 1908; and B. FLETCHER, *A history of architecture on the comparative method, for the student, craftsman, and amateur*, London, 1896; 8th edition, 1928, are convenient text-books.

C. H. CAFFIN, *How to study architecture*, New York, 1917. A. MICHEL, "L'art 'Gothique' oeuvre de France," *R.D.M.*, August, 1917.

G. DEHIO and G. v. BEZOLD, *Die kirchliche Baukunst des Abendlandes*, 2 vols. of text and an atlas in 5 vols. with 601 plates, Stuttgart, 1887–1901. E. S. PRIOR, *English mediaeval architecture*, London, 1900. E. S. PRIOR, *Medieval architecture in England*, Cambridge, 1922. V. MORTET, *Mélanges d'archéologie (antiquité, romaine, et moyen âge)*, 2nd series: *Histoire de l'architecture*, Paris, 1915. ELIZABETH (ROBINS) PENNEL, *French cathedrals, monasteries, abbeys, and sacred sites of France*, New York, 1909. C. WARD, *Mediaeval church vaulting*, Princeton, 1915. C. E. NORTON, *Historical studies of church-building in the middle ages: Venice, Siena, Florence*, New York, 1880. C. A. CUMMINGS, *History of architecture in Italy* (Sections of Romanesque and Gothic) Boston and New York, 1901. T. F. BUMPUS, *Cathedrals and churches of Italy*, New York, 1926. V. LAMPÉREZ Y ROMEA, *Historia de la arquitectura cristiana española en la edad media*, 2 vols., Madrid, 1908–09. G. HUMANN, *Die Beziehungen der Handschriftenornamentik zur romanischen Baukunst erläutert*, Strasburg, 1907. C. A. AUBER, *De l'an mille et de son influence prêtendue sur l'architecture religieuse*, Paris, 1861. E. VIOLLET-LE-DUC, *Dictionnaire raisonné de l'architecture française du XIe au XVIe siècle*, 10 vols., Paris, 1858–68.

Early christian and Byzantine architecture. T. G. JACKSON, *Byzantine and romanesque architecture*, 2 vols., Cambridge, 1913. G. B. BROWN, *From schola to cathedral: a study of early Christian architecture and its relation to the life of the church*, Edinburgh, 1886. H. C. BUTLER, *Early churches in Syria*, edited and completed by E. B. SMITH, Princeton, 1930. A. CHOISY, *L'art de bâtir chez les Byzantins*, Paris, 1883. W. R. LETHABY and H. Swainson, *The church of Santa Sophia, Constantinople; a study of Byzantine building*, London, 1916. A. VAN MILLINGEN, *Byzantine churches in Constantinople, their history and architecture*, London, 1912.

Romanesque architecture. A. K. PORTER, *Lombard architecture*, 4 vols., New Haven, 1915–17. G. T. RIVOIRA, *Lombardic architecture: its origin, development, and derivatives*, translated from the Italian by G. McN. RUSHFORTH, London, 1910. R. CATTANEO, *L'architettura in Italia del secolo VI al mille circa*, Venice, 1888, translated by the Countess ISABEL CURTIS, *Architecture in Italy from the sixth to the eleventh century*, London, 1896. V. RUPRICH-ROBERT, *L'architecture normande en Normandie et en Angleterre*, 2 vols., Paris [1884–1889]. C. MARTIN, *L'art roman en France: l'architecture et la décoration*, Paris, 1910. R. DE LASTEYRIE, *L'architecture religieuse en France à l'époque romane*, Paris, 1912; 2nd edition with a critical bibliography by M. AUBERT, Paris, 1928. J. BAUM, *Romanische Baukunst in Frankreich*, Stuttgart, 1910, edited in English by the author, *Romanesque architecture in France*, London, 1912. E. CORROYER, *L'architecture romane*, Paris, 1888. EDITH A. BROWN, *Romanesque architecture*, New York, 1910; and her *Norman architecture*, London, 1907. L. CLOQUET, *Les cathédrales et basiliques latines, byzantines, et romanes du monde catholique*, Lille, 1912. P. FRANKL, *Die frühmittelalterliche und romanische Baukunst*, Potsdam,

1926. Gómez-Moreno, *Iglesias mozárabes*, Madrid, 1919. C. Ricci, *L'architectura romanica in Italia*, Paris, 1925, English translation, London, 1925. G. G. King, *Mudijar*, London, 1927. F. de Dartein, *Etude sur l'architecture lombarde et sur les origines de l'architecture romano-byzantine*, Paris, 1865–82. J. Puig y Cadafalch, *L'arquitechura romanica a Catalunya*, 3 vols., Barcelona, 1909–18. H. A. Revoil, *Architecture romane du midi de la France*, 3 vols., Paris, 1873.

Gothic architecture. E. Viollet-le-Duc, *Dictionnaire* (there is an index to this work by H. Sabine, *Table analytique*, Paris, 1889); *Entretiens sur l'architecture*, 2 vols., Paris, 1863–72, translated by B. Bucknall, *Discourses on architecture*, 2 vols., London and Boston, 1875. T. F. Bumpus, *A guide to Gothic architecture*, New York, 1914. J. A. Brutails, *Pour comprendre les monuments de la France: notions pratiques d'archéologie à l'usage des touristes*, Paris, 1917. H. Stein, *Les architectes des cathédrales gothiques: étude critique*, Paris, [1909]. L. Gillet, *Histoire artistiques des ordres mendiants, études sur l'art religieux en Europe du XIIIe au XVIIe siècle*, Paris, 1912. E. Corroyer, *L'architecture gothique*, Paris, 1891, translated by W. Armstrong, *Gothic architecture*, New York, 1893. W. H. Goodyear, *Vertical curves and other architectural refinements in the Gothic cathedrals*, New York, 1904; *Illustrated catalogue of photographs and surveys of architectural refinements in medieval buildings*, Edinburgh, 1905, which contains a bibliography on this subject. Villard de Honnecourt, *Album de Villard de Honnecourt architecte du XIII siècle*, Paris, 1906. W. Worringer, *Form problems of the Gothic*, New York, 1920.

A. Rodin, *Les cathédrales de France*, Paris, 1914. C. Martin, *L'art gothique en France*, Paris, 1911, plates without text. E. A. Lefèvre-Pontalis, *L'architecture religieuse dans l'ancien diocèse de Soissons au XIe et au XIIe siècle*, 2 vols., Paris, 1894–96. Elsie W. Rose, *Cathedrals and cloisters of northern France*, 2 vols., London, 1914; *Cathedrals and cloisters of the Isle de France*, 2 vols., New York, 1910. F. Miltoun, *The cathedrals of northern France*, London, 1904. T. F. Bumpus, *The cathedrals of northern France*, New York, 1910; *The cathedrals of southern France*, New York, 1913.

F. Bond, *Gothic architecture in England*, London, 1905; *Cathedrals of England and Wales*, London, 1899; 4th edition, 1912. E. S. Prior, *The cathedral builders in England*, London, 1905; *A history of Gothic art in England*, London, 1900. H. M. Pratt, *The cathedral churches of England*, London, 1910. G. H. West, *Gothic architecture in England and France*, London, 1911. P. H. Ditchfield, *The cathedrals of Great Britain: their history and architecture*, new edition, London, 1916. R. A. Cram, *The ruined abbeys of Great Britain*, London, 1916; revised edition, Boston, 1927. E. Gall, *Die gotische Baukunst in Frankreich und Deutschland*, vol. I: *Die Vorstufen in Nordfrankreich von der Mitte des XI bis gegen Ende des XII. Jahrhunderts*, Leipzig, 1925. S. Gardner, *A guide to English Gothic architecture*, Cambridge, 1922. G. Hume (editor), *Cathedrals, abbeys and famous churches*, 5 vols., London, 1925–26.

W. W. Collins, *Cathedral cities of Italy*, New York, 1911. H. Hartung, *Ziele und Ergebnisse der italienischen Gotik*, Berlin, 1912. A. Haseloff, *Die Bauten der Hohenstaufen in Unteritalien*, I, Leipzig, 1920.

W. W. Collins, *Cathedral cities of Spain*, New York, 1909. C. Rudy, *The cathedrals of northern Spain*, Boston, 1906. G. E. Street, *Some account of Gothic architecture in Spain*, 2nd edition, London, 1869, edited by Georgiana G. King, 2 vols., London, 1914.

T. G. Jackson, *Gothic architecture in France, England, and Italy*, 2 vols., Cambridge, 1915. A. K. Porter, *Medieval architecture: its origins and development*, 2 vols., New York, 1909; new edition, 1912, is not limited to Gothic architecture. C. H. Moore, *The development and character of Gothic architecture*, London, 1890; 2nd edition, enlarged, 1899; reprinted, 1904; *The medieval church architecture of England*, London, 1912. F. Bond, *An introduction to English church architecture, from the eleventh to the sixteenth century*, 2 vols., London and New York, 1913. A. Pugin, *Gothic ornaments, 11th to 16th century: selected from various ancient buildings in England and France*, new edition, London, 1916.

Monographs on Gothic cathedrals. L. Demaison, *Album de la cathédrale de Reims*, 2 vols. [Paris, 1902]; *La cathédrale de Reims: son histoire, les dates de sa construction*, Caen, 1902. L. Bréhier, *La cathédrale de Reims*, Paris, 1916, supplemented by the author's "L'histoire de France à la façade de la cathédrale de Reims," *R.H.*, CXXII (1916), 288–300. C. Schaefer, *Die Kathedrale von Reims*, Berlin, 1898. E. Moreau-Nélation, *La cathédrale de Reims*, Paris [1915]. G. Durand, *Monographie de l'église Notre Dame, cathédrale d'Amiens*, 2 vols., Amiens and Paris, 1903; *Description abrégée de la cathédrale d'Amiens*, Amiens, 1904. E. Lefèvre-Pontalis, *Les architectes et la construction des cathédrales de Chartres*, Paris, 1905. A. Germain, *La cathédrale de Chartres*, Paris, 1914. C. Headlam, *The story of Chartres*, London, 1902 (Mediaeval towns). E. Houvet, *La cathédrale de Chartres*, 5 vols. of plates, Chartres. E. Pottet, *La Sainte-Chapelle de Paris, histoire, archéologie (1246–1912)*, Paris, 1913. Aubert, *Notre-Dame de Paris*. For other books on the churches of Paris see outline XIII. W. R. Lethaby, *Westminster Abbey and the king's craftsmen*, New York, 1906. H. Adams, *Mont-Saint-Michel and Chartres*, with an introduction by R. A. Cram, Boston and New York, 1913. E. Corroyer, *Description de l'abbaye Mont-Saint-Michel et de ses abords*, Paris, 1877, has 130 illustrations. P. Gont, *Le Mont-Saint-Michel: histoire de l'abbaye et de la ville*, Paris, 1911. Margaret and E. Marriage, *The sculptures of Chartres cathedral*, Cambridge, 1909, with text in both English and French.

Medieval sculpture. A. Gardner, *French sculpture of the 13th century*, London, 1915. Louise Pillion, *Les sculpteurs français du XIIIe siècle*, Paris [1912]. R. de Lasteyrie, *Études sur la sculpture française au moyen âge*, Paris, 1902 (Monuments et mémoires publiés par l'Académie des inscriptions et belles-lettres, VIII). L. G. Adams, *Recueil de sculptures gothiques en France depuis le onzième jusqu'au quinzième siècle*, Paris, 1866, 2 vols. of plates, without text. P. Vitry and G. Brière, *Documents de sculpture fran-*

çaise, vol. II, *Moyen âge*, second edition, Paris [1906]. *Le musée de sculpture comparée du palais du Trocadéro du XI au XV siècle*, 3 vols., Paris, n.d. E. S. PRIOR and A. GARDNER, *An account of mediaeval figure sculpture in England*, London, 1912. M. HASAK, *Geschichte der deutschen Bildhauerkunst im 13ten Jahrhundert*, Berlin, 1899. W. H. v. d. MUELBE, *Die Darstellung des jüngsten Gerichts an den romanischen und gotischen Kirchenportalen Frankreichs*, Leipzig, 1911. A. MARQUAND and A. L. FROTHINGHAM, *History of sculpture.* F. PANOFSLAY, *Deutsche Plastik des XI bis XIII Jahrhunderts*, Munich, 1924. A. GOLDSCHMIDT, *Die Elfenbeinskulpturen aus der Zeit der karolingischen und ottonischen Kaiser*, 3 vols., Berlin, 1914–23. CHASE and POST, *History of sculpture.* A. K. PORTER, "The rise of romanesque sculpture," *American journal of archeology*, 2nd series, XXII (1918), 399–427. *Romanesque sculpture of the pilgrimage roads*, 10 vols., Boston, 1923; *Spanish romanesque sculpture*, 2 vols., New York, 1929. V. TERRET, *La sculpture bourguignonne aux XIIe et XIIIe siècles: ses origines et ses inspirations: Cluny*, Paris, 1914. A. FOREL, *Voyage au pays des sculpteurs romans: croquis de route à travers la France*, 2 vols., Paris, 1913–14. W. VÖGE, *Die Anfänge des monumentalen Stiles im Mittelalter*, Strasburg, 1894. P. VITRY and M. AUBERT, *Gothic sculpture in France*, 2 vols., New York, 1929. H. N. FOWLER, *A history of sculpture*, New York, 1916. A. GOLDSCHMIDT, *Die deutschen Bronzetüre des frühen Mittelalters*, Marburg, 1926. E. LÜTHGEN, *Romanische Plastik in Deutschland*, Leipzig, 1923. A. MAYER, *Mittelalterliche Plastik in Italien*, Munich, 1923; *Mittelalterliche Plastik in Spanien*, Munich, 1922. M. AUBERT, *La sculpture française du moyen âge et de la renaissance*, Paris, 1926 (Bibliothèque d'histoire de l'art). H. BEENKEN, *Romanische Skulptur in Deutschland, 11 und 12 Jahrhundert*, Leipzig, 1924.

Medieval painting and illumination. P. D'ANCONA, *La miniature italienne.* A. BOINET, *La miniature carolingienne*, Paris, 1913. P. CLEMEN, *Die romanische Monumentalmalerei in den Rheinlanden*, Düsseldorf, 1916. L. DIMIER, *Les primitifs français*, Paris, 1910. EBERSOLT, *La miniature byzantine.* A. GOLDSCHMIDT, *German illumination*, 2 vols., New York, 1928. J. A. HERBERT, *Illuminated manuscripts*, New York, 1911. MARTIN, *La miniature française du XIIIe au XVIe siècle.* MILLAR, *English illuminated manuscripts from the Xth to the XIIIth century; English illuminated manuscripts of the XIVth and XVth centuries.* S. REINACH, *Repertoire de peinture du moyen âge et de la renaissance*, Paris, 1905. WARNER, *Illuminated manuscripts in the British Museum.* N. H. J. WESTLAKE, *History of design in mural painting from the earliest times to the twelfth century*, London and New York, 1902–05. J. O. WESTWOOD, *Fac-similes of the miniatures and ornaments of Anglo-Saxon and Irish manuscripts*, London, 1868. GERTRUD RICHERT, *Mittelalterliche Malerei in Spanien: katalanische Wand- und Tafelmalerei*, Berlin, 1925. A. LINDBLOM, *La peinture en Suède et en Norvège: étude sur les relations entre l'Europe occidentale et les pays scandinaves*, Stockholm, 1916.

Stained glass. H. ARNOLD, *Stained glass of the middle ages in England and France;* painted by L. B. SAINT, New York, 1913. A. J. DE H. BUSHNELL,

Storied windows, a traveller's introduction to the study of old church glass from the twelfth century to the renaissance, especially in France, London, 1914. H. OIDTMANN, *Die Glasmalerei*, 2 vols., Cologne, 1896–98. J. L. FISCHER, *Handbuch der Glasmalerei*, Leipzig, 1914. F. HARRISON, *Painted glass of York*, S.P.C.K., New York, 1923. P. NELSON, *Ancient painted glass of England*, London, 1913. J. D. LE COUTEUR, *English medieval painted glass* (S.P.C.K. Helps), London, 1926. F. DELAPORTE and E. HOUVET, *Les vitraux de la cathédrale de Chartres*, Chartres, 1926. C. H. SHERRILL, *Stained glass tours in France*, New York, 1908.

Arts and crafts. JULIA ADDISON, *Arts and crafts in the middle ages*, Boston, 1908. A. D. F. HAMLIN, *A history of ornament, ancient and medieval*, New York, 1916. J. TAVENOR-PERRY, *Didanderie: a history and description of medieval art work in copper, brass and bronze*, London, 1910. G. B. BROWN, *The arts in early England* [to 1066], 2 vols., London, 1903. M. KEMMERICH, *Die frühmittelalterliche Porträtplastik in Deutschland bis zum Ende des XIII Jahrhunderts*, Leipzig, 1909. E. VIOLLET-LE-DUC, *Dictionnaire raisonné du mobilier français de l'époque carlovingienne à la renaissance*, Paris, 1875. F. E. HOWARD and F. H. CROSSLEY, *English church woodwork: a study in craftsmanship during the mediaeval period, A. D. 1250–1550*, London, 1917, is illustrated beautifully. E. MOLINIER, *Histoire générale des arts appliqués à l'industrie du Ve à la fin du XVIII siècle*, 5 vols., Paris, 1896–1910. J. J. MARQUET DE VASSELOT, *Bibliographie de l'orfèvrerie et de l'émaillerie françaises*, Paris, 1925.

Bibliographies. The best critical bibliography on medieval architecture, and many an allied subject, is in A. K. PORTER, *Medieval architecture*, I, 335–450, II, 419–70. *Catalogue of books relating to architecture, construction and decoration in the public library of the city of Boston*, 2nd edition, Boston, 1914. R. STURGIS and H. E. KREHBIEL, *Annotated bibliography of fine art*, Boston, 1897. *Internationale Bibliographie der Kunstwissenschaft*, Berlin, 1902ff. E. MÂLE, "L'art du moyen âge en France depuis vingt ans," *R.S.H.*, II (1901), 81–108, is an important review of recent literature. The best collection of books on medieval art is in the Bibliothèque d'art et d'archéologie in Paris, which contains over 100,000 volumes. Excellent bibliography in *Art bulletin*, XI, no. 3 (1929). J. SCHLOSSER, *Die Kunstliteratur: ein Handbuch zur Quellenkunde der neueren Kunstgeschichte*, Vienna, 1924.

Original sources. *Recueil de textes relatifs à l'histoire de l'architecture et à la condition des architectes en France, au moyen âge, XIe–XIIe siècles*, edited by V. MORTET, Paris, 1911, part of no. **968**. *Quellenschriften für Kunstgeschichte und Kunsttechnik des Mittelalters und der Neuzeit*, edited by R. EITELBERGER V. EDELBERG, vols. I–XVIII, Vienna, 1871ff.; new series continued by A. ILG and C. LIST, Vienna, 1883ff.

Periodicals for history of art. *Revue de l'art ancien et moderne*, Paris, 1897ff. *Gazette des beaux-arts*, Paris, 1859ff. *Archivio storico dell' arte*, Rome, 1888ff., since 1898, under the title, *L'arte*. *Revue de l'art chrétien*, Paris, 1857ff. *Zeitschrift für christliche Kunst*, Düsseldorf, 1888ff. *Die christliche Kunst*, Münster, 1904ff. *Art studies, mediaeval, renaissance, and modern*, edited by members of the departments of the fine arts at Harvard and Princeton universities, Cambridge, 1923ff. *The art bulletin*, published quarterly by the College art association of America, New York, 1913ff. *Boletin de la sociédad española, excursiones*, Madrid, 1893ff. *Byzantinische Zeitschrift*, Leipzig, 1892. *Repertorium für Kunstwissenschaft*, Berlin and Leipzig, 1876ff.

II

History of medieval music. *The Oxford history of music*, 7 vols., 2nd edition, London, 1929ff., Introductory vol., and vols. I–II, *The polyphonic period*, by H. E. Wooldridge. E. Dickinson, *Music in the history of the western church*, New York, 1902. H. Riemann, *Handbuch der Musikgeschichte*, 2 vols., 2nd–3rd editions, Leipzig, 1921–22, vol. I, part II, *Mittelalter*, vol. II, part I, *Renaissance*. *Handbuch der Musikgeschichte*, 2 vols., edited by G. Adler, 2nd edition, Berlin, 1930, with important contributions by P. Wagner and F. Ludwig. E. de Coussemaker, *Histoire de l'harmonie au moyen âge*, Paris, 1852; *L'art harmonique aux XIIe et XIIIe siècles*, Paris, 1865. E. Ludwig, "Studien über die Geschichte der mehrstimmigen Musik im Mittelalter," *Sammelbände der Internationalen Musik-Gesellschaft*, IV–VII (1902–06). H. Besseler, "Studien zur Musik des Mittelalters," *Archiv für Musikwissenschaft*, VII–VIII (1925–26). P. Wagner, *Einführung in die gregorianischen Melodien*, 3 vols., 3rd edition, Leipzig, 1911–21. *Scriptores ecclesiastici de musica sacra potissimum*, 3 vols., edited by M. Gerbert, St. Blaise, 1784; reprinted, Graz, 1905. *Scriptorum de musica medii aevi*, 4 vols., edited by E. de Coussemaker, Paris, 1864–76; reprinted, Graz, 1904. *Paléographie musicale*, Tournai, 1889ff. Publications of the Plainsong and medieval music society, London, 1890ff.

XXVIII. DANTE

A. Outline

1. An inspection of the bibliographies listed below will show how stupendous is the amount of literature on Dante. Petrarch and the medieval scholars who shared his enthusiasm for ancient classical literature have also fared well in the modern world of scholarship. The works of Dante have been translated into practically all the modern languages. In the future the best progress in Dante investigations will be made by means of a closer study of the culture of the twelfth and thirteenth centuries which he synthesized even better than did Thomas Aquinas.

2. The life of Dante Alighieri. Born in Florence, 1265. Dante and Beatrice. For Dante's political career in Florence see outline XXXII in part II. In 1302 he was exiled from Florence and never returned. Several years before his exile he married Gemma di Manetto Donati and had four children. Dante was befriended by many powerful persons, including Bartolommeo della Scala, lord of Verona, and his younger brother, Can Grande della Scala. He seems to have gone to Bologna in 1304, and he may possibly have

been in Paris, 1307–09. For his enthusiastic support of the emperor Henry VII see outline XXXI in part II. After many wanderings in Italy he went to Ravenna in 1317 where he completed his great poem. He died in Ravenna in 1321 and was buried there.

3. The writings of Dante. His minor works in Italian: *Canzoniere*, *Vita nuova*, and *Convivio*. His minor works in Latin: *De monarchia*, *De vulgari eloquentia*, *Quaestio de aqua et terra*, *Eclogae*, and *Epistolae*. His great masterpiece in Italian, the *Divina commedia*, in three parts, *Inferno*, *Purgatorio*, and *Paradiso*.

4. Dante's knowledge of theology. His familiarity with the *Vulgate*, with the works of Augustine and with the *Summa theologica* of Thomas Aquinas. Comparison of the *Divina Commedia* with the *Summa*. Dante and the mystics.

5. His knowledge of ancient and medieval philosophy and logic. References in his works to Aristotle and Plato. His scholastic method of reasoning, exemplified especially in the *De monarchia*.

6. His acquaintance with the Latin classical belles-lettres, especially Virgil, Horace, Ovid, Lucan, Statius, and Cicero. The sources of Dante's knowledge of the Latin classics in a period when they were so generally neglected (see outline XVIII). His ignorance of Greek.

7. His interests in history and in political theory. His references to Livy and to Orosius. The sources of his knowledge of the history of his own time. *De monarchia* gives him a very important place in the history of political thought. His ideas of world peace.

8. His acquaintance with the Roman and canon law which were studied so assiduously in Bologna in his day.

9. His knowledge of the natural sciences, especially astronomy and geography.

10. The conflict in Dante's mind concerning the use of Latin and Italian. Evidence from his *De vulgari eloquentia*, *Vita nuova*, and *Convivio*. His decision on the question compared with that of Petrarch. Importance of the influence of these two men in bringing about the decline of Latin and the rise of vernaculars as the learned languages of western Europe.

11. Dante's belated but well-deserved fame as one of the greatest of the world's poets. The influence of his *Divina commedia* on modern learning, literature, and art..

B. Special Recommendations for Reading

Short general books and brief surveys. Taylor, *Mediaeval mind*, II, ch. xliv. J. R. Lowell, "Dante," in his *Among my books*, 2nd series. D. Comparetti, *Vergil*, chs. xiv, xv. E. G. Gardner, *Dante*, London, 1900. P. Toynbee, *Dante Alighieri, his life and works*, New York, 1900; 4th edition, 1910. A. J. Butler, *Dante: his times and his work*, London, 1897; 2nd edition, 1901. L. Ragg, *Dante and his Italy*, New York [1907]. K. Federn, *Dante and his time*, New York, 1902; German original, *Dante und seine Zeit*, 3rd revised edition, Stuttgart, 1921. C. H. Grandgent, *Dante*, New York,

1916 (Master spirits of literature). C. A. DINSMORE, *Life of Dante Alighieri*, Boston, 1919. C. H. GRANDGENT, *The power of Dante*, Boston, 1918; *The ladies of Dante's lyrics*, Cambridge, 1917; *Discourses on Dante*, Cambridge, 1924. J. B. FLETCHER, *Dante*, New York, 1915 (Home university library). J. T. SLATTERY, *Dante, the central man of all the world*, New York, 1920. J. J. CHAPMAN, *Dante*, New York, 1927. F. FLAMINI, *Introduction to the study of the Divine comedy*, translation by JOSSELYN, Boston, 1910. C. FOLIGNO, *Dante*, Bergamo, 1921. B. CROCE, *La poesia di Dante*, Bari, 1921; translation by D. AINSLIE, London, 1922. H. HAUVETTE, *Etudes sur la "Divine Comédie," la composition du poème et son rayonnement*, Paris, 1922; *Dante: introduction à l'étude de la Divine Comédie*, Paris, 1911. J. A. SYMONDS, *Introduction to the study of Dante*, Edinburgh, 1890; 4th edition, London, 1899.

Dante scholarship. E. MOORE, *Studies in Dante*, 4 series, Oxford, 1896–1917; see especially I for his knowledge of books, and III for his astronomy and geography. P. H. WICKSTEED, *Dante and Aquinas: being the substance of the Jowett lectures for 1911*, London and New York, 1913. P. TOYNBEE, *Dante studies and researches*, London, 1902, treats among other things of his relations with the ideas of Albert the Great and Alfraganus. P. TOYNBEE, *Dante studies*, Oxford, 1921. VOSSLER, *Die göttliche Komödie;* English translation with title, *Mediaeval culture: an introduction to Dante and his times*, by W. C. LAWTON, with a bibliography by J. E. SPINGARN. G. SANTAYANA, *Three philosophical poets: Lucretius, Dante, and Goethe*, Cambridge, 1910. For treatises and atlases of medieval geography, which help to explain Dante's ideas of the world and the universe, see the headings "Geographical discoveries," and "Original sources," under outline XXVI in part II.

Dante and the mystics. E. GARDNER, *Dante and the mystics: a study of the mystical aspect of the Divina commedia and its relations with some of its mediaeval sources*, London and New York, 1913.

Early biographies of Dante. *The early lives of Dante* (BOCCACCIO and LIONARDO BRUNI), translated by P. H. WICKSTEED, London, 1907 (King's classics). *The earliest lives of Dante*, translated from the Italian of GIOVANNI BOCCACCIO and LIONARDO BRUNI ARETINO by J. R. SMITH, New York, 1901. E. MOORE, *Dante and his early biographers*, London, 1890.

Original sources. Since all the works of Dante may be read in good English translations, students even if ignorant of Italian and Latin should study his scholarship and his thought by the direct method. Following are some of the best translations: *The Divine comedy* of DANTE ALIGHIERI, translated by C. E. NORTON, 3 vols., Boston, 1891–92 (prose). *The Divine comedy* of DANTE ALIGHIERI translated by H. F. CARY, together with D. G. ROSSETTI's translation of the *New life*, edited by O. KUHNS, New York, 1897. *The Divine comedy* of DANTE ALIGHIERI, translated by H. W. LONGFELLOW, 3 vols., Boston, 1867–71. *La commedia* di DANTE ALIGHIERI: *The Divine comedy*, translated by H. JOHNSON, New Haven, 1916. *The Divina commedia* of DANTE ALIGHIERI, literally translated into English verse in the hendecasyllabic measure of the original Italian, by S. W. GRIFFITH, 3 vols., London [1912]. *The Divine comedy*, translated by C. E. WHEELER, 3 vols., London, 1911. *The Vision: or Hell, Purgatory, and Paradise*, translated by H. F. CARY, with life of Dante, revised, with an introduction by P. TOYNBEE, 3 vols., London, 1900–02 (The little library), also in *Everyman's library*, London, 1910. C. LANGDON, *The Divine comedy of Dante Alighieri:* the Italian text with a translation in English blank verse and a commentary, 3 vols., Cambridge, 1918–21. M. B. ANDERSON, *The Divine comedy of* DANTE ALIGHIERI, Yonkers, 1921 (rhymed verse). (CARY's translation dates from 1809 and is the most generally known in blank verse.) DANTE'S *Divine comedy: The Inferno*, a literal prose translation with the text of the original collated from the best editions, and explanatory notes, by J. A. CARLYLE, New York, 1849; reprinted in the *Temple classics*, London, 1903. *Purgatorio* and *Paradiso* of DANTE ALIGHIERI, translated by P. H. WICKSTEED, with Italian and English on opposite pages, London, 1904 (Temple classics). E. H. PLUMPTREE, *The Divina commedia and Canzoniere of* DANTE ALIGHIERI, 5 vols., Boston, n.d.

The Convivio of DANTE ALIGHIERI, translated by P. H. WICKSTEED, London, 1903 (Temple classics). DANTE'S *Convivio*, translated into English by W. W. JACKSON, Oxford, 1909. *The Banquet* (*Il Convito*) of DANTE ALIGHIERI, translated by KATHERINE HILLARD, London, 1889. *Il Convito: the Banquet of* DANTE ALIGHIERI, translated by ELIZABETH P. SAYER, London and New York, 1887 (Morley's universal library, 49).

DANTE ALIGHIERI, *Vita nuova*, translated into English by D. G. ROSSETTI in his *Dante and his circle*, London, 1874 (also in Temple classics and many other editions). *The New life* of DANTE ALIGHIERI, translated by C. E. NORTON, Boston, 1867; revised edition, 1892. LORNA DE' LUCCHI, *The minor poems of Dante translated into English verse*, Oxford, 1926. TOYNBEE, *The letters of Dante.* P. H. WICKSTEED and GARDNER, *Dante and Giovanni del Virgilio* (Dante's *Eclogues*, text and translation), Westminster, 1902.

The De monarchia of DANTE ALIGHIERI, edited with translation and notes by AURELIA HENRY, Boston and New York, 1904. DANTE, *De vulgari eloquentia*, translated with notes by A. G. F. HOWELL, London, 1890. DANTE, *Quaestio de aqua et terra*, edited and translated, with Latin text and its English translation on opposite pages, by C. L. SHADWELL, Oxford, 1909, who considers it genuine. DANTE ALIGHIERI, *Eleven letters*, translated with notes and historical comments, by C. S. LATHAM, Boston, 1892. *A translation of the Latin works* of DANTE ALIGHIERI, by A. G. F. HOWELL and P. H. WICKSTEED, London, 1904 (Temple classics).

C. BIBLIOGRAPHY

General books. See the general histories of Italian literature, nos. **808–11a,** and the general literature listed under outline XXXIII in part II.

Dante's philosophy. B. NARDI, *Sigieri di Brabante nella Divina commedia e le fonti della filosofia di Dante*, Florence, 1912. G. BUSNELLI, *Cosmogonia e antropogenesi sec. D. Alighieri e le sue fonti*, Rome, 1922. A. F. OZANAM,

Dante et la philosophie catholique au XIIIe siècle, in vol. VI of his *Oeuvres complètes*, Paris, 1872–81, translated as, *Dante and catholic philosophy*, New York, 1897. G. BUSNELLI, *L'Etica nicomachea e l'ordinamento morale dell' "Inferno" di Dante*, Bologna, 1907. W. H. V. READE, *The moral system of Dante's Inferno*, Oxford, 1909. F. FLAMINI, *Il significato e il fine della Divina commedia*, 2 vols., 2nd edition, Livorno, 1916, insists that knowledge of Thomistic philosophy is an essential factor for understanding Dante. GILBERT, *Dante's conception of justice*.

Aids to the study of Dante. E. K. RAND and E. H. WILKINS, *Dantis Alagherii operum latinorum concordantiae*, Oxford, 1912. E. S. SHELDON, *Concordanza delle opere italiane in prosa e del canzoniere di Dante Alighieri*, Oxford, 1905. E. A. FAY, *Concordance of the Divina commedia*, Cambridge, 1888. G. A. SCARTAZZINI, *Enciclopedia dantesca*, 3 vols., Milan, 1896–1905. P. J. TOYNBEE, *A dictionary of proper names and notable matters in the works of Dante*, Oxford, 1898; republished under the title, *Concise dictionary of proper names and notable matters in the works of Dante*, Oxford, 1914. C. A. DINSMORE, *Aids to the study of Dante*, Boston, 1903.

Miscellaneous books. P. TOYNBEE, *Dante in English literature from Chaucer to Cary*, 2 vols., 1909; *Britain's tribute to Dante in literature and art.* "A chronological record of 540 years (c. 1380–1920)," London, 1921. R. T. HOLBROOK, *Portraits of Dante from Giotto to Raffael*, London, 1911. F. J. MATHER, JR., *The portraits of Dante*, Princeton, 1921. M. A. ORR, *Dante and the early astronomers*, London [1914]. E. G. GARDNER, *Dante's ten heavens, a study of the Paradiso*, Westminster, 1898; 2nd edition, 1900. C. MARIOTTI, *S. Francesco, i Francescani e Dante Alighieri*, Quaracchi, 1913. H. BEATTY, *Dante and Virgil*, London, 1905. M. ASÍN Y PALACIOS, *La escatalogia musulmana en la Divina comedia*, Madrid, 1919; translated and abridged by H. SUNDERLAND, *Islam and the Divine comedy*, London, 1926. B. BARBADORO and L. DAMI, *Firenze di Dante*, Florence, 1921. *Dante: essays in commemoration 1321–1921*, edited by A. CIPPICO, et al., London, 1921. F. TORRACA, *I precursori della Divina commedia*, Florence, 1921. M. DODS, *Forerunners of Dante*, Edinburgh, 1903.

Periodicals. *Annual report* of the Dante society, Cambridge, Mass., 1882ff. Società dantesca italiana [of Florence], *Bullettino*, 1894–1921. *Giornale dantesco*, 1893ff. *Studi danteschi*, 1920ff. *Deutsches Dante-Jahrbuch*, 1867ff.

Original texts. Handy one-volume editions of all the works of Dante in the original (without notes) are: *Tutte le opere di* DANTE ALIGHIERI, edited by E. MOORE, Oxford, 1894; reprinted with revisions in 1897, 1904, 1924; and *Le opere di Dante, testo critico della Società dantesca italiana*, Florence, 1921. Editions of *Divina commedia* with Italian notes: by SCARTAZZINI (9th edition, revised by VANDELLI, Milan, 1929); by TORRACA (4th edition, Rome, 1920); by DEL LUNGO (Florence, 1921–26); with English notes by C. H. GRANDGENT (Boston, 1909–13). Editions of *Vita nuova* with Italian notes by D'ANCONA (Pisa, 1884); by CASINI (Florence, 1891); by SCHERILLO (with *Canzoniere;* 2d edition, Milan, 1921); by FLAMINI

(Leghorn, 1910); with English notes by K. McKenzie (Boston, 1922). A. Monti (editor), *Dantis Alagherii epistolae*, Milan, 1921.

Bibliographies. Vossler, *Mediaeval culture*, volume II. T. W. Koch, *Catalogue of the Dante collection presented by W. Fiske to the Cornell university library*, 2 vols., Ithaca, 1898–1900 (supplementary volume by M. Fowler, 1921); and *A list of Danteiana in American libraries, supplementing the catalogue of the Cornell collection*, Boston, 1901. This collection in the Cornell university library is the largest in the world. W. C. Lane, *The Dante collections in the Harvard college and Boston public libraries*, Cambridge, Mass., 1890; *Additions*, 1890ff. *Catalogue of the Dante collection in the library of the University college, London*, Oxford, 1910. For the books on Dante in the British Museum, see no. **3** (also published as separate pamphlet).

INDEX

This index comprises authors, editors, subjects and titles of large collections. The black-faced figures refer to numbers in part I; the light-faced figures to pages in parts II and III. Reference is made only to the place where the title of a work is given in full.